Clinical Neuropsychology

Clinical Neuropsychology

Fifth Edition

Edited by
KENNETH M. HEILMAN, M.D.

The James E. Rooks Jr. Distinguished Professor
Department of Neurology
University of Florida College of Medicine
Gainesville, FL

EDWARD VALENSTEIN, M.D.

Professor
Florida State University College of Medicine
Professor Emeritus
University of Florida
Tallahassee, FL

OXFORD
UNIVERSITY PRESS

OXFORD
UNIVERSITY PRESS

Oxford University Press, Inc., publishes works that further
Oxford University's objective of excellence
in research, scholarship, and education.

Oxford   New York
Auckland   Cape Town   Dar es Salaam   Hong Kong   Karachi
Kuala Lumpur   Madrid   Melbourne   Mexico City   Nairobi
New Delhi   Shanghai   Taipei   Toronto

With offices in
Argentina   Austria   Brazil   Chile   Czech Republic   France   Greece
Guatemala   Hungary   Italy   Japan   Poland   Portugal   Singapore
South Korea   Switzerland   Thailand   Turkey   Ukraine   Vietnam

Copyright © 2012 by Oxford University Press, Inc.

Published by Oxford University Press, Inc.
198 Madison Avenue, New York, New York 10016
www.oup.com

Oxford is a registered trademark of Oxford University Press

Library of Congress Cataloging-in-Publication Data

Clinical neuropsychology / edited by Kenneth M. Heilman, Edward Valenstein. — Fifth Edition.
p. ; cm.
Includes bibliographical references and index.
ISBN 978-0-19-538487-1   1. Neuropsychiatry. 2. Clinical neuropsychology.   I. Heilman, Kenneth M.
(Kenneth Martin), 1938- editor. II. Valenstein, Edward, 1942- editor.
[DNLM: 1. Nervous System Diseases—diagnosis. 2. Neurobehavioral Manifestations.
3. Delirium, Dementia, Amnestic, Cognitive Disorders—diagnosis. 4. Neuropsychology—methods. WL 340]
RC341.C693 2011
616.8—dc22   2010046443

9 8 7 6 5 4 3 2 1
Printed in USA
on acid-free paper

To all of the authors who have contributed to this and former editions.

Preface to the Fifth Edition

Brain injury from any cause may manifest with behavioral symptoms and signs. Clinicians who care for patients with brain injuries from stroke, trauma, tumors, infections, degenerative diseases, and other causes need not only to recognize these behavioral disorders, but also to understand how brain damage may account for them. Thus, as in all former editions of this book, the Fifth Edition focuses on the clinical presentation of the major neurobehavioral syndromes, including symptoms, signs, methods of assessment that are useful for diagnosis, and also on their underlying anatomy, physiology, and pathology. The authors attempt to explain the cognitive mechanisms that can account for specific symptoms and signs, and to provide new information about treatment and management. Authors have also drawn upon information that has become available in the eight years since the Fourth Edition of this text was published.

This edition differs from the previous edition in the addition of a chapter on creativity, since there has been increased interest in creativity, and brain disorders can either enhance or impair creativity. We have chosen not to include a chapter on hallucinations, instead asking authors to discuss hallucinations and delusions when relevant to the subject of their chapters.

We note with deep regret the passing of prior contributors to this text. Dr. Arthur Benton, who died in 2006, enthusiastically supported our original proposal to edit this text, introduced us to Jerry House, then an editor at Oxford University Press, and suggested the title for the book. Arthur was so excited about the publication of a textbook about neuropsychological disorders that he volunteered to be the primary author of two chapters, Disorders of the Body Schema, and Visuoperceptual, Visuospatial, and Visuoconstructive Disorders, for the first three editions of the book. Arthur was one of the founding fathers of modern neuropsychology. He developed many neuropsychological tests that continue to be used. He also trained and mentored many of today's leading neuropsychologists. He died at the age of 97, having had a full life; but he will be missed.

Joseph E. Bogen, M.D., died in 2004. Joe was a neurosurgeon who sectioned the corpus callosum in several patients with seizures refractory to medical treatment. Joe helped to establish a group of investigators in California who performed the critical evaluation of split-brain patients, a group that included Roger Sperry, who won a Nobel Prize in 1981 for his work on commissurotomized animals and humans.

Since our first edition, we have lost other outstanding contributors, including Nelson Butters and D. Frank Benson, but we are fortunate that most of the expert clinician-scientists who wrote chapters for the Fourth Edition have also been able to contribute to this Fifth Edition.

Writing a chapter is financially unrewarding and is generally not held in as high regard as writing papers for peer-reviewed journals. But it is very difficult for students to learn neuropsychology by reading original papers, and reading review chapters is perhaps the most efficient means of learning. Thus, we are fortunate that the authors of our chapters are also educators and know the importance of their efforts. We, the editors, are deeply indebted to them for producing such excellent chapters. and therefore we have dedicated this book to all the people who have written chapters for this and prior editions.

Writing and editing a text is an enormous investment in energy and time. Fortunately, we continue to have the support and loyalty of our families and, for many years, we were fortunate to have as our Department Chair, Dr. Melvin Greer, who provided us with time and encouraged our efforts. Mel died this year, and he will be terribly missed. But his legacy of support and encouragement for the academic pursuits of the faculty have continued with our new Chair, Tetsuo Azhizawa, as well as our many colleagues, friends, and coworkers.

We hope that this Fifth Edition will continue to be of value to clinicians, investigators, and students from a variety of disciplines, including psychology, neurology, psychiatry, speech pathology, and cognitive neuroscience.

Preface to the First Edition

The growth of interest in brain–behavior relationships has generated a literature that is both impressive and bewildering. In teaching neuropsychology, we have found that the reading lists necessary for adequate coverage of the subject have been unwieldy, and the information provided in the reading has been difficult to integrate. We therefore set out to provide a text that comprehensively covers the major clinical syndromes. The focus of the text is the clinical presentation of human brain dysfunction. The authors who have contributed to this volume have provided clinical descriptions of the major neuropsychological disorders. They have discussed methods of diagnosis, and have described specific tests, often of use at the bedside. They have also commented upon therapy. Since the study of pathophysiological and neuropsychological mechanisms underlying these disorders is inextricably intertwined with the definition and treatment of these disorders, considerable space has been devoted to a discussion of these mechanisms, and to the clinical and experimental evidence which bears on them.

A multi-authored text has the advantage of allowing authorities to write about areas in which they have special expertise. This also exposes the reader to several different approaches to the study of brain-behavior relationships, an advantage in a field in which a variety of theoretical and methodological positions have been fruitful. We therefore have not attempted to impose our own views on the contributing authors, but where there were conflicts in terminology, we have provided synonyms and cross-references. Much of brain activity is integrative, and isolated neuropsychological disturbances are rare. Discussions of alexia or agraphia must necessarily include more than a passing reference to aphasia, and so on. Since we wanted each chapter to stand on its own, with its author's viewpoint intact, we have generally allowed some overlap between chapters.

We wish to thank all of the persons who devoted their time and effort to this book. Professor Arthur Benton not only contributed two outstanding chapters, but was instrumental in advising us about authors and content, and in leading us to Oxford University Press. We are grateful to all the other contributing authors, who promptly provided high quality manuscripts; to our secretary, Ann Tison, who typed our manuscripts so many times; and to the editors at Oxford University Press, who helped to improve our grammar and syntax, and, not infrequently, the clarity of our thought. Not least, we are grateful to our families, who have endured many evenings of work with this volume with patience and understanding.

Gainesville, Florida   K.M.H.
March 1979   E.V.

Contents

Contributors

JOHN C. ADAIR, MD
Professor of Neurology
Albuquerque VA Medical Center
and Department of Neurology
University of New Mexico
Albuquerque, New Mexico

STEVEN W. ANDERSON, PHD
Department of Neurology
Division of Behavioral Neurology
& Cognitive Neuroscience
University of Iowa College of Medicine
Iowa City, Iowa

ANNA M. BARRETT, MD
Director, Stroke Rehabilitation Research Laboratory
Kessler Foundation Research Center
Professor of Physical Medicine & Rehabilitation and
Neurology & Neurosciences
University of Medicine and Dentistry
New Jersey Medical School
West Orange, New Jersey

RUSSELL M. BAUER, PHD
Professor and Chair
Department of Clinical and Health Psychology
University of Florida
Gainesville, Florida

STEVEN M. BERMAN, PHD
Center for Addictive Behaviors
UCLA Semel Institute
Los Angeles, California

LEE X. BLONDER, PHD
Sanders Brown Center on Aging and
Department of Behavioral Science
University of Kentucky
Lexington, Kentucky

JOSEPH E. BOGEN, MD
Late Clinical Professor of Neurological Surgery
University of Southern California School of
Medicine
Adjunct Professor of Psychology, University of
California, Los Angeles
Visiting Professor of Biology, California
Institute of Technology
Pasadena, California

DAWN BOWERS, PHD
Professor, Department of Clinical and
Health Psychology
University of Florida
Gainesville, Florida

DAVID CAPLAN, MD, PhD
Professor of Neurology
Neuropsychology Lab
Harvard Medical School
Boston, Massachusetts

H. BRANCH COSLETT, MD
Chief, Section of Cognitive Neurology
William B Kelley Professor of Neurology
University of Pennsylvania School
  of Medicine
Philadelphia, Pennsylvania

ANTONIO R. DAMASIO, MD, PhD
David Dornsife Professor of Neuroscience
Director, Brain and Creativity Institute
University of Southern California
  Los Angeles, California

NATALIE L. DENBURG, PhD
Department of Neurology
Division of Behavioral Neurology & Cognitive
  Neuroscience
University of Iowa College of Medicine
Iowa City, Iowa

VALERIA DRAGO, MD
Laboratorio LENITEM
IRCCS San Giovanni di Dio Fatebenefratelli
Brescia, Italy

RUSSELL A. EPSTEIN, PhD
Associate Professor of Psychology
Department of Psychology and Center for
  Cognitive Neuroscience
University of Pennsylvania
Philadelphia, Pennsylvania

MARTHA J. FARAH, PhD
Director, Center for Neuroscience & Society
Walter H. Annenberg Professor in the Natural
  Sciences
University of Pennsylvania
Philadelphia, Pennsylvania

KENNETH M. HEILMAN, MD
The James E. Rooks Jr. Distinguished Professor
  Department of Neurology
University of Florida College of Medicine
Gainesville, Florida

MARCO IACOBONI, MD, PhD
Professor, Department of Psychiatry and
  Biobehavioral Sciences
Director, Transcranial Magnetic Stimulation Lab
Ahmanson-Lovelace Brain Mapping Center
David Geffen School of Medicine at UCLA
Los Angeles, California

DIANE L. KENDALL, PhD, CCC-SLP
Associate Professor
Department of Speech and Hearing Sciences
University of Washington
Seattle, Washington
Research Investigator VAMC Puget Sound

DAVID KNOPMAN, MD
Professor, Department of Neurology
Mayo Clinic
Rochester, Minnesota

ABHAY KUMAR, MD
Department of Neurology
University of Florida
Gainesville, Florida

BRUCE MILLER, MD
Clausen Distinguished Professor of Neurology
Departments of Neurology and Psychiatry
University of California at San Francisco School
  of Medicine
Los Angeles, California

STEPHEN E. NADEAU, MD
Chief, Neurology Service
Medical Director, Brain Rehabilitation
  Research Center
Malcom Randall VA Medical Center
Professor of Neurology
University of Florida College of Medicine
Gainesville, Florida

GILA Z. RECKESS, MS
Department of Clinical and Health Psychology
University of Florida
Gainesville, Florida

DAVID P. ROELTGEN, MD
Cape Physicians Associates
Cape May Court House, New Jersey

LESLIE J. GONZALEZ ROTHI, PhD
VA Career Research Scientist
Bob Paul Family Professor of Neurology
Associate Chair for Research, Department of
* Neurology*
Professor of Clinical and Health Psychology
* Communicative Processes and Disorders*
Program Director, VA Brain Rehabilitation
* Research Center*
University of Florida
Gainesville, Florida

OLA SELNES, PhD
Professor of Neurology
Johns Hopkins Medical Institutions
Baltimore, Maryland

DANIEL TRANEL, PhD
Professor of Neurology and Psychology
Director of Neuropsychology and
* Cognitive Neuroscience*
University of Iowa College of Medicine
Iowa City, Iowa

LAUREN ULLRICH, BA
Doctoral Student, Department of Neurology
Georgetown University
Washington, D.C.

EDWARD VALENSTEIN, MD
Professor
Florida State University College of Medicine
Professor Emeritus
University of Florida
Tallahassee, Florida

ROBERT T. WATSON, MD
Professor Emeritus
University of Florida
Executive Associate Dean for Clinical Affairs
Professor, Florida State University College of
* Medicine*
Tallahassee, Florida

DAHLIA W. ZAIDEL, PhD
Professor, Department of Psychology
University of California at Los Angeles (UCLA)
Brain Research Institute, UCLA
Los Angeles, California

ERAN ZAIDEL, PhD
Professor, Department of Psychology and
* Brain Research Institute*
University of California
Los Angeles, California

Clinical Neuropsychology

1

Introduction

KENNETH M. HEILMAN AND EDWARD VALENSTEIN

Aristotle thought that the mind, along with its function of thinking, had no relation to the body or the senses and could not be destroyed. The first attempts to localize mental processes to the brain, however, may nevertheless be traced back to antiquity. In the fifth century BC, Hippocrates of Croton claimed that the brain was the organ of intellect and the heart the organ of the senses. Herophilus, in the third century BC, studied the structure of the brain and regarded it as the site of intelligence. He believed that the middle ventricle was responsible for the faculty of cognition and the posterior ventricle was the seat of memory. Galen, in the second century BC, thought that the activities of the mind were performed by the substance of the brain rather than the ventricles, but it was not until the anatomical work of Vesalius in the 16th century AD that this thesis was accepted. Vesalius, however, thought that the brains of most mammals and birds had similar structures in almost every respect and differed only in size, attaining the greatest dimensions in humans. Descartes, in the 17th century, suggested that anatomy predicates function. He reasoned that since all thought, ideas, and actions emanate from the soul, and that all information is consolidated in the soul, the soul had to be located at the anatomic center of the brain. He therefore suggested that the soul resided in the pineal.

The next paradigmatic shift in the understanding of brain–behavior relationships came at the end of the 18th century, when Gall postulated that various human faculties were localized in different organs, or centers, in the brain. This concept of localized function is now called *modularity*. In addition, Gall thought that larger modules would function better than smaller modules. He thought that, although modules are independent, they are able to interact with one another. Unlike Descartes, Gall conceived brain structures as having successive development, with no central point where all nerves unite. He proposed that the vital forces resided in the brainstem and that the intellectual qualities were situated in various parts of the two cerebral hemispheres. The hemispheres were united by the commissures, the largest being the corpus callosum.

Gall was aware that skull size was dependent on the size of the brain, and since bigger is better (as he believed), he also postulated that measurements of a person's skull would allow one to deduce moral and intellectual characteristics. These hypotheses were the foundation of *phrenology*. Unfortunately, phrenologists made many claims that were not based on empirical evidence, and phrenology soon was reduced to the status of a pseudoscience. When phrenology fell into disrepute, many of Gall's original contributions were blighted. His teachings, however, can be considered the foundation of modern neuropsychology.

Noting that students with good verbal memory had prominent eyes, Gall suggested that memory for words was situated in the frontal lobes. He studied two patients who had lost their memory for words and attributed their disorder to frontal lobe lesions. In 1825, Bouillard wrote that he also believed cerebral function to be localized. He demonstrated that discrete lesions could produce paralysis in one limb and not others and cited this as proof of localized function. He also believed that the anterior (frontal) lobe was the center of speech. He observed that the tongue had many functions other than speech and that one function could be disordered (e.g., speech) while others remained intact (e.g., mastication). This observation suggested to him that an effector can have more than one center that controls its actions (Bouillard, 1825).

In 1861, Paul Broca heard Bouillaud's pupil Auburtin speak about the importance of the anterior lobe in speech. Broca had a hospital patient who was being treated for gangrene. This patient had a prior stroke that had resulted in a right hemiplegia, together with loss of speech and writing. The patient was able to understand speech but could articulate only one word: "tan." When this patient died, postmortem inspection of the brain revealed a cavity filled with fluid on the lateral aspect of the left hemisphere. When the fluid was drained, there could be seen a large left hemisphere lesion that included the first temporal gyrus, insula, corpus striatum, and frontal lobe, including the second and third frontal convolutions as well as the inferior portion of the transverse convolution. In 1861, Broca saw another patient who had lost the power of speech and writing but could comprehend spoken language. Autopsy again revealed a left hemisphere lesion involving the second and third frontal convolutions. Broca later saw eight patients who suffered a loss of speech, which he called *aphemia*, but which Trousseau later called *aphasia*.

All eight had left hemisphere lesions. This was the first demonstration of left hemisphere dominance for language (Broca, 1865), and it provided strong evidence to support Gall's hypothesis of brain modularity.

Broca's observations produced great excitement in the medical world. Despite his clear demonstration of left hemisphere dominance, medical opinion appeared to split into two camps, one favoring the view that different functions are exercised by the various portions of the cerebral hemisphere and the other denying that psychic functions are or can be localized. Following Broca's initial observations, a flurry of activity occurred. In 1868, Hughlings Jackson noted that there were two types of aphasic patients—fluent and nonfluent—and in 1869, Bastian argued that there were patients who had deficits not only in the articulation of words but also in their memory for words. Bastian also postulated the presence of a visual and auditory word center and a kinesthetic center for the hand and the tongue. He proposed that these centers were connected and that information, such as language, was processed by the brain in different ways by each of these centers. Lesions in these centers would thus produce distinct syndromes, depending upon which aspect of the processing was disturbed. Bastian thus viewed the brain as a processor. He was the first to describe word deafness and word blindness (Bastian, 1869).

In 1874, Wernicke published his famous *Der Aphasische Symptomenkomplex* (Wernicke, 1874). He was familiar with Meynert's work, which demonstrated that sensory systems project to the posterior portions of the hemispheres, whereas the anterior portions appear to be efferent. Wernicke noted that lesions of the posterior portion of the superior temporal region produced an aphasia in which comprehension was poor. He thought that this auditory center contained sound images of words, whereas Broca's area contained images for the movements need to produce words. He also thought that these areas were connected by a *commissure*, or white matter tract, and that a lesion of this commissure would disconnect the area for sound images from the area for images of movement, resulting in a language disturbance called *conduction aphasia*, in which comprehension was intact, speech was fluent, but repetition was impaired.

Wernicke's scheme could account for motor, conduction, and sensory aphasia with poor repetition. Lichtheim (1885), however, described patients who were nonfluent but repeated normally, and sensory aphasics who could not comprehend but could repeat words. Elaborating on Wernicke's ideas, he devised a complex scheme to explain the mechanism underlying seven types of speech and language disorders. Bastian, Wernicke, and Lichtheim demonstrated that complex behaviors can be fractionated into modular components. They also developed information processing models showing how these components interacted to produce complex behaviors such as speech. These models have had heuristic and clinical value.

Anatomical structure constrains functions. Detailed anatomical studies of the cerebral cortex revealed subtle regional differences in the pattern of cellular organization, and in 1909, Brodmann published the results of anatomic studies defining cytoarchitectonic regions in the cortex of humans and other species. That different areas of the cortex had different architecture supported the postulate that the brain is organized in a modular fashion. When localizing functions, current investigators still refer to Brodmann's areas (Figure 1-1).

Following World War I, the localizationist-information processing approach was abandoned in favor of a holistic approach. Many factors probably underlie this change. The localizationist theory was built on the foundation laid by Gall; thus, when phrenology was discredited, other localizationist theories became suspect. Lashley (1938), using experimental methods (as opposed to the case reports used by the classical neurologists), reported that engrams were not localized in the brain in modules, but rather appeared to be diffusely represented. From these observations, he proposed a theory of mass action: The behavioral result of a lesion depends more on the amount of brain removed than on the location of the lesion. Head (1926) studied the linguistic performance of patients with aphasia and was not satisfied with the classical neurologists' attempts to deduce schemas from clinical observations. Discussing one of Wernicke's case reports, he wrote, "No better example could be chosen of the manner in which the writers of this period were compelled to lop and twist their cases to fit the Procrustean bed of their hypothetical conceptions." Although Freud studied the relationships between the brain and behavior early in his career, he later provided the scientific world with explanations of behavior based on psychodynamic relationships. The Gestalt psychologists abandoned localization in favor of the holistic approach.

Social and political influences were perhaps more important in changing neuropsychological thought than were newer scientific theories. The continental European scientific community was strongly influenced by Kant's *Critique of Pure Reason*, which held that, even though knowledge cannot transcend experience, it is nevertheless in part a priori. According to Kant, the outer world provides only the matter of sensation, whereas the mental apparatus (the brain) orders this matter and supplies the concepts by means of which we understand experience. After World War I, the continental European influence on science waned, while the influence of English-speaking countries blossomed. The American and English political and social systems were strongly influenced by John Locke, a 17th-century liberal philosopher who, unlike Kant, believed that behavior and ideas were not innate but rather derived from experience (the concept of the mind as a "tabula rasa"). If brain organization is primarily dependent on experience (nurture), there was little reason to look at the structure and organization of the brain (nature) in order to understand behavior. This "black box" approach reached its zenith in the 1950s, with the work of the behaviorists such as B. F. Skinner, who focused on how "nurture" controlled behavior.

In the second half of the 20th century, there has been a reawakening of interest in brain–behavior relationships. Many developments contributed to this renaissance. The classical neurologists were rediscovered and their findings replicated. Electronic technology provided researchers with new instruments for observing physiological processes. New statistical

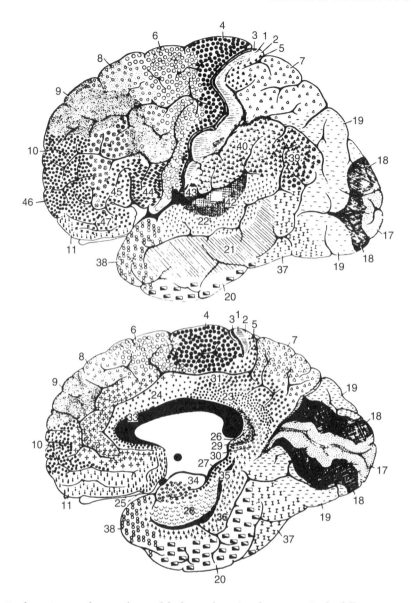

Figure 1–1. Brodmann's cytoarchitectural map of the human brain (Brodmann, 1909). The different areas are defined on the basis of subtle differences in cortical cell structure and organization. Broca's area corresponds roughly to areas 44 and 45 and Wernicke's area to the posterior part of area 22.

procedures enabled investigators to distinguish random results from significant behavior. New behavioral paradigms, such as dichotic listening and lateral visual half-field viewing, permitted psychologists to explore brain mechanisms in normal individuals, as well as in patients with brain injury. Anatomical studies using new staining methods permitted more detailed mapping of connections, and advances in neurochemistry and neuropharmacology ushered in a new form of neuropsychology; one in which, in addition to studying behavioral–structural relationships, investigators can study behavioral–chemical relationships.

Recently, new forms of functional imaging, which will be discussed in more detail below, have allowed cognitive neuroscientists to map some correlates of brain activity during specific behaviors in both normal and brain-injured subjects.

METHODS AND CONCEPTS

The attempt to relate behavior to the brain rests on the assumptions that all behavior is mediated by physical processes and that the complex behavior of higher animals depends upon physical processes in the central nervous system. Changes in complex behavior must therefore be associated with changes in the physical state of the brain. Conversely, changes in the physical state of the brain (such as those associated with brain damage) can alter behavior. The organization of the nervous system, which is to a large extent determined by genetics, but which can also be modified by experience, sets limits on what can be perceived and learned. This organization also determines to a great extent the nature of the behavioral changes that occur in response to brain injury.

The understanding of brain–behavior relationships is aided most by the study of behaviors that can be clearly defined and that are likely to be related to brain processes that can be directly or indirectly observed. Behaviors that can be selectively affected by focal brain lesions or by specific pharmacological agents are therefore most often chosen for neuropsychological study. Conversely, behaviors that are difficult to define or that appear unlikely to be correlated with observable anatomical, physiological, or chemical processes in the brain are poor candidates for study. As techniques for studying the brain improve, more forms of behavior are becoming amenable to study.

Although early in his career Sigmund Freud engaged in behavioral neurology research and even coined the term *agnosia* for patients who had sensory recognition disorders, in his later work he used psychodynamic theory to explain human behavior. Psychodynamic explanations of behavior may be of considerable clinical utility in the evaluation and treatment of certain behavioral disorders, but until some correlation with underlying brain processes is demonstrated, they will not help neuropsychologists understand brain–behavior relationships. Furthermore, psychodynamic explanations of the behavior of brain-damaged patients must be examined critically, so that the emotional response to the injury can be distinguished from emotional changes caused by the brain damage.

Depression, for example, can be seen in brain-damaged persons, such as patients with hemispheric stroke. The obvious psychodynamic explanation is that depression is a "normal" reaction to the loss of function resulting from the brain injury. Evidence that depression correlates less with the severity of functional loss than with the site of the brain lesion, however, suggests that, in some patients, depression may be a direct result of the brain injury and that, in such cases, the psychodynamic explanation may be irrelevant. Similar caveats apply to the better-documented associations of apathy with lesions in the frontal lobes and denial of illness with lesions in the right hemisphere.

There are many valid approaches to the study of brain–behavior relationships, and no morally and intellectually sound approach should be neglected. We will briefly consider the major approaches, emphasizing those that have been used to greatest advantage.

INTROSPECTION

At times, patients' observations of their own mental state may be not only helpful but necessary. How else can one learn of hallucinations or emotional experiences? It is conceivable that people's insights into their own mental processes may be of importance in delineating brain mechanisms. For example, persons with "photographic" memory not surprisingly report that they rely on visual rather than verbal memory, and experiments suggest that visual memory has a greater capacity than verbal memory. Patients may have similarly useful insights, and clinicians would do well to listen carefully to what their patients say. This does not mean, however, that clinicians and researchers must fully accept these explanations. Even in normal persons, introspection is not always valid. In brain-damaged patients, it may be even less reliable. This is particularly true when the language centers have been disconnected from the region of the brain that processes the information the patient is asked about (Geschwind, 1965). For example, sensory information from the left hand projects to the right hemisphere, and thus blindfolded patients with a callosal lesion (separating the left language-dominant hemisphere from the right hemisphere) cannot correctly name an object placed in their left hand. Curiously, such patients usually do not say that they cannot name the object, nor do they explain that their left hand can feel it but they cannot find the right word. Instead, in nearly every such case recorded, the patient confabulates a name. It is clear that, in this situation, the patient's language area, which is providing the spoken "insight," cannot even appreciate the presence of a deficit (until it is later brought to its attention), let alone explain the nature of the difficulty. In other situations, it is apparent that patients make incorrect assumptions about their deficits. Patients with pure word deafness (who cannot understand spoken language but nevertheless can speak well and can hear) often assume that people are deliberately being obscure; the result of this introspection is paranoia. Thus, although a patient's introspection at times can provide useful clues for the clinician, this information must always be analyzed critically and used with caution.

THE BLACK-BOX APPROACH

Behavior can be studied without any knowledge of the nervous system. Just as the electrical engineer can study the function of an electronic apparatus without taking it apart (by applying different inputs and studying the outputs), the brain can be approached and studied as a "black box." The object of the black-box approach is to determine laws of behavior. These laws can then be used to predict behavior, which is one expressed aim of the study of psychology.

To the extent that laws of behavior are determined by the "hardwiring" of the brain, the black-box approach also yields information about brain function. In this regard, the systematic study of any behavior or set of behaviors is relevant to the study of brain function. Psychology, linguistics, sociology, aesthetics, and related disciplines may all reveal a priori principles of behavior. The study of linguistics, for example, has revealed a structure common to all languages (Chomsky, 1967). Since there is no logical constraint that gives language this structure, and since its generality makes environmental influences unlikely, one can assume that the basic structure of language is

hardwired in the brain. Thus, observations of behavior can constrain theories of brain function without any reference to brain anatomy, chemistry, or physiology (see, for example, Caramazza, 1992).

Although the black-box approach yields useful information about brain function, such information is limited because the brain itself is not studied. The study of neuropsychology reflects its origins in 19th-century medical science by emphasizing brain anatomy, chemistry, and physiology as relevant variables: purely cognitive studies are but a part of this endeavor.

BRAIN LESION-ABLATION PARADIGMS

Focal brain lesions change behavior in specific ways. Studies correlating these behavioral changes with the sites of lesions yield information that can be used to predict, from a given behavioral disturbance, the site of the lesions, and vice versa. Such information has great clinical utility.

It is another matter, however, to try to deduce from the behavioral effects of an ablative lesion the normal mechanisms of brain function mediated by the specific area that is damaged. As Hughlings Jackson pointed out over a century ago, the abnormal behavior observed after a brain lesion reflects two functional changes caused by this damage: the loss of the functions mediated by the damaged portion of the brain, and the functioning of the remaining brain tissue after this loss. This remaining brain may react adversely to, or compensate for, the loss of function caused by the lesion, and thus either add to or minimize the behavioral deficit. Acute lesions often disturb function in other brain areas (termed *diaschisis*); these metabolic and physiological changes may not be detectable by neuropathological methods and may thus contribute to an overestimate of the function of the lesioned area. Lesions may also produce changes in behavior by releasing other brain areas from facilitation or inhibition. Thus, it may be difficult to distinguish behavioral effects caused by an interruption of processing normally occurring in the damaged area from effects due to less specific alterations of function in other areas of the brain.

Possible nonspecific effects of a lesion, including mass action effects and reactions to disability or discomfort, can be excluded as major determinants of abnormal behavior by the use of "control" lesions. If lesions of comparable size in other brain areas do not produce similar behavioral effects, one cannot ascribe these effects to nonspecific causes. It is especially elegant to be able to demonstrate that such a control lesion has a different behavioral effect. This has been termed *double-dissociation*: lesion A produces behavioral change *a* but not *b*, whereas lesion B produces behavioral change *b* but not *a* (Teuber, 1955).

Once nonspecific effects have been excluded, one must take into account the various ways in which a lesion may specifically affect behavior. If a lesion in a particular region results in the loss of a behavior, one must not simply ascribe to that region the normal function of performing that behavior. The first step toward making a meaningful statement about brain–behavior relationships is a scrupulous analysis of the behavior in question. For example, if a lesion in a particular area of the brain interferes with writing, it does not mean that the area is the "writing center" of the brain. Writing is a complex process comprising several different components, each of which may be programmed by a different area of the brain. Components include sensorimotor control of the limb, programming of movements necessary for writing, intact language function, mental alertness, and so on. One must study every aspect of behavior that is directly related to the task of writing and define as closely as possible which aspects of the process of writing are disturbed. It may then be possible to make a correlation between the damaged portion of the brain and the component of the writing process that has been disrupted.

It is important to distinguish between lesions that destroy areas of the brain that store specific forms of information (representations) and lesions that disconnect such areas from one another, disrupting processes that require coordination and intercommunication between two or more such areas (Geschwind, 1965). When a person is writing, for example, coordination must exist between areas that contain representations of how words are spelled and areas important in programming the movements needed to write letters. Lesions that disconnect these areas produce agraphia, even though there may be no other language or motor deficit. A lesion in the corpus callosum, for example, may disconnect the language areas in the left hemisphere from the right hemisphere motor area, thus producing agraphia in the left hand.

Significant advances have been made in lesion localization. Until about four decades ago, the anatomic localization of a human brain injury relied primarily on postmortem examination. With the advent of computed tomography (CT) and magnetic resonance imaging (MRI), it became possible to localize brain lesions in live people. More recently, morphometric programs (Sowell et al., 2002) have enabled clinicians and investigators to define the degree and distribution of cortical atrophy in degenerative disorders, extending the localization of function to disorders not traditionally thought of as causing focal lesions. Advances have also been made in the localization of white matter tract lesions. The function of specific cortical areas is determined in part by its cytoarchitecture, but principally by its input and output—its connections. Pioneers such as Liepmann and Maas (1907) and Dejerine (1892) recognized that injury to white matter pathways that connect cortical modules can result in specific behavioral abnormalities. Geschwind's (1965) classic paper on disconnection syndromes revived interest in the syndromes described by the classical neurologists, pointing out the importance of defining the extent of white matter damage, and of understanding in detail the anatomy of brain connections. Standard CT and MR imaging allows investigators to see white matter damage, but diffusion tensor imaging (DTI) tractography can visualize intact and damaged white matter pathways (Filler, 2009).

Partial recovery of function can be attributed to factors such as resolution of edema, increase in blood supply, recovery from ischemia, and resolution of diaschisis. In addition, the brain is not a static organ. It is constantly reorganizing itself, establishing and strengthening connections, as well as pruning underutilized connections. This brain plasticity is most evident in the developing brain, but continues at a slower pace into adult years, persisting even into old age. Brain reorganization can lead to partial or complete recovery from the behavioral effects of brain injury. Therefore, failing to find a deficit in a particular behavior after a brain injury does not prove that the injured portion of the brain does not normally subserve that behavior, particular if time for recovery has elapsed. Brain plasticity especially complicates the study of behavioral disorders in the developing brain, either before or after birth.

Another difficulty in using the ablative paradigm to learn about brain organization is that natural lesions, such as strokes or tumors, do not necessarily respect functional neuroanatomical boundaries. Ischemic strokes occur within the distribution of particular vessels, and these vessels often provide blood to multiple anatomic areas. The association of two behavioral deficits may therefore result not from a functional relationship, but rather from the fact that two brain regions with little anatomical or physiological relation are supplied by the same vessel. For example, the association of a verbal episodic memory disturbance with pure word blindness (alexia without agraphia) merely indicates that the mesial temporal lobe, the occipital lobe, and the splenium of the corpus callosum are all in the distribution of the posterior cerebral artery. Experimental lesions in animals can avoid this problem; however, even within a specific anatomical region many systems may be operating, sometimes with contrasting behavioral functions.

Despite all these problems, the study of brain ablations in humans and animals has yielded more information about brain–behavior relationships than any other approach, and it has been given renewed impetus by the recent development of powerful methods of neural anatomic structural imaging. Lesions as small as 2–3 mm in diameter can be detected by modern x-ray CT. Magnetic resonance imaging scanning gives information about brain structure and blood flow, and can also provide information about metabolic activity.

BRAIN STIMULATION PARADIGMS

Brain stimulation has been used to map connections in the brain and to elicit changes in behavior. One attractive aspect of this method has been that stimulation, as opposed to ablation, is reversible. (Reversible methods of ablation, such as cooling, have also been used to study brain–behavior relationships.) The additional claim that stimulation is more physiologic is open to question: It is highly unlikely that gross electrical stimulation of the brain reproduces any normally occurring physiological state. The stimulation techniques that are usually employed cannot selectively affect only one class of neurons. Furthermore, stimulation disrupts ongoing activity, frequently inhibiting it in a way that resembles the effects of ablation.

Cortical stimulation is often used prior to ablative surgery to remove an epileptic focus or to treat brain tumors, to map the functional properties of brain regions in the operative field. If stimulation of a cortical area produces cognitive dysfunction, such as deficits in speech or memory, the surgeon will try to minimize damage to these regions.

In 1985, Anthony Barker used a magnetic coil held over the scalp to induce currents in motor cortex, resulting in activation of the region of cortex under the coil, with resulting contraction of the muscles controlled by this cortex (Barker, Jalinous, and Freeston, 1985). Subsequently, it was found that slow rates of repetitive transcranial magnetic stimulation (rTMS) inactivate underlying cortex. Repetitive transcranial magnetic stimulation has been used to mimic ablative lesions to learn about the functions of specific portions of the cerebral cortex. Repetitive transcranial magnetic stimulation has also been used to treat neurobehavioral disorders. For example, rTMS over the lateral portion of the left frontal lobe has been used to treat depressed patients who could not be successfully treated with medications, and rTMS of the left hemisphere has been used to treat neglect from right hemisphere strokes. It was posited that the ipsilesional (rightward) attentional bias seen in these patients might be caused by disinhibition of the left hemisphere, resulting from damage to the right hemisphere. Left hemisphere inactivation treatment with TMS has been reported to reduce the severity of neglect by reducing this asymmetrical hemispheric activation (Koch et al., 2008).

For the past 10 years or so, physicians have been placing indwelling electrodes in the brain and attaching stimulators for chronic deep brain stimulation to treat certain neurological and psychiatric conditions. Parkinson disease, dystonia, and tremor have been treated with electrodes placed in the globus pallidus interna, the subthalamic nucleus, and the thalamus. In many of these patients, there is a remission of motor symptoms, but stimulation of deep brain structures also has behavioral effects. Deep brain stimulation is also beginning to be used to treat people with psychiatric disorders. For example, stimulation of the ventral medial frontal lobe has been used to successfully treat depression (Mayberg, 2009), and stimulation of the nucleus accumbens/anterior limb of the internal capsule has been used to treat obsessive-compulsive disorder (Goodman et al., 2010). The cognitive effects of deep brain stimulation are also beginning to be explored.

NEUROCHEMICAL MANIPULATIONS

Neurochemical and immunological methods have identified groups of neurons in the central nervous system that use specific neurotransmitters. The number of neurotransmitters identified continues to increase, and one neuron may express more than one neurotransmitter. The anatomy of major neurotransmitter pathways has been elucidated, and the molecular mechanisms by which some neurotransmitters function is now known is some detail. Drugs given systemically or applied to specific anatomic areas may stimulate, inhibit, or block particular neurotransmitters. There are also drugs that will selective destroy neurons containing specific neurotransmitters, and genetic methods are available to produce animals that lack specific substances. Positron emission tomography (PET) studies can image specific neurotransmitters, such as dopamine, in humans. Using these and other techniques, it is possible to correlate the behavioral effects of pharmacological agents with dysfunction in anatomical areas defined by chemical criteria.

ELECTROPHYSIOLOGICAL STUDIES

The Electroencephalogram

Electrophysiological studies of human behavior have been attempted during brain surgery, and

depth electrode recording may be justified in the evaluation of a few patients (usually in preparation for epilepsy surgery), but most studies rely on the surface-recorded electroencephalogram (EEG). The raw EEG, however, demonstrates changes in amplitude and frequency that are generally nonspecific and poorly localizing. Computer analysis of EEG frequency and amplitude (power spectra) in different behavioral situations (and from different brain regions) has demonstrated correlations between EEG activity and behavior, but only for certain aspects of behavior (such as arousal) or for broad anatomical fields (e.g., between hemispheres). The use of computer averaging has increased our ability to detect electrical events that are time-locked to stimuli or responses. Thus, cortical evoked potentials to visual, auditory, and somesthetic stimuli have been recorded, as have potentials that precede muscle activation. Certain potentials appear to correlate with expectancy (the contingent negative variation and the P300 potential). That potentials can be "evoked" by purely mental events is demonstrated by the recording of potentials time-linked to the nonoccurrence of expected stimuli. Computer algorithms have been developed to trace the spatial and temporal spread of electrical activity associated with specific single events, or with ongoing behaviors, and to assess the coherence of activity from different brain regions. Changes in magnetic fields can also be measured. Although magnetoencephalography (MEG) requires much more elaborate equipment than EEG, it is less affected by intervening skull and scalp, and can detect signals generated at a greater depth. The principal advantage of these physiologic techniques is their temporal resolution, measured in milliseconds. With more powerful computer analysis, the spatial resolution of these physiological measures is improving, with MEG capable of resolving the source of an event within several millimeters to about 2 cm.

Single-unit Recording

Discrete activity of individual neurons can be recorded by inserting microelectrodes into the brain. Obviously, this is largely limited to animal experiments. Much has been learned (and remains to be learned) from the use of this technique in alert, responding animals.

Responses to well-controlled stimuli can be recorded with precision and analyzed quantitatively. Interpretation of single-unit recording presents its own difficulties. The brain activity related to a behavioral event may occur simultaneously in many cells spatially dispersed over a considerable area. Recording from only one cell may not yield a meaningful pattern, but it is now possible to record from arrays of neurons. In addition, single-unit recording may be difficult to analyze in relation to complex behaviors.

FUNCTIONAL NEUROIMAGING

In addition to the electrical and magnetic brain mapping just discussed, the most exciting development in recent years has been the advent of powerful techniques for imaging changes in brain function in the intact organism. Currently, three major forms of brain imaging are used: positron emission tomography (PET), single-photon emission computed tomography (SPECT), and functional MRI (fMRI). Each of these uses a different technique, and each has both positive and negative aspects.

Unfortunately, these three imaging techniques do not have the temporal resolution of electrophysiologic methods, which are measured in milliseconds; however, PET and especially fMRI have much better spatial resolution, and fMRI studies have temporal resolutions of close to 1 second. These three techniques will be very briefly described here (for additional information see Nadeau & Crosson, 1995; D'Esposito 2000; Mazziotta, 2000).

Single-photon emission computed tomography studies employing hexamethyl-propylene-amine-oxime (HMPAO) as the radioactive ligand indirectly measure changes in blood flow. The ligand binds to vascular endothelial membranes over a period of about 2 minutes, and has a half-life of 6 hours, so the behavioral task can be performed outside the scanner and the subject scanned afterward, a distinct advantage over fMRI studies. The spatial resolution of this technique is about 6–7 mm, and the temporal resolution, 3–4 minutes. The dose of radioactivity limits the number of studies that can be done to about three a year.

Positron emission tomography studies using very-short-half-life radiotracers (such as $H_2{}^{15}O$)

provide measures of absolute blood flow. The short half-life (about 2 minutes) allows for relatively brief behavioral trials, and the low radiation exposure enables multiple trials in one sitting. Because of its short half-life, the tracer must be manufactured close to the experiment, a very costly constraint. Also, the experiment must be performed within the scanner; however, the scanner environment is not as constrained or noisy as with fMRI (see below). Positron emission tomography blood flow studies have a temporal resolution of about 2 minutes, and a spatial resolution of from 4 to 16 mm. Because data must be acquired over more than 10 seconds, PET studies usually use blocked trials, and responses to a single event are difficult to discern.

Positron emission tomography studies using fluorodeoxyglucose (^{18}F or FDG) are a more direct measure of brain metabolic activity. FDG is taken up into the brain by the same transporters that take up glucose, but then is metabolized slowly, so that it marks areas of greater metabolic activity for several hours. As with SPECT, the task can be performed outside the scanner, so there are therefore few constraints on the type of behavior that can be studied. The uptake of FDG takes 30–40 minutes, so temporal resolution is very poor.

Functional MRI is faster than PET, and is capable of measuring activity generated by a single behavioral event, so that studies are not restricted to blocked trials. The temporal resolution is as little as 1 second. Functional MRI also has much better spatial resolution, as little as 1 mm. The need to acquire data during the task, however, places constraints on the kind of behavior that can be studied. The subject is confined in a very noisy MRI machine, and movement, speech, and electromagnetic signals can seriously interfere with the quality of the image.

Functional imaging studies of cerebral blood flow assume that a local change in blood flow (that results in a change in measured signal) is related to changes in synaptic activity, and changes in synaptic activity are responsible for specific changes in behavior. Even in the absence of stimuli, the brain is active. Thus, to determine how a behavior influences brain activity, one must subtract irrelevant background signals. Because resting activity is uncontrolled, investigators often use control tasks that resemble the study task in all but a single variable, which then becomes the behavior that is studied.

There are many methodological and theoretic problems with fMRI. At the most fundamental level, the exact means by which the fMRI signal is generated is not entirely understood. The blood oxygen level dependent (BOLD) method used in fMRI studies assumes that blood oxygen levels, reflected by the ratio of oxyhemoglobin to deoxyhemoglobin, are related to synaptic activity in the brain. Synaptic activity uses energy, which consumes oxygen and increases the relative concentration of deoxyhemoglobin to oxyhemoglobin; but within a couple of seconds, a reactive increase in blood flow overcompensates, and the proportion of oxyhemoglobin actually increases over baseline. It is very difficult to detect the initial dip in oxygen levels, and the BOLD technique has relied upon the reactive increase in blood flow and oxyhemoglobin levels.

Single-photon emission computed tomography, PET, and fMRI have all demonstrated reproducible blood flow changes in primary sensory areas in response to stimuli of the appropriate modality. These responses are an order of magnitude larger than behavior-related blood flow changes in association cortex, especially in polymodal and supramodal cortex. One reason is that primary sensory cortex is relatively quiet in the absence of the appropriate sensory stimulus, whereas supramodal cortex is not so dependent upon external stimulation. Therefore, when the control activity is subtracted from the task-related activity, much more of the signal is lost in high-order cortex than in primary sensory cortex. Interpretation of observed changes may be problematic. It is usual to expect that an area that mediates a behavior will become more active and will have greater blood flow with that behavior; however, it is possible that a change in pattern of activity could mediate a behavior without an increase, or perhaps even with an overall decrease, in activity. It has been reasoned that a brain region that is adept at a behavior will be less activated than when involved in a behavior at which it is less adept. If this is true, almost any functional imaging result can have two opposite interpretations: Focal increased activation during an experimental task versus a control task might be interpreted as evidence that the activated region is critical to performance of this task, or it may be interpreted as demonstrating that this region of the brain is not accustomed to performing this activity. In addition, many neurons in the cerebral cortex are inhibitory. During a specific behavior, areas of the brain that might interfere with implementing this behavior must be inhibited. Thus, functional imaging might not be able to distinguish whether the observed changes are related to the neuronal assemblies that are mediating the behavior or to the neurons that are inhibiting other neuronal assemblies. Based on these dichotomies, the interpretation of functional images is often problematic and must be confirmed by convergent evidence using other techniques, such as ablation-lesion studies.

Although in behavioral studies resting activity typically is subtracted from activity during the task, resting patterns of activity have been studied in normal and in disease states, defining a so-called "default mode" of activity, in which certain areas are relatively more active than other brain areas during rest with eyes closed (Raichle et al., 2001). The significance of various default networks and their relationship to states of consciousness and disease states is currently an active area for research (Boly et al., 2008).

COMPUTATIONAL MODELS

Donald Hebb (1949) stated that, "Neurons that fire together wire together," meaning that the strength of connections between neurons is governed by their firing patterns. This idea has led to the attempt to model brain function in terms of computer function. The typical, serially organized computer has not fared well as a model for brain function, but computers that use multiple parallel processors arranged in a network (parallel distributed processors, or PDP networks) have interesting brain-like properties. These include the ability, without further programming, to "learn" associations between coincident stimuli, to behave as if "rules" are learned despite being exposed only to data, and to continue to function in the face of damage to a portion of the network ("graceful degradation")

(Rumelhart & McClelland, 1986). Properties of PDP networks are now often invoked to help explain the nature of neuropsychological deficits occasioned by brain injury, such as interlanguage differences in error rates in patients with aphasia.

Although the brain is highly interconnected, it does not function as a single network, but rather as a collection of many overlapping and interconnecting "modular" networks, each having a specific function. The function of a module depends upon its connections. One can therefore see that network theory can easily be reconciled with the traditional methods of localization of brain function discussed above.

ANIMAL VERSUS HUMAN EXPERIMENTATION

The study of brain–behavior relationships has long relied on experimental research using animals, which allowed investigators to use techniques such as precise anatomic ablations, histological mapping of brain connections, and physiological recordings of behaving subjects that are either not applicable to humans or can be applied only with great difficulty. Despite major differences in anatomy between even the subhuman primates and humans (Figure 1-2), much of this basic research is of direct relevance to human neurobiology. Behavioral studies in animals have yielded a great deal of information, but the applicability of this information to the study of complex human behavior is not always clear. In 1950, nothing in the literature on temporal lobe lesions in animals would have led to the prediction that bilateral temporal lobectomy in humans would result in permanent impairment of episodic memory. Even after the association of medial temporal lobe damage in humans with amnesia had been well established, it took 20 years to develop new testing paradigms that could demonstrate episodic memory impairments in animals with bitemporal ablations (Mishkin, 1978). Conversely, the applicability of behavioral deficits in animals (and especially in nonhuman primates) to syndromes in

humans has also recently been systematically investigated, and some parallels are discernible (Oscar-Berman et al., 1982). Studies of the limbic system and hypothalamus in animals have contributed important information about the relevance of these structures to emotional behavior; however, the emotional content of behavior is difficult to study in animals that cannot report how they feel. Most obviously, animals cannot be used to study behavior that is uniquely human, such as language. Studies of nonlinguistic communication in animals may relate to some aspects of speech in humans, but they do not elucidate the neural mechanisms underlying language. Studies of linguistic behavior in nonhuman primates are controversial, and their relevance to the study of language in humans remains unclear.

CONCEPTUAL ANALYSIS

Many believe that science proceeds by way of careful observation, followed by analysis, which leads to the formation of hypotheses on the basis of the observed data (a posteriori hypothesis). In fact, meaningful observations frequently cannot be made without some sort of a priori hypothesis. How else can one decide which observations to make? An observation can be significant only in terms of a conceptual framework.

Some investigators are loathe to put either a priori or a posteriori hypotheses in print, feeling that they are too tentative. Often encouraged by journal reviewers and editors, they report observations with a minimum of interpretation. This may be unfortunate because tentative hypotheses are the seeds of further observations and hypotheses. Other investigators speculate extensively on the basis of only a few observations. These speculations may lead to clearly stated hypotheses that generate further observations, but there is a risk that observations may be honestly and inadvertently distorted to fit the hypotheses. For example, investigators always discard "irrelevant" information either intentionally or not; however, an investigator with an alternative hypothesis may

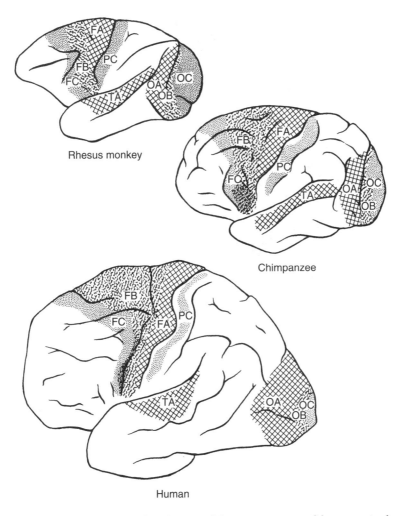

Rhesus monkey

Chimpanzee

Human

Figure 1–2. The primary motor (FA) and visual (OC) areas and the association areas of the motor, visual, somatosensory (PC), and auditory (TA) systems are compared in these lateral views of the hemispheres of the monkey, chimpanzee, and human. Note the expansion of the unshaded areas of cortex, particularly in the frontal lobe and in the area between TA and OA, as one progresses from monkey to human. The latter area is important for language development (see Chapter 2). The significance of the frontal lobes is discussed in Chapter 14.

find observations presumed irrelevant by others to be of critical importance. All hypotheses should be treated as though they were tentative so that, as Head (1926) warned, we do not invite observations to sleep in the Procrustean bed of our hypotheses.

We are still far from fully understanding brain–behavior relationships, and when providing hypotheses and explanations, the use of metaphorical strategies is frequently required. Metaphor is not to be taken literally. Diagrams,

for example, may be used in a metaphorical way to present hypothetical systems. The diagrams found in this book are offered in this spirit: They are meant to be not pictures of the brain but metaphorical representations of hypothetical modular systems.

Similarly, when we speak of the function of specific areas of the brain, it often appears that we assume that the area under discussion operates entirely independently from other modular systems in different areas of the brain. Clearly, this is not true; however, we do often ignore interactions between brain regions in order to discuss the distinguishing features of specific areas.

Overall, we support a flexible approach to the study of brain–behavior relationships. We know too little about the subject to limit our methods of investigation. We must be prepared to analyze data from many sources, make new hypotheses, and test them with the best methods available. Similarly, behavioral testing and methods of treatment must be tailored to the individual situation. Inflexible test batteries, although necessary for obtaining normative data, limit our view of the nervous system if used exclusively. Rigid formulations of therapy similarly limit progress. Changes in testing and therapy, however, should be made not capriciously but rather according to our current understanding of brain–behavior relationships. In this book, therefore, we do not emphasize standardized test batteries; instead, we present the existing knowledge on brain–behavior relationships, which should form the basis of diagnosis and treatment.

ANATOMY BASICS

This text contains many references to neuroanatomic terms, some of which may not be familiar to the reader. The following very brief synopsis may help the reader to understand some of the commonly used anatomic terms. More detailed information is available in texts of neuroanatomy, such as that by Nieuwenhuys, Voogd, and van Huijzen (2008).

The brain is protected by the skull and meningeal membranes. The tentorium cerebelli, a dural membrane structure overlying the cerebellum, divides the skull cavity into the posterior fossa (below the tentorium) and the anterior fossa (above the tentorium). The cerebellum and brainstem (medulla, pons, and midbrain) are in the posterior fossa (see Figure 1-3). The anterior fossa contains the thalamus and hypothalamus, basal ganglia, and the cerebral hemispheres—the cerebral cortex, which contains the cell bodies of nerve cells (neurons), and underlying white matter, which is made up of long neuronal processes (axons) that

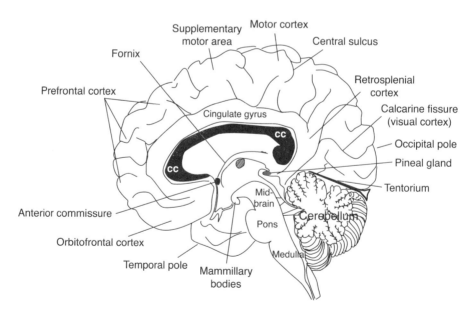

Figure 1–3. Mid-sagittal view of the brain. The brainstem comprises the medulla, pons, and midbrain, and, together with the cerebellum, occupies the posterior fossa within the skull (not shown) beneath the tentorium. The approximate location of important hemispheric landmarks is indicated. CC, corpus callosum.

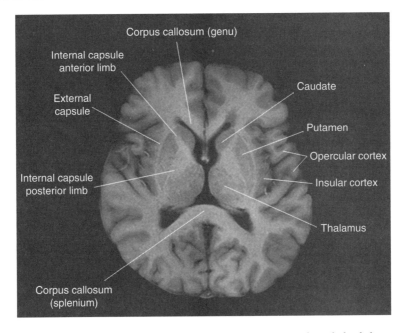

Figure 1–4. Magnetic resonance imaging of the cerebral hemispheres, axial section through the thalamus and basal ganglia. Principal gray matter (nuclear) structures are indicated on the right side of the diagram; white matter structures are indicated by labels on the left side of the diagram. In T1-weighted images, cerebral cortex and other nuclear structures appear darker than white matter structures. The dark ribbon of cerebral cortex is easily distinguished. The portions of frontal and parietal lobes that fold over the insular cortex are called frontal and parietal opercula.

connect gray matter structures. The right and left cerebral hemispheres are connected by the cerebral commissures, the largest of which is the corpus callosum. Neurons are also found in subcortical nuclei, as seen in Figure 1-4. They include the caudate and putamen (together referred to as the striatum), the thalamus, and white matter (connecting) structures including the internal and external capsules and the corpus callosum.

The phylogenetically oldest regions of the cerebral cortex form a ring or *limbus* around the brainstem and diencephalon (which includes the striatum, thalamus, and hypothalamus), and were designated as the *grand lobe limbique* by Paul Broca (see Figure 1-5). These regions, which include the hippocampal cortex, the cingulate and retrosplenial cortex, the orbitofrontal cortex, and the anterior insular cortex, have prominent connections with the hypothalamus, which controls endocrine and autonomic functions related to our internal milieu. Functionally, they are related to autonomic and

emotional behavior, and also, somewhat less intuitively, to memory (see Chapters 15 and 16). The cortex of some limbic structures, such as the hippocampus, has fewer layers than adjacent six-layered neocortex.

Each hemisphere is divided into four lobes: frontal, parietal, temporal, and occipital (Figure 1-6). The frontal lobe is separated from the parietal lobe by the *central sulcus*. Fuster suggests that the anterior–posterior division of the cerebral hemispheres by the central sulcus is analogous to the division of the neural tube (and spinal cord) into posterior (dorsal) and anterior (ventral) halves, such that, in each case, sensory input is to the posterior (dorsal) divisions, and motor output is from the anterior (ventral) divisions. Thus, visual, auditory, and somatosensory input to the cerebral cortex is to primary areas in the occipital, temporal, and parietal lobes, respectively; whereas the primary motor cortex is in the frontal lobe (see Figure 1-7). Primary cortices are surrounded by first-order association cortices that

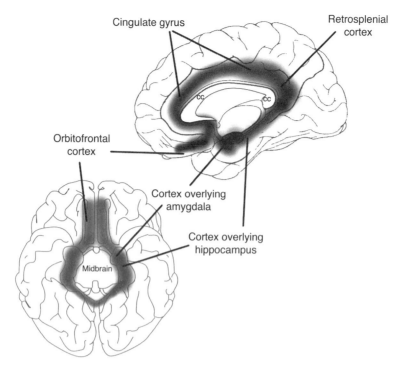

Figure 1–5. Medial and inferior views of the brain with Broca's *grand lobe limbique* shaded. Notice how limbic structures form a ring (or limbus) around the midbrain (on the inferior view below) and the diencephalon (on the medial view above).

process information in the same modality, and these are, in turn, connected to higher-order association cortices. In humans, the most extensive sensory cortical networks subserve vision, with the primary visual cortex (Brodmann's area 17) on the banks of the calcarine fissure in the occipital lobe and many visual association areas occupying adjacent regions in the occipital lobe. Visual association cortex spills over into parietal lobe (for visual spatial functions) and into inferior temporal lobes (for object identification functions), the so-called "where" and "what" pathways (Figure 1-7) (Ungerleider & Mishkin, 1982). Somatosensory and auditory association areas are less extensive, and are principally in parietal and temporal lobes, respectively. Primary association cortices project to multi-modal cortical areas, enabling the association of multiple modalities, and supramodal cortices, another level removed from primary sensory cortex. In the frontal lobes, analogously, the primary motor cortex (Brodmann's area 4) is in the anterior bank of the central sulcus, and

primary motor association cortex, or premotor cortex (Brodmann's area 6, Figures 1-1 and 1-6), is just anterior to primary motor cortex. Broca's area, in the frontal operculum, may be considered a premotor cortex specialized for language production. The supplementary motor area is a premotor region on the medial wall of the hemisphere (also Brodmann's area 6, Figures 1-1 and 1-3) with higher-order motor functions, and is the principal origin of motor projections to the putamen. The cortex anterior to premotor cortex is designated prefrontal cortex. Stimulation of prefrontal cortex, as opposed to stimulation of motor and premotor cortex, does not elicit movement, but prefrontal cortex may be considered, in part, a region of the brain that determines when specific motor plans should be enacted (see Chapter 14). The frontal lobes are dependent upon input from posterior neocortical and limbic regions, and diseases that result in extensive damage to these subcortical pathways manifest with dementias of the frontal type (see Chapter 17).

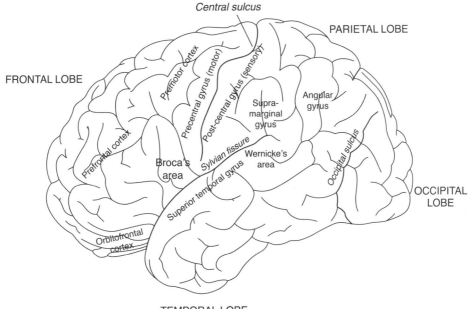

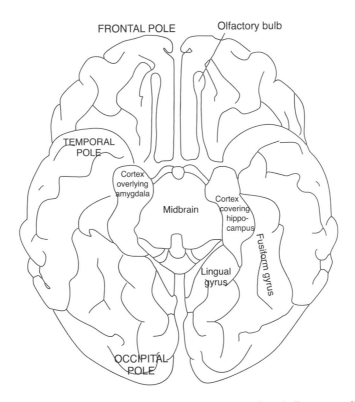

Figure 1–6. Lateral and inferior views of the cerebral hemisphere (brainstem and cerebellum removed). The central sulcus divides the frontal from the parietal lobe; the Sylvian fissure forms the upper border of the temporal lobes. The division between parietal and posterior temporal and occipital lobes is more arbitrary, but the occipital sulcus forms the anterior border of the occipital lobes on the lateral surface. Major landmarks are indicated.

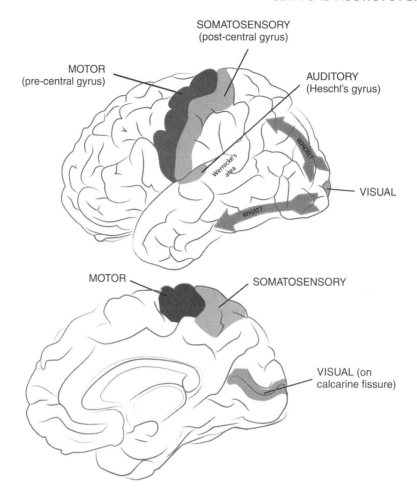

Figure 1–7. Primary cortical motor and sensory areas are indicated on lateral and medial views of the cerebral hemisphere. Primary auditory area (Heschl's gyrus) is on the superior surface of the superior temporal gyrus, buried in the Sylvian fissure: although indicated by a small area of shading on the lateral (upper) view, it is not visible unless the Sylvian fissure is pried open. Similarly, the areas indicated for motor, sensory, and visual cortex do not depict large areas of cortex in the depths of the sulci.

REFERENCES

Barker, A. T., Jalinous, R., & Freeston, I. L. (May 1985). Non-invasive magnetic stimulation of human motor cortex. *The Lancet, 1*(8437), 1106–1107.

Bastian, H. C. (1869). On the various forms of loss of speech in cerebral disease. *British Foreign Medico-Surgical Review, 43,* 470–492.

Boly, M., Phillips, C., Tshibanda, L., Vanhaudenhuyse, A., Schabus, M., Dang-Vu, T. T., et al. (2008). Intrinsic brain activity in altered states of consciousness: How conscious is the default mode of brain function? *Annals of the New York Academy of Science, 1129,* 119–129.

Bouillaud, J. B. (1825). Récherches cliniques propres a démontrer que la perte de la parole correspond à la lésion de lobules anterieurs du cerveau, et à confirmer l'opinion de M. Gall sur le siege de l'organe du langage articulé. *Archives of General Medicine, 8,* 25–45.

Broca, P. (1865). Sur la faculté du langage articulé. *Bulletin Societe Anthropologie Paris, 6,* 337–393.

Brodmann, K. (1909). *Vergleichende Lokalisationslehre der Grosshirnrinde in ihren Prinzipien dargestellt auf Grund des Zellenbaues.* Leipzig: Johann Ambrosius Barth Verlag.

Caramazza, A. (1992). Is cognitive neuropsychology possible? *Journal of Cognitive Neuroscience, 4:* 80–95.

Chomsky, N. (1967). The general properties of language. In C. H. Millikan & F. L. Darley (Eds.), *Brain mechanisms underlying speech and language*. New York: Grune and Stratton.

Dejerine, J. (1892). Contribution a l'etude anatomopathologique et clinique des differentes varietes de cecite verbale. *Compte rendu des seances de la societe de biologie 4*, 61–90.

D'Esposito, M. (2000). Functional neuroimaging in cognition. *Seminars in Neurology, 20*, 487–498.

Filler, A. (2009). Magnetic resonance neurography and diffusion tensor imaging: Origins, history, and clinical impact of the first 50,000 cases with an assessment of efficacy and utility in a prospective 5000-patient study group. *Neurosurgery, 65*(4 Suppl), 29–43.

Geschwind, N. (1965). Disconnexion syndrome in animals and men. I and II. *Brain, 88*, 237–294, 585–644.

Goodman, W. K., Greenberg, B. D., Ricciuti, N., Bauer, R., Ward, H., Shapira, N. A., et al. (2010). Deep brain stimulation for intractable obsessive compulsive disorder: Pilot study using a blinded, staggered-onset design. *Biological Psychiatry, 67*, 535–542.

Head, H. (1926). *Aphasia and kindred disorders of speech*. Cambridge: Cambridge University Press.

Hebb, D.O. (1949). *The organization of behavior*. New York: Wiley.

Koch, G., Oliveri, M., Cheeran, B., Ruge, D., Lo Gerfo, E., Salerno, S., et al. (2008). Hyperexcitability of parietal-motor functional connections in the intact left-hemisphere of patients with neglect. *Brain, 131*, 3147–3155.

Lashley, K. S. (1938). Factors limiting recovery after central nervous lesions. *Journal of Nervous and Mental Disorders, 888*, 733–755.

Lichtheim, L. (1885). On aphasia. *Brain, 7*, 433–484.

Liepmann, H., & Mass, O. (1907). Fall von linksseitiger Agraphie und Apraxie bei rechsseitiger Lahmung. *Z. Psychol. Neurol., 10*, 214227.

Mayberg, H. S. (2009). Targeted electrode-based modulation of neural circuits for depression. *Journal of Clinical Investigation, 119*, 717–725.

Mazziotta, J. C. (2000). Imaging: Window on the brain. *Archives of Neurology, 57*, 1413–1421.

Mishkin, M. (1978). Memory in monkeys severely impaired by combined but not by separate removal of amygdala and hippocampus. *Nature, 273*, 297–298.

Nadeau, S. E., & Crosson, B. (1995). A guide to the functional imaging of cognitive processes. *Neuropsychiatry, Neuropsychology, and Behavioral Neurology, 8*, 143–162.

Nieuwenhuys, R., Voogd, J., & van Huijzen C. (2008). *The human central nervous system*. Berlin: Springer-Verlag.

Oscar-Berman, M., Zola-Morgan, S. M., Oberg, R. G. E., & Bonner, R. T. (1982). Comparative neuropsychology and Korsakoff's syndrome. III: Delayed response, delayed alternation and DRL performance. *Neuropsychologia, 20*, 187–202.

Raichle, M. E., MacLoed, A. M., Snyder, A. Z., Powers, W. J., Gusnard, D. A., & Shulman, G. L. (2001). A default mode of brain function. *Proceedings of the National Academy of Science, U.S.A., 98*, 626–682.

Rumelhart, D. E., McClelland, J. L., & the PDP Research Group (1986). *Parallel distributed processing. Explorations in the microstructure of cognition*. Cambridge, MA: MIT Press.

Sowell, E. R., Thompson, P. M., Rex, D., Kornsand, D., Tessner, K. D., Jernigan, T. L., & Toga, A. W. (2002). Mapping sulcal pattern asymmetry and local cortical surface gray matter distribution in vivo: maturation in perisylvian cortices. *Cerebral Cortex, 12*, 17–26.

Teuber, H. L. (1955). Physiological psychology. *Annual Review of Psychology, 6*, 267–296.

Ungerleider, L. G., & Mishkin, M. (1982). Two cortical visual systems. In D. J. Ingle, M. A. Goodale, & R. J. W. Mansfield (Eds.), *Analysis of visual behavior*, pp. 594–586. Cambridge, MA: MIT Press.

Wernicke, C. (1874). *Des Aphasische Symptomenkomplex*. Breslau: Cohn and Weigart.

2

Aphasic Syndromes

DAVID CAPLAN

Webster's Dictionary defines *syndrome* as "a number of symptoms occurring together and characterizing a particular disease." This definition indicates that a syndrome ties a number of phenomena together. The simplest way for symptoms to be tied together is for them to co-occur (the first feature of a syndrome in Webster's definition). The second feature—that symptoms that co-occur constitute a disease—is more a complex matter. The notion of a disease suggests a common pathogenesis and/or etiology, and/or natural history, and/or response to intervention. Of these features of diseases, some, such as a common natural history and response to intervention, are similar to co-occurrence of symptoms in that they may be simply facts that are observed about symptoms. Others—a common pathogenesis or etiology—require a deeper understanding of a disease, which can only be discovered by studying the mechanisms whereby the disease exerts its effects. From this perspective, calling a set of symptoms a syndrome may be thought of as a step toward understanding pathogenesis and etiology.

Webster's definition, useful as it is, begs a number of important questions. What, exactly, constitutes a symptom? What about the pattern of co-occurrence of symptoms? Polydipsia and polyuria are fairly common—but far from universal—presenting symptoms of diabetes. Neuropathy, retinopathy, nephropathy, and vasculopathy are the major long-term sequelae of diabetes, but they do not all co-occur in any one patient, and many patients with diabetes do not have clinically detectable manifestations of these conditions at all. Conversely, symptoms that occur in a syndrome, or as a manifestation of a disease, very frequently occur in other syndromes and diseases. Reports of cold intolerance, a classic symptom of hypothyroidism, are fairly common; pericardial effusion occurs much more frequently outside of hypothyroidism than as part of the disease. It is not easy to see the pattern of co-occurrence of these symptoms, let alone to relate the symptoms to the disease mechanistically. In some cases, syndromes are only recognized as pathogenesis and etiology are uncovered. Postinfectious and paraneoplastic autoimmune disorders, such as rheumatic fever and Sydenham's chorea following streptococcal pharyngitis, or limbic encephalitis and cerebellar degeneration following lung cancer, are examples of sets of symptoms whose relations to one another emerged only after their etiology was understood.

These observations illustrate the importance of the mechanistic links between symptoms in determining the presence of a syndrome.

Both symptoms and syndromes are linked to taxonomic frameworks in which phenomena are related to one another. As understanding of a set of phenomena increases, the taxonomies to which symptoms and syndromes are related are increasingly determined by the mechanisms that produce and relate the symptoms. Syndromes become more informative, and more valuable scientifically and clinically, as they can be related to more principled taxonomies.

Turning to aphasic syndromes with these considerations in mind, the challenge for neurologists, psychologists, and speech-language pathologists is to determine what aphasic symptoms are, what their co-occurrence patterns are, and to develop explanations for their occurrence and co-occurrence. In this chapter, I briefly review approaches to these questions, and outline questions and challenges that remain.

CLASSICAL CLINICAL
APHASIC SYNDROMES

Aphasic syndromes were first described over 150 years ago (Broca, 1861; Wernicke, 1874, Lichtheim, 1885). The approach to aphasia developed during this period continues to influence the field in two ways: the aphasic disorders identified at that time, which have been called syndromes, are still commonly referred to in both clinical and research work; and the principles enunciated in the early research remain basic to aphasiology. It is therefore appropriate and useful to begin a consideration of aphasic syndromes with those papers.

Broca (1861) described a patient, Leborgne, with a severe speech output disturbance. Leborgne's speech was limited to the monosyllable "tan." In contrast, Broca described as normal Leborgne's ability to understand spoken language, express himself through gestures and facial expressions, and understand nonverbal communication. Broca claimed that Leborgne had lost "the faculty of articulate speech." Broca related this impairment to damaged neural tissue; Leborgne's brain contained a lesion whose center was in the posterior portion of the inferior frontal convolution of the left

hemisphere. The lesion extended posteriorly into the parietal lobe. Broca related the most severe part of the lesion to the expressive language impairment. This area became known as "Broca's area." Broca argued that this was the neural site of the mechanism involved in speech production.

In 1874, Wernicke described a patient with a speech disturbance that was very different from that seen in Leborgne. Wernicke's patient was fluent, but her speech contained words with sound errors, other errors of word forms, and words that were semantically inappropriate. Also unlike Leborgne, Wernicke's patient did not understand spoken language. Wernicke related the two impairments—the one of speech production and the one of comprehension—by arguing that the patient had sustained damage to "the storehouse of auditory word forms." Under these conditions, speech would be expected to contain the types of errors that were seen in this case, and comprehension would be affected. Establishing the location of the lesion in this case was more problematic. Wernicke did not have the opportunity to perform an autopsy on his case. However, he did examine the brain of a second patient whose language had been described prior to her death by her physician in terms that made Wernicke think that she had had a set of symptoms that were the same as those he had seen in his case. The lesion in this second patient occupied the posterior portion of the first temporal gyrus, also on the left. Wernicke suggested that this region, which came to be known as "Wernicke's area," was the locus of the "storehouse of auditory word forms."

Wernicke's paper was the first to describe an *aphasic syndrome*, in the sense of a constellation of symptoms. He had found two deficits—fluent paraphasic speech and poor auditory comprehension—and he related them both to a single functional abnormality: abnormal representations of the sound patterns of words. He further related this abnormality to the location of the lesion he thought produced this deficit. The lesion he thought was responsible for the deficit was in the area of the brain adjacent to the primary auditory cortex (Heschl's gyrus). Basing his ideas on those of his teacher, Meynert, Wernicke argued that a lesion in this location would affect the long-term storage of the sounds of words because the areas of cortex just adjacent to the primary auditory cortex supported higher-order auditory processing, including processing of auditory input as language. Wernicke pointed out that the syndrome he had described was the direct perceptual counterpart to the syndrome that Broca had described, in which a lesion adjacent to the motor cortex produced an impairment of motor speech.

Broca and Wernicke thus enunciated three fundamental principles that underlie the classical aphasic syndromes:

- Language processors are localized (Broca, 1861).
- Diverse language symptoms can be due to an underlying deficit in a single language processor (Wernicke, 1874).
- Language processors are localized in brain regions because of the relationship of the processor to sensory or motor functions (Wernicke, 1874).

A decade later, Lichtheim (1885) applied these principles to a wider range of symptoms. Lichtheim recognized seven syndromes affecting spoken language:

- *Broca's aphasia*, a severe expressive language disturbance reducing the fluency of speech in all tasks (repetition and reading, as well as speaking) and affecting elements of language, such as grammatical words and morphological endings, without an equally severe disturbance of auditory comprehension
- *Wernicke's aphasia*, the combination of fluent speech with erroneous choices of the sounds of words (phonemic paraphasias) and an auditory comprehension disturbance
- *Pure motor speech disorders*—anarthria, dysarthria, and apraxia of speech—output speech disorders due to motor disorders, in which speech is misarticulated but comprehension is preserved
- *Pure word deafness*, a disorder in which the patient does not recognize

spoken words, but spontaneous speech is normal
- *Transcortical motor aphasia*, in which spontaneous speech is reduced but repetition is intact
- *Transcortical sensory aphasia*, in which a comprehension disturbance exists without a disturbance of repetition
- *Conduction aphasia*, a disturbance in spontaneous speech and repetition consisting of fluent paraphasic speech, without a disturbance in auditory comprehension

These syndromes are listed in Table 2-1.

Lichtheim argued that these syndromes followed lesions in those regions of the brain depicted in schematic form on a diagram he published in his paper, reproduced here as Figure 2-1. To understand Lichtheim's view of the relation of lesion locations to the syndromes, we need to note that Lichtheim made the assumption that the meaning of words resided in the superior portion of the parietal lobe (indicated "C," for "concepts," in Figure 2-1), and that he assumed that, in speech production, word meanings activated both word sounds in Wernicke's area and the motor speech planning mechanism in Broca's area; hence, the two arrows originating in the *concept center*, C, in Figure 2-1.

With this background, the relationship of the seven syndromes to lesion sites is quite straightforward. Broca's aphasia, which affects expressive language alone, is due to lesions in Broca's area, the center for motor speech planning adjacent to the motor strip. Wernicke's aphasia follows lesions in Wernicke's area that disturb the representations of word sounds, as we have seen. Pure motor speech disorders arise from lesions interrupting the motor pathways from the cortex to the brainstem nuclei that control the articulatory system. These disorders differ from Broca's aphasic because they are not linguistic; they affect articulation itself, not the planning of speech. Pure word deafness affects the transmission of sound input into Wernicke's area. It therefore disrupts word recognition but not speech, since words themselves are intact and accessible for speech production purposes. Transcortical

Table 2–1. Aphasic Syndromes Described by Lichtheim (1885)

Syndrome	Clinical Manifestations	Hypothetical Deficit	Classical Lesion Location
Broca's aphasia	Major disturbance in speech production with sparse, halting speech, often misarticulated, frequently missing function words and bound morphemes	Disturbances in the speech planning and production mechanisms	Posterior aspects of the 3rd frontal convolution (Broca's area)
Wernicke's aphasia	Major disturbance in auditory comprehension; fluent speech with disturbances of the sounds and structures of words (phonemic, morphological, and semantic paraphasias); poor repetition and naming	Disturbances of the permanent representations of the sound structures of words	Posterior half of the first temporal gyrus and possibly adjacent cortex (Wernicke's area)
Pure motor speech disorder	Disturbance of articulation, apraxia of speech, dysarthria, anarthria, aphemia	Disturbance of articulatory mechanisms	Outflow tracts from motor cortex
Pure word deafness	Disturbance of spoken word comprehension; repetition often impaired	Failure to access spoken words	Input tracts from auditory system to Wernicke's area
Transcortical motor aphasia	Disturbance of spontaneous speech similar to Broca's aphasia with relatively preserved repetition; comprehension relatively preserved	Disconnection between conceptual representations of words and sentences and the motor speech production system	White matter tracts deep to Broca's area connecting it to parietal lobe
Transcortical sensory aphasia	Disturbance in single word comprehension with relatively intact repetition	Disturbance in activation of word meanings despite normal recognition of auditorily presented words	White matter tracts connecting parietal lobe to temporal lobe or portions of inferior parietal lobe
Conduction aphasia	Disturbance of repetition and spontaneous speech (phonemic paraphasias)	Disconnection between the sound patterns of words and the speech production mechanism.	Lesion in the arcuate fasciculus and/or cortico-cortical connections between Wernicke's and Broca's areas

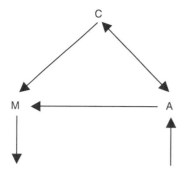

Figure 2–1. The classical Connectionist model (from Lichtheim, 1885). *A* represents the auditory center for the long-term storage of word sounds. *M* represents the motor center for speech planning. *C* represents the concept center. Information flow is indicated by arrows.

motor aphasia results from the interruption of the pathway from the concept center to Broca's area. This affects speech, but not repetition or comprehension. Transcortical sensory aphasia follows lesions between Wernicke's area and the concept center. Repetition of words is intact, but comprehension is affected. Finally, conduction aphasia follows from a lesion between Wernicke's area and Broca's area. Repetition is affected, but comprehension is intact. Speech is also affected, in the same way as it is affected in Wernicke's aphasia, because the sound patterns of words, although activated, are not transmitted properly to Broca's area to be used to plan speech.

The recognition of these syndromes has endured. Benson and Geschwind (1971)

concluded that all researchers recognized the same basic patterns of aphasic impairments, despite using different nomenclature. Along with anomia, global aphasia, and isolation of the speech area, which are directly related to Lichtheim's model (Benson, 1979: see Table 2-2), these syndromes constitute the standard set of aphasic syndromes in clinical use today (Mesulam, 1990, 1998; Damasio, 1992). The anatomical basis for the syndromes Lichtheim described also remains widely accepted in clinical circles, with some modifications. The most important of these is that Geschwind (1965) supplemented the model in Figure 2-1 with the hypothesis that Lichtheim's concept center was located in the inferior parietal lobe. Geschwind argued that the inferior parietal lobe was a tertiary association cortical area that received projections from the association cortex immediately adjacent to the primary visual, auditory, and somesthetic cortices in the occipital, temporal, and parietal lobes. Because of these anatomical connections, the inferior parietal lobe served as a cross-modal association region, associating word sounds with the sensory qualities of objects. This underlay word meaning, in Geschwind's view. Geschwind (1965) and Damasio and Damasio (1980) also specified that the anatomical link between Wernicke's and Broca's areas (in which a lesion caused conduction aphasia) was the white matter tract known as the *arcuate fasciculus*. These extensions and clarifications of Lichtheim's model are shown in Figure 2-2.

Table 2–2. Additional Classical Aphasic Syndromes

Syndrome	Clinical Manifestations	Hypothetical Deficit	Classical Lesion Location
Anomic aphasia	Disturbance in the production of single words, most marked for common nouns. Intact comprehension and repetition	Disturbances of concepts and/or the sound patterns of words	Inferior parietal lobe or connections between parietal lobe and temporal lobe; can follow many lesions
Global aphasia	Major disturbance in all language functions	Disruption of all language processing components	Large portion of the perisylvian association cortex
Isolation of the language zone	Disturbance of both spontaneous speech (sparse, halting speech) and comprehension, with some preservation of repetition; echolalia common	Disconnection between concepts and both representations of word sounds and the speech production mechanism	Cortex just outside the perisylvian association cortex

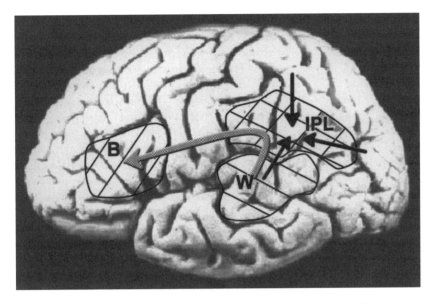

Figure 2–2. The version of the classical model developed by Geschwind (1982). The major addition is that the concept center is eliminated and the inferior parietal lobe is identified as the locus of associations between word forms and sensory properties.

AN ASSESSMENT OF THE CLASSICAL SYNDROMES

As noted above, to assess these syndromes, we must consider how they describe aphasic symptoms, how the symptoms they identify are grouped, and the basis for any such grouping.

With respect to the first of these topics, the classic syndromes have identified the domain of symptoms that form the basis for syndromes. These consist, first and foremost, of the relative preservation of patients' performances in the usual tasks of language use (speaking, understanding spoken language, reading, and writing). Although this might seem like an obvious set of phenomena upon which to base descriptions of aphasia, this focus contrasts with other approaches to the description of aphasia. Jackson, Head, Goldstein, and other pioneers in aphasiology concentrated on the conditions under which language is used. In a famous paper, Hughlings Jackson described a patient, a carpenter, who was mute, but who mustered up the capacity to say "Master's" in response to his son's question about where his tools were. Jackson's poignant comments convey his emphasis on the conditions that

provoke speech, rather than on the form of the speech itself:

The father had left work; would never return to it; was away from home; his son was on a visit, and the question was directly put to the patient. Anyone who saw the abject poverty the poor man's family lived in would admit that these tools were of immense value to them. Hence we have to consider as regards this and other occasional utterances the strength of the accompanying emotional state.

(Jackson, 1878, p. 181)

Goldstein (1948) was concerned about whether patients—both those with and those without aphasia—were capable of abstracting away from the immediacy of a situation to consider longer-term goals, a capacity he called the ability to assume "the abstract attitude."

Both Jackson and Goldstein sought a description of language use as a function of motivational and intellectual states, and tried to describe aphasic disturbances of language in relationship to the factors that drive language production and make for depth of comprehension. This is surely a vital aspect of understanding language impairments. In many ways, it is more humanly relevant than a description of language impairments in terms of which phonemes are produced in spontaneous speech or repetition. Unfortunately, it is a very intractable goal. Wernicke, Lichtheim, Geschwind, and those researchers who conceived and developed the framework of the classical syndromes focused aphasiology on everyday language use, abstracting away from such considerations. To date, this has proven a wise choice.

Second, the description of symptoms in classical aphasic syndromes includes linguistic and psycholinguistic descriptions of language. For instance, Benson and Geschwind (1971) describe Broca's aphasia as follows:

The language output of Broca's aphasia can be described as nonfluent. It is sparse, dysprosodic, and poorly articulated; it is made up of very short phrases and it is produced with effort, particularly in initiation of speech. The output consists primarily of substantive words, i.e., nouns, action verbs, or significant modifiers. The pattern of short phrases lacking prepositions is often termed "telegraphic speech" . . . Comprehension of spoken language is much better than speech but varies, being completely normal in some cases and moderately disturbed in others. (p. 7)

These linguistic and psycholinguistic features are important, because characterizing speech as abnormal is not sufficient to discriminate one classic syndrome from another; as we have seen, speech is abnormal in both Broca's and Wernicke's aphasia, but in different ways. Moreover, given that aphasia is a disturbance of language and its processing, it is obviously desirable to include descriptions of affected language elements and psycholinguistic operations in the data that determine aphasic syndromes.

The classic approach thus established the basic phenomena that are relevant to aphasic syndromes. It encountered serious problems in taking the next steps required by a successful taxonomy: characterizing the symptoms fully and systematically, documenting co-occurrence of symptoms, and accounting for the symptoms and their co-occurrence mechanistically.

The first major failing of the categorization of the classical syndromes is the limited, unsystematic, and atheoretic description provided by its advocates of linguistic representations and psycholinguistic operations that are affected in aphasia. As an example, the abnormalities listed as characteristic of Broca's aphasia by Benson and Geschwind constitute a set of unrelated disturbances affecting speech, each likely due to disturbances of different operations. The symptoms of "dysprosodic" speech, "poorly articulated" speech, and "short phrases lacking prepositions" are likely to reflect disturbances in the assignment of prosody, specifying the articulatory gestures for phonemes, and construction of syntactic forms, respectively. These descriptions are too general: those with Broca's aphasia may have a variety of disturbances affecting each of these aspects of speech planning and production. "Poorly articulated" speech can be dysarthric or apraxic (each of these symptoms has been further subdivided); "telegraphic" speech can take a wide variety forms, not simply be lacking in prepositions. These descriptions are also incomplete: those with Broca's aphasia frequently have some short bursts of fluent speech with substitution of grammatical elements (paragrammatism), not just omission of these elements (de Bleser, 1987).

By ignoring these limitations in the descriptions of aphasic symptoms, the pattern of association of the symptoms that are specified in the syndromes is not established. Cluster analysis has yielded different results, depending on what aphasia test was used (Metter et al., 1984) and the time at which patients were tested (Kertesz & Phipps, 1980). Goodglass and Kaplan (1972, 1982) argued that the pattern of positive and negative weights of tests on factors in a factor analysis of over 250 aphasics tested using the first edition of the Boston Diagnostic Aphasia Examination provided support for the classical syndromes. For instance, they considered a factor on which production of the output features associated with Wernicke's aphasia loaded highly positively and comprehension loaded highly negatively to be one that captured disorders associated with Wernicke's aphasia. If it is reasonable to interpret this factor in this way (alternate analyses are always possible, and alternate ways of doing factor analysis may yield different results), the implication is that every patient is a Wernicke's aphasic to some extent. This is an interesting possibility, quite different from the classical view that patients as a whole fall into one syndrome or another. The presence of a "Wernicke factor" in every patient could result from lesions affecting the area that causes Wernicke's aphasia to different degrees in different patients. This hypothesis could be tested by correlating patients' factor scores with lesion size in Wernicke's area, but these analyses have not been done.

Another way to determine whether the symptoms described in the classical syndromes co-occur frequently is to refer to clinical experience. If the symptoms frequently co-occur, classification of most patients into the clinical syndromes should be relatively easy. In fact, it is not. It is widely appreciated in clinical circles that the classic syndromes do not apply well to many slowly developing diseases, such as brain tumors or Alzheimer disease; to multifocal diseases, such as closed head injury; or in the acute phase of focal disease, such as stroke. Even in the clinical setting, where they can be applied with some success, studies of the chronic phase of single-focal, rapidly developing lesions such as strokes have shown widespread disagreements as to a patient's classification (Holland et al., 1986) and/or that clinicians identify a large number of "mixed" or "unclassifiable" cases (Lecours, Lhermitte, & Bryans, 1983. An unclassifiable case is represented by the patient shown in Figure 2-3, whose scores on the Boston Diagnostic Aphasia Examination do not fit the criteria set out by Goodglass and Kaplan (1972, 1982) for any syndrome. Despite the widespread use of these syndromes in clinical reports, it is truly unclear whether more than a small percentage of patients with language disorders actually fit the criteria for these syndromes.

If the classic syndromes do not divide patients into identifiable groups, and there is little evidence that patterns of performance on aphasia tests produce factors that correspond to the syndromes, one might think to abandon the classification for lack of evidence. However, many clinicians argue that the classic syndromes continue to provide important information about the location of lesions.

In addition, the relation of the syndromes to lesion locations continues to be viewed as providing an explanation for the syndromes, based upon the principles enunciated by Wernicke that relate perceptual processing to unimodal sensory association cortex and motor planning to unimodal motor association cortex. I will discuss the second of these topics below.

With respect to the first, a number of computed tomography (CT) and magnetic resonance imaging (MRI) studies have confirmed a general relationship between the major syndromes and lesion locations. Broca's aphasia is associated with anterior lesions; Wernicke's aphasia is associated with posterior lesions centered in the temporal-parietal juncture (Hayward et al., 1977; Kertesz, 1979; Naeser, 1989; Naeser & Hayward, 1978). Pure motor deficits of speech are associated with subcortical lesions (Alexander et al., 1987; Naeser et al., 1989; Schiff et al., 1983). Pure word deafness is associated with lesions in the auditory association areas and surrounding white matter tracts, often bilaterally (Auerbach et al., 1982; Coslett, et al.,1984; Denes et al., 1975; Metz-Lutz, & Dahl, 1984). Transcortical motor and transcortical sensory aphasia are associated with watershed infarcts between the anterior and middle cerebral arteries (transcortical motor aphasia; Freedman et al., 1984) and middle and posterior cerebral arteries (transcortical sensory aphasia; Kertesz et al., 1982). Conduction aphasia is associated with smaller lesions that appear to often affect the arcuate fasciculus (Damasio & Damasio, 1980).

However, a closer look reveals many limitations of these correlations. Just as the co-occurrence of symptoms into syndromes is unreliable in many types of diseases, so too is the correlation of syndromes with lesions in many (perhaps most) neurological diseases. The studies cited above deal overwhelmingly with chronic stroke patients. As with the co-occurrence of symptoms, even here, at least 15% of patients have lesions that are not predictable from their syndromes (Basso et al., 1985), and some researchers think this number is much higher—as high as 40% or more, depending on what counts as an exception to the rule (de Bleser, 1988). The relationship between lesion location and syndrome is more

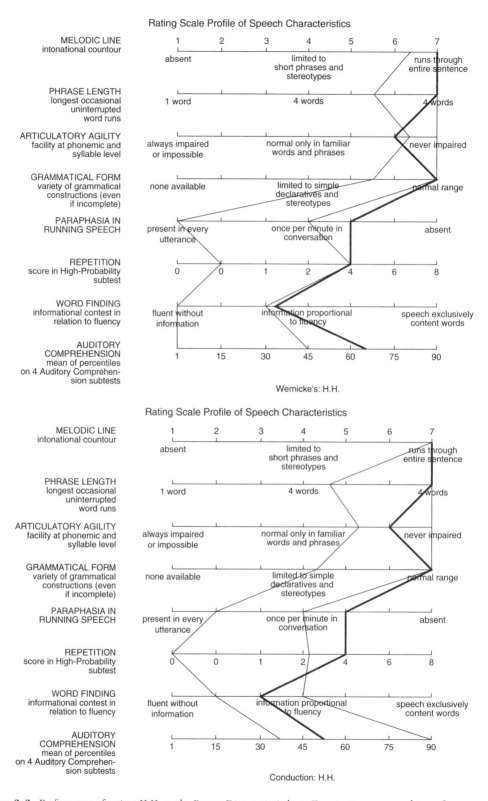

Figure 2–3. Performance of patient H.H. on the Boston Diagnostic Aphasia Examination, compared to performances associated with Wernicke's, conduction, and anomic aphasia.

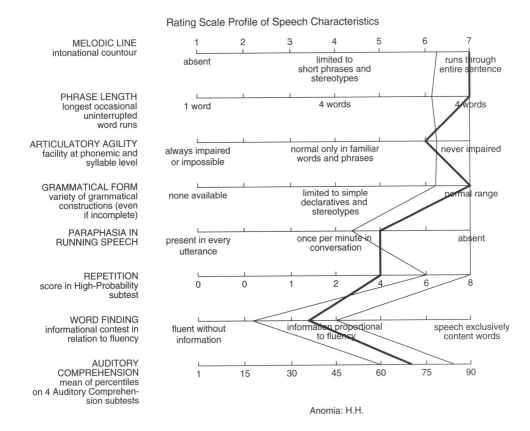

Rating Scale Profile of Speech Characteristics

Anomia: H.H.

Figure 2–3. Continued.

complex than is often claimed, even in cases where the classical localization captures part of the picture. Broca's aphasia, for instance, does not usually occur in the chronic state after lesions restricted to Broca's area, but rather requires much larger lesions (Mohr et al., 1978). When the lesioned brain is imaged metabolically (with, for example, positron emission tomography [PET]), as opposed to structurally, damage following stroke is seen to be more widespread than classically believed (Kempler et al., 1988, 1991; Metter et al., 1983, 1984, 1986, 1988, 1989, 1990, 1992).

To the extent that studies support any relation between classical syndromes and lesion locations, these relations may be due to the effects of brain lesions on motor functions (Caplan, 1987; McNeil & Kent, 1991). If a patient has many and/or severe language function deficits, he has either a global aphasia (if motor speech mechanisms are affected) or

a Wernicke's aphasia (if motor speech mechanisms are not involved). If he has only a few and/or minor language function deficits, he has one of the "nonfluent" aphasias, such as Broca's aphasia, "aphemia," transcortical motor aphasia, or the like (if there are motor speech impairments), or one of the minor "fluent" aphasias, such as anomia, conduction aphasia, transcortical sensory aphasia, or the like (if there are no motor speech impairments). From this point of view, the localizing value of the classical syndromes is due to the invariant location of the motor system, whereas language processing components may vary in their localization in different individuals.

I have belabored the classical syndromes because they remain coin of the realm. Despite all the limitations reviewed above, they continue to exert an influence on ongoing work on language disorders (Damasio, 1992). Aphasic patients are frequently classified in terms provided by these syndromes in clinical reports. In research studies, they continue to exert two types of influence.

One is an effort to relate more specific symptoms to the classical syndromes. For instance, Grodzinsky (2000) has argued that certain disorders affecting syntactically based sentence comprehension are only found in Broca's aphasia; Blumstein et al. (1982) have suggested that Broca's aphasia is associated with abnormalities in "automatic" but not "controlled" semantic processing. A great deal of controversy surrounds such claims (see Chapter 4 for discussion of Grodzinsky's claims). If they are correct, they apply to a very small number of symptoms, and there is no explanation for their occurrence in a particular syndrome. Any such co-occurrences are not a basis for retaining the classic syndromes.

A second way in which the classical syndromes influence contemporary research is through their effect on efforts to characterize newly explored language disorders. An example is the fledgling taxonomy of primary progressive aphasia (PPA). Primary progressive aphasia was first described by Mesulam (1982) as a dementing disease whose primary initial symptom was aphasia. For well over a decade, efforts to subdivide PPA languished, but in recent years a series of clinical-radiological studies have led to partitioning of PPA. Gorno Tempini et al. (2003) distinguished between nonfluent PPA ("nonfluent speech output, 'labored articulation,' agrammatism, difficulty with comprehension of complex syntactic structures, word-finding deficits, and preserved single-word comprehension"), logopenic progressive PPA ("slow rate, grammatically simple but correct [speech], and . . . frequent word-finding pauses") and semantic dementia ("fluent, grammatical speech; confrontation naming deficits; semantic deficits for words and, initially less severely, for objects; surface dyslexia; and relatively spared syntactic comprehension") (all citations from Gorno Tempini et al., 2003. pp 337–338). The similarities of nonfluent PPA to Broca's aphasia, semantic dementia to transcortical sensory aphasia, and of logopenic PPA to anomia or conduction aphasia are striking, and reflect the pervasive influence of the classic syndromes, with

their emphasis on fluency and single-word processing.

The classic syndromes rest on a principle of neural organization that also continues to be influential—the idea that cognitive operations are localized where they are because of their relations to perceptual and motor processes, which has been retained as an explanatory principle (Mesulam 1990, 1998; for a variant view, see Damasio, 1989). The failure of the neuroanatomical model underlying the aphasic syndromes to predict lesion–deficit correlations or the localization of neurovascular or neurophysiological responses to language performances has not been taken as evidence against this principle, only against particular instantiations of it. For instance, the absence of evidence that the meanings of words are represented in the inferior parietal lobe and the results of both activation studies (Martin et al., 1996) and the effects of pathology (Hodges et al., 1992) indicating that concrete nominal concepts are represented in the inferior temporal lobe have led researchers to abandon Geschwind's hypothesis that parietally based cross-modal associations underlie word meaning, but not the more general idea that word meanings are localized in areas of the brain that support particular perceptual or motor processes. In fact, the idea of a neurological basis for "embodied cognition" is enjoying a very productive renaissance (Martin et al., 1996; Pulvermuller, 2003). Even language operations that do not fit into the model of functional neuroanatomy that underlies the classical syndromes—because they are not clearly either perceptual or motor—have been related to the brain through elaborate extensions of the basic principle. Constructing syntactic representations, for instance, is an abstract operation that bears a very distant relation to perceptual and motor processes, and the classical neuroanatomical model makes no predictions about where the neural tissue that supports these processes is localized. However, in an extension of the model that incorporated Luria's (1966) views regarding the role of the dorsolateral frontal lobe in cognitive control, Fiebach and Schubotz (2006) suggested that syntactic analysis of sentences in comprehension is localized in Broca's area because the lateral premotor area, including Broca's area, is involved in the detection of patterns in arbitrary dynamic, temporally extended perceptual events, which includes speech. I shall return to these claims below. The present point is that the principle underlying the classical models continues to exert great intellectual influence in the domain of functional neuroanatomy theories, one, I would say, rivaling the impact of concepts such as neural nets (Arbib, 2002), functional connectivity (Seth, 2005), small worlds (Bassett & Bullmore, 2006), and oscillatory neurophysiological processes (Uhlhass et al., 2008). Given the close connection between explanatory principles and syndromes discussed in the introduction to this chapter, the effect is to reinforce acceptance of the classical syndromes (the "you are known by the company you keep" principle).

NEW APPROACHES

Whatever the impact of the theoretical principles that underlie the classical syndromes, the empirical limitations of these syndromes, briefly reviewed above, require attention. In the past 30 years, these limitations have begun to be addressed. The most significant work has been the development of detailed models of many aphasic abnormalities, ranging from speech planning (Dell et al., 1997) through syntactically based comprehension (see Chapter 4), semantic representations (Caramazza & Mahon, 2003), alexia (Coltheart, 2006), and others. It is well beyond the scope of this chapter to review all this work, but a brief introduction to linguistics and psycholinguistics may allow readers who are unfamiliar with these fields to see the possible scope of work along these lines.

The language code connects particular types of representations to particular aspects of meaning. Words connect phonological units with items, actions, properties, and logical connections. Word formation forms words from existing words. Sentences relate words in hierarchical syntactic structures to each other to determine semantic relationships between them, such as who is accomplishing or receiving

an action. Discourse relates sentences to express temporal order, causation, inferences, and other semantic values. Table 2-3 attempts to systematically describe the levels of the linguistic representations that are basic to language at the word and sentence level. Tables 2-4 and 2-5 and Figures 2-4 and 2-5 present models of how these forms are processed. Tables 2-3 through 2-5 and Figures 2-4 and 2-5 are highly simplified, but they suggest of what language and the language processing system consist.

As seen in these tables and figures, there are many levels of detail at which one can describe language and language processing. Depending on the level of detail at which language impairments are described, there may be hundreds of independent language processing impairments. For instance, we may recognize a disturbance of converting the sound waveform into linguistically relevant units of sound—acoustic-to-phonemic conversion—or we may recognize disturbances affecting the ability to recognize subsets of phonemes, such as vowels, consonants, stop consonants, fricatives, nasals, and the like (Saffran et al., 1976). For many clinical purposes, an adequate way to approach aphasic impairments is at the level of detail that identifies language processing impairments in terms of sets of related operations responsible for activating the major forms of the language code and their associated meanings in the usual language tasks of speaking, comprehending auditorily presented language, writing, and reading. These levels of the language code are listed in Table 2-3. However, for many research purposes, and for some clinical purposes, a more detailed description of linguistic representations and operations is needed.

A psycholinguistic approach to aphasia would describe aphasic symptoms as disorders of specific psycholinguistic operations that have, as a consequence, the failure to normally activate specific linguistic representations in particular tasks. Two obvious ways to identify syndromes within this framework are as individual symptoms that are due to impairments of individual operations and as sets of symptoms that arise from a single impaired operation. With respect to the first type of syndrome, as noted,

Table 2–3. Basic Levels of Language

Level	Form	Associated Semantic Values
Lexical	Words, consisting of sound units (phonemes) organized into higher-order structures (feet, syllables). Syllabic prominence marked by stress or tone. Words have syntactic categories. "Open class," "content" words (noun, verb, adjective) accept new members. "Closed class," "function" words (article, auxiliary, pronoun, etc.) are a fixed set.	Content words: Items, Actions, Features Function words: Logical Connections Words are primarily denotative and related to categories.
Morphological	Words formed from other words by prefixes, suffixes, and infixes. Morphology can be inflectional or derivational.	Inflectional morphology indicates connections between words (e.g., agreement). Derivational morphology changes syntactic category (e.g., changes adjectives to nouns: *happy* → *happiness*). Declension, aspect, and temporal markings, and other phenomena are also morphological in nature.
Sentential	Syntactic structures: hierarchically arranged sets of syntactic categories over which relations are defined (e.g., subject, object, c-command)	Semantic relations between words, such as thematic roles (agent, theme, beneficiary, etc.), attribution of modification, scope of quantification, etc. These "propositional" aspects of meaning describe events and states of affairs. Propositions can have truth values and be used to update semantic memory, to reason, and for other functions.
Discourse	Position in syntactic structures (e.g., first words play important roles in discourse). Intonational contrastive stress	The relationships between propositions–topic, focus, given information, temporal order, causation. The intentions of the participants in the discourse. Some of these semantic features are provided by inferences that go beyond the verbatim content of the discourse.

psycholinguistic analyses potentially identify a large number of aphasic symptoms. With respect to the second type of syndrome, the theories upon which psychologists draw predict and explain certain co-occurrences of symptoms. For instance, semantic dementia (a subtype of PPA, see above) includes both semantic deficits for words and objects and surface dyslexia—an inability to read irregularly spelled words aloud but preserved reading of regular words and nonwords. On the basis of computer models of reading aloud, Patterson and her colleagues (Hodges et al., 1992) have argued that these symptoms co-occur because reading irregular words requires activation of semantic representations to a much greater extent than reading regular words does.

Psycholinguistically characterized syndromes are closely related to models of psycholinguistic operations and linguistic representations, and, in this respect, begin to make contact with a rich body of work in related basic sciences that provide a basis for a taxonomy of aphasic disorders. It is clear, however, that a more detailed and systematic linguistic and psycholinguistic approach to aphasia will provide only part of the basis for developing aphasic syndromes and a taxonomy of aphasic impairments. The reasons for these limitations are important to consider.

First, the psycholinguistic approach, although an advance, is incomplete at the behavioral level. It does not presently deal with the issues that were raised by Jackson, Head, Goldstein, and others regarding the

Table 2–4. Summary of Components of the Language Processing System for Simple Words

Component	Input	Operation	Output
Auditory-Oral Modality			
Input Side			
Acoustic-phonetic processing	Acoustic waveform	Matches acoustic properties to phonetic features	Phonological segments (phonemes, allophones, syllables)
Auditory lexical access	Phonological units	Activates lexical items in long-term memory on basis of sound; selects best fit to stimulus	Phonological forms of words
Lexical semantic access	Words (represented as phonological forms)	Activates semantic features of words	Word meanings
Output Side			
Phonological lexical access	Word meanings ("lemmas")	Activates the phonological forms of words	Phonological form of words
Phonological output planning	Phonological forms of words (and nonwords)	Activates detailed phonetic features of words (and nonwords)	Phonetic values of phonological segments; word stress patterns
Articulatory planning	Phonetic values	Specified articulatory movements	Neural commands for articulation

mechanisms that regulate language use. It has not paid much attention to many aspects of aphasia that are not immediately related to psycholinguistic processing, such as a patient's fluency. For instance, most patients with agrammatism—a speech output disorder that affects function words and morphology—speak slowly, whereas patients whose disturbance affects the choice and ordering of phonemes in content words speak at normal rates. Why does one deficit slow down the speech planning process and the other does not? Is this because of the relationship of the lesions in these disorders to the motor system, or because there is a true functional relationship between the speed of language planning and the level of the language code that is being planned, with difficulties in planning function words, morphology, and syntactic structures slowing down the speech planning process and difficulties in planning the phonemic content words not having this effect? The psycholinguistic approach has not addressed questions such as this.

Second, a purely behavioral approach to aphasia fails to connect aphasic symptoms and syndromes to the normal brain, to pathology, and to genetics. The need to include these factors in an adequate characterization of aphasia stems from the fact that symptoms may co-occur for neurological as well functional reasons: if two operations require the same neural substrate, a lesion in that area will affect both, even if they are functionally unrelated. As an example, there is evidence that visual word forms are recognized in an area of the inferior temporal lobe (Dehaene et al., 2002) adjacent to the area involved in activating the names of visually presented objects (Damasio et al., 1996); the co-occurrence of deficits in visual word recognition and confrontation naming could thus be a syndrome that has its origin in the facts of regional functional neuroanatomy, not functional architecture (as we have suggested might be the case for the co-occurrence of lexical semantic disorders and surface dyslexia). Other reasons for including factors regarding the normal brain, pathology, and genetics in the development of aphasic syndromes come from the purposes for which these syndromes are developed. If aphasic phenomena are to be

Table 2–5. Summary of Components of the Language Processing System for Derived Words and Sentences (Collapsed Over Auditory-oral and Written Modalities)

Component	Input	Operation	Output
Processing Affixed Words			
Input Side			
Morphological analysis	Word forms	Segments words into structural (morphological) units; activates syntactic features of words	Morphological structure; syntactic features
Morphological comprehension	Word meaning; morphological structure	Combines word roots and affixes	Meanings of morphologically complex words
Output Side			
Accessing affixed words from semantics	Word meanings; syntactic features	Activates forms of affixes and function words	Forms of affixes and function words
Sentence-level Processing			
Input Side			
Lexico-inferential comprehension	Meanings of simple and complex words; world knowledge	Infers aspects of sentence meaning on basis of pragmatic plausibility	Aspects of propositional meaning (thematic roles; attribution of modifiers)
Parsing and syntactic comprehension	Word meanings; syntactic features	Constructs syntactic representation and combines it with word meanings	Aspects of propositional meaning
Heuristic sentence completion	Syntactic categories of words	Constructs simplified syntactic structures; combines word meanings in these structures	Aspects of propositional meaning
Output side			
Construction of functional level representation	Messages	Activates content words, assigns thematic roles and other aspects of propositional meaning	Content words, thematic roles, other aspects of propositional meaning
Construction of positional level representation	Content words, syntactic frames, discourse features	Activates syntactic frames in conjunction with function words; inserts phonological forms of content words into syntactic frames	Surface forms of sentences
Phonological output planning	Surface forms of sentences	Combines lexical phonological and sentence-level phonological information	Phonetic values; stress and intonation

useful in diagnosis, they must be related to all three factors: prognosis depends upon pathology and may well depend upon genetic factors; optimally efficacious therapy may differ for similar symptoms as a function of lesion location and type.

Relating symptoms and syndromes to the normal brain, pathology, and genetics is very difficult. Basic features of the neural organization for many aspects of language processing remain unclear and will require considerations that extend well beyond simple localization of specific language operations, including distributed representations and complex patterns of functional connectivity. It is not clear to what extent the principle that the neural substrate for language (and, more generally, cognitive) processing is determined by the role of an area in

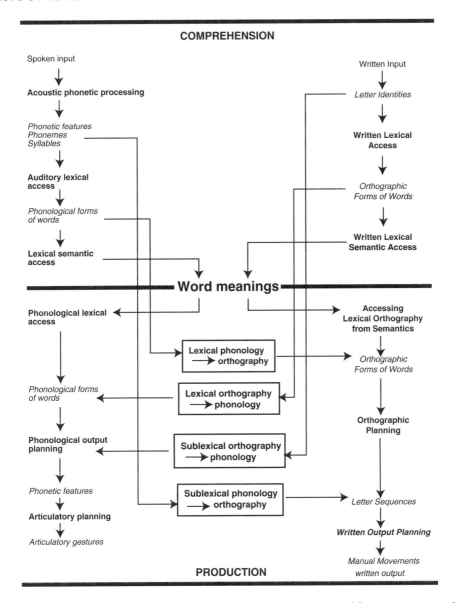

COMPREHENSION

Spoken input

Acoustic phonetic processing

Phonetic features
Phonemes
Syllables

Auditory lexical access

Phonological forms of words

Lexical semantic access

Written Input

Letter Identities

Written Lexical Access

Orthographic Forms of Words

Written Lexical Semantic Access

Word meanings

Phonological lexical access

Lexical phonology → orthography

Lexical orthography → phonology

Phonological forms of words

Sublexical orthography → phonology

Phonological output planning

Phonetic features

Sublexical phonology → orthography

Articulatory planning

Articulatory gestures

Accessing Lexical Orthography from Semantics

Orthographic Forms of Words

Orthographic Planning

Letter Sequences

Written Output Planning

Manual Movements
written output

PRODUCTION

Figure 2–4. Diagrammatic representation of the sequence of activation of components of the processing system for single words. Processing components are presented in boldface; representations are presented in italics. Arrows represent the flow of information (representations) from one processing component to another.

perceptual and motor functions applies. For instance, in the area of syntactically based comprehension, there is evidence that portions of both unimodal sensory and motor association cortex perform the same syntactic operations (see Chapter 4), which is inconsistent with the view that particular operations are supported by particular neural tissue because of their relation to perceptual or motor processing (Caplan, 2006). In addition, aphasic symptoms do not entirely depend on the location of lesioned neural tissue. They differ as a function of the type of lesion and biological factors, such as age, handedness, possibly sex, and others, and change over time after monophasic lesions, such as stoke. To the extent that psycholinguistic features of aphasia differ as a function of such factors, an adequate characterization of aphasic symptoms and syndromes will have to take them into account.

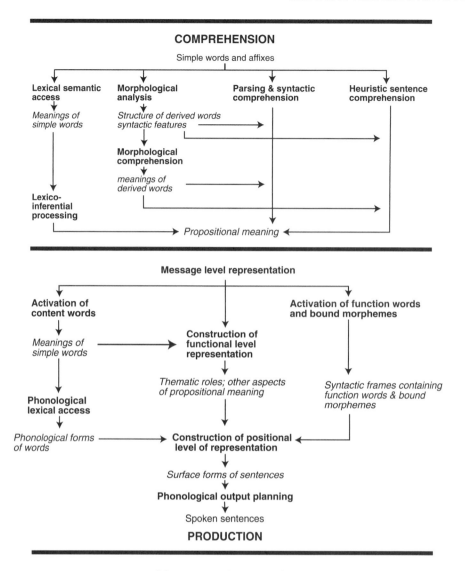

Figure 2–5. Diagrammatic representation of the sequence of operation of components of the language processing system for morphologically complex words and sentences. Processing components are presented in boldface; representations are presented in italics. Arrows represent the flow of information (representations) from one processing component to another.

A good example of the complexity of the relation between psycholinguistically characterized symptoms and syndromes and neurobiological factors can be found in recent studies of PPA. As noted, in recent years, correlations of syndromes based upon psycholinguistic descriptions and radiologically determined sites of cortical thinning have resulted in the beginnings of agreement that PPA can be subdivided, and in suggestions about how to do so. Pathological studies have confirmed that the different PPA syndromes are generally

associated with different cellular pathology—nonfluent PPA mostly with tauopathies and fluent cases, such as semantic dementia, with ubiquitin inclusions (Knibb et al., 2006). However, these associations only account for about half the autopsied cases in each of the PPA syndromes; the remaining 50% of cases contain widely different pathologies, including pathology most commonly seen in other PPA syndromes (in Knibb et al., 13% of fluent PPA cases had tauopathy) and pathology associated with other diseases (ubiquitin inclusions in regions usually associated with motor neuron disease; Rhys Davis et al., 2005; plaque-and-tangle disease indistinguishable from that seen in Alzheimer disease, found in 30% of cases in every PPA syndrome in Knibb et al.'s series of 38 autopsied cases of PPA). These results indicate that there are likely to be multiple etiologies of each of the currently recognized PPA syndromes, and this raises unresolved questions about the determinants of the behavioral manifestations of these diseases. At the genetic level, sibs diagnosed with PPA who carry an identical progranulin mutation have varied in their clinical symptoms and course (Mesulam et al., 2007). Mesulam et al. suggested that variation in the normal allele or unrelated developmental or acquired vulnerabilities of particular neural networks might cause these different phenotypes. Studies such as these show that an integrated psychological-neural-genetic approach to classifying aphasic symptoms and forming aphasic syndromes is needed, and also that it will not be easy to attain.

CONCLUSION

Syndromes are part and parcel of medicine, and the concept of a syndrome has a long history in the study of aphasia. The classical aphasic syndromes established the domain of description of aphasic symptoms and provided principles that underlie the neural basis for language processing that have survived to the present. However, the classic syndromes fail to pursue the descriptions of symptoms and syndromes to the level of detail made possible by work in related scientific areas, and they do not account for basic aspects of the data—the pattern of co-occurrence of symptoms, and the relation of symptoms and syndromes to the brain. Researchers have applied concepts and methods derived from linguistics and psychology to the characterization of aphasic symptoms and syndromes. This approach has yielded a fair number of important results, but is still in its infancy. One area that remains to be addressed is the integration of descriptions of the psychological aspects of aphasia with studies of neurological and genetic factors. The further development and integration of studies

that incorporate these sciences is likely to result in a quite different set of syndromes, whose nature can at present only be foreseen in very general terms.

ACKNOWLEDGMENTS

This work was supported in part by a grant from NIDCD (DC00942).

REFERENCES

Alexander, M. P., Naeser, M. A., & Palumbo, C. L. (1987). Correlations of subcortical CT lesion sites and aphasia profiles. *Brain, 110*, 961–991.

Arbib, M. A. (Ed.). (2002). *The handbook of brain theory and neural networks*, 2nd edition. Cambridge, MA: MIT Press.

Auerbach, S. H., Allard, T., Naeser, M., Alexander, M. P., & Albert, M. L. (1982). Pure word deafness: Analysis of a case with bilateral lesions and a defect at the prephonemic level. *Brain, 105*, 271–300.

Bassett, D.S., & Bullmore, E. (2006). Small-world brain networks. *The Neuroscientist, 12*(6), 512–523.

Basso, A., A. R. Lecours, Anna Basso, Andre Roch Lecours, Silvia Moraschini, & Marie Vanier (1985). Anatomoclinical correlations of the aphasias as defined through computerized tomography: Exceptions. *Brain and Language, 26*, 201–229.

Benson, D. F. (1979). *Aphasia, alexia and agraphia*. London: Churchill Livingstone.

Benson, D. F., & Geschwind, N. (1971). Aphasia and related cortical disturbances. In A. B. Baker & L. H. Baker (Eds.), *Clinical neurology*. New York: Harper & Row.

Blumstein, S. E., Milberg, W., & Shrier, R. (1982). Semantic processing in aphasia: Evidence from an auditory lexical decision task. *Brain and Language, 17*, 301–315.

Broca, P. (1861). Remarques sur le siège de la faculté de la parole articulé, suives d'une observation d'aphémie (perte de parole). *Bulletins de la Société d'Anatomique, 6*, 330–357.

Caplan, D. (1987). *Neurolinguistics and linguistic aphasiology. An introduction Cambridge studies in Speech Science and Communication*. Cambridge: Cambridge University Press.

Caplan, D. (2006). Why is Broca's area involved in syntax? *Cortex 42*, 469–471.

Caramazza, A., & Mahon, B. Z. (2003). The organization of conceptual knowledge: The evidence from category-specific semantic deficits. *Trends in Cognitive Sciences*, 7, 354–361.

Coltheart, M. (2006). Acquired dyslexias and the computational modelling of reading. *Cognitive Neuropsychology*, 23, 96–109.

Coslett, H. B., Brashear, H. R., & Heilman, K. M. (1984). Pure word deafness after bilateral primary auditory cortex infarcts. *Neurology, 34*, 347–352.

Damasio A. R. (1989). Time-locked multiregional retroactivation: A systems-level proposal for the neural substrates of recall and recognition. *Cognition, 33*, 25–62.

Damasio, A. R. (1992). Aphasia. *The New England Journal of Medicine*, 326, 531–539.

Damasio, H., & Damasio, A. R. (1980). The anatomical basis of conduction aphasia. *Brain, 103*, 337–350.

Damasio, H., Grabowski, T. J., Tranel, D., Hichwa, R. D., & Damasio, A. R. (1996). A neural basis for lexical retrieval. *Nature, 380* (April 11, 1996), 499–505.

Davies, R. R., Hodges, J. R., Kril, J., Patterson, K., Halliday, G., Xuereb, J. (2005). The pathological basis of semantic dementia, *Brain, 128*, 1984–1995.

De Bleser, R. (1987). From agrammatism to paragrammatism: German aphasiological traditions and grammatical disturbances. *Cognitive Neuropsychology*, 4, 187–256.

de Bleser, R. (1988): Localization of aphasia: Science or fiction? In D. Denes, C. Semenza, & P. Bisiacchi (Eds.), *Perspectives on cognitive neurology*. Hove, UK: Lawrence Erlbaum.

Dehaene, S., Le Clec, H. G., Poline, J. B., Bihan, D. L., & Cohen, L. (2002). The visual word form area: A prelexical representation of visual words in the left fusiform gyrus. *Neuroreport, 13*(3), 321–325.

Dell, G. S., Schwartz, M. F., Martin, N., Saffran, E. M., & Gagnon, D. A. (1997). Lexical access in aphasic and nonaphasic speakers. *Psychological Review, 104*, 801–838.

Denes, G., & C. Semenza (1975). Auditory modality-specific anomia: Evidence from a case of pure word deafness. *Cortex, 11*, 401–411.

Fiebach, C., & Schubotz, R (2006). Dynamic anticipatory processing of hierarchical sequential events: A common role for Broca's area and ventral premotor cortex across domains? *Cortex, 42*, 499–502.

Freedman, M., Alexander, M. P., Naeser, M. A., & Palumbo, C. (1984). Anatomic basis for transcortical motor aphasia. *Neurology, 34*, 409–417.

Geschwind, N. (1965). Disconnection syndromes in animals and man. *Brain, 88*, 237–294, 585–644.

Geschwind, N. (1982). Language and the brain. *Scientific American, 226*, 76–83.

Goldstein, K. (1948). *Language and language disturbances*. New York: Grune and Stratton.

Goodglass, H., & Kaplan, E. (1972). *Boston Diagnostic Aphasia Examination booklet, the assessment of aphasia and related disorders*, 80 p. Philadelphia: Lea and Febiger.

Goodglass, H., & Kaplan, E. (1982). *The assessment of aphasia and related disorders*, 2nd edition. Philadelphia: Lea & Febiger.

Gorno-Tempini, M. L., Dronkers, N. F., Rankin, K. P., et al. (2004). Cognition and anatomy in three variants of primary progressive aphasia. *Ann Neurol, 55*, 335–346.

Grodzinsky, Y (2000). The neurology of syntax: Language use without Broca's area. *Behavioral and Brain Sciences, 23*, 1–71.

Hayward, R., Naeser, M. A., Zatz. L. M. (1977). Cranial computer tomography in aphasia. *Radiology, 123*, 653–660.

Hodges, J. R., Patterson, K., Oxbury, S., & Funnell, E. (1992). *Semantic dementia: Progressive fluent aphasia with temporal lobe atrophy. Brain, 115*, 1783–1806.

Holland, A. L., Fromm, D., & Swindell, C. S. (1986). The labeling problem in aphasia: An illustrative case. *Journal of Speech & Hearing Disorders, 51*, 176–180.

Jackson, H. H. (1878). On affections of speech from disease of the brain. Reprinted in J. Taylor (Ed.), *Selected writings of John Hughlings Jackson* (1958). New York: Basic Books.

Kempler, D., Curtiss, S., Metter, E., Jackson, C., & Hanson, W. (1991). Grammatical comprehension, aphasic syndromes and neuroimaging. *Journal of Neurolinguistics, 6*.

Kempler, D., Metter, E., Jackson, C., Hanson, W., Riege, W., Mazziotta, J., & Phelps, M. (1988). Disconnection and cerebral metabolism: the case of conduction aphasia. *Archives of Neurology, 45*, 275–279.

Kertesz, A. (1979). *Aphasia and associated disorders: Taxonomy, localization and recovery*. New York: Grune and Stratton.

Kertesz, A., & Phipps, M (1980). The numerical taxonomy of acute and chronic aphasic syndromes. *Psychology Research, 41*, 17–198.

Kertesz, A., Sheppard, A., & MacKenzie, R. (1982). Localization in transcortical sensory aphasia. *Archives of Neurology, 39*, 475–478.

Knibb, J. A., Xuereb, J. H., Patterson, K., & Hodges, J. R. (2006). Clinical and pathological characterization of progressive aphasia. *Annals of Neurology, 59*, 156–165.

Lecours, A. R., Lhermitte, F., & Bryans, B. (1983). *Aphasiology*. London: Balliere Tindall.

Lichtheim, L. (1885). On aphasia. *Brain*, 7, 433–484.

Luria, A. R. (1966). Higher cortical functions in man. B. Haigh (Trans.). New York: Basic Books.

Martin, A., Wiggs, C. L., Ungerleider, L. G., & Haxby, J. V. (1996). Neural correlates of category-specific knowledge. *Nature 379*, 649–652.

McNeil, M. R., & Kent, R. D. (1991). Motoric characteristics of adult aphasic and apraxic speakers. In G. R. Hammond (Ed.), *Advances in psychology: Cerebral control of speech and limb movements* (pp. 317–354). New York: Elsevier/ North Holland.

Mesulam, M. -M. (1982). Slowly progressive aphasia without generalized dementia. *Annals of Neurology*, 11, 592–598.

Mesulam, M. -M. (1990). Large-scale neurocognitive networks and distributed processing for attention, language, and memory. *Annals of Neurology*, 28(5), 597–613.

Mesulam, M. -M. (1998). From sensation to cognition. *Brain*, 121, 1013–1052.

Mesulam M., Johnson, N., Krefft, T. A., Gass, J. M., Cannon, A.D., Adamson, J. L., et al. (2007). Progranulin mutations in primary progressive aphasia: The PPA1 and PPA3 families. *Archives of Neurology*, 64: 43–47.

Metter, E. J., Riege, W. H., Hanson, W. R., Jackson, C. A., Kempler, D., & VanLancker, D. (1983). Comparison of metabolic rates, language and memory, and subcortical aphasias. *Brain and Language*, 19, 33–47.

Metter, E. J., Riege, W. H., Hanson, W. R., Camras, L. R., Phelps, M. E., & Kuhl, D. E. (1984). Correlations of glucose metabolism and structural damage to language function in aphasia. *Brain and Language*, 21, 187–207.

Metter, E. J., Kempler, D., Hanson, R., Jackson, C., Mazziotta, J. C., & Phelps, M. E. (1986). Cerebral glucose metabolism: differences in Wernicke's, Broca's and conduction aphasias. *Clinical Aphasiology*, 16, 97–104.

Metter, E. J., Riege, W. H., Hanson, W. R., Jackson, C. A., Kempler, D., & VanLancker, D. (1988). Subcortical structures in aphasia: an analysis based on (F-18)-fluorodeoxyglucose positron emission tomography and computed tomography. *Archives of Neurology*, 45, 1229–1234.

Metter, E. J., Jackson, C. A., Kempler, D., & Hanson, W. R. (1992). Temporoparietal cortex and the recovery of language comprehension in aphasia. *Aphasiology*, 6, 349–358.

Metter, E. J., Kempler, D., Jackson, C. A., Hanson, W. R., Mazziotta, J. C., & Phelps, M. E. (1989). Cerebral glucose metabolism in Wernicke's, Broca's and conduction aphasia. *Archives of Neurology*, 46, 27–34.

Metter, E. J., Hanson, W. R., Jackson, C. A., Kempler, D., van Lancker, D., Mazziotta, J. C., & Phelps, M. E. (1990). Temporoparietal cortex in aphasia. Evidence from positron emission tomography. *Archives of Neurology*, 47, 1235–1238.

Metz-Lutz, M. -N., & Dahl, E. (1984). Analysis of word comprehension in a case of pure word deafness. *Brain and Language*, 23, 13–25.

Mohr, J. P., Pessin, M. S., Finkelstein, S., Funkenstein, H., Duncan, G. W., & Davis, K. R. (1978). Broca aphasia: Pathologic and clinical. *Neurology*, 28, 311–324.

Naeser, M. (1989). CT scan lesion site analysis and recovery in aphasia. *Brain*, 112, 1–38.

Naeser, M. A., & Hayward, R. W. (1978). Lesion localization in aphasia with cranial computed tomography and the Boston Diagnostic Aphasia Exam. *Neurology*, 28: 545–551.

Naeser, M. A., Palumbo, C. L., Helm-Estabrooks, N., Stiassny-Eder, D., & Albert, M. L. (1990). Late recovery of auditory comprehension in global aphasia: Improved recovery observed with subcortical temporal isthmus lesion versus Wenicke's cortical area lesion. *Arch Neurol*, 47: 425–432.

Naeser, M. A., Palumbo, C. L., Helm-Estabrooks, N., Stiassny-Eder, D., & Albert, M. L. (1989). Severe nonfluency in aphasia: Role of the medial subcallosal fasciculus and other white matter pathology in recovery of spontaneous speech. *Brain*, 112, 1–38.

Pulvermuller, F. (2003). *The neuroscience of language. On brain circuits of words and serial order*. Cambridge, MA: Cambridge University Press.

Saffran, E. M., Marin, O., & Yeni-Komshian, G. (1976). An analysis of speech perception and word deafness. *Brain and Language*, 3, 209–228.

Seth, A. K. (2005). Causal connectivity of evolved neural networks during behavior. *Network: Computation in Neural Systems*, 16, 35–54.

Schiff, H. B., Alexander, M. P., Naeser, M. A., & Galaburda, A. M. (1983). Aphemia: Clinical-anatomic correlates. *Archives of Neurology*, 40, 720–727.

Uhlhaas, P. J., Haenschel, C., Nikoli, D., & Singer, W. (2008). The role of oscillations and synchrony in cortical networks and their putative relevance for the pathophysiology of schizophrenia. *Schizophrenia Bulletin*, 34, 927–943.

Wernicke, C. (1874). *Der Aphasische Symptomenkomplex*. Breslau: Cohn & Weigart. Reprinted in translation in *Boston Studies in Philosophy of Science*, 4, 34–97.

3

Phonology, Semantics, and Lexical Semantics

STEPHEN E. NADEAU AND DIANE L. KENDALL

Phonology involves the structure and systematic patterning of sounds in language (Akmajian et al., 1984; Nadeau, 2001). Semantics involves the representation of meaning. The linkage of meaning to phonology ("lexical semantics") instantiates words. In this chapter, we will rely heavily on evidence from the study of acquired language disorders, but also from studies of slip-of-the-tongue data ("spoonerisms") in normal subjects, and investigations in experimental and computational psychology to elucidate the neurology of phonology, semantics, and lexical semantics.

This chapter begins with a review of disorders of phonological processing. Following this, a theoretical model employing the conceptual framework of parallel distributed processing (PDP) is introduced as a means of both explaining empirical observations in a cogent fashion, and of potentially relating behavior to neural microstructure. On this base, we will then consider semantics. Lexical semantics, the bridge between phonology and semantics, will be considered throughout.

DISORDERS OF PHONOLOGICAL PROCESSING

PHONOLOGICAL SELECTION ERRORS

Phonological selection errors result in the production of incorrect phonemic sequences, easily recognizable when they constitute neologisms. Such errors provide the best evidence that the brain does implicitly recognize phonemes as operational units, and that this sublexical knowledge is accessible from the neural representation of concepts and meaning. Several major types of single phoneme errors may be observed (S. Blumstein, 1973a):

Nonenvironmental:
Substitution: /timz/ "teams" → /kimz/
Simplification: /prIti/ "pretty" → /pIti/
Addition /papa/ "papa" → /papra/

Environmental:
Assimilation within
a word: "Crete" → /trit/

Assimilation across word
boundaries: "roast beef" → /rof bif/
Metathesis (exchange):
"degrees" → /gedriz/

Environmental ("sequential," "contextual")
errors may account for over 70% of errors in
slip-of-the-tongue corpora and for 50%–70%
of phonological errors in the language of subjects with jargon aphasia (Lecours & Lhermitte,
1969; Schwartz et al., 1994).

Several major studies of phonemic selection
errors in aphasic subjects have yielded a wealth
of data on the phenomenological principles
that govern such errors. The relative frequency
of phoneme use is the same in aphasic as in
normal language (S. Blumstein, 1973b). Errors
may occur at any position within a word
(Marquardt et al., 1979; Valdois et al., 1988).
There is considerable variability in the phonemes most prone to selection error. However,
subjects tend to have the least difficulty with
frequently used phonemes, such as vowels and
the consonants /t/, /n/, and /s/, and they tend to
have the most difficulty with consonant clusters,
fricatives (*thin, shoe, then*) and affricates (*chin,
just*), phonemes that occur with the lowest frequency and require more muscles and closer
control of movement than any other class
(Shankweiler & Harris, 1966; Shankweiler
et al., 1968; Johns & Darley, 1970; S. Blumstein,
1973a, 1973b; Dubois et al., 1973; Trost &
Canter, 1974; La Pointe & Johns, 1975; Halpern
et al., 1976; Burns & Canter, 1977; Dunlop &
Marquardt, 1977; Klich et al., 1979; Shewan,
1980; Canter et al., 1985). A similar phenomenon has been noted in slip-of-the-tongue collections (Motley & Baars, 1976; A. W. Ellis,
1980; Levitt & Healy, 1985).

Phoneme selection errors are influenced by
lesion locus. Subjects with Broca's aphasia tend
to replace consonant clusters with a single consonant, whether the cluster is intrasyllabic or
bridges two syllables, and they rarely create
consonant clusters in lieu of a single consonant.
In contrast, whereas subjects with conduction
aphasia alter consonants and consonant clusters just as often, they are more likely to replace
a cluster with a different cluster, or to replace a
single consonant with a cluster (Nespoulous
et al., 1984).

INFLUENCES ON PHONOLOGICAL SELECTION ERRORS

A number of observations, detailed below,
indicate that even when the reliability of phonemic selection is reduced, there are still three
persistent overarching influences that tend
to rein in or modify phonemic selection errors:
(a) regularities in the representations of phonemes themselves; (b) regularities implicit in
knowledge of phonemic sequences (expressed
as environmental influences on phonemic
selection errors, phonemic clumping, and phonotactic constraints); and (c) lexical semantic
input.

Phoneme Representations: Distinctive Features

Many observations regarding phonemic selection errors in aphasic subjects are most usefully
viewed in terms of distinctive features. Distinctive features are the specific states of roughly
18 dimensions of the orofacial-pharyngeal speech
apparatus that, in particular combinations,
operationally define all the phonemes. Some
phonemic selection errors can equally well be
viewed as distinctive feature selection errors
(Lecours & Lhermitte, 1969). For example:

/bat/ → /pat/ (deletion of voice)
/not/ → /dot/ (deletion of nasality)
/fat/ → /pat/ (deletion of continuance)

In these examples, it is impossible to determine whether it is a distinctive feature error
or a phoneme selection error. However, in
some rare cases, it is difficult to conceive that
the error involves anything but a distinctive
feature (Fromkin, 1971; Shattuck-Hufnagel &
Klatt, 1979):

clear blue sky → glear plue sky
(an exchange of the voice feature between
the initial phonemes of the first two words).

In the substitution of one phoneme for
another, the change tends to involve a minimum
number of distinctive features, usually one or
two, rarely more than three (Green, 1969;
Lecours & Lhermitte, 1969; MacKay, 1970;

Poncet et al., 1972; S. Blumstein, 1973b; Burns & Canter, 1977; Keller, 1978; Klich et al., 1979; La Pointe & Johns, 1975; Shinn & Blumstein, 1983; Niemi & Koivuselkä-Sallinen, 1985; Caramazza et al., 1986; Valdois et al., 1988).

Environmental Influences on Phonemic Selection Errors

Phonemic selection errors are frequently influenced by their phonemic environment (S. Blumstein, 1973a). Lecours and Lhermitte (1969) suggested that most phonemic additions, deletions, and substitutions in jargon aphasia can be viewed as sequential errors. These are errors in which a phoneme or phoneme cluster is altered such that, most often, it becomes closer to (in number of distinctive features) a preceding or following phoneme or phoneme cluster that resembles it in terms of distinctive features. The similarity between interacting phonemes observed by Lecours and Lhermitte has also been demonstrated in normal subjects (Garrett, 1975; A. W. Ellis, 1980). Sequential (contextual, environmental) phonemic errors are less common in Broca's aphasia and apraxia of speech than in conduction aphasia, and less common in conduction aphasia than in jargon aphasia (Poncet et al., 1972; Trost & Canter, 1974; La Pointe & Johns, 1975; Burns & Canter, 1977; Shewan, 1980; MacNeilage, 1982; Nespoulous et al., 1984; Canter et al., 1985; D. Miller & Ellis, 1987; Nespoulous et al., 1987; Valdois et al., 1988). This suggests that, as the production of language nears the output phase, the instantiation of phonemes as patterns of activity in articulatory motor representations matures and becomes less susceptible to the effects of perversions of knowledge of the phoneme sequences constituting words or phrases (and lexical semantic influences—see below) on phoneme selection. In contrast, at earlier stages, at which word- and even phrase-level effects are prominent and environmentally linked, phoneme errors are generated, these errors will tend to reflect the properties of the words and multiphoneme sublexical elements rather than the properties of the phoneme.

The occurrence of both anticipatory and perseverative errors reinforces the concept that, as the brain processes phonemes, a number are maintained in a similar state of activity for some time, notwithstanding that they occur sequentially in the output phoneme stream. Thus, a given phoneme may have as much opportunity to influence phonemes later in the stream (perseverative errors) as there is opportunity for later phonemes to influence it (anticipatory errors). The relative frequency of anticipatory and perseverative errors in different types of aphasia may be related in good part to some mix of speech rate effects and impairment of lexical-semantic access (Dell, 1986). Slow speech rates and better lexical-semantic access will tend to correct perseverative errors.

Phonemic Clumping

Phonemic substitutions, additions, deletions, or metatheses, whether in aphasic speech or slip-of-the-tongue errors, may involve phonemic aggregations or clumps of various sizes. These include joint phonemes (e.g., a consonant cluster), syllables, rhymes (e.g., "stop"), affixes, and stems (Lecours & Lhermitte, 1969; Fromkin, 1971; S. E. Blumstein, 1978; Buckingham et al., 1978; Shattuck-Hufnagel, 1979; Shewan, 1980; Stemberger, 1982; Dell, 1986).

Malapropisms (in aphasic speech, often referred to as formal, form-related, or verbal paraphasias) represent substitutions at the word level that are driven by similarity in phonology, number of syllables, stress pattern, and grammatic form, and are unconstrained or only partially constrained by meaning (unlike semantic paraphasias). They provide evidence that spoken word representations exist, independent of meaning, as large phonemic clumps (Fay & Cutler, 1977; Blanken, 1990).

Functors or free grammatical morphemes (closed-class items such as articles, prepositions, and conjunctions) are rarely involved in phonemic paraphasic errors, suggesting that they exist as nearly indissoluble clumps of phonemes (S. Blumstein, 1973a; Garrett, 1975; Lecours, 1982; Stemberger, 1984; Kohn & Smith, 1990). Many have suggested that the relative preservation of functors is a word frequency effect, functors being the most commonly used words (A. W. Ellis et al., 1983; Stemberger & MacWhinney, 1986; A. W. Ellis & Young, 1988).

Neologisms involving major lexical items also exhibit a strong word frequency effect (Strub & Gardner, 1974; Allport, 1984; McCarthy & Warrington, 1984; A. W. Ellis, 1985; D. Bub et al., 1987; D. Miller & Ellis, 1987; Pate et al., 1987; N. Martin & Saffran, 1992).

The size of the units of substitution, addition, deletion, and metathesis is roughly related, like the pattern of environmental influence on phoneme selection errors, to the posterior extent of the lesion responsible for aphasia. Subjects with Broca's aphasia (anterior lesions) are most likely to exhibit literal paraphasias best characterized as single phoneme or distinctive feature alterations. Subjects with posterior lesions with Wernicke's or, even more so, jargon aphasia (Kertesz & Benson, 1970), are most likely to exhibit paraphasias best characterized as joint phoneme, syllable, or morpheme alterations.

Phonotactic Constraints

Sublexical substitutions obey phonetic rules (phonotactic constraints), indicating that rarely in either aphasic or slip-of-the-tongue errors is there evidence of a capability for producing phonemic sequences that are beyond the native speaker (Fromkin, 1971; MacKay, 1972; S. Blumstein, 1973a; Buckingham & Kertesz, 1974; Garrett, 1975; S. E. Blumstein, 1978; Butterworth, 1979; Buckingham, 1980; Niemi & Koivuselkä-Sallinen, 1985). For example:

plant the seed/z/ → plan the seat/s/
*sph*inx in the moonlight → minx in the *sp*oonlight

Failure to modify these selection errors would have resulted in the impermissible sequences seat/z/ and "sphoonlight." Blumstein (S. Blumstein, 1973a) found that only 2.6% of phonemic errors resulted in non-English sequences.

Phonotactic constraints are now defined in terms of phonotactic probabilities (Vitevitch et al., 2004): the frequency with which phonemes and phoneme sequences occur in words in a given language. In picture-naming and nonword repetition tasks, words with high-probability phonemes and phoneme sequences are produced more quickly and accurately than are words with low phonotactic probability, indicating that selection of a phonological word form is influenced not just by semantic factors, but also by the phonological properties of the word (Vitevitch & Rodríguez, 2004; Vitevitch & Luce, 2005). These results suggest that high phonotactic probability, which reflects the extent of the experience of the speaker with phonological sequence production, corresponds to the stronger neural connectivity in phonological networks that provides the basis for faster processing.

Lexical and Semantic Influence

As phonological processing proceeds over time, it continues to be influenced by lexical semantic constraints, even in aphasia. There are four lines of evidence of lexical/semantic constraints on phonological processing:

First, phonemic selection errors are constrained by the lexical target, and both normal subjects and aphasic subjects make more phonological errors repeating nonwords than real words (Brener, 1940; Alajouanine & Lhermitte, 1973; A. D. Martin & Rigrodsky, 1974). Aphasic subjects with relatively good access to lexical targets (e.g., Broca's, conduction) demonstrate *conduite d'approche* (continuous improvement in their effort to zero-in on the target through successive attempts), whereas those with poor lexical-semantic access (e.g., subjects with Wernicke's aphasia) are much less likely to exhibit this phenomenon (Butterworth, 1979; Joanette et al., 1980; D. Miller & Ellis, 1987; Valdois et al., 1989; Gandour et al., 1994; but see also Goodglass et al. 1997). The phonological improvement noted during *conduite d'approche* is seen only with real words, and not with nonwords. Mistakes by subjects who make errors only during nonword repetition tend to reflect lexicalization (D. Bub et al., 1987). Normal subjects are more likely to produce real-word spoonerisms (e.g., barn door → darn boor) than nonword spoonerisms (e.g., dart board → bart doard) (Baars et al., 1975; Garrett, 1976; Dell & Reich, 1981). The likelihood of such real-word spoonerisms can be enhanced by semantic priming. For example, Motley and Baars (1976) found that "get one" is more likely to slip to "wet gun" if preceded by "damp rifle."

Second, in normal subjects, the ultimate selection of a phonological sequence is influenced not just by the semantic representation of the word (which determines the lexical target) and phonotactic probabilities, but also by the effects of phonological neighborhoods. Phonological neighborhood density refers to the number of words that contain phoneme sequences that are similar to phonemic sequences of a given word. For example, a neighbor may be defined as a word that differs by one phoneme from the target word (Vitevitch & Rodríguez, 2004), although a variety of operational definitions has been employed. Words that share sequences with many other words have *dense* neighborhoods, whereas words that share sequences with few other words have *sparse* neighborhoods. The existence of neighborhood density effects provides strong evidence of top-down/bottom-up interactions between semantic and phonological representations in the course of word production, and studies suggest that these interactions occur during repetition as well. Vitevitch and colleagues (Vitevitch, 1997, 2002; Vitevitch & Sommers, 2003), using a series of speech-error elicitation and picture-naming tasks, showed that in English, words with dense neighborhoods were named more quickly and accurately than were those with sparse neighborhoods. This suggests that, during speech production, the many neighbors in dense neighborhoods act to increase engagement of the target phonological form and thereby speed production. However, precisely opposite effects were observed in Spanish (Vitevitch & Stamer, 2006) (for possible explanation, see below: Phonological Decoding). Lipinski and Gupta (2005) examined the effect of neighborhood density on repetition of nonwords. Repetition latencies tended to be shorter for stimuli with low-density neighborhoods. It seems that, in the absence of a semantically driven target, higher neighborhood density leads to slower repetition because all the different words in these neighborhoods, although they share a sequence with the word to be repeated, also include other sequences that engage competing phonological representations. However, Lipinski and

Gupta's experiments also showed that in nonword repetition tasks, phonotactic probability effects trump neighborhood density effects.

Third, observations on abstruse neologisms (neologisms without evident relationship to a plausible target) suggest that lexical-semantic constraints reach deep into the phonological processor, even as excessive noise within that processor interferes with the correct selection of phonemic sequences from concept representations. Neologisms in jargon aphasia have the same number of syllables as the target up to 80% of the time, and they share a greater than chance number of phonemes (and particularly the initial phoneme) with the target, suggesting substantial sublexical access from semantics (concept representations) mediated by connectivity supporting lexical semantics, even when the target is not sufficiently resolved to assure correct output (A. W. Ellis et al., 1983; D. Miller & Ellis, 1987; Valdois et al., 1989; Wilshire, 1998). Neologisms in general reflect disproportionate influence by phonological factors (due to damage to lexical semantic constraints), combined with degradation of phonological sequence knowledge, in the selection of lexical and sublexical components. In jargon aphasia, there is less semantic influence, and the lexical target constantly shifts, so that successive neologisms do not exhibit *conduite d'approche*. In conduction aphasia, relatively greater semantic influence preserves a lexical target most of the time, except in rare malapropisms, thus providing the basis for *conduite d'approche*.

Fourth, in experiments in which normal subjects are given the definition of low-frequency words and develop the "tip-of-the-tongue" (TOT) phenomenon (have a sense that they know the word but cannot actually produce it), there is evidence of sublexical access from concept representations despite unsuccessful lexical access. Despite anomia, subjects are able to guess the number of syllables in the target word with high accuracy; show knowledge of letters within the word, for example guessing the first letter with 57% accuracy; and show knowledge of which syllable in the target is accented (R. Brown & McNeill, 1966; Yarmey, 1973; Koriat & Lieblich, 1974; A. S. Brown, 1991; Burke et al., 1991). In many cases, joint morphemes and syllables are retrieved (Rubin, 1975). Many of the products of naming attempts are phonologically related to the target and many are nonwords that obey the phonotactic rules of the native language and share an affix or root with the target (Kohn et al., 1987). Aphasic subjects are also able to guess the first letter and the number of syllables with far greater than chance accuracy when they develop the TOT phenomenon; however, subjects with conduction or Broca's aphasia are far better than are subjects with Wernicke's or anomic aphasia (Barton, 1971; Goodglass et al., 1976; Laine & Martin, 1996). Even subjects with anomic aphasia may be able to correctly identify the rhyming properties of the names of pictures they cannot actually name (Marin et al., 1976; Feinberg et al., 1986; D. N. Bub et al., 1988). These data suggest that neural activity representing meaning engages phonemes and sublexical clumps of phonemes even when the word representation in aggregate is not sufficiently engaged to elevate it above the threshold for production.

Summary

Studies of phonological selection in normal and aphasic subjects provide evidence of a number of essential properties of the cerebral system instantiating phonological processing: (a) hierarchical structure; (b) simultaneous influence by lexical-semantic and phonological effects; (c) strong influence by phonemic sequence knowledge (phonotactic probabilities); (d) top-down/bottom-up interaction effects in phoneme selection, as reflected in phonological neighborhood effects; (e) simultaneous processing of a chunk of the language stream, such that lexical and sublexical elements influence other elements that both precede and follow them; (f) anatomic distribution, such that lesion locus has major effects on the pattern of breakdown observed; (g) substantial but not absolute similarity between the errors made by aphasic subjects and errors made by normal subjects in slips-of-the-tongue; (h) stochastic function, such that lesions are associated with a reduced probability of correct phonological selection, with actual performance that is variable, and relative preservation of ability to distinguish correct from incorrect.

PHONOLOGICAL DECODING

Errors in acoustic processing exhibit some of the same features as errors in articulatory processing. "Slips-of-the-ear" by normal subjects tend to involve errors of one distinctive feature (Bond & Garnes, 1980). Subjects with aphasias of all types do better with discriminations involving two or more distinctive features relative to discriminations involving a single distinctive feature (S. E. Blumstein et al., 1977; Miceli et al., 1978; Miceli et al., 1980). Neighborhood density effects have been shown in slips of the ear. Vitevitch (2002) analyzed a preexisting corpus containing speech perception errors (Bond, 1999) and found that more slips of the ear tend to occur in words with dense phonological neighborhoods than with words with sparse neighborhoods, suggesting that multiple word forms are activated and compete during spoken word recognition. As for word production, word recognition is influenced by phonological sequence effects: words characterized by higher probability phonemes and phonological sequences are identified more quickly and accurately (Vitevitch & Luce, 1999). Neighborhood density and the frequency of words in the neighborhood also influence word recognition. In English, high neighborhood density and frequency slow lexical decision (determining whether what has been heard is a word or nonword), apparently because the multitude of neighbors compete (Vitevitch & Stamer, 2006). However, as in word production (see above), the results of lexical decision experiments in Spanish are opposite those in English—in Spanish, dense neighborhoods speed recognition. The reasons for these conflicting results are not fully understood. They may have to do with the fact that Spanish is an inflectionally richer language than English (Vitevitch & Stamer, 2006). In Spanish, many of the neighbors are inflectional forms of the same root. In a recognition task, these inflectional derivations facilitate rather than compete. On the other hand, in production, the first part of the word engages many competing inflectional derivations, which then serve to slow completion of production. In contrast, in English, there is little opportunity during recognition tasks for various neighbors to reinforce a common root, and in production tasks, little opportunity for them to engage competing inflectional affixes.

Difficulty in discriminating or labeling bears little relationship to comprehension ability in subjects with aphasia, which is probably defined to a far greater degree by lexical-semantic access; that is, by the integrity of the connections between the substrates for acoustic and concept representations (Baker et al., 1981).

Lexical-semantic effects are evident in auditory perception. Aphasic subjects make more errors with discriminations involving phonemes in nonwords than in real words (S. E. Blumstein et al., 1977; see also Elman & McClelland, 1988). If subjects with Broca's aphasia are faced with difficult phonetic discriminations involving ambiguous stimuli (e.g., indicate whether the first phoneme in "duke" is /d/ or /t/ when the actual /d/ sound is synthesized with voice onset time spanning the range between normal /d/ and /t/), they are unduly biased by lexical effects compared with normal subjects (e.g., more likely to answer /d/ if the word is "duke" than if it is "doot"), consistent with impaired phonetic processing (S. E. Blumstein et al., 1994). Normal subjects will exhibit lexical bias when additional semantic influences are brought to bear. When they hear synthetic words containing acoustically ambiguous phonemes, they will "hear" the form that is semantically congruent. For example, when /b-deIt/ is preceded by "there's the fishing gear and the . . . ," they will hear "bait," whereas when it is preceded by "check the time and the . . . ," they will hear "date"(Bond & Garnes, 1980).

CONDUCTION APHASIA

Conduction aphasia is characterized by impaired repetition, in most cases frequent phonemic paraphasias, occasional semantic and verbal paraphasias, and variable lexical access in spontaneous language and naming to confrontation, with relative sparing of comprehension and grammar (Benson et al., 1973; Dubois et al., 1973; Green & Howes, 1977; Kohn, 1984; Bartha & Benke, 2003). Subjects are not anosognosic and characteristically make extensive attempts to correct their errors. Conduction aphasia is essentially a disorder of phonological processing, and it is caused by a lesion at the core of the neural substrate for phonological processing. On the other hand, because subjects with conduction aphasia have relatively spared lexical access and articulation, they are able to produce voluminous output. For these reasons, conduction aphasia provides an ideal situation for the study of phonological processing, and studies of subjects with conduction aphasia have contributed a great deal to our understanding of phonological processing.

Two different types of conduction aphasia have been defined: repetition conduction aphasia and reproduction conduction aphasia. Repetition conduction aphasia is characterized by relatively normal naming and spontaneous language; no phonemic paraphasias, even in repetition; usually poor phonetic discrimination; impaired auditory-verbal short-term memory; and severely impaired repetition. Reproduction conduction aphasia is characterized by impaired repetition, naming, and spontaneous language with the production of phonemic paraphasic errors in all three. Whether spontaneous language or repetition is more impaired depends on the distribution of the lesion. Auditory verbal short-term memory may be nearly normal. Since many individual subjects exhibit features of both, these two disorders are probably best viewed as defining the two ends of a spectrum.

Repetition Conduction Aphasia and Auditory Verbal Short-term Memory

Warrington and Shallice (1969) suggested that the fundamental problem in repetition conduction aphasia is one of auditory-verbal short-term memory, based on observations that these subjects have auditory digit spans of 1–3; fail to exhibit a recency effect in digit recall (thought to depend on phonological short-term memory stores; see Acheson & MacDonald, 2009); demonstrate a primacy effect, and perform better with familiar, meaningful, and more slowly presented stimuli (suggesting reliance on semantic short term memory stores; Acheson & MacDonald, 2009); and perform poorly on the Brown-Petersen test of memory. In contrast, subjects with reproduction conduction aphasia may have relatively preserved digit spans (H. Damasio & Damasio, 1980; Bartha & Benke, 2003). The auditory-verbal short-term memory hypothesis has been extensively debated (Warrington et al., 1971; Warrington & Shallice, 1972; Strub & Gardner, 1974; Saffran & Marin, 1975; Shallice & Warrington, 1977; Caramazza et al., 1981; Friedrich et al., 1984; Vallar & Baddeley, 1984; Shallice & Vallar, 1990). There are two possible ways in which the neural substrate for phonological processing could support short-term memory: through the transient, sustained activation of the acoustic and articulatory motor phonological networks (phonological working memory); and through the use of linked acoustic and articulatory motor networks for silent rehearsal (the phonological loop posited by Baddeley (Baddeley et al., 1998).

To the extent that auditory-verbal short-term memory deficits reflect impaired ability to silently rehearse, they are a result rather than a cause of the behavior observed. However, to the extent that auditory-verbal short-term memory deficits reflect damage to the neurologic substrate for phonological working memory (the phonological processor itself), it is reasonable to view them as indicative of a genuine deficit in immediate memory (Caramazza et al., 1981). Because damage to articulatory motor representations impairs both silent rehearsal and the substrate for phonological working memory, one would expect auditory-verbal short-term memory deficits in subjects with Broca's aphasia or apraxia of speech, something that has been shown (Goodglass et al., 1970; Heilman et al., 1976; Cermak & Tarlow, 1978; Waters et al., 1992).

Reproduction Conduction Aphasia

Word-length Effects. Longer words pose greater problems for repetition because they increase the number of sublexical elements that are simultaneously being processed. This increases the opportunity for these elements to induce errors by interacting with each other and their various associated sublexical elements. Also, because the lesion reduces the reliability of bringing every one of multiple syllables above production threshold, this increases the opportunity for sublexical omissions (Alajouanine

& Lhermitte, 1973; Dubois et al., 1973; Yamadori & Ikumura, 1975; McCarthy & Warrington, 1984; Caplan et al., 1986; Caramazza et al., 1986; D. Bub et al., 1987; Pate et al., 1987; Valdois et al., 1988; Kohn, 1989; Friedman & Kohn, 1990; Kohn & Smith, 1991, 1995; Gandour et al., 1994). On the other hand, repetition of long words is less likely to result in verbal paraphasias because a single phonemic error is less likely to generate patterns of activity corresponding to other real words.

Variable Lexical Bias Effects. Lexical bias varies with lesion locus. To the extent that the neural substrates for concept representations or the pathways from them are damaged (manifested by anomia) and the substrate for phonological representations is spared, repetition of nonwords will be spared, and lexical bias effects will be reduced. To the extent that the substrate for phonological representations is damaged and pathways from the substrates for concept representations are spared, lexical bias effects will be increased and repetition of nonwords will be impaired.

Frequency Effects. Normal subjects repeat high-frequency words better than low-frequency words (Watkins & Watkins, 1977). Naming errors in aphasia are more likely with low-frequency targets (Kay & Ellis, 1987). Neologistic errors and phonemic paraphasias in jargon and conduction aphasia are more common with low-frequency than high-frequency targets (Strub & Gardner, 1974; Allport, 1984; McCarthy & Warrington, 1984; D. Bub et al., 1987; D. Miller & Ellis, 1987; Pate et al., 1987; N. Martin & Saffran, 1992), as are phonological slips in naturally occurring and experimentally induced slip-of-the-tongue errors (Stemberger, 1984; Dell, 1988; Stemberger & MacWhinney, 1986). In both aphasic and slip-of-the-tongue errors, less common phonemes and phoneme combinations tend to be replaced by more common phonemes and combinations.

Word frequency effects are constrained by the same factors that govern lexical bias. Thus, frequency effects in repetition are maximal when the substrates for concept representations and the pathways that link them to the phonological apparatus are intact and there is damage to the phonological apparatus. On the other hand, if repetition can occur rapidly and accurately, then access to concept representations has minimal impact (still less if there is damage to links to the substrates for concept representations), and frequency effects are much more modest (N. Martin & Saffran, 1997). However, as we have seen in studies of phonotactic constraints, the frequency of phonological sequences also exerts an influence on word production, word repetition, and word recognition.

A MODEL TO ACCOUNT FOR PHONOLOGICAL PROCESSING DISORDERS

Linguistic theories have not yet provided a satisfactory account for the phonological processing disorders observed either in aphasic subjects or in normal subjects demonstrating slips of the tongue. By far the most important reason is that linguistic theories do not enable us to explain behavior in terms of the properties of neural network function or brain organization, or to use what is known about neural network function as an aid to understanding behavior.

Parallel distributed processing models, also called *connectionist models*, offer an alternative approach (McClelland et al., 1986). The greatest source of appeal of PDP models is that they emulate neural networks, enabling us to precisely account for complex behaviors in terms of neural network function—something that behavioral neurologists and neuropsychologists could only dream of before the introduction of this computational approach. Parallel distributed processing models are neural-like in that they incorporate large arrays of simple units that are heavily interconnected with each other, like neurons in the brain. A PDP model that fully emulates neural network principles constitutes a hypothesis not just about the organization of cognitive processes but also about neural organization. The processing sophistication of PDP models stems from the simultaneous interaction of large numbers of units (hundreds or even thousands). The instantiation

of short-term memory (as patterns of unit activity) and long-term memory (as unit interconnection strengths) in the same neural nets that are responsible for processing further emulates brain function. Parallel distributed processing models are particularly appealing in the context of language processing because they involve simultaneous processing at a number of levels and locations, apparently mimicking what is going on in the brain. Finally, pure PDP models (models without incorporated digital devices) implicitly learn the rules governing the data they process in the course of their experience with that data (e.g., Plaut et al., 1996). Thus, in a pure PDP model of phonology, there is no need to build in specific structures to account for specific phonological phenomena. The structure of the model is defined entirely in terms of the domains of information accessible to it and the necessary relationship of these domains to each other. The absence of specific, ad hoc devices motivated by models (e.g., linguistic) designed to account for particular phonological phenomena in an orderly fashion is also crucial to the maintenance of neurological plausibility. In humans, as in PDP models, the phonological phenomena we observe reflect entirely the emergent behavior of the networks.

Parallel distributed processing models incorporate explicitly defined assumptions that are "wired" into them in the mathematical details of their computer implementation. They produce large numbers of predictions that can be (and have been) empirically tested through observations of normal subjects and brain-damaged individuals. They have been remarkably successful in emulating the behavior of these subjects, and systematic analysis of the internal structure of these models has helped us to understand the network basis for behavior. Parallel distributed processing models exhibit properties of graceful degradation and probabilistic selection; that is, when damaged or fed noisy input, they do not produce novel or bizarre output unachievable by an intact network with good input; rather, they tend to produce output that is not so reliably correct but is rule-bound—quite reminiscent of many of the observations that have been made about phonological selection errors.

DISTRIBUTED REPRESENTATION MODELS OF PHONOLOGICAL PROCESSING

Perhaps surprisingly, PDP models can be related in a very direct way to information processing models. The Wernicke-Lichtheim (W-L) information processing model of language function (Figure 3-1) has played a dominant role in understanding aphasic syndromes (Lichtheim, 1885) and has stood the test of time in defining the topographical relationship between the modular domains (acoustic representations, articulatory-motor representations, and concept representations) underlying spoken language function. Unfortunately, the W-L information processing model does not specify the characteristics of the representations within these domains and how they might be stored in the brain. It also does not address the means by which these domains might interact. We have proposed a PDP model that uses the same general topography as the W-L model (Nadeau, 2001; Roth et al., 2006), but also specifies how representations are generated in the modular domains and how knowledge is represented in

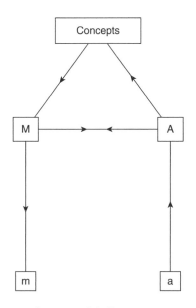

Figure 3–1. The W-L model of language processing. *A* represents acoustic representations, *M* motoric representations, *a* acoustic impulses, and *m* motor impulses. From Lichtheim, L. (1885). On aphasia. *Brain, 7,* 433–484.

the links between these domains (Figure 3-2). Although not tested through simulations, this model is neurally plausible and provides a cogent explanation for a broad range of psycholinguistic phenomena in normal subjects and subjects with aphasia. More generally, connectionist concepts are now deeply embedded in and receive enormous support from mainstream neuroscientific research (e.g., Rolls & Treves, 1998; Rolls & Deco, 2002), and they have become a major generative force in cognitive neuropsychological research.

The PDP modification of the W-L model posits that the acoustic domain (akin to Wernicke's area) contains large numbers of units located in auditory association cortices that represent acoustic features of phonemes.[1] The articulatory domain (analogous to Broca's area) contains units located predominantly in dominant frontal operculum that represent discrete articulatory features of speech, as opposed to continuously variable motor programs (e.g., phonemic distinctive features). The semantic or conceptual domain contains an array of units distributed throughout unimodal, polymodal, and supramodal association cortices that represent semantic features of concepts. For example, the representation of the concept of "house" might correspond to activation of units representing features of houses such as visual attributes, construction materials, contents (physical and human), etc. Each unit within a given domain is connected to many, if not most, of the other units in that same domain (symbolized by the small looping arrow appended to each domain in Figure 3-2). Knowledge within each domain is represented as connection strengths between the units. Thus, semantic knowledge is represented as the pattern of connection strengths throughout the association cortices supporting this knowledge. Within any domain, a representation corresponds to a specific pattern of activity of all the units, hence the term *distributed representation.* Each unit within each of these domains is connected via interposed hidden units to many, if not most, of the units in the other domains.[2] During learning of a language, the strengths of the connections between the units are gradually adjusted, so that a pattern of activity involving the units in one domain elicits the correct

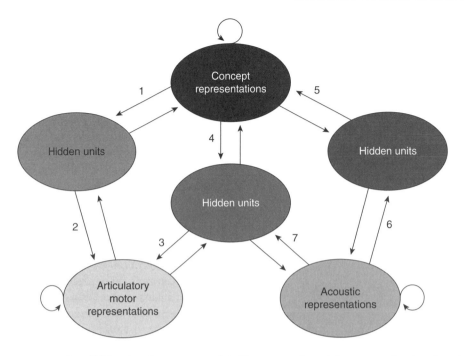

Figure 3–2. Proposed parallel distributed processing model of language. Pathway 6-5 represents the phonological input lexicon. Pathways 1-2 and 4-3 represent the phonological output lexicon.

pattern of activity in the units of another domain. The entire set of connections between any two domains forms a pattern associator network. The hidden unit regions, in conjunction with nonlinear unit properties, enable the systematic association of representations in two connected domains that are arbitrarily related to one another (e.g., word sound and word meaning). During any type of language processing initiated by input to any domain of the network, there will be almost instantaneous engagement of all domains of the network. Thus, linguistic behavior is best viewed as the emergent product of the *entire* network.

We will now focus on particular components of the network in order to provide a more detailed understanding of how they work and the nature of the knowledge they support.

Concept Representations

As noted, the W-L information processing model provides no insight into the nature of the representations in the various domains.

The nature of concept representations (depicted in Figure 3-2) can be best illustrated by a particular model developed by David Rumelhart and his colleagues (Rumelhart et al., 1986). This "rooms in a house" model was comprised of 40 "feature" units, each corresponding to an article typically found in particular rooms or an aspect of particular rooms. Each unit was connected with all the other units in the network—an attribute that defines the model as an *auto-associator network*. Auto-associator networks have the capacity for "settling" into particular states that define representations. Connection strengths were defined by the likelihood that any two features might appear together in a typical house. When one or more units were clamped into the "on" state (as if the network had been shown these particular features or articles), activation spread throughout the model, and the model eventually settled into a steady state that implicitly defined a particular room in a house. Thus, clamping "oven" ultimately resulted in activation of all the items one would expect to find in a kitchen and thereby *implicitly* defined, via a *distributed representation*, the concept of a kitchen. No kitchen unit per se was turned on. Rather, kitchen was defined by the pattern of feature units that were activated. The network contained the knowledge, in the totality of its connections, that enabled this representation to be generated. The 40-unit model actually had the capability of generating distributed representations of a number of different rooms in a house (e.g., bathroom, bedroom, living room, study), subcomponents of rooms (e.g., easy chair and floor lamp, desk and desk-chair, window and drapes), and blends of rooms that were not anticipated in the programming of the model (e.g., clamping both bed and sofa led to a distributed representation of a large, fancy bedroom replete with a fireplace, television, and sofa).

This auto-associator model, simple though it is, has the essential attributes of a network that might be capable of generating the distributed representations of meaning underlying semantics. The brain's semantic auto-associator obviously is comprised of vastly more that 40 features, and enables an enormous repertoire of distributed representations corresponding to the vast number of concepts we are capable of representing (see below: Semantics).

The Acoustic-Articulatory Motor Pattern Associator Network

The knowledge that allows a person to translate heard sound sequences into articulatory-motor sequences, and thereby mediates repetition of both real words and nonwords, is contained in the network that connects the acoustic domain to the articulatory motor domain (the acoustic-articulatory motor pattern associator, Figure 3-2, pathway 7-3). Because this network has acquired, through experience, knowledge of the systematic relationships between acoustic sequences and articulatory sequences, it has learned the sound sequence regularities of the language: the phonemic sequences of joint phonemes, rhymes, syllables, affixes, morphemes, and words characteristic of the language (i.e., phonotactic probabilities) (Nadeau, 2001).

Consideration of the reading model developed by Plaut and colleagues will help to make this more transparent (Seidenberg & McClelland, 1989; Plaut et al., 1996).

This reading model fundamentally recapitulates the acoustic-articulatory motor pathway of Figure 3-2, the major difference (inconsequential to this discussion) being that, in place of acoustic representations, it incorporated orthographic (printed letter) representations. The model was composed of three layers: (a) an input layer of 105 grapheme units grouped into clusters, the first cluster including all possibilities for the one or more consonants of the onset, the second cluster including all the possible vowels in the nucleus, and the third cluster including all possibilities for the one or more consonants in the coda; (b) a hidden unit layer of 100 units; and (c) an output layer of 61 phoneme units grouped into clusters including all the possibilities for onset, nucleus, and coda, respectively (as for the graphemes). Local representations were used for the graphemes and phonemes. There were one-way connections from each of the grapheme input units to each of the hidden units, and two-way connections between each of the hidden units and each of the phoneme output units. Every output unit was connected to every other output unit, providing the network with the auto-associator capability for "settling into" the best solution (as opposed to its own approximate solution). The model was trained using a mathematical algorithm (back propagation) that incrementally alters the strengths of connections in proportion to the contribution they make to the error, which is computed as the difference between the actual output of the network and the desired output of the network. The orthographic representations of 3,000 English, single-syllable words and their corresponding phonological forms were presented, one pair at a time, cycling repeatedly through the entire orpus. In this way, the model ultimately learned to produce the correct pronunciation of all the words it had read. One of the most striking things about the trained model is that it also was able to produce correct pronunciations of plausible English nonwords (i.e., orthographic sequences it had never encountered before). How was this possible?

One might have inferred that the model was simply learning the pronunciation of all the words by rote. If this had been the case, however, the model would have been incapable of applying what it had learned to novel words. In fact, what the model learned was the relationships between *sequences* of graphemes and *sequences* of phonemes that are characteristic of the English language. To the extent that there is a limited repertoire of sequence types, the model was able to learn it and then apply that knowledge to novel forms that incorporated some of the sequential relationships in this repertoire. The information the model acquired through its long experience with English orthographic-phonological sequential relationships went considerably beyond this, however. Certain sequences, those most commonly found in English single-syllable words, were more thoroughly etched in network connectivity. Thus, it was very fast with high-frequency words. It was also very fast with words with an absolutely consistent orthographic-phonologic sequence relationship, such as with words ending in "ust," which are always pronounced /ʌst/ (must, bust, trust, lust, crust, etc.). The model encountered difficulty (reflected in prolonged reading latency) only with low-frequency words, and only to the extent that it had learned different, competing pronunciations of the same orthographic sequence. Thus, it was slow to read "pint" because in every case but "pint," the sequence "int" is pronounced /ɪnt/ (e.g., mint, tint, flint, lint). It was also slow, although not quite so slow, to read words like "shown" because there are two equally frequent alternatives to the pronunciation of "own" (gown, down, town vs. shown, blown, flown). It was very slow with words that are unique in their orthographic-phonologic sequence relationship (e.g., aisle, guide, and fugue). These behaviors precisely recapitulate the behavior of normal human subjects given reading tasks.

The knowledge the model acquires reflects competing effects of type frequency and token frequency. If a single word is sufficiently common (high token frequency), the model acquires enough experience with it that competing orthographic-phonologic sequential relationships have a negligible impact on naming latency. However, if a word is relatively uncommon (e.g., pint), its naming latency will be significantly affected by the knowledge of other words that, although equally uncommon, together belong to a competing type (e.g., mint, flint, tint, sprint).

The implicit knowledge of various regularities captured by the model (and the brain) through experience defines quasi-regular domains. For example, in the case of words ending in "own," orthographic-phonologic regularity exists but it is only quasi-regular because there is not one but two alternatives (shown vs. gown), a particular alternative being determined by the onset cluster. Quasi-regular domains may be composed of more or less equally competing subdomains, each corresponding to a regularity, as in the case of "own" words, or a domain that is regular but for a single member (e.g., mint, tint, splint, etc. vs. pint). In some cases, they may be fully regular (e.g., the "_ust" words). The higher the frequency of a word, the stronger the connectivity between units involved in its production, the less its production is influenced by similarity to neighbors, and the more it approaches a regular domain that has only one member. Whether or not linguistic forms belong to particular quasi-regular domains depends upon the particular regularities that the network is endowed to capture through experience. When a neural network supporting a quasi-regular domain settles into the wrong state, the result is a paraphasic error: phonemic, verbal, or semantic, but also morphologic (paragrammatic) or syntactic, depending on the network.

The capacity of Plaut et al.'s model to read nonwords reflects its ability to capture patterns in the sequential relationships between orthographic and articulatory word forms and to apply this knowledge to novel word forms. Plaut et al. (1996), as well as Seidenberg and McClelland (1989), in their earlier work on this reading model, focused on differences in rhyme components of single-syllable words because these are the major determinants of whether a word is orthographically regular (e.g., mint) or irregular (e.g., pint). However, as Seidenberg and McClelland point out, the network architecture in these models is capable of capturing any kind of regularity in the orthographic and phonological sequences it is exposed to, limited only by the extent of exposure. Such regularities would include joint phonemes other than rhymes (e.g., "str" of stream, street, stray, and strum), and, in a multisyllabic version, syllables and morphemes (affixes and the root forms of nouns and verbs, as well as functors; e.g. articles, auxiliary verbs, conjunctions, and prepositions).

The acoustic-articulatory motor pathway in the model of Figure 3-2 would capture analogous patterns in the sequential relationships between acoustic and articulatory word forms. These sequential relationship patterns (captured in part by measure of phonotactic probabilities—biphone frequencies) potentially involve sequences of varying length, from phoneme pairs (joint phonemes) and syllables, up to and including whole words and possibly multiple word compounds. These patterns represent the repository of knowledge about subword (sublexical) entities in general, as well as our knowledge of phonotactic constraints. As we have seen, this repository of sequence knowledge is additionally influenced by neighborhood effects. Any given phoneme sequence represented in the acoustic-articulatory motor pattern associator comprises part of one or more words. These words define the phonological neighborhood of that sequence. They are engaged through bottom-up/top-down interactions between the acoustic-articulatory motor pattern associator and the domains of concept representations. Thus, the final production of a phoneme sequence is a reflection of the combined effects of input (e.g., acoustic or conceptual), phonotactic effects, neighborhood effects, and noise in the system. Phonotactic effects are seen in tendencies to produce near-miss errors that are off by a small number of phonemic distinctive features (usually one or two); as, for example, /pat/ in lieu of /bat/. Phonological neighborhood effects are seen in often larger errors that substantially reflect regularities in patterns of semantic-phonological knowledge (as in lexical effects, e.g., /rat/ in lieu of /cat/). As we have seen, errors predominantly influenced by phonotactic effects are most often seen in Broca's aphasia, whereas errors substantially influenced by phonological neighborhood effects are most often seen in conduction and Wernicke's aphasia.

Lexicons

Understanding the meaning of a word that is heard is achieved through the connections between the neural domain that contains the sound features of language and the neural domain that contains concept features (the acoustic-concepts representations pattern associator, Figure 3-2, pathway 6-5). This pattern associator network corresponds to the cognitive neuropsychological concept of a phonological input lexicon (A. W. Ellis & Young, 1988). It contains neither knowledge of acoustics nor knowledge of semantics—it serves only to translate a representation in the acoustic domain into a representation in the concepts/semantics domain (where meaning is instantiated). This conceptualization of a lexicon as a vast number of connections between two network domains, although well accepted in the connectionist literature, is not intuitive and is strongly at odds with traditional conceptualizations of lexicons as repositories of abstract local representations of single words. However, it begins to make sense when one recalls that all representations in the central nervous system are distributed (like the "kitchen" representation), not local, and that the knowledge that underlies the capacity to generate a representation lies in connection strengths and is not a piece of data at a memory location (as in a digital computer).

The knowledge that enables a person to translate a concept into a spoken word (the phonological output lexicon (A. W. Ellis & Young, 1988) is presumably contained in two different pattern associator networks that connect the concept representations domain to the articulatory motor domain (Figure 3-2, pathways 1-2 and 4-3). These two pattern associator networks support different forms of knowledge. The indirect concept representations–articulatory motor pathway (pathway 4-3) provides a robust basis for knowledge of sequences and sublexical entities because of the sequence knowledge stored in the acoustic–articulatory motor pattern associator. However, the direct concept representations–articulatory motor pattern associator (pathway 1-2) does not contain much knowledge of sequences and sublexical entities because it translates spatially distributed patterns of activity corresponding to concepts into temporally distributed sequences of activity corresponding to articulated words. This spatial-temporal translation precludes significant acquisition of sequence knowledge and makes this substantially a whole-word pathway. The existence of this direct, whole-word naming route finds support in studies of subjects with repetition conduction aphasia, some of whom appear to have lost most phonological sequence knowledge (pathways 3, 4, and 7; resulting in a severe deficit in auditory verbal short-term memory), but can speak quite well, producing few if any phonological paraphasic errors. They can also repeat real words (with evidence of influence by semantic attributes but little influence of word length). However, they are severely impaired in repeating nonwords and functors (Warrington & Shallice, 1969; Saffran & Marin, 1975; Caramazza et al., 1981; Friedrich et al., 1984). The existence of the direct route is also supported by reports of subjects with conduction aphasia who are able to repeat words better than nonwords (Saffran & Marin, 1975; Friedrich et al., 1984; McCarthy & Warrington, 1984; Caramazza et al., 1986), and who are able to repeat words better when they are given in a sentence context than when given as a single word (thereby increasing the likelihood of engaging concept representations) (McCarthy & Warrington, 1984). However, a model in which the only link from the concept representations domain to the articulatory motor domain is the direct one (pathway 1-2) cannot account for observations that normal subjects exhibit phonological slips of the tongue, and aphasic subjects produce phonemic paraphasias in naming and internally generated spoken language quite comparable to those produced during repetition. To explain these observations, one must posit access from concept representations to phonological sequence knowledge, as indicated in pathway 4-3 of the model. Thus, this PDP model predicts that there should be two pathways enabling naming of concepts.

Further evidence of two pathways supporting naming of concepts has been provided by a patient who, depending upon type of verbal cue provided, could be induced to use either the whole-word (direct) naming route or the phonological (indirect) naming route (Roth et al., 2006). This left-handed man had a Broca's aphasia stemming from a massive infarct involving the entire left middle cerebral artery territory. His language output was largely limited to single words, which he produced quite readily and with good articulation. He tended to pursue a semantic *conduite d'approche*, which, however was successful only about 10% of the time. He made very rare phonological paraphasic errors. When asked to name an object, for example a faucet, and given either no cue or a semantic cue, a typical response would be "dishes . . . chairs . . . dishwasher . . . shut . . . water . . . ready to go . . . water . . . shut . . . hot . . . cold . . . sink . . . water . . . heavy . . . water . . . heavy . . . washer . . . tub." However, when given the phonemic cue "faus," he replied: "fauwash . . . fau . . . fau . . . fauswah . . . thafaush . . . fallshine . . . fallsha . . . fallshvine . . . fallswash . . . fallsh." These patterns of response to bedside testing suggested that he normally used a whole-word route to confrontation naming (as well as in internally generated language) (pathway 1-2, Figure 3-2), but that by providing him with a phonemic cue, we could induce him to employ a phonological route—a route that engaged sublexical representations implicit in his stores of phonological sequence knowledge (pathway 4-3, Figure 3-2). He actually was able to successfully name objects 30% of the time using this pathway, but at the cost of producing large numbers of undesirable nonword errors. The dual-route naming hypothesis was further tested and validated in this patient using systematic cued naming studies.

Phonological Paraphasic Errors

Phonological paraphasic errors are generally thought to reflect damage to dominant hemisphere networks supporting phonological processing. In our model, this would correspond to the dominant hemisphere acoustic–articulatory motor pattern associator network (pathway 7-3, Figure 3-2)—the repository of phonological sequence knowledge. Nonpropositional spoken language, which may be supported by the nondominant hemisphere (Speedie et al., 1993), does reflect sequence knowledge but discrete phrasal, lexical, or sublexical elements of this knowledge cannot be selected at will, as they can be in propositional language processing. The patient with Broca's aphasia described in the previous section (Roth et al., 2006), who could be cued to use one or other of the two concept naming routes (pathways 1-2 or 4-3; Figure 3-1), provides new insight into the neural basis of phonological paraphasic errors. His left hemisphere was nearly completely destroyed. Thus, he must have been speaking using his right hemisphere, which was undamaged, and his performance when naming after phonemic cueing suggests that he was using discretely accessible phonological sequence knowledge represented in his right hemisphere. These observations suggest that deficient development of networks instantiating this knowledge (as contrasted to damage to fully developed

networks) can provide an alternative basis for phonological paraphasic errors.

Factors Influencing Phonological and Lexical Errors in Internally Generated Aphasic Language

In the two-route naming model we have discussed, three factors may influence the pattern of errors observed in internally generated spoken language in perisylvian aphasias (and whether this pattern is marked exclusively by impaired word retrieval, or additionally, by phonemic paraphasic errors). First, given the likely anatomic representation of the network shown in Figure 3-2, most dominant perisylvian lesions probably damage both the whole-word and the phonological output routes (Figure 3-3), and the pattern of spoken output may reflect the relative degree to which these two pattern associator networks are affected. This would explain why subjects with

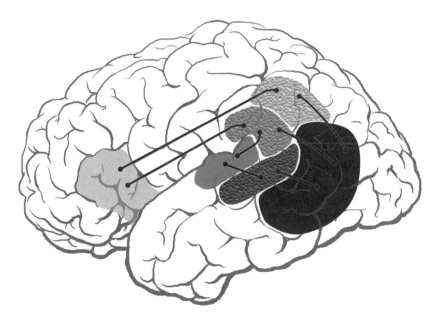

Figure 3–3. Cartoon depicting the network of Figure 3-1 mapped onto the brain. Pattern coding as in Figure 3-1. Concept representations are assumed to be widely distributed across association cortices throughout the brain. In this cartoon, only the region of presumed interface between concept representations and the remainder of the model is depicted. Given the paucity of information about the anatomic organization of the human perisylvian region, the mapping depicted here is, at best, approximate; our goal is primarily to demonstrate the feasibility of mapping a connectionist architecture of phonologic processing to cortical anatomy.

Wernicke's or conduction aphasia apparently do not have the option of relying entirely on the whole-word route. Second, these two output pattern associator networks are likely to be differentially represented in the two hemispheres, with the phonological pathway being more frequently better developed in the dominant hemisphere and the whole-word pathway more equally developed in the two hemispheres. Subjects with dominant hemisphere perisylvian lesions almost invariably demonstrate impaired phonologic sequence knowledge but often exhibit partial sparing of semantic-phonological (lexical) knowledge. Studies of subjects with callosal disconnection demonstrate that the disconnected right hemisphere has a phonological input lexicon and conceptual semantic knowledge but impoverished phonological processing (Zaidel et al., 2003). Third, there may be individual variability in the degree to which connectivity

is developed in these two output routes and this individual variability may vary as a function of hemisphere. Thus, in order to fully understand language production following a left hemisphere lesion, a bihemispheric language model that incorporates both developmental attributes and the impact of the lesion must be considered (Figure 3-4).

As the case of Roth et al. (2006) suggests, in the presence of an extensive left hemisphere perisylvian lesion, deficient development of connectivity in nondominant hemisphere concept representations may lead to the generation of anomia and semantic paraphasic errors, and deficient development of connectivity in the nondominant hemisphere phonological route may lead to the generation of phonemic paraphasic errors. The deficient development of both systems, particularly the phonological one, may be a general characteristic of the right hemisphere, but deficient development of the

Figure 3–4. Cartoon depicting mapping of a bihemispheric model to the brain. This provides the basis for a fuller explanation of the results of left hemisphere lesions on language output in terms of bihemispheric contributions, the effect of the lesion, and the degree to which various networks are developed in each hemisphere. Pattern coding as in Figures 3-2 and 3-3. HU, hidden units.

phonological route might also occur to one degree or another in the left hemisphere as a result of normal variability in phonological network ontogenesis (Goodglass, 1993; Plaut et al., 1996).

Subjects with reproduction conduction or Wernicke's aphasia predominantly use damaged or inadequately developed phonological pathways. Wernicke's aphasia may reflect more severe impairment, hence greater difficulty with word retrieval and more profuse phonemic paraphasic errors than in conduction aphasia. Subjects with Wernicke's aphasia may also have damage to acoustic representations or the acoustic representations–concept representations pathways that enable verbal comprehension. Naming difficulty may arise through mechanisms discussed in the preceding paragraph or in two additional ways. First, damage to Brodmann's areas 37 and 39 in the dominant hemisphere may be associated with word retrieval deficits (Hart & Gordon, 1990; Chertkow et al., 1997; Raymer et al., 1997; Whatmough et al., 2002). These areas may constitute the interface between association cortices throughout the brain supporting concept representations and the core language apparatus (proximal to the point at which the phonological naming route provides differential access to sequence knowledge). Second, dysfunction of conceptual (semantic) networks because of left hemisphere damage and deficient development of right hemisphere networks, as in the patient of Roth et al. (2006), would be expected to yield naming difficulty with production of semantic paraphasic errors.

Processes Occurring During Recovery

The dual-route naming model, as just elaborated, can also account for the patterns of evolution of internally generated spoken language observed during recovery. First, recovery of connectivity in the dominant hemisphere phonological route, or enhancement of deficient connectivity in phonological routes in either hemisphere, would lead to increased naming success and a reduction in phonemic paraphasic errors. Second, because articulatory motor representations normally depend on input from both the whole-word and phonological routes

for activation, damage to either route could lead to anomia as representations fail to reach threshold for activation (a diaschisis effect). Changes may occur in the connectivity within articulatory representations or in surviving connectivity within the two naming routes, such that this diaschisis effect diminishes with time. Third, in normal brain development, neural network connectivity in the two hemispheres presumably evolves such that transcallosal pathways facilitate coordinated bihemispheric activity and do not impede independent unihemispheric activity. A lesion may disrupt this precise interhemispheric coordination (another form of diaschisis), potentially rendering transcallosal input dysfunctional until appropriate readjustment of connectivity within and between hemispheres occurs in the course of recovery. With such readjustment, word retrieval may improve as the nondominant whole-word route achieves a progressively greater transcallosal impact on dominant hemisphere spoken language output. Finally, because phonemic paraphasias have such an invidious effect on communication, patients like that of Roth et al., in order to make themselves more readily understood, may be able to learn a strategy of using only the whole-word route and semantically "boxing in" the concept they are trying to convey.

A RECONSIDERATION OF PHONOLOGY FROM A CONNECTIONIST PERSPECTIVE

This section briefly reviews the disorders of phonological processing discussed earlier in the chapter and shows how the PDP model of phonological processing just introduced can, at least in principle, provide a cogent explanation for most of these observations. Eight fundamental attributes of the model, three of them characteristic of PDP models in general (graceful degradation, top-down/bottom-up processing interactions, and the representation of memory), and five of them specific to this particular model—five repositories of knowledge: phonological articulatory motor, phonological acoustic, and phonological sequence, semantic, and the extensive connectivity between phonological and semantic stores (lexical semantic knowledge), can account for most of the phonological phenomena described above.

Graceful Degradation

Graceful degradation refers to the fact that, although network damage or noisy input enhances the likelihood of errors, the errors themselves reflect the knowledge that was and to some degree, still is represented in the network. Consequently, the errors respect the constraints that were built into the original network. Graceful degradation occurs because the knowledge, represented in the connection strengths, is distributed throughout the model. Thus, a lesion in part of a domain or of some of the connections between two domains leaves intact other portions of the domain and interdomain connectivity that support *all* of the knowledge they have acquired. However, PDP networks are intrinsically probabilistic, and different constraints are instantiated to varying degrees, reflecting the learning experience of the network. Graceful degradation means that damaged or noisy networks are intrinsically self-correcting, but absolutely correct output is rendered less certain in such networks and near misses more likely.

Top-Down/Bottom-Up Processing Interactions

Top-down/bottom-up processing interactions stem from the flow of activation up and down, back and forth, throughout the model, no matter where input occurs (e.g., from the top, during naming or spontaneous language, or from the bottom, during repetition and word perception). Thus, the output of the model is shaped both by the input and by the knowledge existent in connections throughout the model, knowledge whose reliability may have been (gracefully) degraded by injury. Output is also shaped by the distribution of activation throughout the model (in effect: "noise") at the moment that input occurs, hence slip-of-the-tongue errors. Because of top-down/bottom-up processing, for example, in a repetition task, input to acoustic representations will be influenced by the connectivity from concept representations, which will confer lexical frequency and phonological neighborhood effects. Also because of top-down/bottom-up processing, activation will flow up and down through representations of

sequence knowledge, such that in a repetition task, the output will be influenced by representations, perhaps degraded to some extent, of words containing similar phonemes, joint phonemes, rhymes, syllables, and morphemes (i.e., competing representations within quasi-regular sequence domains), as born out in the phonotactic probability effects evident in the experiments of Vitevitch and Luce (2005) and Lipinski and Gupta (2005).

We noted earlier that there is evidence of a hierarchical effect in phonological processing disorders: subjects with Broca's aphasia tend to produce literal paraphasias characterized by single phoneme or distinctive feature errors, whereas those with Wernicke's aphasia more often exhibit slips involving clumps of phonemes. This effect is related to the dominance of semantic and phonological neighborhood effects early in the processing of phonological forms, and the predominance of phonotactic constraints late in processing.

Environmental constraints on phonemic selection reflect the effect of top-down/bottom-up processing effects within the acoustic-articulatory motor pattern associator. A good example of what might be called a top-down/bottom-up/top-down effect is the tendency for repeated phonemes to induce misordering of phonemes around them (Wickelgren, 1969; MacKay, 1970). Dell (1986) elucidated the mechanism of this phenomenon in a spreading activation model of phonological processing (a connectionist model employing entirely local representations). In the model, as in normal subjects, a repeated phoneme such as /æ/ in the phrase "hat pad" could induce either an exchange "pat had," an anticipation "pat pad," or a perseveration "hat had." The /æ/ gets double top-down activation, leading to particularly strong bottom-up activation of all syllables containing /æ/ throughout the time these syllables are being processed (only "hat" and "pad" were in the sequence vocabulary of Dell's model). These, in turn, provide top-down activation of all their constituent consonants, which then compete. In this example, at any one given time, all four component consonant phonemes /h/, /t/, /p/, and /d/ are similarly activated and compete, leading to a significant probability that the wrong one will be selected at a particular instant. Top-down/bottom-up effects are also reflected in the phonemic neighborhood effects observed in word perception, repetition, and production. Recent work employing parallel studies of normal subjects and connectionist simulations has defined further subtleties of top-down/bottom-up effects, even as it has provided new evidence that the brain instantiates such interactive processes, and that connectionist models can fully anticipate psycholinguistic phenomena, as well as elucidate their underlying mechanisms (McClelland et al., 2006).

Malapropisms (formal verbal paraphasias) provide a particularly good illustration of bottom-up/top-down interaction effects. As a lexical item is activated (instantiated as a pattern of neural activity in the phonological apparatus), it activates all of its various sublexical components. These return activation to the lexical target, but also to phonologically similar targets, regardless of their degree of semantic unrelatedness. This pattern of top-down followed by bottom-up spread of activation can have perverse consequences. First, natural noise in the system can lead to selection of a lexical item phonologically similar to the lexical target because its activation level ends up being a little higher—a classic malapropism. Second, in the presence of a lesion of the phonological apparatus, the downward spread of activation from a lexical target may generate patterns of activity corresponding to a phonemic paraphasic error. This error in turn generates bottom-up spread of activation that enhances the likelihood that a phonologically similar word will receive higher activation than the target (Blanken, 1990). This process, the lexicalization of neologisms, adds one or more errors to the original phonological slip. Gagnon et al. (1995) have confirmed that formal paraphasias on average contain a greater number of phonological deviations from the target than do neologisms. Because formal paraphasias in aphasic language reflect an active, top-down mediated lexicalization process, they occur too often to be accounted for by the chance production of real words by single phonemic paraphasias, and they exhibit word frequency and grammatical class effects (greater than chance tendency to be nouns)—phenomena that would never be observed with single phonemic slips alone (Gagnon et al., 1997). A formal paraphasia loses its semantic relationship to the target because words with similar meaning do not generally sound alike.

The Representation of Memory

In neural network models, long-term memories are represented in the strengths of the connections between units (as in the brain, where the units may correspond to neurons), and short-term memory corresponds to the pattern of activation of all the units in the network at any given time. In these models, the neural substrates for memory and processing are one and the same; that is, there are no physically separate memory stores. Functional imaging studies in humans also suggest that long-term memories are represented in the same cortices that process the substance of those memories, and single neuronal studies in monkeys indicate that the short-term or working memory of a cue corresponds either to sustained activity of neurons representing that cue (Ungerleider, 1995), or an alteration in their state, such that they are more susceptible to depolarization by other inputs (Moran & Desimone, 1985). Thus, damage to a processor will inevitably be associated with concomitant impairment in both its short- and long-term mnestic capabilities (N. Martin et al., 1996; N. Martin & Saffran, 1997).

Impairment in phonological short-term memory is most likely to be evident in performance of nonrehearsal tasks, such as the distraction condition of the Brown-Petersen consonant trigram test, on which subjects with repetition conduction aphasia are impaired (Shallice & Warrington, 1977; Caramazza et al., 1981). The ability to use the phonological network for both recall and silent rehearsal is likely to be most important for verbatim repetition of sentences, recall of correct order in word lists (Acheson & MacDonald, 2009), and comprehension of long or grammatically complex sentences. Subjects with repetition conduction aphasia also show impairment on such tasks (Saffran & Marin, 1975; Shallice & Warrington, 1977; Vallar et al., 1990; R. C. Martin et al., 1994; Bartha & Benke, 2003), as do subjects with Broca's aphasia or apraxia of speech (Goodglass et al., 1970; Heilman & Scholes, 1976; Cermak & Tarlow, 1978; Waters et al., 1992).

The long-term memory stored within the connections of the phonological processor corresponds to articulatory motor and acoustic knowledge and knowledge of phonological sequences and provides the substrate for phonological representations. The connections between the units of the phonological processor and concept representations, as we have discussed, instantiate the phonological lexicons and represent our lexical semantic knowledge. Connections within the acoustic-articulatory motor pattern associator provide the basis for knowledge of phonologic sequences in the abstract, devoid of meaning. This sequence knowledge provides the basis for a host of the phonological phenomena reviewed above. These include phonotactic constraints, clumping effects, and environmental constraints on phonemic selection. The connectionist model proposed here, like the brain, would acquire long-term memory through experience with language.

Conduction Aphasias

Finally, a brief explanation of the conduction aphasias in terms of the connectionist model introduced is in order. Repetition conduction aphasia can be attributed to *complete* destruction of pathway 7 and probably the hidden units of the acoustic-articulatory motor pathway and pathways 3 and 4 (the lesions are typically very large; see Figure 3-2). As a result, naming and spontaneous language must take place via pathways 1 and 2, and repetition via pathways 6, 5, 1, and 2. Because these are essentially whole-word pathways, substantially devoid of sequence knowledge, even if they are partially damaged, errors of phonological sequence (phonemic paraphasias) will not occur. Furthermore, because acoustic and articulatory-motor representations have been disconnected, the extent of the neural network capable of supporting phonological short-term memory is vastly reduced (now limited to acoustic representations), with the net result

that these subjects have severely impaired auditory-verbal short-term memory (and thus very short digit spans).

Nearly all the phenomena observed in reproduction conduction aphasia can be accounted for in terms of damage to the hidden units in the acoustic-articulatory motor pattern associator or their various connections to acoustic representations, articulatory representations, or concept representations, or reliance on corresponding but underdeveloped connectivity in the right hemisphere. Consequently, these subjects consistently demonstrate some disorder of sequence knowledge in some aspect of their language, resulting in production of phonemic paraphasic errors. To the extent that the acoustic-articulatory motor pattern associator is spared, repetition will be relatively preserved. To the extent that pathways 4 and 1-2 are spared, lexical access in naming and spontaneous language will be preserved and lexical effects will be evident during repetition as well.

ANATOMY OF PHONOLOGICAL AND LEXICAL PROCESSING

The conceptualization of the language processor developed in this chapter can be reconciled fairly easily with the traditional anatomic mapping of the W-L model (Lichtheim, 1885), in which a center for auditory word images in Brodmann's area 22 (Wernicke's area) is linked, presumably by the arcuate fasciculus, to the area of motor expression in posterior inferior frontal lobe (Broca's area; see Figure 3-1).

Although we have discussed a unitary processor that must implicitly incorporate a hierarchical structure, data from functional imaging studies (Démonet et al., 1992; Paulesu et al., 1993) and from intraoperative electrocortical stimulation studies (Ojemann, 1991) strongly suggest that there is a discontinuity in the perisylvian language cortex that supports phonological processing; that is, there is a posterior language region centered on Brodmann's area 22 in the superior temporal gyrus and extending variably into area 40 (supramarginal gyrus), and an anterior region centered on Broca's area and extending variably backward into frontal opercular areas 4 and 6.

Disconnection theories of conduction aphasia originated with Carl Wernicke and have been a subject of continuous debate ever since (Geschwind, 1965; Palumbo et al., 1992). The long white matter links between Wernicke's and Broca's areas, most importantly the arcuate fasciculus, presumably evolved with the physical separation of these two cortices that developed during evolution. Recent diffusion tensor imaging studies provide evidence of two components of the arcuate fasciculus, one directly linking Broca's and Wernicke's areas, one including the inferior parietal lobule in the pathway, exactly as Wernicke, Lichtheim, and Geschwind hypothesized (Catani et al., 2005).

Reproduction conduction aphasia is produced by lesions in the supramarginal gyrus, posterior aspect of Wernicke's area, and the angular gyrus (Benson et al., 1973; Naeser & Hayward, 1978; H. Damasio & Damasio, 1980; Palumbo et al., 1992). This suggests that these regions comprise part of the acoustic-articulatory motor pattern associator. The insula is also commonly involved in subjects with reproduction conduction aphasia, but it is unlikely that this phylogenetically ancient structure with predominantly orbitofrontal and limbic connectivity participates in language processes (see also Hillis et al., 2004). However, white matter connections from the superior temporal gyrus to the frontal cortex do pass in the extreme capsule, immediately beneath the insula (H. Damasio & Damasio, 1980).

The links between the various networks supporting distributed concept representations and the components of the acoustic-articulatory motor pattern associator likely involve fan-like white matter arrays that coalesce primarily in posterior perisylvian cortex (area 22) and immediately adjacent areas (areas 37 and 39) (Geschwind, 1965). In the view expanded in this chapter, the concept representations–hidden units–acoustic representations pathway instantiates the phonological input lexicon, and the concept representations–hidden units–articulatory motor representations pathways instantiate the phonologic output lexicon. In this way, these lexicons are highly distributed,

and it is only their terminuses that are actually located in the perisylvian cortices of the dominant hemisphere.

SEMANTICS

Concept representations have so far been discussed only in the abstract as distributed representations incorporating defining groups of features (e.g., the rooms in a house model of Rumelhart et al.,1986). In the brain, concept representations reflect patterns of engagement of neural networks in association cortices throughout the brain, where knowledge of the world is stored as synaptic connection strengths. This knowledge constitutes semantic memory (Tulving, 1972, 1983). It provides the basis for meaning. Concept representations, each reflecting some fragment of that vast store of meaning knowledge, are often referred to as *semantic representations*.

The organization of semantic memory is complex, reflecting multiple heterogeneous influences. Perhaps the best place to start in understanding it is with a dementing process that represents almost a pure lesion of cortices supporting world knowledge: *semantic dementia* (Rogers et al., 2006). Semantic dementia is associated with pathology that is maximal in the temporal poles but also involves lateral and inferior temporal cortices through much of their extent (Diehl et al., 2004; Grossman & Ash, 2004; Desgranges et al., 2007), albeit usually sparing the most posterior portions of the temporal cortex (Lambon Ralph et al., 1999) that are associated with object gnosis, visual perceptual processes, and matching object images reflecting different views (Hovius et al., 2003; Rogers et al., 2006). Cortices affected by semantic dementia are visual and auditory association cortices. Temporal polar cortex also provides a major associative link to the amygdala, a core structure of the limbic system. Both hemispheres are affected, but classically left hemisphere pathology is more severe. Semantic dementia is characterized by selective impairment in semantic memory with impoverished knowledge of objects and people, impaired semantic sorting, severe anomia in spontaneous language and naming to confrontation, severely reduced category fluency, and impaired spoken and written word comprehension (Hodges et al., 1992; Rogers et al., 2006). Perceptual skills and nonverbal problem-solving skills are relatively spared, as are grammatic and phonologic function. Because so much of human knowledge of the world is based substantially upon visual and limbic attributes, the impact of semantic dementia on knowledge is pervasive. There may be some involvement of the perirhinal and anterior entorhinal cortex and the hippocampus in semantic dementia, but episodic memory and autobiographic knowledge are relatively preserved until late in the disease course, in contrast to Alzheimer disease.[3]

Knowledge of objects and people is *implicitly* hierarchically organized. Broad superordinate categories, such as animals, include many exemplars, of which dogs is one, and each exemplar may include a number of subordinate types: in the case of dogs, golden retrievers, German shepherds, poodles, etc. The items in each level of the hierarchy are defined by their characteristic features, and the lower the hierarchical level, the more features are required to define an item and the fewer the items that have the additional, more finely discriminating features. Thus, the category animals is for the most part defined by moderate size, four legs, head, eyes, ears, nose, and eating and sexual behavior. To define dogs, one must add features of warm-blooded, carnivorous, furry, and complex social behavior. To define golden retriever, one must add further features of golden color, medium length hair, weight of 50–80 pounds, retriever instincts, and calm demeanor—features shared by relatively few exemplars. The strength with which knowledge of objects and people is instantiated in the brain reflects frequency of exposure, age of knowledge acquisition, and familiarity effects. The resilience of knowledge in face of disease processes reflects these factors interacting with the number of exemplars possessing a given feature.

Semantic dementia provides a prima facie case for neural representation of knowledge in terms of features because the degree to which knowledge of an item is attenuated is: (a) proportional to the number of features required to define that item, which in turn is dependent on the quantity of remaining connections in affected association cortices; and (b) inversely proportional to the strength of the connections between particular features, which is related to the number of concepts that share these features and the frequency with which these concepts are used (McClelland & Rumelhart, 1985; McRae et al., 1997; Devlin et al., 1998; Harm & Seidenberg, 2004; Randall et al., 2004). Items defined by a larger number of relatively distinctive features, shared by fewer other items and used less frequently (with accordingly less redundant interconnectivity), are more susceptible to the effects of pathology. Thus, knowledge supporting superordinate categories is relatively preserved, along with naming of, comprehension of, and ability to sort items into these categories, whereas knowledge of subordinate categories is most severely affected (Hodges et al., 1992, 1995; Rogers et al., 2004; Woollams et al., 2008). Naming errors are either within-category substitutions (e.g., hippopotamus for rhinoceros) or superordinate substitutions (e.g., animal for rhinoceros). Superordinate errors or prototype errors (e.g., "horse" for all large animals) become more common as the disease progresses (Hodges et al., 1995). Low-frequency exemplars are much more severely affected than are high-frequency exemplars (Hodges et al., 1992, 1995), reflecting the relationship between frequency of occurrence in experience and the degree of redundancy with which knowledge born of experience is represented. Subjects with semantic dementia are often able to provide broad superordinate information about an object (e.g., an elephant is an animal) but are unable to answer more specific questions; for example, about an elephant's habitat, size, peculiar features, or disposition (Hodges et al., 1995). The performance of subjects with semantic dementia on animal-drawing tasks is revealing (Bozeat et al., 2003; see also a subject post–herpes simplex encephalitis, Sartori & Job, 1988). Subjects with semantic dementia are very likely to omit features in proportion to the severity of their dementia, and they are most likely to omit highly distinctive features, characterizing only one or a few exemplars. They are most likely to *add* features common to the domain. For example, when asked to draw a rhinoceros, the production typically resembles a pig; the distinctive horns and armor having been omitted because the underlying knowledge has been lost. When asked to draw a duck, the production may be a reasonable facsimile of a duck—except that it has four legs. Thus, as knowledge underlying discriminating features is lost, there is a tendency for all items at a given level of the knowledge hierarchy to assume the features of the prototype. Eventually, even knowledge of the prototype may be lost, relegating the subject to reliance on knowledge supporting the next higher level of the knowledge hierarchy.

The pattern of breakdown of semantic knowledge in PDP models precisely recapitulates the behavior of subjects with semantic dementia (Rogers et al., 2004). The rooms-in-a-house model of Rumelhart et al. (1986) was based on an auto-associator network comprised of 40 features. An auto-associator neural network supporting semantic knowledge would have N features and correspond to an N-dimensional hyperspace. By taking a three-dimensional "slab" of the activity function, we can achieve some insight into its operation (Woollams et al., 2008). Let us take the slab pertaining to animal knowledge. Because we are dealing with an auto-associator network, network activity corresponding to animals will tend to settle into a broad basin—an attractor basin, the central, lowest point of which corresponds to the "centroid" of animal knowledge—the representation of a creature that best defines our sense of animalness. Within the animal basin are innumerable attractor subbasins corresponding to specific animals. Very close to the centroid are subbasins corresponding to animals likely to be very close to the centroid representation (e.g., dogs, cats, cows, horses, etc.). Distant from the centroid are subbasins corresponding to animals that are quite atypical (e.g., platypuses, sea gooseberries, and narwhales). Distance from the centroid is defined by the degree of atypicality (see also Kiran, 2007; Patterson, 2007; Woollams et al., 2008). Within any given subbasin, there may be sub-subbasins

(e.g., corresponding to types of dogs). Within these sub-subbasins may be sub-sub-subbasins corresponding to types within types, perhaps the golden retriever that was our pet and generic golden retrievers. The depth of a basin, relative to that of its subbasins, reflects the degree to which features are shared by the subbasins within that basin. For example, the animal basin is deeper than the tool basin because animals, by and large, share many more features than tools. The topography of the various attractor basins within the semantic field reflects regularities in the knowledge of the relationships between concepts (which are defined by their features), acquired through experience; hence, the effects of frequency, age of acquisition, and familiarity. Similarities between items reflect the number of features they share. Semantic priming occurs to the extent that a stimulus engages features of a concept representation. The more superordinate a concept representation, the greater the number of subordinate representations it shares features with, and the larger the number of subordinate representations that will prime it.

The effect of lesions (focal or diffuse) will be to produce graceful degradation of network performance (Warrington, 1975; Warrington & Shallice, 1984; Shallice, 1988; Hodges et al., 1992). Deep basins will become shallower, and subbasins, particularly those that are shallower and more distant from the centroid—corresponding to more atypical exemplars—will disappear (Woollams et al., 2008). The deeper and therefore more resilient basins are defined by knowledge that is represented in neural connectivity with the greatest degree of redundancy, as a result of stronger connection strengths, which reflect frequency, age of acquisition, and familiarity effects (Hinton & Shallice, 1991; Hodges et al., 1995; Rogers et al., 2004) (see below: Frequency, Age of Acquisition, and Familiarity Effects). As subbasins become shallow or disappear, responses will reflect the settling of the network into surviving neighbors located nearer the centroid—neighbors of higher typicality (yielding coordinate errors; e.g., horse in lieu of donkey); the parent basin (yielding superordinate errors; e.g., animal in lieu of donkey); or failure to settle at all, yielding omission errors (particularly likely to occur with more atypical exemplars that lack near neighbors). This is precisely what has been observed in semantic dementia (Woollams et al., 2008).

CATEGORY-SPECIFIC SEMANTIC KNOWLEDGE

The deficits in semantic knowledge associated with semantic dementia are so pervasive that it is easy to draw the conclusion that there are but two broad, contiguous semantic fields, located in the temporal lobes. However, there is evidence that, in the brain, the meaning of a given word is distributed over a host of networks, depending in part upon the semantic features that are most essential to that meaning, an idea proposed by Lissauer (1988) over a century ago, elaborated by Wernicke (as cited in Eggert, 1977), and in the modern era by Warrington and McCarthy (1987). For example, visual information makes a particularly large contribution to the meaning of living things, and consequently, subjects with damage to visual association cortex due to herpes simplex encephalitis exhibit category-specific naming and recognition deficits for living things (Warrington & Shallice, 1984; Forde & Humphreys, 1999). Subjects with lesions of lateral left hemisphere cortex due to stroke may have particular problems with recognizing and naming artifacts (Warrington & McCarthy, 1987), most likely because the category *artifacts* includes many tools, and tool knowledge is based in a complex of left hemisphere convexity networks that includes representations of movement in peripersonal space that localize in functional imaging studies to the inferior parietal lobule and banks of the intraparietal sulcus (Kemmerer et al., 2008; Tranel et al., 2008) and representations of precise, over-learned, somatosensory and motor processes that are linked to tool movement (Kemmerer et al., 2008). Interestingly, knowledge of musical instruments may or may not be impaired in subjects with impairment in knowledge of living things (Capitani et al., 2003), possibly reflecting the fact that, for nonmusicians, musical instrument knowledge is substantially visual

and limbic, whereas for those who have played an instrument, musical instrument knowledge perforce includes somatosensory and practic components. Subjects with lesions of frontal cortex or Broca's aphasia have particular problems with accessing verbs, something first noted by Fillenbaum et al. (1961) 50 years ago, and subsequently replicated by Luria and Tsvetkova (1967) and countless other investigators.

The distributed representation of the concept "dog" has a crucial component in visual association cortices made available by knowledge of the visual appearance of dogs in general, as well as particular dogs; a component in auditory association cortices corresponding to the sounds that dogs characteristically make; a major component in the limbic system corresponding to one's feelings about dogs in general and about specific dogs; a component in somatosensory cortex corresponding to the feel of dog fur, wet tongue, or cold nose; a major predicative component involving frontal cortex that corresponds to our knowledge of what dogs do, and in turn, to the verbs that can reasonably be paired with "dog" as the agent or patient (the recipient of the verb action) in a sentence (see below: Verbs); a component in olfactory cortex, corresponding to the odors of dogs; and components in perisylvian language cortex that enable us to translate the semantic representation of dog into an articulatory motor representation (so we can say */dawg/*) or an acoustic representation (so we can understand another person saying */dawg/*). The neuroanatomical distribution of semantic memories of various types provides the primary organizing principle in the Lissauer-Wernicke conceptualization and the primary explanation for category-specific deficits. The primacy of the neuroanatomy is often lost in the scientific dialog on category-specific semantic impairments. However, it is fair to say that the various mixes of category-specific deficits that have been observed continue to pose a challenge to any theory, and the debate still rages (Capitani et al., 2003; Mahon & Caramazza, 2009).

The general lack of category-specificity of impairment in semantic dementia (Lambon Ralph et al., 1999; Woollams et al., 2008) likely stems from three major factors: (a) temporal lobe cortices make a crucial contribution to a vast portion of knowledge because of the primacy of the visual and limbic components of human knowledge of the world, including nonliving things such as tools; (b) in semantic dementia, there is extensive involvement of lateral (convexity) temporal cortex involved in the representation of functional attributes of objects (see below) and of temporal pole, affecting limbic connectivity; and (c) as shown in PDP simulations, degradation of one component of a multicomponent knowledge representation will adversely impact the function of the other "normal" components (Farah & McClelland, 1991) because, although the interconnectivity of the components contributes to graceful degradation, it also induces a degree of shared loss. In particular, impairment of a crucial component (e.g., the visual component of animal representations) will have a particularly invidious effect on other, ancillary components (e.g., functional and predicative).

Visual association cortex supports visual processing even as it instantiates visual components of semantic memory (see also Patterson, 2007)—an example of the processing-storage duality of neural network systems in general. The entirety of visual association cortices is involved in visual perceptual processes, explicitly hierarchically organized, as David Marr recognized (Marr, 1982). However, the term "perception" is often used to refer only to more elemental processes subserved in the visual domain by occipital and the most posterior temporal cortices—which are typically largely spared in semantic dementia (Lambon Ralph et al., 1999; Rogers et al., 2006). The artificial separation of perceptual processes from visual semantic memory has also contributed to a popular modern conceptualization of semantic dementia as a disorder of a single, amodal semantic memory system. So too has the perception of semantic dementia as a temporal polar disorder,[4] notwithstanding the visual, auditory, and limbic specificity of the temporal poles; the functional imaging evidence of far more extensive pathology (Diehl et al., 2004; Desgranges et al., 2007); the specific association of lesions of the temporal pole with proper noun naming deficits (H. Damasio et al., 1996; Tranel & Damasio, 2005); and the modest

semantic impairment induced by anterior temporal lobectomy in treatment of epilepsy (Lu et al., 2002).

ABSTRACT WORDS: A FUNDAMENTALLY DIFFERENT FORM OF SEMANTIC REPRESENTATION

Knowledge underlying all concrete nouns appears to be instantiated in the implicitly hierarchical scheme discussed earlier. With either focal or diffuse lesions of association cortices, knowledge degrades in the ways observed in patients with semantic dementia. However, emerging evidence from the comparative study of concrete and abstract words in normal and aphasic subjects suggests that knowledge underlying abstract nouns is configured in a fundamentally different organizational scheme (Crutch & Warrington, 2005, 2007; Crutch et al., 2009). This research suggests that concrete words are related, to the extent that they share *semantic features* ("taxonomic similarity"), as discussed, whereas abstract words are related to the extent to which they share *contextual association*. Thus, in an odd-one-out task, normal subjects are quicker to pick out the concrete word that differs most in semantic features (e.g., yacht, dinghy, *bracelet*, canoe, ferry, barge) than they are to pick out the concrete word that differs most in semantic association (e.g., garden, trellis, weed, rake, lawn, *wallet*) (Crutch et al., 2009). In contrast, normal subjects are quicker to pick out the abstract word that differs most in semantic association (e.g., gamble, casino, poker, chance, luck, *public*) than they are to pick out the abstract word that differs most in semantic features (e.g., attack, raid, strike, *notice*, invasion, assault). The same phenomenon is evident in subjects with aphasia. In subjects with semantic access refractory dysphasia, in whom there is an interference effect between related words processed in close temporal proximity that builds over time, the interference is greater with contextually associated abstract words (e.g., theft, punishment), but it is greater with concrete words sharing semantic features (e.g., tractor, lorry) (Crutch & Warrington, 2005; but see Hamilton & Coslett, 2008). Among patients with aphasia who show semantic facilitation (e.g., subjects with deep dyslexia), facilitation occurs with abstract words only when they are related by contextual association, whereas facilitation occurs with concrete words only when they share semantic features (Crutch & Warrington, 2007). Furthermore, semantic paralexias for concrete words in subjects with deep dyslexia often share semantic features (e.g., coast → seashore), whereas paralexias for abstract words more often involve contextual associates (e.g., evidence → police) (Crutch, 2006).[5]

VERBS

Verbs modify concept representations and do not correspond in and of themselves to concept representations. For example, in the sentence "The old man shot the burglar," "shot" modifies "old man" to become "shooter old man," and it modifies "burglar" to become "shot burglar." The employment of the verb is associated with three types of modification of concept representations. First, there is assignment of thematic roles: the old man has become the agent and the burglar has become the patient or object of the action. Second, the employment of the verb is associated with modification of agent and patient that carries with it the meaning implicit in the verb itself, something we will refer to as verb *flavor*. Consistent with this notion, empirical studies have shown that verbs prime their arguments (Ferretti et al., 2001) and nouns prime plausible verbs (i.e., their permissible predicative components) (McRae et al., 2005). Finally, the verb, as it serves to reciprocally modify the agent and patient, which constitute the arguments of the verb, binds them together in a super-distributed concept representation. Verbs resemble abstract nouns in that they correspond to contextual associations.

It is now possible to roughly define the neuroanatomic basis for these various components of meaning added by verbs to noun concept representations. All verbs have a thematic representational component (because all have argument structures and all connote a plan sustained over time). Some (those involving movement of body parts) have an implementational component. Frontal lobe networks subserve both of these components. Most verbs have one or more flavor components (detailed below) that are based on networks involving postcentral regions (areas posterior to the central sulcus).

Frontal

Thematic. Prefrontal cortex enables volitional formulation of plans that are precisely tailored to the specific demands of the situation—a process that has been defined as intentional intention (Nadeau & Heilman, 2007). Other portions of the hemisphere, *through their connectivity with prefrontal cortex*, provide a repertoire of plans that have been learned through experience and may be released automatically in reactive fashion for execution (reactive intention). Whether intentional or reactive, the final common substrate of intention is prefrontal cortex. The temporal component implicit in plans provides a plausible substrate for dynamic time sense. The role of the frontal lobes in intention also implicitly provides a substrate for instantiation of thematic roles because intention requires the assumption of some role with respect to the action be taken. If you are planning or are engaged in the plans of the actors you are thinking about, then you are no longer an innocent bystander: you are imputing agency and consequence. Because of the potential role of the frontal lobes in providing substrates for both dynamic time sense and the instantiation of thematic roles, one might anticipate that verb production and comprehension might be differentially impaired by frontal lesions—precisely what has been observed. Furthermore, studies of aphasia suggest that subjects with prefrontal lesions are particularly impaired in processing verbs for which thematic role assignment is particularly demanding. Subjects with frontal lesions or Broca's aphasia are able to distinguish perceptual differences between verbs (e.g., between fall and rise, skate and slide); however, they have difficulty with differences substantially contingent on nuances of reciprocal thematic roles (e.g., buy/sell; lead/chase/follow) (Saffran et al., 1980; Byng, 1988; Jones, 1984; S. D. Breedin & Martin, 1996;

Manning & Warrington, 1996; Berndt et al., 2004). On the other hand, subjects with more posterior lesions, particularly lesions implicating visual association cortices, have minimal difficulty with thematic aspects of verb meaning but do poorly when having to make flavor distinctions; as, for example, between verbs such as amble, stroll, saunter, and strut (S. Breedin et al., 1994; Marshall et al., 1995/96; S. D. Breedin & Martin, 1996) (see below).

Implementational. Many verbs connote use of a body part in a very direct way (e.g., to speak, to hit, and to walk). Other verbs, characterizable as practic verbs (e.g., cut with scissors or a knife) implicitly connote use of a body part. Thus, as originally suggested by Damasio (A. R. Damasio & Tranel, 1993), it is plausible that these verb types might have a representational component in premotor and motor cortex. This has been borne out in a particularly elegant functional imaging study of verb meaning by Kemmerer and colleagues (Kemmerer et al., 2008) and finds further support in an extensive body of other work, including functional imaging (positron emission tomography [PET], fMRI, magnetoencephalography) and transcranial magnetic stimulation (TMS) mapping (see Kemmerer et al., 2008, for review). Behavioral studies also provide support for this hypothesis. Reading of sentence segments involving movement (either the verb or an adverb modifying the verb) is slowed when the motion conveyed conflicts with concurrently performed movement—for example, the verb of "he found a new light bulb which he screwed in rapidly," paired with counterclockwise rotation (Taylor & Zwaan, 2008). Subjects with Parkinson disease exhibit robust masked priming[6] of both nouns and verbs when in the on-condition but prime only nouns when in the off-condition, during which they exhibit dysfunction of motor cortex as a result of noisy striatal input (Boulenger et al., 2008). Furthermore, the implementational representation of action verbs in motor cortex appears to be somatotopic—verbs connoting lower extremity movement have a representation component more dorsally in the motor homunculus, in the leg area; verbs connoting upper extremity movement have a representation component more ventrally in the hand–arm knob of the precentral gyrus (see Kemmerer et al., 2008).

Postcentral: Verb Flavor

Verb flavor is usually modality specific. However, most is known about the visual modality, in part because of the extent of our knowledge of this system, in part because of the vast extent of cerebral cortex that is dedicated to visual processing. The latter attribute has provided an opportunity for study of differential lesion effects in experiments of nature, and for functional imaging studies in normal subjects. Thus, this discussion will focus predominantly on the visual representational component.

The varieties of visual verb flavor have a direct correspondence to reasonably well understood neuroanatomy. The most fundamental division of visual systems is into a ventral (largely inferior temporal) "what" system that processes form and color and subserves single object recognition, and a dorsal "where" system (lateral temporal and parietal) that processes location in space and movement (Mishkin et al., 1983).

Movement is of central interest here because the meaning of so many verbs has a movement component. The representation of movement, including movement components of verb meaning, is complex and logically divisible into several domains, each with a neuroanatomic counterpart. An object may be characterized by intrinsic motion (captured by many verbs) that has nothing to do with change in location (e.g., the ball is spinning), or that can occur without a change in location (e.g., he is running [on a treadmill]). Because this particular domain has attributes of an object quality, it is no surprise that it is primarily supported by convexity cortex in the "where" trajectory that is immediately adjacent to "what" system visual object perception cortex on the undersurface of the temporal lobe: posterolateral temporal cortex that corresponds to areas MT and MST of the macaque (area V5, at the junction of the inferior temporal gyrus and the occipital lobe). Deficits in movement perception (Zihl et al., 1983; Zeki, 1991; Gilmour et al., 1994) and action naming (Tranel et al., 2001, 2008) have been observed in subjects with lesions in this region. This region has also been implicated in motion perception and in the representation of meaning of verbs of motion in functional imaging studies of normal subjects (see Kemmer et al., 2008).

Another domain of movement perception involves movement in peripersonal space; that is, in the body-centered spatial coordinates necessary to guide limb and eye movement. Many verbs directly (run, slap) or indirectly—as practic verbs—invoke this domain of movement representation. Because lesions causing persistent deficits in movement perception are typically large, behavior studies have not yet provided much information on fragmentation of movement perception, or on associated deficits in verb meaning. However, functional imaging studies have been quite successful in demonstrating selective engagement of cortex in the vicinity of the left inferior parietal lobule and intraparietal sulcus by verbs of these classes (Kemmerer et al., 2008; Tranel et al., 2008).

The inferior parietal lobule, as Norman Geschwind recognized (Geschwind, 1965), consists of polymodal and supramodal association cortex. For the modality of movement perception in peripersonal space, and the meaning of verbs that describe operations within this space (peripersonal movement verbs like run and slap and practic verbs), the relevant sensory modalities are vision and somesthesis. Practic verbs are likely to be associated with unique and more extensive patterns of engagement because they are associated with very precise, overlearned, somatosensory and motor processes that are linked to visual representations of the tool and the movement. This expectation is born out in the complex but largely orderly patterns of engagement observed in functional imaging studies (Kemmerer et al., 2008).

Components of verb representations that invoke either domains of intrinsic movement or movement in peripersonal space provide the basis for the linguistic component of verb flavor referred to as *manner*. Thus, amble, stroll, saunter, strut, and march all involve variations on the theme of walking, each conveying a particular style of walking. Manner information is characteristically directly encoded by verbs in manner-incorporating languages (e.g., English, German, Russian, Swedish, Chinese) (Kemmerer & Tranel, 2003). Other languages, known as path-incorporating languages (e.g., modern Greek, Spanish, Japanese, Turkish, and Hindi) incorporate *path* information in the verb (e.g., in Greek: *beno* [move in], *ugeno* [move out], *anevveno* [move up], *kateveno* [move down]), whereas manner information is optionally incorporated via a prepositional phrase or gerund (Kemmerer & Tranel, 2003), analogous to the ways in which path information is conveyed in manner-incorporating languages. The data suggesting a postcentral component to action verb meaning representing manner were reviewed above. Presumably, this is a form of movement knowledge instantiated in the cortical network trajectory, beginning with the human homologue of area MT in macaque. It seem likely that the path component of verb representation in path-incorporating languages is similarly represented posteriorly, but more dorsally, in cortices supporting the spatial location components of the "where" system (see below).

Finally, location may change in extrapersonal space, in which case the movement is defined in terms of environmental coordinates, and the principal sensory modality that is brought to bear is vision (although hearing may make a contribution in some circumstances). This type of spatial perception is supported in dorsal occipital and parietal cortical regions. The rare subjects affected by lesions in these regions exhibit either Balint's syndrome (Balint, 1909) or difficulty aligning their personal coordinate system with the environmental coordinate system (Stark et al., 1996). Deficits of this type might be observable in subjects with the syndrome of posterior cortical atrophy. Verb meaning deriving from the knowledge represented in this perceptual system is exemplified by sentences such as the following:

"The bird flew over the house"
as contrasted with:
"The bird flew into the wind."

Note that the adjunctive phrase in the first sentences serves to modify "flew" in a way that incorporates a substantially locative element, whereas "flew" in the second sentence purely characterizes a movement pattern. In a sense, these are two quite different verbs, just as "palatial home" and "Spartan home" are two different noun concepts. Subjects with lesions of ventral visual and parietal cortex should exhibit selective sparing of the comprehension and production of verbs (with or without adjunctive phrases) that connote location in space.

To this point, our focus has been on the nuances of visual verb flavor that are relatable to the ventro-dorsal organization of postcentral cortices supporting perception of various aspects of movement: object movement, movement in peripersonal space, and movement in extrapersonal space. Left out has been a perception that is implicit in the sudden transition of an object from one form to another, the knowledge substrate that supports the meaning of change-of-state verbs (e.g., break, shatter, and crumble, but also sprout, bloom, and wither). Logically, this knowledge should reside in "what" system networks in ventral temporal cortex. This has been borne out by functional imaging studies (Kemmerer et al., 2008).

The visual flavor of a verb may involve a distributed representation that incorporates two or more of the neural domains discussed above. Thus, verbs that incorporate elements of both intrinsic movement and movement in peripersonal space (e.g., hitting, slapping, and practic verbs) may engage both inferior posterolateral temporal cortex and the inferior parietal lobule (Kemmerer et al., 2008). Practic verbs (e.g., cutting) are often associated with a change of state of their associated objects and therefore engage inferior temporal cortex (Kemmerer et al., 2008).

FREQUENCY, AGE OF ACQUISITION, AND FAMILIARITY EFFECTS

Consideration of word frequency is a constant in psycholinguistic, cognitive neuropsychological, and experimental and computational psychological research, and rightfully so, as it seems obvious that the more times one is exposed to a word and its associated concept representation, the better one is going to be able to access it. Simulations involving computational models show that these effects are reflected in stronger interunit connections. However, the evaluation of frequency effects, and control for frequency effects, whether in studies of normal or aphasic subjects, is not straightforward because all language function has multiple components, frequency can affect those components in different ways, and a full understanding of frequency effects has not yet emerged. Frequency of occurrence in major databases, such as that of Francis-Kucera (1982) or CELEX, likely provides a fairly accurate reflection of semantic representations. For example, in these databases, in general, superordinate names have higher frequency than exemplars, and exemplars have a higher frequency than subcategory names. In semantic dementia, an almost pure disorder of knowledge underlying semantic representations, naming performance is strongly correlated with frequency (Lambon Ralph et al., 1998).

On the other hand, frequency of phonological representations depends upon the frequency of the phonemes and the frequency of the phonemic sequences (biphone frequencies) involved. For example, "emu" is an uncommon word, but it is made up of high-frequency phonemes and phoneme sequences that are shared with many other words. The impact of a heard phoneme sequence on the brain is also going to be influenced by the phonological neighborhoods of the involved phonemic sequences. Finally, comprehension and production may be affected by the relative strength of connections between the phonological processor (the acoustic-articulatory motor pattern associator) and cortex supporting concept representations (semantic memory).

Age of acquisition effects reflect evolution in the nature of the changes that occur in neural network connectivity through a network's lifetime of knowledge acquisition. Ellis and Lambon Ralph (2000), in a simulation involving a distributed network computational model of naming, showed that, during early learning, connection strength changes associated with acquisition of new knowledge tended to be large, but as ever more knowledge was accumulated, connection strength changes became ever smaller. As a consequence, network damage differentially affected late-acquired words. They predicted that age of acquisition effects would be most evident in networks that instantiate arbitrary relationships (e.g., between word meaning and sound). However, in domains substantially governed by acquired knowledge of regularities in experience, late-acquired words should be able to exploit the network structure laid down in early word experience, thereby offsetting the loss of plasticity associated with increasing age of acquisition (A. Ellis & Lambon Ralph, 2000; Dent et al., 2008). This prediction was borne out in a subsequent computational simulation of learning to read words, in which there is a high degree of regularity in the mapping between orthography and phonology: minimal age of acquisition effect was evident (Zevin & Seidenberg, 2002). These predictions by computational models have now been fully borne out in a study of normal human subjects (Lambon Ralph & Ehsan, 2006).

A coherent picture of the relationships between word frequency, age of acquisition, and domain regularity is now emerging, supported by parallel findings in computational model simulations and studies of normal human subjects (Lambon Ralph & Ehsan, 2006). High word frequency, early age of acquisition, and domain regularity independently function to speed processing and reduce response latency. In the extreme, each has a dominant effect. Thus, there are modest if any effects of age of acquisition or domain regularity for the highest frequency words; frequency and domain regularity effects are minimized for early-acquired words; and frequency and age of acquisition effects are minimal in highly regular or quasi-regular domains (e.g., networks supporting reading words aloud). However, response latency is increased with low-frequency words, late-acquired words, and in arbitrary domains (e.g., word meaning to word sound), and in these circumstances, there are strong interaction effects in the expected directions. The most prolonged response latencies are observed with words that are low in frequency, late acquired, and in arbitrary domains. In this framework, semantic memory could be viewed as "systematic" (Lambon Ralph & Ehsan, 2006)—it incorporates many regularities, as discussed, but it is not as regular as the relationship between orthography and phonology, even in English. Thus, age of acquisition and frequency effects are

detectable but are not as prominent as in fully arbitrary domains.

Word familiarity is, of course, strongly correlated with word frequency but it comes closer to reflecting the patterns of daily use of words by individual subjects, which may be discrepant from population-based patterns reflected in word-frequency databases. The structure of semantic memory clearly is influenced by familiarity—consider the difference in semantic memory between an Inuit and an Australian aborigine. However, familiarity also affects the pattern of connectivity between semantic and phonologic stores that influences our choice of words in a particular situation (e.g., whether on seeing a Labrador we call it an animal, a dog, or a Labrador).

Recent studies contrasting the behavior of subjects with semantic dementia with that of subjects with large strokes and global aphasia provide experimental data bearing on these issues. Expectably, in word–picture matching tests, subjects with semantic dementia are most accurate in matching superordinate names to pictures (e.g., animal), somewhat less accurate with category names (e.g., dog), and least accurate with subcategory names (e.g., Labrador) (Crutch & Warrington, 2008). This response pattern is entirely consistent with the effects of degradation of the substrate for semantic representations, as discussed above. On the other hand, subjects with large strokes and global aphasia tend to respond most accurately with subcategory names, with intermediate accuracy with category names, and least accurately with superordinate names, notwithstanding that category names are less frequent and subcategory names least frequent (Crutch & Warrington, 2008). Crutch and Warrington (2008) offered a number of potential explanations, but the most straightforward is that, in stroke, damage to white matter connectivity between the substrate for concept representations and perisylvian cortex supporting phonology makes the major contribution to language impairment, and, to varying degrees, language is dependent on underdeveloped semantic-phonologic connectivity in the right hemisphere. These white matter connections reflect in significant part the frequency with which a particular person associates a particular phonological word form with a particular concept—something referred to as the *basic-level effect*, which reflects the impact of experience (and expertise) on our choice of name for a given entity (Rogers & McClelland, 2004). Many people, on seeing a dog, would call it a "dog." However, many would more often produce the name of the type of dog (e.g., "poodle" or "German shepherd"). Very few would respond, "animal." Basic-level names (e.g., "dog" or "poodle") do not bear a consistent relationship to frequency in word databases, although more often than not they are more frequent than more general or more specific terms. This is because they are substantially defined by personal experience and expertise. The basic-level terms employed by a veterinarian might involve, for example, specific types of poodles. Basic-level effects are also strongly reflective of age of acquisition (see above). Basic-level effects interact with the properties of the semantic system. Because atypical exemplars are less susceptible to semantic attractor basin effects (e.g., platypus), the name produced is more likely to reflect basic level effects. On the other hand, with semantic network damage, superordinate categories (e.g., animals) will have an advantage and will be preserved, even as subcategories corresponding to basic level exemplars are lost. Basic-level effects also represent, in part, properties of the semantic system. Expertise affects not just frequency of use of particular terms, but also degree of differentiation in semantic networks.

In the Crutch and Warrington study (2008), when there was damage to semantic-phonologic connectivity, the most redundantly represented connections—those linking the substrate for concepts to the substrate for category or subcategory name representations—were more likely to survive than were those linking concepts to superordinate names. Why the stroke subjects performed best when supplied subcategory names is less clear. Normal subjects show reliably faster reaction times for category names (e.g., dog) and slower responses to subcategory (e.g., Labrador) and superordinate names (e.g., animal) (Crutch & Warrington, 2008). The faster response to category names relative to superordinate names is likely to represent patterns instantiated in semantic-phonologic connectivity, whereas the faster

response to category names relative to subcategory names may additionally reflect the implicitly hierarchical nature of semantic memory representations. Thus, in the word–picture matching comprehension test employed in this study, performance level reflects the interactions of regularities in semantic representations, regularities in semantic-phonologic connectivity, and lesion topography.

Results of studies of the influence of frequency, age of acquisition, and other parameters on performance of various language tasks by subjects with aphasia have often yielded conflicting results (see review by Kittredge et al., 2008). This is quite understandable, given the complex interactive effects of frequency, age of acquisition, domain regularity, and (largely unexplored) familiarity, and the fact that lesions in brain-damaged individuals can be quite variable in their topography and impact. Nevertheless, results of a recent study applying hierarchical multinomial logistic regression analysis to picture naming data from 50 subjects with aphasia due to left-brain strokes (Kittredge 2008) has shed some light, even as they are quite congruent with the foregoing discussion. This statistical approach enables definition of the unique contributions of several independent variables within a single model. In this analysis, word frequency made a significant, unique positive contribution to the production of correct responses and was negatively associated with production of semantic, phonological, and omission errors.

Age of acquisition made a significant unique negative contribution to production of correct responses and a positive contribution to phonological and omission errors, but made no unique contribution to semantic errors. This apparent absence of a relationship between age of acquisition and semantic errors is consistent with the findings of studies of normal subjects reviewed above: that age of acquisition effects should be evident primarily in domains involving arbitrary relationships (e.g., word sound and word meaning), and attenuated in domains instantiating substantial regularity (e.g., semantic memory). Age of acquisition effects have also been found in spoken word recognition. Garlock, Walley, and Metsala (2001) assessed the effects of age of acquisition, word frequency, and neighborhood density on spoken word recognition from a developmental perspective with young children, older children, and adults. Age of acquisition and neighborhood density effects were found for all listeners. In particular, adults showed a greater advantage for the recognition of early-acquired items, consistent with the substantially arbitrary relationships involved in translating acoustic to semantic representations.

TEXTURE

There is a rapidly growing literature on the differential properties of various domains of semantic knowledge—properties we will refer to as semantic *texture*. Little more than a brief sketch of two of the dominant themes is possible here.

The most thoroughly studied difference in texture is that between animals and artifacts, such as tools (Devlin et al., 1998; Forde & Humphreys, 1999; McRae & Cree, 2002; Moss et al., 2002; Rogers et al., 2004). Far more features are held in common by animals overall and by subgroups of animals than by artifacts. Furthermore, the features distinguishing animals from each other tend to be finer than those distinguishing artifacts, and any one feature tends to distinguish a smaller number of exemplars and is hence more fragile. Consequently, in the face of damage to key portions of semantic memory, as in semantic dementia, animal name errors are less likely than tool name errors to be omissions and more likely to be within-category substitutions (e.g., horse for donkey) or superordinate substitutions (e.g., animal for donkey) (Rogers et al., 2004). In the attractor basin conceptualization of activity in semantic space discussed earlier, this texture difference corresponds to greater depth of the animal attractor basin relative to its subbasins when compared to the tool attractor basin in relation to its subbasins—hence our use of the term *texture*. It has been suggested that semantic texture differences between animals and artifacts might fully account for category-specific deficits (Devlin et al., 1998; Forde & Humphreys, 1999). It seems likely that such differences contribute to error profiles associated with category-specific deficits, but they cannot provide the full story because they do not take into account the role of topographic representation of knowledge in the brain, as discussed above.

There is evidence of a comparable phenomenon affecting verb naming in subjects with Alzheimer disease, another disorder predominantly affecting posterior cortices, at least in the early and mid stages of the disease. Verbs have a shallower hierarchy of meaning than do nouns (G. A. Miller & Fellbaum, 1991). For example, to jog is to run, which is to move, whereas a Labrador is a dog, which is a mammal, which is an animal, which is a living thing. Consequently, with damage to posterior cortices, one might expect more nonresponses and descriptive errors and less superordinate errors with verbs relative to nouns. This prediction has been borne out in empirical studies (Robinson et al., 1996; White-Devine et al., 1996).

TREATMENT

Space allows only very brief discussion of treatment of phonological, lexical semantic, and semantic disorders in aphasia. There are literally hundreds of published treatment studies that provide strong proof of principle that the post-stroke brain is plastic, that aphasia treatment can improve language function, and that treatment gains can be enduring. However, the holy grail of aphasia treatment is achievement of maximal generalization—maximal improvement in performance with untrained stimuli or in untrained situations, and in daily verbal communication. Aphasia treatments that focus substantially on enabling subjects to relearn the names of objects—lexical semantic treatments, the most studied and the most commonly used in speech language therapy—are intrinsically nongeneralizing because word meaning, for the most part, bears an arbitrary relationship to word sound. Thus, there is no opportunity during treatment for neural networks to capture commonalities between words (there are none), knowledge of which would enable generalization. We have discussed generalization in aphasia treatment in some detail elsewhere (Nadeau et al., 2008), and here we will focus exclusively on generalization in phonological and semantic treatment.

PHONOLOGICAL TREATMENT

Most subjects with aphasia due to dominant perisylvian lesions exhibit considerable impairment in phonological processing (phonological sequence knowledge; pathway 7-3, Figure 3-2), even as many also exhibit some remnants of this knowledge that might provide a scaffold for treatment. Training of this phonological sequence knowledge (either in the dominant or in the nondominant hemisphere), might enable enhanced naming by the indirect (phonological) naming pathway. Because the same corpus of phonological sequence knowledge underlies all words in the language, if successful, such a treatment would be widely generalizing. A phase I study of such a treatment (Kendall et al., 2008) provided proof of principle of its feasibility and evidence of broad generalization.

SEMANTIC TREATMENT

Treatments of semantic impairment in aphasia are intrinsically generalizing because relearning the features of some exemplars of a domain enhances one's knowledge of other domain members that share those features. In 1996, David Plaut showed that, in semantic retraining of a damaged connectionist model of reading for meaning (incorporating orthographic, semantic, and hidden unit layers), training of atypical exemplars generalized to typical exemplars but not vice versa (Plaut, 1996). This is because training of typical exemplars enhances knowledge underlying the central regions of attractor basins—features prototypic of the semantic category—but has no impact on featural knowledge of atypical exemplars located at the periphery of attractor basins. On the other hand, training of atypical exemplars enhances knowledge relevant to the entire extent of an attractor basin, including the typical exemplars near the center. Studies of semantic treatment of subjects with aphasia have now confirmed this prediction (Kiran & Thompson, 2003).

The great limitation of most semantic treatments is that, although they intrinsically generalize, the scope of generalization is limited to the domains explicitly trained. What is needed is semantic therapies that reach across greater spans of semantic memory. One very promising example of such a treatment, called vNEST (Edmonds et al., 2009), employs verbs to drive the therapy. It takes advantage of the fact that verbs prime their commonly associated arguments (Ferretti et al., 2001), as well as other verbs that share some of their semantic features, and that many verbs admit a very broad range of possibilities for both agent and patient, thereby providing an opportunity for highly diverse modifications of the distributed concept representations of agent and patient, and engagement of atypical exemplars of agent and patient. In this way, the therapy vastly expands the spectrum of semantic features that are incorporated in the training. The therapy also provides subjects the opportunity to draw exemplars from daily life, so long as they are acceptable agents or patients for the verb being presented. Phase one studies of this treatment provide proof of principle of both training effect and broad generalization (Edmonds et al., 2009).

CONCLUSION

A cogent picture of the operation of an integrated system subserving phonological, lexical semantic, and semantic function is starting to emerge. The results are remarkably consistent with PDP conceptualizations, even as simulations employing connectionist models have contributed many insights. The relationship of these linguistic functions to underlying anatomy is also becoming clearer. Cognitive neuropsychology continues to be a major source of new scientific insights, substantially aided by the unique perspectives enabled by certain lesion models, most particularly ischemic perisylvian lesions and semantic dementia. The roles of experimental psychology and computational psychology are growing rapidly, and most notably, we are seeing an increasing number of papers in which simulations involving connectionist models are combined with psycholinguistic studies of normal subjects that test the predictions of the simulations or the hypotheses posed by the models. Functional imaging studies have made a modest contribution but continue to be hobbled by methodologic limitations and susceptibility to artifact. Thanks to the growth in our understanding of phonological, lexical semantic, and semantic systems, as well as improved understanding of principles of neuroplasticity, we are now poised to make significant advances in our treatment of patients with aphasia.

NOTES

1. A unit is the smallest functional entity within a connectionist model. It has a level of activation that is defined as a nonlinear mathematical function of its combined inputs at any one time (in many models, a sigmoid curve that asymptotically approaches a minimum value of 0 or a maximum value of 1). It has an output that is a nonlinear mathematical function of its level of activation, often incorporating a threshold such that, for activation levels below that threshold, there is no output. Each unit is connected to a very large number of other units. The patterns of connectivity within a network define its functional capacity. The precise neural counterpart of a unit is uncertain and may vary with brain region.

2. The interposition of hidden unit layers is a key contributor to the processing power of PDP models and almost certainly to neural networks. In the brain, as in the models, the activity of these hidden units cannot be easily characterized in behavioral terms, but analysis of this activity can provide major insights into mechanisms of processing.

3. In practice, differentiating the cognitive profile of semantic dementia from that of Alzheimer disease may pose some challenges. The strongest differentiating criterion is the ratio of naming performance to delayed recall, which, in the study of Hodges et al. (1999), was eight time greater in Alzheimer disease than in semantic dementia, reflecting the particularly disproportionate memory impairment in Alzheimer disease and naming impairment in semantic dementia. On average, there is also characteristically far more hemispheric asymmetry in semantic dementia than in Alzheimer disease.

4. Voxel-based morphometric (VBM) studies have made a substantial contribution to this misconception. Imaging studies in general and VBM in particular are susceptible to a "tip-of-the-iceberg" effect, in which only the most severe pathology is imaged, even as cognitive deficits may reflect far more extensive disease.

5. For purposes of discussion, we have used a dichotomous classification. In actual fact, the association of abstract and concrete with associative and semantic context is often blurrier. Concrete words may relate to each other substantially by shared contextual association, e.g., dog → cat, rather than coyote, which has greater featural overlap with dog; palm trees with pyramids rather than conifers (Howard & Patterson, 1982); and animals within a geographic context (e.g., farm, zoo, Africa), an association used to advantage in the performance of a category fluency test.

6. Masked priming is identity priming, in which the duration of exposure to the prime is too brief (e.g., 50 ms) for the priming stimulus to be consciously recognized.

REFERENCES

Acheson, D. J., & MacDonald, M. C. (2009). Verbal working memory and language production: Common approaches to the serial ordering of verbal information. *Psychology Bulletin, 135,* 50–68.

Akmajian, A., Demers, R. A., & Harnish, R. M. (1984). *Linguistics: An introduction to language and communication.* Cambridge, MA: MIT Press.

Alajouanine, T., & Lhermitte, F. (1973). The phonemic and semantic components of jargon aphasia. In H. Goodglass, & S. Blumstein (Eds.), *Psycholinguistics and aphasia* (pp. 318–329). Baltimore: Johns Hopkins University Press.

Allport, D. A. (1984). Speech production and comprehension: One lexicon or two? In W. Prinz, & A. F. Sanders (Eds.), *Cognition and motor processes* (pp. 209–228). Berlin/Heidelberg: Springer-Verlag.

Baars, B. J., Motley, M. T., & MacKay, D. G. (1975). Output editing for lexical status in artificially elicited slips of the tongue. *Journal of Verbal Learning and Verbal Behavior, 14,* 382–391.

Baddeley, A., Gathercole, S., & Papagno, C. (1998). The phonological loop as a language learning device. *Psychology Review, 105,* 158–173.

Baker, E., Blumstein, S. E., & Goodglass, H. (1981). Interaction between phonological and semantic factors in auditory comprehension. *Neuropsychologia, 19,* 1–15.

Balint, R. (1909). Seelenlähmung des "Schauens," optische ataxie, raumliche störung der aufmerksamkeit. *Monatsschrift Psychiatrie Neurologie, 25,* 57–71.

Bartha, L., & Benke, T. (2003). Acute conduction aphasia: An analysis of 20 cases. *Brain and Language, 85,* 93–108.

Barton, M. I. (1971). Recall of generic properties of words in aphasic patients. *Cortex, 7,* 73–82.

Benson, D. F., Sheremata, W. A., Bouchard, R., Segarra, J. M., Price, N., & Geschwind, N. (1973). Conduction aphasia. A clinicopathological study. *Archives of Neurology, 28,* 339–346.

Berndt, R. S., Mitchum, C. C., Burton, M. W., & Haendiges, A. N. (2004). Comprehension of reversible sentences in aphasia: The effects of verb meaning. *Cognitive Neuropsychology, 21,* 229–244.

Blanken, G. (1990). Formal paraphasias: A single case study. *Brain and Language, 38,* 534–554.

Blumstein, S. (1973a). *A phonological investigation of aphasic speech*. The Hague: Mouton.

Blumstein, S. (1973b). Some phonologic implications of aphasic speech. In H. Goodglass, & S. Blumstein (Eds.), *Psycholinguistics and aphasia* (pp. 123–137). Baltimore: Johns Hopkins University Press.

Blumstein, S. E. (1978). Segment structure and the syllable in aphasia. In A. Bell, & J. B. Hooper (Eds.), *Syllables and segments* (pp. 189–200). Amsterdam: North-Holland Publishing Company.

Blumstein, S. E., Baker, E., & Goodglass, H. (1977). Phonological factors in auditory comprehension in aphasia. *Neuropsychologia, 15*, 19–30.

Blumstein, S. E., Burton, M., Baum, S., Waldstein, R., & Katz, D. (1994). The role of lexical status on the phonetic categorization of speech in aphasia. *Brain and Language, 46*, 181–197.

Bond, Z. S. (1999). *Slips of the ear: Errors in the perception of casual conversation*. New York: Academic Press.

Bond, Z. S., & Garnes, S. (1980). Misperceptions of fluent speech. In R. A. Cole (Ed.), *Perception and production in fluent speech* (pp. 115–132). Hillsdale, NJ: Lawrence Erlbaum.

Boulenger, V., Mechtouff, L., Thobois, S., Broussolle, E., Jeannerod, M., & Nazir, T. A. (2008). Word processing in Parkinson's disease is impaired for action verbs but not for concrete nouns. *Neuropsychologia, 46*, 743–756.

Bozeat, S., Lambon Ralph, M. A., Graham, K. S., Patterson, K., Wilkin, H., Rowland, J., et al. (2003). A duck with four legs: Investigating the structure of conceptual knowledge using picture drawing in semantic dementia. *Cognitive Neuropsychology, 20*, 27–47.

Breedin, S., Saffran, E. M., & Coslett, H. B. (1994). Reversal of the concreteness effect in a patient with semantic dementia. *Cognitive Neuropsychology, 11*, 617–660.

Breedin, S. D., & Martin, R. C. (1996). Patterns of verb impairment in aphasia: An analysis of four cases. *Cognitive Neuropsychology, 13*, 51–91.

Brener, R. (1940). An experimental investigation of memory span. *Journal of Experimental Psychology, 26*, 467–482.

Brown, A. S. (1991). A review of the tip-of-the-tongue experience. *Psychology Bulletin, 109*, 204–223.

Brown, R., & McNeill, D. (1966). The "tip of the tongue" phenomenon. *Journal of Verbal Learning and Verbal Behavior, 5*, 325–337.

Bub, D., Black, S., Howell, J., & Kertesz, A. (1987). Damage to input and output buffers—what's a lexicality effect doing in a place like that? In E. Keller, & M. Gopnik (Eds.), *Motor and sensory processes of language* (pp. 83–110). Hillsdale, NJ: Lawrence Erlbaum Associates.

Bub, D. N., Black, S., Hamson, E., & Kertesz, A. (1988). Semantic encoding of pictures and words. Some neuropsychological observations. *Cognitive Neuropsychology, 5*, 27–66.

Buckingham, H. W. (1980). On correlating aphasic errors with slips-of-the-tongue. *Applied Psycholinguistics, 1*, 199–220.

Buckingham, H. W., Avakian-Whitaker, H., & Whitaker, H. A. (1978). Alliteration and assonance in neologistic jargon aphasia. *Cortex, 14*, 365–380.

Buckingham, H. W., & Kertesz, A. (1974). A linguistic analysis of fluent aphasia. *Brain and Language, 1*, 43–62.

Burke, D. M., MacKay, D. G., Worthley, J. S., & Wade, E. (1991). On the tip of the tongue: What causes word finding failures in young and older adults? *Journal of Memory and Language, 30*, 542–579.

Burns, M. S., & Canter, G. J. (1977). Phonemic behavior of aphasic patients with posterior cerebral lesions. *Brain and Language, 4*, 492–507.

Butterworth, B. (1979). Hesitation and the production of verbal paraphasias and neologisms in jargon aphasia. *Brain and Language, 8*, 133–161.

Byng, S. (1988). Sentence processing deficits: Theory and therapy. *Cognitive Neuropsychology, 5*, 629–676.

Canter, G. J., Trost, J. E., & Burns, M. S. (1985). Contrasting speech patterns in apraxia of speech and phonemic paraphasia. *Brain and Language, 24*, 204–222.

Capitani, E., Laiacona, M., & Caramazza, A. (2003). What are the facts of semantic category-specific deficits? A critical review of the clinical evidence. *Cognitive Neuropsychology, 20*, 213–261.

Caplan, D., Vanier, M., & Baker, C. (1986). A case study of reproduction conduction aphasia. I: Word production. *Cognitive Neuropsychology, 3*, 99–128.

Caramazza, A., Basili, A. G., Koller, J. J., & Berndt, R. S. (1981). An investigation of repetition and language processing in a case of conduction aphasia. *Brain and Language, 14*, 235–271.

Caramazza, A., Miceli, G., & Villa, G. (1986). The role of the (output) phonological buffer in reading, writing, and repetition. *Cognitive Neuropsychology, 3*, 37–76.

Catani, M., Jones, D. K., & Fytche, D. H. (2005). Perisylvian language networks of the human brain. *Annals of Neurology, 57*, 8–16.

Cermak, L. S., & Tarlow, S. (1978). Aphasic and amnesic patients' verbal vs nonverbal retentive capabilities. *Cortex, 14*, 32–40.

Chertkow, H., Bub, D., Deaudon, C., & Whitehead, V. (1997). On the status of object concepts in aphasia. *Brain and Language, 58*, 203–232.

Crutch, S. J. (2006). Qualitatively different semantic representations for abstract and concrete words: Further evidence from the semantic reading errors of deep dyslexic patients. *Neurocase, 12*, 91–97.

Crutch, S. J., Connell, S., & Warrington, E. K. (2009). The different representational frameworks underpinning abstract and concrete knowledge: Evidence from odd-one-out judgments. *Quarterly Journal of Experimental Psychology, 62*, 1377–1390.

Crutch, S. J., & Warrington, E. K. (2005). Abstract and concrete concepts have structurally different representational frameworks. *Brain, 128*, 615–627.

Crutch, S. J., & Warrington, E. K. (2007). Semantic priming in deep-phonological dyslexia: Contrasting effects of association and similarity upon abstract and concrete word reading. *Cognitive Neuropsychology, 24*, 583–602.

Crutch, S. J., & Warrington, E. K. (2008). Contrasting patterns of comprehension for superordinate, basic-level, and subordinate names in semantic dementia and aphasic stroke patients. *Cognitive Neuropsychology, 25*, 582–600.

Damasio, A. R., & Tranel, D. (1993). Nouns and verbs are retrieved with differently distributed neural systems. *Proceedings of the National Academy of Sciences USA, 90*, 4957–4960.

Damasio, H., & Damasio, A. R. (1980). The anatomical basis of conduction aphasia. *Brain, 103*, 337–350.

Damasio, H., Grabowski, T. J., Tranel, D., Hichwa, R. D., & Damasio, A. R. (1996). A neural basis for lexical retrieval. *Nature, 380*, 499–505.

Dell, G. S. (1986). A spreading-activation theory of retrieval in sentence production. *Psychology Review, 93*, 283–321.

Dell, G. S. (1988). The retrieval of phonological forms in production: Tests of predictions from a connectionist model. *Journal of Memory and Language, 27*, 124–142.

Dell, G. S., & Reich, P. A. (1981). Stages in sentence production: An analysis of speech error data. *Journal of Verbal Learning and Verbal Behavior, 20*, 611–629.

Démonet, J. -F., Chollet, F., Ramsay, S., Cardebat, D., Nespoulous, J. -L., Wise, R., et al. (1992). The anatomy of phonological and semantic processing in normal subjects. *Brain, 115*, 1753–1768.

Dent, K., Johnston, R. A., & Humphreys, G. W. (2008). Age of acquisition and word frequency effects in picture naming: A dual-task investigation. *Journal of Experimental Psychology: Learning, Memory and Cognition, 34*, 282–301.

Desgranges, B., Matuszewski, V., Piolino, P., Chétat, G., Mézenge, F., Langeau, B., et al. (2007). Anatomical and functional alterations in semantic dementia: A voxel-based MRI and PET study. *Neurobiology of Aging, 28*, 1904–1913.

Devlin, J. T., Gonnerman, L. M., Andersen, E. S., & Seidenberg, M. S. (1998). Category-specific semantic deficits in focal and widespread brain damage: A computational account. *Journal of Cognitive Neuroscience, 10*, 77–94.

Diehl, J., Grimmer, T., Drzezga, A., Riemenschneider, M., Förstl, H., & Kurz, A. (2004). Cerebral metabolic patterns at early stages of frontotemporal dementia and semantic dementia. A PET study. *Neurobiology of Aging, 25*, 1051–1056.

Dubois, J., Hécaen, H., Angelergues, R., Maufras de Chatelier, A., & Marcie, P. (1973). Neurolinguistic study of conduction aphasia. In H. Goodglass, & S. Blumstein (Eds.), *Psycholinguistics and aphasia* (pp. 283–300). Baltimore: Johns Hopkins University Press.

Dunlop, J. M., & Marquardt, T. P. (1977). Linguistic and articulatory aspects of single word production in apraxia of speech. *Cortex, 13*, 17–29.

Edmonds, L. A., Nadeau, S. E., & Kiran, S. (2009). Effect of verb network strengthening treatment (vnest) on lexical retrieval of content words in sentences in persons with aphasia. *Aphasiology, 23*, 402–424.

Eggert, G. H. (1977). *Wernicke's works in aphasia: A sourcebook and review*, Vol. 1. The Hague, Netherlands: Mouton.

Ellis, A., & Lambon Ralph, M. A. (2000). Age of acquisition effects in adult lexical processing reflect loss of plasticity in maturing systems: Insights from connectionist networks. *Journal of Experimental Psychology: Learning, Memory and Cognition, 26*, 1103–1123.

Ellis, A. W. (1980). Errors in speech and short-term memory: The effects of phonemic similarity and syllable position. *Journal of Verbal Learning and Verbal Behavior, 19*, 624–634.

Ellis, A. W. (1985). The production of spoken words: A cognitive neuropsychological perspective. In A. W. Ellis (Ed.), *Progress in the psychology of language*, Vol. 2 (pp. 107–145). Hillsdale, NJ: Lawrence Erlbaum Associates.

Ellis, A. W., Miller, D., & Sin, G. (1983). Wernicke's aphasia and normal language processing: A case study in cognitive neuropsychology. *Cognition*, *15*, 111–144.

Ellis, A. W., & Young, A. W. (1988). *Human Cognitive Neuropsychology*. Hillsdale, NJ: Lawrence Erlbaum Associates.

Elman, J. L., & McClelland, J. L. (1988). Cognitive penetration of the mechanisms of perception: Compensation for coarticulation of lexically restored phonemes. *Journal of Memory and Language*, *27*, 143–165.

Farah, M. J., & McClelland, J. L. (1991). A computational model of semantic memory impairment: Modality-specificity and emergent category-specificity. *Journal of Experimental Psychology: General*, *120*(4), 339–357.

Fay, D., & Cutler, A. (1977). Malapropisms and the structure of the mental lexicon. *Linguistic Inquiry*, *8*, 505–520.

Feinberg, T. E., Gonzalez Rothi, L. J., & Heilman, K. M. (1986). "Inner speech" in conduction aphasia. *Archives of Neurology*, *43*, 591–593.

Ferretti, T. R., McRae, K., & Hatherell, A. (2001). Integrating verbs, situation schemas, and thematic role concepts. *Journal of Memory and Language*, *44*, 516–547.

Fillenbaum, S., Jones, L., & Wepman, J. (1961). Some linguistic features of speech from aphasic patients. *Language & Speech*, *4*, 91–108.

Forde, E. M. E., & Humphreys, G. W. (1999). Category specific recognition impairments: A review of important case studies and influential theories. *Aphasiology*, *13*, 169–193.

Francis, W. N., & Kucera, H. (1982). *Frequency analysis of English usage: Lexicon and grammar*. Boston: Houghton Mifflin.

Friedman, R. B., & Kohn, S. E. (1990). Impaired activation of the phonological lexicon: Effects upon oral reading. *Brain and Language*, *38*, 278–297.

Friedrich, F. J., Glenn, C. G., & Marin, O. S. M. (1984). Interruption of phonological coding in conduction aphasia. *Brain and Language*, *22*, 266–291.

Fromkin, V. A. (1971). The non-anomalous nature of anomalous utterances. *Language*, *47*, 27–52.

Gagnon, D. A., Schwartz, M. F., Martin, N., Dell, G. S., & Saffran, E. M. (1995). The origins of form-related word and nonword errors in aphasic naming. *Brain and Cognition*, *28*, 192.

Gagnon, D. A., Schwartz, M. F., Martin, N., Dell, G. S., & Saffran, E. M. (1997). The origin of formal paraphasias in aphasic's picture naming. *Brain and Language*, *59*, 450–472.

Gandour, J., Akamanon, C., Dechongkit, S., Khunadorn, F., & Boonklam, R. (1994). Sequences of phonemic approximations in a Thai conduction aphasic. *Brain and Language*, *46*, 69–95.

Garlock, V. M., Walley, A. C., & Metsala, J. L. (2001). Age of acquisition, word frequency, and neighborhood density effects on spoken word recognition by children and adults. *Journal of Memory and Language*, *45*, 468–492.

Garrett, M. F. (1975). The analysis of sentence production. In G. H. Bower (Ed.), *The psychology of learning and motivation* (pp. 133–177). New York: Academic Press.

Garrett, M. F. (1976). Syntactic processes in sentence production. In R. J. Wales, & E. Walker (Eds.), *New approaches to language mechanisms* (pp. 231–256). Amsterdam: North-Holland.

Geschwind, N. (1965). Disconnexion syndromes in animals and man. *Brain*, *88*, 237–294, 585–644.

Gilmour, G. C., Wenk, H. E., Naylor, L. A., & Koss, E. (1994). Motor perception and Alzheimer's disease. *The Journals of Gerontology. Series B, Psychological Sciences and Social Sciences*, *49*, 52–57.

Goodglass, H. (1993). *Understanding aphasia*. San Diego: Academic Press.

Goodglass, H., Gleason, J. B., & Hyde, M. R. (1970). Some dimensions of auditory language comprehension in aphasia. *Journal of Speech and Hearing Research*, *13*, 595–606.

Goodglass, H., Kaplan, E., Weintraub, S., & Ackerman, N. (1976). The "tip of the tongue" phenomenon in aphasia. *Cortex*, *12*, 145–153.

Goodglass, H., Wingfield, A., Hyde, M. R., Gleason, J. B., Bowles, N. L., & Gallagher, R. E. (1997). The importance of word initial phonology: Error patterns in prolonged naming efforts by aphasic patients. *Journal of the International Neuropsychological Society*, *3*, 128–138.

Green, E. (1969). Phonological and grammatical aspects of jargon in an aphasic patient: A case study. *Language and Speech*, *12*, 103–118.

Green, E., & Howes, D. H. (1977). The nature of conduction aphasia: A study of anatomic and clinical features and of underlying mechanisms. In H. Whitaker, & H. A. Whitaker (Eds.), *Studies in neurolinguistics*, Vol. 3 (pp. 123–156). New York: Academic Press.

Grossman, M., & Ash, S. (2004). Primary progressive aphasia: A review. *Neurocase*, *10*, 3–18.

Halpern, H., Keith, R. L., & Darley, F. L. (1976). Phonemic behavior of aphasic subjects without dysarthria or apraxia of speech. *Cortex*, *12*, 365–372.

Hamilton, A. C., & Coslett, H. B. (2008). Refractory access disorders and the organization of concrete and abstract semantics: Do they differ? *Neurocase, 14*, 131–140.

Harm, M. W., & Seidenberg, M. S. (2004). Computing the meanings of words in reading: Cooperative division of labor between visual and phonological processes. *Psychology Review, 111*, 662–720.

Hart, J., & Gordon, B. (1990). Delineation of single-word semantic comprehension deficits in aphasia, with anatomical correlation. *Annals of Neurology, 27*, 226–231.

Heilman, K. M., Scholes, R., & Watson, R. T. (1976). Defects of immediate memory in Broca's and conduction aphasia. *Brain and Language, 3*, 201–208.

Heilman, K. M., & Scholes, R. J. (1976). The nature of comprehension errors in Broca's, conduction and Wernicke's aphasics. *Cortex, 12*, 258–265.

Hillis, A. E., Work, M., Barker, P. B., Jacobs, M. A., Breese, E. L., & Maurer, K. (2004). Re-examining the brain regions crucial for orchestrating speech articulation. *Brain, 127*, 1479–1487.

Hinton, G. E., & Shallice, T. (1991). Lesioning an attractor network: Investigations of acquired dyslexia. *Psychology Review, 98*, 74–95.

Hodges, J. R., Graham, N., & Patterson, K. (1995). Charting the progression in semantic dementia: Implications for the organization of semantic memory. *Memory, 3*, 463–495.

Hodges, J. R., Patterson, K., Oxbury, S., & Funnell, E. (1992). Semantic dementia. Progressive fluent aphasia with temporal-lobe atrophy. *Brain, 115*, 1783–1806.

Hodges, J. R., Patterson, K., Ward, R., Garrard, P., Bak, T. H., Perry, R., et al. (1999). The differentiation of semantic dementia and frontal lobe dementia (temporal and frontal variants of frontotemporal dementia) from early Alzheimer's disease: A comparative neuropsychological study. *Neuropsychology, 13*, 31–40.

Hovius, M., Kellenbach, M. L., Graham, K. S., Hodges, J. R., & Patterson, K. (2003). What does the object decision task measure? Reflections on the basis of evidence from semantic dementia. *Neuropsychology, 17*, 100–107.

Howard, D., & Patterson, K. (1982). *The pyramids and palm trees test: A test of semantic access from words and pictures.* Bury St. Edmonds, UK: Thames Valley Test Co.

Joanette, Y., Keller, E., & Lecours, A. R. (1980). Sequences of phonemic approximations in aphasia. *Brain and Language, 11*, 30–44.

Johns, D. F., & Darley, F. L. (1970). Phonemic variability in apraxia of speech. *Journal of Speech and Hearing Research, 13*, 556–583.

Jones, E. V. (1984). Word order processing in aphasia: Effect of verb semantics. *Advances in Neurology, 42*, 159–181.

Kay, J., & Ellis, A. W. (1987). A cognitive neuropsychological case study of anomia: Implications for psychologic models of word retrieval. *Brain, 110*, 613–629.

Keller, E. (1978). Parameters for vowel substitutions in Broca's aphasia. *Brain and Language, 5*, 265–285.

Kemmerer, D., Gonzalez Castillo, J., Talavage, T., Patterson, S., & Wiley, C. (2008). Neuronanatomical distribution of five semantic components of verbs: Evidence from fMRI. *Brain and Language, 107*, 16–43.

Kemmerer, D., & Tranel, D. (2003). A double dissociation between the meanings of action verbs and locative prepositions. *Neurocase, 9*, 421–435.

Kendall, D. L., Rosenbek, J. C., Heilman, K. M., Conway, T. W., Klenberg, K., Gsonzalez Rothi, L. J., et al. (2008). Phoneme-based rehabilitation of anomia in aphasia. *Brain and Language, 105*, 1–17.

Kertesz, A., & Benson, D. F. (1970). Neologistic jargon: A clinicopathological study. *Cortex, 6*, 362–386.

Kiran, S. (2007). Complexity in the treatment of naming disorders. *American Journal of Speech-language Pathology, 16*, 18–29.

Kiran, S., & Thompson, C. K. (2003). The role of semantic complexity in treatment of naming deficits: Training semantic categories in fluent aphasia by controlling exemplar typicality. *Journal of Speech, Language, and Hearing Research, 46*, 608–622.

Kittredge, A. K., Dell, G. S., Verkuilen, J., & Schwartz, M. F. (2008). Where is the effect of frequency in word production? Insights from aphasic picture-naming errors. *Cognitive Neuropsychology, 25*, 463–492.

Klich, R. J., Ireland, J. V., & Weidner, W. E. (1979). Articulatory and phonological aspects of consonant substitutions in apraxia of speech. *Cortex, 15*, 451–470.

Kohn, S. E. (1984). The nature of the phonological disorder in conduction aphasia. *Brain and Language, 23*, 97–115.

Kohn, S. E. (1989). The nature of the phonemic string deficit in conduction aphasia. *Aphasiology, 3*, 209–239.

Kohn, S. E., & Smith, K. L. (1990). Between-word speech errors in conduction aphasia. *Cognitive Neuropsychology, 7*, 133–156.

Kohn, S. E., & Smith, K. L. (1991). The relationship between oral spelling and phonological breakdown in a conduction aphasic. *Cortex, 27*, 631–639.

Kohn, S. E., & Smith, K. L. (1995). Serial effects of phonemic planning during word production. *Aphasiology, 9,* 209–222.

Kohn, S. E., Wingfield, A., Menn, L., Goodglass, H., Gleason, J. B., & Hyde, M. (1987). Lexical retrieval: The tip-of-the-tongue phenomenon. *Applied Psycholinguistics, 8,* 245–266.

Koriat, A., & Lieblich, I. (1974). What does a person in a "TOT" state know that a person in a "don't know" state doesn't know? *Memory and Cognition, 2,* 647–655.

La Pointe, L. L., & Johns, D. F. (1975). Some phonemic characteristics in apraxia of speech. *Journal of Communication Disorders, 8,* 259–269.

Laine, M., & Martin, N. (1996). Lexical retrieval deficit in picture naming: Implications for word production models. *Brain and Language, 53,* 283–314.

Lambon Ralph, M. A., & Ehsan, S. (2006). Age of acquisition effects depend on the mapping between representations and the frequency of occurrence: Empirical and computational evidence. *Visual Cognition, 13,* 928–948.

Lambon Ralph, M. A., Graham, K. S., Ellis, A. W., & Hodges, J. R. (1998). Naming in semantic dementia—what matters? *Neuropsychologia, 36,* 775–784.

Lambon Ralph, M. A., Graham, K. S., & Patterson, K. (1999). Is a picture worth a thousand words? Evidence from concept definitions by patients with semantic dementia. *Brain and Language, 70,* 309–335.

Lecours, A. R. (1982). On neologisms. In J. Mehler, E. C. T. Walker, & M. Garrett (Eds.), *Perspectives on mental representation* (pp. 217–250). Hillsdale, NJ: Lawrence Erlbaum Associates.

Lecours, A. R., & Lhermitte, F. (1969). Phonemic paraphasias: Linguistic structures and tentative hypotheses. *Cortex, 5,* 193–228.

Levitt, A. B., & Healy, A. F. (1985). The roles of phoneme frequency, similarity, and availability in the experimental elicitation of speech errors. *Journal of Memory and Language, 24,* 717–733.

Lichtheim, L. (1885). On aphasia. *Brain, 7,* 433–484.

Lipinski, J., & Gupta, P. (2005). Does neighborhood density influence repetition latency for nonwords? Separating the effects of density and duration. *Journal of Memory and Language, 52,* 171–192.

Lissauer, H. (1988). Ein fall von seelenblindheit nebst einem beitrag sur theorie derselven. *Cognitive Neuropsychology, 5,* 157–192.

Lu, L. H., Crosson, B., Nadeau, S. E., Heilman, K. M., Gonzalez Rothi, L. J., Raymer, A. M., et al. (2002). Category-specific naming deficits for objects and actions: Semantic attribute and grammatical role hypotheses. *Neuropsychologia, 40,* 1608–1621.

Luria, A. R., & Tsvetkova, L. S. (1967). Towards the mechanisms of dynamic aphasia. *Acta Neurologica et Psychiatrica Belgica, 67,* 1045–1057.

MacKay, D. G. (1970). Spoonerisms: The structure of errors in the serial order of speech. *Neuropsychologia, 8,* 323–350.

MacKay, D. G. (1972). The structure of words and syllables: Evidence from errors in speech. *Cognitive Psychology, 3,* 210–227.

MacNeilage, P. (1982). Speech production mechanisms in aphasia. In S. Grillner, B. Lindblom, J. Lubker, & A. Persson (Eds.), *Speech Motor Control* (pp. 43–60). London: Pergamon.

Mahon, B. Z., & Caramazza, A. (2009). Concepts and categories: A cognitive neuropsychological perspective. *Annual Review of Psychology, 60,* 27–51.

Manning, L., & Warrington, E. K. (1996). Two routes to naming: A case study. *Neuropsychologia, 34,* 809–817.

Marin, O. M., Saffran, E. M., & Schwartz, M. F. (1976). Dissociation of language in aphasia: Implications for normal function. In H. B. Stekles, S. R. Harnard, & J. Lancaster (Eds.), *Origins and evolution of language and speech.* New York: New York Academy of Sciences.

Marquardt, T. P., Reinhart, J. B., & Peterson, H. A. (1979). Markedness analysis of phonemic substitution errors in apraxia of speech. *Journal of Communication Disorders, 12,* 481–494.

Marr, D. (1982). *Vision: A computational investigation into the human representation and processing of visual information.* San Francisco: W. H. Freeman.

Marshall, J., Chiat, S., Robson, J., & Pring, T. (1995/96). Calling a salad a federation: An investigation of semantic jargon,. Part 2—Verbs. *Journal of Neurolinguistics, 4,* 251–260.

Martin, A. D., & Rigrodsky, S. (1974). An investigation of phonological impairment in aphasia, part 1. *Cortex, 10,* 317–346.

Martin, N., & Saffran, E. M. (1992). A computational account of deep dysphasia: Evidence from a single case study. *Brain and Language, 43,* 240–274.

Martin, N., & Saffran, E. M. (1997). Language and auditory-verbal short-term memory impairments: Evidence for common underlying processes. *Cognitive Neuropsychology, 14,* 641–682.

Martin, N., Saffran, E. M., & Dell, G. S. (1996). Recovery in deep dysphasia: Evidence for a relation between auditory-verbal STM capacity and lexical errors in repetition. *Brain and Language, 52,* 83–113.

Martin, R. C., Shelton, J. R., & Yaffee, L. S. (1994). Language processing and working memory: Neuropsychological evidence for separate phonological and semantic capacities. *Journal of Memory and Language, 33,* 83–111.

McCarthy, R., & Warrington, E. K. (1984). A two-route model of speech production. Evidence from aphasia. *Brain, 107,* 463–485.

McClelland, J. L., Mirman, D., & Holt, L. L. (2006). Are there interactive processes in speech perception? *Trends in Cognitive Sciences, 10,* 363–369.

McClelland, J. L., & Rumelhart, D. E. (1985). Distributed memory and the representation of general and specific information. *Journal of Experimental Psychology: General,114,* 159–188.

McClelland, J. L., Rumelhart, D. E., & PDP Research Group. (1986). *Parallel distributed processing.* Cambridge, MA: MIT Press.

McRae, K., & Cree, G. (2002). Factors underlying category-specific deficits. In E. M. E. Forde, & G. W. Humphreys (Eds.), *Category specificity in brain and mind* (pp. 211–249). Hove, United Kingdom: Psychology Press.

McRae, K., De Sa, V. R., & Seidenberg, M. S. (1997). On the nature and scope of featural representations of word meaning. *Journal of Experimental Psychology: General, 126,* 99–130.

McRae, K., Hare, M., Elman, J. L., & Ferretti, T. R. (2005). A basis for generating expectancies for verbs from nouns. *Memory and Cognition, 33,* 1174–1184.

Miceli, G., Caltagirone, C., Gainotti, C., & Payer-Rigo, P. (1978). Discrimination of voice versus place contrasts in aphasia. *Brain and Language, 6,* 47–51.

Miceli, G., Gainotti, G., Caltagirone, C., & Masullo, C. (1980). Some aspects of phonological impairment in aphasia. *Brain and Language, 11,* 159–169.

Miller, D., & Ellis, A. W. (1987). Speech and writing errors in "neologistic jargonaphasia": A lexical activation hypothesis. In M. Coltheart, G. Sartori, & R. Job (Eds.), *The cognitive neuropsychology of language* (pp. 253–271). Hillsdale, NJ: Lawrence Erlbaum Associates.

Miller, G. A., & Fellbaum, C. (1991). Semantic networks in English. *Cognition, 41,* 197–229.

Mishkin, M., Ungerleider, L. G., & Macko, K. A. (1983). Object vision and spatial vision: Two cortical pathways. *Trends in Neurosciences, 6,* 414–417.

Moran, J., & Desimone, R. (1985). Selective attention gates visual processing in extrastriate cortex. *Science, 229,* 782–784.

Moss, H. E., Tyler, L. K., & Devlin, J. T. (2002). The emergence of category-specific deficits in a distributed semantic system. In E. M. E. Forde, & G. W. Humphreys (Eds.), *Category specificity in brain and mind* (pp. 115–148). Hove, UK: Psychology Press.

Motley, M. T., & Baars, B. J. (1976). Semantic bias effects on the outcomes of verbal slips. *Cognition, 4,* 177–187.

Nadeau, S. E. (2001). Phonology: A review and proposals from a connectionist perspective. *Brain and Language, 79,* 511–579.

Nadeau, S. E., & Heilman, K. M. (2007). Frontal mysteries revealed. *Neurology, 68,* 1450–1453.

Nadeau, S. E., Rothi, L. J. G., & Rosenbek, J. C. (2008). Language rehabilitation from a neural perspective. In R. Chapey (Ed.), *Language intervention strategies in aphasia and related neurogenic communication disorders* (5th ed., pp. 689–734). Philadelphia, PA: Lippincott Williams & Wilkins.

Naeser, M. A., & Hayward, R. W. (1978). Lesion localization in aphasia with cranial computed tomography and the Boston diagnostic aphasia exam. *Neurology, 28,* 545–551.

Nespoulous, J. -L., Joanette, Y., Béland, R., Caplan, D., & Lecours, A. R. (1984). Phonologic disturbances in aphasia: Is there a "markedness effect" in aphasic phonetic errors? *Advances in Neurology, 42,* 203–214.

Nespoulous, J. -L., Joanette, Y., Ska, B., Caplan, D., & Lecours, A. R. (1987). Production deficits in Broca's and conduction aphasia: Repetition versus reading. In E. Keller, & M. Gopnik (Eds.), *Motor and sensory processes of language* (pp. 53–81). Hillsdale, NJ: Lawrence Erlbaum Associates.

Niemi, J., & Koivuselkä-Sallinen, P. (1985). Phoneme errors in Broca's aphasia: Three Finnish cases. *Brain and Language, 26,* 28–48.

Ojemann, G. A. (1991). Cortical organization of language. *Journal of Neuroscience, 11,* 2281–2287.

Palumbo, C. L., Alexander, M. P., & Naeser, M. A. (1992). CT scan lesion sites associated with conduction aphasia. In S. E. Kohn (Ed.), *Conduction aphasia* (pp. 51–75). Hillsdale, NJ: Lawrence Erlbaum Associates.

Pate, D. S., Saffran, E. M., & Martin, N. (1987). Specifying the nature of the production impairment in a conduction aphasic. *Language and Cognitive Processes, 2,* 43–84.

Patterson, K. (2007). The reign of typicality in semantic memory. *Philosophical Transactions of the Royal Society of London. Series B, Biological Sciences, 362,* 813–821.

Paulesu, E., Frith, C. D., & Frackowiak, R. S. J. (1993). The neural correlates of the verbal component of working memory. *Nature, 362,* 342–345.

Plaut, D. C. (1996). Relearning after damage in connectionist networks: Toward a theory of rehabilitation. *Brain and Language, 52,* 25–82.

Plaut, D. C., McClelland, J. L., Seidenberg, M. S., & Patterson, K. (1996). Understanding normal and impaired word reading: Computational principles in quasi-regular domains. *Psychology Review, 103,* 56–115.

Poncet, M., Degos, C., DeLoche, G., & Lecours, A. R. (1972). Phonetic and phonemic transformations in aphasia. *Internation Journal of Mental Health, 1,* 46–54.

Randall, B., Moss, H. E., Rodd, J. M., Greer, M., & Tyler, L. K. (2004). Distinctiveness and correlation in conceptual structure: Behavioral and computational studies. *Journal of Experimental Psychology: Learning, Memory and Cognition, 30,* 393–406.

Raymer, A. M., Foundas, A. L., Maher, L. M., Greenwald, M. L., Morris, M., Rothi, L. J., et al. (1997). Cognitive neuropsychological analysis and neuroanatomic correlates in a case of acute anomia. *Brain and Language, 58,* 137–156.

Robinson, K. M., Grossman, M., White-Devine, T., & D'Esposito, M. (1996). Category-specific difficulty naming with verbs in Alzheimer's disease. *Neurology, 47,* 178–182.

Rogers, T. T., Ivanoiu, A., Patterson, K., & Hodges, J. R. (2006). Semantic memory in Alzheimer's disease and the frontotemporal dementias: A longitudinal study of 236 patients. *Neuropsychology, 20,* 319–335.

Rogers, T. T., Lambon Ralph, M. A., Garrard, P., Bozeat, S., McClelland, J. L., Hodges, J. R., et al. (2004). Structure and deterioration of semantic memory: A neuropsychological and computational investigation. *Psychology Review, 111,* 205–235.

Rogers, T. T., & McClelland, J. L. (2004). *Semantic cognition. A parallel distributed processing approach.* Cambridge, MA: MIT Press.

Rolls, E. T., & Deco, G. (2002). *Computational Neuroscience of Vision.* Oxford: Oxford University Press.

Rolls, E. T., & Treves, A. (1998). *Neural networks and brain function.* New York: Oxford University Press.

Roth, H. L., Nadeau, S. E., Hollingsworth, A. L., Cimino-Knight, A. M., & Heilman, K. M. (2006). Naming concepts: Evidence of two routes. *Neurocase, 12,* 61–70.

Rubin, D. C. (1975). Within word structure in the tip-of-the-tongue phenomenon. *Journal of Verbal Learning and Verbal Behavior, 14,* 392–397.

Rumelhart, D. E., Smolensky, P., McClelland, J. L., & Hinton, G. E. (1986). Schemata and sequential thought processes in PDP models. In J. L. McClelland, D. E. Rumelhart, & the PDP Research Group (Eds.), *Parallel Distributed Processing,* Vol. 2 (pp. 7–57). Cambridge, MA: MIT Press.

Saffran, E. M., & Marin, O. S. M. (1975). Immediate memory for word lists in a patient with deficient auditory short-term memory. *Brain and Language, 2,* 420–433.

Saffran, E. M., Schwartz, M. F., & Marin, O. S. M. (1980). Evidence from aphasia: Isolating the components of a production model. In B. Butterworth (Ed.), *Language production,* Vol. 1 (pp. 221–241). London: Academic Press.

Sartori, G., & Job, R. (1988). The oyster with four legs: A neuropsychological study on the interaction of visual and semantic information. *Cognitive Neuropsychology, 5,* 105–132.

Schwartz, M. F., Saffran, E. M., Bloch, D. E., & Dell, G. S. (1994). Disordered speech production in aphasic and normal speakers. *Brain and Language, 47,* 52–88.

Seidenberg, M. S., & McClelland, J. L. (1989). A distributed, developmental model of word recognition and naming. *Psychology Review, 96,* 523–568.

Shallice, T. (1988). *From Neuropsychology to Mental Structure.* Cambridge: Cambridge University Press.

Shallice, T., & Vallar, G. (1990). The impairment of auditory-verbal short-term storage. In G. Vallar, & T. Shallice (Eds.), *Neuropsychological impairments of short-term memory* (pp. 11–53). Cambridge: Cambridge University Press.

Shallice, T., & Warrington, E. K. (1977). Auditory-verbal short-term memory impairment and conduction aphasia. *Brain and Language, 4,* 479–491.

Shankweiler, D., & Harris, K. S. (1966). An experimental approach to the problem of articulation in aphasia. *Cortex, 2,* 277–292.

Shankweiler, D., Harris, K. S., & Taylor, M. L. (1968). Electromyographic studies of articulation in aphasia. *Archives of Physical Medicine and Rehabilitation, 49,* 1–8.

Shattuck-Hufnagel, S. (1979). Speech errors as evidence for a serial-ordering mechanism in sentence production. In W. E. Cooper, & E. C. T. Walker (Eds.), *Sentence processing: Psycholinguistic studies* (pp. 295–341). Hillsdale, NJ: Lawrence Erlbaum Associates.

Shattuck-Hufnagel, S., & Klatt, D. H. (1979). The limited use of distinctive features and markedness in speech production: Evidence from speech error data. *Journal of Verbal Learning and Verbal Behavior, 18*, 41–55.

Shewan, C. M. (1980). Phonological processing in Broca's aphasics. *Brain and Language, 10*, 71–88.

Shinn, P., & Blumstein, P. (1983). Phonetic disintegration in aphasia: Acoustic analysis of spectral characteristics for place of articulation. *Brain and Language, 20*, 90–114.

Speedie, L. J., Wertman, E., Ta'ir, J., & Heilman, K. M. (1993). Disruption of automatic speech following a right basal ganglia lesion. *Neurology, 43*, 1768–1774.

Stark, M., Coslett, H. B., & Saffran, E. M. (1996). Impairment of an egocentric map of locations: Implications for perception and action. *Cognitive Neuropsychology, 13*, 481–523.

Stemberger, J. P. (1982). The nature of segments in the lexicon: Evidence from speech errors. *Lingua, 56*, 235–259.

Stemberger, J. P. (1984). Structural errors in normal and agrammatic speech. *Cognitive Neuropsychology, 4*, 281–313.

Stemberger, J. P., & MacWhinney, B. (1986). Frequency and the lexical storage of regularly inflected forms. *Memory & Cognition, 14*, 17–26.

Strub, R. L., & Gardner, H. (1974). The repetition defect in conduction aphasia: Mnestic or linguistic? *Brain and Language, 1*, 241–255.

Taylor, L. J., & Zwaan, R. A. (2008). Motor resonance and linguistic focus. *Quarterly Journal of Experimental Psychology, 61*, 896–904.

Tranel, D., Adolphs, R., Damasio, H., & Damasio, A. R. (2001). A neural basis for the retrieval of words for actions. *Cognitive Neuropsychology, 18*, 655–670.

Tranel, D., & Damasio, H. (2005). *Retrieval of unique names depends on neural systems in left temporal polar region*. Paper presented at the 33rd Annual Meeting of the International Neuropsychological Society, St. Louis, MO.

Tranel, D., Manzel, K., Asp, E., & Kemmerer, D. (2008). Naming dynamic and static actions: Neuropsychological evidence. *Journal of Physiology, 102*, 80–94.

Trost, J. E., & Canter, G. J. (1974). Apraxia of speech in patients with Broca's aphasia: A study of phoneme production accuracy and error patterns. *Brain and Language, 1*, 63–79.

Tulving, E. (1972). Episodic and semantic memory. In E. Tulving, & W. Donaldson (Eds.), *Organization of memory* (pp. 381–403). New York: Academic Press.

Tulving, E. (1983). *Elements of episodic memory*. Oxford: Clarendon.

Ungerleider, L. G. (1995). Functional brain imaging studies of cortical mechanisms of memory. *Science, 270*, 769–775.

Valdois, S., Joanette, Y., & Nespoulous, J. -L. (1989). Intrinsic organization of sequences of phonemic approximations: A preliminary study. *Aphasiology, 3*, 55–73.

Valdois, S., Joanette, Y., Nespoulous, J. -L., & Poncet, M. (1988). Afferent motor aphasia and conduction aphasia. In H. A. Whitaker (Ed.), *Phonological processes and brain mechanisms* (pp. 59–92). New York: Springer-Verlag.

Vallar, G., & Baddeley, A. D. (1984). Phonological short-term store, phonological processing and sentence comprehension: A neuropsychological case study. *Cognitive Neuropsychology, 1*, 121–141.

Vallar, G., Basso, A., & Bottini, G. (1990). Phonologic processing and sentence comprehension: A neuropsychological case study. In G. Vallar, & T. Shallice (Eds.), *Neuropsychological impairments of short-term memory* (pp. 448–476). New York: Cambridge University Press.

Vitevitch, M. S. (1997). The neighborhood characteristics of malapropisms. *Language and Speech, 40*, 211–228.

Vitevitch, M. S. (2002). Naturalistic and experimental analyses of word frequency and neighborhood density effects in slips of the ear. *Language & Speech, 45*, 407–434.

Vitevitch, M. S., Armbruster, J., & Chu, S. (2004). Sublexical and lexical representations in speech production: Effects of phonotactic probability and onset density. *Journal of Experimental Psychology: Learning, Memory and Cognition, 30*, 514–529.

Vitevitch, M. S., & Luce, P. A. (1999). Probabilistic phonotactics and neighborhood activation in spoken word recognition. *Journal of Memory and Language, 40*, 374–408.

Vitevitch, M. S., & Luce, P. A. (2005). Increases in phonotactic probability facilitate spoken nonword repetition. *Journal of Memory and Language, 52*, 193–204.

Vitevitch, M. S., & Rodríguez, E. (2004). Neighborhood density effects in spoken word recognition in Spanish. *Journal of Multilingual Communication Disorders, 3*, 64–73.

Vitevitch, M. S., & Sommers, M. S. (2003). The facilitative influence of phonological similarity and neighborhood frequency in speech production in younger and older adults. *Memory & Cognition, 31,* 494–504.

Vitevitch, M. S., & Stamer, M. K. (2006). The curious case of competition in Spanish speech production. *Language and Cognitive Processes, 21,* 760–770.

Warrington, E. K. (1975). The selective impairment of semantic memory. *Quarterly Journal of Experimental Psychology, 27,* 635–657.

Warrington, E. K., Logue, V., & Pratt, R. T. C. (1971). The anatomical localization of selective impairment of auditory verbal short-term memory. *Neuropsychologia, 9,* 377–387.

Warrington, E. K., & McCarthy, R. (1987). Categories of knowledge. Further fractionation and an attempted integration. *Brain, 110,* 1273–1296.

Warrington, E. K., & Shallice, T. (1969). The selective impairment of auditory verbal short-term memory. *Brain, 92,* 885–896.

Warrington, E. K., & Shallice, T. (1972). Neuropsychological evidence of visual storage in short term memory tasks. *Quarterly Journal of Experimental Psychology, 24,* 30–40.

Warrington, E. K., & Shallice, T. (1984). Category specific semantic impairments. *Brain, 107,* 829–854.

Waters, G. S., Rochon, E., & Caplan, D. (1992). The role of high level speech planning in rehearsal - evidence from patients with apraxia of speech. *Journal of Memory and Language, 31,* 54–73.

Watkins, M. J., & Watkins, O. C. (1977). Serial recall and the modality effect: Effects of word frequency. *Journal of Experimental Psychology: Human Learning and Memory, 3,* 712–718.

Whatmough, C., Chertkow, H., Murtha, S., & Hanratty, K. (2002). Dissociable brain regions process object meaning and object structure during picture naming. *Neuropsychologia, 40,* 174–186.

White-Devine, T., Grossman, M., Robinson, K. M., Onishi, K., Biassou, N., & D'Esposito, M. (1996). Verb confrontation naming and word-picture matching in Alzheimer's disease. *Neuropsychology, 10,* 495–503.

Wickelgren, W. A. (1969). Context-sensitive coding, associative memory, and serial order in (speech) behavior. *Psychology Review, 76,* 1–15.

Wilshire, C. E. (1998). Three "abnormal" features of aphasic phonologic errors. *Brain and Language, 65,* 219–222.

Woollams, A. M., Cooper-Pye, E., Hodges, J. R., & Patterson, K. (2008). Anomia: A doubly typical signature of semantic dementia. *Neuropsychologia, 46,* 2503–2514.

Yamadori, A., & Ikumura, G. (1975). Central (or conduction) aphasia in a Japanese patient. *Cortex, 11,* 73–82.

Yarmey, A. D. (1973). I recognize your face but I can't remember your name: Further evidence on the tip-of-the-tongue phenomenon. *Memory & Cognition, 1,* 287–290.

Zaidel, E., Iacoboni, M., Zaidel, D. W., & Bogen, J. (2003). The callosal syndromes. In K. M. Heilman, & E. Valenstein (Eds.), *Clinical Neuropsychology* (4th ed., pp. 347–403). New York: Oxford University Press.

Zeki, S. (1991). Cerebral akinetopsia (visual motion blindness). *Brain, 114,* 811–824.

Zevin, J. D., & Seidenberg, M. (2002). Age of acquisition effects in word reading and other tasks. *Journal of Memory and Language, 47,* 1–29.

Zihl, J., Von Cramon, D. Y., & Mai, N. (1983). Selective disturbance of movement vision after bilateral brain damage. *Brain, 106,* 313–340.

4

Syntactic Aspects of Language Disorders

DAVID CAPLAN

Sentences convey relationships between the meanings of words, such as who is accomplishing an action or receiving it. These aspects of semantic meaning—collectively known as the *propositional content of a sentence*—vastly extend the power of language beyond what is available through single words and word formation processes to allow language to represent events and states of affairs. Propositions can be used to update semantic memory, to reason, and for many other purposes, and thus constitute a vital link between language and other cognitive processes.

Relations between words can be derived logically on the basis of the meanings of words and knowledge about the world. The words "man," "eat," and "cake" can be related in this way to express the proposition that a man ate a cake. Syntactic structures provide a means whereby the meanings of individual words can be combined *arbitrarily* to represent propositional meaning. They thus allow language to express these aspects of meanings when they cannot simply be inferred from the real-world relations between the items and actions in a sentence; that is, to express one of several equally likely relations, or unlikely, false, or impossible relations among items, properties, and actions designated by words in a sentence or a phrase. The ability afforded by syntax to express these relations, free from the constraint that what is conveyed must correspond to likely events and states of affairs in the real world, is crucial to human communication (and possibly human thought). It is the basis for conveying much of the information that is entered into long-term semantic memory (e.g., that John left Susan, rather than vice versa) and to reasoning counterfactually (e.g., "If John were here, he would agree with me"), both of which are important human functions.

Difficulties using syntax to encode or to decode messages are common in aphasia, at least in aphasia secondary to stroke. For instance, Caplan et al. (1985) estimated that 85% of aphasic patients had disturbances affecting their ability to use syntactic structures to determine sentence meaning. Disturbances affecting the ability to construct syntactic structure in production were recognized relatively early, and Pick's study (Brown, 1973) remains a classic both for its description of these disorders and for the model of sentence planning that it contains. That syntactic processing could be disrupted in comprehension was not appreciated until the last quarter of the 20th century. However, research into disorders of syntactic comprehension has made up for lost time, and has been related to theories of syntactic structure and processing much more extensively than has work on syntactic disorders in production. In this chapter, I briefly review behavioral aspects of disorders of syntactic comprehension and production, neural issues related to these disorders, and clinical matters.

SYNTACTIC STRUCTURES

The following layman's view of syntax will provide the first-time reader of this topic with the background needed to follow the issues in this chapter. Syntactic structures are mental entities that relate the meanings of individual words to each other according to a formal (noninferential) system. Individual lexical items are marked for syntactic category (e.g., *cat* is a noun [N]; *kill* is a verb [V]; *a* is a determiner [DET]). These categories combine to create phrasal categories such as noun phrase (NP), verb phrase (VP), sentence (S), etc. Different relations between the syntactic categories in these hierarchical structures determine different aspects of sentence meaning. Consider, for instance, Sentence 4-1, whose syntactic structure is shown in Figure 4-1:

Sentence 4-1. The dog that scratched the cat killed the mouse.

Sentence 4-1 conveys the proposition that the dog killed the mouse. However, the words *the dog* are not adjacent to *killed*. Figure 4-1 shows, however, that they are closely related to *killed* in the hierarchical structure of the sentence. The NP *the dog that scratched the cat* is immediately dominated by the sentence node (S), which also directly dominates the VP *killed the mouse*. An NP immediately dominated by an S is the subject of the sentence, and the subject of the sentence has a thematic role related to the verb of the verb phrase of the sentence. In Sentence 4-1, *the dog* (actually, *the dog that scratched the cat*) is the subject of the sentence and is the agent of the verb *killed*.

Note that there is a sequence of words in Sentence 4-1—*the cat killed the mouse*—in which an NP (*the cat*) is close to a VP in the linear structure of the sentence (*the cat* immediately precedes *killed*) but does not play a thematic role around *killed*. This is because of the

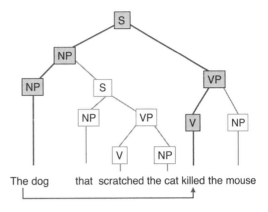

Figure 4–1. Simplified syntactic structure of the sentence, *The dog that scratched the cat killed the mouse*, showing the hierarchical organization of syntactic categories that determine thematic roles.

position of these words in the *hierarchical* syntactic structure of this sentence. *The cat* is the object of the verb *scratched* in the relative clause *that scratched the cat* and is the theme of *scratched*. The path over the hierarchical structure between *the cat* and *killed* has no semantic interpretation (Figure 4-2A).

Sentences convey many different semantic features, and each of these depends upon a different relationship of nodes defined over a syntactic structure. We have briefly considered thematic roles. A second phenomenon that has been extensively studied is co-reference—the relationship of referentially dependent items such as pronouns (e.g., *him*) and reflexives (e.g., *himself*) to referring NPs. Consider Sentence 4-1 with a slight change:

Sentence 4-2. The dog that scratched the cat killed it.

"It" refers to *cat*, not *dog*. The hierarchical structure of Sentences 4-2 and 4-1 are the same, but different relations apply to assign thematic roles and co-reference. The pathway between *the cat* and *it* that determines their co-reference is highlighted in Figure 4-2B. It is very similar to the pathway shown in Figure 4-2A that did *not* apply to assign a thematic role to *the cat* around *killed*.

In summary, syntactic structures are hierarchically organized sets of syntactic categories, over which particular structural relations are

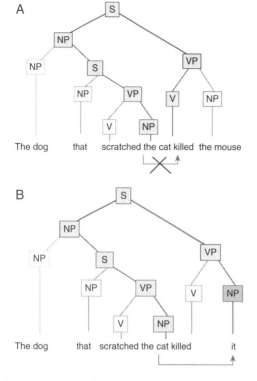

Figure 4–2. A: Simplified syntactic structure of the sentence, *The dog that scratched the cat killed the mouse*, showing the path over the hierarchical organization of syntactic categories that does not determine thematic roles. **B**: Simplified syntactic structure of the sentence, *The dog that scratched the cat killed it*, showing the path over the hierarchical organization of syntactic categories very similar to the one in **A** that is related to co-reference of the pronoun *it*.

defined that determine critical aspects of sentence meaning.

Linguists seek generalizations regarding the relation between syntactic structures and aspects of meaning. The challenge for linguistics is to arrive at the analysis that is simplest overall. This has led many linguists, beginning with Chomsky, to postulate what at first glance seem to be more complex structures than are needed to describe the structure of some sentences. For instance, passive sentences such as Sentence 4-3 are assigned a structure in which the subject (*the cat*) is first located in the position of object of the verb *scratched* and moves to its surface position as the subject of the sentence, as shown in Figure 4-3.

Sentence 4-3. The cat was scratched by the dog.

The simplest way to grasp the rationale for this analysis is to consider that in Sentence 4-3, *the cat* is the theme of *scratched*. In Figure 4-3, *the cat* and *scratch* have the same syntactic relationship as in Sentence 4-1. This allows a generalization to be created that assigns a thematic role to an object of the verb. This generalization does not come without a cost. To form the passive, *the cat* must be copied into its final position and deleted from its position in the structure shown in Figure 4-3. In Chomsky's model, the forms of sentences are derived through a series of insertions, copying, deletions, and other operations. Chomsky and his colleagues argue that, overall, the entire theory of syntax is simpler with these features than without them. For instance, the rule that a verb assigns a thematic role to its object accounts for the fact that *the cat* is the theme of *scratched* in

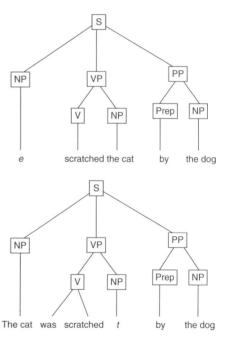

Figure 4–3. Formation of passive sentences, according to Chomsky. The top panel represents the underlying structure of the sentence *The cat was scratched by the dog*. [e] is an empty noun phrase that is a placeholder for the subject of the sentence. The bottom panel represents the surface structure, showing the position of a trace (*t*).

many sentences, such as in Sentences 4-4 through 4-6:

Sentence 4-4. Which cat did the dog scratch?
Sentence 4-5. The cat that the dog scratched ran away.
Sentence 4-6. It was the cat that the dog scratched.

Different features of these sentence lead to copying *the cat* into its surface position in each of the these sentences and in passives, but, Chomsky claims, postulating these rules is both needed (for many, often quite technical, theory-internal, reasons) and simpler than postulating separate rules relating *cat* and *scratched* in all these sentences. Chomsky and his colleagues have built an elaborate theoretical foundation for their models, tying them into considerations regarding the possible forms of human languages and the innate capacity to acquire language. I should emphasize, however, that many researchers do not agree with any of these analyses, and many aspects of Chomsky's theory are highly controversial (see, e.g., Goldberg, 1995, 2006).

Although there is disagreement over the nature of syntactic structures, there is near universal agreement that some form of syntactic structure is constructed from semantic and pragmatic representations as part of the production of spoken, written, and signed language, and from lexical, prosodic, and other perceptual cues in comprehension. There are different models of how this is accomplished. It is reasonable to divide these models into two main groups. The first group consists of models in which syntactic structure is initially computed in relative (or total) isolation from other aspects of sentence structure, and integrated with other linguistic representations after it has been formed (Ferreira & Clifton, 1986). These models are often called "modular" because they postulate an autonomous "module" dedicated to syntactic processing. The second group of models maintains that many different types of information interact at all stages of constructing syntactic structures (Trueswell et al., 1994). These different types of information include the likelihood that a word will occur after another word, the probability that subjects assign to the occurrence of events in the world, the discourse context, and others.

These models view the assignment of syntactic structure as part of a highly interactive process in which different types of information each constrain the possible meaning of a sentence. Recent work has extended the factors that affect the construction of syntactic representations to include completely nonlinguistic elements, such as the nature of the objects a participant must manipulate in an experiment (Tanenhaus et al., 1995, 2000; Altman & Kamide, 2007; Spivey et al., 2005; Farmer et al., 2007). Studies of disorders of syntactic processing have mostly focused on assignment of structures independent of other factors, but, as we shall see, issues related to interactions of parsing with other processes are important to consider.

DISORDERS OF SYNTACTIC COMPREHENSION

I begin with disorders of syntactic comprehension because they have received more theoretically oriented attention.

DOCUMENTING THE EXISTENCE OF DISORDERS OF SYNTACTIC COMPREHENSION

Caramazza and Zurif (1976) first documented the existence of syntactic comprehension in aphasic patients. They tested aphasic patients on a sentence–picture matching test, using the four types of sentences illustrated in Sentences 4-7 through 4-10:

Sentence 4-7. The apple the boy is eating is red.
Sentence 4-8. The boy the dog is patting is tall.
Sentence 4-9. The girl the boy is chasing is tall.
Sentence 4-10. The boy is eating a red apple.

Patients with Broca's aphasia and conduction aphasia made almost no errors when pictures with incorrect adjectives or verbs were used as foils. Their errors were confined to pictures representing reversals of the thematic roles of the nouns in the sentences (so-called *syntactic foils*). Moreover, these patients only made errors on sentences such as Sentences 4-8 and 4-9, in which the syntax of the sentences either indicated an improbable event in the real world or in which the thematic roles are reversible. In the semantically irreversible Sentence 4-7 and Sentence 4-10, these patients made no more errors than normal subjects. Caramazza and Zurif interpreted the results as indicating that some patients (those with Broca's and conduction aphasia) cannot construct syntactic structures. This study established the criteria still in use to diagnose such a disorder—the patient cannot demonstrate understanding of sentences whose meaning cannot be inferred from word meaning and real-world knowledge or by the application of a heuristic (e.g., taking the noun immediately preceding each verb as the agent of that verb).

We should note that this study has loose ends. One problem is that the patients may have performed better on the irreversible sentences than on the reversible ones and made errors on improbable sentences by simply rejecting pictures that depicted impossible events (Grodzinsky & Marek, 1988). A patient's selecting correct pictures over pictures in which lexical semantic foils appeared also does not prove that a patient can understand semantically irreversible sentences, only that he or she understands words. Proving that a patient assigns thematic roles in sentences without assigning syntactic structure is a nontrivial undertaking. One study that took a different step toward documenting such a dissociation is that of Schwartz et al. (1980). In this study, five agrammatic patients did assign thematic roles, but relied heavily on the animacy of nouns in sentences to do so (see also Smith & Mimica, 1984; Smith & Bates, 1987; Bates & Wulfeck, 1989; Bates et al., 1991). The dissociation between the use of animacy and syntax as determinants of thematic roles was not complete, however, and, to my knowledge, an absolute failure to use syntax in a patient who can assign thematic roles has yet to be documented.

If a patient cannot use syntax to determine propositional meaning, the reason for this disorder could be that he or she does not assign syntactic structures, or that he or she does not use such structures to determine meaning. Linebarger et al. (1983) reported results that suggested that some patients have the second of these problems. They found that four agrammatic patients with Broca's aphasia retained the ability to indicate whether sentences were grammatically correct or syntactically ill-formed, despite performing at chance on tests of comprehension of reversible active, passive, and locative sentences. For instance, Linebarger (1990) reported that some patients could indicate that Sentence 4-11 is ill-formed, but not match sentences like Sentence 4-12 and Sentence 4-13 to pictures with thematic role reversal foils.

Sentence 4-11. The woman was watched the man.
Sentence 4-12. The woman was watched by the man.
Sentence 4-13. The woman was watched.

Linebarger and her colleagues interpreted these results as indicating that these patients can assign syntactic structures, but not map them onto propositional semantic features. Supporting evidence for this analysis was published by Schwartz et al. (1985, 1987), who found that their patients were able to judge the ill-formedness of sentences such as Sentence 4-14, but not the anomalous nature of sentences such as Sentence 4-15.

Sentence 4-14. *Who did the teacher smile?
Sentence 4-15. *It was the little boy that the puppy dropped.

In Sentence 4-14, the ill-formedness is created by a syntactic violation—*smile* is an intransitive verb and cannot assign two thematic roles. In Sentence 4-15, the anomaly is created by a violation of real-world probability—puppies are unlikely to drop boys. The fact that patients could detect the ill-formedness of Sentence 4-14 suggests that they built the relevant syntactic structures. The fact that they did not detect the anomaly in Sentence 4-15 suggests that they could not use more complex syntactic structures to assign thematic roles.

These studies suggest that a distinction needs to be made between disorders affecting the construction of syntactic form and those affecting the use of syntactic form to determine aspects of sentence meaning. However, the analysis of these patients' performances is subject to other interpretations; in particular, grammaticality judgments may rely on different semantic information, or use semantic information is a different way, than sentence-picture matching or making anomaly judgments (see discussion of task effects below). Work subsequent to that of Linebarger and her colleagues on the nature of disorders of syntactic comprehension has largely ignored the distinction between constructing and interpreting syntactic structures, perhaps to the detriment of the field. Other questions, however, have received attention.

EXPLORING THE NATURE OF DISORDERS OF SYNTACTIC COMPREHENSION

Whether disturbances of syntactic comprehension exist in isolation or are always accompanied by some form of impairment in nonsyntactic routes to sentence meaning, syntactic disturbances do exist, and their nature has been explored in several ways. In my view, understanding of these disorders has progressed considerably, and I shall present this progress as I see it. It goes without saying that other researchers disagree: The interested reader can consult papers by Y. Grodzinsky, C. Thompson, L. Shapiro (all listed on their websites) and others for alternative views.

Two basic views have been articulated regarding the nature of deficits in syntactically based comprehension. The first is that individual parsing or interpretive operations are selectively affected by brain damage (*specific-deficit models*). The second is that patients lose the ability to apply what have been called "resources" to the task of assigning and interpreting syntactic structure (*resource-reduction models*). The first of these deficits may be likened to a student not being able to calculate π to eight decimal places in his or her head because he or she does not know the formula for calculating π. The second may be likened to a student knowing the formula but not being able to hold the intermediate products of computation in mind.

The first theories of syntactic comprehension deficits were specific-deficit models. My colleagues and I advocated these analyses in our earlier work (see Caplan & Hildebrandt, 1988, for a detailed study of a series of patients within this framework; also Hildebrandt et al., 1987). Researchers who advocate specific-deficit accounts of aphasic disturbances have

claimed that certain patients' patterns of performance indicate that specific representations and processes specified in linguistics and in psycholinguistic models of parsing and sentence interpretation are deficient. For instance, the *trace deletion hypothesis* (Grodzinsky, 2000) maintains that individual patients cannot process sentences that Chomsky's theory maintains contain a certain type of moved item (the term "trace deletion hypothesis" refers to an earlier version of Chomsky's theory in which these items were moved and left a "trace").

Evidence for such deficits would come from the finding that a patient had an impairment restricted to processing those sentences that required that structure or operation to be understood. Proponents of these models have argued that data of this sort are derived from aphasic studies. For instance, Grodzinsky (2000) reviews studies in several languages that he claims show that patients with Broca's aphasia have abnormally low performances on sentences in which these movement/copy operations have taken place, and where simple heuristics cannot lead to a normal interpretation. Such patients have chance performance on sentences such as Sentence 4-16, but above chance performance on the sentences in Sentence 4-17.

Sentence 4-16a. The boy$_i$ was pushed t_i by the girl.
b. It was the boy$_i$ who$_i$ the girl pushed t_i.
c. The boy$_i$ who$_i$ the girl pushed t_i was tall.

Sentence 4-17a. The boy pushed the girl.
b. It was the boy$_i$ who$_i$ t_i pushed the girl.
c. The boy who$_i$ t_i pushed the girl was tall.

According to the trace deletion hypothesis, in both Sentence 4-16 and 4-17, the trace (indicated by t) is absent. Therefore, the noun to which it is normally related (shown by the subscript) is not connected to it in the usual fashion. In these circumstances, Grodzinsky argues, a heuristic assigns the thematic role of Agent to this noun. Therefore, in Sentence 4-16, the aphasic patient constructs a representation of the sentence in which there are two agents, and he chooses one or the other at random when asked to match these sentences to pictures. In Sentence 4-17, only one agent is assigned, and the patient assigns the normal meaning of the sentence. The correct interpretation is achieved by the wrong means: the heuristic, not the usual parsing process.

Although a considerable body of data is consistent with the trace deletion hypothesis, there are serious problems in this analysis, as well as in all other proposals that aphasic deficits affect specific parsing and interpretive operations.

First, adequate linguistic controls have not been run that would show that the deficit is restricted to the structures claimed. For instance, the trace deletion hypothesis maintains that patients with the deficit in question are able to co-index items other than traces, such as pronouns and reflexives. Thus, a patient who has this deficit would not be able to connect *the boy* to the trace in *The boy who the man pushed t bumped him*, but should be able to connect *the man* to *him* in this same sentence. Accordingly, the patient should not know who pushed whom, but should know that the boy bumped the man. None of the papers in the literature that has been taken as supporting the trace deletion hypothesis has reported patients' performance on both sentences with traces and sentences with reflexives (or other referentially dependent items, such as pronouns; see Caplan 1995; Caplan et al. 2007b).

This brings up another issue. Much of the evidence for specific syntactic deficits is not based upon the performance of *individual* patients but rather on the performance of *small groups* of patients with certain diagnoses drawn from the traditional clinical literature on aphasia, such as Broca's aphasia or agrammatic aphasia (for discussion of these syndromes, see Chapter 2). It has been claimed that the objection raised above is answered by these group data. For instance, Grodzinsky (2000) has argued that some agrammatic patients have shown integrity of processing pronouns, thus answering questions about the adequacy of linguistic controls. In my view, these studies do not address the issues raised above. For example, although some agrammatic patients have shown normal performances on sentences with pronouns (Grodzinsky et al. 1993), these patients have not also been tested on sentences with traces; thus, we do not know if they show the deficit specified by the trace deletion hypothesis. Empirical data show that not

all patients with a clinical diagnosis of Broca's aphasia or agrammatism have problems with sentences containing traces (Zurif et al., 1993; Swinney & Zurif 1995; Blumstein et al., 1998; Berndt et al., 1996; Drai & Grodzinsky, 1999; Caramazza et al., 2001; Caplan, 2001a,b) so there is a need to verify the presence of this problem on a patient-by-patient basis.

A second problem with specific-deficit analyses is that the data in support of the analysis overwhelmingly consist of measures of accuracy in one task, usually sentence–picture matching. However, it has been well documented that performance may dissociate over tasks (Cupples & Inglis 1993; Caplan et al. 1997). An inability to perform accurately on a set of sentences in one comprehension task cannot be taken as a reflection of an impairment of a syntactic operation if the patient can perform accurately on those sentences in another comprehension task.

Analysis of the largest series of single cases currently available (Caplan et al., 2006, 2007b) provides data regarding the frequency of occurrence of specific deficits in syntactically based comprehension in aphasia. Forty-two right-handed native English-speaking aphasic patients with single left hemisphere strokes and 25 age- and education-matched controls were tested in object manipulation, sentence–picture matching, and grammaticality judgment tasks; the latter two with whole-sentence auditory and word-by-word self-paced auditory presentation. In each task, three syntactic operations were tested: passivization (Sentence 4-3), object relativization (Sentences 4-4–4-6), and co-indexation of a reflexive. Two constructions instantiating each structure were presented in each task. Deficits were identified as either below-normal or chance performances on sentences containing specific structures or requiring specific operations, and normal or above-chance performance on baseline sentences that did not contain those structures or require those operations. Adjustments were made for speed–accuracy trade-offs, and deficits were determined by response times, as well as by accuracy criteria. Considering only the two comprehension tasks (sentence–picture matching and enactment), four types of deficits could be observed: task-independent, structure-specific deficits (i.e., those affecting the experimental and not the baseline sentences in both constructions in both tasks); task-independent, construction-specific deficits (i.e., those affecting the experimental and not the baseline sentences in one construction in both tasks); task-dependent, structure-specific deficits (i.e., those affecting the experimental and not the baseline sentences in both constructions in one task); and task-dependent, construction-specific deficits (i.e., those affecting the experimental and not the baseline sentences in one construction in one task). Two patients had task-independent, structure-specific deficits, and two others had task-independent, construction-specific deficits; all had other deficits. No patient had task-dependent, structure-specific deficits. Thirty-one patients had task-dependent, construction-specific deficits. Task-dependent, construction-specific deficits were found in both sentence–picture matching and enactment. These results strongly point to most deficits affecting the ability to assign and interpret syntactic structure in one construction in one task. These results are the basis for my current belief that specific deficits affecting a syntactic representation or a parsing/interpretive process postulated by theories such as the trace deletion hypothesis are very rare, if they exist at all.

As noted above, the alternative view is that deficits of aphasic syntactic comprehension consist of reductions of processing capacity. Four arguments have been made in support of this suggestion:

1. Some patients can understand sentences that contain certain structures or operations in isolation but not sentences that contain combinations of those structures and operations (Caplan & Hildebrandt, 1988; Hildebrandt et al., 1987).
2. In large groups of patients, as patients' performances deteriorate, more complex sentence types are affected more than less complex ones (Caplan et al., 1985, 2007b).
3. In factor analyses of performance of such patient groups in syntactic comprehension tasks, first factors on which all sentence types load account for the majority of the variance (Caplan et al., 1985, 1996, 2007b).
4. Simulations of the effect of such reductions on syntactic comprehension in normal subjects through the use of speeded presentation (Miyake et al., 1994), concurrent tasks (King & Just, 1991), and other methods mimic aphasic performance.

These arguments are also not iron-clad. The argument that some patients can understand sentences that contain certain structures or operations in isolation but not sentences containing combinations of those structures and operations suffers from the same limitations of the database discussed above: It is based on a single performance measure (accuracy) in a single task (enactment). Testing the second result (i.e., as patients' performances deteriorate, more complex sentence types are affected to a greater degree than less complex ones) risks circularity unless the effects of resource reduction are modeled and measured; how to do this is a point of contention. Two studies have addressed this issue (Caplan et al., 1985, 2007b) and found this pattern; a third, smaller, study did not (Dick et al., 2001). The data regarding interference effects in normal subjects are complex. Interactions of load and syntactic complexity—and of these factors with subject groups that differ in processing resource capacity—are critical pieces of evidence that would support this model. However, these interactions occur only under special circumstances (Caplan & Waters, 1999; Caplan et al., 2007a), making this argument suggestive at best. The finding that first factors on which all sentence types load account for the majority of the variance is an extremely robust finding, regardless of the task over which factors are extracted or whether they are extracted over several tasks (Caplan et al., 2007b).

Additional evidence regarding the nature of aphasic deficits in syntactic comprehension comes from Rasch models of the performance of the 42 patients reported in Caplan et al. (2007b) on sentence–picture matching and enactment tasks. In a Rasch model, the probability of a correct response to a sentence is modeled as a function of the difficulty of that sentence and the ability of a patient. We explored models in which (a) sentences were grouped by task (i.e., the difficulty of sentences was modeled separately for sentence–picture matching and enactment), (b) sentences were grouped by structural type (i.e., the difficulty of sentences was modeled separately for sentences of different sorts), and (c) patients were clustered on the basis of different clustering algorithms. Seen in terms used above, adding a factor is the equivalent of postulating that difficulty or capacity differs for the sentence types or patients who differ along the lines established by that factor. We found that the introduction of a task factor and a patient grouping factor significantly improved the goodness of fit of the model, but that all sentence groupings either had no effect or made the goodness of fit worse. Results indicate that sentences exert different levels of demand as a function of task but not as a function of specific syntactic structure. This argues against the importance of structure-specific deficits as a major determinant of aphasic performance in syntactic comprehension tasks.

If deficits in aphasic syntactic comprehension consist of a reduction in the processing resources used to support the construction of syntactic representations in particular tasks, a critical question is: What, exactly, are resources? Seen in the most general terms possible, resources are features of a model of a cognitive system that allow certain operations to occur and set limits on their occurrence, but do not themselves enter into computations and are not representations. There are a variety of ways of conceptualizing resources, which are tied to models of the operations that underlie syntactic comprehension itself.

One way to conceive of resources is to see them as intrinsic aspects of the parsing/interpretive process. There are currently two different types of models of this type. In the first type, the operations that underlie syntactic comprehension are algorithms (procedures) that apply to symbolic representations, such as production rules. At least one model that views parsing this way models resources as a cost of each computation and each item stored in a memory system, and sets a limit on the total costs that can be incurred at any point in a computation (Just & Carpenter, 1992). In the second type, the operations that underlie syntactic comprehension are adjustments to weights in connectionist models, and resources are modeled as the number of units in critical positions of the model or as aspects of the weighting process (Rumelhart & McClelland, 1986). An example is the presence and number of hidden units in a Boltzmann machine, whose existence extends the computational power of one-level perceptrons and whose number affects the types of generalizations that the system achieves. Although these types of models differ in fundamental ways, from the point of view of modeling resources, they share the feature that resources—and their limitations—are specified within the models. This is more obviously the case for connectionist models, in which the computational units themselves determine the capacity of the system, than in procedural models, in which the limits on computational capacity are separate from the operations themselves, but in both types, resources are not set by other systems, and the features of the model that determine capacity are imposed arbitrarily.

A second approach to resources is to see them as the effect of cognitive capacities other than the intrinsic operation of the parser/ interpreter. Cognitive functions that have been suggested as resources that support parsing and interpretation include various type of short-term memory (phonological short-term memory: Baddeley, 1986, Caramazza, et al. 1980; working memory: Miyake et al., 1994) and speed of processing capacity (rates of activation and decay: Haarmann & Kolk, 1991, 1994; Haarmann et al., 1997). None of these capacities has been definitely shown to play this role (for discussion, see Caplan & Waters 1990, 1999).

Finally, it is possible that deficits affecting operations that provide input into parsing and interpretation appear as resource reductions in parsing and interpretation. Lowered efficiency of lexical processing can affect syntactic processing by producing delays between the construction of partial parses and interpretations and the presentation of the input to the processes that create these representations, especially in the auditory modality. Again, this possibility has not been adequately explored to discover to what extent it accounts for aphasic performance.

Further insight into and a different perspective on syntactic comprehension disorders come from measures of online syntactic processing— the centisecond-by-centisecond assignment of syntactic structure as a sentence unfolds auditorily or is inspected visually.

One series of online studies uses the cross-modal lexical priming (CMLP) task. In this task, a subject listens to a sentence and, at some point in the sentence, a series of letters appears on a computer screen; the subject must push a button to indicate if the letter string is or is not a word (a lexical decision task). Unbeknown to the subject, in half the cases in which the letter string is a word, it is semantically related or associated with a word that was previously presented in the sentence. In these cases, reaction times are typically faster than when the real-word stimuli are not related to previously presented words.

Swinney and his colleagues (Swinney & Zurif, 1995; Swinney et al., 1996; Zurif et al., 1993) capitalized on this "priming" phenomenon to gain insight into the co-indexation of traces. The normal finding is that cross-modal lexical decisions are speeded for words related to the head noun of a relative clause at the point of the trace in the relative clause and not immediately before that point (for issues regarding this technique, see McKoon et al. 1994; McKoon & Ratcliff, 1994; Nicol et al., 1994). Two studies of aphasic patients found that patients with Broca's aphasia did not show such priming, and these findings were interpreted as consistent with the trace deletion hypothesis (Zurif et al., 1993; Swinney & Zurif, 1995; Swinney et al., 1996). These data are not convincing evidence for a disturbance affecting processing traces, however, for several reasons. One is that the patients' deficit may not have been restricted to traces; performance on sentences with other referentially dependent items, such as reflexives, was not tested (this is the same issue regarding reflexives as was raised above for offline data). Second, the disturbance that was documented

in these patients may have arisen at the lexical, not the syntactic, level. The patients with Broca's aphasia tested in these two studies were not tested for word-to-word priming effects, and the absence of any priming effects may have been due to a failure of these patients to show lexical priming (Milberg & Blumstein, 1981; Blumstein et al., 1982). If the patients reported by Swinney and his colleagues do have a disorder affecting the online processing of "traces," this disorder appears not to be found in all patients with Broca's aphasia (Blumstein et al., 1998).

Two other laboratories have studied online sentence processing in aphasia. Thompson et al. (2004) and Dickey et al. (2005) reported the results of a study using eye tracking to examine the time course of comprehension. Tanenhaus and his colleagues (1995) pioneered the use of eye tracking as a means of exploring this process. They showed that, when subjects listen to sentences while viewing arrays of objects, the pattern of eye movements to objects is revealing about what structures the subjects are building and what they are comprehending online. Thompson et al. (2004) reported the results of this type of eye fixation monitoring in four patients with Broca's aphasia, and reported differences between the eye tracking performance of patients and controls when they heard the verbs in object-extracted structures such as shown in Sentence 4-18.

Sentence 4-18. The cat that the dog chased ran down the street.

In a second report, Dickey et al. (2005) reported that a larger group of 12 patients showed normal eye fixations at the verbs in object-extracted sentence structures, but, later in the sentences, patients tended to look at objects that normal subjects did not look at. Dickey suggested that this pattern suggested that these patients initially always processed the sentences normally, to the point of initially understanding the thematic roles in object-extracted structures in the same way as normal subjects. In his view, errors were due to patients' initial understanding being overridden at a later point in processing by an alternative interpretation of the sentences. The difference between aphasic patients and normal subjects, on this view, is not that aphasic patients' initial comprehension processes are disturbed, but that they are less capable than normal subjects of determining that the syntactically derived meaning, as opposed to the heuristically derived meaning, is correct. A similar possibility was suggested by Caplan and Waters (2003). This deficit would be a failure of some sort of control, or perhaps labeling, process, not of assigning syntactic structure or using it to determine sentence meaning per se.

Our studies suggest this is not always the case. Caplan et al. (2007b) found that the self-paced listening times for syntactically demanding segments in complex sentences were normal when patients responded correctly to the sentences, and deviated from normal (either faster or slower) when those patients responded incorrectly to the sentences. This suggests that the sentence comprehension process provides correct representations on some trials and incorrect representations on others. The deficit—whether in resource availability or in the ability to apply a specific operation—occurs intermittently, not in a fixed fashion. Additional evidence for intermittent disruptions of processing is the finding that, in 7% of comparisons of experimental and baseline sentences, performance on "experimental" sentences was significantly better than performance on baseline sentences (Caplan et al., 2006, 2007b). Assuming that the experimental sentence in the pair requires all the parsing and interpretive operations required in the baseline sentence, plus one or more additional operations, this reversed complexity effect can only be due to random factors occasionally affecting a patient's ability to comprehend a sentence (and to demonstrate that comprehension on a given task).

In summary, the view that deficits in aphasic syntactic comprehension consist of a loss of particular syntactic elements or of the ability to construct (or interpret) certain syntactic structures in a general way, independent of task, does not seem to apply to many patients' disorders in this domain. Rather, patients seem mainly to have a reduction in the processing resources used to support the construction of syntactic representations in particular tasks. Studies of online processing suggest that resource availability varies on a very short time scale; the

physiological basis for a deficit of this sort remains to be understood.

DISORDERS OF SYNTACTIC PRODUCTION

When generating an utterance, speakers must construct phrases and sentences so that information about how the meanings of words are related to one another is properly conveyed. This includes choosing the appropriate words, placing them in the correct order according to grammatically specified constraints, and inflecting them according to language-specific morphological and syntactic requirements. Models of language production agree to a large extent on the major stages of the sentence production process (e.g., Dell, 1986; Levelt, 1989; Garrett, 1975, 1976, 1978, 1980, 1982, 1988; Bock & Levelt, 1994; Vigliocco & Hartsuiker, 2002): (a) formulation of a message, which represents the speaker's intended meaning; (b) grammatical encoding, which translates the nonlinguistic message into an ordered sequence of inflected words; and (c) phonological encoding, which translates the sequence of words into a sequence of sounds to be uttered (Figure 4-4). The following description of these disorders reflects the major types of observations made in this extensive literature, with an emphasis on more recent studies.

DISTURBANCES OF PRODUCTION OF GRAMMATICAL VOCABULARY ELEMENTS

Two aphasic disturbances affect the production of function words—agrammatism and paragrammatism. We will describe each briefly.

Agrammatism is a component of the syndrome of Broca's aphasia. The most noticeable deficit in agrammatism is the widespread omission of function words and affixes and the greater retention of content words. This disparity is always seen in the spontaneous speech of patients termed agrammatic, and often occurs in their repetition and writing as well. The class of words that are affected in agrammatism has been described in two quite different frameworks. The first is a psychological framework, and the second is linguistic. According to

Message (conceptual representation)

GRAMMATICAL ENCODING

I. Functional level representation
Thematic roles:
DOG = Agent
MAN = Theme
BITE = Action
Hierarchical syntactic structure:
[s[NPdog][VP[Vbite][NPman]]].

II. Positional level representation
Constituent assembly: [dog-bite-man]
Inflectional processing: [dog-bites-man]

PHONOLOGICAL ENCODING

/dog/ - /bayts/ - /man/

Figure 4–4. Schematic of standard model of sentence production.

the psychological account, the words that are affected in agrammatism are those that belong to the closed class of vocabulary elements. This set consists of all the vocabulary elements of English other than nouns, verbs, adjectives, and derived adverbs. An adult speaker does not learn new elements of this set, in contrast to the ability to learn new nouns, verbs, and adjectives. The linguistic approach to the characterization of agrammatism has been explored by several researchers. Kean (1977) proposed that the class of elements affected in this syndrome was defined in terms of aspects of their sound pattern—the retained words were ones that could be assigned stress in English. Other linguistic descriptions have also been suggested (Lapointe, 1983; Grodzinsky, 1984; Rizzi, 1985).

Many studies of agrammatic patients (Goodglass, 1973; Luria, 1973; Tissot et al., 1973; Miceli et al., 1983; Berndt, 1987; Parisi, 1987; Miceli et al., 1989; Menn & Obler, 1990) have shown that patients with agrammatism can have different patterns of retention of the function word and bound morpheme vocabulary. For instance, one Italian case showed preservation of free-standing function words but produced incorrect verbal inflections (Miceli et al., 1983). In contrast, one agrammatic English patient correctly inflected verbs (Goodglass, 1976). M.M., a French patient studied by Nespoulous and his colleagues (1988) had trouble producing auxiliary verbs and certain pronouns in French (the "weak" forms of pronouns—*le, la, lui*—but not the "strong" forms—*il, elle, moi, toi*) but considerably less trouble producing other function words. In a famous study, Goodglass and Berko (1960) studied the ability of 21 agrammatic aphasic patients to produce the suffix -*s*. They found that the possessive and third person singular forms of -*s* were more frequently omitted than the plural, and that the third person singular inflectional ending was omitted about as frequently as the possessive. These limited impairments indicate that many patterns of speech have traditionally been included in the category known as agrammatism.

A great deal of research has been directed at the question of what factors determine these patterns. One factor that makes for variation in the manifestations of agrammatic speech is the patient's overall severity (Menn & Obler, 1990). Also, to some extent, the loss of affixes and function words mirrors their developmental sequence of acquisition in reverse, although there are important exceptions to this effect (DeVillers, 1974). Goodglass and Berko's (1960) patients had more trouble producing the nonsyllabic forms (e.g., *bats, cubs*) of the suffix /-s/ than in producing the syllabic form (e.g., *churches*). Kean (1977) pointed out that the differential susceptibility of syllabic and nonsyllabic affixes to omission can be explained in terms of the sonorance hierarchy: The syllabic form of -*s*, found in *churches*, is more sonorant than either of its nonsyllabic forms, /s/ and /z/.

Goodglass (1973) suggested that it is possible to integrate data from a number of experiments to define a class of words that are less "salient" and therefore more difficult for an agrammatic patient. Salience is the "psychological resultant of stress, of the informational significance, of the phonological prominence, and of the affective value of a word" (Goodglass, 1973, p. 204). Kean (1977) proposed that agrammatic patients are constrained to produce real words; this would explain the retention of affixes in languages in which roots without affixes are not well-formed words, such as Hebrew (Grodzinsky, 1984) and Italian (Miceli et al., 1983).

Some variation in the production of function words and bound morphemes reflects control mechanisms. For instance, M.M. could read function words in isolation but not in sentences (Nespoulous et al., 1988).

The second major disturbance of function word production is *paragrammatism*, marked by substitutions of function words and morphological elements. Although separate disorders, agrammatism and paragrammatism often co-occur (Heeschen, 1985; de Bleser, 1987; Menn, Obler, & Goodglass, 1990).

As with omissions in agrammatism, a wide variety of profiles of substitution of function words and bound morphemes can be found in different patients. In some patients, there seems to be some systematicity to the pattern of substitutions. Lapointe (1983) suggested that infinitives and gerunds are the basic forms in the verbal system and that they are produced because they are the first to be accessed by patients with limited resources available for accessing verb forms. In other cases, substitutions are closely related to the inferred target (Miceli et al.,1990). In almost all cases, errors are *paradigm internal*; that is, they do not violate the word formation and even the syntactic processes of the language. Thus, in a language like Italian that has several verb declensions marked by different thematic vowels, substitutions of verb affixes almost always respect the declension of the verb root. In Hebrew, substitutions of the vowels in words are always appropriate to the type of word being produced: Shifts from one

morphological paradigm to another and purely phonological errors do not occur with any frequency in paragrammatism. It thus appears that many constraints on word formation processes are respected in both paragrammatism and agrammatism.

There seem to be two broad sources of paragrammatism and agrammatism: an inability to access these lexical forms per se, and a disturbance of using them in sentence production. Some patients who omit function words and bound morphemes have disturbances affecting the production or processing of these items in isolation. Many patients with agrammatism have *deep dyslexia* and cannot read function words and bound morphemes aloud. Others, such as patient F.S. (Miceli & Caramazza, 1988) have problems repeating some morphological forms. In these cases, several authors have suggested that the omission of function words and bound morphemes seen in sentence production is related to these processing disturbances at the single word level.

In other patients, however, agrammatism occurs only in relationship to sentence planning and production, without any disturbance of processing function words or bound morphemes in isolation. For example, Caramazza and Hillis (1988) reported a patient with this disorder, and, as noted above, M.M., also appears to have trouble with auxiliary verbs and weak pronouns only when he had to produce sentences. In M.M., this phenomenon was quite dramatic. Nespoulous tried an experiment in which he asked M.M. to read words written vertically, one to a page. M.M. did so perfectly, turning the pages over and reading each word, until he quite suddenly realized that the sequence of words formed a sentence. From that point on, he had difficulty with the items in these affected groups of words.

Overall, these studies illustrate the disturbances that patients can have affecting closed-class vocabulary elements in sentence production tasks. Given the connection between the production of function words and bound morphemes and the construction of syntactic form, we might expect that patients with agrammatism and paragrammatism have disturbances of this ability. We now turn to these disturbances.

DISTURBANCES OF GENERATING SYNTACTIC FORM

Disturbances in correctly producing syntactic structures are extremely common in patients with agrammatism. Goodglass et al. (1972) documented the syntactic constructions produced by one agrammatic patient and found virtually no syntactically well-formed utterances. All the agrammatic patients studied in a large contemporary cross-language study showed some impoverishment of syntactic structure in spontaneous speech (Menn & Obler, 1990). The failure to produce complex noun phrases and embedded verbs with normal frequency were the most striking features of the syntactic simplification shown by these patients.

Studies of sentence repetition by agrammatic patients also document their syntactic planning limitations. Ostrin (1982) reported the performance of four agrammatic patients in repeating sentences with a variable number of noun phrases, prepositional phrases, and adjectives modifying nouns. She found that the patients had a strong tendency to repeat either a determiner and a noun (*the man*) or an adjective and a noun (*old man*), but not both (*the old man*). She characterized this finding as showing that the presence of a determiner as a prenominal modifier was not independent of the presence of an adjective in the same position in these patients. Similarly, in sentences with both an NP and a prepositional phrase (PP) in the VP (*The woman is showing the dress to the man*), the patients showed a similar tendency to produce either the NP or the PP but not both. However, the patients' multiple attempts to repeat the target sentences often produced all the elements of the sentence, one on each attempt. Ostrin suggested that these results indicated that the patients retained the entire semantic content of the presented sentence but could not produce all the elements they retained. She suggested that these patients have a reduced number of "planning frames" that they can use.

A second study of the repetition abilities of six agrammatic subjects introduces other considerations into the analysis of what is wrong with these patients. Ostrin and Schwartz (1986) had their patients repeat semantically reversible, semantically plausible, and semantically implausible sentences in the active and passive voice. They found that errors differed for plausible, reversible, and implausible sentences. Errors to plausible sentences were primarily lexical substitutions. Many errors to implausible sentences reversed the thematic roles in the sentence to render the resulting utterance plausible. The patients tended to retain the order of nouns and verbs in the presented sentence, and made many errors that the authors interpreted as efforts to produce passive forms (mixed morphology errors, such as *The bicycle is riding by the boy* for *The bicycle is riding the boy*). The authors argued that the performances of their patients reflected a tendency on their part to produce plausible sentences from an incomplete memory trace that contained the grammatical roles (subject, object) of the noun phrases in the presented sentence.

Friedman and Grodzinsky (1999) have argued that agrammatic patients cannot construct full syntactic trees, and nodes that are higher in a syntactic tree are pruned in agrammatism. Specifically, in some versions of Chomsky's theory, abstract nodes in trees mark subject–verb agreement and tense, with the latter higher than the former (Figure 4-5). The *tree pruning hypothesis* maintains that agrammatics can construct trees with the node for agreement, but not tense; evidence for this comes from observations that tense markers on verbs are more often omitted than are agreement markings. This pattern is not obviously due to the sorts of working memory limitations that were postulated by Ostrin and Schwartz, because agreement requires the verb to be related to the subject noun, whereas tense can be produced on a conceptual basis.

It is not clear whether these disturbances affecting syntactic forms are related to patients' omission of function words and bound morphemes. First, there is no clear connection between the disturbances in production of function words and bound morphemes seen in individual patients and their syntactic abnormalities. Second, although many agrammatic patients show severe reductions in the production of syntactic structures, not all patients

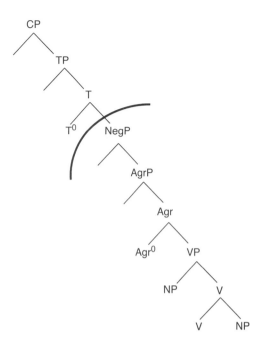

Figure 4–5. Illustration of part of the structure postulated by Chomsky and his colleagues. CP, TP, NegP, and AgrP are Complement Phrase, Tense Phrase, Negative Phrase, and Agreement Phrase, respectively. T^0 and Agr^0 are the nodes at which tense and agreement features are represented. The tense and agreement features of the verb (V) are checked by the features of T^0 and Agr^0. The curved line indicates the positions in the tree that are inaccessible to agrammatic patients, according to Freidman and Grodzinsky (1997).

do so. Miceli et al. (1983), Berndt (1987), and others, have documented patients who omit disproportionally high numbers of function words and bound morphemes, but who produce an apparently normal range of syntactic structures.

Turning to paragrammatic patients, several studies suggest that the syntactic production of these patients differs from that found in agrammatic patients. For instance, Butterworth and Howard (1987) described five paragrammatic patients who each produced many "long and complex sentences, with multiple interdependencies of constituents" (p. 23). Errors in paragrammatism include incorrect tag question formation, illegal noun phrases in relative clauses, and illegal use of pronouns to head relative clauses (Butterworth & Howard, 1987). A particular type of error that has often

been commented on in paragrammatism is a *blend*, in which the output seems to reflect two different ways of saying the same thing. These features of the speech of paragrammatic patients are not found in agrammatic patients—at least not with the same frequency as in paragrammatism—and they suggest that differences exist in the ability of these different patients to construct syntactic structures.

Very few studies of paragrammatic patients' performances on more constrained sentence production tasks have been undertaken. However, one well-known result based on a more constrained test—anagram solution—also indicates differences in the ability of fluent paragrammatic and nonfluent agrammatic patients to construct syntactic structures. Von Stockardt (1972; von Stockhardt & Boder, 1976) found that paragrammatic patients solved anagram tasks according to syntactic constraints, whereas agrammatic patients solved them using semantic constraints. Paragrammatic patients have not been tested as much as agrammatic patients on repetition, picture description, and story completion tasks to ascertain whether they use both basic and more complex syntactic structures to convey specific propositional and discourse-level semantic features. The common belief is that they are much more capable of using a wide range of syntactic structures for these purposes than are agrammatic patients, but make errors in their use.

Butterworth (1982, 1985, Butterworth & Howard, 1987) has argued that the syntactic and morphological errors in paragrammatism result from the failure of these patients to monitor and control their own output. If this is correct, the basic locus of the syntactic errors in paragrammatism may differ from those in agrammatism. Agrammatism would reflect a disturbance of one basic aspect of the sentence building process—the construction of syntactic form—whereas paragrammatism would result from a disturbance of control mechanisms that monitor the speech planning process. Butterworth's analysis assumes that normal subjects often generate erroneous utterances unconsciously, and that these errors are filtered out by control processes.

Several studies indicate that aphasic patients' abilities to utilize syntactic devices to convey aspects of sentence meaning depend upon the devices commonly used in their language. Bates and her colleagues (1989, 1991) have studied the abilities of patients to produce simple sentences in a language that makes extensive use of word order and little use of declensional or inflectional morphology (English), a language that makes extensive use of declensional morphology (German), a language that makes heavy use of inflectional agreement (Italian), and a language that uses both inflectional and declensional forms (Serbo-Croatian) (see Bates & Wulfeck, 1989, for a review of these studies). In each case, the patients tended to produce structures that incorporated the most commonly used syntactic markers in the language, and they had difficulties producing sentences that required the use of less commonly used devices. This finding indicates that the "canonicity" of a structure or a grammatical device—the degree to which it is used in a particular language—influences the ability of a patient to employ that device to express aspects of sentential meaning. These disturbances have been most clearly described in agrammatic patients, and it remains to be seen whether they affect patients with primarily paragrammatic output, as well as patients with other types of aphasic disturbances.

DISTURBANCES AFFECTING THE REALIZATION OF THEMATIC ROLES

Several researchers have suggested that there is a more profound disturbance of sentence production in certain patients. This disturbance has been said to affect the patient's ability to use the basic word order of English to convey propositional features, such as thematic roles. Saffran et al. (1980) presented data regarding the order of nouns around verbs in sentences produced by five agrammatic patients describing simple pictures of actions. The authors noted a strong effect of animacy upon the position of the nouns around the verbs. The authors suggested that thematic roles were not mapped onto the canonical noun-verb-noun word order of English, and that animacy determined the position of nouns around verbs in these patients.

They concluded that agrammatic patients have either lost the basic linguistic notions of thematic roles (Agency, Theme) or else cannot use even the basic word order of the language to express this sentential semantic feature. They argued that this more profound deficit cannot be related to problems with the function word/ inflection vocabulary, and, therefore, that agrammatic patients have more than one impairment affecting sentence planning and production. Although Caplan (1983) argued that the data in Saffran et al.'s study did not support the authors' contention that animacy alone determined word order in the patients' responses, this report raises the question of whether the basic linguistic notions of thematic roles are always preserved in aphasia and whether patients always try to use some sort of structure to convey them. It is possible that some very severely affected patients lose these concepts or do not attempt to convey them. At the least, it appears that some agrammatic patients tend to assign Agency to animate items, even when the task calls for the assignment of another thematic role to an animate noun. As discussed above, similar effects seem to occur in comprehension.

The ability to produce utterances that convey thematic roles is closely linked to the ability to produce verbs. Many agrammatic patients have particular difficulties with the production of verbs. These difficulties do not entirely consist of trouble producing the correct inflectional and derivational forms of a verb in a given context. They also affect the ability to produce verbs themselves, resulting in omissions, paraphrases, and nominalizations of verbs.

Several studies have investigated this disturbance of verb production in agrammatic patients, with similar results. Miceli et al. (1984) compared five agrammatic, five anomic, and ten normal subjects on tests requiring naming objects (The Boston Naming Test; Kaplan, Goodglass, & Weintraub, 1976) or actions (The Action Naming Test; Obler & Albert, 1979). They found that the agrammatic patients were better at naming objects than actions, whereas the anomic patients and normal controls showed the opposite pattern. The agrammatic patients' difficulties in naming actions did not appear to arise at the level of achieving the concept of the action, since many erroneous responses were nouns, phrases, and nominalizations that were related to the intended verbs. Miceli and his colleagues concluded that their agrammatic patients had a sort of anomia for verbs—a disturbance separate from the other aspects of their output.

A recent set of studies has examined unaccusative verbs such as *freeze* (Sentence 4-18), which differ from unergative verb such as *cough* (Sentence 4-20) in assigning the thematic role of theme to their subjects. This has led linguists in the Chomskian framework to posit an underlying structure for sentences with unaccusative verbs, in which the surface subject appears in underlying object position, as for passives. The underlying position is marked with a trace in Sentence 4-18. Sentence 4-19 shows that some unaccusative verbs allow the theme to appear as the object in a transitive sentence; this cannot occur with unergatives (Sentence 4-21 is not a possible sentence related to Sentence 4-20; * indicates an unacceptable sentence). The similarity of unaccusatives to passives, and the fact that both these sentence types have moved constituents in Chomsky's theory, has led researchers to ask if some patients might have specific deficits affecting the ability to produce sentences with unaccusative verbs.

Sentence 4-18. Unaccusative, intransitive: The river$_i$ froze t_i.
Sentence 4-19. Unaccusative, transitive: The cold snap froze the river.
Sentence 4-20. Unergative, intransitive: The boy$_i$ coughed.
Sentence 4-21. Unergative, transitive: *The virus coughed the boy.

Studies have reported on single-word naming of unaccusatives (Thompson, 2003) and unaccusative verb use in sentences (Lee & Thompson, 2004; Bastiaanse & Van Zonneveld, 2005). Thompson (2003) found that agrammatic aphasic subjects were significantly more accurate in a picture-naming task when targets were unergative rather than unaccusative verbs. Lee and Thompson (2004) found that aphasic subjects produced correct sentences at a significantly higher rate for unergative than for unaccusative verbs. Bastiaanse and van Zonneveld (2005) found that agrammatic

aphasic subjects produced unaccusative verbs more accurately in a transitive frame (Sentence 4-19), in which movement does not take place, than in the intransitive form (Sentence 4-18). These authors assumed that the patients had specific deficits affecting the production of sentences with moved constituents, but a study from our lab (McAllister et al., in press) tells a different story. Single-word naming, sentence production, and sentence-picture matching tests using unaccusative, unergative, and passive structures were administered to a group of nine unselected aphasic subjects and 12 age- and education-matched control subjects. The difference between unaccusatives and non-movement constructions was significant for age-matched control subjects, as well as for aphasic patients. This finding supports the hypothesis that the unaccusative construction imposes higher processing costs than non-movement constructions, and that patients do not have the resources needed to meet these costs.

Given the crucial role that verbs play in sentences, one would expect that a disturbance affecting the ability to use information regarding verbs would severely affect many other aspects of sentence production and comprehension. McCarthy and Warrington (1985) have argued that this is the case. Their patient, R.O.X., had a severe disturbance in naming actions and matching verbs to pictures. The authors argued that this disturbance was the result of a category-specific degradation of the meaning of verbs that also resulted in almost no production of verbs in speech and in difficulties in syntactic comprehension. However, the relationship between an inability to produce verbs and other abnormalities in the speech of agrammatic patients is not always so clear. In the Miceli et al. study, patients' inabilities to produce verbs were only partially responsible for the shortened phrase length found in their speech, since the overall correlation between the noun-to-verb ratio and phrase length in the five agrammatic patients was not high. Berndt et al. (1997) also found that disturbances in verb production were variably related to disturbances in producing syntactic structures. It thus appears that some agrammatics have a disturbance affecting their ability to produce verbs, and that this disturbance can affect their ability to accomplish some sentence processing tasks, such as spontaneously producing a normal range of syntactic structures. Other patients can build at least some phrasal structures despite poor verb production, whereas others cannot produce normal phrase structure despite relatively good verb production.

RELATION OF DISORDERS OF SYNTACTIC COMPREHENSION AND PRODUCTION

Studies of aphasic patients are relevant to the question of whether there is a single mechanism that computes syntactic structure in both input and output tasks. The discussion focuses on the fact that patients with expressive agrammatism often have syntactic comprehension disturbances (Heilman & Scholes, 1976; Schwartz et. al., 1980; Grodzinsky, 1986; Caplan and Futter, 1986; etc.). Several authors have argued that the co-occurrence of deficits in sentence production and comprehension seen in these patients indicates the presence of "central" or "overarching" syntactic operations, used in both comprehension and production tasks (Berndt & Caramazza, 1980; Zurif, 1984; Grodzinsky, 1986).

However, although deficits in syntactic comprehension frequently co-occur with expressive agrammatism, it does not appear that the two are due to a single functional impairment. Patients with agrammatism show a wide variety of performances in syntactic comprehension tasks. As noted above, several patients with expressive agrammatism have shown no disturbances of syntactic comprehension whatsoever (Miceli et. al., 1983; Nespoulous et. al., 1984; Kolk & Van Grunsven, 1985), and some patients without agrammatism have syntactic comprehension disorders that are indistinguishable from those seen in agrammatic patients (Caramazza & Zurif, 1976, Caplan et al., 1985, Schwartz et al., 1987, Martin, 1987). To the extent that disturbances of syntactic comprehension and expressive agrammatism can be assessed in terms of degree of severity, there seems to be no correlation between the severity of a syntactic comprehension deficit and the severity of expressive agrammatism in an individual patient. These data constitute an argument against the view that only one impairment produces expressive agrammatism that necessarily entails a disturbance of syntactic comprehension. They are consistent with a model that has separate mechanisms dealing with the construction of syntactic form in input- and output-side processing, and with the view that these mechanisms can be separately disturbed. This conclusion is reflected in the theoretically oriented work of researcher such as Grodzinsky (2000), who has postulated specific deficits in agrammatic production and comprehension—the trace deletion hypothesis and the tree pruning hypothesis—that are unrelated to one another. The different deficits in production and comprehension in agrammatism are not such that one could cause the other; one implication of these analyses, then, is that patients with agrammatism have two deficits, and that the area of the brain in which the lesion occurs supports separate functions in comprehension and production.

APHASIA AND THE FUNCTIONAL NEUROANATOMY OF SYNTACTIC PROCESSING

The two sources of information about the way the brain is organized to support syntactic processing are (a) analysis of effects of lesions on syntactic processing (the lesion approach) and (b) analysis of changes in neural activity that are associated with syntactic functioning (the activation approach). These approaches demonstrate different features of the relation of the brain to a function. Lesions speak to the necessity of an area (or other features) of the brain in performing a function. If a function cannot be performed normally after a lesion, it follows that the area of the brain that is lesioned is necessary for the normal exercise of that function, and if a function can be performed normally after a lesion, it follows that the area of the brain that is lesioned is not necessary for the normal exercise of that function. In contrast, activation studies speak to the sufficiency of an area (or other feature) of the brain in performing a function. If an area of the normal brain is activated by the performance of a function, that area of the brain is part of the neural system sufficient for the performance of that function. Activation and lesion approaches are logically related. In any one individual, the totality of all the areas of the brain that are individually necessary for a function must be the same as the set of areas that are jointly sufficient for the performance of that function. Discrepancies can exist, however, between the results of lesions and activation studies for many reasons. This chapter concludes with a brief review of results from lesion studies and their implications for the neural organization that supports syntactic processing. One note is that all of the detailed work in this area applies to comprehension; clinical studies on production will not be reviewed.

There is good evidence that syntactic processing in sentence comprehension involves the perisylvian association cortex—the pars triangularis and opercularis of the inferior frontal gyrus (Brodmann's areas (BA) 45, 44: Broca's area), the angular gyrus (BA39), the supramarginal gyrus (BA40), and the superior temporal gyrus (BA22: Wernicke's area)—in the dominant hemisphere. We have estimated that over 90% of patients with aphasic disorders who have lesions in this region have disturbances of syntactic comprehension (Caplan, 1987a). Disorders affecting syntactic comprehension after perisylvian lesions have been described in all languages that have been studied, in patients of all ages, with written and spoken input, and after a variety of lesion types, indicating that this cortical region is involved in syntactic processing, independent of these factors (see Caplan, 1987b, for review). Regions outside the perisylvian association cortex that activation studies suggest support syntactic processing include the left inferior anterior temporal lobe (Mazoyer et al., 1993; Bavelier et al., 1997; Noppeney & Price, 2004), the cingulate gyrus and nearby regions of medial frontal lobe (Caplan et al., 1998, 1999, 2000), left superior temporal lobe (Caplan et al., 1998; Carpenter et al., 1999), and left and right posterior inferior temporal lobe (Cooke et al., 2001). The nondominant hemisphere may also be involved in syntactic comprehension (Caplan et al., 1996; Just et al., 1996; Ben Shachar et al., 2003).

A major focus of investigation has been how the perisylvian association cortex is organized to support syntactic comprehension. Different researchers endorse strongly localizationist models (Grodzinsky, 1990, 1995, 2000; Zurif et al. 1993; Swinney & Zurif, l995), distributed net models (Mesulam, 1990, 1998; Damasio, 1992) and models that postulate individual variability in the neural substrate for this function (Caplan et al., 1985, 1996, 2007b; Caplan 1987a, 1994).

To my knowledge, there are five studies in the literature in which radiological images have been analyzed and related to sentence comprehension in aphasic patients. Three only merit brief mention. Kempler et al. (1991) reported computed tomography (CT) and positron-emission tomography (PET) data from a group of 43 aphasic patients. Comprehension performance was correlated with lesion size in Broca's and Wernicke's areas as measured by CT and with hypometabolism throughout the temporal, parietal, and occipital lobes, as measured by fludeoxyglucose (^{18}F; FDG) PET. The problem with this study is that Kempler et al. used the Token Test, which seriously confounds syntactic processing with short-term memory requirements. Tramo et al. (1988) reported three cases in which comprehension of reversible active and passive sentences was studied in a sentence–picture matching task. Comprehension of reversible passives improved to above chance levels in two patients with anterior lesions, but not in the patient with a posterior lesion. This speaks to plasticity and suggests that the posterior perisylvian region has a latent ability to perform the syntactic functions of the anterior region. Caplan et al. (1996) obtained CT scans in 18 patients with left hemisphere strokes. Scans were normalized to the Talairach and Tournoux atlas, and five perisylvian regions of interest defined following the Rademacher et al. (1992) criteria: the pars triangularis and the pars opercularis of the third frontal convolution, the supramarginal gyrus, the angular gyrus, and the first temporal gyrus excluding the temporal tip and Heschl's gyrus. Lesion volume was calculated within each region of interest (ROI). Syntactic comprehension was assessed using an object manipulation task that presented 12 examples of each of 25 sentence types, selected to assess the ability to understand sentences containing only fully referential noun phrases, sentences containing overt referentially dependent NPs (pronouns or reflexives), and sentences containing phonologically empty NPs (PRO, NP-trace, and *wh*-trace; Chomsky 1986, 1995). Multiple analyses failed to find a relation between lesion size in these areas and the magnitude of any syntactic comprehension deficit. Detailed analysis of single cases with small lesions of roughly comparable size, who were tested at about the same time after their strokes, indicated that the degree of variability found in quantitative and qualitative aspects of patients' performances was not related to lesion location or the size of lesions in the anterior or posterior portion of the perisylvian association cortex. Caplan et al. concluded that the syntactic operations examined in this study were not invariantly localized in one small area, but were either distributed or showed variability in localization. This study has the limitations of only scanning 18 participants, not measuring hypoperfusion or hypometabolism in cerebral tissue, normalization that is inadequate by today's standards, and testing syntactic comprehension on a single offline task.

Two more recent studies merit fuller review.

Dronkers et al. (2004) studied 64 patients with left hemisphere strokes as well as eight right hemisphere stroke cases and 15 controls. Patients were scanned using CT or magnetic resonance imaging (MRI). The patients were tested on the Western Aphasia Battery (WAB) and the Curtiss-Yamada Comprehensive Language Evaluation (CYCLE) for sentence comprehension. A voxel-based lesion-symptom mapping (VLSM) approach to analysis of the data was reported. A radiologist identified areas on a template of the brain (consisting of 11 transverse slices) that corresponded to lesions in each patient's brain. Patients were divided into groups with and without lesions at each voxel. For every voxel for which there were at least eight patients with lesions and eight without lesions, the groups were examined for differences in their performance on the CYCLE and on each of its subtests, using Bonferroni-corrected *t*-tests.

The authors created ROIs based upon the presence of significant *t* values. The performance of patients with and without lesions in five areas of the left hemisphere: the middle temporal gyrus (MTG), the anterior banks of the superior temporal sulcus (STS), the STS and the angular gyrus, midfrontal cortex (said to be in BA 46, and what was said to be BA 47) differed on the total CYCLE score. Dronker et al. also divided patients into groups based upon the presence of lesions in "the bulk" of a ROI and compared the scores of the resulting groups on the CYCLE and its subtests using uncorrected *t*-tests. The results were largely similar. The process was repeated for each subtest of the CYCLE. The authors interpreted the pattern of subtests that were different in each of the regions in terms of psycholinguistic processes that were affected in patients with and without lesions in these areas. They suggested that the MTG was involved with lexical processing, the anterior STS with comprehension of simple sentences, the STS and the angular gyrus with short-term memory, and the left frontal cortex with working memory required for complex sentences. Dronker et al. concluded that neither Broca's area nor Wernicke's area contributes to sentence comprehension, and that the apparent involvement of these regions in previous studies is epiphenomenal, due to the role that adjacent cortex plays in these processes.

This study suffers from many limitations. Beginning with the treatment of neurological data, the identification of areas and lesions—including lesion–cerebrospinal fluid (CSF) boundaries—was entirely subjective, and only structural measures of lesions were considered. Unlike the Caplan et al. (1996) study, where ROIs were defined according to the Rademacher system, in the Dronkers' study, no indication is given of how ROIs were defined. It is not clear what the bulk of an (undefined) ROI consisted of, or whether this measurement differed for different ROIs. The decision to eliminate voxels in which seven or fewer patients did or did not have lesions may have eliminated both Broca's area and Wernicke's area (as well as the insula) from consideration, since these regions may have been spared in fewer than eight patients.

The approach of evaluating the effects of lesions at each voxel or at each ROI independently makes no allowance for interactions of lesions in different locations; in particular, effects of total lesion volume were not considered.

With respect to the psycholinguistic analyses, the differences in performance that formed the basis for deficit analyses were those between groups of patients, not differences between patients with lesions in an area and normal subjects. Normal subjects performed at ceiling on all subtests of the CYCLE; accordingly, all the lesions were associated with abnormal performance on all tests. The deficits that underlie these abnormal performances are unclear. CYCLE is a sentence–picture matching test with both syntactic and lexical foils for many items. Errors in which lexical foils are selected provide evidence for lexical deficits, and errors in which syntactic foils are selected provide evidence for sentence-level deficits; however, Dronker et al. did not separate different error types in their analyses. Therefore, the psychological data are inadequate to support any of the conclusions made, beyond the claim that they had abnormal language comprehension.

Caplan et al. (2007c) imaged 32 of the patients and 13 controls reported in Caplan et al. (2007b), using MR and FDG-PET scanning. First-factor scores of principle components analyses of performance on each task were taken as reflections of resource availability of each patient in each task, and differences in accuracy, reaction time, and listening times for words in critical positions (corrected for word length and frequency) in experimental and baseline sentences served as measures of syntactic processing ability for particular structures in particular tasks.

The relation between lesion size and deficits was investigated by regressing MR and PET measures of the extent of the lesion in each seven ROIs against the measures of syntactic processing mentioned above. Because of the small number of cases, regressions were done in series, using general factors and lesion size in larger regions as independent measures in the first analyses and progressing to the effects of lesions in smaller areas. Time since lesion and age did not affect performance. Percent lesion volume on MR and mean PET counts/voxel in a variety of small regions accounted for a significant amount of variance in performance measures, after total lesion size was entered into stepwise regressions. For instance, percent MR lesion in the inferior parietal lobe, the anterior inferior temporal lobe, and superior parietal lobe, and PET counts/voxel in Broca's area accounted for a significant amount of variance in first factor scores for all tasks combined and for object manipulation. Similar patterns (i.e., significant effects of lesion size in several areas on performance measures) were found for other dependent variables. Some areas, such as the anterior inferior temporal region, were significant in several tasks, implying that each of these cortical areas is necessary for multiple functions. Finally, some dependent variables were predicted by lesions in multiple areas, implying that multiple, unrelated cortical areas are necessary for some functions.

The data were also examined on a case-by-case basis to look for evidence of distribution of the functions assessed. The range of performance on five measures (first-factor scores for sentence–picture matching, enactment and grammaticality judgment, syntactic complexity scores for accuracy in sentence–picture matching, and enactment) was examined in patients with lesions within .25 standard deviations (SD) of the mean lesion size in four regions (the entire left hemisphere, the left hemisphere cortex, the perisylvian association cortex, and the combination of the perisylvian association cortex, the inferior anterior temporal lobe, and the superior parietal lobe). In each case, performances of patients with lesions restricted to this small proportion of the total range of lesion sizes covered a wide range of total performance; in some cases almost the entire range, and in one case the entire range, of performance was found. The converse was also considered. The range of lesion sizes in these four regions was examined in patients whose performance fell within .25 SD of the mean performance on these measures. In each case, percent of region lesioned in the selected cases covered a wide portion of the range of percent of region lesioned in all cases. These results argue against models that maintain that the functions which these performance measures assess are evenly distributed across large contiguous brain areas, such as the left hemisphere cortex or the perisylvian association cortex. If this were the case, lesions of equal size in these regions should have led to similar magnitudes of a deficit. The data are consistent with the view that localization of these functions varies across individuals. They are also consistent with the idea that the functions being measured are unevenly distributed throughout large areas, either with the same pattern of unevenness in all individuals (invariant uneven distribution) or with different patterns of uneven distribution in different individuals (variable uneven distribution).

The implications of these results for the neural basis of syntactic processing depends upon the nature of the functions that the behavioral/performance measures measure. As noted above, deficits affecting syntactic comprehension appear to reduce the resource system that is used to support parsing and interpretive operations in a task, not the operations or resource systems that are used to assign and interpret syntactic structures in an amodal, abstract fashion. If this deficit analysis is correct, the data from aphasia provide information about areas that are involved in these interactions, not any that may support amodal parsing and interpretation.

TREATMENT

Given the importance of syntax to the expressive function of language, one might imagine that there would be considerable clinical interest in identifying and treating these disorders. However, this is not the case: Instruments that assess syntactic skills and treatment protocols directed at syntactic disorders are found mostly in research, not clinical, settings. The theoretical orientation of research may reflect the interests of researchers who are trained to investigate these disorders, who have for the most part been trained or heavily exposed to the theory-oriented foci of linguists and psycholinguists who study syntax, but that is not

likely to entirely account for the relative clinical neglect of these disorders. In other areas of aphasia, such as word sound production, vigorous theoretically oriented research (e.g., Dell et al., 1997) coexists with widespread clinical attention to the problem.

What may be a more important factor is the complex relation of syntactic processing to communicative success. In many settings, the propositional content that is required for successful communication can be conveyed through inferences based upon word meanings and knowledge of the world (to which inferences based upon the discourse context may be added). The ability to encode propositional relations grammatically may be more important to successful language use than is the ability to decode propositional meaning on the basis of syntactic structure, but even in production, patients who are quite agrammatic can be very effective in communicating propositional relations if they can access and produce content words. There are many communicative situations, such as reading this chapter, in which syntactic processing is essential, but the focus of clinical rehabilitation is often on much more constrained situations. I shall conclude this chapter with a very brief review of some recent work on treatment.

There is more experience with training syntactic production than comprehension. Several principles that positively affect results seem to emerge from these studies. Training the relationship between the meanings to be expressed and the form of a sentence (Byng, 1988; Nickels, Byng, & Black, 1991; Schwartz et al., 1994; Thompson, et al., 2003; Thompson & Shapiro, 2007) seems to be more effective than training patients to produce particular syntactic forms or grammatical elements, such as inflectional morphology or function words through repetition of target sentences (Holland & Levy, 1971; Naeser, 1975; Helm-Estabrooks, 1981; Helm-Estabrooks et al., 1981; Helm-Estabrooks & Ramsberger, 1986). This may reflect a principle that semantically mediated therapy is more effective than form-based therapy.

Across these more recent studies, however, patients showed variable sentence-specific improvements and generalization to untrained structures, with some notable successes (e.g., Byng, 1988) and other outcomes that were much less favorable. Thompson, Shapiro, and their colleagues (Thompson et al., 1998, 2003; Jacobs & Thompson, 2000; Thompson & Shapiro, 2007) have suggested another principle—the *complexity account of treatment efficacy* (CATE)—that may account for some of these differences in outcome. The CATE maintains that successful training on more complex examples of structures leads to generalization to less complex examples but not vice versa. In Thompson and her colleagues' work, the CATE is associated with a third principle: that successful training generalizes only to syntactic structures that are similar to ones trained. Some of the results that lead to these principles follow.

Thompson et al. (1998) reported that successful training in production of cleft object structures (e.g., "It was the artist who the thief chased") generalized to wh- questions (e.g. "Who did the thief chase?"), but not vice versa. Adopting a version of Chomsky's theory of syntactic structure, these authors argued that these sentences were both examples of a type of movement known as *wh- movement* and that clefts are more complex than wh- questions, accounting for the unidirectional generalization of successful training. Thompson et al. (2003) extended these results to object-relative clauses (e.g., "The man saw the artist who the thief chased"), which are more complex than clefts; the same pattern of generalization only from complex to simple wh- movement structures was found. Thompson et al. (1997) reported a CATE effect in training sentences with the type of movement we described above in passives (NP movement), with generalization from successfully trained "raising" structures (e.g., "The boy seemed to the girl to chase the dog") to passives (which are argued to be less complex). Thompson et al. (1997, 1998) reported that successful training on either wh-movement or NP movement did not generalize to the other type of structure, consistent with Chomsky's view that these types of movements differ and with the view that patients have

specific deficits affecting particular structures and/or parsing operations. The CATE is not perfect in predicting success, however, as not all patients in these studies showed these effects. For instance, patient 2 in Thompson et al. (1997) showed generalization from training on less complex NP movement passives to more complex NP movement subject raising sentences; Jones (1986), Byng (1988), Nickels et al. (1991), and Schwartz et al. (1994) have also reported results in sentence production that run opposite to the CATE.

There are also other many other open questions and much to study in the area of training of sentence comprehension and syntactic production. Other factors that might determine success (age, degree of handedness, level of impairment, lesion factors, among others) have not been systematically examined for their effects on outcome using therapies that incorporate the principles described above. The actual training techniques could be expanded. Many therapies (even those that train comprehension) require some speech production, making them hard (or impossible) to apply in patients with production impairments. Other topics that require study are (a) the best scheduling of therapy for syntactic comprehension deficits; (b) the issue of savings (reduction in time needed to achieve successful training on structures to which generalization has not occurred); (c) maintenance (the extent to which the gains made in therapy are maintained over time); (d) stimulus generalization (change under untrained language conditions—specifically, transfer from sentence comprehension to discourse); and (e) the relevance of any gains to real-world situations. It is to be hoped that additional studies will identify patients whose communicative needs require efficient syntactic processing, and will provide guidelines regarding what therapies are most effective in them.

ACKNOWLEDGMENTS

This work was supported in part by a grant from NIDCD (DC00942).

REFERENCES

Altman, G. T. M. & Kamide, Y. (2007). The real-time mediation of visual attention by language and world knowledge: Linking anticipatory (and other) eye movements to linguistic processing. *Journal of Memory and Language*, 57(4), 502–518.

Baddeley, A. D. (1986). *Working memory*. New York, Oxford University Press.

Bastiaanse, R., & van Zonneveld, R. (2005). Sentence production with verbs of alternating transitivity in agrammatic Broca's aphasia. *Journal of Neurolinguistics*, 18, 57–66.

Bates, E., & Wulfeck, B. (1989). A cross-linguistic approach to language breakdown. *Aphasiology*, 3(2), 111–142.

Bates, E., B. Wulfeck, B., & MacWhinney, B. (1991). Cross-linguistic research in aphasia: An overview. *Brain and Language*, 41, 123–148.

Bavelier, D., Corina, D., & Jezzard, P. (1997). Sentence reading: A functional MRI study at 4 Tesla. *Journal of Cognitive Neuroscience*, 9(5), 664–686.

Berndt, R. S. (1987). Symptom co-occurrence and dissociation in the interpretation of agrammatism. In M. Coltheart, G. Sartori, & R. Job (Eds.), *The cognitive neuropsychology of language* (pp. 221–232). London: Lawrence Erlbaum.

Berndt, R. S., Haendiges, A. N., Mitchum, C. C., & Sandson, J. (1997). Verb retrieval in aphasia 2: Relationship to sentence processing. *Brain and Language*, 56, 107–101.

Berndt, R., Mitchum, C., & Haendiges, A. (1996). Comprehension of reversible sentences in "agrammatism": A meta-analysis. *Cognition*, 58, 289–308.

Berndt, R., & Caramazza, A. (1980). A redefinition of the syndrome of Broca's aphasia. *Applied Psycholinguistics*, 1, 225–278.

Ben-Shachar, M., Hendler, T., Kahn, I., Ben-Bashat, D., & Grodzinsky, Y. (2003). The neural reality of syntactic transformations: Evidence from fMRI. *Psychological Science*, 14, 433–440.

Blumstein, S. E., Milberg, W., & Shrier, R. (1982). Semantic processing in aphasia: Evidence from an auditory lexical decision task. *Brain and Language*, 17, 301–315.

Blumstein, S., Byma, G., Hurowski, K. Huunhen, J., Brown, T. & Hutchison, S. (1998). On-line processing of filler-gap constructions in aphasia. *Brain and Language*, 61(2), 149–169.

Bock, K., & Levelt, P. (1994). Language production: Grammatical encoding. In M. Gernsbacher (Ed.), *Handbook of psycholinguistics* (pp. 945–984). New York: Academic.

Brown, J. W. (1973). *Aphasia*, trans. of A. Pick, Aphasie. Springfield: Thomas.

Butterworth, B., & Howard, D. (1987). Paragrammatisms. *Cognition*, 26, 1–38.

Butterworth, B. L. (1985). Jargon aphasia: Processes and strategies. In S. Newman, & R. Epstein (Eds.), *Current perspectives in dysphasia*. Edinburgh: Churchill Livingstone.

Butterworth, B. (1982). Speech errors: Old data in search of new theories. In A. Cutler (Ed.), *Slips of the tongue in language production* (pp. 73–108). The Hague: Mouton.

Byng, S. (1988). Sentence processing deficits: Theory and therapy. *Cognitive Neuropsychology*, 5(6), 629–676.

Caplan, D. (1983). A note on the "word order problem" in agrammatism. *Brain and Language*, 20(1), 155–165.

Caplan, D. (1987a). Discrimination of normal and aphasic subjects on a test of syntactic comprehension. *Neuropsychologia*, 25, 173–184.

Caplan, D. (1987b). *Neurolinguistics and linguistic aphasiology*. Cambridge, UK: Cambridge University Press.

Caplan, D. (1994). Language and the brain. In M. Gernsbacker (Ed.), *Handbook of psycholinguistics* (pp. 1023–1053). New York: Academic Press.

Caplan, D. (1995). Issues arising in contemporary studies of disorders of syntactic processing in sentence comprehension in agrammatic patients. *Brain and Language*, 50, 325–338.

Caplan, D. (2001a). The measurement of chance performance in aphasia, with specific reference to the comprehension of semantically reversible passive sentences: A note on issues raised by Caramazza, Capitani, Rey and Berndt (2000) and Drai, Grodzinsky and Zurif (2000). *Brain and Language*, 76, 193–201.

Caplan, D. (2001b). Points regarding the functional neuroanatomy of syntactic processing: A response to Zurif (2001). *Brain and Language*, 79, 329–332.

Caplan, D., & Futter, C. (1986). Assignment of thematic roles to nouns in sentence comprehension by an agrammatic patient. *Brain &Language*, 27, 117–134.

Caplan D, & Hildebrandt N. (1988). *Disorders of syntactic comprehension*. Cambridge, MA: MIT Press (Bradford Books).

Caplan, D., & Waters, G. S. (1990). Short-term memory and language comprehension: A critical review of the neuropsychological literature. In G. Vallar, & T. Shallice (Eds.), *Neuropsychological impairments of short-term memory* (pp. 337–389). Cambridge: Cambridge University Press.

Caplan, D., & G. S. Waters. (1999). Verbal working memory and sentence comprehension. *Behavioral and Brain Sciences, 22*, 77–94.

Caplan, D., & Waters, G. S. (2003). On-line syntactic processing in aphasia: Studies with auditory moving windows presentation. *Brain and Language, 84*(2), 222–249.

Caplan, D., Baker, C., & Dehaut, F. (1985). Syntactic determinants of sentence comprehension in aphasia. *Cognition, 21*, 117–175.

Caplan, D., Hildebrandt, N., & Makris, N. (1996). Location of lesions in stroke patients with deficits in syntactic processing in sentence comprehension. *Brain, 119*, 933–949.

Caplan, D., Waters, G., & Hildebrandt, H. (1997). Determinants of sentence comprehension in aphasic patients in sentence-picture matching tasks. *Journal of Speech and Hearing Research, 40*, 542–555.

Caplan, D., Alpert, N., & Waters, G. (1998). Effects of syntactic structure and propositional number on patterns of regional cerebral blood flow. *Journal of Cognitive Neuroscience, 10*, 541–552.

Caplan, D, Albert, N., & Waters, G. S. (1999). PET studies of sentence processing with auditory sentence presentation. *NeuroImage, 9*, 343–351.

Caplan, D., Alpert, N., Waters, G. S. & Olivieri, A. (2000). Activation of Broca's area by syntactic processing under conditions of concurrent articulation. *Human Brain Mapping, 9*, 65–71.

Caplan, D., DeDe, G., & Michaud, J. (2006). Task-independent and task-specific syntactic deficits in aphasic comprehension. *Aphasiology, 20*, 893–920.

Caplan, D., Waters, G., Kennedy, D. Alpert, A., Makris, N, DeDe, G., et al. (2007). A study of syntactic processing in aphasia I: Psycholinguistic aspects. *Brain and Language, 101*, 103–150.

Caplan, D., Waters, G.S., & DeDe, G. (2007b). Specialized verbal working memory for language comprehension. In A. Conway, C. Jarrold, M. Kane, A. Miyake, & J. Towse, J (Eds.) *Variation in working memory.* Oxford, UK: Oxford University Press.

Caplan, D., Waters, G., Kennedy, D., Alpert, A., Makris, N, DeDe, G., et al. (2007c). A study of syntactic processing in aphasia II: Neurological aspects. *Brain and Language, 101*, 151–177.

Caramazza, A., & Hillis, A. (1988). The disruption of sentence production: A case of selected deficit to positional level processing. *Brain and Language, 35*, 625–650.

Caramazza, A., & Zurif, E. B. (1976). Dissociation of algorithmic and heuristic processes in language comprehension: Evidence from aphasia. *Brain and Language, 3*, 572–582.

Caramazza, A., Basili, A. G., & Koller, J. J. (1981). An investigation of repetition and language processing in a case of conduction aphasia. *Brain & Language, 14*, 235–271.

Caramazza, A., Capitani, E., Rey, A., & Berndt, R.S. (2001). Agrammatic Broca's aphasia is not associated with a single pattern of comprehension performance. *Brain and Language, 76*, 158–184.

Carpenter, P. A., Just, M. A., Keller, T. A., Eddy, W. F., & Thulborn, K. R. (1999). Time course of fMRI-activation in language and spatial networks during sentence comprehension. *NeuroImage, 10*, 216–224.

Chomsky, N. (1986). *Knowledge of Language.* New York: Praeger.

Chomsky, N. (1995). *Barriers.* Cambridge, MA: MIT Press.

Cooke, A., Zurif, E. B., DeVita, C., Alsop, D., Koenig, P., Detre, J., et al. (2001). Neural basis for sentence comprehension: Grammatical and short-term memory components. *Human Brain Mapping, 15*, 80–94.

Cupples, L. & Inglis, A. L. (1993). When task demands induce "asyntactic" sentence comprehension: A study of sentence interpretation in aphasia. *Cognitive Neuropsychology, 10*, 201–234.

Damasio, A. R. (1992). Aphasia. *The New England Journal of Medicine, 326*, 531–539.

De Bleser, R. (1987). From agrammatism to para-grammatisms: German aphasiological traditions and grammatical disturbances. *Cognitive Neuropsychology, 4*, 187–256.

De Villiers, J. G. (1974). Quantitative aspects of agrammatism in aphasia. *Cortex, 10*, 36–54.

Dell, G. S. (1986). A spreading activation theory of retrieval in language production. *Psychological Review, 93*, 283–321.

Dell, S., Schwartz, M. F., Martin, N., Saffran, E. M. & Gagnon, D. A. (1997). Lexical access in aphasic and nonaphasic speakers. *Psychological Review, 104*, 801–838.

Dick, F., Bates, E., Wulfeck, B., Utman, J., Dronkers, N., & Gernsbacher, M. (2001). Language deficits, localization, and grammar: Evidence for a distributive model of language breakdown in aphasic patients and neurologically intact individuals. *Psychological Review, 108*, 759–788.

Dickey, M., Thompson, C., & Choy, J. (2005). The on-line comprehension of wh-movement structures in agrammatic Broca's aphasia: Evidence from eyetracking. Paper presented at the Clinical Aphasiology Conference, Sanibel, FL.

Drai, D. & Grodzinksy, Y. (1999). Comprehension regularity in Broca's aphasia? There's more of it than you ever imagined. *Brain and Language, 70*, 139–143.

Dronkers, N., Wilkin, D., Van Valin, R., Redfern, B. & Jaeger, J. (2004). Lesion analysis of the brain areas involved in language comprehension. *Cognition, 92*, 145–177.

Farmer, T. A., Anderson, S. E., & Spivey, M. J. (2007). Gradiency and visual context in syntactic garden-paths. *Journal of Memory and Language, 57*(4), 570–595.

Ferreira, F., & Clifton, C. (1986). The independence of syntactic processing. *Memory and Language, 25*, 348–368.

Friedman, N., & Grodzinsky, Y. (1997). Tense and Agreement in agrammatic production: Pruning the syntactic tree. *Brain and Language, 56*, 397–425.

Garrett, M. F. (1975). The analysis of sentence production. In G. Bower (Ed.), *Psychology of learning and motivation*, Vol. 9 (pp. 137–177). New York: Academic Press.

Garrett, M. F. (1976). Syntactic processes in sentence production. In R. J. Wales, & E. Walker (Eds.), *New approaches to language mechanisms* (pp. 231–255). Amsterdam: North-Holland.

Garrett, M. F. (1978). Word and sentence perception. In R. Held, H. W. Liebowitz, & H. -L. Teuber (Eds.), *Handbook of sensory physiology*, Vol. 8: Perception (pp. 611–623). Berlin: Springer-Verlag.

Garrett, M. F. (1980). Levels of processing in sentence production. In B. Butterworth (Ed.), *Language production*, Vol. 1: Speech and Talk (pp. 177–220). London: Academic Press.

Garrett, M. F. (1982). Production of speech: Observations from normal and pathological language use. In A. W. Ellis (Ed.), *Normality and pathology in cognitive functions* (pp. 19–75). London: Academic Press.

Goldberg, A. (1995). *Constructions: A construction grammar approach to argument structure.* Chicago: University of Chicago Press.

Goldberg. A. (2006). *Constructions at work: The nature of generalization in language.* Oxford: Oxford University Press.

Goodglass, H. (1976). Agrammatism. In H. Whitaker, & H. A. Whitaker (Eds.), *Studies in neurolinguistics*, Vol. 1 (pp. 237–260). New York: Academic Press.

Goodglass, H. (1973). Studies on the grammar of aphasics. In H. Goodglass, & S. Blumstein (Eds.), *Psycholinguistics and aphasia.* Baltimore: John Hopkins University Press.

Goodglass, H., & Berko, J. (1960). Agrammatism and inflectional morphology in English. *Journal of Speech and Hearing Research, 3*, 257–267.

Goodglass, H., Gleason, J. B., Bernholtz, N., & Hyde, M. R. (1972). Some linguistic structures in the speech of a Broca's aphasic. *Cortex, 8*, 191–212.

Grodzinsky, Y. (1984) The syntactic characterization of agrammatism. *Cognition, 16*, 99–120.

Grodzinsky, Y. (1986). Language deficits and the theory of syntax. *Brain and Language, 27*, 135–159.

Grodzinsky, Y. (1990). *Theoretical perspectives on language deficits.* Cambridge, MA: MIT Press.

Grodzinsky, Y. (1995). A restrictive theory of agrammatic comprehension. *Brain and Language, 50*, 27–51.

Grodzinsky, Y. (2000). The neurology of syntax: Language use without Broca's area. *Behavioral and Brain Sciences, 23*, 47–117.

Grodzinsky, Y., & Marek, A. (1988). Algorithmic and heuristic processes revisited. *Brain and Language, 33*, 316–325.

Grodzinsky, Y., Wexler, K., Chien, Y. -C., Marakovitz, S., & Solomon, J. (1993). The breakdown of binding relations. *Brain & Language, 45*, 396–422.

Haarmann, H. J. & Kolk, H. H. (1991). Syntactic priming in Broca's aphasics: Evidence for slow activation. *Aphasiology, 5*, 247–263.

Haarmann, H. J., Just, M. A., & Carpenter, P. A. (1997). Aphasic sentence comprehension as a resource deficit: A computational approach. *Brain and Language, 59*, 76–120.

Heilman, K. M., & Scholes, R. J. (1976). The nature of comprehension errors in Broca's, conduction, and Wernicke's aphasics. *Cortex, 12*, 258–265.

Helm-Estabrooks, N. A., Fitzpatrick, P. M., & Baressi, B. (1981). Response of an agrammatic patient to a syntax stimulation program for aphasia. *Journal of Speech and Hearing Disorders, 47*, 385–389.

Helm-Estabrooks, N. A. & Ramsberger, G. (1986). Treatment of agrammatism in long-term Broca's aphasia. *British Journal of Disorders of Communication, 21*, 39–45.

Heeschen, C. (1985). Agrammatism vs. paragrammatism: A fictitious opposition. In M. -L. Kean (Ed.), *Agrammatism* (pp. 207–248). London: Academic Press.

Hildebrandt, N., Caplan, D., & Evans, K. (1987). The mani lefti without a trace: A case study of aphasic processing of empty categories. *Cognitive Neuropsychology, 4*(3), 257–302.

Holland, A. L., & Levy, C. B. (1971). Syntactic generalization in aphasics as a function of relearning an active sentence. *Acta Symbolica, 2,* 34–41.

Jacobs, B. J., & Thompson, C. K. (2000). Cross-modal generalization effects of training noncanonical sentence comprehension and production in agrammatic aphasia. *Journal of Speech, Language and Hearing Research, 43*(1), 5–20.

Jones, E. (1986). Building the foundations for sentence production in a non-fluent aphasic. *British Journal of Disorders of Communication, 21,* 63–82.

Just, M. A., & Carpenter, P. A. (1992). A capacity theory of comprehension: Individual differences in working memory. *Psychological Review, 99*(1), 122–149.

Just, M. A., Carpenter, P. A., Keller, T. A., Eddy, W. F., & Thulborn, K. R. (1996). Brain activation modulated by sentence comprehension. *Science, 274,* 114–116.

Kaplan, E., Goodglass, H., & Weintraub, S. (1976). *The Boston naming test.* Boston: Veterans Administration.

Kean, M. L. (1977). The linguistic interpretation of aphasic syndromes: Agrammatism in Broca's aphasia, an example. *Cognition, 5,* 9–46.

Kempler, D., Curtiss, S., Metter, E., Jackson, C., & Hanson, W. (1991). Grammatical comprehension, aphasic syndromes and neuroimaging. *Journal of Neurolinguistics, 6,* 301–318.

King, J. W., & Just, M. A. (1991). Individual difference in syntactic processing: The role of working memory. *Journal of Memory and Language, 30,* 580–602.

Kolk, H. H., & van Grunsven, J. J. F. (1985). Agrammatism as a variable phenomenon. *Cognitive Neuropsychology, 2,* 347–384.

Lapointe, S. (1983). Some issues in the linguistic description of agrammatism. *Cognition, 14,* 1–39.

Lee, M., & Thompson, C. (2004). Agrammatic aphasic production and comprehension of unaccusative verbs in sentence contexts. *Journal of Neurolinguistics, 17,* 315–330.

Levelt, W. J. M. (1989). *Speaking: From intention to articulation.* Cambridge, MA: MIT Press.

Linebarger, M. C. (1990). Neuropsychology of sentence parsing. In A. Caramazza (Ed.), *Cognitive neuropsychology and neurolinguistics: Advances in models of cognitive function and impairment* (pp. 55–122). Hillsdale, NJ: Lawrence Erlbaum.

Linebarger, M. C., Schwartz, M. F., & Saffran, E. M. (1983). Sensitivity to grammatical structure in so-called agrammatic aphasics. *Cognition, 13,* 361–392.

Luria, A. R. (1973). *The working brain.* New York: Basic Books.

McAllister, T., Waters, G. S., Caplan, D., & Bachrach, A. (in press). The unaccusative construction in aphasia: Implications for the representation of syntactic movement. *Aphasiology.*

Martin, R. C. (1987). Articulatory and phonological deficits in short-term memory and their relation to syntactic processing. *Brain and Language, 32,* 159–192.

Mazoyer, B. M., Tzourio, N., Frak, V., Syrota, A., Murayama, N., Levrier, O., et al. (1993). The cortical representation of speech. *Journal of Cognitive Neuroscience, 5*(4), 467–479.

McCarthy, R., & Warrington, E. M. (1985). Category specificity in an agrammatic patient: The relative impairment of verb retrieval and comprehension. *Neuropsychologia, 23,* 709–727.

McKoon, G. & R. Ratcliff. (1994). Sentential context and on-line lexical decision. *Journal of Experimental Psychology: Learning, Memory, and Cognition, 20,* 1239–1243.

McKoon, G., Ratcliff, R., & Ward, G. (1994). Testing theories of language processing: An empirical investigation of the on-line lexical decision task. *Journal of Experimental Psychology: Learning, Memory, and Cognition, 20,* 1219–1228.

Menn, L., & Obler, L. (1990). Agrammatic aphasia: a cross-language narrative sourcebook. Johns Benjamins.

Menn, L., Obler, L., & Goodglass, H. (Eds.). (1990). *A Cross-Language Study of Agrammatism.* Philadelphia: John Benjamins.

Mesulam, M. M. (1990). Large-scale neurocognitive networks and distributed processing for attention, language, and memory. *Annals of Neurology, 28*(5), 597–613.

Mesulam, M. -M. (1998). From sensation to cognition. *Brain, 121,* 1013–1052.

Miceli, G., Guistolisi, L., & Caramazza, A. (1990). *The interaction of lexical and non-lexical processing mechanisms: Evidence from anomia.* Baltimore: The Cognitive Neuropsychology laboratory, The Johns Hopkins University.

Miceli, G., Silveri, M. C., Romani, C., & Caramazza, A. (1989). Variation in the pattern of omissions and substitutions of grammatical morphemes in the spontaneous speech of so-called patients. *Brain and Language, 36,* 447–492.

Miceli, G., & Caramazza, A. (1988). Dissociation of inflectional and derivational morphology. *Brain and Language, 35,* 24–65.

Miceli, G., Silveri, M., Villa, G., & Caramazza, A. (1984). On the basis for the agrammatic's difficulty in producing main verbs. *Cortex, 20,* 207–220.

Miceli, G., Mazzucchi, A., Menn, L., & Goodglass, H. (1983). Contrasting cases of Italian agrammatic aphasia without comprehension disorder. *Brain and Language, 19,* 65–97.

Milberg, W., & Blumstein, S. E. (1981). Lexical decision and aphasia: Evidence for semantic processing. *Brain and Language, 14,* 371–385.

Miyake, A. K., Carpenter, P., & Just, M. (1994). A capacity approach to syntactic comprehension disorders: Making normal adults perform like brain-damaged patients. *Cognitive Neuropsychology, 11,* 671–717.

Naeser, M. A. (1975). A structured approach to teaching aphasics basic sentence types. *British Journal of Disorders in Communication, 10,* 70–76.

Nespoulous, J. -L., Dordain, M., Perron, C., Ska, B., Bub, D., Caplan, D., et al. (1988). Agrammatism in sentence production without comprehension deficits: Reduced availability of syntactic structures and/or of grammatical morphemes? A case study. *Brain and Language, 33,* 273–295.

Nespoulous, J. L., Joanette, Y., Beland, R., Caplan, D., & Lecours, A. R. (1984). Phonological disturbances in aphasia: Is there a "markedness" effect in aphasic phonemic errors? In F. C. Rose (Ed.), *Progress in aphasiology: Advances in neurology,* Vol. 42. New York: Raven Press.

Nickels, L., Byng, S., & Black, M. (1991). Sentence processing deficits: A replication of therapy. *British Journal of Disorders of Communication, 26*(2), 175–199.

Nicol, J., Fodor, J., & Swinney, D. (1994). Using cross-modal lexical decision tasks to investigate sentence processing. *Journal of Experimental Psychology: Learning, Memory, and Cognition, 20,* 1229–1238.

Noppeney, U. & Price, C. J. (2004) An fMRI Study of Syntactic Adaptation. *Journal of Cognitive Neuroscience, 16,* 702–713.

Obler, L. K., & Albert, M. L. (1979). *Action naming test.* Unpublished manuscript, Boston.

Ostrin, R., & Schwartz, M. F. (1986). Reconstructing from a degraded trace: A study of sentence repetition in agrammatism. *Brain and Language, 28,* 328–345.

Ostrin, R. (1982). *Framing the production problem in agrammatism.* Unpublished paper, Psychology, University of Pennsylvania.

Parisi, D. (1987). Dual coding: Theoretical issues and empirical evidence. In J. M. Scandura, & C. J. Brainerd (Eds.), *Structure/process models of complex human behavior.* Leiden, Netherlands: Nordhoff.

Rademacher, J., Galaburda, A. M., Kennedy, D. N., Filipek, P. A., & Caviness, Jr., V. S. (1992). Human cerebral cortex: Localization, parcellation, and morphometry with magnetic resonance imaging. *Journal of Cognitive Neuroscience, 4,* 352–374.

Rizzi, L. (1985). Two notes on the linguistic interpretation of Broca's aphasia. In M. -L. Kean (Ed.), *Agrammatism* (pp. 153–164). London: Academic Press.

Rumelhart, D. E., & McCelland, J. L. (Eds.). (1986). *Parallel distributed processing,* Vol. I. Cambridge, MA: Foundations MIT Press.

Saffran, E. M., Bogyo, L. C., Schwartz, M. F., & Marin, O. S. M. (1980). Does deep dyslexia reflect right-hemisphere reading? In M. Coltheart, K. Patterson, & J. C. Marshall (Eds.), *Deep dyslexia* (pp. 381–406). London: Routledge.

Schwartz, M., Saffran, E., Marin, O. (1980). The word order problem in agrammatism. I: Comprehension. *Brain and Language, 10,* 249–262.

Schwartz, M. F., Linebarger, M. C., & Saffran, E. M. (1985). The status of the syntactic deficit theory of agrammatism. In M. -L. Kean (Ed.), *Agrammatism* (pp. 83–124). New York: Academic Press.

Schwartz, M. F., Linebarger, M. C., Saffran, E. M., & Pate, D. S. (1987). Syntactic transparency and sentence interpretation in aphasia. *Language and Cognitive Processes, 2,* 85–113.

Schwartz, M. F., Saffran, E. M., Fink, R. B., Myers, J. L., & Martin, N. (1994). Mapping therapy: A treatment program for agrammatism. *Aphasiology, 8*(1), 19–54.

Smith, S., & Mimica, I. (1984). Agrammatism in a case-inflected language: Comprehension of agent-object relations. *Brain and Language, 13,* 274–290.

Smith, S., & Bates, E. (1987). Accessibility of case and gender contrasts for assignment of agent-object relations in Broca's aphasics and fluent anomics. *Brain and Language, 30,* 8–32.

Swinney, D., & Zurif, E. (1995). Syntactic processing in aphasia. *Brain and Language, 50,* 225–239.

Swinney, D., Zurif, E., Prather, P., & Love, T. (1996). Neurological distribution of processing resources underlying language comprehension. *Journal of Cognitive Neuroscience, 8,* 174–184.

Spivey, M., Grosjean, M., & Knoblich, G. (2005). Continuous attraction toward phonological competitors. *Proceedings of the National Academy of Sciences, 102*(29), 10393–10398.

Tanenhaus, M., Magnuson, J., Dahan, D., & Chambers, C. (2000). Eye movements and lexical access in spoken-language comprehension: Evaluating a linking hypothesis between fixations and linguistic processing. *Journal of Psycholinguistic Research, 29*, 557–580.

Tanenhaus, M. K., Spivey-Knowlton, M. J., Eberhard, K. M., & Sedivy, J. E. (1995). Integration of visual and linguistic information in spoken language comprehension. *Science, 268*, 1632–1634.

Thompson, C. (2003). Unaccusative verb production in agrammatic aphasia: The argument structure complexity hypothesis. *Journal of Neurolinguistics, 16*, 151–167.

Thompson, C. K., Ballard, K. J., & Shapiro, L. P. (1998). The role of syntactic complexity in training wh-movement structures in agrammatic aphasia: Optimal order for promoting generalization. *Journal of the International Neuropsychological Society, 4*(6), 661–674.

Thompson, C. K., & Shapiro, L. P. (2005). Treating agrammatic aphasia within a linguistic framework: Treatment of Underlying Forms. *Aphasiology, 19*(10–11), 1021–1036.

Thompson, C. K., & Shapiro, L. P. (2007). Complexity in treatment of syntactic deficits. *American Journal of Speech Language Pathology, 16*(1), 30–42.

Thompson, C. K., Shapiro, L. P., Ballard, K. J., Jacobs, B. J., Schneider, S. S., & Tait, M. E. (1997). Training and generalized production of wh- and NP-movement structures in agrammatic aphasia. *Journal of Speech, Language and Hearing Research, 40*(2), 228–244.

Thompson, C. K., Shapiro, L. P., Kiran, S., & Sobecks, J. (2003). The role of syntactic complexity in treatment of sentence deficits in agrammatic aphasia: The complexity account of treatment efficacy (CATE). *Journal of Speech, Language, and Hearing Research, 46*(3), 591–607.

Thompson, C., Dickey, M., & Choy, J (2004). Complexity in the comprehension of wh-movement structures in agrammatic Broca's aphasia: Evidence from eyetracking. *Brain and Language, 91*, 124–125.

Tissot, R. J., Mounin, G., & Lhermitte, F. (1973). *L'agrammatisme*. Brussels: Dessart.

Tramo, M. J., Baynes, K., & Volpe, B. T. (1988). Impaired syntactic comprehension and production in Broca's aphasia: CT lesion localization and recovery patterns. *Neurology, 38*, 95–98.

Trueswell, J. C., Tanenhaus, M. K., & Garnsey, S. M. (1994). Semantic influence on syntactic processing: Use of thematic information in syntactic disambiguation. *Journal of Memory and Language, 33*, 285–318.

von Stockhardt, T. R., & Bader, L. (1976). Some relations of grammar and lexicon in aphasia. *Cortex, 12*, 49–60.

Von Stockardt, T. R. (1972). Recognition of syntactic structure in aphasic patients. *Cortex, 8*, 322–334.

Zurif, E. B. (1984). Psycholinguistic interpretation of the aphasias. In D. Caplan, A. R. Lecours, & A. Smith (Eds.), *Biological Perspectives on Language* (pp. 158–171). Cambridge, MA: MIT Press.

Zurif, E., Swinney, D., Prather, P., Solomon, J., & Bushell, C. (1993). An on-line analysis of syntactic processing in Broca's and Wernicke's aphasia. *Brain and Language, 45*, 448–464.

5

Acquired Dyslexia

H. BRANCH COSLETT

Disorders of reading are frequently encountered in patients with acquired cerebral lesions. Investigations in the past few decades have improved our understanding of these disorders. In this chapter, we review the peripheral dyslexias, including neglect dyslexia, attentional dyslexia, and pure alexia (or alexia without agraphia), as well as the "central" dyslexias, including deep, surface, and phonological dyslexia. Current accounts of acquired dyslexia are also discussed. Finally, we briefly describe the reading tasks that serve to differentiate the different reading disorders.

INTRODUCTION

Investigations of acquired dyslexia commenced in the late 19th century, a time at which a number of now classical disorders were first described (Fruend, 1889; Liepman & Maas, 1907). Perhaps the most influential early contributions to the understanding of dyslexia were provided by Dejerine, who described two patients with quite different patterns of reading impairment. Dejerine's first patient (Dejerine, 1891) manifested impaired reading and writing subsequent to an infarction involving the left parietal lobe. Dejerine termed this disorder *alexia with agraphia* and attributed

the disturbance to a disruption of the "optical image for words," which he thought to be supported by the left angular gyrus. In an account that, in some respects, presages contemporary psychological accounts, Dejerine concluded that reading and writing required the activation of these "optical images" and that the loss of the images resulted in the inability to recognize or write even familiar words.

Dejerine's second patient (Dejerine, 1892) was quite different. This patient exhibited a right homonymous hemianopia and was unable to read aloud or for comprehension, but could write. This disorder, designated *alexia without agraphia* (also known as agnosic alexia and pure alexia), was attributed by Dejerine to a "disconnection" between visual information presented to the right hemisphere and the left angular gyrus, which he assumed to be critical for the recognition of words.

After the seminal contributions of Dejerine, the study of acquired dyslexia languished for decades during which the relatively few investigations that were reported focused primarily on the anatomic underpinnings of the disorders. Although a number of interesting observations were reported, they were often either ignored or their significance not appreciated. For example, Akelaitis (1944) reported that patients whose corpus callosa had been severed were unable to read aloud stimuli presented in the left visual field; this observation provided powerful support for Dejerine's interpretation of alexia without agraphia as a disconnection syndrome, but was reported only in passing in a series of contributions that failed to demonstrate a substantial role of the corpus callosum in behavior.

The study of acquired dyslexia was subsequently revitalized by the elegant and detailed analyses by Marshall and Newcombe (1966, 1973), which demonstrated that, by virtue of a careful investigation of the pattern of reading deficits exhibited by dyslexic subjects, distinctly different and reproducible types of reading deficits could be elucidated. Thus, these investigators described a patient (GR) who read approximately 50% of concrete nouns but was severely impaired in the reading of abstract nouns and all other parts of speech. The most striking aspect of G.R.'s performance, however, was his tendency to produce errors that appeared to be semantically related to the target word (e.g., the word "speak" read as "talk"). Marshall and Newcombe (1973) designated this disorder *deep dyslexia*. These investigators also described two patients whose primary deficit appeared to be an inability to reliably apply grapheme–phoneme correspondences. Thus, JC, for example, rarely applied the "rule of e" (which lengthens the preceding vowel in words such as *like*) and experienced great difficulties in deriving the appropriate phonology for consonant clusters and vowel digraphs. The disorder characterized by impaired application of print-to-sound correspondences was termed *surface dyslexia*.

On the basis of these data, Marshall and Newcombe (1973) concluded that the meaning of written words could be accessed by two distinct procedures. The first was a direct procedure whereby familiar words activated the appropriate stored representation (or visual word form) that, in turn, activated meaning directly; reading in deep dyslexia was assumed to involve this procedure. The second procedure was assumed to be a phonologically based process in which grapheme-to-phoneme or print-to-sound correspondences were employed to derive the appropriate phonology (that is, "sound out" the word); the reading of surface dyslexics was assumed to be mediated by this nonlexical procedure. Although a number of Marshall and Newcombe's specific hypotheses have subsequently been criticized, their argument that reading may be mediated by two distinct procedures has received considerable empirical support.

The conceptual framework developed by Marshall and Newcombe motivated many subsequent studies of acquired dyslexia; indeed, the information-processing or verbal models of reading, one of which is illustrated in Figure 5-1, have been based to a considerable degree on the insights provided by these investigators. As an information-processing model will serve as the basis for the discussion of specific forms of acquired dyslexia, the model illustrated in Figure 5-1 will be briefly described. A number of current accounts of acquired dyslexia, one of which is a direct descendant of the model proposed by Marshall and Newcombe, will be discussed below.

The information-processing model of reading depicted in Figure 5-1 provides three distinct procedures for oral reading. Two of these procedures correspond to those described by Marshall and Newcombe. The first (labeled "A" in Figure 5-1) involves the activation of a stored

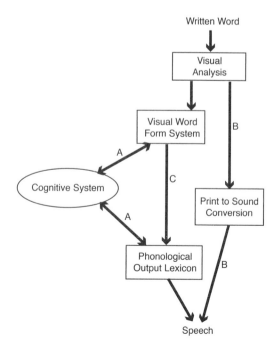

Figure 5–1. An information-processing model of the processes involved in reading.

entry in the visual word form system and the subsequent access to semantic information and ultimately activation of the stored sound of the word at the level of the phonologic output lexicon. The second ("B" in Figure 5-1) involves the nonlexical grapheme-to-phoneme or print-to-sound translation process; this procedure does not entail access to any stored information about words, but rather is assumed to be mediated by access to a catalog of correspondences stipulating the pronunciation of phonemes. Many information-processing accounts of the language mechanisms subserving reading incorporate a third reading procedure. This mechanism ("C" in Figure 5-1) is lexically based, in that it is assumed to involve the activation of the visual word form system and the phonologic output lexicon. The procedure differs from the lexical procedure described above, however, in that there is no intervening activation of semantic information. This procedure has been called the *direct reading mechanism* or route. Support for the direct lexical mechanism comes from a number of sources, including observations that some subjects read aloud words that they do not appear to comprehend (Schwards, Saffran, & Marin, 1979; Coslett, 1991). More recently, Law and colleagues (2006, 2009) have provided evidence for an independent semantic route in reading. They reported two Chinese patients who had suffered strokes, but whose performance on tests of phonology and access to semantic representations for verbal materials argued for independent lexical mechanisms.

Although most recent reports of acquired dyslexia involve English-speaking subjects, acquired dyslexias have been reported in many different languages, including Spanish (Ferreres, Cultiño, & Olmedo, 2005), Japanese (kana and kanji; Sato et al., 2008), Chinese (Cheung, Cheung, & Chan, 2004; Yin & Weekes, 2005), Turkish (Raman & Weekes, 2005) and others.

PERIPHERAL DYSLEXIAS

A useful starting point in the discussion of the alexias is the distinction offered by Shallice and Warrington (1980) between peripheral and central dyslexias. The former are conditions characterized by a deficit in the processing of visual aspects of the stimulus, which prevents the patient from reliably matching a familiar word to its stored visual form or *visual word form*. In contrast, central dyslexias reflect impairment to the deeper or higher reading functions by which visual word forms mediate access to meaning or speech production mechanisms. Next, the major types of peripheral dyslexia are briefly described.

ALEXIA WITHOUT AGRAPHIA

The classical syndrome of alexia without agraphia or pure alexia is perhaps the prototypical peripheral dyslexia. As noted above, the traditional account (Dejerine, 1892; Geschwind & Fusillo, 1966) of this disorder attributes the syndrome to a "disconnection" of visual information, which is restricted to the right hemisphere, from the left hemisphere word recognition system.

Although these patients do not appear to be able to read in the sense of fast, automatic word recognition, many are able to use a compensatory strategy that involves naming the letters of the word in serial fashion; they read, in effect, "letter-by-letter" (Patterson & Kay, 1982). Using the slow and inefficient letter-by-letter procedure, patients with pure alexia typically exhibit significant effects of word length, requiring more time to read long as compared to short words. In contrast to those with central dyslexia, performance is typically not influenced by factors such as part of speech (e.g., noun vs. functor), the extent to which the referent of the word is concrete (e.g., "table") or abstract (e.g., "destiny"), or whether the word is orthographically regular (i.e., can be "sounded out").

A number of alternative accounts of the processing deficit in pure alexia have been proposed. Thus, some investigators have proposed that the impairment is attributable to a limitation in the transmission of letter identity information to the visual word system (Patterson & Kay, 1982) or an inability to directly encode visual letters as abstract orthographic types (Bub & Arguin, 1995). Farah and Wallace (1991) and Chialant and Caramazza (1996) have suggested that pure alexia is attributable to a low-level visual disorder that adversely impacts complex visual stimuli such as printed words (see also Raman & Weekes, 2005; Buxbaum & Coslett, 1996). Other investigators have argued that the disorder is attributable to a disruption of the visual word form system itself (Warrington & Shallice, 1980). As with many syndromes defined on the basis of a single, cardinal deficit, there is reason to believe that pure alexia may be attributable to different processing impairments in different subjects. Consistent with this view, Rosazza et al. (2007) recently reported that two patients with pure alexia exhibited different patterns of impairment. They suggested that the syndrome of pure alexia may reflect damage to different levels of processing in different subjects.

Although most reports of pure alexia have emphasized the profound nature of the reading deficit, often stating that patients were utterly incapable of reading without recourse to a letter-by-letter procedure (Geschwind & Fusillo, 1966; Patterson & Kay, 1982), a number of investigators have reported data demonstrating that pure alexic patients are able to comprehend words that they are unable to explicitly identify (Coslett & Saffran, 1989a; Landis, Regard, & Serrat, 1980; Shallice & Saffran, 1986). The interpretation of these data remains controversial. Behrmann and colleagues (1998) have suggested that the preserved reading in pure alexia is mediated by the (lesioned) normal reading system. On this account, the imageability and part of speech effects, as well as the implicit nature of the reading performance, are assumed to be attributable to weak activation of stored word forms by the visual input. Alternatively, we (Coslett & Saffran, 1989a; Saffran & Coslett, 1998) and others (Landis, Regard, & Serrat, 1980) have argued that implicit reading in pure alexia reflects the lexical processing of the right hemisphere. We shall return to a consideration of the implications of these data in a later discussion of reading and the right hemisphere.

The anatomic basis of pure alexia has been extensively investigated. Although rarely associated with lesions that "undercut" or disconnect the posterior perisylvian cortex on the left (Greenblatt, 1976), the disorder is typically associated with a lesion in the posterior portion of the dominant hemisphere, which compromises visual pathways in the dominant hemisphere, as well as white matter tracts (such as the splenium of the corpus callosum or forceps major)

critical for the interhemispheric transmission of visual information (Binder & Mohr, 1994; Damasio & Damasio, 1983). The disconnection account originally offered by Dejerine has recently received support from an elegant neuroimaging study of a subject who was studied before and after a surgical procedure that resulted in dyslexia (Epelbaum et al., 2008). Their analysis supported the long-hypothesized role of the inferior longitudinal fasciculus in normal reading.

Finally, an important contribution to the understanding of the anatomic basis of pure alexia has recently come from the comparison of eye movements during reading of subjects with pure alexia and subjects with right hemianopic dyslexia who did not exhibit the full syndrome of pure alexia (Pflugshaupt et al., 2009). They found that, whereas all subjects exhibited low-amplitude rightward saccades during text reading, substantial increases in fixation frequency and viewing time were specific to pure alexia. Furthermore, they found that the region corresponding to the visual word form system in the left fusiform gyrus was disrupted in pure alexia, but not in hemianopic subjects without dyslexia. Thus, these data are consistent with claims (e.g., 24) that pure alexia is associated with a disruption of a system that is specialized for the recognition of visually presented words.

NEGLECT DYSLEXIA

Neglect dyslexia, which is most commonly encountered in patients with left-sided neglect, is characterized by a failure to explicitly identify the initial portion of a letter string. Interestingly, the performance of patients with neglect dyslexia is often influenced by the nature of the letter string; thus, patients with this disorder may fail to report the "ti-" in nonwords such as "tiggle" but read the word "giggle" correctly (Sieroff, Pollatsek, & Posner, 1986). The fact that performance is affected by the lexical status of the stimulus suggests that neglect dyslexia is not attributable to a failure to register letter information, but rather reflects an attentional impairment at a higher level of representation (Behrman et al., 1990; Ladavas, Shallice, & Zanella, 1997). Consistent with this view, Arduino, Vallar, and Burani (2006) recently contrasted the reading of three subjects with attentional dyslexia with brief and untimed presentation of stimuli. They found that, with untimed presentation, subjects exhibited the typical pattern of errors disproportionately involving the beginning of letter strings. In contrast, with brief presentation, errors involved all portions of the letter strings. These data are consistent with a number of lines of evidence from neglect (see Chapter 12) demonstrating that early processing of sensory information may be relatively intact in neglect and that "neglect" arises at a later stage of processing.

Finally, it should be noted that neglect dyslexia for the right side of letter strings is occasionally observed in subjects with left hemisphere lesions. As demonstrated by Petrich, Greenwald, and Berndt (2007), this deficit may be severe for written words yet not evident for any other type of stimulus.

ATTENTIONAL DYSLEXIA AND RELATED DISORDERS

Perhaps the least studied of the acquired dyslexias, attentional dyslexia is characterized by the relative preservation of single-word reading in the context of a gross disruption of reading when words are presented as text or in the presence of other words or letters (Price & Humphreys, 1993; Saffran & Coslett, 1996; Warrington, Cipolotti, & McNeal, 1993). Patients with this disorder may also exhibit difficulties identifying letters within words, even though the words themselves are read correctly (Saffran & Coslett, 1996) and be impaired in identifying words flanked by extraneous letters (e.g., "lboatm"). Finally, we (Saffran & Coslett, 1996) have investigated a patient with attentional dyslexia secondary to autopsy-proven Alzheimer disease who produced frequent "blend" errors, in which letters from one word of a two-word display intruded into the other word. Although several accounts for this disorder have been proposed, it has been attributed by several investigators to an impairment in visual attention or a loss of location information, such that the position of letters within or between words appears to shift.

A number of investigators have explored reading deficits in subjects with degenerative disorders such as the visual variant of Alzheimer disease (Price & Humphreys, 1993). Crutch and Warrington (2007) reported data from three subjects in whom the effects of visual "crowding" were systematically investigated. They found that the proximity (but not identity) of flanking letters significantly influenced the report of a target letter; this represents an important step in the direction toward a more nuanced understanding of the specific deficits that fall under the general rubric of early or prelexical reading deficits.

CENTRAL DYSLEXIAS

DEEP DYSLEXIA

Deep dyslexia, initially described by Marshall and Newcombe in 1973, is perhaps the most extensively investigated of the central dyslexias (see, for example, Coltheart, Patterson, & Marshall, 1980) and, in many respects, the most compelling. The allure of deep dyslexia is due in large part to the intrinsically interesting hallmark of the syndrome, the production of semantic errors. Shown the word *castle*, a deep dyslexic may respond "knight;" shown the word *bird*, the patient may respond "canary." At least for some deep dyslexics, it is clear that these errors are not circumlocutions. Semantic errors may represent the most frequent error type in some deep dyslexics, whereas in other patients they comprise only a small proportion of reading errors. Deep dyslexics also typically produce frequent "visual" errors (e.g., *skate* read as "scale") and morphological errors in which a prefix or suffix is added, deleted, or substituted (e.g., *scolded* read as "scolds"; *governor* read as "government").

Additional features of the syndrome include a greater success in reading words of high as compared to low imageability. Thus, words such as *table*, *chair*, *ceiling*, and *buttercup*, the referent of which is concrete or imageable, are read more successfully than words such as *fate*, *destiny*, *wish*, and *universal*, which denote abstract concepts.

Another characteristic feature of deep dyslexia is a part-of-speech effect, such that nouns are typically read more reliably than modifiers (adjectives and adverbs) which are, in turn, read more accurately than verbs. Deep dyslexics manifest particular difficulty in the reading of functors (a class of words that includes pronouns, prepositions, conjunctions, and interrogatives including *that, which, they, because, under*, etc.) The striking nature of the part-of-speech effect may be illustrated by the patient reported by Saffran and Marin (1977) who correctly read the word *chrysanthemum* but was unable to read the word *the*. Most errors to functors involve the substitution of a different functor (*that* read as "which") rather than the production of words of a different class, such as nouns or verbs. As functors are in general less imageable than nouns, verbs, or adjectives, some investigators have claimed that the apparent effect of part of speech is in reality a manifestation of the pervasive imageability effect (Allport & Funnell, 1981). We have reported a patient, however, whose performance suggests that the part-of-speech effect is not simply a reflection of a more general deficit in the processing of low-imageability words (Coslett, 1991).

Finally, all deep dyslexics exhibit a substantial impairment in the reading of nonwords. When confronted with letter strings such as *flig* or *churt*, deep dyslexics are typically unable to employ print-to-sound correspondences to derive phonology; nonwords frequently elicit "lexicalization" errors (e.g., *flig* read as "flag"), perhaps reflecting a reliance on lexical reading in the absence of access to reliable print-to-sound correspondences.

How can deep dyslexia be accommodated by the information-processing model of reading illustrated in Figure 5-1? Several alternative explanations have been proposed. Some investigators have argued that the reading of deep dyslexics is mediated by a damaged form of the left hemisphere–based system employed in normal reading (Caramazza & Hillis, 1990; Morton & Patterson, 1980). On such an account, multiple processing deficits must be hypothesized to accommodate the full range of symptoms characteristic of deep dyslexia. First, the strikingly impaired performance in reading nonwords and other tasks assessing phonologic

function suggest that the print-to-sound conversion procedure is disrupted. Second, the presence of semantic errors and the effects of imageability (a variable thought to influence processing at the level of semantics) suggest that these patients also suffer from a semantic impairment. Last, the production of visual errors suggests that these patients suffer from impairment in the visual word form system or in the processes mediating access of the stimulus to the visual word form system. An alternative account is that the syndrome reflects postsemantic deficits (Caramazza & Hillis, 1990). Buchanan and colleagues (2003) and Colangelo and Buchanan (2007) provide substantial evidence for this hypothesis.

Other investigators (Coltheart, 1980; Saffran et al., 1980) have argued that deep dyslexics' reading is mediated by a system not normally used in reading—that is, the right hemisphere. We will return to the issue of reading with the right hemisphere below.

Although deep dyslexia has occasionally been associated with posterior lesions, the disorder is typically encountered in association with large perisylvian lesions extending into the frontal lobe (Coltheart, Patterson, & Marshall, 1980). As might be expected given the lesion data, deep dyslexia is usually associated with global or Broca's aphasia but may rarely be encountered in patients with fluent aphasia.

PHONOLOGICAL DYSLEXIA: READING WITHOUT PRINT-TO-SOUND CORRESPONDENCES

First described by Derouesne and Beauvois (1979), phonologic dyslexia is, perhaps, the "purest" of the central dyslexias in that the syndrome appears to be attributable to a selective deficit procedure mediating the translation from print to sound. Thus, although in many respects less arresting than deep dyslexia, phonological dyslexia is of considerable theoretical interest (see Coltheart, 1996, for a discussion of this disorder).

Phonologic dyslexia is a relatively mild disorder in which reading of real words may be nearly intact or only mildly impaired. Patients with this disorder, for example, correctly read 85%–95% of real words (Bub et al., 1987;

Funnell, 1983). Some patients with this disorder read all different types of words with equal facility (Bub et al., 1987), whereas other patients are relatively impaired in the reading of functors (Glosser & Friedman, 1990). Unlike patients with surface dyslexia (described below), the regularity of print-to-sound correspondences is not relevant to their performance; thus, phonologic dyslexics are as likely to correctly pronounce orthographically irregular words such as *colonel* as they are words with standard print-to-sound correspondences, such as *administer*. Most errors in response to real words bear a visual similarity to the target word (e.g., *topple* read as "table").

The striking and theoretically relevant aspect of the performance of phonologic dyslexics is a substantial impairment in the oral reading of nonword letter strings. We have examined patients with this disorder, for example, who read more than 90% of real words of all types, yet correctly pronounce only approximately 10% of nonwords. Most errors involve the substitution of a visually similar real word (e.g., *phope* read as "phone") or the incorrect application of print-to-sound correspondences (e.g., *stime* read as "stim" [to rhyme with "him"]).

Within the context of the reading model depicted in Figure 5-1, the account for this disorder is relatively straightforward. Good performance with real words suggests that the processes involved in normal "lexical" reading—that is, visual analysis, the visual word form system, semantics, and the phonological output lexicon—are at least relatively preserved. The impairment in nonword reading suggests that the print-to-sound translation procedure is disrupted.

Explorations of the processes involved in nonword reading have identified a number of distinct procedures involved in this task (Coltheart, 1996). If these distinct procedures may be selectively lesioned by brain injury, one might expect to observe different subtypes of phonologic dyslexia. Although the details are beyond the scope of this chapter, it should be noted that Coltheart (1996) has reviewed evidence suggesting that such subtypes may be observed. A recent review of this issue was provided by Tree (2008).

Some investigators have emphasized the role of a general phonologic deficit in the genesis of

phonological dyslexia (e.g., Crisp & Lambon Ralph, 2006; Farah, Stowe, & Levinson, 1996). Although most patients with this disorder are impaired on a wide range of tasks assessing phonologic processing, a number of otherwise typical and well-studied patients with the disorder do not exhibit phonologic deficits except in reading (Coltheart, 2006; Tree & Kay, 2006). These data argue strongly that phonological dyslexia cannot simply be attributed to a modality independent deficit in phonology that is manifest in reading. As the issue is central to debates regarding computational as opposed to dual-route accounts of dyslexia (see below), the question continues to be controversial.

As noted above, there are numerous similarities between phonological and deep dyslexia; the major difference, of course, is that deep dyslexia is characterized by semantic errors, whereas these are not present in phonological dyslexia. Friedman (1996) noted that as subjects with deep dyslexia recover, they often stop making semantic errors, thereby meeting criteria for phonologic dyslexia (see also Glosser & Friedman, 1990). More recently Crisp and Lambon Ralph (2006) reported data from 12 patients with phonological or deep dyslexia that are consistent with this view. Thus, a number of investigators argue that a continuum exists between deep and phonologic dyslexia, with the former representing a more severe impairment.

Phonologic dyslexia has been observed in association with lesions in a number of sites in the dominant perisylvian cortex, and on occasion, with lesions of the right hemisphere (e.g., Patterson, 1982). Damage to the superior temporal lobe and angular and supramarginal gyri in particular is found in most but not all patients with this disorder. Although quantitative data are lacking, the lesions associated with phonological dyslexia appear, on average, to be smaller than those associated with deep dyslexia.

SURFACE DYSLEXIA: READING WITHOUT LEXICAL ACCESS

Surface dyslexia, first described by Marshall and Newcombe (1973), is a disorder characterized by the inability to read words with "irregular" or exceptional print-to-sound correspondences.

Patients with surface dyslexia are thus unable to read aloud words such as *colonel, yacht, island, have,* and *borough,* the pronunciation of which cannot be derived by sounding-out strategies. In contrast, these patients read words containing regular correspondences (e.g., *state, hand, mosquito, abdominal*), as well as nonwords (e.g., *blape*), quite well.

As noted above, some accounts of normal reading postulate that familiar words are read aloud by matching the letter string to a stored representation of the word and retrieving the pronunciation by means of a mechanism linked to semantics or by means of a "direct" route. A critical point to note is that, as reading involves stored associations of letter strings and sounds, the pronunciation of the word is not computed by rules but is retrieved and, therefore, whether the word contains regular or irregular correspondences does not appear to play a major role in performance.

The fact that the nature of the print-to-sound correspondences significantly influences performance in surface dyslexia demonstrates that the deficit in this syndrome is in the mechanisms mediating lexical reading—that is, in the semantically mediated and "direct" reading procedures. Similarly, the preserved ability to read words and nonwords demonstrates that the procedures by which words are "sounded out" are at least relatively preserved.

What, then, is the level at which the processing impairment giving rise to surface alexia is located? Scrutiny of the model depicted in Figure 5-1 suggests that the lexical mechanisms mediating reading may be disrupted at a number of different levels; thus, for example, surface dyslexia may be associated with disruption of the visual word form system, with a disruption of semantics (in conjunction with a deficit in the "direct" route) (Schwartz, Saffran, & Marin, 1979; Shallice, Warrington, & McCarthy, 1983), or with a lesion involving the phonologic output lexicon (Howard & Franklin, 1987). Using the traditional logic of neuropsychology, the putative locus of the processing disturbance is inferred on the basis of the overall pattern of deficits. Consider the patient described by Marshall and Newcombe (1973), who, in response to the word *listen,* said "Liston" (a former heavyweight champion

boxer) and added "that's the boxer." The fact that the patient knew the word Liston suggests that the problem was not at the semantic level, at which information about the meaning of the word would be stored.

Surface dyslexia is infrequently observed in patients with focal lesions. The disorder is most often encountered in patients with progressive, degenerative dementias. Surface dyslexia is characteristic of semantic dementia, a variant of frontotemporal dementia associated with atrophy that is typically most pronounced in the anterior portions of the temporal lobes, sometimes with a left-sided predominance (Hodges et al., 1992; Woollams et al., 2007; see also, Chapter 17). In this disorder, subjects slowly but inexorably lose knowledge of the world; the severity of the surface dyslexia often parallels the loss of semantic knowledge.

READING AND THE RIGHT HEMISPHERE

One important and controversial issue regarding reading concerns the putative reading capacity of the right hemisphere. For many years, investigators argued that the right hemisphere was "word blind" (Dejerine, 1892; Geschwind, 1965). In recent years, however, several lines of evidence have suggested that the right hemisphere may possess the capacity to read (Coltheart, 1980; Saffran et al., 1980). One seemingly incontrovertible line of evidence comes from the performance of a patient who underwent a left hemispherectomy at age 15 for treatment of seizures caused by Rasmussen's encephalitis (Patterson, Vargha-Khadem, & Polkey, 1989). After the hemispherectomy, the patient was able to read approximately 30% of single words and exhibited an effect of part of speech; she was also utterly unable to use a grapheme-to-phoneme conversion process. Thus, in many respects, this patient's performance was similar to that of acquired deep dyslexia, a pattern of reading impairment that has been hypothesized to reflect the performance of the right hemisphere (Coltheart, 1980; Saffran et al., 1980).

The performance of some split-brain patients is also consistent with the claim that the right hemisphere is literate. These patients may, for example, be able to match printed words presented to the right hemisphere with an appropriate object (Zaidel, 1978; Zaidel & Peters, 1983; see also Chapter 13). Interestingly, the patients are apparently unable to derive sound from the words presented to the right hemisphere; thus, they are unable to determine if a word presented to the right hemisphere rhymes with an auditorally presented word.

Another line of evidence supporting the claim that the right hemisphere is literate comes from the evaluation of the reading of patients with pure alexia and optic aphasia (Coslett & Saffran, 1989a, 1989b). We reported data, for example, from four patients with pure alexia who performed well above chance on a number of lexical decision and semantic categorization tasks with briefly presented words that they could not explicitly identify. Three of the patients who regained the ability to explicitly identify rapidly presented words exhibited a pattern of performance consistent with the right hemisphere reading hypothesis. These patients read nouns better than functors and words of high imageability (e.g., *chair*) better than words of low imageability (e.g., *destiny*). Additionally, both patients for whom data are available demonstrated a deficit in the reading of suffixed (e.g., "eating") as compared to pseudo-suffixed (e.g., "ceiling") words. These data are consistent with a version of the right hemisphere reading hypothesis postulating that the right hemisphere lexical-semantic system primarily represents high-imageability nouns. On this account, functors, affixed words and low-imageability words are not adequately represented in the right hemisphere.

Finally, we reported data from an investigation with a patient with pure alexia whose recovered reading was disrupted by transcranial magnetic stimulation (TMS) to the right but not the left hemisphere (Coslett & Monsul, 1994). This pattern of performance is, of course, consistent with the hypothesis that the right hemisphere is capable of mediating reading.

Although a consensus has not yet been achieved, there is mounting evidence that, at least for some people, the right hemisphere is not word-blind, but may support the reading of some types of words. The full extent of this reading capacity and whether it is relevant to normal reading, however, remains unclear. A comprehensive account of the role of the right hemisphere in reading and other language abilities has recently been published by Lindell (2006).

Finally, we note that functional imaging studies in subjects with acquired (Coltheart, 2000; Price et al., 1998; Weekes, Coltheart, & Gordon, 1997) and developmental (Pitchfort et al., 2007) deep dyslexia have suggested that the right hemisphere may support reading.

COMPUTATIONAL MODELS OF READING

Our discussion to this point has focused on an information processing or "verbal model" account of reading disorders. In recent years, fundamentally different types of reading models have been proposed. One account, originally developed by Seidenberg and McClelland (1989) and subsequently elaborated by Plaut (1997), as well as by Harm and Seidenberg (2004) belongs to the general class of *parallel distributed processing* or *connectionist* models. These models differ from information processing accounts in that they do not incorporate word-specific representations (e.g., visual word forms, output phonologic representations). On this account, subjects are assumed to learn how written words map onto spoken words through repeated exposure to familiar and unfamiliar words. Learning of word pronunciations is achieved by means of the development of a mapping between letters and sounds generated on the basis of experience with many different letter strings. The probabilistic mapping between letters and sounds is assumed to provide the means by which both familiar and unfamiliar words are pronounced. This model not only accommodates many of the classic findings in the literature on normal reading but has been "lesioned" in an attempt to reproduce the patterns of reading impairment characteristic of surface (Patterson, Seidenberg, & McClelland, 1989; Rogers et al., 2004; Woollams et al., 2007) and deep dyslexia (Plaut & Shallice, 1993). The adequacy of these simulations remains a topic of substantial debate. Coltheart (2006) has recently argued that "lesioned" versions of these models do not faithfully reproduce the pattern of deficits observed in phonological or surface dyslexia, whereas Woollams et al. (2007) provide compelling evidence that the "triangle" connectionist model accommodates many aspects of the performance of surface dyslexia exhibited by patients with semantic dementia. Welbourne and Ralph (2007) recently reported an attempt to model phonologic dyslexia with the triangle connectionist model. Reasoning that the performance of subjects with acquired dyslexia reflects not only the effect of the lesion but also the effects of recovery, they retrained a lesioned version of the Plaut et al. (1996) connectionist model; they argue that "recovery" of the network was crucial and that it was only when this plasticity-related recovery was implemented computationally that the pattern of deficits characteristic of phonological dyslexia was observed.

An alternative computational account of reading has been developed by Coltheart and colleagues (Coltheart, 2005; Coltheart & Rastle, 1994; Rastle & Coltheart, 1999). The *dual-route cascaded* or DRC model represents a computationally instantiated version of the dual-route theory presented in Figure 5-1. This "localist" (as opposed to "distributed") account incorporates a lexical route (similar to "C" in Figure 5-1), as well as a nonlexical route by which the pronunciation of graphemes is computed on the basis of position-specific correspondence rules. Like the parallel distributed processing model described above, the DRC model accommodates a wide range of findings from the literature on normal reading. For example, Coltheart and colleagues (Coltheart, 2005; Coltheart et al., 2001) demonstrated that the DRC model incorporating distinct but interactive lexical and nonlexical routes generates quantitative predictions regarding reading that have been supported in studies involving young normal readers, children with developmental dyslexia, and children with stroke. More recently, Rapcsak et al. (2007) extended this work to a heterogeneous but well-studied group of adults with acquired dyslexia. They found that an equation derived from dual-route theory that includes information about reading

of nonwords and irregular words accurately predicts overall reading performance. Finally, Nickels et al. (2008) reported successful simulations of the data from three subjects with phonological dyslexia with the DRC model. Interestingly, no single lesion generated adequate simulations for all three subjects; consistent with the basic principle that different sites of pathology are likely to generate different processing deficits, different types of "lesions" to the model were required to reproduce the specific pattern of deficits exhibited by the different patients.

A computationally instantiated model of reading aloud, based on Glushko's *reading by analogy*" hypothesis, has also been developed (Dampert et al., 1999). On this account, there is a single procedure for deriving the pronunciation of letter strings that is based on analogy to familiar words (Baron, 1977; Glushko, 1979; Kay & Marcel, 1981). This account proposes that, when confronted with the nonword "paze," subjects generate a response that rhymes with gaze because the letter string "-aze" has a single phonological instantiation in English; when presented the letter string "tave," in contrast, subjects are both slower to respond and more variable, as the "-ave" letter string has multiple phonological instantiations in English words (e.g., have vs. gave). Marchand and Friedman (2005) recently demonstrated that a computationally implemented version of the analogy account can be lesioned to account for the data of two dyslexic subjects with unusual patterns of performance. The debate regarding the relative merits of these and other (Van Orden et al., 1997) reading models continues.

ASSESSMENT OF READING

As previously noted, the specific types of dyslexia are distinguished on the basis of performance with different types of stimuli. For example, deep dyslexia is characterized by impaired performance on nonwords, an effect of part of speech, such that nouns are read better than modifiers or functors, and an effect of imageability, such that words denoting more abstract objects or concepts are read less well than are words of high imageability. The assessment of patients with dyslexia should include stimuli varying along the dimensions discussed below.

The effect of imageability or concreteness should be assessed by presenting words of high (e.g., *desk, frog, mountain*) and low (e.g., *fate, universal, ambiguous*) imageability. Part of speech should be assessed by presenting nouns (e.g., *table, meatloaf*), modifiers (e.g., *beautiful, early*), verbs (e.g., *ambulate, thrive*), and functors (e.g., *because, their*). The effect of orthographic regularity should be assessed by presenting regular words that can be "sounded out" (e.g., *flame, target*) and irregular words that cannot (e.g., *come, tomb*). The ability to "sound out" words is also assessed by presenting nonword letter strings that may either sound like a real word (e.g., *phish*) or not (e.g., *blape*).

As word frequency is typically an important determinant of performance, a wide range of word frequencies should also be employed. Finally, in order to obtain a reliable assessment of performance, testing should include at least ten words of each of the stimulus types noted above. The compilation of the appropriate lists of stimuli may be time-consuming; consequently, many investigators employ published word lists, some of which are commercially available (Kay, Lesser, & Coltheart, 1996).

TREATMENT

Finally, it should be noted that there is an emerging literature on the treatment of acquired reading disorders. Whereas there is no widely recognized and effective treatment for any of the acquired dyslexias, there have been a number of reports of theoretically motivated interventions that appear to offer promise (see Leff & Behrmann, 2008, for a recent review).

ACKNOWLEDGMENTS

This work was supported by the National Institute of Deafness and Other Communication Disorders (RO1 DC2754).

REFERENCES

Allport, D. A., & Funnell, E. (1981). Components of the mental lexicon. *Philosophical Transactions of the Royal Society of London B, 295,* 397–410.

Arduino, L. S., Vallar, G., & Burani, C. (2006). Left neglect dyslexia and the effect of stimulus duration. *Neuropsychologia, 44,* 662–665.

Baron, J. (1977). Mechanisms for pronouncing printed words: Use and acquisition. In D. LaBerge, & S. Samuels (Eds.), *Basic processes in reading: Perception and comprehension* (pp. 175–216). Hillsdale, NJ: Lawrence Erlbaum Associates.

Behrman, M., Moscovitch, M., Black, S. E., & Mozer, M. (1990). Perceptual and conceptual mechanisms in neglect dyslexia. *Brain, 113,* 1163–1183.

Behrmann, N., Plaut, D. C., & Nelson, J. (1998). A literature review and new data supporting an interactive account of letter-by-letter reading. *Cognitive Neuropsychology, 15,* 7–52.

Binder, J. R., & Mohr, J. P. (1994). The topography of callosal reading pathways: A case control analysis. *Brain, 115,* 1807–1826.

Bub, D., & Arguin, M. (1995). Visual word activation in pure alexia. *Brain and Language, 49,* 77–103.

Bub, D., Black, S. E., Howell, J., & Kertesz, A. (1987). Speech output processes and reading. In M. Coltheart, G. Sartori, & R. Job (Eds.), *Cognitive neuropsychology of language.* Hillsdale, NJ: Erlbaum.

Buchanan, L., McEwen, S., Westbury, C., & Libben, G. (2003). Semantic and semantic error: Implicit access to semantic information from words and nonwords in deep dyslexia. *Brain and Language* (Special Issue: Meaning in Language), *84,* 65–83.

Buxbaum, L. J., & Coslett, H. B. (1996): Deep dyslexic phenomenon in pure alexia. *Brain and Language, 54,* 136–167.

Caramazza, A., & Hillis, A. E. (1990). Where do semantic errors come from? *Cortex, 26,* 95–122.

Chailant, D., & Caramazza, A. (1996): Perceptual and lexical factors in a case of letter-by-letter reading. *Cognitive Neuropsychology, 15,* 167–202.

Cheung. R.W., Cheung, M., & Chan, A. S. (2004). Confrontation naming in Chinese patients with left, right or bilateral brain damage. *Journal of the International Neuropsychological Society, 10,* 46–53.

Colangelo, A., & Buchanan, L. (2007): Localizing damage in the functional architecture: The distinction between implicit and explicit processing in deep dyslexia. *Journal of Neurolinguistics*, *20*, 111–144.

Coltheart, M. (1980). Deep dyslexia: A right hemisphere hypothesis. In M. Coltheart, K. Patterson, & J. C. Marshall (Eds.), *Deep Dyslexia* (pp. 326–380). London: Routledge and Kegan Paul.

Coltheart, M. (1996). Phonological dyslexia: Past and future issues. *Cognitive Neuropsychology*, *13*, 749–762.

Coltheart, M. (2000). Deep dyslexia is right-hemisphere reading. *Brain and Language*, *71*, 299–309.

Coltheart, M. (2005). Modelling reading: The dual route approach. In M. J. Snowling, & C. Hulme (Eds.), *The science of reading*. Oxford, UK: Blackwell Publishing.

Coltheart, M. (2006). Acquired dyslexias and the computational modeling of reading. *Cognitive Neuropsychology*, *23*, 96–109.

Coltheart, M., Patterson, K., & Marshall, J. C. (Eds.). (1980). *Deep Dyslexia*. London: Routledge and Kegan Paul.

Coltheart, M., & Rastle, K. (1994). Serial processing in reading aloud: Evidence for dual-route models of reading. *Journal of Experimental Psychology: Human Perception and Performance*, *20*, 1197–1211.

Coltheart, M., Rastle, K., Perry, C., Langdon, R., & Ziegler, J. (2001). DRC: A dual route cascaded model of visual word recognition and reading aloud. *Psychological Review*, *108*, 204–256.

Coslett, H. B. (1991). Read but not write "idea": Evidence for a third reading mechanism. *Brain and Language*, *40*, 425–443.

Coslett, H. B., & Monsul, N. (1994). Reading and the right hemisphere: Evidence from transcranial magnetic stimulation. *Brain and Language*, *46*, 198–211.

Coslett, H. B., & Saffran, E. M. (1989a). Evidence for preserved reading in pure alexia. *Brain*, *112*, 327–359.

Coslett, H. B., & Saffran, E. M. (1989b). Preserved object identification and reading comprehension in optic aphasia. *Brain*, *112*, 1091–1110.

Crisp, J., & Lambon Ralph, M. A. (2006). Unlocking the nature of the phonological-deep dyslexia continuum: The keys to reading aloud are in phonology and semantics. *Journal of Cognitive Neuroscience*, *18*, 348–362.

Crutch, S. J., & Warrington, E. K. (2007). Foveal crowding in posterior cortical atrophy: A specific early-visual-processing deficit affecting word reading. *Cognitive Neuropsychology*, *24*, 843–866.

Damasio, A., & Damasio, H. (1983). The anatomic basis of pure alexia. *Neurology*, *33*, 1573–1583.

Damper, R. I., Marchand, Y., Adamson, M. J., & Gustafson, K. (1999). Evaluating the pronunciation component of text-to-speech systems for English: A performance comparison of different approaches. *Computer Speech and Language*, *13*, 155–176.

Dejerine, J. (1891). Sur en case de cecite verbal avec agraphie, suivi d'autopsie. *Compte Rendu des Seances de la Societe de Biologie*, *3*, 197–201.

Dejerine, J. (1892). Contribution a l'etude anatomo-pathologique et clinique des differentes varietes de cecite verbale. *Compte Rendu des Seances de la Societe de Biologie*, *4*, 61–90.

Derouesne, J., & Beauvois, M. -F. (1979). Phonological processing in reading: Data from Dyslexia. *Journal of Neurology, Neurosurgery and Psychiatry*, *42*, 1125–1132.

Epelbaum, S., Pinel, P., Gaillard, R., Delmaire, C., Perrin, M., Dupont, S., et al. (2008). Pure alexia as a disconnection syndrome: New diffusion imaging evidence for an old concept. *Cortex*, *44*, 962–974.

Farah, M. J., Stowe, R. M., & Levinson, K. L. (1996). Phonological dyslexia: Loss of a reading-specific component of the cognitive architecture? *Cognitive Neuropsychology*, *13*, 849–868.

Farah, M. J., & Wallace, M. A. (1991). Pure alexia as a visual impairment: A reconsideration. *Cognitive Neuropsychology*, *8*, 313–334.

Ferreres, A. R., & Cuitiño Olmedo, A. (2005). Acquired surface alexia in Spanish: A case report. *Behavioural Neurology*, *16*, 71–84.

Freund, D. C. (1889). Uber optische aphasia und seelenblindheit. *Archiv Psychiatrie und Nervenkrankheiten*, *20*, 276–297.

Friedman, R. B. (1996). Recovery from deep alexia to phonological alexia: Points on a continuum. *Brain and Language*, *52*, 114–128.

Funnell, E. (1983). Phonological processes in reading: New evidence from acquired dyslexia. *British Journal of Psychology*, *74*, 159–180.

Geschwind, N. (1965). Disconnection syndromes in animals and man. *Brain*, *88*, 237–294, 585–644.

Geschwind, N., & Fusillo, M. (1966). Color-naming defects in association with alexia. *Archives of Neurology*, *15*, 137–146.

Glosser, G., & Friedman, R. (1990). The continuum of deep/phonological dyslexia. *Cortex*, *25*, 343–359.

Glushko, R. J. (1979). The organization and activation of orthographic knowledge in reading aloud. *Journal of Experimental Psychology: Human Perception and Performance*, *5*, 674–691.

Greenblatt, S. H. (1976). Subangular alexia without agraphia or hemianopsia. *Brain and Language*, 3, 229–245.

Harm, M. W., & Weidenberg, M. S. (2004). Computing the meaning of words in reading: Cooperative division of labor between visual and phonological processes. *Psychological Review*, 111, 662–720.

Hodges, J. R., Patterson, K., Oxbury, S., & Funnell, E. (1992). Semantic dementia: Progressive fluent aphasia with temporal lobe atrophy. *Brain*, 115, 1783–1806.

Howard, D., & Franklin, S. (1987). Three ways for understanding written words, and their use in two contrasting cases of surface dyslexia (together with an odd routine for making "orthographic" errors in oral word production). In A. Allport, D. Mackay, W. Prinz, & Scheerer, E. (Eds.), *Language Perception and Production*. New York: Academic Press.

Kay, J., Lesser, R., & Coltheart, M. (1996). Psycholinguistic assessments of language processing in aphasia: An introduction. *Aphasiology*, 10, 159–180.

Kay, J., & Marcel, A. (1981). One process, not two, in reading aloud. *Quarterly Journal of Experimental Psychology*, 33A, 397–413.

Ladavas, E., Shallice, T., & Zanella, M. T. (1997). Preserved semantic access in neglect dyslexia. *Neuropsychologia*, 35, 257–270.

Landis, T., Regard, M., & Serrat, A. (1980). Iconic reading in a case of alexia without agraphia caused by a brain tumor: A tachistoscopic study. *Brain and Language*, 11, 45–53.

Law, S., Wong, W., & Chiu, K. M. Y. (2009). Preserved reading aloud with semantic deficits: Evidence for a non-semantic lexical route for reading Chinese. *Neurocase*, 11, 167–175.

Law, S., Wong, W., & Kong, A. (2006). Direct access from meaning to orthography in Chinese: A case study of superior written to oral naming. *Aphasiology*, 20, 565–578.

Leff, A. P., & Behrmann, M. (2008). Treatment of reading impairment after stroke. *Current Opinion in Neurology*, 21, 644–648.

Liepmann, H., & Maas, O. (1907). Fall von linksseitiger Agraphie und Apraxie bei reshsseitiger Lahmung. *Z Psychology Neurology*, 10, 214–227.

Lindell, A. K. (2006). In your right mind: Right hemisphere contributions to language processing and production. *NeuroPsychological Review*, 16, 131–148.

Marchand, Y., Friedman, R. B. (2005). Impaired oral reading in two atypical dyslexics: A comparison with a computational lexical-analogy model. *Brain and Language*, 93, 255–266.

Marshall, J. C., & Newcombe, F. (1966). Syntactic and semantic errors in paralexia. *Neuropsychologia*, 4, 169–176.

Marshall, J. C., & Newcombe, F. (1973). Patterns of paralexia: A psycholinguistic approach. *Journal of Psycholinguistic Research*, 2, 175–199.

Morton, J., & Patterson, K. E. (1980). A new attempt at an interpretation, or, an attempt at a new interpretation. In M. Coltheart, K. Patterson, & J. C. Marshall (Eds.), *Deep Dyslexia* (pp. 91–118). London: Routledge and Kegan Paul.

Nickels, L., Biedermann, B., Coltheart, M., & Saunders, S. (2008). Computational modeling of phonological dyslexia: How does the DRC model fare? *Cognitive Neuropsychology*, 25, 165–193.

Patterson, K. (1982). The relation between reading and phonological coding: Further neuropsychological observations. In A. W. Ellis (Ed.), *Normality and pathology in cognitive functions*. London: Academic Press.

Patterson, K., & Kay, J. (1982). Letter-by-letter reading: Psychological descriptions of a neurological syndrome. *Quarterly Journal of Experimental Psychology*, 34A, 411–441.

Patterson, K. E., Seidenberg, M. S., & McClelland, J. L. (1989). Connections and disconnections: Acquired dyslexia in a computational model of reading processes. In R. G. M. Morris (Ed.), *Parallel Distributed Processing: Implications for psychology and neurobiology*. Oxford: Oxford University Press.

Patterson, K., Vargha-Khadem, F., & Polkey, C. F. (1989). Reading with one hemisphere. *Brain*, 112, 39–63.

Petrich, J. A. F., Greenwald, M. L., & Berndt, R. S. (2007). An investigation of attentional contributions to visual errors in right "neglect dyslexia." *Cortex*, 43, 1036–1046.

Pflugshaupt, T., Gutbrod, K., Wurtz, P., von Wartburg, R., Nyffeler, T., de Haan, B., et al. (2009). About the role of visual field deficits in pure alexia. *Brain*, 132, 1907–1917.

Plaut, D. C. (1997). Structure and function in the lexical system: Insights from distributed models of word reading and lexical decision. *Language and Cognitive Processes*, 12, 765–805.

Plaut, D. C., McClelland, J. L., Seidenberg, M. S., & Patterson, K. (1996). Understanding normal and impaired word reading: Computational principles in quasi-regular domains. *Psychological Review*, 103, 56–115.

Plaut, D. C., & Shallice, T. (1993). Deep dyslexia: A case study in connectionist neuropsychology. *Cognitive Neuropsychology*, 10, 377–500.

Price, C. J., Howard, D., Patterson, K., Warburton, E. A., Friston, K. J., & Frackowiak, R. S. J. (1998). A functional neuroimaging description of two deep dyslexic patients. *Journal of Cognitive Neuroscience, 10,* 303–315.

Price, C. J., & Humphreys, G. W. (1993). Attentional dyslexia: The effect of co-occurring deficits. *Cognitive Neuropsychology, 10,* 569–592.

Raman, I., & Weekes, B. S. (2005). Acquired dyslexia in a Turkish-English speaker. *Annals of Dyslexia, 55,* 79–104.

Rapcsak, S. Z., Henry, M. L., Teague, S. L., Carnahan, S. D., & Beeson, P. M. (2007). Do dual-route models accurately predict reading and spelling performance in individuals with acquired alexia and agraphia? *Neuropsychologia, 45,* 2519–2524.

Rastle, K., & Coltheart, M. (1999). Serial and strategic effects in reading aloud. *Journal of Experimental Psychology: Human Perception and Performance, 25,* 482–503.

Rogers, T. T., Lambon Ralph, M. A., Garrard, P., Bozeat, S., McClelland, J. L., Hodges, J. R., & Patterson, K. (2004). Structure and deterioration of semantic memory: A neuropsychological and computational investigation. *Psychological Review, 111,* 205–235.

Rosazza, C., Appollonio, I., Isella, V., & Shallice, T. (2007). Qualitatively different forms of pure alexia. *Cognitive Neuropsychology, 24,* 393–418.

Saffran, E. M., Bogyo, L. C., Schwartz, M. F., & Marin, O. S. M. (1980). Does deep dyslexia reflect right-hemisphere reading? In M. Coltheart, K. Patterson, J. C. Marshall (Eds.), *Deep Dyslexia* (pp. 381–406). London: Routledge and Kegan Paul.

Saffran, E. M., & Coslett, H. B. (1996). Attentional dyslexia in Alzheimer's disease: A case study. *Cognitive Neuropsychology, 13,* 205–228.

Saffran, E. M., & Coslett, H. B. (1998). Implicit vs. letter-by-letter reading in pure alexia: A tale of two systems. *Cognitive Neuropsychology, 15,* 141–166.

Saffran, E. M., & Marin, O. S. M. (1977). Reading without phonology: Evidence from aphasia. *Quarterly Journal of Experimental Psychology, 29,* 515–525.

Sato, H., Patterson, K., Fushimi, T., Maxim, J., & Bryan, K. (2008). Deep dyslexia for kanji and phonological dyslexia for kana: Different manifestations from a common source. *Neurocase, 14,* 508–524.

Schwartz, M. F., Saffran, E. M., & Marin, O. S. M. (1979). Dissociation of language function in dementia: A case study. *Brain and Language, 7,* 277–306.

Seidenberg, M. S., & McClelland, J. L. (1989). A distributed, developmental model of word recognition and naming. *Psychological Review, 96,* 523–568.

Shallice, T. (1987). *From neuropsychology to mental structure.* Cambridge: Cambridge Univ. Press.

Shallice, T., & Saffran, E. M. (1986). Lexical processing in the absence of explicit word identification: Evidence from a letter-by-letter reader. *Cognitive Neuropsychology, 3,* 429–458.

Shallice, T., & Warrington, E. K. (1980). Single and multiple component central dyslexic syndromes. In M. Coltheart, K. Patterson, J. C. Marshall (Eds.), *Deep dyslexia* (pp. 119–145). London: Routledge and Kegan Paul.

Shallice, T., Warrington, E. K., & McCarthy, R. (1983). Reading without semantics. *Quarterly Journal of Experimental Psychology, 35A,* 111–138.

Sieroff, E., Pollatsek, A., & Posner, M. (1988). Recognition of visual letter strings following injury to the posterior visual spatial attention system. *Cognitive Neuropsychology, 5,* 427–449.

Tree, J. J. (2008). Two types of phonological dyslexia– A contemporary review. *Cortex, 44,* 698–706.

Tree, J. J., & Kay, J. (2006). Phonological dyslexia and phonological impairment: An exception to the rule? *Neuropsychologia, 44,* 2861–2873.

Van Orden, G. C., Jansen op de Haar, M. A., & Bosman, A. M. (1997). Complex dynamic systems also predict dissociations but they do not reduce to autonomous components. *Cognitive Neuropsychology, 14,* 131–165.

Warrington, E. K., Cipolotti, L., & McNeal, J. (1993). Attentional dyslexia: A single case study. *Neuropsychologia, 31,* 871–885.

Warrington, E., & Shallice, T. (1980). Word-form dyslexia. *Brain, 103,* 99–112.

Weekes, B., Coltheart, M., & Gordon, E. (1997). Deep dyslexia and the right-hemisphere reading–a regional cerebral blood flow study. *Aphasiology, 11,* 1139–1158.

Welbourne, S. R., & Lambon Ralph, M. A. (2007). Using parallel distributed processing models to simulate phonological dyslexia: The key role of plasticity-related recovery. *Journal of Cognitive Neuroscience, 19,* 1125–1139.

Woollams, A. M., Ralph, M. A. L., Plaut, D. C., & Patterson, K. (2007). SD-Squared: On the association between semantic dementia and surface dyslexia. *Psychological Review, 114,* 316–339.

Yin, W., He, S., & Weekes, B. S. (2005). Acquired dyslexia and dysgraphia in Chinese. *Behavioural Neurology, 16*, 159–167.

Zaidel, E. (1978). Lexical organization in the right hemisphere. In P. Buser, & A. Rougeul-Buser (Eds.), *Cerebral correlates of conscious experience* (pp. 177–197). Amsterdam: Elsevier.

Zaidel, E., & Peters, A. M. (1983). Phonological encoding and ideographic reading by the disconnected right hemisphere: Two case studies. *Brain and Language, 14*, 205–234.

6

Agraphia

LAUREN ULLRICH AND DAVID P. ROELTGEN

Benedikt(1865) applied the term *agraphia* to disorders of writing in 1865. Ogle (1867) found that, although aphasia and agraphia usually occur together, they were separable. He concluded that there were distinct cerebral centers for writing and speaking that were anatomically proximate. In contrast, Lichtheim (1885) proposed that disorders of writing usually were the same as disorders of speech. The exception was agraphia due to disruption of the "center from which the organs of writing are innervated. (pg 437)" Lichtheim proposed that agraphia and aphasia were similar because the acquisition of writing (and spelling) was superimposed on speech, and therefore utilized previously acquired speech centers. Head (1926) also stressed this relationship. Goldstein (1948) emphasized two types of agraphia: primary agraphia resulting from disruption of the motor act of writing, and secondary agraphia, resulting from disturbances of speech.

Nielson's classification (1946) reflected his view that writing is closely associated with speech, but functionally and anatomically separable from it (a view similar to Ogle's). Nielson described three types of agraphia: apractic (apraxic), aphasic, and isolated. Apractic agraphia was characterized by poorly formed letters and was associated with limb apraxia.

Aphasic agraphia was a reflection of a co-occurring aphasic disturbance. Isolated agraphia occurred without associated neuropsychological signs and resulted from a lesion of the frontal writing center (Exner's area). Nielson thought that isolated agraphias were rare. He suggested that both functional and anatomic connections accounted for the frequent association of agraphia and aphasia.

Classifications of agraphia up until the late 1970s continued in this vein, focusing on the relationships between agraphia and other cognitive and linguistic faculties. Leischner (1969), Hecaen and Albert (1978), Benson (1979), and Kaplan and Goodglass (1981), who derived their classifications from clinical evaluations of agraphic patients, used a taxonomic approach, generally distinguishing five types of agraphia: pure agraphia, aphasic agraphia, agraphia with alexia (also called *parietal agraphia*; Kaplan & Goodglass, 1981), apraxic agraphia, and spatial agraphia. More recent analyses of agraphia differ from these approaches in that they focus on questions of spelling processes and representations. Information-processing (IP) or cognitive neuropsychological models are most often used to represent the results obtained by this approach.

NEUROPSYCHOLOGICAL MODELS OF WRITING

In the last three decades, IP or cognitive neuropsychological models containing two apparently dissociable systems have been proposed to explain the ability to write (and spell aloud; Ellis, 1982; Margolin, 1984; Roeltgen, 1985; Roeltgen & Heilman, 1985; Patterson, 1986; Lesser, 1990; Rapcsak & Rubens, 1990; Roeltgen & Rapcsak, 1993). These models contain many similar cognitive components, although the terms used to describe the components and the subtleties of functional capacities among them often differ. Attempts have also been made to determine brain regions important for these cognitive functions (Henry et al., 2007; Roeltgen & Heilman, 1985; Roeltgen & Rapcsak, 1993; Rapcsak et al., 2008).

Some authors have argued that a modular model is not the best representation of brain function (Harm & Seidenberg, 2004; Plaut et al., 1996; Seidenberg & McClelland, 1989). An alternative approach, the use of distributed network (connectionist) models, has been proposed to better mimic cognitive processing. The debate is theoretically important and will be addressed later in the chapter. However, the clinical utility of the IP models is such that it will be emphasized.

For convenience, this chapter will refer to the general output of both writing and oral spelling systems as "spelling." "Writing" will refer to written production (handwriting) and "oral spelling" will refer to oral production.

DUAL-ROUTE MODEL

Linguistic Components

There are at least two routes adults can use to spell words. The *lexical* route (also called lexical-orthographic or orthographic; Figure 6-1, components 4-5-6), processes words holistically, by accessing a store of learned word forms (the orthographic output lexicon). The lexical route therefore cannot process unfamiliar or nonwords, since there are no stored representations of these words, but is able to process words with irregular (for example, "calm") or inconsistent/ambiguous spellings (for example, "phone") in addition to regular words. The *nonlexical* route (or sublexical or phonological) (Figure 6-1, components 7-8-9) processes words on a subword level, fractionating them into phonological component and then converting them into graphemes. One way that this may occur is through what has been termed *sublexical sound-letter* or *phoneme-grapheme* conversion. It has been suggested, however, that the phonological system is lexically based and spells unknown words by analogy to known words (Campbell, 1985). Regardless of mechanism, the nonlexical route can process unfamiliar regular words and nonwords, but cannot correctly process irregular words. Although there is debate about how the outputs from these two systems compete or interact to produce a single spelling (Ward, 2003), it is probable that the lexical system dominates the output unless it is dysfunctional or there is no available lexical item for the word that is to be spelled (e.g. an unfamiliar word).

Evidence in support of these two routes comes from studies of patients whose spelling of irregular and nonwords dissociate. Dysfunction in the nonlexical route results in *phonological agraphia*. These patients have an impaired ability to spell nonwords, but the spelling of regular and irregular words is intact. Dysfunction in the lexical route results in *lexical agraphia*, which is characterized by an inability to spell irregular words, although regular and nonword spelling remains relatively preserved.

PHONOLOGICAL AGRAPHIA

As mentioned, damage to the nonlexical route is manifest as phonological agraphia. This disorder is characterized by impaired ability to spell nonwords and preserved ability to spell familiar words, both regular and irregular. Spelling errors by patients with phonological agraphia are usually phonologically incorrect. They may have a high degree of visual resemblance to the stimulus, thus supporting a role of visual word images in the lexical system (Roeltgen et al., 1983a).

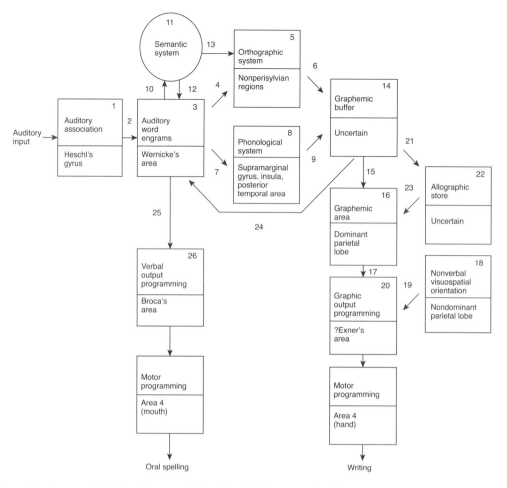

Figure 6–1. An anatomically based neuropsychological model of writing and spelling.

Roeltgen and colleagues (Roeltgen et al., 1982; Roeltgen et al., 1983a; Roeltgen & Heilman, 1984) originally proposed that the anatomic basis of phonological agraphia was the supramarginal gyrus or the insula medial to it. Subsequent studies have demonstrated that lesions occurring within other perisylvian regions may also result in phonological agraphia (Alexander et al., 1992; Baxter & Warrington, 1986; Bolla-Wilson et al., 1985; Bub & Kertesz, 1982; Henry et al., 2007; Kim et al., 2002; Nolan & Caramazza, 1982; Rapcsak et al., 2008; Rapcsak & Beeson, 2002; Roeltgen, 1989; Shallice, 1981). The reason for this heterogeneity is not known, but may be due to functional diversity, as well as to known individual variations in cerebral architecture and functional representation (Henry et al., 2007).

Co-occurrence with Other Neuropsychological Disorders

Phonological agraphia frequently co-occurs with aphasia; of 21 reported patients with phonological agraphia (Baxter & Warrington, 1985; Bolla-Wilson et al., 1985; Bub & Kertesz, 1982; Goodman-Schulman & Caramazza, 1987; Hatfield, 1985; Roeltgen, 1983; Roeltgen et al., 1983a; Roeltgen & Heilman, 1984; Shallice, 1981), 19 had aphasia, typically those types that occur with perisylvian lesions. Although phonological agraphia is commonly associated with aphasia, as noted by Nielson, this disorder may be dissociated from aphasia, and in aphasic patients, the pattern of writing disturbance may be different from the pattern of speech disturbance (Assal et al., 1981; Balasubramanian, 2005; Nielson, 1946; Roeltgen et al., 1983a).

Similarly, phonological alexia (dyslexia), shares many characteristics with phonological agraphia, specifically, an inability to transcode nonwords. Roeltgen and colleagues (1983a) and Roeltgen and Heilman (1984) studied four patients with phonological agraphia. Although one patient had no alexia, and one had lexical (or surface) alexia, two had phonological alexia. This suggests that, in some patients, phonological agraphia and phonological alexia may be related, and may share neuropsychological mechanisms that mediate the conversion between phonemes and graphemes. A single lesion affecting this conversion mechanism would disrupt both phonological spelling and reading, but lesions that disrupt information as it enters or exits the conversion system would affect either reading or writing in isolation.

LEXICAL (SURFACE) AGRAPHIA

Damage in the lexical route is manifest as lexical agraphia. These patients are unable to spell irregular words, although regular and nonword spelling is relatively preserved. This set of symptoms has also been termed *surface agraphia* (Behrmann, 1987; de Partz et al., 1992). Beauvois and Derouesne (1981) were the first to describe lexical agraphia. Since then, other cases have been reported (Alexander et al., 1990; Friedman & Alexander, 1989; Goodman-Shulman & Caramazza, 1987; Hatfield & Patterson, 1983; Croisile et al., 1989; Rapcsak et al., 1988, 1990; Rapp et al., 2002; Roeltgen & Heilman, 1984; Roeltgen & Rapcsak, 1993). Although the lexical route (and thus irregular word spelling) is impaired, regular and nonword spelling are relatively spared because the nonlexical route can be used. Accordingly, these patients usually spell phonologically, making regularization errors on irregular words (yacht →YAT).

Roeltgen and Heilman (1984) were the first to attempt delineation of the anatomy underlying lexical agraphia. They argued that the junction

of the posterior angular gyrus and the parieto-occipital lobule is an important anatomic substrate for lexical agraphia. Subsequent studies have demonstrated that cortical or subcortical lesions that are outside the perisylvian region are most commonly associated with lexical agraphia (Alexander et al., 1990; Croisile et al., 1989; Rapcsak & Beeson, 2004; Rapcsak et al., 1988; Roeltgen & Rapcsak, 1993; Roeltgen, 1989; Rothi et al., 1987).

Functional imaging studies also support the existence of separate phonological and lexical systems. Areas outside the perisylvian region are activated when normal spellers spell known words (Beeson et al., 2003), a task that can be mediated by the lexical route. Activation in the perisylvian region occurs when spelling nonwords (Rapcsak et al., 2008), a task that requires the phonological route.

Although the studies discussed above were performed in participants who wrote in English, similar dual-route models have been applied to other Western languages. The presence of kanji (morphograms) and kana (phonograms) has enabled Japanese investigators to develop similar dual-route models (Iwata, 1984; Nakamura et al., 2002; Sakurai et al., 1997; Soma et al., 1989).

One issue that has been infrequently investigated is whether lexical agraphia can occur in transparent languages that have regular orthography without irregular words, such as Italian. Luzzi and colleagues (2003) studied a patient with a degenerative disorder. Their patient inserted inappropriate apostrophes into words, consistent with the loss of orthographic knowledge. More striking was a study by Luzzatti and colleagues (1998), who evaluated 54 aphasic Italian subjects and showed that 18 of them displayed a pattern of lexical agraphia with good spelling of nonwords but phonologically plausible errors on words with ambiguous phoneme-to-grapheme transcription, as well as irregular words borrowed from other languages.

Co-occurrence with Other Neuropsychological Disorders

Lexical agraphia is frequently associated with aphasia. As is the case with phonological agraphia, the associations of lexical agraphia with aphasia appear to depend on the underlying pathological anatomy of the syndromes. Lexical agraphia, a disorder that frequently is caused by lesions of structures outside the perisylvian region, is associated with aphasic disorders caused by lesions outside the perisylvian region (Roeltgen & Rapcsak, 1993).

There are also reports of lexical agraphia co-occurring with alexia. This can be explained because disrupted flow of information out of the orthographic lexicon would produce lexical agraphia, and disrupted flow into this lexicon would produce lexical (surface) alexia. Dysfunction of the system itself would produce both lexical agraphia and alexia.

Lexical agraphia also frequently co-occurs with Gerstmann syndrome. Given that angular gyrus lesions cause Gerstmann syndrome and ideomotor apraxia (Gerstmann, 1940; Nielson, 1938; Roeltgen et al., 1983b), it is not unexpected that lexical agraphia, a disorder commonly due to angular gyrus lesions, occurs with the three other signs of Gerstmann syndrome.

SEMANTIC AGRAPHIA

Degradation of semantic-conceptual networks (Figure 6-1, component 11), or a disconnection of semantics from the lexical system used in spelling (Figure 6-1, component 13), is a specific form of dysfunction in the lexical route that has been termed *semantic agraphia* (Roeltgen et al., 1986). This term has not found consistent use: Some patients with semantic impairments are still diagnosed as having surface agraphia (Macoir & Bernier, 2002), but there is a distinction between lexical and semantic impairments.

Patients with semantic agraphia lose their ability to spell and write with meaning. They may produce semantic jargon when writing a sentence (Rapcsak & Rubens, 1990). Also, they write and orally spell semantically incorrect but correctly spelled dictated homophones. For example, when asked to write "doe" as in "the doe ran through the forest," these patients may write "dough." They may write nonwords and irregular words correctly, demonstrating intact phonological and lexical routes that are separate from semantics. The pathology of the reported

patients with semantic agraphia is variable but frequently involves anatomic substrates important for accessing meaning in speech (Roeltgen & Rapcsak, 1993). Semantic agraphia is a common finding in Alzheimer's disease (Forbes et al., 2004; Niels & Roeltgen, 1995a) and semantic dementia (Reilly & Peelle, 2008).

Co-occurrence with Other Neuropsychological Disorders

Patients with semantic agraphia commonly have aphasia, alexia, or both. In some patients, the associations appear to be related to a generalized semantic impairment. These patients produce frequent homophone errors in writing and have impaired comprehension of speech and reading, with preserved oral repetition and oral reading. The speech and reading disabilities of other patients appear to reflect the anatomic diversity of semantic agraphia. Consequently, patients with semantic agraphia may have no additional impairments, or they may have any of the commonly described aphasias or alexias (Roeltgen et al., 1986), as well as elements of Gerstmann syndrome and ideomotor apraxia.

LEXICAL AGRAPHIA WITH SEMANTIC PARAGRAPHIA

Many patients with lexical agraphia have difficulty utilizing semantic information when writing (Hatfield & Patterson, 1983; Macoir & Bernier, 2002). These patients, when asked to spell dictated homophones, frequently spell the semantically incorrect homophone (as do patients with semantic agraphia). They differ from patients with semantic agraphia in that they are able to comprehend the meaning of the words when they read or hear them. Therefore, general semantic knowledge (Figure 6-1, component 11) is preserved, but interacts poorly with spelling. This is presumably because of a disturbance of the direct semantic influence on spelling (through the lexical system).

DEEP AGRAPHIA

Bub and Kertesz (1982), Roeltgen and colleagues (1983a), and Hatfield (1985) described patients who, like those with phonological agraphia, had trouble spelling nonwords, but also had more trouble spelling function words than nouns. There was no effect of ambiguity in sound-to-spelling translation. They spelled nouns of high imageability (e.g., "arm") better than nouns of low imageability (e.g., "law"). They also made semantic paragraphic errors. These are spelling errors that consist of real words related in meaning to the target word, but with little phonological or visual resemblance to the target. For example, one patient wrote "flight" when the stimulus was "propeller" (Roeltgen et al., 1983a). Bub and Kertesz (1982) termed this disorder *deep agraphia*.

The general consensus is that this constellation of impairments is indicative of degraded semantics plus an abolished nonlexical route (Cipolotti et al., 2004; Glasspool et al., 2006). However, some patients with deep agraphia demonstrate spared comprehension. They have been shown to have a disruption in a different part of the lexical route: access from semantics to the orthographic output lexicon (Hillis et al., 1999).

A TEST OF THE DUAL-ROUTE MODEL

This chapter emphasizes a dual-route IP model because of its utility in the clinical setting due to the relatively straightforward predictability of functional deficits from performance (Laine & Martin, 2006). Although models of language such as the one described here are commonly called *dual*-route models, they actually propose three routes for processing words: two lexical routes and one nonlexical. Because semantic information is automatically activated, but is not obligatory for accurate reading or spelling, familiar words can be spelled using a lexical route that goes through semantics or by a route that bypasses semantics. The third route, the nonlexical route, is represented in the model by sublexical grapheme-to-phoneme correspondence rules. The lexical and nonlexical routes are largely independent, but share input and output modules. This allows for the different routes to be separately or jointly affected, depending on at what step the deficit is located.

To prospectively test the dual-route model, Roeltgen (1989, 1991) examined 43 consecutive

right-handed patients with left hemisphere lesions and compared them with controls matched for handedness, age, and education. In this study, classification was based on the strict definitions of the agraphic disorders described here. Phonological agraphia required preserved ability to write real words, whereas some previous studies (Roeltgen et al., 1983a; Roeltgen & Heilman, 1984) required only a relatively better ability to write real as opposed to nonsense words. Using this stricter criterion, the model presented in Figure 6-1 successfully classified 33 of the 43 patients. Eight had no agraphia, five had lexical agraphia, four had phonological agraphia, ten had semantic agraphia, and six had global agraphia (severely impaired performance on all word types). Most patients with semantic agraphia also had an additional linguistic impairment involving the phonological or lexical systems, or the graphemic buffer (see below). Therefore, the number of patients classified as having a specific type of agraphia exceeds the number of patients studied.

Three important conclusions were drawn from the analysis of these patients. First, educational level significantly affected spelling performance after stroke. Better-educated subjects had better overall spelling ability after stroke and were less likely to have difficulty spelling nonwords.

Second, eight patients had normal or nearly normal spelling performance when spelling nonwords but impaired performance when spelling real words, with an equal degree of impairment for both regular and irregular words. It is likely that these patients, like patients with lexical agraphia, had impairment of the lexical system, but, unlike patients with lexical agraphia, they did not use the relatively preserved phonological system to compensate for difficulty spelling real words. This lack of compensation may be explained by the finding that patients with this type of agraphia were less likely to have chronic lesions than were patients with lexical agraphia. This pattern of performance may be termed *noncompensated lexical agraphia*.

Third, the study correlated the type of agraphias with the locus of cerebral lesion. Although approximately 50% of the patients had acute lesions, the lesion locations of patients with lexical, phonological, and semantic agraphias were similar to those described previously in chronic patients. Patients with lexical agraphia had lesions sparing the mid-perisylvian region, specifically the insula, the anterior supramarginal, and the posterior superior temporal gyri. In contrast, the patients with phonological agraphia had lesions involving these structures. The patients with semantic agraphia had various left hemisphere lesions. Therefore, the left hemispheric anatomic localizations for phonological, lexical, and semantic agraphia are similar for both chronic and acute lesions. The issues of education, chronicity, and localization may be important variables to consider in written language rehabilitation (addressed later in the chapter).

OTHER MODELS OF SPELLING

The dual-route model described above has shown practical and theoretical strengths. However, there are other models with different frameworks. These include the dual-route cascaded model (DRC; see Coltheart, 2001, for review) and the parallel distributed processing (PDP) models (connectionist models; Plaut et al., 1996; Seidenberg & McClelland, 1989). Although these models are superficially different from each other and from the dual-route model, they are conceptually similar.

DUAL-ROUTE CASCADED MODEL

The DRC model is similar to the standard dual-route model previously described, but with a few differences. The main difference is the assumption that information "cascades" through the model, proceeding to the next module in the pathway before processing has finished in the previous module. It also incorporates excitatory and inhibitory feedback systems (Figure 6-2). This model has been represented computationally (Coltheart et al., 2001).

In this model, the smallest symbolic parts in each module (e.g., words in the lexicon or letters in the letter unit module) are represented as discrete units. Coltheart (2001)

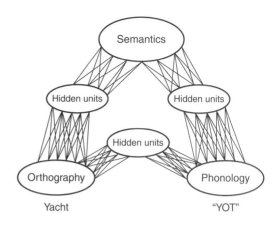

Figure 6–2. The dual-route cascaded (DRC) model of visual word recognition and reading aloud. Adapted from M. Coltheart, B. Curtis, P. Atkins, & M. Haller. (1994). Models of reading aloud: Dual-route and parallel-distributed-processing approaches. *Psychological Review, 100*(4), 598. With permission of the publisher, the American Psychological Association.

argues that a computational model constructed in this way is preferable to the "learning algorithm" approach used by connectionist models (detailed below) because the functional architecture is decided from the outset based on empirical data from previous research on language as opposed to letting it develop as the network "learns."

Attempts to model language processes must be able to account for both normal and impaired performance. The DRC model can make quantitative predictions about regular word reading/ spelling ability based on measures of the proportion of irregular words and nonwords read and spelled. This is because irregular words can be processed only by the lexical route, whereas nonwords can be processed only by the nonlexical route; thus, the ability of a patient to read/spell each kind of word provides a relatively pure measure of the preservation of each route. Since regular words can be processed by both routes, preserved regular word reading (REG) should be predictable from reading/spelling accuracy of irregular words (IRR) and nonwords (NWD) using a simple equation: REG = IRR + (1–IRR) * NWD. Put simply, the equation states that the nonlexical route will be able to process a proportion of the regular words that cannot be processed by the lexical route. The sum of the proportion of regular words processed by the lexical route and the proportion of the remaining words processed by the nonlexical route will equal the total proportion of regular words that can be read or spelled.

The resulting predictive equation has been used to predict regular word reading ability in normal readers, children with developmental dyslexia, and children with brain damage due to stroke (Castles at al., 2006; Coltheart et al., 2001). Rapcsak and colleagues (2007) used this formula to predict reading and spelling performance of patients with acquired alexia and agraphia. They found that the dual-route equation explains 88.8% of the variance in regular word reading scores and 92.1% of the variance in regular word spelling scores. Using a multiple regression analysis, they also found that the lexical and nonlexical routes made significant unique contributions to predictions of regular word reading and spelling. However, irregular word spelling was a more powerful predictor of regular word spelling, which suggests that the lexical route dominates reading and spelling of regular words. Other studies by Rapcsak and colleagues have also applied the DRC model to agraphia, with good results (Henry et al., 2007; Rapcsak et al., 2008).

In summary, there is considerable support for some form of a dual-route model that utilizes separate systems for spelling irregular and nonwords. However, support for this model has not elucidated the functional organization of those routes; for example, whether the semantic system is necessary for lexical spelling. However, evidence from patients with semantic agraphia suggests that correct spellings of irregular words can be produced even in the face of degraded semantics.

CONNECTIONIST MODELS

Another approach uses computational principles to model written language. These models have almost exclusively been applied to reading, but here we will use them as an alternative approach to model normal and impaired spelling. In the place of modules, connectionist models follow the principles of distributed representations, distributed relationships, and interactivity.

Two schools of thought exist regarding connectionist models in language modeling. One regards connectionist models as a challenge to classical IP models, arguing that the dissociations seen in aphasia and agraphia may result from different types of damage to a single system rather than to distinct systems (Van Orden et al., 2001). The other views connectionist models as a tool for elaborating on IP models and developing theories about the internal workings of the modules within IP theories. In this view, connectionist models allow for concrete theorizing at a finer level of detail. We take the latter position; that connectionist and IP models are two ways of looking at the same thing.

PARALLEL DISTRIBUTED PROCESSING MODEL

The most widely accepted connectionist model is the PDP model (Figure 6-3). Instead of parsing out separate modules for each language function, the PDP model includes only three components, representing orthography, phonology, and semantics (Harm & Seidenberg, 2001, 2004). Originally, the PDP model

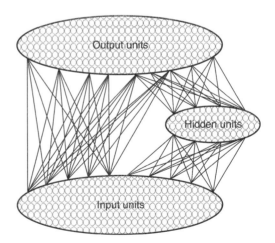

Figure 6–3. Parallel distributed processing (PDP) model based on Seidenberg and McClelland's (1989) general framework of lexical processing. Each oval represents a group of units, and each line represents a group of connections. Adapted from Seidenberg, M. S., & McClelland, J. L. (1989). A distributed, developmental model of word recognition and naming. *Psychological Review, 96*, 526. With permission of the publisher, the American Psychological Association.

implemented only the connection between phonology and orthography (Harm & Seidenberg, 2004; Plaut et al., 1996; Plaut & Shallice, 1993; Seidenberg & McClelland, 1989), making it much more distinct from the IP model. These two components did not prove sufficient to model patient data, and thus semantics was added. Although it has been used understand reading, it can also be conceptually applied to spelling.

In the PDP model, words are represented not by single nodes, but as patterns of activity across the units that make up each component. Each component is connected to the other through a set of hidden units that acts to extract higher-order patterns from this activity. The model is trained on a corpus of words, and the model slowly gathers statistical regularities from the words presented to it.

When applied to reading, the PDP model has been able to learn to read regular and irregular words and also generalize to nonwords, which are read through the use of componential attractors that can recombine to support nonword reading. The PDP model can also predict the reading performance of normal and impaired individuals (Plaut et al., 1996). Impaired reading is simulated by selectively "lesioning" parts of the model.

Connectionist models assume distributed representations that are driven by underlying statistical regularities in its learned vocabulary, as opposed to set rules for phoneme-to-grapheme conversion. Accordingly, the two routes for reading in a connectionist model do not align perfectly onto the classical lexical and nonlexical distinction. Most notably, the nonlexical route (the direct connection between orthography and phonology) can read certain high-frequency irregular words as well as regular and nonwords (Plaut et al., 1996). One area in which connectionist models have different predictions from dual-route models is that the latter predicts that irregular word (lexical) reading may occur without semantic activation, whereas the connectionist models would only make that prediction for high-frequency irregular words. Regardless of these differences, conceptually, the connectionist models are not that different from dual-route models. In both, irregular words and nonwords

are read by different routes and can be impaired separately.

Of the few connectionist spelling models that exist, most are based on a three-layer feedforward network similar to the original Seidenberg and McClelland (1989) reading model, with a phonology layer, a layer of hidden units, and an orthography layer (Brown & Loosemore, 1994; Bullinaria, 1994, 1997; Olson & Caramazza 1994). Much like the original Seidenberg and McClelland (1989) reading model, these single-route spelling models had limited success in reproducing normal spelling.

DUAL-ROUTE MULTILAYER MODEL

The most successful connectionist model of spelling is a hybrid connectionist–dual-route model by Houghton and Zorzi (2003). They created a multilayer network that contains a phonology layer and an orthography layer connected by two separate routes: a direct route and an indirect route mediated by hidden units. In this model, the nonlexical route is represented by the direct connection and comes to act like a sublexical spelling-to-sound conversion system (nonwords spelled plausibly, regular words spelled correctly, irregular words are regularized), while the lexical route is represented by the indirect connection (irregular words spelled correctly). This model is able to reproduce spelling patterns in normal spellers and lexical (surface) agraphics.

OUTPUT MECHANISMS

Up to this point we have discussed only central language processes. However, there are many steps between central processing and behavioral output. The first step is deciding between alternative spellings produced by the phonological and lexical systems. Output from the two routes must converge prior to motor output, since most patients with disorders of either spelling system usually produce the same errors in oral spelling as in writing.

Since the lexical and phonological systems need not produce the same spellings, there must be some way of choosing which spelling is to be produced. For example, in attempting to spell "comb" the lexical system, if familiar with the word, will produce "c-o-m-b." The phonological system, however, may produce "k-o-m" or "c-o-m," since the silent "b" does not conform to the rules of English orthography. Alternatively, "k-o-m-e" could be produced by analogy with "home." These alternative spellings will converge on the graphemic buffer (see below), which must transfer the correct spelling to the motor output systems. Because the lexical system produces only one response (which is dependent on prior experience), whereas the phonological system has the potential to produce multiple letter sequences for a single phonemic sequence, it is reasonable to assume that, under normal circumstances, the output of the lexical system is preferentially incorporated into written or oral spelling.

This assumption is supported by both patient and modeling data. In the dual-route multi-layer model (Houghton & Zorzi, 2003), output from the lexical route dominates the nonlexical route. However, when the lexical route is partially damaged (as when modeling surface agraphia), the response is typically a mixture of the output from both routes (i.e., the lexical output "tough" and the phonological output "tuff" result in the response TUGH). This result clearly mimics the errors of the surface agraphic patient LAT, who, for example, spelled the word "bouquet" as BOUKET (reported in Rapp et al., 2002). Data from patients with semantic agraphia also support this contention (Roeltgen et al., 1986). Patterns of response obtained from these patients suggest that the phonological system is probably only used for spelling nonwords and unfamiliar regular words. Rarely, normal writers produce "slips of the pen" (spontaneous writing errors) that are phonologically correct (Hotopf, 1980). These errors (responses such as "k-o-m" for "comb") suggest that, although most normal spelling utilizes the lexical system, the phonological system continues to function in the background.

GRAPHEMIC BUFFER

The outputs of the linguistic systems converge on what has been termed the *graphemic* or *orthographic* buffer (Caramazza et al., 1987; Hillis and Caramazza, 1989; Lesser, 1990; Margolin, 1984; Figure 6-1, component 14). This component is thought to be a temporary store of abstract letters, and is responsible for letter selection and assembly (Kan et al., 2006). Impairment of the graphemic buffer results in errors in spontaneous writing, writing to dictation, written naming, and delayed copying. Errors are not affected by linguistic factors (i.e., word class, regularity, and imageability) but are influenced by word length, with errors being more common in longer words (Cantagallo & Bonazzi, 1996) and at the ends of words (Sage & Ellis, 2004). Errors tend to be substitutions, deletions, transposition, and insertions of single letters (Caramazza et al., 1987; Cipolotti et al., 2004; Miceli et al., 1985), but complex graphemes (ck) may function as single units (Tainturier & Rapp, 2004). Finally, nonwords are spelled in a roughly similar fashion to words, but are less accurate (Caramazza et al., 1987; Shallice et al., 1995). Spelling also appears to be under certain orthographic constraints. For example, some patients with graphemic buffer impairment have selected impairment of vowels, or respect vowel and consonant positions, substituting vowels for vowels and consonants for consonants (Cubelli, 1991).

Glasspool and colleagues (2006) presented an elegant account of graphemic buffer impairment by developing a connectionist model based on dissociation and association, as well as error data, and set inside an IP model framework. Their model of the graphemic buffer is based on a class of models called *competitive queuing* that has been successful in modeling serial behavior like spelling. They used their model to compare dysfunction that would result from an impairment of the graphemic buffer itself versus impairment of information reaching the graphemic buffer (deep dysgraphia), and were able to reproduce many key features of both patient error profiles.

Despite the fact that only a few reports have described patients with agraphia due to impairment of the graphemic buffer, the lesion loci have varied widely. These have included the left frontal parietal region (Hillis & Caramazza, 1989; Lesser, 1990), the left parietal region (Annoni et al., 1998; Cubelli, 1991; Miceli et al., 1985; Posteraro et al., 1988), and the right frontal parietal and basal ganglia region (Hillis & Caramazza, 1989). We (unpublished observation) and M. Laine (personal communication) have each observed patients with apparent agraphia due to impairment of the graphemic buffer; these patients had relatively discrete lesions of the left posterior dorsal lateral frontal lobe. Cubelli (1991) described an instance of this disorder from a subcortical left frontal lesion. Also, Niels and Roeltgen (1995b) described impairment of the graphemic buffer in early Alzheimer disease.

The variability in pathology (frontal and parietal lesions) suggests impairment of what Nadeau and Crosson (1997) have termed "selective engagement" (also called working memory). Nadeau argues that interaction of frontal and parietal mechanisms is important for selecting and maintaining a behavior, which in this case is spelling. He also posits that these processes are influenced by the thalamus; thus, we would predict that certain thalamic lesions should show impairment of the graphemic buffer. Some support for this was found in the prospective study by Roeltgen (1989, 1991). Four of the nine patients with lesions involving the thalamus had generalized spelling impairments consistent with disruption of the graphemic buffer; the other five had lexical agraphia.

MOTOR COMPONENTS

Motor output of spelled words may be either manual (written letters or graphemes) or oral (oral spelling). The dominant or nondominant hand may perform writing. Writing includes motor and visuospatial skills, as well as knowledge of graphemes. There is some understanding of the neuropsychological bases of these skills, but considerably less is known about the components underlying oral spelling.

DISORDERS OF WRITING

Apraxic Agraphia

In addition to the pyramidal and extrapyramidal motor systems (which will not be discussed here), knowledge of purposeful skilled movements and postures (praxis) is necessary for writing (see Chapter 11). Praxis includes the ability to properly hold a pen or pencil, as well as the ability to perform the other learned movements necessary for forming written letters (graphemes). Apraxia usually results from lesions in the hemisphere opposite the preferred hand. In most right-handers this is also the hemisphere dominant for language, and consequently apraxia is often associated with aphasia. In apraxic patients who are also aphasic, it may not be possible to clearly separate the apraxic from the aphasic elements of agraphia.

Several patients have been described who have had language in the hemisphere ipsilateral to the preferred hand. When the hemisphere controlling the preferred hand was damaged, they developed ideomotor apraxia without aphasia (Heilman et al., 1973, 1974; Valenstein & Heilman, 1979). Patients with such disorders have illegible writing, both spontaneously and to dictation. Their oral spelling is preserved. Their writing typically improves with copying. They should be able to type or use anagram letters (Valenstein & Heilman, 1979). This syndrome may be termed *apraxic agraphia with ideomotor apraxia and without aphasia*. Rothi and Heilman (1981) termed the functional region important for producing strokes in writing the *graphemic area* (Figure 6-1, component 16).

Damage resulting in apraxic agraphia without aphasia is typically located in the parietal lobe opposite the hand dominant for writing. Within the parietal lobe, lesions specific to the postcentral gyrus, the intraparietal sulcus, and the anterior intraparietal sulcus may be associated with clinically distinct types of apraxic agraphia (Sakurai et al., 2007). Such results emphasize the complexities of nosologic descriptions. Individual variation within basic syndromes is common. This chapter emphasizes basic disorders as having the most clinical importance, but recognizes that individual variations within these disorders may be marked.

Apraxic Agraphia Without Apraxia (Ideational Agraphia)

This disorder is characterized by damage to the graphemic area, the cognitive system necessary for performing handwriting, and thought to store the knowledge of the spatial features of letters (Rothi & Heilman, 1981). Patients with injury to the graphemic area produce poorly formed graphemes but have normal praxis, including the ability to imitate holding a pen or pencil (Roeltgen & Heilman, 1983). In the absence of these spatial representations, seeing letters might help to guide movements, and in this disorder grapheme production improves with copying. The initial patients described by Roeltgen and Heilman (1983) and Margolin and Binder (1984) also had disturbed visual-spatial skills and therefore copying was moderately impaired; however, subsequent patients have presented with intact visuospatial skills (Baxter & Warrington, 1986, who termed it *ideational agraphia*; Croisile et al., 1990). Carey and Heilman (1988) described this form of agraphia in a patient with impaired letter imagery despite normal reading, suggesting impaired visual-spatial letter engrams. In a study of a similar patient, analysis of errors suggested that this type of agraphia may also occur from a disconnection of the motor engrams from the motor output systems (Otsuki et al.,1999; Figure 6-1, pathway 17). This patient had a selective disorder of writing stroke sequences when writing. However, he was able to orally express the correct sequences.

The anatomic substrate for apraxic agraphia without apraxia appears to be the parietal lobe, perhaps the superior parietal lobule, either in the hemisphere contralateral to the hand used for writing (Baxter & Warrington, 1986; Carey & Heilman, 1988; Del Grosso Destreri et al., 2000; Margolin and Binder, 1984; Otsuki et al., 1999) or in the ipsilateral hemisphere (Roeltgen & Heilman, 1983). However, there is at least one patient reported who had a dominant frontal lesion (Hodges, 1991).

Spatial Agraphia

These patients have an impairment of visuospatial skills and produce malformed letter components (strokes) characterized by (a) reiteration of strokes, (b) inability to write on a straight horizontal line, and (c) insertion of blank spaces between graphemes. Disruption of this ability has been termed *visuospatial agraphia*, *constructional agraphia*, or *afferent dysgraphia* (Ellis et al., 1987; Figure 6-1, component 18). In patients with this disorder, the ability to copy is usually disturbed.

Spatial agraphia is usually due to nondominant parietal or frontal lobe lesions (Ardila & Rosselli, 1993). Although lesions of this region produce spatial agraphia, this area may not be activated on functional magnetic resonance imaging (fMRI) in normal writing to dictation (Menon & Desmond, 2001). Spatial agraphia may also be part of a neglect syndrome (see Chapter 12). Ellis and colleagues (1987) suggested that this relationship may result from a failure to utilize visual and kinesthetic feedback. Silveri and colleagues (1997) provided support for this hypothesis in a patient with spatial agraphia from a cerebellar lesion. Their patient performed much better with his eyes open than with his eyes closed. A study by Chary and colleagues (2004) further described interactions between graphemic strokes and perception, showing a loss of the basic motor principles that govern graphemic stroke production.

Agraphia Due to Impaired Allographic Store

These patients make frequent case and style errors, or can write correctly in one case, but not another. The allographic stores (Black et al., 1987; Debastiani & Barry, 1989; Figure 6-1, component 22) are thought to be important for directing the handwriting systems in the production of correct case (upper and lower) and style (script [cursive] or manuscript [print]). Dissociations of ability to write in different cases and styles support the contention that graphic programs for these are dissociable (Del Grosso Destini et al., 2000; Kartounis, 1992; Menichelli et al., 2008; Trojano & Chichio, 1994). Further evidence indicates that orthographic constraints, such as length, are present in patients with this disorder, indicating preservation of the linguistic information despite peripheral breakdown (Chialant et al., 2002).

Unilateral (Callosal) Agraphia

Unilateral agraphia occurs from lesions of the neo-commissures. The spelling and grapheme systems of the left hemisphere have access via the neocommissures to the right hemisphere motor system responsible for controlling the nondominant (left) hand. Disruption of this interhemispheric transfer results in unilateral agraphia (Bachoud-Levi et al., 2000; Bogen, 1969; Geschwind & Kaplan, 1962; Levy et al., 1971; Liepmann & Maas, 1907; Rubens et al., 1977; Tanaka et al., 1990). Most patients with this type of agraphia make unintelligible scrawls when they attempt to write with their left hands, but most improve with copying, consistent with apraxic agraphia with apraxia. However, there is variability, usually related to the part of the corpus callosum affected (Kazui & Sawada, 1993; Watson & Heilman, 1983). Some patients have apraxic agraphia without apraxia (Sugishita et al., 1980; Yamadori et al., 1980), others may have apraxia without agraphia (Kazui & Sawada, 1993), and others have unilateral linguistic agraphia (Gersh & Damasio, 1981). Studies of Japanese patients (Sugishita et al., 1980; Yamadori et al., 1980) have shown dissociations between kana (phonograms) and kanji (morphograms), interpreted by Rothi et al. (1987) as showing right hemispheric ability to support the more ideographic kanji characters.

DISORDERS OF ORAL SPELLING

The mechanisms for oral spelling are not as well defined as those for writing. Two possible mechanisms exist. One mechanism would utilize the area of auditory word images or engrams (Wernicke's area) to guide the anterior perisylvian speech regions (e.g., Broca's area) to produce oral letters (Figure 6-1, pathway 25-26). The other mechanism would utilize an independent area of oral motor engrams (letter name conversion as defined by Ward, 2003) for letters to guide or program Broca's area. Evidence at this time supports the first mechanism.

One patient with relatively spared writing but disturbed oral spelling has been described (Kinsbourne & Warrington, 1965). This patient also had difficulty saying words spelled to him. This finding suggests that the system of auditory word images (Wernicke's area) is necessary for both perception of aurally perceived

spelled words and the production of oral letters. Alternatively, there may be a close anatomic proximity between the area of auditory word images and the area of oral motor engrams for letters. If the latter interpretation is correct, both systems were damaged in the patient seen by Kinsbourne and Warrington. Additionally, this hypothesis would predict that patients with destruction of auditory word images (Wernicke's aphasia) could have preserved oral spelling. Although patients with Wernicke's aphasia and preserved written spelling have been described (Hier & Mohr, 1977; Roeltgen et al., 1983a), no patients with Wernicke's aphasia and preserved oral spelling have been described.

TESTING FOR AGRAPHIA

Testing for agraphia can provide insight into specific disorders caused by focal dysfunction. Tests of writing can also help detect global cognitive impairment, such as confusional states (Chedru & Geschwind, 1972). In the evaluation of a patient with agraphia, both linguistic and motor components should be evaluated. The linguistic component includes the choice of the correct letters (spelling) and the choice of the correct word (meaning). The motor component includes those neuropsychological functions necessary for producing the correct letter form and the correct word form. In order to evaluate patients for different forms of agraphia, three types of tests should be used: spontaneous writing, writing to dictation, and copying.

To test spontaneous writing, the patient is asked to write sentences or words about a familiar topic. We recommend having the patient write about a picture, as the same picture can then be used with different patients and at different times with the same patient to compare performance. Spontaneous writing assesses conceptual generative abilities, word selection, and syntax, as well as the patient's ability to spell and produce letters.

Writing to dictation, usually limited to single words or phrases, allows one to evaluate the effects of particular variables on writing, such as word length and frequency. The word type can also be varied to test specific hypotheses based on models of agraphia, such as those presented in this chapter. These models predict, for example, that certain patients may have more difficulty with a word depending on the class (noun, verb, adjective, adverb, or function word, i.e., conjunctions and prepositions), imageability (high or low), abstractness (high or low), regularity (regular or irregular), or lexicality (real or nonword). The mode of the patient's response may also be varied: the patient can be asked to write, using print or script, to spell orally, type, or spell using anagram letters (blocks with single letters written on them). This enables the examiner to distinguish motor or apraxic agraphias, in which typing and spelling are spared, from linguistic agraphias, in which letter choice is impaired.

The third group of writing tests evaluates copying. The examiner can have the subject copy letters, words, sentences, or paragraphs. The examiner should observe the patient's technique to distinguish among three potential copy methods; slavish or "stroke-by-stroke" copying (drawing letters), "letter-by-letter" copying, and transcribing, in which the material is written fluently. Techniques that may help to distinguish these copying methods include: (a) varying the length of material to be copied (increased length usually decreases slavish and letter-by-letter copying), (b) increasing the distance between the stimulus and the response (it is difficult to slavishly copy material from across the room), (c) having the patient copy nonsense figures (limiting the patient to slavish copying), and (d) performing delayed copying (showing the stimulus to the patient, removing the stimulus, and then having the patient write it, generally limiting the patient to transcribing).

Important information may be gleaned from the analysis of the patient's writing. It is important to analyze performance related to specific word types (i.e., comparing performance when writing regular, irregular, and nonwords; see Lexical Agraphia, above). It may also be important to analyze syntax, content, and sentence length in spontaneous sentences or paragraphs (Rapcsak & Rubens, 1990).

It is also important to assess the patient's semantic system. Semantics are most often tested by word–picture or picture–picture matching. The most common form of this type of task is Pyramids and Palm Trees (PPT; Patterson & Howard, 1992). In this task, patients must choose which of several pictures is most closely related in meaning to a target picture or word, written and/or spoken. Other tests of semantic ability include the Kissing and Dancing test, a test of action semantics similar to the PPT (Bak & Hodges, 2003), and tests of category fluency ("in one minute, list as many animals as you can"), and synonym judgment task (word–word matching).

Analysis of handwriting form is necessary in assessing patients for apraxic agraphia. The patient's ability to spell orally, type, and use anagram letters should be compared to his or her writing. Letter imagery should also be tested: for example, have the patient name all the capital letters composed of only straight lines. The patient should be asked to copy, and to convert printed words to script and vice versa, to assess allographic representations. Patients should also be evaluated for ideomotor and limb-kinetic apraxia.

In addition to these detailed tests of writing, it is important to evaluate patients for neurological or neuropsychological disorders that may interfere with writing, oral spelling, or copying. These include disorders of speech, reading, praxis, visuoperceptual, visuospatial, constructional abilities, attention, and elementary motor and sensory functions.

REHABILITATION

Effective means for the successful rehabilitation of aphasia are still being devised. Rehabilitation of aphasia is still relatively in its infancy, and of agraphia even more so. It has only recently been accepted that rehabilitation can be effective in reducing the disabilities caused by chronic stroke, but an increasing number of studies are showing therapy gains even years post-onset (Nickels, 2002). Although early rehabilitation studies were only loosely guided by theory, current research into rehabilitation is now more often based on cognitive models. These models can be very useful in guiding a clinician to what aspects of a patient's disability should be investigated in more detail (Laine & Martin, 2006), what impairment needs to be treated, and how best to treat these impairments. Although most rehabilitation studies use IP models to structure rehabilitation, other approaches have been described (Horner & Loverso, 1991). It is also important to keep in mind that individual variability is such that no one treatment will be effective for all patients, even if the underlying impairment seems to be the same (Beeson & Rapcsak, 2002).

One of the major questions in aphasia rehabilitation is whether to try to rehabilitate the deficit or to focus on preserved functions to encourage compensatory strategies. The majority of studies take the former approach, focusing on treating the deficit. Few studies have compared the efficacy of targeting different rehabilitation strategies within patients who have a specific form of agraphia to learn if different forms of agraphia are best treated with different strategies that target specific processing impairments (Schmalzl & Nickels, 2006).

In many cases, treatment is aimed at relearning or reaccessing orthographic representations of words by repeated practice of specific items. These strategies often incorporate cuing hierarchies that increase or decrease support for correct spelling as treatment continues (Beeson et al., 2002; Carlomagno et al., 1994; Hillis, 1989). Several case studies of patients with agraphia have reported successful rehabilitation of the orthographic representations of trained items (Aliminosa et al., 1993; Beeson, 1999; Hillis & Caramazza, 1987; Rapp & Kane, 2002; Rapp, 2005; Raymer et al., 2003; Schmalzl & Nickels, 2006; Seron et al., 1980). One example of a successful treatment is the copy and recall treatment (CART), which has been used to successfully rehabilitate a number of patients (Beeson, 1999; Beeson et al., 2002, 2003; Beeson & Egnor, 2006; Beeson & Hirsch, 1998). Following successful treatment focused on orthographic representations, generalization to untrained items is generally low, and maintenance of learning, when tested, has been mixed.

The semantic system has also been a target of therapy. In patients with semantic deficits, explicit clarification of the distinguishing features of an object has been successfully used to treat agraphia (Hillis, 1991). Word–picture matching has also been used successfully to improve written naming in one patient (Hillis & Caramazza, 1994). In some cases, the entire lexical–semantic route is targeted, with rehabilitation focused on reestablishing a link between meaning and spelling (Behrmann, 1987; Carlomagno et al., 1991; de Partz et al., 1992)

Conway and colleagues (1998) used a phonological rehabilitation treatment called the Auditory Discrimination in Depth Program to treat a patient with mild phonological alexia and mixed agraphia. After 2 months (101 hours) of treatment, large gains in phonological awareness and reading and spelling of words and nonwords were demonstrated and maintained 2 months post-treatment. However, this patient had only a mild deficit, which might have made the deficit more treatable. Multiple case studies have reported success with related strategies for teaching sound-to-letter correspondences. These include the "key word" (/b/ is for "baby"; Hillis & Caramazza, 1994; Hillis Trupe, 1986) and "lexical analogy" (/ro/ is for "Roma"; Carlomagno & Parlato, 1989; Carlomagno et al., 1991, 1994; Hatfield, 1983) approaches, which take advantage of preserved spelling knowledge.

There have been reports of attempts to rehabilitate the graphemic buffer. However, improvement in spelling from these therapies seems to come from compensatory strategies (such as self-correction) or strengthening of orthographic representations so they are more resistant to degradation, rather than to improvement in the graphemic buffer itself (Hillis, 1989; Hillis & Caramazza, 1987). Support for this interpretation is demonstrated by a study that specifically targeted orthographic representations for strengthening and found that word-length effects were eliminated on trained items (Aliminosa et al., 1993). However, one group found that patients with a graphemic buffer deficit seemed to have more generalization to untrained items after treatment than did patients with an orthographic lexicon deficit who received the same treatment (Rapp, 2005; Rapp & Kane, 2002; Raymer et al., 2003). Because the graphemic buffer is a working memory component that is used in the spelling of all words and nonwords, rehabilitation of this component would be expected to generalize to untrained words more than the relearning of an item-specific entry in the lexicon would. This is evidence that the graphemic buffer can, in fact, be improved by therapy.

Rehabilitation efforts can also be focused on strengthening existing language facilities and teaching compensatory strategies. One such strategy teaches patients with lexical agraphia to take advantage of their relatively preserved phonological route and "sound out" words. Patients are trained to generate possible spelling alternatives and use residual lexical knowledge to find the spelling that "looks right." They then check their response with an electronic spell checker that provides feedback to correct misspellings (Beeson et al., 2000). As demonstrated by the previous treatment, technology can be an effective crutch for those with writing impairments (see also Mortley et al., 2001). Difficulty with handwriting may be overcome through the use of a keyboard and computer. These strategies are focused more on functional communication (Horner & Loverso, 1991), making pragmatic concerns a priority.

Other treatments have focused on teaching self-correcting strategies. One such patient, DH, predominantly made single-letter errors on the ends of words (Hillis & Caramazza, 1987). Once taught to use a search strategy focused on the end of words, he was able to detect and correct errors. Similarly, a few attempts have been made to use self-dictation to remediate written spelling when oral spelling is preserved. Results have been positive, with three out of four reported cases improving (Lesser, 1990; Mortley et al., 2001; Pound, 1996; Ramage et al., 1998).

CONCLUSION

The neuropsychological approach to the agraphias offers a promising method of classifying these disorders. It complements, rather than supplants, the traditional classifications that rely on associated neurological findings, such as aphasia, alexia, or visuospatial disorders, rather than on the strict analysis of writing. Other approaches, including connectionist models, can also be combined with the neuropsychological models. Neuropsychological analysis may be of use not only in classifying agraphias, but also in designing treatment strategies and in helping elucidate underlying brain functions.

REFERENCES

Alexander, M. P., Friedman, R., LoVerso (*sic*), F., & Fischer, R. (1990). Anatomic correlates of Lexical Agraphia. Presented at the Academy of Aphasia, Baltimore, MD.

Alexander, M. P., Friedman, R. B., Loverso, F., & Fischer, R. S. (1992). Lesion localization of phonological agraphia. *Brain Language*, *43*, 83–95.

Aliminosa, D., McCloskey, M., Goodman-Schulman, R., & Sokol, S. M. (1993). Remediation of acquired dysgraphia as a technique for testing interpretations of deficits. *Aphasiology*, *7*(1), 55–69.

Annoni, J. M., Lemay, M. A., de Mattos Fimenta, M. A., & Lecours, A. R. (1998). The contribution of attentional mechanisms to an irregularity effect at the grapheme buffer level. *Brain Language*, *63*, 64–78.

Ardila, A., & Rosselli, M. (1993). Spatial agraphia. *Brain Cognition*, *22*, 137–147.

Assal, G., Buttet, J., & Jolivet, R. (1981). Dissociations in aphasia: A case report. *Brain Language*, *13*, 223–240.

Bachoud-Levi, A. C., Ergis, A. M., Cesaro, P., & Degos, J. D. (2000). Dissociation between distal and proximal left limb agraphia and apraphethesia in a patient with a callosal disconnection syndrome. *Cortex*, *36*(3), 351–363.

Bak, T. H., & Hodges, J. R. (2003). Kissing and dancing—A test to distinguish the lexical and conceptual contributions to noun/verb and action/object dissociation. Preliminary results in patients with frontotemporal dementia. *Journal of Neurolinguistics*,*16*,169–181.

Balasubramanian, V. (2005). Dysgraphia in two forms of conduction aphasia. *Brain Cognition*, *57*(1), 8–15.

Baxter, D. M., & Warrington, E. K. (1985). Category specific phonological dysgraphia. *Neuropsychologia*, *23*, 653–666.

Baxter, D. M., & Warrington, E. K. (1986). Ideational agraphia: A single case study. *Journal of Neurology, Neurosurgery and Psychiatry*, *49*, 369–374.

Beauvois, M. F., & Derouesne, J. (1981). Lexical or orthographic agraphia. *Brain*, *104*, 2–49.

Beeson, P. M. (1999). Treating acquired writing impairment: Strengthening graphemic representations. *Aphasiology, 13*, 367–386.

Beeson, P. M., & Egnor, H. (2006). Combining treatment for written and spoken naming. *Journal of the International Neuropsychological Society, 12*(6), 816–827.

Beeson, P. M., & Hirsch, F.M. (1998). Writing treatment for severe aphasia. Presentation at the Annual Convention of the American Speech-Language-Hearing Association, San Antonio, TX.

Beeson, P. M., & Rapcsak, S. Z. (2002). Clinical diagnosis and treatment of spelling disorders. In A. E. Hillis (Ed.), *The handbook of adult language disorders: Integrating cognitive neuropsychology, neurology, and rehabilitation* (pp. 101–120). New York: Psychology Press.

Beeson, P. M., Hirsch, F. M., & Rewega, M. A. (2002). Successful single-word writing treatment: Experimental analyses of four cases. *Aphasiology, 16*(4/5/6), 473–491.

Beeson, P. M., Rewega, M., Vail, S., & Rapcsak, S. Z. (2000). Problem-solving approach to agraphia treatment: Interactive use of lexical and sublexical spelling routes. *Aphasiology, 14*, 551–565.

Beeson, P. M., Rising, K., & Volk, J. (2003). Writing treatment for severe aphasia: Who benefits? *Journal of Speech, Language and Hearing Research, 46*, 1038–1060.

Behrmann, M. (1987). The rites of righting writing: Homophone mediation in acquired dysgraphia. *Cognitive Neuropsychology, 4*, 365–384.

Benedikt, M. (1865). *Uber aphasie, agraphie und venwndte pathologische Zustande* (Chapter 6, 897–899, 923–926). Vienna: Wiener Medizische Presse.

Benson, D. F. (1979). *Aphasia, alexia and agraphia.* New York: Churchill Livingston.

Black, S. E., Behrmann, M., Bass, K., & Hacker, P. (1987). Selective writing impairment: Beyond the allographic code. *Aphasiology, 3*(3), 265–277.

Bogen, J. E. (1969). The other side of the brain. I. Dysgraphia and dyscopia following cerebral commissurotomy. *Bulletin of the Los Angeles Neurological Society, 34*, 3–105.

Bolla-Wilson, K., Speedie, J. J., & Robinson, R. G. (1985). Phonologic agraphia in a left-handed patient after a right-hemisphere lesion. *Neurology, 35*, 1778–1781.

Brown, G. D. A., & Loosemore, R. P. W. (1994). Computational approaches to normal and impaired spelling. In G. D. A. Brown, & N. C. Ellis (Eds.), *Handbook of spelling: Theory, process and intervention* (pp. 319–335). Chichester: John Wiley.

Bub, D., & Kertesz, A. (1982). Deep agraphia. *Brain Language, 17*, 146–165.

Bullinaria, J. (1994). Connectionist modeling of spelling. In *Proceedings of the Sixteenth Annual Conference of the Cognitive Science Society* (pp. 78–83). Hillsdale, NJ: Lawrence Erlbaum.

Bullinaria, J. (1997). Modeling reading, spelling and past tense learning with artificial neural networks. *Brain Language, 59*, 236–266.

Campbell, R. (1985). When children write nonwords to dictation. *Journal of Experimental Child Psychology, 40*, 133–151.

Cantagallo, A., & Bonazzi, S. (1996). Acquired dysgraphia with selective damage to the graphemic buffer: A single case report. *Italian Journal of Neurological Sciences, 17*, 249–254.

Caramazza, A., Miceli, G., Villa, G., & Romani, C. (1987). The role of the graphemic buffer in spelling: Evidence from a case of acquired dysgraphia. *Cognition, 26*, 59–85.

Carey, M. A., & Heilman, K. M. (1988). Letter imagery deficits in a case of pure apraxic agraphia. *Brain Language, 34*, 147–156.

Carlomagno, S., & Parlato, V. (1989). Writing rehabilitation in brain damaged adult patients: A cognitive approach. In G. Deloche (Ed.), *Cognitive approaches in neuropsychological rehabilitation* (pp. 175–205). Hillsdale, NJ: Lawrence Erlbaum.

Carlomagno, S., Colombo, A., Casadio, A., Emanuelli, S., & Razzano, C. (1991). Cognitive approaches to writing rehabilitation in aphasics: Evaluation of two treatment strategies. *Aphasiology, 5*(4–5), 355–360.

Carlomagno, S., Ivavrone, A., & Colombo, A. (1994). Cognitive approaches to writing rehabilitation: From single case to group studies. In M. J. Riddoch, & G. W. Humphreys (Eds.), *Cognitive neuropsychology and cognitive rehabilitation* (pp.485–502). Hillsdale, NJ: Lawrence Erlbaum.

Castles, A., Bates, T. C., & Coltheart, M. (2006). John Marshall and the developmental dyslexias. *Aphasiology, 20*, 871–892.

Chary, C., Meary, D., Orliaguet, J. -P., David, D., Moreaud, O., & Kandel, S. (2004). Influence of motor disorders on the visual perception of human movements in a case of peripheral dysgraphia. *Behavioral Neurology, 10*(3), 223–232.

Chedru. F., & Geschwind, N. (1972). Writing disturbances in acute confusional states. *Neuropsychologia, 10*, 343–354.

Chialant, D., Domoto-Reilly, K., Proios, H., & Caramazza, A. (2002). Preserved orthographic length and transitional probabilities in written spelling in a case of acquired dysgraphia. *Brain Language*, *82*(1), 30–46.

Cipolotti, L., Bird, C., Glasspool, D., & Shallice, T. S. (2004). The impact of deep dysgraphia on graphemic output buffer disorders. *Neurocase*, *10*(6), 405–419.

Coltheart, M., Rastle, C., Perry, C., Langdon, R., & Ziegler, J. (2001). DRC: A dual route cascaded model of visual word recognition and reading aloud. *Psychology Review*, *108*, 204–258.

Conway, T. W., Heilman,P., Rothi, L. J. G., Alexander, A. W., Adair, J., Crosson, B. A., & Heilman, K. M. (1998) Treatment of a case of phonological alexia with agraphia using the auditory discrimination in depth (ADD) program. *Journal of the International Neuropsychological Society*, *4*, 608–620.

Croisile. B., Trillet, M., Laurent, B., Latombe, D., & Schott, B. (1989). Agraphie lexicale par hematome temporo-parietal gauche. *Revista Neurologia (Paris)*, *145*, 287–292.

Croisille, B., Laurent, B., Michel, M., & Trillet, M. (1990). Pure agraphia after deep left hemisphere hematoma. *Journal of Neurology, Neurosurgery and Psychiatry*, *53*, 263–265.

Cubelli, R. (1991). A selective deficit for writing vowels in acquired dysgraphia. *Nature*, *353*, 258–260.

de Partz, M. -P., Seron, X., & Van der Linden, M. V. (1992). Re-education of surface dysgraphia with a visual imagery strategy. *Cognitive Neuropsychology*, *9*, 369–401.

Debastiani, P. & Barry, C. (1989). A cognitive analysis of an acquired dysgraphic patient with an "allographic" writing disorder. *Cognitive Neuropsychology*, *6*, 45–41.

Del Grosso Destreri, N., Farina, E., Alberoni, M., Pomati, S., Nichelli, P., & Mariani, C. (2000). Selective uppercase dysgraphia with loss of visual imagery of letter forms: A window on the organization of graphomotor patterns. *Brain Language*, *71*(3), 353–372.

Ellis, A. W. (1982). Spelling and writing (and reading and speaking). In A. W. Ellis (Ed.), *Normality and Pathology in Cognitive Functions*. London: Academic Press.

Ellis, A. W., Young, W. W., & Flude, B. M. (1987). "Afferent dysgraphia" in a patient and in normal subjects. *Cognitive Neuropsychology*, *4*, 465–487.

Forbes, K. E., Shanks, M. F., & Venneri, A. (2004). The evolution of dysgraphia in Alzheimer's disease. *Brain Research Bulletin*, *63*, 19–24.

Friedman, R. B., & Alexander, M. P. (1989). Written spelling agraphia. *Brain Language*, *36*, 5063–5517.

Gersh, F., & Damasio, A. R. (1981). Praxis and writing of the left hand may be served by different callosal pathways. *Archives of Neurology*, *38*, 634–636.

Gerstmann, J. (1940). Syndrome of finger agnosia, disorientation for the right and left, agraphia and acalculia. *Archives of Neurology and Psychiatry*, *44*, 398–408.

Geschwind. N., & Kaplan E. (1962). A human cerebral disconnection syndrome. *Neurology*, *12*, 675–685.

Glasspool, D. W., Shallice, T., & Cipolotti, L. (2006) Towards a unified process model for graphemic buffer disorder and deep dysgraphia. *Cognitive Neuropsychology*, *23*(3), 479–512.

Goldstein, K. (1948). *Language and language disturbances*. New York: Grune and Stratton.

Goodman-Schulman, R., & Caramazza, A. (1987). Patterns of dysgraphia and the nonlexical spelling process. *Cortex*, *23*, 143–148.

Harm, M. W. & Seidenberg, M. (2001). Are there orthographic impairments in phonological dyslexia? *Cognitive Neuropsychology*, *18*(1), 71–92.

Harm, M. W. & Seidenberg, M. (2004). Computing the meaning of words in reading: Cooperative division of labor between visual and phonological processes. *Psychology Review*, *111*(3), 662–720.

Hatfield, F. M. (1983). Aspects of acquired dysgraphia and implication for re-education. In C. Code, & D. J. Muller (Eds.), *Aphasia Therapy* (pp. 157–169). London: Edward Arnold Publisher.

Hatfield, F. M. (1985). Visual and phonological factors in acquired dysgraphia. *Neuropsychologia*, *23*, 13–29.

Hatfield, F. M., & Patterson, K. E. (1983). Phonological spelling. *Quarterly Journal of Experimental Psychology*, *35A*, 451–468.

Head, H. (1926). *Aphasia and kindred disorders of speech*. Cambridge, UK: Cambridge University Press.

Hecaen, H., & Albert, M. L. (1978). *Human neuropsychology*. New York: John Wiley and Sons.

Heilman, K. M, Coyle, J. M., Gonyea, E. F., & Geschwind, N. (1973). Apraxia and agraphia in a left hander. *Brain*, *96*, 21–28.

Heilman, K. M., Gonyea, E. F., & Geschwind, N. (1974). Apraxia and agraphia in a right hander. *Cortex*, *10*, 284–288.

Henry, M. L., Beeson, P. M., Stark, A. J., & Rapcsak, S. Z. (2007). The role of left perisylvian cortical regions in spelling. *Brain Language*, *100*(1), 44–52.

Hier, D. B., & Mohr, J, P. (1977). Incongruous oral and written naming. *Brain Language*, *4*, 115–126.

Hillis Trupe, A. E. (1986). Effectiveness of retraining phoneme to grapheme conversion. In R. H. Brookshire (Ed.), *Clinical Aphasiology* (pp. 163–171). Minneapolis, MN: BRK Publishers.

Hillis, A. E. (1989). Efficacy and generalization of treatment for aphasic naming errors. *Archives of Physical Medicine and Rehabilitation*,*70*, 632–636.

Hillis, A. E. (1991). Effects of separate treatments for distinct impairments within the naming process. *Clinical Aphasiology*, *19*, 255–265.

Hillis, A. E., & Caramazza, A. (1987). Model-driven treatment of dysgraphia. In R. H. Brookshire (Ed.), *Clinical aphasiology* (pp. 84–105). Minneapolis, MN: BRK Publishers.

Hillis, A. E., & Caramazza, A. (1989). The graphemic buffer and attentional mechanisms. *Brain Language*, *36*, 208–235.

Hillis, A. E., & Caramazza, A. (1994). Theories of lexical processing and rehabilitation of lexical deficits. In M. J. Riddoch, & G. W. Humphreys (Eds.), *Cognitive neuropsychology and cognitive rehabilitation* (pp. 449–484). Hillsdale, N. J: Lawrence Erlbaum.

Hillis, A. E., Rapp, B., C., & Caramazza, A. (1999). When a rose is a rose in speech but a tulip in writing. *Cortex*, *35*, 337–356.

Hodges, J. R. (1991). Pure apraxic agraphia with recovery after drainage of a left frontal cyst. *Cortex*, *27*, 469–473.

Horner, J., & Loverso, F. L. (1991). Models of aphasia treatment in Clinical Aphasiology 1972–1988. *Clinical Aphasiology*, *20*, 61–75.

Hotopf, N. (1980). Slips of the pen. In V. Frith (Ed.), *Cognitive Processes in Spelling* (pp. 287–307). London: Academic Press.

Houghton, G. & Zorzi, M. (2003). Normal and impaired spelling in a connectionist dual-route architecture. *Cognitive Neuropsychology*, *20*(2), 115–162.

Iwata, M. (1984). Neuropsychological correlates of the Japanese writing system. *Trends In Neurosciences*, *7*, 290–293.

Kan, I., Biran, I., Thompson-Schill, S. L., & Chatterjee, A. (2006). Letter selection and letter assembly in acquired dysgraphia. *Cognitive and Behavioral Neurology*, *19*(4), 225–236.

Kaplan. E., & Goodglass, H. (1981). Aphasia-related disorders. In M. T. Sarno (Ed.), *Acquired Aphasia*. New York: Academic Press.

Kartsounis, L. D. (1992). Selective lower-case letter ideational agraphia. *Cortex*, *28*, 145–150.

Kazui, S. & Sawada, T. (1993) Callosal apraxia without agraphia. *Annals of Neurology*, *33*(4), 401–403.

Kim, H. -J., Chu, K., Lee, K. -M., Kim, D. W., & Park, S. -H. (2002). Phonological agraphia after superior temporal gyrus infarction. *Archives of Neurology*, *9*(8), 1314–1316.

Kinsbourne, M. & Warrington, E. K. (1965). A case showing selectively impaired oral spelling. *Journal of Neurology, Neurosurgery, and Psychiatry*, *28*, 563–566.

Laine, M. & Martin, N. (2006). *Anomia: Theoretical and clinical aspects*. New York: Psychology Press.

Leischner, A. (1969). The agraphias. In P. J. Vinken, & G. W. Bruyn (Eds.), *Disorders of Speech, Perception and Symbolic Behavior* (pp. 141–180). Amsterdam: North Holland.

Lesser, R. (1990). Superior oral to written spelling: Evidence for separate buffers? *Cognitive Neuropsychology*, *7*, 347–366.

Levy, J., Nebes, R. D., & Sperry, R. W. (1971). Expressive language in the surgically separated minor hemisphere. *Cortex*, *7*, 49–58.

Lichtheim, L. (1885). On aphasia. *Brain*, *7*, 433–485.

Liepmann, H., & Maas, O. (1907). Ein Fall von linksseitiger Agraphie und Apraxie bei rechtsseitiger Lahmumg. *Journal of Psychological Neurology*, *10*, 214–227.

Luzzatti, C., Laiacona, M., Allamano, N., De Tanti, A., & Inzaghi, M. G. (1998). Writing disorders in Italian aphasic patients: A multiple single-case study of dysgraphia in a language with shallow orthography. *Brain*, *121*(9), 1721–1734.

Luzzi, S., Bartolini, M., Coccia, M., Provinciali, L., Piccirilli, M., & Snowden, J. S. (2003). Surface dysgraphia in a regular orthography: Apostrophe use by an Italian writer. *Neurocase*, *9*(4), 285–296.

Macoir, J., & Bernier, J. (2002). Is surface dysgraphia tied to semantic impairment? Evidence from case of semantic dementia. *Brain Cognition*, *48*(2–3), 452–457.

Margolin, D. I. (1984). The neuropsychology of writing and spelling: Semantic phonological, motor, and perceptual processes. *Quarterly Journal of Experimental Psychology*, *36A*, 459–489.

Margolin, D. I., & Binder, L. (1984). Multiple component agraphia in a patient with atypical cerebral dominance: An error analysis. *Brain Language*, *22*, 26–40.

Menichelli, A., Rapp, B., & Semenza, C. (2008). Allographic agraphia: A case study. *Cortex*, *44*(70), 861–868.

Menon, V., & Desmond, J. E. (2001). Left superior parietal cortex involvement in writing: Integrating fMRI with lesion evidence. *Cognitive Brain Research*, *12*(2), 337–340.

Miceli, G., Silveri, M. C., & Caramazza, A. (1985). Cognitive analysis of a case of pure dysgraphia. *Brain Language*, *25*, 187–212.

Mortley, J., Enderby, P., & Petheram, B. (2001). Using a computer to improve functional writing in a patient with severe *dysgraphia*. *Aphasiology*, *15*(5), 443–461.

Nadeau, S. E. & Crosson, B. (1997). Subcortical Aphasia. *Brain Language*, *58*(3), 355–402.

Nakamura, K., Honda, M., Hirano, S., Oga, T., Sawamoto, N., Hanakawa, T., et al. (2002). Modulation of the visual word retrieval system in writing: A functional MRI study on the Japanese orthographies. *Journal of Cognitive Neuroscience*, *14*(1), 104–115.

Nickels, L. (2002).Therapy for naming disorders: Revisiting, revising, and reviewing. *Aphasiology*, *16*(10–11), 935–980.

Niels, J., & Roeltgen, D. P. (1995a). Decline in homophone spelling associated with loss of semantic influence on spelling in Alzheimer's disease. *Brain Language*, *49*(27), 49.

Niels, J., & Roeltgen. D. P. (1995b). Spelling and attention in early Alzheimer's disease: Evidence for impairment of the graphemic buffer. *Brain Language*, *49*, 241–262.

Nielson, J. M. (1938). Gerstmann syndrome: Finger agnosia, agraphia, confusion of right and left acalculia. *Archives of Neurological Psychiatry*, *39*, 536–559.

Nielson, J. M. (1946). *Agnosia, apraxia, aphasia: Their value in cerebral localization*. New York: Paul B. Hoeber.

Nolan, K. A., & Caramazza, A. (1982). Modality-independent impairments in word processing in a deep dyslexic patient. *Brain Language*, *16*, 236–264.

Ogle, J. W. (1867). Aphasia and agraphia. *Rep. Mod. Res. Counsel St. George's Hospital (Land.)*, *2*, 83–122.

Olson, A. & Caramazza, A. (1994). Representation and connectionist models: The NETspell experience. In G. D. A. Brown, and N. C. Ellis (Eds.), *Handbook of spelling: Theory, process and intervention* (pp. 337–363). Chichester: John Wiley.

Otsuki, M., Soma, Y., Aral, T., Otsuka, A., & Tsuji, S. (1999). Pure apraxic agraphia with abnormal writing stroke sequences: Report of a Japanese patient with a left superior parietal hemorrhage. *Journal of Neurology, Neurosurgery and Psychiatry*, *66*, 233–237.

Patterson, K. (1986). Lexical but nonsemantic spelling? *Cognitive Neuropsychology*, *3*, 341–367.

Patterson, K., & Howard, D. (1992). Pyramids and Palmtrees: A test of semantic access from words and pictures. Bury St. Edmunds, Suffolk: Thames Valley Test Company.

Plaut, D. C., McClelland, J. L., Seidenberg, M., & Patterson, K. (1996). Understanding normal and impaired reading: Computational principles in quasi-regular domains. *Psychological Review*, *103*, 56–115.

Plaut, D. C., & Shallice, T. T. (1993). Deep dyslexia: A case study of connectionist neuropsychology. *Cognitive Neuropsychology*, *10*(5), 377–500.

Posteraro, L., Zinelli, P., & Mazzucci, A. (1988). Selective impairment of the graphemic buffer in acquired dysgraphia. *Brain Language*, *35*, 274–286.

Pound, C. (1996). Writing remediation using preserved oral spelling: A case for separate output buffers. *Aphasiology*, *10*, 283–296.

Ramage, A., Beeson, P. M., & Rapcsak, S. Z. (1998). Dissociation between oral and written spelling: Clinical characteristics and possible mechanisms. Presentation at the Clinical Aphasiology Conference, June. In A. E. Hillis (Ed.), *The handbook of adult language disorders: Integrating cognitive neuropsychology, neurology, and rehabilitation* (p. 116). New York: Psychology Press.

Rapcsak, S. Z., & Beeson, P. M. (2002). Neuroanatomical correlates of spelling and writing. In A. E. Hillis (Ed.), *Handbook on adult language disorders: Integrating cognitive neuropsychology, neurology, and Rehabilitation* (pp. 71–99). New York: Psychology Press.

Rapcsak, S. Z., & Beeson, P. M. (2004). The role of left posterior inferior temporal cortex in spelling. *Neurology*, *62*, 2221–2229.

Rapcsak, S. Z., & Rubens, A. B. (1990). Disruption of semantic influence on writing following a left prefrontal lesion. *Brain Language*, *38*, 334–344.

Rapcsak, S. Z., Arthur, S. A., & Rubens, A. B. (1988). Lexical agraphia from focal lesion of the left precentral gyms. *Neurology*, *38*, 1119–1123.

Rapcsak, S. Z., Henry, M. L., Teague, S. L., Carnahan, S. D., & Beeson, P. M. (2007). Do dual-route models accurately predict reading and spelling performance in individuals with acquired alexia and agraphia? *Neuropsychologia*, *45*(11), 2519–2524.

Rapcsak, S. Z., Beeson, P. M., Henry, M. L., Leyden, A., Kim, E., Rising, K., et al. (2008). Phonological dyslexia and dysgraphia: Cognitive mechanisms and neural substrates. *Cortex*, doi:10.1016/j.cortex.2008.04.006.

Rapp, B. (2005). The relationship between treatment outcomes and the underlying cognitive deficit: Evidence from the remediation of acquired dysgraphia. *Aphasiology*, *19*(10), 994–1008.

Rapp, B., Epstein, C., & Tainturer, M. J. (2002). The integration of information across lexical and sublexical processes in spelling. *Cognitive Neuropsychology*, *19*(1), 1–29.

Rapp, B., & Kane, A. (2002). Remediation of deficits affecting different components of the spelling process. *Aphasiology*, *16*, 439–454.

Raymer, A., Cudworth, C., & Haley, M. (2003) Spelling treatment for an individual with dysgraphia: Analysis of generalisation to untrained words. *Aphasiology*, *17*(6), 607–624.

Reilly, J., & Peelle, J. E. (2008). Effects of semantic impairment on language processing in semantic dementia. *Seminars in Speech and Language*, *29*(1), 32–43.

Roeltgen, D. P. (1983). *The neurolinguistics of writing: Anatomic and neurologic correlates*. Presented at the International Neuropsychological Society, Pittsburgh, PA.

Roeltgen, D. P. (1985). Agraphia. In K. M. Heilman, & E. Valenstein (Eds.), *Clinical Neuropsychology* (2nd ed., pp. 75–96). New York: Oxford University Press.

Roeltgen, D. P. (1989). *Prospective analysis of a model of writing, anatomic aspects*. Presented at the Academy of Aphasia, Santa Fe, NM.

Roeltgen, D. P. (1991). Prospective analysis of writing and spelling. Part II. Results not related to localization. *Journal of Clinical Experimental Neuropsychology*, *13*, 48.

Roeltgen, D. P., & Heilman, K. M. (1983). Apraxic agraphia in a patient with normal praxis. *Brain Language*, *18*, 35–46.

Roeltgen, D. P., & Heilman, K. M. (1984). Lexical agraphia, further support for the two system hypothesis of linguistic agraphia. *Brain*, *107*, 811–827.

Roeltgen, D. P., & Heilman, K. M. (1985). Review of agraphia and proposal for an anatomically based neuropsychological model of writing. *Applied Psycholinguistics*, *6*, 205–220.

Roeltgen, D. P., & Rapcsak, S. (1993). Acquired disorders of writing and spelling. In G. Blanken (Ed.), *Linguistic disorders and pathologies* (pp. 262–278). Berlin: Walter de Gruyter.

Roeltgen, D. P., Rothi, L. J. G., & Heilman, K. M. (1982). Isolated phonological agraphia from a focal lesion. Presented at the Academy of Aphasia, New Paltz, NY.

Roeltgen, D. P., Rothi, L. J. G., & Heilman. K. M. (1986). Linguistic semantic agraphia. *Brain Language*, *27*, 257–280.

Roeltgen, D. P., Sevush, S., & Heilman. K. M. (1983a). Phonological agraphia: Writing by the lexical-semantic route. *Neurology*, *33*, 733–757.

Roeltgen, D. P., Sevush, S., & Heilman. K. M. (1983b). Pure Gerstmann syndrome from a focal lesion. *Archives of Neurology*, *40*, 46–47.

Rothi, L. J. G., & Heilman. K. M. (1981). Alexia and agraphia with spared spelling and letter recognition abilities. *Brain Language*, *12*, 1–13.

Rothi, L. J. G., Roeltgen, D. P., & Kooistra, C. A. (1987). Isolated lexical agraphia in a right-handed patient with a posterior lesion of the right cerebral hemisphere. *Brain Language*, *301*, 181–190.

Rubens, A. B., Geschwind, N., Mahowald, M. W., & Mastri, A. (1977). Posttraumatic cerebral hemispheric disconnection syndrome. *Archives of Neurology*, *34*, 750–755.

Sage, K., & Ellis, A. (2004) Lexical influences in graphemic buffer disorder. *Neuropsychology*, *21*, 381–400.

Sakurai, Y., Matsumura, K., Iwatsubo, T., & Mornose, T. (1997). Frontal pure agraphia for kanji or kana: Dissociation between morphology and phonology. *Neurology*, *49*, 946–952.

Sakurai, Y., Onuma, Y., Nakazawa, G., Ugawa, Y., Momose, T., Tsuji, S., & Mannen, T. (2007). Parietal dysgraphia: Characterization of abnormal writing stroke sequences, character formation and character recall. *Behavioral Neurology*, *18*(2), 99–114.

Schmalzl, L., & Nickels, L. (2006), Treatment of irregular word spelling in acquired dysgraphia: Selective benefit from visual mnemonics. *Neuropsychological Rehabilitation*, *16*(1), 1–37.

Seidenberg, M. S., & McClelland, J. L. (1989) A distributed, developmental model of word recognition and naming. *Psychology Review*, *96*(4), 523–568.

Seron, X., Deloche, G., Moulard, G., & Rousselle, M. (1980). A computer-based therapy for the treatment of aphasic subjects with writing disorders. *Journal of Speech and Hearing Disorders*, *45*, 45–58.

Shallice, T. (1981). Phonological agraphia and the lexical route in writing. *Brain*, *104*, 412–429.

Shallice, T., Glasspool, D. W., & Houghton, G. (1995). Can neuropsychological evidence inform modeling? Analyses of spelling. *Language and Cognitive Processes*, *10*, 195–225.

Silveri, M. C., Misciagna, S., Leggio, M. C., & Moliriari, M. (1997). Spatial dysgraphia and cerebellar lesion: A case report. *Neurology*, *48*, 1529–1532.

Soma, Y., Sugishita, M., Kitamura, K., Maruyama, S., & Imanaga, H. (1989). Lexical agraphia in the Japanese language: Pure agraphia for Kanji due to left posteroinferior temporal lesions. *Brain*, *112*(6), 1549–1561.

Sugishita, M., Toyokura, Y., Yoshioka, M., & Yamada, R. (1980). Unilateral agraphia after section of the posterior half of the truncus to the corpus callosum. *Brain Language*, *9*, 212–223.

Tainturier, M. J., & Rapp, B. C. (2004). Complex graphemes as functional spelling units: Evidence from acquired dysgraphia. *Neurocase*, *10*(2), 122–131.

Tanaka, Y., Iwasa, H., & Obayashi, T. (1990). Right hand agraphia and left hand apraxia following callosal daiTiage in a right-hander. *Cortex*, *26*, 665–671.

Trojano, L., & Chiacchio, L. (1994). Pure dysgraphia with relative sparing of lower-case writing. *Cortex*, *30*, 499–501.

Valenstein, E., & Heilman, K. M. (1979). Apraxic agraphia with neglect-induced paragraphia. *Archives of Neurology*, *67*, 44–56.

Van Orden, G. C., Pennington, B. F., & Stone, G. O. (2001). What do double dissociations prove? *Cognitive Science*, *25*, 111–172.

Ward, J. (2003). Understanding oral spelling: A review and synthesis. *Neurocase*, *9*(1), 1–14.

Watson, R. T., & Heilman, K. M. (1983). Callosal apraxia. *Brain*, *106*, 391–404.

Yamadori, A., Osumi, Y., Ikeda, H., & Kanazawa, Y. (1980). Left unilateral agraphia and tactile anomia. Disturbances seen after occlusion of the anterior cerebral artery. *Archives of Neurology*, *37*, 88–91.

7

Disorders of Visual-Spatial Perception and Cognition

MARTHA J. FARAH AND RUSSELL A. EPSTEIN

Humans are visual creatures, and our brain organization reflects this. Vision is the main function of the occipital cortex and occupies much of the parietal and temporal cortex as well. Even in the most anterior parts of the brain, as physically distant as possible from primary visual cortex, are areas dedicated to eye movement programming and visual working memory. One consequence of this organization is that lesions to many different parts of the brain can affect vision. The nature of the visual disturbance depends on the particular contribution that the damaged area would normally have made to vision.

This chapter reviews disorders of visual processing in an order roughly corresponding to the stages of visual processing affected, beginning with the earliest stages of cortical visual processing. For each disorder, its main features, associated lesion site, and implications for our understanding of normal vision will be discussed.

DISORDERS OF EARLY AND INTERMEDIATE VISION

VISUAL FIELD DEFECTS AND CORTICAL BLINDNESS

After the visual signal leaves the eye, where it receives some initial filtering, it projects to the thalamus, where it receives further processing, and then on to the primary visual cortex, situated at the very back of the brain. Total destruction of the primary visual cortex causes cortical blindness. Partial destruction causes partial blindness, and the location of the lesion within the primary visual cortex corresponds to the location of the visual field defect, in a highly systematic way that reflects the retinotopic arrangement of the primary visual cortex. With vascular lesions, it is common for some or all of the primary cortex in one hemisphere to be damaged, whereas the opposite hemisphere is unaffected. This results in blindness restricted to one half of the visual field, or *hemianopia*. It sometimes called *homonymous hemianopia* to indicate that the blind regions are the same regardless of which eye is used to see.

In the days before computed tomography (CT) scanning, the anatomy of the primary visual cortex and the pathways from thalamus to visual cortex allowed lesions to be roughly localized from visual field defects. As shown in Figure 7-1, homonymous visual field defects imply that the lesion is posterior, because input from the two eyes merges anteriorly at the optic chiasm (location B of the figure). Because the left optic radiation projecting to the left visual cortex represents only the right visual

field, and vice versa, visual field defects also reveal the side of the lesion. The altitude of the visual field defect is also informative, with lower quadrant blindness suggesting a parietal or superior occipital lesion because of the dorsal course of the pathways from thalamus to cortex, and upper quadrant blindness suggesting a temporal or inferior occipital lesion because of the ventral course. An early and classic generalization about the anatomy of face recognition was based on this type of analysis. J.C. Meadows (1974) reviewed the visual field charts of a large number of cases of *prosopagnosia*, or face recognition impairment, and found a preponderance of left upper quadrant defects, often with

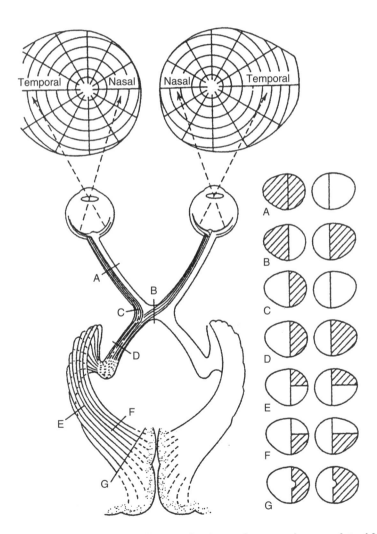

Figure 7–1. Correspondences between location of lesion within the visual system and pattern of visual field defects. From J. Homans. (1945). *A textbook of surgery.* Springfield IL: Charles C. Thomas.

defects in the upper right as well. From this, he was able to infer that the critical substrates for face recognition are in the right temporal cortex or bilateral temporal cortices in most people, a conclusion that has been confirmed with the advent of structural and functional brain imaging in recent years.

DISORDERS OF COLOR PROCESSING

Surrounding the primary visual cortex is a set of cortical regions that receive their input principally from the primary visual cortex. They maintain a retinotopic organization, although it is somewhat less precise than in primary visual cortex, and they carry out additional processing on the visual signal. The nature of this processing is not thoroughly understood, but at least one area, on the ventral surface of the brain, is known to play an important role in color perception.

The existence of a specialized cortical visual area for color was first suggested by patients with acquired cortical color blindness, also called acquired *cerebral achromatopsia* (see Zeki, 1990, for a review). Such patients report that the world seems drained of color, like a black-and-white movie. In other respects, their vision may be roughly normal. For example, they may have good acuity, motion and depth perception, and object recognition. However, when examined carefully, they have been found to have subtle impairments of form vision, for example a disturbance in the ability to discriminate spiral forms that differ only slightly from one another (Gallant et al., 2000). It should be added that frank problems with face, object, and printed word recognition often accompany achromatopsia, although they may be transient and are likely to be caused by impairment to areas neighboring the color area. Cases in which the color vision impairment is the only clinically apparent problem lend support to the existence of a brain area specialized for color perception. The co-occurrence of subtle impairments in non-color vision suggest that this specialization is not absolute, but only relative, consistent with findings from single-unit recordings in monkeys that show a degree of shape selectivity along with color selectivity in extrastriate cortex (Solomon & Lennie, 2007).

The sudden loss of color vision impacts on patients' lives in numerous ways. In one case, for example, a man was stopped by the police for running red lights. He could no longer select his own clothes each day, and required that food be placed in set positions, so that he could discriminate mayonnaise and mustard from jam and ketchup. He found the changed appearance of food unappetizing, and began to eat only those foods that are naturally black and white: rice, olives, black coffee, and yogurt (Sacks & Wasserman, 1987).

In some cases, a unilateral lesion will result in color loss in just one hemifield, consistent with retinotopic mapping of the area responsible for color vision. A particularly selective and well-studied case of this was described by Damasio, Yamada, Damasio, Corbett, and McKee (1980). Although acuity, depth perception, motion perception, and object recognition were roughly normal in both hemifields, there was a striking asymmetry for color perception: "He was unable to name any color in any portion of the left field of either eye, including bright reds, blues, greens, and yellows. As soon as any portion of a colored object crossed the vertical meridian, he was able instantly to recognize and accurately name its color. When an object such as a red flashlight was held so that it bisected the vertical meridian, he reported that the hue of the right half appeared normal while the left half was gray." The problem was not with color naming but with perception, as he was also unable to match colors in the left visual field.

The lesions in achromatopsia are usually on the inferior surface of the temporo-occipital region, in the lingual and fusiform gyri. The most recent meta-analysis of lesion locations for patients with full-field, hemifield, or quadrantic achromatopsia showed that right ventral occipitotemporal cortex was damaged in the majority of cases, along with roughly similarly localized left hemisphere lesions in many of the full-field cases (Bouvier & Engle, 2006). This localization is consistent with functional neuroimaging studies in which the substrates of color perception have been isolated by comparing cerebral activation patterns while subjects view colored displays to patterns resulting when gray-scale versions of the same displays are viewed (e.g., Wade et al., 2008).

Achromatopsia should be distinguished from three other color-related disorders that sometimes follow brain damage in humans. *Color anomia* refers to an impairment in producing the names of colors. It is sometimes seen in isolation from anomia for other types of words (Goodglass, Wingfield, Hyde, & Theurkauf, 1986), but it is not a disorder of color perception. There is no difficulty performing nonverbal tests of color perception and no subjective loss of color perception. This disorder is often caused by left ventral temporal lesions.

Color-object association is a task that has been used with a variety of different neuropsychological populations, from visually impaired to language impaired (DeRenzi & Spinnler, 1967). In a pure *disorder of color-object association*, the patient sees colors normally and knows how to use color names in the context of overlearned or abstract associations ("lemon yellow" or "green is the color of envy"). But knowledge of the typical colors of objects in the absence of a verbal association is impaired. Such knowledge is typically accessed with the help of mental imagery (e.g., when retrieving the color of a U.S. mailbox or an ear of corn, most people report forming a mental image of the queried object and "looking" at it to see its color). Therefore, this type of color processing impairment could be a specific result of a more general impairment in visual image generation, to be discussed later in this chapter.

Color agnosia is a less clearly defined entity, said to involve a loss of knowledge about colors, and distinct from the other disorders reviewed here. Different authors seem to have different meanings in mind when they use this term (Farah, 2000). At least some of the data on color agnosia seem to require an explanation that is neither perceptual nor linguistic per se: Kinsbourne and Warrington (1964) showed that their patient could learn arbitrary associations between pairs of objects, noncolor names, and numbers, but could not learn associations between colors and noncolor names or numbers, nor between color names and other things. Furthermore, in these and other tasks, both the "colors" black, white and gray, and the names "black," "white," and "gray" were spared. A case with carefully studied perceptual and cognitive

abilities, consistent with loss of nonperceptual color knowledge, was described by Miceli et al. (2001).

DISORDERS OF MOTION PERCEPTION

A small number of cases have described acquired cerebral motion blindness or *cerebral akinetopsia* (see Zeki, 1993 for a review). By far the best-studied case is that of Zihl, Von Cramon, and Mai (1983). This was case L.M., a 43-year-old woman who, following bilateral strokes in the posterior parietotemporal and occipital regions, was left with but one major impairment: namely the complete inability to perceive visual motion. Zihl et al. (1983) tested L.M.'s visual perception in a variety of simple experimental tasks and compared her performance with that of normal subjects. In her color and depth perception, object and word recognition, and a variety of other visual abilities tested by these authors, L.M. did not differ significantly from normal subjects. In addition, her ability to judge the motion of a tactile stimulus (wooden stick moved up or down her arm) and an auditory stimulus (tone-emitting loudspeaker moved through space) was also normal. In contrast, her perception of direction and speed of visual motion in horizontal and vertical directions within the picture plane and in depth was grossly impaired.

In her everyday life, she was profoundly affected by her visual impairment. When pouring tea or coffee the fluid appeared to be frozen, like a glacier. Without being able to perceive movement, she could not stop pouring at the right time and frequently filled the cup to overflowing. Following conversations was difficult without being able to see the facial and mouth movements of each speaker, and gatherings of more than two other people left her feeling unwell and insecure. She complained that "people were suddenly here or there but I have not seen them moving." The patient could not cross the street because of her inability to judge the speed of a car. "When I see the car at first, it seems far away. But then, when I want to cross the road, suddenly the car is very near." She gradually learned to estimate the distance of moving vehicles by means of the sound becoming louder.

As with achromatopsia, the existence of akinetopsia implies a high degree of cerebral specialization for a single dimension of visual information. Although L.M.'s lesions were fairly large and encompassed both parietal and temporal cortex, the critical lesion site has been inferred to be the posterior middle temporal gyrus. Functional neuroimaging studies of motion perception, comparing brain activation patterns to moving and static displays, show their maximum in this same region (Zeki et al., 1991).

Recent studies have documented even further division of labor within the overall task of visual motion perception. In one series of case studies, Vaina and colleagues (2005) found different patterns of relative impairment for the perception of different aspects of motion in different patients. For example the ability to integrate long-range displacements of an object into a percept of object motion was dissociable from the ability to discriminate velocity of motion. A distinct set of areas appears to be required for the perception of biological motion, that is, patterns of movement characteristic of naturally locomoting humans and animals. Saygin (2007) found that patients who were impaired at biological motion perception but not a simpler motion detection task tended to have damage to specific regions in the frontal and temporal cortex, coincident with the regions implicated for biological motion perception in functional imaging studies (Saygin et al., 2004).

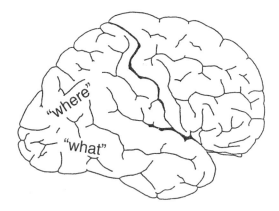

Figure 7–2. The two cortical visual systems: Dorsal visual areas are particularly important for spatial or "where" processing, and ventral visual areas are particularly important for appearance or "what" processing.

DISORDERS OF HIGHER-LEVEL VISUAL-SPATIAL FUNCTION

AN ORGANIZING FRAMEWORK: THE TWO CORTICAL VISUAL SYSTEMS

Higher-level vision has two main goals, the identification of stimuli and their localization. Although a bit of an oversimplification, this dichotomy of function has provided a useful organizing framework for the neuropsychology of high-level vision. The two goals, sometimes abbreviated as "what" and "where," are achieved by relatively independent and anatomically separate systems, located in the ventral and dorsal visual cortices, respectively, as shown in Figure 7-2. These have been termed *the two cortical visual systems* (Ungerleider & Mishkin, 1972).

The earliest evidence for the existence of two cortical visual systems came from neurological case reports. Neurologists noted that some patients were selectively impaired at object recognition but retained good spatial abilities, and others were impaired at spatial vision but failed in object recognition (Potzl, 1928; Lange, 1936). Given the subjectively seamless experience of knowing what and where an object is when we look at it, these dissociations are striking. Dorsal simultanagnostic patients, with bilateral posterior parietal damage, may quickly and easily recognize an object (at least, once they have found it), but cannot point to it or describe its location relative to other objects in the scene (Holmes, 1918). Conversely, agnosic patients, with bilateral inferior occipitotemporal damage, may perform well on these simple localization tests, as well as on more complex tests of spatial cognition, while failing to recognize simple drawings of familiar objects, short printed words, or the faces of loved ones (Farah, 2004).

The same dissociation, in a weaker form, is found after unilateral right hemisphere brain damage. Newcombe and Russell (1969) tested World War II veterans with penetrating head wounds on two kinds of task. In the "closure" task, designed to tax visual recognition, patients had to judge the age and gender of faces rendered as fragmentary regions of light and shadow. In the maze task, designed to tax spatial processing, patients had to learn, by trial and error, the correct path through a matrix. Two subgroups of patients were defined, corresponding to the lowest 20% of scores on each of the two tests. The resulting subgroups were nonoverlapping, and indeed each group performed on a par with the remaining subjects on the other test, supporting the idea that "what" and "where" are processed independently. Furthermore, the men with poor closure performance all had posterior temporal lesions, whereas the men with poor maze performance all had posterior parietal lesions. Experimental studies of animals, using both lesions and single-unit recordings, add further support to the idea of a dorsal spatial visual system and a ventral pattern recognition system.

The clearest case of a visual disorder due to ventral system damage is *visual agnosia*, the impairment of visual recognition not due to more elementary visual problems or more general intellectual problems. Depending upon the precise location of damage, and whether it is confined to the left or right hemisphere, or is bilateral, a patient may be agnosic for some kinds of object and not others. Face recognition may be primarily or perhaps even exclusively impaired (*prosopagnosia*), and the ability to recognize printed words may also be affected selectively (*pure alexia*). Visual agnosia, in its many forms, is the subject of Chapter 11 in this volume, and a book by Farah (2004).

The most common form of visual disorder due to dorsal system damage is *hemispatial neglect*, a fascinating condition in which patients lose awareness of stimuli contralateral to a dorsal system lesion, but have no problem perceiving those same stimuli if moved to a non-neglected region of space. Neglect is also the subject of Chapter 12 in this volume. In addition to neglect, several other distinct problems with visual-spatial perception and cognition can follow lesions of the dorsal visual system. Three general types of visual-spatial disorder are briefly reviewed here. Visual-spatial disorders that are manifest primarily in perceiving and recognizing aspects of large-scale environmental space will be discussed in the next section.

In *impaired perception of location*, the loss of ability to perceive the location of a single object results in a condition known as *visual disorientation*. Whether asked to point to or describe an object's location, the patient is grossly inaccurate. This is, not surprisingly, a disabling problem. The critical lesion site is the occipital-parietal junction, and in some cases a unilateral form of the disorder is observed after damage to either the left or right hemisphere alone (Riddoch, 1935).

Impaired perception of line orientation is a subtler impairment of spatial perception, generally brought out by testing. A widely used test of orientation perception is that of Benton, Varney, and Hamsher (1978), illustrated in Figure 7-3. The spatial nature of the judgment and the minimal nature of the shape information involved suggest that this ability would depend strongly on the parietal cortex, and indeed that is the case. There is also a pronounced asymmetry

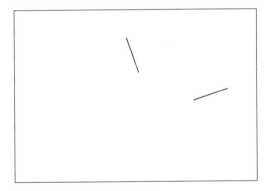

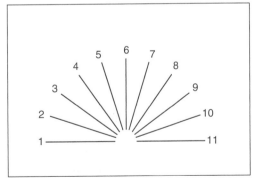

Figure 7–3. A typical item from the Benton, Varney, and Hamsher (1978) test of orientation perception. The patient's task is to match the orientations of the test lines, above, with lines from the response set, below.

in favor of greater right hemisphere involvement in this ability (DeRenzi, 1982).

Although it can be difficult to disentangle impairments of visual localization from impairments of visually guided reaching, a number of careful studies have done so (DeRenzi, 1982). The *impairment of visually guided reaching,* also known as *optic ataxia,* is usually observed in unilateral form, but this generality covers a surprising array of variants. The left–right division may pertain to the hemispace, the reaching limb, or both, as when the left arm's reaches into the left hemispace are disproportionately less accurate than other limb–space combinations. In addition, some patients with unilateral

lesions show a milder level of optic ataxia on the ipsilesional side of space. Optic ataxia usually follows damage high in the parietal lobe, anterior to the regions most likely to cause visual disorientation. The precise scope of the impairment presumably depends on what parts of parietal gray and underlying white matter are damaged. Figure 7-4 shows how different combinations of hemispace and limb selectivity could result from interruption of the pathways from visual to motor cortex at different points.

The *impaired drawing and building* category has persisted in the clinical neuropsychology literature, under the label *constructional apraxia,* for many decades, probably because drawing

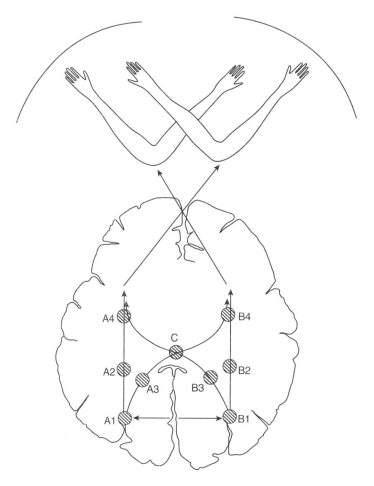

Figure 7–4. Schematic diagram of different possible lesions interrupting visuomotor control, which would result in different patterns of limb and visual field differences in visually guided reaching. Lesions at points marked 1 and 4 would result in pure field selectivity and limb selectivity, respectively. Lesions at points marked 2 and 3 would result in both field and limb selectivity, contralateral and ipsilateral, respectively. A lesion at C would result in a different pattern of field and limb selectivity, with contralateral combinations of limb and field, on either side, impaired (as in callosotomy patients). From E. ReRenzi. (1982). *Disorders of space exploration and cognition.* New York: Wiley and Co.

and assembling objects are handy bedside tasks and are effective at revealing a range of spatial impairments. However, it is such a heterogeneous category that it is hardly a category at all. An enormous number of different underlying impairments can cause poor drawings or disorganized arrangements of puzzle parts, including motor and executive impairments as well as spatial impairments. Even for constructional apraxia following posterior lesions, there are pronounced differences between the effects of left and right hemisphere lesions, with the former generally resulting in spare, impoverished constructions and the latter resulting in abundantly detailed but disorganized constructions, as illustrated in Figure 7-5 (McFie & Zangwill, 1960).

DISORDERS OF SPATIAL NAVIGATION

Patients can lose the ability to navigate their environment following damage to regions as diverse as the posterior parietal cortex, cingulate, parahippocampal, and lingual gyri. Their associated impairments are likewise variable.

A review by Aguirre and D'Esposito (1999) used cognitive theories of topographic orientation and information about lesion localization to arrive at a useful taxonomy of topographic disorders, which is summarized here. The different forms of topographic disorientation are informative about the organization of topographic knowledge in the normal brain. The patterns of preserved and impaired abilities described here suggest that spatial orientation in the environment involves both specialized topographic representations and more general spatial abilities, that spatial and landmark knowledge of the environment are subserved by partially dissociable systems, and that the acquisition of topographic knowledge may be carried out by a specialized learning system (see Epstein, 2008, for a review).

Egocentric disorientation is the term used to describe patients whose topographic disorientation is secondary to visual disorientation (described in the previous section). Not surprisingly, patients who cannot localize objects in space are severely handicapped in navigating both familiar and unfamiliar terrain. Of course, this form of topographic impairment is not

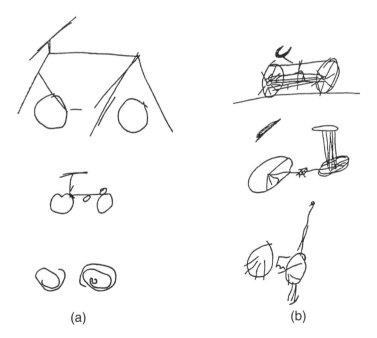

(a)   (b)

Figure 7–5. Examples of constructional apraxia in a bicycle drawing task following (a) left and (b) right hemisphere lesions. From McFie, J., & Zangwill, O.L. (1960). Visual-constructive disabilities associated with lesions of the left cerebral hemisphere. *Brain, 83,* 243–261.

specific to topographic knowledge: These patients have difficulty localizing *any* object relative to their body (hence the term "egocentric" disorientation). A representative case, described by Levine, Warach, and Farah (1985), was unable even to find his way around his own home, despite intact recognition of objects and landmarks. The critical lesion site, as noted earlier, is the posterior parietal lobe bilaterally.

Heading disorientation is a more specific impairment in spatial representation. These patients are oriented within their immediate environment and can localize objects relative to their body, but cannot understand the relationship between the immediate environment and locations beyond it that are not currently visible. Often, the onset of the impairment is quite dramatic. For example, Ino and colleagues (2007) reported that their patient suddenly became lost while returning home from work: "He could recognize buildings and the landscape and therefore understand where he was, but the landmarks that he recognized did not provoke directional information about any other places with respect to those landmarks. Consequently, he could not determine which direction to proceed." Note that this patient was able to identify the buildings around him without difficulty, but was unable to situate these landmarks within a larger spatial scheme that allowed him to know which way to go to reach his goal. The buildings were stripped of their navigational relevance, thus robbing the patient of his sense of direction.

The critical lesion site appears to be the posterior cingulate/retrosplenial region, in either the left or right hemisphere. Interestingly, the concomitant navigational problems often clear up after a few months in cases of unilateral damage but not in cases of bilateral damage, possibly because the undamaged hemisphere begins to compensate in the unilateral case. Burgess (2008; see also Byrne et al., 2007) has proposed that the retrosplenial cortex plays a key role in mediating between egocentric spatial representations in the parietal lobe and allocentric spatial relationships in the medial temporal region. Under this hypothesis, lesions to this region lead to a profound deficit in one's ability to implement a route, because it is impossible to translate long-term knowledge about

the spatial relationship between landmarks into local knowledge about which way to turn at any particular point on the route.

Landmark agnosia is an impairment of visual recognition that is selective or disproportionate for those objects in the environment that normally serve as landmarks. These include many kinds of large topographical entities, such as buildings, monuments, squares, vistas, intersections and so on. Patients with landmark agnosia, such as Pallis's classic (1955) case, often retain their spatial knowledge of the environment, as evidenced by good descriptions of routes, layouts, and maps. However, without the ability to discriminate one landmark from another, they cannot apply this knowledge. The typical lesions in landmark agnosia are similar to those of other visual agnosias, especially prosopagnosia—that is, the inferior surface of the occipitotemporal regions, either bilateral or right-sided. The lingual gyrus and posterior parahippocampal cortex appear to be particularly involved.

Although at first glance the visual perception of these patients may appear to be unimpaired (with the common exception of a visual field cut), they often complain that some global organizing aspect of the scene is missing (Habib & Sirigu, 1987; Epstein et al., 2001). For example, a patient described by Hecaen (1980) reported that "it's the whole you see, in a very large area I can identify some minor detail or places but I don't recognize the whole." This inability to perceive scenes as unified entities is also evident in a compensatory strategy that is often observed: Rather than identifying places in a normal manner, landmark agnosia patients will often focus on minor visual details (for example, a distinctive mailbox or door knocker). Mendez and Cherrier (2003) examined a patient for which this whole scene–specific object distinction was particularly acute. When asked to identify photographs of locations from a previously learned route, he was especially impaired for scenes that could only be recognized based on their overall configuration. Interestingly, if he was able to recognize a landmark or scene, he knew which direction to go from the landmark; indeed, he reported that he retained the equivalent of a "street guide" of his hometown in his head.

Anterograde disorientation refers to a topographic impairment that is selective for the acquisition of new topographical knowledge. Such patients often present with symptoms similar to that of landmark agnosia, but eventually regain normal topographic abilities for environments that were familiar before their brain injury. Habib and Sirigu (1987) describe a typical case. The critical lesion site for anterograde disorientation appears to be the right parahippocampal gyrus, just anterior to the region impacted in landmark agnosia (Takahashi & Kawamura, 2002). Indeed, anterograde disorientation and landmark agnosia are often found in the same patients.

OTHER TOPOGRAPHICAL DISORDERS

Navigational problems are sometimes reported that do not easily fit under the four major symptoms listed by Aguirre and D'Esposito. Of particular interest are a small number of patients who are reported to be impaired at both acquisition *and* retrieval of spatial knowledge but are relatively unimpaired on nonspatial materials. For example, Luzzi and colleagues (2000) describe a patient who could recognize buildings but could not produce a floor plan of the apartment that he had lived in for many years. Damage in this case was in the right medial temporal lobe, anterior to the region typically damaged in anterograde disorientation. Burgess and colleagues (2006) report a similar phenomenon in a patient with possible early Alzheimer disease, who was not amnestic. She could recognize buildings but was unable to remember the route to a local restaurant where she had dined regularly for the past 10 years. The converse phenomenon—preserved topographical memory but impaired verbal/episodic memory—has also been described (Maguire & Cipolotti, 1998).

DISORDERS OF MENTAL IMAGERY

The most obvious function of the cortical visual system is the analysis of retinal inputs. Yet, it is also used to represent visual and spatial information in the absence of triggering stimuli.

When we imagine the appearance of an object or the layout of a scene from memory, we are using some of the same mechanisms in the occipital, temporal, and parietal lobes that are used when we recognize and localize physically present and visible stimuli.

Disorders of mental imagery can be grouped into three main categories: Disorders of image representation, disorders of image generation, and disorders of image transformation. The first set includes imagery problems that appear secondary to loss of the underlying representations used in both imagery and perception. The second and third categories include problems with imagery per se, either the ability to activate intact visual representations for the purpose of forming a mental image, or the ability to manipulate an image once formed.

DISORDERS OF IMAGE REPRESENTATION

If imagery and perception are both impaired after brain damage, this suggests that the functional locus of damage is the representations of visual appearance used by both. There are many reports of parallel impairments of imagery and perception, and these have attracted interest for what they can tell us about mental image representation. Specifically, they imply that mental imagery shares representations with the cortical visual system. A representative sample of these reports is presented here.

Color

Disorders of color imagery have often been noted, and the nature of the imagery impairment is generally similar to the perceptual impairment. For example, DeRenzi and Spinnler (1967) investigated various color-related abilities in a large group of unilaterally brain-damaged patients and found an association between impairment on color vision tasks, such as the Ishihara test of color blindness, and on color imagery tasks, such as verbally reporting the colors of common objects from memory. Beauvois and Saillant (1985) studied the imagery abilities of a patient with a visual–verbal disconnection syndrome. The patient could perform purely visual color tasks (e.g., matching color samples) and purely verbal color tasks (e.g., answering questions such as "What color is associated with envy?") but could not perform tasks in which a visual representation of color had to be associated with a verbal label (e.g., color naming). When the patient's color imagery was tested purely visually, by selecting the color sample that represents the color of an object depicted in black and white, she did well. However, when the equivalent problems were posed verbally (e.g., "What color is a peach?"), she did poorly. In other words, mental images interacted with other visual and verbal task components as if they were visual representations. De Vreese (1991) reported two cases of color imagery impairment, one of whom had left occipital damage and displayed the same type of visual–verbal disconnection as the patient just described, and the other of whom had bilateral occipital damage and parallel color perception and color imagery impairments.

Hemispatial Attention

In one of the best-known demonstrations of parallel impairments in imagery and perception, Bisiach and Luzzatti (1978) found that patients with hemispatial neglect for visual stimuli also neglected the contralesional sides of their mental images. Their two right parietal–damaged patients were asked to imagine a well-known square in Milan, shown in Figure 7-6. When they were asked to describe the scene from vantage point A on the map, they tended to name more landmarks on the east side of the square (marked with lower case a's in the figure); that is, they named the landmarks on the right side of the imagined scene. When they were then asked to imagine the square from the opposite vantage point, marked B on the map, they reported many of the landmarks previously omitted (because these were now on the right side of the image) and omitted some of those previously reported.

"What" and "Where"

Levine, Warach, and Farah (1985) studied the roles of the two cortical visual systems in mental imagery. One patient had visual disorientation following bilateral parieto-occipital damage, and the other had visual agnosia following bilateral inferior temporal damage. We found that the preserved and impaired aspects of visual imagery paralleled the patients' visual abilities: The first case could neither localize visual stimuli in space nor accurately describe the locations of familiar objects or landmarks from memory. However, he was good at both perceiving object identity from appearance and describing object appearance from memory. The second was impaired at perceiving object identity from appearance and describing object appearance from memory, but was good at localizing visual stimuli and at describing their locations from memory. In subsequent testing of the second patient, we found that he was impaired relative to control subjects on tasks that require imagining visual appearance (such as imagining animals and reporting whether they had long or short tails, imagining common objects and reporting their colors, and imagining triads of states within the United States and reporting which two are most similar in outline shape), but he performed well on tasks that require imagining spatial properties (such as paths through a matrix, mental rotation, and imagining triads of states and reporting which two are closest to one another; Farah, Hammond, Levine, & Calvanio, 1988).

Visual Field

Shared representations for imagery and perception exist within the occipital cortex as well. This was demonstrated by a patient with hemianopia for images and percepts following occipital resection. Our patient was a woman with epilepsy who was undergoing right occipital lobectomy. By testing her before and after her surgery, she could serve as her own control. If mental imagery consists of activating representations in the occipital lobe, then it should be impossible to form images in regions of the visual field that are blind due to occipital lobe destruction. This predicts that patients with homonymous hemianopia should have a smaller maximum image size, or visual angle of the mind's eye. By asking her to report the distance of imagined objects such as a horse, bread box, or ruler when they are visualized as close as possible without "overflowing" her imaginal

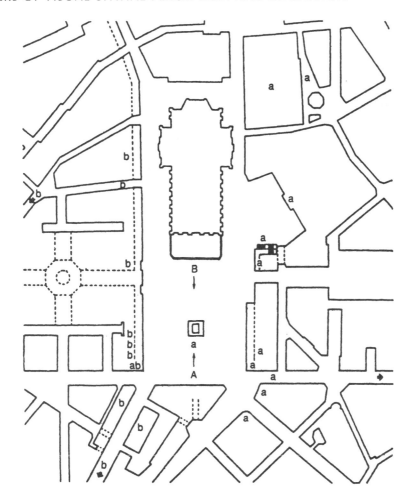

Figure 7–6. A map of the Piazza Del Duomo in Milan. When patients with left neglect were asked to imagine themselves standing at point A looking toward the cathedral, and to report what they saw in their "mind's eye," the locations they mentioned were those marked with an "a." When they repeated the procedure from the vantage point of B, they then mentioned the locations marked with a "b." From Farah, M. J. (1996). In M.S. Gazzaniga (Ed.), *The cognitive neurosciences.* Cambridge: MIT Press.

visual field, we could compute the visual angle of that field. We found that the size of her biggest possible image was reduced after surgery, as represented in Figure 7-7. Furthermore, by measuring maximal image size in the vertical and horizontal dimensions separately, we found that only the horizontal dimension of her imagery field was significantly reduced. These results provide strong evidence for the use of occipital visual representations during imagery.

Exceptions

Although patients with cortical visual damage usually manifest parallel impairments in their

mental imagery, this is not always the case. For example, Bartolomeo, D'Erme, and Gianotti (1994) have described preserved attention to the left sides of mental images in the presence of left visual neglect. Behrmann, Winocur, and Moscovitch (1994) and Servos and Goodale (1995) describe severely agnosic patients who demonstrate good visual mental imagery abilities. Such cases have been reported with increasing frequency as researchers have come to recognize their relevance to theories of mental imagery (e.g., Bartolomeo, 2008). These observations conflict with the hypothesis that imagery and visual perception share representations. However, earlier levels of representation in the

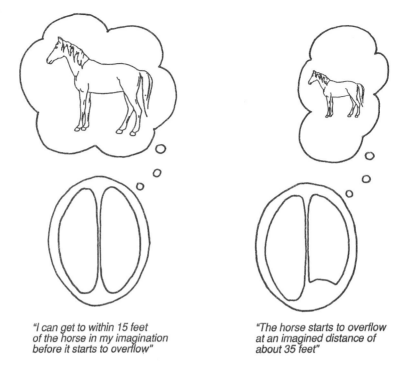

"I can get to within 15 feet
of the horse in my imagination
before it starts to overflow"

"The horse starts to overflow
at an imagined distance of
about 35 feet"

Figure 7–7. Depiction of the effects of unilateral occipital lobectomy on the visual angle of the mind's eye. From Farah, M. J. (1996). In M.S. Gazzaniga (Ed.), *The cognitive neurosciences.* Cambridge: MIT Press.

central visual system may be less engaged by, and needed for, imagery than later levels, and it is possible that these cases of preserved imagery suffered damage to relatively early stages of processing. Even in the patient with the seemingly highest-level impairment, Behrmann et al.'s agnosic, there is evidence that the locus of damage is relatively early in visual segmentation and grouping processes. A more detailed consideration of these discrepant findings and their implications is provided in Farah (2000).

To conclude, in most cases of selective visual impairments following damage to the cortical visual system, patients manifest qualitatively similar impairments in mental imagery and perception. Central impairments of color perception tend to co-occur with impairments of color imagery. Spatial attention impairments for the left side of the visual scene also affect the left side of mental images. Higher-order impairments of visual spatial orientation, sparing visual object recognition, and the converse, are associated with impairments of spatial imagery sparing imagery for object appearance, and the converse. Finally, hemianopia resulting from

surgical removal of one occipital lobe is associated with a corresponding loss of half the mind's eye's visual field. Taken together, these findings imply that at least some cortical visual representations perform "double duty," supporting both imagery and perception.

DISORDERS OF IMAGE GENERATION

If imagery consists of activating some of the same cortical visual areas used for perception, do these representations become activated in the absence of a stimulus? Whereas one cannot see a familiar object without recognizing it, one can think about familiar objects without inexorably calling to mind a visual mental image. This suggests that the activation of visual representations in imagery is a separate, voluntary process, needed for image generation but not for visual perception and object recognition.

Farah (1984) reviewed the neurological literature on imagery and identified a set of cases in which the underlying impairment seemed to be in image generation per se. In these cases, perception was grossly intact, yet the patients complained of difficulty visualizing objects and scenes from memory. A few years later, my colleagues and I encountered such a patient ourselves (Farah, Levine, & Calvanio, 1988). The imagery impairment was demonstrated in a number of ways, including a sentence verification task developed by Eddy and Glass (1981). Half of the sentences required the use of visual imagery to verify (e.g., "A grapefruit is larger than a cantaloupe") and half did not (e.g., "The U.S. government functions under a two-party system"). Eddy and Glass had shown that normal subjects find the two sets of questions equally difficult (as did right hemisphere-damaged control subjects tested by Farah et al.), and that performance on the imagery questions was selectively impaired by visual interference, thus validating them as imagery questions. R.M. showed a selective deficit for imagery on this validated task: He performed virtually perfectly on the nonimagery questions, and performed significantly worse on the imagery questions.

R.M. was also tested on imagery for the colors of objects, using black-and-white drawings of characteristically colored objects (e.g., a cactus, an ear of corn) for which he was to select the appropriate colored pencil. His imagery was further tested with drawing tasks. By these measures, too, his imagery was poor.

To infer a problem with image generation per se, as opposed to shared image–percept representations, R.M.'s object recognition and perceptual abilities were also tested. R.M. was not agnosic, and passed a stringent test of object recognition designed to assess long-term visual memory of the same items he was asked to image. In this test, R.M. was asked to select the correct drawing of an object from a pair. For example, a fish was either the correct shape or peanut-shaped. He performed this test perfectly. To assess color perception and long-term memory for object colors, different colored versions of each drawing were presented, and R.M. had to recognize which drawing was correctly colored. Although he did not perform perfectly on the color perception control condition, he did significantly better in this condition than in the imagery condition, using the same objects and colors.

The pattern of preserved and impaired abilities in R.M. is consistent with an impairment of

mental image generation. In subsequent years, a small number of additional cases of selectively impaired imagery have been reported (e.g., Grossi, Orsini, & Modafferi, 1986; Riddoch, 1990; Goldenberg, 1992; Morro et al., 2008), as well as similar but weaker dissociations in subgroups of patients in group studies (Bowers, Blonder, Feinberg, & Heilman, 1991; Goldenberg, 1989; Goldenberg & Artner, 1991; Stangalino, Semenza, & Mondini, 1995).

What parts of the brain carry out image generation? This question has evoked controversy. Although mental imagery was for many years assumed to be a function of the right hemisphere, Ehrlichman and Barrett (1983) pointed out that there was no direct evidence for this assumption. Farah (1984) noted a trend in the cases she reviewed for left posterior damage. Farah et al. (1988) suggested that the left temporo-occipital area may be critical. This idea has met with a range of reactions.

Sergent (1990) argued against the hypothesis of left hemisphere specialization for image generation, concluding that "in spite of recent claims that the left hemisphere is specialized for the generation of visual mental images, an examination of the relevant data and experimental procedures provides little support for this view, and suggests that both hemispheres simultaneously and conjointly contribute to this process" (p. 98). Her conclusions followed persuasively from her reading of the literature, although one could take issue with this reading at a number of points. For example, our case study of patient R.M., whose performance on tests of image generation, object recognition, and color perception were described in the previous section, was discounted on the grounds that his object recognition and color perception were not tested.

Tippett (1992) arrived at a less extreme conclusion, declaring that "what is striking in this area is the pervasiveness of findings (especially with brain-damaged patients) that seem to implicate the left hemisphere in the image generation process" (p. 429) and concludes that "support is found for the involvement of the left hemisphere, although many researchers claim that the posterior regions of both hemispheres contribute to image generation" (p. 415).

A third view was expressed by Trojano and Grossi (1994), who reviewed the case report literature on mental imagery defects with and without accompanying visual recognition impairments. Of the latter type of imagery defect, corresponding to the hypothesized image generation defect, they conclude that "mental imagery relies on dissociable processes which are localized in left hemisphere posterior areas" (p. 213). A more recent summary concludes that, when visual imagery is impaired without obvious perceptual impairment "damage to the left temporal lobe seems to be the rule in these cases" (Bartolomeo, 2008, p. 108). The recent focally damaged cases mentioned above (Grossi, et al., 1986; Farah et al., 1988; Riddoch, 1990; Goldenberg, 1992; Morro et al., 2008) have supported this suggestion, as have the group studies to varying degrees (most clearly Goldenberg & Artner, 1991; Stangalino et al., 1995). The rarity of cases of image generation deficit suggests that this function may not be strongly lateralized in most people; however, when impairments are observed after focal unilateral damage, the left or dominant hemisphere is implicated.

DISORDERS OF IMAGE TRANSFORMATION

The ability to visualize the spatial transformation of an object, whether currently in view or purely imaginary, allows one to simulate mentally the translation, enlargement, or rotation of the object. This ability is frequently called into play by our everyday spatial problem solving, for example figuring out how to fit a big suitcase into a car trunk. Mental rotation is the most intensively studied mental image transformation, and virtually the only one studied in neurological patients.

As might be expected, given the fundamentally spatial character of mental rotation, the parietal lobes appear to be essential for this ability. Group studies of focally brain-damaged patients have invariably localized mental rotation to the parietal lobes, with some supporting a predominantly right parietal locus (Ratcliff, 1979; Ditunno & Mann, 1990) and another suggesting left parietal superiority (Mehta & Newcombe, 1991). Consistent with these localizations, many functional neuroimaging studies have mapped the anatomy of mental rotation and almost invariably find bilateral parietal activation, greater on the right (e.g., see Corballis, 1997, for a review).

REFERENCES

Aguirre, G. K., & D'Esposito, M. (1999). Topographical disorientation: A synthesis and taxonomy. *Brain, 122,* 1613–1628.

Bartolomeo, P. (2008). The neural correlates of visual mental imagery: An ongoing debate. *Cortex, 44,* 107–108.

Bartolomeo, P., D'Erme, P., & Gainotti, G. (1994). The relationship between visuospatial and representational neglect. *Neurology, 44,* 1710–1714.

Beauvois, M. F., & Saillant, B. (1985). Optic aphasia for colours and colour agnosia: A distinction between visual and visuo-verbal impairments in the processing of colours. *Cognitive Neuropsychology, 2,* 1–48.

Behrmann, M., Winocur, G., & Moscovitch, M. (1992). Dissociation between mental imagery and object recognition in a brain-damaged patient. *Nature, 359,* 636–637.

Behrmann, M., Winocur, G., & Moscovitch, M. (1994). Intact visual imagery and impaired visual perception in a patient with visual agnosia. *Journal of Experimental Psychology. Human Perception and Performance, 20,* 1068–87.

Benton, A. L., Varney, N. R., & Hamsher, K. (1978). Visuospatial judgment: A clinical test. *Archives of Neurology, 35,* 364–367.

Bisiach, E., & Luzzatti, C. (1978). Unilateral neglect of representational space. *Cortex, 14,* 129–133.

Bouvier, S. E., & Engel, S. A. (2006). Behavioral deficits and cortical damage loci in cerebral achromatopsia. *Cerebral Cortex, 16,* 183–191.

Bowers, D., Blonder, L. X., Feinberg, T., & Heilman, K. M. (1991). Differential impact of right and left hemisphere lesions on facial emotion and object imagery. *Brain, 114,* 2593–2609.

Burgess, N. (2008). Spatial cognition and the brain. *Annals of the New York Academy of Science, 1124,* 77–97.

Burgess, N., Trinkler, I., King, J., Kennedy, A., & Cipolotti, L. (2006). Impaired allocentric spatial memory underlying topographical disorientation. *Review of Neuroscience, 17,* 239–251.

Byrne, P., Becker, S., & Burgess, N. (2007). Remembering the past and imagining the future: A neural model of spatial memory and imagery. *Psychological Review, 114,* 340–375.

Corballis, M. C. (1997). Mental rotation and the right hemisphere. *Brain and Language,* 100–21.

Damasio, A. R., Yamada, T., Damasio, H., Corbett, J., & McKee, J. (1980). Central achromatopsia: Behavioral, anatomic, and physiologic aspects. *Neurology, 30,* 1064–1071.

Davidoff, J., & Wilson, B. (1985). A case of visual agnosia showing a disorder of pre-semantic visual classification. *Cortex, 21,* 121–134.

De Renzi, E. (1982). *Disorders of space exploration and cognition.* New York: John Wiley & Sons.

De Renzi, E., & Spinnler, H. (1967). Impaired performance on color tasks in patients with hemispheric lesions. *Cortex, 3.*

De Vreese, L. P. (1991). Two systems for color naming defects. *Neuropsychologia, 29,* 1–18.

Ditunno, P. L., & Mann, V. A. (1990). Right hemisphere specialization for mental rotation in normal and brain damaged subjects. *Cortex, 26,* 177–188.

Eddy, P., & Glass, A. (1981). Reading and listening to high and low imagery sentences. *Journal of Verbal Learning and Verbal Behavior, 20,* 333–345.

Ehrlichman, H., & Barrett, J. (1983). Right hemispheric specialization for mental imagery: A review of the evidence. *Brain and Cognition, 2,* 55–76.

Epstein, R. A. (2008). Parahippocampal and retrosplenial contributions to human spatial navigation. *Trends in Cognitive Sciences, 12,* 388–396.

Epstein, R., DeYoe, E. A., Press, D. Z., Rosen, A. C., Kanwisher, N. (2001). Neuropsychological evidence for a topographical learning mechanism in parahippocampal cortex. *Cognitive Neuropsychology, 18,* 481–508.

Farah, M. J. (1984). The neurological basis of mental imagery: A componential analysis. *Cognition, 18,* 245–272.

Farah, M. J. (2004). *Visual agnosia* (2nd ed.). Cambridge, MA: MIT Press/Bradford Books.

Farah, M. J. (2000). *The cognitive neuroscience of vision.* Oxford: Blackwell Publishers.

Farah, M. J., Hammond, K. L., Levine, D. N., & Calvanio, R. (1988). Visual and spatial mental imagery: Dissociable systems of representation. *Cognitive Psychology, 20,* 439–462.

Gallant, J. L., Shoup, R. E., & Mazer, J. A. (2000). A human extrastriate area functionally homologous to macaque v4. *Neuron, 27*(2), 227–235.

Goldenberg, G. (1992). Loss of visual imagery and loss of visual knowledge - A case study. *Neuropsychologia, 30,* 1081–1099.

Goldenberg, G., & Artner, C. (1991). Visual imagery and knowledge about the visual appearance of objects in patients with posterior cerebral artery lesions. *Brain and Cognition, 15,* 160–186.

Goodglass, H., Wingfield, A., Hyde, M. R., & Theurkauf, J. C. (1986). Category-specific dissociations in naming and recognition by aphasic patients. *Cortex, 22,* 87–102.

Grossi, D., Orsini, A., & Modafferi, A. (1986). Visuoimaginal constructional apraxia: On a case of selective deficit of imagery. *Brain and Cognition, 5,* 255–267.

Kinsbourne, M., & Warrington, E. K., (1964). Observations on color agnosia. *Journal of Neurology, Neurosurgery, & Psychiatry, 27,* 296.

Habib, M., & Sirigu, A. (1987). Pure topographical disorientation and anatomical basis. *Cortex, 23,* 73–85.

Hecaen, H. (1980). Development and perspectives of neuropsychology. *Acta Neurologica Latinoamericana, 26,* 75–102.

Holmes, G. (1918). Disturbances of visual orientation. *British Journal of Ophthalmology, 2,* 449–468, 506–518.

Ino, T., Doi, T., Hirose, S., Kimura, T., Ito, J., & Fukuyama, H. (2007). Directional disorientation following left retrosplenial hemorrhage: A case report with fMRI studies. *Cortex, 43*(2), 248–254.

Lange, J. (1936). Agrosien und apraxien. In O. Bunke, & O. Foerster (Eds.), *Handbuch der neurologie.* Berlin: Springer.

Levine, D. N., Warach, J., & Farah, M. J. (1985). Two visual systems in mental imagery: Dissociation of "what" and "where" in imagery disorders due to bilateral posterior cerebral lesions. *Neurology, 35,* 1010–1018.

Luzzi, S., Pucci, E., Di Bella, P., & Piccirilli, M. (2000). Topographical disorientation consequent to amnesia of spatial location in a patient with right parahippocampal damage. *Cortex, 36,* 427–434.

Maguire, E. A., & Cipolotti, L. (1998). Selective sparing of topographical memory. *Journal of Neurology, Neurosurgery and Psychiatry, 65,* 903–909.

McFie, J., & Zangwill, O. L. (1960). Visual constructive disabilities associated with lesions of the left cerebral hemisphere. *Brain, 83.*

Meadows, J. C. (1974). The anatomical basis of prosopagnosia. *Journal of Neurology, Neurosurgery, and Psychiatry, 37,* 489–501.

Mehta, Z., & Newcombe, F. (1991). A role for the left hemisphere in spatial processing. *Cortex, 27,* 153–67.

Mendez, M. F., & Cherrier, M. M. (2003). Agnosia for scenes in topographagnosia. *Neuropsychologia, 41,* 1387–1395.

Miceli, M., Fouch, E., Capasso, R., Shelton, J. R., Tomaiuoli, F., & Caramazza, A. (2001). The dissociation of color from form and function knowledge. *Nature Neuroscience, 4*, 662–667.

Moro, V., Berlucchi, G., Lerch, J., Tomaiuolo, F., & Aglioti, S. M. (2008). Selective deficit of mental visual imagery with intact primary visual cortex and visual perception, *Cortex, 44*, 109–118.

Newcombe, F., & Russell, R. (1969). Dissociated visual perceptual and spatial deficits in focal lesions of the right hemisphere. *Journal of Neurology, Neurosurgery, & Psychiatry, 32*, 73–81.

Pallis, C. A. (1955). Impaired identification of faces and places with agnosia for colors. *Journal of Neurology, Neurosurgery and Psychiatry, 18*, 218–224.

Potzl, O. (1928). *Die aphasielehre voma standpunkte der kliniscen psychitrie.* Leipzig: FranzDeudicte.

Ratcliff, G. (1979). Spatial thought, mental rotation and the right cerebral hemisphere. *Neuropsychologia, 17*, 49–54.

Riddoch, G. (1935). Visual disorientation in homonymous. Hemifields. *Brain, 57*, 100–121.

Riddoch, J. M. (1990). Loss of visual imagery: A generation deficit. *Cognitive Neuropsychology, 7*, 249–273.

Sacks, O., & Wasserman, R. (1987). The case of the colorblind painter. *New York Review of Books*, 25–34.

Saygin, A. P. (2007). Superior temporal and premotor brain areas necessary for biological motion perception. *Brain, 130*, 2452–2461.

Saygin, A. P., Wilson, S. M., Hagler, Jr., D. J., Bates, E., & Sereno, M. I. (2004). Point-light biological motion perception activates human premotor cortex. *Journal of Neuroscience, 24*, 6181–6188.

Sergent, J. (1990). The neuropsychology of visual image generation: Data, method, and theory. *Brain and Cognition, 13*, 98–129.

Servos, P., & Goodale, M. A. (1995). Preserved visual imagery in visual form agnosia. *Neuropsychologia, 33*, 1383–1394.

Solomon, S. G. & Lennie, P. (2007). The machinery of colour vision. *Nature Reviews Neuroscience, 8*, 276–286.

Stangalino, C., Semenza, C., & Mondini, S. (1995). Generating visual mental images: Deficit after brain damage. *Neuropsychologia, 33*, 1473–1483.

Takahashi, N., & Kawamura, M. (2002). Pure topographical disorientation—the anatomical basis of landmark agnosia. *Cortex, 38*(5), 717–725.

Tippett, L. J. (1992). The generation of visual images: A review of neuropsychological research and theory. *Psychological Bulletin, 112*, 415–432.

Trojano, L., & Grossi, D. (1994). A critical review of mental imagery defects. *Brain and Cognition, 24*, 213–243.

Tranel, D. (1997). Disorders of color processing (perception, imagery, recognition, and naming). In T. E. Feinberg, & M. J. Farah (Eds.), *Behavioral Neurology and Neuropsychology.* (pp. 257–265). New York: McGraw Hill.

Ungerleider, L. G., & Mishkin, M. (1982). Two cortical visual systems. In D. J. Ingle, M. A. Goodale, & R. J. W. Mansfield (Eds.), *Analysis of Visual Behavior.* Cambridge, MA: MIT Press.

Vaina, L. M., Cowey, A., Jakab, M., & Kikinis, R. (2005). Deficits of motion integration and segregation in patients with unilateral extrastriate lesions. *Brain, 128*, 2134–2145.

Wade, A., Augath, M., Logothetis, N., & Wandell, B. (2008). fMRI measurements of color in macaque and human. *Journal of Vision, 8*(10), 1–19.

Zeki, S. (1990). A century of cerebral achromatopsia. *Brain, 113*, 1721–1777.

Zeki, S. (1993). *A vision of the brain.* Oxford: Blackwell Scientific Publications.

Zeki, S., Watson, J. D. G., Lueck, C. J., Friston, K., Kennard, C., & Frackowiak, R. S. (1991). A direct demonstration of functional specialization in human visual cortex. *Journal of Neuroscience, 11*, 641–649.

Zihl, J., von Cramon, D., & Mai, N. (1983). Selective disturbance of movement vision after bilateral brain damage. *Brain, 106*, 313–340.

8

Acalculia and Disturbances of the Body Schema

NATALIE L. DENBURG AND DANIEL TRANEL

In this chapter, we review the recent literature on *acalculia* and *body schema disturbances*. Neither of these conditions has been consistently defined, and there is little consensus about their neuropsychological and neuroanatomical correlates. These conditions are uncommon, and there is a paucity of well-standardized and validated assessment procedures. Nevertheless, there has been a resurgence of interest in various aspects of the neural basis of number (cf. Butterworth, 1999) and body schema processing (cf. Damasio, 1999), many utilizing functional imaging approaches (e.g., Arzy, Thut, Mohr, Michel, & Blanke, 2006; Downing, Chan, Peelen, Dodds, & Kanwisher, 2006; Morris, Pelphrey, & McCarthy, 2006; Peelen & Downing, 2007), that have tackled basic questions about the neural substrates of number processing (e.g., Lee, 2000; Dehaene, Molko, Cohen, & Wilson, 2004) and body representation (e.g., Schwoebel & Coslett, 2005; Peelen & Downing, 2007; Hodzic, Muckli, Singer, & Stirn, 2009). This work has added considerably to our understanding of what might go awry in the conditions of acalculia and body schema disturbances.

The disorders of acalculia, finger agnosia (FA), and right–left disorientation (RLD) have the (mis)fortune of being part of the tetrad of manifestations which comprise Gerstmann syndrome (Gerstmann, 1940) (the other being agraphia), the existence and significance of which has been repeatedly and forcefully questioned (e.g., Benton, 1961, 1977, 1992; Critchley, 1966). In fact, many studies of acalculia have taken place in the context of broader investigations of Gerstmann syndrome (e.g., Wingard, Barrett, Crucian, Doty, & Heilman, 2002; Martory et al., 2003).

Although close to a century of literature deals with acalculia and body schema disturbances, our review focuses on more recently published studies. The majority of investigations are case studies of patients with a wide range of neurological conditions, including focal vascular lesions, head injuries, cerebral tumors, degenerative diseases, and many others. To give the reader an appreciation of the wide variety of disturbances of number and math processing, as well as body schema processing that can develop in connection with brain injury, we will review a somewhat bewildering array of different lesion types, lesion loci, and profiles of neuropsychological dysfunction. We will attempt a synthesis of the main findings, insofar as possible, with regard to each of the main topics.

ACALCULIA

Acalculia refers to an acquired neuropsychological condition in which patients with previously normal calculation abilities develop impairments in processing numbers as a consequence of acquired brain dysfunction. In terms of localization, the classic notion is that acalculia is caused by a left inferior parietal lobe lesion. Acalculia is frequently accompanied by aphasia. However, as the studies reviewed below indicate, it is evident that acalculia can result from damage to numerous brain regions, in either hemisphere, and even from damage to subcortical structures. As alluded to earlier, the difficulty of establishing the brain–behavior correlates of acalculia are likely attributable to a multitude of issues, including how the condition is defined, strategies employed in clinical and research studies, and the complex, multifaceted nature of the neural and cognitive processes involved in calculation. Furthermore, acalculia can arise in connection with a variety of neurological conditions that cause cerebral lesions, including stroke, tumor, traumatic brain injury, and degenerative conditions.

TERMINOLOGY

In 1919, Henschen coined the term "akalkulia" to refer to an acquired calculation disturbance. Berger (1926) and later Grewel (1952) offered and further refined, respectively, the terms "primary" and "secondary" acalculia. Primary (also known as pure) acalculia refers to acalculia that cannot be attributed to defects in other cognitive domains. In secondary acalculia, calculation disturbances are attributable, at least in part, to defects of attention, memory, or language. Hécaen, Angelergues, and Houillier (1961) proposed a heuristically useful tripartite system for classifying patients with acalculia. Their classification entailed:

- *Acalculia with alexia and agraphia for numbers*, which may or may not be accompanied by aphasia. Here, calculation disturbances occur as a result of impaired reading or writing of numbers. This form of acalculia is thought to be caused primarily by left hemisphere (especially inferior parietal)

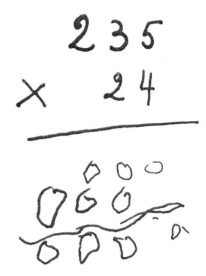

Figure 8–1. Example of agraphia for numbers. (From Hécaen et al., 1961. Reprinted from Hécaen, H., Angelergues, R., & Houillier, S. (1961). Les varietes cliniques des acalculies au cours des lesions retrorolandiques: Approche statistique du probleme. *Reviews Neurologique*, 105, 85–103, with permission of the publisher.

lesions. An example of this type of impairment is shown in Figure 8-1.
- *Acalculia of the spatial type* refers to disordered spatial organization of numbers, related to visual neglect, misalignment of numbers, and number inversions. This form of acalculia is thought to be caused primarily by right hemisphere lesions. An example of this type of impairment is shown in Figure 8-2.
- *Anarithmetria* is diagnosed when acalculia does not conform to either of the above two classifications. The term denotes a primary acalculia. This form of acalculia is thought to be caused primarily by left hemisphere lesions, but can occur, albeit with less frequency, following right hemisphere lesions.

The two classification systems outlined above have considerable overlap. That is, Hécaen et al.'s (1961) first two classifications fit nicely with Berger (1926) and Grewel's (1952) term *secondary acalculia*, whereas Hécaen et al.'s third classification is more or less synonymous with *primary acalculia* (Berger, 1926; Grewel, 1952).

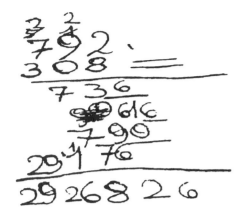

Figure 8–2. Example of disordered spatial alignment of numbers. From Semenza, C., Miceli, L., & Girelli, L. (1997). A deficit for arithmetical procedures: Lack of knowledge or lack of monitoring? *Cortex, 33,* 483–498, with permission of the publisher.

Acalculia was comprehensive reviewed by Ardila and Rosselli in 2002, and by Denburg and Tranel in 2003. In the current review, we have included the most consistent and definitive of the studies covered in these previous reviews, and have added a review of important studies that have appeared in the literature since then. The section on relevant findings from functional imaging has also been brought up to date. For earlier reviews of the historical literature, the reader is referred to Boller and Grafman (1983) and Levin, Goldstein, and Spiers (1993). We have adapted from McCloskey and associates (McCloskey, Caramazza, & Basili, 1985; McCloskey, 1992) a framework to organize our review. We will outline a number of notable dissociations, which suggest that a significant degree of modularity exists for number processing and calculation in the human brain. We begin by reviewing case studies, and then turn our attention to group studies.

CASE STUDIES

SELECTIVE IMPAIRMENT OF SYNTACTIC PROCESSING IN ARABIC NUMERAL PRODUCTION

This refers to impairments in syntactic processing of numbers in the context of intact lexical processing. Singer and Low (1933) present the unusual case of a patient who developed acalculia following carbon monoxide poisoning. When verbal numbers (e.g., two hundred forty-two) were presented aurally and the patient was asked to write the Arabic equivalents, he produced responses in which the individual digits were correct but the order of magnitude was incorrect (e.g., "two hundred and forty-two" was written as 20042). However, intact comprehension was assumed, given that the patient was accurate in his judgment of which of two spoken verbal numbers was larger. Macoir, Audet, and Breton (1999) observed a similar deficit in a patient with acalculia and language disturbances following a left inferior/posterior parietal cerebral vascular accident (CVA). The patient demonstrated a selective impairment in number transcoding (e.g., "nine thousand nine hundred and one" was written as 90901), in the context of intact numerical comprehension abilities. A similar case was reported by Cipolotti, Butterworth, and Warrington (1994).

SELECTIVE IMPAIRMENT OF OPERATION SYMBOL COMPREHENSION

This refers to a selective deficit in the comprehension of written operation symbols. Ferro and Botelho (1980) presented two cases that illustrate this condition. One patient suffered an intracerebral hematoma in the left occipito-temporal junction, and the other sustained a left hemisphere stroke. Both patients manifested a disturbance of processing arithmetical signs (e.g., they could not differentiate + from −) as their only symptom of acalculia. The authors termed this condition *asymbolic acalculia.* Although both of these patients were also aphasic, their asymbolic acalculia could not, according to the authors, be accounted for by their aphasia.

SELECTIVE IMPAIRMENT OF CALCULATION ABILITY

This refers to a dissociation between fact retrieval (intact) and calculation ability (impaired). Warrington (1982) described a patient with severe acalculia following a left parietal intracerebral hematoma. Although the patient demonstrated preserved counting and estimation of quantity and knowledge of number facts (e.g., "What is the boiling point of water?"), simple calculations were impaired. Similarly, Hittmair-Delazer, Sailer, and Benke (1995) studied a patient who demonstrated severe problems with basic arithmetic following a bone marrow transplant with extensive irradiation and chemotherapy. Although the patient was unable to answer very simple arithmetic problems (2 + 3 =?), he maintained intact processing of algebraic expressions and an understanding of complex arithmetic text problems. Semenza, Miceli, and Girelli (1997) followed a 17-year-old boy who suffered from some prenatal or early developmental neurological insult that began to reveal itself at 6 months of age (asymmetry in posture and movement). Computed tomography (CT) scans revealed hydrocephalus with atrophy of the right dorsolateral prefrontal cortex as well as the right superior parietal lobe. These authors report a specific deficit for calculation ability, in the context of intact number and magnitude knowledge (e.g., counting dots, transcoding from spoken to Arabic numerals, magnitude estimation, personal and nonpersonal number facts, such as calendar dates).

MULTIPLE DEFICITS IN CALCULATION

Delazer and Benke (1997) assessed a patient with severe calculation problems (as well as agraphia, FA, RLD, and apraxia) resulting from a left parietal lobe tumor. The patient maintained some "memorized fact knowledge" described as superficial (times tables, as well as some additions and subtractions), although she completely lost conceptual knowledge of arithmetic and performed very poorly on most calculation tasks. In terms of conceptual knowledge, the patient lost all ability to implement "back-up strategies" when faced with a calculation task for which she was unable to work out the answer. That is, when offered strategies such as using paper and pencil, a written number line, a pile of tokens, or her fingers, the patient was unable to take advantage of these strategies effectively. Similarly, the patient demonstrated an inability to derive unknown facts

from known ones; for example, two arithmetic problems were presented in pairs so that the answer for one problem could be inferred from the other (commutativity; "If 13 + 9 = 22, what is 9 + 13?"). The authors noted that the patient's ability to reason verbally, as measured by tasks of conceptualization and matrix reasoning, was preserved, despite impaired conceptual knowledge of arithmetic. Ashkenazi, Henik, Ifergane, and Shelef (2008) studied the case of an individual with an infarct to the left intraparietal sulcus who presented with multiple calculation deficits.

DISSOCIATION OF ARITHMETIC OPERATIONS

This refers to the ability to execute particular, but not all arithmetic operations. Benson and Weir (1972) presented the case of a patient with a generally isolated calculation disturbance resulting from left parietal lobe pathology. An intriguing dissociation was demonstrated in that the patient maintained the ability to complete addition and subtraction problems accurately, while displaying grave difficulty with multiplication and division problems. Grafman, Kampen, Rosenberg, Salazar, and Boller (1989) studied the case of a patient with Alzheimer disease who presented with primary calculation complaints. Two years of periodic follow-up evaluations revealed an ensuing dissolution of his arithmetic abilities. This patient showed the functional dissociation of being able to add and subtract accurately, but not being able to multiply or divide. A similar case, albeit resulting from a left frontal infarction, demonstrated intact addition and subtraction in the context of impaired multiplication (Tohgi et al., 1995). Lampl, Eshel, Gilad, and Sarova-Pinhas (1994) examined a patient with acalculia following a left parietotemporal hemorrhage. The patient retained the ability to subtract, without being able to perform any other arithmetic operations. These reports support the idea that different processing systems may underlie each of the basic arithmetic operations. Finally, an illustrative case of acalculia of the spatial type, secondary to right hemisphere damage and specific to multiplication, was presented by Grana, Hofer, and Semenza (2006).

OTHER CASE STUDIES

Dehaene and Cohen (1997) reported two patients with "pure anarithmetria." Case 1 sustained a left subcortical lesion and Case 2 sustained a right inferior parietal lesion. Both patients could read Arabic numerals and write them to dictation, but the patients manifested a notable calculation deficit. In addition, Case 1 demonstrated a selective deficit of rote verbal knowledge (e.g., arithmetic tables) despite intact semantic knowledge of numerical quantities. Case 2 showed the opposite pattern. This double dissociation suggests that there are distinct neural processing systems for numbers and calculations.

GROUP STUDIES

Group studies have been utilized primarily to study the relationship between hemispheric impairment and calculation abilities, and to further validate findings from case studies. Many aspects of calculation involve verbal processing, and not surprisingly, acalculia is commonly associated with aphasia. However, as suggested by Hécaen et al. (1961), acalculia can also be caused by right hemisphere lesions. According to Cohn (1961), right hemisphere damaged individuals may demonstrate left hemispatial neglect and visuospatial defects, including difficulties in horizontal positioning, vertical columnar alignment, and transportation of numbers, that contribute to calculation disturbances.

One of the first large-scale studies to compare left and right hemisphere damaged patients on the same battery of calculation tasks was undertaken by Grafman, Passafiume, Faglioni, and Boller (1982). These investigators studied the presence of two of Hécaen et al.'s (1961) three acalculia classifications (i.e., anarithmetria and acalculia of the spatial type) in left and right hemisphere damaged patients. Seventy-six patients with intact ability to read and write numbers and 26 healthy comparisons were administered a written calculation task and a brief neuropsychological battery. The patients were further divided into the following groups: Left anterior without visual field defect, left posterior with visual field defect, right anterior without visual field defect, and right posterior

with visual field defect. The calculation task was scored both quantitatively and qualitatively. The patients with left hemisphere lesions committed the greatest number of errors; furthermore, the left posterior lesion group performed the most poorly relative to the other experimental groups for qualitative errors. The results were unchanged when these investigators employed age-, education-, and neuropsychological-group adjustments. Therefore, this study demonstrates that acalculia is particularly salient in left posterior lesions irrespective of language and visuospatial abilities.

Jackson and Warrington (1986) studied acalculia in 56 left hemisphere damaged patients, 67 right hemisphere damaged patients, and 100 healthy comparison subjects. All subjects were administered the Graded Difficulty Arithmetic Test (GDA; Jackson & Warrington, 1986), which is a speeded test of addition and subtraction abilities. The left hemisphere group was significantly impaired on the GDA relative to the right hemisphere group and comparison participants. In contrast, the right hemisphere group's performance did not differ from that of the comparison participants.

Dahmen, Hartje, Büssing, and Sturm (1982) compared 20 patients with Wernicke's aphasia, 20 patients with Broca aphasia, 20 patients with right retro-Rolandic lesions, and 40 normal comparison subjects on a calculation task that involved items differing in the degree of spatial and linguistic processing required for successful completion. Wernicke aphasics performed significantly worse than the other subjects on calculation tasks with a spatial component (e.g., alignment of numbers). The investigators summarized their findings as being consistent with the lesion location in Wernicke's aphasia, involving the temporoparietal cortices, and suggested that spatial visualization plays an important role in the calculation disorders of patients with Wernicke's aphasia.

Given the high comorbidity between language disorders and acalculia, Deloche and Seron (1982) investigated whether these two disorders are the result of damage to a cognitive component shared by the two conditions, or from damage to two different components. Seven patients with Broca's aphasia and seven patients with Wernicke's aphasia were administered two tasks, involving the transcoding of written numerals (e.g., two hundred and forty eight) into digit strings (248), and the error types of each aphasic group were compared. It was hypothesized that those with Broca's aphasia would evidence faulty calculation as a result of syntactic errors, whereas those with Wernicke's aphasia would demonstrate acalculia as a result of lexical and serial order errors. As hypothesized, the authors found distinct error patterns in the two groups. It was concluded that the number processing disorders in patients with Broca's and Wernicke's aphasias were parallel to their language deficits, thus suggesting that the disorders result from damage to a shared cognitive component. In a follow-up study, Seron and Deloche (1983) reversed their task to the transcoding of digit strings (248) into written numerals (two hundred and forty eight), and found results comparable to the Deloche and Seron (1982) findings.

Rosselli and Ardila (1989) examined the calculation deficits of 41 left hemisphere and 21 right hemisphere brain-damaged patients. Patients with left hemisphere lesions were further subdivided into seven subgroups: Prefrontal, Broca's aphasia, conduction aphasia, Wernicke's aphasia, anomic aphasia, alexia without agraphia, and global aphasia. Right hemisphere patients were subdivided into anatomical groups of pre-Rolandic and retro-Rolandic. As in other studies, the aphasic subgroups performed worse on a calculation task, evincing discrete degrees and types of errors. More specifically, the patients with global aphasia displayed the greatest number of calculation disturbances. In contrast, prefrontal patients performed better on the calculation task. Finally, patients with Wernicke's aphasia demonstrated relatively greater difficulty on tasks that required spatial abilities.

Delazer, Girelli, Semenza, and Denes (1999) studied the calculation abilities of 50 patients with focal left hemisphere lesions and of 15 healthy comparison subjects. On the basis of aphasia testing, patients were placed in one of five groups: amnesic aphasias, Broca's aphasia, global aphasia, Wernicke's aphasia, and nonaphasic subjects. Calculation error rates correlated with the severity of the language deficit: Patients with global aphasia displayed the most severe defects, whereas those with amnesic aphasia displayed the mildest impairments. In all patient groups, addition was the strongest operation while multiplication proved the most difficult. Additionally, patients with Broca's aphasia displayed a number of interesting findings, including particularly poor reading of Arabic numerals (relative to number words, e.g., "23" vs. "twenty-three"), a high incidence of syntactic errors that was thought to reflect a more general impairment in syntactic processing, and disordered multiplication as compared to subtraction. The authors concluded that calculation abilities are mediated to a significant degree by linguistic functions.

Basso, Burgio, and Caporali (2000) compared the calculation performance of 50 left hemisphere damaged patients, 26 right hemisphere damaged patients, and 211 healthy subjects using the Assessment Battery for Calculation and Number Processing (Deloche et al., 1994), which consists of 13 tasks and numerous subtasks. On the basis of performance on language tests, the left hemisphere group was further divided into the following experimental groups: those with Broca's aphasia (16), those with Wernicke's aphasia (18), and nonaphasic subjects (16). Using the number of tasks failed by normal controls as a marker, these authors were able to classify patients as "clinically acalculic" if they failed three or more tasks on the Calculation Battery. Eight patients with Broca's (50%) and 11 with Wernicke's (61%) aphasia fell into this acalculic classification. However, the authors underscored that a high percentage of aphasic patients were not clinically acalculic. Utilizing this same criterion, only two of the nonaphasic subjects (13%), three of the right hemisphere damaged (12%), and four of the comparison subjects (2%) were deemed acalculic. The relationship between acalculia and spatial disorders was less clear cut, with the exception of finding that the three right brain damaged acalculic patients also had constructional apraxia.

Our group studied clock drawing performance in a large group of patients ($N = 133$) with focal damage to either the left or right hemisphere (Tranel, Rudrauf, Vianna, & Damasio, 2008). Impairments in clock drawing were most strongly associated with damage to right parietal cortices (supramarginal gyrus) and left inferior frontoparietal opercular cortices (Figure 8-3A–C). Visuospatial errors were predominant in patients with right hemisphere damage. Of particular relevance to the current review, a subset of patients failed the clock drawing test because of basic problems in processing (comprehending and/or executing) the instruction to set the clock hands to a particular time (e.g., "Set the clock to twenty 'til four"), in the setting of a well-drawn clock and normal placement of clock numbers. In this subgroup, left hemisphere lesions were most common (11 of 13 patients), and the lesions were concentrated in the inferior frontal gyrus, the ventral peri-Rolandic regions, the anterior supramarginal gyrus, the insula, and the superior temporal gyrus. (Figure 8-3A–C). This finding is consistent with the literature reviewed above, pointing to the importance of left perisylvian language cortices for processing many aspects of numerical information.

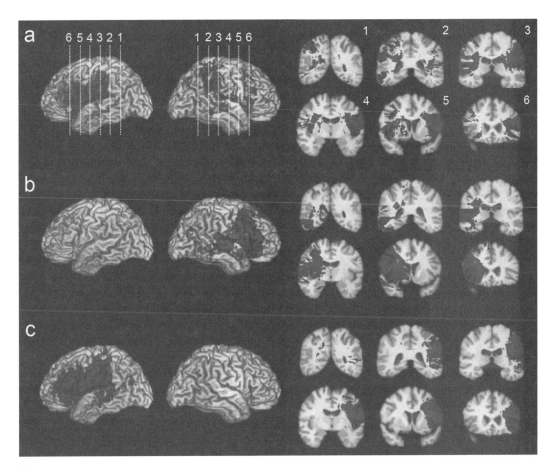

Figure 8–3. Lesion-deficit relationships for the Clock Drawing Test. The three Maps (A–C) show in dark gray regions of the brain, where significant effects of lesion-deficit relationship were found at a threshold of $p < 0.05$ (uncorrected). For A–C, the left and right lateral hemispheres are shown on the left side, and coronal slices at the levels indicated by 1–6 (on the left and right hemispheres in [A]) are shown on the right side of the Figure (the left hemisphere is on the right in the coronal slices). **A:** Map for clock drawing impairments, irrespective of error type. **B:** Map for impairments in spatial organization and number placement. **C:** Map for impairments in time setting. From Tranel, D., Rudrauf, D., Vianna, E.P.M., & Damasio, H. (2008). Does the Clock Drawing Test have focal neuroanatomical correlates? *Neuropsychology,* *22,* 553–562, with permission of the publisher.

EXPERIMENTAL INVESTIGATION OF THE NEURAL CORRELATES OF NUMBER PROCESSING

The aforementioned review highlights the widespread distribution of calculation processes in the brain. The case studies, in particular, additionally suggest that there exist dissociable brain networks for different aspects of number processing. However, the precise functional role of particular brain regions in calculation remains uncertain, and researchers have recently employed a number of other methods to corroborate and extend lesion studies conducted in acalculic patients. These methods include cortical stimulation, electrophysiology (ERPs), metabolic studies, functional neuroimaging (positron emission tomography [PET], functional magnetic resonance imaging [fMRI]), and repetitive transcranial magnetic stimulation (rTMS).

Whalen, McCloskey, Lesser, and Gordon (1997) studied a cognitively and intellectually intact young patient with a left parasagittal parietal region brain tumor and associated seizure disorder. At the age of 9, the patient underwent surgery to remove the tumor; however, recurrence was noted at the age of 16. Prior to a second neurosurgery, electrodes were placed in the patient's left hemisphere in an effort to localize the seizure focus and to map the cognitive functions that may be affected by the resection. In doing so, the researchers were able to examine the effects of mild stimulation of localized brain regions on sensory, motor, and cognitive tasks, including calculation. After determining that stimulation of particular sites did not affect the patient's attentional or expressive speech abilities, the results revealed that multiplication was significantly disrupted relative to addition. More specifically, stimulation at a left parietal site impaired performance on single-digit multiplication problems, likely also disrupting the retrieval of stored multiplication facts.

Using PET, Dehaene et al. (1996) examined the regional cerebral blood flow patterns underlying two simple mental calculation tasks, single-digit multiplication and number comparison (i.e., selection of which of two numbers is largest), relative to a resting condition, in eight healthy participants. For the comparison task, there was an absence of activation of critical brain regions with the exception of those areas necessary for basic stimulus identification and response selection. However, a trend for bilateral inferior parietal region activity was noted. Regarding multiplication, the inferior parietal region was activated bilaterally, as were the left fusiform/lingual region and left lenticular nucleus, suggesting a role for these structures in multiplication. Of note, the authors underscore that no activation was found in the left and right angular gyri for either task. Finally, the rather distinct neuroanatomical activation involved in number comparison versus multiplication suggested that these two arithmetic functions may be subserved by distinct neural networks.

Burbaud et al. (1995) investigated the role of the right and left prefrontal cortices in calculation using fMRI. Eight right-handed and eight left-handed subjects participated in the study, and the subjects were asked to complete two numerical tasks (mental recitation of numbers and mental calculation). Recitation of numbers resulted in little cerebral activation. Mental calculation, on the other hand, with its working memory demands, activated prefrontal brain regions. Furthermore, in right-handed subjects, activation was clearly lateralized to the left dorsolateral prefrontal cortex, whereas bilateral activation was found in left-handed subjects. In another fMRI study, Rueckert et al. (1996) measured activation in 12 right-handed subjects performing a mental calculation task involving subtraction by serial sevens. All subjects showed significant activation in left prefrontal cortex, left posterior parietal cortex (angular and/or supramarginal gyri), and bilateral motor/premotor cortex. Additional areas of activation varied from subject to subject (e.g., right prefrontal, left temporal lobe), suggesting a great deal of individual variability. Rueckert et al. (1996) concluded that their findings corroborated the important role of the posterior parietal area in calculation, while not supporting a differential role for the angular gyrus.

Chochon, Cohen, van de Moortele, and Dehaene (1999; see also Dehaene, Spelke, Pinel, Stanescu, & Tsivkin, 1999) attempted to distinguish between calculation tasks lateralized to the left parietal lobe from calculation tasks lateralized to the right parietal lobe. Eight healthy subjects underwent fMRI while completing tasks of digit naming, number comparison, subtraction, and multiplication. Based on the fMRI results, the four tasks could be ordered hierarchically with each higher task causing additional activation: Naming < Comparison < Multiplication < Subtraction. With the exception of digit naming, all of the tasks activated the parieto-occipital and cingulate regions. In terms of differential parietal lobe activity, number comparison relied more heavily on right parietal and prefrontal activation; the opposite pattern (i.e., left hemisphere activation) was suggested by the multiplication task. Finally, bilateral activation occurred during the subtraction task. These authors concluded that distinct parietal pathways exist for different arithmetic operations.

Using fMRI and normal participants, Lee (2000) examined the neural substrates of number processing, following the identification of a patient who suffered an intracranial hemorrhage at the left parieto-temporal junction, resulting in selective acalculia (i.e., impaired multiplication but intact subtraction) . During fMRI, the multiplication task performed by the normal participants elicited activation at the border between the angular gyrus and supramarginal gyrus, as well as the superior frontal gyrus, of the left hemisphere. These areas of activation foci in normal subjects were similar to areas of brain damage in the patient. By contrast, activation in intraparietal sulcus, superior and inferior frontal gyri, and posterior inferior temporal gyri, all bilaterally, were observed during the subtraction task. Taken together, these data support the notion that different cognitive and neuronal mechanisms underlie multiplication and subtraction computations.

Also using fMRI, Rickard et al. (2000) explored the patterns of neural activation for two relatively simple arithmetic tasks, multiplication verification and magnitude judgment, in eight right-handed healthy adult participants. The authors attempted to improve on prior functional imaging studies by utilizing simple arithmetic tasks rather than complex ones, given that complex tasks may engage ancillary cognitive

processes that are not directly associated with arithmetic per se. For the multiplication verification task, bilateral activation in multiple brain regions was demonstrated, involving Brodmann's area 44 (left greater than right), dorsolateral prefrontal cortex (areas 9 and 10), inferior and superior parietal areas (left greater than right), and lingual and fusiform gyri. Regarding magnitude judgment, the results were even more variable, with the greatest and most consistent activation in the bilateral inferior parietal cortex. Like Dehaene et al. (1996), these investigators found no activation (and actually detected deactivation) in angular and supramarginal gyri, a finding that appears inconsistent with the neuropsychological literature.

Rusconi, Walsh, and Butterworth (2005) observed that, in normal participants, rTMS over the left angular gyrus disrupted both number processing and finger gnosis, suggesting a common neuronal network for numbers and body knowledge (and consistent, in a general sense, with the Gerstmann syndrome phenomenon).

The additional experimental approaches, especially fMRI, have confirmed and extended findings from lesion studies regarding the neural basis for number processing and mathematical operations. Although the complexities and nuances of the literature are many, the basic story line is fairly consistent with earlier work, highlighting in particular the importance of the left inferior parietal region (although functional imaging studies, as a rule, have called more attention to left frontal and right hemisphere homologues—parietal and frontal—as participating in number processing). From a broad perspective, though, we are more impressed by the overall similarity of the story line, and it would be hard to conclude that functional imaging has "revolutionized" our current understanding of brain–behavior relationships for numbers and math.

NEUROPSYCHOLOGICAL EVALUATION OF ACALCULIA

Paying bills, balancing a checkbook, addressing letters, counting out money for a purchase, and understanding the measurement aspects of a recipe are just a few examples of how meaningful calculation is to our daily life. Ideally, assessment of calculation skills should be varied, and should cover aural and written calculation, the comprehension and use of operations, and the spatial components of arithmetic.

COMPREHENSIVE ASSESSMENT

One especially comprehensive calculation test battery is that of Benton (1963), which comprises 12 tasks (see Table 8-1). Other comprehensive tests include the VESPAR (Langdon & Warrington, 1995), which measures arithmetic reasoning while minimizing attention and language contributions. An experimental battery discussed previously is the EC301 Assessment Battery for Calculation and Number Processing (Deloche et al., 1993, 1994). Subsequent research (Deloche, Dellatolas, Vendrell, & Bergego, 1996) demonstrated that the EC301 has strong ecological validity, as demonstrated by strong correlations with an activities in daily life (ADL) questionnaire that measured daily numerical activities (e.g., reading time on a digital clock).

DIAGNOSTIC ASSESSMENT

Numerous diagnostic tests of calculation are available for purchase from commercial sources. Although widely utilized, these tests do not provide evaluation of all facets of calculation disturbances discussed in this chapter. We have summarized the most useful tests in Table 8-2. All tests reviewed in this section, with the exception of Wechsler Adult Intelligence Scale-IV (WAIS-IV) Arithmetic, have available two parallel forms, which helps minimize practice effects in repeat assessments.

QUALITATIVE ASSESSMENT

Error analyses are often a very useful addition to traditional assessment. Grafman et al. (1982) utilized the Benton Visual Retention Test scoring criteria (Sivan, 1992) to examine calculation errors qualitatively. Specifically, they scored six types of errors: misplacement, size error, distortion, rotation, omission, and perseveration. Qualitative assessment is particularly important when addressing spatial forms of calculation disorders.

Table 8–1. Benton's Battery of Arithmetic Tests

1. Appreciation of number values when presented verbally with a pair of numbers such as 28 and 31, where the task is to say which is greater.

2. Appreciation of number values when presented visually, and the response is either oral or pointing to the larger of two numbers.

3. Reading numbers aloud.

4. Pointing to written numbers that are named by the examiner.

5. Writing numbers to dictation.

6. Writing numbers from copy.

7. Counting out loud from 1 to 20, from 20 to 1, and from 1 to 20 by 2's.

8. Estimating the number of items in a series of continuous dots and again in a discontinuous series of dots (e.g., four groups of five dots each arranged horizontally).

9. Oral arithmetic calculation in which simple examples are given using each of the four basic operations.

10. Written arithmetic calculation in which the examples are similar to those given orally.

11. Arithmetic reasoning ability via the Arithmetic Reasoning subtest of the Wechsler Adult Intelligence Scale (IV).

12. Immediate memory for calculation problems. This measure is a component of test #9 and serves as a control to ascertain whether a memory deficit is responsible for inability to perform calculation problems given orally.

Table 8–2. Diagnostic Assessment of Calculation Ability

---

1. KeyMath Diagnostic Arithmetic Test-Revised (KeyMath-R; Connolly, 1991):
   a. Thirteen subtests in three major areas:
      i.   Basic Concepts: Measurement of basic mathematical knowledge; contains three subtests (numeration, rational numbers, and geometry)
      ii. Operation: Measurement of computation; contains five subtests (addition, subtraction, multiplication, division, and mental computation)
      iii. Applications: Measurement of mathematics that are encountered in everyday life; contains five subtests (measurement, time and money, estimation, interpreting data, and problem solving)
   b. Normative data: Upper limit of 15 years, 5 months, but may prove useful with older individuals

2. Peabody Individual Achievement Test-Revised/Normative Update (PIAT-R/NU; Markwardt, 1997):
   a. One hundred multiple-choice items that range in difficulty from simple matching tasks to high school arithmetic. The examiner reads each item aloud while visually displaying the question and response options to the examinee.
   b. Normative data have an upper limit of 22 years, 11 months, but may prove useful with older individuals.

3. WAIS-IV Arithmetic subtest (Wechsler, 2008):
   a. Tests range from the counting of visually displayed objects to verbally presented mathematical problems involving fractions and proportions. A time limit is instituted for all problems. Use of pencil and paper to complete the problems is not allowed.
   b. Excellent normative date, with norms through 90 years 11 months of age.

4. Wechsler Individual Achievement Test-2nd Edition (WIAT-II, 2001) subtests:
   a. Two subtests address calculation and, together, they can be combined to form a composite Mathematics score:
      i. Mathematics Reasoning: Covers assessment of quantitative concepts; problem solving; money, time, and measurement; geometry; reading and interpreting charts and graphs; statistics
      ii. Numerical Operations: Covers numerical identification and writing; addition, subtraction, multiplication, division; fractions, decimals, and algebra.
   b. Normative data have an upper limit of 19 years, 11 months, but may prove useful with older individuals. (The WIAT-III is scheduled for release in August of 2009, and this version has normative data from 4 years through 19 years.)

5. Wide Range Achievement Test (Fourth Edition) (WRAT-4; Wilkinson, 2006)–Math Computation subtest:
   a. A timed (15-minute) test of written calculation. Problems on the typical adult level involve simple and complex written calculation, in addition to questions that could be found in college-level mathematics courses.
   b. Normative data are excellent, with norms from 5 years 0 months through 94 years 11 months of age.

6. The Woodcock-Johnson Tests of Achievement-III/Normative Update (WJ-III/NU; Woodcock, Shrank, McGrew, & Mather, 2005):
   a. Three calculation subtests:
      i.   Calculation: Measurement of the ability to perform written calculation problems ranging from simple addition to calculus-based problems;
      ii. Applied Problems: Measurement of the ability to solve practical problems; the complex problems necessitate written calculation; covers oral and math "word problems"
      iii. Quantitative Concepts: Measurement of knowledge of mathematical concepts and vocabulary; covers oral questions about mathematic factual information, operations, and signs
      iv. There is also a Math Fluency subtest, which assesses the speed of performing simple calculations for 3 minutes.
   b. Normative data: A Broad Mathematics Cluster score can be calculated following the administration of the Calculation and Applied Problems subtests; in addition, the Applied Problems subtest allows for a Mathematics Reasoning Cluster score. WJ-III/NU normative data are excellent, with norms from 24 through 90 years of age.

OTHER ISSUES IN ASSESSMENT

It is critically important to gain a sense of the patient's premorbid calculation abilities, in order to rule out developmental problems, relatively undeveloped math skills, or lack of opportunity to learn calculation skills. Furthermore, one must keep in mind the presence of gender typical discrepancies in mathematical reasoning abilities, which tend to favor males (Benbow & Stanley, 1983; Hyde, Fennema, & Lamon, 1990). Consideration of the aforementioned concerns can be accomplished in a number of ways, including examination of academic records, knowledge of the patient's occupation and job responsibilities, or discussion with the patient and family members. Furthermore, given the high comorbidity between aphasia and acalculia, it is essential to evaluate the patient's language abilities thoroughly. Finally, calculation tasks should be administered as part of a full neuropsychological battery, as calculation disturbances may arise secondary to defects in attention, memory, or executive functions.

RECOVERY

Recovery from acquired defects in mathematical processing has not been investigated very extensively, but a few recent studies have provided some preliminary information on this issue. Caporali, Burgio, and Basso (2000) studied the natural course of acalculia in 51 patients with left hemisphere damage, and found—not surprisingly—that the great majority of recovery occurs in the initial days and weeks following a vascular event. Interestingly, they also found that initial severity of acalculia does not predict recovery, although initial severity did predict recovery of auditory comprehension. Basso, Caporali, and Faglioni (2005) examined an unselected series of 92 patients with left hemisphere damage, using assessments of calculation conducted in the acute/periacute (days and weeks after lesion onset) and chronic (on average, 5 months after lesion onset) epochs. Of the 92, the great majority displayed comorbid acalculia and aphasia. As in Caporali et al. (2000), the majority of recovery from acalculia was observed to occur in the first several months following the vascular event.

SUMMARY AND COMMENT

It is evident from this review that acquired disturbances of mathematical ability can appear in many different forms, in the setting of many different types of neurological disease, and in connection with many different lesion sites. Nonetheless, the preponderance of the evidence indicates that left-sided lesions to the parietal region, especially in the inferior parietal lobule,

are most consistently associated with acalculia, especially the "primary" type. It has even been suggested that the left parietal region constitutes the "mathematical brain" in humans (Butterworth, 1999). Although acalculia has often been reported in patients who also manifest disturbances of language processing, this association is not a necessary one, as some cases have been described in whom acalculia occurred without an accompanying aphasia. The neuroanatomical separation of mathematical and language processing is supported further by cases of the reverse dissociation—that is, impaired processing of linguistic information with preserved processing of numbers and mathematical calculations (e.g., Anderson, Damasio, & Damasio, 1990). Finally, there is evidence from fMRI that, although "exact" types of mathematical knowledge (e.g., number facts, math tables) may depend on language and on inferior prefrontal structures that are also used for word association tasks, "approximate" arithmetic (e.g., quantity manipulation, approximation of magnitudes) may be language-independent and rely on bilateral areas of the parietal lobes that are also involved in visuospatial processing (Dehaene et al., 1999). In our view, the distinction between exact and approximate types of arithmetic reasoning has considerable appeal, and may prove very fruitful in future attempts to define the neural correlates of mathematical capacity.

Studies of acalculia have provided several important insights into the neural basis of calculation. Studies based on the lesion method have furnished testable hypotheses, some of which have been pursued with group studies and functional imaging techniques. Furthermore, studies of normal individuals and brain-damaged patients with acalculia have been essential to the development of theoretical models of number comprehension and production (e.g., McCloskey, Caramazza, & Basili, 1985; Ashcraft, 1987; Dehaene, 1992; McCloskey, 1992; Dehaene & Cohen, 1995; Butterworth, 1999). Such models will undoubtedly help in the creation of effective rehabilitation techniques for children with learning disorders and adults with acquired brain damage. Work along these lines is already under way (Sullivan, Macaruso, & Sokol, 1996; Guyard, Masson, Quiniou, & Siou, 1997).

DISTURBANCES OF THE BODY SCHEMA

THE CONCEPT OF BODY SCHEMA

It is not especially controversial to assert that human bodies, compared to virtually all other kinds of objects, are special. To begin with, the experience of our own bodies occurs through both exteroceptive (e.g., vision) and interoceptive (e.g., nociception) channels. The stream of afferent information is more or less continuous and constant, giving rise to the sense that our bodies are "always there." An essential foundation associated with this sense is the *body schema,* which is comprised by a dynamic, online representation of the relative locations of one's body parts in space. The body schema is built up from the integration of many different types of signals (e.g., proprioceptive, vestibular, tactile). The body schema is a fundamental component of corporeal awareness and the self (e.g., Damasio, 1999).

Body schema disturbances is a broad term that, in principle, can be applied to a wide variety of disorders of processing related to the representation and spatial location of the body, including conditions such as anosognosia, somatoparaphrenia (disownership of body parts), autoscopia, tactile extinction, out-of-body experiences, supernumerary phantom limbs, and the phantom limb phenomenon (e.g., Frederiks, 1985; Denes, 1989; Halligan, Marshall, & Wade, 1995; McGonigle et al., 2002; Blanke & Arzy, 2005). Here, following the tradition of previous authors (e.g., Benton, 1985; Benton & Sivan, 1993), we focus on three specific manifestations of body schema disturbance: autotopagnosia (AT), FA, and RLD. Two of these—FA and RLD—are part of the tetrad of signs included under the classic Gerstmann syndrome, and thus they are to some extent cognate to the condition of acalculia described earlier. And, as we will highlight below, all of the body schema disturbances reviewed here tend to be related neuroanatomically to structures in the left parietal region, although the relationship is far less robust and reliable than many of the more well-studied neuropsychological syndromes (e.g., aphasia).

Several factors may explain the rather murky status of body schema disturbances in the neuropsychological literature. As Benton and Sivan (1993) noted, the term "body schema" has never received a standard, widely accepted definition, with different authors offering their own, often fairly idiosyncratic, explications. Also, the explanatory value of the concept of body schema has been repeatedly questioned (Benton, 1958, 1959; Poeck & Orgass, 1971; Denes, 1989). Some authors have argued that the term is useful in explaining the so-called *phantom limb phenomenon,* but newer studies have provided the basis for more parsimonious and compelling formulations of this condition (Ramachandran, 1998; Ramachandran & Rogers-Ramachandran, 2000). Perhaps of greatest importance, there has been a marked paucity of theoretical frameworks within which the concept of body schema could be properly situated and interpreted. This situation may finally be changing, though, as several groups of investigators have (mainly based on fMRI) developed more elaborate and cohesive frameworks for understanding the body schema (e.g., Maravita & Iriki, 2004; Braun, Desjardins, Gaudelet, & Guimond, 2007; Corradi-Dell'Acqua, Tomasino, & Fink, 2009).

LOCALIZATION: THE EXTRASTRIATE BODY AREA

Images of human bodies rapidly capture the focus of attention, even when nothing is expected (Downing et al., 2004; Ro et al., 2007). Functional imaging studies have shown that such perceptual processes may be mediated by the *extrastriate body area* (EBA), located in the inferior lateral portion of Brodmann area 19. The EBA responds preferentially to the sight of stationary (Downing et al., 2001, 2006a, 2007; Peelen & Downing, 2005; Morris et al., 2006; Spiridon et al., 2006) and moving (Bartels & Zeki, 2004; Downing et al., 2006b; Kable & Chatterjee, 2006) human bodies and nonfacial body parts. The EBA is engaged during the planning, execution, and imagination of goal-directed movements, and may be involved in the production of actions with different limbs (Astafiev et al., 2004; Jackson et al., 2006). In addition, the visual perception of human bodies and nonfacial body parts elicits a distinctive electrophysiological component that has been linked with the EBA

(Thierry et al., 2006; Pourtois et al., 2007). Finally, rTMS over the EBA interferes with the discrimination of bodily forms (Urgesi et al., 2004, 2007a, 2007b). Thus, insofar as the visual perception of body parts is concerned, the EBA has been reliably associated with this function, especially in functional neuroimaging studies.

AUTOTOPAGNOSIA

Autotopagnosia can be defined as an inability to identify body parts, either on one's self, on the examiner, or on a human picture. The deficit may encompass both verbal and nonverbal modalities; that is, the patient can be asked to point to a named body part, or nonverbally, the patient can be asked to point to the same part of his or her own body as the examiner is pointing to on him- or herself. In strict terms, AT should occur in relationship to both sides of the body (cf. Benton & Sivan, 1993), that is, as a bilateral condition; however, some authors have allowed a broader conceptualization, in which unilateral manifestations (e.g., hemisomatognosia) are considered. Autotopagnosia has been reported as the result of dementia (Pick, 1922) and focal left hemisphere damage (e.g., Selecki & Herron, 1965; Sauguet, Benton, & Hécaen, 1971), usually involving the parietal lobe. Autotopagnosia is usually accompanied by aphasia, reaching disorders, apraxia, neglect, or visuospatial disturbances, and, according to Benton and Sivan (1993), a "pure" case of AT has never been reported in the literature.

CASE AND GROUP STUDIES

Many explanations for AT have been posited, perhaps nearly as many as there are cases reported in the literature. First, the patient's inability to name body parts may be due to an underlying language disturbance (e.g., anomia). Related to aphasia, another explanation is that AT is attributable to a category-specific comprehension deficit in which the patient has difficulty in understanding the names of body parts (Goodglass, Klein, Carey, & Jones, 1966; but see Kemmerer & Tranel, 2008, for a different conclusion). Third, a parts–whole hypothesis has been raised, which suggests that the affected patient has an inability to separate a

whole into its component parts (De Renzi & Faglioni, 1963; De Renzi & Scotti, 1970).

Semenza and Goodglass (1985) examined 32 brain-damaged patients and underscored the important role of language in body part identification. They found that the likelihood of success or failure in body part identification was a function of a single factor: lexical frequency. That is, accuracy of body part identification increased with frequency of use in the respective language ($r = .69$ for Italian- and $r = .75$ for English-speaking patients).

Ogden (1985) reported the case of a patient with a left parietal lobe tumor that resulted in AT. The patient's AT could neither be attributed to language or mental status abnormalities nor to an inability to separate a whole into its component parts. Although this patient is one of the purest cases of AT to be reported to date, he demonstrated all aspects of Gerstmann syndrome, in addition to ideomotor apraxia, dressing apraxia, and visuospatial deficits. Evaluation of the patient for AT was complex and thorough, and his deficits fell into the classic dissociation discussed by Denes (1989): Intact "what tasks," which involve understanding, naming, and describing the functions of the body and body parts singled out by the examiner, in the context of impaired "where tasks," which involve pointing to a specific body part on verbal command or imitation or describing the precise location of a specific body part in relation to other body parts. Similar findings were demonstrated for Semenza's (1988) examination of a patient with a left parieto-occipital tumor.

Sirigu, Grafman, Bressler, and Sunderland (1991) carried out a unique experiment to discern whether the ability to identify body parts could be dissociated from the ability to identify inanimate objects placed on the body. The investigators studied a patient with probable dementia of the Alzheimer type who was roughly 3 years into the progression of the disease. As would be expected, she presented on neuropsychological testing with a broad array of cognitive impairments, including the full tetrad of Gerstmann syndrome and dressing apraxia. Twenty-five body parts distributed over the entire body were chosen for study. In terms of body part identification in verbal and nonverbal conditions, the patient displayed difficulty localizing body parts on herself and on others, but was able to demonstrate naming and functional comprehension of body parts. When ten inanimate objects were placed on her body at roughly the same locations as the body identification task (e.g., a figurine placed on the left knee), she successfully and reliably pointed to these objects and even recalled their position after their removal. The results of this study led the investigators to conclude that two systems of body knowledge exist, one for semantic and lexical information (intact in this patient) and the other for storing a body-specific visuospatial representation (impaired in this patient).

Denes, Cappelletti, Zilli, Porta, and Gallana (2000) studied two AT patients who presented with somewhat complicated neurological pictures. Case 1 suffered a left posterior parietal lobe hemorrhage accompanied by significant calculation and writing disturbances, as well as mild language disturbances. Case 2, a left-handed woman, suffered a vascular lesion of the right temporoparietal region and demonstrated aphasia and mild apraxia. Both patients were administered a comprehensive battery of body-knowledge tasks, which involved body part naming on a human picture, self, and others, as well as body part localization. Both patients performed at ceiling in naming body parts. However, localization proved much more difficult, although their errors were meaningful and demonstrated some degree of body knowledge. For example, "vicinity" errors, in which the patient pointed to a body part close in location to the target, were common. These authors also found a lack of support for the proposal that AT is a function of an inability to separate a whole into its component parts. Rather, the investigators hypothesized that AT was attributable to an impairment in the ability to encode body position information for self and others. In a same–different matching task, patients decided whether two pictures of static body positions and two pictures of building block figures were the same or different. In contrast to controls, who found the matching of body positions easier than the blocks, the patients demonstrated a comparable performance for the two tasks, suggesting a lack of the usual proclivity for body positions. The investigators concluded that lesions of the parietal lobe of the language-dominant hemisphere can impair the ability to locate body parts on verbal command and to detect changes in body position in a model.

We conducted a large-scale lesion study to investigate the neural substrates of body part terms (Kemmerer & Tranel, 2008). A battery of 12 tests assessing lexical and conceptual aspects of body part knowledge was administered to 104 brain-damaged patients. We found that:

1. Impaired naming of body parts was associated with lesions in the left frontal opercular and anterior/inferior parietal opercular cortices, and in the white matter underlying these regions (Figure 8-4).

2. Knowledge of the meanings of body part terms was remarkably resistant to impairment, regardless of lesion site; in fact, we did not find a single patient who exhibited significantly impaired understanding of the meanings of body part terms. Also, we found that one patient with body part anomia had a left occipital lesion that included the EBA. This study focused mainly on the production and comprehension of body part terms (as opposed to body schema knowledge per se), but it demonstrates very clearly the robust nature of knowledge for body part terms.

Laiacona, Allamano, Lorenzi, and Capitani (2006) reported a patient with a left hemisphere lesion who presented with a disproportionate impairment in knowledge for body parts, but without AT per se. The patient's deficit involved the lexical-semantic representations of body parts, and was most severe for limbs. The authors suggested that limbs are the most vulnerable component of the overall category of body parts. Another lesion study reported two patients who had dissociated performance in pointing to human body parts (Felician, Ceccaldi, Didic, Thinus-Blanc, & Poncet, 2003). One patient had a selective deficit in pointing to his own body parts, but preserved ability to point to the body parts of others. The other patient had the reverse pattern—impaired ability to point to the body parts of others, but preserved ability

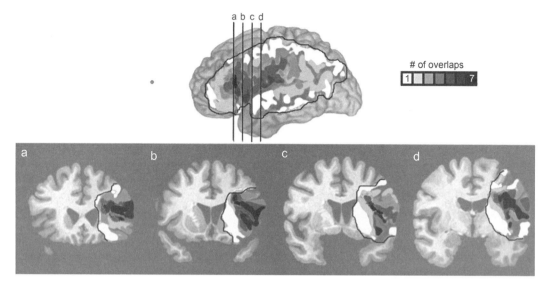

Figure 8–4. Lesion overlap map for seven patients with impaired naming of body parts. The top panel depicts a lateral view of the left hemisphere, and the bottom panels show four coronal cuts (a, b, c, d) through the posterior frontal region (with left hemisphere on the right). The area of lesions is within the middle cerebral artery territory, designated by a black outline. The degree of lesion overlap is indicated by the color bar, with black corresponding to greatest overlap (all seven patients), down to white for the least overlap (only one patient). Adapted from Kemmerer, D., & Tranel, D. (2008). Searching for the elusive neural substrates of body part terms: A neuropsychological study. *Cognitive Neuropsychology*, 25, 601–629, with permission of the publisher.

to point to her own body parts. The authors proposed that the left superior and inferior parietal regions are parts of networks involved in the respective processing of somatosensory and visuospatial representations of bodies.

A so-called "pure" case of AT associated with a left subcortical lesion was reported by Guariglia, Piccardi, Puglisi Allegra, and Traballesi (2002). The patient was studied thoroughly, and in the context of normal language and general cognitive functioning, demonstrated a selective impairment in performing tasks of body part representation. The patient's performances were especially defective on tests relying on visuospatial body representation, whereas her semantic and linguistic knowledge of body parts was spared. The authors suggested that their case supported the notion that AT can result from a deficit in a system that processes the structural properties and relative position of single body parts. They went on to argue that their case, as perhaps the purest case of AT ever reported, indicates that there is a neural system specifically dedicated to body part representation.

However, it is challenging to reconcile this claim, based on a single patient with a subcortical lesion, with the rather vast literature pointing to various cortical structures (especially parietal) as important for body part processing.

Another lesion study compared recognition of self versus others' body parts (Frassinetti, Maini, Romualdi, Galante, & Avanzi, 2008). Patients with left hemisphere lesions and healthy comparison participants performed better on tasks that required processing of one's own body parts, compared to tasks requiring processing of the body parts of others. By contrast, patients with right hemisphere lesions did not show this advantage for self body parts, and the authors interpreted this finding as consistent with the notion that the right hemisphere may be important for the recognition of self body parts, through a frontoparietal network.

Using fMRI, Corradi-Dell'Acqua, Hesse, Rumiati, and Fink (2008) found that the left posterior intraparietal sulcus (IPS) region was activated when participants were engaged in a task that required them to judge the distance between body parts (as compared to a task requiring identification of body parts per se). The authors suggested that their findings showed that the left posterior IPS specifically processes information about spatial relationships among body parts; this, in turn, is consistent with the notion that damage to this region tends to be associated with AT.

OTHER CONSIDERATIONS

As the studies reviewed above illustrate, there is considerable confusion in the literature regarding the extent to which language disturbances play a role in AT. In our view, a strict definition of AT would exclude a role for language entirely; that is, AT should be considered a disturbance of the knowledge of body parts that cannot be attributed to or explained by an impairment of language, and especially, an impairment in retrieving and comprehending words for body parts. This formulation of AT is more in keeping with the notion that the core feature of the disorder is a disturbance of the body schema, and with the idea that AT can be classified as a disturbance of knowledge retrieval: that is, an "agnosia." Our concerns here are not just specious; in fact, a number of studies have demonstrated that the naming of body parts can be impaired quite independently of body part knowledge (De Renzi & Scotti, 1970; Ogden, 1985); moreover, it has been shown that naming and comprehending of body parts can be impaired or preserved quite selectively in relationship to naming items from other conceptual categories (e.g., Goodglass et al., 1966; Yamadori & Albert, 1973; McKenna & Warrington, 1978; Suzuki, Yamadori, & Fujii, 1997; Kemmerer & Tranel, 2008).

NEUROPSYCHOLOGICAL EVALUATION OF AUTOTOPAGNOSIA

Virtually no systematic approaches to the neuropsychological assessment of AT exist. A review of common neuropsychological assessment and neurological exam texts revealed little attention to the topic. Research studies, however, have tended to use or adapt the approach set forth by Semenza and Goodglass (1985). Their battery includes 18 body parts (i.e., nose, knee, chest, eye, shoulder, ear, hip, wrist, toe, neck, elbow, hair, thigh, chin, ankle, cheek, thumb, and lips), and their localization is required in each of nine experimental conditions involving verbal or nonverbal processing.

We (Kemmerer & Tranel, 2008) adapted and expanded this approach, and developed a battery of 12 tests that provides comprehensive assessment of the production, comprehension, and nonverbal processing of body part terms and body part information, which are outlined in Table 8-3.

FINGER AGNOSIA

Finger agnosia can be defined as a finger localization deficit (Benton, 1959). Patients with FA demonstrate a loss of the ability to name fingers, show fingers on verbal command, or localize fingers following tactile stimulation. They are typically able to use their fingers for everyday life activities, often with an added degree of clumsiness. Of the body schema disturbances reviewed in this chapter, FA occurs with the greatest frequency (Frederiks, 1985), and is considered a hallmark feature of Gerstmann syndrome. Finger agnosia is most commonly considered a bilateral condition, in which both hands are affected. Finally, FA is most pronounced on examination of the middle three fingers (Frederiks, 1985).

Whether FA can occur as an isolated phenomenon continues to be an issue of great debate. Many believe it is actually a component of AT, or secondary to aphasia, dementia, or visuospatial dysfunction (e.g., Shenal, Jackson, Crucian, & Heilman, 2006; see Benton, 1992, for a review). Morris, Lüders, Lesser, Dinner, and Hahn (1984) demonstrated that stimulation of perisylvian cortical areas elicits FA unaccompanied by other defects, suggesting that, in principle, FA could exist in isolation. The most common neural correlate of FA is left parietal-occipital dysfunction. However, a sizeable minority of the literature reviewed below suggests that FA can occur with lesions on either side of the brain (e.g., Kinsbourne & Warrington, 1962; Moro, Pernigo, Urgesi, Zapparoli, & Aglioti, 2008).

Table 8–3. Twelve Tests for the Comprehensive Assessment of the Production, Comprehension, and Nonverbal Processing of Body Part Terms and Body Part Information

1. Production Tests

Each of the four production tests requires retrieval of the phonological output forms of the same 30 words (or synonyms for them), which refer to body parts distributed across the major corporeal regions in the following manner: head (*N* = 13): *head, face, neck, chin, cheek, forehead, ear, earlobe, eye, eyelash, nose, mouth, lip*; torso (*N* = 3): *chest, belly/stomach/abdomen, back*; upper extremities (*N* = 8): *shoulder, arm, elbow, wrist, hand, finger, knuckle, fingernail*; lower extremities (*N* = 6): *leg, thigh, knee, ankle, foot, toe.*

Test 1: *Name own body parts (visual input)*: The examiner points to 30 of the subject's body parts, and the task is to produce the colloquial spoken name for each one.

Test 2: *Name own body parts (tactile input)*: The examiner touches 30 of the subject's body parts while the subject is blindfolded, and the task is to produce the colloquial spoken name for each one.

Test 3: *Name examiner's body parts*: The examiner points to 30 of his or her own body parts, and the task is to produce the colloquial spoken name for each one.

Test 4: *Name isolated body parts*: The subject is shown 30 pictures of isolated body parts, and the task is to produce the colloquial spoken name for each one. The pictures consist of a mixture of photographs and line drawings, and each one includes not only the relevant body part but also its immediate spatial context—e.g., the picture of a cheek shows the right profile of a man's face with a black circle around the cheek.

2. Comprehension Tests

The first six comprehension tests evaluate, in different ways, knowledge of the shape, location, and function components of body part terms. The last comprehension test assesses knowledge of how these terms are sometimes applied to the parts of inanimate objects.

Test 5: *Point to own named body parts*: The examiner says the names of 30 body parts (the same terms as in Tests 1–4), and the subject's task is to point to the corresponding parts of his or her own body. Failure on this type of test is the major symptom of autotopagnosia (e.g., Felician et al., 2003).

Test 6: *Point to examiner's named body parts*: The examiner says the names of 30 body parts (the same terms as in Tests 1–4), and the subject's task is to point to the corresponding parts of the examiner's body. Failure on this type of test is the major symptom of heterotopagnosia (e.g., Felician et al., 2003).

Test 7: *Word-picture matching*: This test is made up of 25 sets of three pictures. The task is to choose which picture in each set best represents the meaning of a printed body part term. For each set, one picture shows the target body part (e.g., a forehead), another picture shows a distractor body part that is related to the target with respect to either shape, position, or function (e.g., a cheek), and the third picture shows a distractor body part that is unrelated to the target (e.g., an elbow).

Test 8: *Word-picture verification*: The subject is shown 30 pictures of isolated body parts (just like in Test 4), each of which is associated with a single printed body part term. The task is to indicate whether or not the term accurately refers to the depicted body part. For example, in one item the word is *shoulder* and the picture shows a man's shoulder with a circle around it.

Test 9: *Locations of body parts*: The subject is asked ten questions about the relative spatial positions of body parts and must answer "Yes" or "No" for each one. Examples: "Is the elbow a part of the arm?" "Is the head connected to the waist?" Unlike Test 5 and Test 6, this test does not require the subject to point to named parts of either his or her own body or the examiner's body. Instead, it probes knowledge of the location component of body part terms in a somewhat more abstract manner.

Test 10: *Functions of body parts*: The subject is asked six questions about the characteristic functions of particular body parts. Examples: "What is the nose for?" "What do the feet do?" Acceptable answers included one-word responses (e.g., "smelling") or short phrases (e.g., "help you walk") that matched responses given by normal participants.

Test 11: *Body part terms applied to the parts of inanimate objects*: The subject is shown 20 pictures of inanimate objects, and in each picture, a specific part of the object is highlighted by an arrow or circle. For each item, the picture is presented together with three printed body part terms, and the task is to indicate which term is conventionally used to refer to the highlighted part of the object. Examples (with the correct term underlined): the *teeth/claws/face* of a comb; the *head/back/foot* of a hammer; the *arm/leg/foot* of a chair; the *mouth/nose/face* of a cave; the *nose/head/foot* of an airplane. Although this test involves fixed linguistic collocations, it nevertheless provides a useful measure of the subject's knowledge of how English body part terms are sometimes applied to the parts of inanimate objects.

(Continued)

Table 8–3. Continued

3. Nonlinguistic Test

The last test was designed to probe conceptual knowledge of body parts independently of lexical-phonological processing of body part terms.

Test 12: Odd one out: This test is comprised of 20 sets of three pictures. For each set, two of the pictures show body parts that are related with respect to either function (e.g., an eye and an ear, which are both senses) or location (e.g., a back and a chest, which are both parts of the torso), whereas the third picture shows a body part that is unrelated to the other two (e.g., a shoulder or a cheek, for the two examples above, respectively) (Figure 8-5). The task is to indicate which picture is unrelated to the other two.

From Kemmerer, D., & Tranel, D. (2008). Searching for the elusive neural substrates of body part terms: A neuropsychological study. Cognitive *Neuropsychology* 25: 601–629.

CASE AND GROUP STUDIES

Benton (1959) took the view that finger localization involves a language function or a symbolic process, and that FA is due to "an impairment of language function in which the patient has lost the ability to handle the symbols that related to the fingers (p. 159)." Benton's hypothesis was tested by Kinsbourne and Warrington (1962). They administered verbal and nonverbal tests of finger localization to 12 patients with elements of Gerstmann syndrome (one-third of whom had bilateral lesions, one-third left hemisphere lesions, and one-third right hemisphere lesions) and 20 brain-damaged comparison patients without any Gerstmann symptoms. Results revealed that all patients with elements of Gerstmann syndrome failed at least three of five finger localization tests administered. Moreover, the performance of target patients was significantly worse on the nonverbal finger localization tests than on verbal tasks of finger localization. In summary, these authors concluded that their findings challenge Benton's view that language disturbance is essential to FA.

Gianotti, Cianchetti, and Tiacci (1972) studied finger localization in 162 unselected patients with unilateral brain damage (88 left and 74 right hemisphere brain-damaged). The results demonstrated that the incidence of FA did not differ significantly in right and left brain-damaged patients when nonverbal procedures and larger samples are used. What did play a significant role in FA, however, was the presence of aphasia and/or general mental impairment: The poor performance of the right brain-damaged group was associated with general mental impairment, whereas the left brain-damaged group showed a relatively higher incidence of aphasia and sensory impairment.

Benke, Schelosky, and Gerstenbrand (1988) studied FA in groups of right brain-damaged, left brain-damaged without aphasia, and aphasic patients. The investigators confirmed the high frequency of FA in aphasic patients, but also noted its occurrence in nonaphasic patients. In all the groups, the presence of FA was related to the severity of the defect in visuospatial, language-related cognitive functions, and mental imagery. The authors concluded that, rather than being the direct expression of a focal lesion, FA reflects impairment in higher-level cognitive systems.

Tucha, Steup, Smely, and Lange (1997) studied a patient with a tumor of the left angular gyrus. The patient presented with Gerstmann syndrome. Neuropsychological evaluation was unremarkable except for acalculia, agraphia, and spelling impairments. Neurological testing revealed that she additionally manifested toe agnosia. These investigators suggest that patients should more regularly be evaluated for toe agnosia, and, if common, a new term, *digit agnosia*, is recommended. However, Fein (1987) warns that normal adults misidentify toes with great regularity.

A right-handed patient with a right hemisphere lesion presented with Gerstmann syndrome and was found to have an association

Function (senses)

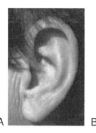
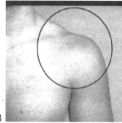

A   B

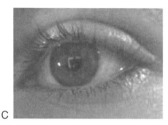

C

Location (torso)

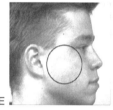

D   E

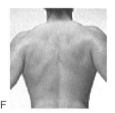

F

Figure 8–5. Examples of the types of stimuli used in the Odd One Out test. For each set of three pictures, the subject is asked to determine which body part is *un*related to the other two with respect to either function (*top panel*, with the shoulder being the correct answer because it does not pertain to the senses) or location (*bottom panel*, with the cheek being the correct answer because it does not pertain to the torso). Note that the relevant dimension of comparison is not provided by the examiner, but must be discovered by the subject. From Kemmerer, D., & Tranel, D. (2008). Searching for the elusive neural substrates of body part terms: A neuropsychological study. *Cognitive Neuropsychology, 25,* 601–629, with permission of the publisher.

between FA and gesture imitation deficits (Moro, Pernigo, Urgesi, Zapparioli, & Aglioti, 2008). No language deficits were noted. The patient's gestural imitation deficit specifically involved finger movements and postures. The authors made the intriguing suggestion that Gerstmann syndrome is a disorder of body representation that involves hands and fingers—that is, nonfacial body parts most involved in social interactions.

Three patients with angular gyrus lesions and FA were reported by Anema, Kessels, de Haan, Kappelle, et al. (2008). The patients had intact somatosensory processing. They performed normally when pointing to the touched finger on their own hand, but failed to indicate this finger on a drawing of a hand or to name it. The deficit was confined to fingers and did not extend to other body parts. The authors suggested that these cases provide additional evidence for the dissociation between body image and body schema.

A case of left-hand FA following a hemorrhagic lesion encroaching on the posterior third of the corpus callosum, but sparing the splenium, was reported by Balsamo, Trojano, Giamundo, and Grossi (2008). The patient also demonstrated a striking tactile agnosia with the left hand. The authors interpreted the findings as an example of a disconnection syndrome.

NEUROPSYCHOLOGICAL EVALUATION OF FINGER AGNOSIA

Benton (1959) and Benton et al. (1994) developed a 60-item test consisting of three parts (i.e., 10 items for each part below for each of the hands) to assess FA:

1. With the hand visible, localization of single fingers touched by the examiner
2. With the hand hidden from view, localization of single fingers touched by the examiner
3. With the hand hidden from view, localization of pairs of fingers simultaneously touched by the examiner

Mode of response on the part of the examinee can take a number of forms, including naming, pointing on a drawing, or referring to the fingers with numbers (Figure 8-6).

RIGHT–LEFT DISORIENTATION

Right–left orientation refers to the ability to identify the right and left sides of one's own body, and to identify the right and left sides of a person seated oppositely or in a photo/drawing. It additionally necessitates both spatial and symbolic elements for successful performance. Individuals with RLD often demonstrate the sparing of other spatial concepts, such as up–down and front–back (Denes, 1989). As noted earlier, RLD is one of the Gerstmann signs, and it has been described most frequently in connection with at least some of the other components of Gerstmann syndrome. Right–left disorientation may develop consequently to broader disturbances of body schema or language processing, but it can exist as a fairly isolated symptom (Gold, Adair, Jacobs, & Heilman, 1995), suggesting that it is useful to retain RLD as a meaningful neuropsychological entity. As we have alluded to, the most common neural correlate of RLD is left parietal dysfunction.

Studies

It is not altogether uncommon to observe some degree of right–left confusion in healthy adults. Wolf (1973) examined the incidence of right–left confusion in a sample of physicians and their spouses. Results revealed that 17.5% of women and 8.8% of men sampled admitted to "frequent" right–left confusion. Harris and Gitterman (1978) assessed the frequency of right–left confusion in a sample of 364 university faculty members, and found greater error rates among females, especially left-handed females. These results are consistent with the premise that women generally have inferior spatial skills relative to men (De Renzi, 1982). In children, this ability appears to follow a developmental trajectory with own body right–left orientation developing before the ability to identify right from left on an opposing individual (Benton, 1959; Clark & Klonoff, 1990; Benton & Sivan, 1993). Assessment of RLD is evident on developmental tests of adaptive behavior, such as the Vineland Adaptive Behavior Scales (Sparrow, Balla, & Cicchetti, 1984). By the age of 12, however, most children show an adult level of success in right–left opposing

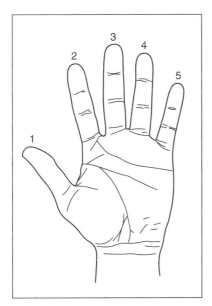
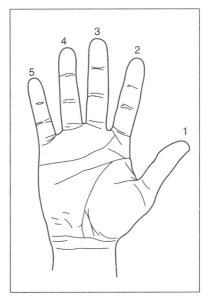

Figure 8–6. Examples of hand/finger stimuli used in the Figure Localization Test of Benton. From Benton, A. L., Sivan, A. B., Hamsher, K. S., Varney, N. S., & Spreen, O. (1994). *Contributions to neuropsychological assessment: A clinical manual.* New York: Oxford, with permission of the publisher.

orientation tasks (Clark & Klonoff, 1990). At the other end of the spectrum, it has been shown that right–left discrimination ability begins to decline after about age 50 (Ofte & Hugdahl, 2002).

Although RLD is classically thought of as being related to left hemisphere damage, work by Ratcliff (1979) suggests some right hemisphere contribution to right–left orientation. Ratcliff (1979) found that patients with right parietal-temporal-occipital lesions were impaired in making right–left judgments about inverted (upside down) figures, but not with upright figures. Ratcliff (1979) summarized his findings as lending support to the notion that the right posterior cortex was specialized for mental rotation. Consistent with this, an fMRI study showed that right–left discrimination predominantly activated right hemisphere structures, including structures in the region of the temporal-parietal-occipital junction (Auer, Schwarcz, Aradi, et al., 2008).

In one of the few group studies conducted on this topic, Sauguet, Benton, and Hécaen (1971) examined 31 patients with right hemisphere lesions and 49 patients with left hemisphere lesions. The left hemisphere group was divided into 21 patients with "sensory" aphasia and 28 patients without aphasia. All patients completed, among other tasks, right–left orientation in four formats: (1) right–left orientation of one's own body, (2) confronting front view of examiner and model, (3) confronting back view of examiner, and (4) imitation of a three step movement. For Format 1, nonaphasic patients, regardless of side of lesion, performed relatively strongly; however, two-thirds of left hemisphere patients with aphasia performed defectively. For Formats 2 and 3, 50% of left hemisphere patients with aphasia performed defectively, as did 13% of nonaphasic patients with right hemisphere lesions. Interestingly, all left hemisphere nonaphasic subjects performed relatively strongly. For Format 4, 48% of left hemisphere patients with aphasia performed defectively, as did 32% of nonaphasic patients with right hemisphere lesions and 14% of left hemisphere nonaphasic subjects. This study suggests that the relationship of RLD with side-of-lesion and the presence or absence of aphasia is not a simple one; rather, the performance

of different unilateral lesion groups is dependent on what aspect of RLD is assessed. The study additionally suggests that right hemisphere damage contributes to RLD, especially during imitation tasks.

Fischer, Marterer, and Danielczyk (1990) examined whether patients with probable dementia of Alzheimer type (DAT) would show RLD, suggestive of left parietal dysfunction. Eighteen patients with DAT were matched on age, education, and dementia severity with 18 multi-infarct dementia (MID) patients. All participants were administered a shortened version of the Right–Left Orientation Test involving six questions addressing right–left orientation on own body and six questions addressing right–left orientation on a confronting doll (Benton, 1959; Benton, Sivan, Hamsher, Varney, & Spreen, 1994). Participants were also administered tests of language and visuospatial ability. The investigators found that DAT and MID groups did not differ on own body right–left orientation. In contrast, the DAT group performed significantly more poorly than the MID group on right–left orientation on a confronting doll, and this impairment was independent of language and visuospatial dysfunction. The authors suggest that their findings are consistent with the biparietal hypometabolism commonly seen in PET studies of DAT patients.

Neuropsychological Evaluation of Right–Left Disorientation

Formal examination of RLD makes demands on numerous cognitive abilities, including auditory comprehension, verbal expression of the labels "left" and "right," short-term memory for the instructions, sensory discrimination, and mental rotation. Furthermore, the mode of response is varied, including naming, executing movements in response to verbal command, and imitation of movement (Benton & Sivan, 1993). Finally, identification of "right" and "left" may occur on own body, confronting examiner/picture, or a combination of the two.

Benton and Sivan (1993) underscore the importance of taking a hierarchical approach to the assessment of RLD in which the execution of each lower level is a prerequisite for successful performance at higher levels. Table 8-4 demonstrates that a basic premise of examining RLD is that the ability to execute double uncrossed commands (I-C) is a prerequisite for success on double crossed commands (I-D). Occasional exceptions to the rule do occur with failures on an easier item (I-D), while success occurs for an apparently more difficult item (III-B). According to Benton et al. (1994), successful completion of III-A and III-B requires a rotation of 180 degrees in orientation.

Diagnostic Assessment

The following tests allow one to determine the presence or absence of a clinically significant RLD. If RLD is present, it is important to get a notion of whether the patient had an unusual premorbid weakness of these capacities. Furthermore, aphasic patients present a particularly challenging puzzle since their RLD may be driven by primary language factors such as comprehension deficits; anomia, which could cause confusion in the use of the "right" and "left" labels; and deficits in auditory retention.

The Right–Left Orientation Test (RLOT; Benton, 1959; Benton, Sivan, Hamsher, Varney, & Spreen, 1994) is a 20-item test of simple (e.g., show me your right hand) and complex (e.g., touch your right ear with your right hand) verbal commands to assess right–left orientation. The first 12 items involve discerning right from left on the subject's own body. The final eight questions necessitate right–left discrimination on the examiner or on a model that is at least 15 inches in height. Alternative forms of this test exist.

The Standardized Road-Map Test of Direction Sense (Money, 1976) is a test of right–left orientation in extrapersonal space. On an unmarked road map, the examiner draws a dotted pathway and the subject is asked to tell the direction (right or left) at each turn. Normative data for subjects 18 years of age and younger do not exist; however, for individuals older than 18, a cutoff value has been established to categorize the subject as intact or impaired.

The Laterality Discrimination Test (LDT; Culver, 1969) is a speeded task of laterality judgment and spatial perception. The stimuli consist of 32 line drawings of body parts (16 hands, eight feet, four eyes, and four ears). Subjects are shown one card at a time, and are asked to judge whether the picture is a right or left body part.

Table 8–4. Components of Right–Left Orientation

I. Orientation Toward One's Own Body
    A. Naming single lateral body parts touched by examiner
    B. Pointing to single lateral body parts on verbal command
    C. Executing double-uncrossed movements on verbal command (e.g., touching left ear with left hand)
    D. Executing double-crossed movements on verbal command (e.g., touching right ear with left hand)

II. Orientation Toward One's Own Body Without Visual Guidance (Blindfolded or Eyes Closed)
    A. Naming single lateral body parts touched by examiner
    B. Pointing to single lateral body parts on verbal command
    C. Executing double-uncrossed movements on verbal command (e.g., touching left ear with left hand)
    D. Executing double-crossed movements on verbal command (e.g., touching right ear with left hand)

III. Orientation Toward Confronting Examiner or Picture
    A. Naming single lateral body parts touched by examiner
    B. Pointing to single lateral body parts on verbal command
    C. Imitating uncrossed movements of examiner (e.g., left hand on left ear)
    D. Imitating crossed movements of examiner (e.g., left hand on right ear)

IV. Combined Orientation Toward One's Own Body and Confronting Person
    A. Placing either left or right hand on specified part of confronting person on verbal command (e.g., placing right hand on confronting person's left ear)

From Benton, A. L., & Sivan, A. B. (1993). Disturbances of the body schema. In K. M. Heilman & E. Valenstein (Eds.), *Clinical neuropsychology*. New York: Oxford.

As can be seen from the above diagnostic tests, the availability of nonverbal tests is lacking. However, most can be adapted for a nonverbal administration that involves pointing responses and imitation. Inclusion of a few nonverbal tasks seems important, given the dissociation in performance on verbal and nonverbal right–left orientation that was revealed in a case of a patient with a left anterior temporal lobe tumor (Dennis, 1976).

SUMMARY

Our review indicates that the neural basis of body schema representation remains poorly understood. The specific disorders of AT, FA, and RLD appear to be linked primarily to dysfunction of the left parietal regions, and as suggested by other authors (e.g., Denes, 1989), seem to depend on an altered conceptual representation of the body and body parts. Much of this alteration seems attributable in many cases to linguistic factors. Insofar as clinical practice is concerned, though, it is our impression that the utility of these constructs—and of the entire Gerstmann syndrome for that matter—remains viable, and we would encourage the continued use and teaching of these terms in clinical neuropsychology.

ACKNOWLEDGMENTS

This chapter is supported by Program Project Grant NINDS NS19632 and NIDA DA022549.

REFERENCES

Anderson, S. W., Damasio, A. R., & Damasio, H. (1990). Troubled letters but not numbers. *Brain, 113*, 749–766.

Anema, H. A., Kessels, R. P., de Haan, E. H., Kappelle, L. J., Leijten, F. S., van Zandvoort, M. J., & Dijkerman, H. C. (2008). Differences in finger localisation performance of patients with finger agnosia. *Neuroreport, 19*, 1429–1433.

Ardila, A., & Rosselli, M. (2002). Acalculia and dyscalculia. *Neuropsychology Review, 12*, 179–231.

Arzy, S., Thut, G., Mohr, C., Michel, C. M., & Blanke, O. (2006). Neural basis of embodiment: Distinct contributions of temporoparietal junction and extrastriate body area. *Journal of Neuroscience, 26*, 8074–8081.

Ashcraft, M. H. (1987). Children's knowledge of simple arithmetic: A developmental model and simulation. In J. Bisanz, C. J. Brainerd, & R. Kail (Eds.), *Formal methods in developmental psychology: Progress in cognitive developmental research*. New York: Springer-Verlag.

Ashkenazi, S., Henik, A., Ifergane, G., & Shelef, I. (2008). Basic numerical processing in left intraparietal sulcus (IPS) acalculia. *Cortex, 44*, 439–438.

Astafiev, S. V., Stanley, C. M., Shulman, G. L., & Corbetta, M. (2004). Extrastriate body area in human occipital cortex responds to the performance of motor actions. *Nature Neuroscience, 7*, 542–548.

Auer, T., Schwarcz, A., Aradi, M., Kalmar, Z., Pendleton, C., Janszky, I., et al. (2008). Right-left discrimination is related to the right hemisphere. *Laterality, 13*, 427–438.

Balsamo, M., Trojano, L., Giamundo, A., & Grossi, D. (2008). Left hand tactile agnosia after posterior callosal lesion. *Cortex, 44*, 1030–1036.

Bartels, A., & Zeki, S. (2004). Functional brain mapping during fee viewing of natural scenes. *Human Brain Mapping, 21*, 75–85.

Basso, A., Burgio, F., & Caporali, A. (2000). Acalculia, aphasia, and spatial disorders in left and right brain-damaged patients. *Cortex, 36*, 265–280.

Basso, A., Caporali, A., & Faglioni, P. (2005). Spontaneous recovery from acalculia. *Journal of the International Neuropsychological Society, 11*, 99–107.

Benbow, C. P., & Stanley, J. C. (1983). Sex differences in mathematical reasoning ability: More facts. *Science, 222*, 1029–1031.

Benke, T., Schelosky, L., & Gerstenbrand, F. (1988). A clinical investigation of finger agnosia. *Journal of Clinical and Experimental Neuropsychology, 10*, 335.

Benson, D. F., & Weir, W. F. (1972). Acalculia: Acquired anarithmetia. *Cortex, 8*, 465–472.

Benton, A. L. (1958). Significance of systematic reversal in right-left discrimination. *Acta Psychiatrica Neurologica Scandinavica, 33*, 129–137.

Benton, A. L. (1959). *Right-left discrimination and finger localization: Development and pathology*. New York: Hoeber-Harper.

Benton, A. L. (1961). The fiction of the "Gerstmann syndrome." *Journal of Neurology, Neurosurgery, and Psychiatry, 24*, 176–181.

Benton, A. L. (1963). *Assessment of number operations*. Iowa City: University of Iowa Hospital, Department of Neurology.

Benton, A. L. (1977). Reflections on the Gerstmann syndrome. *Brain and Language, 4*, 45–62.

Benton, A. L. (1985). Body schema disturbances: Finger agnosia and right-left disorientation. In K. M. Heilman, & E. Valenstein (Eds.), *Clinical neuropsychology*. New York: Oxford.

Benton, A. L. (1992). Gerstmann's syndrome. *Archives of Neurology, 49*, 445–447.

Benton, A. L., & Sivan, A. B. (1993). Disturbances of the body schema. In K. M. Heilman, & E. Valenstein (Eds.), *Clinical neuropsychology*. New York: Oxford.

Benton, A. L., Sivan, A. B., Hamsher, K. S., Varney, N. S., & Spreen, O. (1994). *Contributions to neuropsychological assessment. A clinical manual*. New York: Oxford.

Berger, H. (1926). Ueber Rechenstorgungen bei herderkrankungen des grosshirns. *Archiv für Psychiatrie und Nervenkrankheiten, 78*, 238–263.

Blanke, O., & Arzy, S. (2005). The out-of-body experience: Disturbed self-processing at the temporo-parietal junction. *Neuroscientist, 11*, 16–24.

Boller, F., & Grafman, J. (1983). Acalculia: Historical development and current significance. *Brain and Cognition, 2*, 205–223.

Braun, C. M., Desjardins, S., Gaudelet, S., & Guimond, A. (2007). Psychic tonus, body schema and the parietal lobes: A multiple lesion case analysis. *Behavioral Neurology, 18*, 65–80.

Burbaud, P., Degreze, P., Lafon, P., Franconi, J-M., Bouligand, B., Bioulac, B., et al. (1995). Lateralization of prefrontal activation during internal mental calculation: A functional magnetic resonance imaging study. *Journal of Neurophysiology, 74*, 2194–2200.

Butterworth, B. (1999). *What counts: How every brain is hardwired for math*. New York: The Free Press.

Caporali, A., Burgio, F., & Basso, A. (2000). The natural course of acalculia in left-brain-damaged patients. *Neurological Sciences, 21*, 143–149.

Chochon, F., Cohen, L., van de Moortele, P. F., & Dehaene, S. (1999). Differential contributions of the left and right inferior parietal lobules to number processing. *Journal of Cognitive Neuroscience, 11*, 617–630.

Cipolotti, L., Butterworth, B., & Warrington, E. K. (1994). From "one thousand nine hundred and forty-five" to 1000,945. *Neuropsychologia, 32*, 503–509.

Clark, C. M., & Klonoff, H. (1990). Right and left orientation in children aged 5 to 13 years. *Journal of Clinical and Experimental Neuropsychology, 12*, 459–466.

Cohn, R. (1961). Dyscalculia. *Archives of Neurology, 4*, 301–307.

Connolly, A. J. (1991). *KeyMath diagnostic arithmetic test-Revised*. Toronto: PsyCan Corporation.

Corradi-Dell'Acqua, C., Hesse, M. D. Rumiati, R. I., & Fink, G. R. (2008). Where is a nose with respect to a foot? The left posterior parietal cortex processes spatial relationships among body parts. *Cerebral Cortex, 18*, 2879–2890.

Corradi-Dell'Acqua, C., Tomasino, B., & Fink, G. R. (2009). What is the position of an arm relative to the body? Neural correlates of body schema and body structural description. *Journal of Neuroscience, 29*, 62–71.

Critchley, M. (1966). The enigma of Gerstmann's syndrome. *Brain, 89*, 183–198.

Culver, C. M. (1969). Test of right-left discrimination. *Perceptual and Motor Skills, 29*, 863–867.

Dahmen, W., Hartje, W., Büssing, A., & Sturm, W. (1982). Disorders of calculation in aphasic patients–Spatial and verbal components. *Neuropsychologia, 20*, 145–153.

Damasio, A. R. (1999). *The Feeling of what happens: Body and emotion in the making of consciousness*. Orlando: Harcourt/Brace.

Dehaene, S. (1992). Varieties of numerical abilities. *Cognition, 44*, 1–42.

Dehaene, S., Molko, N., Cohen, L., & Wilson, A. J. (2004). Arithmetic and the brain. *Current Opinion in Neurobiology, 14*, 218–224.

Dehaene, S., Tzourio, N., Frak, V., Raynaud, L., Cohen, L., Mehler, J., & Mazoyer, B. (1996). Cerebral activations during number multiplication and comparison: A PET study. *Neuropsychologia, 34*, 1097–1106.

Dehaene, S., & Cohen, L. (1995). Towards an anatomical and functional model of number processing. *Mathematical Cognition, 1*, 83–120.

Dehaene, S., & Cohen, L. (1997). Cerebral pathways for calculation: Double dissociation between rote verbal and quantitative knowledge of arithmetic. *Cortex, 33*, 219–250.

Dehaene, S., Spelke, E., Pinel, P., Stanescu, R., & Tsivkin, S. (1999). Sources of mathematical thinking: Behavioral and brain-imaging evidence. *Science, 284*, 970–974.

Delazer, M., & Benke, T. (1997). Arithmetic facts without meaning. *Cortex, 33*, 697–710.

Delazer, M. Girelli, L., Semenza, C., & Denes, G. (1999). Numerical skills and aphasia. *Journal of the International Neuropsychological Society, 5*, 213–221.

Deloche, G., Dellatolas, G., Vendrell, J., & Bergego, C. (1996). Calculation and number processing: Neuropsychological assessment and daily life activities. *Journal of the International Neuropsychological Society*, 2, 177–180.

Deloche, G., & Seron, X. (1982). From three to 3: A differential analysis of skills in transcoding quantities between patients with Broca's and Wernicke's aphasia. *Brain*, 105, 719–733.

Deloche, G., Seron, X., Baeta, E., Basso, A., Salinas, D. C., Gaillard, F., et al. (1993). Calculation and number processing: The EC301 assessment battery for brain-damaged adults. In F. J. Stachowiak (Ed.), *Developments in the assessment and rehabilitation of brain damaged patients*. Tubingen: Gunter Narr Verlag.

Deloche, G., Seron, X., Larroque, C., Magnien, C., Metz-Lutz, M. N., Noel, M. N., et al. (1994). Calculation and number processing: Assessment battery; Role of demographic factors. *Journal of Clinical and Experimental Neuropsychology*, 16, 195–208.

Denburg, N. L., & Tranel, D. (2003). Acalculia and disturbances of the body schema. In K. M. Heilman, & E. Valenstein (Eds.), *Clinical Neuropsychology* (4th ed., pp. 161–184). New York: Oxford.

Denes, G. (1989). Disorders of body awareness and body knowledge. In F. Boller, & J. Grafman (Eds.), *Handbook of Neuropsychology*, Vol. 2. Amsterdam: Elsevier.

Denes, G., Cappelletti, J. Y., Zilli, T., Porta, F. D., & Gallana, A. (2000). A category-specific deficit of spatial representation: The case of Autotopagnosia. *Neuropsychologia*, 38, 345–350.

Dennis, M. (1976). Dissociated naming and locating of body parts after left anterior temporal lobe resection: An experimental case study. *Brain and Language*, 3, 147–163.

De Renzi, E. (1982). *Disorders of space exploration and cognition*. New York: Wiley.

De Renzi, E., & Faglioni, P. (1963). L'autotopagnosia. *Arch. Psicol. Neurol. Psychiatr.* 24: 1–34.

De Renzi, E., & Scotti, G. (1970). Autotopagnosia: Fiction or reality? *Archives of Neurology (Chicago)*, 23, 221–227.

Downing, P. E., Bray, D., Rogers, J., & Childs, C. (2004). Bodies capture attention when nothing is expected. *Cognition*, 93, B27–B38.

Downing, P. E., Chan, A. W., Peelen, M. V., Dodds, C. M., Kanwisher, N. (2006) Domain Specificity in Visual Cortex. *Cerebral Cortex*, 16, 1453–1461.

Downing, P. E., Chan, A. W. -Y., Peelen, M. V., Dodds, C. M., & Kanwisher, N. (2006a). Domain specificity in visual cortex. *Cerebral Cortex*, 16, 1453–1461.

Downing, P. E. Jiang, Y., Shuman, M., & Kanwisher, N. (2001). A cortical area selective for visual processing of the human body. *Science*, 293, 2470–2473.

Downing, P. E., Peelen, M. V., Wiggett, A. J., & Tew, B. D. (2006b). The role of the extrastriate body area in action perception. *Social Neuroscience*, 1, 52–62.

Downing, P. E., Wiggett, A. J., & Peelen, M. V. (2007). Functional magnetic resonance imaging investigation of overlapping lateral occipitotemporal activations using multi-voxel pattern analysis. *Journal of Neuroscience*, 27, 226–233.

Fein, D. (1987). Systematic misidentification of toes in normal adults. *Neuropsychologia*, 25, 293–294.

Felician, O., Ceccaldi, M., Didic, M., Thinus-Blanc, C., & Poncet, M. (2003). Pointing to body parts: A double dissociation study. *Neuropsychologia*, 41, 1307–1316.

Ferro, J. M., & Botelho, M. A. S. (1980). Alexia for arithmetical signs. A cause of disturbed calculation. *Cortex*, 16, 175–180.

Fischer, P., Marterer, A., & Danielczyk, W. (1990). Right-left disorientation in dementia of the Alzheimer type. *Neurology*, 40, 1619–1620.

Frassinetti, F., Maini, M., Romualdi, S., Galante, E., & Avanzi, S. (2008). Is it mine? Hemispheric asymmetries in corporeal self-recognition. *Journal of Cognitive Neuroscience*, 20, 1507–1516.

Frederiks, J. A. M. (1985). Disorders of the body schema. In P. J. Vinken, & G.W. Bruyn (Eds.), *Handbook of clinical neurology*, Vol. 4. Amsterdam: North-Holland.

Gainotti, G., Cianchetti, C., & Tiacci, C. (1972). The influence of the hemispheric side of lesion on non verbal tasks of finger localization. *Cortex*, 8, 364–381.

Gerstmann, J. (1940). Syndrome of finger agnosia, disorientation for right and left, agraphia, and acalculia. *Archives of Neurology and Psychiatry*, 44, 398–408.

Gold, M., Adair, J. C., Jacobs, D. H., & Heilman, K. M. (1995). Right-left confusion in Gerstmann's syndrome: A model of body centered spatial orientation. *Cortex*, 31, 267–283.

Goodglass, H., Klein, B., Carey, P., & Jones, K. (1966). Specific semantic word categories in aphasia. *Cortex*, 2, 74–89.

Grafman, J., Kampen, D., Rosenberg, J., Salazar, A. M., & Boller, F. (1989). The processing breakdown of number processing and calculation ability: A case study. *Cortex*, 25, 121–133.

Grafman, J., Passafiume, D., Faglioni, P., & Boller, F. (1982). Calculation disturbances in adults with focal hemispheric damage. *Cortex*, *18*, 37–50.

Grana, A., Hofer, R., & Semenza, C. (2006). Acalculia from a right hemisphere lesion dealing with "where" in multiplication procedures. *Neuropsychologia*, *44*, 2972–2986.

Grewel, F. (1952). Acalculia. *Brain*, *75*, 397–407.

Guariglia, C., Piccardi, L., Puglisi Allegra, M. C., & Traballesi, M. (2002). Is autopagnosia real? EC says yes. A case study. *Neuropsychologia*, *40*, 1744–1749.

Guyard, H., Masson, V., Quiniou, R., & Siou, E. (1997). Expert knowledge for acalculia assessment and rehabilitation. *Neuropsychological Rehabilitation*, *7*, 419–439.

Halligan, P. W., Marshall, J. C., & Wade, D. T. (1995). Unilateral somatoparaphrenia after right hemisphere stroke: A case description. *Cortex*, *31*, 173–182.

Harris, L. J., & Gitterman, S. R. (1978). University professors' self-descriptions of left-right confusability: Sex and handedness differences. *Perceptual and Motor Skills*, *47*, 819–823.

Hécaen, H., Angelergues, R., & Houillier, S. (1961). Les varietes cliniques des acalculies au cours des lesions retrorolandiques: Approche statistique du probleme. *Revue. Neurologique. 105*: 85–103.

Henschen, S. E. (1919). Uber sparch-, musik-, und rechenmechanismen und ihre lokalisation im Grosshirm. *Zeitscrift für die gesamte Neurologie und Psychiatrie*, *52*, 273–298.

Hittmair-Delazer, M., Sailer, U., & Benke, T. (1995). Impaired arithmetic facts but intact conceptual knowledge–A single-case study of dyscalculia. *Cortex*, *31*, 139–147.

Hodzic, A., Muckli, L., Singer, W., & Stirn, A. (2009). Cortical responses to self and others. *Human Brain Mapping*, *30*, 951–962.

Hyde, J. S., Fennema, E., & Lamon, S. J. (1990). Gender differences in mathematics performance: A meta-analysis. *Psychological Bulletin*, *107*, 139–155.

Jackson, M., & Warrington, K. (1986). Arithmetic skills in patients with unilateral cerebral lesions. *Cortex*, *22*, 611–620.

Jackson, P. L., Meltzoff, A. N., & Decety, J. (2006). Neural circuits involved in imitation and perspective taking. *Neuroimage*, *31*, 429–439.

Kable, J. W., & Chatterjee, A. (2006). Specificity of action representations in the lateral occipitotemporal cortex. *Journal of Cognitive Neuroscience*, *18*, 1498–1517.

Kemmerer, D., & Tranel, D. (2008). Searching for the elusive neural substrates of body part terms: A neuropsychological study. *Cognitive Neuropsychology*, *25*, 601–629.

Kinsbourne, M., & Warrington, E. K. (1962). A study of finger agnosia. *Brain*, *85*, 47–66.

Laiacona, M., Allamano, N., Lorenzi, L., & Capitani, E. (2006). A case of impaired naming and knowledge of body parts. Are limbs a separate sub-category? *Neurocase*, *12*, 307–316.

Lampl, Y., Eshel, Y., Gilad, R., & Sarova-Pinhas, I. (1994). Selective acalculia with sparing of the subtraction process in a patient with left parietotemporal hemorrhage. *Neurology*, *44*, 1759–1761.

Langdon, D. W., & Warrington, E. W. (1995). *The VESPAR: A verbal and spatial reasoning test*. Hove, England: Erlbaum.

Lee, K. M. (2000). Cortical areas differentially involved in multiplication and subtraction: A functional magnetic resonance imaging study and correlation with a case of selective acalculia. *Annals of Neurology*, *48*, 657–661.

Levin, H. S., Goldstein, F. C., & Spiers, P. A. (1993). Acalculia. In K. M. Heilman, & E. Valenstein (Eds.), *Clinical neuropsychology*. New York: Oxford.

Macoir, J., Audet, T., & Breton, M. -F. (1999). Code-dependent pathways for number transcoding: Evidence from a case of selective impairment in written verbal numeral to arabic transcoding. *Cortex*, *35*, 629–645.

Maravita, A., & Iriki, A. (2004). Tool for the body (schema). *Trends in Cognitive Science*, *8*, 79–86.

Markwardt, F. C. (1997). *Peabody Individual Achievement Test-Revised/normative update*. Circle Pines, MN: American Guidance Service.

Martory, M. D., Mayer, E., Pegna, A. J., Annoni, J. M., Landis, T., & Khateb, A. (2003). Pure global acalculia following a left subangular lesion. *Neurocase*, *9*, 319–328.

McCloskey, M. (1992). Cognitive mechanism in numerical processing: Evidence from acquired dyscalculia. *Cognition*, *44*, 107–157.

McCloskey, M., Caramazza, A., & Basili, A. (1985). Cognitive mechanisms in number processing and calculation: Evidence from dyscalculia. *Brain and Cognition*, *4*, 171–196.

McGonigle, D. J., Haninen, R., Salenius, S., Hari, R., Frackowiak, R. S. J., & Frith, C. D. (2002). Whose arm is it anyway? An fMRI case study of supernumerary phantom limb. *Brain*, *125*, 1265–1274.

McKenna, P., & Warrington, E. K. (1978). Category-specific naming preservation: A single case study. *Journal of Neurology, Neurosurgery, and Psychiatry, 41*, 571–574.

Money, J. A. (1976). *Standardized road map of direction sense*. San Rafael, CA: Academic Therapy Publications.

Moro, V., Pernigo, S., Urgesi, C., Zapparoli, P., & Aglioti, S. M. (2008). Finger recognition and gesture imitation in Gerstmann's syndrome. *Neurocase, 15*, 13–23.

Morris, H. H., Lüders, H., Lesser, R. P., Dinner, D. S., & Hahn, J. (1984). Transient neuropsychological abnormalities (including Gerstmann's syndrome) during cortical stimulation. *Neurology, 34*, 877–883.

Morris, J. P., Pelphrey, K. A., & McCarthy, G. (2006). Occipitotemporal activation evoked by the perception of human bodies is modulated by the presence or absence of the face. *Neuropsychologia, 44*, 1919–1927.

Ofte, S. H., & Hugdahl, K. (2002). Right-left discrimination in male and female, young and old subjects. *Journal of Clinical and Experimental Neuropsychology, 24*, 82–92.

Ogden, J. A. (1985). Autotopagnosia. *Brain, 108*, 1009–1022.

Peelen, M. V., & Downing, P. E. (2007). The neural basis of visual body perception. *Nature Reviews Neuroscience, 8*, 636–648.

Peelen, M. V., & Downing, P. E. (2005). Within-subject reproducibility of category-specific visual activation with functional MRI. *Human Brain Mapping, 25*, 402–408.

Pick, A. (1922). Storung der orientierung am eigenen korper. *Psychologische Forschung, 1*, 303–318.

Poeck, K., & Orgass, B. (1971). The concept of the body schema: A critical review and some experimental results. *Cortex, 7*, 254–277.

Pourtois, G., Peelen, M., Spinelli, L., Seeck, M., & Vuilleumier, P. (2007). Direct intracranial recording of body-selective responses in human extrastriate visual cortex. *Neuropsychologia, 45*, 2621–2625.

Ramachandran, V. S. (1998). Consciousness and body image: Lessons from phantom limbs, Capgras syndrome, and pain asymbolia. *Philosophical Transactions of the Royal Society of London–Series B: Biological Sciences, 353*, 1851–1859.

Ramachandran, V. S., & Rogers-Ramachandran, D. (2000). Phantom limbs and neural plasticity. *Archives of Neurology, 57*, 317–320.

Ratcliff, G. (1979). Spatial thought, mental rotation and the right cerebral hemisphere. *Neuropsychologia, 17*, 49–54.

Rickard, T. C., Romero, S. G., Basso, G., Wharton, C., Flitman, S., & Grafman, J. (2000). The calculating brain: An fMRI study. *Neuropsychologia, 38*, 325–335.

Ro, T., Friggel, A., & Lavie, N. (2007). Attentional biases for faces and body parts. *Visual Cognition, 15*, 322–348.

Rosselli, M., & Ardila, A. (1989). Calculation deficits in patients with right and left hemisphere damage. *Neuropsychologia, 27*, 607–617.

Rueckert, L., Lange, N., Partiot, A., Appollonio, I., Litvan, I, Le Bihan, D., & Grafman, J. (1996). Visualizing cortical activation during mental calculation with functional MRI. *Neuroimage, 3*, 97–103.

Rusconi, E., Walsh, V., & Butterworth, B. (2005). Dexterity with numbers: rTMS over left angular gyrus disrupts finger gnosis and number processing. *Neuropsychologia, 43*, 1609–1624.

Sauguet, J., Benton, A. L., & Hécaen, H. (1971). Disturbances of the body schema in relation to language impairment and hemispheric locus of lesion. *Journal of Neurology, Neurosurgery, and Psychiatry, 34*, 496–501.

Schwoebel, J., & Coslett, H.B. (2005). Evidence for multiple, distinct representations of the human body. *Journal of Cognitive Neuroscience, 17*, 543–553.

Selecki, B. R., & Herron, J. T. (1965). Disturbances of the verbal body image: A particular syndrome of sensory aphasia. *Journal of Nervous and Mental Disease, 141*, 42–52.

Semenza, C. (1988). Impairment in localization of body parts following brain damage. *Cortex, 24*, 443–449.

Semenza, C., & Goodglass, H. (1985). Localization of body parts in brain injured subjects. *Neuropsychologia, 23*, 161–175.

Semenza, C., Miceli, L., & Girelli, L. (1997). A deficit for arithmetical procedures: Lack of knowledge or lack of monitoring? *Cortex, 33*, 483–498.

Seron, X., & Deloche, G. (1983). From 4 to four. A supplement to "From three to 3." *Brain, 106*, 735–744.

Shenal, B. V., Jackson, M. D., Crucian, G. P., & Heilman, K. M. (2006). Finger agnosia in Alzheimer's disease. *Cognitive and Behavioral Neurology, 19*, 202–203.

Singer, H. D., & Low, A. A. (1933). Acalculia (Henschen): A clinical study. *Archives of Neurology and Psychiatry, 29*, 467–498.

Sirigu, A., Grafman, J., Bressler, K., & Sunderland, T. (1991). Multiple representations contribute to body knowledge processing. *Brain, 114*, 629–642.

Sivan, A. B. (1992). *Benton Visual Retention Test* (5th Edition). San Antonio, TX: The Psychological Corporation.

Sparrow, S. S., Balla, D. A., & Cicchetti, D. V. (1984). *Vineland adaptive behavior scales*. Circle Pines, MN: American Guidance Services.

Spiridon, M., Fischl, B., & Kanwisher, N. (2006). Location and spatial profile of category-specific regions in human extrastriate cortex. *Human Brain Mapping, 27*, 77–89.

Sullivan, K. S., Macaruso, P., & Sokol, S. M. (1996). Remediation of arabic numeral processing in a case of developmental dyscalculia. *Neuropsychological Rehabilitation, 6*, 27–53.

Suzuki, K., Yamadori, A., & Fujii, T. (1997). Category-specific comprehension deficit restricted to body parts. *Neurocase, 3*, 193–200.

Thierry, G., Pegna, A. J., Dodds, C., Roberts, M., Basan, S., & Downing, P. (2006). An event-related potential component sensitive to images of the human body. *Neuroimage, 32*, 871–879.

Tohgi, H., Saitoh, K., Takahashi, S., Takahashi, H., Utsugisawa, K., Yonezawa, H., et al. (1995). Agraphia and acalculia after a left prefrontal (F1, F2) infarction. *Journal of Neurology, Neurosurgery, and Psychiatry, 58*, 629–632.

Tranel, D., Rudrauf, D., Vianna, E. P. M., & Damasio, H. (2008). Does the Clock Drawing Test have focal neuroanatomical correlates? *Neuropsychology, 22*, 553–562.

Tucha, O., Steup, A., Smely, C., & Lange, K. W. (1997). Toe agnosia in Gerstmann syndrome. *Journal of Neurology, Neurosurgery, and Psychiatry, 63*, 399–403.

Urgesi, C., Berlucchi, G., & Aglioti, S. M. (2004). Magnetic stimulation of extrastriate body area impairs visual processing of nonfacial body parts. *Current Biology, 14*, 2130–2134.

Urgesi, C., Calvo-Merino, B., Haggard, P., & Aglioti, S. M. (2007a). Transcranial magnetic stimulation reveals two cortical pathways for visual body processing. *Journal of Neuroscience, 27*, 8023–8030.

Urgesi, C., Candidi, M., Ionta, S., & Aglioti, M. (2007b). Representation of body identity and body actions in extrastriate body area and ventral premotor cortex. *Nature Neuroscience, 10*, 30–31.

Warrington, E. K. (1982). The fractionation of arithmetical skills: A single case study. *Quarterly Journal of Experimental Psychology, 34A*, 31–51.

Wechsler, D. (2008). *Wechsler adult intelligence scale-IV*. New York: The Psychological Corporation.

Wechsler, D. (2001). *Wechsler individual achievement test* (2nd ed.). San Antonio: The Psychological Corporation.

Whalen, J., McCloskey, M., Lesser, R. P., & Gordon, B. (1997). Localizing arithmetic processes in the brain: Evidence from a transient deficit during cortical stimulation. *Journal of Cognitive Neuroscience, 9*, 409–417.

Wilkinson, G. S. (2006). *WRAT-4 Administration manual*. Wilmington, DE: Wide Range.

Wingard, E. M., Barrett, A. M., Crucian, G. P., Doty, L., & Heilman, K. M. (2002). The Gerstmann syndrome in Alzheimer's disease. *Journal of Neurology, Neurosurgery, and Psychiatry, 72*, 403–405.

Wolf, S. M. (1973). Difficulties in right-left discrimination in a normal population. *Archives of Neurology, 29*, 128–129.

Woodcock, R. W., Shrank, F. A., McGrew, K. S., & Mather, N. (2005). *Woodcock-Johnson tests of achievement-III–Normative update*. Allen, TX: DLM Teaching Resources.

Yamadori, A., & Albert, M. L. (1973). Word category aphasia. *Cortex, 9*, 112–125.

9

Anosognosia

JOHN C. ADAIR AND ANNA M. BARRETT

Anosognosia refers to a condition in which brain-injured patients deny or fail to acknowledge their deficits. The term was originally used to describe lack of awareness or recognition of hemiparesis (Babinski, 1914). Subsequent reports applied the term more broadly to unawareness of any neurological or neuropsychological deficit (Fisher, 1989) including hemianesthesia, visual loss (hemianopia or cortical blindness), prosopagnosia, amnesia, dementia, aphasia, cortical deafness, involuntary movements, apraxia, and thought disorder due to schizophrenia.

This chapter focuses on anosognosia for hemiparesis (AHP), reviewing its clinical characteristics and anatomic correlates. The putative mechanisms of AHP are discussed, as well as issues pertinent to treatment and rehabilitation.

CLINICAL CHARACTERISTICS

Anosognosia is among the more dramatic cognitive conditions, since typically the causative lesions are large, and the neurological deficits that patients deny or fail to acknowledge are severe. For example, patients with new-onset hemiplegia, when asked to explain why they have come to the hospital, may mention trivial, unrelated problems, such as

indigestion (Bisiach & Geminiani, 1991). They may displace their illness, claiming, for example, that they are accompanying a sick relative, or they may offer rationalizations that can range from the plausible (e.g., attributing left upper extremity weakness to right-handedness) to the fantastical (e.g., claiming they work at the hospital).

Whereas some patients with anosognosia fail to acknowledge or explicitly deny hemiparesis or hemiplegia, they make little or no attempt to use the weak or paralyzed limbs, and they may avoid activities that require the use of the limb, suggesting that they may have subconscious insight about their disability. Other patients with anosognosia may attempt activities that they are unable to perform, such as getting out of bed and walking. When anosognosic patients learn to acknowledge their deficits, they often appear unconcerned about the severity or ramifications of their disability. This admission of disability in the absence of concern is called *anosodiaphoria* (Critchley, 1953). The same patient may alternate between anosognosia and anosodiaphoria, acknowledging hemiparesis at one point and denying it at others (Ramachandran, 1995; Nardone et al., 2007).

Although many patients are anosognosic for all of their deficits, this condition can also be selective. Most commonly, double dissociations occur between AHP and anosognosia for hemianopia or hemianesthesia (Bisiach et al., 1986). Patients may also deny sensorimotor symptoms while retaining awareness of cognitive disorders, or vice versa (Brier et al., 1995; Berti et al., 1996; Jehkonen et al., 2000). The severity of AHP may differ between affected limbs: For example, patients may be aware of leg paresis but fail to acknowledge arm weakness.

Confronting patients with AHP about their motor deficits often elicits statements at odds with the facts, sometimes frankly delusional. Asked why their paretic extremity failed to move, patients may blame fatigue or lack of interest (Orfei et al., 2007). Patients may say they are clapping their hands when they move only one, and they can tenaciously insist that they moved a disabled limb as instructed (Berti et al., 1998). Such "productive" features suggest that AHP may be associated with alternative, delusional perceptions of somatic state (i.e., illusory/phantom limb movements). Other patients may use their intact extremity to move their paralyzed extremity and appear satisfied that they demonstrated "normal" movement (Bisiach & Geminiani, 1991). More extreme forms of somatic delusions include patients who express hatred of their plegic limbs, known as *misoplegia*, or assert that weak extremities belong to someone else. Even when confronted with blatant contradictions between their statements and actions, AHP patients appear indifferent and reveal no trace of embarrassment about logical inconsistencies. Accordingly, AHP must be considered in terms of both the deficits patients fail to observe as well as the alternative "experience" that many claim to experience (Vuilleumier, 2004).

ASSESSMENT OF ANOSOGNOSIA FOR HEMIPARESIS

Determining the presence of AHP remains, in essence, a clinical judgment. The most basic assessments indicate whether AHP is present or absent, but fail to capture its magnitude or scope. Some recent assessment techniques consider AHP along a continuum of severity (Marcel et al., 2004; Baier & Karnath, 2005).

According to some investigators, unequivocal identification of AHP requires severe weakness; any residual motor function compromises diagnostic confidence (Berti et al., 2008).

No particular assessment procedure can be endorsed as a gold standard. Nearly all measures employ structured interviews that ask the patient progressively more specific questions about their health and physical status (Orfei et al., 2007). Some scales incorporate elements of the physical examination to directly confront patients with their deficits. A frequently used technique ranks AHP on a four-point Likert scale (Bisiach et al., 1986). Grades range from the spontaneous reporting of a deficit in response to general questions about health (grade 0), to persistent denial of weakness even after explicit demonstration (grade 3). Recent research, however, calls into question the validity of "mild" (grade 1) AHP. Patients with grade 1 AHP in one study showed considerable similarity on several clinical variables (e.g., severity of weakness, neglect) to patients without AHP, and provided reasonable alternative responses to general questions about their health (Baier & Karnath, 2005). Accordingly, patients judged as mild or grade 1 AHP may simply assign a lower priority to paresis than to other concurrent symptoms.

Other tools include the Denial of Illness Scale (Starkstein et al., 1993a), which uses a semistructured interview to rank a patient's insight into ongoing symptoms as well as their consequences (e.g., fear of death or invalidism). The scale extends the range of scores (0–16), and scores discriminate reliably between patients with and without AHP. Cutting's Anosognosia Questionnaire (1978) assesses whether patients manifest associated phenomena such as illusory limb movements. Most recently, Marcel and colleagues (2004) developed the Structured Awareness Interview. The questionnaire consists of eight items scored in an ordinal fashion, as well as questions that ask patients to estimate their ability to perform unimanual, bimanual, and bipedal tasks.

All of the foregoing scales require patients to take a "first person" perspective. Recent research indicates, however, that whether patients acknowledge limb weakness may depend on how examiners pose the questions.

One approach asked a patient with severe AHP to rate his own performance on tasks using his weak upper extremity from 0 (very badly performed) to 10 (very well performed). Despite obstinate denial of weakness on standard interview, the patient gave low (but not 0) ratings for most of the tasks (Berti et al., 1998). More recently, Marcel and associates (2004) asked patients with unilateral stroke how well they could perform a variety of tasks compared to their usual ability, then inquired how well someone else would fare if they were in the patient's "present state." Nearly half of right brain-injured patients claimed they could accomplish the tasks, but judged that another person in their condition could not. Such findings suggest that some AHP patients may have implicit insight into their disability. Furthermore, some degree of awareness may be expressed if patients are asked to assume a "third person" perspective.

Other methods demonstrate how patients who acknowledge motor dysfunction during interview may still fail to appreciate the consequences of their deficits. One study segregated patients with regard to AHP based on standard scales and asked them to judge their ability to perform bimanual or bipedal tasks compared with their "normal ability" (Nimmo-Smith et al., 2005). Of 29 right brain-injured patients considered aware of weakness based on structured interview, a substantial proportion (12 of 29) consistently overestimated their ability to complete bimanual tasks. Hence, future research on AHP after focal cerebral damage may benefit from methods used for traumatic brain injury that focus less on awareness of focal deficits than their functional implications (Orfei et al., 2007). For example, the Prigatano competency rating scale requires patients to rate the relative ease of behaviors relevant to self-care, interpersonal abilities, cognition, and emotional status (Prigatano et al., 2005). The same scale completed by caregivers or therapists can be subtracted from patient ratings to gauge deficit underestimation. Note, however, that factors other than a patient's deficit may influence caregiver ratings, undermining the validity of subtraction techniques. Furthermore, difference scores may confound anosognosia assessment if analysis methods yield summary data rather than individual item discrepancies (Hartman-Maeir et al., 2003). Because patient–observer differences may result in deficit underestimation (difference >0) or overestimation (difference <0), summary scores may obscure findings through combining items with opposite values.

ANATOMIC CORRELATES

Clinical studies spanning more than 50 years indicate that AHP most frequently follows injury to the right or nondominant hemisphere (Cutting, 1978; Stone et al., 1993; Starkstein et al., 1992; Pia et al., 2004). When Prigatano and colleagues (1996) examined patients with right or left hemisphere injury, however, both groups tended to similarly overestimate their abilities. But although the incidence of AHP following left or right hemisphere stroke may be similar, AHP was more severe following right hemisphere lesions (Hartman-Maeir et al., 2003). Similarly, Baier and Karnath (2005) found no right–left asymmetry for mild AHP, whereas moderate and severe grades occurred most often after right brain injury.

Selection bias might partly account for right–left asymmetry because aphasia with dominant hemisphere injury may confound a patient's ability to report deficit awareness. Thus, many investigations exclude such cases as "unassessable." Friedlander (1967) estimated the frequency of AHP after left brain injury by assuming that AHP was as common among those with severe aphasia as among patients without severe aphasia. Including severely aphasic patients reduced but did not negate asymmetry that favored the right hemisphere, a finding reported by others (Cutting, 1978; Starkstein et al., 1992). Bisiach and colleagues (1991) observed that even aphasic patients may provide nonverbal indications of deficit awareness. A newly developed assessment method that relies less on verbal communication than structured interviews indicates that AHP may be more common after left brain injury than previously believed (Cocchini et al., 2009).

Other support for right–left asymmetry in AHP comes from experimentally induced hemiplegia during intracarotid barbiturate infusion (Gilmore et al., 1992; Buchtel et al., 1992; Kaplan et al., 1993; Durkin et al., 1994; Carpenter et al., 1995; Dywan et al., 1995, Lu et al., 1997). By testing patients shortly after recovery from anesthesia, aphasia no longer influences assessment of deficit awareness. Although AHP prevalence during Wada testing varies considerably between studies, the overall conclusion remains that AHP occurs more frequently during right hemisphere inactivation.

Radiographic studies have largely failed to identify specific injury sites within the right hemisphere that are characteristic of AHP. One early study mapped lesions from computerized tomographic (CT) scans after right hemisphere stroke (Bisiach et al., 1986). Qualitative analysis indicated that AHP was associated with damage to the inferoposterior parietal region and thalamus. Another CT-based investigation reported that patients with AHP had marginally larger lesions and greater atrophy of the uninjured hemisphere than did patients without AHP (Levine et al., 1991). Starkstein et al. (1992) observed that patients with AHP had a higher frequency of right hemisphere lesions, primarily involving the temporoparietal junction, thalamus, and basal ganglia, and that they had more subcortical white matter atrophy than did patients without AHP. Multiple other researchers subsequently replicated the association of AHP with larger injuries, both for ischemic stroke and intracerebral hemorrhage (Jehkonen et al., 2000; Hartman-Maeir et al., 2003).

Cases of AHP following isolated subcortical damage have also been described. For example, AHP can occur after pontine infarction or hemorrhage (Evyapan & Kumral, 1999; Bakchine et al., 1997). Case reports also document AHP following caudate hemorrhage (Jacome, 1986; Healton et al., 1982) or infarction (House & Hodges, 1998), as well as focal thalamic injury (Watson & Heilman, 1979; Graff-Radford et al., 1984; Liebson, 2000). It must be kept in mind, however, that these subcortical regions have anatomical connections to the cortex, and lesions may result in cortical dysfunction.

A recent meta-analysis of 85 cases confirmed a variety of cortical and subcortical lesions associated with AHP (Pia et al., 2004). Frontal and/or parietal regions were involved significantly more often than other areas, either alone or in combination. Other common sites included basal ganglia, insula, and thalamus. Isolated subcortical damage most frequently involved the striate nuclei and thalamus.

Other investigations using magnetic resonance imaging (MRI) and detailed image analysis have provided novel results. Berti and colleagues (2005) examined brain MRI scans with image subtraction methods and reported that severe AHP was most consistently associated with damage to premotor cortical regions (Brodmann areas 6, 44, and 46) and the insula. Findings concur with a single-case study documenting reduced prefrontal blood flow remote from primary injuries in a patient with AHP 2 years after a hemorrhagic stroke (Venneri & Shanks, 2004). Conversely, another recent study reported discrepant findings. Karnath and associates (2005) compared MRI scans from patients with right hemisphere stroke, comparing patients with moderate to severe AHP with patients without AHP matched for age, time since injury, and relevant clinical variables. Image subtraction revealed that the posterior insula was involved in all AHP patients, compared with only 38% of control patients, whereas differential involvement of prefrontal structures was not replicated.

MECHANISMS UNDERLYING ANOSOGNOSIA FOR HEMIPARESIS

A unifying explanation of AHP in psychobiological terms remains elusive. One general class of hypothesis posits that AHP results from psychological defense adaptations that moderate the impact of impairment on a patient's ego. This type of theory, termed "global" by some authors, accounts for AHP through a single overarching basis. Other examples of global hypotheses consider AHP as a consequence of cognitive impairment. Another class of theories invokes modular and dissociable processes that can be discretely disrupted. Modular hypotheses thus regard AHP as a direct consequence of focal injury, surmising that AHP emerges as part of other concurrent neuropsychological or neurological conditions, either alone or in combination. Such accounts propose malfunction of feedback to systems that normally monitor sensorimotor capacities, interhemispheric disconnection, and defective or misinterpreted feedforward processes.

PSYCHOLOGICALLY MOTIVATED DENIAL

Anosognosia for hemiparesis has been attributed to an unconscious defense mechanism that reduces the distress of functional loss (Wortis & Datner, 1942; Sandifer, 1946). In their book *Denial of Illness*, Weinstein and Kahn (1955) provided detailed observations of patients with anosognosia. They hypothesized that "denial . . . was a continuation of a preexisting personality trend." In support, Weinstein and Kahn (1953) compared premorbid personality traits between two patient groups who differed regarding whether or not they explicitly denied deficits. Patients with anosognosia regarded infirmity as shameful or embarrassing, and had denied symptoms of prior illnesses. Although patients who acknowledged symptoms varied considerably, no premorbid tendency to deny or ignore illness was observed.

A number of observations are not consistent with psychologically motivated denial as an explanation for AHP. First, AHP typically manifests soon after injury, with resolution in the ensuing days or weeks. In contrast, motivated coping strategies should evolve over time (Bisiach & Geminiani, 1991; Vuilleumier, 2004). Second, psychological defense presumably requires high-level cognitive processes. Accordingly, AHP should most frequently accompany small, deep injuries involving motor pathways (e.g., posterior internal capsule) that minimally impact cognition. As described above, however, AHP most frequently develops after extensive, cortically based injuries. Third, deficits such as hemianopia cause relatively minor disability or disfigurement, thereby posing minimal threat to self-esteem. Because patients may deny such deficits as resolutely as those with more overt disorders, the relationship between ego preservation and injury effect appears tenuous. Last, psychological defense mechanisms provide no a priori reason for AHP to develop more often following right

versus left brain injuries (Heilman, 1991; Bisiach & Geminiani, 1991).

Several lines of research also provide evidence against psychologically motivated denial. More contemporary studies using personality questionnaires or inventories failed to reveal distinctive temperaments or dispositions associated with AHP (Levine et al., 1991; Small & Ellis, 1996). Starkstein and colleagues (1992) reasoned that if psychological coping strategies protect patients from negative reactions, then individuals with AHP should show less depression. They studied a large cohort of left and right hemisphere stroke patients, however, and found no difference in affective symptoms as a function of AHP. Other data showing dissociations between adverse psychological outcomes and AHP pose a formidable challenge to the defense mechanism hypothesis. For example, AHP during intracarotid barbiturate infusion contradicts motivated denial because inquiry about symptom awareness follows recovery (Heilman et al., 1998; Meador et al., 2000). Patients with resolved symptoms should have no compelling motivation to deny prior deficits.

Although ego defense appears an inadequate sole explanation for AHP, psychological factors may modulate rather than motivate anosognosia. Whereas individuals who fail to appraise contralesional body function might either underestimate or overestimate deficits, self-judgment errors in AHP appear skewed toward a presumption of normality. It is possible that previously developed attitudes and beliefs about one's body may bias or condition self-efficacy judgments (Vuilleumier, 2004). Alternatively, brain injury may influence patients' emotional response. Patients with right hemisphere injury frequently exhibit abnormal expression of affective states or fail to interpret the affect of others (Heilman et al., 2003). Hence, inadequate affective valuation of symptoms could contribute to AHP, potentially through attenuating the impetus to react to uncertainty about bodily function. Empirical support for such conjecture remains to be established. Spalletta and colleagues (2007) found no association between AHP and alexithymia (awareness of emotion). Patients with AHP experience the same range of emotions as control subjects (Turnbull & Solms, 2007). Patients with AHP may differ in how they "manage" negative emotions, however. When recounting emotion-inducing incidents, for example, one AHP patient provided anecdotes related to the experience of others, whereas normal controls and patients without anosognosia referenced their own experiences.

COGNITIVE IMPAIRMENT

Anosognosia for hemiparesis has been attributed to failure of cognitive processes needed to appraise body function (Levine, 1990). The earliest descriptions of AHP described affected patients as "confused," although cognitive impairment was minor compared to the severity of anosognosia (Vallar & Ronchi, 2006). More recently, Cutting (1978) found "disorientation" in 71% of patients with AHP compared to only 6% in those aware of weakness. Other authors suggest that AHP results from loss of sensory feedback and the mental flexibility that would allow these patients to make the necessary observations to critically assess self-efficacy (Levine et al., 1991), or from a disturbance of memory processes that incorporate ongoing self-observations into long-term self-knowledge of motor ability (Cocchini et al., 2002; Marcel et al., 2004).

Several investigators have tried to define a cognitive profile associated with AHP. Levine et al. (1991) found that individuals with AHP scored lower on most measures of memory and intellect. Starkstein and colleagues (1993b) examined the cognitive correlates of AHP after right and left hemisphere injury. Patients with AHP performed worse on a measure of general cognition and on tasks sensitive to frontal brain injury. However, no between-group differences were found for attention, verbal comprehension, constructional abilities, or memory. Another recent study found a significant relationship between improvement in one measure of executive function and resolution of AHP (Narushima et al., 2008).

Arguments cited against the psychological defense mechanism hypothesis pertain to explanations of AHP based on cognitive dysfunction. First, cognitive impairment cannot easily account for differences in anosognosia across modalities (Bisiach et al., 1986): Cognitive impairment should reduce awareness of all deficits to a similar degree. Second, observations of AHP in Wada test subjects also argue against cognitive dysfunction as a cause of AHP. Whereas with right hemisphere anesthesia patients often have no language or verbal memory deficits, when these same patients undergo left hemisphere anesthesia they are usually globally aphasic and have impaired episodic memory; however, after left hemisphere anesthesia, patients are more likely to recall their hemiplegia than after right hemisphere anesthesia.

SENSORY DEFECTS, NEGLECT, AND ASOMATOGNOSIA

One "modular" account of AHP, termed the *feedback hypothesis*, attributes faulty deficit awareness to inadequate sensory information. As noted by Heilman (1991), individuals mainly derive information about bodily integrity through somatic sensation, visual inspection, or both. Because lesions most often associated with AHP also result in interruption of visual or somatic afference from the contralesional side of the body, several authors emphasize the relationship between elemental sensory disorders, particularly defective proprioception, and AHP (Gerstmann, 1942; Levine et al., 1991). According to such feedback accounts, AHP may result from primary sensory defects or higher-order perceptual–attentional disturbances (e.g., neglect) that preclude patients from detecting their motor deficits.

There is clinical evidence against the deafferentation hypothesis of AHP. Specifically, patients with severe sensory loss can be aware of and acknowledge their neurological deficits, and patients with anosognosia often have lesions that spare sensory systems (Small & Ellis, 1996; Marcel et al., 2004). Furthermore, peripheral nerve or spinal cord injuries that cause profound weakness and tactile sensory impairment rarely lead to anosognosia. Some advocates of the deafferentation hypothesis question whether standard clinical examinations of patients with AHP can detect the type of sensory loss that may cause this disorder and note that simple ordinal measures, used in all clinical research to date, do not provide a sufficiently precise characterization of sensory disruption (Vuilleumier, 2004).

Other researchers consider AHP as one component of a more pervasive disorder of processing information from contralesional space, called the *neglect syndrome* (Bisiach & Berti, 1987). The neglect syndrome comprises a family of conditions that preclude normal awareness or orientation to contralesional stimuli despite the presence of intact basic sensorimotor function (see Chapter 12). Neglect behaviors may involve far extrapersonal space, the immediate extrapersonal environment (peripersonal space), or personal space itself. Personal neglect or hemiasomatognosia, refers to a state in which patients disregard contralesional body parts and fail to acknowledge the existence of half of their body (Feinberg et al., 1990). Neglect for personal (or peripersonal) space might thus plausibly contribute to AHP by impeding self-assessment of contralesional bodily functions, a feedback hypothesis.

Levine and colleagues (1991), advocates of the feedback hypothesis, assessed right hemispheric stroke patients with and without AHP on tests of extrapersonal neglect and reported that patients with AHP manifested more consistent and severe neglect than did patients with transient or no AHP. In contrast, Bisiach and colleagues (1986) reported that, although both personal neglect and extrapersonal neglect frequently co-occurred with AHP, double dissociations were not uncommon, a finding subsequently replicated by numerous researchers (Small & Ellis, 1996; Jehkonen et al., 2000; Marcel et al., 2004; Spalleta et al., 2007; Appelros et al., 2007). Recently, Baier and Karnath (2008) examined "abnormal attitudes" toward paretic limbs in patients after right brain infarction. Although patients with moderate to severe AHP frequently exhibited abnormal "sensation of limb ownership," (p. 487) there were patients with AHP who did not.

Additional evidence that personal neglect cannot entirely account for AHP comes from studies of Wada testing. During right hemisphere anesthesia, patients were asked to distinguish their own hands from those of the examiners (Adair et al., 1995). Only a minority of patients developing AHP failed to acknowledge ownership of paretic extremities. A more recent study documented a high coincidence of AHP and asomatognosia during right carotid amobarbital injection (Meador et al., 2000); however, these disorders were dissociable, particularly as the effects of barbiturate resolved and AHP persisted in the absence of asomatognosia.

DISCONNECTION, CONFABULATION, AND ILLUSORY LIMB MOVEMENT

Geschwind (1965) attributed AHP to disconnection of the left hemibody's "self-monitor" in the right hemisphere from language centers in the left hemisphere. Deprived of information, the intact left hemisphere confabulates in response to questions about the left hemibody's function. The disconnection hypothesis received indirect support from Feinberg and associates (1994). During forced-choice identification of objects presented to the impaired left visual hemifield, AHP patients produced random (i.e., confabulatory) responses whereas the group without AHP more readily admitted their failure to identify stimuli. A later study further demonstrated a strong statistical relationship between confabulatory or illusory limb movements and AHP in patients with right hemisphere stroke (Feinberg et al., 2000).

Several lines of research discredit interhemispheric disconnection with confabulation as a primary explanation for AHP. In one experiment, AHP patients could select either physically feasible unimanual tasks resulting in small rewards or physically impossible bimanual tasks producing large rewards (Ramchandran, 1995). Assuming that AHP resulted from disconnection, the right hemisphere should still choose achievable tasks; however, in nearly all trials, AHP patients selected the unachievable bimanual tasks. Because subjects indicated preferences with their ipsilesional hand, results may have alternatively indicated that the left hemisphere "confabulated nonverbally." Hence, another study tested the disconnection hypothesis directly during Wada procedures (Adair et al., 1997). If interhemispheric disconnection caused AHP, then providing the left hemisphere with visual and kinesthetic feedback about the paretic limb should enhance motor deficit awareness. But providing feedback by positioning the weak left upper extremity in the right visual hemispace failed to modify AHP in most subjects.

Further investigations also failed to confirm a one-to-one relationship between confabulation and AHP. Following right intracarotid barbiturate infusion, examiners apposed the fingertips of the paretic hand against different textures (Lu et al., 1997). Catch trials, in which no tactile stimulus was delivered, provided opportunities for confabulation. Findings established dissociations between confabulation and AHP: Some subjects acknowledged weakness but confabulated on catch trials, whereas some AHP patients never made confabulatory responses. Another study that assessed the relationship of AHP to illusory limb movements failed to demonstrate a link between phantom percepts and AHP (Lu et al., 2000). Although several subjects reported illusory movements in their paretic extremity, most retained deficit awareness. Conversely, others failing to report illusory movements showed AHP. Despite evidence of dissociation between confabulation and AHP on an individual basis, some data indicates relatively impaired reality monitoring in stroke survivors with AHP. Hence, confabulation may promote or maintain AHP, even if it is not the major causative factor (Venneri & Shanks, 2004; Jenkinson et al., 2009).

FEEDFORWARD HYPOTHESES: THE INFLUENCE OF INTENTION

Recent hypotheses of AHP frame the disorder in terms of cognitive psychological accounts of motor control (Figure 9-1). Current theory posits that, prior to volitional movement, the brain issues two distinct messages (Frith et al., 2000). One message dictates the sequence, duration, and force of muscle contractions necessary to move a limb from its current state to an intended or target state. The other message, issued concurrently, generates a "forward model" that predicts the somatosensory outcome of the subsequent action and provides signals that modulate the perception of movement (Coslett, 2005). Such action predictions are considered to form the basis of motor awareness, and also contribute to the correct

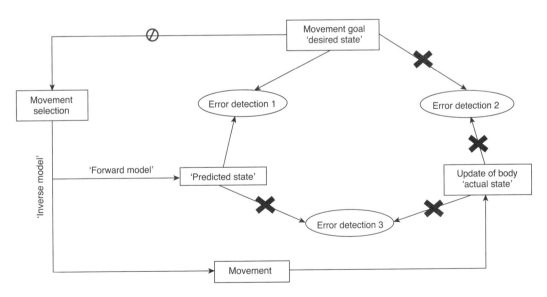

Figure 9–1. Accounts of AHP related to a computational model of motor control. The ⊘ depicts how defective motor intention leads to no mismatch within the system, whereas the ✖ illustrates the hypothesis that preserved intention in AHP may result in illusory movement experience due to failure to modify awareness of discrepancy at other error detection levels.

attribution of movement to the self (i.e., intention) or to an external agent (Blakemore & Frith, 2003).

For hemiplegic patients to be aware of weakness or an absence of movement, brain processes associated with intention set a hypothetical "comparator" regarding forthcoming movements. When the comparator is expecting a change in afferent feedback resulting from the intended movement, a failure of movement creates a mismatch that makes the subject aware of weakness. AHP might result when defective intention fails to prepare the comparator. Then, a lack of movement in the paretic extremity would fail to generate a mismatch. Accordingly, Heilman (1991) speculated that AHP may originate from defective intentional processes.

Experimental evidence provides limited evidence regarding abnormal intentional processing in AHP. In one study, surface potentials were recorded from proximal muscles during maximal unimanual effort (Gold et al., 1994). Normal control subjects and hemiparetic patients without AHP activated trunk muscles bilaterally when attempting maximal power grip with either hand. In contrast, an AHP patient activated proximal muscles only during maximal grip with the nonparetic hand; no muscle activity on either side accompanied attempted grip with the weak hand. Investigators interpreted findings as consistent with loss of motor intention associated with AHP. Hildebrandt and Zieger (1995) recorded motor responses from the plegic extremity in another AHP patient and were able to evoke responses when the subject recalled past experiences of movement or attempted bimanual tasks. Attempting to move the plegic hand in isolation, however, failed to generate muscle activity, consistent with the earlier study.

Clinical observations also support an association between AHP and defective intention. For example, when Chatterjee (1996) asked patients to recall their experience of deficit unawareness shortly after AHP resolved, individuals reported that they realized weakness only after attempts to move were prompted. Similar findings were obtained during Wada testing (Adair et al., 1997). While visually inspecting the weak limb failed to alter AHP, individuals who acknowledged plegia did so only after commands to move the paralyzed limb.

Berti and colleagues (2008) proposed an alternative hypothesis that intact intentional systems actually contribute to AHP. Defective intention might account for why AHP patients might deny or not recognize weakness, but fails to explain why they may report illusory movement. Berti et al. (2008) recorded the surface electromyogram from proximal muscles during attempted movements in hemiplegic patients and controls. In contrast to earlier findings, their patient with severe AHP activated proximal muscles during attempts to reach with the plegic extremity, consistent with preserved intentional processing. Berti interpreted this as indicating that there was an intention to action, but that the patients fail to compare this intention with sensory feedback indicating the action has not occurred. To test this comparator hypothesis directly, Fotopolou et al. (2008) used a prosthetic left hand to create false visual feedback about the paretic limb moving or not moving, and manipulated intention by instructing patients to attempt self-generated movement on some trials versus being told that an experimenter would lift their hand in others. When self-generated movement attempts were not matched by prosthetic hand movement, the participants with AHP made erroneous judgments. They reported that they had moved their hand when they had not. Sensory feedback about the failure to move was thus "selectively ignored" when AHP patients generated a forward model or action prediction. Of note, hemiplegic participants' awareness of their hemiplegia was suspended during attempted movements that were matched by prosthetic hand motion, with patients claiming inexplicably to experience moving their paretic limbs. This suggests that a match between the intended movement and the predicted limb position (error detection 1 in Figure 9-1) is sufficient to experience an appropriate movement, even when there is a failure to match between the kinesthetic feedback of the actual state, and the intended movement (error detection 2 in Figure 9-1). Why patients fail to register such discrepancies is unclear, although proponents of Berti's hypothesis resort to mechanisms discussed previously, such as neglect or confabulation (Frith et al., 2000). The neural substrates of the comparator also remain unspecified, although results of functional imaging research provide preliminary information about brain regions related to such processes.

FUNCTIONAL NEUROIMAGING

In contrast to other domains of cognitive neuroscience, functional imaging data relevant to AHP are limited. Indirect insights might be afforded, however, through studies of the physiological correlates of self-evaluation, motor awareness, and the detection of discrepancies between actions and their consequences. A substantial literature exists with regard to brain activity evoked when normal subjects judge their own personal characteristics (Johnson et al., 2002). Such tasks increase activity in anterior medial prefrontal cortex and posterior cingulate/precuneus region. To what extent these areas contribute to appraisal of one's own motor function is not clear, because prior studies asked subjects to consider only nonmotor aspects of themselves (e.g., physical appearance, temperament).

More relevant information may be gathered from investigations into the generation of motor intention and awareness. A number of functional imaging studies demonstrate that preparation for action increases activity in the anterior supplementary motor area (pre-SMA). Although specific neurobiological determinants of intention awareness remain unclear, preliminary evidence indicates that similar regions are involved. For example, when normal individuals become aware of their intention to move, cerebral blood flow increases selectively in the pre-SMA (Lau et al., 2004). Inactivation of this region with transcranial magnetic stimulation also delays normal subjects' judgments of movement onset relative to their actual reaction time (Haggard & Magno, 1999).

Patients with AHP fail to register discrepancies between intended and actual motor states. Accordingly, research into brain activity during tasks that provoke discordance between intended and realized movements in normal

subjects may also be relevant to the neurobiological basis of AHP. Fink et al. (1999) measured cerebral blood flow during a paradigm that induced conflict between expectations of intended movement and what subjects actually observed (in a mirror box) during execution (Figure 9-2). Incongruity between intention and perceived movement selectively increased cerebral blood flow in the right dorsolateral prefrontal cortex (Brodmann's area 9/46), regardless of which hand was observed. Using a different paradigm, Farrer et al. (2003) evaluated relative cerebral blood flow while subjects controlled via joystick a "virtual hand" viewed on a computer monitor. Investigators parametrically varied congruence between the subjects' actual intended movements and the virtual hand's trajectory. Results showed that activity in the right posterior insula correlated directly and the right inferior parietal lobe correlated inversely with the degree of congruence between performed and viewed movement (Figure 9-3).

Although functional imaging information regarding AHP thus remains incomplete, brain regions implicated in motor awareness and the detection of intention/action discrepancies concord with human lesion studies (Berti et al., 2005; Karnath et al., 2005). Damage to frontal lobe systems, especially the pre-SMA, may speculatively constitute one basis for AHP related to defective motor intention, while a network involving premotor (Brodmann's area 9/46), insula, and inferior parietal sites might represent discrepancies between intended and consequent action in a manner consistent with the comparator process affected in other AHP patients.

TREATMENT AND REHABILITATION

Understanding and managing AHP may improve patient outcomes for several reasons. First, current treatments for acute ischemic stroke depend critically on initiation shortly after onset of injury. Although little data on this point exist, deficit unawareness may be one reason why stroke patients or their families delay seeking care (Di Legge et al., 2005). Second, AHP patients may fail to comprehend

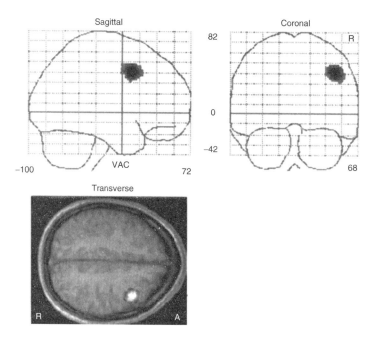

Figure 9–2. Region in right dorsolateral prefrontal cortex shows a significant relative increase in cerebral blood flow in a task in which intended movements were discordant with realized sensorimotor outcomes. From Fink, G., Marshall, J. C., Halligan, P. W., Frith, C. D., Driver, J., Frackowiak, R. S. J., & Dolan, R. J. (1999). The neural consequences of conflict between intention and the senses. *Brain, 122,* 497–512, with permission of the publisher.

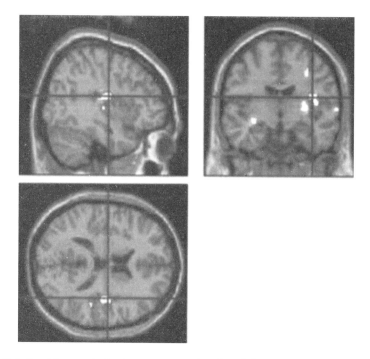

Figure 9–3. Activity in the right posterior insula activity varies directly with the congruence between intended and actual movement. From Farrer, C., Franck, N., Georgieff, N., Frith, C. D., Decety, J., & Jeannerod, M. (2003). Modulating the experience of agency: A positron emission tomography study. *Neuroimage, 18,* 324–333, with permission of the publisher.

the rationale for rehabilitation treatment. Lack of motivation to participate in physical, occupational, or speech therapies may account for the observation that AHP patients recover incompletely and take longer to attain therapeutic benefit (Gialanella & Mattioli, 1992; Maeshima et al., 1997). Gialanella and colleagues (2005) recently reported rehabilitation outcomes of patients with isolated neglect compared to a group with both neglect and AHP. Despite matching subjects for age and scan characteristics, treatment effectiveness and efficiency was significantly poorer in the AHP group. Third, caregivers for AHP patients may be particularly burdened. One study reported that AHP persisting at discharge predicted reduced activity level, even after accounting for severity of initial disability (Hartmann-Maeir et al., 2003). Finally, AHP may preclude patients from making necessary concessions to residual disability, thereby exposing themselves to further harm (e.g., falling when they fail to use assist devices). Research demonstrates that increase in deficit awareness correlates with improved occupational performance (Ekstam et al., 2007). Hence, measures to reduce AHP may be particularly beneficial with regard to reducing caregiving demands and need for further medical care related to accidents.

Studies indicate that standard rehabilitation measures influence AHP recovery. In one large series, inpatient therapy after first stroke (mean duration 96 days) reduced the overestimation of ADL capacity from 53% to 27% for right hemisphere injuries and from 42% to 23% for left hemisphere injuries (Hartman-Maeir et al., 2003). Other studies indicate that self-awareness training leads to improved functional outcomes (Toglia & Kirk, 2000). A recent trial asked their intervention group to predict performance before attempting instrumental activities of daily living, and then judge actual performance after execution (Goverover et al., 2007). Compared to controls undergoing conventional practice, patients receiving "awareness training" significantly improved performance of activities.

Certain maneuvers that ameliorate neglect also improve deficit awareness, at least for AHP. For example, in many patients with neglect,

cold caloric stimulation of the right ear temporarily reduces spatial bias. Cappa et al. (1987) were the first to report that vestibular stimulation can also increase awareness of hemiparesis. In contrast to the effect on neglect behaviors, the influence on AHP outlasted the immediate stimulation period in this study. However, even patients who gained insight during stimulation would relapse shortly thereafter, indicating that memory of the transient experience could not override anosognosia. In another report, caloric stimulation corrected both AHP and somatoparaphrenic delusions about the paretic extremity (Bisiach et al., 1991). How other pharmacological and behavioral interventions employed in the treatment of neglect syndrome might also modify AHP remains unknown.

At least one study capitalized on the observation that some AHP patients retain awareness of weakness from a third-person perspective. A patient with persistent AHP was asked to view a video tape of herself during a structured interview during which she reported to move her plegic left arm as instructed (Fotopoulou et al., 2009). After watching herself, the patient immediately gained insight into her hemiplegia, an effect that persisted for at least 6 months. As with other approaches mentioned above, further research will be necessary to confirm the applicability of self-observation to a broader spectrum of AHP patients.

CONCLUSION

Substantial research has so far failed to reduce AHP to a single mechanism associated with damage to a specific brain region. Furthermore, AHP cannot be readily explained by specific combinations of individual psychological or cognitive disorders (Marcel et al., 2004). Multiple dissociations suggest that AHP may arise from multiple causes, making each proposed explanation valid for only a subgroup of patients (Meador et al., 2000). Furthermore, awareness of motor dysfunction may not be a unitary function occurring at a single instant (Dennett & Kinsbourne, 1992). Accordingly, deficit awareness may fractionate based on the temporal context of self-appraisal. In other words, patients' responses to questions about their weakness may depend on the dynamic interactions of prospective knowledge-based predictions ("Will I move?"), "online" or concurrent experiences ("Am I moving?"), or retrospective recollection, either immediate or more remote ("Did I move?").

Framing AHP research within the cognitive neuropsychological model of motor control appears a valid strategy for future investigation. Other questions may be framed from an ecological perspective. The adaptive value of deficit awareness is clear when damage does not affect the nervous system. For example, pain states result in motivations to resolve injury and reduce distress; malaise due to systemic illness has a protective effect on reducing metabolism and conserving energy. When the injury affects the central nervous system, however, the neuronal networks that normally allow deficit detection may fail, resulting in anosognosia. Although unawareness of deficits may reduce stress, anosognosia can delay treatment, diminish a person's ability to cope with a deficit, and reduce motivation for rehabilitation.

REFERENCES

Adair J. C., Na, D. L., Schwartz, R. L., Fennell, E. M., Gilmore, R. L., & Heilman, K. M. (1995). Anosognosia for hemiplegia: Test of the personal neglect hypothesis. *Neurology, 45*, 2195–2199.

Adair, J. C., Schwartz, R. L., Na D. L., Fennell, E. B., Gilmore, R. L., & Heilman, K. M. (1997). Anosognosia: Examining the disconnection hypothesis. *Journal of Neurology, Neurosurgery, and Psychiatry, 63*, 798–800.

Appelros, P., Karlsson, G. M., & Hennerdal, S. (2007). Anosognosia versus unilateral neglect. Coexistence and their relations to age, stroke severity, lesion site and cognition. *European Journal of Neurology, 14*, 54–59.

Babinski, J. (1914). Contribution a l'etude dies troubles mentaux dans l'hemiplegie organique cerebrale (anosognosie). *Revue Neurologie, 27*, 845–847.

Baier, B., & Karnath, H. O. (2005). Incidence of anosognosia for hemiparesis revisited. *Journal of Neurology, Neurosurgery, and Psychiatry, 76*, 358–361.

Baier, B., & Karnath, H. O. (2008). Tight link between our sense of limb ownership and self-awareness of actions. *Stroke, 39*, 486–488.

Bakchine, S., Crassard, I., & Seilhan, D. (1997). Anosognosia for hemiplegia after a brainstem haematoma: A pathological case. *Journal of Neurology, Neurosurgery, and Psychiatry, 63*, 686–687.

Berti, A., Ladavas, E., & Corte, M. D. (1996). Anosognosia for hemiplegia, neglect dyslexia, and drawing neglect: Clinical findings and theoretical considerations. *Journal of the International Neuropsychological Society, 2*, 426–440.

Berti, A., Ladavas, E., Stracciari, A., Gianarelli, C., & Ossola, A. (1998). Anosognosia for motor impairment and dissociations with patients' evaluation of the disorder: Theoretical considerations. *Cognitive Neuropsychology, 3*, 21–43.

Berti, A., Bottini, G., Gandola, M., Pia, L., Smania, N., Stracciari, A., et al. (2005). Shared cortical anatomy for motor awareness and motor control. *Science, 309*, 488–491.

Berti, A., Spinazzola, L., Pia, L., & Rabuffetti, M. (2008). Motor awareness and motor intention in anosognosia for hemiplegia. In P. Haggard, Y. Rossetti, & M. Kawato (Eds.), *Sensorimotor foundations of higher cognition* (pp. 163–182). New York: Oxford University Press.

Bisiach, E., Vallar, G., Perani, D., Papagno, C., & Berti, A. (1986). Unawareness of disease following lesions of the right hemisphere: Anosognosia for hemiplegia and anosognosia for hemianopia. *Neuropsychologia, 24*, 471–482.

Bisiach, E., & Berti, A. (1987). Consciousness in dyschiria. In M. S. Gazzaniga (Ed.), *The cognitive neurosciences* (pp. 1131–1340). Cambridge, MA: MIT Press.

Bisiach, E., & Geminiani, G. (1991). Anosognosia related to hemiplegia and hemianopia. In G.P. Prigatano, & D.L. Schacter (Eds.), *Awareness of deficit after brain injury* (pp. 17–52). New York: Oxford University Press.

Blakemore, S. J., & Frith, C. (2003). Self-awareness and action. *Current Opinion in Neurobiology, 13*, 219–224.

Breier, J. I., Adair, J. C., Gold, M., Fennell, E. B., Gilmore, R. L., & Heilman, K. M. (1995). Dissociation of anosognosia for hemiplegia and aphasia during left-hemisphere anesthesia. *Neurology, 45*, 65–67.

Buchtel, H., Henry, T., & Abou-Khalil, B. (1992). Memory for neurological deficits during the intracarotid amytal procedure: A hemispheric difference. *Journal of Clinical and Experimental Neuropsychology, 14*, 96–97.

Cappa, S., Sterzi, R., Vallar, G., & Bisiach, E. (1987). Remission of hemineglect and anosognosia during vestibular stimulation. *Neuropsychologia, 25,* 775–782.

Carpenter, K., Berti, A., Oxbury, S., Molyneaux, A. J., Bisiach, E., & Oxbury, J. M. (1995). Awareness of and memory for arm weakness during intracarotid sodium amytal testing. *Brain, 18,* 243–251.

Chatterjee, A. (1996). Anosognosia for hemiplegia: Patient retrospections. *Cognitive Neuropsychiatry, 1,* 221–237.

Cocchini, G., Beschin, N., & Della-Salla, S. (2002). Chronic anosognosia: A case report and theoretical account. *Neuropsychologia, 40,* 2030–2038.

Cocchini, G., Beschin N., Cameron, A., Fotopoulou, A., & Della Sala, S. (2009). Anosognosia for motor impairment following left brain damage. *Neuropsychology, 23,* 223–230.

Coslett, H. B. (2005). Anosognosia and body representations forty years later. *Cortex, 41,* 263–270.

Critchley, M. (1953). *The parietal lobes.* London: Edward Arnold.

Cutting, J. (1978). Study of anosognosia. *Journal of Neurology, Neurosurgery, and Psychiatry, 41,* 548–555.

Dennett, D. C., & Kinsbourne, M. (1992). Time and the observer: the when and where of consciousness in the brain. *Behavioral and Brain Sciences, 15,* 183–201.

Di Legge, S., Fang, J., Saposnik, G., & Hachinski, V. (2005). The impact of lesion side on acute stroke treatment. *Neurology, 65,* 81–86.

Durkin, M. W., Meador, K. J., Nichols, M. E., Lee, G. P., & Loring, D. W. (1994). Anosognosia and the intracarotid amobarbital procedure (Wada Test). *Neurology, 44,* 978–979.

Dywan, D. A., McGlone, J., & Fox, A. (1995). Do intracarotid barbiturate injections offer a way to investigate hemispheric models of anosognosia? *Journal of Clinical and Experimental Neuropsychology, 17,* 431–438.

Ekstam, L., Uppgard, B., Kottorp, A., & Tham, K. (2007). Relationship between awareness of disability and occupational performance during the first year after stroke. *American Journal of Occupational Therapy, 61,* 503–511.

Evyapan, D., & Kumral, E. (1999). Pontine anosognosia for hemiplegia. *Neurology, 53,* 647–649.

Farrer, C., Franck, N., Georgieff, N., Frith, C. D., Decety, J., & Jeannerod, M. (2003). Modulating the experience of agency: A positron emission tomography study. *Neuroimage, 18,* 324–333.

Feinberg, T. E., Haber, L. D., & Leeds, N. E. (1990). Verbal asomatognosia. *Neurology, 40,* 1391–1394.

Feinberg, T. E., Roane, D. M., Kwan, P. C., Schindler, R. J., & Haber, L. D. (1994). Anosognosia and visuoverbal confabulation. *Archives of Neurology, 51,* 468–473.

Feinberg, T. E., Roane, D. M., & Ali, J. (2000). Illusory limb movements in anosognosia for hemiplegia. *Journal of Neurology, Neurosurgery, and Psychiatry, 68,* 511–513.

Fink, G., Marshall, J. C., Halligan, P. W., Frith, C. D., Driver, J., Frackowiak, R. S. J., & Dolan, R. J. (1999). The neural consequences of conflict between intention and the senses. *Brain, 122,* 497–512.

Fisher, C. M. (1989). Neurologic fragments. II. Remarks on anosognosia, confabulation, memory, and other topics; and an appendix on self-observation. *Neurology, 39,* 127–132.

Fotopoulou, A., Tsakiris, M., Haggard, P., Vagopoulou, A., Rudd, A., & Kopelman, A. (2008). The role of motor intention in motor awareness: An experimental study on anosognosia for hemiplegia. *Brain, 131,* 3432–3442.

Fotopoulou, A., Rudd, A., Holmes, P., & Kopelman, M. (2009). Self-observation reinstates motor awareness in anosognosia for hemiplegia. *Neuropsychologia, 47,* 1256–1260.

Friedlander, W. J. (1967). Anosognosia and perception. *American Journal of Physical Medicine and Rehabilitation, 46,* 1394–1408.

Frith, C. D., Blakemore, S. J., & Wolpert, D. M. (2000). Abnormalities in the awareness and control of action. *Philosophical Transactions of the Royal Society B: Biological Sciences, 355,* 1771–1788.

Gerstmann, J. (1942). Problems of imperception of disease and of impaired body territories with organic lesions. *Archives of Neurology and Psychiatry, 48,* 890–913.

Geschwind, N. (1965) Disconnexion syndromes in animals and man. *Brain, 88,* 237–294.

Gialanella, B., & Mattioli, F. (1992). Anosognosia and extrapersonal neglect as predictors of functional recovery following right hemisphere stroke. *Neuropsychological Rehabilitation, 2,* 169–178.

Gialanella, B., Monguzzi, V., Santoro, R., & Rocchi, S. (2005). Functional recovery after hemiplegia in patients with neglect: The rehabilitative role of anosognosia. *Stroke, 36,* 2687–2690.

Gilmore, R. L., Heilman, K. M., Schmidt, R. P., Fennell, E. M., & Quisling, R. (1992). Anosognosia during Wada testing. *Neurology, 42,* 925–927.

Gold, M., Adair, J. C., Jacobs, D. H., & Heilman, K. M. (1994). Anosognosia for hemiplegia: An electrophysiological investigation of the feed-forward hypothesis. *Neurology, 44,* 1804–1808.

Goverover, Y., Johnston, M. V., Toglia, J., & Deluca, J. (2007). Treatment to improve self-awareness in persons with acquired brain injury. *Brain Injury, 21*, 913–923.

Graff-Radford, N. R., Eslinger, P. J., Damasio, A. R., & Yamada, T. (1984). Nonhemorrhagic infarction of the thalamus: Behavioral, anatomic, and physiologic correlates. *Neurology, 34*, 14–23.

Haggard, P., & Magno, E. (1999). Localising awareness of action with transcranial magnetic stimulation. *Experimental Brain Research, 127*, 102–107.

Hartman-Maier, A., Soroker, N., Oman, S. D., & Katz, N. (2003). Awareness of disabilities in stroke rehabilitation-A clinical trial. *Disability and Rehabilitation, 25*, 35–44.

Healton, E. B., Navarro, C., Bressman, S., & Brust, J. C. M. (1982). Subcortical neglect. *Neurology, 32*, 776–778.

Heilman, K. M. (1991). Anosognosia. Possible neuropsychological mechanisms. In G. P. Prigatano, & D. L. Schacter (Eds.), *Awareness of deficit after brain injury* (pp. 53–62). New York: Oxford University Press.

Heilman, K. M., Barrett, A. M., & Adair, J. C. (1998) Possible mechanisms of anosognosia: A defect in self-awareness. *Philosophical Transactions of the Royal Society B: Biological Sciences, 353*, 1903–1909.

Heilman K. M., Blonder, L. X., Bowers, D., & Valenstein, E. (2003). *Emotional disorders associated with neurological disease.* In Clinical Neuropsychology, K. M. Heilman & E. Valenstein (Eds.). New York: Oxford University Press, pp. 447–478.

Hildebrandt, H., & Zieger, A. (1995). Unconscious activation of motor responses in a hemiplegic patient with anosognosia and neglect. *European Archives of Psychiatry and Clinical Neuroscience, 246*, 53–59.

House, A., & Hodges, J. R. (1998). Persistent denial of handicap after infarction of the right basal ganglia: A case study. *Journal of Neurology, Neurosurgery, and Psychiatry, 41*, 112–115.

Jacome, D. E. (1986). Case report: Subcortical prosopagnosia and anosognosia. *American Journal of Medical Sciences, 292*, 386–388.

Jehkonen, M., Ahonen, J. P., Dastidar. P., Laippala, P., & Vilkki, J. (2000). Unawareness of deficits after right hemisphere stroke: Double-dissociations of anosognosias. *Acta Neurologica Scandinavica, 102*, 378–384.

Jenkinson, P. M., Edelstyn, N. M. J., Drakeford, J. L., & Ellis, S. J. (2009). Reality monitoring in anosognosia for hemiplegia. *Consciousness and Cognition, 18*, 458–470.

Johnson, S. C., Baxter, L. C., Wilder, L. S., Pipe, J. G., Heiserman, J. E., & Prigatano, G. P. (2002). Neural correlates of self-reflection. *Brain, 125*, 1808–1814.

Kaplan, R. F., Meadows, M. E., Cohen, R. A., Bromfield E. B., & Ehrenberg, B. L. (1993). Awareness of deficit after the sodium amobarbital (Wada) test. *Journal of Clinical and Experimental Neuropsychology, 15*, 383.

Karnath, H. O., Baier, B., & Nägele, T. (2005). Awareness of the functioning of one's own limbs mediated by the insular cortex? *Journal of Neuroscience, 5*, 7134–7138.

Lau, H. C., Rogers, R. D., Haggard, P., & Passingham, R. E. (2004). Attention to intention. *Science, 303*, 1208–1210.

Levine, D. N. (1990). Unawareness of visual and sensorimotor defects: A hypothesis. *Brain and Cognition, 13*, 233–281.

Levine, D. N., Calvanio, R., & Rinn, W. E. (1991). The pathogenesis of anosognosia for hemiplegia. *Neurology, 41*, 1770–1781.

Liebson, E. (2000). Anosognosia and mania associated with right thalamic hemorrhage. *Journal of Neurology, Neurosurgery, and Psychiatry, 68*, 107–108.

Lu, L. H., Barrett, A. M., Schwartz, R. L., Cibula, J. E., Gilmore, R. L., Uthman, B. M., & Heilman, K. M. (1997). Anosognosia and confabulation during the Wada test. *Neurology, 49*, 1316–1322.

Lu, L. H., Barrett, A. M., Cibula, J. E., Gilmore, R. L., Fennell, E. B., & Heilman, K. M. (2000). Dissociation of anosognosia and phantom movement during the Wada test. *Journal of Neurology, Neurosurgery, and Psychiatry, 69*, 820–823.

Maeshima, S., Dohi, N., Funahashi, K., Nakai, K., Itakura, T., & Komai, N. (1997). Rehabilitation of patients with anosognosia for hemiplegia due to intracerebral haemorrhage. *Brain Injury, 11*, 691–697.

Marcel, A. J., Tegner, R., & Nimmo-Smith, I. (2004). Anosognosia for plegia: Specificity, extension, partiality and disunity of bodily unawareness. *Cortex, 40*, 19–40.

Meador, K. J., Loring, D. W., Feinberg, T. E., Lee, G. P., & Nichols, M. E. (2000). Anosognosia and asomatognosia during intracarotid amobarbital injection. *Neurology, 55*, 816–820.

Nardone, I. B., Ward, R., Fotopoulou, A., & Turnbull, O. H. (2007). Attention and emotion in anosognosia: Evidence of implicit awareness and repression? *Neurocase, 13*, 438–445.

Narushima, K., Moser, D. J., & Robinson, R. G. (2008). Correlation between denial of illness and executive function following stroke: A pilot study. *Journal of Neuropsychiatry and Clinical Neurosciences, 20*, 96–100.

Nimmo-Smith, I., Marcel, A. J., & Tegnér, R. (2005). A diagnostic test of unawareness of bilateral motor task abilities in anosognosia for hemiplegia. *Journal of Neurology, Neurosurgery, and Psychiatry, 76*, 1167–1169.

Orfei, M. D., Robinson, R. G., Prigatano, G. P., Starkstein, S., Rusch, N., Bria, P., et al. (2007). Anosognosia for hemiplegia after stroke is a multifaceted phenomenon: A systematic review of the literature. *Brain, 130*, 3075–3090.

Pia, L., Neppi-Modona, M., Ricci, R., & Berti, A. (2004). The anatomy of anosognosia for hemiplegia: A meta-analysis. *Cortex, 40*, 367–377.

Ramachandran, V. S. (1995). Anosognosia in parietal lobe syndrome. *Consciousness and Cognition, 4*, 22–51.

Sandifer, P. H. (1946). Anosognosia and disorders of body scheme. *Brain, 39*, 122–137.

Small, M., & Ellis, S. (1996). Denial of hemiplegia: An investigation into the theories of causation. *European Neurology, 36*, 353–363.

Spalletta, G., Serra, L., Fadda, L., Ripa, A., Bria, P., & Caltagirone, C. (2007). Unawareness of motor impairment and emotions in right hemisphere stroke: A preliminary investigation. *International Journal of Geriatric Psychiatry, 22*, 1241–1246.

Starkstein, S. E., Fedoroff, J. P., Price, T. R., Leiguarda, R., & Robinson, R. G. (1992). Anosognosia in patients with cerebrovascular lesions: A study of causative factors. *Stroke, 23*, 1446–1453.

Starkstein, S. E., Fedoroff, J. P., Price, T. R., & Robinson, R. G. (1993a). Denial of illness scale: A reliability and validity study. *Neuropsychiatry Neuropsychology, and Behavioral Neurology, 6*, 93–97.

Starkstein, S. E., Fedoroff, J. P., Price, T. R., Leiguarda, R., & Robinson, R. G. (1993b). Neuropsychological deficits in patients with anosognosia. *Neuropsychiatry Neuropsychology, and Behavioral Neurology, 6*, 43–48.

Stone, S. P., Halligan, P. W. & Greenwood, R. J. (1993). The incidence of neglect phenomena and related disorders in patients with an acute right of left hemisphere stroke. *Age and Aging, 22*, 46–52.

Toglia, J., & Kirk, U. (2000). Understanding awareness deficits following brain injury. *NeuroRehabilitation, 15*, 57–80.

Turnbull, O. H., & Solms, M. (2007). Awareness, desire, and false beliefs: Freud in the light of modern neuropsychology. *Cortex, 43*, 1083–1090.

Vallar, G., & Ronchi, R. (2006). Anosognosia for motor and sensory deficits after unilateral brain damage: A review. *Restorative Neurology and Neuroscience, 24*, 247–257.

Venneri, A., & Shanks, M. F. (2004). Belief and awareness: Reflections on a case of persistent anosognosia. *Neuropsychologia, 42*, 230–238.

Vuilleumier, P. (2004). Anosognosia: The neurology of beliefs and uncertainties. *Cortex, 40*, 9–17.

Watson, R. T., & Heilman, K. M. (1979). Thalamic neglect. *Neurology, 29*, 690–694.

Weinstein, E. A., & Kahn, R. L. (1953). Personality factors in denial of illness. *American Medical Association Archives of Neurology and Psychiatry, 69*, 355–367.

Weinstein, E. A., & Kahn, R. L. (1955). *Denial of illness: Symbolic and physiological aspects.* Springfield, IL: Charles C. Thomas.

Wortis, H., & Dattner, B. (1942). Analysis of a somatic delusion: A case report. *Psychosomatic Medicine, 4*, 319–323.

10

Apraxia

KENNETH M. HEILMAN AND LESLIE J. GONZALEZ ROTHI

INTRODUCTION

The motor system, which includes the corticospinal system together with motor neurons, is capable of directing muscles to make an almost infinite variety of movements. To perform skilled movements, the brain must acquire the knowledge through experience to program the motor system, so that these movements can be made correctly. Additionally, the brain must, through experience, learn to link motor plans to their meaning, thus providing purpose to each unique movement. The failure to correctly perform skilled, purposeful movement is called *apraxia*, a term originally coined by Steinthal (1871), but derived from Greek and literally meaning *without action*.

Many abnormalities of movements can be associated with dysfunction of the central nervous system. Since apraxia is a cognitive-motor disorder, abnormalities of movement should not be called apraxic if they can be attributed to weakness, dystonia, tremor, chorea, athetosis, ballismus, seizures, positive or negative myoclonus, ataxia, or sensory defects. In addition, impairments of purposeful movements can also be caused by nonmotor cognitive disorders, such as impairments of language comprehension, agnosia, or inattention.

Although apraxia is in part defined by exclusion of the disorders mentioned above, apraxia is not a homogenous disorder, and a wide variety of apraxic errors may characterize the motor performance of a patient who has apraxia. The different forms of apraxia are defined by the types of errors made by the patient and the conditions that elicit these errors. The term apraxia has been used to describe abnormal movements in many portions of the body and during many actions. For example, some abnormalities of walking have been called "gait apraxia," other patients might have what has been called "apraxia of eye opening," and some patients when attempting to speak cannot correctly program their articulatory muscles, a disorder called "apraxia of speech." This review of apraxia will be primarily limited to those apraxic disorders that are associated with forelimb and oral movements.

At least two types of forelimb apraxia exist: those that are specific to certain acts, such as drawing (constructional apraxia) or dressing (dressing apraxia), and those are that are not related to a specific activity. Since constructional apraxia and dressing apraxia are usually primarily caused by visuospatial disorders such as neglect, rather than by disorders of movement programming, they will not be discussed in this chapter, but are discussed in Chapters 7 and 12. The forms of general limb apraxia that we will discuss include limb-kinetic apraxia, ideomotor apraxia, and disconnection or disassociation apraxias, as well as conduction, ideational, and conceptual apraxias.

EXAMINATION

GENERAL NEUROLOGICAL EXAMINATION

Since apraxia is in part defined by the exclusion of other motor, sensory-perceptual, attentional, and cognitive disorders (such as aphasia) that may obscure apraxic errors, a careful and thorough neurological examination is required. Patients with stroke and degenerative diseases can have weakness, sensory deficits, and abnormal movements (such as tremor, chorea, athetosis, ballismus, myoclonus, and ataxia) limited to one upper limb. In these patients, the normal side can still be tested for apraxia. If the abnormality is mild enough to permit use of the affected extremity, or both upper extremities, they should also be tested, but the examiner must make allowances for the effects of these disorders on test results.

Many apraxic patients have cognitive deficits such as aphasia, and when testing these patients their ability to understand commands should be determined. Patients with comprehension disorders can be tested by attempting to have them imitate a correct or nonsense pantomime, or by showing them tools or implements, or the objects with which these tools work, and encouraging them either to pantomime the correct transitive action or to use the actual tools. As will be discussed below, apraxic patients may use body parts as tools or implements, as well as make spatial and temporal errors, but often these movements can be recognized as having the correct intent, providing evidence that the verbal or nonverbal command has been understood. Such movement errors should therefore not be attributed to aphasia.

TESTING FOR APRAXIA

Patients rarely complain of apraxia and often appear unaware of their defect, a form of anosognosia (Rothi et al., 1990). Some patients who are aware of their performance deficits make excuses and appear to be unconcerned about their disability, a form of anosodiaphoria. For example, patients with right hemiparesis often attribute their motor disabilities to the use of their nondominant left arm and hand. They think their movements are clumsy because, even before their brain injury, their left forelimb was not as well coordinated as their right. Furthermore, apraxia is usually mildest when a patient uses actual tools or objects and most apparent when pantomiming. Since patients at home are rarely called upon to use pantomime, these patients and their families are often not aware of this disorder. Therefore, when assessing for apraxia the clinician cannot rely on history but must test patients.

The following are suggested procedures for apraxia testing. The diagnosis of specific forms of apraxia is based on relative performance across these tasks and on the type of errors that patients make. After discussing testing methods, the different forms of apraxia will be discussed.

The examiner should test both forelimbs when possible. Even if one hand is severely paretic, the nonparetic hand should be tested. In addition to observing a patient's performance, the clinician should ascertain if a patient is disturbed by his errors or if he can even recognize that he has made errors.

Gestures-Pantomimes to Command

Gesture-to-command should involve both pantomiming the use of tools or implements (transitive gestures) such as, "Show me how you would use a pair of scissors to cut a piece of paper in half," as well as performing intransitive gestures, which are arbitrarily coded nonverbal communications, such as waving good-bye. In general, patients are more likely to make errors when attempting to perform transitive gestures than when performing

Table 10–1. Tests for Apraxia

Intransitive Limb Gestures	*Intransitive Buccofacial Gestures*
1. Wave good-bye	1. Stick out tongue
2. Hitchhike	2. Blow a kiss
3. Salute	
4. Beckon "come here"	*Transitive Buccofacial Gestures*
5. Stop	1. Blow out a match
6. Go	2. Suck on a straw
Transitive Limb Gestures	*Serial Acts*
1. Open a door with a key	1. Show how you would make a sandwich.
2. Flip a coin	2. Show how you would write and mail a letter.
3. Open a catsup bottle	
4. Use a screwdriver	
5. Use a hammer	
6. Use scissors	

intransitive gestures. Although it was thought that transitive pantomimes are more difficult because they are more motorically complex than intransitive gestures, Mozaz et al. (2002) demonstrated that normal subjects make more errors in recognizing correct versus incorrect transitive than intransitive postures. These results suggest that complexity cannot account for the greater difficulty performing transitive than intransitive gestures. Perhaps the representations of intransitive gestures are more strongly formed than those of transitive gestures because normally people communicate with intransitive rather than transitive gestures. The gestures we use to test patients are listed in Table 10-1.

Frequently, when patients pantomime, they use a body-part-as-tool. They may perform in this manner either because they do not understand that they are supposed to pantomime (i.e., they are using the body part as a symbol of the tool) or because they cannot perform the task even though they understand the task. If a patient uses a body-part-as-tool, his or her performance should be corrected (e.g., "Do not use your finger as a key. Make believe you are really holding a key and use it to open a locked door").

- *Gesture-Pantomime Imitation.* Having patients pantomime transitive acts to command is often the most sensitive test for detecting certain forms of apraxia, therefore gesture imitation alone, if performed normally, is not an adequate test for apraxia. However, there are patients who can perform well to command who fail on imitation. This pattern is seen, for example, in patients with visual pantomime agnosia and in patients with conduction apraxia (discussed below). It is therefore important to test the imitation of transitive and intransitive movements. In addition, it may be useful to test meaningless gestures, which can only be assessed by imitation, since patients with pantomime agnosia and conduction apraxia may be more impaired imitating meaningless than meaningful gestures.

- *Gestures-Pantomimes in Response to Seeing Tools.* This test may be especially useful when a patient has a language comprehension deficit, and it is unclear if the failure to correctly gesture to command results from a language or apraxic disorder.

- *Gestures-Pantomimes in Response to Seeing Objects upon which Tools Work.* This test may also be helpful when a comprehension disorder is present. It is performed by showing the patient objects that receive the action of specific tools (e.g., a nail partially driven into block of wood) and having the patient pantomime using the appropriate tools (e.g., a hammer). Because seeing a tool before pantomiming how this tool should be used may provide cues as how to posture the hand, the object viewing test may be more sensitive in demonstrating apraxia.

- *Using tools.* This task is performed by providing a series of tools to the patient (e.g., a hammer) and requesting the patient to demonstrate how she would use each tool. These tests may be performed with or without the object (e.g., nail) upon which the tool works.
- *Gesture Pantomime Discrimination.* In this test, the examiner tells the patient what tool he will be using, and after the examiner correctly or incorrectly pantomimes the use of the tool, the patient tells the examiner if the action was correct or incorrect.
- *Comprehending Pantomimes and Gestures.* In this test, the examiner makes a series of pantomimes of transitive movements and after each pantomime asks, "What tool am I using?" or "Am I using a hammer or a saw?"
- *Serial Acts.* In this test, the patient is provided the materials to complete a multistep task and is asked to complete this task. (e.g., "Show me, how would you make a sandwich?").
- *Action–Tool Associations.* In this test, the examiner displays an array of tools (e.g., hammer, screwdriver, knife, pliers, etc.) and then pantomimes a target action (e.g., cutting). After each act, he or she asks the patient to point to the tool in the array that is associated with this action.
- *Tool–Object Associations.* The examiner displays a series of objects. After each object is displayed (e.g., a partially driven nail) the examiner asks the subject to select from an array of tools the tool that was used to accomplish this action.
- *Mechanical Knowledge.* If the subject performs well on the tool–object association test, the tool is taken away and the patient is asked to select an alternative tool that could accomplish the same goal. For example, if the patient is shown a partially driven in nail and the patient selects a hammer, the hammer is removed, and

the patient can select another appropriate tool, such as a pair of pliers to complete this task.

VARIETIES OF LIMB APRAXIA

Although, as mentioned, the term apraxia was initially used by Steinthal (1871), it was primarily Hugo Liepmann who described and brought attention to these disorders in the early part of the 20th century. Liepmann (1920) described three forms of limb apraxia: limb-kinetic, ideomotor, and ideational. We subsequently described three additional forms of apraxia: disassociation, conduction, and conceptual. In the subsequent sections, we will describe the clinical aspects of these forms of apraxia as well as the pathophysiology that might account for these disorders.

LIMB-KINETIC APRAXIA

Clinical

To perform many skilled acts, especially those performed by the hand and fingers, a person needs be able to make dexterous movements. Since the term *dexterity* can also mean right-handedness, we use the term *deftness.* Liepmann called the loss of the ability to make deft movements, limb-kinetic apraxia. This movement abnormality can be seen when the patient pantomimes or imitates, but the most sensitive tests involve the manipulation of actual objects with the fingers. Neuropsychologists often assess patients using rapid finger tapping, but this test does not assess the coordination between fingers and may be abnormal because of bradykinesia. Neuropsychologists also use the pegboard test, but in some patients, spatial disorders, such as optic ataxia, can also impair performance in this test. In the clinic, we ask patients to rotate a coin (such as a nickel) between their thumb, index, and middle fingers of each hand, as rapidly as possible for 20 revolutions. (Hanna-Pladdy, Mendoza, Apostolos, & Heilman, 2002). This test is easy to perform and very sensitive.

Typically, patients with hemispheric damage have a loss of deftness in their contralateral hand. Heilman, Meador, and Loring (2000) as well as Hanna-Pladdy and colleagues (2002), have found that people with right hand preference and left hemisphere lesions are also likely to have a loss of deftness in their ipsilesional left hand. In contrast, right-handed people with right hemisphere lesions will usually perform normally with their ipsilesional (right) hand.

Pathophysiology

Liepmann (1920) postulated that injury to the sensorimotor cortex may induce this disorder. Support for this postulate came from the work of Lawrence and Kuypers (1968), who demonstrated a loss of precision (pincer) grasp in monkeys with corticospinal tract lesions. Other studies, however, suggest that portions of the convexity of the premotor cortex are also important for programming deft movements (Freund & Hummelsheim, 1985; Fogassi et al., 2001). In addition, using fMRI, Nirkko and coworkers (2001) provided converging evidence for the role of premotor cortex in the programming of deft movements. They found that discrete unilateral distal finger movements were associated with activation of the contralateral convexity premotor cortex.

As mentioned, left, but not right hemisphere injury in right-handed people can induce ipsilateral limb-kinetic apraxia (Heilman et al., 2000; Hanna-Pladdy et al., 2002). There are at least two means by which the left hemisphere's motor systems might influence the deftness of the left hand in right-handed people. Studies of humans have revealed that there are asymmetries of the corticospinal system, with the left hemisphere influencing the ipsilateral left hand more than the right hemisphere influencing the right hand. Thus, the left hemisphere might have more ipsilateral projections than does the right hemisphere. It is also possible that the left hemisphere's motor programming system might influence the right hemisphere's motor system by transferring information by way of the corpus callosum. Watson and Heilman (1983) reported a woman who had an infarct of her corpus callosum. She was tested for limb-kinetic apraxia, but despite having an ideomotor apraxia of her left (but not right) hand, she was able to make precise independent but coordinated finger movements with

her left hand, such as being able to lift a dime off a table with a pincer grasp. Gazzaniga and coworkers (1967) noted that the right and left hands were equally clumsy after surgical interhemispheric disconnection for the treatment of intractable seizures. In contrast, Verstichel and Meyrignac (2000) reported a right-handed man who suffered an infarct that involved the anterior and middle parts of his corpus callosum. This patient demonstrated loss of agility (deftness) of his left hand. These investigators diagnosed that this patient had a "melokinetic" (limb-kinetic) apraxia of his left hand, postulating a disconnection limb-kinetic apraxia.

Limb-kinetic apraxia can be induced by almost all diseases that injure the cerebral cortex, including stroke, trauma, and tumors. However, limb-kinetic apraxia can often be seen in patients with Parkinson disease (Quencer et al., 2007) and is commonly seen with corticobasal degeneration.

IDEOMOTOR APRAXIA

Clinical

Whereas patients with limb-kinetic apraxia have a loss of deftness, patients with ideomotor apraxia make primarily spatial errors, but also can make temporal errors (Poizner et al., 1989; Rothi et al., 1988). In addition, the severity of the ideomotor apraxia is independent of manual dexterity. Patients with ideomotor apraxia have the greatest difficulty when attempting to pantomime the use of a tool or instrument (Goodglass & Kaplan, 1963). Although they may improve their performance with imitation, gesture to imitation is frequently still defective. Similarly, improvement may be noted when the actual object is used, but performance often remains defective (Poizner et al., 1989).

One of the most common errors made by patients with ideomotor apraxia is what Goodglass and Kaplan, 1963 called *body-part-as-object errors*. Since these patients are using their body part as a tool, we call these errors *body-part-as-tool errors*. At first, normal subjects often also use a body part as a tool. For example, when asked to pantomime the use of a pair of scissors, normal subjects will often use their forefinger and middle finger as if they were the blades of the scissors. However, when asked to act as if they were actually holding and using this tool rather than using their hand and fingers as if they *are* the tool, normal subjects will stop using their body part as a tool (Raymer et al., 1997). When patients with ideomotor apraxia are asked to pantomime the use of tools, they will also frequently use their body parts as the tools, but unlike normal people when corrected, patients with ideomotor apraxia will either continue to use the body part as a tool or demonstrate postural errors.

In addition to making body-part-as-tool errors, when pantomiming transitive acts, patients with ideomotor apraxia often make spatial errors. Patients with ideomotor apraxia demonstrate three forms of spatial errors: incorrect forelimb postures, spatial movement errors, and spatial orientation errors (Rothi et al., 1988b; Poizner et al., 1990). Postural errors entail the failure to position the fingers, hand, and arm so that they can properly hold the imagined utensil or tool. Since holding the actual tool or implement constrains hand and finger position, postural errors are seen primarily with pantomime and imitation and not with actual object use. When patients make spatial orientation errors, their hand holding the imagined tool fails to correctly approach the imagined object upon which the tool works. For example, when asked to pantomime the use of scissors, apraxic patients may move the scissors laterally instead of forward, or when asked to cut a slice of bread with a knife, they may fail to keep the imaginary knife in a constant sagittal plane.

Patients can make spatial movement errors because they move the incorrect joint or joints. For example, when asked to pantomime the use of a screwdriver, the normal subjects usually fix their wrist and shoulder joints and rotate (pronate-supinate) the forearm, so that the imaginary screwdriver rotates on its axis. The apraxic patient may fix the shoulder and forearm and rotate the wrist, so that the screwdriver moves incorrectly in arc-like motions. Movement errors can also occur when performing an action in which the patient must make multiple joint movements, such as using a knife to slice bread. Normally, when slicing a loaf of bread with a knife, as the arm at the shoulder joint is brought forward, the forearm at the elbow joint

is extended, and when the arm at the shoulder joint is brought back, the forearm at the elbow is flexed. With each successive cutting movement, the forearm at the elbow is flexed less, so that the knife moves downward. Patients with ideomotor apraxia primarily use one joint movement, usually the more proximal movement (shoulder), or they fail to coordinate the two movements (Poizner et al., 1990).

When performing skilled purposeful movements, people must move their limbs at different speeds; patients with apraxia may move their limbs at incorrect speeds (Poizner et al., 1990). There also may be a delay in the initiation of movement or occasional pauses, especially when the spatial trajectory must be changed. Patients with ideomotor apraxia may also fail to coordinate the speed of movement with its spatial components. For example, when cutting bread with a knife, a person normally slows the speed of the forelimb movement when they are about to reverse the direction of the cut; once the direction has been changed, the speed of movement increases. Patients with ideomotor apraxia do not demonstrate this pattern of movement.

Pathophysiology

Callosal Lesions. Liepmann and Maas (1907) studied a patient with right hemiplegia who performed poorly when attempting to carry out verbal commands with his left forelimb. On postmortem examination, he was found to have a lesion in the left basis pontis, which accounted for his right hemiplegia, and a lesion of the anterior four-fifths of the corpus callosum, which Liepmann and Maas thought accounted for his left-hand apraxia. Although it could be postulated that the callosal lesion resulted in apraxia because it disconnected the language areas in the left hemisphere from the areas in the right hemisphere that control the movements of the left forelimb, Liepmann and Maas did not believe that a language–motor disconnection could fully explain their patient's movement deficits, because their patient also failed on nonverbal tasks. Using his nonparetic left forelimb, he could not correctly imitate skilled movements or manipulate actual tools. These deficits could not be accounted for by a primary sensorimotor disorder, because primary visual, visual association, primary somesthetic, somesthetic association, premotor, and motor areas in the right hemisphere were all intact. Liepmann and Maas concluded that the left hemisphere must contain "movement formulas" that control purposeful skilled movements of both hands. Their patient's apraxia resulted from the inability of the right hemisphere's sensorimotor areas to access the movement representations (movement formula) stored in this patient's left hemisphere.

Liepmann (1920) proposed that these "movement formulas" contain the "time-space-form picture of the movement" (see Kimura, 1979). In order to perform a skilled, learned act, one must place particular body parts in certain spatial positions in a specific order at specific times. The spatial positions assumed by the relevant body parts depend not only on the nature of the act but also on the position and size of an external object with which the body parts must interact. Skilled acts also require orderly changes in the spatial positions of the body parts over time. These movement formulas command the motor systems to adopt the appropriate spatial positions of the relevant body parts over time.

According to Liepmann's postulate, a callosal lesion in a right-handed patient who has both movement and language representations in her or his left hemisphere would not interfere with the ability of the patient to carry out commands, imitate, and use actual tools correctly with her or his right hand, but would result in the patient having difficulty with all these tasks when using his or her left hand. These predictions, however, were not completely supported by subsequent cases. Geschwind and Kaplan (1962) described a patient with a left hemisphere glioblastoma who underwent surgery and postoperatively was found to have an infarction in the distribution of the left anterior cerebral artery. This infarction caused destruction of the anterior four-fifths of the corpus callosum. Their patient could not carry out verbal commands with his left forelimb but, unlike the patient reported by Liepmann and Maas, he could correctly imitate and he could use actual tools with his left hand. He was also agraphic with the left hand and could not type

or use anagram letters with the left hand, but performed all these tasks flawlessly with the right hand. A language–motor disconnection, induced by this callosal infarction, could explain both the left-hand aphasic agraphia and the left-hand apraxia to verbal command.

Praxis has also been studied in epileptic patients who underwent a surgical lesion of the corpus callosum to help control seizures. Gazzaniga and his coworkers (1967) reported that these callosal disconnections were not associated with impaired imitation or ability to correctly use tools with the left forelimb. These reports did not support Liepmann and Mass' postulate that, in people who are right-handed, the left hemisphere contains movement formula and callosal disconnection not only prevents verbal commands from gaining access to the right hemisphere, which controls the left forelimb, but also prevents these movement representations from gaining access to the right hemisphere.

Subsequently, Watson and Heilman (1983) and Graff-Radford et al. (1987) reported patients with acute naturally occurring callosal lesions who, unlike the patient of Geschwind and Kaplan (1962), had severe apraxia of their left forelimb when tested by command, imitation, and even the use of actual tools and implements. These reports provided support for Liepmann's callosal motor disconnection hypothesis.

Why do some patients with callosal injury demonstrate errors consistent with an ideomotor apraxia when imitating and using objects with the left forelimb, while others do not? One possible reason is that the patients with surgical callosal lesions had a history of poorly controlled seizures and either the developmental abnormality that induced this seizure disorder or the seizures themselves might have induced alterations of brain organization; however, Geschwind and Kaplan's patient did not have a long history of poorly controlled seizures, suggesting that the absence of left-hand ideomotor apraxia with imitation and actual object use cannot be entirely explained by brain reorganization. Extracallosal damage can also not explain the difference between patients, since Geschwind and Kaplan's patient had considerable extracallosal damage, but could imitate and use actual tools; however Watson and Heilman's patient (1983) did not show any extracallosal damage. The reported discrepancies in praxis following callosal lesions might be explained by intersubject variability in the capability of the two hemispheres to subserve praxis. Whereas in the majority of people left hemisphere injury induces aphasia, in some people, the right hemisphere appears to mediate language, and in others, both hemispheres appear to mediate language. Similarly, it is possible that in some people, movement representations are either stored in the right hemisphere or both hemispheres. In right-handed people, right hemisphere lesions have only been rarely reported to produce ideomotor apraxia; however, left hemisphere lesions that damage cortical areas known to induce both aphasia and apraxia more often induce aphasia than ideomotor apraxia. In one study, only 57% (20 of 35) of aphasic patients were also apraxic (Heilman, 1975), suggesting that movement formula or space–time movement representations are bilaterally represented in a considerable minority of right-handed people (Heilman, 1979). Since, in these patients, language representations are stored in the left hemisphere, when the left hemisphere is disconnected from the motor areas of the right hemisphere and the patient is verbally requested to make a specific gesture, the verbal message cannot access the right hemisphere to activate the specific movement representations stored in the right hemisphere. In contrast, these right hemisphere movement representations can be accessed when the subject observes the examiner make a gesture or when they see a tool; therefore, under these circumstances, the patients can correctly imitate and use actual objects. Those patients who demonstrate this clinical picture do not have ideomotor apraxia, but rather have a language–movement representation disconnection, or a dissociation apraxia. These forms of apraxia are discussed later in this chapter.

In contrast, the patients of Watson and Heilman (1983) and Graff-Radford et al. (1987) probably had language and movement representations restricted to their left hemispheres, and when these patients sustained a callosal injury, they disconnected both language and movement representations from the right hemisphere

motor systems. These patients were impaired in gesturing to command, imitating gestures, and using actual objects, making spatial and temporal errors typical of ideomotor apraxia.

Most left-handed people, like right-handed people, are left hemisphere dominant for speech and language. However, since these patients are left-handed, they are likely to have movement representations stored in the right hemisphere. Consistent with this postulate, we have seen two left-handed patients who were apraxic but not aphasic following right hemisphere lesions (Heilman et al., 1973; Valenstein & Heilman, 1979). The dissociation between praxis and speech deficits in these patients suggests that movement representations in these two patients were stored in the right hemisphere, whereas language was mediated by the left hemisphere. We can speculate that, had these patients also had a lesion of their corpus callosum, their left hemisphere would be deprived of access to movement representations, and their right hand would perform poorly to command, to imitation, and with the use of the actual objects; that is, they would have a right ideomotor apraxia. However, the right hemisphere would have access to movement representations but would be deprived of language by callosal disconnection; therefore, the left hand would appear apraxic when requested to gesture in response to verbal command but would perform well with imitation and with an actual objects: It would demonstrate a dissociation apraxia.

Left Hemisphere Lesions (Intrahemispheric). In right-handed patients, almost all cases of apraxia are associated with left hemisphere lesions (Goodglass & Kaplan, 1963; Hecaen & Ajuriaguerra, 1964; Geschwind, 1965; Hecaen & Sanguet, 1971). In right-handed people, the left hemisphere is also dominant for language. Apraxia therefore is commonly associated with aphasia. This has led to the suggestion that apraxia and aphasia may both be manifestations of a primary defect in symbolization: Aphasia is a disturbance of verbal symbolization, whereas apraxia is a defect of nonverbal symbolization (e.g., emblem and pantomime) (Goldstein, 1948). The observation that patients with apraxia perform poorly to command and imitation but improve with the use of the actual object (Goodglass & Kaplan, 1963) lends support to Goldstein's asymbolia postulate. In addition, Dee et al. (1970) and Kertesz and Hooper (1982) found a close relationship between language impairment and apraxia.

Several studies, however, lend support to Liepmann's hypothesis that the left hemisphere controls skilled movements and that destruction of the movement representations or separation of these representations from the motor areas controlling the extremity causes abnormalities of skilled movement. Goodglass and Kaplan (1963) tested apraxic and nonapraxic aphasic subjects with the Wechsler Adult Intelligence Scale and used the performance-scaled score as a measure of intellectual ability. They also tested their subjects' ability to gesture and perform simple and complex pantomimes. Although apraxic aphasic patients performed less well on these motor skills than did their intellectual counterparts in the control groups, no clear relationship emerged between the severity of aphasia and the degree of gestural-praxis disorder. Apraxic aphasic patients were also less able to imitate than were nonapraxic aphasic controls. Although Goodglass and Kaplan believed that their results supported Liepmann's "movement formula" hypothesis, versus Goldstein's asymbolia hypothesis, they noted that their apraxic subjects did not have any difficulty in handling tools. Liepmann, however, thought apraxic patients were clumsy with tools, and Poizner et al. (1989) observed and quantified motor and spatial errors of apraxic patients' use of actual tools and implements. Kimura and Archibald (1974) studied the ability of left hemisphere–impaired aphasic patients and right hemisphere–impaired controls to imitate unfamiliar and meaningless motor sequences. The performance of aphasic apraxic patients with left hemisphere impairment was poorer than that of the controls, again supporting Liepmann's hypothesis. Strong support for the postulate that apraxia is a disorder of skilled movements rather than a symbolic defect comes from Liepmann's own observations that six of the 20 patients with apraxia whom he reported were not aphasic. Goodglass and Kaplan (1963) and Heilman et al. (1973, 1974) have also

described similar patients. In addition, aphasic patients are often not apraxic (Heilman, 1975). The dissociation between symbolic disorders (aphasia) and disorders of skilled movements observed in patients with left hemisphere disease and the observation that even nonsymbolic movements are poorly performed by apraxic patients provides evidence to support the hypothesis that apraxia is a disorder of skilled movements and not a form of asymbolia.

Disconnection Hypothesis

Geschwind (1965) proposed that language elicits motor behavior by using a neural substrate similar to that proposed by Wernicke (1874) to explain language processing (see Figure 10-1). Auditory stimuli travel along auditory pathways and reach Heschl's gyrus (primary auditory cortex). From Heschl's gyrus, the auditory message is relayed to the posterior superior portion of the temporal lobe (auditory association cortex). In the left hemisphere, this is called Wernicke's area, and is important in language comprehension. Wernicke's area is connected to premotor areas by the arcuate fasciculus, and the convexity premotor area on the left is connected to the left primary motor area. According to Geschwind, when someone is told to carry out a command with their right hand, this perisylvian pathway is used. To carry

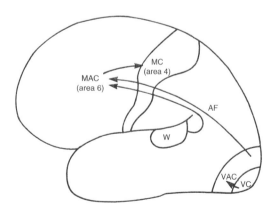

Figure 10–1. Geschwind's schema. Lateral view of the left side of the brain. AF, arcuate fasciculus; MAC, motor association cortex; MC, motor cortex; VAC, visual association cortex; VC, visual cortex; W, Wernicke's area. The arrows indicate major connections of the areas shown.

out a verbal command with the left hand, information must be carried to the right premotor cortex. Since it is rare to find fibers that run obliquely in the corpus callosum, fibers either cross from Wernicke's area in the left hemisphere to the contralateral auditory association area in the right hemisphere or cross from the left hemisphere's premotor area to the premotor area on the right. The information is then conveyed to the primary motor cortex on the same side as the premotor cortex. Geschwind (1965) postulated that when a person uses her or his left hand in response to a verbal command, the information reaches the right hemisphere by way of the connections between the left and right premotor cortical areas. Support for the hypothesis that the interhemispheric communication for carrying out verbal commands with the left hand crosses the corpus callosum anteriorly comes from the observation of a patient who had a selective anterior callosal section (to remove a colloid cyst). This anterior callosal section induced an ideomotor apraxia of the left hand (personal observation by KMH).

Geschwind believed that disconnection explained most apraxic disturbances. As we have already discussed, according to Geschwind, callosal lesions produce unilateral ideomotor apraxia by disconnecting the left premotor region from the right. Lesions that destroy the left convexity premotor cortex also cause ideomotor apraxia, because the cell bodies of neurons that cross the corpus callosum are destroyed. Therefore, a lesion in the left convexity premotor cortex would cause a defect similar to that induced by a lesion in the body of the corpus callosum. Lesions of the left convexity premotor cortex are often associated with right hemiplegia, so the right limb frequently cannot be tested. If these patients were not hemiplegic, however, they would probably also make apraxic errors when using their right forelimb.

According to Geschwind's model (1965), lesions of the arcuate fasciculus should disconnect the posterior language areas, important for language comprehension, from the convexity premotor cortex, important for implementing motor programs. Therefore, patients with injury to the arcuate fasciculus, sparing convexity premotor cortex, should be able to comprehend verbal commands but not be able to perform skilled movements in response to these commands. More posterior lesions, affecting the primary auditory cortex, Wernicke's area, or the connections between them, cause abnormalities in language comprehension, but not apraxia. These patients fail to carry out commands because they cannot understand the command, not because they have difficulty performing skilled movements.

Patients with a left arcuate fasciculus lesion have a normal right hemisphere. Thus, when attempting to imitate using the left hand, patients with left parietal-arcuate lesions should be able to imitate normally with their left forelimb since imitation does not require language comprehension and the right hemisphere of these patients has normal connections between the visual association areas and the right hemisphere premotor area. One major problem with Geschwind's model is that patients with left parietal lesions that involve the arcuate fasciculus often cannot normally imitate with their left forelimb. Geschwind attempted to explain this discrepancy by noting that the arcuate fasciculus also contains fibers passing from visual association cortex to premotor cortex. He proposed that the arcuate fasciculus of the left hemisphere is dominant for visuomotor connections, but there is no evidence to support this hypothesis. Even if one assumes that the left arcuate fasciculus is dominant for visuomotor connections and interruption of this dominant pathway explains why patients cannot imitate, it could not explain why these patients are more clumsy than normal people even when they use actual tools with their left forelimb. One would have to assume that the arcuate fasciculus also carries somesthetic-motor impulses and that the left arcuate fasciculus is also dominant for this function. There is, however, no evidence to support this postulate.

Representational Hypothesis

After a person learns a skilled motor behavior, future behaviors that require that same movement are expedited. In addition, even in the absence of specific movement instructions or cues, one can pantomime the transitive and intransitive movement either to command or spontaneously. These observations indicate that the nervous system stores knowledge of the spatial and temporal parameters of learned, skilled acts. When this knowledge is required to program a skilled act, these movement representations are retrieved from storage and implemented rather than being constructed de novo. A hypothesis that may explain why patients with a dominant parietal lesion cannot properly pantomime or imitate transitive actions or correctly demonstrate the correct use of actual tools and implements is that the "movement formulas" or learned time–space movement representations are stored in the dominant parietal cortex (Heilman, 1979; Kimura, 1979). These movement representations (or praxicons) help program the premotor cortex, which in turn helps to implement the required movements by selectively activating the motor cortex, which innervates the specific muscle motor neuron pools needed to carry out the skilled act (Figure 10-2).

The ideomotor apraxia caused by destruction of the inferior parietal areas, where these movement representations or praxicons are stored, differs from the apraxia caused by either disconnection from the premotor cortex or injury to the premotor cortex that implements these movement representations. With disconnection of the parietal lobe from the premotor areas or with destruction of the premotor areas, the movement representations (praxicons) can be intact and, therefore, these patients still have the information characterizing distinctive features of learned, skilled movements. Although patients with either disorder experience difficulty in performing purposeful skilled acts in response to commands, imitation, or use of tools/implements, patients whose representations for skilled acts are retained but whose premotor areas are disconnected or destroyed are able to discriminate a correctly performed skilled act from an incorrectly performed act. In contrast, patients with parietal lesions that have destroyed these representations (praxicons) are not able to perform this analysis (Heilman et al., 1982; Rothi et al., 1985). Converging evidence for the postulate that movement representations or praxicon are stored in the dominant inferior parietal lobe

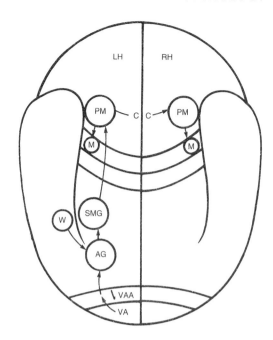

Figure 10–2. Author's schema. View from top of brain. W, Wernicke's area; VA, primary visual area; VAA, visual association area; AG, angular gyrus; SMG, supramarginal gyrus; PM, premotor area (motor association cortex); M, motor cortex; CC, corpus callosum; LH, left hemisphere; RH, right hemisphere. The arrows show major connections of the areas shown.

comes from functional imaging studies of normal subjects who, when pantomiming the use of tools, activated their left parietal cortex (Moll et al., 1998) and when imitating gestures-pantomimes also activated the inferior parietal lobe (Mühlau et al., 2005).

If ideomotor apraxia results from destruction of the cortex that stores movement representations or praxicons, patients with this form of ideomotor apraxia should be impaired at acquiring new motor skills and retaining new gestures in memory. In regard to the former, Heilman et al. (1975) studied right-handed patients with apraxia and aphasia and compared them to control participants who had aphasia but not ideomotor apraxia. These subjects were given six trials on a rotary pursuit apparatus (five acquisition trials and one retention trial). Since most of these subjects had a right hemiparesis, all subjects used their left, nonparetic forelimb. The performance of the control group on the sixth trial was significantly better than on the first trial; however, there was no significant difference between the first and sixth trials in the apraxic group, suggesting that these patients with ideomotor apraxia had a defect in motor learning. The defect appeared to be caused by a combined impairment of acquisition as well as retention, and is thought to be caused by the degradation of the region of the brain where this information normally is stored. Wyke (1971) studied patients with either right or left hemisphere lesions, and gave these subjects a motor acquisition task that required bimanual coordination. Although patients with left hemisphere disease demonstrated acquisition, it was below the level of skill demonstrated by patients with right hemisphere disease. Since Wyke did not separate the subjects with left hemisphere injury into apraxic and nonapraxic participants, it is not certain if the patients with apraxia would have demonstrated poorer learning than nonapraxic left hemisphere–damaged patients. Rothi and Heilman (1985) used a modified Buschke (1973) learning-memory testing paradigm to study apraxic subjects' ability to learn a list of gestures and noted significantly more consolidation errors in the apraxic than control groups, suggesting apraxic patients have a memory consolidation deficit. Pistarini and coworkers (1991) also studied gesture and skill learning in patients with ideomotor apraxia and found that these patients were impaired. Visual imagery is thought to be dependent on activation of representation of seen or felt stimuli. If patients with ideomotor apraxia have a loss of movement representations (praxicons), it might be expected that they would also demonstrate imagery deficits of previously seen transitive and intransitive movements. Ochipa et al. (1997) demonstrated that ideomotor apraxia may be associated with deficits in movement imagery.

Innervatory Patterns

The dominant inferior parietal lobe stores the praxicons in a three-dimensional spatial-temporal supramodal code that has to be translated into a motor plan before the target movement can be made. Although Geschwind (1965) thought that lesions in convexity premotor cortex might induce apraxia, the role of the convexity premotor cortex in praxis is unclear.

Many complex movements, however, require the simultaneous movement of multiple joints. Barrett et al. (2002) suggested that convexity premotor cortex may be important in binding or coordinating these movement programs. The convexity premotor cortex may also be important in adapting the motor program so that the upper extremity can guide the tool/implement to the object with which it will interact. Many purposeful skilled acts require a sequence of movements. For example, if asked to demonstrate how to unlock a door with a key, normally a person would make the hand posture needed to hold the key (e.g., thumb adducted against flexed forefinger), then extend the arm at the elbow and shoulder so that he could place the key in the door lock, and then he or she would rotate his hand by making a rotatory movement at the elbow joint. Hlustík et al. (2002) using functional imaging, demonstrated that the convexity premotor cortex might also be important in sequencing these movements.

The premotor cortex in the medial frontal lobe is called the supplementary motor area (SMA). This part of the premotor cortex might play a different role than the convexity premotor cortex. Whereas stimulation of the primary motor cortex (Brodmann's area 4) induces simple single movements, SMA stimulation induces complex movements of the fingers, arms, and hands (Penfield & Welch, 1951). The SMA receives projections from parietal neurons and projects to the primary motor neurons. The SMA neurons discharge before neurons in the primary motor cortex (Brinkman & Porter, 1979). Studies of cerebral blood flow, an indicator of cerebral metabolism, reveal that a single, simple, repetitive movement increases activation of the contralateral motor cortex. However, complex movements increase flow in contralateral motor cortex and bilaterally in the SMA. When subjects think about making complex movements but do not move, blood flow is increased to the SMA but not to the primary motor cortex (Orgogozo & Larsen, 1979). These observations suggest that the SMA is important in translating the temporal-spatial movement programs stored in the parietal lobe into a motor program, and this program helps to selectively activate motor neurons in the motor cortex.

Support for this postulate comes from the report of Watson et al. (1986), who described several patients with left-sided medial frontal lesions that included the SMA, and who had bilateral ideomotor apraxia. However, unlike patients with parietal lesions, these patients could both comprehend and discriminate well-performed from incorrectly performed pantomimes. Because the SMA has efferent connections with the primary motor cortex and receives projections from the parietal lobe, is activated before motor cortex, becomes activated with complex learned movements, and, when ablated, induces apraxia, we believe the SMA is the major site at which movement representations are translated into motor programs or innervatory patterns that selectively activate motor cortex.

Whereas basal ganglia dysfunction is thought to induce alterations of muscle tone (e.g., plastic or cogwheel rigidity), abnormal movements (e.g., tremor or choreoathetosis), decreased spontaneous movements (e.g., akinesia), and slowing of movements (bradykinesia), the role of basal ganglia dysfunction in apraxia remains unclear. There have been several reports of patients who demonstrated ideomotor apraxia from lesions that involved the basal ganglia and/or thalamus (Basso et al., 1980; Agostini et al., 1983). Rothi et al. (1988a) described two patients with left-sided lenticular infarctions that did not involve cerebral cortex or associative pathways. Both patients had spatial movement errors that were similar to errors seen in patients with cortical lesions. However, both patients also showed frequent preservative errors.

Alexander et al. (1986) described five discrete cortical striatal-pallidal-thalamic-cortical circuits. We have already provided evidence that lesions of the left SMA are associated with apraxia. The SMA is a part of the motor circuit that includes the putamen. The SMA projects to the putamen, which in turn projects to the globus pallidus, and the globus pallidus projects to the ventrolateral nucleus of the thalamus. Finally, the ventrolateral nucleus projects back to the SMA. This discrete "motor loop" may control the flow of information into the SMA. Therefore, lesions of the loop may cause dysfunction of the SMA, and SMA dysfunction may lead to apraxia.

Support for the postulate that the basal ganglia are important in praxis also comes from reports of patients with degenerative basal ganglia diseases. For example, Shelton and Knopman (1991) reported that apraxia was associated with Huntington disease, and Leiguarda et al. (1997) reported that 27% of patients with Parkinson disease have ideomotor apraxia. Ideomotor apraxia has also been reported in the Parkinson-plus syndromes of progressive supranuclear palsy (PSP) (Leiguarda et al., 1997) and corticobasal degeneration (Jacobs et al., 1999 and Merians et al., 1999). In addition, patients with basal ganglia disease (such as Parkinson disease) may be impaired at learning new motor skills. However, even nondemented patients with basal ganglia disease may have cortical dysfunction. Pramstaller and Marsden (1996) performed a detailed review and meta-analysis of the relationships between basal ganglia injury and apraxia and concluded that diseases confined to the basal ganglia "rarely, if ever, cause apraxia."

CONDUCTION (IMITATION) APRAXIA

Clinical

Although most patients with ideomotor apraxia imitate transitive gestures better than they do pantomime transitive gestures to command, Ochipa et al. (1990) described a patient whose imitation of learned transitive and symbolic movements was worse than his pantomime of these same movements to command. This patient had no difficulty comprehending the examiners' pantomimes and gestures. Subsequently, Politis (2004) reported a similar case.

This disorder is called *conductional apraxia* because this gestural disorder is parallel to the aphasic disorder called conduction aphasia, in which patients are very impaired in speech repetition.

Pathophysiology

Unfortunately, the model we have developed thus far (Figure 10-3) cannot account for these findings. Such findings suggest that there are two independent sets of motor representations or praxicons, one for input (input praxicon) and one for output (output praxicon) (Rothi et al., 1991)

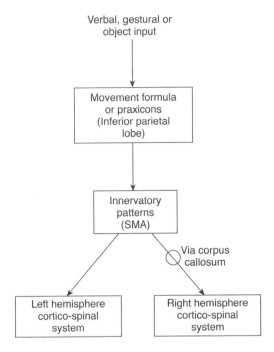

Verbal, gestural or
object input

Movement formula
or praxicons
(Inferior parietal
lobe)

Innervatory
patterns
(SMA)

Via corpus
callosum

Left hemisphere
cortico-spinal
system

Right hemisphere
cortico-spinal
system

Figure 10–3. Diagrammatic model of ideomotor apraxia. SMA, supplementary motor area.

(see Figure 10-4). A preserved ability to comprehend gesture in conjunction with impaired imitation would suggest that the input praxicon remains intact and that the impairment occurs after observed stimuli are processed by the input praxicon. Because the patient was better able to pantomime to command, this would suggest that verbal language is capable of activating the output praxicon (bypassing processing by the input praxicon). Thus the impairment in imitation would be caused by a disconnection between the input and output praxicons (see Figure 10-4). Unfortunately, the localization of lesions that cause conduction (imitative) apraxia is unknown.

VERBAL-MOTOR DISSOCIATION APRAXIA

Clinical

Heilman (1973) described patients who, when asked to gesture, hesitated to make any movements and appeared as if they did not understand the command. In other domains, however, speech comprehension was intact. They could demonstrate that they understood the command both verbally and by picking out the correct act from several performed by the examiner. Unlike patients with ideomotor apraxia, they were able to imitate and to use actual tools flawlessly. When patients with this disorder see a tool, see the object upon which a tool acts (e.g., nail), or hold a tool, they are able to make the correct movements. Because of these preserved skills, it appears that they have intact movement representations. What seems to be defective is their ability to elicit or activate the correct movement representation (praxicon) in response to language.

Pathophysiology

Although we hypothesized that the lesions were in, or deep to, the parietal region (angular gyrus), we never learned the exact locations of the left hemisphere lesions that induce this form of apraxia.

The patients with callosal lesions described by Geschwind and Kaplan (1962) and Gazzaniga et al. (1967) could not perform with their left hand in response to command, but they could imitate and use tools. Performance with the left hand was similar to the performance with both hands of patients with the left hemisphere lesions described above (Heilman, 1973). If normal performance on imitation and use-of-object tasks suggests that movement representations (praxicons) are intact and connected to premotor area, then patients with callosal lesions and patients with subcortical lesions, deep in the parietal lobe, must have a dissociation between language areas and the area where motor representations are stored. In patients with callosal lesions, these movement representations were presumed to be in both hemispheres, whereas comprehension of commands was being mediated by the left hemisphere. In patients with left hemisphere lesions, both speech comprehension and the learned motor skills were being mediated by the left hemisphere, and the lesion disassociated language areas important in comprehension of speech from the area of the brain that stores the praxicons, such that language was not able to activate the appropriate praxicon (see Figure 10-4). An alternative hypothesis is that in patients with left hemisphere lesions, the right hemisphere was mediating language comprehension, the left hemisphere contained

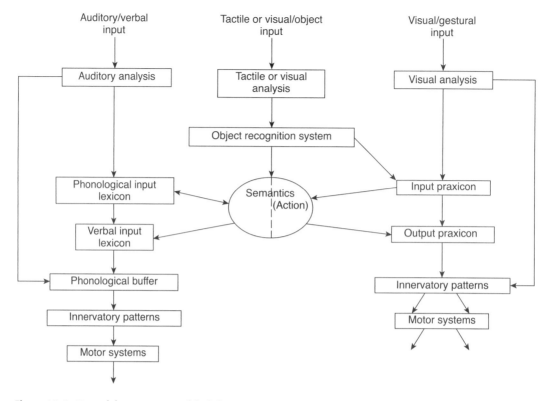

Figure 10–4. Revised diagrammatic model of ideomotor apraxia.

the praxic representations, and the lesions disconnected the language areas from these representations.

VISUAL–MOTOR AND TACTILE–MOTOR DISSOCIATION APRAXIA

Clinical

De Renzi et al. (1982) replicated Heilman's (1973) observations of a verbal–motor dissociation apraxia and also described a patient who performed in the opposite manner. The patient failed to correctly perform gestures with visual stimuli, but performed well to verbal command. Although most patients perform skilled actions better with tactile stimuli than by command, the authors described two patients who performed better with visual and verbal stimuli than with tactile stimuli.

Pathophysiology

The mechanism proposed by De Renzi et al. to explain these modality-specific apraxias was

similar to that proposed by Heilman (1973); namely, a disconnection between modality-specific pathways and the network where movements are programmed.

PANTOMIME AGNOSIA

Clinical

Agnosia is a failure of recognition that cannot be attributed to deafferentation (e.g., blindness) or a naming disorder (e.g., anomic aphasia). Disorders of gesture or pantomime discrimination (correct vs. incorrect) and recognition associated with ideomotor apraxia from posterior lesions (described above) are not considered to be forms of agnosia because of the associated production deficits. Rothi et al. (1986), however, reported two patients who could not comprehend or discriminate visually presented gestures, but who performed gestures normally to command. These patients could be considered to have pantomime agnosia. Both patients could imitate better than they could comprehend or discriminate gestures. Because they could imitate, their inability to discriminate or comprehend gestures could not be accounted for by a defect in vision or perception. These patients had left-sided temporo-occipital lesions that may have disconnected visual input from the input praxicon. Schwartz et al. (1998) reported patients who could not recognize tools but could recognize pantomimes. These patients were the opposite of those reported by Rothi, in that they had object agnosia without pantomime agnosia.

Pathophysiology

Whereas Rothi et al. (1986) thought that the ventral occipital-temporal "what" visual stream is important for gesture comprehension, the loss of the ability to name tools, with a preserved ability to comprehend gestures reported by Schwartz et al. (1998) suggests that it may be the dorsal "where" visual stream that is important for gesture recognition, whereas the ventral stream "what" stream is important for object recognition.

In regard to the neuropsychological mechanism, a parallel model from the classical aphasia literature might help us to understand the mechanisms underlying pantomime agnosia. Patients with Wernicke's aphasia and pure word deafness can neither comprehend spoken language nor repeat. Wernicke's aphasia is thought to be related to destruction of the phonological lexicon (representations of learned word sounds), and pure word deafness is thought to be related to an inability of auditory input to gain access to this lexicon. Patients with transcortical sensory aphasia, however, can repeat (i.e., imitate) in spite of being unable to comprehend, demonstrating that comprehension and imitation are dissociable. This comprehension–imitation disassociation suggests that these two processes are at least in part divergent and are mediated by different parts of the brain. Lichtheim (1885) suggested that, whereas repetition is mediated by a phonological–lexical system that is still functional in patients with transcortical sensory aphasia, comprehension also requires semantic processing. Thus, in transcortical sensory aphasia, the systems that mediate semantic processing of language are impaired, or auditory input cannot gain access to these semantic systems

(Heilman et al., 1976). The neuropsychological mechanisms underlying impaired gesture comprehension with spared imitation reported by Rothi et al. could be similar. Perhaps, these patients can gain access to the input praxicon, but the activated praxic representations cannot access semantics (see Figure 10-4).

Several authors have suggested that speech repetition (i.e., imitation) may be performed either by using stored word representations (lexical) or by using a nonlexical route (McCarthy & Warrington, 1984; Coslett et al., 1987). Just as we can repeat words we have not previously heard, we can also mimic movements we have never seen or previously learned to perform. Perhaps imitation, like repetition, can take place without having to access stores of previously learned skilled movements (see Figure 10-4). Support for this alternative imitation system comes from the observation of a patient whose deficit was limited to the imitation of nonfamiliar limb movements (Mehler, 1987). Since there are no memory stores for unfamiliar movements, the praxicon could not be accessed and the patient had to rely on an impaired, nonrepresentational route. Some patients with ideomotor apraxia imitate better than they perform to verbal commands, but others do not. Perhaps the patients with ideomotor apraxia who improve with imitation can use this nonrepresentational route, whereas those who do not improve may have an additional deficit in this nonrepresentational route. Functional imaging research has suggested that gesture imitation might use the same or a similar network as speech imitation (Kuhn & Brass, 2008). However, the anatomic differences between the two routes discussed above are not entirely known.

IDEATIONAL APRAXIA

Clinical

There has been much confusion about the term *ideational apraxia*. The disassociation apraxias discussed above were unfortunately originally called ideational apraxia (Heilman, 1973). The inability to carry out a series of acts, an ideational plan, has also been called ideational apraxia (Marcuse, 1904; Pick, 1905). These patients have difficulty sequencing acts. For example, when attempting to make a sandwich, the patient with ideational apraxia may cut each slice of bread in half, before putting on the ham, cheese, and mustard. As noted by Pick (1905), most patients with this type of ideational apraxia have a degenerative dementia (such as Alzheimer disease) or a confusional state.

Most patients with ideomotor apraxia improve with actual object use; however, De Renzi et al. (1968) reported patients who made gross errors with the use of actual tools. De Renzi et al. considered the inability to use actual tools a sign of ideational apraxia. Although the inability to use actual tools may be induced by a conceptual disorder (see below), Zangwell (1960) noted that failure to use actual tools may be related to a severe production disorder, ideomotor apraxia. However, as we will discuss in the next section, the nature of the error may reveal if the patient is suffering from a production or conceptual disorder.

Pathophysiology

Most patients with ideational apraxia are suffering from some form of dementia. Both lesion (Mateer, 1999) and functional imaging studies (Wildgruber et al., 1999) suggest that the frontal lobes are critical for sequencing. Vascular or arteriosclerotic dementia is more often associated with frontal dysfunction than is early Alzheimer disease and vascular dementia is more often associated with sequencing deficits (Starkstein et al., 1996). No studies, however, have attempted to determine which forms of dementia are most frequently associated with ideational apraxia. Although most of the apraxic disorders discussed in the chapter are associated primarily with left hemisphere injury, it appears that the lesions that cause ideational apraxia, such as those associated with degenerative dementias, are not lateralized (Jason, 1983). The loci of lesions that induce ideational apraxia, however, remain to be determined.

CONCEPTUAL APRAXIA

Loss of Tool–Action Associative Knowledge

Whereas patients with ideomotor apraxia make production (e.g., spatial and temporal) errors when pantomiming, imitating, or even using actual tools, patients with conceptual apraxia make content errors resulting from an inability to select the correct actions associated with the use of specific tools, utensils, or objects (tool–object action knowledge) (Ochipa et al., 1989). For example, when asked to pantomime how to use a screwdriver, the patient may pantomime a hammering movement, or when provided with a screwdriver, the patient might use the screwdriver as if it were a hammer. In contrast, patients with ideomotor apraxia may make circular arcs rather than twisting their hand on a fixed axis, but despite their spatial and temporal errors, they still may demonstrate the knowledge that screwdrivers need to be turned. Patients with conceptual apraxia appear to have lost or to be unable to access this knowledge.

Content–action errors, such as hammering when shown a screwdriver, can be a manifestation of object agnosia. However, Ochipa et al. (1989) reported a patient who could name tools but used them inappropriately. For example, when attempting to brush his teeth, he used a tube of toothpaste as a toothbrush, and when attempting to eat he used a knife to stir his iced tea. Because this patient could name the tool, he was not agnosic. However, because he could not associate the correct action with the tool, he was considered to have a conceptual apraxia.

Loss of Tool–Object Associative Knowledge

Patients with conceptual apraxia may also be unable to recall which tool is associated with an object (tool–object association knowledge). For example, when shown a nail that has been partially driven into a piece of wood, patients with this disorder may select a screwdriver instead of a hammer from an array of other tools. This conceptual defect may also be in the verbal domain: The patient may be unable to name or point to a tool when its function is described, even though he or she can name the actual tool and also point to the correct tool when named by the examiner. He or she might also be unable to describe verbally the function of a particular tool.

Loss of Mechanical Knowledge

Patients with conceptual apraxia may also be unaware of the mechanical advantage afforded by tools (mechanical knowledge). Therefore, when they are presented with a partially driven-in nail and are expected to complete the task without an available hammer, these patients may not select an alternate tool that is hard, rigid, and heavy, such as a wrench or pliers. Instead, they may select an alternative tool that is flexible and lightweight, such as a handsaw.

One of the highest levels of mechanical knowledge is the ability to invent or construct tools. Patients with conceptual apraxia may also be unable to construct tools (tool fabrication).

Because patients with Alzheimer disease may have impaired semantic memory even early in the course of the disease, Ochipa et al. (1992) studied patients with degenerative dementia of the Alzheimer type for the three components of conceptual apraxia: (a) tool–action knowledge (e.g., screwdrivers are twisted); (b) object–tool knowledge (e.g., nails are pounded in by a hammer; and (c) mechanical knowledge, such as selecting an effective alternative tool (a wrench can be used to pound in a nail) or making a tool. These investigators found that patients with Alzheimer disease often do have conceptual apraxia. When compared to controls, they were impaired on all three components. This study also revealed that some or all of these three elements of conceptual apraxia may be present in patients who have neither ideomotor apraxia nor a semantic language impairment.

Heilman et al. (1997) demonstrated that conceptual apraxia can also be caused by focal cerebral diseases, such as cerebral infarction. In right-handed patients the responsible lesions were primarily in the left hemisphere. Further evidence that these representations are lateralized comes from the observation of a patient who had a callosal disconnection and demonstrated conceptual apraxia of the nonpreferred (left) hand (Watson & Heilman, 1983). The patient with callosal injury described by Liepmann and Maas (1907) also appears to have had elements of conceptual apraxia.

Not all people have conceptual representations confined to their left hemisphere. A patient with conceptual apraxia investigated by Ochipa et al. (1989) was left-handed and rendered conceptually apraxic by a lesion in the right hemisphere, suggesting that both production and conceptual representations have lateralized

representations, and that such representations are usually contralateral to the preferred hand. Left hemisphere lesions associated with conceptual apraxia are found in both the frontal lobe and the inferior parietal lobe, suggesting that the network mediating conceptual knowledge of tools is widely distributed (Heilman et al., 1997). Functional imaging studies of tool conceptual knowledge has also revealed a distributed pattern of activation that includes the inferior frontal lobe and the inferior parietal-posterior temporal area, as well as other regions (i.e., dorsal premotor, cuneus, and inferior temporal areas) (Ebisch et al., 2007).

Pathophysiology

It is not known if the three subtypes of conceptual apraxia (loss of tool–object action knowledge, loss of tool–object association knowledge, and loss of mechanical knowledge, including tool fabrication) are associated with different loci of dysfunction. The lesion associated with conceptual apraxia when testing tool use (tool–object action and tool–object association knowledge) has been localized to the posterior regions of the left hemisphere. Liepmann (1920) thought that this knowledge was stored in the caudal parietal lobe. De Renzi and Lucchelli (1988) thought that the critical area was in the temporoparietal junction. Although Heilman et al. (1997) found that, in right-handed subjects, conceptual apraxia was most frequently associated with left hemisphere lesions, they did not find a critical intrahemispheric locus.

Although ideomotor and conceptual apraxia often co-occur, the finding that there are patients with ideomotor apraxia who do not demonstrate conceptual apraxia and patients with conceptual apraxia who do not demonstrate ideomotor apraxia provides evidence for the postulate that the conceptual and production systems are independent (Rapcsak et al., 1995; Heilman et al., 1997). However, in order to perform skilled acts to command or to visual presentation of tools or objects, conceptual and production systems must interact. The recognition and naming of gestures also requires that these systems interact. This is diagrammatically depicted in Figure 10-4 (Rothi et al., 1991).

BUCCOFACIAL APRAXIA (ORAL APRAXIA)

Clinical

Hughlings Jackson (cited by Taylor, 1932) was the first to describe buccofacial or oral apraxia, which he called "non-protrusion of the tongue." Patients with oral apraxia have difficulty performing purposeful learned skilled movements with the face, lips, tongue, cheeks, larynx, and pharynx. For example, when they are asked to pretend to blow out a match, suck on a straw, lick a sucker, or blow a kiss, they will make incorrect movements. Poeck and Kerschensteiner (1975) described several types of errors. Verbal descriptions may be substituted for the movement: The patient with oral apraxia, when asked to pantomime blowing out a match, may respond by saying, "blow." Other types of errors include movement substitutions and perseverations. Raade et al. (1991) noted that patients with buccofacial apraxia make content, spatial, and temporal errors. Mateer and Kimura (1977) demonstrated that imitation of meaningless movements was also impaired, providing evidence that oral apraxia is not a form of asymbolia. Although many of these patients do not improve with imitation, they often dramatically improve when seeing or using an actual object (e.g., a burning match).

Pathophysiology

To learn if impairment of the same system could account for both buccofacial and limb ideomotor apraxia, Raade et al. (1991) studied the co-occurrence of these apraxias, the type of errors made by apraxic patients, and lesion sites. Forty percent of their subjects had only one type of apraxia. Basso et al. (1980) reported dissociations in 23% of their subjects, and De Renzi et al. (1968) in 28% of theirs. Raade et al. (1991) also found different types of error. Whereas patients with limb apraxia made more errors with transitive than with intransitive oral-facial movements, Raade and colleagues found no difference in errors between transitive versus intransitive movements in patients with buccofacial apraxia.

Tognola and Vignolo (1980) studied patients who were unable to imitate oral gestures. The critical areas where they found lesions included

the frontal and central opercula, anterior insula, and a small area of the first temporal gyrus (adjacent to the frontal and central opercula). Tognola and Vignolo (1980) and Kolb and Milner (1981) found that parietal lesions were not associated with oral apraxia, but they did not test performance to command. Benson et al. (1973), however, described patients with parietal lesions who exhibited oral apraxia to command.

Some authors have classified the phonological selection and sequencing deficit of nonfluent aphasia as "apraxia of speech" (Johns & Darley, 1970; Deal & Darley, 1972). Although Pieczuro and Vognolo (1967) noted that 90% of patients with Broca's aphasia have oral apraxia, it would seem unlikely that buccofacial apraxia causes this phonological disturbance because there are patients with nonfluent aphasia who do not have oral apraxia. It can be argued, however, that oral and verbal apraxias are points along a continuum, sharing a common underlying mechanism. It could be posited that speech requires finer coordination than does response to a command such as, "Blow out a match." Therefore, the effortful, phonologically inaccurate speech of the nonfluent aphasic patient may still be caused by an apraxic disturbance affecting speech more than oral, nonverbal movement. Oral apraxia and the speech production deficits associated with Broca's aphasia often coexist, but they can also be completely dissociated (Heilman et al., 1974), suggesting that, at least in part, the anatomic system that mediates facial praxis is not the same as those that mediate the movements used in speech. Furthermore, because patients may have conduction aphasia with or without oral apraxia (Benson et al., 1973), oral apraxia may coexist with fluent speech. If one attributes the nonfluent disorders of speech, in disorders such as Broca's aphasia, to a generalized oral motor programming deficit, one cannot explain how oral apraxia may be associated with the fluent speech seen in conduction aphasia. In addition, we have examined a patient with aphemia (nonfluent speech with intact writing skills) who did not have oral apraxia. If the speech deficits exhibited by left hemisphere–impaired patients are induced by motor defects, this motor programming defect is strongly linked to the language and phonological systems and is not a generalized oral motor programming deficit.

DISEASES THAT MAY INDUCE APRAXIA

Any disease that destroys or injures portions of the cerebral cortex or portions of the thalamus (Nadeau et al., 1994) may induce apraxia, including stroke (infarctions and hemorrhages), trauma, and tumors. These diseases can cause all the forms of apraxia discussed above. Apraxia may also be associated with a wide variety of degenerative diseases. For example, ideomotor, ideational, and conceptual apraxias are often seen in patients with Alzheimer disease (Ochipa et al., 1989; Rapcsak et al., 1989). Patients with corticobasal degeneration can demonstrate an asymmetrical or even a unilateral ideomotor and limb kinetic apraxia, often as the first symptoms or signs of this disorder (Jacobs et al., 1999). Leiguarda et al. (1997) reported that ideomotor apraxia may be associated with Parkinson disease. We have found that many patients with Parkinson disease have limb-kinetic apraxia (Quencer et al., 2007). Ideomotor apraxia has also been reported to be frequently associated with Huntington disease (Shelton & Knopman, 1991). Finally, apraxia may also be the sign and symptom of developmental disorders and is often observed with autism.

RECOVERY AND TREATMENT

After a stroke, spontaneous recovery from apraxia may occur over a period of months. However, some degree of apraxia may persist (Sunderland, 2000) and may cause disability, as it can interfere with activities of daily living (ADLs; Bjorneby & Reinvang, 1985). Basso et al. (1987) demonstrated that patients with apraxia from anterior lesions recover better than those with posterior lesions. In addition, the presence of a right hemisphere lesion did not appear to retard recovery, suggesting that recovery was mediated by uninjured portions of the left hemisphere. The portions of brain that are responsible for recovery are unknown. There are several options. Damaged areas may recover. Undamaged portions of the hemisphere dominant for praxis may take over function for the damaged areas. Possibly, the nondominant hemisphere may also have a residual ability to compensate for the damaged hemisphere.

Stroke patients are often anosognosic for their apraxic disability (Rothi et al., 1990) or attribute their disabilities to right hemiparesis and inexperience using their left arm. Therefore, these patients often do not request therapy. In addition, little information is presently available on methods for treatment of apraxia, or their efficacy. However, information from animal recovery models (Rothi & Horner, 1983) suggests that therapy should be aimed initially at restitution of function: treating the underlying disorder, so that maximum function can be achieved within the limits set by the recovery process. Smania et al. (2000, 2006) studied treatment of ideomotor apraxia from stroke. Their treatment consisted of a behavioral training program consisting of gesture production exercises made up of gestures with or without symbolic value and related or unrelated to the use of objects. They had 35 sessions, each lasting 50 minutes. With this treatment, they found that the severity of apraxia predicted the ability to perform ADLs. With treatment, there was improvement in apraxia and in the ability to perform ADLs. In addition, compensatory strategies can help apraxic patients develop the skills needed to perform ADLs (van Heugten et al., 1998). Apraxic patients should be taught alternative strategies for performing tasks that pose difficulty for them.

Although many of the symptoms and signs associated with degenerative diseases such as Parkinson disease or even Alzheimer disease can be pharmacologically treated, we could not find reports of the successful pharmacological treatment of apraxia in degenerative disorders. For example, as mentioned above, patients with Parkinson disease have limb-kinetic apraxia (Quencer et al., 2007). Although dopaminergic treatments reduce many of the symptoms and signs of Parkinson disease, treatment with dopaminergic agents does not appear improve apraxia (Gebhardt et al., 2008). Buxbaum and coworkers (2008) have noted in a treatment review paper that, although limb apraxia is a common and disabling disorder of skilled purposeful movements frequently associated with degenerative diseases and stroke, surprisingly few studies have focused on the development of treatment paradigms. Hopefully, in the next edition of this text, we will report additional successful treatment paradigms.

REFERENCES

Agostoni, E., Coletti, A., Orlando, G., & Fredici, G. (1983). Apraxia in deep cerebral lesions. *Journal of Neurology, Neurosurgery, and Psychiatry, 46,* 804–808.

Alexander, G. E., DeLong, M. R., & Strick, P. L. (1986). Parallel organization of functionally segregated circuits linking basal ganglia and cortex. *Annual Review of Neuroscience, 9,* 357–381.

Barrett, A. M., Dore, L. S., Hansell, K. A., & Heilman, K. M. (2002). Speaking while gesturing: The relationship between speech and limb praxis. *Neurology, 58*(3), 499–500.

Basso, A., Capitani, E., Della-Sala, S., Laiacona, M., Spinnler, H. (1987). Recovery from ideomotor apraxia. A study on acute stroke patients. *Brain, 110*(3), 747–760.

Basso, A., Luzzatti, C., & Spinnler, H. (1980). Is ideomotor apraxia the outcome of damage to well-defined regions of the left hemisphere? Neuropsychological study of CT correlation. *Journal of Neurology, Neurosurgery, and Psychiatry, 43,* 118–126.

Benson, F., Shermata, W., Bouchard, R., Segarra, J., Prie, D., & Geschwin, N. (1973). Conduction aphasia. A clinicopathological study. *Archives of Neurology, 28,* 339–346.

Bjorneby, E. R., & Reinvang, I. R. (1985). Acquiring and maintaining self-care skills after stroke. The predictive value of apraxia. *Scandinavian Journal of Rehabilitation Medicine, 17*(2), 75–80.

Brinkman, C., & Porter, R. (1979). Supplementary motor area in the monkey: Activity of neurons during performance of a learned motor task. *Journal of Neurophysiology, 42,* 681–709.

Buschke, H. (1973). Selective reminding for analysis of memory and learning. Journal of Verbal Learning and Verbal Behavior, *12,* 543–550.

Buxbaum, L. J., Haaland, K. Y., Hallett, M., Wheaton, L., Heilman, K. M., Rodriguez, A., & Gonzalez Rothi, L. J. (2008). Treatment of limb apraxia: Moving forward to improved action. *American Journal of Physical Medicine and Rehabilitation, 87*(2), 149–61.

Coslett, H. B., Roeltgen, D. P., Rothi, L. G., & Heilman, K. M. (1987). Transcortical sensory

aphasia: Evidence for subtypes. *Brain Language,* 32, 362–378.

Deal, J. L., & Darley, F. L. (1972). The influence of linguistic and situational variables on phonemic accuracy in apraxia of speech. *Journal of Speech and Hearing Research, 15,* 639–653.

Dee, H. L., Benton, A., & Van Allen, M. W. (1970). Apraxia in relation to hemisphere locus lesion, and aphasia. *Transactions of the American Neurological Association, 95,* 147–150.

De Renzi, E., Faglioni, P., & Sorgato, P. (1982). Modality-specific and supramodal mechanisms of apraxia. *Brain, 105,* 301–312.

De Renzi, E., & Lucchelli, F. (1988). Ideational apraxia. *Brain, 113,* 1173–1188.

De Renzi, E., Pieczuro, A., & Vignolo, L. (1968). Ideational apraxia: A quantitative study. *Neuropsychologia, 6,* 41–52.

Ebisch, S. J., Babiloni, C., Del Gratta, C., Ferretti, A., Perrucci, M. G., Caulo, M., et al. (2007). Human neural systems for conceptual knowledge of proper object use: A functional magnetic resonance imaging study. *Cerebral Cortex, 17*(11), 2744–51.

Fogassi L, Gallese V, Buccino G, Craighero L, Fadiga L, Rizzolatti G. (2001) Cortical mechanism for the visual guidance of hand grasping movements in the monkey: A reversible inactivation study. Brain. Mar; 124(Pt 3): 571–86.

Freund, H., & Hummelsheim, H. (1985). Lesions of premotor cortex in man. *Brain, 108,* 697–733.

Gazzaniga, M., Bogen, J., & Sperry, R. (1967). Dyspraxia following diversion of the cerebral commissures. *Archives of Neurology, 16,* 606–612.

Gebhardt, A., Vanbellingen, T., Baronti, F., Kersten, B., & Bohlhalter, S. (2008). Poor dopaminergic response of impaired dexterity in Parkinson's disease: Bradykinesia or limb kinetic apraxia? *Movement Disorders, 23,* 1701–1706.

Geschwind, N. (1965). Disconnection syndromes in animals and man. *Brain, 88,* 237–294, 585–644.

Geschwind, N., & Kaplan, E. (1962). A human cerebral disconnection syndrome. *Neurology, 12,* 65–685.

Goldstein, K. (1948). *Language and language disturbances.* New York: Grune and Stratton.

Goodglass, H., & Kaplan, E. (1963). Disturbance of gesture and pantomime in aphasia. *Brain, 86,* 703–720.

Graff-Radford, N. R., Welsh, K., & Godersky, J. (1987). Callosal apraxia. *Neurology, 37,* 100–105.

Hanna-Pladdy, B., Mendoza, J. E., Apostolos, G. T., Heilman K. M. (2002) Lateralised motor control: hemispheric damage and the loss of deftness. *J Neurol Neurosurg Psychiatry.* Nov; 73(5):574–7.

Hecaen, H., & de Ajuriaguerra, J. (1964). *Left handedness*. New York: Grune and Stratton.

Hecaen, H., & Sanguet, J. (1971). Cerebral dominance in left-handed subjects. *Cortex, 7*, 19–48.

Haaland, K. Y., Harrington, D. L., & Knight, R. T. (1999). Spatial deficits in ideomotor limb apraxia. A kinematic analysis of aiming movements. *Brain, 122*(6), 1169–1182.

Heilman, K. M. (1973). Ideational apraxia— A re-definition. *Brain, 96*, 861–864.

Heilman, K. M. (1975). A tapping test in apraxia. *Cortex, 11*, 259–263.

Heilman, K. M. (1979). Apraxia. In K. M. Heilman, & E. Valenstein (Eds.), *Clinical Neuropsychology*. New York: Oxford University Press.

Heilman, K. M., Coyle, J. M., Gonyea, E. F., & Geschwind, N. (1973). Apraxia and agraphia in a left-hander. *Brain, 96*, 21–28.

Heilman, K. M., Gonyea, E. F., & Geschwind, N. (1974). Apraxia and agraphia in a right-hander. *Cortex, 10*, 284–288.

Heilman, K. M., Maher, L. M., Greenwald, M. L. & Rothi, L. J. (1997). Conceptual apraxia from lateralized lesions. *Neurology, 49*(2), 457–464.

Heilman, K. M., Meador, K. J., & Loring, D. W. (2000). Hemispheric asymmetries of limb-kinetic apraxia: A loss of deftness. *Neurology, 55*, 523–526.

Heilman, K. M., Rothi, L. J., & Valenstein, E. (1982). Two forms of ideomotor apraxia. *Neurology, 32*, 342–346.

Heilman, K. M., Schwartz, H. D., & Geschwind, N. (1975). Defective motor learning in ideomotor apraxia. *Neurology, 25*, 1018–1020.

Heilman, K. M., Tucker, D. M., & Valenstein, E. (1976). A case of mixed transcortical aphasia with intact naming. *Brain, 99*, 415–426.

Hlustík, P., Solodkin, A., Gullapalli, R. P., Noll, D. C., & Small, S. L. (2002). Functional lateralization of the human premotor cortex during sequential movements. *Brain and Cognition, 49*(1), 54–62.

Jacobs, D. H., Adair, J. C., Macauley, B., Gold, M., Gonzalez-Rothi, L. J., & Heilman, K. M. (1999). Apraxia in corticobasal degeneration. *Brain and Cognition, 40*(20), 336–354.

Jason, G. W. (1983). Hemispheric asymmetries in motor function: II. Ordering does not contribute to left-hemisphere specialization. *Neuropsychologia, 21*(1), 47–58.

Johns, D. F., & Darley, F. L. (1970). Phonemic variability in apraxia of speech. *Journal of Speech and Hearing Research, 13*, 556–583.

Kertesz, A., & Hooper, P. (1982). Praxis and language: The extent and variety of apraxia in aphasia. *Neuropsychologia, 20*, 275–286.

Kimura, D. (1979). Neuromotor mechanisms in the evolution of human communication. In H. D. Steklis, & M. J. Raleigh (Eds.), *Neurobiology of social communication in primates: An evolutionary perspective*. New York: Academic Press.

Kimura, D., & Archibald, Y. (1974). Motor function of the left hemisphere. *Brain, 97*, 337–350.

Kleist, K. (1934). *Gehirnpathologie*. Leipzig: Barth.

Kolb, B., & Milner, B. (1981). Performance of complex arm and facial movements after focal brain lesions. *Neuropsychologia, 19*, 491–503.

Kühn, S., Brass, M. (2008). Testing the connection of the mirror system and speech: How articulation affects imitation in a simple response task. *Neuropsychologia, 46*(5), 1513–21.

Lawrence, D. G., & Kuypers, H. G. J. M. (1968). The functional organization of the motor system in the monkey. *Brain, 91*, 1–36.

Leiguarda, R. C., Pramstaller, P. P., Merello, M., Starkstein, S., Lees, A. J., & Marsden, C. D. (1997). Apraxia in Parkinson's disease, progressive supranuclear palsy, multiple system atrophy and neuroleptic-induced parkinsonism. *Brain, 120*(1), 75–90.

Lichtheim, L. (1885). On aphasia. *Brain, 7*, 733–784.

Liepmann, H. (1920). Apraxia. *Ergbn. Ges. Med., 1*, 516–543.

Liepmann, H., & Mass, O. (1907). Fall von linksseitiger agraphie und apraxie bei rechsseitiger lahmung. *Zeitschrift fur Psychologie und Neurologie, 10*, 214–227.

Marcuse, H. (1904). Apraktiscke symotome bein linem fall von seniler demenz. *Zentralbl. Mervheik. Psychiatrie, 27*, 737–751.

Mateer, C. A. (1999). Executive function disorders: Rehabilitation challenges and strategies. *Seminars in Clinical Neuropsychiatry, 4*(1), 50–59.

Mateer, K., & Kimura, D. (1977). Impairment of nonverbal movements in aphasia. *Brain and Language, 4*, 262–276.

McCarthy, R., & Warrington, E. K. (1984). A two route model of speech production: Evidence from aphasia. *Brain, 107*, 463–485.

Mehler, M. F. (1987). Visuo-imitative apraxia. *Neurology, 37*, 129.

Merians, A. S., Clark, M., Poizner, H., Jacobs, D. H., Adair, J. C., Macauley, B., et al. (1999). Apraxia differs in corticobasal degeneration and left-parietal stroke: A case study. *Brain and Cognition, 40*, 314–35.

Moll, J., De-Oliveira-Souza, R., De-Souza-Lima, F., & Andreiuolo, P. A. (1998). Activation of left intraparietal sulcus using fMRI conceptual praxis paradigm. *Arquivos de neuro-psiquiatria, 56*(4), 808–811.

Mozaz, M., Rothi, L. J., Anderson, J. M., Crucian, G. P., & Heilman, K. M. (2002). Postural knowledge of transitive pantomimes and intransitive gestures. *Journal of the International Neuropsychological Society, 8*(7), 958–62.

Mühlau, M., Hermsdörfer, J., Goldenberg, G., Wohlschläger, A. M., Castrop, F., Stahl, R., et al. (2005). Left inferior parietal dominance in gesture imitation: An fMRI study. *Neuropsychologia, 43*(7), 1086–98.

Nadeau, S. E., Roeltgen, D. P., Sevush, S., Ballinger, W. E., & Watson, R. T. (1994). Apraxia due to a pathologically documented thalamic infarction. *Neurology, 44*(11), 2133–2137.

Nirkko, A. C., Ozdoba, C., Redmond, S. M., Bürki, M., Schroth, G., Hess, C. W., Wiesendanger, M. (2001). Different ipsilateral representations for distal and proximal movements in the sensorimotor cortex: activation and deactivation patterns. Neuroimage. May; 13(5): 825–35.

Ochipa, C., Rapcsak, S. Z., Maher, L. M., Rothi, L. J., Bowers, D., & Heilman, K. M. (1997). Selective deficit of praxis imagery in ideomotor apraxia. *Neurology, 49*(2), 474–480.

Ochipa, C., Rothi, L. J. G., & Heilman, K. M. (1989). Ideational apraxia: A deficit in tool selection and use. *Annals of Neurology, 25*, 190–193.

Ochipa, C., Rothi, L. J. G., & Heilman, K. M. (1990). Conduction apraxia. *Journal of Clinical and Experimental Neuropsychology, 12*, 89.

Ochipa, C., Rothi, L. J. G., & Heilman, K. M. (1992). Conceptual apraxia in Alzheimer's disease. *Brain, 115*, 1061–1071.

Orgogozo, J. M., & Larsen, B. (1979). Activation of the supplementary motor area during voluntary movement in man suggests it works as a supramotor area. *Science, 206*, 847–850.

Penfield, W., & Welch, K. (1951). The supplementary motor area of the cerebral cortex. *Archives of Neurology and Psychiatry, 66*, 289–317.

Pick, A. (1905). *Studien uber motorische apraxia und ihre mahestenhende erscheinungen*. Leipzig: Deuticke.

Pieczuro, A., & Vignolo, L. A. (1967). Studio sperimentale sull'aprassia ideomotoria. *Sisterna Nervoso, 19*, 131–143.

Pistarini, C., Majani, G., Callegari, S., Viola, L. (1991). Multiple learning tasks in patients with ideomotor apraxia. *Rivista de Neurologia, 61*(2), 57–61.

Poeck, K., & Kerschensteiner, M. (1975). Analysis of the sequential motor events in oral apraxia. In K. Zulch, O. Kreutzfeld, & G. Galbraith (Eds.),

Otfried Foerster symposium (pp. 98–109). Berlin: Springer.

Poizner, H., Mack, L., Verfaellie, M. Rothi, L. J. G., & Heilman, K. M. (1990). Three dimensional computer graphic analysis of apraxia. *Brain, 113*, 85–101.

Poizner, H., Soechting, J. F., Bracewell, M., Rothi, L. J. G., & Heilman, K. M. (1989). Disruption of hand and joint kinematics in limb apraxia. *Abstracts - Society for Neuroscience, 15*, 196.2.

Politis, D. G. (2004). Alterations in the imitation of gestures (conduction apraxia). *Revue Neurologique (Paris), 38*(8), 741–5.

Pramsmtaller, P. P., Marsden, C. D. (1996). The basal ganglia and apraxia. *Brain, 119*(1), 319–340.

Quencer, K., Okun, M. S., Crucian, G., Fernandez, H. H., Skidmore, F., & Heilman, K. M. (2007). Limb-kinetic apraxia in Parkinson's disease. *Neurology, 68*(2), 150–151.

Raade, A. S., Rothi, L. J. G., & Heilman, K. M. (1991). The relationship between buccofacial and limb apraxia. *Brain and Cognition, 16*, 130–146.

Rapcsak, S. Z., Croswell, S. C., Rubens, A. B. (1989). Apraxia in Alzheimer's disease. *Neurology, 39*, 664–8.

Rapcsak, S. Z., Ochipa, C., Anderson, K. C., & Poizner, H. (1995). Progressive ideomotor apraxia: Evidence for a selective impairment of the action production system. *Brain and Cognition, 27*(2), 213–236.

Raymer, A. M., Maher, L. M., Foundas, A. L., Heilman, K. M., & Rothi, L. J. (1997). The significance of body part as tool errors in limb apraxia. *Brain and Cognition, 34*(2), 287–292.

Rothi, L. J. G., & Heilman, K. M. (1985). Ideomotor apraxia: Gestural learning and memory. In E. A. Roy (Ed.), *Neuropsychological studies in apraxia and related disorders* (pp. 65–74). New York: Oxford University Press.

Rothi, L. J. G., Heilman, K. M., & Watson, R. T. (1985). Pantomime comprehension and ideomotor apraxia. *Journal of Neurology, Neurosurgery, and Psychiatry, 48*, 207–210.

Rothi, L. J. G., & Horner, J. (1983). Restitution and substitution: Two theories of recovery with application to neurobehavioral treatment. *Journal of Clinical Neuropsychology, 5*, 73–82.

Rothi, L. J. G., Kooistra, C., Heilman, K. M., & Mack, L. (1988a). Subcortical ideomotor apraxia. *Journal of Clinical and Experimental Neuropsychology, 10*, 48.

Rothi, L. J. G., Mack, L., & Heilman, K. M. (1986). Pantomime agnosia. *Journal of Neurology, Neurosurgery, and Psychiatry*, 49, 451–454.

Rothi, L. J. G., Mack, L., & Heilman, K. M. (1990). Unawareness of apraxic errors. *Neurology*, 40 (Suppl. 1), 202.

Rothi, L. J. G., Mack, L., Verfaellie, M., Brown, P., & Heilman, K. M. (1988b). Ideomotor apraxia: Error pattern analysis. *Aphasiology*, 2, 381–387.

Rothi, L. J. G., Ochipa, C., & Heilman, K. M. (1991). A cognitive neuropsychological model of limb praxis. *Cognitive Neuropsychology*, 8, 443–458.

Schwartz, R. L., Barrett, A. M., Crucian, G. P., & Heilman, K. M. (1998). Dissociation of gesture and object recognition. *Neurology*, 50(4), 1186–1188.

Shelton, P. A., & Knopman, D. S. (1991). Ideomotor apraxia in Huntington's disease. *Archives of Neurology*, 48(1), 35–41.

Smania, N., Girardi, F., Domenicali, C., Lora, E., & Aglioti, S. (2000). The rehabilitation of limb apraxia: A study in left-brain-damaged patients. *Archives of Physical Medicine and Rehabilitation*, 81(4), 379–88.

Smania, N., Aglioti, S. M., Girardi, F., Tinazzi, M., Fiaschi, A., Cosentino, A., & Corato, E. (2006). Rehabilitation of limb apraxia improves daily life activities in patients with stroke. *Neurology*, 67(11), 2050–2052.

Starkstein, S. E., Sabe, L., Vazquez, S., Teson, A., Petracca, G., Chemerinski, E., et al. (1996). Neuropsychological, psychiatric, and cerebral blood flow findings in vascular dementia and Alzheimer's disease. *Stroke*, 27(3), 408–14.

Steinthal, P. (1871) Abris der Sprachwissenschift. Berlin Krager.

Sunderland, A. (2000). Recovery of ipsilateral dexterity after stroke. *Stroke*, 31(2), 430–433.

Taylor, J. (1932). *Selected writings*. London: Hodder and Stoughton.

Tognola, G., & Vignolo, L. A. (1980). Brain lesions associated with oral apraxia in stroke patients: A cliniconeuroradiological investigation with the CT scan. *Neurophysiologica*, 18, 257–272.

Valenstein, E., & Heilman, K. M. (1979). Apraxic agraphia with neglect induced paragraphia. *Archives of Neurology*, 36, 506–508.

Van-Heugten, C. M., Dekker, J., Deelman, B. G., Van-Dijk, A. J., Stehmann-Saris, J. C., & Kinebanian, A. (1998). Outcome of strategy training in stroke patients with apraxia: A phase II study. *Clinical Rehabilitation*, 12(4), 294–303.

Verstichel, P., & Meyrignac, C. (2000). Left unilateral melokinetic apraxia and left dynamic apraxia following partial callosal infarction. *Revue Neurologique (Paris)*, 156(3), 274–277.

Watson, R. T., Fleet, W. S., Rothi, L. J. G., & Heilman, K. M. (1986). Apraxia and the supplementary motor area. *Archives of Neurology*, 43, 787–792.

Watson, R. T., & Heilman, K. M. (1983). Callosal apraxia. *Brain*, 106, 391–403.

Wernicke, E. (1874). *Der aphasische symptomenkomplex*. Breslau: Cohn and Weigart.

Wildgruber, D., Kischka, U., Ackermann, H., Klose, U., & Grodd, W. (1999). Dynamic pattern of brain activation during sequencing of word strings evaluated by fMRI. *Cognitive Brain Research*, 7(3), 285–294.

Wyke, M. (1971). The effects of brain lesions on the learning performance of a bimanual coordination task. *Cortex*, 7, 59–71.

Zangwell, O. L. (1960). L'apraxie ideatorie. *Nerve Neurologie.*, 106, 595–603.

11

Agnosia

RUSSELL M. BAUER

Agnosia is a rare neuropsychological symptom defined in the classical literature as a failure of recognition that cannot be attributed to elementary sensory defects, mental deterioration, attentional disturbances, aphasic misnaming, or to unfamiliarity with external stimuli (Frederiks, 1969). Agnosia is characteristically modality-specific; the patient who fails to recognize material presented through a particular sensory channel (e.g., vision) can do so successfully in another channel (e.g., touch, hearing). In this chapter, we will review agnosias in the visual, auditory, and tactile modalities.

One of the most vexing questions about agnosia is whether it is best thought of as an impairment of perception or memory access. Many agnosic patients have obvious perceptual abnormalities, but others do not and instead seem to fail only when the task requires them to access and use stored knowledge about objects. In his classic definition, Teuber (1968) stated that "two limiting sets of conditions: failure of processing and failure of naming . . . bracket . . . the alleged disorder of recognition per se, which would appear in its purest form as a normal percept that has somehow been stripped of its meaning." Teuber's definition implies that, in its purest form, agnosia is a modality-specific disorder of access to meaning-based or semantic memory.

An early observation of agnosia-like phenomena was provided by Munk (1881), who observed that dogs with bilateral occipital lobe excisions neatly avoided obstacles placed in their paths, but failed to react appropriately to objects that had previously frightened or attracted them. Similar observations were made by Horel and Keating (1969, 1972) in the macaque with lesions of the occipital lobe and its projections to temporal lobe. Munk felt that his dogs' behavior resulted from a loss of memory images from previous visual experience and termed the condition *Seelenblindheit* (mind blindness). Nine years later, Lissauer (1890) provided the first detailed report of a recognition disturbance in man, and his views on different varieties of the disturbance have had important historical impact on theory and practice. The term *agnosia* was introduced by Freud (1891), eventually replacing "mind blindness" and related terms such as "asymbolia" (Finkelnburg, 1870) and "imperception" (Jackson, 1876). As with most neurobehavioral syndromes, significant debate has existed regarding the functional mechanisms responsible for, or even the existence of, agnosic phenomena (Bay, 1953).

Interpretation of agnosic syndromes has evolved over time. In the early 20th century, when Gestalt psychology guided perceptual theory, published cases of agnosia were conceptualized with Gestalt concepts in mind (cf. Goldstein & Gelb, 1918; Brain, 1941; Goldstein, 1943). With the reemergence of *disconnection theory* (Geschwind, 1965), cases of agnosia during the 1960s and 1970s were largely viewed as examples of sensory–verbal or sensory–limbic disconnections. More recently, agnosias have increasingly been interpreted within the framework of cognitive neuropsychology (Farah, 1990). A brief review of four broad explanatory models will be undertaken before discussing the major agnosic syndromes.

MODELS OF RECOGNITION

STAGE MODELS

The earliest neuropsychological ideas of the process of object recognition were embodied in *stage models*, which held that the cortex first built up a percept from elementary sensory impressions, and then achieved recognition in a subsequent stage where the percept was "matched" to stored information about the object. Lissauer (1890) argued that recognition proceeds in two stages: apperception and association. By apperception, he meant the conscious perception of a sensory impression; the construction of separate visual attributes into a whole. By association, he meant the imparting of meaning to the content of perception by matching and linking it to a previous experience. A central idea in Lissauer's work is that object or face recognition depends not just upon the integrity of early perceptual processes, but also upon a later, culminating "gnostic" stage, in which perception accesses an internal representation. Only after such a stage has been reached will conscious recognition occur. Patients with defects at the apperceptive stage should show impairments in visual processing, including copying and matching of objects, whereas patients with associative defects should be relatively free of such impairments because their defect is "post-perceptual."

Although Lissauer's two-stage model has been historically important, recent analyses of normal and disordered perception have raised serious questions about its ability to accommodate the clinical data. The apperceptive stage is itself further divisible into a number of constituent visual abilities that can be selectively impaired with appropriately placed lesions (Humphreys & Riddoch, 1987; Farah, 1990; Kaas, 1995). Also, it is now clear that perception is not entirely normal in the vast majority of so-called associative agnosic patients (Bauer & Trobe, 1984; Humphreys & Riddoch, 1987; Levine & Calvanio, 1989). Despite these problems, the apperceptive–associative distinction remains a useful descriptive framework, and will be used to organize the presentation of clinical material in this chapter.

DISCONNECTION MODELS

In 1965, Geschwind, in his classic paper on disconnection theory, defined agnosia in a different way. In Geschwind's view, agnosia resulted from a disconnection between visual perception and the language system. Geschwind cited anatomic evidence from the syndrome of visual object agnosia which, in his view, was most often seen in the context of left mesial occipital lobe damage. According to Geschwind, this lesion not only induced a right homonymous hemianopia, but also affected the callosal splenium, preventing information perceived in the intact right hemisphere from reaching the left hemisphere language areas. In advancing this hypothesis, Geschwind described patients who failed to identify or name objects on formal testing but later used or interacted normally with the object in vivo. In bringing attention to these phenomena, Geschwind provided clear evidence that recognition is not a unitary phenomenon. He wrote,

A fundamental difficulty has been in the acceptance of a special class of defects of "recognition," lying somewhere between defects of "perception" and "naming." What indeed are the criteria for recognition and is it a single function? I believe that there is no single faculty of recognition, but that the term covers the totality of all the associations aroused by any object. Phrased another way, we "manifest" recognition by responding appropriately; to the extent that any appropriate response occurs, we have shown "recognition." But this view abolishes the notion of a unitary step of "recognition"; instead, there are multiple parallel processes of appropriate response to a stimulus. To describe the behavior correctly we must describe the pattern of loss and preservation of responses to each particular type of stimulus.

(Geschwind, 1965)

It is now clear that disconnection theory cannot, by itself, account for the fact that most agnosic patients show abnormal verbal *and nonverbal* processing of viewed objects. However, the idea that "recognition" manifests itself in multiple, sometimes dissociable, ways is a critical concept. The answer to the basic question, "Did the patient recognize?" depends on input, processing, and output requirements of the task used to assess recognition performance.

COMPUTATIONAL MODELS

The models proposed by Lissauer and Geschwind received significant impetus from the study of visual recognition disorders. An alternative approach is to begin by accounting for normal perceptual phenomena and to then determine whether such an account can explain recognition failures observed in the clinic. This approach begins by specifying the tasks that sensory/perceptual systems must perform in order to achieve the kind of powerful and flexible recognition abilities we as humans possess. We are able to recognize everyday objects and faces with remarkable ease across wide ranges in viewing distance, orientation, and illumination. We are able to "infer" depth, volume, and structure from relatively impoverished two-dimensional stimuli such as photographs and line drawings. We can determine with immediate certainty whether a pictured and real object are the same or different, or whether they would be used together. Thus, from perceptual analysis, we can derive an enormous amount of structural and semantic information about the world around us.

What is required to perform all these remarkable functions? In his attempt to answer this question, Marr (1982) started with the assumption that the brain must store some form of codified, symbolic description (a "representation") of known objects/faces that is sufficiently flexible to accommodate the perceptual variations inherent in everyday recognition tasks. His analysis led him to postulate three types

of representations, which he referred to as the primal sketch, the viewer-centered or 2½-dimensional (2½-D sketch, and the object-centered or three-dimensional (3-D) sketch. The *primal sketch* represents intensity changes across the field of vision, resulting in a way of specifying the two-dimensional geometry (shape) of the image. The *2½-D sketch* represents the spatial locations of visible surfaces from the point of view of the observer. This type of representation is computed on the basis of the spatial relationship between viewer and object, and is therefore referred to as a "viewer-centered" or "viewpoint-dependent" description. The *3-D sketch* specifies the configuration of object surfaces, features, and shapes in an object-centered/viewpoint-independent coordinate frame. That is, this frame (in which shapes and features are represented in terms of their location *on the object*), yields a description that is not dependent upon the observer's point of view since simple rotation would not alter the spatial relationships among features of the object. Presumably, achieving this kind of description is essential to flexible object recognition, although it is obvious that specific objects could be sometimes be recognized using only a 2½-D sketch (see below).

Marr's theoretical position is important because it provides an a priori conceptual approach to the study of object recognition disturbances. Indeed, we will see that Marr's ideas about multiple object representations provides an useful framework within which to understand the various ways that recognition can become disordered. Marr's ideas have led to the development of new, more refined, clinical assessment tools, and have clarified some of the intractable problems in this area. They also remind us that the various tests used to tap the apperceptive and associative stages of object recognition impose different demands on the recognition apparatus.

A computational model set in neural terminology has been proposed by Damasio (1989). Like its ancestors in the parallel-distributed processing framework (McClelland & Rumelhart, 1986; Goldman-Rakic, 1988), Damasio's model suggests that perception involves the evocation of a neural activity pattern in primary and first-order association cortex that corresponds to the various perceptual features extracted from viewed objects. Downstream, these features come together in so-called *local convergence zones*, which serve to bind the pattern of features into an "entity" (e.g., object). Damasio specifically rejects the view that recognition involves the activation of a "packaged," locally stored memory representation of the stimulus. Instead, recognition occurs when the neural pattern defining a specific entity is reactivated in a time-locked fashion (in response to stimulation). The most important feature of this approach is that *no fundamental distinction between perception and memory is made*. That is, information about previously encountered items is stored in a pattern of neural activity, not in a localized representation. In this sense, recognition is indeed "re-cognition." Because the memory–perception distinction is abolished, this model renders irrelevant the question: "Is agnosia a perceptual or memory deficit?" Damasio's model predicts that there can be no disorder of object recognition without attendant perceptual dysfunction. As we shall see, this seems entirely consistent with the behavior of most associative agnosics.

COGNITIVE NEUROPSYCHOLOGICAL MODELS

Cognitive neuropsychological models attempt to outline, in cognitive terms, the functional components involved in object recognition. Such models have received significant attention only in the context of visual recognition. One representative model of object recognition, proposed by Ellis and Young (1988) is depicted in Figure 11-1. In this model, the initial, viewer-centered, and object-centered representations correspond to Marr's three levels of object description. According to Ellis and Young, the process of recognition begins by comparing viewer-centered and object-centered representations to stored structural descriptions of known objects (so-called *object recognition units* [ORUs]). The ORU acts as an interface between visual representations (which describes what an object looks like) and semantic information (which describes the object's functional properties and attributes). When information in viewer- and object-centered representations adequately match structural information in some ORU, the ORU becomes activated. This gives rise to a sense of familiarity and

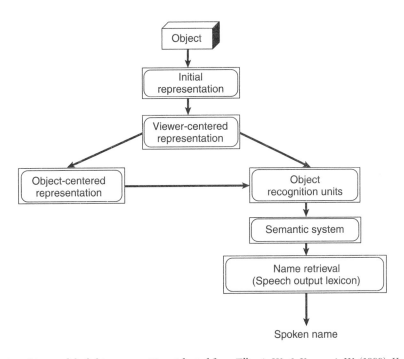

Figure 11–1. A working model of object recognition. Adapted from Ellis, A. W., & Young, A. W. (1988). *Human cognitive neuropsychology*. Hillsdale NJ: Lawrence Erlbaum, with permission of the publisher.

unlocks semantic information about the object. Since the ORU receives independent input from viewer- and object-centered representations, it can be activated by either independently if a sufficient match is obtained. Name retrieval occurs in the final stage of the model. Its position at the bottom of the model assumes that the semantic system does not contain a record of the object's name, but can retrieve the name from a separate store or lexicon. There is no direct link between ORU and speech output lexicon; all retrieval of object names occurs via the semantic representation. Deficits prior to the level of the ORU roughly correspond to Lissauer's apperceptive agnosic classification; defects subsequent to this point are more or less associative.

CRITERIA OF RECOGNITION

In the literature, three classes of responses have been used to provide evidence that an object has been recognized. First, the patient's ability to *overtly identify the stimulus* can be assessed. Responses in this category include confrontation naming, pointing, and demonstrating the use of the object in its presence. The second class involves *responses that indicate semantic knowledge about the object*. Tasks eliciting responses of this type include sorting and grouping objects on the basis of functional characteristics. It is obviously important to know whether an agnosic patient can group unrecognized objects with other semantically similar objects. If the patient can do this, some degree of meaningful information is being extracted from the stimulus. Third, the presence or absence of *discriminative responses adequate to the stimulus* (e.g., correct object use in the absence of direct naming or recognition, physiological or behavioral discrimination, and similar effects) can be assessed. These three response classes measure different levels of performance in tasks of object recognition, and may be dissociated in specific instances. For example, a patient may "recognize" an object (by emitting a discriminative response to it or by sorting it with other like objects), without being able to identify it. Dissociations *within* a class (e.g., a patient who cannot name an object but who can demonstrate how it is used) are also informative.

CLINICAL PHENOMENA

VISUAL AGNOSIA

The patient with visual agnosia cannot identify visually presented material even though language, memory, and general intellectual functions are preserved at sufficient levels, so that their impairment cannot account singly or in combination for the failure to recognize. The recognition defect is modality-specific; identification is immediate and certain when the patient is presented the stimulus in other sensory modalities.

When the patient fails to name but can indicate visual recognition by verbal description or demonstrating the object in use, the failure is usually considered to be "anomic" in nature. Unlike the agnosic patient, the anomic patient generally does not improve when the material is presented through another sensory modality (Spreen, Benton, & Van Allen, 1966; Goodglass, Barton, & Kaplan, 1968), and is less apt to perform normally when asked to produce lists of words in specific categories, to complete open-ended sentences, or to respond to definitions. The conversational speech of the anomic patient may alert the examiner to the possibility of difficulty on visual confrontation naming because it contains word-finding pauses, circumlocutions, semantic paraphasias, and a general lack of substantives (see Chapter 2, on Aphasia).

Visual agnosia has been classified in a number of different ways. The most widely known classification is Lissauer's (1890) apperceptive–associative distinction discussed earlier, which, from a clinical perspective, is based primarily on the severity of perceptual impairment. Visual agnosia has also been classified according to the specific category of visual material that cannot be recognized. Impairments in the recognition of faces (prosopagnosia), colors (color agnosia), objects (object agnosia), and an agnosic inability to read (agnosic alexia) have been described in isolation and in various combinations (Farah, 1991). The co-occurrence of associative visual object agnosia with alexia, color agnosia, and prosopagnosia is common, although not obligatory.

Some types of agnosia (e.g., visual object agnosia) prevent the recognition not only of the *specific identity* of an object, but also of the general *semantic class* to which it belongs. Other forms of agnosia (e.g., prosopagnosia) allow the ability to recognize the general nature of the object (e.g., a face), but prevent appreciation of its *individual identity within that class*. It is not yet clearly established that this distinction has direct biological relevance. It is possible that specific identity discriminations (e.g., "That's *my* wallet"), are more visually or semantically demanding than more general ones (e.g., "That's *a* wallet") and that certain classes of objects (e.g., faces) place special demands on sensory/perceptual systems (Damasio, Damasio, & Van Hoesen, 1982; Warrington & Shallice, 1984). It is also possible that certain classes of objects demand qualitatively different types of processing that differ in kind, rather than degree, from processes involved in recognizing other objects (Farah, Wilson, Drain, & Tanaka, 1998). We will consider these issues later when we describe some strikingly specific agnosias.

Apperceptive Visual Agnosia

The term *apperceptive agnosia* has been applied to a broad spectrum of patients who have in common some measurable impairment at the perceptual level, but whose elementary sensory functions appear to be relatively intact. Farah (1990) points out that the term has been applied to a heterogeneous range of disabilities from patients whose visual impairments prevent them from negotiating their surroundings (Luria, Pravdina-Vinarskaya, & Yarbuss, 1963) to those without in vivo impairments in object recognition who fail specialized perceptual tests that require patients to match stimuli across different views (Warrington & Taylor, 1973). The majority of cases have resulted from carbon monoxide poisoning (Adler, 1944; Benson & Greenberg, 1969; Mendez, 1988; Milner & Heywood, 1989; Milner, Perrett, Johnston, et al., 1991), bilateral cerebrovascular accident (CVA; Stauffenberg, 1914), basilar artery occlusion (Caplan, 1980), or bilateral posterior cortical atrophy (Benson, Davis, & Snyder, 1988; Mendez, Mendez, Martin, et al., 1990). The behavior of these patients suggests severe visual difficulties. Many are recovering from a state of cortical blindness. Because of their helplessness in the visual environment, many are considered blind until they report that they can indeed see or until they are observed avoiding obstacles in their environment. Standard testing then reveals normal or near normal acuity in the spared visual field. Preservation of sufficient field and acuity to allow for recognition distinguishes the apperceptive agnosic from the patient with Anton' syndrome (Anton, 1899), which includes the denial of cortical blindness.

Apperceptive agnosic patients may have defects in early perceptual organization, and may fail tests that require grouping based on similarity or proximity or that depend on integration of multiple stimuli. They cannot draw misidentified items or match them to sample. They are generally unable to point to objects named by the examiner. The impairment most often involves elements of the visual environment that require shape and pattern perception. The recognition of even the simplest of line drawings may be impossible. However, bright and highly saturated colors may be better recognized. Some patients can trace the outlines of letters, objects, or drawings but often retrace them over and over because they lose the starting point. Many patients behave as if they are unaware or unconcerned about their deficit until they are given a visual recognition task. They will then acknowledge that they do not see clearly. Others are aware of their difficulty but try to conceal it by complaining that they need new glasses or that the lighting or quality of the line drawings used for recognition is poor.

Many patients complain that their visual environment changes or disappears as they try to scrutinize it. Recognition may improve when visual stimuli are moved or, in the case of reading, if letters are traced (Botez, 1975). This condition, known as *visual static agnosia* may reflect residual capacity of the subcortical (tectopulvinar) visual system (Denny-Brown & Fischer, 1976; Zihl & Von Cramon, 1979; Celesia, Archer, Kuroiwa, & Goldfader, 1980). Patients may claim they need new glasses, or may complain about poor lighting. One of our patients, a retired architect, remarked condescendingly about the poor quality of our line-drawn stimuli. It has always been difficult to characterize the visual performance of these patients because of large inter- and intraindividual variability; in fact, there may be multiple forms of deficit (Shelton, Bowers, Duara, & Heilman, 1994). Cognizant of this variability, Farah (1990) attempted to bring order out of chaos by subdividing apperceptive agnosic patients into four behaviorally meaningful categories.

Narrow. Apperceptive Agnosia. Representative cases in this category include patients reported by Adler (1944), Alexander & Albert (1983), Benson & Greenberg (1969), Campion & Latto (1985), Gelb & Goldstein (1918), and Milner et al. (1991). These patients all have "seemingly adequate" elementary visual function (acuity, visual fields, luminance detection, color vision, depth and movement perception) but display a striking inability to recognize, match, copy, or discriminate simple visual forms. Benson and Greenberg's patient is a case in point.

The patient was a 25-year-old victim of accidental carbon monoxide poisoning. For several months, he was thought to be blind, but one day he was seen navigating the corridor in his wheelchair. He could name colors and could often follow moving visual stimuli, but could not identify by vision alone objects placed before him. He could occasionally identify the letters "x" and "o" if allowed to see them drawn, or if they were moved slowly before his eyes. Visual acuity was at least 20/100 measured by his ability to indicate the orientation of the letter "E." He could detect the movement of small objects at standard distances and could reach for fine threads on a piece of paper. Optokinetic nystagmus was elicited bilaterally with fine 1/8-inch marks on a tape. Visual fields were normal to 3 mm wide objects with minimal inferior constriction bilaterally to 3 mm red and green objects. There was an impersistence of gaze with quasi-random searching movements, particularly when inspecting an object. His recognition deficit included objects, photographs, body parts, letters, and numbers, but not colors. He could tell which of two objects was larger and could detect very small movements of small targets. He easily identified and named objects when he could touch them or hear the sounds

they made. He was totally unable to match or copy material that he could not identify. However, he was taught to apply a name to each object in a small group of objects that were presented to him one at a time on a piece of white paper. For instance, after he was repeatedly shown the back of a red and white playing card and informed of its identity, he was able on later exposures to identify it. He was thus able to use color and size cues to learn and remember the names of various objects in a closed set. However, when these objects were placed out of context, he was no longer able to name them. His recent and remote memory, spontaneous speech, comprehension of spoken language, and repetition were intact. On psychophysical testing, he was able to distinguish small differences in the luminance (0.1 log unit) and wavelength (7–10 microns) of a test aperture subtending a visual angle of approximately 2 degrees, but was unable to distinguish between two objects of the same luminance, wavelength, and area when the only difference between them was shape. Thus, the patient seemed to have specific impairments in shape perception, with some sparing of perception of other visual attributes. Benson and Greenberg (1969) referred to the patient's defect as a "visual form agnosia."

Many of these patients develop compensatory strategies, such as tracing of the outline of stimuli or executing small head movements as they explore their visual environment, perhaps as an attempt to use movement cues to aid form detection. The patient reported by Landis, Graves, Benson, and Hebben (1982), developed an apperceptive visual agnosia secondary to mercury intoxication, and presented with a clinical picture similar to that of the famous patient *Schn.* (Goldstein & Gelb, 1918). The patient developed a strategy whereby he would trace letters, parts of letters, or words with the left hand alone or with both hands. He could trace simple geometric figures if the point of departure for tracing was unimportant. With more complex figures, irrelevant lines misled him. He developed a sophisticated system of codes that aided in the identification of individual letters. Goldstein and Gelb's (1918) patient *Schn.* also developed a tracing strategy by using both his head and hand. Both patients' recognition abilities deteriorated instantly if they were prevented from using kinesthetic feedback. The relative impairment in form and orientation perception with relative sparing of visuomotor capability has recently been reframed in terms of Milner and Goodale's (1995) reformulated ventral-dorsal visual stream concept (Karnath et al., 2009). Karnath's patient had a visual form agnosia resulting from a bilateral posterior cerebral artery (PCA) stroke that involved the medial aspects of the occipitotemporal cortex, including the fusiform and lingual gyri and the posterior cingulated gyrus. In the right hemisphere, the parahippocampal gyrus and cuneus was also affected. The authors suggested that the recognition defect arose from ventral visual stream damage, whereas preserved visuomotor capacity was attributed to intact dorsal stream structures.

Dorsal Simultanagnosia. The term *simultanagnosia* was introduced by Wolpert (1924) to refer to a condition in which the patient is unable to appreciate the meaning of a whole picture or scene even though the individual parts are "well-recognized." Luria (1959) used the term literally to indicate the inability to see or attend to more than one object at a time. Representative cases have been reported by Hecaen & de Ajuriaguerra (1954), Holmes (1918), Luria et al. (1963), and Tyler (1968). Most of these patients sustained bilateral parieto-occipital damage, although cases with superior occipital (Rizzo & Hurtig, 1987) or inferior parietal damage (Kase et al., 1977, Case 1) have been reported. Simultanagnosia can also present in the context of generalized or localized degenerative disease (Graff-Radford et al., 1993; Ardila, Rosselli, Arvizu, & Kuljis, 1997; Beversdorf & Heilman, 1998; Mendez, 2000; Tang-Wai, Graff-Radford, Boeve, et al., 2004).

As a result of their visual defect, these patients are impaired in counting tasks (Holmes, 1918) and on tasks that require the naming of a number of objects presented together (Luria et al., 1963). The disorder may also be evident in a dramatic inability to interpret the overall meaning of a line drawing or picture, with performance on such tasks often being a haphazard, inferred reconstruction of fragmented picture elements. Based on the study of such

patients, Luria (Luria, 1959; Luria et al., 1963) concluded that simultanagnosia represents a complex perceptuomotor breakdown of the active, serial feature-by-feature analysis necessary for processing elements of a visual scene or pattern. In the most severe cases, prominent features available in the stimulus array may themselves be fragmented and distorted.

Luria equated simultanagnosia with a perceptual defect often found as part of Balint syndrome (Balint, 1909; Husain & Stein, 1988), which consists of: (a) psychic paralysis of fixation with an inability to voluntarily look into the peripheral field (Tyler, 1968; Karpov, Meerson, & Tonkongii, 1979); (b) optic ataxia, manifested by clumsiness or inability to manually respond to visual stimuli, with mislocation in space when pointing or reaching to visual targets (Boller et al., 1975; Haaxma & Kuypers, 1975; Levine, Kaufman, & Mohr, 1978; Damasio & Benton, 1979), and (c) a disturbance of visual attention mainly affecting the periphery of the visual field resulting in a dynamic concentric narrowing of the effective field (Hecaen & Ajuriaguerra, 1954; Levine & Calvanio, 1978; DeRenzi, 1982). Balint syndrome is almost invariably associated with *large* biparietal lesions (but see Watson & Rapcsak, 1987), and is especially severe when frontal lobe lesions are also found (Hecaen & Ajuriaguerra, 1954). Frontal lobe involvement may lead to particularly severe psychic paralysis and optic ataxia, presumably because of disruption in visual-motor mechanisms and because of the role played by frontal eye fields and surrounding prefrontal cortex in the control of saccadic eye movements and visual attention (Lynch & McClaren, 1989). Some of these patients may represent the "flip side" of visual form agnosia in that they show severe impairment in the dorsal visual pathway (and associated impairment in action vision) with relative sparing of the ventral stream.

Visual fields may be normal by standard perimetric testing, but shrink to "shaft vision" when the patient concentrates on the visual environment. Performance may be worse in one hemifield, more often on the left. A striking example of narrowing of the effective visual field is given by Hecaen and Ajuriaguerra (1954; Case 1). While their patient's attention was focused on the tip of a cigarette held between his lips, he failed to see a match flame offered him and held a few inches away. The three subjects described by Rizzo and Hurtig (1987) reported intermittent disappearance of a light target during electro-oculography (EOG)-verified fixation, suggesting that a disorder of attentional mechanisms that permit sustained awareness of visual targets is involved. Verfaellie, Rapcsak, and Heilman (1990), using Posner's attentional cueing task, found that their patient with Balint syndrome had difficulty shifting attention to the left or right visual field, and benefited only from cues directing attention to the upper visual field. This patient also demonstrated a loss of spontaneous blinking, which may normally participate in a complex system mediating saccadic eye movement, sensory relay, and attentional deployment (Watson & Rapcsak, 1987). Denberg, Jones, and Tranel (2009) reported a patient with dorsal simultanagnosia as a visual variant of Alzheimer disease who showed covert psychophysiological recognition of complex, emotionally charged pictures despite a total inability to verbally recognize picture content, suggesting spared nonconscious recognition.

Simultanagnosia-like phenomena sometimes occur in normal vision under the right circumstances. When visual or auditory stimuli are presented in rapid succession, the second instance of a stimulus will sometimes not be seen (or heard) if it occurs within 80–150 ms of the first presentation. This phenomenon is known as *repetition blindness* (RB). Theoretical accounts of RB suggest that recognition/awareness depends on linking an input representation of a stimulus (a "type") to representation that specifies its spatiotemporal context (a "token"). By this account, processing of tokens takes time and consumes processing capacity. Repetition blindness occurs when the visual system fails to individuate the second type–token link (Kanwisher, 1987). A recent study has shown that a patient with dorsal simultanagnosia shows RB for pictures, letters, and drawings that was diminished by semantic relatedness, but not affected by the extent of visual similarity between objects (Coslett & Lie, 2008). These findings indicate that the patient was able to compute object identity, but was unable to link the results of that computation

to a representation coding spatial location. The patient had suffered multiple strokes and had become unable to "see" after right parietal infarction. Magnetic resonance imaging (MRI) revealed small areas of old infarction involving the left middle temporal gyrus, the left middle frontal gyrus, both parietal lobes, and underlying white matter. Coslett and colleagues suggest, in a variant of type–token theory, simultanagnosia may entail a defect at the point at which information computed in the ventral visual pathway (object-based perceptual information) is bound together with information on object location computed in the dorsal stream (Coslett & Saffran, 1991; Coslett & Lie, 2008). Similarly extensive evidence of perceptual and semantic processing in neglected or extinguished field in other disorders of perceptual awareness have been documented (Driver & Vuillemeir, 2001).

Ventral Simultanagnosia. A second group of simultanagnosias appears to have lesions restricted to the left occipitotemporal junction. The primary feature that distinguishes these patients from dorsal simultanagnosic patients is that they succeed on dot-counting tasks and seem less impaired in negotiating their natural environment. Whether the disorder is one of degree or kind is debatable, although the anatomic pathology of this group is clearly distinct from that seen in dorsal simultanagnosia. The patients of Kinsbourne and Warrington (1962), Levine and Calvanio (1978), and Warrington and Rabin (1971), all presenting as letter-by-letter readers, are representative cases.

Kinsbourne and Warrington (1962) described a defect in simultaneous form perception, which they believed accounted for the reading disturbance in these patients. Levine and Calvanio (1978) found that patients with simultanagnosia would report only one or two letters when presented with three letters simultaneously. If told in advance which letter to name, they successfully reported any single letter; if told after the exposure which letter to name, they performed poorly. The authors interpreted the defect as impairment in the perceptual analysis of compound visual arrays. Patients with this form of simultanagnosia thus do not perceive more than one object at a time. Their problem is compounded by an inability to relate small portions of what they see to the remainder of the stimulus by scanning.

Perceptual Categorization Deficit. This category includes patients who have no problem with real-life recognition of objects but whose defect must be elicited experimentally. These patients, most of whom have unilateral posterior right hemisphere lesions, have difficulties matching different views of two- or three-dimensional objects. Such cases have been reported by DeRenzi, Scotti, and Spinnler (1969), Warrington and Taylor (1973), and Warrington and James (1988). Because they may recognize real-life objects, these patients are usually not considered agnosic, but are included in Farah's (1990) classification system because they appear to have a special kind of perceptual defect. Although Warrington's studies had localized the defect to the posterior right hemisphere, patients with unilateral left hemisphere lesions may also have the defect (Mulder, Bouma, & Ansink, 1995). In Marr's (1982) terms, these patients fail to achieve a viewpoint-independent description of objects, and thus are impaired whenever an object identification or matching task requires them to match stimuli across views or to recognize a stimulus presented from a highly unconventional or noncanonical viewpoint.

Most of the controversy regarding the existence of agnosia has involved the apperceptive types, and some have suggested that agnosia as a distinct entity does not exist (Bay, 1953). These criticisms are weakened by the fact that severe sensory abnormalities in the context of visual field defects, perceptual derangement, and dementia do not necessarily lead to agnosic symptoms (Ettlinger, 1956). The converse also seems true; one of Ettlinger's patients with prosopagnosia, performed at a higher level on visuosensory tests than did most of the nonagnosic patients. Studies by Levine and Calvanio (1978) suggest that patients with agnosia do not differ from normal subjects in sensation time or susceptibility to backward masking. It is evident, therefore, that visual sensory abnormalities in elementary visual processing (e.g., sensation time and local adaptation time) are often insufficient in themselves to produce an agnosia-like recognition defect. It is true, however, that many patients with visual agnosia have elements of this type of disturbance and many also have abnormalities in visual attention, search, and exploration. Studies in which stimulus manipulations seek to mimic apperceptive agnosia in normal subjects point to the special importance of perceptual grouping processes in producing the defect (Vecera & Gilds, 1998). In some cases, a combination of impaired feature recognition and limited cognitive resources available for processing demanding visual material may be present (Grossman, Galetta, & D'Esposito, 1997).

Although each of the four types of apperceptive agnosia has a relatively consistent lesion profile, it is premature to fully specify a unifying functional anatomy underlying all forms of visual apperceptive agnosia. It is clear that there is no singular entity called "apperceptive visual agnosia." However, it seems reasonable, on clinical and experimental grounds, to conclude that complex visual abilities are made up of dissociable information-processing channels, including segmentation, grouping, figure–ground, form discrimination, color perception, luminance, size, movement, spatial localization, feature integration, and object-location binding (Maunsell & Newsome, 1987; DeYoe & Van Essen, 1988) and that the variability among apperceptive agnosics reflects the fact that these channels can be impaired singly or in combination at the individual case level.

Associative Visual Agnosia

Associative visual agnosia is defined by the presence of a modality-specific object identification defect in the context of a preserved ability to copy and/or match stimuli presented in the affected modality. The degree of perceptual disturbance in this class of patients is different in degree and kind from that seen in apperceptive agnosia, although when tested, visual perception is rarely normal. A number of well-documented cases meeting the above criteria have appeared in the literature, leaving no doubt about the existence of this form of agnosia (Rubens & Benson, 1971; Taylor & Warrington, 1971; Lhermitte, Chedru, & Chain, 1973; Benson, Segarra, & Albert, 1974; Hecaen, Goldblum, Masure, & Ramier, 1974; Newcombe & Ratcliff, 1974; Mack & Boller,

1977; Albert, Soffer, Silverberg, & Reches, 1979; Pillon, Signoret, & Lhermitte, 1981; Davidoff & Wilson, 1985; Feinberg, Schindler, Ochoa, McCarthy & Warrington, 1986; Riddoch & Humphreys, 1987a; Kwan & Farah, 1994).

Pointing to objects named by the examiner, while characteristically impaired, may be better than identifying objects verbally or gesturally. This may reflect the fact that pointing takes place in the context of a closed set, whereas naming an object involves an almost infinite list of potential names. Also, pointing to a named object is an easier task because it does not involve speaking and therefore reduces the chances that an incorrect verbal response will adversely affect nonverbal aspects of stimulus recognition. Picture identification is often more impaired than is the identification of real objects. Identification of line drawings is more impaired than either of these, and impaired identification of drawings or pictures may be the only residual defect after the acute disturbance has cleared. This dissociation is not seen in the naming performance of aphasics (Corlew & Nation, 1975), and may serve as a way of distinguishing agnosia and aphasia.

Impairment of face recognition (prosopagnosia), color recognition (so-called *color agnosia*), and of comprehending written material (alexia) are frequently but not invariably found with associative object agnosia (Farah, 1991). Object agnosia itself is more rare than these other conditions, each of which may occur in isolation or in various combinations. Some authors believe that symptom co-occurrence is a simple "neighborhood sign," while others believe it reflects the fact that certain classes of objects (e.g., objects and faces) share visual processing demands. Tactile and auditory recognition are typically intact, although two patients of Newcombe and Ratcliff (1974) and the patients of Taylor and Warrington (1971) and Feinberg, Gonzalez-Rothi, and Heilman (1986) were unable to identify objects by touch or vision.

The associative agnosic patient not only cannot name seen objects, but also typically fails when asked to demonstrate semantic knowledge about the stimulus or its functional properties. The failure to sort objects and pictures into categories (e.g., articles of clothing, tools, etc.) or to match two different representations

of the same object (a small line drawing of a wrist watch with a real watch) are typical examples. Some agnosic patients can classify objects according to their basic level (Rosch et al., 1976) category (e.g., prosopagnosic patients always identify faces as faces) but are unable to identify the object at a more specific, individual level ("John's face" or "my wallet"). Others can identify neither the general class nor the individual-within-class. Such differences may signal important differences among agnosic syndromes or may more simply reflect the fact that different recognition tasks demand different levels of specificity.

The role played by perceptual factors in associative agnosia has received recent attention. On the one hand, these patients are capable of remarkable visual achievements given the severity of their object recognition disturbances. The patients of Rubens and Benson, Taylor and Warrington, and Newcombe and Ratcliff (Case 1) matched to sample and produced strikingly accurate drawings of pictures and objects they could not identify (Figure 11-2). The patients of Rubens and Benson, and Taylor and Warrington were able to find hidden figures in figure–ground tests. Case 1 of Newcombe and Ratcliff showed no deficits on psychophysical tests of visual function.

On the other hand, two lines of evidence have suggested that perceptual abilities are not normal in many of these patients and that such abnormalities may play a causative role in at least some aspects of the recognition disorder. First, although these patients may be capable of achieving normal scores on tests of copying and matching, qualitative data suggest remarkably consistent evidence of slow, feature-by-feature, or "slavish" drawing and of a reliance on local detail at the expense of the more global aspects of the stimulus (Humphreys & Riddoch, 1987; Levine & Calvanio, 1989; Farah, 1990). For example, Humphreys and Riddoch (1987) provide an exquisitely detailed report of a patient H.J.A., who took hours to complete remarkably accurate drawings of objects he could not identify. Our own experience with the prosopagnosic patient L.F. reveals that performance on difficult facial matching tests (e.g., Benton Test of Facial Recognition), although quantitatively normal, proceeds in a

Figure 11–2. Copies of line drawings by a patient with associative visual agnosia. After copies were made, the patient still misidentified drawings as follows: A: "I still don't know." B: "Could be a dog or any other animal." C: "Could be a beach stump." D: "A wagon or a car of some kind. The larger vehicle is being pulled by the smaller one." (From Rubens and Benson, 1971.)

feature-by-feature manner resulting in extremely prolonged response times. Indeed, convincing evidence exists of often subtle perceptual deficits in at least some well-documented cases of associative visual agnosia (Delvenne, Seron, Coyette, & Rossion, 2004; Duchaine & Nakayama, 2004). Second, changes in perceptual variables can significantly affect the "recognizability" of stimuli (Levine & Calvanio, 1978, 1989; Riddoch & Humphreys, 1987a). Stimulus complexity (e.g., presence of color, morphological similarity between items) appears to exert a strong effect on the frequency of semantic and morphological errors on object naming tasks. Presence of fine-grained visual information contributes to ease of identification (Levine &

Calvanio, 1978). A frequently reported finding is that associative agnosics appear deficient in "gestalt perception," although they may perceive local details relatively normally. Partially covering an item or placing it in unusual context hinders identification. Levine and Calvanio (1989) reported that their associative agnosic patient, L.H., was severely impaired on tasks of "visual closure," the ability to perceive shape, and identity of an object that has been degraded by visual noise (cf. also Farah, 1990). H.J.A., the patient reported by Humphreys and Riddoch (1987) performed poorly on a feature integration task requiring him to detect an upside down T among a group of upright T's. Unlike normal subjects, H.J.A. did not show faster detection when the stimuli were arranged in a discrete circular configuration (as opposed to random presentation), suggesting a defect in integrating local feature details into an overall "gestalt." These findings illustrate why there is growing discontent with the apperceptive–associative distinction, at least in its "strong" form. They also illustrate why models of object recognition that posit no fundamental distinction between perception and memory/association (cf. Goldman-Rakic, 1988; Damasio, 1989) have enjoyed increased attention.

The cases of Kertesz (1979) and Wapner, Judd, and Gardner (1978) further complicate the apperceptive–associative distinction. Kertesz' patient presents a challenge since she had elements of Balint syndrome, visual static agnosia (Botez, 1975), alexia without agraphia, prosopagnosia, and amnestic syndrome. The patient performed poorly on copying tasks (her reproductions were poorly executed and contained only fragmented elements of the associated target stimuli), but matched real objects, line drawings, colors, letters, and geometric figures better than she named or pointed to them. Verbal responses were marked by perseverations and form confusions. The patient had 20/20 acuity (open E method). Computed tomography (CT) scan revealed right frontal and deep left occipital lobe lesions.

Wapner, Judd, and Gardner (1978) presented a case report of visual agnosia in an artist whose drawing skills were assessed in detail. Their patient suffered a cerebral infarction with resulting variable right hemianopia, visual recognition defect, and amnesia. Brain scan revealed bilateral medial occipital infarctions. Visual acuity was 20/70. The patient showed poor visual recognition of objects and drawings in the context of moderately impaired design copying. Interestingly, the patient showed a striking dissociation in qualitative drawing performance between objects he could and could not recognize. With unrecognized objects, his drawings revealed piecemeal, slavish reproduction of recognized elements. Describing his drawing of a telephone dial, he said, "a circle, another circle, a square . . . things keep coming out . . . and this is as though it hooks into something." In contrast, when drawing an object he could identify, the patient relied on preserved structural knowledge of the essential components of the object, producing

a sketch that was faithful to the specific target. He remarked, "can't help but use your natural knowledge in drawing the thing." These two cases are important for two reasons. First, they both showed dissociations *among* various tests classically used to tap the apperceptive level. Second, their combined defects at the levels of perception and recognition underscore the fact that agnosia is the final outcome of many different defects. These considerations lead to the conclusion that associative agnosia, like apperceptive agnosia, is a label that subsumes a continuum of defects. On one end of the continuum are patients who have complex impairments in perceptual integration insufficient to impair copying or basic matching skills (Riddoch & Humphreys, 1987). On the other are patients who are apparently free of even subtle visual impairment, whose defect represents an inability of the visual system to access semantic information about viewed objects (Anaki, Kaufman, Freedman, & Moscovitch, 2007).

Clinicians should be aware of complexities in examining these patients. There is evidence that the initial verbalized response to visual presentation can adversely affect recognition ability in at least some patients. Identification errors are usually morphological confusions or perseverations, although semantic errors are not uncommon. The tendency to perseverate previous naming errors and the disruptive influence of visual naming on tactile identification are examples of this. One might expect that a visual agnosic patient with normal blindfolded tactile naming would perform at least as well when he simultaneously inspects and handles an object. However, the otherwise superior tactile identification of the patients of Ettlinger and Wyke (1961) and Rubens et al. (1978, cited in Rubens, 1979) fell to the much lower level of visual identification alone when the patients were allowed to simultaneously view and handle the objects.

Preventing the contaminating effect of verbal responses is not always easy. Many patients insist on speaking despite strict instructions to remain silent. Case 1 of Oxbury et al. (1969) who was specifically instructed to demonstrate in silence the use of objects shown to her, continued to name them aloud and then to produce an incorrect gesture that corresponded to her verbal misidentification. This same patient, when asked to match a line drawing to one of three real objects, would misname the drawing and then search vainly for the named object. It has been claimed that perseverations represent verbal reports of a lingering visual sensory experience of previously viewed material (Critchley, 1964; Cummings et al., 1982). However, when a patient is asked to draw an object on which such perseverative errors occur, he or she draws the item he or she is viewing, not the item whose name has been perseverated (Rubens & Benson, 1971; Lhermitte & Beauvois, 1973). Successfully copying a misidentified picture generally does not facilitate identification of that picture. This suggests that the motor system generally does not have the ability to cue the visual identification process in most patients, although requiring the patient to write the name (Lhermitte & Beauvois, 1973) or to supply a description (Newcombe & Ratcliff, 1974) instead of naming aloud normalized recognition in one case and enhanced it in the other.

The most common visual field defect in associative agnosia is a dense, right homonymous hemianopia or an upper right quadrantanopia (Albert, Reches, & Silverberg, 1975a). Two left-handed patients with left homonymous hemianopia have been reported (Newcombe & Ratcliff, 1974 [Case 2]; Levine, 1978). Interestingly, reading was spared in these patients. Normal visual fields have also been reported (Davidenkov, 1956; Taylor & Warrington, 1971; Newcombe & Ratcliff, 1974 [Case I]).

The marked variability of performance of patients in the natural setting as opposed to the test setting was noted by Geschwind (1965), who viewed misidentifications as confabulated responses elaborated by the intact speech area pathologically disconnected from intact visual sensory area. Failure to supply the correct gesture results from concomitant disconnection between motor and sensory areas. The common association of visual object agnosia with right homonymous hemianopia, alexia, and color agnosia, a triad occurring in the context of damage to mesial left occipital lobe and nearby posterior callosal fibers, supports the visual–verbal disconnection hypothesis. Authors arguing against the disconnection hypothesis cite (a) the occasional finding of normal visual fields or left

homonymous hemianopia (Cambier et al., 1980), (b) the occasional absence of color agnosia and alexia in the same patient (Newcombe & Ratcliff, 1974 [Case 1]; Levine, 1978), and (c) the question of why a left occipital-splenial lesion produces the syndrome of alexia without agraphia commonly but object agnosia only rarely. The pathology in some cases is inconsistent with a visual–verbal disconnection view. For example, Levine's (1978) patient had a unilateral right occipital lobe resection and was, in fact, able to verbally code some visually presented stimuli with remarkable accuracy (e.g., "Something with 'U' in it," when looking at a padlock). A series of recent cases of associative visual agnosia found consistent damage to the dominant parahippocampal, fusiform, and lingual gyri, but inconsistent damage to the callosal splenium (Feinberg et al., 1994).

Strictly speaking, the imperfect correlation between color agnosia, alexia, and visual object agnosia does not, by itself, invalidate the visual–verbal disconnection hypothesis. It remains possible that there may be highly specific forms of visual–verbal disconnection, and that unilateral or bilateral intrahemispheric disconnection and/or selective destruction of independent pathways mediating various elements of visual recognition play a role (cf. Ratcliff & Ross, 1981). There is, for example, evidence for the specificity of neural pathways for color (Meadows, 1974b; Zeki, 1973, 1977). This kind of specificity is also implicit in the classical work of Hubel and Wiesel (1977). However, more damaging for the visual–verbal disconnection view is the fact that many associative agnosic patients fail on tasks that require *nonverbal* identification, such as functional classification or gesturing.

Since associative agnosia is a heterogeneous disorder, it is not surprising that there is disagreement with regards to its anatomic localization. Some authors (Warrington, 1985) suggest that diffuse damage may be involved, but that a lateralized left hemisphere lesion may be sufficient. Alexander and Albert (1983) argue for a bilateral occipitotemporal localization (cf. also Benson et al., 1974). Geschwind's (1965) visual–verbal disconnection model is based on unilateral damage to the left mesial occipital region and callosal splenium, and other left-sided cases include the patients of Warrington and

McCarthy (1987) and Feinberg et al. (1986, 1994). Levine's (1978) patient shows that associative agnosia can result from a unilateral right occipital lesion. It thus seems likely that multiple forms of associative visual agnosia exist. Patients such as those of Taylor and Warrington (1971) and Newcombe and Ratcliff (1974 [Cases 1 and 2]) with diffuse bilateral disease processes, tactile agnosia, and normal visual fields probably form a group separate from those with right homonymous hemianopia associated with infarction in the territory of the left posterior cerebral artery.

Optic Aphasia

Optic aphasia refers to the condition in which the patient is unable to name visually presented objects but is able to show that he or she recognizes the object by indicating its use, by pointing to it when it is named, or by otherwise demonstrating knowledge of object meaning. Tactile and auditory naming are preserved. Representative cases have been reported by Lhermitte and Beauvois (1973), Riddoch and Humphreys (1987b), Larrabee, Levin, Huff et al. (1985), and Coslett and Saffran (1989a). Whether optic aphasia and associative agnosia differ in degree or kind remains a matter of controversy (De Renzi & Saetti, 1997; Chanoine, Ferreira, Demonet, Nespoulous, & Poncet, 1998), although the recent trend is to consider it a separate entity. The term was introduced by Freund (1889) to describe the deficit of one of his patients with a right homonymous hemianopia and aphasia due to a left parieto-occipital tumor. The patient's naming ability was impaired primarily for visually presented objects. Freund hypothesized a left speech area–right occipital disconnection as the basis for the visual naming deficit in the intact visual field.

The patient of Lhermitte and Beauvois (1973) represents a good example of the syndrome. Their patient suffered a left posterior cerebral artery territory infarction and presented with right homonymous hemianopia, moderately severe amnesia, and alexia. The most striking feature of his presentation was an inability to name visually presented objects. Naming errors consisted of perseverations of previously presented objects, semantic errors (in which an object was given the name of a semantically related object), and, less frequently, visual errors. At the same time, he could demonstrate that he knew what the object was by demonstrating how it would be used. Drawing of viewed objects was normal even when the object was misnamed. He showed normal tactile naming in both right and left hands, and could name environmental sounds without difficulty. Also, when given the name of an object he was viewing, he could provide an accurate definition of the object and its functional properties. Although he was aware of his visual field defect and his reading disturbance, he was not aware of his difficulty in visual naming.

Optic aphasia is important because its existence challenges the widely held view that object naming is based on a common set of semantic representations that can be accessed from any sensory modality. The problem is this: Why should a patient who shows intact verbal semantics (as evidenced, for example, by his good performance on the definitions task) and intact visual semantics (as evidenced by his accurate miming of object use) be able to name only those objects that are held in the hand? There have been several different answers to this question. Beavois (1982) suggested that, in J.F., visual and verbal semantics became disconnected from each other, and that only tactile input had preserved access to verbal semantics. This view assumes the existence of multiple, modality-specific semantic systems, segregated according to the modality in which constituent information is represented (Warrington, 1985; Shallice, 1988).

Riddoch and Humphreys (1987b) suggest a different answer based on their analysis of another case of optic aphasia. Riddoch and Humphreys presented an object decision task, in which the patient had to decide whether a series of individual line drawings represented real objects or not. Their patient performed normally on this task, suggesting that he had preserved knowledge of object structure. However, the patient was impaired in grouping semantically related objects (e.g., hammer and nail), and could not draw named objects from memory. Thus, in either direction, the patient could not link semantic and visual information. Based on these results, Riddoch and Humphreys describe optic aphasia as a modality-specific semantic access problem. They further postulate that the knowledge of how to use objects is linked to structural rather than to semantic properties, and suggest that the patient may be able to demonstrate object use by a direct connection between visual object recognition units and motor action systems.

A third answer was provided by Coslett and Saffran (1989a). They suggested that at least some patients with optic aphasia are able to access semantic information contained in the right hemisphere but are unable to access the semantic system and speech production mechanisms within the left hemisphere. Like Warrington (1975) and Shallice (1987), these authors posit multiple semantic systems, but argue that these systems are differentiated not by the modality of input, but by their anatomic locus in the right or left hemisphere. The patient described by Coslett and Saffran was a 67-year-old man with a large left occipital lobe infarct and a lacunar infarct in the right internal capsule. The patient was unable to name visually presented objects but was able to name them to palpation and visual description, and could point to them when they were named. This latter ability is not easily accommodated by a model that dissociates all visual and verbal input. The patient could correctly categorize unnamed pictures and words and could group unrecognized objects according to their functional similarity and semantic association. This provides good evidence that the patient was able to access detailed semantic information from visually presented objects, which Coslett and Saffran argue reflects an intact right hemisphere semantic system.

Although the mechanisms discussed above all invoke deficits of semantic access, Shuren et al. (1993) suggested that an important factor may be lexical access. They reported three patients who named visually presented stimuli normally, but could not name the same objects when given a definition, nor could they demonstrate or describe the use of the objects. They called this disorder *nonoptic aphasia* and suggested that, although percepts could access an intact lexicon, the semantic representations were degraded. In contrast, patients with optic aphasia may be able to access semantics, but not the lexicon.

Although optic aphasia appears to be distinct from associative agnosia, the possibility remains that, at least in some patients, the distinction may be a matter of degree (De Renzi & Saetti, 1997; Chanoine et al., 1998). Clinical lore suggests that patients may evolve into optic aphasia during recovery from classical associative visual agnosia. The fact that some patients can be made to oscillate between optic aphasia and visual agnosia by varying the instructions given them on a particular task blurs, at least in some cases, the distinction between a naming disorder and a disturbance of recognition.

Disorders of Color Recognition and Naming

The term *color agnosia* presents something of a conceptual dilemma. Unlike objects, colors cannot be heard or palpated, and cannot be shown in use; they can only be known through vision or visual representation (imagery). It is difficult to imagine a clinical tool to assess color recognition in other modalities, and thus it is hard to establish the modality-specificity of the deficit, although "conceptual" color tasks (e.g., "What color is associated with feelings of envy"?) have utility in assessing semantic aspects of color processing. Still, acquired anomalies of color vision and color performance do occur as a result of lesions to the posterior cortex (DeRenzi & Spinnler, 1967). Five syndromes of color disturbance have been described: (a) *central achromatopsia/dyschromatopsia* (MacKay & Dunlop, 1899; Meadows, 1974b; Green & Lessell, 1977; Pearlman et al., 1979; Damasio et al., 1980; Young & Fishman, 1980); (b) *color agnosia* and *color amnesia* (Farah, Levine, & Calvanio, 1988; Luzzatti & Davidoff, 1994; DeRenzi, 2000); (c) *color anomia*, found in association with pure alexia and right homonymous hemianopia, and attributable to visual–verbal disconnection (Geschwind & Fusillo, 1966; Meadows, 1974b; Oxbury, Oxbury, & Humphrey, 1969 [Case I]; Beauvois & Saillant, 1985); (d) a *specific color aphasia*, in which the patient has linguistic defects, but the impairment in utilizing color names is disproportionately severe (Kinsbourne & Warrington, 1964; Oxbury et al., 1969 [Case 2]); and (e) *color naming and color association defects concomitant with aphasia* (DeRenzi et al., 1972, 1973;

Cohen & Kelter, 1979). We will review the first four of these defects below.

Central Achromatopsia/Dyschromatopsia. Although acquired loss of color vision can occur in diabetes, ocular hypertension, glaucoma, cataracts, and other diseases, central achromatopsia refers to a loss of color vision due to central nervous system (CNS) disease. The causative lesions can be in the optic nerve, chiasm, or in one or both of the cerebral hemispheres (Green & Lessell, 1977). The disorder can be hemianopic (Albert, Reches, & Silverberg, 1975b), or can exist throughout the visual fields. The defect may be subtotal or selective, and can rarely affect one color more than others. Critchley (1965) described a patient with *xanthopsia* who suddenly felt as if all objects around him were covered with gold paint.

Patients with achromatopsia notice their loss of color vision, and describe their visual world as "black-and-white," "all gray," "washed out," or "dirty." Damasio et al. (1980) reported that one of their patients had every drapery in her house laundered because she thought they were soiled (in fact, she was initially admitted through the psychiatry service because she was thought to be obsessively preoccupied with cleaning). Such patients perform poorly on tasks of color perception (Ishihara plates, Medmont C-100 Test, Farnsworth D-15 Test, hue discrimination, color matching), but do well on verbal-verbal tasks (e.g., "What color is blood?," "Name three blue things"). Performance on visual–verbal tasks (naming, pointing, color-object naming, and pointing) varies with the severity of the disorder.

There is agreement in the literature that achromatopsia results from unilateral or bilateral lesions in the inferior ventromedial sector of the occipital lobe, involving the lingual and fusiform gyri (Meadows, 1974b; Green & Lessell, 1977; Damasio et al., 1980). Superior field defects are the rule. Prosopagnosia and topographical memory loss are found in the bilateral, but not the unilateral cases (Damasio et al., 1980). Two patients (Green & Lessell, 1977 [Case 4]; Pearlman et al., 1979) who each had two separate unilateral posterior cerebral artery infarctions, did not become achromatopsic until their second strokes. At least one case

of reversible achromatopsia and prosopagnosia associated with migraine has been reported (Lawden & Cleland, 1993). Visual evoked responses to alternating green and red checkerboard patterns may be abnormal (Damasio et al., 1980), although chromatic contrast sensitivity has been reportedly normal (Heywood, Kentridge, & Cowey, 1998).

The physiologic work of Zeki (1973, 1977) has revealed that the rhesus monkey has specialized areas (V-4 complex and an additional region in the superior temporal sulcus) containing "color-coded" cells that selectively respond to specific wavelengths of light. Haywood and colleagues have shown that lesions anterior to V4, but completely sparing it, can lead to achromatopsia in monkeys (Heywood, Gaffan, & Cowey, 1995). Damasio et al. (1980) speculate that the lingual and fusiform gyri in man may be the human homologues of V-4. The exact location is not currently known, although recent functional imaging evidence points to the fusiform gyrus (Sakai et al., 1995). What does seem clear from clinical data is that a single area in each hemisphere controls color processing for the entire hemifield (Damasio et al., 1980).

Color Agnosia and Color Amnesia. Once a color is appropriately perceived, it has to be categorized as belonging to a given region of hue, such as red or blue. This process implies the existence of an internal color space that stores abstract mental representations of color. Some patients appear to have defects in categorizing colors despite the ability to perceptually discriminate them. The patient with this defect may fail complex color sorting tests, may err in assigning the appropriate color to common objects, either in coloring or naming tests, or may fail purely "verbal" color tests ("What color is associated with envy?") because of a defect in color categorization (DeRenzi, 2000). In these patients, color naming may be spared (Farah, Levine, & Calvanio, 1988; Luzzatti & Davidoff, 1994). Luzzatti and Davidoff suggested that, once a color has been categorized, it accesses the semantic memory store and the phonological output lexicon separately, and that selective lesions of one of these pathways can result in a differential impairment of memory and language skills. The disorder was labeled agnosia, but DeRenzi (2000) suggested that the term *color amnesia* might be more appropriate.

A fascinating dissociation between color perception and color categorization was reported by Marangolo, DeRenzi, DiPace, Ciurli, and Castriota-Skanderberg (1998). Their patient had a paracallosal lesion in the left hemisphere that produced left tactile agnosia, ideomotor apraxia, and agraphia, and right constructional apraxia. Matching to sample of colors and letters was normal in both hands, but was impaired *only in the left hand* when the sample was removed and matching took place after a short delay. The hand effect was not seen for objects or faces. Marangolo et al. suggested that matching from memory demands color categorization and that this is a predominantly left hemisphere function. Because of the callosal lesion, the patient was not able to transmit color categorization information to the right hemisphere/left hand. Although speculative, the association of color categorization and left hemisphere functioning may help explain why other defects of color processing are more frequent after left hemisphere lesions.

Color Anomia. The patient with color anomia succeeds on visual–visual (e.g., color matching) and verbal–verbal (e.g., naming colors from memory) tasks, but is unable to name visualized colors, a visual–verbal task. The disorder is classically associated with the syndrome of alexia without agraphia (Stengel, 1948; Geschwind & Fusillo, 1966; Carlesimo, Casadio, Sabbadini, & Caltagirone, 1998), and frequently exists in the context of right homonymous hemianopia. The underlying neurobehavioral mechanism is a visual–verbal disconnection resulting from infarction in the left PCA distribution, wherein information from the intact right hemisphere/left visual field cannot access the naming area due to damage to the callosal splenium. The patients of Geschwind and Fusillo (1966) and Oxbury et al. (1969 [Case I]) are classic examples of this syndrome.

These patients may show impairment on some tasks related to color perception, such as coloring pictures or detecting errors in wrongly colored stimuli. This impairment is exacerbated if the patient attempts to verbalize his answers. Damasio, McKee, and Damasio (1979) suggest that the type of stimuli, the demands of the task, and the patient's problem-solving approach can strongly influence the extent of visual–verbal dissociation. In their analysis, visual–verbal dissociation is maximized when, at the perceptual level, stimuli are purely visual (such as color), structurally less rich (such as line drawings), or low in association value. Visual–verbal dissociation is maximized at the verbal end when a specific name, rather than the name of a broad category, is required (Boller & Spinnler, 1967). If the patient's verbalizations about the stimulus are incorrect, they may interfere with attempts to assign it the correct color.

Specific Color Aphasia. Patients with this syndrome are distinguished from color anomics by their poor performance on verbal–verbal tasks. The patients of Oxbury et al. (1969 [Case 2]) and Kinsbourne and Warrington (1964) are among the best documented cases. Aphasic symptoms are usually present, but the difficulty with color names and other color-associative skills is disproportionately severe. Oxbury's patient had head trauma (and probable bilateral lesions) with complete right homonymous hemianopia and mild right hemiparesis. Kinsbourne and Warrington's patient had a left posterior parietal subdural hematoma. These patients can generally sort colors by hue and category, and can appropriately match colors. These deficits are similar to those reported in aphasic patients by DeRenzi et al. (1972).

Prosopagnosia

The term *prosopagnosia* was formally introduced by Bodamer (1947) to describe an acquired inability to recognize previously familiar faces. Patients with this disorder often present with a dramatic and recognizable disability that comes to the attention of the clinician by the report of family members who are distressed about the patient's inability to recognize them. An inability to become familiar with newly encountered individuals (e.g., health care workers and hospital personnel) is also present (Beyn & Knyazeva, 1962). The patient reports, and demonstrates in everyday behavior, an inability to recognize the identity of individuals by their facial features. However, the patient is capable of recognizing others by voice or some other nonfacial cue. This is usually a disabling condition to which some patients adjust through compensations. For example, some patients become able use extrafacial cues, including clothing, characteristic gait, length of hair, height, or distinguishing birthmark, to achieve recognition. In most cases, the patient realizes that he or she has a defect, and is distressed by it, although there are exceptions (Young, de Haan, & Newcombe, 1990). Prosopagnosia typically presents as an acquired disorder, although convincing cases of developmental prosopagnosia have been reported (De Haan, 1991; Kracke, 1994; Ariel & Sadeh, 1996; Behrmann & Aridan, 2005; Duchaine, 2000), including some familial cases that suggest the heritability of the developmental form of the syndrome (Schmalzl, Palermo, & Coltheart, 2008; Lee, Duchaine, Wilson, & Nakayama, 2009).

The inability to recognize family members, friends, and hospital staff may lead to the mistaken conclusion that the patient is suffering from a severe memory defect or a generalized dementia. The disorder should be distinguished from Capgras syndrome, a disturbance in which the patient believes that familiar persons have been replaced by imposters (Alexander et al., 1979; Ellis & Young, 1990). When formally tested, patients with prosopagnosia may score normally on face discrimination and matching tasks (Warrington & James, 1967; Benton & Van Allen, 1972). They almost invariably recognize faces as faces, and can often succeed at perceptually demanding tasks of age, gender, and expression discrimination (Tzavaras et al., 1970; Benton & Van Allen, 1972). Their primary defect is in identifying and recognizing whose face they are viewing. Such patients may be unable to recognize their own face in a mirror, although they often correctly infer that it must be themselves. The defect also prevents the identification of famous personalities, family members, and other familiar persons.

Clinical examination often reveals additional neuropsychological deficits including central achromatopsia, constructional disability, topographical memory loss, and dressing apraxia, and the patient may or may not show signs of object agnosia (Hecaen & Angelergues, 1962). There is evidence that prosopagnosia may take apperceptive and associative forms (Gloning et al., 1970;

Levine, 1978; Bauer & Trobe, 1984, DeRenzi et al., 1991), and recent evidence suggests that subtle impairments in the ability to use shading in figure–ground segmentation for face processing may be present in some cases (Hefter, Jerksey, & Barton, 2008). Thus, patients with prosopagnosia should be examined with basic tests of facial discrimination, facial learning, and perceptual function to determine whether the recognition defect results from impairments in basic perceptual processes or is at the stage in which perceptual inputs are compared with stored information about faces.

Although patients with prosopagnosia deny any familiarity with the faces they view and fail miserably on tests of facial identification, many are able to demonstrate some degree of recognition ability if such ability is measured indirectly. This has been referred to as "covert recognition," and includes a number of distinct behavioral phenomena. For example, prosopagnosic patients can autonomically discriminate facial identity (Bauer, 1984) and facial familiarity (Tranel, 1985) despite a total inability to recognize faces overtly. They can show crossdomain semantic priming using faces and names (Young, Hellawell, & DeHaan, 1988). They show normal interference in name classification ("Is Brad Pitt a politician or an actor?") when a face from a different semantic category is presented (DeHaan, Young, & Newcombe, 1987a; De Haan, Bauer, & Greve, 1992). All of these data suggest that prosopagnosic patients can extract information from faces that is not reflected in their verbal report. There are two main explanations of this effect, one based on the idea that covert recognition reflects the residual activity within a damaged face processing system (Schweinberger & Burton, 2003), the other based on a dissociation between the face processing system and conscious awareness (Bauer, 1984).

Lesions causing prosopagnosia are usually bilateral and involve the cortex and white matter in the mesial occipitotemporal region. Although bilateral lesions are typical, there are now several well-documented cases of prosopagnosia with CT evidence of damage restricted to the right hemisphere (DeRenzi, 1986a; Landis, Cummings, Christen, Bogen, & Imhof, 1986; Michel, Poncet, & Signoret, 1989; Benton, 1990;

Tohgi et al., 1994; Evans, Heggs, Antoun, & Hodges, 1995). The anatomic facts suggest that impairment in the right occipitotemporal junction is necessary, and at times sufficient, to produce prosopagnosia, although the paradigmatic lesion profile is bilateral in nature (Meadows, 1974a; Cohn, Newmann, & Wood, 1977; Whiteley & Warrington, 1977; Damasio, Damasio, & Van Hoesen, 1982; Ettlin et al., 1992). Some authors believe that unilateral right hemisphere damage restricted to the inferior occipitotemporal does not produce full-blown prosopagnosia; for this to occur, more extensive superior damage, often extending into the parietal lobe, must be present (Damasio, Tranel, & Damasio, 1990). Damasio et al. (1990) described three subtypes: an associative type characterized by bilateral damage in Brodmann areas 18, 19, and 37; an amnestic-associative type resulting from damage to the hippocampus and surrounding cortex; and an apperceptive type resulting from extensive right hemisphere damage involving Brodmann areas 18, 19, 37, and 39. Superior field defects (either altitudinal hemianopia or superior quadrantanopia) are most common, suggesting that causative lesions tend to occur inferiorly in the occipitotemporal region (Meadows, 1974a).

The occipitotemporal projection system (OTPS) is a series of short U fibers that course beneath the cortical mantle to connect adjacent regions in striate, prestriate, and inferior temporal cortex (Tusa & Ungerleider, 1985). This system, which serves as the functional interface between visual association cortices in the occipital and temporal lobes, has been particularly implicated in prosopagnosia (Benson, Segarra, and Albert, 1974; Meadows, 1974a; Bauer, 1982). The regions in the temporal lobe served by the OTPS subsequently project to the limbic system. Accordingly, prosopagnosia has been interpreted as an element of a visual–limbic disconnection syndrome (Benson, Segarra, & Albert, 1974; Bauer, 1982). Evidence that prosopagnosic patients suffer from reductions in emotional responsivity to visual stimuli seems to support this idea (Bauer, 1982; Habib, 1986). Although disconnection may be responsible for this latter effect, lesion localization in the occipitotemporal cortex seems critical because OTPS lesions anterior to the occipitotemporal

area (which, if complete, also produce visual–limbic disconnection) do not typically result in prosopagnosia (Meadows, 1974a). It is possible that intrinsic damage to the occipitotemporal region destroys the association cortex in which the neural substrates of face processing and other forms of complex visual form recognition reside (Iversen & Weiskrantz, 1964, 1967; Kuypers et al., 1965; Gross et al., 1972; Damasio et al., 1982; Perrett, Rolls, & Caan, 1982; Perrett, Mistlin, & Chitty, 1987).

Prosopagnosia has stimulated strong interest because it apparently represents a category-specific defect and thus may shed light on the manner in which perceptual representations are stored and organized in the brain. One important historical question is whether face recognition is special in some way, or whether it is simply distinct because of its complexity (Valentine, 1988; Nachson, 1995; Farah, 1996; Kreiman, Koch, & Fried, 2000; Park, Newman, & Polk, 2009).

In the past decade, cognitive models of the face recognition process have been constructed as a way of understanding the various steps involved in extracting identity information from people's faces. One such model, similar to that proposed by Marr, and adapted from Ellis and Young (1988), is depicted in Figure 11-1. According to the model, faces are first subjected to complex visual analysis of the facial structure, including both featural and configural elements. This "structural encoding" step includes the construction of two kinds of structural representations. The first, the "viewer-centered description" represents the image of the face from the viewer's perspective. Many such descriptions of each face are possible, depending upon point of view, momentary facial expression, lighting, and other factors. The second is a "viewpoint-independent description," which is a general structural description of the face that is not dependent upon either viewpoint or expression. The viewpoint-independent description allows us to recognize that two pictures of faces, seen from different points of view, may belong to the same person. Although the structural encoding step is a critical first step in analyzing facial identity, other kinds of non–identity-based visual processing are going on simultaneously. The face may be analyzed for its emotional expression (expression analysis) or might be visually inspected in such a way as to allow lip-reading (facial speech analysis). These two processes are depicted as outside the structural encoding box to emphasize that they are not involved in identity processing. In fact, many severely impaired prosopagnosic patients perform normally on emotion-recognition or lip-reading tasks (Campbell, Landis, & Regard, 1986; Tranel, Damasio, & Damasio, 1988). Once a structural representation of the face is constructed, other forms of directed visual processing (e.g., gender, age discrimination, same–different judgments) are possible. Associative prosopagnosic patients succeed at this type of processing, whereas those with an apperceptive defect may have difficulty in performing complex facial discriminations.

An important component of the model is the *face recognition unit* (FRU). The FRU receives input from structural encoding and contains the visual structural descriptions that allow a particular known face to be discriminated from other familiar and unfamiliar faces. According to the model, each familiar face has its own FRU. Activation of the FRU leads to a sense of familiarity, but not to individual identification, since the FRU contains structural, but not semantic information. Activation of the FRU normally leads to the activation of a *person identity node* (PIN) that contains semantic information about the owner of the face. After activation of the FRU and PIN, a name might be assigned to the individual face. According to the model, naming occurs only after an appropriate PIN is activated.

This kind of model has been useful in organizing a large body of empirical findings on face recognition in normal subjects and is helpful in understanding patterns of impairment in face processing that occur after brain injury. As applied to prosopagnosia, the model is useful in describing the various stages at which a face-recognition defect can occur. Some patients have difficulty at the structural encoding level, and thus, have difficulty with a broad range of face discrimination and perception tasks. Others have defects much later in the processing chain. In some patients, the face recognition units themselves appear to be damaged,

while in others, access to otherwise intact FRUs, or from the FRU to the PIN, appears to be impaired. Evidence of intact FRUs comes from case studies in which patients more easily learn correct face–name matches than incorrect ones (Bruyer, 1991; De Haan, Young, & Newcombe, 1991) and from studies demonstrating intact access to person information in semantic priming paradigms (Young et al., 1988).

Recent computational studies have attempted to evaluate the degree to which impairments at particular stages of a cognitive model could account for the pattern of spared and impaired face identification abilities in at least some prosopagnosic patients. Computational approaches are valuable because they provide dynamic, hypothesis-driven tests of models derived from clinical cases. Using an interactive activation model patterned after similar models in word recognition, Burton et al. (1990) attempted to simulate the behavior of their prosopagnosic patient, P.H. This patient failed at all conventional tests of facial identification, but showed intact semantic priming of familiarity decisions with both faces and names. That is, when Prince Charles' face was presented as a prime, he was more likely to regard Princess Diana's face as familiar than when an unrelated face preceded Diana's face. Thus, despite a complete failure of overt recognition, P.H. showed that he could access some semantic information from viewed faces. Burton et al. attempted to simulate this finding by "lesioning" their interactive activation model. The basic architecture of the model, patterned after the Bruce and Young (1986) face recognition model, contained a number of distinct pools of units corresponding to names, faces (FRUs) persons (PINs), and semantic information. In their simulation, input was applied to an individual name or FRU, and activation of associated units was measured. The normal behavior of the model accurately simulated cross-domain (face–name) and within-domain (name–name) semantic priming. For example, when input was applied to the Prince Charles PIN, increased activation (priming) occurred at the Diana FRU. Based on their behavioral data, Burton et al. hypothesized that P.H.'s lesion damaged the links between FRUs and PINs. In the normal simulation described above, all connections were equally weighted. In order to simulate damaged links between the face recognition units and the person identity notes, the weights assigned to these links were halved and model was run again. Results from the simulations showed (a) normal name–name priming (expected in prosopagnosia, since the disorder does not affect the patient's ability to recognize names), and (b) intact cross-domain (face–name) priming for names despite the fact that activation at the FRU never reached recognition threshold. Thus, this computational model successfully simulated both normal and disordered face recognition performance.

Other researchers have utilized computational approaches to address the issue of whether the pattern of spared and impaired recognition abilities in prosopagnosia implies impaired access to an intact face recognition processor (Farah, O'Reilly, & Vecera, 1993). Contrary to the view of covert recognition in prosopagnosia as reflecting failure of the face processor to access conscious awareness, these researchers argued that covert recognition reflected damage to the face processor itself. They argued that the damaged neural network would manifest residual knowledge in the kinds of tasks used to measure covert recognition. They constructed a three-layer model consisting of face, name, and semantic (occupational) information for 16 units. The model contained face input and name units on the first level, face- and name-hidden units on the second level, and semantic units on the third level. Using a contrastive Hebbian learning algorithm, the network was first trained to associate an individual's face, name, and semantics whenever one of these was presented. The network was then lesioned by removing between two and 14 units from the 16-item face input pool and from the 16-item face-hidden unit pool. In four simulations measuring face-name learning, speed of visual perception, semantic priming, and face recognition, their lesioned model displayed behavior remarkably similar to that reported in experimental studies of prosopagnostic patients, showing "covert" without "overt" recognition.

Neuroimaging and electrophysiological investigations with humans and primates have also yielded important information about the neural basis of face recognition. A long line of electrophysiological work in the macaque has revealed populations of cells that respond selectively to faces, in some cases to particular faces (Perrett, Rolls, & Caan, 1982; Baylis, Rolls, & Leonard, 1985; Desimone, 1991). These findings have led to speculation that the temporal cortex contains the hardware that supports face-specific "modules" or at least dedicated face-specific perceptual mechanisms. Although this view seems widely accepted, it has been observed that lesions to these regions do not clearly produce a serious impairment in face recognition ability (Baylis et al., 1985). Nevertheless, findings from electrophysiological and functional neuroimaging studies have continued to inform and constrain cognitive models of the face recognition process.

Some electrophysiological data from humans have yielded similar results. Studies with implanted electrodes have revealed patches of cells in extrastriate visual cortex that selectively respond to faces. Evidence suggests that these cells are intermixed with others that are not face-responsive, rather than forming a localized "face region" (Allison et al., 1994). In a study of facial repetition effects, scalp potential and current density maps revealed maximum activity in the inferotemporal and fusiform gyri (from 50 to at least 250 ms), mainly on the right, for both faces and shapes, and in the hippocampus and adjacent areas (around 300 ms), specifically for faces (George et al., 1997).

Electrophysiological analyses of prosopagnosic performance on face recognition tests have yielded evidence for defects in structural encoding. In one study, unfamiliar faces, inverted faces, and houses were shown to a prosopagnosic and controls. The controls showed consistent early negativity (N170) at the lateral temporal electrode sites, but the prosopagnosic patient did not (Eimer & McCarthy, 1999). The N170 is thought to reflect a late stage in structural encoding (Bentin Allison, Puce, Perez, et al., 1996) that appeared to be deficient in the prosopagnosic patient. However, other studies have shown normal N170 (e.g., Harris, Duchaine, & Nakayama, 2005), probably reflecting heterogeneity in the patients studied. In a recent study of developmental prosopagnosia, three of four patients showed absent

P1 to faces and N170 to faces and bodies (Righart & deGelder, 2007).

Neuroimaging studies have generally confirmed conclusions about functional location of face processing learned from patient studies, but with additional complexities. In general, neuroimaging studies have evolved from initial studies of specific brain regions to reveal a complex distributed network involved in "person knowledge" (Gobbini & Haxby, 2007). This network includes a core system dedicated to visual appearance (occipitotemporal regions, posterior superior temporal sulcus, fusiform gyrus), a system important for "person knowledge" (anterior paracingulate, anterior temporal cortex, precuneus/posterior cingulate), and a system dedicated to processing emotional responses and reward states evoked when processing faces (amygdala, insula, striatum) (Haxby, Hoffman, & Gobbini, 2000). The inferior occipital and fusiform gyri (the so-called *occipital face area* [OFA] and *fusiform face area* [FFA]) appear to be critical parts of the network for processing invariant features of faces necessary for person identification (Kanwisher, Chun, McDermott, & Ledden, 1996; Kanwisher, Tong, & Nakayama, 1998; Gobbini & Haxby, 2007). However, nonfacial stimuli can activate FFA (Tarr & Gauthier, 2000), and the effects of facial familiarity on activations within this region are not straightforward (Gobbini & Haxby, 2007). In contrast, facial familiarity appears to exert a monotonic effect on activations in the anterior paracingulate cortex, the posterior superior temporal sulcus, and the precuneus. Personal familiarity evokes additional activation in limbic regions, including the amygdala and insula (Gobbini & Haxby, 2007). These findings may be relevant in light of the apparent impairment of visual–limbic connectivity involved in prosopagnosia.

Some consider prosopagnosia as one of a number of category-specific agnosias. Although in prosopagnosia the defect in identifying individuals on the basis of their facial features is disproportionately impaired (compared, for example, to the identification of objects), the balance of available data suggest that, in most cases, impairment in recognizing other classes of objects coexists with the face agnosia. Doubt is cast on a purely category-specific view by

reports of prosopagnosic patients who concurrently lost the ability to recognize specific chairs (Faust, 1955) or automobiles (Lhermitte & Pillon, 1975), and by functional imaging studies showing that FFA activation occurs when bird and car experts view specific exemplars from their respective areas of interest (Gauthier, Skudlarski, Gore, & Anderson, 2000; Turk, Rosenblum, Gazzaniga, & Macrae, 2005). Bornstein and colleagues have reported two prosopagnosic patients, one a birdwatcher, the other a farmer, who concurrently lost the ability to recognize individual birds or cows, respectively (Bornstein & Kidron, 1959; Bornstein, 1963; Bornstein, Sroka, & Munitz, 1969). Additional issues regarding the concept of category specificity are discussed below.

One prominent view of the disorder is that the underlying defect prevents the identification of individual items within a class of objects that are visually similar (Damasio et al., 1982). According to this view, recognition proceeds normally at the superordinate level (i.e., the patient concludes correctly that she is looking at a face) but breaks down at subordinate levels. Several relevant factors, including the similarity in physical structure among facial exemplars, the number of faces one must recognize, and familiarity with specific exemplars can influence recognition in such a way as to make it appear category-specific (Damasio et al., 1990). Contrary to this view, prosopagnosic patients show disproportionate difficulty recognizing faces even when other visual discrimination tasks (e.g., objects) are made to be of comparable difficulty (Farah, Levinson, & Klein, 1995). This finding is relevant to the question of whether faces are special or unique as an object category, and the related issue of whether the brain has evolved a special-purpose module for face recognition.

Evidence for a special-purpose face processor comes from the single-unit studies described above and from behavioral research showing unique perceptual effects found only with faces. The best example of the latter type of evidence is the "face inversion effect" (Yin, 1969; Valentine, 1988). Compared to upright faces, recognizing and discriminating upside-down faces is much harder for normal subjects, and appears to proceed using different visual processes. This vastly inferior performance with inverted faces has been taken to suggest the presence of specialized recognition processes (or at least the development of special expertise) for upright faces. It has been reported that prosopagnosic patients may not show a normal face inversion effect (Busigny & Rossion, 2009), and, in fact, may show better performance with upside-down faces (i.e., an "inversion superiority effect"; Farah, Wilson, Drain, & Tanaka, 1995b). Although this finding has been taken as support for the existence of a specialized face processor, a subsequent report (de Gelder, Bachoud Levi, & Degos, 1998) found an inversion superiority effect for faces *and shoes* in a prosopagnosic patient. Thus, the debate about whether face recognition is unique has not yet been fully resolved, although a likely answer to this important question is that face recognition involves some unique abilities that do not completely overlap with other visual recognition abilities (Yin, 1970).

Other Category-specific Recognition Defects. Before leaving the topic of visual agnosia, it is important to mention other cases in which visual recognition disorders appear to be limited to a specific semantic category or class of objects (Warrington & Shallice, 1984; Farah, Hammond, Mehta, & Ratcliff, 1989; Damasio, 1990; Farah, 1991). As indicated earlier, questions regarding category specificity arose in the context of evaluating the significance of other selective forms of agnosia, such as prosopagnosia. Although some prosopagnosic patients have a relatively "pure" face recognition defect (DeRenzi, 1986b), others have difficulty in recognizing objects in other semantic classes such as animals (Bornstein & Kidron, 1959; Damasio et al., 1982), plants (Shuttleworth, Syring, & Allen, 1982), or foods (Damasio et al. 1982; Michel, Perenin, & Sieroff, 1986). When these problems have been considered together, it has been suggested that a supercategorical defect in recognizing living things might be involved (cf. Farah, McMullen, & Meyer, 1991), reflecting primary neural organization along an animate–inanimate dimension (Caramazza & Shelton, 1998). However, it is unclear how other category-specific deficits involving, for example, musical instruments (Gainotti & Silveri, 1996), medical

implements (Crosson, Moberg, Boone, Rothi, & Raymer, 1997), or cars (Forde, Francis, Riddoch, Rumiati, & Humphreys, 1997) can be accommodated in this framework (Dixon, 2000; Dixon, Piskopos, & Schweizer, 2000).

Two general explanations for such category specificity have been offered. One is that these disorders represent localized impairment in a categorically organized semantic system. Another view suggests that living things are more visually complex (Gloning et al., 1970), more visually similar one to another (Forde et al., 1997) or require, for identification, more specific names than do nonliving things (cf. Farah, McMullen, & Meyer, 1991). The former explanation suggests that a selective disruption in the recognition of living things reveals something basic about the structure of semantic memory; the latter implies that such selective disruption results from task, processing, or response factors that have been confounded in the usual clinical tasks of object recognition (Dixon, 2000).

With these alternative explanations in mind, Farah, McMullen, and Meyer (1991) devised a series of object-naming tasks that took account of visual complexity, similarity among items, and response specificity (e.g., table vs. picnic table) and gave them to two patients who became agnosic after sustaining severe closed head injury. They found that, despite efforts to control for these variables, living things remained selectively impaired relative to nonliving things. Their data do not allow them to specifically discern the locus of impairment (i.e., whether it is in a categorically organized semantic system or within a modularly organized visual system specialized for the recognition of living things), but they concluded that some level of visual or semantic representations specific to living things appeared to be involved.

The patient PSD reported by Damasio (1990) shows a similar, although apparently more complicated dissociation. This patient was able to visually recognize man-made tools, although his recognition of most natural stimuli was less than 30% accurate. At the same time, he showed normal recognition of some natural stimuli (e.g., body parts) and poor recognition of some man-made stimuli (e.g., musical instruments).

Computational models have been applied to the problem of category specificity in visual recognition and naming (Farah & McClelland, 1991; Small, Hart, Nguyen, & Gordon, 1995; Devlin, Gonnerman, Andersen, & Seidenberg, 1998). In these accounts, stimuli are represented by sets of perceptual features that are then "lesioned" in an attempt to produce results analogous to human neurological syndromes. Although a detailed review of these models is beyond the scope of this chapter, the basic result that emerges from these simulations is that damage to feature-based computational models can accurately simulate category-specific naming and recognition deficits without having to postulate hierarchical or categorical organization within the semantic system itself. A more recent computational investigation (Lambon Ralph, Lowe, & Rogers, 2007) showed that the type and distribution of pathology within the semantic system may be critical in determining category specificity. When semantic representations within their model were degraded (by removing them), a generalized semantic deficit emerged, but when representations were distorted (by changing the model's connection weights), a category-specific defect emerged. These data are intriguing in that they may suggest that category specificity in visual processing represents a complex interplay between a partially or completely damaged perceptual processing system that sends distorted information about object identify to the semantic network.

AUDITORY AGNOSIA

The term *auditory agnosia* refers to impaired capacity to recognize sounds in the presence of otherwise adequate hearing as measured by standard audiometry. The term has been variably applied to refer to (a) an generalized impairment in recognizing both speech and nonspeech sounds, and (b) a specific deficit in the recognition of nonverbal sounds only, reserving the term *pure word deafness* (PWD) for a selective impairment in speech sound recognition. We prefer the second approach, and in this section we will discuss PWD and auditory agnosia separately. The term *cortical deafness* generally has been applied to those patients whose daily activities and auditory behavior indicate an extreme lack of awareness of auditory

stimuli of any kind, and whose audiometric pure tone thresholds are markedly abnormal. *Receptive (sensory) amusia* refers to loss of the ability to appreciate various characteristics of heard music. *Phonagnosia* refers to the loss of the ability to recognize familiar persons by voice.

Cortical Auditory Disorder and Cortical Deafness

In the large majority of cases, impairment of nonverbal sound recognition is accompanied by some degree of impairment in the recognition of speech sounds. The relative severity of these impairments may reflect premorbid lateralization of linguistic and nonlinguistic processes in the individual patient, and may depend upon which hemisphere is more seriously, or primarily, damaged (Ulrich, 1978). Terminological confusion has arisen with regard to these "mixed" forms, with such terms as "cortical auditory disorder" (Kanshepolsky et al., 1973; Miceli, 1982) "auditory agnosia" (Oppenheimer & Newcombe, 1978; Rosati et al., 1982), "auditory agnosia and word deafness" (Goldstein, Brown, & Hollander, 1975), and "congenital aphasia" (Landau & Kleffner, 1957; Landau, Goldstein, & Kleffner, 1960) all being used to describe similar phenomena. We will refer to these mixed forms as cortical auditory disorders, and will discuss them together with cortical deafness. Cortical auditory disorders frequently evolve from a state of cortical deafness, and it is often difficult to define a clear separation between the two.

Patients with these disorders have difficulty recognizing auditory stimuli of many kinds, verbal and nonverbal (Vignolo, 1969; Lhermitte et al., 1971). Aphasic signs, if present, are mild, and do not prevent the patient from recognizing incoming information provided audition is not required. Difficulties in temporal auditory analysis and localization of sounds in space are common. These disorders are rare, and their underlying neuroanatomic basis is poorly understood (Rosati et al., 1982). Some case reports have questioned the distinctive nature of "true" cortical deafness (Vignolo, 1969; Lhermitte et al., 1971; Kanshepolsky et al., 1973).

Distinguishing between cortical deafness and auditory agnosia continues to be problematic. It has been suggested that a diagnosis of cortical deafness requires a demonstration that brainstem auditory evoked responses are normal, but cortical evoked potentials (EPs) are not (Coslett, Brashear, & Heilman, 1984). One distinction that is frequently cited is that the cortically deaf patient feels deaf and seems to be so, whereas the auditory agnosic patients insists that he is not deaf (Michel et al., 1980). This turns out to be a poor criterion. Although it was originally believed that bilateral cortical lesions involving the primary auditory cortex resulted in total hearing loss, evidence from animal experiment (Massopoust & Wolin, 1967), cortical mapping of the auditory area (Celesia, 1976), and clinicopathological studies in man (Wohlfart et al., 1952; Mahoudeau et al., 1956) indicate that complete destruction of primary auditory cortex does not lead to substantial permanent loss of audiometric sensitivity. It is more likely, however, for an asymptomatic patient with old unilateral temporal lobe pathology to suddenly become totally deaf with the occurrence of a second contralateral lesion in the auditory region.

A neuroanatomic distinction between cortical deafness and auditory cortical disorders has been tentatively offered by Michel et al. (1980). Recognizing the hazards of such a dichotomy, they distinguish between lesions of auditory koniocortex (41–52 of Brodmann) and lesions of pro- and para-konio cortex (22, 52 of Brodmann), respectively. Although this distinction may prove useful, naturally occurring lesions do not typically obey architectonic boundaries (Michel et al., 1980).

In their paper on cortical deafness, Michel et al. (1980) considered the possibility that the two syndromes could be differentiated on the basis of auditory evoked potentials (AEPs). Several studies (e.g., Jerger et al., 1969; Michel et al., 1980) have found either totally absent cortical AEPs or absent late components of AEP in patients with cortical auditory disorders. However, AEPs have been found to be present in other cases (Albert et al., 1972 [PWD]; Assal & Despland 1973 [auditory agnosia]), and in at least one case of cortical deafness (Adams et al., 1977), normal late AEPs were found. Although

results to date are conflicting, this remains a promising area of research. Such variability may be due in part to differing pathologies and recording methods. Michel et al. (1980) offer methodological suggestions designed to increase comparability among patients.

Cortical deafness is most commonly seen in bilateral cerebrovascular disease, in which the course is commonly biphasic with a transient deficit (often aphasia and hemiparesis) related to unilateral damage followed by a second deficit associated with sudden transient total deafness (Jerger et al., 1969; Adams, Rosenberger, Winter, & Zollner, 1977; Earnest et al., 1977; Liecester, 1980). A biphasic course is also typical of cases of auditory cortical disorder.

In cortical deafness, bilateral destruction of the auditory radiations or the primary auditory cortex has been a constant finding (Leicester, 1980). The anatomic basis of auditory cortical disorder is more variable. Although lesions can be quite extensive (cf. Oppenheimer and Newcombe, 1978), the superior temporal gyrus (i.e., efferent connections of Heschl's gyrus) is frequently involved. Some cases (Motomura et al., 1986; Kazui et al., 1990) suggest that generalized auditory agnosia can result from relatively circumscribed bilateral subcortical lesions that impinge upon the auditory radiations.

Pure Word Deafness (Auditory Agnosia for Speech, Auditory Verbal Agnosia)

The patient with PWD is unable to comprehend spoken language although reading, writing, and speaking are relatively normal (Buchman, 1986). By definition, comprehension of nonverbal sounds is relatively spared. The syndrome is "pure" in that it is *comparatively* free of aphasic symptoms found in other disorders of language comprehension, such as Wernicke's and transcortical sensory aphasia. The disorder was first described by Kussmaul (1877). Lichtheim (1885), who called the disorder "subcortical sensory aphasia," defined it as "the inability to understand spoken words as an isolated deficit unaccompanied by disturbance of spontaneous speech or by severe disturbance in writing or understanding of the printed word." With few exceptions, PWD has been associated with bilateral, symmetric cortical-subcortical lesions in the anterior part of the superior temporal gyri, with some sparing of Heschl's gyrus, particularly on the left. Some patients have unilateral lesions located subcortically in the dominant temporal lobe, presumably destroying the ipsilateral auditory radiation as well as callosal fibers from the contralateral auditory region (e.g., Liepmann and Storch, 1902; Schuster & Taterka, 1926; Kanter, Day, Heilman, & Gonzalez-Rothi, 1986). Cases of PWD after right hemisphere lesions (Roberts, Sandercock, & Ghadiali, 1987; Bhaskaran, Prakash, Kumar, & Srikumar, 1998; Kitayama, Yamazaki, Shibahara, & Nomura, 1990) are quite rare and may be related to atypical cerebral dominance. The neuroanatomic substrate is generally conceived as a bilateral disconnection of Wernicke's area from auditory input (Geschwind, 1965; Hecaen & Albert, 1978). The low incidence of PWD is explained by the fact that it takes a circumscribed and unusually placed lesion of the superior temporal gyrus to involve Heschl's gyrus or its connections and still selectively spare Wernicke's area.

Cerebrovascular disease is by far the most common cause of PWD, although neurodegenerative disease has also been implicated (Otsuki, Soma, Sato, Homma, & Tsuji, 1998; Jorgens et al., 2008). Developmental auditory verbal agnosia coincident with seizures or retardation are also recognized syndromes in child neurology (Gascon, Victor, Lambroso, & Goodglass, 1973; Rapin, Mattis, Rowan, & Golden, 1977; Cooper & Ferry, 1978; Lamberts, 1980). The adult patient, when first seen, may be recovering from cortical deafness (Mendez & Geehan, 1988) or from a full-blown Wernicke's aphasia, although occasionally PWD may actually evolve to a Wernicke's aphasia (Klein and Harper, 1956; Gazzaniga et al., 1973; Albert and Bear, 1974). As the paraphasias and reading disturbances disappear, the patient still does not comprehend spoken language but can communicate by writing. Deafness can be ruled out by normal pure-tone thresholds on audiometry. At this stage, the patient may experience auditory hallucinations or exhibit transient euphoric or paranoid ideation (Reinhold, 1950; Shoumaker et al., 1977). The inability to repeat speech stimuli that are not comprehended distinguishes PWD (generally viewed as a disturbance at the perceptual-discriminative level; Jerger et al., 1969; Kanshepolsky et al., 1973), from transcortical sensory aphasia, in which word sounds are perceived normally, but in which sound is estranged from meaning. The absence of florid paraphasia and of reading and writing disruption distinguishes the disorder from Wernicke's aphasia.

The patient with PWD may complain that speech is muffled or sounds like a foreign language, and some complain of dramatic, sometimes aversive, changes in their subjective experience of speech (dysacusis; cf. Mendez & Geehan, 1988). Hemphill and Stengel's patient (1940) stated that "voices come but no words." The patient of Klein and Harper (1956) described speech as "an undifferentiated continuous humming noise without any rhythm" and "like foreigners speaking in the distance." Albert and Bear's (1974) patient said "words come too quickly," and, "they sound like a foreign language." Spontaneous speech may contain occasional word-finding pauses and paraphasias and is often slightly louder than normal. Performance on speech perception tests is inconsistent and highly dependent upon context (Caplan, 1978) and the linguistic structure of the material (Auerbach et al., 1982). Patients do much better when they are aware of the category under discussion, or when they can lipread. Comprehension often drops suddenly when the topic is changed. Words embedded in sentences are more easily identified than are isolated words. Slowing the presentation rate of words in sentences sometimes facilitates comprehension.

Most studies of patients with PWD have emphasized the role of auditory-perceptual processing in the genesis of the disorder (Jerger et al., 1969; Kansepolsky et al., 1973; Albert & Bear, 1976; Auerbach et al., 1982; Mendez & Geehan, 1988). Temporal resolution (Albert and Bear, 1974; Jörgens et al., 2008), and phonemic discrimination (Denes & Semenza, 1975; Saffran et al., 1976; Nakakoshi, Kashino, Mizobuchi, Fukada, & Katori, 2001) have also received attention. Auerbach et al. (1982) suggest that the disorder may take two forms: (a) a prephonemic temporal auditory acuity disturbance associated with bilateral temporal lesions, or (b) a disorder of phonemic discrimination attributable to left temporal lesions.

Albert and Bear (1974) suggested that the problem in PWD is one of temporal resolution of auditory stimuli rather than specific phonetic impairment. Their patient demonstrated abnormally long click-fusion thresholds (time taken to perceive two clicks as one), and improved in auditory comprehension when speech was presented at slower rates. This may lessen the impact of abnormally slow temporal auditory analysis or may allow the patient to reconstruct the message strategically (Niesser, 1967). Saffran, Marin, and Yeni-Komshian (1976) showed that informing their patient of the nature of the topic under discussion (indicating the category of words to be presented or giving the patient a multiple-choice array just before presentation of words) significantly facilitated comprehension. Words embedded in a sentence were better recognized, particularly when they occurred in the latter part of the sentence. Whereas a temporal auditory acuity disorder was likely present in Albert and Bear's (1974) patient, the patient of Saffran et al. (1976) displayed linguistic discrimination deficits that appeared to be independent of a disorder in temporal auditory acuity.

Several studies have reported brainstem and cortical auditory evoked responses in patients with PWD (see Michel et al., 1980 for review). Brainstem EPs are almost universally reported as normal, suggesting normal processing up to the level of the auditory radiations (Albert & Bear, 1974; Stockard & Rossiter, 1977; Auerbach et al., 1982). Results from studies of cortical AEPs are more variable, probably consistent with variable pathology (Auerbach et al., 1982). For example, the patient of Jerger et al. (1969) had no appreciable AEP, yet heard sounds. The patient of Auerbach et al. (1982) showed normal P1, N1, and P2 to right ear stimulation, but minimal response over either hemisphere to left ear stimulation. A recent study using magnetoencephalography (MEG; Jörgens et al., 2008) found prolonged M100 responses with activation delayed nearly threefold to 600–700 ms compared to controls, with the primary source located in the left planum temporale and the right Heschl's gyrus.

On tests of phonemic discrimination, patients with bilateral lesions tend to show distinctive deficits for the feature of place of articulation

(Naeser, 1974; Auerbach et al., 1982). Those with unilateral left hemisphere disease showed either impaired discrimination for voicing (Saffran et al., 1976) or no distinctive pattern (Denes & Semeneza, 1975).

On dichotic listening, some patients show extreme suppression of right ear perception (Albert & Bear, 1974; Saffran et al., 1976) suggesting that the left hemisphere phonetic decoding area (Wernicke's area) is inaccessible to auditory material that has already been acoustically processed by the right hemisphere. However, the patient of Auerbach et al. (1982) showed marked *left ear* extinction, which the authors attribute to spared auditory processing in the left temporal lobe.

Patients with PWD perform relatively well with environmental sounds, although the appreciation of music is sometimes disturbed (Buchman, Garron, Trost-Cardamone, Wichter, & Schwartz, 1986). Some patients may recognize foreign languages by their distinctive prosodic characteristics, and others can recognize *who* is speaking, but not what is said, suggesting preserved paralinguistic speech comprehension. Coslett, Brashear, and Heilman (1984) described a PWD patient who showed a remarkable dissociation between the comprehension of neutrally and affectively intoned sentences. He was asked to point to pictures of males and females depicting various emotional expressions. When verbal instructions were given in a neutral voice, he performed poorly. When instructions were given with affective intonations appropriate to the target face, he performed significantly better, at a level commensurate to his performance with written instructions. This patient had bilateral destruction of primary auditory cortex with some sparing of auditory association cortex, suggesting at least some direct contribution of the auditory radiations directly to cortex without initial decoding in Heschl's gyrus (Coslett et al., 1984). These authors speculate that one reason why patients with PWD improve their auditory comprehension with lipreading is that face-to-face contact allows them to take advantage of visual cues (gesture and facial expression) that are processed by different brain systems. An alternative explanation is that lipreading provides information about place of articulation, a linguistic feature that can be used to markedly reduce the available cohort of possible words, and which is markedly impaired in the bilateral cases of PWD (Auerbach et al., 1982). In either instance, the finding of preserved comprehension of paralinguistic aspects of speech further reinforces the notion that comprehension of speech and nonspeech sounds are dissociable.

There is evidence that unilateral left-sided lesions, particularly those producing Wernicke's aphasia with impaired auditory comprehension, are also associated with impaired ability to match nonverbal sounds with pictures (Vignolo, 1969). However, resulting errors are almost exclusively semantic, not acoustic, and thus do not suggest that unilateral left hemispheric temporal lobe damage produces a perceptual-discriminative sound recognition disturbance. For that reason, the finding of impaired ability to discriminate nonverbal speech sounds in a patient with PWD suggests bilateral disease, even in the absence of other bilateral neurological signs. Since many of these patients have, by history, successive strokes, the primary and secondary side of damage may be important in producing a picture dominated either by PWD or by auditory sound agnosia (Ulrich, 1978).

Although distinctions have been made between basic defects in auditory perception versus defects in linguistic processing, few studies of PWD have analyzed the defect in terms of the apperceptive–associative distinction so prominent in discussing visual agnosia (Polster & Rose, 1998). One study suggests that this distinction may describe the difference between PWD and a very rare and ill-defined disorder called *pure word meaning deafness*, in which the patient can hear and repeat words, but does not know their meaning (Franklin, Turner, Ralph, Morris, & Bailey, 1996).

Auditory Sound Agnosia (Auditory Agnosia for Nonspeech Sounds)

Auditory agnosia for nonspeech sounds is by far less common than PWD. This may be because such a defect may be less noticeable and less disabling than a disorder of speech comprehension, and also because nonspecific auditory complaints may be discounted when pure tone audiometric and speech discrimination thresholds are normal. This is unfortunate, since normal

or near-normal audiometric evaluation does not rule out the possible role played by primary auditory perceptual defects (Goldstein, 1974; Buchtel & Stewart, 1989).

Vignolo (1969) argued that there may be two forms of auditory sound agnosia: (a) a perceptual-discriminative type associated mainly with right hemisphere lesions involving Brodmann's areas 41, 42, and 52, and (b) an associative-semantic type associated with lesions of the left hemisphere involving Brodmann's areas 37, 20, and closely linked to Wernicke's aphasia. This anatomic distinction is by no means settled. The former group makes predominantly acoustic (e.g., "man whistling" for birdsong) errors on picture–sound matching tasks, whereas the latter group makes predominantly semantic (e.g., "cat" for barking dog) errors. This division follows the original classification of Kliest (1928), who distinguished between the ability to perceive isolated sounds or noises and the inability to understand the meaning of sounds. It also resembles the apperceptive–associative dichotomy made by Lissauer (1890). In the verbal sphere, the analogous distinction is between PWD (perceptual–discriminative) and transcortical sensory aphasia (semantic–associative).

Few stable cases of "pure" auditory sound agnosia have been reported in the literature (Nielsen & Sult, 1939; Wortis & Pfeffer, 1948; Spreen, Benton, & Fincham, 1965; Albert et al., 1972; Fujii et al., 1990; Schnider, Benson, Alexander, & Schnider-Klaus, 1994; Saygin, Leech, & Dick, 2010). Sometimes a patient evolves into auditory sound agnosia from a more generalized agnosia for both verbal and nonverbal sounds (Motomura, Yamadori, Mori, & Tamaru, 1986). The patient of Spreen et al. was a 65-year-old right-handed male whose major complaint when seen 3 years after a left hemiparetic episode was that of "nerves" and headache. Audiometric testing demonstrated moderate bilateral high-frequency loss and speech reception thresholds of 12 dB for both ears. There was no aphasia. The outstanding abnormality was the inability to recognize common sounds; understanding of language was fully retained, and there were no other agnosic defects. Sound localization was normal. Scores on the pitch subtest of the Seashore Tests of Musical Talent were at chance level. The patient claimed no experience or talent with music and refused to cooperate with further testing of musical ability. The patient could match previously heard but misidentified sounds with one of four tape-recorded choices, suggesting an associative defect. Postmortem examination revealed a sharply demarcated old infarct of the right hemisphere involving the superior temporal and angular gyri, as well as a large portion of the inferior parietal, inferior and middle frontal, and long and short gyri of the insula. This case represents one of the few examples of auditory sound agnosia with unilateral pathology. The lesion is too large to allow for precise anatomical–clinical correlation. Other cases with unilateral pathology include those reported by Fujii et al. (small posterior right temporal hemorrhagic lesion that involved the middle and superior temporal gyri), Neilsen and Sult (right thalamus and parietal lobe), and Wortis and Pfeffer (large lesion of the right TPO junction). The case reported by Fujii (1990) is informative because he was completely free of aphasic symptoms and because of the relatively small size of his lesion. In this patient, pure tone audiometry was within normal limits in spite of a 30 dB high-frequency hearing loss in the left ear. He showed marked suppression of the left ear during dichotic listening tests involving digits and words. Brainstem auditory evoked responses (BAERs) were normal, and sound localization was intact. The patient was selectively impaired in identification of non-speech sounds, and his errors consisted primarily of acoustic confusions. Saygin, Leech, and Dick (2010) reported a right-handed patient with auditory sound agnosia secondary to a stroke in *left posterior temporal and parietal cortices* who showed no impairment of language comprehension. Although the patient showed no signs of right hemisphere speech dominance prior to stroke, functional imaging showed post-stroke activation of the *right* temporal cortex and left anterior superior temporal gyrus to speech sounds, suggesting cortical reorganization.

Albert et al. (1972) described a patient with auditory sound agnosia with minimal dysphasia. Clinical evidence suggested bilateral involvement. The patient could attach meaning to word sounds, but not to nonverbal sounds.

Albert et al. also demonstrated marked extinction of the left ear to dichotic listening; impaired perception of pitch, loudness, rhythm, and time; and abnormally delayed and attenuated cortical AEPs, worse on the right. They concluded that the sound agnosia in their patient resulted from "an inability to establish the correspondence between the perceived sound and its sensory or motor associations" (associative defect), and suggested that the dissociation between verbal and nonverbal sound recognition in their patient reflected different processing mechanisms for linguistic and nonlinguistic aspects of acoustic input.

Sensory (Receptive) Amusia

Musical ability is a complex domain of functions in which selective impairments can occur after brain damage. Several distinct disorders have been identified, including vocal amusia, loss of skilled instrumental ability (instrumental amusia; McFarland & Fortin, 1982), loss of the ability to read write music (musical alexia and agraphia; Brust, 1980; Midorikawa & Kawamura, 2000), impaired recognition of music (receptive amusia; Procopis, 1983; Piccirilli, Sciarma, & Luzzi, 2000; Schuppert, Munte, Wieringa, & Altenmuller, 2000), and disorders of rhythm (Berman, 1981). In recent years, extensive analysis of congenital amusia ("tone deafness") has been undertaken by Peretz and colleagues (Peretz, 2001, 2008). Analysis of the patient with reported musical impairments should take into account the multicomponential nature of musical abilities.

The subject of amusia has been reviewed in detail by Wertheim (1969), Critchley and Henson (1977), and Gates and Bradshaw (1977). Sensory (receptive) amusia refers to an inability to appreciate various characteristics of heard music. It occurs to some extent in all cases of auditory sound agnosia, and in the majority of cases of aphasia and pure word deafness, but can occur independently of these other deficits (Piccirilli et al., 2000). As is the case with auditory sound agnosia, the loss of musical perceptual ability may be underreported because a specific musical disorder rarely interferes with everyday life. A major obstacle to systematic study of acquired amusia is the extreme variability of pre-illness musical abilities, interests, and skills. It was

Wertheim's (1969) opinion that receptive amusia corresponds more frequently with a lesion of the left hemisphere, whereas expressive musical disabilities are more apt to be associated with right hemisphere dysfunction. Recent evidence indicates that cerebral organization of musical ability is dependent on degree of experience, skill, and musical sophistication. Musically skilled and trained individuals may be more likely to perceive music "analytically" and to rely more heavily on the dominant hemisphere. Dichotic listening studies show that the right hemisphere plays a more important role than the left in the processing of musical and non-linguistic sound patterns (Blumstein & Cooper, 1974; Gordon, 1974). However, the left hemisphere appears to be of major importance in the processing of sequential (temporally organized) material of any kind, including musical series. According to Gordon (1974), melody recognition becomes less of a right hemisphere task as time and rhythm factors become more important for distinguishing tone patterns (see also Mavlov, 1980), although it has been argued that rhythm and interval processing may be vulnerable to right hemisphere damage (Schuppert et al., 2000). Such complexities contribute to a lack of definition of the entity of receptive amusia and the difficulty of localizing the deficit to a particular brain region. Further complicating the picture is the fact that pitch, harmony, timbre, intensity, and rhythm may be affected to different degrees and in various combinations in the individual patient. Furthermore, there is evidence that aspects of musical denotation (the-so-called "real-world" events referred to by lyrics) and musical connotation (the formal expressive patterns indicated by pitch, timbre, and intensity) are selectively vulnerable to focal brain lesions (Gardner et al., 1977). For instance, on tests of musical denotation, right hemisphere-damaged patients perform well on items where acquaintance with lyrics is required; in contrast, aphasic patients with anterior lesions are superior to both right hemisphere patients and to aphasic patients with posterior lesions on items where knowledge of lyrics is unnecessary. On tests of musical connotation, right hemisphere patients do better in matching sound patterns to temporally sequenced designs than to simultaneous gestalten.

Aphasic patients with posterior lesions perform relatively well on tests of musical connotation. Comprehensive tests of musical ability that separate these many subskills are now available (Schuppert et al., 2000; Peretz, Champod, & Hyde, 2003).

Peretz and colleagues (1994) applied comprehensive nonverbal auditory testing to two patients with bilateral lesions of auditory cortex. In their patients, the perception of speech and environmental sounds was spared, but the perception of tunes, prosody, and voice was impaired. Based on these behavioral dissociations, a modular organization of auditory processing has been proposed that contains, in the least, separate modules for speech and music (Piccirilli et al., 2000; Peretz & Coltheart, 2003). Peretz and Coltheart (2003) distinguish between pitch organization (tonal, interval, and contour analysis) and temporal organization (rhythm and meter analysis), and further highlight the importance of emotional expression analysis in music comprehension. Further, skills in distinguishing different voices or instruments (which is timbre-dependent) and in recognizing tunes may be dissociable. In contrast, the notion that nominally distinct classes of auditory material (e.g., melodies, prosody, and voice) share common processes may be critically important in developing a functional taxonomy of auditory recognition disorders in general, and of amusia in particular (Schuppert et al., 2000).

This suggestion points out certain significant deficiencies in the evaluation of amusic patients. Although theories linking brain function to music perception have long been available (Hecaen, 1962; Bever & Chiarello, 1974), such theories do not often contain sufficient process-specificity to guide the clinical evaluation of amusic patients. Thus, for example, relatively little is known regarding which musical features will be most informative in constructing a neuropsychological model of music perception. Another obstacle to systematic study of acquired amusia is the variability of pre-illness musical abilities, interests, and experience (see Wertheim [1969] for a system of classifying musical ability level). The cerebral organization of musical perception has been suggested to be dependent upon on the degree of these pre-illness characteristics (Bever & Chiarello, 1974).

One key aspect of musical processing that deserves increased attention is its emotional aspect, which is part of the cognitive model of musical abilities proposed by Peretz and Coltheart (2003). Listening to music might thus be expected to engage areas of the brain associated with emotion processing, and conversely, damage to these regions might be expected to lead to defects in the experience of pleasure and tension occasioned by musical stimuli. In normal subjects, the nucleus accumbens (NAc), ventral tegmental area (VTA), hypothalamus, and insula have demonstrated increased perfusion when subjects reported experiencing music-related pleasure in a functional MRI (fMRI) paradigm (Menon & Levitin, 2005).

Paralinguistic Agnosias: Auditory Affective Agnosia and Phonagnosia

Heilman, Scholes, and Watson (1975) showed that patients with right temporoparietal lesions and the neglect syndrome were impaired in the comprehension of affectively intoned speech, but showed normal comprehension of speech content. Patients with left temporoparietal lesions and fluent aphasia comprehended both affective (paralinguistic) and content (linguistic) aspects of speech normally. Whether this defect represents a "true" agnosia remains to be determined, since auditory sensory/perceptual skills were not assessed. It is possible that auditory affective agnosia is a variant of auditory sound agnosia (i.e., that it represents a category-specific auditory agnosia).

Van Lancker and colleagues (Van Lancker, Cummings, Kreiman, & Dobkin, 1988; Van Lancker, Kreiman, & Cummings, 1989) have revealed another type of paralinguistic deficit after right hemisphere disease. In their studies, patients with unilateral right hemispheric damage showed deficits in discriminating and recognizing familiar voices, whereas patients with left hemispheric damage were impaired only on a task that required discrimination between two famous (but not personally familiar) voices. Computed tomographic evidence suggested that right parietal damage was significantly correlated with voice recognition impairment, whereas temporal lobe damage in either hemisphere led to deficits in voice discrimination.

The authors refer to this deficit as "phonagnosia," but, like auditory affective agnosia, it remains to be seen whether it is truly agnosic in nature. A distributed cortical network may be involved in the processing of familiar visual and vocal stimuli (Shah et al., 2001). In this fMRI study, subjects viewed familiar and unfamiliar faces and listened to personally familiar and unfamiliar voices. Changes in neural activity associated with stimulus modality irrespective of familiarity were observed in regions known to be important for face recognition (bilateral fusiform gyrus) and voice recognition (superior temporal gyrus bilaterally), whereas familiarity of faces and voices (relative to unfamiliar faces and voices) was associated with increased neural activity in the posterior cingulate cortex, including the retrosplenial cortex.

Whether these defects are agnosic in nature is uncertain, but the discovery of seemingly specific impairments in the comprehension of affectively intoned speech and speaker identity is important in light of the fact that paralinguistic abilities may be spared in cases of PWD (Coslett et al., 1984). As indicated above, patients with PWD frequently report that they are able to recognize the speaker of the message and, less frequently, the language in which it is transmitted. These findings lend further support to the idea that linguistic and nonlinguistic processing of auditory signals are based on different neuropsychological mechanisms and, in fact, may be preferentially processed by different hemispheres. Further research is needed to provide more precise neuroanatomic correlates of auditory affective agnosia and phonagnosia.

SOMATOSENSORY AGNOSIA

Compared to visual agnosia, somatosensory (tactile) agnosias have received less attention and are poorly understood. However, it is likely that loss of higher-order tactual recognition in the absence of elementary somatosensory loss is probably at least as common as visual or auditory agnosia. Several distinct disorders have been identified, and many classifications of somatosensory agnosia have been offered. A reasonable descriptive framework was proposed by Delay (1935) who identified (a) impaired recognition of the size and shape of objects (*amorphognosia*); (b) impaired discrimination of the distinctive qualities of objects such as density, weight, texture, and thermal properties (*ahylognosia*); and (c) impaired recognition of the identity of objects in the absence of amorphognosia and ahylognosia (*tactile asymboly*). Delay's scheme is similar to that of Wernicke (1895), who distinguished between primary agnosia and secondary agnosia, or asymboly. For Wernicke, primary agnosia involved a loss of primary identification because of a destruction of "tactile images." In contrast, secondary agnosia resulted from the inability of intact tactile images to be associated with other sensory representations, resulting in a loss of appreciation of the object's significance.

The systematic study of tactile recognition disturbances has been beset by terminological confusion. The terms "tactile agnosia" and "astereognosis" have been used interchangeably by some authors, whereas others draw a sharp distinction between them. Astereognosis has been used to denote loss of the ability to distinguish three-dimensional forms (Hoffman, 1884; cited by Gans, 1916), the inability to make shape or size discriminations (Roland, 1976), and the inability to identify objects by touch (Delay, 1935). This is confusing, since Hoffman and Roland use the term to describe *discrimination* defects, while Delay and others use the term to denote defects of object *identification*. It is clear that defects in two-point discrimination, point localization, and position sense can impair tactile form perception, and thus object identification, without producing concomitant defects in sensitivity to light touch, temperature, or pain (Gans, 1916; Campora, 1925; Corkin, 1978). However, significant defects in discriminative ability need not accompany disorders of tactual identification (Corkin, 1978). Thus, clinical data suggest that tactile discrimination and identification are dissociable. Unfortunately, the vast majority of the physiological and anatomic data on somatosensory agnosia has come from animal research almost exclusively using discrimination, rather than identification paradigms.

With these considerations in mind, we will use the term *cortical tactile disorders* to refer to a diverse spectrum of defects in somatosensory discrimination or recognition of distinct object qualities. We will reserve the term *tactile agnosia* for those rare cases in which there is an inability to identify the nature of tactually presented objects despite adequate sensory, attentional, intellectual, and linguistic capacities. Although debatable, we will discuss *astereognosis* as an apperceptive form of tactile agnosia, recognizing that it represents a failure of complex perceptual processing that has, as an outcome, an impairment in tactile object recognition (TOR).

Before discussing disorders of tactile recognition, some comments about the functional anatomy of the somatosensory systems are necessary. An exhaustive review of this vast literature will not be undertaken here; the interested reader is referred to excellent reviews by Hecaen and Albert (1978), Corkin (1978), Mountcastle and Powell (1959a,b) and Werner and Whitsel (1973).

Two relatively distinct somatosensory systems have been identified. One is the spinothalamic system: Cutaneous nerve endings → spinothalamic tract → reticular formation → intrinsic thalamic nuclei → superior bank of Sylvian fissure [SII] (Hecaen & Albert, 1978; Brodal, 1981). This system is primarily responsible for the less precise aspects of somesthetic perception, and seems especially important in nociception and perception of thermal properties. The other system is centered on the medial lemniscus: cutaneous and subcutaneous receptors → medial lemniscal tract → ventroposterolateral thalamic nuclei → postcentral gyrus [SI]). The postcentral gyrus corresponds to Brodmann Areas 3, 1, 2. This system appears responsible for more precise discriminative aspects of touch, and carries information regarding form, position, and temporal change (Mountcastle, 1961). The two cortical somatosensory "receiving areas" (SI, SII) contain complex representations (homunculi) of body parts, with SI arranged somatotopically, and SII less so. The postcentral gyrus (SI) receives innervation from contralateral body parts, whereas SII receives bilateral input. It should be noted that other areas of cortex, including supplementary motor area and superior parietal lobe (Areas 5, 7), also receive direct input from somatosensory thalamus (Brodal, 1981).

In the sections on visual agnosia, we made mention of the fact that certain visual tasks place strong motor-exploratory demands on the visual system. This motor theme is also a striking characteristic of the somatosensory system. In a report of the results of cortical stimulation during craniotomy, Penfield (1958) found significant overlap between sensory and motor regions, in that 25% of stimulation points giving rise to somatosensory experiences were located in the precentral region. Woolsey (1964) found similar results in his electrophysiological studies of the alert monkey. Because of these and related findings, it has become common to speak of the sensorimotor cortex. Anatomic interconnections of SI and SII attest to the sensorimotor nature of these regions. Both SI and SII have reciprocal connections with thalamic nuclei, supplementary motor cortex, Area 4, and with each other (Hecaen & Albert, 1978; Brodal, 1981). In addition, SI projects heavily to Area 5 (the superior parietal lobule) (Jones & Powell, 1969; Corkin, 1978), important for motor pursuit of motivationally relevant targets in extrapersonal space (Mountcastle, Lynch, Georgopoulos, Sakata, & Acuna, 1975).

Thus, the functional interconnections of cortical somatosensory areas involve regions that, from numerous other studies, have been found to subserve motor, proprioceptive, and spatial functions. The existence of such a complex system in the human brain is important for intentional, spatially guided motor movements that bring us into contact with tactile stimuli. Reciprocal connections among somatosensory, motor, proprioceptive, and spatial components of the system provide the mechanisms whereby regulation of the perceptual act can be achieved. The complex functional organization of the somatosensory systems underscores the idea that perception is an active process and involves more than the mere passive processing of environmental input.

Although patients with lesions of the afferent somatosensory pathways frequently cannot identify tactually presented objects, this is due to a severe sensory loss, sometimes referred to as *stereoanesthesia*. Lesions of the primary visual and auditory areas produce specific disorders of sensation that can vary in severity depending on the extent and location of the lesion. Total ablation of primary visual and auditory areas results in cortical blindness or deafness, respectively.

In contrast, complete anesthesia for touch, temperature, pain, and vibration are rare following cortical lesions (Hecaen & Albert, 1978). Redundancy in representation seems to be an especially important characteristic of somatosensory systems. Paul et al. (1972) explored units in anatomic subdivisions of SI, and found multiple representations of the monkey's hand, one in each subdivision (cf. also Powell & Mountcastle, 1959; Mountcastle & Powell, 1959a,b). Randolph and Semmes (1974) selectively ablated each of the SI subregions (3b, 2, 1). Area 3b excisions resulted in impairment of all aspects of tactile discrimination learning. Lesions of Area 1 produced loss of hard–soft and rough–smooth (texture) discrimination, but spared complex–concave and square–diamond (shape) discriminations. The opposite pattern was seen in Area 2 lesions. Thus, the hand appears to be represented and re-represented within specific subdivisions of somatosensory cortex according to sensory submodality.

The notion of sensory submodality dates back at least to von Frey (1895), who divided the tactile sense into light touch, pressure, temperature, and pain sensitivity. Head (1918) divided sensory functions into three categories: recognition of spatial relations (passive movement, two-point discrimination, and point localization); relative sensitivity to touch, temperature, and pain; and recognition of similarity and difference (size, shape, weight, and texture). Submodalities may be selectively impaired, but others spared, by circumscribed cortical lesions. Head's (1918) framework, for example, suggests dissociations between the discrimination of texture and weight versus spatial relations, touch, temperature, or pain (cf. Corkin, 1978). Head, Rivers, and Sherrer (1905), based on studies of recovery from peripheral nerve injuries, distinguished between protopathic and epicritic sensation. The epicritic system subserves local point sensibility, while the protopathic system is more diffuse. The protopathic–epicritic distinction has been widely accepted by anatomists and physiologists (Rose & Woolsey, 1949; Mountcastle, 1961). As implied previously, the epicritic aspects of touch are more directly subserved by the medial lemniscal–SI system, whereas the protopathic dimension relates more closely to the functions of the bilaterally represented SII, although there is considerable functional overlap between the two systems.

Cortical Tactile Disorders

The brief review of the somatosensory systems has been designed to emphasize the complexity of this sensory modality, and to enable the reader to anticipate the enormous variability with which patients suffering from tactile recognition and identification disorders present. Historically, there have been two views regarding the nature and functional localization of disorders of tactile sensation. The first, more traditional, view is that sensory defects are associated with the contralateral primary somatosensory projection area in the postcentral gyrus (Head, 1920). The other perspective is that more extensive aspects of cortex (e.g., posterior parietal lobe) are involved in somatosensory perception (Semmes, Weinstein, Ghent, & Teuber, 1960). In a series of studies, Corkin and colleagues (Corkin, 1964; Corkin et al., 1970; Corkin, Milner, & Taylor, 1973) administered quantitative tasks of pressure sensitivity, two-point discrimination, point localization, position sense, and tactual object recognition to patients who had been operated on for relief of focal epileptic seizures. Lesions in the contralateral postcentral gyrus produced the most severe disorders of cortical tactile sensation. Also, clear demonstration was made of the existence of bilateral sensory defects associated with a unilateral cortical lesion, as had been previously reported by Semmes et al. (1960) and Oppenheim (1906).

Corkin found that the most severe defects occurred in patients whose lesions encroached on the hand area. This is consistent with the findings of Roland (1976) in his studies of tactual shape and size discrimination impairment with focal cortical lesions. Corkin et al. (1970) also found that disorders of tactual object recognition were restricted to the contralateral hand in patients with lesions that involved the hand area in SI. Importantly, defects of TOR were always associated with significant defects in pressure sensitivity, two-point discrimination, and other elementary sensory functions. Patients with parietal lobe lesions sparing SI did not show object identification disturbances.

Twenty of 50 patients with parietal lobe involvement showed additional sensory defects ipsilateral to the damaged hemisphere (Corkin et al., 1970). This effect was found with equal frequency after left and right hemisphere excisions, in contrast to previous studies that had found the incidence of ipsilateral sensory impairment to be much more frequent following left hemisphere damage (Semmes et al., 1960). Differences in the extent of lesions in the samples used by Corkin et al. (circumscribed cortical excisions) and Semmes et al. (penetrating missile wounds) may account for some of these discrepancies. An important anatomic fact is that, in patients with bilateral sensory defects of the hand, the postcentral hand area needs not be involved (Corkin, Milner, & Taylor, 1973). The area of damage implicated in these patients was tentatively offered as SII. In summarizing this data, Corkin (1978) suggests that unilateral SI hand area lesions produce severe contralateral sensory defects, while unilateral SII lesions may produce milder defects that affect both hands.

There is growing evidence of hemispheric specialization for certain higher somesthetic functions. Data on this issue can be found in cerebral laterality studies, examinations of patients following brain bisection, and in studies of performance on complex somatosensory tasks after unilateral hemispheric lesions (Milner & Taylor, 1972; Corkin, 1978). Although laterality studies have failed to show hemispheric specialization for elementary somesthetic functions such as pressure sensitivity (Fennell, Satz, & Wise, 1967), vibration sensitivity (Seiler & Ricker, 1971; cited in Corkin, 1978), two-point discrimination (McCall & Cunningham, 1971), or point localization (Semmes et al., 1960; Weinstein, 1968), results of complex sensory tasks requiring spatial exploration of figures or fine temporal analysis reveal evidence of hemispheric specialization. The left hand–right hemisphere combination appears especially proficient at tasks in which a spatial factor is important, such as in ciphering Braille (Rudel, Denckla, & Spalten, 1974) or perceiving the spatial orientation of tactually presented rods (Benton, Levin, & Varney, 1973). Results from studies of split-brain patients (Corkin, 1978) are consistent with these conclusions; the left hand–right hemisphere combination is better able to perform complex, spatially patterned discriminations although the right hand–left hemisphere can succeed if familiar stimuli are presented, if a small array of objects is involved, or in other situations in which linguistic processing can be effectively used (Milner & Taylor, 1972).

Thus, patients with right hemisphere disease do worse than left hemisphere-damaged patients in tasks requiring the perception of complexly organized spatial stimuli, although any patient with elementary somatosensory dysfunction, regardless of hand, can be expected to do poorly in that hand (Corkin, 1978). Semmes (1965) has identified a group of patients without primary sensory tactile impairment who fail in tests of object shape discrimination. These patients were unimpaired in roughness, texture, and size discrimination, but showed profound impairments on tests of spatial orientation and route finding. These patients suffered from lesions of the superior parietal lobe. Semmes concluded that a nontactual factor has an effect in these discriminative defects that transcended sensory modality. According to her view, what is "spatial" for vision is represented in touch by the temporal exploration of object qualities. Teuber (1965a,b) interprets the difficulty as a special form of spatial disorientation rather than one of agnosia for shape.

To summarize, no hemispheric specialization appears to exist for elementary somatosensory function, although there is growing evidence that the right hemisphere is more strongly involved in processing the highly spatial character of some tactile discrimination and identification tasks. Postcentral gyrus lesions frequently result in severe and long-lasting defects in the contralateral hand, whereas lesions of SII result in less severe, bilateral defects. A general conclusion from this extensive and complex literature is that the central regions (so-called sensorimotor cortex) are more directly involved in elementary somatosensory function, whereas complex somatosensory tasks possessing strong spatial or motor exploratory components involve additional structures posterior or anterior to the sensorimotor region (Corkin, 1978). This distinction makes it possible to see a higher somatosensory disorder in the absence of elementary sensory loss. Whether this higher disorder deserves to be called an "agnosia" is a subject to which we now turn.

Tactile Agnosia

The patient with tactile agnosia cannot appreciate the nature or significance of objects placed in the hand despite elementary somatosensory function, intellectual ability, attentional capacity, and linguistic skill adequate to the task of object identification. The terms "astereognosis" or "pure astereognosis" have been sometimes used synonymously with "tactile agnosia," and sometimes used to describe basic defects in the appreciation of size, shape, and texture. Delay (1935) asserted that astereognosis was a complex disorder comprised of amorphagnosis, ahylognosia, *and* tactile agnosia. In our view, astereognosis, as it has been described in the literature, essentially refers to apperceptive tactile agnosia. We will use the term in this fashion, and will reserve the term "associative tactile agnosia" for cases in which a deficit of TOR exists without concomitant sensory-perceptual defects.

Clinical case reports of pure astereognosis are rare (Raymond & Egger, 1906; Campora, 1925; Hecaen & David, 1945; Newcombe & Ratcliff, 1974. Frequently, obvious sensory defects do appear at some point in the clinical course of these patients, although not necessarily coincident with the identification disturbance. The astereognosic patient frequently has defects limited to one hand, usually the left, although patients with defects limited to the right hand have been reported (Hecaen & David, 1945). In some cases, the asymbolic hand can eventually achieve recognition of the object, although only after protracted linguistic analysis of the separate features.

Many astereognosic patients do not normally palpate the object when it is placed in the hand for identification (Oppenheim, 1906, 1911). This suggests a defect in the mechanism whereby tactile impressions are collected to form an integrated percept of the whole object, or a defect in stored structural tactile representations. Motor and sensory information is highly integrated in the act of palpating an object; motor commands are issued that direct the hand in ongoing exploration. Roland and Larsen (1976),

in a series of experiments using regional cerebral blood flow (rCBF) during astereognostic
testing in man, have shown that local rCBF
increases occur most strongly in the contralateral sensorimotor hand area and the premotor
region. Although sensorimotor integration and
proprioception are crucial components in tactile identification, it should be noted that the
motor component probably has a complex role
and is not obligatory in any simple sense. This
conclusion is warranted by two clinical facts:
(a) motor paralysis does not necessarily cause
tactile identification disturbances (Caselli, 1991b),
and (b) objects can often be identified if they
are passively moved across the subject's hand,
independent of active manipulation. Still, the
fact that true astereognosic patients do not palpate objects suggests that elementary sensory
function is not actively brought to bear, nor is it
adequately integrated with motor information,
in the perceptual processing of the stimulus.

Evidence for an associative defect exists
when elementary somatosensory defects are
either absent or too mild to account for a TOR
disturbance and when the patient can draw or
match tactually presented stimuli. For example,
the patient of Hecaen and David (1945) could
not name an object placed in the hand, but
could draw an accurate picture of the object
and could then name the picture. The patients
of Ratcliff and Newcombe (1974) could tactually match to sample even though they had a
disturbance in recognition of the nature of
objects.

As in other forms of agnosia, there has been
significant debate regarding the existence of
"true" tactile agnosia. Three general disclaimers
have been proposed. The first is the familiar
argument that all disturbances of tactile object
identification can be traced to defects of elementary somatosensory dysfunction. The second
states that the defect is not an agnosia, but
instead represents a modality-specific anomia.
Third, there are those who do not deny the
existence of higher defects of tactile identification in the context of normal elementary somatosensory function, but who say that the defect
of function in astereognosis is spatial and supramodal, involving both tactile and visual disturbances. Because one of the hallmarks of the
agnosia concept is its modality specificity, this

third view rejects the notion that tactile object
identification disturbances are agnosic in nature.
Each of these views is capable of handling some,
but not all, of the data. We will briefly examine
the status of each of these arguments below.

The possible role of subtle somatosensory
defects in producing disorders of tactile identification has been raised by several authors
(Head & Holmes, 1911; Bay, 1944; Corkin
et al., 1970). Bay (1944) stated that most putative cases of tactile agnosia had been inadequately tested for elementary somatosensory
dysfunction, and specifically implicated labile
thresholds and defects in performing complex
sensory discriminations. Head and Holmes
(1911) also stressed the importance of incon-
stant thresholds, and found that rapid local
fatigue and abnormal persistence of sensations
frequently accompanied defects of tactile
object identification. Semmes (1953) mentions
the possible contributory role of tactile extinction revealed by the method of double simultaneous stimulation, and states that, "if one stimulus
'extinguishes' or 'obscures' the perception of
another, or displaces the subjective position,
the resultant impression might be sufficiently
different from normal perception to make recognition impossible" (p. 144). In a recent study,
somatosensory evoked potentials were measured as an index of early sensory/perceptual
function and were found to be abnormal in
every case of putative tactile agnosia (Mauguiere
& Isnard, 1995).

Most studies fail to evaluate elementary sensory function to effectively refute the sensory
argument. One exception is a careful study by
Caselli (1991) that examined TOR disturbances
in 84 patients with a variety of peripheral and
CNS diseases. Using an extensive battery of tests
of somatosensory function and two tests of
TOR, Caselli found a number of patients who,
despite normal or only mildly compromised
somatosensory function, had disproportionate
TOR impairment. According to Caselli, this
type of impairment can result from unilateral
damage (in either hemisphere) involving parietotemporal cortices, possibly affecting SII.
Hecaen (1972) paid careful attention to somatosensory function in examining his agnosic
patient, revealing neither lability of threshold
nor sensory perseveration. Although only one

hand was agnosic, tactile discrimination, touch, and thickness discrimination was equal in both hands. There did appear to be a subtle defect in shape discrimination in the affected hand, as the patient could not accurately judge a series of objects on a continuum from ovoid to sphere, but, like many of Caselli's patients, this defect seemed insufficient in severity to account for the TOR disturbance. Delay (1935) found no differences between the hands for pain, temperature, pressure, kinesthesis, or vibration sense, although tactile localization and position sense were poorer in the affected hand (cf. Hecaen & Albert, 1978). Nakamura et al. (1998) found a bilateral impairment in recognizing palpated objects despite normal hylogonosis and morphognosis. This case had bilateral subcortical angular gyrus lesions, leading the authors to speculate that there was a bilateral disconnection of the somatosensory regions from semantic memory (Endo, Miyasaka, Makishita, Yanagisawa, & Sugishita, 1992; Nakamura, Endo, Sumida, & Hasegawa, 1998). Thus, there are cases in which defects in elementary somatosensory function cannot fully account for the observed defects in object identification.

Although the existence of tactile agnosia seems now established, the possibility that a modality-specific anomia might account for some instances of TOR impairment is raised by the landmark patient of Geschwind and Kaplan (1965). This patient underwent surgical extirpation of a left hemisphere glioblastoma and postoperatively developed a left anterior cerebral artery infarction involving the anterior four-fifths of the corpus callosum. He was unable to name or to supply verbal descriptions of items placed in his left hand but could draw misidentified objects with the left hand and could tactually choose a previously presented object from a larger group.

It is important to emphasize the differences between Geschwind and Kaplan's patient and other patients with deficient tactile object identification. First, because their patient could demonstrate recognition nonverbally, the defect was not a tactile agnosia in the true sense, but instead represented a disconnection of right hemisphere (left hand) tactual input from the speech area in the left hemisphere. Second, their patient, who had bilateral lesions, demonstrated

an object naming defect confined to the left hand (see also Gazzaniga, Bogen, & Sperry, 1963; Geschwind & Kaplan, 1965; Lhermitte, et al., 1976; McKeever & et al., 1981; Watson & Heilman, 1983; Boldrini, Zanella, Cantagallo, & Basaglia, 1992). This is in contrast to patients with bilateral impairments in TOR after a unilateral lesion insufficient in size or location to cause a complete tactile–verbal disconnection syndrome (Lhermitte & Ajuriaguerra, 1938). It also contrasts with the patient reported by Beauvois et al. (1978) who, after surgical removal of a large left parieto-occipital tumor, developed a modality-specific inability to name or verbally describe objects placed in either hand. When blindfolded, the patient could demonstrate the use of tactually presented objects. Naming errors were frequently semantic confusions. The authors interpret the deficit as a bilateral tactile aphasia, and suggest that it represents the tactile analogue of optic aphasia (Lhermitte & Beauvois, 1973). A third difference is that Geschwind and Kaplan's patient showed normal tactual exploration of objects, whereas patients with apperceptive tactile agnosia (astereognosis) show deficient palpation of objects, characterized either by a reluctance to manipulate the object or by a stereotypic pattern of manipulation that is independent of specific object qualities.

Supramodal Spatial Defects

Some patients with tactile recognition disorders also have profound defects in spatial localization, route-finding, and other visuospatial tasks (Semmes, 1965; Corkin, 1978). In concluding her review of somatosensory function, Corkin (1978) states that it is "possible to observe an impairment of high tactile functions in an individual whose elementary sensory status is preserved. It is inappropriate, however, to call this impairment an agnosia, because the higher-order deficits seen are not specific to somethesis" (p. 145). Recent evidence suggests that tactile recognition may be dependent upon spatial and visual processing, perhaps representing the assembly of an object's structural description (Platz, 1996; Saetti, De Renzi, & Comper, 1999; Zangaladze, Epstein, Grafton, & Sathian, 1999). This is a persuasive and important argument, but does not conclusively rule out the existence of an associative tactile agnosia in some patients. It is possible, for example, to suffer from an isolated deficit in tactile shape perception without the contribution of apparent spatial disability (Reed, Caselli, & Farah, 1996). It is likely that, in many cases, large lesions involving parietal cortex and underlying white matter affect spatial networks in addition to specifically involving the second somatosensory system. What may result from this kind of lesion is a sort of mixed defect in which somatosensory and spatial factors combine in unspecified amounts.

Although the anatomic and clinical evidence is far from clear, it seems reasonable to distinguish four defects of somatosensory recognition: cortical tactile disorders, astereognosis, tactile agnosia, and disorders of tactile naming secondary to tactile–verbal disconnection. Cortical tactile disorders involve defects in basic and intermediate somatosensory function, the end result of which will be pervasive somatosensory impairment in addition to defects in TOR. We believe that astereognosis is a more specific defect, that it deserves a designation as an apperceptive tactile agnosia (but see Tranel, 1991). It is primarily caused by a lesion in the functional system subserved by the middle third of the postcentral gyrus (the hand area) and its cortical and subcortical connections. Tactile agnosia, in contrast, seems to result from parietotemporal lesions that primarily involve SII (Caselli, 1991a) and involve connections between somatosensory regions and semantic memory stores (Endo et al., 1992).

Understanding complex somatosensory function in the individual patient requires a systematic neuropsychological evaluation of the task of tactual object identification as well as an evaluation of elementary and intermediate somatosensory function (Caselli, 1991a). When an object is palpated, sensory and proprioceptive cues received by postcentral gyrus interact with premotor region to direct a series of coordinated movements necessary to construct a tactile image of the object. Most TOR tasks contain components which could be described as sensory, spatial, proprioceptive, constructive and motor. The functional interconnections between SI, premotor region, and more posterior portions

of the parietal cortex highlight the challenges in functionally separating these task dimensions in tasks of TOR.

AGNOSIA AND CONSCIOUS AWARENESS

Despite a profound disability in direct identification of objects or faces, many agnosic patients are able to demonstrate some knowledge about the stimulus if appropriate tests of recognition are used. Such knowledge is demonstrated on tasks that do not require the patient to make a direct identification or naming response. Instead, the task is structured such that knowledge is demonstrated in an indirect or "implicit" way.

Dissociations of this type have received substantial discussion in literatures on amnesia and hemispatial neglect (see Chapters 16 and 12, this volume). For example, it has been shown that severely amnesic patients are able to acquire new motor or perceptual skills, and can demonstrate intact perceptual and conceptual priming of previously presented information (Roediger, Guynn, & Jones, 1994; Verfaellie & Keane, 1997). Similarly, patients with hemispatial neglect are capable of perceiving unattended information and, in some cases, engaging in high-level semantic processing of neglected stimuli despite being unaware of their perceptions (McGlinchey-Berroth et al., 1993; Farah & Feinberg, 1997). Other findings include lexical access without awareness in acquired alexia (Landis et al., 1980; Shallice & Saffran, 1986; Coslett & Saffran, 1989b), preserved visual identification capacity in hemianopic fields ("blindsight"; Weiskrantz et al., 1974, Weiskrantz, 1986), and preserved semantic priming in Wernicke's aphasia (Milberg & Blumstein, 1981; Blumstein et al., 1982). In all of these examples, evidence exists that the cognitive system thought to be impaired in these patients is capable of residual processing. However, the results of such processing cannot, or do not, reach the level of conscious awareness.

The best evidence for "covert recognition" in agnosia has come from studies of patients with prosopagnosia. Bruyer et al. (1983) provided the first behavioral evidence of covert recognition when they showed that their prosopagnosic could more readily match unrecognized faces with their real names than with arbitrary names. DeHaan, Young, and Newcombe (1987b) found that their prosopagnosic, like normal controls, performed same–different judgments more rapidly when the task involved famous faces than they did when unknown faces were presented. In these two examples, performance benefited from familiarity even though the patients never recognized specific faces as familiar.

In an elegant series of studies, DeHaan et al. (1987a,b) used the face–name interference (FNI) task to explore preserved semantic processing of faces in prosopagnosia. In FNI, subjects are asked to make a semantic classification judgment (e.g., "Is this an actor or politician?") when presented with printed names. Presented along with the name, but irrelevant for the name classification task, is a face that is (a) the same person as the printed name, (b) from the same semantic category as the printed name, or (c) from a different category. In normal subjects, name classification is slowed by the presence of a face from a different category, presumably based on a Stroop-like phenomenon. Prosopagnosic patients also show this effect, even though they fail to recognize a single face (DeHaan et al., 1987a,b, 1992), suggesting that, at some level, they can extract semantic information from faces and can thus become distracted by it when they perform the name classification task.

Covert recognition in prosopagnosia has also been demonstrated using psychophysiological (Bauer, 1984; Bauer & Verfaellie, 1986; Tranel & Damasio, 1985, 1988), electrophysiological (Debruille et al., 1989; Renault et al., 1989), and oculomotor (Rizzo et al., 1987) measures. Bauer (1984) showed that electrodermal responses to correct face–name matches were greater than to incorrect matches, whereas Tranel and Damasio (1985) showed a similar effect for face familiarity. Bauer and Verfaellie (1986) replicated this effect with a second prosopagnosic, but failed to show covert learning of new faces.

Renault et al. (1989) recorded evoked potentials while their prosopagnosic performed familiarity judgments to a series of faces in which the proportion of familiar and unfamiliar faces was varied. They found that, despite poor explicit recognition, P300 amplitude varied inversely

with stimulus probability (e.g., was higher on series containing few familiar faces) and latency varied positively with face familiarity.

Rizzo et al. (1987) evaluated exploratory eye movements in two prosopagnosic patients while they viewed famous and unfamiliar faces. Like normal subjects, these patients examined the whole face when encountering unfamiliar faces, but concentrated on internal features when viewing famous faces. Thus, the manner of visual exploration reveals that, at some level, facial familiarity is detected by the visual system although it is not reflected in the patient's verbal report.

Similar techniques have been applied to the question of whether prosopagnosic patients can learn new faces. Sergent and Poncet (1990) asked their prosopagnosic patient to inspect a series of famous and novel faces in preparation for a subsequent recognition task. Afterward, some of these faces (old) were combined with series of new faces, and subjects were asked to perform an old/new discrimination. Although the patient was generally unable to discriminate between old and new faces, face familiarity led to increased accuracy in episodic recognition. Remarkably, the patient was able to directly recognize faces on some trials.

Greve and Bauer (1990) used a variant of Zajonc's "mere exposure" paradigm to demonstrate covert learning of faces in their prosopagnosic. The patient was shown a series of faces that were each later paired with a novel distractor for forced-choice recognition and preference judgments. In forced-choice recognition, the patient was asked to indicate which of the two faces had been previously presented. In the preference-judgment task, the patient was asked which of the two faces he liked better. He performed at chance in forced-choice recognition, but "liked" significantly more of the target faces than predicted by chance. Thus, both of these studies suggest that prosopagnosic patients can learn some aspects of new faces provided that such learning is assessed indirectly.

In a few patients, psychophysiological (Bauer, 1986) and behavioral (Newcombe et al., 1989) measures have failed to reveal evidence of covert recognition (cf. Bruyer, 1991 for review). These patients had significant apperceptive defects, suggesting cognitive impairment prior to the level of the face recognition unit. This suggests that covert recognition is a characteristic of associative prosopagnosia.

These findings, and those in the literature on amnesia, alexia, aphasia, neglect, and blindsight, suggest that a substantial amount of perceptual and semantic processing must be intact in these patients, prior to, or independent of, the process that generates contextual or autobiographical recognition (Damasio, 1989; Schacter, 1989). Second, they imply that autobiographical recognition or appreciation of the nature of a stimulus involves mechanisms that are different from, or additional to, the mechanisms that process stimulus attributes.

One important issue concerns the implication such findings have for the functional architecture of object recognition. One of the dominant viewpoints is that such findings imply a dissociation between stimulus processing and consciousness. Schacter (1989) offers a general account of such dissociations by proposing that implicit and explicit domains reflect parallel, nonoverlapping outputs of early, modular cortices dedicated to processing specific types of information. In this view, one set of outputs links the outputs from sensory cortex with motor, verbal, and visceroautonomic response systems that are themselves capable of reading out cortical activity without conscious or executive control. Another independent set of outputs links modular cortices with a conscious awareness system responsible, in the case of object recognition, for explicit stimulus identification. According to this model, covert recognition in agnosia would result when functional interaction between modular cortices is selectively interrupted or disconnected while modular outputs to motor, verbal, and autonomic response systems remain intact. This impairment of functional interaction between modular cortices and the awareness system would lead to the kind of deficit one sees in agnosia: a domain-specific impairment in conscious identification without a global impairment in conscious awareness.

An alternative model, not requiring a disconnection mechanism, posits that dissociations between implicit and explicit forms of object/ face identification are the natural result of a damaged object recognition processor (Farah et al., 1993). This general approach was outlined above in the section on prosopagnosia, and is useful because (a) it begins to specify the nature of information processing taking place at different levels of the nervous system, and (b) it supplements lesion work in a way that informs and constrains the analysis of individual cases.

EXAMINATION OF THE PATIENT WITH AGNOSIA

Two basic principles should guide the examination of the agnosic patient. First, care should be taken to rule out the possibility that the recognition disorder is attributable to sensory-perceptual dysfunction, inattention, aphasia, generalized memory loss, or dementia. Second, an extensive analysis of the scope and limits of the patient's defect is required to characterize its functional locus.

RULING OUT ALTERNATIVE EXPLANATIONS

At the outset, it is important to remember that agnosic recognition failures are classically modality-specific. Patients who exhibit multimodal defects are more likely to be suffering from amnesic syndrome, language disturbance, dementia, or, in rarer cases, generalized impairments in semantic access. The nonaphasic agnosic patient will not usually manifest word-finding difficulty in spontaneous speech, and will generally succeed in generating lists of words in specific categories, in completing open-ended sentences, and in supplying words that correspond with definitions. Except in the rare case of optic aphasia, the agnosic will not be able to identify the misnamed objects by means of circumlocution, or by indicating function. It is thus important to determine whether the patient is able to demonstrate the use of objects not in his presence and to follow commands not requiring objects (e.g., salute, wave goodbye, make a fist, etc.). Failures of this type in the presence of otherwise intact auditory comprehension indicate apraxia; subsequent failure to demonstrate the use of objects presented on visual confrontation may therefore be apraxic, not agnosic.

In pointing and naming tasks, it is important to be certain that the patient is visually fixating on the objects to be identified and that pointing errors are not due to mislocation in space. Recognition should be examined both in the context of normal surroundings and in the formal test setting, taking care to ensure that the patient is familiar with target objects.

As a start, comprehensive neuroimaging, neurologic and neuropsychological assessment of intellectual skill, memory function, language, constructional/perceptual ability, attention, problem solving, and personality/emotional factors should be undertaken to determine the location of the lesion and to rule out bracketing conditions.

CHARACTERIZING THE NATURE OF THE DEFECT

In the visual sphere, the recognition of objects, colors, words, geometric forms, faces, and emblems and signs should be evaluated. In the event of failure to recognize, the patient should be allowed to match misidentified items to sample and to produce drawings of objects not identified. Quantitative achievement *and qualitative performance* on these tasks should be carefully noted, keeping in mind that quantitatively correct matching and accurate drawing does not necessarily suggest intact perceptual processing. Poor drawing does not necessarily implicate an apperceptive defect, since visuomotor or constructional defects may also be present. For this reason, it is important to use tasks in addition to drawing to document intact perception, if possible. Cross-modal matching and matching objects across different views should be evaluated. Line drawings to be copied should contain sufficient internal detail so that slavish tracing of an outline can, if present, be elicited.

Other perceptual functions, such as figure–ground perception (hidden figures), perceptual grouping, closure and synthetic ability, topographical orientation, route-finding, and visual counting (counting dots on a white paper, picking up pennies spread over a table top) should also be evaluated. Visual memory for designs, objects,

faces, and colors should be assessed by delayed recall (drawing from memory) and multiple-choice recognition tasks. The ability to categorize, sort misidentified objects, and pair similar objects that are not morphologically identical should be tested.

The patient should be asked to identify pictures of well-known people and to identify hospital staff by face. If recognition does not occur, the patient should be asked to determine whether the face is of a male or female or whether the face is of a human or animal. In the acutely hospitalized patient, ability to recognize visiting family can be assessed by dressing the family member in a white coat or other appropriate hospital garb to minimize the use of extrafacial cues by the patient. If face recognition impairment exists, it is important to demonstrate intact semantic (nonvisual) knowledge about persons that cannot be recognized visually. Failure to name a particular face should, therefore, be further examined by asking the subject to provide information (e.g., "Who is Tiger Woods?") about unrecognized personalities. Discrimination of faces across different viewpoints should be evaluated with matching tasks (e.g., Benton Facial Recognition Test).

Color perception should be tested with pseudoisochromatic plates and with the Medmont C-100 or Farnsworth D-15 ("visual" color tasks). The patient should be asked to respond to verbal tasks such as "What is the color of a banana?," to list as many colors as possible in a minute, or to name as many items as possible of a certain color. Other visual tasks, including coloring line drawings with crayons, should be given. Finally, visual–verbal color tasks such as naming colors pointed out by the examiner or pointing to named colors should be routinely presented.

The possibility of confabulation interfering with identification performance should be kept in mind. Therefore, test performance when the patient is allowed to verbalize should be compared with performance when he is prohibited from verbalizing by asking him to count backward or by having him place his tongue between his teeth. Comparing naming in the tactile modality alone with simultaneous visual and tactile presentation is also important.

Careful visual fields and visual acuity measures are crucial. It may be necessary, in testing patients who cannot read, to construct tests of acuity that use nonverbal targets, such as the orientation of lines of various lengths and distances from the viewer, or the detection of two points at variable distances from each other and from the patient. If equipment is available, detailed psychophysical tests should be employed including absolute threshold determination, local adaptation time, flicker fusion, contrast and spatial frequency sensitivity, movement aftereffect, and the brief presentation of single and multiple items. In patients with associated alexia without agraphia, rapid presentation of words and letters, as well as a neurobehaviorally oriented reading battery should be given. Depth perception using Julesz figures should be tested. Luminance discrimination should also be assessed. The use of an eye-movement monitor may be useful in describing visual scanning behavior. In settings where such sophisticated equipment is not available, careful observational analysis of visual exploratory behavior, manifested in eye movements, head-turning, and step-by-step feature comparisons, should nonetheless be conducted.

In the auditory sphere, standard audiometric testing using speech reception and pure tone audiometry should be conducted. The ability to localize sounds in space should also be examined by using both absolute and relative localization tasks. It should be remembered that patients with acquired auditory sound agnosia do not ordinarily complain about their problems. Recognition of nonverbal sounds should be tested preferably with the use of a series of tape-recorded environmental sounds that are sufficiently familiar to unimpaired subjects to yield nearly perfect recognition. The Seashore Tests of Musical Talent may be used with the understanding that in the absence of history of proven musical ability and interest, results may be difficult to interpret.

In the tactile sphere, each hand should be assessed separately in the performance of basic somatosensory function (touch, pain, temperature, vibration, kinesthesia, proprioception, two-point discrimination, double simultaneous stimulation, as well as discrimination of weight, texture, shape, and substance. In assessing TOR, verbal, pointing, and matching tasks should be used. Cross-modal matching (tactual–verbal,

tactual–visual) are also important in evaluating the scope of the recognition defect. It is important to allow the patient to draw misidentified objects or to after-select them from a group tactually. Tactual exploratory behavior (palpating of objects) should also be carefully observed.

CONCLUSION

Over the past 20 years, significant advances have been made toward an understanding of the complex components of recognition processes. It is now clear that "recognition" is not a simple process. Much of the historic debate about the existence of agnosia can be attributed to the fact that our models of recognition have generated some incorrect assumptions about what should happen when the recognition system becomes damaged. The best example is the debate over whether agnosia is a perceptual or memory access problem. Historically, the major problem with this question has been our assumption that it is the proper question to ask in the first place. We now know better, and significant advances have been made as a result in the last decade. The concept of recognition encompasses a broad range of behaviors, including attention, feature extraction, exploratory behavior, pattern and form perception, temporal resolution, and memory. New data on sensory and perceptual systems have revealed the exquisite complexity of the cortical and subcortical systems that support sensory and perceptual activities. Because of these advances, we have transcended the notion of a two-stage recognition process comprised of "apperception" and "association." Instead, recognition of sensory stimuli is now understood as a complex outcome of parallel processing occurring simultaneously at cortical and subcortical levels.

These complexities make it extremely unlikely that a core defect responsible for all agnosic phenomena exists. It now seems more fruitful to specify the conditions under which stimuli can and cannot be recognized and to more precisely specify the input, processing, and output requirements of specific tasks of identification and recognition. By doing this, and by correlating the emerging clinical findings with available neuropathological data, a meaningful understanding of the spectrum of agnosic deficits, and of normal recognition abilities, is rapidly emerging.

REFERENCES

Adams, A. E., Rosenberger, K., Winter, H., & Zollner, C. (1977). A case of cortical deafness. *Archiv fur Psychiatrie und Nervenkrankheiten, 224,* 213–220.

Adler, A. (1944). Disintegration and restoration of optic recognition in visual agnosia. *Archives of Neurology and Psychiatry, 51,* 243–259.

Albert, M. L., & Bear, D. (1974). Time to understand: A case study of word deafness with reference to the role of time in auditory comprehension. *Brain, 97,* 373–384.

Albert, M. L., Reches, A., & Silverberg, R. (1975a). Associative visual agnosia without alexia. *Neurology, 25,* 322–326.

Albert, M. L., Reches, A., & Silverberg, R. (1975b). Hemianopic colour blindness. *Journal of Neurology, Neurosurgery, and Psychiatry, 38,* 546–549.

Albert, M. L., Soffer, D., Silverberg, R., & Reches, A. (1979). The anatomic basis of visual agnosia. *Neurology, 29,* 876–879.

Albert, M. L., Sparks, R., von Stockert, T., & Sax, D. (1972). A case study of auditory agnosia: Linguistic and nonlinguistic processing. *Cortex, 8,* 427–433.

Alexander, M. P., & Albert, M. L. (1983). The anatomical basis of visual agnosia. In A. Kertesz (Ed.), *Localization in neuropsychology.* New York: Academic Press.

Alexander, M. P., Stuss, D. T., & Benson, D. F. (1979). Capgras syndrome: A reduplicative phenomenon. *Neurology, 29,* 334–339.

Allison, T., Ginter, H., McCarthy, G., Nobre, A. C., Puce, A., Luby, M., & Spencer, D. D. (1994). Face recognition in human extrastriate cortex. *Journal of Neurophysiology, 71,* 821–825.

Anaki, D., Kaufman, Y., Freedman, M., & Moscovitch, M. (2007). Associative (prosop) agnosia without (apparent) perceptual deficits: A case study. *Neuropsychologia, 45,* 1658–1671.

Anton, G. (1899). Ueber die selbstwahrnehmungen der herderkrankungen des gehirns durch den kranken bei rindenblindheit und rindentaubheit. *Archiv für Psychiatrie, 32,* 86–127.

Ardila, A., Rosselli, M., Arvizu, L., & Kuljis, R. O. (1997). Alexia and agraphia in posterior cortical atrophy. *Neuropsychiatry, Neuropsychology and Behavioral Neurology, 10,* 52–59.

Ariel, R., & Sadeh, M. (1996). Congenital visual agnosia and prosopagnosia in a child: A case report. *Cortex, 32,* 221–240.

Assal, G., & Despland, P. A. (1973). Présentation d'un cas d'agnosie auditive. *OtoNeuro-Ophtalmologie, 45,* 353–355.

Auerbach, S. H., Allard, T., Naeser, M., Alexander, M. P., Albert, M. L. (1982). Pure word deafness: Analysis of a case with bilateral lesions and a defect at the prephonemic level. *Brain, 105,* 271–300.

Balint, R. (1909). Seelenlahmung des "schauens," optische ataxie, raumliche storung der aufmerksamkeit. *Monatsschrift fur Psychiatrie und Neurologie, 25,* 57–71.

Bauer, R. M. (1982). Visual hypoemotionality as a symptom of visual-limbic disconnection in man. *Archives of Neurology, 39,* 702–708.

Bauer, R. M. (1984). Autonomic recognition of names and faces in prosopagnosia: A neuropsychological application of the Guilty Knowledge Test. *Neuropsychologia, 22,* 457–469.

Bauer, R. M. (1986). The cognitive psychophysiology of prosopagnosia. In H. Ellis, M. Jeeves, F. Newcombe, & A. Young (Eds.), *Aspects of face processing.* Dordrecht: Martinus Nijhoff.

Bauer, R. M., & Trobe, J. (1984). Visual memory and perceptual impairments in prosopagnosia. *Journal of Clinical Neuro-Ophthalmology, 4,* 39–46.

Bay, E. (1953). Disturbances of visual perception and their examination. *Brain, 76,* 515–550.

Bay, E. (1944). Zum problem der taktilen agnosie. *Der Zeitschrift fur Nervenk, 156,* 1–3, 64–96.

Baylis, G. C., Rolls, E. T., & Leonard, C. M. (1985). Selectivity between faces in the responses of a population of neurons in the cortex in the superior temporal sulcus of the monkey. *Brain Research, 342,* 91–102.

Beauvois, M. F. (1982). Optic aphasia: A process of interaction between vision and language. *Philosophical Transactions of the Royal Society of London (Biology), 298,* 35–47.

Beauvois, M. F., Saillant, B., Meininger, V., & Lhermitte, F. (1978). Bilateral tactile aphasia: A tacto-verbal dysfunction. *Brain, 101,* 381–401.

Beauvois, M. F., & Saillant, B. (1985). Optic aphasia for colors and color agnosia: A distinction between visual and visuo-verbal impairments in the processing of colors. *Cognitive Neuropsychology, 2,* 1–48.

Behrmann, M., & Avidan, G. (2005). Congenital prosopagnosia: Face-blind from birth. *Trends in Cognitive Sciences, 9,* 180–187.

Benson, D. F., & Greenberg, J. P. (1969). Visual form agnosia. *Archives of Neurology, 20,* 82–89.

Benson, D. F., Davis, R. J., & Snyder, B. D. (1988). Posterior cortical atrophy. *Archives of Neurology, 45,* 789–793.

Benson, D. F., Segarra, J., & Albert, M. L. (1974). Visual agnosia-prosopagnosia. *Archives of Neurology*, *30*, 307–310.

Bentin, S., Allison, T., Puce, A., Perez, E., & McCarthy, G. (1996). Electrophysiological studies of face perception in humans. *Journal of Cognitive Neuroscience*, *8*, 551–565.

Benton, A. (1990). Facial recognition 1990. *Cortex*, *26*, 491–499.

Benton, A. L., & Van Allen, M. W. (1972). Prosopagnosia and facial discrimination. *Journal of Neurological Sciences*, *15*, 167–172.

Benton, A. L., Levin, A., & Varney, N. (1973). Tactile perception of direction in normal subjects. *Neurology*, *23*, 1248–1250.

Berman, I. W. (1981). Musical functioning, speech lateralization and the amusias. *South African Medical Journal*, *59*, 78–81.

Bever, T. G., & Chiarello, R. J. (1974). Cerebral dominance in musicians and nonmusicians. *Science*, *185*, 137–139.

Beversdorf, D. Q., & Heilman, K. M. (1998). Progressive ventral posterior cortical degeneration presenting as alexia for music and words. *Neurology*, *50*, 657–659.

Beyn, E. S., & Knyazeva, G. R. (1962). The problem of prosopagnosia. *Journal of Neurology, Neurosurgery, and Psychiatry*, *25*, 154–158.

Bhaskaran, R., Prakash, M., Kumar, P. N., & Srikumar, B. (1998). Crossed aphasia leading to pure word deafness. *Journal of Association of Physicians of India*, *46*, 824–826.

Blumstein, S., & Cooper, W. (1974). Hemispheric processing of intonation contours. *Cortex*, *10*, 146–158.

Bodamer, J. (1947). Prosopagnosie. *Archiv fur Psychiatrie und Nervenkrankheiten*, *179*, 6–54.

Boldrini, P., Zanella, R., Cantagallo, A., & Basaglia, N. (1992). Partial hemispheric disconnection syndrome of traumatic origin. *Cortex*, *28*, 135–143.

Boller, F., & Spinnler, H. (1967). Visual memory for colors in patients with unilateral brain damage. *Cortex*, *3*, 395–405.

Boller, F., Cole, M., Kim, Y., et al. (1975). Optic ataxia: Clinical-radiological correlations with the EMIscan. *Journal of Neurology, Neurosurgery, and Psychiatry*, *38*, 954–958.

Bornstein, B. (1963). Prosopagnosia. In L. Halpern (Ed.), *Problems of dynamic neurology*. New York: Grune & Stratton.

Bornstein, B., & Kidron, D. P. (1959). Prosopagnosia. *Journal of Neurology, Neurosurgery, and Psychiatry*, *22*, 124–131.

Bornstein, B., Sroka, H., & Munitz, H. (1969). Prosopagnosia with animal face agnosia. *Cortex*, *5*, 164–169.

Botez, M. I. (1975). Two visual systems in clinical neurology: Readaptive role of the primitive system in visual agnosic patients. *European Neurology*, *13*, 101–122.

Brain, W. R. (1941). Visual object agnosia with special reference to the gestalt theory. *Brain*, *64*, 43–62.

Brodal, A. (1981). *Neurological anatomy in relation to clinical medicine* (3rd ed.). New York: Oxford University Press.

Brown, J. W. (1972). *Aphasia, apraxia, and agnosia—clinical and theoretical aspects*. Springfield, IL: Charles C. Thomas.

Brust, J. C. (1980). Music and language: Musical alexia and agraphia. *Brain*, *103*, 367–392.

Bruyer, R. (1991). Covert face recognition in prosopagnosia: A review. *Brain and Cognition*, *15*, 223–235.

Bruyer, R., Laterre, C., Seron, X., Feyereisen, P., Strypstein, E., Pierrard, E., & Rectem, D. (1983). A case of prosopagnosia with some preserved covert remembrance of familiar faces. *Brain and Cognition*, *2*, 257–284.

Buchman, A. S., Garron, D. C., Trost-Cardamone, J. E., Wichter, M. D., & Schwartz, M. (1986). Word deafness: One hundred years later. *Journal of Neurology, Neurosurgery, and Psychiatry*, *49*, 489–499.

Buchtel, H. A., & Stewart, J. D. (1989). Auditory agnosia: Apperceptive or associative disorder? *Brain and Language*, *37*, 12–25.

Burton, A. M., Bruce, V., & Johnston, R. A. (1990). Understanding face recognition with an interactive activation model. *British Journal of Psychology*, *81*, 361–380.

Busigny, T., & Rossion, B. (in press, 2009). Acquired prosopagnosia abolishes the face inversion effect. *Cortex*.

Cambier, J., Masson, M., Elghozi, D., et al. (1980). Agnosie visuelle sans hemianopsie droite chez un sujet droitier. *Revue Neurologique (Paris)*, *136*, 727–740.

Campbell, R., Landis, T., & Regard, M. (1986). Face recognition and lipreading. A neurological dissociation. *Brain*, *109*(Pt 3), 509–521.

Campion, J. & Latto, R. (1985). Apperceptive agnosia due to carbon monoxide poisoning. An interpretation based on critical band masking from disseminated lesions. *Behavioral Brain Research*, *15*, 227–240.

Campora, G (1925). Astereognosis: Its causes and mechanism. *Brain*, *18*, 65–71.

Caplan, L. R. (1978). Variability of perceptual function: The sensory cortex as a categorizer and deducer. *Brain and Language*, *6*, 1–13.

Caplan, L. R. (1980). "Top of the basilar" syndrome. *Neurology, 30*, 72–79.

Caramazza, A., & Shelton, J. R. (1998). Domain-specific knowledge systems in the brain the animate-inanimate distinction. *Journal of Cognitive Neuroscience, 10*, 1–34.

Carlesimo, G. A., Casadio, P., Sabbadini, M., & Caltagirone, C. (1998). Associative visual agnosia resulting from a disconnection between intact visual memory and semantic systems. *Cortex, 34*, 563–576.

Caselli, R. J. (1991a). Rediscovering tactile agnosia. *Mayo Clinic Proceedings, 66*, 129–142.

Caselli, R. J. (1991b). Bilateral impairment of somesthetically mediated object recognition in humans. *Mayo Clinic Proceedings, 66*, 357–364.

Celesia, G. G. (1976). Organization of auditory cortical areas in man. *Brain, 99*, 403–414.

Celesia, G. G., Archer, C. R., Kuroiwa, Y., & Goldfader, P. R. (1980). Visual function of the extrageniculo-calcarine system in man. *Archives of Neurology, 37*, 704–706.

Chanoine, V., Ferreira, C. T., Demonet, J. F., Nespoulous, J. L., & Poncet, M. (1998). Optic aphasia with pure alexia: A mild form of visual associative agnosia? A case study. *Cortex, 34*, 437–448.

Cohen, R., & Kelter, S. (1979). Cognitive impairment of aphasics in color to picture matching tasks. *Cortex, 15*, 235–245.

Cohn, R., Neumann, M. A., & Wood, D. H. (1977). Prosopagnosia: A clinico-pathological study. *Annals of Neurology, 1*, 177–182.

Cooper, J. A., & Ferry, P. C. (1978). Acquired auditory verbal agnosia and seizures in childhood. *Journal of Speech and Hearing Disorders, 43*, 176–184.

Corkin, S. (1978). The role of different cerebral structures in somesthetic perception. In C. E. Carterette, & M. P. Friedman (Eds.), *Handbook of perception* (pp. 105–155). New York: Academic Press.

Corkin, S. (1964). *Somesthetic function after focal cerebral damage in man.* Unpublished doctoral dissertation, McGill University, Montreal.

Corkin, S., Milner, B., & Rasmussen, T. (1970). Somatosensory thresholds: Contrasting effects of postcentral-gyrus and posterior parietal-lobe excision. *Archives of Neurology, 23*, 41–58.

Corkin, S., Milner, B., & Taylor, L. (1973). *Bilateral sensory loss after unilateral cerebral lesions in man.* Presented at the joint meeting of the American Neurological Association and the Canadian Congress of Neurological Sciences, Montreal.

Corlew, M. M., & Nation, J. E. (1975). Characteristics of visual stimuli and naming performance in aphasic adults. *Cortex, 11*, 186–191.

Coslett, H. B., & Lie, E. (2008). Simultanagnosia: Effect of semantic category and repetition blindness. *Neuropsychologia, 46*, 1853–1863.

Coslett, H. B., & Saffran, E. (1991). Simultanagnosia: To see but not two see. *Brain, 114*, 1523–1545.

Coslett, H. B., & Saffran, E. (1989a). Preserved object recognition and reading comprehension in optic aphasia. *Brain, 112*, 1091–1110.

Coslett, H. B., & Saffran, E. (1989b). Evidence for preserved reading in "pure alexia." *Brain, 112*, 327–360.

Coslett, H. B., Brashear, H. R., & Heilman, K. M. (1984). Pure word deafness after bilateral primary auditory cortex infarcts. *Neurology, 34*, 347–352.

Critchley, M. N. (1964). The problem of visual agnosia. *Journal of Neurological Sciences, 1*, 274–290.

Critchley, M. N. (1965). Acquired anomalies of colour perception of central origin. *Brain, 88*, 711–724.

Critchley, M. M., & Henson, R. A. (1977). *Music and the brain: Studies in the neurology of music.* Springfield, IL: Charles C. Thomas.

Crosson, B., Moberg, P. J., Boone, J. R., Rothi, L. J., & Raymer, A. (1997). Category-specific naming deficit for medical terms after dominant thalamic/capsular hemorrhage. *Brain and Language, 60*, 407–442.

Cummings, J. L., Syndulko, K., Goldberg, Z., & Treiman, D. M. (1982). Palinopsia reconsidered. *Neurology, 32*, 331–341.

Damasio, A. R. (1989). Time-locked multiregional retroactivation: a systems-level proposal for the neural substrates of recall and recognition. *Cognition, 33*, 25–62.

Damasio, A. R., & Benton, A. L. (1979). Impairment of hand movements under visual guidance. *Neurology, 29*, 170–174.

Damasio, A. R., & Damasio, H. (1982). Cerebral localization of complex visual manifestations: Clinical and physiological significance (Abst). *Neurology, 32*, A96 (Suppl).

Damasio, A. R., Damasio, H., & Van Hoesen, G. W. (1982). Prosopagnosia: Anatomic basis and behavioral mechanisms. *Neurology, 32*, 331–341.

Damasio, H., McKee, H., & Damasio, A. R. (1979). Determinants of performance in color anomia. *Brain and Language, 7*, 74–85.

Damasio, A. R., Tranel, D., & Damasio, H. (1990). Face agnosia and the neural substrates of memory. *Annual Review of Neuroscience, 13*, 89–109.

Damasio, A. R., Yamada, T., Damasio, H., Corbett, J., McKee, J. (1980). Central achromatopsia: Behavioral, anatomic, and physiologic aspects. *Neurology, 30,* 1064–1071.

Davidenkov, S. (1956). Impairments of higher nervous activity: Lecture 8, visual agnosias. In *Clinical lectures on nervous diseases.* Leningrad: State Publishing House of Medical Literature.

Davidoff, J., & Wilson, B. (1985). A case of visual agnosia showing a disorder of presemantic visual classification. *Cortex, 21,* 121–134.

Debruille, B., Breton, F., Robaey, P., Signoret, J. L., & Renault, B. (1989). Potentiels evoques cerebraux et reconnaisance consciente et non consciente des visages: Application a l'étude de prosopagnosie. *Neurophysiologie Clinique, 19,* 393–405.

de Gelder, B., Bachoud Levi, A. C., & Degos, J. D. (1998). Inversion superiority in visual agnosia may be common to a variety of orientation polarised objects besides faces. *Vision Research, 38,* 2855–2861.

De Haan, E. H., Bauer, R. M., & Greve, K. W. (1992). Behavioural and physiological evidence for covert face recognition in a prosopagnosic patient. *Cortex, 28*(1), 77–95.

De Haan, E. H., Young, A. W., & Newcombe, F. (1991). Covert and overt recognition in prosopagnosia. *Brain, 114*(Pt 6), 2575–2591.

DeHaan, E. H. F., Young, A., & Newcombe, F. (1987a). Faces interfere with name classification in a prosopagnosic patient. *Cortex, 23,* 309–316.

DeHaan, E. H. F., Young, A., & Newcombe, F. (1987b). Face recognition without awareness. *Cognitive Neuropsychology, 4,* 385–415.

Delay, J. (1935). *Les astereognosies. Pathologie due toucher. Clinique, physiologie, topographie.* Paris: Masson.

Delvenne, J. F., Seron, X., Coyette, F., & Rossion, B. (2004). Evidence for perceptual deficits in associative visual (prosop)agnosia: A single case study. *Neuropsychologia, 42,* 597–612.

Denberg, N. L., Jones, R. D., & Tranel, D. (2009). Recognition without awareness in a patient with simultanagnosia. *International Journal of Psychophysiology, 72,* 5–12.

Denes, G., & Semenza, C. (1975). Auditory modality-specific anomia: Evidence from a case of pure word deafness. *Cortex, 11,* 401–411.

Denny-Brown, D., & Fischer, E. G. (1976). Physiological aspects of visual perception II: The subcortical visual direction of behavior. *Archives of Neurology, 33,* 228–242.

DeRenzi, E. (2000). Disorders of visual recognition. *Seminars in Neurology, 20,* 479–485.

DeRenzi, E. (1982). *Disorders of space exploration and cognition.* New York: John Wiley and Sons.

De Renzi, E. (1986a). Prosopagnosia in two patients with CT scan evidence of damage confined to the right hemisphere. *Neuropsychologia, 24,* 385–389.

DeRenzi, E. (1986b). Current issues in prosopagnosia. In H. D. Ellis, M. A. Jeeves, F. Newcombe, & A. Young (Eds.), *Aspects of Face Processing.* Dordrecht: Martinus Nijhoff.

DeRenzi, E., Faglioni, P., Grossi, D., & Nichelli, P. (1991). Apperceptive and associative forms of prosopagnosia. *Cortex, 27,* 213–221.

DeRenzi, E., Faglioni, P., Scotti, G., & Spinnler, H. (1972). Impairment in associating colour to form, concomitant with aphasia. *Brain, 95,* 293–304.

DeRenzi, E., Faglioni, P., Scotti, G., & Spinnler, H. (1973). Impairment of color sorting: An experimental study with the Holmgren Skein test. *Cortex, 9,* 147–163.

De Renzi, E., & Saetti, M. C. (1997). Associative agnosia and optic aphasia: Qualitative or quantitative difference? *Cortex, 33,* 115–130.

DeRenzi, E., Scotti, G., & Spinnler, H. (1969). Perceptual and associative disorders of visual recognition. *Neurology, 19,* 634–642.

DeRenzi, E., & Spinnler, H. (1967). Impaired performance on color tasks in patients with hemispheric damage. *Cortex, 3,* 194–217.

Desimone, R. (1991). Face-selective cells in the temporal cortex of monkeys. *Journal of Cognitive Neuroscience, 3,* 1–8.

Devlin, J. T., Gonnerman, L. M., Andersen, E. S., & Seidenberg, M. S. (1998). Category-specific semantic deficits in focal and widespread brain damage: A computational account. *Journal of Cognitive Neuroscience, 10,* 77–94.

DeYoe, E. A., & Van Essen, D. C. (1988). Concurrent processing streams in monkey visual cortex. *Trends in Neurosciences, 11,* 219–226.

Dixon, M. J. (2000). A new paradigm for investigating category-specific agnosia in the new millennium. *Brain and Cognition, 42,* 142–145.

Dixon, M. J., Piskopos, M., & Schweizer, T. A. (2000). Musical instrument naming impairments: The crucial exception to the living/nonliving dichotomy in category-specific agnosia. *Brain and Cognition, 43,* 158–164.

Driver, J., & Vuillemier, P. (2001). Perceptual awareness and its loss in unilateral neglect and extinction. *Cognition, 79,* 39–88.

Duchaine, B. C. (2000). Developmental prosopagnosia with normal configural processing. *Neuroreport, 11,* 79–83.

Duchaine, B., & Nakayama, K. (2004). Developmental prosopagnosia and the Benton facial recognition test. *Neurology, 62,* 1219–1220.

Earnest, M. P., Monroe, P. A., & Yarnell, P. A. (1977). Cortical deafness: Demonstration of the pathologic anatomy by CT scan. *Neurology, 27,* 1175–1175.

Eimer, M., & McCarthy, R. A. (1999). Prosopagnosia and structural encoding of faces: Evidence from event-related potentials. *Neuroreport, 10,* 255–259.

Ellis, A. W., & Young, A. W. (1988). *Human cognitive neuropsychology.* Hillsdale, NJ: Lawrence Erlbaum.

Ellis, A. W., & Young, A. W. (1990). Accounting for delusional misidentifications. *British Journal of Psychiatry, 157,* 239–248.

Endo, K., Miyasaka, M., Makishita, H., Yanagisawa, N., & Sugishita, M. (1992). Tactile agnosia and tactile aphasia: Symptomatological and anatomical differences. *Cortex, 28,* 445–469.

Ettlin, T. M., Beckson, M., Benson, D. F., Langfitt, J. T., Amos, E. C., & Pineda, G. S. (1992). Prosopagnosia: A bihemispheric disorder. *Cortex, 28,* 129–134.

Ettlinger, G. (1956). Sensory deficits in visual agnosia. *Journal of Neurology, Neurosurgery, and Psychiatry, 19,* 297–307.

Ettlinger, G., & Wyke M. (1961). Defects in identifying objects visually in a patient with cerebrovascular disease. *Journal of Neurology, Neurosurgery, and Psychiatry, 24,* 254–259.

Evans, J. J., Heggs, A. J., Antoun, N., & Hodges, J. R. (1995). Progressive prosopagnosia associated with selective right temporal lobe atrophy. A new syndrome? *Brain, 118*(Pt 1), 1–13.

Farah, M. J. (1990). *Visual agnosia: Disorders of object vision and what they tell us about normal vision.* Cambridge, MA: MIT Press/Bradford Books.

Farah, M. J. (1991). Patterns of co-occurrence among the associative agnosias: Implications for visual object representation. *Cognitive Neuropsychology, 8,* 1–19.

Farah, M. J. (1996). Is face recognition "special"? Evidence from neuropsychology. *Behavioral Brain Research, 76*(1–2), 181–189.

Farah, M. J., & Feinberg, T. E. (1997). Consciousness of perception after brain damage. *Seminars in Neurology, 17,* 145–152.

Farah, M. J., Hammond, K. M., Mehta, Z., & Ratcliff, G. (1989). Category-specificity and modality-specificity in semantic memory. *Neuropsychologia, 27,* 193–200.

Farah M. J., Levine D. N., & Calvanio R. (1988). A case study of mental imagery deficit. *Brain & Cognition, 8,* 147–164.

Farah, M. J., & McClelland, J. L. (1991). A computational model of semantic memory impairment: Modality specificity and emergent category specificity. *Journal of Experimental Psychology: General, 120,* 339–357.

Farah, M. J., O'Reilly, R. C., & Vecera, S. P. (1993). Dissociated overt and covert recognition as an emergent property of a lesioned neural network. *Psychological Review, 100,* 571–588.

Farah, M. J., Wilson, K. D., Drain, H. M., & Tanaka, J. R. (1995). The inverted face inversion effect in prosopagnosia: Evidence for mandatory, face-specific perceptual mechanisms. *Vision Research, 35,* 2089–2093.

Farah, M. J., Wilson, K. D., Drain, M., & Tanaka, J. N. (1998). What is "special" about face perception? *Psychological Review, 105,* 482–498.

Faust, C. (1955). *Die zerebralen herderscheinungen bei hinterhauptsverletzungen und ihre beurteilung.* Stuttgart: Thieme Verlag.

Feinberg, T. E., Gonzalez-Rothi, L. J., & Heilman, K. M. (1986). Multimodal agnosia after unilateral left hemisphere lesion. *Neurology, 36,* 864–867.

Feinberg, T. E., Schindler, R. J., Ochoa, E., Kwan, P. C., & Farah, M. J. (1994). Associative visual agnosia and alexia without prosopagnosia. *Cortex, 30,* 395–411.

Fennell, E., Satz, P., & Wise, R. (1967). Laterality differences in the perception of pressure. *Journal of Neurology, Neurosurgery, and Psychiatry, 30,* 337–340.

Finkelnburg, F. C. (1870). Niederrheinische gesellschaft in Bonn. Medicinische section. *Berliner klinische Wochenschrift, 7,* 449–450, 460–461.

Forde, E. M. E., Francis, D., Riddoch, M. J., Rumiati, R. L., & Humphreys, G. W. (1997). On the links between visual knowledge and naming: A single case study of a patient with a category-specific impairment for living things. *Cognitive Neuropsychology, 14,* 403–458.

Franklin, S., Turner, J., Ralph, M., Morris, J., & Bailey, P. L. (1996). A distinctive case of word-meaning deafness. *Cognitive Neuropsychology, 13,* 1139–1162.

Frederiks, J. A. M. (1969). The agnosias. In P. J. Vinken, & G. W. Bruyn (Eds.), *Handbook of clinical neurology,* Vol. 4. Amsterdam: North Holland.

Freud, S. (1891). *Zur auffasun der aphasien. Eine kritische studie.* Vienna: Franz Deuticke.

Freund, D. C. (1889). Ueber optische aphasie und seelenblindheit. *Archiv fur Psychiatrie und Nervenkrankheiten, 20,* 276–297, 371–416.

Fujii, T., Fukatsu, R., Watabe, S., Ohnuma, A., Teramura, K., Kimura, I., et al. (1990). Auditory sound agnosia without aphasia following a right temporal lobe lesion. *Cortex, 26,* 263–268.

Gainotti, G., & Silveri, M. C. (1996). Cognitive and anatomic locus of lesion in a patient with a category-specific semantic impairment for living beings. *Cognitive Neuropsychology, 13,* 352–389.

Gans, A. (1916). Uber tastblinheit and uber storungen der raumlichen wahrenhmungen der sensibilitat. *Zietschrift fur die gesamte Neurologie und Psychiatrie, 31,* 303–428.

Gardner, H., Silverman, H., Denes, G., Semenza, C., & Rosenstiel, A. K. (1977). Sensitivity to musical denotation and connotation in organic patients. *Cortex, 13,* 242–256.

Gascon, G., Victor, D., Lombroso, C., & Goodglass, D. (1973). Language disorder, convulsive disorder, and electroencephalographic abnormalities. *Archives of Neurology, 28,* 156–162.

Gates, A., & Bradshaw, J. L. (1977). The role of the cerebral hemispheres in music. *Brain and Language, 4,* 403–431.

Gauthier, I., Skudlarski, P., Gore, J. C., Anderson, A. W. (2000). Expertise for cars and birds recruits brain areas involved in face recognition. *Nature Neuroscience, 3,* 191–197.

Gazzaniga, M. S., Bogen, J. E. & Sperry, R. W. (1963). Laterality effects in somesthesis following cerebral commisurotomy in man. *Neuropsychologia, 1,* 209–215.

Gazzaniga, M., Glass, A. V., & Sarno, M. T. (1973). Pure word deafness and hemispheric dynamics: A case history. *Cortex, 9,* 136–143.

George, N., Jemel, B., Fiori, N., & Renault, B. (1997). Face and shape repetition effects in humans: A spatio-temporal ERP study. *Neuroreport, 8,* 1417–1423.

Geschwind, N. (1965). Disconnexion syndromes in animals and man. *Brain, 88,* 237–294, 585–644.

Geschwind, N., & Fusillo, M. (1966). Color-naming defects in association with alexia. *Archives of Neurology, 15,* 137–146.

Geschwind, N., & Kaplan, E. F. (1962). A human disconnection syndrome. *Neurology, 12,* 675–685.

Gloning, I., Gloning, K., Jellinger, K., & Quatember, R. (1970). A case of prosopagnosia" with necropsy findings. *Neuropsychologia, 8,* 199–204.

Gobbini, M. I., & Haxby, J. V. (2007). Neural systems for recognition of familiar faces. *Neuropsychologia, 45,* 32–41.

Goldman-Rakic, P. S. (1988). Topography of cognition: Parallel distributed networks in primate association cortex. *Annual Review of Neuroscience, 11,* 137–156.

Goldstein, K. (1943). Some remarks on Russell Brain's article concerning visual object-agnosia. *Journal of Nervous and Mental Disease, 98,* 148–153.

Goldstein, K., & Gelb, A. (1918). Psychologische analysen hirnpathologischer falle auf grund von untersuchungen hirnverletzter. *Zetischrift fur die gesamte Neurologie und Psychiatrie, 41,* 1–142.

Goldstein, M. N. (1974). Auditory agnosia for speech ("pure word deafness"): A historical review with current implications. *Brain and Language, 1,* 195–204.

Goldstein, M. N., Brown, M., & Holander, J. (1975). Auditory agnosia and word deafness: Analysis of a case with three-year follow up. *Brain and Language, 2,* 324–332.

Goodglass, H., Barton, M. I., & Kaplan, E. F. (1968). Sensory modality and object-naming in aphasia. *Journal of Speech and Hearing Research, 11,* 488–496.

Gordon, H. W. (1974). Auditory specialization of the right and left hemispheres. In M. Kinsbourne, & W. L. Smith (Eds.), *Hemispheric disconnection and cerebral function.* Springfield, IL: Charles C. Thomas.

Graff-Radford, N. R., Bolling, J. P., Earnest, F. T., Shuster, E. A., Caselli, R. J., & Brazis, P. W. (1993). Simultanagnosia as the initial sign of degenerative dementia. *Mayo Clinic Proceedings, 68,* 955–964.

Green, G. L., & Lessell, S. (1977). Acquired cerebral dyschromatopsia. *Archives of Ophthalmology, 95,* 121–128.

Greve, K. W., & Bauer, R. M. (1990). Implicit learning of new faces in prosopagnosia: An application of the mere-exposure paradigm. *Neuropsychologia, 28,* 1035–1041.

Gross, C. G., Rocha-Miranda, C. E., & Bender, D. B. (1972). Visual properties of neurons in inferotemporal cortex of the macaque. *Journal of Neurophysiology, 35,* 96–111.

Grossman, M., Galetta, S., & D'Esposito, M. (1997). Object recognition difficulty in visual apperceptive agnosia. *Brain and Cognition, 33,* 306–342.

Haaxma, R., & Kuypers, H. G. J. M. (1975). Intrahemispheric cortical connections and visual guidance of band and finger movements in the rhesus monkey. *Brain, 98,* 239–260.

Habib, M. (1986). Visual hypoemotionality and prosopagnosia associated with right temporal lobe isolation. *Neuropsychologia, 24,* 577–582.

Harris, A. M., Duchaine, B. C., & Nakayama, K. (2005). Normal and abnormal face selectivity of the N170 response in developmental prosopagnosics. *Neuropsychologia, 43,* 25–36.

Haxby, J. V., Ungerleider, L. G., Horwitz, B., Maisog, J. M., Rapoport, S. I., & Grady, C. L. (1996). Face encoding and recognition in the human brain. *Proceedings of the National Academy of Sciences USA, 93,* 922–927.

Haxby, J. V., Hoffman, E. A., & Gobbini, M. I. (2000). The distributed human neural system for face perception. *Trends in Cognitive Science, 46,* 223–233.

Head, H. (1918). Sensation and the cerebral cortex. *Brain, 41,* 57–253.

Head, H., & Holmes, G. (1911). Sensory disturbances from cerebral lesions. *Brain, 34,* 102–254.

Head, H., Rivers, W. H. R., & Sherren, J. (1905). The afferent system from a new aspect. *Brain, 28,* 99.

Hecaen, H. (1972). *Introduction a la neuropsychologie.* Paris: Larousse.

Hecaen, H. (1962). Clinical symptomatology in right and left hemispheric lesions. In V. B. Mountcastle (Ed.), *Interhemspheric relations and cerebral dominance.* Baltimore, MD: Johns Hopkins University Press.

Hecaen, H., & Angelergues, R. (1962). Agnosia for faces (prosopagnosia). *Archives of Neurology, 7,* 92–100.

Hecaen, H., & David, M. (1945). Syndrome parietale traumatique: Asymbolie tactile et hemi-asomatognosie paroxystique et douloureuse. *Revue Neurologique, 77,* 113–123.

Hecaen, H. & de Ajuriaguerra, J. (1954). Balint's syndrome (psychic paralysis of visual fixation) and its minor forms. *Brain, 77,* 373–400.

Hecaen, H. & de Ajuriaguerra, J. (1956). Agnosie visuelle pour les objets inanimes par lesion unilaterale gauche. *Revue Neurologique, 94,* 222–233.

Hecaen, H., Goldblum, M. C., Masure, M. C., & Ramier, A. M. (1974). Une nouvelle observation dagnosie d'objet. Déficit de l'association ou de la catégorisation, spécifique de la modalité visuelle? *Neuropsychologia, 12,* 447–464.

Hefter, R., Jerksey, B. A., & Barton, J. J. (2008). The biasing of figure-ground assignment by shading cues for objects and faces in prosopagnosia. *Perception, 37,* 1412–1425.

Heilman, K. M., Scholes, R., & Watson, R. T. (1975). Auditory affective agnosia. Disturbed comprehension of affective speech. *Journal of Neurology, Neurosurgery, and Psychiatry, 38,* 69–72.

Hemphill, R. C., & Stengel, E. (1940). A study of pure word deafness. *Journal of Neurology and Psychiatry, 3,* 251–262.

Heywood, C. A., Gaffan, D., & Cowey, A. (1995). Cerebral achromatopsia in monkeys. *European Journal of Neuroscience, 7,* 1064–1073.

Heywood, C. A., Kentridge, R. W., & Cowey, A. (1998). Form and motion from colour in cerebral achromatopsia. *Experimental Brain Research, 123*(1–2), 145–153.

Hoffman, H. (1884). Stereognostiche versuche, angesllellf zue ermi helangder elemente des gefahlssinnes, aus denen die vorstellungen des korps vin raume gebildet werden. *Deutsches Archiv für klinische Medizin, 36,* 398–426.

Holmes, G. (1918). Disturbances of visual orientation. *British Journal of Ophthalmology, 2,* 449–468.

Horel, J. A., & Keating, E. G. (1969). Partial Kluver-Bucy syndrome produced by cortical disconnection. *Brain Research, 16,* 281–284.

Horel, J. A., & Keating, E. G. (1972). Recovery from a partial Kluver-Bucy syndrome induced by disconnection. *Journal of Comparative and Physiological Psychology, 79,* 105–114.

Hubel, D. H., & Weisel, T. N. (1977). Functional architecture of macaque monkey visual cortex. *Proceedings of the Royal Society of London (Biology), 198,* 1–59.

Humphreys, G. W., & Riddoch, M. J. (1987). *To see but not to see: A case study of visual agnosia.* London: Lawrence Erlbaum.

Husain, M., & Stein, J. (1988). Rezso Balint and his most celebrated case. *Archives of Neurology, 45,* 89–93.

Iversen, S. D., & Weiskrantz, L. (1967). Perception of redundant cues by monkeys with inferotemporal lesions. *Nature, 214,* 241–243.

Iversen, S. D., & Weiskrantz, L. (1964). Temporal lobe lesions and memory in the monkey. *Nature, 201,* 740–742.

Jackson, J. H. (1932). *Case of large cerebral tumour without optic neuritis and with left hemiplegia and imperception. R. Lond Ophthal. Hosp. Rep. 8, 434.* In I. Taylor (Ed.), *Selected Writings of John Hughlings Jackson* Vol. 2. London: Hodder & Stoughton. (Originally published 1876).

Jerger, J., Weikers, N., Sharbrough, F., & Jerger, S. (1969). Bilateral lesions of the temporal lobe. A case study. *Acta Oto-Laryngologica,* Suppl. *258,* 1–51.

Jones, E. G., & Powell, T. P. S. (1969). Connections of the somatic sensory cortex of the rhesus monkey. I. Ipsilateral cortical connections. *Brain, 92,* 477–502. II. Contralateral connections. Brain, *92,* 717–730.

Jörgens, S., Biermann-Ruben, K., Jurz, M. W., Flügel, C., Daehli-Kurz, K., Antke, C., et al. (2008). Word deafness as a cortical auditory processing deficit: A case report with MEG. *Neurocase, 14,* 307–316.

Kaas, J. H. (1995). Human visual cortex. Progress and puzzles. *Current Biology, 5*(10), 1126–1128.

Kanshepolsky, J., Kelley, J., & Waggener, J. (1973). A cortical auditory disorder. *Neurology, 23,* 699–705.

Kanter, S. L., Day, A. L., Heilman, K. M., & Gonzalez-Rothi, L. J. (1986). Pure word deafness: A possible explanation of transient deterioration after extracranial-intracranial bypass grafting. *Neurosurgery, 18,* 186–189.

Kanwisher, N. (1987). Repetition blindness: Type recognition without token individuation. *Cognition, 27,* 117–143.

Kanwisher, N., Chun, M. M., McDermott, J., & Ledden, P. J. (1996). Functional imagining of human visual recognition. *Cognitive Brain Research, 5*(1–2), 55–67.

Kanwisher, N., Tong, F., & Nakayama, K. (1998). The effect of face inversion on the human fusiform face area. *Cognition, 68,* B1–11.

Karnath, H. -O, Rüter, J., Mandler, A., & Himmelbach, M. (2009). The anatomy of object recognition - Visual form agnosia caused by medial occipitotemporal stroke. *Journal of Neuroscience, 29,* 5854–5862.

Karpov, B. A., Meerson, Y. A., & Tonkonogii, I. M. (1979). On some peculiarities of the visuomotor system in visual agnosia. *Neuropsychologia, 17,* 231–294.

Kase, C. S., Tronscoso, J. F., Court, J. E., Tapia, F. J., & Mohr, J. P. (1977). Global spatial disorientation. *Journal of Neurological Sciences, 34,* 267–278.

Kazui, S., Naritomi, H. Sawada, T., & Inque, N. (1990). Subcortical auditory agnosia. *Brain and Language, 38,* 476–487.

Kertesz, A. (1979). Visual agnosia: The dual deficit of perception and recognition. *Cortex, 15,* 403–419.

Kim, J. J., Andreasen, N. C., O'Leary, D. S., Wiser, A. K., Ponto, L. L., Watkins, G. L., & Hichwa, R. D. (1999). Direct comparison of the neural substrates of recognition memory for words and faces. *Brain, 122*(Pt 6), 1069–1083.

Kinsbourne, M., & Warrington, E.K. (1962). A disorder of simultaneous form perception. *Brain, 85,* 461–486.

Kinsbourne, M., & Warrington, E. K. (1964). Observations on color agnosia. *Journal of Neurology, Neurosurgery, and Psychiatry, 27,* 296–299.

Kitayama, I., Yamazaki, K., Shibahara, K., & Nomura, J. (1990). Pure word deafness with possible transfer of language dominance. *Japanese Journal of Psychiatry and Neurology, 44,* 577–584.

Klein, R., & Harper, J. (1956). The problem of agnosia in the light of a case of pure word deafness. *Journal of Mental Sciences, 102,* 112–120.

Kliest, K. (1928). Gehirnpathologische und iokalisatorische ergebnisse uber horstorungen, geruschtaubheiten und amusien. *Monatsschrift fur Psychiatrie und Neurologie, 68,* 853–860.

Kracke, I. (1994). Developmental prosopagnosia in Asperger syndrome: Presentation and discussion of an individual case. *Developmental Medicine and Child Neurology, 36,* 873–886.

Kreiman, G., Koch, C., & Fried, I. (2000). Category-specific visual responses of single neurons in the human medial temporal lobe. *Nature Neuroscience, 3,* 946–953.

Kussmaul, A. (1877). Disturbances of speech. In H. vonZiemssien (Ed.), *Cyclopedia of the practice of medicine.* New York: William Wood & Co.

Kuypers, H. G. J. M., Szwarcbart, M. K., Mishkin, M., & Rosvold, H. E. (1965). Occipitotemporal corticocortical connections in the rhesus monkey. *Experimental Neurology, 11,* 245–262.

Lamberts, F. (1980). Developmental auditory agnosia in the severely retarded: A further investigation. *Brain and Language, 11,* 106–118.

Lambon Ralph, M. A., Lowe, C., & Rogers, T. T. (2007). Neural basis of category-specific semantic deficits for living things: Evidence from semantic dementia, HSVE and a neural network model. *Brain, 130,* 1127–1137.

Landau, W. U., & Kleffner, F. R. (1957). Syndrome of acquired aphasia with convulsive disorder in children. *Neurology, 7,* 523–530.

Landau, W. U., Goldstein, R., & Kleffner, F. R. (1960). Congenital aphasia: A clinicopathologic study. *Neurology, 10,* 915–921.

Landis, T., Cummings, J. L., Christen, L., Bogen, J. E., & Imhof, H. G. (1986). Are unilateral right posterior cerebral lesions sufficient to cause prosopagnosia? Clinical and radiological findings in six additional patients. *Cortex, 22,* 243–252.

Landis, T., Graves, R., Benson, D. F., & Hebben, N. (1982). Visual recognition through kinaesthetic mediation. *Psychological Medicine, 12,* 515–531.

Landis, T., Regard, M., & Serrant, A. (1980). Iconic reading in a case of alexia without agraphia caused by a brain tumor: A tachistoscopic study. *Brain and Language, 11,* 45–53.

Larrabee, G. J., Levin, H. S., Huff, F. J., Kay, M. C., & Guinto, F. C. (1985). Visual agnosia contrasted with visual-verbal disconnection. *Neuropsychologia, 23*, 1–12.

Lawden, M. C., & Cleland, P. G. (1993). Achromatopsia in the aura of migraine. *Journal of Neurology, Neurosurgery, and Psychiatry, 56*, 708–709.

Lee, Y., Duchaine, B., Wilson, H. R., & Nakayama, K. (2009). Three cases of developmental prosopagnosia from one family: Detailed neuropsychological and psychophysical investigation of face processing. *Cortex 46*, 949–964.

Leicester, J. (1980). Central deafness and subcortical motor aphasia. *Brain and Language, 10*, 224–242.

Levine, D. N. (1978). Prosopagnosia and visual object agnosia: A behavioral study. *Brain and Language, 5*, 341–365.

Levine, D. N., & Calvanio, R. (1978). A study of the visual defect in verbal alexia-simultanagnosia. *Brain, 101*, 65–81.

Levine, D. N., & Calvanio, R. (1989). Prosopagnosia: A defect in visual configural processing. *Brain and Cognition, 10*, 149–170.

Levine, D. N., Kaufman, K. J., & Mohr, J. P. (1978). Inaccurate reaching associated with a superior parietal lobe tumor. *Neurology, 28*, 556–561.

Lhermitte, F., & Beauvois, M. F. (1973). A visual-speech disconnection syndrome. *Brain, 96*, 695–714.

Lhermitte, J. & de Ajuriaguerra, I. (1938). Asymbolie tactile et hallucinations du toucher. Etude anatomoclinique. *Revue Neurologique, 70*, 492–495.

Lhermitte, F., Chedru, J., & Chain, F. (1973). A propos d'une cas d'agnosie visuelle. *Revue Neurologique, 128*, 301–322.

Lhermitte, F., Chain, F. Chedru, J., & Penet, C. (1976). A study of visual processes in a case of interhemispheric disconnexion. *Journal of Neurological Sciences, 25*, 317–330.

Lhermitte, F., Chain, F. Escourolle, R., et al. (1971). Etude des troubles perceptifs auditifs dans les lesions temporales bilaterales. *Revue Neurologique, 128*, 329–351.

Lhermitte, F., & Pillon, B. (1975). La prosopagnosie: Role de l'hemisphere droit dans la perception visuelle. *Revue Neurologique, 131*, 791–812.

Lichteim, L. (1885). On aphasia. *Brain, 7*, 433–484.

Liepmann, H., & Storch, E. (1902). Der mikroskopische gehirnbefund bei dem fall gorstelle. *Monatsschrift fur Psychiatrie und Neurologie 11*, 115–120.

Lissauer, H. (1890). Ein fall von seeienblindheit nebst conem beitrage zur theorie derselben. *Archiv fur Psychiatrie, 21*, 222–270.

Luria, A. R. (1959). Disorders of "simultaneous perception" in a case of bilateral occipitoparietal brain injury. *Brain, 83*, 437–449.

Luria, A. R., Pravdina-Vinarskaya, E. N., & Yarbus, A. L. (1963). Disorders of ocular movement in a case of simultanagnosia. *Brain, 86*, 219–228.

Luzzatti C., & Davidoff, J. (1994). Impaired retrieval of object-colour knowledge with preserved colour naming. *Neuropsychologia, 32*, 933–950.

Lynch, J. C., & McClaren, J. W. (1989). Deficits of visual attention and saccadic eye movements after lesions of parietooccipital cortex in monkeys. *Journal of Neurophysiology, 61*, 74–90.

Mack, J. L., & Boller, F. (1977). Associative visual agnosia and its related deficits: The role of the minor hemisphere in assigning meaning to visual perceptions. *Neuropsychologia, 15*, 345–349.

MacKay, G., & Dunlop, J. C. (1899). The cerebral lesions in a case of complete acquired colour-blindness. *Scottish Medical Surgical Journal, 5*, 503–512.

Mahoudeau, D., Lemoyne, J., Dubrisay, J., & Caraes, J. (1956). Sur un cas dagnosie auditive. *Revue Neurologique, 95*, 57.

Makino, M., Takanashi, Y., Iwamoto, K., Yoshikawa, K., Ohshima, H., Nakajima, K., et al. (1998). Auditory evoked magnetic fields in patients of pure word deafness. *No To Shinkei, 50*, 51–55.

Marangolo, P., DeRenzi, E., DiPace, E., Ciurli, P., & Castriota-Skanderberg, A. (1998). Let not thy left hand know what thy right hand knoweth: The case of a patient with an infarct involving the callosal pathways. *Brain, 121*, 1459–1467.

Marr, D. (1982). *Vision: A computational investigation into the human representation and processing of visual information.* New York: W. H. Freeman.

Massopoust, L. C., & Wolin, L. R. (1967). Changes in auditory frequency discrimination thresholds after temporal cortex ablation. *Experimental Neurology, 19*, 245–251.

Mauguiere, F., & Isnard, J. (1995). Tactile agnosia and dysfunction of the primary somatosensory area. Data of the study by somatosensory evoked potentials in patients with deficits of tactile object recognition. *Revue Neurologique Paris, 151*(8–9), 518–527.

Maunsell, J. H. R., & Newsome, W. T. (1987). Visual processing in monkey extrastriate cortex. *Annual Review of Neuroscience, 10*, 363–401.

Mavlov, L. (1980). Amusia due to rhythm agnosia in a musician with left hemi-sphere damage: A non-auditory supramodal defect. *Cortex, 16*, 331–338. 87

McCall, G. N., & Cunningham, N. M. (1971). Two-point discrimination: Asymmetry in spatial discrimination on the two sides of the tongue, a preliminary report. *Perceptual and Motor Skills*, 32, 368–370.

McCarthy, R. A., & Warrington, E. K. (1986). Visual associative agnosia: A clinico-anatomical study of a single case. *Journal of Neurology, Neurosurgery, and Psychiatry*, 49, 1233–1240.

McClelland, J. L., & Rumelhart, D. E. (1986). *Parallel distributed processing: Explorations in the microstructure of cognition II. Psychological and biological models*. Cambridge, MA: MIT Press.

McFarland, H. R., & Fortin, D. (1982). Amusia due to right temporoparietal infarct. *Archives of Neurology*, 39, 725–727.

McGlinchey Berroth, R., Milberg, W. P., Verfaellie, M., Alexander, M., & et al. (1993). Semantic processing in the neglected visual field: Evidence from a lexical decision task. *Cognitive Neuropsychology*, 10, 79–108.

McIntosh, A. R., Grady, C. L., Ungerleider, L. G., Haxby, J. V., Rapoport, S. I., & Horwitz, B. (1994). Network analysis of cortical visual pathways mapped with PET. *Journal of Neuroscience*, 14, 655–666.

McKeever, W. F., Larrabee, G. J., Sullivan, K. F., Johnson, H. J., Furguson, S., & Rayport, M. (1981). Unimanual tactile anomia consequent to corpus callosotomy: Reduction of anomic deficit under hypnosis. *Neuropsychologia*, 19(2), 179–190.

Meadows, J. C. (1974a). The anatomical basis of prosopagnosia. *Journal of Neurology, Neurosurgery, and Psychiatry*, 37, 489–501.

Meadows, J. C. (1974b). Disturbed perception of colours associated with localized cerebral lesions. *Brain*, 97, 615–632.

Mendez, M. F. (2000). Corticobasal ganglionic degeneration with Balint's syndrome. *Journal of Neuropsychiatry and Clinical Neuroscience*, 12, 273–275.

Mendez, M. F., & Geehan, G. R., Jr. (1988). Cortical auditory disorders: Clinical and psychoacoustic features. *Journal of Neurology, Neurosurgery, and Psychiatry*, 51, 1–9.

Mendez, M. F., Mendez, M. A., Martin, R., Smyth, K. A., & Whitehouse, P. J. (1990). Complex visual disturbances in Alzheimer's disease. *Neurology*, 40, 439–443.

Menon, V., & Levitin, D. J. (2005). The rewards of music listening: Response and physiological connectivity of the mesolimbic system. *Neuroimage*, 28(1), 175–184.

Miceli, G. (1982). The processing of speech sounds in a patient with cortical auditory disorder. *Neuropsychologia*, 20, 5–20.

Michel, F., Perenin, M. T., & Sieroff, E. (1986). Prosopagnosie sans hemianopsie apres lesion unilateralie occipito-temporale droite. *Revue Neurologique*, 142, 545–549.

Michel, J., Peronnet, F., & Schott, B. (1980). A case of cortical deafness: Clinical and electrophysiological data. *Brain and Language*, 10, 367–377.

Michel, F., Poncet, M., & Signoret, J. L. (1989). Are the lesions responsible for prosopagnosia always bilateral?. *Revue Neurologique Paris*, 145, 764–770.

Midorikawa, A., & Kawamura, M. (2000). A case of musical agraphia. *Neuroreport*, 11(13), 3053–3057.

Milner, A. D., & Goodale, M. A. (1995) *The visual brain in action*. Oxford: Oxford University Press.

Milner, A.D. & Heywood, C.A. (1989). A disorder of lightness discrimination in a case of visual form agnosia. *Cortex*, 25, 489–494.

Milner, A. D., Perrett, D. I., Johnston, R. S., Benson, P. J., Jordan, T. R., Heeley, D. W., et al. (1991). Perception and action in "visual form agnosia." *Brain*, 114, 405–428.

Milner, B., & Taylor, L. B. (1972). Right-hemisphere superiority in tactile pattern recognition after cerebral commisurotomy: Evidence for nonverbal memory. *Neuropsychologia*, 10, 1–15.

Motomura, N., Yamadori, A., Mori, E., & Tamaru, F. (1986). Auditory agnosia: Analysis of a case with bilateral subcortical lesions. *Brain*, 109, 379–391.

Mountcastle, V. B. (1961). Some functional properties of the somatic afferent system. In W. A. Rosenblith (Ed.), *Sensory communication* (pp. 403–436). Cambridge, MA: MIT Press.

Mountcastle, V. B., & Powell, T. P. S. (1959a). Neural mechanisms subserving cutaneous sensibility, with special reference to the role of afferent inhibition in sensory perception and discrimination. *Bulletin of the Johns Hopkins Hospital*, 105, 201–232.

Mountcastle, V. B., & Powell, T. P. S. (1959b). Central nervous mechanisms subserving position sense and kinesthesis. *Bulletin of the Johns Hopkins Hospital*, 105, 173–200.

Mountcastle, V. B., Lynch, J. C., Georgopoulos, A., Sakata, H., & Acuna, C. (1975). Posterior parietal association cortex of the monkey: Command functions for operations within extrapersonal space. *Journal of Neurophysiology*, 38, 871–908.

Mulder, J. L., Bouma, A., & Ansink, B. J. (1995). The role of visual discrimination disorders and neglect in perceptual categorization deficits in right and left hemisphere damaged patients. *Cortex, 31,* 487–501.

Munk, H. (1881). Ueber die functionen der grosshirnrinde. In *Gesammelte mittheilungenaus den iahren 1877–1880.* Berlin: Hirschwald.

Nachson, I. (1995). On the modularity of face recognition: The riddle of domain specificity. *Journal of clinical and Experimental Neuropsychology, 17,* 256–275.

Naeser, M. (1974). *The relationship between phoneme discrimination, phoneme/picture perception, and language comprehension in aphasia.* Presented at the 12th Annual Meeting of the Academy of Aphasia, Warrenton, Virginia.

Nakakoshi, S., Kashino, M., Mizobuchi, A., Fukada, Y., & Katori, H. (2001). Disorder in sequential speech perception: A case study on pure word deafness. *Brain and Language, 76,* 119–129.

Nakamura, J., Endo, K., Sumida, T., & Hasegawa, T. (1998). Bilateral tactile agnosia: A case report. *Cortex, 34,* 375–388.

Neisser, U. (1967). *Cognitive psychology.* New York: Appleton-Century-Crofts.

Neisser, U. (1976). *Cognition and reality.* San Francisco: W. H. Freeman.

Newcombe, F., & Ratcliff, G. (1974). Agnosia: A disorder of object recognition. In F. Michel, & B. Schott (Eds.), *Les syndromes de disconnexion calleuse chez l'homme.* Colloque International de Lyon.

Newcombe, F., Young, A. W., & DeHaan, E. H. F. (1989). Prosopagnosia and object agnosia without covert recognition. *Neuropsychologia, 27,* 179–191.

Nielsen, J. M., & Sult, C. W., Jr. (1939). Agnosia and the body scheme. *Bulletin of the Los Angeles Neurological Society, 4,* 69–81.

Oppenheim, H. (1911). *Textbook of nervous diseases for physicians and students.* Edinburgh: Darien Press.

Oppenheimer, D. R., & Newcombe, F. (1978). Clinical and anatomic findings in a case of auditory agnosia. *Archives of Neurology, 35,* 712–719.

Otsuki, M., Soma, Y., Sato, M., Homma, A., & Tsuji, S. (1998). Slowly progressive pure word deafness. *European Neurology, 39,* 135–140.

Oxbury, J., Oxbury, S., & Humphrey, N. (1969). Varieties of color anomia. *Brain, 92,* 847–860.

Pallis, C. A. (1955). Impaired identification of faces and places with agnosia for colors. *Journal of Neurology, Neurosurgery, and Psychiatry, 18,* 218–224.

Park, J., Newman, L. I., & Polk, T. A. (2009). Face processing: The interplay of nature and nurture. *Neuroscientist, 15,* 445–449.

Paul, R. L., Merzenich, M., & Goodman, H. (1972). Representation of slowly and rapidly adapting cutaneous mechanoreceptors of the hand in Brodmann's areas 3 and 1 of Macaca mulatta. *Brain Research, 36,* 229–249.

Pearlman, A. L., Birch, J., & Meadows, J. C. (1979). Cerebral color blindness: An acquired defect in hue discrimination. *Annals of Neurology, 5,* 253–261.

Penfield, W. (1958). *The excitable cortex in conscious man.* Springfield, IL: Charles C. Thomas.

Peretz, I. (2001). Brain specialization for music. New evidence from congenital amusia. *Annals of the New York Academy of Sciences, 930,* 153–65.

Peretz, I. (2008). Musical disorders: From behavior to genes. *Current Directions in Psychological Science, 17,* 329–33.

Peretz, I., Champod, A. S., & Hyde, K. (2003) Varieties of amusia: The Montreal battery of evaluation of amusia. *Annals of the New York Academy of Sciences, 999,* 58–75.

Peretz, I., & Coltheart, M. (2003). Modularity of musical processing. *Nature Neuroscience, 6,* 688–691.

Peretz, I., Kolinsky, R., Tramo, M., Labrecque, R., Hublet, C., Demeurisse, G., & Belleville, S. (1994). Functional dissociations following bilateral lesions of auditory cortex. *Brain, 117*(Pt 6), 1283–1301.

Perrett, D., Mistlin, A. J., & Chitty, A. J. (1987). Visual cells responsive to faces. *Trends in Neuroscience, 10,* 358–364.

Perrett, D., Rolls, E. T., & Caan, W. (1982). Visual neurons responsive to faces in the monkey temporal cortex. *Experimental Brain Research, 47,* 329–342.

Piccirilli, M., Sciarma, T., & Luzzi, S. (2000). Modularity of music: Evidence from a case of pure amusia. *Journal of Neurology, Neurosurgery, and Psychiatry, 69,* 541–545.

Pillon, B., Signoret, J. L., & Lhermitte, F. (1981). Agnosie visuelle associative. Role del hemisphere gauche dans la perception visuelle. *Revue Neurologique, 137,* 831–842.

Platz, T. (1996). Tactile agnosia. Casuistic evidence and theoretical remarks on modality-specific meaning representations and sensorimotor integration. *Brain, 119*(Pt 5), 1565–1574.

Polster, M. R., & Rose, S. B. (1998). Disorders of auditory processing: Evidence for modularity in audition. *Cortex, 34,* 47–65.

Powell, T. P. S., & Mountcastle, V. B. (1959). Some aspects of the functional organization of the cortex of the postcentral gyrus of the monkey: A correlation of findings obtained in a single unit analysis with cyto-architecture. *Bulletin of the Johns Hopkins Hospital, 105,* 123–162.

Procopis, P. G. (1983). A case of receptive amusia with prominent timbre perception defect. *Journal of Neurology, Neurosurgery, and Psychiatry, 46,* 464.

Randolph, M., & Semmes, J. (1974). Behavioral consequences of selective subtotal ablations in the postcentral gyrus of Macaca mulatta. *Brain Research, 70,* 55–70.

Rapin, I., Mattis, S., Rowan, A. J., & Golden, G. G. (1977). Verbal auditory agnosia in children. *Developmental Medicine and Child Neurology, 19,*192–207.

Ratcliff, G., & Ross, J. E. (1981). Visual perception and perceptual disorder. *British Medical Bulletin, 37,* 181–186.

Raymond, F., & Egger, M. (1906). Un cas d'aphasie tactile. *Revue Neurologique, 14,* 371–375.

Reed, C. L., Caselli, R. J., & Farah, M. J. (1996). Tactile agnosia. Underlying impairment and implications for normal tactile object recognition. *Brain, 119,* 875–888.

Reinhold, M. (1950). A case of auditory agnosia. *Brain, 73,* 203–223.

Riddoch, M. J., & Humphreys, G. W. (1987a). A case of integrative visual agnosia. *Brain, 110,* 1431–1462.

Riddoch, M. J., & Humphreys, G. W. (1987b). Visual object processing in optic aphasia: A case of semantic access agnosia. *Cognitive Neuropsychology, 4,* 131–185.

Righart, R., & de Gelder, B. (2007). Impaired face and body perception in developmental prosopagnosia. *Proceedings of the National Academy of Sciences, 104,* 17234–17238.

Rizzo, M., & Hurtig, R. (1987). Looking but not seeing: Attention, perception, and eye movements in simultanagnosia. *Neurology, 37,* 1642–1648.

Rizzo, M., Hurtig, R., & Damasio, A. R. (1987). The role of scanpaths in facial recognition and learning. *Annals of Neurology, 22,* 41–45.

Roberts, M., Sandercock, P., & Ghadiali, E. (1987). Pure word deafness and unilateral right temporo-parietal lesions: A case report. *Journal of Neurology, Neurosurgery, and Psychiatry, 50,* 1708–1709.

Roediger, H. L., III, Guynn, M. J., & Jones, T. C. (1994). Implicit memory: A tutorial review. In G. d'Ydewalle, & P. Eelen (Eds.), *International perspectives on psychological science, Vol. 2: The state of the art.* (pp. 67–94). Hove, UK: Lawrence Erlbaum.

Roland, P. E. (1976). Astereognosis. *Archives of Neurology, 33,* 543–550.

Roland, P. E., & Larsen, B. (1976). Focal increase of cerebral blood flow during stereognostic testing in man. *Archives of Neurology, 33,* 551–558.

Rosati, G., DeBastiani, P., Paolino, E., et al. (1982). Clinical and audiological findings in a case of auditory agnosia. *Journal of Neurology, 227,* 21–27.

Rosch, E., Mervis, C. B., Gray, W., Johnson, D., & Boyes-Braem, P. (1976). Basic objects in natural categories. *Cognitive Psychology, 8,* 382–439.

Ross, E. D. (1980). Sensory-specific and fractional disorders of recent memory in man. I. Isolated loss of visual recent memory. *Archives of Neurology, 37,* 193–200.

Ross, E. D. (1980b). The anatomic basis of visual agnosia [letter]. *Neurology, 30,* 109–110.

Rubens, A. B. (1979). Agnosia. In K.M. Heilman, & E. Valenstein (Eds.), *Clinical neuropsychology.* New York: Oxford University Press.

Rubens, A. B., & Benson, D. F. (1971). Associative visual agnosia. *Archives of Neurology, 24,* 304–316.

Rudel, R.G., Denckla, M. B., & Spalten, E. (1974). The functional asymmetry of Braille letter learning in normal, sighted children. *Neurology, 24,* 733–738.

Saetti, M. C., De Renzi, E., & Comper, M. (1999). Tactile morphagnosia secondary to spatial deficits. *Neuropsychologia, 37,* 1087–1100.

Saffran, E. B., Marin, O. S. M., & Yeni-Komshian, G. H. (1976). An analysis of speech perception in word deafness. *Brain and Language, 3,* 255–256.

Sakai, K., Watanabe, E., Onodera, Y., Uchida, I., Kato, H., Yamamoto, E., et al. (1995). Functional mapping of the human colour centre with echo-planar magnetic resonance imaging. *Proceedings of the Royal Society of London: Basic Biological Sciences, 261*(1360), 89–98.

Saygin, A. P., Leech, R., & Dick, F. (2010). Nonverbal auditory agnosia with lesion to Wernicke's area. *Neuropsychologia, 48,* 107–113.

Schacter, D. L. (1989). On the relation between memory and consciousness: Dissociable interactions and conscious experience. In H. L. Roediger, & F. I. M. Craik (Eds.), *Varieties of memory and consciousness: Essays in honour of Endel Tulving* (pp. 355–389). Hillsdale, NJ: Lawrence Erlbaum.

Schmalzl, L., Palermo, R., & Coltheart, M. (2008). Cognitive heterogeneity in genetically based prosopagnosia: A family study. *Journal of Neuropsychology*, 2, 99–117.

Schnider, A., Benson, D. F., Alexander, D. N., & Schnider-Klaus, A. (1994). Non-verbal environmental sound recognition after unilateral hemispheric stroke. *Brain*, 117, 281–287.

Schuppert, M., Munte, T. F., Wieringa, B. M., & Altenmuller, E. (2000). Receptive amusia: Evidence for cross-hemispheric neural networks underlying music processing strategies. *Brain*, 12, 546–559.

Schuster, P., & Taterka, H. (1926). Beitrag zur anatomie und klinik der reinen worttaubbit. *Zeitschrift fur der Gesamte Neurologie und Psychiatrie*, 105, 494.

Schweinberger, S. R., & Burton, A. M. (2003). Covert recognition and the neural system for face processing. *Cortex*, 39, 9–30.

Seiler, J., & Ricker, K. (1971). Das vibrationsempfinden. Eine apparative schwellenbestimmung. *Zeitschrift fur Neurologie*, 200, 70–79.

Semmes, J. (1965). A non-tactual factor in astereognosis. *Neuropsychologia*, 3, 295–314.

Semmes, J. (1953). Agnosia in animal and man. *Psychological Review*, 60, 140–147.

Semmes, J., Weinstein, S., Ghent, L., & Teuber, H. -L. (1960). *Somatosensory changes after penetrating brain wounds in man*. Cambridge, M A: Harvard University Press.

Sergent, J., Ohta, S., & MacDonald, B. (1992). Functional neuroanatomy of face and object processing. A positron emission tomography study. *Brain*, 115, 15–36.

Sergent, J., & Poncet, M. (1990). From covert to overt recognition of faces in a prosopagnosic patient. *Brain*, 113, 989–1004.

Sergent, J., & Villemure, G. (1989). Prosopagnosia in a right hemispherectomized patient. *Brain*, 112, 975–995.

Shah, N. J., Marshall, J. C., Zafiris, O., Schwab, A., Zilles, K., Markowitsch, H. J., & Fink, G. R. (2001). The neural correlates of person familiarity: A functional magnetic resonance imaging study with clinical implications. *Brain*, 124, 804–815.

Shallice, T. (1988). *From neuropsychology to mental structure*. Cambridge: Cambridge University Press.

Shallice, T., & Saffran, E. (1986). Lexical processing in the absence of explicit word identification: Evidence from a letter-by-letter reader. *Cognitive Neuropsychology*, 3, 429–458.

Shelton, P. A., Bowers, D., Duara, R., & Heilman, K. M. (1994). Apperceptive visual agnosia: A case study. *Brain and Cognition*, 25, 1–23.

Shoumaker, R. D., Ajax, E. T., & Schenkenberg, T. (1977). Pure word deafness (auditory verbal agnosia). *Diseases of the Nervous System*, 38, 293–299.

Shraberg, D., & Weitzel, W. D. (1979). Prosopagnosia and the Capgras Syndrome. *Journal of Clinical Psychiatry*, 40, 313–316.

Shuren, J. Geldmacher, D., & Heilman, K. M. (1993). Nonoptic aphasia: Aphasia with preserved confrontation naming in Alzheimer's disease. *Neurology*, 43, 1900–1907.

Shuttleworth, E. C., Syring, V., & Allen, N. (1982). Further observations on the nature of prosopagnosia. *Brain and Cognition*, 1, 307–322.

Small, S. L., Hart, J., Nguyen, T., & Gordon, B. (1995). Distributed representations of semantic knowledge in the brain. *Brain*, 118, 441–453.

Sparr, S. A., Jay, M., Drislane, F. W., & Venna, N. (1991). A historic case of visual agnosia revisited after 40 years. *Brain*, 114, 789–800.

Sprague, J. M., Levy, J. D., & Berlucci, C. (1977). Visual cortical areas mediating form discrimination in the rat. *Journal of Comparative Neurology*, 172, 441–488.

Spreen, O., Benton, A. L., & Fincham, R. (1965). Auditory agnosia without aphasia. *Archives of Neurology*, 13, 84–92.

Spreen, O., Benton, A. L., & Van Allen, M. W. (1966). Dissociation of visual and tactile naming in amnesic aphasia. *Neurology*, 16, 807–814.

Stauffenburg, V. (1914). *Uber Seelenblindheit. Arbeiten aus dem Hirnatomischen Institut in Zurich Heft 8*. Wiesbaden: Bergman.

Stengel, E. (1948). The syndrome of visual alexia with color agnosia. *Journal of Mental Sciences*, 94, 46–58.

Stockard, J. J., & Rossiter, V. S. (1977). Clinical and pathologic correlates of brainstem auditory response abnormalities. *Neurology*, 27, 316–325.

Tang-Wai, D. F., Graff-Radford, N. R., Boeve, B. F., Dickson, D. W., Parisi, J. E., Crook, R., Caselli, R. J., Knopman, D. S., & Petersen, R. C. (2004). Clinical, genetic, and neuropathologic characteristics of posterior cortical atrophy. *Neurology*, 63, 1168–1174.

Tarr, M. J., Gauthier, I. (2000). FFA: A flexible fusiform area for subordinate level visual processing automatized by expertise. *Nature Neuroscience*, 3, 764–769.

Taylor, A., & Warrington, E. K. (1971). Visual agnosia: A single case report. *Cortex*, 7, 152–164.

Teuber, H.-L (1965a). Somatosensory disorders due to cortical lesions. *Neuropsychologia*, 3, 287–294.

Teuber, H. -L. (1965b). Postscript: Some needed revisions of the classical views of agnosia. *Neuropsycholgia*, *3*, 371–378.

Teuber, H. -L. (1968). Alteration of perception and memory in man. In L. Weiskrantz (Eds.), *Analysis of behavioral change*. New York: Harper & Row. 91

Tohgi, H., Watanabe, K., Takahashi, H., Yonezawa, H., Hatano, K., & Sasaki, T. (1994). Prosopagnosia without topographagnosia and object agnosia associated with a lesion confined to the right occipitotemporal region. *Journal of Neurology*, *241*, 470–474.

Torres, J. R., Sanders, C. V., Strub, R. L., & Black, R. W. (1978). Cat-scratch disease causing reversible encephalopathy. *Journal of the American Medical Association*, *240*, 1628–1629.

Tranel, D. (1991). What has been rediscovered in "rediscovering tactile agnosia"? *Mayo Clinic Proceedings*, *66*, 210–214.

Tranel, D., & Damasio, A. R. (1985). Knowledge without awareness: An autonomic index of facial recognition by prosopagnosics. *Science*, *228*, 1453–1454.

Tranel, D., Damasio, A. R., & Damasio, H. (1988). Intact recognition of facial expression, gender, and age in patients with impaired recognition of face identity. *Neurology*, *38*, 690–696.

Turk, D. J., Rosenblum, A. C., Gazzaniga, M. S., & Macrae, C.N. (2005). Seeing John Malkovich: The neural substrates of person categorization. *Neuroimage*, *24*, 1147–1153.

Tusa, R. J., & Ungerleider, L. G. (1985). The inferior longitudinal fasciculus: A reexamination in humans and monkeys. *Annals of Neurology*, *18*, 583–591.

Tyler, H. R. (1968). Abnormalities of perception with defective eye movements (Balint's syndrome]. *Cortex*, *4*, 154–171.

Tzavaras, A., Hecaen, H., & LeBras, H. (1970). Le probleme de la specificite du deficit de la reconnaisance du visage humans lors des lesions hemispheriques unilaterales. *Neuropsychologia*, *8*, 403–416.

Ulrich, G. (1978). Interhemispheric functional relationships in auditory agnosia: An analysis of the preconditions and a conceptual model. *Brain and Language*, *5*, 286–300.

Valentine, T. (1988). Upside down faces: A review of the effects of inversion upon face recognition. *British Journal of Psychology*, *79*, 471–491.

Van Lancker, D. R., Cummings, J. L., Kreiman, L., & Dobkin, B. H. (1988). Phonagnosia: A dissociation between familiar and unfamiliar voices. *Cortex*, *24*, 195–209.

Van Lancker, D. R., Kreiman, J., & Cummings, J. (1989). Voice perception deficits: Neuroanatomical correlates of phonagnosia. *Journal of Clinical and Experimental Neuropsychology*, *11*, 665–674.

Vecera, S. P., & Gilds, K. S. (1998). What processing is impaired in apperceptive agnosia? Evidence from normal subjects. *Journal of Cognitive Neuroscience*, *10*, 568–580.

Verfaellie, M., & Keane, M. M. (1997). The neural basis of aware and unaware forms of memory. *Seminars in Neurology*, *17*, 153–161.

Verfaellie, M., Rapcsak, S. Z., & Heilman, K. M. (1990). Impaired shifting of attention in Balint's syndrome. *Brain and Cognition*, *12*, 195–204.

Vignolo, L. A. (1969). Auditory agnosia: A review and report of recent evidence. In A.L. Benton (Ed.), *Contributions to clinical neuropsychology*. Chicago: Aldine.

Von Frey, M. (1895). Bietrage zur Sinnes physiologie der Haut Berichle u.d. Verhandlungen d.k. Sachs. *Gesellschaft d. Wissensch* 2 S: 166.

Wapner, W., Judd, T., & Gardner, H. (1978). Visual agnosia in an artist. *Cortex*, *14*, 343–364.

Warrington, E. K. (1985). Agnosia: The impairment of object recognition. In P.J. Vinken, G.W. Bruyn, & H.L. Klawans (Eds.), *Handbook of clinical neurology*. Amsterdam: Elsevier.

Warrington, E. K., & James, M. (1967). An experimental investigation of facial recognition in patients with unilateral cerebral lesions. *Cortex*, *3*, 317–326.

Warrington, E. K., & James, M. (1988). Visual apperceptive agnosia: A clinico-anatomical study of three cases. *Cortex*, *24*, 13–32.

Warrington, E. K., & McCarthy R. (1987). Categories of knowledge: Further fractionation and an attempted integration. *Brain*, *110*, 1273–1296.

Warrington, E. K., & Rabin, P. (1971). Visual span of apprehension in patients with unilateral cerebral lesions. *Quarterly Journal of Experimental Psychology*, *23*, 423–431.

Warrington, E. K. & Shallice, T. (1984). Category-specific semantic impairments. *Brain*, *107*, 829–854.

Warrington, E. K., & Shallice, T. (1980). Word-form dyslexia. *Brain*, *103*, 391–403.

Warrington, E. K., & Taylor, A. M. (1973). The contribution of the right parietal lobe to visual object recognition. *Cortex*, *9*, 152–164.

Watson, R. T., & Heilman, K. M. (1983). Callosal apraxia. *Brain*, *106*, 391–403.

Watson, R. T., & Rapcsak, S. Z. (1987). Loss of spontaneous blinking in a patient with Balint's syndrome. *Archives of Neurology*, *46*, 567–570.

Weinstein, S. (1968). Intensive and extensive aspects of tactile sensitivity as a-function of body part, sex, and laterality. In D. R. Kenshalo (Ed.), *The skin senses*. Springfield, IL: Charles C. Thomas, pp. 195–222.

Weiskrantz, L. (1986). *Blindsight: A case study and implications*. New York: Oxford University Press.

Weiskrantz, L., Warrington, E. K., Sanders, M. D., & Marshall, J. (1974). Visual capacity in the hemianopic field following a restricted occipital ablation. *Brain, 97*, 709–728.

Werner, G., & Whitsel, B. (1973) Functional organization of the somatosensory cortex. In A Iggo (Ed.), *Somatosensory systems, handbook of sensory physiology*, Vol. 2. New York: Springer-Verlag, pp. 621–700.

Wernicke, C. (1895). Zwei falle von rindenlasion. *Arbeiten aus der psychiatrischen Klinik in Breslau, 11*, 35.

Wertheim, N. (1969). The amusias. In P. J. Vinken & G.W. Bruyn (Eds.), *Handbook of clinical neurology* (Vol. 4). Amsterdam: North-Holland.

Whiteley, A. M., & Warrington, E. K. (1977). Prosopagnosia: A clinical, psychological, and anatomical study of three patients. *Journal of Neurology, Neurosurgery, and Psychiatry, 40*, 395–403.

Wilbrand, H. (1887). *Die Seelenblindheit als Herderscheinung*. Wiesbaden: Bergmann.

Wohlfart, G., Lindgren, A., & Jernelius, B. (1952). Clinical picture and morbid anatomy in a case of "pure word deafness." *Journal of Nervous and Mental Disease, 116*, 818–827.

Wolpert, I. (1924). Die Simultanagnosie: Storung der gesamtauffassung. *Zeitschrift fur der Gesamte Neurologie und Psychiatrie, 93*, 397–413.

Woolsey, C. N. (1952). Cortical localization as defined by evoked potential and electrical stimulation studies. In G. Schaltenbrand & C. N. Woolsey (Eds.), *Cerebral localization and organization*. Madison: University of Wisconsin Press, pp. 17–26.

Wortis, S. B., & Pfeffer, A. Z. (1948). Unilateral auditory-spatial agnosia. *Journal of Nervous and Mental Disease, 108*, 181–186.

Yin, R. K. (1970). Face recognition by brain-injured patients: A dissociable ability? *Neuropsychologia, 8*, 395–402.

Yin, R. K. (1969). Looking at upside-down faces. *Journal of Experimental Psychology, 81*, 141–145.

Young, A. W., de Haan, E. H., & Newcombe, F. (1990). Unawareness of impaired face recognition. *Brain and Cognition, 14*, 1–18.

Young, A. W., Hellawell, D., & DeHaan, E. H. F. (1988). Cross-domain semantic priming in normal subjects and a prosopagnosic patient. *Quarterly Journal of Experimental Psychology, 40A*, 561–580.

Young, R. S., & Fishman, G. A. (1980). Loss of color vision and Stiles II, mechanism in a patient with cerebral infarction. *Journal of the Optical Society of America, 170*, 1301–1305.

Zangaladze, A., Epstein, C. M., Grafton, S. T., & Sathian, K. (1999). Involvement of visual cortex in tactile discrimination of orientation. *Nature, 401*(6753), 587–590.

Zeki, S. M. (1973). Colour coding in rhesus monkey prestriate cortex. *Brain Research, 53*, 422–427.

Zeki, S. M. (1977). Colour coding in the superior temporal sulcus of rhesus monkey visual cortex. *Proceedings of the Royal Society of London Biology, 197*, 195–223.

Zihl, J. & Von Cramon, D. (1979). The contribution of the "second" visual system to directed visual attention in man. *Brain, 102*, 835–856.

12

Neglect and Related Disorders

KENNETH M. HEILMAN, ROBERT T. WATSON,
AND EDWARD VALENSTEIN

Unilateral neglect is the failure to report, respond, or orient to novel or meaningful stimuli presented in a specific location, when this failure cannot be attributed to either sensory or motor defects (Heilman, 1979). Neglect may be spatial or personal. Hemispatial neglect may occur in three spatial reference frames: body centered, environmentally centered, and object centered. One may be inattentive to stimuli in space or on the person (attentional or sensory neglect). A person might fail to act in a portion of space, in a spatial direction, or to use a portion of one's body (intentional or motor neglect). Many specific disorders have been described, distinguished by their presumed underlying mechanisms, the distribution of the abnormal behavior, and the means of eliciting the behavior. Different behavioral manifestations may occur at different times, and in some patients certain manifestations are never seen.

The major behavioral manifestations that we will discuss in this chapter include: (a) inattention or sensory neglect, both spatial and personal as well as allesthesia; (b) sensory extinction to simultaneous stimuli; (c) spatial neglect, including contralesional and ipsilesional hemineglect, as well as vertical and radial spatial neglect; (d) intentional or motor neglect, including limb and spatial akinesia, impersistence and allokinesia; (e) asomatognosia; and (f) representational neglect, both antegrade and retrograde. Although anosognosia (unawareness of contralateral weakness) and anosodiaphoria are commonly associated with the signs of the neglect syndrome, in this volume, this neurobehavioral disorder will be covered in a separate chapter. The first section of this chapter will define specific disorders and describe clinical tests that may be used to assess them. The second section will discuss pathophysiology, and the third, recovery and treatment.

DEFINITIONS AND TESTS

INATTENTION

Sensory Neglect

Definition. Sensory neglect or inattention refers to a deficit in awareness of stimuli presented contralateral to a lesion that does not involve sensory projection systems or the primary cortical sensory areas to which they project. The distribution of attentional deficits varies from patient to patient, and may vary in the same patient depending on the method of testing. Patients may fail to attend to visual, auditory, or to tactile stimuli, and their inattention may be to stimuli in space or to stimuli presented on the body. It is not unusual for patients with neglect also to be inattentive to stimuli that are ipsilateral to their lesion, but ipsilateral inattention is usually not as severe as contralateral. In addition to being unaware of stimuli, patients with hemispheric lesions may have difficulty disengaging attention or shifting attention, especially in a contralesional direction.

When the locus of the lesion is not known, it can be difficult to distinguish sensory neglect from sensory loss. Sometimes instructional cues, novel stimuli, or stimuli with strong motivational value may elicit a response, demonstrating that the primary sensory pathways are intact and that the prior failure to detect stimuli was an attentional deficit. The clinician's difficulty in distinguishing sensory neglect from an afferent deficit varies with sensory modality. This discrimination is easiest with auditory deficits, in which, except for stimuli delivered very close to one ear, failure to report unilateral stimuli usually results from unilateral auditory inattention. There are two reasons for this observation. First, patients with unilateral hearing loss will usually detect stimuli presented on the side of deaf ear because the sound will project to the good ear. Second, unilateral cerebral lesions do not cause unilateral hearing loss, because the auditory pathways carrying information from each ear project to both cerebral hemispheres. Therefore, patients who neglect or are inattentive to unilateral auditory stimuli most often have unilateral inattention rather than a primary afferent defect. However, auditory inattention is often mild and can be difficult to detect. Patients with hemianesthesia from unilateral cortical lesions also are most likely suffering from inattention rather than deafferentation. Elementary somatic sensation can probably be subserved by the thalamus. Lesions of the ventral posterolateral and ventral posteromedial thalamic nuclei can result in hemianesthesia, but lesions in somatosensory cortex should not. Some patients with cortical lesions who appear to have tactile anesthesia can detect contralesional stimuli when cold water is injected into the contralesional ear (Vallar et al., 1990). The reason why cold water injected into an ear improves sensory inattention is not entirely known. Some have posited that cold water stimulation increases arousal and this increased arousal allows patients to detect contralesional sensory stimuli (Storrie-Baker et al., 1997). Cold water also activates the vestibular system, inducing nystagmus and a feeling of body rotation. In patients with left-sided neglect, moving objects toward the right can improve detection (Heilman & Valenstein, 1979), and cold water caloric stimulation might alter egocentric perceptual systems in a similar manner. To discriminate between deafferentation and inattention, the clinician can also use psychophysiological procedures, such as evoked potentials, demonstrating intact early components and reduced late components in patients with inattention (Watson et al., 1977).

The distinction between unilateral inattention and deafferentation can be most difficult in the visual modality. Hemianopia is commonly caused by lesions affecting the calcarine (primary visual) cortex or the geniculocalcarine pathways that carry visual information from the thalamus to the cerebral cortex. Patients with hemisphere lesions that spare these structures, but produce severe neglect, may behave as if they have a hemianopia. The ability to point to the location of a stimulus in the blind field or to avoid objects in the hemianopic field does not necessarily indicate an attentional deficit, since patients with hemianopia have been reported to have these abilities, presumably on the basis of subcortical (collicular) visual processing (Sanders et al., 1974)

It is sometimes possible to demonstrate that that an apparent hemianopia actually results from inattention. The method used takes advantage of discrepancies between retinotopic and body frames of reference. The distribution of attention in space depends not only on the position of the stimulus in the visual field, but also on the relative position of the stimulus to the patient's body. The retinotopic visual field and the spatial fields defined by head or body position are only congruent when the subject is looking straight ahead. Moving the eyes to one side will result in the retinotopic visual field being different from the head or body spatial field, and moving the head and eyes will result in three noncongruent fields. True hemianopia is not influenced by eye movements, but visual inattention can vary with direction of gaze. For example, patients with body-centered inattention may fail to detect contralesional visual stimuli when they gaze straight ahead or to contralesional hemispace, but when their gaze is directed toward ipsilesional hemispace, placing the contralateral visual field within the ipsilesional head or body hemispace, patients might be able to detect stimuli, even though the stimuli remain at the same retinotopic locations (Kooistra & Heilman, 1989; Nadeau & Heilman, 1991).

Testing. Inattention is detected by asking patients if they were stimulated and if stimulated, where they were stimulated. Language-impaired patients may respond nonverbally, but failure to respond nonverbally may reflect akinesia rather than inattention. Stimuli should be given in each of three modalities: visual, somesthetic, and auditory. These visual, somesthetic, and auditory stimuli should be randomly presented to the abnormal (contralesional) side, to the normal side of the body, and these stimuli should be intermixed with nonstimuli in a random order. The examiner instructs the patient, "When I say 'now' tell me if you felt, or heard or saw a stimulus and if so, on which side it was located."

Visual stimuli are presented to each half-field with the eyes directed straight ahead, away from the lesion, and toward the lesion. Perimetry and tangent screen examination can be used; however, for bedside testing, confrontation techniques are adequate. Either a cotton-tipped applicator or a finger can be used as the stimulus. The patient may be asked to detect finger movements, or to count fingers in one or both visual fields. To test for somesthetic neglect at the bedside, the patient can be touched with a finger, a cotton applicator, or, if better control of stimulus intensity is desired, von Frei hairs. More elaborate equipment can be used for better control of stimulus intensity, if this is needed for research purposes. Other somatosensory modalities (pin, temperature, etc.) can also be tested. Auditory stimuli for bedside testing may consist of rubbing or snapping the fingers. Audiometric techniques are preferable for rigorous testing.

Extinction to Simultaneous Stimulation

Definition. As patients with sensory inattention improve, they become able to correctly detect and correctly localize (right vs. left) stimuli even contralateral to their lesion, but when presented with bilateral simultaneous stimuli they often fail to report contralesional stimuli. This phenomenon, which can also be seen in patients without prior sensory inattention, was first noted by Loeb (1885) and Oppenheim (1885) in the tactile modality and by Anton (1899) and Poppelreuter (1917) in the visual modality. It has been called "extinction to double simultaneous stimulation" (or just "extinction"). It may also be seen in the tactile (Bender, 1952) and auditory (Heilman et al., 1970) modalities. A patient may have extinction in several modalities (multimodal extinction) or in one modality. Extinction is usually mildest in the auditory modality. Although extinction is most severe when a stimulus presented to the side contralateral to the lesion is paired with a stimulus on the other side of midline, extinction may also occur when both stimuli are on the same side, even when they are both ipsilateral to the lesion (Rapcsak et al., 1987; Feinberg et al., 1990). In this testing condition, the patient extinguishes the stimulus that is closer to the contralesional side.

Testing. If the patient responds normally to unilateral stimulation, bilateral simultaneous stimulation should be given, interspersed with unilateral stimuli, Visual, tactile, or auditory stimuli are presented to the right and left visual fields, sides of the body, or sides of the head, respectively. As mentioned, it is sometimes possible to demonstrate visual or tactile extinction when two stimuli are delivered to the same hemifield or on the same side of the body. Bender (1952) noted that normal subjects may show extinction to simultaneous stimulation when stimuli are delivered to two different (asymmetrical) parts of the body (simultaneous bilateral heterologous stimulation). For example, if the right side of the face and the left hand are stimulated simultaneously, normal subjects sometimes report only the stimulus on the face. Normal subjects do not extinguish symmetrical simultaneous stimuli (simultaneous bilateral homologous stimulation). Simultaneous bilateral heterologous stimulation can sometimes be used to test for milder forms of extinction. For example, when the right face and left hand are stimulated, the patient with left-sided neglect might not report the stimulus on the left hand, but when the left face and right hand are stimulated, the patient reports both stimuli.

Defective Vigilance

Definition. When testing for sensory inattention or extinction some patients will initially be able to detect contralesional stimuli; however, with repeated stimulation they eventually fail to detect these stimuli.

Testing. Testing for defects in vigilance is similar to that performed for extinction, only in this case the testing is prolonged.

Allesthesia

Definition. When patients without right–left confusion are touched on the side opposite their lesion, they may report that they were touched on the same side as their lesion (Obersteiner, 1882). This has been called *allesthesia*. A similar defect may be seen in other sensory modalities.

Testing. Testing is the same as that described for sensory inattention. However, to make certain that the defect is one of allesthesia rather than allokinesia, the patient should respond verbally rather than by moving the limb.

INTENTIONAL (MOTOR) NEGLECT

Patients may fail to respond to a stimulus even though they are aware of it, and even when they have the strength to respond. We call the failure to respond in the absence of unaware-ness or weakness an action-intentional disorder. In the following sections, we discuss five types of action-intentional disorders: akinesia, motor extinction, hypokinesia, motor impersis-tence and allokinesia.

Akinesia

Definitions. Akinesia is a failure of initiation of movement that cannot be attributed to dysfunc-tion in upper or lower motor neuron systems or unawareness of the imperative stimulus.

Akinesia may involve the eyes, the head, a limb, or the whole body. It may vary depending upon where in space the body part is moved, or in what direction it is moved. In directional akinesia, there is a reluctance to move in the direction contralateral to the lesion. Certain forms of gaze palsy are directional akinesias, and there are directional akinesias of the head and even of the arms. Directional akinesia may be associated with a directional motor bias. The patient's eyes may deviate toward the side of the lesion, and, when asked to point to a spot opposite the sternum with the eyes closed, the patient's arm may also deviate to the side of the lesion (Heilman et al., 1983b).

Akinesia may also depend upon the side in which the action is taken. In the patient described by Meador et al. (1986), the arm contralateral to the lesion was less akinetic in ipsilesional than in contralesional hemispace, independent of the direction of movement.

Movements can be produced in response to an external stimulus or they can occur even in the absence of a stimulus. The failure of move-ment in the former condition we call exoge-nously evoked (exo-evoked) akinesia and a failure of movement in the latter condition, endogenously evoked (endo-evoked) akinesia. A patient may have either exo- or endo-evoked akinesia or both.

Testing. Because akinesia may affect different body parts, one should assess movements of the eyes, head, trunk and limbs. To detect endo-evoked akinesia, it is important to observe spon-taneous behavior. Patients with endo-evoked akinesia often have symptoms of abulia (decreased drive, with psychomotor retardation). Patients whose akinesia is principally endo-evoked may respond normally to external stimuli. This has been called *kinesia paradoxica*, and is frequently associated with Parkinson disease.

Exo-evoked akinesia or motor neglect results in failure to move in response to a stimulus, when this failure to respond is not the result of an elemental sensory defect or sensory inat-tention. To distinguish these deficits, Watson et al. (1978) devised the crossed-response task. Although originally used in monkeys, it can also be used with humans. Monkeys were trained to respond with the right arm to a left-sided stimulus and with the left arm to a right-sided stimulus. An animal with a unilateral hemispheric lesion was considered to have a sensory deficit or sensory neglect if it did not respond to a con-tralesional stimulus using the "normal" (ipsile-sional) arm. It was considered to have exo-evoked akinesia if it failed to move the contralesional extremity in response to stimulation of the "normal" (ipsilesional) side, despite intact spontaneous movements and normal strength of the contralesional arm. One can use the crossed-response task to test for exo-evoked akinesia of the limbs, the eyes, or the head.

To assess whether the spatial coordinates of actions influence akinesia, the examiner needs to observe directional and hemispatial movements that are both endo-evoked (spontaneous) and exo-evoked (in response to stimuli). When attempting to determine if there is an endo-evoked directional akinesia of the eyes, one should observe spontaneous eye movements to detect eye deviation or bias toward the side of the lesion, or a paresis of gaze to the side opposite the lesion (a failure to look spontaneously into contralesional space). An exo-evoked directional akinesia of the eyes can be assessed by a modification of the Watson et al. (1978) paradigm, in which the patient must look either toward or away from ipsi- and contralesional stimuli. The examiner stands directly in front of a patient and positions one hand in the patient's right visual field and the other in the left visual field, at eye level. The patient is instructed to fixate on the examiner's nose, and to look away from a finger if it moves downward and toward the finger if it moves upward. A failure to look at the contralesional finger when it moves upward may be related to sensory defect (e.g., hemianopia), sensory neglect, or directional akinesia. A failure, however, to look toward the contralesional finger when the ipsilesional finger moves downward suggests an exo-evoked ocular directional akinesia (Butter et al., 1988b).

Similar tests can be used to detect directional and hemispatial akinesia of the head or arm. To test for a directional bias of an arm (similar to eye deviation), patients are asked to close their eyes and point to their sternum. If they are able to point to the sternum, they are then asked to point with their index finger to the position in space that is perpendicular to their sternum (the midsagittal plane). Patients with a directional motor (intentional) bias will deviate in the direction of their lesioned hemisphere (Heilman et al., 1983b).

To test for exo-evoked hemispatial akinesia of the arm, the examiner must test the patient with arms crossed and uncrossed. In uncrossed conditions, each hand is placed on a table in compatible hemispace. In the crossed condition, each hand is placed in the opposite hemispace. The patient is instructed to lift the hand that is positioned on the same side as the examiner's moving finger when the examiner's finger moves up, but to move the hand on the opposite side when the examiner's finger moves down. After the patient is trained on this paradigm (up-same, down-opposite), the examiner randomly moves his right or left index finger up or down. When a patient fails to move the contralesional arm when it is in contralesional hemispace but moves the arm when it crosses into ipsilesional hemispace, the patient is considered to have hemispatial limb akinesia (Meador et al., 1986).

To distinguish exo-evoked directional akinesia, hemispatial akinesia, or directional hypometria from an ipsilesional attentional bias, Na et al. (1998) used a video apparatus. When using this apparatus the subjects could not directly see their own hand, but instead observed their hand and the stimulus (a line) on a video monitor. In the direct condition, the hand movements and the line are accurately portrayed; however, in the indirect condition right and left on the monitor are reversed, so that leftward movements in actual work space appear to be rightward on the monitor and vice versa. Using this paradigm, patients with an ipsilesional attentional bias will reverse the spatial error in the indirect condition, but patients with primarily directional akinesia (hypometria) will continue to err in the same direction. Using this same paradigm, Schwartz et al. (1998) demonstrated that many patients have a combination of attentional and intentional neglect.

To dissociate hemispatial akinesia from hemispatial inattention, Coslett et al. (1990) also had patients view the stimulus (a line) and their own responding hand on a TV monitor. The patient was prevented from viewing the line directly. Both the line (where the action takes place) and the TV monitor were independently placed in either hemispace. A greater ipsilesional bias of line bisection with the TV monitor in contralesional as compared with ipsilesional hemispace, independent of line placement, indicates a contribution of hemispatial inattention.

A greater ipsilesional bias of line bisection when the line is placed in contralesional hemispace as compared with ipsilesional hemispace, independent of monitor placement, suggests a contribution of a hemispatial or directional akinesia. Other investigators have used other procedures to dissociate hemispatial and directional akinesia or directional hypometria from hemispatial sensory neglect or an attention bias. For example Bisiach et al. (1990) used a pulley with a string, and Tegner and Levander (1991) used a mirror apparatus.

De Renzi et al. (1970) developed a simple task that can be used to test for endo-evoked directional and hemispatial limb akinesia. In our modification, the patient is blindfolded and small objects such as pennies are randomly scattered on a table to the left and right of the patient's midsagittal plane (both hemispatial fields) and within arm's reach. The patient is asked to retrieve as many pennies as possible. The task is endo-evoked because the patient cannot see the pennies and must initiate exploratory behavior in the absence of an external stimulus. Patients with an endo-evoked directional or hemispatial akinesia of the arm may fail to move their arms fully into contralateral hemispace to explore for pennies.

Motor Extinction

Definition. Some patients who do not demonstrate akinesia when they move one limb at a time may demonstrate contralesional akinesia when they must simultaneously move both limbs (Valenstein & Heilman, 1981). We call this motor extinction.

Testing. Motor extinction is tested by using a method similar to that used to test for sensory extinction; however, the examiner not only requests verbal report as to where the patient was stimulated (e.g., right, left, both, or none), but in other trials, the examiner requests that the subject move the body part (e.g., hand or arm) on the same side that was stimulated (right, left, both) and not to report the side on which they were stimulated. Patients with sensory extinction will fail to report the contralesional stimulus with simultaneous stimulation and will also fail to move the contralesional limb. Patients with

motor extinction will report stimulation of both sides, but either move only the ipsilesional limb or move the contralesional limb after they have lifted the ipsilesional limb.

Hypokinesia

Definition. Patients with mild defects in action-intentional systems may not fail to initiate responses, but may initiate them after an abnormally long delay. We have called this *hypokinesia*. Since the patient must respond to a stimulus to judge whether or not the response is slow, hypokinesia is by definition exo-evoked. Motor impersistence can also influence performance on the cancellation task.

Testing. The same paradigms that are used to test for akinesia of the eyes and limbs can be used to test for hypokinesia. Although some patients with hypokinesia have such markedly slowed initiation times that hypokinesia can be detected easily, others have more subtle defects, necessitating reaction-time paradigms to observe their defects. Reaction times can be slowed for a variety of reasons, including impaired attention, bradyphrenia, or hypokinesia. To detect hypokinesia, one should use simple reaction times that do not require cognition and cannot, therefore, be impaired by bradyphrenia. Similarly, to test for hypokinesia, one has to use stimulus parameters that ensure that inattention cannot masquerade as hypokinesia.

Hypokinesia can be seen both in the limbs and eyes and may be either independent of direction or directionally specific such that there is a greater delay initiating movements in a contralesional direction than in an ipsilesional direction (Heilman et al., 1985). Hypokinesia can also be hemispatial: Movements with the same limb may be more slowly initiated in contralesional hemispace than in ipsilesional hemispace (Meador et al., 1986).

Motor Impersistence

Definition. Motor impersistence is the inability to sustain an act. It is the intentional equivalent of the attentional disorder of impaired vigilance. It can be demonstrated in a variety of body parts, including the limbs, eyes, eyelids, jaw, and tongue. Like akinesia, it may also be directional (Kertesz et al., 1985) or hemispatial (Roeltgen et al., 1989).

Testing. Limb impersistence can be tested by asking a patient to maintain a limb posture such as arm extension for 20 seconds. Since limb impersistence can be hemispatial (Roeltgen et al., 1989), one can test each limb in its own and in opposite hemispace. To test for directional impersistence, the examiner requests patients to keep their eyes directed, or their head turned, to the left or right for 20 seconds. Directional impersistence may be worse in one hemispace than the other. Patients with directional impersistence usually have more difficulty in maintaining motor activation in contralesional hemispace or in the contralesional direction. Whereas all persistence tasks are initially exo-evoked, the examiner can use a signal or instructions to initiate the activity, and then either withdraw the stimulus or allow it to persist throughout the trial.

Allokinesia

Definition. Patients with allokinesia move the incorrect (ipsilesional) extremity or move in the incorrect direction (toward ipsilesional rather than contralesional hemispace).

Testing. When testing subjects for allokinesia one should make certain that the patient does not have right–left confusion or allesthesia. The patient could be asked to raise the arm touched, or to look at the examiner's moving finger, or to look toward the source of a sound. Although patients will correctly verbally localize these stimuli correctly to the left or right, they will raise the incorrect (ipsilesional arm), look ipsilaterally, or turn their head ipsilaterally.

SPATIAL NEGLECT

Definitions. When patients with spatial neglect are asked to perform a variety of tasks in space, they most often neglect the hemispace

Figure 12–1. Example of hemispatial neglect (visuospatial agnosia). Patient asked to draw a man. (Provided by Anna Barrett.)

contralateral to their lesion. For example, when asked to draw a picture, they may fail to draw portions of the picture that are in contralesional hemispace (Figure 12-1). When asked to bisect a line, they may quarter it instead (Figure 12-2), or they may fail to cross out lines distributed over a page (Figure 12-3). The patients appear to be neglecting one-half of visual space. This has been variously termed hemispatial neglect, visuospatial agnosia, hemispatial agnosia, visuospatial neglect, and unilateral spatial neglect.

Although several authors (Battersby et al., 1956; Gainotti et al., 1972) have attributed the original description of hemispatial neglect to Holmes (1918), Holmes actually reported six patients with disturbed visual orientation from bilateral lesions. It was Riddoch (1935) who reported two patients without any disturbance of central vision who had visual disorientation limited to homonymous half-fields. Brain (1941)

Figure 12–2. Performance of patient with hemispatial neglect on line bisection task.

Figure 12–3. Performance by patient with hemispatial neglect on crossing out task.

also described three patients who had visual disorientation limited to homonymous half-fields not caused by defects in visual acuity. Brain attributed this disorder to inattention of the left half of external space and thought it was similar to the "amnesia" for the left half of the body that may follow a lesion of the right parietal lobe. Paterson and Zangwill (1944), McFie et al. (1950), and Denny–Brown and Banker (1954) demonstrated that patients with spatial neglect also omitted material on one side of drawings and failed to eat from one side of their plate.

Patients with hemispatial neglect may fail to read part of a word or a portion of a sentence. For example, they may read the word "cowboy" as "boy." This has been called *neglect paralexia* (Benson & Geschwind, 1969). Patients may write on only one side of a page, or they may make errors typing letters on the side of a keyboard contralateral to their lesion (Figure 12-4). This has been termed neglect paragraphia (Valenstein & Heilman, 1978).

In addition to horizontal neglect, neglect of lower (Rapcsak et al., 1988) and upper (Shelton et al., 1990) vertical space and neglect of near and far radial space (Shelton et al., 1990) have been reported. Mark and Heilman (1998) demonstrated that many patients with spatial neglect have a combination of horizontal, vertical, and radial neglect. One most commonly encounters left-sided, lower vertical, and proximal radial neglect. Halligan and Marshall (1991) reported a patient who had horizontal neglect when the stimuli were near the body, but did not have neglect when the stimuli were placed far from the body. In contrast, Vuilleumier et al. (1998) reported a patient with a right temporal hematoma who had neglect in far space but no neglect in near space. Neglect may be viewer- (body-) centered, object-centered (allocentric), or environment-centered. Viewer-centered neglect may be defined by the trunk, the head or the eyes.

Testing. There are many tests for spatial neglect, but the three most commonly used are the cancellation, line bisection, and drawing tasks. In the cancellation test described by Albert (1973), lines are drawn in random positions on a sheet of paper. The patient is asked to cancel or cross out all the lines (Figure 12-3). Patients with spatial neglect may fail to cancel lines on the contralesional side of the page. On this cancellation task, patients often fail to cancel more targets on the lower than upper part of the left side of the page (Mark & Heilman 1998). The cancellation task can be made more difficult and sensitive by asking patients to discriminate between targets

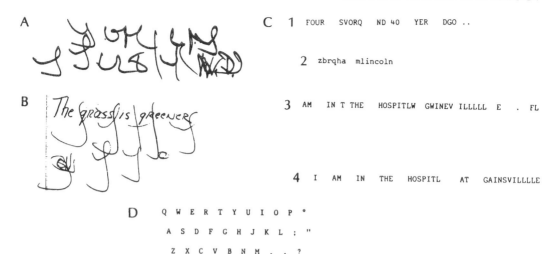

Figure 12–4. A: Attempting to write, "You are a doctor." **B:** Copying. **C:** Typing. (1–3) Typewriter directly in front of patient; (4) typewriter moved to patient's right. **D:** The typewriter keyboard. Note that the letters missed (A, S, E) are at the left of the keyboard.

and distracting stimuli. The more difficult it is to discriminate targets from distracting stimuli, the more sensitive the task (see Rapcsak et al., 1989). Increasing the number of stimuli and randomly distributing stimuli can also increase the sensitivity of this test (Chatterjee et al.,1999). Stimuli that activate the left hemisphere (Heilman & Watson, 1978), and stimuli that require computations, can also increase left sided neglect in a cancellation test (Mennemeier et al., 2004) patients with right hemisphere lesions.

Many patients when performing the cancellation task repeatedly cancel the same target (Na et al., 1999), but it is unclear if this perseveration, which might indicate an inability to disengage, influences the severity of hemispatial neglect. The cancellation test can also be used to detect object-centered neglect (Rapcsak et al., 1989) by using stimuli with lateralized distinctive features. For example, in an array of triangles distributed over a page, some triangles have openings on the left side, some on the right side, and some have no openings. The patient is requested to cancel all the triangles with openings. Patient with left-sided object-centered neglect will fail to cancel the triangles with left-sided opening, and these errors can in some patients be distributed on both sides of the page (Figure 12-5).

The line bisection task is also commonly used to assess patients for spatial neglect.

Some patients who perform normally on cancellation tests will perform poorly on line bisection, and vice versa (Schubert & Spatt, 2001). A line 6–10 inches long is drawn on a sheet of paper that is placed before the patient. The patient is then asked to bisect this line ("Make a mark in the middle of the line"). Patients with spatial neglect will usually displace their mark to the ipsilesional side (contralateral neglect). Neglect is usually more apparent when longer lines are used (Bisiach et al., 1983; Butter et al., 1988a). Errors in bisection are reduced or even reversed when very short lines are used (Halligan & Marshall, 1991). Neglect is also usually more apparent when the line is placed in contralesional body or head hemispace (Heilman & Valenstein, 1979). There have been reports of patients who bisect even very long lines toward contralesional hemispace (Kwon & Heilman, 1991; Na et al., 1998). This has been called *ipsilateral* or *ipsilesional neglect*.

Although most often patients are tested with horizontal lines (at the intersection of the coronal and transverse planes), vertical and radial neglect has been reported (Shelton et al., 1990; Rapcsak et al., 1988). Thus, lines can also be presented vertically (at the intersection of the midsagittal and coronal planes) or radially (at the intersection between the midsagittal and transverse planes).

Figure 12–5. Performance by a patient with object-centered neglect. Some of the triangles have gaps on either the right or left sides; the patient is instructed to put an "x" through each gap. The examiner has circled the four stimuli with gaps that the patient neglected: all had gaps on the left side of the stimulus. In contrast, this patient found all of the triangles with gaps on the right side of the object, even when they were on the left side of the page.

As will be discussed, spatial neglect can be caused by action-intentional disorders as well as by perceptual-attentional disorders. One means of dissociating action-intentional from perceptual-attentional disorders is to prevent patients from seeing the actual page or their hands, and instead to have them perform the line bisection by viewing the stimuli on a monitor (Na et al., 1998). The monitor can also be placed in either hemispace. When the monitor reverses the image, the patient who has attentional neglect of left hemispace, with rightward deviation on line bisection, will now bisect the actual line to left of midline. If, however, this patient has intentional neglect even when the monitor right-left reverses the image, the attempted bisections will continue to be deviated to the right. In another test, called the Landmark Test (Harvey et al., 1995), patients are shown pre-bisected lines and asked

to determine if the bisection is actually at the midpoint of the line or if it is deviated to the right or left of center. Since patients are not performing the actual bisection, if these patients demonstrate a perceptual bias, their deficit is attentional and not intentional.

Spatial neglect can also be assessed by asking patients to copy a drawing (Figure 12-1) or to draw spontaneously. Drawing to command, rather than copying, may be more of a test for representational spatial neglect (see below). A failure to draw one side of the object or one side of a scene, may indicate the presence of spatial neglect. Ogden (1985) had patients copy a picture that contained a house, with a fence and two trees. This test can detect viewer-centered neglect such that all stimuli on the left half of the page are not drawn, or object-centered neglect wherein all the objects in the scene are drawn, but only the right half of each object. Since patients with right hemisphere lesions commonly have visuospatial defects and associated constructional apraxia, they may have difficulty with spontaneous drawing.

Experimental paradigms that change the position of the body in relation to gravity may be able to dissociate body- and environment-centered reference systems. If patients who neglect left-sided stimuli in the upright position lie on their right side and continue to neglect stimuli to the left of the body's midsagittal plane, they have body-centered neglect; but if in this recumbent position they are presented with a line oriented parallel to the body's midsagittal plane, and they neglect the side of the line closer to their feet, which is the left side of the line with respect to the environment, they would have environmental-centered neglect. Patients can neglect stimuli both to the left of the body (body- or viewer-centered) and on the left side of the environment (environment-centered) (Ladavas 1987; Farah et al., 1990).

Patients with neglect may also demonstrate a combination of body- and object-centered neglect. Rapcsak et al. (1989) asked subjects with left hemispatial neglect to perform a selective cancellation test. On one half of the trials, the subjects were asked to cancel only those stimuli that had a distinctive feature on the left. On the other half of the trials, subjects were asked only to cancel those stimuli that had a distinctive feature on the right. As expected, subjects canceled more stimuli on the right side of the page than on the left, but in addition, they canceled more stimuli with distinctive features on the right than on the left, suggesting that, in addition to viewer- or environmentally centered neglect, they also had object-centered neglect.

PERSONAL NEGLECT AND ASOMATOGNOSIA

Definition. Patients with asomatognosia may fail to recognize that their own contralesional extremities belong to them, and they may complain that someone else's arm or leg is in bed with them. They may persist in this denial even when confronted with objective evidence. Patients with personal neglect, even without asomatognosia, may fail to dress or groom the

abnormal side. Although this may be considered a form of dressing apraxia, the pathophysiology may be different from the dressing apraxia seen in patients with visuospatial deficits.

Testing. One of the best means of determining if a patient has personal neglect is to observe their dressing and grooming behavior. One can also blindfold a patient and attach small self-stick notes to the left and right side of their trunk and ask them to remove all the pieces of paper. One can also use body bisections (Mark et al., 1990) by putting a large horizontal line in front of the patient and asking them to put a mark directly across from their left shoulder, right shoulder, right nipple, left nipple, and sternum. To determine if a patient has asomatognosia, the examiner can ask the patient if his arm or leg belongs to him or to someone else. Some patients will recognize that their arm belongs to them but they may give it a name (personification) or demonstrate negative feelings toward this limb (misoplegia).

REPRESENTATIONAL NEGLECT

Anterograde

Definition. Patients with neglect may be unable to recall stimuli in contralesional hemispace even though they perceive these stimuli. This memory deficit has been reported in several modalities.

Testing. We randomly presented consonants through earphones to patients on either the neglected or non-neglected side and asked them to report the stimulus either immediately or after a distraction-filled interval. We found that distraction induced a greater recall deficit for the stimuli presented on the contralesional side (e.g., left ear) (Heilman et al., 1974). In the visual modality, Samuels et al. (1971) tested patients with right parietal lesions and found a similar phenomenon, but unfortunately, they did not evaluate their subjects for neglect.

Retrograde-Representational

Definition, Description, and Testing. Denny-Brown and Banker (1954) described a patient who could not describe from memory the details of the side of a room that was opposite her cerebral lesion. Bisiach and Luzzatti (1978) also described patients with neglect who, while in the hospital, were asked to image a square in Milan after coming out of a cathedral in this square. These patients were unable to recall left-sided details of this image. However, when imagining themselves facing the cathedral from the opposite side of this square in Milan, they could recall details that had been on the left side but now were on the right. However, from this imagined prospective, these patients did not recall the details that were now on their left side. Whereas most patients with hemispatial representational neglect have hemispatial neglect, there have been reports of patients who have hemispatial neglect but do not appear to have representational neglect, and there have been reports of patients who have representational neglect who do not appear to have hemispatial neglect (Coslett, 1998). Coslett (1998) also reported a person who had problems recognizing images of his left hand in different positions, but could recognize images of his right hand. Thus, this patient appeared to have personal representational neglect.

MECHANISMS UNDERLYING NEGLECT AND RELATED DISORDERS

Most of the defects associated with neglect can be attributed to one or more of three basic mechanisms: disorders of attention, disorders of action or intention, and representational or memory disorders. Although the various behavioral manifestations of the neglect syndrome often coexist, patients may not display all of the manifestations, and different manifestations may be present at different times in the same patient. In this section, the mechanisms of these disorders will be discussed.

MECHANISMS UNDERLYING INATTENTION (SENSORY NEGLECT)

As noted above, patients with neglect may be unaware of novel or meaningful stimuli in one or more modalities. This unawareness of contralesional stimuli has been attributed to disorders of sensation, to complex perceptual deficits including abnormalities of the "body schema," and to disorders of attention.

Sensory Hypotheses

Battersby and associates (1956) thought that neglect in humans resulted from decreased sensory input superimposed on a background of decreased mental function. Sprague et al. (1961) concluded that neglect was caused by loss of patterned sensory input to the forebrain, particularly to the neocortex. Eidelberg and Schwartz (1971) similarly proposed that neglect was a passive phenomenon due to quantitatively asymmetrical sensory input to the two hemispheres. They based this conclusion on the finding that neglect resulted from neospinothalamic lesions, but not from medial lemniscal lesions. They claimed that the neospinothalamic tract carries more tactile information to the hemisphere than does the medial lemniscus. However, since lesions in the cerebral cortex may also produce neglect, they postulated that the syndrome could also be caused by a reduced functional mass of one cortical area concerned with somatic sensation relative to another.

Body Schema

Brain (1941) believed that the parietal lobes contain the body schema and mediate spatial perception. Parietal lesions therefore caused a patient to fail to recognize not only half of his body but also half of space. Brain thought that allesthesia resulted from severe damage to the schema for one-half of the body, causing events occurring on that half, if perceived at all, to be related in consciousness to the surviving schema representing the normal half.

Amorphosynthesis

Denny-Brown and Banker (1954) proposed that the parietal lobes were important in cortical sensation and that the phenomenon of inattention belonged to the whole class of cortical disorders of sensation: "a loss of fine discrimination . . . an inability to synthesize more than a few properties of a sensory stimulus and a disturbance of synthesis of multiple sensory stimuli." The neglect syndrome was ascribed to a defect in spatial summation that they called *amorphosynthesis*.

Attentional Hypotheses

Because patients with neglect and related disorders often appear to be unaware of contralesional stimuli, and this unawareness cannot be accounted for by deafferentation, it is thought that many of the symptoms of neglect are related to attentional deficits.

It has been said that everyone knows what attention is, but no one can fully define it. Perhaps this is so because attention is a mental process rather than a thing or object, and processes are more difficult to define than objects. Brains have a limited capacity to process stimuli. Under many circumstances, the brain receives more afferent stimuli than it can possibly process. In addition to external stimuli, humans can activate internal representations. The processing of these internal representations may further tax a limited capacity system and reduce a person's ability to process afferent stimuli. Since organisms, including humans, have a limited processing capacity, they need a means to triage incoming information. Attention is the mental process that permits humans to triage afferent input.

Normally, triage depends upon the potential importance of the incoming information to the organism. Significance is determined by two major factors: goals or sets and biological drives or needs. Because one cannot know the potential importance of novel stimuli, one must, at least temporarily, attend to novel stimuli until their significance is determined. Therefore, stimuli that are novel or important for a person's goals, sets, needs or drives will be triaged at a higher level than irrelevant stimuli.

To triage stimuli, organisms must direct their attention to significant stimuli and away from irrelevant stimuli. There are at least two means to direct attention: by sensory modality, and by spatial location. One sensory modality may be attended over others. For example, visual information can be attended rather than information carried by touch or audition. Spatial location can be used to direct attention either between sensory modalities or within a sensory modality.

Some of the first papers about the neglect syndrome referred to defects of attention.

For example, Poppelreuter (1917) introduced the word *inattention*. Brain (1941) and Critchley (1966) were also strong proponents of this view. However, Bender and Furlow (1944, 1945) challenged the attentional theory; they felt that inattention could not be important in the pathophysiology of the syndrome because neglect could not be overcome by having the patient "concentrate" on the neglected side.

Heilman and Valenstein (1972) and Watson and associates (1973, 1974) again postulated an attention-arousal hypothesis. These authors argued that the sensory and perceptual hypotheses could not explain all cases of neglect, since neglect was often produced by lesions outside the traditional sensory pathways. Evoked potential studies in animals with unilateral neglect have demonstrated a change in late waves (that are known to be influenced by changes in attention and stimulus significance) but no change in the early (sensory) waves (Watson et al., 1977). Furthermore, neglect is often multimodal and therefore cannot be explained by a defect in any one sensory modality.

Anatomical Basis of Attention. Unilateral neglect in humans and monkeys can be induced by lesions in many different brain regions. These include cortical areas such as the temporoparietal-occipital junction (Critchley, 1966; Heilman et al., 1970, 1983a) (Figure 12-6), limbic areas such as the cingulate gyrus (Heilman & Valenstein, 1972; Watson et al., 1973), and subcortical areas such as the thalamus (Figure 12-7) and mesencephalic reticular formation (MRF; Figures 12-7 and 12-8) (Watson et al., 1974). As we will discuss below, these subcortical areas have been shown to be important in mediating arousal, and the cortical areas are regions that are probably specifically involved in the analysis of the behavioral significance of stimuli and their spatial location. We have proposed that inattention or sensory neglect is an attentional-arousal disorder induced by dysfunction in a cortical (frontal and temporoparietal)-limbic (cingulate)-reticular formation network (Heilman & Valenstein, 1972; Watson et al., 1973, 1981; Heilman, 1979). Mesulam (1981) subsequently put forth a similar proposal. We will review the evidence for our view, and propose a model or schema to explain the neglect syndrome (Figures 12-9 and 12-10).

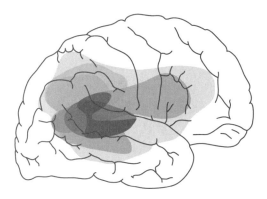

Figure 12–6. Lateral view of the right hemisphere. Lesions (as determined by computed tomography scan) of ten patients with the neglect syndrome are superimposed.

NEGLECT AND RELATED DISORDERS

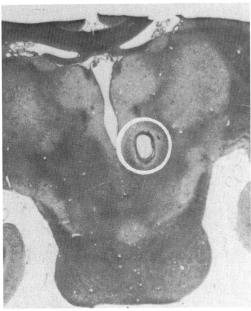

Figure 12–8. Electrolytic lesion in the mesencephalic reticular formation of a monkey who had developed unilateral neglect after the lesion was made.

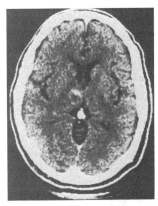

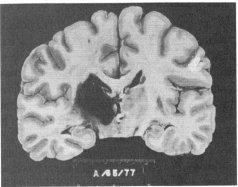

Figure 12–7. *Top*: Computed tomography scan demonstrating a contrast-enhancing right thalamic infarction in a patient with the neglect syndrome. *Bottom*: Right thalamic hemorrhage at postmortem examination of a patient who had the neglect syndrome.

In monkeys and cats, profound sensory neglect results from discrete lesions of the MRF (Reeves & Hagaman, 1971; Watson et al., 1974). Stimulation of the MRF is associated with behavioral arousal and also with desynchronization of the electroencephalogram (EEG), a physiological measure of arousal (Moruzzi & Magoun, 1949). In humans, the performance of attention-demanding tasks increases the activation of the MRF and the thalamic intralaminar nuclei, as determined by positron emission tomography (PET; Kinomura et al., 1996). Unilateral stimulation of the reticular activating system induces greater EEG desynchronization in the ipsilateral than in the contralateral hemisphere (Moruzzi & Magoun, 1949). Arousal is a physiological state that prepares the organism for sensory and motor processing. Whereas bilateral MRF lesions result in coma, unilateral lesions result in contralateral neglect, which is probably due to unilateral hemispheric hypoarousal (Watson et al., 1974).

Many neurons that ascend from the mesencephalic reticular activating system and its environs are monoaminergic. The area of the mesencephalon stimulated by Moruzzi and

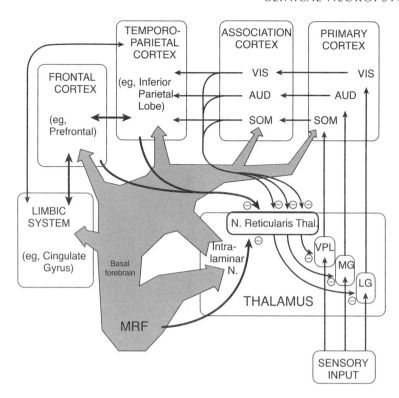

Figure 12–9. Schematic representation of pathways important in sensory attention and tonic arousal. MRF, mesencephalic reticular formation; VIS, visual; AUD, auditory; SOM, somesthetic. Within the thalamus, sensory relay nuclei are indicated: VPL, ventralis posterolateralis; MG, medial geniculate; LG, lateral geniculate.

Magoun (1949) contains ascending catecholamine systems, including the noradrenergic system that projects diffusely from the locus ceruleus to the cortex. Although this norepinephrine system would appear to be ideal for mediating cortical arousal (Jouvet, 1977), studies have revealed that this system appears not to be critical for tonic arousal and is primarily active in response to external noxious stimuli (Aston-Jones & Bloom, 1981). As mentioned above, Moruzzi and Magoun (1949) demonstrated that unilateral stimulation of the mesencephalic reticular activating system induced greater desynchronization ipsilaterally than contralaterally. We have shown that unilateral lesions in the region of the MRF induce EEG and behavioral changes suggestive of unilateral coma (Watson et al., 1974). Unilateral locus coeruleus lesions do not induce similar behavioral or EEG changes (Deuel, personal communication).

Although unilateral injury to the dopaminergic (DA) system may induce neglect because dopamine is critical for mediating intention (see section below on intention), dopamine does not appear to be important in arousal because blockade of dopamine synthesis or of dopamine receptors does not appear to affect EEG desynchronization (Robinson et al., 1978).

Acetylcholine appears to have a role in the mediation of arousal. Shute and Lewis (1967) described an ascending cholinergic reticular formation. Stimulation of the midbrain mesencephalic reticular activating system not only induces the arousal response but also increases the rate of acetylcholine release from the neocortex (Kanai & Szerb, 1965). Acetylcholine makes some neurons more responsive to sensory input (McCormick, 1989). Cholinergic agonists induce neocortical desynchronization, whereas antagonists abolish desynchronization (Bradley, 1968). Unfortunately, however, although cholinergic blockers such as atropine interfere with EEG desynchronization, they do not dramatically affect behavioral arousal. Vanderwolf and Robinson (1981) suggested that there may be two types of cholinergic input to the neocortex from the

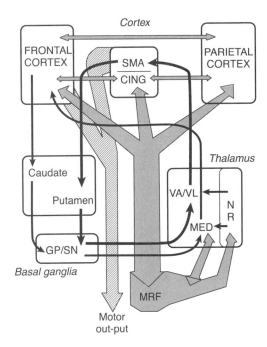

Figure 12–10. Schematic representation of pathways important for motor activation and preparation to respond. Two basal ganglia "loops" are indicated: one (*thick black arrows*) from the supplementary motor area (SMA) to putamen to globus pallidus (GP)/substantia nigra (SN) to VA/VL (ventralis anterior and ventralis lateralis) of thalamus back to the SMA; the other (*thin black arrows*) from prefrontal cortex to caudate to GP/SN to the medial thalamic nuclei (MED) back to prefrontal cortex. NR, nucleus reticularis thalami; CING, cingulate gyrus.

reticular formation, only one of which is atropine sensitive. Therefore, the non–atropine-sensitive cholinergic input may be responsible for behavioral arousal. It is believed that cholinergic projections from the nucleus basalis are responsible for increasing neuronal responsivity (Sato et al., 1987). The nucleus basalis receives a projection from the peripeduncular area of the mesencephalon, which, in turn, receives a projection from the cuneiform area of the mesencephalon (Arnault & Roger, 1987). Mesencephalic stimulation may thus influence cortical cholinergic activity via the nucleus basalis.

The mesencephalic reticular activating system may project to the cortex in a diffuse polysynaptic fashion (Schiebel & Schiebel, 1967) (see Figure 12-8) and thereby influence cortical processing of sensory stimuli. Steriade and Glenn (1982) found that the centralis lateralis and paracentralis thalamic nuclei also project to widespread cortical regions. Other neurons from these thalamic areas project to the caudate. Thirteen percent of neurons with cortical or caudate projections could be activated by mesencephalic reticular activating system stimulation.

There is an alternative means whereby the mesencephalic reticular activating system may affect cortical processing of sensory stimuli. Sensory information that reaches the cortex is relayed through specific thalamic nuclei. Somatosensory information is transmitted from the ventralis posterolateralis (VPL) to the postcentral gyrus, auditory information is transmitted through the medial geniculate nucleus (MGN) to the supratemporal plane (Heschl's gyrus), and visual information is transmitted through the lateral geniculate nucleus (LGN) to the occipital lobe (area 17) (Figure 12-9). The nucleus reticularis (NR) thalami, a thin reticular nucleus enveloping the thalamus, projects to the thalamic relay nuclei and appears to inhibit thalamic relay to the cortex (Schiebel & Schiebel, 1966) (Figure 12-9). The mesencephalic reticular activating system also projects to the NR. Rapid mesencephalic reticular activating system stimulation or behavioral arousal inhibits the NR and is thereby associated with enhanced thalamic transmission to the cerebral cortex (Singer, 1977). Therefore, unilateral lesions of MRF may induce neglect not only because the cortex is unprepared for processing sensory stimuli in the absence of MRF-mediated arousal, but also because the thalamic sensory relay nuclei are being inhibited by the NR.

Lesions of thalamic relay nuclei or of primary sensory cortex induce a sensory defect rather than neglect. Primary cortical sensory areas project to unimodal association cortex (see Figure 12-9). Association cortex synthesizes multiple features of a complex stimulus within a single sensory modality. Lesions of unimodal association cortex may induce perceptual deficits in a single modality (for example, apperceptive agnosia). Modality-specific association areas may also detect stimulus novelty (modeling) (Sokolov, 1963). When a stimulus is neither novel nor significant, corticofugal projections to the NR may allow habituation to occur by selectively influencing thalamic relay. When a stimulus is novel or significant, corticofugal projections might inhibit the NR and thereby allow the thalamus to relay additional sensory input. This capacity for selective control of sensory input is supported by a study revealing that stimulation of specific areas within NR related to specific thalamic nuclei (e.g., NR lateral geniculate, NR medial geniculate, or NR ventrobasal complex) results in abolition of corresponding (visual, auditory, or tactile) cortical evoked responses (Yingling & Skinner, 1977). Physiologic imaging studies reveal that selectively attending to tactile stimuli may activate primary (somesthetic) cortex (Meyer et al., 1991). This activation may be mediated by corticofugal projections that inhibit the inhibition NR exerts on thalamic relay nuclei such as ventral posterior lateral (VPL).

Primary sensory areas project to unimodal sensory association cortex. In the visual system, there are many different unimodal association areas, but in general, areas located in ventral occipitotemporal regions are important in processing the visual properties of objects (the "what" system), whereas visual association areas in dorsal (superior) occipitoparietal regions are important in processing the spatial position of stimuli (the "where" system) (Haxby et al., 1991). Patients with ventral (what system) lesions may be impaired at recognizing objects (visual object agnosia) and faces (prosopagnosia). In contrast, patients with dorsal (where system) lesions may have problems locating objects in space in relation to their body (for example, optic ataxia). Unimodal association areas converge upon polymodal association areas (Figure 12-9). In the monkey, these are the prefrontal cortex and both banks of the superior temporal sulcus (STS) (Pandya & Kuypers, 1969). Unimodal association areas may also project directly to the caudal inferior parietal lobule (IPL) or, alternatively, may reach the IPL after a synapse in polymodal convergence areas (e.g., prefrontal cortex and both banks of the STS) (Mesulam et al., 1977). Polymodal convergence areas may subserve cross-modal associations and polymodal sensory synthesis. Polymodal sensory synthesis may also be important in "modeling" (detecting stimulus novelty) and detecting significance. In contrast to the unimodal association cortex that projects to specific parts of the NR and thereby gates sensory input in one modality, these multimodal convergence areas may have a more general inhibitory action on NR and provide

further arousal after cortical analysis. These convergence areas also may project directly to the MRF, which either may induce a general state of arousal because of diffuse multisynaptic connections to the cortex or may increase thalamic transmission via connections with NR, as discussed above, or both.

Evidence that polymodal parietal cortex may be important in enhancing thalamic transmission by inhibiting the inhibitory thalamic reticular nucleus comes from the observation that patients with Balint syndrome from biparietal lesions note that after a few seconds visual stimuli, unless moving, disappear. Mennemeier et al. (1994), suggested and provided support for the hypothesis that visual stimuli disappear because the parietal lobes can no longer inhibit this inhibitory thalamic nucleus. Mennemeier et al. also suggested that, whereas the parietal lobes inhibit the inhibitory thalamic reticular nucleus and thereby enhance stimulus transmission, the frontal lobes excite the inhibitory NR, diminish transmission, and promote habituation. To test this hypothesis Mennemeier et al. studied visual habituation using the Troxlar paradigm. In this paradigm, the subject looks at a central fixation point and notes when a dot on the right or left of this fixation point fades from vision. Mennemeier et al., found that contralateral to parietal lesions there was enhanced habituation (rapid fading) and contralateral to frontal lesions there was delayed habituation.

Evidence that polymodal areas of cortex modulate arousal comes from neurophysiological studies showing that stimulation of select cortical sites induces a generalized arousal response. These sites in monkeys include the frontal prearcuate region and both banks of the STS that is the precursor of human's inferior parietal lobe (Segundo et al., 1955). When similar sites are ablated, there is EEG evidence of ipsilateral hypoarousal (Watson et al., 1977).

Although determination of stimulus novelty may be mediated by sensory association cortex, stimulus significance is determined in part by the needs of the organism (motivational state). Limbic system input into brain regions important for determining stimulus significance might provide information about biological needs. The frontal lobes might provide input about needs related to goals that are neither directly

stimulus dependent nor motivated by an immediate biological need, since the frontal lobes do
play a critical role in goal-mediated behavior
and in developing sets (see Chapter 14).

Polymodal (e.g., STS) and supramodal (IPL)
areas have prominent limbic and frontal connections. In humans, lesions in the right posterior superior temporal lobe (Karnath et al., 2001)
as well as the inferior parietal lobe can induce
elements of the neglect syndrome (Heilman
et al., 1983) Polymodal and supramodal cortices project to the cingulate gyrus (a portion of
the limbic system), and the cingulate gyrus also
projects to these areas (Figure 12-9). The prefrontal cortex, STS, and IPL have strong reciprocal connections. The posterior cingulate cortex
(Brodmann's area 23) has more extensive
connections with polymodal association areas
(prefrontal cortex and STS) and the IPL than
does the anterior cingulate cortex (Brodmann's
area 24) (Vogt et al., 1979; Baleydier &
Maugierre, 1980). These connections provide
an anatomic substrate by which motivational
states (e.g., biological needs, sets, and long-term
goals) may influence stimulus processing.

*Physiological Properties of Neurons in the
Inferior Parietal Lobe.* Investigators have been
able to study the physiological function of specific areas of the nervous system by recording
from single neurons in awake animals. In this
experimental situation, the firing characteristics of individual neurons can be measured in
relation to specific sensory stimuli or motor
behaviors. For example, a single neuron in the
visual cortex may respond maximally to a contrast
border in a specific region of the visual field, sometimes in a specific orientation. By varying the
nature of the stimulus and by training the animal
to respond in specific ways, the characteristic
patterns of firing of individual neurons can be
defined in terms of the optimal stimulus and/or
response parameters that cause a maximal change
in firing rate. In this fashion, investigators have
defined the properties of neurons in the parietal
lobe (areas 5 and 7) of the monkey (Mountcastle
et al., 1975, 1981; Goldberg & Robinson, 1977;
Robinson et al., 1978; Bushnell et al., 1981;
Lynch, 1980; Motter & Mountcastle, 1981).
Unlike single cells in primary sensory cortex,
the activity of many parietal neurons correlates

best with stimuli or responses of importance to
the animal, whereas similar stimuli or responses
that are unimportant are associated with either
no change or a lesser change in neuronal activity (Colby & Goldberg, 1999).

Early investigations identified parietal
neurons that responded to visual stimuli of
biologic significance, aversive as well as reward-
ing, suggesting activity that might mediate
selective attention (Goldberg & Robinson,
1977; Robinson et al., 1978). Some neurons
were active with fixation of nonmoving stimuli,
some only when the animal was tracking a
moving stimulus, and others responded only
when stimuli were moving in a specific direction. Most had receptive fields in the contralateral visual field (i.e., they responded only to
stimuli in a portion of the contralateral visual
field), but other neurons had large receptive
fields, sometimes spanning both visual fields
(Mountcastle, 1981).

Subsequent work has revealed a striking specialization of subregions of areas 5 and 7 related
to spatial organization (Colby & Goldberg, 1999).
Within the intraparietal (IP) sulcus of the monkey,
a lateral region (LIP) contains exclusively visually responsive neurons that are specialized to
respond to objects that are beyond the animal's
reach and that can only be explored by eye
movements. Many neurons in LIP fire in relation to eye movements, either in anticipation of
them, during a delay in a task that entails an eye
movement, or after an eye movement has been
made. On the opposite bank of the IP sulcus,
in the medial IP (MIP) area, neurons are found
that respond principally to visual or tactile stimuli
from objects that are within reach of the animal
(Colby & Duhamel, 1991). Ventral to this, in
ventral IP (VIP), neurons respond to stimuli
in near personal space, which the animal can
reach with the mouth. Some bimodal neurons
in this region fire in response to tactile stimuli
in a region on the face, and to moving visual
stimuli only when the trajectory of the stimuli
would bring them into contact with that region
of the face (Colby et al., 1993). Still more anteriorly, in anterior IP (AIP), neurons respond to
the shape and orientation of visual or tactile stimuli. These neurons also fire in conjunction with
hand movements that grasp the object (Colby
& Goldberg, 1999). Thus, within parietal lobe,

multiple representations of space differ with regard to the activity that will target stimuli: eye movements (LIP), touching with the hand (MIP) or face (VIP), or grasping (AIP). Although these spatial representations are used in the planning of movements, in most instances studied, they appear not to program movements directly. Enhancement of response is often independent of the kind of response. Thus, neurons in LIP will respond equally to a stimulus if the response is an eye movement toward the stimulus or a bar press without visual fixation (Colby et al., 1996). Since many of the neurons in these regions respond differentially to objects that are significant to the organism, lesions in these areas can reduce awareness of objects in far or near space, suggesting an anatomic and physiologic basis for the spatial direction of attention. Damage to these areas may therefore result in various distributions of hemispatial neglect. This may be relevant to the production of restricted forms of the neglect syndrome in humans, such as, for example, Vuilleumier et al.'s (1998) report of neglect for far but not near space.

Studies using functional imaging have provided converging evidence that the right posterior temporoparietal region is important for allocating attention. For example, Fink et al. (2001) demonstrated activation of this area during the Landmark test, in which normal subjects were attempting to learn if the presented line has been correctly bisected.

Summary of the Attentional Model. The human brain has a limited capacity to process information, and therefore, the brain must triage or select information based on its biological significance. To process information, the cortex has to be in a physiological state of readiness, called arousal. The mesencephalic-diencephalic reticular system mediates arousal. Unilateral inattention will follow unilateral mesencephalic reticular activating system lesions because the MRF does not prepare the cortex for sensory processing, and/or because it no longer inhibits the ipsilateral NR, which then inhibits thalamic transmission of sensory input to the cortex. Corticothalamic collaterals from association cortex to the NR may serve unimodal orienting or habituation. Unilateral lesions of multimodal sensory convergence areas that project to mesencephalic

reticular activating system and NR, such as the posterior-superior temporal and inferior parietal region, induce contralateral inattention because the subject cannot be aroused by or process contralateral stimuli. To selectively attend to a biologically significant stimulus, one must recognize the stimulus and know its spatial location. The sensory association systems that mediate "what" and "where" sensory analyses converge in the inferior parietal cortex. Biological significance is determined by immediate needs or drives, mediated by portions of the limbic system such as the cingulate gyrus, or by long-term goals and sets, mediated by dorsolateral frontal lobes. The posterior superior temporal and inferior parietal region, the cingulate gyrus, and the dorsolateral frontal lobe are all highly interconnected, and, with the reticular (arousal) systems, form an attentional network, illustrated in Figure 12-9. A lesion affecting any one of these modules or the connections between them (Burcham et al., 1997) can result in unilateral sensory neglect.

MECHANISMS UNDERLYING EXTINCTION

The patient with extinction reports a stimulus presented in isolation, but does not report the same stimulus when another stimulus is presented simultaneously. Most often, the two stimuli are presented on opposite sides of the body, and it is the stimulus contralateral to the lesion that is extinguished. Extinction may be induced by stimuli in the same or different modalities. The nature and complexity of a stimulus may also affect extinction.

Extinction can be seen in normal subjects as well as in patients with central nervous system (CNS) lesions (Kimura, 1967; Benton & Levin, 1972). The lesions causing extinction are usually in the same areas as lesions that cause inattention. Also, extinction, like inattention, is more commonly associated with right than left hemisphere dysfunction (Meador et al., 1988). However, certain forms of extinction may also occur after lesions of the corpus callosum (Sparks & Geschwind, 1968; Milner et al., 1968), and left-sided extinction has even been reported to follow left hemisphere lesions (Schwartz et al., 1979). Extinction in normal subjects, extinction in patients with callosal lesions, and extinction in patients with hemisphere lesions may all have different mechanisms. In this section, we primarily discuss the extinction seen with hemisphere lesions.

Extinction in humans is most often reported with parietotemporal lesions (Heilman et al., 1983). Multimodal extinction may also occur in monkeys with parietotemporal lesions (Heilman et al., 1970). Whereas the ipsilateral extinction reported by Schwartz et al. (1979) required complex stimuli, extinction after parietotemporal lesions can be demonstrated using simple stimuli.

In general, despite many published reports, especially about dichotic listening in normal subjects, the mechanisms underlying extinction are not entirely understood. We will discuss several hypotheses that have been advanced to explain extinction.

Sensory Hypothesis

Extinction has been reported to be induced by lesions that affect purely sensory systems. Because patients with partial deafferentation may exhibit extinction, several authors have postulated a sensory mechanism to explain extinction. Psychophysical methods have been used to demonstrate that, in normal subjects, the sensory threshold increases on one side when the opposite side is stimulated. This has been called *obscuration*, and has been attributed to reciprocal inhibition (Benton & Levin, 1972). If obscuration occurs in patients with an elevated threshold from an afferent lesion, it would appear similar to extinction in patients without deafferentation.

Suppression and Reciprocal Inhibition

Nathan (1946) and Reider (1946) suggested that extinction results from suppression, mediated by transcallosal inhibition. A similar mechanism was proposed by Kinsbourne (1970). Normally, each hemisphere inhibits the other, but the inhibition becomes unbalanced when one hemisphere is damaged. The damaged hemisphere is inhibited more than the undamaged hemisphere. Consequently, stimuli delivered to the side of the body opposite the damaged hemisphere are not perceived when the normal side is stimulated.

The notion of transcallosal inhibition thus has bearing on theories of inattention. This is discussed further below (mechanisms of hemispatial neglect).

One can also explain extinction and obscuration on the basis of asymmetric inhibition of thalamic relay. As discussed above, NR thalami normally inhibits thalamic relay nuclei, decreasing sensory transmission to the ipsilateral cortex. The NR is inhibited by ipsilateral sensory association cortex and multimodal cortex (inferior parietal lobe), facilitating sensory transmission to ipsilateral cortex. There may be reciprocal facilitation of the contralateral NR, resulting in decreased sensory transmission to the contralateral cortex. Therefore, even under normal conditions, a stimulus on one side would increase the threshold for stimuli on the other side. Lesions of association cortex would decrease inhibition of NR, which in turn would inhibit the thalamic sensory nuclei, thus making the thalamus less sensitive to contralateral stimuli. With bilateral simultaneous stimuli, activated attentional cells in the intact hemisphere would increase contralateral NR activity even more, further inhibiting thalamic sensory nuclei and thereby inducing extinction.

Interference Theory

Birch et al. (1967) proposed that the damaged hemisphere processes information more slowly than the intact hemisphere. Because of this inertia, the damaged side is more subject to interference from the normal side. To support their hypothesis, the authors demonstrated that stimulating the abnormal side (contralesional side) before stimulating the normal side (ipsilateral side) reduced extinction; however, stimulating the normal side before the abnormal side had no effect on extinction.

Limited Attention or Capacity Theory

According to the limited attention or capacity theory, bilateral simultaneous stimuli are normally processed simultaneously, each hemisphere processing the contralateral stimulus and having an attentional bias toward contralateral space or body. However, a damaged hemisphere (usually the right) may be unable to attend to contralateral stimuli. Recovery from unilateral inattention may be mediated by the normal (left) hemisphere. This hemisphere, however, may not only have an attentional bias toward contralateral space and body, but also may have a limited attentional capacity. Therefore, with bilateral simultaneous stimulation, the normal hemisphere's attentional mechanism, biased toward the contralateral stimulus, may be unable to attend to an ipsilateral stimulus (Heilman, 1979).

Evidence for the Different Theories of Extinction

Here, we briefly review studies that have some bearing on the various theories of extinction. We should note that these theories may not be mutually exclusive: Because extinction can be caused by lesions in a variety of anatomically and functionally different areas, the reciprocal inhibition, limited attention, and interference theories could each be correct, but for different lesions.

Benton and Levin (1972) reported that, in normal subjects, threshold is raised by presenting a simultaneous stimulus. Because normal persons do not have lesions, Benton and Levin's findings cannot be explained readily by the limited attention or interference models. Their findings appear to support the reciprocal inhibition model. The findings of Birch et al. (1967) that extinction is reduced when a contralesional stimulus precedes an ipsilesional stimulus, but not when an ipsilesional stimulus precedes a contralesional stimulus, are compatible with both the reciprocal inhibition and limited attention theories. Support for the reciprocal NR gating model comes from the work of Staines et al. (2000), who used fMRI to study patients with tactile extinction and found a reduction of activation in the primary somatosensory cortex. However, Volpe et al. (1979) asked patients with visual extinction to tell if objects projected into the contralesional field were or were not the same as those presented to the ipsilateral field. Although subjects were unaware of the contralesional stimulus when it was presented simultaneously with the ipsilesional stimulus, when forced to respond, they could determine if the objects were the same or different. In addition, Beversdorf et al. (2008) performed fMRI on

a patient with tactile extinction and on matched controls. Although the patient was unaware of the contralesional tactile stimulus, when presented with an ipsilesional tactile stimulus, the somatosensory cortex demonstrated activation, suggesting that extinction can not be entirely explained by thalamic sensory inhibition in all patients. Sevush and Heilman (1981) and Kaplan et al. (1990) showed that a unilateral stimulus preceding a trial with bilateral simultaneous stimuli may alter the pattern of extinction in patients with unilateral hemisphere lesions. The subject is more likely to show extinction when a bilateral trial is preceded by a contralesional (e.g., left) stimulus than when a bilateral trial is preceded by an ipsilesional (e.g., right) stimulus. In addition, Rapcsak et al. (1987) observed that extinction can occur even within a visual field. These findings cannot be explained by the interference model.

Heilman et al. (1984) provided additional support for the model of limited attentional capacity. Patients who exhibited extinction were asked to report where on their body they were given a tactile stimulus: on the right, the left, both, or neither. In this "neither" stimulation condition, the subject was not stimulated, but was still asked to give a response. Subjects erred by reporting "both" when the arm ipsilateral to the damaged hemisphere was stimulated more often than they reported "both" when the contralateral arm was stimulated. Using a similar paradigm, Schwartz et al. (personal communication) found that a patient with left-sided extinction would often report being touched on the left when they were not. One interpretation of these findings is that patients were not sufficiently attentive to their contralesional extremities to realize when they had not been touched. Since the errors consisted of reporting stimulation that did not occur rather than failing to report stimuli, these results cannot be explained by the suppression, reciprocal inhibition, or interference theories and are most compatible with the limited attention or capacity theory. Rapcsak et al. (1987) demonstrated that capacity is most limited in the contralesional field and becomes progressively reduced as one moves laterally toward the ipsilesional field. However, with right hemisphere lesions, capacity may be so reduced that even when two stimuli are given ipsilaterally in either the visual (Rapcsak et al., 1987) or tactile modality (Feinberg et al., 1990), one stimulus is extinguished. This extinguished stimulus is usually the one that is closest to the contralesional side.

An extinction-like phenomenon might also play a role in the bias observed with line bisection. Riestra et al. (2001) studied patients with spatial neglect, using two tasks. In one task pre-bisected lines were presented in which the bisection marks were off center; in the second task, the right and left segments of the bisected lines were presented independently and sequentially. In the pre-bisected line task, subjects were asked to report the position of the bisection, but in the segments task, subjects compared the length of the line segments. The subjects with neglect were more accurate with the sequential presentation of line segments than they were in the pre-bisected line task. These results suggest that an extinction-like phenomenon plays a role in line bisection bias. In addition, Mark et al. (1988) using a cancellation test had patients either cross out targets or erase targets. They found that hemispatial neglect was more severe in the cancellation than in the erase conditions, again providing support that extinction like phenomena might induce hemispatial neglect. However, an alternative explanation of these results—a failure of disengagement—will be discussed below.

MECHANISMS UNDERLYING ACTION-INTENTIONAL DISORDERS

Unilateral neglect has been described following unilateral lateral frontal lesions in monkeys (Bianchi, 1895; Kennard & Ectors, 1938; Welch & Stuteville, 1958) and man (Heilman & Valenstein, 1972). Watson et al. (1978) recognized that, in most testing paradigms, the animal is required to respond to a stimulus contralateral to the lesion either by orienting to the stimulus or by moving the limbs on the side of the stimulus. Since these animals with frontal lobe lesions were not weak, it was assumed that their failure to make the appropriate response resulted from sensory neglect. Watson et al. (1978) suggested that it could be explained equally well by unilateral or hemispatial akinesia. They therefore trained monkeys to use the

left hand to respond to a tactile stimuli on the right leg, and the right hand to respond to a left-sided tactile stimuli. After unilateral frontal arcuate lesions (lateral prefrontal lobe), the monkeys showed contralateral neglect, but when stimulated on their neglected side, they responded normally with the limb on the side of the lesion. When stimulated on the side ipsilateral to the lesion, however, they often failed to respond with the contralateral limb, or responded by moving the limb ipsilateral to the lesion. These results cannot be explained by sensory, perceptual, or attentional hypotheses, and are thought to reflect a defect of intention: an inability to initiate a response by the contralateral limb or a response in contralesional hemispace.

Anatomic and Physiological Mechanisms

The region of the arcuate gyrus (periarcuate region) in monkeys contains the frontal eye field. Stimulation of the frontal eye field elicits contralateral eye movement, head rotation, and pupillary dilation resembling attentive orienting (Wagman & Mehler, 1972). The connections of the periarcuate region are important in understanding its possible role in motor activation or intention. The periarcuate region has reciprocal connections with auditory, visual, and somesthetic association cortex (Chavis & Pandya, 1976). Evoked potential studies have confirmed this as an area of sensory convergence (Bignell & Imbert, 1969). The periarcuate region is also reciprocally connected with the cortex on the banks of the STS, another site of multimodal sensory convergence, and with the cortex on the banks of the intraparietal sulcus, an area of somatosensory and visual convergence. There are also connections with prearcuate cortex. The periarcuate cortex has reciprocal connections with subcortical areas: the paralamellar portion of dorsomedial nucleus (DM) and the adjacent centromedian-parafascicularis (CM-Pf) complex (Kievet & Kuypers, 1977; Akert & Von Monakow, 1980). Just as the periarcuate region is transitional in architecture between agranular motor cortex and granular prefrontal cortex, the paralamellar-CM-Pf complex is situated between medial thalamus, which projects to granular cortex, and lateral thalamus, which projects to agranular cortex. Projections to MRF (Kuypers and Lawrence, 1967) as well as nonreciprocal projections to caudate also exist. Lastly, the periarcuate region also receives input from the limbic system, mainly from the anterior cingulate gyrus (Baleydier & Mauguiere, 1980).

The neocortical sensory association and sensory convergence areas connections provide the frontal lobes with information about external stimuli that may call the individual to action. Limbic connections (from the anterior cingulate gyrus) may provide the frontal lobe with motivational information. Connections with the MRF may be important in arousal.

Because this area of the lateral frontal lobe has connections with sensory association cortex, limbic, and reticular formation connections, it would appear to be an ideal candidate for mediating a response to a stimulus to which the subject is attending (Figure 12-9). Although this area may not be critical for mediating how to respond (e.g., providing instruction for the spatial trajectory and temporal patterns), it may control when one responds. There is evidence from physiological studies to support this hypothesis. Recordings from single cells in the posterior frontal arcuate gyrus reveal responses similar to those of the superior colliculus, a structure also important in oculomotor control (Goldberg & Bushnell, 1981). These visually responsive neurons show enhanced activity time-locked to the onset of stimulus and preceding eye movement. This differs from IPL neurons that respond to visual input independent of behavior: An IPL neuron whose activity enhances in a task that requires a saccade also enhances with tasks that do not require a saccade. Therefore, the IPL neurons seem to be responsible for selective spatial attention, which is independent of behavior, and any neuron that is enhanced to one type of behavior will also be enhanced to others (Bushnell et al., 1981). The frontal eye field neurons, however, are linked to behavior, but only to movements that have motivational significance. Responses to other stimulus modalities (e.g., audition) may be controlled by an adjacent group of neurons in the arcuate gyrus (Whittington & Hepp-Reymond, 1977).

The dorsolateral frontal lobe has extensive connections with CM-Pf, one of the "nonspecific" intralaminar thalamic nuclei. Nonsensory

or motor-intentional neglect has also been reported in monkeys after CM-Pf lesions (Watson et al., 1978) and in a patient with an intralaminar lesion (Bogousslavsky et al., 1986). An akinetic state (akinetic mutism) is seen with bilateral CM-Pf lesions in humans (Mills & Swanson, 1978). We have postulated a possible role for CM-Pf in behavior (Watson et al., 1981). This role is based on behavioral, anatomic, and physiological evidence that CM-Pf and periarcuate cortex are involved in mediating responses to meaningful stimuli.

Low-frequency stimulation of CM-Pf induces cortical recruiting responses (Jasper, 1949) and activates the inhibitory NR through a CM-Pf-frontocortical-NR system (Yingling & Skinner, 1975). This NR activation elicits inhibitory postsynaptic potentials in the ventrolateral thalamic nucleus (VL), and thus blocks VL transmission to motor cortex (Purpura, 1970). Transmission in VL has been shown to be inversely proportional to NR activity (Filion et al., 1971). The VL projects to motor cortex, and may be important in the control of movement initiation.

High-frequency stimulation of the CM-Pf induces inhibition of NR, desynchronization of the EEG, and behavioral arousal (Moruzzi & Magoun, 1949; Yingling & Skinner, 1975). These manifestations elicited by high-frequency CM-Pf stimulation are predominantly mediated via the MRF-NR system, since they are blocked by a lesion between the CM-Pf and MRF (Weinberger et al., 1965). A lesion of the CM-Pf-frontocortical-NR system also prevents inhibition of the NR response to rapid CM-Pf stimulation, whereas rapid MRF stimulation during this blockade will continue to inhibit the NR (Yingling & Skinner, 1977). This indicates that the NR can be inhibited by either an MRF-NR system or a CM-Pf-frontocortical-NR system and suggests that different types of behavior may be mediated independently by these systems.

Novel or noxious stimuli, or anticipation of a response to a meaningful stimulus, produce inhibition of the NR and a negative surface potential over the frontal cortex (Yingling & Skinner, 1977). This surface-negative potential occurs if a stimulus has acquired behavioral significance (Walter, 1973). Specifically, when a warning stimulus precedes a second imperative stimulus that requires a motor response, a negative waveform appears between stimuli. This has been called the *contingent negative variation* (CNV) and is thought to reflect motivation, attention, or expectancy.

Skinner and Yingling (1976) demonstrated that, in a conditional tone/shock expectancy paradigm, both the frontal negative wave and inhibition of NR elicited by the tone were abolished by blockade of the CM-Pf-frontocortical-NR system, although primitive orienting persisted. Novel or noxious stimuli or rapid MRF stimulation continued to inhibit NR. In an operant task involving alternate bar press for reward, cooling of the CM-Pf-frontocortical-NR loop sufficient to block cortical recruitment induced incorrect responses to the previously reinforced bar press (i.e., perseveration) (Skinner & Yingling, 1977). Further cooling caused the subject to cease responding altogether. These behavioral observations demonstrated that an appropriate response to a meaningful stimulus in an aroused subject requires an intact CM-Pf-frontocortical-NR system, whereas primitive behavioral orienting elicited by novel or noxious stimuli depends on an intact MRF-NR system. Responding to basic survival stimuli (e.g., food when hungry) may also depend on an MRF-NR system.

Skinner and Yingling (1977) interpreted their data as supporting a role for the MRF-NR system in tonic arousal and the CM-Pf-frontocortical-NR system in "selective" attention. We agree with the hypothesized role of the MRF-NR system in tonic arousal but suggest that the role of the CM-Pf-frontocortical-NR system is preparing the aroused organism to respond to a meaningful stimulus. The demonstration that intralaminar neurons have activity time-locked to either sensory or motor events, depending on the experimental condition, supports the pivotal role of this structure in sensory-motor integration (Schlag-Rey & Schlag, 1980).

The periarcuate region and thalamic zone around the lateral aspect of the dorsomedial nucleus and intralaminar nucleus share common anatomic features. In addition to reciprocal connections, there is a complex arc from periarcuate cortex, motor cortex, and CM-Pf to the neostriatum (caudate and putamen), from the neostriatum to globus pallidus to CM-Pf and VL, and from CM-Pf and VL back to premotor and motor cortex. Not surprisingly, lesions of structures within this loop, including arcuate gyrus (Watson et al., 1978), basal ganglia (Valenstein & Heilman, 1981), VL (Velasco & Velasco, 1979), and CM-Pf (Watson et al., 1978), have induced a deficit in responding to multimodal sensory stimuli (Figure 12-9).

Neurotransmitter Deficits in Intentional Disorders

Much evidence suggests DA neurons play an important role in the mediation of intention. Intentional deficits are prominent in patients with Parkinson disease, which is characterized pathologically by degeneration of ascending DA neurons. In animals, unilateral lesions in these pathways (Marshall et al., 1971) and unilateral destruction of the DA system by a toxin (Schneider et al., 1992), cause many of the signs of unilateral neglect.

Three related DA pathways have been defined. The nigrostriatal pathway originates in the pars compacta of the substantia nigra (SN), and projects to the neostriatum (caudate and putamen). The mesolimbic pathway originates principally in the ventral tegmental area (VTA) of the midbrain (area A10), just medial to the SN, and terminates in the limbic areas of the basal forebrain (nucleus accumbens septi and olfactory tubercle). The mesocortical pathway originates principally in DA neurons located more laterally in the midbrain (areas A8 and A9) and project to the frontal and cingulate cortex (Ungerstedt, 1971a; Lindvall et al., 1974; Williams & Goldman-Rakic, 1998).

Ascending DA fibers course through the lateral hypothalamus (LH) in the median forebrain bundle. Bilateral lesions in the lateral hypothalamus of rats induce an akinetic state (Teitelbaum & Epstein, 1962). Unilateral LH lesions cause unilateral neglect, as these rats circle toward the side of their lesion and fail to respond to sensory stimuli delivered to the contralateral side (Marshall et al., 1971). There is considerable evidence the LH lesions cause neglect by damaging DA fibers passing through the hypothalamus. Neglect occurs with 6-hydroxydopamine (6-OHDA) lesions of LH that damage DA fibers relatively selectively (Marshall et al., 1974), but not with kainic acid lesions that damage cell bodies but not fibers of passage (Grossman et al., 1978). Unilateral damage to the same DA fibers closer to their site of origin in the midbrain also causes unilateral neglect (Ljungberg & Ungerstedt, 1976; Marshall, 1979). Conversely, unilateral stimulation in the area of ascending DA fibers (Arbuthnott & Ungerstedt, 1975) or of the striatum (Pycock, 1980) causes animals to turn away from the side of stimulation, as if they are orienting to the opposite side. Normal (nonlesioned) rats spontaneously turn more in one direction. They also have an asymmetry in striatal dopamine concentration, and their direction of turning is generally away from the side of the brain with more dopamine (Glick et al., 1975).

Lesions of the ascending DA pathways affect the areas of termination of these pathways in at least two ways. First, degeneration of dopamine-containing axons depletes these areas of dopamine. Marshall (1979) has shown that the neglect induced in rats by ventral tegmental 6-OHDA lesions is proportional to the depletion of dopamine in the neostriatum. These DA target areas attempt to compensate for the depletion of DA afferents by increasing their responsiveness to dopamine. This is mediated, at least in part, by an increase in the number of DA receptors (Heikkila et al., 1981), which correlates with behavioral recovery from neglect (Neve et al., 1982).

Changes in DA innervation and in DA receptor sensitivity and number of receptors can explain many effects of pharmacological manipulation in animals with unilateral lesions of the ascending DA pathways. Such lesions result in degeneration of DA axon terminals on the side of the lesion. Drugs such as L-dopa or amphetamines, which increase the release of dopamine from normal DA terminals, will therefore cause more dopamine to be released on the unlesioned side than on the lesioned side, resulting in orientation or turning toward the lesioned side (Ungerstedt, 1971b, 1974). Several days after the lesion, when DA receptors on the side of the lesion begins to increase, drugs that directly stimulate DA receptors, such as apomorphine, cause the animal to turn away from the side of the lesion (Ungerstedt; 1971b, 1974).

Although rats have been used in most studies, lesions that probably involve the ascending DA systems have also induced unilateral neglect in cats (Hagamen et al., 1977) and monkeys (Deuel, 1980; Apicella et al., 1991). As mentioned above, bilateral degeneration of the nigrostriatal fibers in humans is associated with parkinsonism, in which akinesia and hypokinesia are prominent symptoms. Ross and Stewart (1981) described a patient with akinetic mutism secondary to bilateral damage to the anterior hypothalamus. This patient responded to treatment with bromocriptine, a direct DA receptor agonist. Since the lesion was probably anterior to the site at which nigrostriatal fibers diverge from the median forebrain bundle, the authors suggested that damage to the mesolimbic and mesocortical pathways was critical in causing their patient's hypokinesia.

The evidence summarized above indicates the importance of DA pathways in mediating intention. Although the neglect induced by LH or VTA lesions has been called "sensory" neglect or inattention, rats trained to respond to unilateral stimulation by turning to the side opposite the side of stimulation respond well to stimulation of their "neglected" side (the side opposite the lesion) but fail to turn when stimulated on their "normal" side (Hoyman et al., 1979). This paradigm is similar to that used by Watson et al. (1978), and demonstrates that lesions in ascending DA pathways cause a defect of intention.

Following unilateral frontal lesions, rats demonstrated contralateral neglect that was reversed by the dopamine agonist apomorphine (Corwin et al., 1986). This apomorphine-induced reduction of neglect was blocked by the prior administration of the dopamine blocker spiroperidol. Rats who had neglect induced by ablation of the frontal cortex recover; however, a dopamine blocker administered to these animals can again induce neglect (Vargo, 1999). Humans with neglect have also been treated with dopamine agonists. This will be discussed in the treatment section.

Physiological studies of striatal DA neurons reveal short-latency phasic responses to stimuli that are novel or signal a reward (Shultz, 1998; Redgrave, Prescott, & Gurney, 1999). These neurons may also fire in relation to the preparation, initiation, or execution of movements related to significant stimuli (Shultz, Tremblay, & Hollerman, 2000). These physiologic studies provide evidence that the activity of DA neurons is related to the regulation of actions that are triggered by significant environmental stimuli.

MECHANISMS UNDERLYING MEMORY AND REPRESENTATIONAL DEFECTS

Patients with neglect may have a hemispatial anterograde memory deficit, such that stimuli presented on the contralesional side are not recalled as well as those presented ipsilesionally. William James (1890) noted that "an object once attended will remain in the memory whilst one inattentively allowed to pass will leave no trace behind." The concept of arousal and its relation to learning and retention has been intensely investigated (for a review see Eysenck, 1976). For example, direct relationships have been found between phasic skin conductance response amplitude during learning and accuracy of immediate and delayed recall (Stelmack et al., 1983). As discussed in an earlier section, neglect may be associated with an attention-arousal deficit. Stimuli presented in the hemispace contralateral to a hemispheric lesion may receive less attention and be associated with less arousal than stimuli presented in ipsilateral hemispace. Because these stimuli are poorly attended and do not induce arousal, they may be poorly encoded. Patients with neglect may therefore demonstrate a hemispatial anterograde memory deficit (Heilman et al., 1974).

Denny-Brown and Banker (1954) asked a patient with spatial neglect to describe a room from memory and this patient failed to recall items from one side of the room. Bisiach and Luzzatti (1978) asked two patients with right hemisphere damage to describe from memory a familiar scene (the main square in Milan) from two different spatial perspectives, one facing the cathedral and the other facing away from the cathedral. Regardless of the patients' orientation, more left- than right-sided details were omitted. On the basis of these findings and those of a second study (Bisiach et al., 1979), these investigators postulated that the mental representation of the environment is structured topographically and is mapped across the brain. That is, the mental picture of the environment may be split between the two hemispheres (like the projection of a real scene). Therefore, with right hemisphere damage, there is a representational disorder for the left half of this image. The representational map postulated by Bisiach may be hemispatially organized, so that left hemispace is represented in the right hemisphere and right hemispace is represented in the left hemisphere.

There are at least three reasons why one side of a mental image could not be envisioned:

- Part (e.g., the left half) of the representation may have been destroyed, as suggested by Bisiach and Luzzatti (1978), and this damage might cause both antegrade and retrograde amnesia.
- The representation may have been intact but could not be activated so that an image was formed.
- The image was formed, but it was not attended and therefore not correctly inspected.

If the representation is destroyed, attentional manipulation should not affect retrieval, but if patients with neglect have an activational or attentional deficit, attentional manipulation may affect retrieval. Meador et al. (1987) replicated Bisiach and Luzzatti's observations and also provided evidence that behavioral manipulations could affect performance. When normal subjects are asked to recall objects in space, they move their eyes to the position the object occupied in space (Kahneman, 1973). Although it is unclear why normal subjects move their eyes during this type of recall task, having patients move their eyes toward neglected hemispace may aid recall because the eye movement induces hemispheric activation or helps direct attention or both. Meador et al. (1987) asked a patient with left hemispatial neglect and defective left hemispatial recall to move his eyes to either right or left hemispace during recall. The patient's recall of left-sided detail was better when he was looking toward the left than toward the right. Although this finding provides evidence that hemispatial retrograde amnesia may be induced by an exploratory-attentional deficit or an activation deficit, it does not exclude the possibility that, in other cases, the representation had been destroyed.

MECHANISMS UNDERLYING HEMISPATIAL NEGLECT

Patients with hemispatial neglect fail to perform on the side of space opposite their lesion, even when using their "normal" ipsilesional hand. For example, they may draw only half a picture, or bisect lines to one side (see Figures 12-1, 12-2). Although hemianopia may enhance the symptoms of hemispatial neglect, hemianopia by itself cannot entirely account for this deficit, because some patients with hemispatial neglect are not hemianopic (McFie et al., 1950), and some hemianopic patients do not demonstrate hemispatial neglect. Although neglect can be allocentric (left half of stimuli can be neglected even in ipsilateral hemispace), it also can be environmental or viewer- or body-centered (Heilman & Valenstein, 1979). The abnormal performance of patients in viewer-centered contralateral space suggests that each hemisphere is responsible not only for receiving stimuli from contralateral space and for controlling the contralateral limbs, but also for attending and intending in contralateral hemispace independent of which hand is used (Heilman, 1979; Bowers & Heilman, 1980).

Hemispace can be defined according to several frames of reference, including the visual half-field (retinotopic), eye position, head position, or trunk position. With the eyes and head facing directly ahead, the hemispaces defined by the eyes, head and trunk are all congruent. But if the eyes are directed to the far right, for example, the left visual field falls in large part in the right hemispace, as defined by the head and body midline. Similarly, if the head and eyes are turned far to the right, left head and eye hemispace can both be in body right hemispace. Evidence suggests that the body frame of reference is of greatest importance in determining the symptoms of hemispatial neglect (Heilman & Valenstein, 1979; Bowers & Heilman, 1980).

Experimental evidence in normal subjects supports the hypothesis that each hemisphere is organized, at least in part, to interact with stimuli in contralateral hemispace. If a subject fixes his gaze at an object that is in the midsagittal plane, keeps his right arm in right hemispace and his left arm in left hemispace, and receives a stimulus delivered in his right visual half-field, he will respond more rapidly with his right hand than with his left hand. Similarly, if a stimulus is delivered in his left visual half-field, he will respond more rapidly with his left hand than with his right (Anzola et al., 1977).

These results were traditionally explained by an anatomic pathway transmission model, in which the reaction times are longer when the hand opposite the stimulated field responds because, in this situation, information must be transmitted between hemispheres, and this takes more time than when information can remain in the same hemisphere. But if a choice reaction time paradigm is used, and the hands are crossed so that the left hand is in right hemispace and the right hand is in left hemispace, then the faster reaction times are made by the hand positioned in the same side of space as the stimulus (Anzola et al., 1977), even though in this situation the information must cross the corpus callosum. Clearly, these results cannot be explained by a pathway transmission model.

Cognitive theorists have attributed the stimulus–response compatibility in these crossed-hand studies to a "natural" tendency to respond to a lateralized stimulus with the hand that is in a corresponding spatial position (Craft & Simon, 1970). Alternatively, each hemisphere may be important for intending in the contralateral hemispatial field, independently of which hand is used to respond (Heilman & Valenstein, 1979; Heilman, 1979). According to this hemispatial hypothesis, when each hand works in its own hemispace, the same hemisphere mediates both the sensorimotor system and the intentional system; however, when a hand works in the opposite hemispace, different hemispheres mediate the sensorimotor and intentional systems.

If the cerebral hemispheres are organized hemispatially, a similar compatibility may exist between the visual half-field in which a stimulus is presented and the side of hemispace in which the visual half-field is aligned. Our group (Bowers et al., 1981) has found a hemispace–visual half-field compatibility suggesting that each hemisphere may not only be important for intending to the contralateral hemispatial field, independent of hand, but may also be important in attending or perceiving stimuli in contralateral hemispace independent of the visual field to which these stimuli are presented.

According to these hypotheses and results, when each hand works in its own spatial field, the same hemisphere mediates both the sensorimotor systems and the attentional-intentional systems. However, when a hand (e.g., right) operates in the opposite spatial field (e.g., left), the hemisphere that is contralateral to this hand (e.g., left) controls the sensorimotor apparatus, but the hemisphere ipsilateral to the hand (e.g., right) mediates attention and intention because the hand is crossed and is in left hemispace. Under these conditions, the sensorimotor and attention-intentional system must communicate through the corpus callosum. Support for this postulate comes from the observation that, when patients with callosal disconnection bisect lines in opposite hemispace, each hand errs by gravitating toward its "own" (compatible) hemispace (Heilman et al., 1984).

Microelectrode studies in alert monkeys support the hypothesis that the brain may be hemispatially organized. Researchers have identified cells with high-frequency activity while the monkey is looking at an interesting target (fixation cells). The activity of these cells depends not only on an appropriate motivational state, but also on an appropriate oculomotor state. That is, certain cells become active only when the animals are looking into contralateral hemispace (Lynch, 1980).

Although these studies support the hypothesis that each hemisphere mediates attention and intention in contralateral viewer-centered hemispace independent of the sensory hemifield or the extremity used, the neural substrate underlying this viewer-centered hemispatial organization of the hemispheres remains unknown. One would expect, for example, that with a right lateral gaze there should be a corollary discharge to activate or alert left hemisphere attentional networks that process stimuli in the right visual field.

To determine if patients with left sided neglect have a body-centered hemispatial deficit, we placed lines in either right, center, or left hemispace. Even when subjects were required to look to the left end of the line before bisecting this line, ensuring that they saw the entire line, performance was significantly better when the line was placed in right than left hemispace (Heilman & Valenstein, 1979). These observations indicate that patients with hemispatial neglect have a hemispatial defect rather than a hemifield defect.

Several neuropsychological mechanisms have been hypothesized to account for this

hemispatial deficit: attentional, intentional, exploratory gaze, and representational map.

Attentional Hypothesis

At least four attentional hypotheses have been proposed to explain spatial neglect: (a) inattention or unawareness, (b) ipsilesional attention bias, (c) inability to disengage from ipsilesional stimuli, and (d) reduced sequential attentional capacity or premature habituation. These four hypotheses are not necessarily mutually contradictory.

The inattention hypothesis states that patients with left hemispatial neglect fail to act in left hemispace because they are unaware of stimuli in left hemispace. Objects that receive greater attention appear to have greater magnitude than those that receive less attention. Thus, because patients are unaware of or inattentive to stimuli or portions of stimuli in left hemispace they may fail to interact with these stimuli, or they may perceive that the objects or parts of objects in left hemispace have a relative reduced magnitude when compared to objects or parts of objects in right hemispace. For example, in the cancellation task, patients with neglect fail to cancel targets in left hemispace because they are unaware of them. In the line bisection task, they might be unaware of a portion of the left side of the line and only bisect the portion of the line of which they are aware, or because they are inattentive to the neglected side of the line, this part of the line appears to be shorter than its actual size and they deviate their attempted line bisection ipsilesionally to correct for their reduced perception of line length on the contralesional side.

Several observations support these attentional hypotheses. The severity of left-sided neglect may be decreased by instructions to attend to a contralesional stimulus, and increased by instructions to attend to an ipsilesional stimulus (Riddoch & Humphreys, 1983). These instructions may modify attention in a "top-down" manner. The severity of neglect may also be modified by novelty. Novelty may influence attention in a "bottom-up" manner. Butter et al. (1990) showed that novel stimuli presented on the contralesional side also reduced spatial neglect. Cues may also be intrinsic to the stimulus. Kartsounis and Warrington (1989) have shown that neglect is less severe when one is drawing meaning-fulpictures than when drawing meaningless pictures.

Normal people who read European languages usually begin searching on the left side of the page. On the line cancellation task, however, patients with left-sided neglect often begin to search for targets on the right side of the page. Ladavas et al. (1990) demonstrated that patients with right parietal lesions have shorter reaction times to right-sided stimuli than to left-sided stimuli, providing evidence of an attentional bias. Kinsbourne (1970) posited that each hemisphere inhibits the opposite hemisphere. When one hemisphere is injured, the other becomes hyperactive, and attention is biased contralaterally. Heilman and Watson (1977) agree that an ipsilesional bias exists, but believe that the bias is not being induced by a hyperactive hemisphere. If, normally, each hemisphere orients attention in a contralateral direction, and one hemisphere is hypoactive there will also be an attentional bias. A seesaw or teeter-totter may tilt one way because one child is either too heavy (hyperactive hypothesis of Kinsbourne) or because the other child is too light (hypoactive hypothesis of Heilman and Watson, 1977).

Support for the hypoactive (vs. Kinsbourne's hyperactive) hemisphere hypothesis comes from both behavioral and physiological studies. Ladavas et al. (1990) found that attentional shifts between vertically aligned stimuli were slower when stimuli were in left (contralesional) hemispace than when they were in right (ipsilesional) hemispace. This slowing cannot be explained by the hyperactive hemisphere hypothesis, which predicts only slowing in the horizontal axis (i.e., left directional shifts of attention should be slower than right shifts) and is therefore supportive of the hypoactive hemisphere theory. Additional support for the hypoactive hypothesis comes from the finding of EEG slowing in the nonlesioned (left) hemisphere (Heilman, 1979) of patients with neglect, and from PET studies that show lower energy metabolism in the uninjured hemisphere (Fiorelli et al., 1991).

Posner et al. (1984) proposed a three-stage model of attention. When people are called upon to shift their attention to another portion of space, they must first disengage attention from the stimulus to which they are currently attending, move their attention to the new stimulus, and

then engage that stimulus. Posner et al. (1984) studied patients with parietal lesions by providing visual cues as to which side of space the imperative (reaction time) stimulus would appear. The cues could be either valid correctly, indicating the side that the stimulus would actually appear, or invalid incorrectly, indicating the side on which the stimulus would appear. The valid cues occurred much more frequently than the invalid cues. In normal subjects, valid cues reduce reaction times and invalid cues increase reaction times. Posner et al. found that in patients with parietal lobe lesions, invalid cues (indicating that the reaction time stimulus is to appear ipsilesionally) resulted in abnormal prolongation of reaction times to contralesional stimuli. These results suggest that one of the functions of the parietal lobe is to disengage attention. Patients may have spatial neglect because they cannot disengage from ipsilesional stimuli.

Mark et al. (1988) tested the disengagement and bias hypothesis of spatial neglect by comparing the performance of patients on a cancellation task in which the subjects were required to mark each detected target with their performance on another cancellation task in which the subject erased the targets. If a target is erased and cannot be seen, the subject should have little or no difficulty disengaging from this target and thus erasing targets should systematically reduce bias. They observed that, on the standard cancellation task, subjects with neglect would first start canceling targets on the side of the sheet that is ipsilateral to their lesion (right side). Although they could disengage from specific targets, they often returned to these targets and canceled them again. When erasing targets, patients' performance improved (they erased more targets); however, they continued to neglect some targets on the left. These observations suggest a bias rather than a problem with "disengagement." The bias hypothesis accounts for the distribution of neglect. Even in the absence of right-side stimuli the subjects with left neglect continue to have a right-sided attention bias and are unable to move their attentional focus fully leftward.

Chatterjee et al. (1992) requested that a patient who demonstrated left-sided neglect on standard cancellation tasks alternately cancel targets on the right and left side of an array.

Using this procedure, the patient was able to overcome her right-sided bias, but she did not cancel more targets. Instead, she now neglected targets in the center of the array. This observation suggests that there might also be a limited action-intentional capacity for sequential exploratory actions (impersistence), or inappropriately rapid habituation or both.

Motor Intentional Hypothesis

When a person attends to a specific spatial location, she/he also prepares to act in that direction. Therefore, sensory attention and motor intention should be closely linked. However, a patient tested by Heilman and Howell (1980) provides evidence that these processes may be dissociable. This patient with intermittent right parieto-occipital seizures was monitored by an EEG while he received right, left, and bilateral stimuli. Interictally, the patient did not have inattention or extinction; however, while the right hemispheric seizure focus was active, he had left-sided extinction. When asked to bisect lines during right hemispheric seizures, however, rather than neglecting left space, the patient attempted to make a mark to the left of the entire sheet of paper. When asked to bisect lines immediately after a seizure, he bisected the line to the right of midline, suggesting left hemispatial neglect. However, at this stage no sensory extinction was present. This case illustrates that attention to contralateral stimuli and intention to perform in this contralateral hemispatial field can be dissociated.

The action-intention hypothesis of hemispatial neglect states that, although patients may be aware of stimuli in contralateral hemispace, they fail to act on these stimuli because they have either a reduced ability to act (or sustain action) in contralesional hemispace or they have an action-intentional bias to act ipsilesionally. Several observations support these hypotheses.

De Renzi et al. (1970) asked blindfolded patients with hemispatial neglect to search a maze for a target. The subjects failed to explore the left side of the maze. When using the tactile modality to explore, one can only attend to stimuli in a new spatial position after one has moved to this new location. Therefore, the failure to explore the left (contralesional) side of the maze cannot be attributed to an attentional deficit and may provide evidence for a hemispatial action-intentional deficit.

The results of a study by Heilman et al. (1983b) suggest that, in addition to a hemispatial action-intentional deficit, patients with unilateral spatial neglect have a rightward motor-intentional bias. Control subjects and patients with left-sided hemispatial neglect were asked to close their eyes, point with their right index finger to their sternum (breast bone), and then point to an imaginary spot in space in their midsagittal plane (directly in front of their sternum). The patients with left hemispatial neglect pointed to the right of midline, whereas the controls pointed slightly to the left of midline. Because this task did not require visual input from left hemispace, the defective performance could not be attributed to hemispatial inattention or an attentional bias. Heilman et al. (1983b) also tested the ability of patients with left-sided hemispatial neglect to move a lever toward or away from the side of their lesion. These subjects needed more time to initiate movements toward the neglected left hemispace than to initiate movements toward right hemispace, thus demonstrating a directional hypokinesia. These asymmetries were not found in brain-lesioned controls without neglect. This directional hypokinesia may be related to a motor intentional bias or to an inability for the motor-intentional system to disengage from right stimuli in right hemispace. Sapir et al. (2007) found that patients with directional hypokinesia often had lesions of the basal ganglia, including the ventral lateral putamen, the claustrum, and the white matter underlying the frontal lobe. However, many patients with subcortical strokes also have cortical damage that might not be seen on structural imaging.

To learn if defective attention or defective intention was primarily responsible for the abnormal performance of patients with spatial neglect, Coslett et al. (1990) had patients bisect lines that they could only see displayed on a TV monitor connected to a video camera focused on the patient's hand and line. Using this technique, motor-action and sensory feedback could be dissociated such that the action could take place in left hemispace, but the feedback could take place in right hemispace or vice versa. Independent of the position of the line, two of the four subjects improved when the monitor was moved from left (contralesional) to right (ipsilesional) hemispace, suggesting their primary disturbance was attentional. The two other subjects were not improved by moving the monitor into right hemispace but were primarily affected by the hemispace in which the action took place, performing better when the line was in right (ipsilesional) hemispace than in left (contralesional) hemispace, suggesting that they had primarily a motor-intentional deficit. The two patients who had primarily intentional neglect had frontal lesions, and those with attentional neglect had parietal lesions.

That spatial neglect can be associated with a motor-intentional bias is also supported by the work of Bisiach et al. (1990). They used a loop of string stretched around two pulleys. The string was positioned horizontally, with one pulley on the left and the other on the right. An arrow was attached to the top segment of string. Subjects with neglect and control subjects were asked to place the arrow midway between the two pulleys. In the congruent condition, the subject held the arrow on the upper string to move it. In the noncongruent condition, the subject moved the arrow by lateral displacement of the lower string, which moved the arrow in the opposite direction. If neglect was caused by a directional hypokinesia, the error in the congruent and noncongruent conditions should be in opposite directions. Six of 13 subjects showed a significant reduction of neglect in the noncongruent condition, suggesting that they had a significant motor-intentional bias.

Na and coworkers (1998) attempted to dissociate attentional and intentional aspects of neglect by having subjects view their performance of a line bisection task on a video monitor on which the task was displayed either normally (direct condition) or right–left reversed (indirect condition). Subjects could not view the workspace directly, but only could see their hand and the line on the monitor. In the indirect condition, hand movements on the right side of the line in the actual workspace appeared on the monitor as being on the left and vice versa. In the indirect condition, the performance of patients with primarily attentional neglect should be influenced by the monitor, so that when viewed on the monitor they will be inattentive to the left side and will bisect lines toward the right, even though in actual work space, the line is bisected to the left, a reversal of their usual error. In contrast, the performance of patients with intentional spatial neglect will be influenced primarily by the motor aspects of the task, and the subjects with left-sided neglect would continue to bisect lines toward the right in the indirect condition, even though on the monitor this bisection would appear as a leftward bias. This technique allows the investigator to determine the relative contribution of attentional and intentional biases in the same subject. For example, if a patient reverses his deviation in the indirect condition, but the deviation is less than it was in the direct condition, it would suggest that the patient has an attentional bias, with some lesser contribution of a rightward intentional bias. Using this apparatus, Na et al. (1998) found that most patients with spatial neglect could be demonstrated to have both intentional and attentional biases, but in patients with frontal lesions, the intentional bias dominated, whereas in patients with temporoparietal lesions, the attentional bias predominated. The finding of mixed attentional and intentional bias is consistent with the idea that the networks subserving attention and intention influence one another.

Representational Hypothesis

We have already mentioned Denny-Brown's and Banker's (1954) as well as Bisiach and Luzzatti's (1978) observations that patients can have a deficit in body-centered hemispatial memory or imagery. Bisiach attributed this deficit to destruction of the representation of left space stored in the right hemisphere. Destruction of a representation may account not only for a deficit in imagery and memory but also for hemispatial neglect.

The construct of attention derives from the knowledge that the human brain has a limited capacity to simultaneously process information. The organism, therefore, must select which stimuli to process. Except for stimuli that will be attended regardless of their significance, such as unexpected moving objects, loud sounds, or bright lights, attention is directed in a top-down fashion. Therefore, knowledge or representations must direct the selection process. At least two representations are needed to perform a spatial task, such as a cancellation task: a representation of the target and a representation of the environment. Because patients with left-sided spatial neglect are able, in a cancellation task, to detect target stimuli on the right side, their failure to detect stimuli on the left cannot be attributed to a loss of the representation of the target. If the knowledge of left space is stored in the right hemisphere, and these representations are destroyed, attention may not be directed to left space because the person has no knowledge of this space.

In a similar fashion, mental representations may also direct action. The number of independent actions one can simultaneously perform is also limited. Therefore, just as one selects stimuli to process, one must also select actions to perform. At least two pieces of knowledge guide action: how to move, and where to act. Since patients with spatial neglect know how to act in ipsilesional space, their failure to act in contralesional space cannot be attributed to a loss of the "how" or movement representation. However, if knowledge of contralesional space is lost, one may fail to act in or toward that portion of space.

Therefore, both intentional and attentional defects may be induced by a representational defect. The loss of a representation (knowledge) of one-half of space should be manifested by all the signs we discussed: an attentional deficit, an intentional deficit, a memory deficit, and an imagery deficit. Unless a patient has all these deficits, hemispatial neglect cannot be attributed to a loss of the spatial representation.

In the clinic, we see patients who have primarily a motor-intentional disorder, as well as others who have primarily a sensory-attentional disorder. Not all patients with neglect have imagery defects, and some patients with imagery defects do not have hemispatial neglect (Guariglia et al., 1993). Therefore, a representational deficit cannot account for all cases of spatial neglect. However, there are patients who are severely inattentive to contralesional stimuli, fail to explore contralesional space, and have a profound contralesional spatial memory defect. Although these patients may have defects in multiple systems, their representation for contralesional space may be destroyed, so that they no longer know of its existence.

Exploratory Hypothesis

Chedru et al. (1973) recorded eye movements of patients with left-sided spatial neglect and demonstrated failure to explore the left side of space. This failure to explore could not be accounted for by paralysis, since these patients could voluntarily look leftward. If patients fail to explore the left side of a line, they may never learn the full extent of the line, bisecting only the portion they have explored. Similarly, if they do not fully explore the left side of a sheet, they may fail to cancel targets on the part of the sheet they have failed to explore. However, these defects of visual exploration may all be attributed to the attentional, intentional, or representational defects previously discussed.

MECHANISMS OF IPSILATERAL NEGLECT

Some patients with right hemispheric lesions show a leftward rather than a rightward bias when attempting to bisect lines (ipsilateral or ipsilesional neglect). The mechanisms of ipsilateral neglect have not been entirely elucidated. Butter et al. (1988b) studied the eye movements of a patient with left-sided neglect from a right dorsolateral frontal lesion. In the acute stages of the illness, the patient was able to make rightward but not leftward saccades. To try to determine if this asymmetry in gaze was due to left-sided inattention or to directional ocular akinesia toward the left, Butter et al. adapted the crossed-response task of Watson et al. (1978) by asking the patient to move his eyes in the direction opposite a lateralized stimulus. When presented with left-sided visual stimuli, this patient could move his eyes to the right, but when presented with right-sided stimulus the patient could not move his eyes to the left, suggesting a directional akinesia. As the patient recovered, this directional akinesia abated, and the patient was able to look leftward to right-sided stimuli. However in this crossed response task, now when presented with a left-sided stimulus, instead of looking rightward, the patient first looked leftward. This has been termed a *visual grasp*. The patient with ipsilateral neglect reported by Kwon and Heilman (1991) also had a visual grasp from a frontal lesion. Kim et al. (1999) studied a series of patients with ipsilateral neglect and demonstrated that most had frontal lesions. Denny-Brown and Chambers (1958) proposed that the parietal lobes mediate approach behaviors, and the frontal lobes mediate avoidance behaviors. Injury to the frontal lobes may disinhibit the parietal lobes and induce aberrant approach behaviors. Kwon and Heilman suggested that the left-sided visual grasp and ipsilateral neglect may both be manifestations of inappropriate approach behaviors (i.e., attentional or action-intentional grasp responses). Robertson et al. (1994) replicated Kwon and Heilman's observations, but suggested that ipsilateral neglect was related to a learned compensatory strategy. However, some of the patients with ipsilateral neglect reported by Kim et al. (1999) demonstrated this phenomenon almost immediately after their stroke, suggesting that ipsilateral neglect could not be attributed entirely to a compensatory strategy. Kim et al. (1999) also demonstrated that ipsilateral neglect, like contralateral neglect, can be induced by both a contralesional attentional bias and a contralesional intentional bias. Finally, ipsilateral neglect is more commonly observed with line bisection than cancellation tasks. Na et al. (2000) studied five patients who demonstrated ipsilateral neglect on line bisection. These subjects were given a character line bisection task (horizontally aligned characters), in which the subjects were instructed to mark a target character at or closest to the true midpoint of the simulated line, as well as a traditional line bisection task. Four of their five patients showed a dissociation, such that ipsilateral neglect occurred with attempted solid line bisections, whereas contralateral neglect was present with the character lines. The character line bisection depends more heavily on focal attention than does the standard straight line bisection task and focal attention is primarily mediated by the left hemisphere. These contrasting results with two different forms of stimuli suggest that ipsilateral neglect cannot be entirely explained by a compensatory strategy. Two patients who had ipsilateral neglect on the normal line bisection task were also tested for a visual grasp, and both demonstrated a visual grasp. These results suggest that an attentional grasp response might have a greater influence on tasks that require right hemisphere

mediated global attention than on tasks that require focal attention.

HEMISPHERIC ASYMMETRIES OF NEGLECT

Many early investigators noted that the neglect syndrome was more often associated with right than left hemisphere lesions (Brain, 1941; McFie et al., 1950; Critchley, 1966). Although Battersby et al. (1956) thought this preponderance of right hemisphere-lesioned patients was the result of a sampling artifact caused by the exclusion of aphasic subjects, subsequent studies confirmed that lesions in the right hemisphere more often induce elements of the neglect syndrome. Albert (1973), Gainotti et al. (1972), and Costa et al. (1969) demonstrated that hemispatial neglect is more frequent and more severe after right than after left hemisphere lesions. Meador et al. (1988) showed that extinction is more common in right than in left hemisphere dysfunction, and Becker and Karnath (2007) recently replicated this result. Studies of limb akinesia (Coslett et al., 1989) and studies of eye movements (De Renzi et al., 1982; Meador et al., 1989) revealed that limb akinesia and directional akinesia are also more common after right than after left-hemisphere lesions.

Inattention

Most of the attentional cells (or comparator neurons) found in the parietal lobe of monkeys by Lynch (1980) and Robinson et al. (1978) had contralateral receptive fields, but some of these neurons had bilateral receptive fields, and thus responded to stimuli presented in either visual half-field. To account for hemispheric asymmetry of attention in humans, we suggested that the temporoparietal regions of the human brain also have attentional or comparator neurons, but that the cells in the right hemisphere are more likely than cells in the left hemisphere to have bilateral receptive fields (Heilman & Van Den Abell, 1980). Thus, cells in the left hemisphere would be activated predominantly by novel or significant stimuli in right hemispace or in the right hemifield, but cells in the right hemisphere would be activated by novel or significant stimuli presented in either visual field or on either side of hemispace (or both). Thus, when the left hemisphere is damaged, the right can attend to ipsilateral stimuli, but the left hemisphere cannot attend to ipsilateral stimuli after right-sided damage, and this asymmetry might account for the finding that right hemisphere lesions would cause contralateral inattention more often than left hemisphere lesions.

Activation of attentional neurons induces local EEG desynchronization (Sokolov, 1963), and if the right hemisphere is dominant for attention, the right hemisphere should desynchronize to stimuli presented in either field, whereas the left hemisphere would desynchronize primarily to right-sided stimuli. We therefore presented lateralized visual stimuli to normal subjects while recording EEG from the scalp. We found that the right parietal lobe desynchronized almost equally to right- or left-sided stimuli, whereas the left parietal lobe desynchronized mainly to right-sided stimuli. These observations are compatible with the hypothesis that the right hemisphere (parietal lobe) dominates the attentional processes (Heilman & Van Den Abell, 1980). A similar phenomenon has been demonstrated using PET (Pardo et al., 1991). These electrophysiological and imaging studies provide evidence for a special role of the right hemisphere in attention and may also help explain why inattention is more often caused by right hemisphere lesions.

Neglect of environmental stimuli may occur even when stimuli are presented to the side ipsilateral to right hemisphere lesions (Albert, 1973; Heilman & Valenstein, 1979; Weintraub & Mesulam, 1987). Although less severe and less frequent, extinction within ipsilesional visual and tactile fields may be seen with right hemisphere lesions (Rapcsak et al. 1987; Feinberg et al., 1990). These observations suggest that, although the left hemisphere can attend rightward, when compared to the right hemisphere, the left hemisphere's attentional capacity to attend contralaterally is limited.

Arousal

Using the galvanic skin response as a measure of arousal, it has been demonstrated that patients with right temporoparietal lesions have a reduced response when compared to patients with left temporoparietal lesions (Heilman et al., 1978; Schrandt et al., 1989). Yokoyama et al. (1987) obtained similar results using heart rate as a measure of arousal. We also compared the EEG from the nonlesioned hemisphere of awake patients with right or left temporoparietal infarctions. Patients with right-sided lesions showed more theta and delta activity over their nonlesioned left hemisphere than patients with left-sided lesions showed over their right hemisphere. These studies suggest that the right hemisphere may have a special role in mediating both arousal.

Intention

Patients with right hemisphere lesions more often have contralateral limb akinesia (limb motor neglect) than do patients with left hemisphere lesions (Coslett & Heilman, 1989). Patients with cerebral lesions confined to a single hemisphere have slower reaction times with the hand ipsilateral to the lesion than do nonlesioned controls using the same hand (Benton & Joynt, 1959). De Renzi and Faglioni (1965) used a simple reaction time task to study patients with unilateral cerebral lesions. Although lesions of either hemisphere slowed the reaction times of the hand ipsilateral to the lesion, right hemisphere lesions caused greater slowing than did left hemisphere lesions. DeRenzi and Faglioni assumed that this difference in reaction times indicated that patients with right hemisphere injuries had larger lesions that those with left hemisphere injury. Unfortunately, at the time this study was performed, brain imaging such as CT or MRI was not available. Howes and Boller (1975), however, confirmed that patients with right hemisphere lesions had slower reaction times, and found that the right hemisphere lesions associated with these deficits were not larger than the left hemisphere lesions. Although Howes and Boller alluded to a loss of topographical sense as perhaps being responsible for these asymmetries, they did not draw any conclusions about why right hemisphere lesions produced slower reaction times. Unfortunately, they did not mention whether the patients with profound ipsilateral slowing had unilateral neglect.

In monkeys, no hemispheric asymmetries in the production of the neglect syndrome have been noted; however, we (Valenstein et al., 1987) found that monkeys with lesions inducing neglect had slower ipsilateral reaction times than monkeys with lesions of equal size that did not induce neglect.

It has been shown that warning stimuli may prepare an individual for action and thereby reduce reaction times (Lansing et al., 1959). Pribram and McGuiness (1975) used the term *activation* to define physiological readiness to respond to environmental stimuli. Because patients with right hemisphere lesions have been shown to have reduced behavioral evidence of activation, we have postulated that in humans, the right hemisphere may also be dominant for mediating the activation process. That is, the left hemisphere prepares the right extremities for action, but the right hemisphere prepares both sides. Therefore, with left-sided lesions, left-side limb akinesia is minimal, but with right-sided lesions there is severe left-limb akinesia. In addition, because the right hemisphere is more involved than the left hemisphere in activating ipsilateral extremities, there will be more ipsilateral hypokinesia with right hemisphere lesions than with left hemisphere lesions.

If the right hemisphere dominates mediation of activation or intention (physiological readiness to respond), normal subjects may show more activation (measured behaviorally by the reaction time) with warning stimuli delivered to the right hemisphere than with warning stimuli delivered to the left hemisphere. We, therefore, gave normal subjects lateralized warning stimuli followed by central reaction time stimuli. Warning stimuli projected to the right hemisphere reduced reaction times of the right hand more than warning stimuli projected to the left hemisphere reduced left-hand reaction times. Warning stimuli projected to the right hemisphere reduced reaction times of the right hand even more than did warning stimuli projected directly to the left hemisphere. These results support the hypothesis that the right hemisphere dominates motor activation (Heilman & Van Den Abell, 1979). As we have discussed, motor bias, directional akinesia, and hypokinesia are more common with right than with left hemisphere lesions. This would suggest that the right hemisphere can prepare movements for both hands and in both directions, but the left hemisphere prepares only the right hand and rightward directed movements.

Hemispatial Neglect

Gainotti et al. (1972), Albert (1973), and Costa et al. (1969) have shown that hemispatial neglect is both more frequent and more severe with right-sided than with left-sided lesions. In the preceding sections, we discussed some of the mechanisms that may underlie hemispatial neglect. The same hypotheses we put forward to explain attentional and intentional asymmetries may also be extended to a representational hypothesis, such that the right hemisphere contains representations for both sides of space and the left hemisphere for right space. The right hemisphere has a special role in visuoperceptive, visuospatial, and visuoconstructive processes, and several authors (McFie et al., 1950; Albert, 1973) have proposed that the asymmetries of hemispatial neglect are related to disorders of these processes.

Kinsbourne (1970) proposed that language-induced left hemisphere activation makes neglect more evident with right than with left hemisphere lesions. Behavioral and psychophysiological studies have shown that language may induce left hemisphere activation (Kinsbourne, 1974; Bowers & Heilman, 1976). Patients are usually tested for hemispatial neglect using verbal instructions, and, not being aphasic, they usually think and communicate verbally. To test Kinsbourne's hypothesis, we (Heilman & Watson, 1978) had patients with left-sided hemispatial neglect perform a cancellation task in which the subject was asked either to cross out words or to cross out lines oriented in a specific direction (e.g., horizontal). In the verbal condition, the target words were mixed with two others that were foils, and in the visuospatial condition, the target lines were mixed with other lines (e.g., vertical and diagonal) that acted as foils. All the subjects tested crossed out more lines and went farther to the left on the paper in the nonverbal condition than in the verbal condition. These results give partial support to Kinsbourne's hypothesis. However, Caplan (1985) could not obtain similar results, suggesting the difference found by Heilman and Watson may be related to differences in attentional demands of the two types of stimuli used in this task (see Rapcsak et al., 1989). However, additional support of Kinsbourne's hypothesis comes from the observation that neglect is less severe when the left hand is used to perform cancellation tasks than when the right hand is used (Halligan & Marshall, 1989).

We have previously discussed the proposal that hemispatial neglect can be induced by hemispatial or directional akinesia, or by hemispatial or directional inattention. In the preceding section, we postulated that the right hemisphere is dominant for intention and attention. That hemispatial neglect occurs more often after right hemisphere lesions may be explained by a similar phenomenon.

NEUROPATHOLOGY OF NEGLECT

Neglect in man can accompany lesions in the following areas: (a) inferior parietal lobe (IPL) (Critchley, 1966), (b) dorsolateral frontal lobe (Heilman & Valenstein, 1972), (c) cingulate gyrus (Heilman & Valenstein, 1972), (d) thalamus, and (3) MRF (Watson & Heilman, 1979). It has been reported that striatal lesions can also induce neglect (Heir et al., 1977). On the basis of brain imaging, Heilman et al. (1983) and Vallar et al. (1994) concluded that neglect is probably seen most frequently after temporoparietal lesions. However, more recent studies have suggested that posterior temporal lesions and inferior parietal lesions might induce different forms of neglect, lesions in the temporal lobe being more likely to induce object-centered or allocentric neglect and lesions of the parietal lobe more likely to induce viewer-centered or egocentric neglect (Hillis et al., 2005). Lissauer (1890) demonstrated that ventral posterior temporo-occipital lesions induce object agnosia, and Balint (1909) demonstrated that more dorsal lesions induced deficits of determining spatial location (i.e., optic ataxia and psychic paralysis of gaze). More recently, Mishkin et al. (1982) demonstrated this same dichotomy in monkeys, calling the ventral visual stream the "what" system and the dorsal stream the "where "system. The finding that temporal lesions are more likely to induce object-centered or allocentric neglect and the parietal lesions induce viewer-centered or egocentric neglect is compatible with this "where" and "what" dichotomy. Studies of rodents have revealed that, not only do parietal and frontal lesions induce neglect, but a disconnection of

these areas also produce neglect (Burcham et al., 1997). More recently, He et al. (2007) demonstrated in humans that lesions of the white matter tracts between the frontal and parietal lobes was associated with severe neglect.

The most common cause of neglect from cortical lesions is cerebral infarction (from either thrombosis or embolus), and the most common cause of subcortical neglect is intracerebral hemorrhage. Neglect can also be seen with tumors. Rapidly growing malignant tumors (e.g., metastatic or glioblastoma) are more likely to produce neglect than are slowly growing tumors. It is unusual to see neglect as the result of a degenerative disease, because the degeneration is most often bilateral and insidious. However, we and others have seen neglect with focal atrophy, and neglect has also been reported with Alzheimer disease (Ishiai et al., 1996; Mendez et al., 1997; Bartolomeo et al., 1998; Venneri et al., 1998). The akinesia seen with degenerative diseases may be bilateral neglect (Heilman & Valenstein, 1972; Watson et al., 1973), which we believe is the cause of akinetic mutism. We have also seen a transient neglect syndrome as a postictal phenomenon in a patient with idiopathic right temporal lobe seizures, and the transient bilateral akinesia seen with other types of seizures may also be induced by similar mechanisms (Watson et al., 1974). Neglect may also be seen after unilateral (right) electroconvulsive therapy (ECT) (Sackeim, personal communication, 1983).

RECOVERY OF FUNCTION AND TREATMENT

NATURAL HISTORY

After a cerebral infarction, some patients acutely demonstrate a characteristic syndrome that includes asomatognosia and personal neglect, limb akinesia, profound sensory inattention or allesthesia, hemispatial neglect, head and eye deviation, and anosognosia for hemiplegia. In a period of weeks to months, many of these signs and symptoms abate, but extinction can be demonstrated with bilateral simultaneous stimulation, and extinction might persist for years. Hemispatial neglect also diminishes. Often, the motor-intentional deficits persist and can be chronically disabling.

Unlike humans, who recover from the neglect syndrome slowly and often incompletely, monkeys with surgical ablation rarely show evidence of neglect after 1 month. The neural mechanisms underlying this recovery are poorly understood. One hypothesis is that the undamaged hemisphere plays a role in recovery. It may receive sensory information from the side of the body opposite the lesion, either via ipsilateral sensory pathways or from the damaged hemisphere via the corpus callosum. The uninjured hemisphere might also enhance the injured hemisphere's ability to attend to contralateral sensory information and to initiate contralateral limb movements. In either case, a corpus callosum transection should worsen symptoms of neglect. Crowne et al. (1981) showed that neglect from frontal ablations was worse if the corpus callosum was simultaneously sectioned than if the callosum was intact. Watson et al. (1984) showed that monkeys receiving a frontal arcuate gyrus ablation several months after a corpus callosum transection also had worse neglect than did animals with an intact callosum. These results suggest that the hemispheres are mutually excitatory or compensatory through the corpus callosum.

Although callosal section worsened the severity of neglect, both groups of investigators found that it did not influence the rate of recovery. These animals with callosal transections also recovered completely. This suggests that recovery is an intrahemispheric rather than an interhemispheric process. If the intact hemisphere is responsible for recovery, then a callosal transection, after recovery, should not reinstate neglect. Crowne et al. (1981) did reinstate neglect in three animals undergoing corpus callosum transections. It is possible, however, that extracallosal damage during surgery might be responsible for reinstating neglect. We performed a similar callosal section after a monkey recovered from neglect and did not reinstate neglect. If the intact hemisphere is responsible for recovery in an animal with divided hemispheres, the recovery would have to be mediated through ipsilateral pathways. To test this hypothesis, we have made a unilateral spinal cord lesion to

interrupt ipsilateral sensory pathways in one of our recovered monkeys without reinstating neglect (Watson et al., 1984). Our observations suggest that recovery is occurring within the injured hemisphere. Positron emission tomography studies have also supported the postulate that recovery from neglect is primarily intrahemispheric (Pizzamiglio et al., 1998).

Hughlings Jackson (Jackson, 1932) postulated that functions could be mediated at several levels of the nervous system (hierarchical representation). Lesions of higher areas (such as the cerebral cortex) would release phylogenetically more primitive areas, which may assume some of the function of the lesioned cortical areas. After cortical lesions disrupt the cortical (frontoparietal)-limbic (cingulate)-reticular network, important in mediating attention, it is possible that subcortical areas become responsible for mediating orienting responses. Ideally, the area that substitutes for the lesioned area must have similar characteristics. It must have multimodal afferent input, reticular connections, and be capable of inducing activation with stimulation. Last, ablation of this area should induce the neglect syndrome, even if transiently. The superior colliculus not only receives visual input but also receives somesthetic projections from the spinotectal tract (Sprague & Meikle, 1965), as well as fibers from the medial and lateral lemnisci and the inferior colliculus (Truex & Carpenter, 1964). Sprague and Meikle believe that the superior colliculus is a sensory integrative center, not just a reflex center controlling eye movements. Tectoreticular fibers project to the MRF, and ipsilateral fibers are more abundant than contralateral fibers (Truex & Carpenter, 1964). Stimulation of the colliculus, like stimulation of the lateral frontal lobe (arcuate gyrus) or the posterior temporoparietal region produces an arousal response (Jefferson, 1958). Unilateral lesions of the superior colliculus produce a multimodal unilateral neglect syndrome, and combined cortical-collicular lesions produce a more profound disturbance regardless of the order of removal (Sprague & Meikle, 1965). Therefore, it is possible that after injury to the cortico-limbic-reticular network mediating attention, a collicular-reticular system functionally compensates.

Unlike the neglect induced by cortical lesions in monkeys, the neglect associated with lesions of ascending DA projections in rats can be permanent (Marshall, 1982). The severity and persistence of neglect induced by 6-OHDA injections into the VTA of rats is correlated with the amount of striatal DA depletion: Those with more than 95% loss of striatal dopamine have a permanent deficit. The extent of recovery of these animals is also directly related to the quantity of neostriatal dopamine present at sacrifice. Unrecovered rats show pronounced contralateral turning after injections of apomorphine, a dopamine receptor stimulant. Recovered rats given methyl-p-tyrosine, a catecholamine synthesis inhibitor, or spiroperidol, a dopamine receptor blocking agent, had their deficits reappear. These results suggest that restoration of dopaminergic activity in dopamine-depleted rats is sufficient to reinstate orientation (Marshall, 1979). Further investigation of these findings indicates that a proliferation of dopamine receptors may contribute to pharmacological supersensitivity and recovery of function (Neve et al., 1982). Finally, implanting DA neurons from the ventral tegmental area of fetal rats adjacent to the ipsilesional striatum will induce recovery in rats having unilateral neglect from a 6-OHDA lesion in the ascending dopamine tracts (Dunnett et al., 1981). This recovery is related to growth of dopamine-containing neurons into the partially denervated striatum. Corwin et al. (1986) induced neglect in rats by ablating frontal cortex unilaterally. After the rats had recovered from neglect, spiroperidol reinstituted their neglect.

C-14,2-deoxyglucose (2-DG) with PET permits investigators to measure metabolic activity. In rats with 6-OHDA lesions of the VTA that had shown no recovery from neglect, the uptake of 2-DG into the neostriatum, nucleus accumbens septi, olfactory tubercle, and central amygdaloid nucleus was significantly less on the denervated side than on the normal side. Rats recovering by 6 weeks showed equivalent 2-DG uptake in the neostriatum and central amygdaloid nucleus on the two sides. Recovery is therefore associated with normalization of neostriatal metabolic activity (Kozlowski & Marshall, 1981).

Similar results have been found in monkeys recovering from frontal arcuate gyrus–induced neglect (Deuel et al., 1979). Animals with neglect showed depression of deoxyglucose in ipsilateral subcortical structures, including the thalamus and basal ganglia. Recovery from neglect occurred concomitantly with a reappearance of symmetrical metabolic activity.

It is possible that cortical lesions in animals induce only transient neglect because these lesions affect only a small portion of a critical neurotransmitter system. Critically placed small subcortical lesions, on the other hand, can virtually destroy all of a transmitter system, and can cause a permanent syndrome.

Recovery from cortically induced neglect might also depend on the influence of cortical lesions on subcortical structures. It is likely that, just as certain homologous cortical structures are thought to be mutually inhibitory via the corpus callosum, certain pairs of subcortical structures may also be mutually inhibitory. For example, in the study of Watson et al. (1984), a prior corpus callosal lesion worsened neglect from a frontal arcuate lesion. Although this could be explained by loss of an excitatory or compensatory influence from the normal frontal arcuate region on the lesioned hemisphere, it could also be interpreted as a loss of excitation from cortex on a subcortical structure, such as the basal ganglia, that in turn inhibits the contralateral basal ganglia. The latter is supported by a study showing that anterior callosal section in rats enhances the normal striatal dopamine asymmetry and increases amphetamine-induced turning (Glick et al., 1975). In addition, Sprague (1966) showed that the loss of visually guided behavior in the visual field contralateral to occipitotemporal lesions in cats could be restored by a contralateral superior colliculus removal or by transection of the collicular commissure. The only way to explain this observation is to assume that the superior colliculi are mutually inhibitory.

It appears that recovery from a CNS insult can occur within the injured hemisphere. For the neglect syndrome, this may be secondary to activation of perilesional cortex or to subcortical structures and to alterations of neurotransmitter systems such as the DA systems. An understanding of interhemispheric cortical and subcortical interactions, and intrahemispheric cortical and subcortical interactions in the normal state and during recovery of function, is one of the most intriguing aspects of the neglect syndrome and holds great promise for pharmacological and possibly even surgical intervention in this syndrome.

TREATMENTS

The neglect syndrome is a behavioral manifestation of underlying cerebral disease. The evaluation and treatment of the underlying disease are of primary importance. In addition, in the management of patients with neglect, so long as a patient has neglect syndrome, he or she should not be allowed to drive, or to work with anything that, if neglected, could cause injury to him- or herself or to others. The following is a review of the treatments, both behavioral and pharmacological, that have been used to treat this disabling disorder.

Behavioral Therapies

Forced Use. During the acute stages when patients have anosognosia, rehabilitation is difficult; however, in most patients, anosognosia is transient. In addition, because patients with neglect remain inattentive to their left side and in general are poorly motivated, training is laborious and in many cases unrewarding. Kunkle et al. (1999) treated patients who had a hemiparesis by binding their nonparetic arm and forcing them to use the hemiparetic arm. They found that this procedure induced recovery. It is possible that some of their patients' motor deficit was related to limb akinesia (motor neglect), rather than to weakness associated with corticospinal damage. In the last decade, studies, primarily in animals, have demonstrated that experience can change neuronal networks. Therefore, it is possible that stimulation of the contralesional side may induce functional reorganization and thereby reduce the severity of neglect.

Patients with neglect of left hemispace can be forced to look to the left by wearing glasses in which the right half of the two lenses are made opaque. Thus, if the patient wants to see something, he has to look to the left. This treatment appears to help some patients (Arai et al., 1997).

Directing Attention Contralesionally. In one of the first attempts to behaviorally treat neglect, Diller and Weinberg (1977) trained patients with neglect to look to their neglected side. Although this is one of the most commonly used rehabilitation strategies, it is not clear that these top-down attentional-exploratory treatments generalize to other situations. In contrast to this top-down treatment, Butter et al. (1990) used a bottom-up treatment. Brainstem structures, such as the superior colliculus, may play an important role in recovery from neglect. Butter et al. (1990) recognized that since dynamic stimuli readily summon attention in normal subjects and are potent activators of brain structures such as the colliculi, perhaps they could be used to reduce neglect. He tested patients with neglect on a line bisection task and demonstrated that dynamic stimuli presented to the contralesional (left) side reduced neglect. Neglect patients with hemianopia also improved, suggesting that these stimuli affect subcortical structures. Polanowska et al. (2008) used a combination of top-down (visual scanning) and bottom-up (stimulation of the left hand) methods to treat patients with unilateral neglect, and demonstrated that the patients who received the combination treatment appeared to improve more than those who just received visual scanning training. Robertson and North (1994) demonstrated that having patients move their contralesional hand in contralesional hemispace can reduce the severity of hemispatial neglect, and these investigators have therefore used a hand movement strategy to manage neglect. Finally, Sturm et al. (2006) attempted to treat patients with neglect using alertness training. Although the patients showed some improvement, it was short lived.

Caloric Stimulation. Asymmetrically activating the vestibular system in normal subjects may induce a spatial bias similar to that observed in neglect (Shuren et al., 1998). Rubens (1985) induced asymmetrical vestibular activation in patients with left-sided neglect by injecting cold water into the left ear and noting that unilateral spatial neglect abated. Valler et al. (1995) reported that vestibular stimulation could help sensory inattention, and Rode et al. (1992) found that vestibular stimulation even helped motor neglect. Adair et al. (2003) found that caloric stimulation improved sensory-attentional more than motor-intentional neglect. However, the benefits of caloric stimulation last only a few minutes after the stimulation has been discontinued.

Opticokinetic Stimulation. Inducing optokinetic nystagmus by having patients look at series of stimuli moving in a contralesional direction (Pizzamigialo et al., 1990) improved neglect. Kerkoff et al. treated subjects with neglect within a week of stroke onset. One group of subjects were given five treatment sessions with repetitive optokinetic stimulation (OKS), and another group was treated with visual scanning training, in which subjects were instructed to scan the stimuli in a systematic fashion, starting at the left top and ending at the right bottom. Both groups were tested 2 weeks after treatment. These investigators found that OKS was an effective treatment. In contrast, no improvements were seen in subjects using the visual scanning task. Choi et al. (2007) demonstrated that healthy elderly can selectively fixate on a line projected against a moving background, and they perceive the line moving in the opposite direction of the background. They show a line-bisection bias in the direction opposite to the moving background. In contrast, patients with neglect are primarily influenced by the direction of the moving background, and their line bisection deviates in the same direction as the moving line.

Neck Vibration. Karnath and coworkers (1995) demonstrated that left-sided neglect could be reduced by vibrating the left posterior neck muscles, as well as by turning the trunk 15 degrees to the left. These results suggest that afferent information about lengthening of the left posterior neck muscles (produced by turning the trunk or vibration) reduces the severity of neglect. Johannsen et al. (2003) gave patients daily vibration treatment to the left posterior neck muscles for 20 minutes on 10 consecutive days. During these vibration treatments, these patients did not perform any specific activities. These investigators reported amelioration of spatial neglect after terminating the vibration therapy that lasted more than a year.

Prisms. As we discussed, Coslett et al. (1990) demonstrated that patients with spatial neglect induced by attentional disorders improved when feedback was presented to the ipsilesional side. Persons with neglect have an ipsilateral (e.g., rightward) shift of spatial midline. Rossi et al. (1990) used 15-diopter Fresnel prisms to shift images toward ipsilesional space (e.g., further to the right side). After using the prisms for 4 weeks, the treated group performed better than the control group in tasks such as line bisection or cancellation. However, activities of daily living did not improve. Rossetti et al. (1998) had subjects with neglect adapt to prisms by having them repeatedly point straight ahead while wearing the prisms. After this treatment, patients showed a reduction of their ipsilesional bias on tests of neglect. Subsequent studies have suggested that prism treatment has long-term effects (Shiraishi et al., 2008), but other studies have not been able to demonstrate this (Nys et al., 2008).

Eye Patching. Neglect associated with cortical lesions may be reduced by destroying the contralesional colliculus or the intercollicular commissure (Sprague, 1966). These findings suggested that the colliculus contralateral to the cortical lesion may be inhibiting the ipsilesional colliculus. Each colliculus receives greater input from the retina of the contralateral eye than it does from the ipsilateral eye. Posner and Rafal (1987) suggest that patching the ipsilesional eye may reduce neglect because it would deprive the superior colliculus contralateral to the lesioned hemisphere of retinal input, and this reduced input may reduce collicular activation. Although some have found this ipsilesional patching procedure useful in reducing the signs of neglect (Butter & Kirsh, 1992) others have found that ipsilateral patching can make neglect more severe (Barrett et al., 2001). Therefore, each eye should be tested before deciding which eye should be patched. The mechanisms underlying reduction in neglect from collicular lesions remain uncertain. Recent studies suggest that interruption of fibers from the substantia nigra pars reticulata to the opposite superior colliculus may account for the reduction in neglect (Wallace, Rosenquist, & Sprague, 1989, 1990). Reduction in neglect from lesions in the contralesional superior colliculus may therefore not result from tecto-tectal inhibition; however, the underlying mechanisms, remain to be more fully elucidated.

Transcranial Magnetic Stimulation

Transcranial magnetic stimulation (TMS) of the undamaged (left) hemisphere in the posterior parietal region has been used to treat neglect. Slow stimulation, which appears to induce inhibition of the stimulated cortex, has been reported to alleviate the symptoms of neglect for several weeks (Brighina et al., 2003; Shindo et al., 2006). In the neglect syndrome, there are hemispheric asymmetries of activation, and this treatment might be effective because it reduces this hemispheric activation asymmetry.

Pharmacological Treatments

Neglect in rats with unilateral frontal (Corwin et al., 1986) and parietal lesions (Corwin et al., 1996) were treated with apomorphine, a dopamine agonist. Dopamine agonist therapy significantly reduced neglect in these animals. Spiroperidol, a dopamine receptor blocking agent, blocked the therapeutic effect of apomorphine. Fleet et al. (1987) treated two neglect patients with bromocriptine, a dopamine agonist. Both showed dramatic improvements. Subsequently, other investigators have also shown that dopamine agonist therapy may be helpful in the treatment of neglect (Hurford et al., 1998; Geminiani et al., 1998,). In addition, Geminiani et al. found that dopamine agonist treatment helped both the sensory attentional and motor intentional forms of spatial neglect, but Barrett et al. (1999, 2001) demonstrated that dopamine agonist treatment helped intentional more than attentional neglect. Mukand et al. (2001) treated four patients with neglect using levodopa/carbidopa and found that three of the four improved. Treatment with levodopa increases levels of dopamine, as well as increasing levels of norepinephrine. One study reported that treatment with guanfacine, a noradrenergic agonist that modulates the dorsolateral prefrontal cortex, ameliorates neglect (Malhotra et al., 2006), but the influence of medications that influence brain norepinephrine has to be further explored.

Although dopamine therapy appears to help patients with neglect, Barrett et al. (1999) and Grujic et al. (1998) found that, in some patients, dopamine agonist therapy increased rather than decreased the severity of neglect. Barrett et al.'s patient had striatal injury, and these researchers suggested that the paradoxical effect seen in their patient may be related to involvement of the basal ganglia. In patients with striatal injury, dopamine agonists may be unable to activate the striatum on the injured side but instead activate the striatum on the uninjured side, thereby increasing the ipsilesional orientation bias.

REFERENCES

Adair, J. C., Na, D. L., Schwartz, R. L., & Heilman, K. M. (1998). Analysis of primary and secondary influences on spatial neglect. *Brain and Cognition*, 37(3), 351–367.

Adair, J. C., Na, D. L., Schwartz, R. L., & Heilman, K. M. (2003). Caloric stimulation in neglect: Evaluation of response as a function of neglect type. *Journal of the International Neuropsychological Society*, 9(7), 983–988.

Akert, K., & Von Monakow, K. H. (1980). Relationship of precentral, premotor, and prefrontal cortex to the mediodorsal and intralaminar nuclei of the monkey thalamus. *Acta Neurobiologiae Experimentalis (Warsaw)*, 40, 7–25.

Albert, M. D. (1973). A simple test of visual neglect. *Neurology*, 23, 658–664.

Anderson, M., & Yoshida, M. (1977). Electrophysiological evidence for branching nigral projections to the thalamus and superior colliculus. *Brain Research*, 137, 361–364.

Anton, G. (1899). Über die selbstwahrnehmung der herderkrankungen des gehirns durch den kranken der rindenblindheit und rindentaubheit. *Archiv für Psychiatrie und Nervenkrankheiten*, 32, 86–127.

Anzola, G. P., Bertoloni, A., Buchtel, H. A., & Rizzolatti, G. (1977). Spatial compatibility and anatomical factors in simple and choice reaction time. *Neuropsychologia*, 15, 295–302.

Apicella, P., Legallet, E., Nieoullon, A., & Trouche, E. (1991). Neglect of contralateral visual stimuli in monkeys with unilateral dopamine depletion. *Behavioural Brain Research*, 46, 187–195.

Arbuthnott, G. W., & Ungerstedt, U. (1975). Turning behavior induced by electrical stimulation of the nigro-striatal system of the rat. *Experimental Neurology, 27,* 162–172.

Arai, T., Ohi, H., Sasaki, H., Nobuto, H., & Tanaka, K. (1997). Hemispatial sunglasses: Effect on unilateral spatial neglect. *Archives of Physical Medicine and Rehabilitation, 78*(2), 230–232.

Arnault, P., & Roger, M. (1987). The connections of the peripeduncular area studied by retrograde and anterograde transport in the rat. *Journal of Comparative Neurology, 258,* 463–478.

Aston-Jones G, Bloom F.E. (1981). Norepinephrine-containing locus coeruleus neurons in behaving rats exhibit pronounced responses to non-noxious environmental stimuli. *Journal of Neuroscience, 1*(8): 887–900.

Avemo, A., Antelman, S., & Ungerstedt, U. (1973). Rotational behavior after unilateral frontal cortex lesions in the rat. *Acta Physiologica Scandinavica, Suppl. 396,* 77.

Babinski, J. (1914). Contribution a l'etude des troubles mentaux dans l'hemiplegie organique cerebrale (agnosognosie). *Revue Neurologique (Paris), 27,* 845–847.

Baleydier, C., & Mauguiere, F. (1980). The duality of the cingulate gyrus in monkey–neuroanatomical study and functional hypothesis. *Brain, 103,* 525–554.

Balint, R. (1909). Seelenlähmung des "Schauens," optische ataxia, räumliche störung der aufmerksamkeit. *Monatsschrift für Psychiatrie und Neurologie, 5,* 51–81.

Barrett, A. M., Crucian, G. P., Schwartz, R. L., & Heilman, K. M. (1999). Adverse effect of dopamine agonist therapy in a patient with motor-intentional neglect. *Archives of Physical Medicine and Rehabilitation, 80*(5), 600–603.

Barrett, A. M., Crucian, G. P., Beversdorf, D. Q., & Heilman, K. M. (2001). Monocular patching may worsen sensory-attentional neglect: A case report. *Archives of Physical Medicine and Rehabilitation, 82*(4), 516–518.

Bartolomeo, P., Dalla Barba, G., Boisse, M. F., Bachout-Levi, A. C., Degos, J. D., & Boller, F. (1998). Right-side neglect in Alzheimer's disease. *Neurology, 51,* 1207–1209.

Battersby, W. S., Bender, M. B., & Pollack, M. (1956). Unilateral spatial agnosia (inattention) in patients with cerebral lesions. *Brain, 79,* 68–93.

Becker, E., Karnath, H. O. (2007). Incidence of visual extinction after left versus right hemisphere stroke. *Stroke, 38*(12), 3172–3174.

Bender, M. B. (1952). *Disorders of perception.* Springfield, Ill.: C. C. Thomas.

Bender, M. B., & Furlow, C. T. (1944). Phenomenon of visual extinction and binocular rivalry mechanism. *Transactions of the American Neurological Association, 70,* 87–93.

Bender, M. B., & Furlow, C. T. (1945). Phenomenon of visual extinction and homonymous fields and psychological principals involved. *Archives of Neurology and Psychiatry, 53,* 29–33.

Benson, F., & Geschwind, N. (1969). The alexias. In P. J. Vinken, & G. W. Bruyn (Eds.), *Handbook of neurology* Vol. 4. Amsterdam: North-Holland.

Benton, A. L., & Joynt, R. J. (1959). Reaction times in unilateral cerebral disease. *Confinia Neurologica, 19,* 147–256.

Benton, A. L., & Levin, H. S. (1972). An experimental study of obscuration. *Neurology, 22,* 1176–1181.

Beversdorf, D. Q., Hughes, J. D., Heilman, K. M. (2008). Functional MRI of the primary somatosensory cortex in extinction to simultaneous bilateral tactile stimuli due to right temporal lobe stroke. *Neurocase, 14*(5), 419–424.

Bianchi, L. (1895). The functions of the frontal lobes. *Brain, 18,* 497–522.

Bignall, K. E., & Imbert, M. (1969). Polysensory and cortico-cortical projections to frontal lobe of squirrel and rhesus monkey. *Electroencephalography and Clinical Neurophysiology, 26,* 206–215.

Birch, H. G., Belmont, I., & Karp, E. (1967). Delayed information processing and extinction following cerebral damage. *Brain, 90,* 113–130.

Bisiach, E., & Luzzatti, C. (1978). Unilateral neglect of representational space. *Cortex, 14,* 29–133.

Bisiach, E., Luzzatti, C., & Perani, D. (1979). Unilateral neglect, representational schema and consciousness. *Brain, 102,* 609–618.

Bisiach, E., Bulgarelli, C., Sterzi, R., & Vallar, G. (1983). Line bisection and cognitive plasticity of unilateral neglect of space. *Brain and Cognition, 2,* 32–38.

Bisiach, E., Geminiani, G., Berti, A., & Rusconi, M. L. (1990). Perceptual and premotor factors of unilateral neglect. *Neurology, 40,* 1278–1281.

Bisiach, E., Vallar, G., Perani, D., Papagno, C., & Buti, A. (1986). Unawareness of disease following lesions of the right hemisphere: Anosognosia for hemiplegia and anosognosia for hemianopsia. *Neuropsychologia, 24,* 471–482.

Bogosslavsky, J., Miklossy, J., Deruaz, J. P., Regli, F., & Assai, G. (1986). Unilateral left paramedian infarction of thalamus and midbrain: A clinico-pathological study. *Journal of Neurology, Neurosurgery, and Psychiatry, 49,* 686–694.

Bowers, D., & Heilman, K. M. (1976). Material specific hemispheric arousal. *Neuropsychologia, 14,* 123–127.

Bowers, D., & Heilman, K. M. (1980). Effects of hemispace on tactile line bisection task. *Neuropsychologia*, *18*, 491–498.

Bowers, D., Heilman, K. M., & Van Den Abell, T. (1981). Hemispace-visual half field compatibility. *Neuropsychologia*, *19*, 757–765.

Bradley, P. B. (1968). The effect of atropine and related drugs on the EEG and behavior. *Progress in Brain Research*, *28*, 3–13.

Brain, W. R. (1941). Visual disorientation with special reference to lesions of the right cerebral hemisphere. *Brain*, *64*, 224–272.

Brighina, F., Bisiach, E., Oliveri, M., Piazza, A., La Bua, V., Daniele, O., & Fierro, B. (2003). 1 Hz repetitive transcranial magnetic stimulation of the unaffected hemisphere ameliorates contralesional visuospatial neglect in humans. *Neuroscience Letters*, *336*(2), 131–133.

Brown, R. M., Crane, A. M., & Goldman, P. S. (1979). Regional distribution of monamines in the cerebral cortex and subcortical structures of the rhesus monkey: Concentrations and in vivo synthesis rates. *Brain Research*, *168*, 133–150.

Burcham, K. J., Corwin, J. V., Stoll, M. L., & Reep, R. L. (1997). Disconnection of medial agranular and posterior parietal cortex produces multimodal neglect in rats. *Behavioural Brain Research*, *86*(1), 41–47.

Burcham, K. J., Corwin, J. V., & Van-Vleet, T. M. (1998). Light deprivation produces a therapeutic effect on neglect induced by unilateral destruction of the posterior parietal cortex in rats. *Behavioural Brain Research*, *90*(2), 187–197.

Bushnell, M. C., Goldberg, M. E., & Robinson, D. L. (1981). Behavioral enhancement of visual responses in monkey cerebral cortex: I. Modulation if posterior parietal cortex related to selected visual attention. *Journal of Neurophysiology*, *46*, 755–772.

Butter, C. M., Kirsch, N. (1992). Combined and separate effects of eye patching and visual stimulation on unilateral neglect following stroke. *Archives of Physical Medicine and Rehabilitation*, *73*(12), 1133–1139.

Butter, C. M., Kirsch, N. L., & Reeves, G. (1990). The effect of lateralized dynamic stimuli on unilateral spatial neglect following right hemisphere lesions. *Restorative Neurology and Neuroscience*, *2*, 39–46.

Butter, C. M., Mark, V. W., & Heilman, K. M. (1988a). An experimental analysis of factors underlying neglect in line bisection. *Journal of Neurology, Neurosurgery, and Psychiatry*, *51*, 1581–1583.

Butter, C. M., Rapcsak, S. Z., Watson, R. T., & Heilman, K. M. (1988b). Changes in sensory inattention, direction hypokinesia, and release of the fixation reflex following a unilateral frontal lesion: a case report. *Neuropsychologia*, *26*, 533–545.

Caplan, B. (1985). Stimulus effects in unilateral neglect. *Cortex*, *21*, 69–80.

Chatterjee, A., Mennemeier, M., & Heilman, K. M. (1992). Search patterns in neglect. *Neuropsychologia*, *30*, 657–672.

Chatterjee, A., Thompson, K. A., & Ricci, R. (1999). Quantitative analysis of cancellation tasks in neglect. *Cortex*, *35*(2), 253–262.

Chavis, D. A., & Pandya, D. N. (1976). Further observations on corticofrontal connections in the rhesus monkey. *Brain Research*, *117*, 369–386.

Chedru, F., Leblanc, M., & Lhermitte, F. (1973). Visual searching in normal and brain-damaged subjects. *Cortex*, *9*, 94–111.

Choi, K. M., Lee, B. H., Lee, S. C., Ku, B. D., Kim, E. J., Suh, M. K., et al. (2007). Influence of moving background on line bisection performance in the normal elderly versus patients with hemispatial neglect. *American Journal of Physical Medicine and Rehabilitation*, *86*(7), 515–526.

Colby, C. L., & Duhamel, J.-R. (1991). Heterogeneity of extrastriate visual areas and multiple parietal areas in the macaque monkey. *Neuropsychologia*, *29*, 517–537.

Colby, C. L., Duhamel, J.-R., & Goldberg, M. E. (1993). Ventral intraparietal area of the macaque: anatomic location and visual response properties. *Journal of Neurophysiology*, *69*, 902–914.

Colby, C. L., Duhamel, J.-R., & Goldberg, M. E. (1996). Visual, presaccadic and cognitive activation of single neurons in monkey lateral intraparietal area. *Journal of Neurophysiology*, *76*, 2841–2852.

Colby, C. L., & Goldberg, M. E. (1999). Space and attention in parietal cortex. *Annual Review of Neuroscience*, *22*, 319–349.

Corbett, D., & Wise, R. A. (1980). Intracranial self-stimulation in relation to the ascending dopaminergic systems of the midbrain: moveable electrode mapping study. *Brain Research*, *185*, 1–15.

Corwin, J. V., Burcham, K.J., & Hix, G. I. (1996). Apomorphine produces an acute dose-dependent therapeutic effect on neglect produced by unilateral destruction of the posterior parietal cortex in rats. *Behavioural Brain Research*, *79*(1–2), 41–49.

Corwin, J. V., Kanter, S., Watson, R. T., Heilman, K. M., Valenstein, E., & Hashimoto, A. (1986).

Apomorphine has a therapeutic effect on neglect produced by unilateral dorsomedial prefrontal cortex lesions in rats. *Experimental Neurology, 36*, 683–698.

Corwin, J. V., & Vargo, J. M. (1993). Light deprivation produces accelerated behavioral recovery of function from neglect produced by unilateral medial agranular prefrontal cortex lesions in rats. *Behavioural Brain Research, 56*(2), 187–196.

Coslett, H. B., & Heilman, K. M. (1989). Hemihypokinesia after right hemisphere strokes. *Brain and Cognition, 9*, 267–278.

Coslett, H. B., Bowers, D., Fitzpatrick, E., Haws, B., & Heilman, K. M. (1990). Directional hypokinesia and hemispatial inattention in neglect. *Brain, 113*, 475–486.

Coslett, H. B. (1997). Neglect in vision and visual imagery: A double dissociation. *Brain, 120*(Pt 7), 1163–1171.

Coslett, H. B. (1998). Evidence for a disturbance of the body schema in neglect. *Brain and Cognition, 37*(3), 527–544.

Costa, L. D., Vaughan, H. G., Horowitz, M., & Ritter, W. (1969). Patterns of behavior deficit associated with visual spatial neglect. *Cortex, 5*, 242–263.

Craft, J., & Simon, J. (1970). Processing symbolic information from a visual display: interference from an irrelevant directional clue. *Journal of Experimental Psychology, 83*, 415–420.

Critchley, M. (1966). *The parietal lobes*. New York: Hafner.

Crossman, A. R., Sambrook, M. A., Horwitz, M., & Ritter, W. (1977). The neurological basis of motor asymmetry following unilateral 6-hydroxy-dopamine lesions in the rat: The effect of motor decortication. *Journal of the Neurological Sciences, 34*, 407–414.

Crowne, D. P., Yeo, C. H., & Russell, I. S. (1981). The effects of unilateral frontal eye field lesions in the monkey: Visual–motor guidance and avoidance behavior. *Behavioural Brain Research, 2*, 165–185.

Dalsass, M., & Karuthamer, G. M. (1981). Behavioral alterations and loss of caudate modulation in the CM–PF complex of the cat after electrolytic lesions of the substantia nigra. *Brain Research, 208*, 67–79.

De Renzi, E., Colombo, A., Faglioni, P., & Gilbertoni, M. (1982). Conjugate gaze paralysis in stroke patients with unilateral damage. *Archives of Neurology, 39*, 482–486.

De Renzi, E., Faglioni, P., & Scott, G. (1970). Hemispheric contribution to the exploration of space through the visual and tactile modality. *Cortex, 1*, 410–433.

De Renzi, E., & Faglioni, P. (1965). The comparative efficiency of intelligence and vigilance test detecting hemispheric change. *Cortex, 1*, 410–433.

Denny–Brown, D., & Banker, B. Q. (1954). Amorphosynthesis from left parietal lesions. *Archives of Neurology and Psychiatry, 71*, 302–313.

Denny-Brown D., & Chambers, R. A. (1958). The parietal lobes and behavior. *Research Publications Association for Research in Nervous and Mental Disease, 36*, 35–117.

Deuel, R. K. (1980). Sensorimotor dysfunction after unilateral hypothalamic lesions in rhesus monkeys. *Neurology, 30*, 358.

Deuel, R. K., Collins, R. C., Dunlop N., & Caston, T. V. (1979). Recovery from unilateral neglect: behavioral and functional anatomic correlations in monkeys. *Society for Neuroscience. Abstract 5, 624*.

Diller, L., & Weinberg, J. (1977). Hemi–inattention in rehabilitation: the evolution of a rational remediation program. In E. A. Weinstein, & R. R. Friedland (Eds.), *Advances in neurology* Vol. 18. New York: Raven Press.

Divac, I., Fonnum, F., & Storm-Mathison, J. (1977). High affinity uptake of glutamate in terminals of corticostriatal axons. *Nature, 266*, 377–378.

Dunnet, S. B., Bjorklund, A. Stenevi, U., & Iverson, S. D. (1981). Behavioral recovery following transplantation of substantia nigra in rats subjected to 6-OHDA lesions of the nigrostriatal pathway. I. Unilateral lesions. *Brain Research, 215*, 147–161.

Eidelberg, E., & Schwartz, A. J. (1971). Experimental analysis of the extinction phenomenon in monkeys. *Brain, 94*, 91–108.

Eysenck, M. W. (1976). Arousal, learning and memory. *Psychological Bulletin, 83*, 389–404.

Farah, M. J., Brunn, J. L., Wong, A. B., Wallace, M. A., & Carpenter, P. A. (1990). Frames of reference for locating attention to space: evidence from neglect syndrome. *Neuropsychologia, 28*, 335–347.

Feeney, D. M., & Wier, C. S. (1979). Sensory neglect after lesions of substantia nigra on lateral hypothalamus: Differential severity and recovery of function. *Brain Research, 178*, 329–346.

Feinberg, T. E., Habor, L. D., & Stacy, C. B. (1990). Ipsilateral extinction in the hemineglect syndrome. *Archives of Neurology, 47*, 803–804.

Filion, M., Lamarre, Y., & Cordeau, J. P. (1971). Neuronal discharges of the ventrolateral nucleus of the thalamus during sleep and wakefulness in the cat. Evoked activity. *Experimental Brain Research, 12*, 499–508.

Fink, G. R., Marshall, J. C., Weiss, P. H., Zilles, K. (2001). The neural basis of vertical and horizontal line bisection judgments: An fMRI study of normal volunteers. *Neuroimage, 14*(1 Pt 2), S59–67.

Fiorelli, M., Blin, J., Bakchine, S., LaPlane, D., & Baron, J. C. (1991). PET studies of cortical diaschisic in patients with motor hemi–neglect. *Journal of the Neurological Sciences, 104*, 135–142.

Fleet, W. S., Valenstein, E., Watson, R. T., & Heilman, K. M. (1987). Dopamine agonist therapy for neglect in humans. *Neurology, 37*, 1765–1771.

Fonnum, F., & Walaas, I. (1979). Localization of neurotransmitter candidates in neostriatum. In I. Divac, & R. G. E. Oberg (Eds.), *The neostriatum* (pp. 53–69). Oxford: Pergamon Press.

Gainotti, G., Messerli, P., & Tissot, R. (1972). Qualitative analysis of unilateral and spatial neglect in relation to laterality of cerebral lesions. *Journal of Neurology, Neurosurgery, and Psychiatry, 35*, 545–550.

Geminiani, G., Bottini, G., & Sterzi, R. (1998). Dopaminergic stimulation in unilateral neglect. *Journal of Neurology, Neurosurgery, and Psychiatry, 65*(3), 344–347.

Geschwind, N. (1965). Disconnexion syndromes in animals and man. *Brain, 88*, 237–294.

Glick, S. D. (1972). Changes in amphetamine sensitivity following cortical damage in rats and mice. *European Journal Pharmacology, 20*, 351–356.

Glick, S. D., Cran, A. M., Jerussi, T. P., Fleisher, L. N., & Green, J. P. (1975). Functional and neurochemical correlates to potentiation of striatal asymmetry by callosal section. *Nature, 254*, 616–617.

Goldberg, M. E., & Bushnell, M. C. (1981). Behavioral enhancement of visual responses in monkey cerebral cortex: II Modulation in frontal eye fields specifically related saccades. *Journal of Neurophysiology, 46*, 773–787.

Goldberg, M. E., & Robinson, D. C. (1977). Visual responses of neurons in monkey inferior parietal lobule. The physiological substrate of attention and neglect. *Neurology, 27*, 350.

Grofova, I. (1979). Extrinsic connections of neostriatum. In I. Divak, & R. G. E. Oberg (Eds.), *The neostriatum* (pp. 37–51). Oxford: Pergamon Press.

Grossman, S. P., Dacey, D., Halaris, A. E., Collier, T., & Routtenberg, A. (1978). Aphagia and adipsia after preferential destruction of nerve cell bodies in the hypothalamus. *Science, 202*, 537–539.

Grujic, Z., Mapstone, M., Gitelman, D. R., Johnson, N., Weintraub, S., Hays, A., et al. (1998). Dopamine agonists reorient visual exploration away from the neglected hemispace. *Neurology, 51*(5), 1395–1398.

Guariglia, C., Padovani, A., Pantano, P., & Pizzamiglio, L. (1993). Unilateral neglect restricted to visual imagery. *Nature, 364* (6434), 237–237.

Hagamen, T. C., Greeley, H. P., Hagamen, W. D., & Reeves, A. G. (1977). Behavioral asymmetries following olfactory tubercle lesions in cats. *Brain, Behavior and Evolution, 14*, 241–250.

Halligan, P. W., & Marshall, J. C. (1989). Laterality of motor response in visuo-spatial neglect: A case study. *Neuropsychologia, 27*, 1301–1307.

Halligan, P. W., Marshall, J. C. (1991). Recovery and regression in visuo-spatial neglect: A case study of learning in line bisection. *Brain Injury, 5*(1), 23–31.

Halligan, P. W., & Marshall, J. C. (1991). Left neglect for near but not far space in man. *Nature, 350*(6318), 498–500.

Harvey, M., Milner, A. D., & Roberts, R. C. (1995). An investigation of hemispatial neglect using the Landmark Task. *Brain and Cognition, 27*(1), 59–78.

Haxby, J. V., Grady, C. L., Horwitz, B., Ungerleider, L. G., Mishkin, M., Carson, R. E., et al. (1991). Dissociation of object and spatial visual processing pathways in human extrastriate cortex. *Proceedings of the National Academy of Science U.S.A. 88*(5), 1621–1625.

He, B. J., Snyder, A. Z., Vincent, J. L., Epstein, A., Shulman, G. L., Corbetta, M. (2007). Breakdown of functional connectivity in frontoparietal networks underlies behavioral deficits in spatial neglect. *Neuron, 53*(6), 905–918.

Head, H., & Holmes, G. (1911). Sensory disturbances from cerebral lesions. *Brain, 34*, 102–254.

Heikkila, R. E., Shapiro, B. S., & Duvoisin, R. C. (1981). The relationship between loss of dopamine nerve terminals, striatal; s3H spiroperidol binding and rotational behavior in unilaterally 6-hydroxdopamine-lesioned rats. *Brain Research, 211*, 285–307.

Heilman, K. M. (1979). Neglect and related disorders. In K. M. Heilman, & E. Valenstein (Eds.), *Clinical neuropsychology.* (pp. 268–270). New York: Oxford University Press.

Heilman, K. M., Bowers, D., & Watson, R. T. (1983b). Performance on hemispatial pointing task by patients with neglect syndrome. *Neurology, 33*, 661–664.

Heilman, K. M., Bowers, D., & Watson, R. T. (1984). Pseudoneglect in patients with partial callosal disconnection. *Brain*, *107*, 519–532.

Heilman, K. M., Bowers, D., Coslett, H. B., Whelan, H., & Watson, R. T. (1985). Directional hypokinesia: Prolonged reaction times for leftward movements in patients with right hemisphere lesions and neglect. *Neurology*, *35*, 855–860.

Heilman, K. M., & Howell, F. (1980). Seizure-induced neglect. *Journal of Neurology, Neurosurgery, and Psychiatry*, *43*, 1035–1040.

Heilman, K. M., Odenheimer, G. L. Watson, R. T., & Valenstein, E. (1984). Extinction of non-touch. *Neurology*, *34*(Suppl. 1), 188.

Heilman, K. M., Pandya, D. N., & Geschwind, N. (1970). Trimodal inattention following parietal lobe ablations. *Transactions of the American Neurological Association*, *95*, 259–261.

Heilman, K. M., Schwartz, H. D., & Watson, R. T. (1978). Hypoarousal in patients with neglect syndrome and emotional indifference. *Neurology*, *28*, 229–232.

Heilman, K. M., & Valenstein, E. (1972). Frontal lobe neglect in man. *Neurology*, *22*, 660–664.

Heilman, K. M., & Valenstein, E. (1979). Mechanisms underlying hemispatial neglect. *Annals of Neurology*, *5*, 166–170.

Heilman, K. M., Valenstein, E., & Watson, R. T. (1983). Localization of neglect. In A. Kertesz (Ed.), *Localization in neurology* (pp. 471–492). New York: Academic Press.

Heilman, K. M., & Van Den Abell, T. (1979). Right hemispheric dominance for mediating cerebral activation. *Neuropsychologia*, *17*, 315–321.

Heilman, K. M., & Van Den Abell, T. (1980). Right hemisphere dominance for attention: The mechanisms underlying hemispheric asymmetries of inattention (neglect). *Neurology*, *30*, 327–330.

Heilman, K. M., & Watson, R. T. (1977). The neglect syndrome–a unilateral defect of the orienting response. In S. Hardned, R. W. Doty, L. Goldstein, J. Jaynes, & G. Kean Thamer (Eds.), *Lateralization in the nervous system*. New York: Academic Press.

Heilman, K. M., & Watson, R. T. (1978). Changes in the symptoms of neglect induced by changes in task strategy. *Archives of Neurology*, *35*, 47–49.

Heilman, K. M., Watson, R. T., & Schulman, H. (1974). A unilateral memory deficit. *Journal of Neurology, Neurosurgery, and Psychiatry*, *37*, 790–793.

Heir, D. B., Davis, K. R., Richardson, E. T., et al. (1977). Hypertensive putaminal hemorrhage. *Annals of Neurology*, *1*, 152–159.

Herkenham, M. (1979). The afferent and efferent connections of the ventromedial thalamic nucleus in the rat. *Journal of Comparative Neurology*, *183*, 487–518.

Hillis, A. E., Newhart, M., Heidler, J., Barker, P. B., Herskovits, E. H., & Degaonkar, M. (2005). Anatomy of spatial attention: Insights from perfusion imaging and hemispatial neglect in acute stroke. *Journal of Neuroscience*, *25*(12), 3161–3167.

Holmes, G. (1918). Disturbances of vision from cerebral lesions. *British Journal of Ophthalmology*, *2*, 253–384.

Howes, D., & Boller, F. (1975). Evidence for focal impairment from lesions of the right hemisphere. *Brain*, *98*, 317–332.

Hoyman, L., Weese, G. D., & Frommer, G. P. (1979). Tactile discrimination performance deficits following neglect–producing unilateral lateral hypothalamic lesions in the rat. *Physiology and Behavior*, *22*, 139–147.

Hyvarinen, J., & Poranen, A. (1974). Function of the parietal associative area 7 as revealed from cellular discharge in alert monkeys. *Brain*, *97*, 673–692.

Ishiai, S., Okiyama, R., Koyama, Y., & Seki, K. (1996). Unilateral spatial neglect in Alzheimer's disease. *A line bisection study. Acta Neurologica Scandinavica*, *93*, 219–224.

Ishiai S, Koyama, Y., Seki, K., Orimo, S., Sodeyama, N., Ozawa, E., et al. (2000). Unilateral spatial neglect in AD: Significance of line bisection performance. *Neurology*, *55*(3), 364–370.

Iverson, S. D., Wilkinson, S., & Simpson, B. (1971). Enhanced amphetamine responses after frontal cortex lesions in the rat. *European Journal of Pharmacology*, *13*, 387–390.

Jackson, J. Hughlings. (1932). In J. Taylor (Ed.), *Selected writings of John Hughlings Jackson*. London: Hodder and Stoughton.

James, W. (1890). *The principles of psychology*, Vol. 2. New York: Holt.

Jasper, H. H. (1949). Diffuse projection systems: The integrative action of the thalamic reticular system. *Electroencephalography and Clinical Neurophysiology*, *1*, 405–419.

Jefferson, G. (1958). Substrates for integrative patterns in the reticular core. In M. N. E. Scheibel, & A. B. Scheibel (Eds.), *Reticular formation*. Boston: Little, Brown.

Johannsen, L., Ackermann, H., Karnath, H. O. (2003). Lasting amelioration of spatial neglect by treatment with neck muscle vibration even without concurrent training. *Journal of Rehabilitation Medicine*, *35*(6), 249–253.

Jouvet, M. (1977). Neuropharmacology of the sleep waking cycle. In L. L. Iverson, S. D. Iverson, & S. H. Snyder (Eds.), *Handbook of psychopharmacology* (pp. 233–293). New York: Plenum Press.

Kahneman, D. (1973). *Eye movement attention and effort*. Englewood Cliffs, NJ: Prentice-Hall.

Kaplan, R. F., Verfaellie, M., DeWitt, D., & Caplan, L. R. (1990). Effects of changes in stimulus contingency on visual extinction. *Neurology*, *40*, 1299–1301.

Kanai, T., & Szerb, J. C. (1965). Mesencephalic reticular activating system and cortical acetylcholine output. *Nature*, *205*, 80–82.

Karnath, H. O. (1995). Transcutaneous electrical stimulation and vibration of neck muscles in neglect. *Experimental Brain Research*, *105*(2), 321–324.

Karnath, H. O., Ferber, S., Himmelbach, M. (2001). Spatial awareness is a function of the temporal not the posterior parietal lobe. *Nature*, *411*(6840), 950–953.

Kartsounis, L. D., & Warrington, E. K. (1989). Unilateral visual neglect overcome by ones implicit in stimulus arrays. *Journal of Neurology, Neurosurgery, and Psychiatry*, *52*, 1253–1259.

Kennard, M. A., & Ectors, L. (1938). Forced circling movements in monkeys following lesions of the frontal lobes. *Journal of Neurophysiology*, *1*, 45–54.

Kerkhoff, G., Keller, I., Ritter, V., & Marquardt, C. (2006). Repetitive optokinetic stimulation induces lasting recovery from visual neglect. *Restorative Neurology and Neuroscience*, *24*(4–6), 357–369.

Kertesz, A., Nicholson, I., Cancelliere, A., Kassa, K., & Black, S. E. (1985). Motor impersistence: A right-hemisphere syndrome. *Neurology*, *35*, 662–666.

Kievet, J., & Kuypers, H. G. J. M. (1977). Organization of the thalamo-cortical connections to the frontal lobe in the rhesus monkey. *Experimental Brain Research*, *29*, 299–322.

Kim, M., Na, D. L., Kim, G. M., Adair, J. C., Lee, K. H., & Heilman K. M. (1999). Ipsilesional neglect: Behavioural and anatomical features. *Journal of Neurology, Neurosurgery, and Psychiatry*, *67*(1), 35–38.

Kimura, D. (1967). Function asymmetry of the brain in dichotic listening. *Cortex*, *3*, 163–178.

Kinomura, S., Larsson, J., Gulyas, B., & Roland, P. E. (1996). Activation by attention of the human reticular formation and thalamic intralaminar nuclei. *Science*, *271*(5248), 512–515.

Kinsbourne, M. (1970). A model for the mechanism of unilateral neglect of space. *Transactions of the American Neurological Association*, *95*, 143.

Kinsbourne, M. (1974). Direction of gaze and distribution of cerebral thought processes. *Neuropsychologia*, *12*, 270–281.

Kooistra, C. A., & Heilman, K. M. (1989). Hemispatial visual inattention masquerading as hemianopsia. *Neurology*, *39*, 1125–1127.

Kozlowski, M. R., & Marshall, J. F. (1981). Plasticity of neostriatal metabolic activity and behavioral recovery from nigrostriatal injury. *Experimental Neurology*, *74*, 313–323.

Kunkel, A., Kopp, B., Muller, G., Villringer, K., Villringer, A., Taub, E., & Flor, H. (1999). Constraint-induced movement therapy for motor recovery in chronic stroke patients. *Archives of Physical Medicine and Rehabilitation*, *80*(6), 624–628.

Kuypers, H. G. J. M., & Lawrence, D. G. (1967). Cortical projections to the red nucleus and the brain stem in the rhesus monkey. *Brain Research*, *4*, 151–188.

Kwon, S. E., & Heilman, K. M. (1991). Ipsilateral neglect in patient following a unilateral frontal lesion. *Neurology*, *41*(12), 2001–2004.

Ladavas, E. (1987). Is the hemispatial deficit produced by right parietal damage associated with retinal or gravitational coordinates. *Brain*, *110*, 167–180.

Ladavas, E., Petronio, A., & Umicta, C. (1990). The deployment of visual attention in the intact field of hemineglect patients. *Cortex*, *26*, 307–312.

Lansing, R. W., Schwartz, E., & Lindsley, D. B. (1959). Reaction time and EEG activation under alerted and nonalerted conditions. *Journal of Experimental Psychology*, *58*, 1–7.

Lindvall, O., Bjorklund, A., Morre, R. Y., & Stenevi, U. (1974). Mesencephalic dopamine-neurons projecting to the neocortex. *Brain Research*, *81*, 325–331.

Lissauer, H. (1890). Ein fall vol seelenblindheit nebst einem beitrag zur theorie derselben [A case of visual agnosia with a contribution to theory]. *Archiv fur Psychiatrie*, *21*, 222–270. Translated in.Shallice, T., & Jackson, M. (1988). Lissauer on agnosia. *Cognitive Neuropsychology*, *5*, 153–192.

Ljungberg, T., & Ungerstedt, U. (1976). Sensory inattention produced by 6-hydroxydopamine-induced degeneration of ascending dopamine neurons in the brain. *Experimental Neurology*, *53*, 585–600.

Loeb, J. (1885). Die elementaren storunger eirfacher functionennach oberflachlicher umschriebener verletzung des grosshirns Pfluger's. *Archives of Physiology*, *37*, 51–56.

Lynch, G. S., Ballantine, P., & Campbell, B. A. (1969). Potentiation of behavioral arousal after cortical damage and subsequent recovery. *Experimental Neurology, 23*, 195–206.

Lynch, J. C. (1980). The functional organization of posterior parietal association cortex. *Behavioral and Brain Sciences, 3*, 485–534.

Malhotra, P. A., Parton, A. D., Greenwood, R., & Husain, M. (2006). Noradrenergic modulation of space exploration in visual neglect. *Annals of Neurology, 59*(1), 186–190.

Mark, V. W., & Heilman, K. M. (1990). Bodily neglect and orientational biases in unilateral neglect syndrome and normal subjects. *Neurology, 40*(4), 640–643.

Mark, V. W., & Heilman, K. M. (1998). Diagonal spatial neglect. *Journal of Neurology, Neurosurgery, and Psychiatry, 65*(3), 348–352.

Mark, V. W., Kooistra, C. A., & Heilman, K. M. (1988). Hemispatial neglect affected by nonneglected stimuli. *Neurology, 38*, 1207–1211.

Marshall, J. F. (1979). Somatosensory inattention after dopamine-depleting intracerebral 6-OHDA injections: spontaneous recovery and pharmacological control. *Brain Research, 177*, 311–324.

Marshall, J. F. (1982). Neurochemistry of attention and attentional disorders. *Annual course 214, Behavioral Neurology.* Presented at the American Academy of Neurology, April 27, 1982.

Marshall, J. F., Richardson, J. S., & Teitelbaum, P. (1974). Nigrostriatal bundle damage and the lateral hypothalamic damage. *Journal of Complementary Physiology and Psychology, 87*, 808–830.

Marshall, J. F., Turner, B. H., & Teitelbaum, P. (1971). Sensory neglect produced by lateral hypothalamic damage. *Science, 174*, 523–525.

Mattingley, J. B., Bradshaw, J. L., Phillips, J. G. (1992). Impairments of movement initiation and execution in unilateral neglect. Directional hypokinesia and bradykinesia. *Brain, 115* (Pt 6), 1849–1874.

Mattingley, J. B., Husain, M., Rorden, C., Kennard, C., Driver, J. (1998). Motor role of human inferior parietal lobe revealed in unilateral neglect patients. *Nature, 392* (6672), 179–182.

McCormick, D. A. (1989). Cholinergic and noradrenergic modulation of thalamocortical processing. *Trends in Neurology, 12*, 215–221.

McFie, J., Piercy, M. F., & Zangwell, O. L. (1950). Visual spatial agnosia associated with lesions of the right hemisphere. *Brain, 73*, 167–190.

Meador, K., Hammond, E. J., Loring, D. W., Allen, M., Bowers, D., & Heilman, K. M. (1987). Cognitive evoked potentials and disorders of recent memory. *Neurology, 37*, 526–529.

Meador, K., Loring, D. W., Lee, G. P., Brooks, B. S., Thompson, W. O., & Heilman, K. M. (1988). Right cerebral specialization for tactile attention as evidenced by intracarotid sodium amytal. *Neurology, 38*, 1763–1766.

Meador, K., Loring, D. W., Lee, G. P., Brooks, B. S., Nichols, T. T., Thompson, E. E., Thompson, W. O., & Heilman, K. M. (1989). Hemisphere asymmetry for eye gaze mechanism. *Brain, 112*, 103–111.

Meador, K., Watson, R. T., Bowers, D., & Heilman, K. M. (1986). Hypometria with hemispatial and limb motor neglect. *Brain, 109*, 293–305.

Mehler, W. R. (1966). Further notes of the center median nucleus of Luys. In *The Thalamus*, D. P. Purpura, & M. D. Yahr (Eds.). New York: Columbia University Press, pp. 109–122.

Mendez, M. F., Cherrier, M. M., & Cymerman, J. S. (1997). Hemispatial neglect on visual search tasks in Alzheimer's disease. *Neuropsychiatry Neuropsychology and Behavioral Neurology, 10*, 203–208.

Mennemeier, M. S., Chatterjee, A., Watson, R. T., Wertman, E., Carter, L. P., & Heilman, K. M. (1994). Contributions of the parietal frontal lobes to sustained attention and habituation. *Neuropsychologia, 32*(6), 703–716.

Mennemeier MS, Morris M, & Heilman KM. (2004). Just thinking about targets can aggravate neglect on cancellation tests. *Neurocase, 10*(1), 29–38.

Mesulam, M. M. (1981). A cortical network for directed attention and unilateral neglect. *Annals of Neurology, 10*, 309–325.

Mesulam, M., Van Hesen, G. W., Pandya, D. N., & Geschwind, N. (1977). Limbic and sensory connections of the inferior parietal lobule (area PG) in the rhesus monkey: a study with a new method for horseradish perosidase histochemistry. *Brain Research, 136*, 393–414.

Meyer, E., Ferguson, S.S.G., Zarorre, R. J., Alivisatos, B., Marrett, S., Evans, A. C., & Hakim, A. M. (1991). Attention modulates somatosensory cerebral blood flow response to vibrotactile stimulation as measured by positron emission tomography. *Annals of Neurology, 29*, 440–443.

Mills, R. P., & Swanson, P. D. (1978). Vertical oculomotor apraxia and memory loss. *Annals of Neurology, 4*, 149–153.

Milner, B., Taylor, L., & Sperry, R. W. (1968). Lateralized suppression of dichotically presented digits after commissural section in man. *Science*, *161*, 184–186.

Mishkin, M., Ungerleider, L. G., & Macko, K. A. (1982). Object vision and spatial vision: Two cortical pathways. *Trends in Neurosciences*, *6*, 414–417.

Moruzzi, G., & Magoun, H. W. (1949). Brainstem reticular formation and activation of the EEG. *Electroencephalography and Clinical Neurophysiology*, *1*, 455–473.

Motter, B. C., & Mountcastle, V. B. (1981). The functional properties of the light sensitive neurons of the posterior parietal cortex studied in waking monkeys: foveal sparing and opponent vector organization. *Journal of Neuroscience*, *1*, 3–26.

Mountcastle, V. B., Anderson, R. A., & Motter, B. C. (1981). The influence of attentive fixation upon the excitability of the light sensitive neurons of the posterior parietal cortex. *Journal of Neuroscience*, *1*, 1218–1245.

Mountcastle, V. B., Lynch, J. C., Georgopoulos, A., Sakata, H., & Acuna, C. (1975). Posterior parietal association cortex of the monkey: command function from operations within extrapersonal space. *Journal of Neurophysiology*, *38*, 871–908.

Mukand JA, Guilmette TJ, Allen DG, Brown LK, Brown SL, Tober KL, & Vandyck WR. (2001). Dopaminergic therapy with carbidopa L-dopa for left neglect after stroke: a case series. *Archives of Physical Medicine and Rehabilitation*, *82*(9), 1279–1282.

Na, D. L., Adair, J. C., Kim, G. M., Seo, D. W., Hong, S. B., & Heilman, K. M. (1998). Ipsilateral neglect during intracarotid amobarbital test. *Neurology*, *51*(1), 276–279.

Na, D. L., Adair, J. C., Williamson, D. J., Schwartz, R. L., Haws, B., & Heilman, K. M. (1998). Dissociation of sensory-attentional from motor-intentional neglect. *Journal of Neurology, Neurosurgery, and Psychiatry*, *64*(3), 331–338.

Na, D. L., Adair, J. C., Kang, Y., Chung, C. S., Lee, K. H., & Heilman, K. M. (1999). Motor perseverative behavior on a line cancellation task. *Neurology*, *52*(8), 1569–1576.

Na, D. L., Adair, J. C., Choi, S. H., Seo, D. W., Kang, Y., & Heilman, K. M. (2000). Ipsilesional versus contralesional neglect depends on attentional demands. *Cortex*, *36*(4), 455–467.

Na, D. L., Adair, J. C., Choi, S. H., Seo, D. W., Kang, Y., & Heilman, K. M. (2000). Ipsilesional versus contralesional neglect depends on attentional demands. *Cortex*, *36*(4), 455–467.

Nadeau, S. E., & Heilman, K. M. (1991). Gaze-dependent hemianopia without hemispatial neglect. *Neurology*, *41*, 1244–1250.

Nathan, P. W. (1946). On simultaneous bilateral stimulation of the body in a lesion of the parietal lobe. *Brain*, *69*, 325–334.

Neve, K. A., Kozlowski, M. R., & Marshall, J. F. (1982). Plasticity of neostriatal dopamine receptors after nigrostriatal injury: relationship to recovery of sensorimotor functions and behavioral supersensitivity. *Brain Research*, *244*, 33–44.

Nieoullon, A., Cheramy, A., & Glowinski, J. (1978). Release of dopamine evoked by electrical stimulation of the motor and visual areas of the cerebral cortex in both caudate nuclei and in the substantia nigra in the cat. *Brain Research*, *15*, 69–83.

Nys, G. M., de Haan, E. H., Kunneman, A., de Kort, P. L., & Dijkerman, H. C. (2008). Acute neglect rehabilitation using repetitive prism adaptation: a randomized placebo-controlled trial. *Restorative Neurology and Neuroscience*, *26*(1), 1–12.

Obersteiner, H. (1882). On allochiria–a peculiar sensory disorder. *Brain*, *4*, 153–163.

Ogden, J. A. (1985). Anterior-posterior interhemispheric differences in the loci of lesions producing visual hemineglect. *Brain and Cognition*, Jan *4*(1), 59–75.

Olds, J., & Milner, P. (1954). Positive reinforcement produced by electrical stimulation of septal area and other regions of the rat brain. *Journal of Complementary Physiology and Psychology*, *47*, 419–427.

Oppenheim, H. (1885). Ueber eine durch eine klinisch bisher nicht verwertete Untersuchungsmethode ermittelte Form der Sensibitatsstorung bei einseitigen Erkrankunger des Grosshirns. *Neurol Zentrabl. 4*, 529–533. Cited by Benton A. L. (1956). Jacques Loeb and the method of double stimulation. *Journal of the History of Medicine and Allied Sciences*, *11*, 47–53.

Pandya, D. M., & Kuypers, H. G. J. M. (1969). Cortico-cortical connections in the rhesus monkey. *Brain Research*, *13*, 13–36.

Pardo, J. V., Fox, P. T., & Raichle, M. E. (1991). Localization of a human system for sustained attention by positron emission tomography. *Nature*, *349*, 61–64.

Paterson, A., & Zangwill, O. L. (1944). Disorders of visual space perception associated with lesions of the right cerebral hemisphere. *Brain*, *67*, 331–358.

Polanowska, K., Seniow, J., Paprot, E., Leśniak, M., & Członkowska, A. (2008). Left-hand somatosensory stimulation combined with visual scanning training in rehabilitation for post-stroke hemineglect: A randomised, double-blind study. *Neuropsychological Rehabilitation*, *1*. [Epub ahead of print].

Posner, M. I., & Rafal, R. D. (1987). Cognitive theories of attention and rehabilitation of attentional deficits. In M. J. Mier, A. L. Benton, & L. Diller (Eds.), *Neuropsychological rehabilitation*. New York: Guilford.

Posner, M. I., Walker, J., Friedrich, F. J., & Rafal, R. D. (1984). Effects of parietal lobe injury on covert orienting of visual attention. *Journal of Neuroscience, 4*, 163–187.

Poppelreuter, W. L. (1917). Die psychischen Schadigungen durch Kopfschuss Krieg im 1914–1916: Die Storungen der niederen und hoheren Leistkungen durch Verletzungen des Oksipitalhirns. Vol. 1. *Leipzig: Leopold Voss*. Referred to by M. Critchley (1949). *Brain, 72*, 540.

Pibram, K. H., & McGuiness, D. (1975). Arousal, activation and effort in the control of attention. *Psychology Reviews, 182*, 116–149.

Pizzamiglio, L., Frasca, R., Guariglia, C., Incoccia, C., & Antonucci, G. (1990). Effect of optokinetic stimulation in patients with visual neglect. *Cortex, 26*(4), 535–540.

Pizzamiglio L., Perani D., Cappa SF., Vallar G., Paolucci S., Grassi F., Paulesu E., Fazio F. (1998). Recovery of neglect after right hemispheric damage: H2(15)O positron emission tomographic activation study. *Archives of Neurology*. 55(4):561–8.

Purpura, D. P. (1970). Operations and processes in thalamic and synaptically related neural subsystemes. In F. O. Schmidt (Ed.), *The neurosciences, second study program*. (pp. 458–470). New York: Rockefeller University Press.

Pycock, C. J. (1980). Turning behavior in animals. *Neuroscience, 5*, 461–514.

Rapcsak, S. Z., Watson, R. T., & Heilman, K. M. (1987). Hemispace-visual field interactions in visual extinction. *Journal of Neurology Neurosurgery and Psychiatry, 50*, 1117–1124.

Rapcsak, S. Z., Cimino, C. R., & Heilman, K. M. (1988). Altitudinal neglect. *Neurology, 38*, 277–281.

Rapcsak, S. Z., Fleet, W. S., Verfaellie, M., & Heilman, K. M. (1989). Selective attention in hemispatial neglect. *Archives of Neurology, 46*, 178–182.

Redgrave, P., Prescott, T. J., & Gurney, K. (1999). Is the short-latency dopamine response too short to signal reward error? *Trends in Neuroscience, 22*, 146–151.

Reeves, A. G., & Hagamen, W. D. (1971). Behavioral and EEG asymmetry following unilateral lesions of the forebrain and midbrain of cats. *Electroencephalography and Clinical Neurophysiology, 39*, 83–86.

Reider, N. (1946). Phenomena of sensory suppression. *Archives of Neurology and Psychiatry, 55*, 583–590.

Riddoch, G. (1935). Visual disorientation in homonymous half-fields. *Brain, 58*, 376–382.

Riddoch, M. J., & Humphreys, G. (1983). The effect of cuing on unilateral neglect. *Neuropsychologia, 21*, 589–599.

Riestra, A. R., Crucian, G. P., Burks, D. W., Womack, K. B., & Heilman K. M. (2001). Extinction, working memory, and line bisection in spatial neglect. *Neurology, 57*(1), 147–149.

Robertson, I. H., Halligan, P. W., Bergego, C., Homberg, V., Pizzamiglio, L. Weber, E., & Wilson, B.A. (1994). Right neglect following right hemisphere damage? *Cortex, 30*(2), 199–213.

Robertson, I. H., & North, N. T. (1994). One hand is better than two: motor extinction of left hand advantage in unilateral neglect. *Neuropsychologia, 32*(1), 1–11.

Robinson, D. L., Goldberg, M. E., & Stanton, G. B. (1978). Parietal association cortex in the primate sensory mechanisms and behavioral modulations. *Journal of Neurophysiology, 41*, 910–932.

Rode, G., Charles, N., Perenin, M.T., Vighetto, A., Trillet, M., & Aimard, G. (1992). Partial remission of hemiplegia and somatoparaphrenia through vestibular stimulation in a case of unilateral neglect. *Cortex, 28* (2), 203–208.

Roeltgen, M. G., Roeltgen, D. P., & Heilman, K. M. (1989). Unilateral motor impersistence and hemispatial neglect from a striatal lesion. *Neuropsychiatry Neuropsychology and Behavioral Neurology, 2*, 125–135.

Ross, E. D., & Stewart, R. M. (1981). Akinetic mutism from hypothalamic damage: successful treatment with dopamine agonists. *Neurology, 31*, 1435–1439.

Rossi, P. W. Kheyfets, S., & Reding, M. J. (1990). Fresnel prisms improve visual perception in stroke patients with homonymous hemianopia unilateral visual neglect. *Neurology, 40*, 1597–1599.

Rossetti, Y., Rode, G., Pisella, L., Farne, A., Ling, L., Boisson, D., & Perenin, M. (1998). Prism adaptation to a rightward optical deviation rehabilitates left hemispatial neglect. *Nature, 395*, 166–169.

Rubens, A. B. (1985). Caloric stimulation and unilateral visual neglect. *Neurology, 35*(7), 1019–1024.

Samuels, I., Butters, N., & Goodglass, H. (1971). Visual memory defects following cortical limbic lesions: effect of field of presentation. *Physiology and Behavior, 6*, 447–452.

Sanders, M. D., Warrington, E. K., Marshall, J., & Wieskrantz, L. (1974). "Blindsight": Vision in a field defect. *Lancet*, *1*(7860), 707–708.

Sapir, A., Kaplan, J. B., He, B. J., & Corbetta, M. (2007). Anatomical correlates of directional hypokinesia in patients with hemispatial neglect. *Journal of Neuroscience*, *27*(15), 4045–4051.

Sato, H., Hata, Y. Hagihara, K., & Tsumoto, T. (1987). Effects of cholinergic depletion on neuron activities in the cat visual cortex. *Journal of Neurophysiology*, *58*, 781–794.

Scheibel, M. E., & Scheibel, A. B. (1967). Structural organization of nonspecific thalamic nuclei and their projection toward cortex. *Brain*, *6*, 60–94.

Scheibel, M. E., & Scheibel, A. B. (1966). The organization of the nucleus reticularis thalami: a Golgi study. *Brain Research*, *1*, 43–62.

Schlag–Rey, M., & Schlag, J. (1980). Eye movement neurons in the thalamus of monkey. *Investigations in Ophthalmology and Vision Science ARVO*, supplement, 176.

Schneider, J. S., McLaughlin, W. W., & Roeltgen, D. P. (1992). Motor and nonmotor behavioral deficits in monkeys made hemiparkinsonian by intracarotid MPTP infusion. *Neurology*, *42* (8), 1565–1572.

Schrandt, N. J., Tranel, D., & Domasio, H. (1989). The effects of total cerebral lesions on skin conductance response to signal stimuli. *Neurology*, *39* (Suppl. 1), 223.

Schubert, F., & Spatt, J. (2001). Double dissociations between neglect tests: Possible relation to lesion site. *European Neurology*, *45*(3), 160–164.

Schultz, W. (1998). Predictive reward signal of dopamine neurons. *Journal of Neurophysiology*, *80*, 1–27.

Schultz, W., Tremblay, L., & Hollerman, J. R. (2000). Reward processing in primate orbitofrontal cortex and basal ganglia. *Cerebral Cortex*, *10*, 272–284.

Schwartz, A. S., Marchok, P. L., Kreinick, C. J., & Flynn, R. E. (1979). The asymmetric lateralization of tactile extinction in patients with unilateral cerebral dysfunction. *Brain*, *102*, 669–684.

Segundo, J. P., Naguet, R., & Buser, P. (1955). Effects of cortical stimulation on electrocortical activity in monkeys. *Neurophysiology*, *1B*, 236–245.

Sevush, S., & Heilman, K. M. (1981). Attentional factors in tactile extinction. Presented at a meeting of the International Neuropsychological society, Atlanta, Georgia.

Shelton, P. A., Bowers, D., & Heilman, K. M. (1990). Peripersonal and vertical neglect. *Brain*, *113*, 191–205.

Shindo, K., Sugiyama, K., Huabao, L., Nishijima, K., Kondo, T., & Izumi, S. (2006). Long-term effect of low-frequency repetitive transcranial magnetic stimulation over the unaffected posterior parietal cortex in patients with unilateral spatial neglect. *Journal of Rehabilitation Medicine*, *38*(1), 65–67.

Shiraishi, H., Yamakawa, Y., Itou, A., Muraki, T., & Asada, T. (2008). Long-term effects of prism adaptation on chronic neglect after stroke. *NeuroRehabilitation*, *23*(2), 137–151.

Shuren, J., Hartley, T., & Heilman, K. M. (1998). The effects of rotation on spatial attention. *Neuropsychiatry Neuropsychology and Behavioral Neurology*, *11*(2), 72–75.

Shute, C.C.D., & Lewis, P. R. (1967). The ascending cholinergic reticular system, neocortical olfactory and subcortical projections. *Brain*, *90*, 497–520.

Singer, W. (1977). Control of thalamic transmission by corticofugal and ascending reticular pathways in the visual system. *Physiology Review*, *57*, 386–420.

Skinner, J. E., & Yingling, C. D. (1976). Regulation of slow potential shifts in nucleus reticularis thalami by the mesencephalic reticular formation and the frontal granular cortex. *Electroencephalography and Clinical Neurophysiology*, *40*, 288–296.

Skinner, J. E., & Yingling, C. D. (1977). Central gating mechanisms that regulate event-related potentials and behavior–a neural model for attention. In J. E. Desmedt (Ed.), *Progress in clinical neurophysiology*, Vol. 1 (pp. 30–69). New York: S. Karger.

Sokolov, Y. N. (1963). *Perception and the conditioned reflex*. Oxford: Pergmon Press.

Sparks, R., & Geschwind N. (1968). Dichotic listening in man after section of the neocortical commissures. *Cortex*, *4*, 3–16.

Sprague, J. M. (1966). Interaction of cortex and superior colliculus in mediation of visually guided behavior in the cat. *Science*, *153*, 1544–1547.

Sprague, J. M., & Meikle, T. H. (1965). The role of the superior colliculus in visually guided behavior. *Experimental Neurology*, *11*, 115–146.

Sprague, J. M., Chambers, W. W., & Stellar, E. (1961). Attentive, affective and adaptive behavior in the cat. *Science*, *133*, 165–173.

Stelmack, R. M., Plouffe, L. M., & Winogron, H. W. (1983). Recognition memory and the orienting response. An analysis of the encoding of pictures and words. *Biological Psychology*, *16*, 49–63.

Staines, R. T., McIlroy, W. E., Graham, S. J., Gladstone, D. J., & Black, S. E. (2000).

Somatosensory extinction of simultaneous stimuli is associated with decreased activation of somatosensory cortices. *Neurology, 54*(Suppl 3), A104.

Steriade, M., & Glenn, L. (1982). Neocortical and caudate projections of intralaminar thalamic neurons and their synaptic excitation from the midbrain reticular core. *Journal of Neurophysiology, 48,* 352–370.

Storrie-Baker, H. J., Segalowitz, S. J., Black, S. E., McLean, J. A., Sullivan, N. (1997). Improvement of hemispatial neglect with cold-water calorics: An electrophysiological test of the arousal hypothesis of neglect. *Journal of the International Neuropsychological Society, 3*(4), 394–402.

Sturm, W., Thimm, M., Küst, J., Karbe, H., & Fink, G. R. (2006). Alertness-training in neglect: Behavioral and imaging results. *Restorative Neurology and Neuroscience, 24*(4–6), 371–384.

Tegner, R., & Levander, M. (1991). Through a looking glass. A new technique to demonstrate direction hypokinesia in unilateral neglect. *Brain, 114*(Pt 4), 1943–1951.

Teitelbaum, P., & Epstein, A. N. (1962). The lateral hypothalamic syndrome: Recovery of feeding and drinking after lateral hypothalamic lesions. *Psychology Review, 69,* 74–90.

Truex, R. C., & Carpenter, M. B. (1964). *Human neuroanatomy*. Baltimore: Williams and Wilkins.

Ungerstedt, U. (1971a). Striatal dopamine release after amphetamine or nerve degeneration revealed by rotational behavior. *Acta Physiologica Scandinavica, Suppl. 82,* 49–68.

Ungerstedt, U. (1971b). Post-synaptic supersensitivity of 6-hydroxydopamine induced degeneration of the nigro-striatal dopamine system in the rat brain. *Acta Physiologica Scandinavica, Suppl. 82,* 69–93.

Ungerstedt, U. (1974). Brain dopamine neurons and behavior. In F. O. Schmidt, & F. G. Woren (Eds.), *Neurosciences,* Vol. 3 (pp. 695–703). Cambridge, MA: MIT Press.

Vallar, G., Rusconi, M. L., Bignamini, L., Geminiani, G., & Perani, D. (1994). Anatomical correlates of visual and tactile extinction in humans: A clinical CT scan study. *Journal of Neurology, Neurosurgery, and Psychiatry, 57*(4), 464–470.

Vallar, G., Sterzi, R., Bottini, G., Cappa, S., & Rusconi, L. (1990). Temporary remission of left hemianesthesia after vestibular stimulation: A sensory neglect phenomenon. *Cortex, 26,* 123–131.

Valenstein, E., & Heilman, K. M. (1978). Apraxic agraphia with neglect induced paragraphia. *Archives of Neurology, 38,* 506–508.

Valenstein, E., & Heilman, K. M. (1981). Unilateral hypokinesia and motor extinction. *Neurology, 31,* 445–448.

Valenstein, E., Van den Abell, T., Tankle, R., & Heilman, K. M. (1980). Apomorphine-induced turning after recovery from neglect induced by cortical lesions. *Neurology, 30,* 358.

Valenstein, E., Van den Abell, T., Watson, R. T., & Heilman, K. M. (1982). Nonsensory neglect from parietotemporal lesions in monkeys. *Neurology, 32,* 1198–1201.

Valenstein, E., Watson, R. T., Van den Abell, T., Carter, R., & Heilman, K. M. (1987). Response time in monkeys with unilateral neglect. *Archives of Neurology, 44,* 517–520.

Vallar, G., Papagno, C., Rusconi, M. L., & Bisiach, E. (1995). Vestibular stimulation, spatial hemineglect and dysphasia, selective effects. *Cortex, 31*(3), 589–593.

Vanderwolf, C. H., & Robinson, T. E. (1981). Reticulo-cortical activity and behavior: A critique of arousal theory and new synthesis. *Behavioral and Brain Sciences, 4,* 459–514.

Vargo, J. M., Lai, H. V., & Marshall, J. F. (1998). Light deprivation accelerates recovery from frontal cortical neglect: Relation to locomotion and striatal Fos expression. *Behavioral Neuroscience, 112*(2), 387–398.

Vargo, J. M., Richard-Smith, M., & Corwin, J. V. (1989). Spiroperidol reinstates asymmetries in neglect in rats recovered from left or right dorsomedial prefrontal cortex lesions. *Behavioral Neuroscience, 103*(5), 1017–1027.

Velasco, F., & Velasco, M. (1979). A reticulothalamic system mediating proprioceptive attention and tremor in man. *Neurosurgery, 4,* 30–36.

Venneri, A., Pentore, R., Cotticelli, B., & Della Sala, S. (1998). Unilateral spatial neglect in the late stages of Alzheimer's disease. *Cortex, 34,* 743–752.

Vogt, B. A., Rosene, D. L., & Pandya, D. N. (1979). Thalamic and cortical afferents differentiate anterior from posterior cingulate cortex in the monkey. *Science, 204,* 205–207.

Volpe B.T., Ledoux J.E., Gazzaniga, M.S. (1979). Information processing of visual stimuli in an "extinguished" field. *Nature, 282*(5740): 722–4.

Vuilleumier, P., Valenza, N., Mayer, E., Reverdin, A., & Landis, T. (1998). Near and far visual space in unilateral neglect. *Annals of Neurology, 43,* 406–410.

Wagman, I. H., & Mehler, W. R. (1972). Physiology and anatomy of the cortico-oculomotor mechanism. *Progress in Brain Research, 37,* 619–635.

Wallace, S. F., Rosenquist, A. C., & Sprague, J. M. (1989). Recovery from cortical blindness mediated by destruction of nontectotectal fibers in the commissure of the superior colliculus in the cat. *Journal of Comparative Neurology, 284,* 429–450.

Wallace, S. F., Rosenquist, A. C., & Sprague, J. M. (1990). Ibotenic acid lesions of the lateral substantia nigra restore visual orientation behavior in the hemianopic cat. *Journal of Comparative Neurology, 296,* 222–252.

Walter, W. G. (1973). Human frontal lobe function in sensory-motor association. In K. H. Pribram, & A. R. Luria (Eds.), *Psychophysiology of the frontal lobes* (pp. 109–122). New York: Academic Press.

Watson, R. T., & Heilman, K. M. (1979). Thalamic neglect. *Neurology, 29,* 690–694.

Watson, R. T., Andriola, M., & Heilman, K. M. (1977). The EEG in neglect. *Journal of the Neurological Sciences, 34,* 343–348.

Watson, R. T., Heilman, K. M., Cauthen, J. C., & King, F. A. (1973). Neglect after cingulectomy. *Neurology, 23,* 1003–1007.

Watson, R. T., Heilman, K. M., Miller, B. D., & King, F. A. (1974). Neglect after mesencephalic reticular formation lesions. *Neurology, 24,* 294–298.

Watson, R. T., Miller, B. D., & Heilman, K. M. (1977). Evoked potential in neglect. *Archives of Neurology, 34,* 224–227.

Watson, R. T., Miller, B. D., & Heilman, K. M. (1978). Nonsensory neglect. *Annals of Neurology, 3,* 505–508.

Watson, R. T., Valenstein, E., & Heilman, K. M. (1981). Thalamic neglect: The possible role of the medical thalamus and nucleus reticularis thalami in behavior. *Archives of Neurology, 38,* 501–507.

Watson, R. T., Valenstein, E., Day, A. L., & Heilman, K. M. (1984). The effects of corpus callosum section on unilateral neglect in monkeys. *Neurology, 34,* 812–815.

Watson, R. T., Valenstein, E., Day, A., & Heilman, K. M. (1994). Posterior neocortical systems subserving awareness and neglect. Neglect after superior temporal sulcus but not area 7 lesions. *Archives of Neurology, 51*(10), 1014–1021.

Weinberger, N. M., Velasco, M., & Lindsley, D. B. (1965). Effects of lesions upon thalamically induced electrocortical desynchronization and recruiting. *Electroencephalography and Clinical Neurophysiology, 18,* 369–377.

Weinstein, E. A., & Kahn, R. L. (1955). *Denial of Illness. Symbolic and physiological aspects.* Springfield, IL: C. C. Thomas.

Weintraub, S., & Mesulam, M. M. (1987). Right cerebral dominance in spatial attention: Further evidence based on ipsilateral neglect. *Archives of Neurology, 44,* 621–625.

Welch, K., & Stuteville, P. (1958). Experimental production of neglect in monkeys. *Brain, 81,* 341–347.

Whittington, D. A., & Hepp-Reymond, M. C. (1977). Eye and head movements to auditory targets. *Neurosciences Abstract, 3,* 158.

Williams, S. M., & Goldman-Rakic, P. S. (1998). Widespread origin of the primate mesofrontal dopamine system. *Cerebral Cortex, 8,* 321–245.

Yingling, C. D., & Skinner, J. E. (1975). Regulation of unit activity in nucleus reticularis thalami by the mesencephalic reticular formation and the frontal granular cortex. *Electroencephalography and Clinical Neurophysiology, 39,* 635–642.

Yingling, C. D., & Skinner, J. E. (1977). Gating of thalamic input to cerebral cortex by nucleus reticularis thalami. In J. E. Desmedt (Ed.), *Progress in clinical neurophysiology,* Vol. 1 (pp. 70–96). New York: S. Karger.

Yokoyama, K. Jennings, R., Ackles, P., Hood, P., & Boller, F. (1987). Lack of heart rate changes during an attention demanding task after right hemisphere lesions. *Neurology, 37,* 624–630.

13

Callosal Syndromes

ERAN ZAIDEL, MARCO IACOBONI, STEVEN M. BERMAN,
DAHLIA W. ZAIDEL, AND JOSEPH E. BOGEN[‡]

Since the publication of the fourth edition of *Clinical Neuropsychology*, there have been relatively few papers published on the split brain. This in part reflects the dwindling population of patients with complete cerebral commissurotomy (CCC) who also have relatively intact intelligence. The trend also reflects a growing emphasis on laterality experiments in normal subjects. Nonetheless, the disconnection syndrome continues to guide laterality research in the normal brain, motivating new research questions, suggesting new methodologies, and testing the limits of interhemispheric relations.

The major recent contributions to the study of the disconnection syndrome do not consist of dramatic new discoveries of "what it is like to be a split-brain." Rather, they qualify and revise earlier claims about alterations of action, perception, and attention. Recent research also highlights variability within and across split-brain patients. Such variability can be measured both behaviorally and physiologically. One sorely neglected domain remains the neurophysiology of the disconnection syndrome; what data are available are reviewed here briefly as well.

ORGANIZATION OF THIS CHAPTER

In this chapter, following some introductory notes and a description of the acute and stable effects of commissurotomy, the chronic human split-brain syndrome will be analyzed in its various domains. Within each domain, patients' behavior can reflect lack of interhemispheric transfer, hemisphere specialization, or compensatory phenomena. There follow discussions of electrophysiological correlates of the disconnection syndrome, of interhemispheric transfer following cerebral commissurotomy, and of partial disconnection syndromes. Next, a methodological and theoretical overview of the contribution of the "split brain" to research on hemispheric relations in the normal brain will be presented. The chapter concludes with a discussion of dual consciousness in the split brain. To make room for new sections, the excellent historical section present in previous editions has been omitted.

Most of the data discussed in this chapter derive from studies on patients with surgical disconnections, usually performed for treatment of intractable epilepsy. Because these patients have structural or physiological abnormalities

---

[‡] Deceased

that lead to epilepsy, and because epilepsy may also affect behavior, the effects of surgical disconnection may differ in degree or quality from naturally occurring callosal lesions occurring in previously normal persons. Naturally occurring callosal lesions are mentioned in this chapter, but not analyzed separately, and are also described in other chapters in this volume.

ANATOMY: THE CEREBRAL COMMISSURES

The collections of nerve fibers that directly connect one cerebral hemisphere with the other, called the *cerebral commissures*, include the corpus callosum (CC), the anterior commissure, and the hippocampal commissures. Of these, the CC is by far the largest, with at least 200 million fibers. The 2×10^8 estimate of Tomasch (1954) was based on light microscopy of a few cases. According to Innocenti (personal communication, 1991), measurement by electron microscopy will at least triple the previous estimate (see also Clarke et al., 1989). Aboitiz et al. (1992) conducted a comprehensive analysis of the human CC with light microscopy and a limited analysis with electron microscopy and estimated the total number of fibers in the human CC to be over 200 million.

The posterior and the habenular commissures, as well as other commissures of the spinal cord and brainstem, are not included among the cerebral commissures.

TERMINOLOGY

Surgical section of all of the cerebral commissures is called *commissurotomy*, whereas that of the CC alone is called *callosotomy*. It is now common to use the term "split-brain" to refer to cases of callosotomy as well as complete cerebral commissurotomy (CCC), since both groups of patients manifest most of the same signs and symptoms. The Los Angeles split-brain patients (Bogen and Vogel, 1962, 1975; Bogen et al., 1965, 1988) had CCC (including not only the CC, but also the anterior commissure, dorsal and ventral hippocampal commissures and, in some cases, the massa intermedia). In the experimental animal, split-brain preparations often include section of all of the cerebral commissures plus the optic chiasm; this makes it possible to restrict visual information to one hemisphere

merely by covering one eye. In the human with an intact chiasm, restriction of visual input to one hemisphere requires restriction of the visual stimuli to one or the other visual hemifield.

ETIOLOGY OF CALLOSAL LESIONS

Surgical section of all or part of the CC, with or without section of the other cerebral commissures, has been used for the treatment of medically intractable, multifocal epilepsy (Reeves, 1984; Spencer et al., 1987). Some seizure disorders respond well to section of only the anterior half or anterior two-thirds of the callosum (the "partial split-brain"). Surgeons may also approach deep midline tumors or arteriovenous malformation (AVMs) by sectioning a portion of the CC. Examples are genu section for anterior communicating aneurysm clipping, trunk sections for access to the third ventricle and environs, and splenial section for approaching the pineal region.

Lesions of the CC also occur naturally. Ischemic strokes affecting the territory of the anterior cerebral artery can destroy the anterior four-fifths of the CC (Foix & Hillemand, 1925; Critchley, 1930; Ethelberg, 1951), and posterior cerebral artery strokes can affect the posterior one-fifth (splenium). Tumors (usually gliomas) can occur anywhere in the callosum, the best studied being tumors of the genu or of the splenium. Multiple sclerosis can cause disconnection signs. Head trauma has also been associated with callosal injury. Toxic (such as Marchiafava-Bignami disease) and/or infectious lesions of the callosum occasionally occur. From time to time, an anterior cerebral artery aneurysm rupture results in hemorrhagic dissection of the CC or spasm with infarction of the CC. These naturally occurring lesions usually result in fractions of the complete callosotomy syndrome that improve over time. Familiarity with the complete syndrome makes identification of the partial varieties easier. Congenital absence of the CC (callosal agenesis) has been intensively studied; it is, for the most part, not accompanied by disconnection signs, a perplexity that remains elusive to date.

Callosal lesions are often accompanied by damage to neighboring structures. As a result, neighborhood signs may overshadow signs of callosal disconnection. Although any sign after cortical damage (in a region giving rise to cal-losal fibers) could be suspected of being partially callosal in origin, small lesions of the callosum are only rarely reliably correlated with any behavioral deficit.

DISCONNECTION SYNDROME FOLLOWING COMPLETE CEREBRAL COMMISSUROTOMY

SYNOPSIS OF THE HUMAN SPLIT-BRAIN SYNDROME

When patients who have had a complete callo-sotomy have recovered from the acute opera-tive effects and reach a fairly stable state, they manifest a variety of phenomena that can be grouped under four headings:

- *Social ordinariness.* One of the most remarkable results is that, in ordinary social situations, the patients are indistin-guishable from normal individuals. Special testing methods, usually involving the lat-eralization of input, are needed to expose their deficits.
- *Lack of interhemispheric transfer.* A wide variety of situations (described below) have been contrived to show that the human subjects are in this respect the same as split-brain cats and monkeys. A typical example is the inability to identify with one hand an object palpated with the other.
- *Hemispheric specialization effects.* The hemispheric specialization typical of human subjects results in phenomena not seen in split-brain animals. A typical example is the inability of right-handers to name or describe an object in the left hand, even when it is being appropriately manipulated.
- *Compensatory phenomena.* Split-brain subjects progressively acquire a variety of strategies for circumventing their inter-hemispheric transfer deficits. A common example is for the patient to speak out loud the name of an object palpated in the right hand; because the right hemisphere can recognize many individual words, the object can then be identified with the left hand.

In this and subsequent sections, frequent reference is made to specific split-brain patients. The case histories of the most com-monly studied patients are summarized in Table 13-1.

ACUTE EFFECTS OF COMMISSUROTOMY

In the immediate postoperative period and diminishing for weeks after, behavioral deficits may be related to injury to the right hemi-sphere from retraction during surgery, such as left-sided weakness and focal chronic sei-zures; to *diaschisis*, the dysfunction of undam-aged brain regions related to the loss of contact with other regions resulting from the sudden destruction of millions of commissural fibers; and to disconnection effects that will eventu-ally be compensated. It may be difficult to know which factor or factors account for any specific deficit.

During the first few days after CCC, in right-handers operated on from the right side, patients commonly respond reasonably well with their right limbs to simple commands. But they are easily confused by three- or even two-part commands, each part of which is obviously understood. These patients often lie quietly and may seem mildly "akinetic," although they cooperate when stimulated. There is some-times an imperviousness resembling that often seen with naturally occurring genu lesions. The patients are often mute, even when willing to write short (usually one-word) answers (Bogen, 1976). Failure of left-side responses to verbal command is usually severe and can be mistaken for hemiplegia. With improvement, well-coordinated but repetitive reaching, grop-ing, and grasping with the left hand sometimes resembles a grasp reflex; grasp reflexes may actually be present bilaterally for a day or two after surgery. When forced grasping cannot be elicited (by inserting two fingers into the patient's palm and drawing them out across the web between the thumb and index finger), it is nev-ertheless possible in most cases to demonstrate a proximal traction response; that is, the patient is unable to relax the hand grip when the exam-iner pulls so as to exert traction on the elbow and shoulder flexors (Twitchell, 1951). As the patient improves, there may be competitive movements between the left and right hands.

Table 13–1. Summary of Case Histories

| Patient | Gender | Handedness | Surgery | Age at Surgery (years) | Age at Onset of Symtomes (years) | IQ HISTORY | | Lesion Localization | Predominant Extracallosal Damage |
						Preoperative	Postoperative		
N.G	F	R	Complete cerebral commissurotomy: single-stage midline section of anterior commissure, corpus callosum, massa intermedia, and right fornix. Surgical approach by retraction of RH	30	18	Weschler-Bellvue 76 (79, 74) at age 30	WAIS, 77 (83, 71) at age 35	L posterior temporal R central	RH (BI)
L.B.	M	R	As above, but massa intermedia was not visualized	13	3:6	WISC 113 (119, 108) at age 13	WAIS, 106 (110, 100) at age 16	R central	RH (BI)
R.Y.	M	R	As above (normal cerebral development until age 13)	43	17	—	WAIS, 90 (99, 79) at age 45	R posterior?	RH
N.W.	F	R	As above. Massa intermedia divided. Partial damage to left fornix	36	8	WAIS 93 (97, 89) at age 36	WAIS, 93 (97, 89) at age 36	R temporal, parietal	RH (BI)
C.C.	M	R	As above. Surgical approach by LH retraction. Very difficult operation and slow recovery	13	10	WISC 76 (73, 83) at age 13	WAIS, 72 (72, 75) at age 16:8	L temporal, parietal	LH
A.A.	M	R	As above. Difficult operation	14	5:6	WAIS 74 (80, 72) at age 14	WAIS, 78 (77, 82) at age 17:8	L frontoparietal; birth injury to R arm area R frontal	LH (BI)

	Sex	Hemisphere	Procedure					Lesion	
P.S.	M	R	Callosotomy, two-stage, anterior first	15	2	WAIS 89 (83, 99)	WAIS, 89	L temporal	LH
V.P.	F	R	Callosotomy, two-stage, anterior first	27	6	—	WAIS-R 91	Bilateral L temporal	LH (BI)
D.R.	F	R	Callosotomy, single-stage	38	17	WAIS 117 (114, 100) at age 52	WAIS-R 89 (105, 72)	R temporal	RH
J.W.	M	R	Callosotomy, two-stage, posterior first	25	19	—	WAIS-R 95 (97, 95) at age 34	R anterior L frontoparietal	BI
V.J.	F	L	Callosotomy, two-stage, anterior first	42	16	WAIS-R 80 (88, 75)	WAIS-R 88 (96, 73)	—	BI

BI, bilateral; L, left; LH, left hemisphere; R, right; RH, right hemisphere; WAIS, Wechsler Adult Intelligence Scale; WISC, Wechsler Intelligence Scale for Children. WAIS-R, Wechsler Intelligence Scale Revised.

These patients commonly have bilateral Babinski signs, as well as bilaterally absent superficial abdominal reflexes.

Left arm hypotonia, left arm positive traction response, bilateral Babinski responses, and mutism were regularly observed in the Los Angeles series of cases. However, there was considerable variation from one patient to another, both in this series and in others (Wilson et al., 1975, 1977; Holtzman et al., 1981; McKeever et al., 1981; Ferguson et al., 1985; Reeves, 1991; Sass et al., 1991). At one extreme, the first patient, W.J., had preoperative right-frontal atrophy, was oldest at the time of brain injury (age 30) and at the time of operation (45), and subsequently showed the most severe apraxic and related symptoms. At the other end of the spectrum, L.B., a 13-year-old boy (see Bogen et al., 1988, for magnetic resonance imaging [MRI] status), had relatively little brain damage before surgery, had brain injury at birth, was youngest at the time of operation, and subsequently had the smoothest postoperative course and minimal left hand apraxia.

Within a few months after operation, there was a remarkable reduction in symptoms of hemispheric disconnection. The patient's personality and behavior in social situations and during most of a routine neurologic examination, appear much as before the operation. However, with appropriate tests using lateralized input, the disconnected hemispheres can be shown to operate independently to a large extent. Each of the hemispheres appears to have its own learning processes and its own separate memories, many of which are largely inaccessible to the other hemisphere.

THE CHRONIC, STABILIZED SYNDROME OF HEMISPHERIC DISCONNECTION: DISSOCIATIVE PHENOMENA

Volitional Ambivalence and Alexithymia

In split-brain patients, phenomena that suggest volitional ambivalence may be elicited by history or, less commonly, observed in the clinic. There may be a disparity between facial expression and verbalization, or between what the left

hand is doing and what the patient is saying. Or, there may be a dissociation between general bodily actions (rising, walking, etc.) and what is being done by either hand or what is being said. Such dissociations have occurred sufficiently often following callosal section in animals (Trevarthen, 1965) and humans that, in patients without CCC, the presence of these signs should arouse suspicion of hemispheric disconnection. Perhaps such conative or volitional ambivalence, when it occurs in normal subjects, might be attributable, at least on some occasions, to altered information transfer by anatomically intact commissures (Galin, 1974; Hoppe, 1977).

In contrast with volitional ambivalence, emotional ambivalence (such as the report by the patient of simultaneously possessing two conflicting internal feelings) has not been a symptom of commissurotomy nor of most reported natural cases of callosal lesions. Individuals with cerebral commissurotomy are less apt than normal individuals to discuss their feelings, conflicting or otherwise (Hoppe & Bogen, 1977). This condition, *callosal alexithymia* (TenHouten et al., 1986), may be explained by a defect in right to left hemisphere communication (Speedie et al., 1984; Klouda et al., 1988). Extending this hypothesis to persons without brain lesions, it would be predicted that individuals with higher scores on an alexithymia scale would show a greater right hemisphere deficit and weaker callosal transfer in an emotionality judgment task. However, Tabibnia et al. (2001) found that this was not the case.

Intermanual Conflict

The dissociative phenomenon most clearly identifiable with hemispheric disconnection is intermanual conflict, in which the hands act at cross-purposes. Almost all of the CCC patients in the Los Angeles series manifested some degree of intermanual conflict in the early postoperative period. For example, a few weeks after one patient (R.Y.) underwent surgery, his physiotherapist said, "You should have seen R.Y. yesterday—one hand was buttoning up his shirt and the other hand was coming along right behind it undoing the buttons!" (Bogen, 1979).

Another patient (A.M.) exhibited similar conflicts during Bogen's follow-up examination in February 1973: "When attempting a Jendrassik reinforcement, the patient reached with his right hand to hold his left, but the left hand actually pushed his right hand away. While testing finger-to-nose test (with the patient sitting), his left hand suddenly started slapping his chest like Tarzan."

Similar phenomena after callosotomy have been observed by others (Wilson et al., 1977; Ferguson et al., 1985; Reeves, 1991; Sass et al., 1991) as well as by Akelaitis (1944-45), who called it "diagnostic dyspraxia." Intermanual conflict has been described in many individual case reports of callosal infarcts or tumors (Fisher, 1963; Schaltenbrand, 1964; Joynt, 1977; Barbizet et al., 1978; Beukelman et al., 1980; Watson & Heilman, 1983; Sine at al., 1984; Degos et al., 1987; Levin et al., 1987; Tanaka et al., 1990; Della Sala et al., 1991, 1994; Schwartz et al., 1991; Baynes et al., 1997).

Intermanual conflict usually subsides soon after callosotomy, probably because other integrative mechanisms supplement or replace commissural function. In rare cases, it may persist for years, for reasons still poorly understood (Ferguson et al., 1985; Reeves, 1991).

The Anarchic (Alien) Hand

Related to intermanual conflict is a circumstance in which one of the patient's hands, usually the left hand in the right-handed patient, behaves in a way that the patient finds "foreign," "alien," or at least uncooperative. Della Sala et al. (1991) point out that such patients rarely deny that the troublesome hand belongs to them; hence, they prefer the term "anarchic" to "alien." The anarchic hand often leads to intermanual conflict, and has been seen consequent to callosal lesions at least since the report of Goldstein (1908). Even patient L.B., who was the youngest patient in the California series and had no long-term appreciable apraxia to verbal command, manifested this phenomenon 3 weeks after surgery. For example, while doing the block design test unimanually with his right hand, his left hand came up from beneath the table and was reaching for the blocks when he slapped it with his right hand and said, "That will keep it quiet for a while." Anarchic hand has been most persistent in N.W. a patient with a rather flamboyant personality, which may have contributed to her frequent complaints about "my little sister" in referring to whomever or whatever it was that made her left hand behave peculiarly. Evidence has been steadily accumulating that the anarchic hand, to be persistent, depends upon medial frontal cortical dysfunction (Goldberg et al., 1981; McNabb et al., 1988; Banks et al., 1989; Leiguarda et al., 1989; Starkstein et al., 1990; Tanaka et al., 1990).

The term "alien hand" was erroneously introduced (Bogen, 1979) as the result of Bogen's misreading of Brion and Jedynak (1975). However, Bogen later disapproved of the use of this term. A recent rereading makes clear that Brion and Jedynak used the term *la main étrangère* to describe a misidentification resulting from failure of interhemispheric *sensory* transfer, whereas they used the term *l'autocritique interhémisphérique* to describe seemingly purposeful actions disavowed by the patients.

The emphasis by Brion and Jedynak (1975) and by Bogen (1979) on callosal disconnection as the cause of anarchic hand was challenged by Goldberg et al. (1981), who reported two right-handed patients with a right anarchic hand subsequent to left medial frontal infarction. The role of medial frontal damage is difficult to evaluate since such lesions typically also involve the CC. The necessity for callosal disconnection (particularly for persisting cases) thus resulting in hemispheric independence would be disproved if anarchic hand emerged in hemispherectomized individuals suffering subsequent frontal damage. This debate is unresolved. It has been suggested (Feinberg et al., 1992) that there are two forms of anarchic hand: one callosal and the other mediofrontal. To the extent that a callosal lesion is essential (Geschwind et al., 1995), the anarchic hand supports the idea of an "other mind" (Bogen, 2000). Alternatively, it may be that the behavioral dissociation (between hand action and verbalization) is the result of interhemispheric disconnection of visually guided motor planning from verbal awareness (Milner & Goodale, 1995; Bogen, 1997).

Marchetti and Della Sala (1998) argue that the anarchic hand is not associated with an (anterior) callosal lesion, but is attributable to damage to the contralateral supplementary motor area (SMA) in the medial frontal lobe. In this view, the SMA converts intentions to self-initiated actions, and damage to this area leads to failure to modulate and inhibit externally triggered actions generated by the convexity premotor area on the same side. This account of neglect in terms of loss of frontal inhibition can help us understand anarchic behavior of either hand, or even of both hands (Mark et al., 1991).

Whereas a variety of forms of "alien hand" share the occurrence of involuntary movements, the inciting stimulus and the types of movement differ. In the callosal form, there are purposeful complex movements of the non-dominant hand. In the frontal form, there is grasping and utilization behavior of the dominant hand. Forced grasping occurs equally often with either the right or the left hand; it is usually a stereotyped response following stimulation, and it is typically a sign of contralateral frontal lobe dysfunction, requiring no direct callosal injury. The alien hand associated with cortical-basal degeneration is characterized by what appears to be spontaneous elevations of an arm, and a better term for this phenomenon might be "wayward" or "wandering" hand. It is misleading to describe any form of anarchic hand as alien if (as pointed out by Della Sala et al., 1994) the patients do not ascribe the hand to someone else, but recognize it as their own, although out of control. While all three forms (callosal, frontal, basal-ganglionic) involve loss of motor control, only the callosal form involves denial of purposeful movement and the occurrence of intermanual conflict, which can be termed "alien." Therefore, it is proposed that the different forms represent distinct syndromes and should be so named. For the type of movement that is well-coordinated, seemingly purposeful, and commonly effective, the term "autonomous hand" is preferred.

Autocriticism

In a related phenomenon, described by Brion and Jedynak (1975), which they called *l'autocritique interhémisphérique*, the patient expresses fairly frequent astonishment at the capacity of the left hand to behave independently. When the left hand makes some choice among objects, the patient may say that "my hand did that," rather than taking the responsibility. A patient was described by Sweet (1945) as saying, "Now you want me to put my left index finger on my nose." She then put that finger into her mouth and said, "That's funny; why won't it go up to my nose?" (p. 88).

Split-brain patients soon accept the idea that they have capacities of which they are not aware, such as left hand retrieval of objects not nameable. They may quickly rationalize such acts, sometimes in a transparently erroneous way (Gazzaniga & LeDoux, 1978). Even many years after surgery, these patients will occasionally be surprised or even irritated when some well-coordinated or obviously well-informed act has just been carried out by the left hand. This is particularly common under conditions of continuously lateralized input (E. Zaidel, 1977, 1978a; E. Zaidel & Peters, 1981). Praised by the examiner following successful performance by his disconnected right hemisphere on difficult language tasks, L.B. would sometimes exclaim: "How can I be correct when I don't know what I just did?" But it occurs even in social situations. In the summer of 1989, L.B. (then 24 years postoperative) was having lunch between testing sessions with two investigators. One of them asked about his attitude toward his left hand. He replied, "I hardly ever use it." The other examiner (Bogen) then pointed out that he was, at that moment, holding up a cup of juice in his left hand and had just taken a drink from the cup. "Sure enough," he said, looking at it, "I guess it is good for something."

SYMPTOMS, SIGNS, TESTING, AND COGNITIVE NEUROSCIENCE OF SPECIFIC DOMAINS IN CHRONIC, STABILIZED SYNDROME OF HEMISPHERIC DISCONNECTION

The testing of split-brain patients in the psychology laboratory has become progressively more sophisticated, and is often unfamiliar even to otherwise experienced neuropsychologists

(Zaidel et al., 1990). Thus, simple maneuvers that can be used in the clinic when hemispheric disconnection is suspected are emphasized. The general logic for studying hemispheric specialization in split-brain patients is to restrict sensory input to one hemisphere at a time, to require a response from the same or opposite hemisphere, and to compare latency or accuracy in the two conditions. In the case of visual and somesthetic input, predominantly contralateral innervation guarantees that left visual field (LVF) and left hand stimulation, respectively, will reach the right hemisphere, whereas right visual field (RVF) and right hand input will reach the left hemisphere. In the case of auditory stimuli, contralateral input can be assumed only when two acoustically similar, but not identical, stimuli reach both ears simultaneously (dichotic listening). For motor responses, it is assumed that each hemisphere has better control of the contralateral hand, especially for distal movements, but in the chronic disconnection syndrome, both hemispheres develop ipsilateral motor control sufficient for simple actions, such as binary choices. Consequently, experiments should rely on complete or partial lateralization at the input side. Given the emergence of speech in some disconnected right hemispheres, it should not be assumed without further testing that verbal output reflects responses by the disconnected left hemisphere.

The descriptions provided here apply to right-handers. In left-handers, the situation is rarely a simple reversal. Usually, it is quite complex, as can be seen in the case histories described in the literature (Liepmann, 1900; Hécaen & Ajuriaguerra, 1964; Botez & Crighel, 1971; Tzavaras et al., 1971; Heilman et al., 1973, 1981; Schott et al., 1974; Aptman et al., 1977; Hirose et al., 1977; Poncet et al., 1978; Herron, 1980; Gur et al., 1984; Joseph, 1986; Baynes et al., 1998; Spencer et al., 1988).

OLFACTION: UNILATERAL VERBAL ANOSMIA

Unlike most other sensory pathways, the olfactory pathways are almost exclusively uncrossed. Berlucchi and Aglioti (1999) describe the pathways as follows: "Information from primary sensory neurons in the olfactory epithelium of each nostril is transmitted to the olfactory bulb of the same side. The axons of the projection neurons of the olfactory bulb form the lateral olfactory tract that reaches the ipsilateral olfactory cortex consisting of paleocortical (prepiriform and periamygdaloid areas) and mesocortical components (entorhinal area)" (p. 656). The anterior olfactory nucleus, which receives input from the second-order bulbar neurons, may then send information across the anterior commissure, and cortical olfactory areas, such as the piriform cortex, may also project across the splenium of the CC. Berlucchi and Aglioti (1999) believe that "the interhemispheric transmission of olfactory information does not involve the CC and relies upon the anterior and hippocampal commissures" (p. 656).

Following CCC, the patient is unable to name odors presented to the right nostril, even when they can be named quite readily when presented to the left nostril. This is not a unilateral deficit of smell, since the patient can select, by feeling with the left hand, an object that corresponds to the odor presented to the right nostril, such as selecting a plastic banana or a plastic fish after having smelled the related odor (Gordon & Sperry, 1969).

The original study of commissurotomy subjects found that odor identification (using a nonlinguistic task and response mode) was superior using the left nostril as compared to using the right (Gordon & Sperry, 1969). A subsequent study of callosotomy patients found left hemispheric specialization for odor memory, although not for odor identification (Eskenazi et al., 1988). Other populations, however, suggest the opposite pattern of laterality. Some studies show more impairment in olfactory ability among patients with right- rather than left-sided brain damage or temporal lobectomy (e.g., West & Doty, 1995), although others have found no differences (Zatorre & Jones-Gotman, 1991). Tasks designed to measure the olfactory ability of each hemisphere in normal subjects have also suggested right hemisphere specialization (e.g., Hummel et al., 1998), but brain activation studies are conflicting (Zald & Pardo, 1997; Dade et al., 1998; Sobel et al., 1999).

There is evidence that the hemispheres normally work together in olfaction. Patients who lack interhemispheric fibers suffer olfactory deficits in odor discrimination and identification (Eskenazi et al, 1988; West & Doty, 1995). Is it possible for olfactory information to transfer between the hemispheres at all in the absence of the CC and anterior commissure? Of the two interhemispheric connections in the olfactory system, the anterior commissure appears to be more important. Gordon and Sperry (1969) found that four out of five complete commissurotomy patients could name odors presented to the left nostril, but not those presented to the right. Risse et al. (1978) and Eskenazi et al. (1988) found that callosotomy patients, on the other hand, were all able to name odors presented to the right nostril.

Patients with callosotomy (Eskanazi, 1988), with callosal agenesis (Kessler et al., 1991), and with CCC, all showed that there was a consistent impairment of odor identification among individuals lacking the CC. The data do not show hemispheric specialization for olfaction. The data from some patients do suggest that some subcallosal routes may be able to convey information about odors. Subcallosal routes exist for other sensory modalities as well, and these routes appear to vary across individual patients (Clarke & Zaidel, 1989).

TASTE

The lateral organization of the gustatory pathway in humans is incompletely understood. Most studies support an uncrossed projection from each side of the tongue to the cortex, but reports of a crossed organization continue to appear. The afferent gustatory fibers from each half of the tongue are known to travel via the VIIth and IXth cranial nerves to the ipsilateral nucleus of the solitary tract (NST). This projects to the parvocellular part of the ventroposteromedial nucleus of the thalamus (VPMpc), which in turn projects ipsilaterally to the primary gustatory cortex in the frontal operculum and anterior insula (Kobayakawa et al., 1996). The unsolved question is whether the projection from the NST to the VPMpc is crossed or uncrossed. Following unilateral brain lesions, gustatory impairments such as ageusias, hypogeusias, or dysgeusias can be localized to one side of the tongue, but both subcortical and

cortical lesions give conflicting results (reviewed in Aglioti et al., 2001).

Aglioti et al. (2000) studied the lateral organization of the gustatory pathway in a man with a complete callosal agenesis, in another man with a complete section of the CC who had a right anterior frontal lesion and language in the left hemisphere, and in normal controls. Sapid solutions were applied to one or the other side of the tongue and subjects reported the taste of the stimulus either verbally or by manually pointing to the name of the taste. There were no differences in accuracy and reaction time (RT) between the right and left hemitongues of the controls and the acallosal subject. By contrast, the callosotomy subject showed a constant marked advantage of the left hemitongue over the right for both accuracy and speed of response, although performance with right stimuli was clearly above chance. Assuming left hemisphere control of speech in the callosotomy patient, the results reject an exclusively crossed organization of the gustatory pathway from tongue to cortex, and favor a bilaterally distributed organization of this pathway, with a marked predominance of the uncrossed over the crossed component. These results, however, cannot rule out an exclusively uncrossed organization.

Berlucchi (personal communication, 2000) has since confirmed these results in two more callosotomy patients without cortical lesions. Still needed is a demonstration that the uncrossed gustatory component is stronger than the crossed one in the disconnected right hemisphere as well. There may also be individual differences in the relative magnitude of the uncrossed and crossed gustatory components, and these differences might explain the conflicts in the neurological literature.

VISION

Methodology

The bulk of research on hemispheric relations in the split brain has used visual stimuli. The visual system permits relatively easy lateralization of the input. To restrict sensory visual information to one hemisphere, lateralized visual stimuli are presented for less than 150 msec.

This prevents the confounding effects of involuntary saccadic eye movements, which have a latency of about 180 msec. To avoid possible confounds due to the predominance of crossed over uncrossed fibers at the chiasm, binocular vision is used. Although humans are believed to show negligible bihemispheric anatomic overlap around the vertical meridian (on the order of minutes of arc), it is prudent to present stimuli with their outermost edge at least 1–2 degrees away from fixation. Although electroencephalographic (EEG) recording is often used to monitor eye movements (Jordan et al., 1998), adequate fixation can usually be ascertained by video taping or direct inspection. Currently, hemifield tachistoscopy is usually implemented on personal computers.

To study the processing of dynamic visual stimuli restricted to one hemisphere, E. Zaidel (1973) developed a contact lens system that is effective, but requires individual fitting. Other investigators used part-opaque contact lenses (Dimond et al., 1975) or goggles (Francks et al., 1985), which are imprecise. Instead of yoking the hemifield occluder directly to the eye via a contact lens, it is possible to track eye movements noninvasively and use the horizontal component of the eye movements to control hemifield occlusion, either optically–mechanically (Zaidel & Frazier, 1977) or on a video monitor (Wittling, 1990). The critical needs are to separate eye movements from head movements, obtain an accurate measure of eye movements (with an error of <30 minutes of arc) within a relatively wide visual scanning area (about 10 degrees of arc), and ensure occlusion in real time. No fully operational eye tracker-based system for simulating hemianopia currently exists.

Failure of Interhemispheric Transfer: Double Hemianopia

Stimuli confined to one visual hemifield will reach only the contralateral hemisphere. Callosal section will prevent the hemisphere ipsilateral to the stimulus from having access to this stimulus. Therefore, only one hemisphere can reliably report the presence of the stimulus. Although tachistoscopic presentation is ideal for confining the stimulus to one hemisphere, the disconnection can sometimes be demonstrated with simple confrontation testing of the visual fields (VFs). The patient is allowed to have both eyes open but does not speak, and is allowed to use only one hand to respond (sitting on the other hand, for example). Using the free hand, the subject indicates the onset of a stimulus, such as the wiggling of the examiner's fingers. With such testing, there may appear to be an homonymous hemianopia contralateral to the indicating hand (the patient reliably points to the right hemifield stimulus with the right hand but not to a left hemifield stimulus). When the patient is tested with the other hand, there seems to be a homonymous hemianopia in the other hemifield. One can also test for this deficit by holding up one or more fingers in one hemifield, and asking the patient to show the same number of fingers using the hand ipsilateral or contralateral to the stimulus, or by asking the patient to demonstrate a hand posture shown to only one hemisphere.

Recent experiments with split-brain monkeys elucidate the role of callosal transfer in updating visual information in response to eye movements. Updating is the process by which neurons that represent a stimulus location after an eye movement receive information from neurons that represented the same location prior to the eye movement, a process necessary to preserve spatial constancy. After callosal section, split-brain monkeys exhibit a selective impairment of updating on eye movement sequences that require computing location across the visual hemifields. This selective impairment quickly partially recovered, suggesting that indirect cortico-subcortical pathways may play a role in updating visuospatial representations across the visual hemifields (Berman et al., 2005). Single-cell recordings from neurons in the lateral intraparietal cortex (LIP) of split-brain monkeys demonstrate that LIP neurons can update across hemifields without direct cortico-cortical connections. However, the magnitude and timing of responses in LIP neurons during updating across hemifields was reduced and delayed compared to within-hemifields responses (Heiser et al., 2005), even at the level of single neuron activity in LIP (Berman et al., 2007). Thus, although direct interhemispheric cortico-cortical connections are not necessary for updating visual representations across the hemifields, they are still the most efficient pathways for this functional process.

Compensatory Strategies

Most patients eventually achieve a condition in which no field defect can be demonstrated by the confrontation technique. This depends mainly upon the ability of each hemisphere to direct the head and eyes toward the visual target; this can signal the hemisphere ipsilateral to the stimulus to respond. If turning of the head is prevented, a lateral glance will suffice to cue the patient. Some patients learn to "cheat:" For example, as soon as it is apparent that there is no suitable stimulus in the right visual hemifield, the right hand may point to the left visual hemifield. This cheating can sometimes be detected by providing no stimulus at all on some trials.

Each hemisphere, especially the left, can exert a modicum of ipsilateral control, especially for gross arm movements. As a result, stimuli in the right hemifield (seen only by the left hemisphere) may be pointed to when the patient is using only the left hand, and similarly for the left hemifield stimuli when only the right hand is available. But such pointing is less reliable and accurate, as compared with the dependable response and precise localization possible when the patient is using the hand contralateral to the stimulated hemisphere.

Visual Deficits Related to
Hemispheric Specialization

Verbal Report of Left Visual Field Stimuli: Left Hemianomia. Since verbal output is mediated almost entirely by the left hemisphere, patients with CC may not verbally report stimuli confined to the left hemifield, which access only the right hemisphere. If stimuli are presented simultaneously in both visual hemifields, only the stimulus in the right hemifield is described by the patient, that is, by the left hemisphere. There is usually no verbal response to the stimulus in the left visual hemifield until the left hemisphere realizes that the patient's left hand is also in action, pointing to the left hemifield stimulus. Split-brain patients may be unable to name aloud objects presented in the left hemifield. This problem is usually not evident in patients with left hemialexia from acquired splenial lesions (usually with right hemianopia from a left posterior cerebral artery territory infarction), but see Poeck (1984), whose patient with alexia was also unable to name objects (i.e., had optic anomia as well as hemialexia).

Left hemialexia. Subjects with left hemialexia cannot read individual words flashed to the left hemifield even in the absence of hemianopia. This is true not only for complete callosotomy, but also for patients with section of only the splenium (Trescher & Ford, 1937; Maspes, 1948; Gazzaniga & Freedman, 1973; Damasio et al., 1980; Sugishita et al., 1986; Sugishita & Yoshioka, 1987). It is sometimes possible to demonstrate left hemialexia by the brief presentations of cards, showing printed letters or short words, in the left hemifield. Patients are often unable to read a card presented this way, although they can readily read it when it is presented in the right hemifield. When presented with a compound word, such as "houseboat," patients with injury to the splenium may read only the right half of the word ("boat"). Although eye movements are usually too active for such simple testing methods, hemialexia was, in fact, observed using such methods, long before its demonstration by tachistoscopic presentation (Trescher & Ford, 1937). Hemialexia has been intensively studied with both tachistoscopic and computerized techniques by Sugishita et al. (1986, 1987; see also Gruesser & Landis, 1991).

Compensation. There is some apparent recovery over the years, part of which is attributable to semantic transfer; that is, the word in the LVF is recognized by the right hemisphere and this semantic information somehow transfers to the speaking left hemisphere, which can then approximate the stimulus word. Reading a word in the LVF is most likely to be successful if the stimuli are known and not too numerous, and the diffusely distributed semantic information may be used to identify the word (Myers and Sperry, 1985; Sidtis et al., 1981a; Cronin-Golomb, 1986b; Sugishita et al., 1986; Zaidel et al., 1990).

AUDITION

Left Hemisphere Suppression of Ipsilateral Verbal Input in Dichotic Listening

Auditory information to each ear crosses at the level of the superior olive and the midbrain (inferior colliculus); however, there are also ipsilateral projections, so that even in the split-brain patient, each hemisphere receives input from both ears. Monaural stimulation therefore projects to both hemispheres. Dichotic stimulation, in which distinct but acoustically similar stimuli are presented simultaneously to each ear, suppresses the ipsilateral projections (extinction) and reveals an advantage for the contralateral ear-hemisphere projections in normal subjects. Which of the competing two contralateral stimuli is identified depends upon the degree to which the ipsilateral stimulus is suppressed by the stronger contralateral auditory projections, and also upon hemisphere specialization for processing the specific type of auditory input. Thus, when verbal stimuli are used, there is a right ear advantage in normal subjects, because the left hemisphere preferentially analyzes the verbal stimuli, and contralateral (right ear) projections to the left hemisphere dominate weaker ipsilateral (left ear) or cross-callosal projections. In split-brain subjects, this right ear advantage becomes much more pronounced (Milner et al., 1968; Sparks & Geschwind, 1968; Gordon, 1975; Springer & Gazzaniga, 1975; Zaidel, 1976, 1983; Zaidel et al., 1990), suggesting that interruption of callosal transfer prevents the left hemisphere from accessing auditory information from the left ear via the right hemisphere. Both ipsilateral suppression and hemispheric competence can be assessed in the split-brain patient by using lateralized visual probes to be matched with the sound in either ear (Zaidel, 1983). Although left ear words are poorly reported verbally, their perception by the right hemisphere is occasionally evidenced by appropriate actions of the left hand (Gordon, 1973).

Left ear extinction has also been found in patients with lesions of the left hemisphere when the lesions are fairly deep and are apt to interrupt commissural fibers. Since left hemisphere lesions are usually associated with perceptual degradation of stimuli presented to the right ear, the suppression of the left ear by a left hemisphere lesion has been called "paradoxical ipsilateral extinction" (Sparks et al., 1970). Further observations support the conclusion that lesions close to the midline in either hemisphere cause suppression of left ear stimuli by interrupting interhemispheric pathways (Michel & Peronnet, 1975; Damasio & Damasio, 1979; Cambier et al., 1984; Rubens et al., 1985; Rao et al., 1989; Pujol et al., 1991). Because paracallosal lesions can also result in right ear extinction for nonverbal material, such as that used in a complex pitch discrimination task, it has been suggested that the so-called paradoxical loss would better be termed "callosal extinction" (Sidtis et al., 1989).

Right Hemisphere Suppression of Nonverbal Ipsilateral Auditory Input in Dichotic Listening

Patient L.B. was tested on a verbal identification version of Ley and Bryden's (1982) dichotic words/emotions test. This test consists of four rhyming consonant-vowel-consonant (CVC) words spoken using four different emotional prosodic intonations. The word identification task yielded a massive right ear advantage, whereas the emotional identification test yielded a massive left ear advantage, consistent with (a) right hemispheric suppression of the ipsilateral nonverbal emotional prosodic auditory input, (b) left hemisphere suppression of the ipsilateral verbal auditory input, (c) right hemisphere specialization for recognition of emotional prosody, and (d) complementary left hemisphere specialization for words. This complementary specialization is observed in the normal brain as well (Ley & Bryden, 1982). The simplest account of this pattern of results is that (a) there is good ipsilateral suppression for both tasks in both hemispheres; (b) the left hemisphere specializes for and dominates the identification of the words, exhibiting an expected massive right ear advantage; (c) the right hemisphere specializes for and dominates the identification of emotional prosody, yielding a massive left ear advantage; and (d) verbal identification of the emotions reflects either right hemisphere speech or else left hemisphere verbalization of the emotion or a code identifying it, which is transferred subcallosally from the right hemisphere to the left hemisphere.

Sidtis (1988) demonstrated that apparent advantage also exists in the disconnected right hemisphere for complex pitch discrimination. Tramo and Barucha (1991) further found an advantage for the disconnected right hemisphere for harmonic progression and associative auditory function.

SOMESTHESIS

Somatosensory projections to the hemispheres are more lateralized than auditory projections, but not as completely contralateral as visual projections. The medial lemniscus system, which is mainly involved in the transmission of tactile and proprioceptive input, and even more the spinothalamic system, which mainly transmits thermal and pain sensations, both project not only contralaterally, but also ipsilaterally. Although ipsilateral connections from distal body parts are almost absent, those from axial and proximal body parts are dense. Somesthetic afferents from the face go to both ipsi- and contralateral cortical areas (Berlucchi & Aglioti, 1999).

Failure of Interhemispheric Transfer

The lack of interhemispheric transfer following CCC can be demonstrated with respect to somestheses (including touch, pressure, and proprioception) in a variety of ways.

Cross-retrieval of Small Test Objects. The patient is given an object to feel with one hand, and then asked to retrieve the same object from among a number of objects. Such a collection is most conveniently placed in a paper plate about 15 cm in diameter, around which the subject can shuffle the objects with one hand while exploring for the test object. What distinguishes the split-brain patients from normal subjects is that their excellent same-hand retrieval (with either hand) is not accompanied by ability to retrieve with one hand objects felt with the other.

Cross-replication of Hand Postures. Specific postures impressed on one (unseen) hand by the examiners cannot be mimicked by the patient's opposite hand. But if more proximal

stimuli are used, it may be difficult to demonstrate any failure of interhemispheric communication, probably because of ipsilateral hemispheric projections of sensory stimuli.

Intermanual Point Localization. After CCC, there is a partial loss of the ability to name exact points stimulated on the left side of the body. This defect is least apparent, if at all, on the face and it is most apparent on the distal extremities, especially the fingertips. This deficit is not dependent on language, as it can be done in a nonverbal fashion and in both directions (right to left and vice versa).

Young children also have difficulty in cross-localizing or cross-matching (Galin et al., 1977, 1979; but cf. Pipe, 1991), possibly because their commissures are not yet fully functioning (Yakovlev & Lecours, 1967; but cf. Brody et al., 1987; Baierl et al., 1988). Immaturity of transcallosal inhibition has been suggested as the source of unnecessary duplication during simple reaching (Lehman, 1978).

Hemispheric Specialization and Tactile Anomia

One of the most convincing ways to demonstrate hemispheric disconnection is to ask the patient to feel with one hand and then to name various small, common objects, in the absence of vision. Unilateral anomia is a reliable and persistent sign following callosotomy. Of the many maneuvers developed in the laboratory to test split-brain patients, this is the principal one to be adopted as part of a routine neurological examination.

Patients with extensive callosal lesions are commonly unable to name or describe an object held in the left hand, although they readily name objects held in the right hand. Sometimes a recovering patient can give a vague description of the object, but still be unable to name it. After a patient with a callosal lesion has regained the ability to name objects in the left hand, this ability may extinguish (Mayer et al., 1988) with dichaptic stimulation (i.e., by placing an object in each hand simultaneously) (Witelson, 1974).

To establish hemispheric disconnection, it is necessary to exclude other causes of unilateral anomia, particularly astereognosis (or even a gross sensory deficit), as may occur with a right parietal lesion. The best way to exclude astereognosis or tactile agnosia (Caselli, 1991) is to show that the object has in fact been recognized, even though it cannot be verbally identified or described, by retrieving it correctly from a collection of similar objects, as described above.

Compensatory Mechanisms

When testing for anomia, the examiner must be aware that certain clever patients may have strategies for circumventing their deficit. For example, the patient may drop an object or may manipulate it in some other way (such as running a fingernail down the teeth of a comb) to produce a characteristic noise by which the object can be identified. In the same vein, a subject may identify a pipe or some other object by a characteristic smell and thus circumvent the inability of the left hemisphere to identify, by palpation alone, an object in the left hand.

With time, it may be increasingly difficult to demonstrate any hemispheric disconnection, even using distal stimuli. E. Zaidel (1998b) found that persisting deficits in tests of stereognosis often reflected extracallosal damage rather than failure of interhemispheric transfer.

Neuroimaging

Fabri et al. (1999) imaged normal controls and callosotomy patients from the Ancona series with functional MRI (fMRI) during unilateral somatosensory stimulation. Normal subjects showed contralateral activation in SI, posterior parietal cortex, and parietal opercular cortex, as well as ipsilateral activation in homologous posterior parietal and parietal opercular cortex. In patients with anterior callosal section up to and including the posterior body, ipsilateral activation was missing, indicating that the posterior third of the body of the CC is critical in the interhemispheric transfer of somatosensory information.

MOTOR FUNCTIONS

Simple Reaction Time and the Crossed–Uncrossed Difference

Simple reaction time (SRT) may be the simplest complete cognitive task that can be specified in either cognitive or neuroscientific terms. Subjects press a button with the right or left hand when they detect a light patch in the left or the right visual hemifield. The most common approach for measuring interhemispheric transfer time is the SRT task of Poffenberger (1912). When subjects respond with the hand ipsilateral to the visual stimulus (uncrossed), the same hemisphere processes the visual stimulus and initiates the motor response, and therefore there is no need for transfer of information through the CC. In contrast, when the stimulus is contralateral to the responding hand (crossed), the hemisphere opposite to the one controlling the responding hand receives the visual stimulus, and thus a transfer of information through callosal fibers is needed. The difference in reaction times between the two crossed responses (LVF targets with right hand responses, and RVF targets with left hand responses) and the two uncrossed responses (LVF targets with left hand responses, and RVF targets with right hand responses) (divided by 2) is an estimate of interhemispheric conduction time. Typically, in normal subjects this, difference, called the *crossed–uncrossed difference* (CUD), is 3–4 msec, whereas in split–brain patients it is 30–60 msec, and in callosal agenesis patients it is 15–20 msec (Clarke & Zaidel, 1989; Marzi et al., 1991). Motor transfer is sensitive to the motor demands of the reaction time paradigm, and changing or alternating response finger can change reaction times. By the same token, visual transfer is sensitive to visual parameters, such as brightness or eccentricity. Many experiments support the conclusion that information in the crossed conditions is transferred through callosal motor channels. For example, Iacoboni et al. (1994) studied a patient before and after partial callosotomy sparing the splenium of the CC. They found evidence for motor transfer before surgery and for visual transfer following it. In a later study, Iacoboni and Zaidel (1995) manipulated motor and visual parameters in both normal subjects and split-brain patients with results supporting the same conclusions.

In a recent study, however, Mooshagian et al. (2009) found that the CUD can be influenced by attentional factors (spatial compatibility), not only in normal subjects, but also in patients with split and acallosal brains. This suggests that the CUD may not represent a pure index of interhemispheric conduction delay and that attentional factors may have to be measured and "subtracted out" to obtain an accurate estimate of interhemispheric conduction. Saron et al. (2003) has event-related potential (ERP) evidence that, in the Poffenberger SRT task, the motor code transfers back and forth between hemispheres several times before the response. However, control over the response appears to remain in the hemisphere of input (Zaidel, 1986).

Bimanual Motor Control

If the left hemisphere controls the right hand and the right hemisphere controls the left hand, how then does a person perform bimanual motor activities, and what is the role of the CC in their organization? Classic as well as recent studies on callosal involvement in bimanual motor control suggest that overlearned bimanual motor sequences, including either parallel or alternating sequences, do not require intact callosal fibers, whereas novel bimanual motor sequences, such as those requiring interdependent bimanual control, cannot be learned with or without visual guidance if callosal fibers are transected (D. Zaidel & Sperry, 1977; Franz et al., 2000).

Are the temporal and spatial characteristics of bimanual movements dissociable? Franz et al. (1996) have shown that normal subjects produce trajectory errors when the spatial demands of the task differ between the two hands. Remarkably, callosal patients were not impaired in this task. Temporal synchrony, however, was similar in normal subjects and in split-brain patients, suggesting that spatial control and temporal synchronization are dissociable. In an earlier study, Tuller and Kelso (1989) demonstrated that phase-locked bimanual movements are very stable in split-brain patients, whereas intermediate states between in-phase and antiphase coordinated patterns are severely affected. This, again, suggests that the desynchronization of complex temporal patterns between the two hands requires callosal connections. More recently, Ivry and Hazeltine (1999) looked at the synchronization of manual responses to acoustic timing signals in a callosotomy patient. The task required the

patient to synchronize bimanual or unimanual responses to auditory tones. Both normal subjects and the patient demonstrated less temporal variability in the bimanual condition, suggesting that motor commands are not integrated by callosal fibers in this task.

Motor "Dominance"

Two recent studies have investigated motor representations in split-brain subjects. One study used transcranial magnetic stimulation (TMS) to investigate corticospinal facilitation during action observation in the left and right motor cortex of a split-brain patient (Fecteau et al., 2005). The rationale behind this study is that mirror neurons—premotor neurons that activate during action observation (for a review, see Iacoboni & Dapretto, 2006)—should "prime" the motor cortex and facilitate the corticospinal motor system. Transcranial magnetic stimulation on this split-brain subject demonstrated corticospinal facilitation restricted to the left hemisphere, whereas in control subjects the effect was bilateral. These results need to be confirmed in other split-brain patients, but they suggest that, in the split-brain patient, premotor mirroring mechanisms may be restricted to the left hemisphere.

Another recent study investigated the relationships between tool use skills and hand dominance in callosotomy patients (Frey et al., 2005). In right-handers, tool use representations are also lateralized to the left hemisphere. Are tool use representations restricted to the hemisphere that controls the dominant hand? In callosotomy patients with both right and left hand preference, tool use representations were lateralized to the left hemisphere, thus demonstrating that these motor representations are not anchored to manual preference.

Deficits Due to Hemispheric Specialization

Following callosal section, right-handed patients are often unable to correctly execute verbal commands with the left hand movements that they can readily and accurately execute with the right hand. Historically, this was the first callosal symptom described. In the absence of an elemental motor deficit, a pronounced inability to perform certain movements with the left hand in response to verbal command is strong evidence for a callosal lesion. There are two explanations for this deficit, not mutually exclusive. First, it can reflect right hemispheric disconnection from left hemisphere language comprehension: The right hemisphere (left hand) cannot perform the commanded movement because it does not comprehend the command. Second, it may reflect left hemisphere dominance for motor control: The disconnected right hemisphere may understand the command, but may not have the ability to execute the command correctly. Nonverbal tasks, such as imitation or the use of three-dimensional objects, may help separate verbal comprehension from motor programming deficits (see also Chapter 10).

The study of motor control in the absence of the CC is important to better understand theoretical aspects of motor behavior and to design better interventions in clinical populations. The first systematic study of motor control in the split-brain patient was reported by D. Zaidel and Sperry (1977) for patients in the Los Angeles series. Tachistoscopic presentations of drawings of hand postures to the two visual hemifields of split-brain patients have shown that they can actually imitate hand postures with either hand, as long as the hand used for imitation is ipsilateral to the visual hemifield of presentation (Sperry, 1974). Studies of patients with unilateral brain damage, however, suggest that, in right-handers, the left hemisphere plays a dominant role in posture execution (see Chapter 10).

Apraxia. Early split-brain studies suggested that left hand apraxia in commissurotomy patients is restricted to apraxia to verbal commands. Those studies found no substantial difference in imitative performance between the right and the left hand (Sperry, 1974; Volpe, 1982). However, more recently, Lausberg et al. (2003) found selective left hand apraxia in split-brain patients asked to pantomime visually presented objects. These deficits did not occur in the left hand with the use of actual objects. The authors' analysis of "concept errors" by the left hand led them to conclude that the errors reflected right hemisphere control, rather than ipsilateral left

hemisphere control. Working with hemisphere-damaged patients, Lausberg and Cruz (2004) showed that imitation of the positions of the hand relative to the head is strongly lateralized to the left hemisphere, whereas imitation of finger configurations can be performed competently in either hemisphere. Furthermore, Lausberg and Cruz (2004) performed an experiment that required callosotomy and commissurotomy patients to imitate hand–head positions and finger configurations presented in free vision or in each visual hemifield. Some split-brain patients did, and some did not, show a right hemisphere deficit in imitating hand–head positions, but none showed a deficit in imitating finger configurations. Withdrawal of visual input deteriorated imitation of finger configurations in the split-brain patients, but not in the control subjects. Moreover, in split-brain patients, lateralized presentations deteriorated performance relative to free vision. These findings highlight several methodological and theoretical caveats. First, individual differences exist in performance across patients. Second, the performance of the disconnected hemispheres is sensitive to the method of assessment (free vision vs. hemifield tachistoscopy vs. continuously lateralized presentations with free scanning). Third, differences often exist between the performance of patients with hemispheric damage and of patients with disconnection. Fourth, differences often exist between behavioral laterality effects in normal subjects and in patients with disconnection.

Compensatory Mechanisms

Immediately after surgery, all of the patients were unable to perform correctly actions to verbal commands using their left limbs, such as "Wiggle your left toes," or "Make a fist with your left hand." The degree of left hand (and left foot) deficit is subject to individual differences. The left limb dyspraxia is attributable to the simultaneous presence of two deficits: poor comprehension by the right hemisphere (which has good control of the left hand), and poor ipsilateral control by the left hemisphere (which understands very well). Subsidence of the dyspraxia can therefore result from two compensatory mechanisms: increased right hemisphere comprehension of words, and increased left hemisphere control of the left hand. The capacity of either hemisphere, and particularly of the left hemisphere, to control the ipsilateral hand varies from one patient to another, both in the immediate postoperative period and many years later. The extent of ipsilateral motor control can be tested by flashing to the right or left visual hemifield sketches of thumb and fingers in different postures, for the subject to mimic with one or the other hand. Responses are poor with the hand on the side opposite the visual input, with simple postures such as a closed fist or an open hand being attainable after further recovery. As recovery proceeds, good ipsilateral control is first attained for responses carried out by the more proximal musculature. After several months, most of these patients can form a variety of hand and finger postures with either hand to verbal instructions such as "Make a circle with your thumb and little finger."

Subsidence of the apraxia continues, but even after many years, left-sided apraxia to verbal command can still be demonstrated (Zaidel & Sperry, 1977; Trope et al., 1987), sometimes under paradoxical circumstances. Thus, using visual hemifield tachistoscopy throughout, split-brain patients are sometimes unable to follow verbal commands with the left hand even though they can demonstrate, separately, good recognition of the printed verb and of the pictured action (E. Zaidel, 2001a). Detailed models of the underlying compensatory neural–behavioral processes remain to be developed. Such models need to account for the type of movement that is imitated and the method of presentation.

LANGUAGE

The split-brain person provides a unique perspective on the independent contribution of each cerebral hemisphere to language processing and on the role of interhemispheric interaction in normal language function. However, although the absence of the CC reduces interhemispheric facilitation, inhibition, and cooperation, it does not eliminate them completely. Descriptive clinical observations of language in the acute and chronically split-brain patient

are presented, followed by an analysis of right hemisphere capacities in language comprehension and production.

Clinical Presentation

Postcallosotomy Mutism. It was first thought that mutism following callosotomy was simply a neighborhood sign, a partial form of akinetic mutism (without the akinesia) that resulted from retraction around the anterior end of the third ventricle during section of the anterior commissure (Cairns, 1952; Ross & Stewart, 1981; Lebrun, 1990) or retraction of medial frontal lobe (Fuiks et al., 1991; Reeves, 1991). However, there is evidence to suggest that more persistent mutism may in fact result from hemispheric disconnection rather than from medial frontal extracallosal damage. Bogen (1998) had a number of patients who did not have mutism, despite extensive retraction of either anterior third ventricle or mesial right frontal cortex or both. In these patients, commissural section spared the splenium. Rayport et al. (1983; personal communication to J.E. Bogen from S. Ferguson in 1991) observed in three of eight cases with staged callosotomy a marked decrease in spontaneous speech without paraphasia, comprehension deficit, or an inability to sing. This deficit occurred only after the second stage of surgery. Notable was the absence of any mutism after the first stage (rostrum, genu, and most of the trunk); the mutism appeared only after the second stage (splenium and remainder of the trunk). It had been proposed that hemispheric disconnection may lead to mutism because of an unusual interdependence of the hemispheres in language function secondary to early brain injury or abnormal development. This may lead to anomalous (including bilateral) speech representation (Bogen & Vogel, 1975; Bogen, 1976; Sussman et al., 1983; Sass et al., 1990), and particularly to discordant manual and speech dominance (Ferguson et al., 1985; Spencer et al., 1988), which creates unusual dependence on interhemispheric interaction for speech programming. Mutism may thus result from interhemispheric conflict (possibly at a brainstem level) or from a bilateral diaschisis that affects speech much more than writing (Bogen, 1976; Ferguson et al., 1985).

Quattrini et al. (1997) reviewed postcallosotomy mutism in 36 patients of the Ancona series. Two out of eight patients with complete two-stage sections and eight out of 27 with anterior callosotomies had transient mutism lasting from 4 to 25 days. One patient with a splenial section had no mutism. The two patients with complete callosotomy had mutism after both the initial anterior and the subsequent posterior callosal sections. Mutism was accompanied by good speech comprehension (following of verbal commands) and writing. Recovery from mutism was always complete. Mutism was not associated with left-handedness, but it was associated with more complex surgical manipulation.

Mild Pragmatic Deficit. Although seemingly normal on clinical aphasiological tests, more subtle observation reveals persistent lacunae in the language repertoires of patients with cerebral commissurotomy. These lacunae include chronic impoverishment of verbal description of personal emotional experience (alexithymia, cf. TenHouten et al., 1986), failure to sustain adequate comprehension when reading paragraphs or extended text (Zaidel, 1982), and deficits in conversational interaction. The lacunae involve pragmatics, rather than phonology and syntax, and are highly variable across patients. They include social inappropriateness by failing to follow leads, using inappropriate rules of politeness, and a tendency to rationalize mistakes and confabulate reasons for strange behavior.

Formal testing of the pragmatic ability of (the left hemisphere of) commissurotomy patients L.B., N.G., A.A., and R.Y. with the Right Hemisphere Communication Battery (Gardner and Brownell, 1986) showed consistently severe deficits across all patients in three tests: appreciation of prosody, the understanding of pictorial metaphors, and the retelling of stories, reflecting impaired recognition of emotion, nonliteral language, and integrative processes (discourse), respectively. This suggests selective normal right hemisphere contribution to those subtests (Spence et al., 1990). To varying degrees, however, all four patients showed a consistent and frequent use of humor in conversation. They also used common idioms and proverbs appropriately and frequently, and their gestures and intonation seemed normal.

Clinical and Experimental Assessment of Language in the Disconnected Right Hemisphere

Auditory comprehension of nouns by the disconnected right hemisphere is suggested by the subject's ability to retrieve with the left hand various objects named aloud by the examiner. Comprehension of printed words by the disconnected right hemisphere is often present, especially for short, concrete, high-frequency words. For example, after a printed noun is flashed to the left visual hemifield, the subjects are typically able to retrieve with the left hand the designated item from among an array of objects hidden from view. Ipsilateral control by the disconnected left hemisphere in these tests is excluded because incorrect verbal descriptions given by the subject immediately after a correct response by the left hand show that only the disconnected right hemisphere knew the answer.

There follows a more detailed consideration of observations in two series of callosotomy patients: the Los Angeles series (Zaidel's lab) and the Dartmouth-Toledo series (Gazzaniga's lab). The two laboratories use different patients and somewhat different methodologies, and one should exercise caution in making comparisons between them.

The Los Angeles, California Series. L.B. and N.G. have been the focus of the most comprehensive experimental studies of right hemisphere language in patients with complete commissurotomy. These studies employed a contact lens system for presenting extended displays and permitting free ocular scanning by one hemisphere at a time (Zaidel, 1975). Some language competence in the disconnected right hemisphere has been reported in other patients, including auditory comprehension by A.A. (Nebes, 1971; Nebes & Sperry, 1971), right hemisphere execution of verbal commands by

R.Y. (Gordon, 1980), phonological encoding in the right hemisphere of C.C. (Levy & Trevarthen, 1977), and auditory comprehension by the right hemisphere in N.W. and RM. (Bogen, 1979).

Phonetics/phonology, syntax, lexical semantics, and pragmatics. The DRHs have poor auditory discrimination (Zaidel, 1978b) and poor phonetic identification (Zaidel, 1983) (e.g., in dichotic listening to nonsense stop consonant-vowel [CV] syllables). They also have a poor short-term verbal memory (Token Test; Zaidel, 1977) with a capacity of 3 ± 1 items, similar to anterior aphasics. The disconnected right hemisphere cannot match words for rhyming—that is, it has no grapheme–phoneme conversion rules (Zaidel & Peters, 1981)—and must read words through a whole-word lexical route (Zaidel, 1998a).

The disconnected right hemisphere has access to some rudimentary syntactic structures, such as passives or negatives; it finds grammatical categories easier than syntactic structures; and it finds lexicalized morphological constructions easier than inflected ones. When processing syntax, it seems particularly constrained by memory load (Zaidel, 2001a).

The disconnected right hemisphere has a rich and diverse auditory lexicon, and it recognizes a variety of semantic relations. It has linguistic access to both episodic and semantic information, and its semantic network is organized connotatively. The visual lexicon is smaller and organized differently than in the disconnected left hemisphere. The disconnected right hemisphere has abstract letter identities (Eviatar & Zaidel, 1994). It can perform lexical decision, and it exhibits sensitivity to word frequency (Zaidel, 2001a) and concreteness (Eviatar et al., 1990) but not to grapheme–phoneme regularity (Zaidel & Peters, 1981; Zaidel, 2001a). It is sensitive to format distortion (zigzag, vertical), especially for words (Zaidel, 2001a).

Developmental profile. The disconnected right hemisphere does not exhibit a uniform mental age profile in a sample of auditory language functions (Zaidel, 1978b). Its competence tends to be in the range of normal 3- to 6-year-olds, but it has little or no speech, and

its auditory vocabulary can reach an adult level (Zaidel, 1976).

The Dartmouth-Toledo Series.

Phonetics/phonology, syntax, and lexical semantics. Patient V.P. showed a right hemisphere ability to discriminate CV syllables (Sidtis et al., 1981b), and patient J.W. showed phonetic competence in the disconnected right hemisphere by being able to combine visual and auditory cues to produce the McGurk Illusion (Baynes et al., 1994). All five patients (P.S., V.P., J.W., D.R., and V.J.) showed good comprehension of single spoken words by the disconnected right hemisphere. Those tested (P.S., V.P., J.W.) showed some grammatical competence. V.P. and J.W. could perform grammaticality judgments and disambiguate syntactically ambiguous sentences but not identify passive sentences. Similar to the California patients, their disconnected right hemispheres have some grammatical competence but poor grammatical performance.

All five patients could read single words, some (I.W., D.R.) as many as they could comprehend aurally. P.S. and V.P., but not J.W., had grapheme–phoneme conversion in the disconnected right hemisphere. All five patients displayed considerable lexical semantic flexibility in the disconnected right hemisphere.

Writing. The acute disconnection syndrome usually includes left hand agraphia. Only P.S. and V.P. could write with the left hand. V.J.'s most severe postoperative language deficit was bilateral agraphia (Baynes et al., 1998). V.J. was left-handed and left hemisphere dominant for speech. She had two-stage callosotomy at age 41 with loss of writing in either hand (Baynes et al., 1998). Although V.J. was left hemisphere dominant for speech, she had reduced speech output after callosotomy. Agraphia has been reported as a consequence of callosotomy in other patients discordant for speech and manual dominance (Spencer et al., 1988), but not universally (Gur et al., 1984). V.J.'s left hemisphere could speak and understand, read and spell aloud. Thus, it could control both spoken and written language. V.J.'s right hemisphere could not speak, but it could understand spoken and written language and it could make lexical decisions (i.e., it was similar to the disconnected right hemisphere of L.B.). It could copy but not write spontaneously to dictation or give the name of a picture in the LVF. Thus, the writing deficit of the left hemisphere appears peripheral, at the level of "allographs." V.J.'s right hemisphere, in turn, had no "output graphemic buffer" (Margolin, 1984).

Right hemisphere speech. One of the most important recent developments in the study of language in the disconnected right hemisphere is arguably the emergence of right hemisphere speech. The data on right hemisphere speech in relation to other language functions in the California and Dartmouth-Toledo series can be summarized as follows (see Table 13-2):

- Right hemisphere speech is most likely to occur soon after surgery and to show the greatest range in patients with early damage to language cortex in the left hemisphere.
- Evidence for apparent right hemisphere speech is more likely to occur in patients who show evidence for linguistic transfer between the hemispheres.
- In most patients right hemisphere speech never emerges or develops at all.

A convenient, but not definitive, method of establishing the presence of speech in the right hemisphere of a split-brain patient is to require the subject to read aloud words presented in the LVF with and without word/nonword distractors presented in the opposite VF. Briefly, if reading aloud of LVF words is indifferent to RVF distractors, then it is concluded that the right hemisphere does the actual "reading" (Zaidel, 1998a).

Left hand agraphia. Normal right-handers can write legibly, if not fluently, with the left hand. This ability is commonly lost with callosal lesions, especially (but not always) those that cause unilateral apraxia (Gersh & Damasio, 1981). Inability to write to dictation is common with left hemisphere lesions (also see Chapter 7), but the deficit is almost always present in both hands. In contrast, patients with callosal disconnection are able to copy simple or even complex geometric figures with their left hand, despite being unable to write with the left hand or even copy writing previously made with their own right hand (Bogen & Gazzaniga, 1965; Bogen, 1969a; Kumar, 1977; Zaidel & Sperry, 1977; Della Sala et al., 1991). Copying of block letters may be present when the copying of cursive writing is not; this may not represent printing with the left hand, but rather only copying of geometric figures that happen also to have linguistic content.

Summary. Whereas more behavioral data are needed to characterize right hemisphere speech and more physiological data are needed to delineate the conditions under which it is expressed, the overwhelming neuropsychological evidence suggests that the disconnected right hemisphere has a unique linguistic profile, although different experimental populations yield somewhat different profiles, and there are considerable individual differences. When the right hemisphere is disconnected from the left hemisphere, the emerging right hemisphere language profile is characterized by (a) much better language comprehension than speech; (b) better auditory comprehension than reading; (c) visual word recognition that proceeds via (abstract) ideography or through orthographic rules, but without grapheme–phoneme translation, so that lexical representations are "addressed" rather than "assembled"; (d) a rich lexical semantic system, but poor phonology and an impoverished syntax; and (e) paralinguistic competence in appreciating the communicative significance of emotional prosody and facial expressions.

Table 13-3 shows four patterns of lexical language in the disconnected right hemisphere. All patients have a substantial auditory lexicon and at least a moderate reading vocabulary. The difference in patterns across individual patients is in terms of speech and writing. First, some patients, such as P.S. and V.P., have early evidence for rich right hemisphere speech and writing. Second, some patients, such as L.B. and J.W., develop intermittent right hemisphere control of speech. Third, most patients, such as N.G., R.Y., A.A., and D.R., never develop right hemisphere speech. Finally, left-handed patients with left hemisphere language

Table 13–2. Summary of Language Abilities of Right Hemispheres of Split-brain Patients from the California and Dartmouth-Toledo Series

Patient	AUDITORY LANGUAGE COMPREHENSION			READING						ACTIONS WITH LEFT HAND				
	Phonetics	Words	Sentences	Words	Sentences	GPC	Lex. Dec.	Lexical Semantics	Grammar	Pictures	Auditory	Written	Writing	Speech
L.B.	+[a]	+	−	+	−	−	+	+	+[d]	+	+[d]	+[d]	−	+[f]
N.G.	+[a]	+	−	+	−	−	+[d]	+	+[d]	+	+[d]	+[d]	−	−
R.Y.	−	+	0	+	−	−	+[d]	0	0	0	+[d]	0	−	−
A.A.	−	+	0	+	−	−	+[d]	0	0	0	+[d]	0	−	−
N.W.	0	+	0	0	0	0	0	0	0	0	+[d]	0	−	−
C.C.	0	0	0	0	0	0	0	0	0	0	+[d]	0	−	−
P.S.	0	+	+	+	0	+	0	+	+	+[c]	+[c]	+	+	+
V.P.	+[a]	+	0	+	0	+	+[d]	+	+[e]	0	+[c]	+	+	+
J.W.	+	+	0	+	0	−	+[d]	+	+[d,e]	+	+[c]	+[d]	−	+[f]
D.R.	0	+	0	+[b]	−[c]	0	+[d]	+	0	0	−[f]	−[c]	−	−
V.J.	0	+	0	+	0	0	+	0	0	0	0	0	−	−

GPC, grapheme–phoneme correspondance rules; +, present; −, absent; 0, not tested.
[a]Phoneme discrimination, not identification. [b]Slow. [c]Assumed. [d]Limited. [e]Grammatically judgment but not grammatical comprehension. [f]Occasionally.

Table 13–3. Lexical Language in the Disconnected Right Hemisphere

Patients	Auditory Comprehension	Reading	Speech	Writing
Early RH speech: P.S., V.P.	+	+	+	+
Late, occasional RH speech: L.B., J.W.	+	+	~+	−
No RH speech: N.G., R.Y., A.A., D.R.	+	+	−	−
Left-handed, LH dominant for speech: V.J.	+	+	−	−

RH, right hemisphere; +, present; −, absent.

dominance, such as V.J., may suffer some loss of fluency and may be agraphic in both hands. The fact that all disconnected right hemispheres understand at least some spoken language is important to the clinician: Testing of the disconnected right hemisphere can be facilitated with verbal instructions. However, every effort should be made to illustrate the task nonverbally, so as not to bias the results in favor of the disconnected left hemisphere.

Gesture. Kimura (1973) believes that the linguistically dominant (left) hemisphere is exclusively specialized for language as well as for motor control (cf. Liepmann & Maas, 1907) and therefore also for the production of spontaneous speech-accompanying gestures. This view was challenged by Lausberg et al. (2007) in a series of systematic studies with complete commissurotomy patients, callosotomy patients, and normal participants. They concluded that communicative gestures with each hand, with and without speech production, reflect the specialization of the contralateral hemisphere for the type of gesture. In one study, Kita and Lausberg (2008) examined gestures based on spatial imagery (i.e., iconic gestures with observer viewpoint) and compared them to abstract deictic gestures. They found that patients with complete commissurotomy or with callosotomy produced spatial imagery gestures with the left as well as with the right hand. In another study, Lausberg et al. (2007) examined hand preferences in gesture types in spontaneous gesticulation during standardized interviews. Patients exhibited a reliable left hand preference for spontaneous communicative gestures despite left hand agraphia and apraxia. Specifically, the patients displayed baton-tosses and shrugs more often with the left hand, but exhibited a right hand preference for pantomime gestures. The authors proposed that left hand gestures reflect the specialization of the right hemisphere for functions such as prosody or emotion. These findings are important for several reasons: first, they reflect complementary hemispheric specialization during communication; second, they demonstrate that each hemisphere can automatically control the contralateral hand to support its own cognitive repertoire; and third, they show that continuity between action and language is consistent with evolutionary theories that hypothesize the gestural origin of the hemispheric specialization of language.

VISUOSPATIAL, VISUOPERCEPTUAL, AND VISUOCONSTRUCTIVE FUNCTIONS

Binocular Rivalry

Binocular rivalry refers to the suppression of an image presented to one eye when a different image is presented simultaneously to the other eye. The results of a recent study of binocular rivalry in a split-brain patient (O'Shea & Corballis, 2005) suggest that rivalry is fully processed independently in each cerebral hemisphere. These findings are consistent with the idea of independent consciousnesses in each hemisphere (Bogen, 2000).

Stereopsis

Only midline stereopsis requires interhemispheric integration. Thus, off the midsagittal plane in front of or behind the fixation point, callosal section does not affect stereopsis

(Gazzaniga et al., 1965). Split-brain patients show significant midline deficits with random dot stereograms, with disparities ranging from 15 to 180 minute arc within 1 to 3 degrees off the vertical meridian (Hamilton & Vermeire, 1986). In contrast, Lassonde (1986) described a deficit in tachistoscopic depth perception in commissurotomy patients over the entire field, attributable to loss of nonspecific diffuse callosal contributions (but see Rivest et al., 1994).

Space

The disconnected right hemisphere was found to be superior to the disconnected left hemisphere in part/whole and gestalt completion tasks (Nebes, 1974); on modified forms of standardized spatial relations tests, such as the Differential Aptitude Test (Levy, 1974; Kumar, 1977); on the use of perspective cues to assist in accurate perception (Cronin-Golomb, 1986a); and on tests of geometric invariance (Euclidean, Affine, projective, and topological) (Franco & Sperry, 1977). The disconnected left hemisphere was found to be superior in figure–ground disembedding (Zaidel, 1978a).

More recently, Funnell et al. (1999) found that the disconnected right hemisphere of callosotomy patient J.W. from the Dartmouth-Toledo series was superior to the disconnected left hemisphere in matching of mirror-reversed stimuli. From their findings, they concluded that both disconnected hemispheres can perform pattern recognition, but that the disconnected right hemisphere is specialized for processing spatial information. Corballis et al. (1999) studied illusory contours and amodal completion in two callosotomy patients from the Dartmouth-Toledo series (J.W. and V.P.) and found equal bilateral perception of illusory contours in the disconnected hemispheres, but better amodal completion in the disconnected right hemisphere. They concluded that illusory contours might be attributed to low-level visual processes common to both hemispheres, whereas amodal completion reflects a higher-level, lateralized process.

Because of large individual differences, results obtained from a few patients should be interpreted with caution until they are confirmed in larger samples of callosum-sectioned patients, or better, in lateralized paradigms with normal subjects.

Visual Imagery

Different components of visual imagery are differentially lateralized. Mental rotation shows superiority in the disconnected right hemisphere (Farah et al., 1985; Corballis & Sergent, 1988). Image generation shows superiority in the disconnected left hemisphere (Farah et al., 1985; Corballis & Sergent, 1988).

Hierarchic Perception

It has been suggested that the left hemisphere is specialized for local processing (details) or the analysis of patterns with relatively high spatial frequency, whereas the right hemisphere is specialized for global processing (wholes) or the analysis of patterns with relatively low spatial frequency (Hellige, 1993). Left hemisphere perception then proceeds bottom-up, right hemisphere perception proceeds top-down, and the two streams are integrated via the CC. This conceptualization is often operationalized in the Navon paradigm (Navon, 1977), in which large H's or S's, made up of small H's or S's, are presented peripherally to normal subjects who are required to identify the large (global) or small (local) letter (H or S). Subjects exhibit three effects: (a) it is easier to identify the large letters than the small letters ("global precedence" or "the level effect"); (b) consistent stimuli in which the large and small elements are the same (e.g., a large H made up of small H's) are easier to identify than inconsistent stimuli in which the large and small elements are different (e.g., a large S made up of small H's) ("the consistency effect"); and (c) the consistency effect is stronger for local identification ("global interference") than for global identification ("local interference"). The latter is referred to as the *asymmetric consistency effect*, and it is reflected in a significant Level × Consistency interaction. In normal subjects, some find RVF specialization for identifying local targets and, less frequently LVF specialization for global targets (van Kleek, 1989). On the basis of findings in patients with unilateral temporoparietal lesions, Robertson et al. (1988)

speculated that the consistency effect, and particularly the asymmetric consistency effect, is mediated by the CC. This predicts that the effect should be absent in patients with CCC (Robertson & Lamb, 1991).

Robertson et al. (1993) presented hierarchic patterns in the LVF or RVF, or the same pattern simultaneously in both VFs (BVF), of commissurotomy patients L.B., N.G., and A.A. Weekes et al. (1997) conducted a follow-up study with two of the same commissurotomy patients, using very similar stimuli and conditions. Together, the two studies found instances of unilateral consistency effects and of unilateral asymmetric consistency effects. Three conclusions can be drawn from these results. First, the absence of a Level × VF interaction is not a necessary consequence of disconnection. Second, consistency effects can occur in the absence of the CC. Third, the asymmetric consistency effect can occur in the split brain. Both disconnected hemispheres could process both local and global stimuli and each could therefore exhibit consistency effects. Similar observations were made in a patient with complete or "functional" left or right hemispherectomies (Weeks, Ptito, & Zaidel, unpublished data). Thus, the behavior of the split-brain patients is unlikely to reflect the effects of subcallosal interhemispheric transfer.

Right Constructional Apraxia

By *constructional praxis*, the ability to put together a meaningful configuration, such as an object (three dimensions) or a complex drawing (two dimensions), is implied. Constructional dyspraxia is the inability to organize several parts into a configuration despite a normal ability to handle or draw the individual parts (Benton, 1962; Benton & Fogel, 1962; Warrington, 1969; De Renzi, 1982). Constructional dyspraxia can occur from lesions in either hemisphere. Left lesions may result in an absence of some of the parts and in simplified versions of a model, and right hemisphere lesions tend to result in inappropriate relationships among the parts, including a loss of perspective in drawings intended to represent three dimensions (Paterson & Zangwill, 1944; Warrington et al., 1966; Benton, 1967; Hécaen & Assal, 1970; Gainotti et al., 1977).

Constructional apraxia can be quite prominent in the right hand of right-handers with callosal lesions. Hemispheric disconnection (in a right-hander) is strongly suggested if the patient can copy designs better with the left hand than with the right (Bogen, 1969b; Yamadori et al., 1983).

Left Hemineglect

Early studies of unilateral neglect of space in patients from the California series using standard clinical tests disclosed no evidence for frank neglect (Plourde & Sperry, 1984). Zaidel (1979) tested visual search of pictorial scenes using continuously lateralized visual presentations while permitting ocular scanning by one hemisphere at a time and found no difference between targets located on the left or right part of a scene. However, more recent studies by Lausberg et al. (2003) required patients to demonstrate the content of animated scenes with two moving objects, and found that right hand performance was restricted to the right half of space, whereas left hand performance extended over both the right and left halves of space. Whereas a clinical level of neglect can be observed in the split-brain patients, it seems highly variable across patients and even within the same patient at different times (Corballis et al., 2007).

Spatial Acalculia

Because of spatial disability when using the right hand, the patient with hemispheric disconnection may have difficulties using pencil and paper to solve arithmetic problems (Dahmen et al., 1982). The patients with CCC had some difficulty with written arithmetic, a deficit that progressively receded (Bogen, 1969a, p. 92). Surprisingly, sometimes following complete commissurotomy a patient would have difficulty in doing arithmetic on paper whereas comparable problems could be done by mental calculation. Colvin et al. (2005) studied the abilities of the disconnected hemisphere to perform subitizing and magnitude comparisons. Both hemispheres were equally able to perform both tasks, including comparisons across different numerical representations (Arabic numerals, number words, or dot arrays).

Both hemispheres also exhibited the "distance effect." Funnell et al. (2007) found that the disconnected left hemisphere was superior to the disconnected right hemisphere in simple calculations. The disconnected right hemisphere showed some ability for calculations with small numbers, and it was more accurate in proximate than in exact operations.

REASONING

Abstract Concepts

The disconnected right hemisphere was superior on a tactile version of a concept formation test (Kumar, 1977), and it was able to process abstract concepts (Cronin-Golomb, 1995). The disconnected left hemisphere was superior on both a tactile and a visual version of the Raven Color Progressive Matrices, which requires the coordination of abstract rules (D.W. Zaidel & Sperry, 1974; Zaidel et al., 1981). The disconnected left hemisphere was also superior on the more difficult Raven Standard Progressive Matrices. A form-board version of the test, which permits a trial-and-error strategy, showed that only the disconnected left hemisphere benefitted from error correction. Research on mathematics in the split brain to date has emphasized simple arithmetic instead of more abstract number concepts and mathematical reasoning, including proofs. This is unfortunate, and it reflects the state of the field in general. The area of abstract mathematical reasoning deserves more attention in modern cognitive neuroscience.

Probability Matching

Wolford et al. (2000) conducted a probability guessing experiment and concluded that the disconnected right hemisphere used an "animal-like" strategy of choosing the options that occur most commonly (maximizing), whereas the disconnected left hemisphere tends to discern patterns based on previous occurrences (frequency matching). The authors argue that frequency matching represents a more advanced strategy of searching for patterns in events. This strategy may represent, instead, the specialization of the disconnected left hemisphere for

coordinating two rules at the same time (Zaidel et al., 1981).

Nonverbal Piagetian Tests

Nonverbal Piagetian tests for spatial development (stereognosis, localization of topographical positions) at the preoperational and concrete operational stages showed mixed hemispheric superiorities across tests and across patients, and did not succeed in characterizing each hemisphere as performing at some consistent developmental stage (Zaidel, 1978b; Fugelsang et al., 2005)

Everyday "Semantics"

The disconnected right hemisphere has rich pictorial semantics. It recognizes objects, scenes, landmarks and personally relevant people and events (e.g., Sperry et al., 1979). In contrast to the disconnected left hemisphere, the disconnected right hemisphere shows a selective advantage for stereotypical exemplars of natural categories and for conventionally organized scenes (D.W. Zaidel, 1995).

ATTENTION

Attention in the split brain can be viewed more generally as a model system for the problem of intermodular communication. How can anatomically and functionally separate "modules" maintain their independence to permit parallel processing at one time, but communicate at other times?

Vigilance

There is some controversy about whether the split-brain syndrome includes abnormal gaps in vigilance and about whether the disconnected right hemisphere is more vigilant than the disconnected left hemisphere (Dimond, 1979) or not (Ellenberg & Sperry, 1979).

Focused Attention in Dichotic Listening

Zaidel (1983) has administered to commissurotomy patients a dichotic listening test with CV syllables (bee, dee, gee, pee, tee, kee) and with lateralized visual probes and attention instructions (left ear, right ear, divided). The results showed (a) exclusive left hemisphere specialization for the task, and (b) ipsilateral suppression of the left ear signal in the left hemisphere. The authors thus inferred (c) that, in the normal brain, the left ear signal is relayed from the right hemisphere to the left hemisphere via the CC prior to processing. There were no effects of focused attention to either ear on the right ear advantage in normal subjects, but a substantial effect in a split-brain patient (L.B.). In the disconnected left hemisphere, attention to the right ear had no effect, but attention to the left ear increased the left ear score and decreased the right ear score. Similarly, in the disconnected right hemisphere, attention to the left ear had no effect, but attention to the right ear reduced the left ear score and increased the right ear score. Taken together, the data suggest that focused attention in the split brain activates attention-specific subcallosal interhemispheric auditory channels. In the normal brain, these subcallosal channels are presumably superseded by callosal channels that are less sensitive to spatial attention.

Dichotic listening tests vary widely in the degree of temporal and acoustic overlap between left and right ear signals. The greater the overlap, the greater the ipsilateral suppression and the less susceptible the ear advantage is to modulation by focused attention.

Covert Orienting of Spatial Attention

If each cerebral hemisphere is an independent cognitive system, then each has an independent control system—an independent attentional mechanism that regulates the resources and operations of the hemisphere. But split-brain patients largely behave as well-integrated and coordinated organisms, and this suggests that there is an overall, shared attentional system that coordinates the interaction of the two disconnected hemispheres. This creates a puzzle: Is attention in the split brain divided or shared? Four interrelated solutions have been proposed:

1. *Stage of processing.* The two disconnected hemispheres can select stimuli, encode

and decode them, and select responses independently, but they share response execution mechanisms to avoid behavioral conflict. Thus, early stages of processing show attentional disconnection, whereas late stages of processing are unified (Reuter-Lorenz, 2002).

2. *Automatic vs. controlled attention.* One distinguishes fast automatic orienting due to peripheral cues that are not informative from slow strategic orienting due to central cues when valid cues predominate (cf. Briand & Klein, 1987). Automatic orienting of spatial attention is believed to be controlled by the parietal-putamen-superior colliculus complex (Posner & Dehaene, 1994). By contrast, controlled orienting of spatial attention may also engage the frontal lobe in an executive role (Mesulam, 1990). Reuter-Lorenz (2002) argues that, when spatial attention is oriented automatically in response to a peripheral cue, there is evidence for independent and parallel attentional systems in the two disconnected hemispheres, whereas when attention is oriented strategically in response to a central cue, there is evidence for a shared attentional system.

3. *Location- vs. object-based attention.* Corballis (1995) argues that location-based attention, as in covert orienting in space, is unified, whereas object-based attention is divided. He argues that location-based attention is mediated subcortically by the superior colliculus and the second visual system, also believed to mediate unconscious "blind sight" and projecting via the pulvinar to extra striate cortex. In the split brain, this system applies to spatial information in the periphery as well as close to fixation, and it does not require sustained input. Object-based attention, by contrast, is cortically mediated via the geniculostriate system and is necessary for the conscious identification of form information.

4. *Cortically vs. subcortically mediated attention.* The subcortical system is unified via the intercollicular commissure or perhaps via the diencephalon, midbrain, or cerebellum

(Trevarthen, 1991), whereas the cortical system is divided. The cortical–subcortical distinction applies both to attention and to perception (Corballis, 1995). Thus, it is not the case simply that attention is integrated in the split brain while perception is divided, as originally suggested (Gazzaniga, 1987). None of the four views completely accounts for all available data. Some key experiments are reviewed below.

Spatial Cueing

Simple Reaction Time. In Posner's cueing paradigm (1980), two or more positions across the vertical meridian are predesignated as potential target locations. One of these locations is cued centrally (symbolically, e.g., a letter L or R) or peripherally (at the location of the target, e.g., a box around the stimulus location) before the onset of the imperative target. The task is an SRT with unimanual button presses. Responses to cued targets are usually faster than responses to uncued targets. Cued targets usually yield a small facilitation (benefit) relative to a neutral cue. Miscued targets usually exhibit a (larger) inhibition (cost) relative to the neutral cue. The cost and benefit are often conceptualized as being due to shifts of attention in space. Recall that one distinguishes fast (<300 msec between cue and target) automatic priming due to uninformative peripheral cues from controlled slow priming (>300 msec) due to central informative (mostly valid) cues. What could be predicted about valid versus invalid cueing across the vertical meridian in the split brain? If the two hemispheres have independent attentional systems, then the most straightforward prediction is that when the side of the miscue is opposite that of the response cue, there should be no benefit or cost to such cues. Any validity–invalidity effect across the vertical meridian in the split brain is presumably mediated by a unified attentional system that represents both VFs, a system that has access to ipsilateral visual cue information or to other subcallosal interhemispheric cue information. But would such validity–invalidity, benefits–costs be greater or smaller in the split brain

than in the normal brain? The simplest prediction is that they should be smaller. Otherwise, subcallosal channels must have spatial orienting functions that are normally suppressed by the CC, but that are released following callosal section.

Reuter-Lorenz and Fendrich (1990) used a Posner paradigm with informative peripheral cues and long cue-to-target stimulus onset asynchrony (SOAs) and observed unified attention in patients with complete callosotomies. By contrast, Arguin et al. (2000) used informative central cues and intermediate SOAs and found that (a) some, but not all, callosotomy patients showed attentional disconnection, and (b) some anterior callosotomy patients also showed attentional disconnection. Thus, conflict in the literature exists, and there is a need for a common methodology. Nonetheless, two conclusions emerge. First, attention in the disconnection syndrome can be split. Second, some subcallosal channels can mediate attentional interactions in split-brain subjects.

Passarotti et al. (unpublished data; Zaidel, 1994) administered to commissurotomy patients L.B. and N.G. from the California series, and to normal controls, different versions of the Posner experiment with both peripheral and semicentral informative cues and SOAs ranging from 150 to 250 msec. Targets appeared in one of four boxes in the corners of a square centered at fixation. In this way, they could compare neutral and valid trials to invalid trials crossing the horizontal meridian, invalid trials crossing the vertical meridian, and invalid trials crossing both meridians. The results with both peripheral and semicentral cues showed complex attentional interactions between the two VFs, both facilitatory and inhibitory, consistent with unified attention. These data are consistent with a model that assumes that (a) the right hemisphere has as attentional map that includes both VFs, whereas the left hemisphere has an attentional map that includes only the RVF; (b) the left hemisphere controls attention to RVF targets, and the right hemisphere controls attention to LVF targets; (c) the two hemispheres show different patterns of costs and benefits, with the right hemisphere more likely than the left to show costs due to invalid cues; (d) the two attentional systems can maintain independence in the normal brain; (e) the attentional system in the right hemisphere has both callosal and subcallosal access to RVF information; (f) both the callosal and subcallosal interhemispheric attentional effects include facilitatory as well as inhibitory components; and (g) large individual differences exist across split-brain patients in the nature of subcallosal attention effects. In particular, the data from L.B., together with the data from normal subjects, suggest that there is an asymmetric, *callosally* mediated mirror image facilitation from the RVF to the LVF, as well as a *subcallosally* mediated mirror image inhibition in the same direction. In the normal brain, callosal facilitation dominates, whereas the split-brain data unmask subcallosal inhibition. The data suggest that, contrary to Reuter-Lorenz's hypothesis, automatic attention can be unified between the two disconnected hemispheres. Displays with multiple target locations reveal more complex spatial-orienting mechanisms than inferred from the original Posner paradigm, which were restricted to left and right target locations only.

Spatial Cueing in Choice Reaction Time. Similar discrepancies are reported for spatial cueing in choice RT tasks. Thus, Holtzman (1984) found evidence for shared attention, whereas Mangun et al. (1994) found evidence for independent attentional systems in the disconnected hemispheres. In both experiments, subjects made binary choices of cued lateralized targets. Holtzman used central cues and large (1,500 msec) SOAs, whereas Mangun et al. used peripheral cues and shorter SOAs (150–600 msec). Thus, different attentional systems may have been engaged in the two tasks. It is important to note that, even though invalid cues crossing the vertical meridian had an effect, demonstrating some unification of attention between the two disconnected hemispheres, it is nonetheless the case that invalid cues crossing the midline affected target detection in the other hemisphere rather differently (more extremely) than invalid cues within the same hemisphere as the target. Thus, unification is far from normal. The CC appears to be necessary for modulating some of the extreme effects of orienting to peripheral stimuli in the split brain.

Visual Search. Search of visual targets among distractors engages controlled attention, and its speed is negatively correlated with the number of distractors when it requires feature conjunction (i.e., when the target is composed of a conjunction of features that are also present in the distractors) (Treisman & Gelade, 1980). Is visual search in one visual hemifield sensitive to distractors in the other visual hemifield? Luck et al. (1989) showed that, unlike normal subjects, one callosotomy patient (J.W.) and one commissurotomy patient (L.B.) exhibited search times for targets in one VF that were independent of the number of distractors in the other. This, then, is an example of divided, controlled attentional systems, arguing against the automatic–divided, controlled–unified hypothesis of Reuter-Lorenz. The results are consistent with the location- versus object-based and subcortical–cortical hypotheses of Corballis (1995), since the visual search task of Luck et al. is most likely object-based and cortically mediated.

An opposite result was obtained by Pollmann and Zaidel (1998), who studied the effects of ipsilateral and contralateral distractors on lateralized visual search in two commissurotomy patients N.G. and L.B. Targets and distractors varied in relative salience. In general, distractors slowed down the search for contralateral targets, showing that, contrary to Luck et al., the search was not independent in the two hemispheres. This effect was equally true for low-salience targets with high-salience distractors and for high-salience targets with low-salience distractors, arguing against the automaticity hypothesis of Reuter-Lorenz. However, the response arrangement was unique: Patients were asked to press a button with their left finger if a target was present in the LVF and to press another button with the right hand if a target was present in the RVF. Thus, both hemispheric response systems were poised to respond, and this may have activated interhemispheric interaction to prevent conflict. By contrast, Luck et al. (1989) used bimanual responses, which may not invoke a strategic response competition (Reuter-Lorenz, 2002).

Pollmann (1996) had demonstrated earlier an extinction-like asymmetry in the search task using low-salience targets and high-salience distractors in the normal brain: RVF distractors interfered with LVF targets, but not vice versa. This effect was reversed in commissurotomy patient L.B., who is not able to transfer visual form information between the hemispheres, but not in N.G., who is able to transfer such information. This is another example of attentional interdependence, albeit abnormal, between the disconnected hemispheres. Pollmann and E. Zaidel, moreover, proposed a model for the interdependence. They considered two competing models for the contralateral distractor asymmetry in normal subjects: (a) Kinsbourne and Bruce's (1987) proposal that the left hemisphere orienting system is dominant, and (b) Heilman et al.'s (1987) and Mesulam's (1981) proposal that the right hemisphere has a more bilateral coverage in space, together with (c) the proposal that the right hemisphere is dominant for spatial orienting (Heilman & Van Den Abell, 1980). The search data in split-brain patients support elements from both of the earlier proposals. They are consistent with a model of an attentional gradient for the whole field in each hemisphere, but one that is steeper in the left hemisphere. This explains the reversed contralateral distractor asymmetry in L.B. by absence of ipsilateral visual information rather than by subcallosal inhibition. The model assumes that there are independent attentional systems in the two disconnected hemispheres, but it does not assume that they interact directly. The model suggests that the CC has a limited role in spatial orienting during search, which may help explain the absence of neglect phenomenon in the disconnected hemispheres (Plourde & Sperry, 1984). (Several split-brain studies have even reported leftward attentional biases in visual tasks; see Proverbio et al., 1994; Reuter-Lorenz et al., 1995; Berlucchi et al., 1995).

Hemispheric Specialization. Pollmann and E. Zaidel's (1998) controlled visual search experiments (with targets, nontargets, and distractors) revealed a left hemisphere advantage in L.B. for both low- and high-effort searching, with and without ipsilateral distractors. N.G. showed no hemispheric difference. By contrast, Pollmann and E. Zaidel's (1999) controlled visual search experiments (with targets and nontargets only) suggested an right hemisphere advantage in L.B. and an left hemisphere

advantage for N.G. for both low- and high-effort searching. Kingstone et al. (1995) asked whether a consistent hemispheric specialization is present for guided visual search, where (effortful, controlled) conjunction search is constrained to a subset of items that share a target feature, thus rendering the search more efficient. They used "congruent responding" (press a right hand key when a target is present in the RVF, etc.) and long presentations while monitoring eye fixation. The task was administered to callosotomy patients J.W., V.P., and D.R. All patients scanned bilateral arrays twice as fast as unilateral arrays with the same number of stimuli, thus confirming Luck et al.'s (1989) evidence of divided attention. J.W. and D.R. exhibited a RVF advantage for the standard conjunction search and a selective RVF benefit from guided search. V.P. exhibited an LVF advantage for standard search and no advantage from the guided search. Kingstone et al. concluded that guided search is specialized in the left hemisphere and attribute V.P.'s discrepancy to individual differences. Taken together, the data from both series of patients suggest dramatic individual differences in hemispheric specialization for attentional tasks and individual shifts across tasks. Generalization from a limited group of patients and tasks is therefore unwise.

In sum, there is abundant evidence for interhemispheric attentional effects in the split brain. It appears that some levels of processing automatically engage interhemispheric integration by interactions between the two hemispheric attentional systems, even in the split brain. Other levels of processing permit hemispheric independence in cognition by segregating the attentional systems of the two hemispheres, not only in the split brain, but also in the normal brain.

Dual Tasks. Two early experiments showed that hemispheric disconnection can produce superior performance on two concurrent tasks. Gazzaniga and Sperry (1966) required subjects to perform two different visual discriminations separately or concurrently in the two VFs. Unlike normal subjects, whose responses were slower when required to perform the discriminations concurrently, commissurotomy patients performed the tasks equally well concurrently and alone. Ellenberg and Sperry (1979) reported similar results from a tactile sorting task performed either unimanually or bimanually without visual guidance, even when opposite sorting rules applied for the two VF-response hand combinations. Franz et al. (1996) showed an analogous effect in a drawing task.

Other studies of dual tasks show dominance by the hemisphere that is specialized for processing the stimuli or by the hemisphere that controls the response mode (Levy et al., 1972). This is consistent with the stage-of-processing hypothesis of Reuter-Lorenz (early–separate; late–unified).

Experiments on the psychological refractory period (PRP), however, suggest that the attentional systems of the two disconnected hemispheres are unified. In the typical PRP paradigm, subjects are required to perform two different tasks in a fixed order. Typically, the RT for task 2 increases as the SOA between stimuli in the two tasks decreases. It is believed that the PRP effect reflects a bottleneck in response selection or movement production for task 2 (Reuter-Lorenz, 2002). Contrary to expectation, the PRP in callosotomy patient J.W. was robust and similar to that in normal subjects (Pashler et al., 1995), even when the tasks were felicitous for each hemisphere (Ivry et al., 1998). Unlike normal subjects, however, the PRP in J.W. was not affected by the consistency of stimulus–response (S–R) mapping in the two VFs (Ivry et al., 1998). Taken together, this implies that each disconnected hemisphere can maintain distinct rules for S–R mapping and can select the appropriate response without interference from the other hemisphere, but that the two hemispheres cannot initiate independent responses (Reuter-Lorenz, 2002). This pattern would also be consistent with the stage-of-processing hypothesis of Reuter-Lorenz.

Redundant Target Effects. Detection or identification of targets is faster with multiple copies of the target than when a single stimulus is presented. This phenomenon is called the *redundant target effect* (RTE). There are at least two possible mechanisms for the RTE: (a) independent attentional processes exist for each target, and the fastest process determines the onset of

response (probability summation operating at the stage of response generation); and (b) neural interaction or co-activation occurs among the stimulus copies at an early processing stage, leading to hyperpriming of the response (neural summation) (Miller, 1982). One would predict that, when stimuli are confined to one VF, the RTE would be similar in normal subjects and split-brain subjects; and when the stimuli are distributed between VFs, split-brain patients would have a reduced RTE compared to normal subjects. Surprisingly, when the redundant targets occur in both VFs, there can be a paradoxically large RTE in the split-brain patient (hyper-RTE). This was shown both for SRT (Reuter-Lorenz et al., 1995) and for controlled visual search (Pollmann & E. Zaidel, 1999).

Corballis (1998) observed a hyper-RTE in split-brain patients when the targets and background were different in luminance, but it reduced to a "standard" RTE with equiluminant targets and background. This implicates the superior colliculus in the hyper-RTE because that structure is believed to modulate luminance. By contrast, fMRI of the standard RTE in the normal brain was associated with bilateral premotor activation (Iacoboni & E. Zaidel, 2003), consistent with the view that probability summation occurs at a late stage of response programming. Three recent studies on callosal patients performing RTE tasks are consistent with the phenomenon being mediated by cortico-subcortical interaction (Ouimet et al., 2009; Roser & Corballis, 2002; Roser & Corballis, 2003).

The Effect of Response Mode. Lateralized hemifield testing of split-brain patients in simple or choice RT tasks usually takes one of three forms: blocked unimanual responses; congruent field–hand responses, in which subjects respond to LVF targets with the left hand and to RVF targets with the right hand; and (c) simultaneous bimanual responses. These different modes can be expected to engage different degrees of attentional interhemispheric interaction. One may expect congruent responding to increase hemispheric independence and bimanual responding to increase interhemispheric interaction. Instead, Luck et al. (1989) found evidence for divided attention during visual search using bimanual responses, whereas Pollmann and E. Zaidel (1998) found evidence for unified attention during visual search using congruent responses. Thus, task demands can override response mode in engaging independent attentional systems in the two disconnected hemispheres. However, one may expect blocked unimanual responses (with stimuli on both sides) to increase interhemispheric interaction, and that is what was found. Pollmann and E. Zaidel (1999) found an interhemispheric hyper-RTE in L.B. using visual search with high attentional demands when employing unimanual responses but not when employing congruent responses (Pollmann & E. Zaidel, unpublished data). Taking the interhemispheric hyper-RTE as an index of unified attention, this means that unimanual responses increase interhemispheric interaction relative to congruent responses. Thus, it is concluded that the three response modes engage unified attention decreasingly in the following order: unimanual > congruent > bimanual.

Brain Imaging of Response Selection. A different perspective on motor control issues in the split brain is derived from neuroimaging studies. Deoxyglucose mapping of the macaque brain has shown that reaches toward visual targets in split-brain monkeys are largely controlled by the contralateral hemisphere and involve a large network of visual, motor, and integrative areas (see review in Savaki & Dalezios, 1999). With regard to the role played by callosal fibers in transhemispheric motor inhibition, a series of studies had previously shown that primary motor activation in one hemisphere is associated with primary motor inhibition in the opposite hemisphere (Meyer et al., 1998; Allison et al., 2000, and references therein). An fMRI study was conducted on a chronic commissurotomy patient and on normal controls. Subjects were required to perform unimanual movements with the right hand in response to visual stimuli. Normal subjects demonstrated the expected pattern of activation of the contralateral motor cortex and inhibition of the ipsilateral motor cortex. In the split-brain patients, however, only a contralateral primary motor activation during unimanual right hand movements was observed (Iacoboni et al., unpublished observation). This suggests

that the transhemispheric motor inhibition observed during unimanual movements in normal subjects is callosally mediated.

MEMORY

Short- and Long-term Memory in Complete and Partial Commissurotomy Patients

The first systematic study of memory following surgical section of the CC, and to date still the one with the greatest number of cases (N = 10), was of eight patients with single-stage, complete commissurotomy (CC, anterior, and hippocampal commissures) and two with partial commissurotomy of the CC (splenium left intact and anterior commissure sectioned) in the Bogen-Vogel (Caltech) series (D. Zaidel & Sperry, 1974; D. Zaidel, 1990b). Prior to any systematic studies, patients' families had noted a mild though persistent recent memory impairment following the surgery, but not severe amnesia. Memory for personal or historical events occurring prior to surgery continued to be intact after surgery (Sperry et al., 1979; D. Zaidel, 1993). Milner and Taylor (1972) found memory deficits on specific memory tests in the same patients, even when stimuli were confined to one hemisphere, and even when presented to the hemisphere dominant for the material (Milner & Taylor, 1972; Milner et al., 1990). These patients were given six standardized tests of recent memory postoperatively, including the Wechsler Memory Scale (WMS). This battery tested memory for pictured objects, nonverbal visual designs, sequential and temporal-spatial order, verbal paired-associates, digit span, and other related measures (for a detailed review, see D. Zaidel, 1990b). The findings revealed that the most substantial decrement in recent memory was seen in patients with complete commissurotomy, but even when the disconnection syndrome was absent, as was the case with the two partial commissurotomy patients, memory scores were below normal. There were no systematic tests of memory preoperatively in this group. However, because patients suffer from a high rate of epileptic seizures and receive high doses of anticonvulsant medication preoperatively, and surgery often reduces both the need for anticonvulsant medication and the frequency of seizures, it is unlikely that comparison of pre- vs. post-operative testing can validly assess the contribution of commissurotomy to memory loss.

Mild to moderate memory impairments have also been documented in patients who have undergone callosotomy (CC section alone) to control intractable epilepsy (LeDoux et al., 1977; Ferguson et al., 1985; Phelps et al., 1991). In the Wilson-Dartmouth series, a case report was published of a 15-year-old boy with right hemisphere atrophy and substantial right temporal lobe damage incurred at age 10 with reportedly no memory impairment (LeDoux et al., 1977). Close scrutiny of this report, however, reveals below-normal performance on the story passages of the WMS, the scores being closely similar to those obtained by the two partial commissurotomy patients in the Bogen-Vogel series described above.

Standardized memory tests were administered to a few patients in the Wilson-Dartmouth series, some with partial and some with complete callosotomy (Phelps et al., 1991). The patients with complete callosotomy and those with posterior callosal sections were found to have consistent memory deficits, but not those with anterior callosotomy. In contrast to these findings, a published report described seven patients with anterior callosotomy due to aneurysms of the anterior communicating and pericallosal arteries who developed memory disturbances following surgery (Simernitskaia & Rurua, 1989).

The cause of memory disturbances following section of some or all of the cerebral commissures remains uncertain. Possible explanations include damage to the fornix, damage to the hippocampal commissure, damage to the anterior commissure, or interference with interhemispheric communication required for some kinds of memory.

Fornix Damage

It has been suggested that memory loss following CC section may result from damage to the fornix (LeDoux et al., 1977; Clark & Geffen, 1989; Berlucchi & Aglioti, 1999). According to the judgment of the surgeons in Bogen-Vogel bilateral damage to the fornix was seen in none of the 10 cases in this series; in several cases there is no damage at all, and in some there is only partial unilateral interruption. In our judgment it is therefore not likely that fornix damage explains amnesia in these cases.

Damage to the Hippocampal Commissure

The hippocampal commissure connects the left and right hippocampi. It is just beneath the posterior portion of the CC. In humans it is relatively much smaller than in monkeys, cats, or rats (Amaral et al., 1984) and its functionality in humans has been questioned (Wilson et al., 1987). It was sectioned in the eight complete commissurotomy patients, but not in partial commissurotomy cases or in partial callosotomy patients in whom the splenium was left intact. Yet memory deficits were found in two patients with partial commissurotomy. Thus, attributing anterograde memory problems in callosum-sectioned patients to the status of the hippocampal commissure (Clarke et al., 1989; Phelps et al., 1991; Berlucchi et al., 1995; Baynes & Gazzaniga, 2000) may not be justified.

Damage to the Anterior Commissure

The role of the anterior commissure alone in the memory scores is difficult to assess in the Bogen-Vogel cases since it was sectioned in all cases, and there are few reports of sections restricted to this commissure. However, judging from the split brain work with monkeys by Doty et al. (1994), this commissure alone does not seem to play a critical role in human memory.

Conclusions About the Role of the Corpus Callosum in Memory

When posterior regions of the callosum are damaged, memory for visual material suffers, regardless of whether the patients have had complete callosal section (D. Zaidel & Sperry, 1974; D. Zaidel, 1990a) or only section of the posterior callosal regions (Phelps et al., 1991; Rudge & Warrington, 1991). Multiple variables may affect scores on memory tests. Even so, three observations are worth pointing out:

- Some memory decrement, varying in severity from mild to substantial, is often present following section of the CC alone, or following only a small lesion in the CC.

- Single, as opposed to serial, section does not appear to affect occurrence of memory impairment.
- The word association and story passages subtests of the WMS appear to be sensitive to partial or complete forebrain commissurotomy. These tasks most likely depend on intact interhemispheric integration. The mechanism for the integration is a matter for speculation at this point.

In humans, unilateral hemisphere lesions may be associated with memory loss, whereas in animals bilateral lesions are required. It may be speculated that, in humans, asymmetry in the memory functions of the two hemispheres (see D. Zaidel, 1990a, 1994; Beardsworth & D. Zaidel, 1994) increases the need for mechanisms of integration between the hemispheres. Whereas evidence suggests a progressive phylogenetic reduction in hippocampal commissural connections from rats to cats to monkeys and to humans (Amaral et al., 1984; Pandya & Rosene, 1985; Rosene & Van Hoesen, 1987; Wilson et al., 1990), it is suggested that the CC may function to integrate the specialized memory functions of the two hemispheres.

FUNCTIONAL BRAIN ACTIVITY: EPs AND ERPs

Behavioral laterality effects have limited spatial and temporal resolution. Combining behavioral responses with simultaneous electrophysiological information, and in recent years, with other measures of cerebral activity (EEG, fMRI, PET, magnetoencephalography [MEG], and near-infrared spectroscopy [NIRS]), provides a more detailed picture of brain function. Electrical activity that is volume-conducted to the scalp (EEG) can be noninvasively recorded while subjects perform experimental tasks. When the EEG is averaged in response to repeated stimuli, nonspecific activity is diminished, leaving invariant positive (P) and negative (N) deflections in the electrical wave form of voltage potential change over time. Deflections automatically evoked by sensory stimuli are called *evoked potentials* (EPs), and

those elicited by task-specific stimulus categories are called *event-related potentials* (ERPs). We focus here on what has been learned from EP and ERP studies of patients with compromised cerebral commissures, and close by discussing a few studies that use newer functional brain imaging tools.

CONTINGENT NEGATIVE VARIATION

The contingent negative variation (CNV) is an electronegative deflection that increases in amplitude during the period between a cue and a later imperative target stimulus. In an early ERP study, Gazzaniga and Hillyard (1973) reported that warning signals lateralized to one hemisphere of commissurotomy patients elicited a broadly distributed scalp-recorded negativity, with normal bilateral symmetry. They concluded that this CNV potential, and the preparatory processing it is thought to represent, were controlled by a widespread projection system originating in the brainstem. It should be noted, however, that one of their three patients did have a 28% larger CNV over the warned hemisphere. Subsequent studies on patients with prefrontal lesions have been consistent with the conclusion that the CNV originates in the brainstem and has broad bilateral symmetry (Rosahl & Knight, 1995).

VISUAL EVOKED POTENTIAL

An early study by Gott et al. (1975) showed evidence of independent functioning of the two hemispheres. They correlated the posterior scalp visual ERP waveforms between and within the hemispheres of five commissurotomy patients in response to words (rhyme judgment) and shapes (matching judgment). There were greater within-hemisphere correlations and smaller between-hemisphere correlations in patients as compared to controls. In addition, words presented to the RVF produced the same within-hemisphere correlations between the left hemisphere O1 and P3 scalp sites for patients and controls ($r = .83$). In contrast, words presented to the LVF produced an equivalent level of correlation between O2 and P4 in the right hemisphere of patients ($r = .89$), but a much lower correlation in controls ($r = .55$). The authors suggest that intact subjects use callosal channels to send rhyme information presented to the right hemisphere to the left hemisphere for processing, decreasing the correlations within the right hemisphere. In contrast, callosotomy patients must manage with the isolated right hemisphere, thereby increasing the time-locked synchrony of visual processing within that hemisphere. If replicable, this approach could be an important source of evidence for identification of tasks that can be performed by either hemisphere, and it may show relative specialization (direct access) versus those that are exclusively specialized in one hemisphere (callosal relay) (E. Zaidel et al., 1990). Also, see the section on the split brain as a model.

Early Visual Evoked Potentials

In normal subjects, the early P1 (~100 msec) and N1 (~150 msec) VEPs are generally larger and reach maximum amplitude earlier over the hemisphere contralateral to the VF where a unilateral visual stimulus is presented. The N1 and P1 recorded over the ipsilateral hemisphere are delayed by 10–30 msec. This timing disparity has been used as a measure of interhemispheric transfer time (IHTT). The ERP IHTT is quite a bit longer than the 3–4 msec difference between the mean reaction time of crossed trials in SRT (in which the responding hand is contralateral to the VF stimulated) and uncrossed trials (CUD IHTT). The ERP results have been used to argue that the traditional CUD measure of callosal transfer time either represents only one of many callosal channels of information transfer (Rugg et al., 1984) or is a statistical artifact (Saron et al., 2003). The strongest evidence that these potentials are transmitted across the hemispheres via the CC is the fact that the most consistent ERP finding in patients with a compromised CC is normal P1/N1 over the hemisphere contralateral to a visual stimulus, but deficient or missing P1/N1 over the ipsilateral hemisphere. This has been reported in acallosals (Rugg et al., 1985; Saron et al., 1997; Brown et al., 1998, 1999), commissurotomy patients (Mangun et al., 1991; Tramo et al., 1995; Brown et al., 1998), and patients with callosal injury (Satomi et al., 1995; Marzi et al., 2000; Zaidel & Iacoboni, 2003).

The splenium is particularly implicated in interhemispheric transfer. Although Marzi et al. (2000) report ipsilateral P1/N1 decrements in head trauma patients with damage to both the middle and posterior third of the CC, their Figure 4 shows essentially normal N1/P1 at all parietal sites for a patient with an intact splenium. In contrast, a patient with damage only to the splenium shows no ipsilateral P1/N1. Additionally, Tramo et al. (1995) demonstrated normal ipsilateral potentials after an initial surgery that transected the anterior two-thirds of the CC but spared the splenium. Only after resection of the splenium were the ipsilateral potentials abolished.

Tramo et al. (1995) found that the splenium also permitted interhemispheric shifts in attention, which suggests that one functional significance of the transcallosal propagation of early sensory potentials may be coordination of attention across the vertical meridian. In general, channels of the CC that mediate attention to particular sensory stimuli are close to the channels that mediate interhemispheric transfer of those stimuli.

P3 or P300

Kutas et al. (1990) recorded EEG from five commissurotomy patients while they pressed a button in response to rare visual targets (their own first name) and concluded that interhemispheric integration of P300 amplitude is subcortically mediated. Whenever the visual information was presented to the right hemisphere, P300 was larger over that hemisphere, consistent with a right hemisphere dominance for attention. The subcortical account of the P300 was strengthened by the report in the same paper of a bilateral auditory oddball task in which commissurotomy patients, in contrast to controls, had larger P300 over right than left parietal scalp. This suggests that the intact CC modulates the P300. Supporting this reasoning, Proverbio et al. (1994) reported that a callosotomy patient had a strong rightward attentional bias, as reflected in shorter reaction times and larger P300s in response to stimuli in rightmost space. They concluded that selectively reduced left hemisphere amplitudes in response to LVF stimuli resulted from a left hemisphere bias to direct attention to right hemispace, whereas the right hemisphere could direct attention to both hemifields. This suggests the transient appearance of neglect after callosotomy may be due to a loss of callosal connections that allow the two hemispheres to maintain attentional equilibrium between left and right hemispace, and also maintain symmetry of the P300.

Bereitschaftspotential

A temporary asymmetry of the *Bereitschaftspotential* (BP, a motor preparatory potential) after destruction of the anterior two-thirds of the CC was described by Tanaka et al. (1990). For several months following subarachnoid hemorrhage from a right anterior cerebral artery aneurysm, the patient developed signs of diagnostic dyspraxia and intermanual conflict. Recordings of movement-related potentials revealed a marked attenuation of the BP over the right hemisphere, observed only when the patient initiated voluntary activity with the right hand. Since the BP is believed to represent a cerebral cortical activity preparatory for voluntary movement, we infer that the level of dysfunction in this patient is at the motor preparatory level, caused by a disconnection of the right hemisphere from the left.

N400

Kutas et al. (1988) presented auditory sentences ending in a pair of lateralized visual words to five callosotomy patients. Each word was congruent or incongruent with the meaning of the sentence. (e.g.,"He spread his toast with SOCKS/BUTTER"). The amplitude of a negative potential appearing about 400msec after the word (the N400 potential) is larger when the word is unexpected. This is believed to result from the more extensive semantic processing elicited by unprimed lexical items. The N400 showed an increase in amplitude in response to incongruous words presented to both VFs in patients P.S. and V.P., but was absent in response to LVF incongruous words in J.W., L.B., and N.G. Patient P.S. was able to quickly name objects presented to the LVF. V.P. also developed full right hemisphere object naming over the 2 years between testing and publication.

The authors interpret the symmetrical N4 elicited from either VF in P.S. and V.P. as indicative of bilateral subcortical control, but suggest that, in patients lacking right hemisphere expressive language, only the isolated left hemisphere could activate the lexical search process.

OTHER TOOLS FOR ASSESSING FUNCTIONAL BRAIN ACTIVITY

Some authors have studied the coherence between the hemispheres in callosotomy patients. TenHouten et al. (1987, 1988) assessed the relationship between an index of alexithymia (difficulty in expressing emotions) and interhemispheric coherence of α-band activity in eight split-brain patients and control subjects watching a short film. Alexithymic individuals showed less coherence between homologous frontal, temporal, and parietal electrode pairs than did nonalexithymic subjects, suggesting that alexithymia is associated with poor interhemispheric communication.

The EEG activity in the high-frequency γ band (>30 Hz), which has been associated with temporal percept attribute binding, was recently examined in two complete commissurotomy patients during tachistoscopically presented lateralized lexical decision (Weems & Zaidel, 2004; Weems et. al., unpublished). Both patients showed poor discrimination and a strong behavioral word bias (70%–80%). In contrast to studies of normal subjects, in which words produced more left hemisphere γ than did nonwords, both patients showed more γ response to nonwords as compared to words. The electrophysiological response in both patients was dissociable from conscious perception and more sensitive to lexical category, suggesting subliminal processing.

Positron emission tomography was used to study regional cerebral blood flow during a simple speeded visuomotor task (responding to lateralized light flashes; Marzi et al., 1999). In normal subjects, anterior brain regions were activated in the uncrossed condition and posterior brain regions in the crossed condition. These findings do not support a simple model of interhemispheric transfer, in which the cortical routes differ in the crossed condition only by the addition of a callosal transfer route. Marzi et al. also studied a single split-brain patient and found that the crossed condition activated the left frontal lobe and insula. They speculated that, in this patient, visual information may be transferred by the intact anterior commissure or by subcortical commissures.

Because of the lack of risk from radiation and greater potential spatial resolution, fMRI is becoming the technique of choice in most functional brain mapping studies. Fabri et al. have applied fMRI to study transfer of somatosensory information in callosotomy patients (Fabri et al., 1999, 2001, 2006). Eight callosotomized subjects demonstrated that midline trunk skin regions are represented bilaterally in primary somatosensory cortex, and that ipsilateral activation is not dependent on the CC (Fabri et al., 2006).

In contrast, 12 callosotomized patients and control subjects demonstrated that normal identification (tactile naming) of objects palpated in the left hand requires that the posterior third of the body of the CC be intact (Fabri et al., 1999). Only when this region was undamaged did fMRI activation develop in ipsilateral cortices. Such ipsilateral activations were not necessary, however, for efficient left hand naming. In an elegant subsequent study, a thirteenth patient underwent callosal section first of the anterior two-thirds of the CC, and 15 months later of the posterior third of the CC (Fabri et al., 2001). Naming of objects palpated by the left hand and ipsilateral activation in secondary somatosensory and posterior parietal cortices were intact before the second operation, but not at 6 months or 1 year after the posterior section.

Although standard EEG coherence analyses lack the anatomical resolution to discriminate specific networks, recently developed functional connectivity measures applied to fMRI data can measure interhemispheric coherence with greater specificity. Uddin et al. (2008) recently applied independent components analysis (ICA) and seed-based functional connectivity measures to resting state fMRI data and demonstrated residual functional connectivity in complete commissurotomy patient N.G. Interhemispheric correlation scores fell within the normal range (defined by 42 neurologically intact participants) for two of three assessed regions, suggesting that commissural

connections are not the only fibers involved in maintaining interhemispheric coherence and that cortical brain networks can be coordinated by subcortical mechanisms. The connectivity data are consistent with intact interhemispheric transfer of visual shapes in this patient.

INTERHEMISPHERIC TRANSFER IN PATIENTS WITH CALLOSAL SECTION

RESIDUAL INTERHEMISPHERIC TRANSFER

Despite complete disconnection, residual transfer of information, ranging from sensory to abstract, has been repeatedly reported. The classic test of transfer is verbalization of stimuli presented to the nonverbal (right) hemisphere. There are many possible explanations for this, including: (a) ipsilateral projection of sensory information from the LVF to the left hemisphere where verbalization occurs; (b) improper lateralization of stimuli; (c) transfer of cognitive information sufficient to identify the stimulus to the left hemisphere following recognition by the right hemisphere; (d) cross-cueing from the right hemisphere to the left hemisphere, using shared perceptual space (e.g., the right hemisphere may fixate on a related item in the room, thus identifying it to the left hemisphere, or it may trace the shape of the object in question with the head, so that the movement can be "read off" by the left hemisphere) (Bogen, 1998); or (e) if all other alternatives are ruled out, right hemisphere speech (see above).

Sensory Information

Ambient (Peripheral) Vision. Trevarthen and Sperry (1973) described residual transfer following CCC of gross peripheral changes in movement, orientation, position, size, and brightness. They attributed it to a subcortically mediated, "second," extrageniculostriate and primitive ambient visual system. This system, which is dedicated to space around the body, involves projections from the superior colliculus to the pulvinar and visual association areas of the cortex, and allows for transfer between sides via brainstem commissures following cerebral commissurotomy. Trevarthen contrasted the subcortical, peripheral, space-based ambient system with the cortical, foveal, object-based focal geniculostriate system, which mediates shape perception and is disconnected by the surgery. Use of the contact lens for hemispheric scanning (Zaidel, 1975) provides optimal conditions to test for interhemispheric transfer and did disclose shape transfer (verbalization of LVF stimuli) of simple binary sensory features, such as curved versus straight, long or short, single or two parts.

Focal (Parafoveal) Vision. More recent experiments suggest that foveal visuospatial information can also transfer in the split brain. Holtzman (1984) showed that callosotomized patients could direct their eyes to a location in one VF on the basis of a location cue in the other VF. However, they could not direct their eyes to a shape in one VF on the basis of a shape cue in the other VF. Sergent (1987) showed transfer of orientation, alignment (location + orientation), and angle, and Corballis (1984) refined these findings. Ramachandran et al. (1986) found that commissurotomized subjects experienced apparent motion when two stimuli in different locations were presented in rapid succession, even when the stimuli were distributed across the midline. This finding was disputed by Gazzaniga (1987), but confirmed by Naikar and Corballis (1996). Naikar (1999) showed that the direction, but not the color, of bilateral apparent motion stimuli can be perceived in the split brain, arguing for a superior-collicular mediation of apparent motion across the vertical meridian. Apparent motion is presumably inferred from subcortically based shifts of attention (Naikar & Corballis, 1996).

Sergent (1991) also showed transfer of area size (large–small), and spatial direction (left–right, above–below), but the task included only three levels in each stimulus dimension, and the results can be explained by subcortical transfer or cross-cueing of one bit of information. For example, the cue may be a subtle raising or lowering of the tongue inside the mouth (Corballis, 1995).

Transfer of Abstract Concepts

There are many examples of subcortical transfer of abstract semantic features of the stimulus, generally without making complete identification possible. Those features include affective and connotative information (e.g., happy, sad) (E. Zaidel, 1976; Sperry et al., 1979); associative features, both perceptual and semantic (Myers & Sperry, 1985); categorical information (e.g., "animals that go in the water," where one picture is shown to each VF simultaneously); functional features (e.g., "shoe-sock"); and abstract semantic relations (e.g., communication: envelope-telephone; Cronin-Golomb, 1986b).

Sergent argued that some commissurotomy patients could transfer the concept of a "vowel" (Sergent, 1983), of "green" (Sergent, 1986), "odd or even" (Sergent, 1987), or "add up to less than 10" (Sergent, 1987). But these can all be explained by a simple guessing strategy based on the information in one VF, or by the transfer of binary information (Corballis, 1995). Sergent (1987) also found that split-brain patients could determine whether four-letter strings straddling the midline were words or not, although they could not identify them. However, Corballis and Trudel (1993) could not replicate this with a larger set of stimuli that precluded cross-cueing. Sergent (1990) further reported that commissurotomy patients could compare digits across the vertical meridian under certain instructions (press one key if either digit is higher than the other, and press another key if they are equal) but not with other instructions (same–different judgment). Again, appropriate strategies and binary transfer can explain some success, but Corballis (1995) failed to replicate the findings with the same patients, and Seymour et al. (1994) failed to replicate them with others. Overall, then, there is little support for the interhemispheric transfer of high-level information about shape or quantity.

For one of the patients tested by Sergent, N.G., there is now evidence that, although she cannot name stimuli presented to the LVF, N.G. can integrate surprisingly complex form information across the midline. She was able to compare meaningless Vanderplas shapes just as well between, as within the hemispheres (Zaidel, 1994), independent of the visual complexity of the stimuli (Clarke, 1990). She could compare letters across the midline by shape (A-A or a-a) but not by name (A-a) (Eviatar & Zaidel, 1994). She could compare primary colors or shades of colors between the two hemifields, but only when luminance was not equal (Weems & Zaidel, unpublished data). Finally, she could match across the two VFs two faces with identical views, but not with rotated views (Weems & Zaidel, unpublished data). Thus, she seemed unable to transfer person identity nodes. It can be assumed that N.G.'s transfer is automatic and unconscious (correct same–different judgment, but no identification) and thus identify the information processing locus of attention/consciousness. In N.G., that locus is quite late or deep.

Variability Within and Across Patients

Double Dissociation Between Left Hemianomia and Cross-hemisphere Comparisons. The two classical symptoms of the disconnection syndrome, namely, LVF anomia and failure of cross-integration across the midline, can show double dissociation in the chronic condition. On the one hand, L.B. can name some LVF pictures, letters, or words without being able to make same–different judgments about the same stimuli across the vertical meridian (see right hemisphere speech). On the other hand, N.G. can make accurate same–different judgments about visual stimuli in the two visual hemifields, without being able to name the same stimuli in the LVF.

It is important to recognize that neither misnaming of LVF stimuli alone, nor failure at cross-matching alone, is sufficient to establish complete disconnection. For example, cross-matching may fail in the absence of disconnection because of a tendency to neglect one hemifield with bilateral presentation, even while accurate verbalizing of LVF stimuli is preserved. Conversely, verbalizing of stimuli presented in the LVF may fail in the absence of disconnection, where cross-matching is present, because the transferred code may be so degraded as to be sufficient only for visual pattern matching, but not for stimulus identification.

Intriligator et al. (1995) reported a pattern similar to L.B.'s in A.C., a patient who had a lesion of the posterior third of his CC. He could name unilateral or bilateral stimuli in both VFs, ranging in complexity from sine wave gratings to faces and objects. He could not, however, compare (same–different) the same stimuli across the vertical meridian, although he could compare them within either VF. These results imply that interhemispheric transfer for visual comparisons and for naming is carried out by different callosal channels, the former more posterior than the latter.

Implicit Transfer

Interhemispheric transfer in the split brain is defined as being implicit if both verbalization of LVF stimuli and cross-matching on demand fail (i.e., disconnection is present), but there is nonetheless some automatic influence of the unattended stimulus in one VF (the distractor) on a conscious decision of an attended stimulus in the other VF (the target). Given L.B.'s and J.W.'s ability to name some LVF pictures or words (see right hemisphere speech) and N.G.'s ability to compare shapes across the vertical meridian, the preconditions for implicit transfer may not be satisfied and may need to be assessed for each task and patient on a case-by-case basis. The canonical case for implicit priming in the split brain would require (a) evidence for failure of explicit transfer, (b) information about priming within each disconnected hemisphere, and (c) evidence for significant priming between the disconnected hemispheres. Converging evidence from the normal brain may also be required. Several examples of alleged implicit priming follow.

Lambert (1993) showed presumed negative priming of a RVF target by a LVF prime in a lexical categorization task in both normal subjects and L.B. However, this result awaits confirmation because the targets that showed inhibition were different from those that did not, and various control conditions were not reported.

Iacoboni and E. Zaidel (1996) used a lateralized lexical decision task with simultaneous bilateral stimulus strings and with unilateral targets cued peripherally. Normal subjects exhibit three distinct distractor effects of a letter string in the unattended field on the decision of the target in the attended field. First, there is a lexicality priming effect, such that unattended word distractors enhance decision of word targets relative to unattended nonword distractors, especially in the LVF (Iacoboni & Zaidel, 1996). This effect persists in the split-brain patient (L.B.), although it is mediated by different, subcallosal channels (Zaidel, 1994). Second, lexical decision of unilateral word targets is more accurate than of word targets accompanied by different word or nonword distractors (Iacoboni & Zaidel, 1996). This effect is absent or dramatically reduced in the split-brain patient (L.B.). Third, bilateral presentation of the same target speeds up RVF decisions of word targets in normal subjects (Mohr et al., 1994b), but not in L.B. (Mohr et al., 1994a). Taken together, the results suggest that the split brain prevents the normal implicit sharing of lexical resources between the two hemispheres, but nonetheless permits implicit transfer of postlexical decision codes.

Weekes and E. Zaidel (1996) used a version of the Stroop task with spatially separate color patches and color words and with unimanual rather than verbal responses. The spatial separation permits a comparison of the Stroop effects within and between the hemispheres, and unimanual responses (pressing one of three keys) permit probing of either hemisphere. Both the spatial separation and the unimanual responses dilute the Stroop effect, but do not eliminate it (Weekes & Zaidel, 1996). Both N.G. and L.B. showed significant Stroop effects within and between the hemispheres (Zaidel, 1994; Weekes & Zaidel, unpublished data).

Complex implicit facilitatory and inhibitory subcallosal effects occur in covert orienting of spatial attention using the Posner paradigm of cueing in SRT (see Attention, above).

Finally, perhaps the most dramatic example of implicit transfer in the split brain is the enhanced redundant target effects (hyper-RTE) in SRT and choice RT (see Attention, above). Some callosal patients show coactivation of detection or identification of unilateral targets by bilateral copies in the other VF, and this fails to occur in the normal brain. It appears that the CC normally serves to modulate or inhibit some of these automatic interactions.

In sum, CCC allows explicit and implicit interhemispheric transfer of information about location, orientation, size, and movement through the collicular visual system. Large individual differences exist, however, in the transfer of object (shape) information. Color information is least likely to transfer. Response codes in choice tasks can also transfer, even for abstract decisions.

Some semantic, especially affective, information can transfer. Thus, it is critical for the investigator to assess transfer before measuring hemispheric competence along some experimental variable in the disconnected hemispheres on a case-by-case basis.

PARTIAL DISCONNECTION

CALLOSAL CHANNELS

The effects of partial disconnection are not yet completely understood. Some conflict exists between the symptoms following surgical disconnection and those following disconnection due to traumatic or cerebrovascular accidents. Symptoms tend to be more dramatic with natural lesions, perhaps because of associated extracallosal damage (see Figure 13-1).

Anatomical (Aboitiz et al., 1992), physiological (Chen, 1986), and behavioral data support the view that the CC contains modality-, material-, and function-specific channels for communication and control that interconnect homotopic regions in the two cerebral hemispheres (Zaidel et al., 1990; Zaidel & Iacoboni, 2003). The anteroposterior arrangement of those channels respects the anteroposterior arrangement of the corresponding cortical regions: going in a caudal-rostral direction, the splenium interconnects visual cortices, the isthmus probably interconnects auditory cortices and superior temporal lobes, the posterior midbody interconnects somatosensory cortices, the anterior midbody interconnects motor cortices, and the genu interconnects frontal cortices. Aboitiz et al. (1992) compared the number of small unmyelinated fibers that predominantly interconnect association cortex with the number of myelinated fibers that predominantly interconnect sensory motor cortex. They found complementary distributions for the two types of fibers: Small fibers predominated in anterior and posterior callosal regions, whereas large fibers predominated in the posterior midbody and locally in the posterior splenium. Assignment of callosal channels to specific tasks has barely been attempted. Clarke and E. Zaidel (1994) explored the conjecture (Galaburda et al., 1990) that the connectivity of

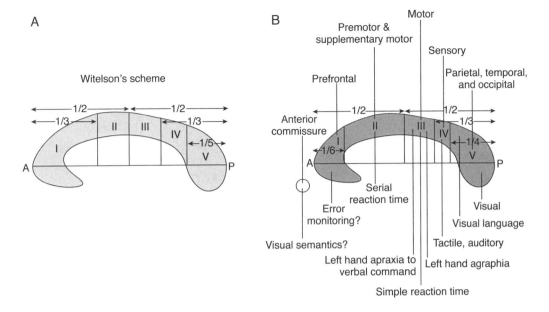

Figure 13–1. A: Witelson's scheme of dividing the corpus callosum. I–V: Anterior-to-posterior partition of the midsagittal view of the corpus callosum. The fractions (1/2, 1/3, 1/4, 1/5, 1/6) denote proportions along the longest straight line connecting the anterior (A) to posterior (P) ends of the corpus callosum. **B:** The partition of the corpus callosum based on DTI imaging (Hofer & Frahm, 2006; Zarei et al., 2006) and the clinical symptoms associated with lesions to different regions. The figure shows the likely portions of the corpus callosum that transfer different kinds of information (shown below the figure) to and from corresponding cortical regions (shown above the figure).

a callosal channel is inversely proportional to the asymmetry of the modules that it interconnects. They also examined correlations in normal subjects between lexical decision or phonetic perception asymmetries and morphometric callosal measures, and concluded that lexical access is processed in superior–posterior temporal regions that interconnect through the isthmus, whereas phonetic perception is processed in frontal regions that interconnect through the anterior callosum.

THE ANTERIOR COMMISSURE

Patients with complete callosotomy sparing the anterior commissure are said to exhibit a generalized but not the complete disconnection syndrome (Sidtis et al., 1981b). They exhibit somatosensory, auditory, and, usually, but not always, visual disconnection. Left hemialexia/hemianomia may (Risse et al., 1978) or may not (McKeever et al., 1981) be present. They do not exhibit olfactory disconnection (Risse et al., 1989).

DiVirglio et al. (1999) found interhemispheric inferotemporal and occipital projections through the anterior commissure in humans and suggested that they may mediate visuosemantic information. Indeed, Lauro-Grotto et al. (submitted) describe a callosotomy patient, M.E., with a right prefrontal lesion who was unable to read LVF words but could name some LVF pictures and make semantic decisions about LVF pictures. The authors attributed these symptoms to visuosemantic transfer via the anterior commissure in a patient with left hemisphere speech.

THE SPLENIUM

Complete section of the splenium is necessary and sufficient for visual disconnection (Maspes, 1948), but hemianomia or hemialexia are not invariably present. The splenium appears to contain several different channels. The posterior splenium may transfer nonverbal visual information, whereas the anterior splenium may transfer verbal visual information (Damasio &

Damasio, 1983). The posterior splenium (and genu) was severed in a Japanese patient who attempted suicide with an ice pick (Abe et al., 1986). This resulted in a more severe left hemi-alexia for kana (phonological script) than for kanji (logographical script). Cohen and Dehaene (1996) described a patient with an infarct in the posterior half of the CC; this patient had a dis-connection for Arabic digits and for numeros-ity, but transfer for approximate magnitude of the digits.

The Isthmus

Section of the isthmus of the CC usually (Alexander & Warren, 1988), but not always (Sugishita et al., 1995), results in auditory dis-connection. This is best demonstrated by mas-sive right ear advantage (left ear suppression) in dichotic listening to stop consonant-vowel syllables (see Audition). The anterior splenium may subserve auditory interhemispheric trans-fer in some subjects (Sugishita et al., 1995).

The Body

Lesions in the body of the CC often result in more or less severe tactile or motor disconnec-tion (Jeeves, 1979; Bentin et al., 1984; Mayer et al., 1988). Tactile disconnection consists of failure of interhemispheric tactile transfer and results in left hand tactile anomia. Section of the anterior body may result in left hand apraxia to verbal command (see above). Section of the posterior body may result in left hand agraphia.

Anterior Callosotomy Sparing the Splenium

Surgical section of the anterior two-thirds of the CC may paradoxically result in few or no disconnection symptoms. Auditory disconnec-tion may be present, depending on the poste-rior extent of the lesion. There may be mild deficit in bimanual coordination and in tactile or motor transfer. Memory for new events may also be impaired (Gordon, 1990). This con-trasts with natural lesions to those parts, which may prevent cross-modal associations and may result in left unilateral agraphia and apraxia (see Chapter 10).

THE SPLIT BRAIN AS A MODEL FOR BEHAVIORAL LATERALITY EFFECTS IN THE NORMAL BRAIN

In the past 100 years, research on hemispheric specialization and interhemispheric interaction has made dramatic twists and turns, driven largely by technological advances in neurosci-ence and consequent ebbs and flows in local-izationist versus holistic approaches to brain and behavior. Lichtheim (1885), Leipmann and Maas (1907), and Dejerine (1892) articu-lated influential localizationist theoretical models of behavior based on neurological patients with focal hemispheric lesions, which emphasized cognitive deficits due to intra- and interhemispheric disconnection. These models were met with strong resistance by influential holists such as Pierre Marie (1906), and by the young and ambitious pediatric neurologist Sigmund Freud (1891), and were largely ignored in the early 20th century (see Chap-ter 1, Introduction). This neglect was rein-forced when a study of surgical callosotomy for treatment of epilepsy in humans failed to show evidence of postoperative functional hemi-spheric disconnection (Akalaitis, 1944–45). In the middle of the 20th century, experiments in normal humans and animals reawakened interest in disconnection syndromes (Mishkin & Forgay, 1952; Myers & Sperry, 1958), and the work of Geschwind (1965) and the California split-brain researchers (Sperry, Bogen, & Gazzaniga, 1969) documented that corpus callosal lesions had specific behavioral effects related to hemispheric disconnection.

Beginning with Broca's discovery of left hemisphere specialization for speech (1865), the common view was that the left hemisphere is dominant for all cognitive functions in right-handers and that the right hemisphere is domi-nant in left-handers. It was not until the 1930s and 1940s that neurologists recognized and accepted that the two hemispheres have com-plementary specialization. The first paper to describe experimental evidence for hemispheric specialization for higher functions (reading) in the normal brain was published by Shepherd Ivory Franz at UCLA, in 1933. He used hemi-field tachistoscopy to demonstrate hemispheric specialization (a visual hemifield advantage) for reading, but was misled by the attentional effects of reading scanning habits. Although he was aware of the implications of his findings for hemispheric specialization in the normal brain, Franz was a holist, and he therefore de-emphasized the significance of his own findings. It was not until 1952 that Mishkin and Forgays ran a similar experiment in Hebb's lab and also initially misinterpreted the findings as due to reading scanning habits. Hebb's lab followed up the intriguing hemispheric leads and eventually pioneered studies hemispheric relations in the normal brain.

Roger Sperry's research on the split brain was enormously influential because it was backed by meticulous animal work, it confirmed more dramatically earlier observations from neurological patients on complementary hemispheric specialization, and it introduced the concept of "hemispheric independence" (see below). In this way, the split brain had motivated a productive "research industry" on hemispheric specialization in the normal brain between 1970 and 1990. Unfortunately, it also motivated facile generalizations about the duality of human nature that penetrated the public media and resulted in a scientific backlash between 1990 and 2000. It was not until the turn of the century that imaging studies of human cognition revealed consistent bilateral activations that differed as a function of task and stage of processing. There was some initial tension between the localizationist focus of neuroimaging and the growing focus on interhemispheric integration in behavioral laterality experiments. However, recent research in neuroimaging is showing an increasing focus on functional connectivity. Consequently, behavioral experiments on hemispheric specialization, and especially on interhemispheric interaction, are gaining momentum again. The split brain serves as a powerful model system for how components (modules) of the mind/brain maintain information processing independence on the one hand, but communicate and affect each other on the other.

HEMISPHERIC INDEPENDENCE

The split-brain model conceives the two hemispheres as two separate cognitive systems that maintain independence on some occasions and interact on others. Each hemisphere has its own attention system for coordinating its own perceptual and cognitive operations. Following the emergence of the modern split-brain experiments, the concept of hemispheric independence was extended, with little change, from the split brain to the normal brain. It was found that many tasks can be performed by each normal hemisphere alone, albeit with a different information processing style and varying efficiency. Thus, the split brain remains a potent model system for behavioral laterality effects in the normal brain. It operationalizes the concept of "degree of hemispheric specialization" by demonstrating independent processing of the same task in each hemisphere. Further, research on the split brain has suggested useful distinctions in behavioral laterality effects in normal subjects among "callosal relay" tasks that are exclusively specialized in one hemisphere, "direct access" tasks that can be processed independently in each hemisphere, and "interhemispheric" tasks that routinely require hemispheric integration. Most important, the disconnection syndrome motivates recent inquiries into degrees of hemispheric independence in the normal brain (E. Zaidel, 1994).

Response Hand × Target Visual Hemifield Interactions

Hemispheric specialization and interhemispheric interaction in the normal brain are usually studied with tasks that separate the sensory input and/or the motor output of the two hemispheres. These are exactly the procedures followed in studying the split brain. Most commonly, the input is flashed to one visual hemifield (VF) at a time and responses are controlled by one hand at a time. A surprising amount of information about the hemispheric processing of a task can be garnered from measuring accuracy and latency of responses in the four stimulus VF by response hand (rh) conditions. If a task can be performed in either hemisphere ("direct access," cf. E. Zaidel et al., 1990), then a statistically significant VF × rh interaction would be expected, such that the ipsilateral VF-rh conditions are faster and/or more accurate than the contralateral VF-rh conditions. If the task is exclusively specialized to one hemisphere ("callosal relay"), then a significant main effect of VF together with a significant main effect of the ipsilateral response hand would be expected. As the task increases in difficulty (Zaidel et al., 1988) and resources are taxed (Coto, 2009), the contralateral VF-rh conditions become more efficient than the ipsilateral ones. Usually, the laterality of the input VF, rather than laterality of the responding hand, determines the hemisphere in control.

Interhemispheric Interaction

The cerebral cortex in each hemisphere communicates mostly through the CC, which, by and large, is organized homotopically. Different "modules" interact through different channels of the callosum. The CC serves to transfer sensorimotor information between primary sensorimotor cortices, cognitive information between association cortices, and control signals, both facilitatory and inhibitory, between prefrontal cortices (Zaidel & Iacoboni, 2003). There are also channel-specific control signals to coordinate the transfer of specific higher level codes between the corresponding modules.

Several modes of interhemispheric interactions have been described in the normal brain.

- *Shifting control dynamically to the specialized hemisphere at each stage of information processing* (Zaidel & Iacoboni, 2003). The dominant hemisphere may actually inhibit performance in the other hemisphere in order to minimize interference.
- *Division of labor and parallel processing of different components of the task in each hemisphere* (Zaidel et al., 1988; Luck et al., 1989). In this case, parallel processing in the two hemispheres is more effective than processing in one hemisphere alone. For example, there may be parallel processing in the two hemispheres during early stages and sharing during later stages of processing (Pollmann & Zaidel, 1998; Copeland & Zaidel, 1997). Thus, some perceptual tasks that require comparisons of two stimuli are more efficient when each hemisphere receives a different

stimulus than when either hemisphere receives both—the *bilateral distribution advantage* (BDA) (Banich & Belger, 1990; Copeland & Zaidel, 1996). The BDA requires not only efficient parallel processing, but also an effective callosal channel for transferring the comparison code (Pollmann et al., 2003).

- *Initial processing in the specialized hemisphere and performance monitoring in the other* (Iacoboni et al., 1997; Kaplan & Zaidel, 2001). For example, the left hemisphere is specialized for lexical decision, but the right hemisphere is specialized for detecting errors during that task, both implicitly and in response to explicit error feedback (Kaplan & Zaidel, 2001). Thus, failure of error monitoring may be due to callosal disconnection of the relevant channel. Indeed, split-brain patients show selective inability to monitor errors (Kaplan, 2002), and this inability can be task-channel specific (Hochman et al., submitted).

These examples illustrate how split-brain research can inform us about interhemispheric interactions, and not just about differences between the hemispheres. The analysis of interhemispheric interaction in the normal brain is currently making major advances in two domains: the analysis of functional connectivity between modules using fMRI and EEG measures, and the analysis of the structure and function of the partitions of the CC using diffusion tensor imaging.

Executive Control

Since each cerebral hemisphere is, in part, an independent cognitive system, each may process information differently and produce conflicting results. Consequently, there is a need for an overall executive control system that coordinates activities, establishes priorities, and resolves conflict. The dominance of the control system may be studied by comparing conditions in which one or the other hemisphere receives the input with conditions in which both hemispheres receive the same input simultaneously. Depending on the nature of the stimulus and the task, bilateral copies of the targets sometime yield the "average" of the performance of the two sides, sometime yields better performance than either hemisphere alone, and sometime yields the same performance as one of the hemispheres (Zaidel & Rayman, 1994). In the latter case, the hemisphere was "in control" or "dominant."

Complexity of Information Processing

It is useful to measure complexity of a task by the volume of the cortical networks selectively engaged by the task. Consequently, when resources are limited, as during fatigue, performance benefits from marshalling resources from both hemispheres (Coto, 2009).

Functional Plasticity

Many cognitive functions can be performed by either hemisphere, often in a manner complementary to each other. Control is usually vested in a "dominant module" on one side, but when that module is overloaded, inhibited, or damaged, the other hemisphere may be able to take over. Such shifts of control provide a model of cortical plasticity. The split brain can demonstrate the limits of such shifts, but not the shifts themselves. A lesion in one hemisphere can inhibit residual function in the other hemisphere. In such cases, it may be possible to compensate for hemispheric damage and adjust the hemispheric equilibrium by deactivating the damaged hemisphere, thereby regaining some of the lost function.

Behavioral Laterality Effects Depend on Context

Standard hemifield tachistoscopic or dichotic listening studies of hemispheric specialization involve discrete stimuli, arranged in a pseudo-random sequence. Such sequences introduce momentum effects that interact with the observed laterality effects. Thus, it has been argued that the right hemisphere is sensitive to the overall frequency of occurrence of target type, whereas the left hemisphere is more sensitive to the local context in which the target occurs (Wolford, 2000). Moreover, test sequences often repeat stimulus types, if not tokens, and the two

hemispheres may be selectively sensitive to such repetitions (Weems & Zaidel, 2004). In particular, significant momentum effects occur from trial to trial as a function of target type, stimulus VF, and correctness of the previous trial (Iacoboni et al., 1997). The picture is further complicated by the fact that task complexity or subject fatigue may cause readjustment of hemispheric interaction in order to optimize limited resources, thereby changing the observed laterality effects. Emotionality of the stimuli and their congruence with the emotionality of the subject also plays a role and affects measures of hemispheric specialization. All these factors need to be taken into account and either controlled or randomized in large samples.

OTHER THEORETICAL CONSIDERATIONS

Early theories of hemispheric specialization were material-specific, with left hemisphere specialization for language and right hemisphere specialization for spatial functions. Later accounts emphasized modality specificity, with predominant left hemisphere specialization for auditory and somesthetic inputs and predominant right hemisphere specialization for visual input. However, both accounts quickly gave way to process-specific models of hemispheric specialization. Especially influential is the account of the left hemisphere as being analytic and the right hemisphere as being synthetic (Levy, 1974; Zaidel, 2001b). This borrows the distinction between two perceptual styles (visual closure) in factorial theories of intelligence (Thurstone, 1950). A more recent process-specific characterization of hemispheric specialization describes the left hemisphere as being specialized for processing local information (bottom-up) and the right hemisphere as being specialized for processing global information (top-down) (see Hierarchic Perception, above). One particularly attractive model describes the left hemisphere as being specialized for processing novel stimuli, using rule-based reasoning and deduction. By contrast, the right hemisphere is described as being specialized for processing familiar stimuli, using inductive, experience-based learning and forming conventional concepts (MacLeod, personal communication, September 20, 2009; D. Zaidel,

1990). This is true at the perceptual level (MacLeod, personal communication, September 20, 2009) and the semantic level (the sterotypicality effect; semantic organization in pictures, D. Zaidel, 1990), as well as at the level of social conventions. There has also been a popular application of hemispheric specialization to social and clinical conditions. The left hemisphere is then described as emphasizing the individual concept of self in the environment, whereas the right hemisphere emphasizes the group self-concept. A popular clinical model borrows the characterization of hemispheric specialization in birds and attributes to the frontal left hemisphere the affective style of "approach" and to the frontal right hemisphere the affective style of "avoidance" (MacNeilage et al., 2009).

CONVERGENCE OF EVIDENCE FROM THE NORMAL AND SPLIT BRAIN

Competence Versus Performance

Experiments with split-brain patients often disclose greater hemispheric competence than would be inferred from neurological patients with unilateral lesions. Further, experiments with normal subjects often disclose greater hemispheric competence than observed in split-brain patients. This apparent contradiction can be resolved by regarding the disconnected hemispheres as demonstrating the limits of competence for a given function. In contrast, real-time monitoring of brain activation during cognition can reveal actual performance of that function. Thus, imaging data often describes more extreme hemispheric asymmetries than are observed with lateralized behavioral testing. Behavioral asymmetries in the normal brain represent the real-time division of labor between the hemispheres, which changes frequently as a function of task demands and available resources.

The split-brain paradigm provides a measure of positive hemispheric competence, rather than inferring hemispheric specialization from deficits. However, in the case of hemispheric interaction, the split brain provides an indirect inference from deficits. In this case, the normal brain provides converging evidence of positive competence. Still, it is not the case that the split brain allows for no interhemispheric interaction

at all. Often, subcortical commissures do provide communication between the two sides and occasionally, such communication is magnified in the split brain and reduced by the normal CC. Thus, the CC often serves to modulate, inhibit, and desynchronize the two sides. Examples include effect of attention on the left ear advantage in dichotic listening, the hyper-redundant target effect, and thalamic oscillations of the EEG.

In fact, systematic discrepancies exist between profiles of hemispheric specialization observed in the normal brain (Bradshaw & Nettleton, 1983, Bryden, 1982), in the split brain (e.g., Zaidel et al., 1999), and in hemisphere-damaged patients (Denes & Pizzamiglio, 1999; Heilman & Valenstein, 2011). Laterality effects are typically smallest in the normal brain and largest in the damaged brain. Thus, unilateral lesions can lead to devastating cognitive deficits not mirrored in the disconnected, let alone the normal, hemispheres (Benson & Zaidel, 1985). For example, large perisylvian left hemisphere lesions can lead to global aphasia, and yet the disconnected right hemisphere is neither word deaf nor word blind. Similarly, right posterior lesions can lead to neglect of the left half of space and denial of illness (anosognosia), and yet the disconnected left hemisphere does not exhibit full-blown neglect or denial. Rather, it exhibits subtle neglect that is task- and hemisphere-specific. In general, it seems that unilateral lesions reflect the additive effects of loss of function in diseased tissue, diaschisis, and pathological inhibition of residual competence in the healthy hemisphere. Those effects are minimized in split-brain patients and absent in normal persons. Consequently, the disconnected hemispheres exhibit greater functional competence than inferred from lesion studies. The normal hemispheres, in turn, evince even greater competence than the disconnected hemisphere because they can borrow resources from each other, even when each maintains independent control of information processing. Hemispheric representation for language is illustrative. Phonological and syntactic deficits tend to mirror lesions restricted to the left hemisphere, semantic deficits follow predominantly left hemisphere lesions, and pragmatic deficits follow predominantly right hemisphere lesions. But the disconnected right hemisphere has substantial auditory language comprehension, including some knowledge of grammar, a modicum of lexical (but not sublexical) reading, and on occasion even some speech (Zaidel, 1998). Consequently, appeal is often made to right hemisphere language in trying to account for perplexing symptoms in aphasic syndromes, including covert reading in pure alexia, semantic errors in deep dyslexia, or good miming in the presence of misnaming written words in optic aphasia. The normal brain suggests that right hemisphere language competence is even richer, including grapheme–phoneme correspondence. The challenge for future research is to release latent right hemisphere language capacities for clinical recovery in aphasia, and to modulate the degree of hemispheric specialization in the normal brain for cognitive optimization.

Generalizability and Individual Differences

The Los Angeles series of commissurotomy patients is unique because (a) the patients were relatively high functioning; (b) they suffered from relatively minor extracallosal damage rather than from massive early lesions causing hemispheric functional reorganization; (c) these patients have diverse neurological histories, yet even after years of intensive testing, they show similar functional hemispheric profiles; and (d), in general, the predominant hemisphericity of extracallosal damage in these patients does not correlate with behavioral laterality effects. Thus, it is unlikely that the disconnection syndrome observed in these patients represents an abnormal state of cerebral dominance. However, even this group shows large individual differences in hemispheric organization. For example, as mentioned above, complete commissurotomy patient L.B. showed no evidence of cortical interhemispheric transfer, but did show evidence for sporadic right hemisphere speech. Conversely, complete commissurotomy patient N.G. showed facile interhemispheric transfer in some callosal channels, but showed no evidence of right hemisphere speech. Furthermore, the ability of patient L.B. with CCC to name LVF words switched from session to session, perhaps as a function of available resources, fatigue, information processing load, or subclinical epilepsy in the left hemisphere. Similar within-patient variability was observed

in hemineglect symptoms in a commissurotomized man from the Ancona series (Corballis et al., 2007). Indeed, the presence of right hemisphere speech is a major demarcation line among patients with CCC. The majority of such patients do not have expressive speech (see above). Moreover, there are large individual differences in specialization and transfer between patients with similar callosal sections. Indeed, there are large interindividual differences in the structure and function of the CC. Such individual differences are larger than group differences, such as a function of sex or handedness. For example, covert orienting of spatial attention across the vertical meridian sometimes does and sometimes does not show evidence of disconnection in patients with corpus callosotomy (Arguin et al., 2000).

The chronically disconnected left hemisphere does not show frank neglect of the left half of space or prosopagnosia, and the disconnected right hemisphere is not globally aphasic. It is neither word deaf nor word blind. In fact, the language profile of the disconnected right hemisphere can explain some paradoxical syndromes in clinical neurology, such as covert reading in pure alexia, semantic errors in deep dyslexia, or misnaming with good miming in optic aphasia. In all those cases, the symptoms can be interpreted as reflecting the contributions of the intact right hemisphere. It is likely that focal lesions involve both diaschisis and pathological inhibition of residual competence in the healthy hemisphere. Consequently, the disconnected hemispheres often exhibit greater hemispheric capabilities than inferred from lesion studies. At the same time, the competence and range of abilities in the normal hemispheres is greater than seen in the disconnected hemispheres, due to information processing enabled by interhemispheric interaction. For example, some normal cognitive effects, such as the consistency effect in hierarchic perception (global interference with local decisions), the Stroop effect, discourse processing, or verbal access to emotions may be inherently interhemispheric, and hence reduced in the split brain. Even the split brain permits some interhemispheric exchange through multiple subcortical pathways, so that the competence of the disconnected hemispheres may in turn overestimate the overall competence of residual hemispheres following hemispherectomy for lesions of late onset.

Patients with CCC can respond with one hand to a light flash in the opposite visual hemifield in the absence of the CC. However, their responses are slow, highly variable across patients, and appear to rely on different subcallosal routes. Some patients with CCC appear to use motor pathways, whereas others use visual pathways (Clarke & Zaidel, 1989). Moreover, spatial orienting across the vertical midline in patients with CCC sometimes exhibits mirror-image facilitation and sometimes mirror-image inhibition, neither one of which is apparent in the normal brain (Zaidel, 1994).

In spite of half a century of accumulating research, the structural/functional components of the human cerebral commissures are still not known. In particular, the role of the anterior commissure is unclear, and there is increasing evidence that it plays an important role in interhemispheric transfer of higher cognitive codes, including semantic information. The functional role of specific callosal channels is likely to be clarified by emerging technologies, such as diffusion tensor imaging, for relating structural and functional connectivity. These technologies promise to extend human potential by modulating the physiology of hemispheric relations. The disconnection syndrome remains an indispensable guide for such a program.

CONSCIOUSNESS

Investigators who study split-brain patients for the first time are often struck by the degree to which the cognitions of the patient's two hemispheres are separate from each other. Soon, these scientists start using sentences such as, "the right hemisphere was very good today," or "the left hemisphere was especially obnoxious during the testing," or "the left hemisphere got very upset when I praised the performance of the right hemisphere." Behaviorists and philosophers often become irate at this formulation. As Irv Maltzman commented to E. Zaidel once, "Hemispheres don't do things, people do things." Zaidel's response was, "To say that the right hemisphere did 'X' is shorthand for "when the patient received the stimulus in the LVF and responded with the left hand, he was able

to do 'X.'"" But the use of the words "the right hemisphere did 'X,'" or "the left hemisphere denied 'Y'" represents an overwhelming phenomenological impression that the behavior of each hemisphere represents a person and that the two hemispheres are two different people. Each disconnected hemisphere seems to be conscious, but not to be aware of the other.

FROM HEMISPHERIC SPECIALIZATION TO HEMISPHERIC INDEPENDENCE

Split-brain research has verified in a particularly dramatic and direct way that the two cerebral hemispheres have complementary specializations. The disconnected right hemisphere excels in tasks that involve attention, space, and emotion, and that require synthesis. The disconnected left hemisphere is specialized for tasks that involve language and symbolic manipulation and require analysis. However, the split brain has also demonstrated that each cerebral hemisphere constitutes a separate cognitive system. Each has its own sensory apparatus, a different perceptual style, a distinct memory system, unique problem solving strategies, distinct concept of the self, as well as different emotions and language. Furthermore, each disconnected hemisphere appears to have separate networks of attention, which coordinate its own information processing, both internally and with the external world. Indeed, the two disconnected hemispheres appear to have two *distinct personalities*; each separately, independently, and simultaneously conscious, and each possessing a distinctive mode of interaction with the external world.

OPERATIONAL CRITERIA FOR CONSCIOUSNESS

Intuitively, phenomenally, it is required that an organism has consciousness if, and only if, the following five criteria are satisfied:

- The organism is capable of adaptive behaviors and novel problem solving.
- The organism has a concept of oneself as distinct from others (i.e., a theory of mind), including an internal model of the self in relationship to the external world.

- The organism can monitor its own performance and correct its own errors.
- The organism has feelings or emotions, both basic and social.
- The organism has direct phenomenal or subjective experience (i.e., qualia).

Each disconnected hemisphere appears to satisfy all five criteria to a greater or lesser extent.

Adaptive Problem Solving

Each disconnected hemisphere can adapt to new situations and solve complex reasoning problems, such as the Raven Progressive Matrices (Zaidel, 1981), although sometimes using alternative strategies. However, there remain cognitive domains that can be processed in one hemisphere, but not in the other. These domains are not available to the other hemisphere, and their absence limits the cognitive repertoire, which is normally made possible by interhemispheric integration. The range of adaptive problem solving in the split brain is therefore more limited than in the normal brain. This view introduces the concept of "degrees of cognitive competence" in individuals with normally variable degrees of callosal connectivity. In this sense, the concept of normal consciousness also admits of degrees.

The disconnection syndrome suggests that interhemispheric integration increases the range of cognitions in some domains, but restricts it in others. Thus, split-brain patients are especially skillful at visual–motor tasks that require independent actions in the two sides. For example, the split-brain patient is better able than a normal person to perform asynchronous actions in the two hands at the same time. Similarly, in dichotic listening to, say, verbal material, split-brain patients have unusually high scores in the ear contralateral to the specialized hemisphere. This is because the processing of that ear is free from cross-callosal interference by processing information in the ear ipsilateral to the specialized hemisphere. Conversely, the split-brain patient is impaired on tasks that require integration across the vertical midline or interhemispheric cooperation. For example, the split-brain patient is unable to correct her own errors when resources are limited and the natural division of labor is to relegate processing to one hemisphere and error-monitoring to the other. It that sense, the split-brain patient is both less and more conscious than a normal person, given the criteria above.

Using the split brain as a model for the normal mind, a normal individual's consciousness can then be viewed as the net result of an interaction between at least two distinct states of consciousness. The question next arises as to why the normal person with an intact brain experiences consciousness as unified rather than dual. Sperry reasoned that normal consciousness is a higher emergent entity that transcends the separate awareness in the connected left hemisphere and right hemisphere, supersedes them in controlling thought and action, and integrates their activity. Instead, it is argued that normal consciousness is also dual, with partially separate parallel processing in the two hemispheres that sometimes results in subjective feelings of conflict. This implies a duality of the mechanisms for consciousness (Bogen, 1995a, 1995b, 1997, 2000). In fact, some normal subjects behave like split-brain patients during some lateralized tests (Iacoboni et al., 1996), and most normal subjects probably modulate their callosal connectivity during cognition (Zaidel et al., 1990), thus demonstrating spontaneous or dynamic functional disconnection (Zaidel, 1986). In particular, the ability to "separate" the two normal hemispheres enough to permit parallel processing is critical for adjustment to increased information processing load due to fatigue (Coto, 2009), task complexity (Zaidel et al., 1988), or emotional stress (Tabibnia & Zaidel, 2005).

Concept of Intentional Self

Each disconnected hemisphere has a distinct concept of self. In fact, the two hemispheres have similar, but not identical, self-concepts with a similar sense of past, present and future, family, social culture, and history. Sperry et al. (1979) studied the reactions of the two disconnected hemispheres of L.B. and N.G. to pictures of self, relatives, pets, and belongings, and of public, historical, and religious figures and personalities from the entertainment world. They found a characteristic social, political, personal, and self-awareness roughly comparable in the two sides of the same subject. Uddin et al. (2008) found that the two disconnected hemispheres are equally sensitive in discriminating one's own face from that of a familiar other, measured using a continuum of morphed images from the patients own face and that of a familiar other. However, Schiffer et al. (1998) probed more deeply into the psychological status of the two hemispheres of L.B. and A.A. and found that they have different perspectives on the world, especially with regard to self-image and childhood memories. Informal testing (E. Zaidel, unpublished data) suggests that the disconnected right hemisphere has a rather conventional self-image ("super ego"), akin to right hemisphere affinity for conventional scenes and stereotypical concepts (D.W. Zaidel, 1990a; see Memory, above).

Introspective Report

Introspective, especially linguistic, report is often regarded as the defining feature of consciousness. However, the disconnected right hemisphere has neither the speech nor constructed "nonverbal" narratives, so characteristic of human adults. It is neither spontaneously generative nor constructive. Nonetheless, the disconnected right hemisphere does comprehend sequences of pictures that make up narratives about the self in relationship to the world, and it can judge how applicable they are to itself. In this way, the examiner can probe the self-image of each hemisphere by offering alternative scenarios and let each disconnected hemisphere select the most appropriate ones. This has rarely been done. The disconnected left hemisphere routinely denies that the disconnected right hemisphere is cognitively competent and tends to confabulate about intentional behavior initiated by the disconnected right hemisphere (cf. Gazzaniga's left hemisphere "interpreter"). However, there is no reason to believe that the disconnected right hemisphere would not be able to similarly comment about intentional behavior initiated by the disconnected left hemisphere by selecting from appropriate choices. Unfortunately, the opportunity for the disconnected right hemisphere to "confabulate" about stimuli that were generated by the disconnected left hemisphere was never systematically provided by experimenters.

Error Monitoring

An important component of self-awareness is the ability to assess the success or effectiveness of one's actions. Can each disconnected hemisphere monitor its own performance, detect its errors when they occur, and proceed to correct them? There is evidence from behavioral laterality effects using hemifield tachistoscopy in the normal brain that, when resources are limited, error monitoring is most effective when one (presumably the specialized) hemisphere performs the task while the other monitors the performance for errors (Iacoboni et al., 1997); this presupposes that both hemispheres can perform the task and that the elements of the computations can transfer from one hemisphere to the other through the CC. In those cases, callosal disconnection should result in failure of error monitoring. That is just what was observed in patients with complete and partial disconnection (Hochman et al., submitted). Thus, complete commissurotomy patient N.G was able to perform an Eriksen Flanker task in either hemisphere, but she was unable to correct her errors in either. Further, Hochman et al. studied patients with anterior and posterior partial callosal lesions to the posterior midbody and to the anterior splenium, respectively. They administered a motor learning task (the serial reaction time task of M.J. Missen) and a visual comparison task to each patient. The patients with anterior callosal lesions were able to learn the motor task in either hand, but were not able to transfer learning from either hand to the other. They were also unable to correct their own errors in the motor learning task in either hemisphere. At the same time, they were able to match visual face stimuli in either hemisphere, as well as between the hemispheres, and were able to correct their errors in the matching task in either hemisphere. By contrast, the patient with posterior callosal disconnection was able to learn the motor task in either hemisphere, was able to transfer learning from one hemisphere to the other, and was able to correct his errors in either hemisphere. However, although he was able to match faces within either hemisphere, he was unable to match faces between the two hemispheres, and he was unable to correct his errors on the visual matching task in either hemisphere.

Thus, effective error monitoring may require the interhemispheric integration of task-specific information. Consciousness of one's own errors is therefore sometimes dependent on interhemispheric integration that is not available to the split-brain patient.

Emotion

It is clear from overt behavior and self-report that the disconnected left hemisphere is capable of experiencing basic emotions, including sadness, joy, anger, and disgust. The disconnected left hemisphere also exhibits more complex and nuanced emotions, including embarrassment, jealousy, and humor. It is more difficult to determine emotions experienced by the disconnected right hemisphere. However, there are unmistakable cases in which a picture (of a nude) restricted to the right hemisphere generated a blushing response in N.G. and where a foul smell restricted to the right (uncrossed) nostril elicits a facial expression of disgust. In both cases, the disconnected left hemisphere was aware of the emotional response, but not of its cause. The full range of human emotional responses undoubtedly calls for extensive interhemispheric integration. For example, it is sometimes claimed that the experience of anxiety leads to defense reactions of functional disconnection, and therefore patients with CCC may not experience intense anxiety. More generally, the split-brain patients from the California series were diagnosed by psychiatrists (Klaus Hoppe) as being alexithymic (Hoppe & Bogen, 1977). They tend to have flat affect and seem to be verbally "unaware" or "indifferent" to the significance of strong emotional experiences, such as the painful death of one's mother (L.B.).

The Turing Test Versus the Empathy Test. One common criterion for consciousness has been passing the Turing test of human intelligence, experience, and emotions. In this test, a person communicates with a human or a machine by typing in questions and receiving sentences back. If the investigator cannot discriminate between the responses from the human versus the machine, the machine has intelligence and is conscious. This test highlights the role of language in consciousness, but it should not imply

that organisms without language are not conscious. Thus, other criteria were formulated (adaptive cognition, feelings, self-representations with intentionality). Interestingly, similar criteria were described in the movie *Blade Runner*, based on Philip K. Dick's "Do Androids Dream of Electric Sheep?" (1968) and directed by Ridley Scott (1982). In the book and movie, androids are initially identified by their lack of empathy, and the presence of empathy is measured with the fictional Voight-Kampff test. This procedure gives feelings, and therefore the right hemisphere, a special role in consciousness.

Qualia

There is evidence from vision, taste, smell, and touch that both disconnected hemispheres have distinct subjective experiences. Both hemispheres appear to experience pain. *Qualia* may be characterized as the result of processing emotions and sensory experiences at a "meta level" of cognition. A way of accounting for the intersubjective understanding of qualia is in terms of mirror neurons, innate or acquired, that correspond to the phenomenal experience, such as pain.

SOME IMPLICATIONS

Localized Consciousness: Simultaneity and Restricted Mutuality

Phenomenologically, there is no question that the disconnected hemispheres are differently, independently, and simultaneously conscious. Each hemisphere can have a distinct and unique self-concept, different long-term preferences, likes and dislikes, and different intentions at any moment. Each can solve complex problems using different strategies, and each reacts to errors differently. This is rarely, if ever, denied by an observer of the split brain "in action." Thus, the split brain demonstrates that consciousness can be restricted to a particular cortical space, namely a hemisphere. Bogen (1995a) further believed that consciousness can be localized to the intralaminar nuclei of the thalamus in each hemisphere. This region is heavily and reciprocally connected to cortical and subcortical regions (especially the basal ganglia), and bilateral lesions to these regions result in loss of consciousness. The hemispheres may have restricted "mutuality" (i.e., incomplete awareness) of each other's cognitive range, desires, and intentions.

Unity of Consciousness

In spite of many years of behavioral testing, in which the patients repeatedly experience disconnection symptoms, such as the inability to name experiences in the left sensory field, the split-brain patients consistently verbally deny or fail to acknowledge the actions and experiences of the disconnected right hemisphere. Thus, even with verbal introspection, the disconnected left hemisphere still denies awareness of the disconnected right hemisphere. Even in the presence of apparent conflict between the two sides, the patients continue to verbally express a strong phenomenological sense of unity. MacKay and MacKay (1982) tried, but failed, to engage the two disconnected hemispheres in direct competition. Thus, from the point of view of subjective experience, there is a need to preserve a sense of unified self, even at the expense of contradictory behavior. The fact that the two disconnected hemispheres generally don't engage in overt conflict is explained in part by right hemisphere passivity, in part by left hemisphere dominance, and in part by a unified system of motor control, as well as shared subcortical structures.

However, the split brain does demonstrate that two simultaneous and different spheres of consciousness can coexist in the same individual. Incidents of an anarchic left hand in patients with complete and partial commissurotomy do occur, especially in the acute stage, rare and short-lived though they are. The anarchic hand demonstrates that both streams of consciousness can proceed in parallel all the way from sensory registration to response. In other words, dual consciousness exists.

It is important to know whether the two normal cerebral hemispheres are ever simultaneously and independently conscious of conflicting events generated, say, by the two hands. Supposing the two normal hemispheres do have conflicting intentions, it is commonplace to believe that different intentions to act generate different perceptual streams and that there must be an algorithm for determining the "winning" intention. It could be that the algorithm operates early enough to shut off one of the two systems before conflict can occur.

Moral Responsibility

The two disconnected hemispheres appear to exhibit different perceptual, cognitive, and social styles. Thus, the right hemisphere is less likely to change its perceptual interpretation of an ambiguous figure (MacLeod, personal communication, September 20, 2009), it is more sensitive to perceptual stereotypes, and it is more socially conventional (D.W. Zaidel, 1995; E Zaidel, personal communication). Is the right hemisphere "more morally responsible" in the normal brain? Suppose the disconnected left hemisphere is responsible for a moral transgression that is legally recognized. Can the disconnected right hemisphere share responsibility for the act? How can the disconnected left hemisphere be punished without punishing the disconnected right hemisphere?

The Role of Language in Consciousness

Recognizing that the disconnected right hemisphere is conscious provides evidence that language is not necessary for human consciousness.

Dynamic Modularity

The disconnection syndrome exhibits a wide range of interactions between the two hemispheres, ranging from parallel and independent processing in each hemisphere to a close cooperation between the two. Thus, the hemispheres are sometimes "modular" and sometimes unified. Each hemisphere has a model of the self and the environment, and includes the complement of cognitions, ranging from sensation and perception to memory and language. Therefore, the disconnected hemisphere does not satisfy Fodor's criteria for modularity (context independence). Nonetheless, they are sometime independent of each other and are best characterized as a system with dynamic mutual modularity. This revises Fodor's definition and makes it more "neuroscientifically friendly."

Dreams

The experience of dreams may be affected by commissurotomy. E. Zaidel found that N. G. and L.B. from the Los Angeles series do not report dreams (unpublished data), but Greenwood et al. (1977) found normal dream report in some callosotomy patients from the Dartmouth series. Hoppe (1977) interviewed 12 commissurotomy patients and found that their dreams lacked condensation, displacement, and symbolization, and that their fantasies were unimaginative, utilitarian, and tied to reality. Their symbolizations were concrete, discursive, and rigid.

WHAT IT IS LIKE TO HAVE A SPLIT BRAIN

The story of Clever Hans, the horse who could "perform" complex arithmetical calculations, is well known. What is perhaps less well known, is that a committee of experts, including the famous Swiss cognitive psychologist Clapperred, investigated the event and found it to be "authentic." It was later found, of course, that the trainer provided unconscious cues for the horse, and that in his absence, Hans was unable to show his "skill." The committee also recommended that, instead of asking Clever Hans to find the square root of a seven-digit number, it would be more interesting to ask "What is it like to be a horse?" Similarly, researchers who have studied the split brain quickly realized that instead of asking which hemisphere is better at say, perceiving faces, a more interesting question would be "What is it like to be a right hemisphere?" Since the right hemisphere does not spontaneously generate answers to this question, the examiner has to develop alternative hypotheses and put them to the disconnected right hemisphere and let it choose between them (cf. Sperry et al., 1979). Unfortunately, precious few of these experiments were actually carried out. The disconnected left hemisphere seems to be surprisingly unaware of its "special condition," vis a vis the relative separation from half of the body and the apparent purposeful behavior of its sister right hemisphere. In fact, the disconnected left hemisphere seems to go to great lengths to deny independent cognition in the disconnected right hemisphere, at the expense of confabulation and self-contradiction.

What emerges is a surprising mix of the need to assert unity of self and consciousness on one hand, and unawareness and denial of the other half. There is no reason to believe that the disconnected right hemisphere is very different in that regard, even in the absence of expressive language, although this was never tested. Due to the absence of spontaneously generated self-referential commentary by the disconnected right hemisphere, and together with its clearly well-integrated, purposeful, and intentional behavior, one tends to associate with it a "mystique of reticence." However, a coherent self-narrative of the disconnected left hemisphere is still to be elicited.

In sum, each disconnected hemisphere is a model of a whole brain, complete with representations of the self and of the environment and with the perceptual-cognitive repertoire to manipulate them. Each disconnected hemisphere is also separately conscious. How and where their separate sets of consciousness are integrated remains a major challenge for cognitive neuroscience.

REFERENCES

Abe, T., Nakamura, N., Sugishita, M., Kato, Y., & Iwata, M. (1986). Partial disconnection syndrome following penetrating stab wound of the brain. *European Neurology*, 25, 233–239.

Aboitiz, F., Scheibel, A. B., Fisher, R. S., & Zaidel, E. (1992). Fiber composition of the human corpus callosum. *Brain Research*, 598, 143–153.

Aglioti, S., Tassinari, G., Corballis, M. C., & Berlucchi, G. (2000). Incomplete gustatory lateralization as shown by analysis of taste discrimination after callosotomy. *Journal of Cognitive Neuroscience*, 12, 238–245.

Aglioti, S., Tassinari, G., Fabri, M., Del Pesce, M., Quattrini, A., Manzoni, T., & Berlucchi, G. (2001). Taste laterality in the split brain. *European Journal of Neuroscience*, 13, 1–8.

Akelaitis, A. J. (1945). Studies on the corpus callosum, IV: Diagnostic dyspraxia in epileptics following partial and complete section of the corpus callosum. *European Journal of Neuroscience*, 101, 594–599.

Alexander, M. P., & Warren, R. L. (1988). Localization of callosal auditory pathways: A CT case study. *Neurology*, 38, 802–804.

Allison, J. D., Meador, K. J., Loring, D. W., Figueroa, R. E., & Wright, J. C. (2000). Functional MRI cerebral activation and deactivation during finger movement. *Neurology, 54*, 135–142.

Amaral, D. G., Insausti, R., & Cowan, W. M. (1984). The commissural connections of the monkey hippocampal formation. *Journal of Comparative Neurology, 224*, 307–336.

Aptman, M., Levin, H., & Senelick, R. C. (1977). Alexia without agraphia in a left-handed patient with prosopagnosia. *Neurology, 27*, 533–536.

Arguin, M., Lassonde, M., Quattrini, A., Del Pesce, M., Foschi, N., & Papo, I. (2000). Divided visuospatial attention systems with total and anterior callosotomy. *Neuropsychologia, 38*, 283–291.

Baierl, P., Förster, C., Fendel, H., Naegele, M., Fink, D., & Kenn, W. (1988). Magnetic resonance imaging of normal and pathological white matter maturation. *Pediatric Radiology, 18*, 183–189.

Banich, M. T., & Belger, A. (1990). Interhemispheric interaction: How do the hemispheres divide and conquer a task? *Cortex, 26*(1), 77–94.

Banks, G., Short, P., Martinez, A. J., Latchaw, R., Ratcliff, G., & Boller, F. (1989). The Alien hand syndrome: Clinical and postmortem findings. *Archives of Neurology, 46*, 456–459.

Barbizet, J., Degos, J. D., Leeune, A., & Leroy, A. (1978). Syndrome de dysconnection interhémisphérique avec dyspraxie diagonistique aucours d'une maladie de Marchafava-Bignami. *Revue Neurologique (Paris), 134*, 781–789.

Baynes, K., Eliassen, J. C., Lutsep, H. L., & Gazzaniga, M. S. (1998). Modular organization of cognitive systems masked by interhemispheric integration. *Science, 280*, 902–905.

Baynes, K., Funnell, M. G., & Fowler, C. A. (1994). Hemispheric contributions to the integration of visual and auditory information in speech perception. *Perception and Psychophysics, 55*, 633–641.

Baynes, K., & Gazzaniga, M. S. (2000). Callosal disconnection. In M. J. Farah, & T. E. Feinberg (Eds.), *Patient-based approaches to cognitive neuroscience* (pp. 327–333). Cambridge, MA: MIT Press.

Baynes, K., Tramo, M. J., Reeves, A. G., & Gazzaniga, M. S. (1997). Isolation of a right hemisphere cognitive system in a patient with anarchic (alien) hand sign. *Neuropsychologia, 8*, 1159–1173.

Beardsworth, E., & Zaidel, D. W. (1994). Memory for faces in epileptic children before and after unilateral temporal lobectomy. *Journal of Clinical and Experimental Neuropsychology, 16*, 738–748.

Benson, D. F., & Zaidel, E. (Eds.) (1985). *The dual brain: Hemispheric specialization in humans.* *The UCLA medical forum series*. New York: Guilford.

Bentin, S., Sahar, A., & Moscovitch, M. (1984). Interhemispheric information transfer in patients with lesions in the trunk of the corpus callosum. *Neuropsychologia, 22*, 601–611.

Benton, A. L. (1962). The visual retention test as a constructional praxis task. *Confinia Neurologica, 22*, 141–155.

Benton, A. L. (1967). Constructional apraxia and the minor hemisphere. *Confinia Neurologica, 29*, 1–16.

Benton, A. L., & Fogel, M. L. (1962). Three-dimensional constructional praxis. *Archives of Neurology, 7*, 347–354.

Berlucchi, G., & Aglioti, S. (1999). Interhemispheric disconnection syndrome. In G. Denes, & L. Pizzamiglio (Eds.), *Handbook of clinical and experimental neuropsychology* (pp. 635–670). East Sussex: Psychology Press.

Berlucchi, G., Aglioti, S., Marzi, C. A., & Tassinari, G. (1995). Corpus callosum and simple visuomotor integration. *Neuropsychologia, 33*, 923–936.

Berman, R. A., Heiser, L. M., Dunn, C. A., Saunders, R. C., & Colby, C. L. (2007). Dynamic circuitry for updating spatial representations. III. From neurons to behaviors. *Journal of Neurophysiology, 98*, 105–121.

Berman, R. A., Heiser, L. M., Saunders, R. C., & Colvin, C. L. (2005). Dynamic circuitry for updating spatial representations. I. Behavioral evidence for interhemispheric transfer in the split-brain macaque. *Journal of Neurophysiology, 94*, 3228–3248.

Beukelman, D. R., Flowers, C. R., & Swanson, P. D. (1980). Cerebral disconnection associated with anterior communicating artery aneurysm: Implications for evaluation of symptoms. *Archives of Physical Medicine and Rehabilitation, 61*, 18–23.

Bogen, J. E. (1969a). The other side of the brain. I: Dysgraphia and dyscopia following cerebral commissurotomy. *Bulletin of the Los Angeles Neurological Society, 34*, 73–105.

Bogen, J. E. (1969b). The other side of the brain. II: An appositional mind. *Bulletin of the Los Angeles Neurological Society, 34*, 135–162.

Bogen, J. E. (1976). Language function in the short term following cerebral commissurotomy. In H. Avakian-Whitaker, & N. A. Whitaker (Eds.), *Current trends in neurolinguistics* (pp. 193–224). New York: Academic Press.

Bogen, J. E. (1979). A systematic quantitative study of anomia, tactile cross-retrieval and verbal cross-cueing in the long term following complete cerebral commissurotomy. Invited address, Academy of Aphasia, San Diego.

Bogen, J. E. (1995a). On the neurophysiology of consciousness. Part 1: Overview. *Consciousness and Cognition, 4,* 52–62.

Bogen, J. E. (1995b). On the neurophysiology of consciousness. Part 2: Constraining the semantic problem. *Consciousness and Cognition, 4,* 137–158.

Bogen, J. E. (1997). Some neurophysiologic aspects of consciousness. *Seminars in Neurology, 17,* 95–103.

Bogen, J. E. (1998). Physiological consequences of complete or partial commissural section. In M. L. J. Apuzzo (Ed.), *Surgery of the third ventricle* (2nd ed., pp. 167–186). Baltimore: Williams and Wilkins.

Bogen, J. E. (2000). Split-brain basics: Relevance for the concept of one's other mind. *Journal of the American Academy of Psychoanalysis, 28*(2), 341–369.

Bogen, J. E., Fisher, E. D., & Vogel, P. J. (1965). Cerebral commissurotomy: A second case report. *Journal of the American Medical Association, 194,* 1328–1329.

Bogen, J. E., & Gazzaniga, M. S. (1965). Cerebral commissurotomy in man: Minor hemisphere dominance for certain visuospatial functions. *Journal of Neurosurgery, 23,* 394–399.

Bogen, J. E., Schultz, D. H., & Vogel, P. J. (1988). Completeness of callosotomy shown by magnetic resonance imaging in the long term. *Archives of Neurology, 45,* 1203–1205.

Bogen, J. E., & Vogel, P. J. (1962). Cerebral commissurotomy in man. *Bulletin of the Los Angeles Neurological Society, 27,* 169–172.

Bogen, J. E., & Vogel, P. J. (1975). Neurologic status in the long term following cerebral commissurotomy. In F. Michel, & B. Schott (Eds.), *Les syndromes de disconnexion calleuse chez l'homme* (pp. 227–251). Lyon: Hopital Neurologique.

Botez, M. I., & Crighel, E. (1971). Partial disconnexion syndrome in an ambidextrous patient. *Brain, 94,* 487–494.

Bradshaw, J. L., & Nettleton, N. C. (1983). *Human cerebral asymmetry.* Englewood Cliffs, NJ: Prentice Hall.

Briand, K. A., & Klein, R. M. (1987). Is Posner's "beam" the same as Treisman's "glue?" On the relation between visual orienting and feature integration theory. *Journal of Experimental Psychology. Human Perception and Performance, 13,* 228–241.

Brion, S., & Jedynak, C. P. (1975). *Les troubles du transfert interhémisphérique.* Paris: Masson.

Broca, P. (1865). Du siège de la faculté *du* langage articulé. *Bulletins et mémoires de la Société d'anthropologie de Paris, 6,* 377–393.

Brody, B. A., Kinney, H. C., Kloman, A. S., & Gilles, F. H. (1987). Sequence of central nervous system myelination in human infancy. I. An autopsy study of myelination. *Journal of Neuropathology and Experimental Neurology, 46,* 283–301.

Brown, W. S., Bjerke, M. D., & Galbraith, G. C. (1998). Interhemispheric transfer in normals and acallosals: Latency adjusted evoked potential averaging. *Cortex, 34*(5), 677–692.

Brown, W. S., Jeeves, M. A., Dietrich, R., & Burnison, D. S. (1999). Bilateral field advantage and evoked potential interhemispheric transmission in commissurotomy and callosal agenesis. *Neuropsychologia, 37,* 1165–1180.

Bryden, M. P. (1982). *Laterality: Functional asymmetry in the intact brain.* New York: Academic Press.

Cairns, H. R. (1952). Disturbances of consciousness with lesions of the brain stem and diencephalon. *Brain, 75,* 109–146.

Cambier, J., Elghozi, D., Graveleau, P., & Lubetzki, C. (1984). Hemisomatagnosie droite et sentiment d'amputation par lésion gauche sous-corticale. Rôle de la disconnexion calleuse. *Revue Neurologique (Paris), 140,* 256–262.

Caselli, R. J. (1991). Rediscovering tactile agnosia. *Mayo Clinic Proceedings, 66,* 129–142.

Chen, B. H. (1986). Selective corpus callosotomy for the treatment of intractable generalized epilepsy. *Chinese Journal of Neurosurgery, 1,* 197.

Clark, C. R., & Geffen, G. M. (1989). Corpus callosum surgery and recent memory. *Brain, 112,* 165–175.

Clarke, J. M. (1990). Interhemispheric functions in humans: Relationships between anatomical measures of the corpus callosum, behavioral laterality effects and cognitive profiles. Unpublished doctoral dissertation, University of California, Los Angeles.

Clarke, J. M., & Zaidel, E. (1989). Simple reaction times to lateralized flashes: Varieties of interhemispheric communication routes. *Brain, 112,* 849–870.

Clarke, S., Kraftsik, R., Van Der Loos, H., & Innocenti, G. M. (1989). Forms and measures of adult and developing human corpus callosum: Is there sexual dimorpism? *Journal of Comparative Neurology, 280,* 213–230.

Cohen, L., & Dehaene, S. (1996). Cerebral networks for number processing: Evidence from a case of posterior callosal lesion. *Neurocase, 2,* 155–174.

Colvin, M. K., Funnell, M. G., & Gazzaniga, M. S. (2005). Numerical processing in the two hemispheres: Studies of a split-brain patient. *Brain and Cognition, 57*(1), 43–52.

Copeland, S. A., & Zaidel, E. (1996). Contributions to the bilateral distribution advantage. *Journal of the International Neuropsychological Society,* 2, 29.

Copeland, S. A., & Zaidel, E. (1997). Callosal channels and the bilateral distribution advantage: Patterns in agenesis and partial section of the corpus callosum. *Journal of the International Neuropsychological Society, 3,* 50.

Corballis, M. C. (1984). Human laterality: Matters of pedigree. *Behavioral and Brain Sciences, 7,* 734–735.

Corballis, M. C. (1995). Visual integration in the split brain. *Neuropsychologia, 33,* 937–959.

Corballis, M. C. (1998). Interhemispheric neural summation in the absence of the corpus callosum. *Brain, 121,* 1795–1807.

Corballis, M. C., & Sergent, J. (1988). Imagery in a commissurotomized patient. *Neuropsychologia, 26,* 13–26.

Corballis, M. C., & Trudel, C. I. (1993). The role of the forebrain commissures in interhemispheric integration. *Neuropsychology, 7,* 306–324.

Corballis, M. C., Corballis, P. M., Fabri, M., Paggi, A., & Manzoni, T. (2007). Now you see it, now you don't: Variable hemineglect in a commissurotomized man. *Cognitive Brain Research, 25,* 521–530.

Corballis, P. M., Fendrich, R., Shapley, R. M., & Gazzaniga, M. S. (1999). Illusory contour perception and amodal boundary completion: Evidence of a dissociation following callosotomy. *Journal of Cognitive Neuroscience,11,* 459–466.

Coto, M. (2009). *The effects of fatigue and biological rhythms on hemispheric attention.* Unpublished doctoral dissertation, University of California, Los Angeles.

Critchley, M. (1930). The anterior cerebral artery and its syndromes. *Brain, 53,* 120–165.

Cronin-Golomb, A. (1986b). Subcortical transfer of cognitive information in subjects with complete forebrain commissurotomy. *Cortex, 22,* 499–519.

Cronin-Golomb, A. (1986a). Figure-background perception in right and left hemispheres of human commissurotomy subjects. *Perception, 15,* 95–109.

Cronin-Golomb, A. (1995). Semantic networks in the divided cerebral hemispheres. *Psychological Science, 6,* 212–218.

Dade, L. A., Jones-Gotman, M., Zatorre, R. J., & Evans, A. C. (1998). Human brain function during odor encoding and recognition. A PET activation study. *Annals of the New York Academy of Science, 855,* 572–574.

Dahmen, W., Hartje, W., Bussing, A., & Sturm, W. (1982). Disorders of calculation in aphasic patients: Spatial and verbal components. *Neuropsychologia, 20,* 145–153.

Damasio, A. R., Chui, H. C., Corbett, J., & Kassel, N. (1980). Posterior callosal section in a nonepileptic patient. *Journal of Neurology, Neurosurgery, and Psychiatry, 43,* 351–356.

Damasio, A. R., & Damasio, H. (1983). The anatomic basis of pure alexia. *Neurology (Cleveland), 33,* 1573–1583.

Damasio, H., & Damasio, A. (1979). "Paradoxic" ear extinction in dichotic listening: Possible anatomic significance. *Neurology, 29,* 644–653.

Degos, J. D., Gray, F., Louarn, F., Ansquer, J.C., Poirier, J., & Barbizet, J. (1987). Posterior callosal infarction. *Brain, 110,* 1155–1171.

Dejerine, J. (1892). Contributions a l'etude anatomio-pahtologique et clinique des differented varietes de cecite verbale. *Comptes rendurs des séances et memories de la Soc. De Biol.* Vol. 44 (vol. 4 of Series 9) (Second section-Memoires, pp. 61–90).

Della Sala, S., Marchetti, C., & Spinnler, H. (1991). Right-sided anarchic (alien) hand: A longitudinal study. *Neuropsychologia, 29,* 1113–1127.

Della Sala, S., Marchetti, C., & Spinnler, H. (1994). The anarchic hand: A fronto-mesial sign. In F. Boller, & J. Grafman (Eds.), *Handbook of neuropsychology,* Vol. 9 (pp. 233–255). Amsterdam: Elsevier Science.

Denes, G., & Pizzamiglio, L. (1999). *Handbook of clinical and experimental neuropsychology.* East Sussex, England: Psychology Press.

De Renzi, E. (1982). *Disorders of space exploration and cognition.* New York: John Wiley and Sons.

Dick, P. K. (1968). *Do androids dream of electric sheep?* New York: Ballantine Books.

Dimond, S. J. (1979). Performance by split-brain humans on lateralized vigilance tasks. *Cortex, 15,* 43–50.

Dimond, S. J., Bures, J., Farrington, L. J., & Brouwers, E. Y. M. (1975). The use of contact lenses for the lateralization of visual input in man. *Acta Psychologica, 39,* 341–349.

DiVirglio, G., Clarke, S., Pizzolato, G., & Schaffner, T. (1999). Cortical regions contributing to the anterior commissure in man. *Experimental Brain Research,124,* 1–7.

Doty, R. W., Ringo, J. L., & Lewine, J. D. (1994). Interhemispheric sharing of visual memory in macaques. *Behavioral Brain Research, 20,* 79–84.

Ellenberg, L., & Sperry, R. W. (1979). Capacity for holding sustained attention following commissurotomy. *Cortex, 15,* 421–438.

Eskenazi, B., Cain, W. S., Lipsitt, E. D., & Novelly, R. A. (1988). Olfactory functioning and callosotomy: A report of two cases. *Yale Journal of Biology and Medicine, 61*, 447–456.

Ethelberg, S. (1951). Changes in circulation through the anterior cerebral artery. *Acta Psychiatrica. Neurology*, Suppl., *75*, 3–2ll.

Eviatar, Z., Menn, L., & Zaidel, E. (1990). Concreteness: Nouns, verbs and hemispheres. *Cortex, 26*, 611–624.

Eviatar, Z., & Zaidel, E. (1994). Letter matching within and between the disconnected hemispheres. *Brain and Cognition, 25*,128–137.

Fabri, M., Polonara, G., Quattrini, A., Salvolini, U., Del Pesce, M., & Manzoni, T. (1999). Role of the corpus callosus in the somatosensory activation of the ipsilateral cerebral cortex: An fMRI study of callosotomized patients. *European Journal of Neuroscience, 11*, 3983–3994.

Fabri, M., Polonara, G., Del Pesce, M., Quattrini, A., Salvolini, U., & Manzoni, T. (2001). Posterior corpus callosum and interhemispheric transfer of somatosensory information: An fMRI and neuropsychological study of a partially callosotomized patient. *Journal of Cognitive Neuroscience, 13*(8), 1071–1079.

Fabri, M., Polonara, G., Mascioli, G., Paggi, Al, Salvolini, U., & Manzoni, T. (2006). Contribution of the corpus callosum to bilateral representation of the trunk midline in the human brain: An fMRI study of callosotomized patients. *European Journal of Neuroscience, 23*, 3139–3148.

Farah, M. J., Gazzaniga, M. S., Holtzman, J. D., & Kosslyn, S. M. (1985). A left hemisphere basis for visual mental imagery? *Neurapsychologia, 23*,115–118.

Fecteau, S., Lassonde, M., & Theoret, H. (2005). Modulation of motor cortex excitability during action observation in disconnected hemispheres. *Cognitive Neuroscience and Neuropsychology, 16*(4), 1591–1594.

Feinberg, T. E., Schindler, R. J., Glanagan, N. G., & Haber, L. D. (1992). Two alien hand syndromes. *Neurology, 42*, 19–24.

Ferguson, S. M., Rayport, M., & Corrie, W. S. (1985). Neuropsychiatric observations on behavioral consequences of corpus callosum section for seizure control. In M. A. Reeves (Ed.), *Epilepsy and the corpus callosum* (pp. 501–514). New York: Plenum Press.

Fisher, C. M. (1963). Symmetrical mirror movements and left ideomotor apraxia. *Transactions of the American Neurological Association, 88*, 214–216.

Foix, C., & Hillemand, P. (1925). Les syndromes de l'artère cérébrale antérieure. *Encéphale, 20*, 209–232.

Francks, J. B., Smith, S. M., & Ward, T. M. (1985). The use of goggles for testing hemispheric asymmetry. *Bulletin of the Psychonomic Society, 23*, 487–488.

Franco, L., & Sperry, R. W. (1977). Hemisphere lateralization for cognitive processing of geometry. *Neuropsychologia, 15*, 107–114.

Franz, E. A., Eliassen, J. C., Ivry, R. B., & Gazzaniga, M. S. (1996). Dissociation of spatial and temporal coupling in the bimanual movements of callosotomy patients. *Psychological Science, 7*, 306–310.

Franz, E. A., Waldie, K. E., & Smith, M. J. (2000). The effect of callosotomy on novel versus familiar bimanual actions: A neural dissociation between controlled and automatic processes? *Psychological Science, 11*, 82–85.

Franz, S. I. (1933). The inadequacy of the concept of unilateral cerebral dominance in learning. *Journal of Experimental Psychology, 16*(6), 873.

Frey, S. H., Funnell, M. G., Gerry, V. E., & Gazzaniga, M. S. (2005). A dissociation between the representation of tool-use skills and hand dominance; Insights from left- and right-handed callosotomy patients. *Journal of Cognitive Neuroscience, 17*(2), 262–272.

Freud, S. (1891). *Zur auffassung der aphasien: Eine kritishce studie*. Vienna: Franz Deuticke.

Fugelsang, J. A., Roser, M. E., Corballis, P. M., Gazzaniga, M. S., & Dunbar, K. N. (2005). Brain mechanisms underlying perceptual causality. *Cognitive Brain Research, 24*, 41–47.

Fuiks, K. S., Wyler, A. R, Hermann, B. P., & Somes, G. (1991). Seizure outcome from anterior and complete corpus callosotomy [see comments]. *Journal of Neurosurgery,74*, 573–578.

Funnell, M. G., Colvin, M. K., & Gazzaniga, M. S. (2007). The calculating hemispheres: Studies of a split-brain patient. *Neuropsychologia, 45*(10), 2378–2386.

Funnell, M. G., Corballis P. M., & Gazzaniga, M. S. (1999). A deficit in perceptual matching in the left hemisphere of a callosotomy patient. *Neurapsychologia, 37*, 1163–1154.

Gainotti, G., Miceli, G., & Caltagirone, C. (1977). Constructional apraxia in left brain-damaged patients: A planning disorder? *Cortex, 13*, 109–118.

Galaburda, A. M., Rosen, G. D., & Sherman, G. F. (1990). Individual variability in cortical organization: Its relationship to brain laterality and implications to function. *Neuropsychologia, 28*, 529–546.

Galin, D. (1974). Implications for psychiatry of left and right cerebral specialization. *Archives of General Psychiatry, 31*, 572–583.

Galin, D., Diamond, R, & Herron, J. (1977). Development of crossed and uncrossed tactile localization on the fingers. *Brain and Language*, *4*, 588–590.

Galin, D., Johnstone, J., Nakell, L., & Herron, J. (1979). Development of the capacity for tactile information transfer between hemispheres in normal children. *Science, 204*, 1330–1332.

Gardner, H., & Brownell, H. H. (1986). *Right Hemisphere Communication Battery*. Boston Psychology Service, VAMC.

Gazzaniga, M. S. (1987). Perceptual and attentional processes following callosal section in humans. *Neuropsychologia, 25*, 119–133.

Gazzaniga, M. S., Bogen, J. E., & Sperry, R. W. (1965). Observations on visual perception after disconnexion of the cerebral hemispheres in man. *Brain, 88*, 221–236.

Gazzaniga, M. S., & Freedman, H. (1973). Observations on visual processes after posterior callosal section. *Neurology, 23*, 1126–1130.

Gazzaniga, M. S., & Hillyard, S. A. (1973). Attention mechanisms following brain bisection. In S. Kornblum (Ed.), *Attention and performance IV* (pp. 221–238). New York: Academic Press.

Gazzaniga, M. S., & LeDoux, J. E. (1978). *The integrated mind*. New York: Plenum Press.

Gazzaniga, M. S., & Sperry, R. W. (1966). Simultaneous double discrimination response following brain bisection. *Psychonomic Science, 4*, 261–262.

Gersh, F., & Damasio, A. R. (1981). Praxis and writing of the left hand may be served by different callosal pathways. *Archives of Neurology,38*, 634–636.

Geschwind, N. (1965). Disconnexion syndromes in animals and man. *Brain, 88*(2), 237.

Geschwind, D. H., Iacoboni, M., Mega, M. S., Zaidel, D. W., Cloughesy, T., & Zaidel, E. (1995). The alien hand syndrome: Interhemispheric motor disconnection due to a lesion in the midbody of the corpus callosum. *Neurology, 45*, 802–808.

Goldberg, G., Mayer, N. H., & Toglia, J. U. (1981). Medial frontal cortex infarction and the alien hand sign. *Archives of Neurology, 38*, 683–686.

Goldstein, K. (1908). Zur lehre von der motorischen apraxie. *Journal of Physiology and Neurology, 11*(4/5), 169–187. (Cited by Brion & Jedynak, 1975).

Gordon, H. W. (1973). *Verbal and non-verbal cerebral processing in man for audition*. Thesis, California Institute of Technology.

Gordon, H. W. (1975). Comparison of ipsilateral and contralateral auditory pathways in callosum-sectioned patients by use of a response-time technique. *Neuropsychologia, 13*, 9–18.

Gordon, H. W. (1980). Right hemisphere comprehension of verbs in patients with complete forebrain commissurotomy: Use of the dichotic method and manual performance. *Brain and Language, 11*, 76–86.

Gordon, H. W. (1990). Neuropsychological sequelae of partial of partial commissurotomy. In F. Boller, & J. Grafman (Eds.), *Handbook of neuropsychology* Vol. 4 (pp. 85–97). Amsterdam: Elsevier.

Gordon, H. W., & Sperry, R. W. (1969). Lateralization of olfactory perception in the surgically separated hemispheres of man. *Neuropsychologia, 7*, 111–120.

Gott, P. S., Rossiter, V. S., Galbraith, G. C., & Saul, R. E. (1975). Visual evoked responses in commissurotomy patients. In K. J. Zulch, O. Creutzfeldt, & G. C. Galbraith (Eds.), *Cerebral localization* (pp. 144–149). New York: Springer-Verlag.

Greenwood, P., Wilson, D. H., & Gazzaniga, M. S. (1977). Dream report following commissurotomy. *Cortex, 13*, 311–316.

Gruesser, O. J., & Landis, T. (1991). *Visual agnosias and other disturbances of visual perception and cognition*. London: Macmillan Press.

Gur, R. E., Gur, R. C., Sussman, N. M., O'Connor, M. J., & Vey, M. M. (1984). Hemispheric control of the writing hand: The effect of callosotomy in a left-hander. *Neurology, 34*, 904–908.

Hamilton, C. R., & Vermeire, B. A. (1986). Localization of visual functions with partially split-brain monkeys. In F. Lepore, M. Ptito, & H. H. Jasper (Eds.),*Two hemispheres-one brain: Functions of the corpus callosum* (pp. 315–333). New York: Alan R. Liss.

Hécaen, H., & Ajuriaguerra, J. (1964). *Left handedness*. New York: Grune and Stratton.

Hécaen, H., & Assal, G. (1970). A comparison of constructive deficits following right and left hemispheric lesions. *Neuropsychologia, 8*, 289–303.

Hécaen, H., De Agostini, M., & Monzon-Montes, A. (1981). Cerebral organization in left-handers. *Brain and Language, 12*, 261–284.

Heilman, K. M., Bowers, D., Valenstein, K, & Watson, R. T. (1987). Hemispace and hemispatial neglect. In K. M. Jeannerod (Ed.), *Neurophysiological and neuropsychological aspects of spatial neglect* (pp. 115–150). Amsterdam: North Holland.

Heilman, K. M., Coyle, J. M., Gonyea, K. F., & Geschwind, N. (1973). Apraxia and agraphia in a left-hander. *Brain, 96*, 21–28.

Heilman, K. M., & Valenstein, E. (In press). *Clinical Neuropsychology* (5th ed.). New York: Oxford University Press.

Heilman, K.M., and Valenstein, E., Eds. (2011). Clinical Neuropsychology, Fifth Edition. Oxford University Press: New York, New York.

Heilman, K. M., & Van Den Abell, T. (1980). Right hemisphere dominance for attention: The mechanisms underlying hemispheric asymmetries of inattention (neglect). *Neurology, 30*, 327–330.

Heiser, L. M., Berman, R. A., Saunders, R. C., & Colby, C. L. (2005). Dynamic circuitry for updating spatial representations II: Physiological evidence for interhemispheric transfer in area LIP of the split-brain macaque. *Journal of Neurophysiology, 94*, 3249–3258.

Hellige, J. B. (1993). *Hemispheric asymmetry: What's right and what's left*. Cambridge, MA: Harvard University Press.

Herron, J. (Ed.) (1980). *Neuropsychology of left handedness*. New York: Academic Press.

Hirose, G., Kin, T., & Murakami, E. (1977). Alexia without agraphia associated with right occipital lesion. *Journal of Neurology, Neurosurgery, and Psychiatry, 40*, 225–227.

Hochman, E. Y., Eviatar, Z., Barnea, A., Zaaroor, M., & Zaidel, E. (submitted). My brother's keeper: Channel-specific interhemispheric integration enables error monitoring.

Hofer, S., & Frahm, J. (2006). Topography of the human corpus callosum revisited-Comprehensive fiber tractography using diffusion tensor magnetic resonance imaging. *NeuroImage, 32*(3), 989–994.

Holtzman, J. D. (1984). Interactions between cortical and subcortical visual areas: Evidence from human commissurotomy patients. *Vision Research, 24*, 801–813.

Holtzman, J. D., Sidtis, J. J., Volpe, B. T., Wilson, D. H., & Gazzaniga, M. S. (1981). Dissociation of spatial information for stimulus localization and the control of attention. *Brain, 104*, 861–872.

Hoppe, K. D. (1977). Split-brains and psychoanalysis. *Psychoanalysis Quarterly, 46*, 220–244.

Hoppe, K., & Bogen, J. K. (1977). Alexithymia in 12 commissurotomized patients. *Psychotherapy and Psychosomatics, 28*, 148–155.

Hummel, T., Mohammadian, P., & Kobal, G. (1998). Handedness is a determining factor in lateralized olfactory discrimination. *Chemical Senses, 23*, 541–544.

Iacoboni, M., & Dapretto, M. (2006). The mirror neuron system and the consequences of its dysfunction. *Nature Reviews Neuroscience, 7*, 942–951.

Iacoboni, M., Fried, I., & Zaidel, K. (1994). Callosal transmission time before and after partial commissurotomy. *Neuroreport, 5*, 2521–2524.

Iacoboni, M., Rayman, J., & Zaidel, E (1996). Left brain says yes, right brain says no: Normative duality in the split brain. In S. R. Hameroff, A. W. Kasniak, & A. C. Scott (Eds.), *Toward a scientific basis of consciousness* (pp. 197–202). Cambridge, MA: MIT Press.

Iacoboni, M., Rayman, J., & Zaidel, E. (1997). Does the previous trial affect lateralized lexical decision? *Neuropsychologia, 35*, 81–88.

Iacoboni, M., & Zaidel, E. (1995). Channels of the corpus callosum: Evidence from simple reaction times to lateralized flashes in the normal and the split brain. *Brain, 118*, 779–788.

Iacoboni, M., & Zaidel, E. (1996). Hemispheric independence in word recognition: Evidence from unilateral and bilateral presentations. *Brain and Language, 53*, 121–140.

Iacoboni, M., & Zaidel, E. (2003). Stable and variable aspects of callosal channels: Lessons from partial disconnection. In E. Zaidel, & M. Iacoboni (Eds.), *The parallel brain: The cognitive neuroscience of the corpus callosum* (pp. 301–306). Cambridge, MA: MIT Press.

Ivry, R. B., Franz, E. A., Kingstone, A., & Johnston, J. C. (1998). The PRP effect following callosotomy: Uncoupling of lateralized response codes. *Journal of Experimental Psychology. Human Perception and Performance, 24*, 463–480.

Ivry, R. B., & Hazeltine, E. (1999). Subcortical locus of temporal coupling in the bimanual movements of a callosotomy patient. *Human Movement Science, 18*, 345–375.

Jeeves, M. A. (1979). Some limits to interhemispheric integration in cases of callosal agenesis and partial commissurotomy. In I. S. Russell, M. W. van Hof, & G. Berlucchi (Eds.), *Structure and function of cerebral commissures* (pp. 449–474). Baltimore: University Park Press.

Jordan, T. R., Patching, G. R., & Milner, A. D. (1998). Central fixations are inadequately controlled by instructions alone: Implications for studying cerebral asymmetry. *Quarterly Journal of Experimental Psychology, 51A*, 371–391.

Joseph, R. (1986). Reversal of cerebral dominance for language and emotion in a corpus callosotomy patient. *Journal of Neurology, Neurosurgery, and Psychiatry, 49*, 628–634.

Joynt, R. J. (1977). Inattention syndromes in split-brain man. In E. A. Weinstein, & R. P. Friedland (Eds.), *Hemi-inattention and hemisphere specialization* (pp. 33–39). New York: Raven Press.

Kaplan, J. T. (2002). *The neuropsychology of executive function: Hemispheric contributions to error monitoring and feedback processing.* Unpublished doctoral dissertation, University of California, Los Angeles.

Kaplan, J. T., & Zaidel, E. (2001). Error monitoring in the hemispheres: The effect of lateralized feedback on lexical decision. *Cognition 82*(2), 157–178.

Kessler, J., Huber, M., Pawlik, G., Heiss, W. D., & Markowitsch, H. J. (1991). Complex sensory cross-integration deficits in a case of corpus callosum agenesis with bilateral language representation: Positron-emission-tomography and neuropsychological findings. *International Journal of Neuroscience, 58,* 275–282.

Kimura, D. (1973). The asymmetry of the human brain. *Scientific American, 228*(3), 70–78.

Kingstone, A., Enns, J. T., Mangun, G. R., & Gazzaniga, M. S. (1995). Guided visual search is a left-hemisphere process in split-brain patients. *Psychological Science, 6,* 11–121.

Kinsbourne, M., & Bruce, R. (1987). Shift in visual laterality within blocks of trials. *Acta Psychologica, 66,* 159–166.

Kita, S., & Lausberg, H. (2008). Generation of co-speech gestures based on spatial imagery from the right-hemisphere: Evidence from split-brain patients. *Cortex, 44*(2), 131–139.

Klouda, R. V., Robin, D. A., Graff-Radford, N. R., & Cooper, W. E. (1988). The role of callosal connections in speech prosody. *Brain and Language, 35,* 154–171.

Kobayakawa, T., Endo, H., Ayabe-Kanamura, S., Kumagai, T., Yamaguchi, Y., Kikuchi, Y., et al. (1996). The primary gustatory area in human cerebral cortex studied by magnetoencephalography. *Neuroscience Letters, 212,* 155–158.

Kumar, S. (1977). Short-term memory for a nonverbal tactual task after cerebral commissurotomy. *Cortex, 13,* 55–61.

Kutas, M., Hillyard, S.A., Volpe, B.T. and Gazzaniga, M.S. (1990). Late positive event-related potentials after commissural section in humans. *Journal of Cognitive Neuroscience 2*(3), 258–271.

Kutas, M., Hillyard, S.A., and Gazzaniga, M.S. (1988.) Processing of semantic anomaly by right and left hemispheres of commissurotomy patients: Evidence from event-related potentials. *Brain 111*(3), 553–576.

Lambert, A. J. (1993). Attentional interaction in the split-brain: Evidence from negative priming. *Neuropsychologia, 31,* 313–324.

Lassonde, M. (1986). The facilitatory influence of the corpus callosum on intrahemispheric processing. In F. Lepore, M. Ptito, & H. H. Jasper (Eds.), *Two hemispheres-one brain: Functions of the corpus callosum* (pp. 385–401). New York: Alan R. Liss.

Lauro-Grotto, R., Tassinari, G., & Shallice, T (submitted). Interhemispheric transfer of visual semantic information in the callostomized brain.

Lausberg, H., & Cruz, R. F. (2004). Hemispheric specialization for imitation of hand-head positions and finger configurations: A controlled study in patients with complete callosotomy. *Neuropsychologia, 42*(3), 320–334.

Lausberg, H., Cruz, R. F., Kita, S., Zaidel, E., & Ptito, A. (2003). Pantomime to visual presentation of objects: Left hand dyspraxia with complete callosotomy. *Brain, 126,* 343–360.

Lausberg, H., Zaidel, E., Cruz, R. F., & Ptito, A. (2007). Speech-independent production of communicative gestures: Evidence from patients with complete callosal disconnection. *Neuropsychologia, 45*(13), 3092–9104.

Lebrun, Y. (1990). *Mutism.* London: Whurr.

LeDoux, J. E., Risse, G. L., Springer, S. P., Wilson, D. H., & Gazzaniga, M. S. (1977). Cognition and commissurotomy. *Brain, 100,* 87–104.

Lehman, R. A. W. (1978). The handedness of rhesus monkeys. II: Concurrent reaching. *Cortex, 14,* 190–196.

Leiguarda, R., Starkstein, S., & Berthier, M. (1989). Anterior callosal haemorrhage: A partial interhemispheric disconnection syndrome. *Brain, 112,* 1019–1037.

Levin, H. S., Goldstein, F. C., Ghostine, S. Y., Weiner, R. L., Crofford, M. J., & Eisenberg, H. M. (1987). Hemispheric disconnection syndrome persisting after anterior cerebral artery aneurysm rupture. *Neurosurgery, 21,* 831–838.

Levy, J. (1974). Cerebral asymmetries as manifested in split-brain man. In M. Kinsbourne, & W. L. Smith (Eds.), *Hemispheric disconnection and cerebral function* (pp. 165–183). Springfield, IL: C. C. Thomas.

Levy, J., & Trevarthen, C. (1977). Perceptual, semantic and phonetic aspects of elementary language processes in split-brain patients. *Brain, 100,* 105–118.

Levy, J., Trevarthen, C., & Sperry, R. W. (1972). Perception of bilateral chimeric figures following hemispheric deconnection. *Brain, 95,* 61–78.

Ley, R. G., & Bryden, M. P. (1982). A dissociation of right and left hemispheric effects for recognizing emotional tone and verbal content. *Brain and Cognition, 1,* 3–9.

Lichtheim, L. (1885). On aphasia. *Brain*, 7(4), 433.

Liepmann, H. (1900). Das Krankheitsbild der apraxie (motorische asymbolie) auf grund eines falles von einseitiger apraxie. *Monatsschrift fur Psychiatrie und Neurologie*, 8, 182–197.

Liepmann, H., & Maas, O. (1907). Fall von links-seitiger agraphie und apraxie bei rechtsseitiger lahmung. *Journal of Psychology and Neurology*, 10, 214–227.

Luck, S. J., Hillyard, S. A., Mangun, G. R, & Gazzaniga, M. S. (1989). Independent hemispheric attentional systems mediate visual search in split-brain patients. *Nature*, 342, 543–545.

MacKay, D. M., & MacKay, V. (1982). Explicit dialogue between left and right half-systems of split brains. *Nature*, 295, 690–691.

MacNeilage, P. F., Rogers, L. J., & Vallortigara, G. (2009). Origins of the left and right brain. *Scientific American*, 301, 60–67.

Mangun, G. R., Luck, S. J., Plager, R., & Loftus, W. (1994). Monitoring the visual world: Hemispheric asymmetries and subcortical processes in attention. *Journal of Cognitive Neuroscience*, 6, 267–275.

Mangun, G. R., Luck, S. J., Plager, R., Loftus, W., Hillyard, S. A., Handy, T., et al. (1991). Monitoring the visual world: Hemispheric asymmetries and subcortical processes in attention. *Journal of Cognitive Neuroscience*, 6, 267–275.

Marchetti, C., & Della Sala, S. (1998). Disentangling alien hand and anarchic hand. *Cognitive Neuropsychiatry*, 3(3), 191–207.

Margolin, D. I. (1984). The neuropsychology of writing and spelling: Semantic, phonological, motor, and perceptual processes. *Quarterly Journal of Experimental Psychology*, 36, 459–489.

Marie, P. (1971). The third left frontal convolution plays no special role in the function of language. In M. F. Cole, & M. Cole (Eds.), *Pierre Marie's papers on speech disorders* (pp. 57–71). New York: Hafner. (Original work published 1906, *Semaine Mid*, 26, 241–247).

Mark, V. W., McAlaster, R, & Laser, K. L. (1991). Bilateral alien hand. *Neurology*, 41(Supp. 1), 302.

Marzi, C. A., Bisiacchi, P., & Nicoletti, R (1991). Is interhemispheric transfer of visuomotor information asymmetric? Evidence from a metaanalysis. *Neuropsychologia*, 29, 1163–1177.

Marzi, C. A., Girelli, M., Miniussi, C., Smania, N., & Maravita, A. (2000). Electrophysiological correlates of conscious vision: Evidence from unilateral extinction. *Journal of Cognitive Neuroscience*, 12, 869–877.

Marzi, C. A., Perani, D., Tassinari, G., Colleluori, A., Maravita, C., Miniussi, C., et al. (1999).

Pathways of interhemispheric transfer in normals and in a split-brain subject: A positron emission tomography study. *Experimental Brain Research*, 126, 451–458.

Maspes, P. K. (1948). Le syndrome experimental chez l'homme de la section du splenium du corps calleux: Alexie visuelle pure heminnopisque. *Revue Neurologique (Paris)*, 80, 100–113.

Mayer, K., Koenig, O., & Panchaud, A. (1988). Tactual extinction without anomia: Evidence of attentional factors in a patient with a partial callosal disconnection. *Neuropsychologia*, 26, 851–868.

McKeever, W. F., Sullivan, K. F., Ferguson, S. M., & Rayport, M. (1981). Typical cerebral hemisphere disconnection deficits following corpus callosum section despite sparing of the anterior commissure. *Neuropsychologia*, 19, 745–755.

McNabb, A. W., Carroll, W. M., & Mastaglia, F. L. (1988). "Alien hand" and loss of biomanual coordination after dominant anterior cerebral artery territory infarction. *Journal of Neurology, Neurosurgery, and Psychiatry*, 51, 218–222.

Mesulam, M. M. (1981). A cortical network for directed attention and unilateral neglect. *Annals of Neurology*, 10, 309–325.

Mesulam, M. M. (1990). Large-scale neurocognitive networks and distributed processing for attention, language, and memory. *Annals of Neurology*, 28, 597–613.

Meyer, B. U., Roricht S., & Woiciechowsky, C. (1998). Topography of fibers in the human corpus callosum mediating interhemispheric inhibition between the motor cortices. *Annals of Neurology*, 43, 360–369.

Michel, F., & Peronnet, F. (1975). Extinction gauche au test dichotique: Lesion hemispherique ou lesion commissurale? In F. Michel, & B. Schott (Eds.), *Les syndromes de disconnexion calleuse chez l'homme* (pp. 85–117). Lyon: Hopital Neurologique.

Miller, J. (1982). Divided attention: Evidence for coactivation with redundant signals. *Cognitive Psychology*, 14, 247–279.

Milner, A. D., & Goodale, M. A. (1995). *The visual brain in action*. Oxford, UK: Oxford University Press.

Milner, B., & Taylor, L. (1972). Right-hemisphere superiority in tactile pattern-recognition after cerebral commissurotomy: Evidence for nonverbal memory. *Neuropsychologia*, 10, 1–15.

Milner, B., Taylor, L., & Jones-Gorman, M. (1990). Lessons from cerebral commissurotomy: Auditory attention, haptic memory, and visual images in verbal associative learning. In C. B. Trevarthen (Ed.), *Brain functions and circuits of the mind* (pp. 293–303). Cambridge, UK: Cambridge University Press.

Milner, B., Taylor, L., & Sperry, R. W. (1968). Lateralized suppression of dichotically presented digits after commissural section in man. *Science*, *161*, 184–186.

Mishkin, M, & Forgays, D. G. (1952). The tachistoscopic recognition of English and Jewish words. *Journal of Experimental Psychology*, *65*, 555.

Mohr, B., Pulvermuller, F., Rayman, J., & Zaidel, E. (1994a). Interhemispheric cooperation during lexical processing is mediated by the corpus callosum: Evidence from a split-brain patient. *Neuroreport*, *181*, 17–21.

Mohr, B., Pulvermuller, F., & Zaidel, E. (1994b). Lexical decision after left, right and bilateral presentation of function words, content words and non-words: Evidence for interhemispheric interaction. *Neuropsychologia*, *32*, 105–124.

Mooshagian, E., Iacoboni, M., & Zaidel, E. (2009). Spatial attention and interhemispheric visuomotor integration in the absence of the corpus callosum. *Neuropsychologia*, *47*(3), 933–937.

Myers, R. E., & Sperry, R. W. (1958). Interhemispheric communication through the corpus callosum: Mnemonic carry-over between the hemispheres. *Archives of Neurology and Psychiatry*, *80*, 298–303.

Myers, J. J., & Sperry, R. W. (1985). Interhemispheric communication after section of the forebrain commissures. *Cortex*, *21*, 249–260.

Naikar, N. (1999). Same/different judgements about the direction and colour of apparent-motion stimuli after commissurotomy. *Neuropsychologia*, *37*, 485–493.

Naikar, N., & Corballis, M. C. (1996). Perception of apparent motion across the retinal midline following commissurotomy. *Neuropsychologia*, *34*, 297–309.

Navon, D. (1977). Forest before trees: The precedence of global features in visual perception. *Cognitive Psychology*, *9*, 353–383.

Nebes, R. D. (1971). Priority of the minor hemisphere in commissurotomized man for the perception of part-whole relations. *Cortex*, *11*, 333–349.

Nebes, R. D. (1974). Hemispheric specialization in commissurotomized man. *Psychology Bulletin*, *81*, 1–14.

Nebes, R. D., & Sperry, R. W. (1971). Hemispheric deconnection syndrome with cerebral birth injury in the dominant arm area. *Neuropsychologia*, *9*, 247–259.

O'Shea, R.P., and Corballis, P.M. (2005). Visual grouping on binocular rivalry in a split-brain observer. *Vision Research* *45*(2), 247–261.

O'Shea, R. P., & Corballis, P. M. (2004). Visual grouping on binocular rivalry in a split-brain observer. *Vision Research*, *45*(2), 247–261.

Ouimet, C., Jolicoeur, P., Miller, J., Ptito, A., Paggi, A., Foschi, N., et al. (2009). Sensory and motor involvement in the enhanced redundant target effect: A study comparing anterior- and totally split-brain individuals. *Neuropsychologia*, *47*(3), 684–692.

Pandya, D. N., & Rosene, D. F. (1985). Some observations on trajectories and topography of commissural fibers. In A. G. Reeves (Ed.), *Epilepsy and the corpus callosum* (pp. 21–39). New York: Plenum Press.

Pashler, H., Luck, S. L., Hillyard, S. A., Mangun, G. R., O'Brien, S., & Gazzaniga, M. S. (1995). Sequential operation of disconnected cerebral hemispheres in split-brain patients. *Neuroreport*, *5*, 2381–2384.

Paterson, A., & Zangwill, O. L. (1944). Disorders of visual space perception associated with lesions of the right cerebral hemisphere. *Brain*, *67*, 331–358.

Phelps, E. A., Hirst, W., & Gazzaniga, M. S. (1991). Deficits in recall following partial and complete commissurotomy. *Cerebral Cortex*, *1*, 492–498.

Pipe, M. (1991). Developmental changes in finger localization. *Neuropsychologia*, *29*, 339–342.

Plourde, G., & Sperry, R. W. (1984). Left hemisphere involvement in left spatial neglect from light-sided lesions: A commissurotomy study. *Brain*, *107*, 95–106.

Poeck, K. (1984). Neuropsychological demonstration of splenial interhemispheric disconnection in a case of "optic anomia." *Neuropsychologia*, *22*, 707–713.

Poffenberger, A. T. (1912). Reaction time to retinal stimulation: with special reference to the time lost in conduction through nerve centers. The Science Press.

Pollmann, S. (1996). A pop-out induced extinction-like phenomenon in neurologically intact subjects. *Neuropsychologia*, *34*, 413–425.

Pollmann, S., & Zaidel, E. (1998). The role of the corpus callosum in visual orienting: Importance of interhemispheric visual transfer. *Neuropsychologia*, *36*, 763–774.

Pollmann, S., & Zaidel, E. (1999). Redundancy gains for visual search after complete commissurotomy. *Neuropsychology*, *13*, 246–258.

Pollmann, S., Zaidel, E., and Cramon, D.Y. (2003). The neural basis of bilateral distribution advantage. *Experimental Brain Research* *153*(3), 322–333.

Pollmann, S., Zaidel, E., & von Cramon, D. Y. (2004). The neural basis of the bilateral distribution advantage. *Experimental Brain Research, 153*(3), 322–333.

Poncet, M., Ali Chérif, A., Choux, M., Boudouresques, J., & Lhermitte, F. (1978). Étude neuropsychologique d'un syndrome de déconnexion calleuse totale avec hémianopsie latéterale homonyme droite. *Revue Neurologique (Paris), 11*, 633–653.

Posner, M. I. (1980). Orienting of attention. *Quarterly Journal of Experimental Psychology, 32*, 3–25.

Posner, M. I., & Dehaene, S. (1994). Attentional networks. *Trends in Neuroscience, 17*, 75–79.

Proverbio, A. M., Zani, A., Gazzaniga, M. S., & Mangun, G. R. (1994). ERP and RT signs of a rightward bias for spatial orienting in a split-brain patient. *Neuroreport, 5*, 2457–2461.

Pujol, J., Junqué, C., Vendrell, P., Garcia, P., Capdevila, A., & Martí-Vilalta, J. L. (1991). Left-ear extinction in patients with MRI periventricular lesions. *Neuropsychologia, 29*, 177–184.

Quattrini, A., Del Pesce, M., Provinciali, L., Cesarano, R, Ortenzi, A., Paggi, A., et al. (1997). Mutism in 36 patients who underwent callosotomy for drug-resistant epilepsy. *Journal of Neurosurgical Sciences, 41*, 93–96.

Ramachandran, V. S., Cronin-Golomb, A., & Myers, J. J. (1986). Perception of apparent motion by commissurotomy patients. *Nature, 320*, 358–359.

Rao, S. M., Bernardin, L., Leo, G. J., Ellington, L., Ryan, S. B., & Burg, L. S. (1989). Cerebral disconnection in multiple sclerosis: Relationship to atrophy of the corpus callosum. *Archives of Neurology, 46*, 918–920.

Rayport, M., Ferguson, S. M., & Corrie, W. S. (1983). Outcomes and indications of corpus callosum section for intractable seizure control. *Applied Neurophysiology, 46*, 47–51.

Reeves, A. G. (Ed.) (1984). *Epilepsy and the corpus callosum*. New York: Plenum Press.

Reeves, A. G. (1991). Behavioral changes following corpus callosotomy. In D. Smith, D. Treiman, & M. Trimble (Eds.), *Advances in neurology* Vol. 55 (pp. 293–300). New York: Raven Press.

Reuter-Lorenz, P. A. (2002). Parallel processing in the bisected brain: Implications for callosal functions. In E. Zaidel, & M. Iacoboni (Eds.), *The Parallel Brain: The cognitive neuroscience of the corpus callosum* (pp. 341–354). Cambridge, MA: MIT Press.

Reuter-Lorenz, P. A., & Fendrich, R. (1990). Orienting attention across the vertical meridian: Evidence from callosotomy patients. *Journal of Cognitive Neuroscience, 2*, 232–238.

Reuter-Lorenz, P. A., Nozawa, G., Gazzaniga, M. S., & Hughes, H. C. (1995). Fate of neglected targets: A chronometric analysis of redundant target effects in the bisected brain. *Journal of Experimental Psychology. Human Perception And Performance, 21*, 211–230.

Risse, G., Gates, J., Lund, G., Maxwell, R., & Rubens, A. (1989). Interhemispheric transfer in patients with incomplete section of the corpus callosum. *Archives of Neurology, 46*, 437–443.

Risse, G. L., LeDoux, J., Springer, S. P., Wilson, D. H., & Gazzaniga, M. S. (1978). The anterior commissure in man: Functional variation in a multisensory system. *Neuropsychologia, 16*, 23–31.

Rivest, J., Cavanagh, P., & Lassonde, M. (1994). Interhemispheric depth judgment. *Neuropsychologia, 32*, 69–76.

Robertson, L. C., & Lamb, M. R. (1991). Neuropsychological contributions to theories of part/whole organization. *Cognitive Psychology, 23*, 299–330.

Robertson, L. C., Lamb, M. R, & Knight, R. T. (1988). Effects of lesions of temporal-parietal junction on perceptual and attentional processing in humans. *Journal of Neuroscience, 8*, 3757–3769.

Robertson, L. C., Lamb, M. R, & Zaidel, E. (1993). Interhemispheric relations in processing hierarchical patterns: Evidence from normal and commissurotomized subjects. *Neuropsychology, 7*, 325–342.

Rosahl, S. K., & Knight, R. T. (1995). Role of prefrontal cortex in generation of the contingent negative variation. *Cerebral Cortex, 5*, 123–134.

Rosene, D. L., & Van Hoesen, G. W. (1987). The hippocampal formation of the primate brain. In E.G. Jones, & A. Peters (Eds.), *Cerebral cortex* (pp. 345–456). New York: Plenum Press.

Roser, M., & Corballis, M. C. (2002). Interhemispheric neural summation in the split brain with symmetrical and asymmetrical displays. *Neuropsychologia, 40*(8), 1300–1312.

Roser, M., & Corballis, M. C. (2003). Interhemispheric neural summation in the split brain: Effect of stimulus color and task. *Neuropsychologia, 41*(7), 830–846.

Ross, E. D., & Stewart, R. M. (1981). Akinetic mutism from hypothalamic damage: Successful treatment with dopamine agonists. *Neurology, 31*, 1435–1439.

Rubens, A. B., Froehling, B., Slater, G., & Anderson, D. (1985). Left ear suppression on verbal dichotic tests in patients with multiple sclerosis. *Annals of Neurology, 18*, 459–463.

Rudge, P., & Warrington, E. K. (1991). Selective impairment of memory and visual perception in splenial tumours. *Brain*, *114*, 349–360.

Rugg, M. D., Lines, C. R., & Milner, A. D. (1984). Visual evoked potentials to lateralized visual stimuli and the measurement of interhemispheric transmission time. *Neuropsychologia*, *22*(2), 215–225.

Rugg, M. D., Milner, A. D., & Lines, C. R. (1985). Visual evoked potentials to lateralized stimuli in two cases of callosal agenesis. *Journal of Neurology, Neurosurgery and Psychiatry*, *48*(4), 367–373.

Saron, C. D., Foxe J. J., Schroeder C. E., & Vaughan H. G. (2003). Complexities of interhemispheric communication in sensorimotor tasks revealed by high-density event-related potential mapping. In K. Hugdahl, & R. J. Davidson (Eds.), *The asymmetrical brain* (pp. 341–408). Cambridge, MA: MIT Press.

Saron, C. D., Lassonde, M., Vaughan, H. G., Foze, J. J., Alfhors, S. P. & Simpson, G. V. (1997). Interhemispheric visuomotor interaction in callosal agenesis: Spatiotemporal patterns of cortical activation. *Society for Neuroscience - Abstracts*, *23*(2), 1949.

Sass, K. J., Lencz, T, Westerveld, M., Novelly, R. A., Spencer, D. D., & Kim, J. H. (1991). The neural substrate of memory impairment demonstrated by the intracarotid amobarbital procedure. *Archives of Neurology*, *48*, 48–52.

Sass, K. J., Novelly, R. A., Spencer, D. D., & Spencer, S. S. (1990). Postcallosotomy language impairments in patients with crossed cerebral dominance. *Journal of Neurosurgery*, *72*, 85–90.

Satomi, K., Horai, T., Kinoshita, Y., & Wakazono, A. (1995). Hemispheric asymmetry of event-related potentials in a patient with callosal disconnection syndrome: A comparison of auditory, visual and somatosensory modalities. *Electroencephalography and Clinical Neurophysiology*, *94*(6), 440–449.

Savaki, H., & Dalezios, Y. (1999). 14C-deoxyglucose mapping of the monkey brain during reaching to visual targets. *Progress in Neurobiology*, *58*, 473–540.

Schaltenbrand, G. (1964). Discussion. In G. Schaltenbrand, & C. N. Woolsey (Eds.), *Cerebral localization and organization* (p. 41). Madison: University of Wisconsin Press,.

Schiffer, F., Zaidel, E., Bogen, J., & Chasan-Taber, S. (1998). Different psychological status in the two hemispheres of two split-brain patients. *Neuropsychiatry Neuropsychology, and Behavioral Neurology*, *11*, 151–156.

Schott, B., Trillet, M., Michel, F., & Tommasi, M. (1974). Le syndrome de disconnexion calleuse chez l'ambidextre et le gaucher. In F. Michel, & B. Schott (Eds.), *Les syndromes de disconnexion calleuse chez l'homme* (pp. 343–346). Lyon: Hopital Neurologique.

Schwartz, M. F., Reed, E. S., Montgomery, M., Palmer, C., & Mayer, N. H. (1991). The quantitative description of action disorganisation after brain damage: A case study. *Cognitive Neuropsychology*, *8*, 381–414.

Scott, R. (Producer). (1982). *Blade Runner* [Motion picture]. United States: The Ladd Company.

Sergent, J. (1983). Unified response to bilateral hemispheric stimulation by a split-brain patient. *Nature*, *305*, 800–802.

Sergent, J. (1986). Subcortical coordination of hemisphere activity in commissurotomized patients. *Brain*, *109*, 357–369.

Sergent, J. (1987). A new look at the human split brain. *Brain*, *110*, 1375–1392.

Sergent, J. (1990). Furtive incursions into bicameral minds: Integrative and coordinating role of subcortical structures. *Brain*, *113*, 537–568.

Sergent, J. (1991). Processing of spatial relations within and between the disconnected cerebral hemispheres. *Brain*, *114*, 1025–1043.

Seymour, S. E., Reuter-Lorenz, P. A., & Gazzaniga, M. S. (1994). The disconnection syndrome: Basic findings reaffirmed. *Brain*, *117*, 105–115.

Sidtis, J. J. (1988). Dichotic listening after commissurotomy. In K. Hugdahl (Ed.), *Handbook of dichotic listening: Theory, methods and research* (pp. 161–184). New York: John Wiley and Sons.

Sidtis, J. J., Sadler, A. E., & Nass, R. D. (1989). Double disconnection effects resulting from infiltrating tumors. *Neuropsychologia*, *27*, 1415–1420.

Sidtis, J. J., Volpe, B. T., Holtzman, J. D., Wilson, D. H., & Gazzaniga, M. S. (1981a). Cognitive interaction after staged callosal section: Evidence for transfer of semantic activation. *Science*, *212*, 344–346.

Sidtis, J. J., Volpe, B. T., Wilson, D. H., Rayport, M., Gazzaniga, M. S. (1981b). Variability in right hemisphere language function after callosal section: Evidence for a continuum of generative capacity. *Journal of Neuroscience*, *1*, 323–331.

Simernitskaia, E. G., & Rurua, V. G. (1989). Memory disorders in lesions of the corpus callosum in man [in Russian]. *Zhurnal vyssheĭ nervnoĭ deiatelnosti imeni I P Pavlova*, *39*, 995–1002.

Sine, R. D., Soufi, A., & Shah, M. (1984). The callosal syndrome: Implications for stroke. *Archives of Physical Medicine and Rehabilitation, 65,* 606–610.

Sobel, N., Prabhakaran, V., Hartley, C. A., Desmond, J. E., Glover, G. H., Sullivan, E. V., & Gabrieli, J. D. (1999). Blind smell: Brain activation induced by an undetected air-borne chemical. *Brain, 122*(Pt 2), 209–217.

Sparks, R., & Geschwind, N. (1968). Dichotic listening in man after section of neocortical commissures. *Cortex, 4,* 3–16.

Sparks, R., Goodglass, H., & Nickel, B. (1970). Ipsilateral versus contralateral extinction in dichotic listening from hemispheric lesions. *Cortex, 6,* 249–260.

Speedie, L. J., Coslett, H. B., & Heilman, K. M. (1984). Repetition of affective prosody in mixed transcortical aphasia. *Archives of Neurology,41,* 268–270.

Spence, S. J., Zaidel, E., & Kasher, A. (1990). The light hemisphere communication battery: Results from commissurotomy patients and normal subjects reveal only partial right hemisphere contribution. *Journal of Clinical and Experimental Neuropsychology, 12,* 42–43.

Spencer, S. S., Gates, J. R., Reeves, A. R., Spencer, D. D., Maxwell, R. E., & Roberts D. (1987). Corpus callosum section. In J. Engel, Jr. (Ed.), *Surgical treatment of the epilepsies* (pp. 425–444). New York, Raven Press.

Spencer, S. S., Spencer, D. D., Williamson, P. D., Sass, K. J., Novelly, R. A., & Mattson, R. H. (1988). Corpus callosotomy for epilepsy. II. Neuropsychological outcome. *Neurology, 38,* 2428.

Sperry, R. W. (1974). Lateral specialization in the surgically separated hemispheres. In F. O. Schmitt, & F. G. Worden (Eds.), *Neuroscience:Third study program* (pp. 5–19). Cambridge, MA: MIT Press.

Sperry, R. W., Gazzaniga, M. S., & Bogen, J. E. (1969). Interhemispheric relationships: The neocortical commissures; syndromes of hemispheric disconnection. *Handbook of Clinical Neurology, 4,* 273–290.

Sperry, R.W., Zaidel, E., & Zaidel, D. (1979). Self recognition and social awareness in the deconnected minor hemisphere. *Neuropsychologia, 17,* 153–166.

Springer, S. P., & Gazzaniga, M. S. (1975). Dichotic testing of partial and complete split-brain subjects. *Neuropsychologia, 13,* 341–346.

Starkstein, S. E., Berthier, M. L., Fedoroff, P., Price, T. R., & Robinson, R. G. (1990). Anosognosia and major depression in 2 patients with cerebrovascular lesions. *Neurology, 40,* 1380–1382.

Sugishita, M., Otomo, K., Yamazaki, K., Shimizu, H. Yoshioka, M., & Shinohara, A. (1995). Dichotic listening in patients with partial section of the corpus callosum. *Brain, 118,* 417–427.

Sugishita, M., & Yoshioka, M. (1987). Visual processes in a hemialexic patient with posterior callosal section. *Neuropsychologia, 25,* 329–339.

Sugishita, M., Yoshioka, M., & Kawamura, M. (1986). Recovery from hemialexia. *Brain, and Language, 29,* 106–118.

Sussman, N. M., Gur, R. C., Gur, R. E., & O'Connor, M. J. (1983). Mutism as a consequence of callosotomy. *Journal of Neurosurgery, 59,* 514–519.

Sweet, W. H. (1945). Seeping intracranial aneurysm simulating neoplasm: Syndrome of the corpus callosum. *Archives of Neurology and Psychiatry, 45,* 86–104.

Tabibnia, A., Kee-Rose, K., Rickels, W., & Zaidel, E. (2001). Hemispheric specialization, emotion, and alexithymia. *Cognitive Neuroscience Society - Abstract, 8,* 30.

Tabibnia, G., & Zaidel, E. (2005). Alexithymis, interhemispheric transfer, and right hemispheric specialization: A critical review. *Psychotherapy and Psychosomatics, 74*(2), 81–92.

Tanaka, Y., Iwasa, H., & Yoshida, M. (1990). Diagnostic dyspraxia: Case report and movement related potentials. *Neurology, 40,* 657–661.

TenHouten, W. D., Hoppe, K. D., Bogen, J. E., & Walter, D. O. (1986). Alexithymia: An experimental study of cerebral commissurotomy patients and normal control subjects. *American Journal of Psychiatry, 143,* 312–316.

TenHouten, W. D., Hoppe, K. D., Bogen, J.E., & Walter, D. O. (1987). Alexithymia and the split brain. 5. EEG alpha-band interhemispheric coherence analysis. *Psychotherapy and Psychosomatics, 47,* 1–10.

TenHouten, W. D., Hoppe, K. D., Bogen, J. E., & Walter, D. O. (1988). Alexithymia and the split brain. 6. Electroencephalographic correlates of alexithymia. *Psychiatric Clinics of North America, 11*(3), 317–329.

Thurstone, L. L. (1950). Some primary abilities in visual thinking. *Proceeding of the American Philosophical Society, 94*(6), 517–521.

Tomasch, J. (1954). Size, distribution, and number of fibres in the human corpus callosum. *Anatomical Record, 119,* 7–19.

Tramo, M. J., & Bharucha, J. J. (1991). Musical priming by the right hemisphere post-callosotomy. *Neuropsychologia, 29,* 313–325.

Tramo, M. J., Baynes, K., Fendrich, R., Mangun, G. R., Phelps, E. A., Reuter-Lorenz, P. A., &

Gazzaniga, M. S. (1995). Hemispheric specialization and interhemispheric integration: Insights from experiments with commissurotomy patients. In A.G. Reeves, & D. W. Roberts (Eds.), *Epilepsy and the corpus callosum II* (pp. 263–295). New York: Plenum Press.

Treisman, A. M., & Gelade, G. (1980). A feature integration theory of attention. *Cognitive Psychology, 12*, 97–136.

Trescher, H. H., & Ford, F. R. (1937). Colloid cyst of the third ventricle; report of a case: Operative removal with section of posterior half of corpus callosum. *Archives of Neurology, Psychiatry, 37*, 959–973.

Trevarthen, C. (1965). Functional interactions between the cerebral hemispheres of the split-brain monkey. In E.C. Ettlinger (Ed.), *Functions of the corpus callosum* (pp. 24–40). London: Churchill.

Trevarthen, C. (1991). Integrative functions of the cerebral commissures. In R.D. Nebes (Ed.), *Handbook of neuropsychology, Vol. 4: The commissurotomized brain* (pp. 49–83). Oxford: Elsevier.

Trevarthen, C., & Sperry, R. W. (1973). Perceptual unity of the ambient visual field in human commissurotomy patients. *Brain, 96*, 547–570.

Trope, I., Fishman, B., Cur, R. C., Sussman, N. M., & Gur, R. E. (1987). Contralateral and ipsilateral control of fingers following callosotomy. *Neuropsychologia, 25*, 287–291.

Tuller, B., & Kelso, J. A. (1989). Environmentally specified patterns of movement coordination in normal and split-brain subjects. *Experimental Brain Research,75*, 306–316.

Twitchell, T. E. (1951). The restoration of motor function following hemiplegia in man. *Brain, 74*, 443–480.

Tzavaras, A., Hécaen, H., & Le Bras, H. (1971). Troubles de la reconnaissance du visage humain et lateralisation hemispherique lesionnelle chez les sujets gauchers. *Neuropsychologia, 9*, 475–477.

Uddin, L. Q., Mooshagian, E., Zaidel, E., Scheres, A., Margulies, D. S., Kelly, A. M. C, et al. (2008). Residual function connectivity in the split-bran revealed with resting-state functional MRI. *Neuroreport, 19*(7), 703–709.

Van Kleek, M. (1989). Hemisphere differences in global versus local processing of hierarchical visual stimuli by normal subjects: New data and a meta-analysis of previous studies. *Neuropsychologia, 27*, 1165–1178.

Volpe, B. T. (1982). Cortical mechanisms involved in praxis: Observations following partial and complete section of the corpus callosum in man. *Neurology, 32*, 645–650.

Warrington, E. K. (1969). Constructional apraxia. In P. J. Vinken, & C. W. Bruyn (Eds.), *Handbook of clinical neurology* Vol. 4 (pp. 67–83). Amsterdam: North Holland.

Warrington, E. K., James, M., & Kinsbourne, M. (1966). Drawing disability in relation to laterality of cerebral lesion. *Brain, 89*, 53–82.

Watson, R. T., & Heilman, K. M. (1983). Callosal apraxia. *Brain, 106*, 391–403.

Weekes, N., Ptito, A., & Zaidel, E. (submitted). Perceptual and hemispheric relationships in a hierarchical perception task.

Weekes, N. Y., Carusi, D., & Zaidel, E. (1997). Interhemispheric relations in hierarchical perception: A second look. *Neuropsychologia, 35*, 37–44.

Weekes, N. Y., & Zaidel, E. (1996). The effects of procedural variations on lateralized Stroop effects. *Brain and Cognition, 31*, 308–330.

Weems, S., & Zaidel, E. (2004). The relationship between reading ability and lateralized lexical decision. *Brain & Cognition, 55*(3), 507–515.

Weems, S., Zaidel, E., Berman, S., & Mandelkern, M. (unpublished). Gamma response to lexical stimuli in the split-brain: Electrophysiological response in the absence of behavioral competency.

West, S. E., & Doty, R. L. (1995). Influence of epilepsy and temporal lobe resection on olfactory function. *Epilepsia, 36*, 531–542.

Wilson, C. L., Isokawa-Akesson, M., Babb, T. L., & Crandall, P. H. (1990). Functional connections in the human temporal lobe: 1. Analysis of limbic system pathways using neuronal activity evoked by electrical stimulation. *Experimental Brain Research, 82*, 279–292.

Wilson, C. L., Isokawa-Akesson, M., Babb, T. L., Engle, J. J., Cahan, L. D., Crandall, & P. H. (1987). A comparative view of local and interhemispheric limbic pathways in humans: An evoked potential analysis. In J. Engle, Jr. (Ed.), *Fundamental mechanisms of human brain function* (pp. 27–38). New York: Raven Press.

Wilson, D. H., Culver, C., Waddington, M., & Gazzaniga, M. (1975). Disconnection of the cerebral hemispheres. *Neurology, 25*, 1149–1153.

Wilson, D. H., Reeves, A., Gazzaniga, M., & Culver, C. (1977). Cerebral commissurotomy for control of intractable seizures. *Neurology, 7*, 708–715.

Witelson, S.F. (1974). Hemispheric specialization for linguistic and nonlinguistic tactual perception using a dichotomous stimulation technique. Cortex 10(1), 3–17.

Wittling, W. (1990). Psychophysiological correlates of human brain asymmetry: Blood pressure changes during lateralized presentation of an emotionally laden film. *Neuropsychologia, 28*, 457–470.

Wolford, G., Miller, M. B., & Gazzaniga, M. (2000). The left hemisphere's role in hypothesis formation. *Journal of Neuroscience, 20*(6), 64.

Yakovlev, P. I., & Lecours, A. R. (1967). The myelogenetic cycles of regional maturation of the brain. In A. Minkowski (Ed.), *Regional development of the brain in early life* (pp. 3–70). Edinburgh: Blackwell.

Yamadori, A., Nagashima, T., & Tamaki, N. (1983). Ideogram writing in a disconnection syndrome. *Brain and Language, 19*, 346–356.

Zaidel, D., & Sperry, R. W. (1974). Memory impairment after commissurotomy in man. *Brain, 97*, 263–272.

Zaidel, D., & Sperry, R. W. (1977). Some long-term motor effects of cerebral commissurotomy in man. *Neuropsychologia, 15*, 193–204.

Zaidel, D. W. (1995). A view of the world from a split-brain perspective. In E. Critchley (Ed.), *The neurological boundaries of reality*. New Jersey: Aronson.

Zaidel, D. W. (1990a). Long-term semantic memory in the two cerebral hemispheres. In C. Trevarthen (Ed.), *Brain circuits and functions of the mind* (pp. 266–280). New York: Cambridge University Press.

Zaidel, D. W. (1990b). Memory and spatial cognition following commissurotomy. In F. Boller & J. Grafman (Eds.), *Handbook of neuropsychology* Vol. 4 (pp. 151–166). Amsterdam: Elsevier.

Zaidel, D. W. (1993). View of the world from a split-brain perspective. In E. Critchley (Ed.), *Neurological boundaries of reality* (pp. 161–74). London: Farrand Press.

Zaidel, D. W. (1994). Worlds apart: Pictorial semantics in the left and right cerebral hemispheres. *Current Directions in Psychological Science, 3*, 5–8.

Zaidel, E. (1973). *Linguistic competence and related functions in the right hemisphere of man following commissurotomy and hemispherectomy.* Ph. D. thesis, California Institute of Technology. Dissertation Abstracts International. 34:2350B (University Microfilms 73–26, 481).

Zaidel, E. (1975). A technique for presenting lateralized visual input with prolonged exposure. *Vision Research, 15*, 283–289.

Zaidel, E. (1976). Auditory vocabulary of the right hemisphere following brain bisection or hemidecortication. *Cortex, 12*, 191–211.

Zaidel, E. (1977). Unilateral auditory language comprehension on the token test following cerebral commissurotomy and hemispherectomy. *Neuropsychologia, 15*, 1–17.

Zaidel, E. (1978a). Concepts of cerebral dominance in the split-brain. In P. Buser, & A. Rougeul-Buser (Eds.), *Cerebral correlates of conscious experience* (pp. 263–284). Amsterdam: Elsevier.

Zaidel, E. (1978b). Lexical organization in the right hemisphere. In P. Buser, & A. Rougeul-Buser (Eds.), *Cerebral correlates of conscious experience* (pp. 177–197). Amsterdam: Elsevier.

Zaidel, E. (1979). Performance on the ITPA following cerebral commissurotomy and hemispherectomy. *Neuropsychologia, 17*(3–4), 259–280.

Zaidel, E. (1981). Hemispheric intelligence: The case of the Raven Progressive Matrices. In M. P. Friedman, J. P. Das, & N. O'Connor (Eds.), *Intelligence and learning* (pp. 531–552). New York: Plenum Press.

Zaidel, E. (1982). Reading in the disconnected right hemisphere: An aphasiological perspective. In Y. Zotterman (Ed.), *Dyslexia: Neuronal, cognitive and linguistic aspects* (pp. 67–91). Oxford: Pergamon Press.

Zaidel, E. (1983). Disconnection syndrome as a model for laterality effects in the normal brain. In J. Hellige (Ed.), *Cerebral hemisphere asymmetry: Method, theory and application* (pp. 95–151). New York: Praeger.

Zaidel, E. (1986). Callosal dynamics and right hemisphere language. In F. Lepore, M. Ptito, & H. H. Jasper (Eds.), *Two Hemispheres-One Brain: Functions of the corpus callosum* (pp. 435–459). New York: Alan R. Liss.

Zaidel, E. (1994). Interhemispheric transfer in the split-brain: long-term status following complete cerebral commissurotomy. In R. J. Davidson, & K. Hughdal (Eds.), *Brain asymmetry* (pp. 491–531). Cambridge, MA: MIT Press.

Zaidel, E. (1998a). Language in the right hemisphere following callosal disconnection. In B. Stemmer, & H. Whitaker (Eds.), *Handbook of neurolinguistics* (pp. 369–383). San Diego: Academic Press.

Zaidel, E. (1998b). Stereognosis in the chronic split brain: Hemispheric differences, ipsilateral control and sensory integration across the midline. *Neuropsychologia, 36*, 1033–1047.

Zaidel, E. (2001a). Hemispheric specialization for language in the split brain. In F. Boller, & J. Grafman (Series Eds.) & R. Berndt (Vol. Ed.), *Handbook of neuropsychology* (2nd ed.) Vol. 2, *Language and aphasia* (pp. 393–418). Amsterdam: Elsevier.

Zaidel, E. (2001b). Brain asymmetry. In N. J. Smelser, & P. B. Baltes (Series Eds.) & R. F. Thompson (Vol. Ed.), *International encyclopedia of the social & behavioral sciences:* Vol. 2. *Behavioral and cognitive neuroscience* (pp. 1321–1329). Amsterdam, New York: Elsevier.

Zaidel, E., Clarke, J. M., & Suyenobu, B. (1990). Hemispheric independence: A paradigm case for cognitive neuroscience. In A. B. Scheibel, & A. F. Wechsler (Eds.), *Neurobiology of higher cognitive functions* (pp. 297–355). New York: Guilford Press.

Zaidel, E., & Frazer, R. E. (1977). A universal half-field occluder for laterality research. *Caltech Biology Annual Report*, 137–138.

Zaidel, E., & Iacoboni, M. (2003). Sensory-motor integration in the spilt-brain. In E. Zaidel, & M. Iacoboni (Eds.), *The parallel brain: The cognitive neuroscience of the corpus callosum* (pp. 319–336). Cambridge, MA: MIT Press.

Zaidel, E., & Peters, A. M. (1981). Phonological encoding and ideographic reading by the disconnected light hemisphere: Two case studies. *Brain and Language, 14*, 205–234.

Zaidel, E., & Rayman, J. (1994). Interhemispheric control in the normal brain: Evidence from redundant bilateral presentations. In C. Umilta, & M. Moscovitch (Eds.), *Attention & performance XV: Conscious and nonconscious processes* (pp. 477–504). Cambridge, MA: MIT Press.

Zaidel, E., White, H., Sakurai, E., & Banks, W. (1988). Hemispheric locus of lexical congruity effects: Neuropsychological reinterpretation of psycholinguistic results. In C. Chiarello (Ed.), *Right hemisphere contributions to lexical semantics* (pp. 71–88). New York: Springer.

Zaidel, E., Zaidel, D. W, & Bogen, J. E. (1990). Testing the commissurotomy patient. In A. A. Boulton, G. B. Baker, & M. Hiscock (Eds.) *Neuromethods,* Vol. 15 *Neuropsychology* (pp. 147–201). Clifton, NJ: Humana Press.

Zaidel, E., Zaidel, D. W, & Sperry, R. W. (1981). Left and right intelligence: Case studies of Raven's Progressive Matrices following brain bisection and hemidecortication. *Cortex, 17*, 167–186.

Zaidel, E., Zaidel, D. W., & Bogen, J. E. (1999). The split brain. In G. Adelman, & B. Smith (Eds.), *Encyclopedia of neuroscience* (2nd ed., pp. 1930–1936). Amsterdam: Elsevier.

Zald, D. H., & Pardo, J. V. (1997). Emotion, olfaction, and the human amygdala: Amygdala activation during aversive olfactory stimulation. *Proceedings of the National Academy of Sciences USA, 94*, 4119–4124.

Zarei, M., Johansen-Berg, H., Smith, S., Ciccarelli, O., Thompson, A. J., & Matthews, P.M. (2006). Functional anatomy of interhemispheric cortical connections in the human brain. *Journal of Anatomy, 209*, 311–320.

Zatorre, R. J., & Jones-Gotman, M. (1991). Human olfactory discrimination after unilateral frontal or temporal lobectomy. *Brain, 114*(Pt. lA), 71–84.

14

The Frontal Lobes

ANTONIO R. DAMASIO, STEVEN W. ANDERSON,
AND DANIEL TRANEL

Although this is a time of unprecedented progress in cognitive neuroscience, clinicians who evaluate and treat frontal lobe dysfunction still face many of the frustrations encountered by prior generations. Damage to the frontal lobes can disrupt in various ways a set of very complex neuroanatomical and functional systems, which for the most part remain incompletely understood. The frontal lobes make up over one-third of the human cerebral cortex and have diverse anatomical units, each with distinct connections to other cortical and subcortical regions and to each other. Although progress has been made in elucidating the connectional pattern and physiology of some of its subregions in nonhuman primates (see below), the means have not existed to map equivalent complexity in the human brain. Paralleling the challenges presented by the anatomical complexity of the frontal lobes are those that stem from the nature of the signs and symptoms of frontal damage, and most saliently, the fact that such signs and symptoms do not lend themselves easily to quantitative analysis in a laboratory setting. Nonetheless, new findings on frontal lobe dysfunction are appearing regularly and have provided support for some long-held suppositions, as well as new ideas regarding the operations of the frontal lobes. For example, the central role of the frontal lobes in higher cognitive activities is not in question, and there is also growing evidence that frontal dysfunction may contribute to certain psychiatric disorders.

The purpose of this chapter is to review important cognitive and behavioral changes that result from damage to the human frontal lobes. Selected findings from research with nonhuman primates and functional imaging studies of normal persons are also included. In light of the limited sensitivity and specificity of established clinical neuropsychological probes to the cognitive and behavioral defects that result from frontal lobe damage, it is particularly important for clinicians to be aware of experimental findings regarding frontal lobe dysfunction. Attention to such research will not only allow for more sophisticated understanding of the behavioral problems seen in patients with damage to frontal networks, but may also provide clues to help guide development of the next generation of clinical measures.

NEUROANATOMICAL OVERVIEW

Knowledge of neuroanatomy is helpful in understanding the functions of the frontal lobe, and is also a prerequisite for the interpretation of the investigations discussed later in this chapter. For that reason, we present here a brief review of frontal lobe morphology.

FRONTAL CORTEX

Inspection of the external surface of the lobe reveals three important natural borders—the Rolandic sulcus, the Sylvian fissure, and the corpus callosum—and three large expansions of cortex—in the lateral convexity, in the mesial

flat aspect that faces the opposite lobe, and in the inferior concave aspect that covers the roof of the orbit. Traditional anatomy has divided the frontal cortex into the following principal regions: the precentral cortex, the prefrontal cortex, and the limbic cortex (Figure 14-1).

The precentral cortex corresponds to the long gyrus immediately anterior to the Rolandic sulcus, forming its anterior bank and depth. This area continues over the mesial lip of the

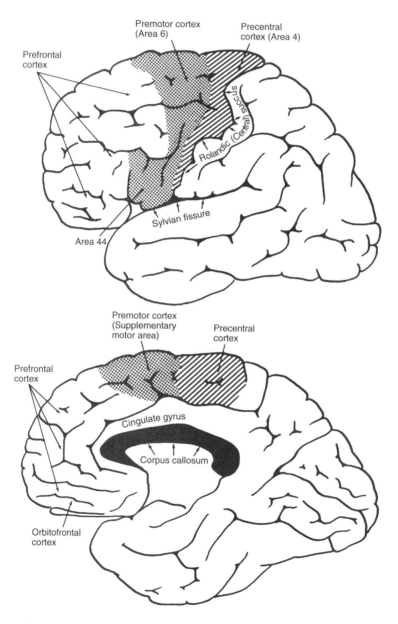

Figure 14–1. Lateral (*top*) and medial (*bottom*) views of the human cerebral hemisphere.

lobe, forming the anterior part of the paracentral lobule. Histologically, it is a region of agranular cortex, and its function as the primary motor area is well known. The presence of Betz cells is a distinguishing feature. In Brodmann's map (Figure 14-1), it corresponds to field 4. Anterior and parallel to this region lies the premotor cortex, which in humans corresponds to the posterior portion of the three horizontally placed frontal gyri. Histologically, this is a transitional cortex, the function of which is closely related to motor activity. For the most part, this is field 6 in Brodmann's map, but the lower region, which comprises a portion of the third (inferior) frontal gyrus, is referenced as field 44 and corresponds to Broca's area. Field 45 is closely connected to 44, both anatomically and functionally. In the mesial prolongation of the premotor zone, which also approximates the cingulate sulcus, lies the supplementary motor area. A cingulate motor area with a topographically organized body map lies in the depths and lower bank of the cingulate sulcus. Like the primary and supplementary motor cortices, it gives rise to corticospinal axons.

Anterior to both the precentral and premotor regions lies the prefrontal cortex, which makes up most of the frontal cortex and encompasses the pole of the lobe. Macroscopically, three major aspects may be distinguished: mesial, dorsolateral, and orbital. Histologically much of this is granular cortex that corresponds in Brodmann's map to fields 8, 9, 10, 11, 12, 47, and 46. This is the enigmatic area that most authors have in mind when they speak of the frontal lobe in relation to behavior. Little is known about the contribution of each of these separate areas, with the exception of area 8, the so-called eye field, which presumably serves a central role in relation to eye and head movements. The limbic system parts of the frontal lobe correspond to areas 24, 25, and 32 (the anterior and subgenual portions of the cingulate gyrus) and to areas 13 and 14 (the posterior parts of the orbitofrontal area and the gyrus rectus). Technically, these are agranular cortices; however, they are probably related in essential ways to both the granular and agranular cortices.

FRONTAL LOBE CONNECTIONS

Understanding the prefrontal lobe depends upon knowledge of its afferent and efferent connections. Some of these connections are with other neocortical structures, mainly from and to association areas in the temporal, parietal, and occipital lobes, including special areas of multimodal convergence. The prefrontal cortex is also connected to the premotor region and thus indirectly to motor cortex. There are significant connections with limbic and motor subcortical structures, as well as with the cingulate motor area, giving prefrontal cortex direct access to neurons that give rise to corticobulbar and corticospinal axons. Some projections are unidirectional, such as those to the caudate and putamen. Some seem to be bidirectional, such as those with the nucleus medialis dorsalis of the thalamus. The latter is a particularly important connection, so much so that some authors have defined the prefrontal cortex as that region which is coextensive with projections from the nucleus medialis dorsalis. The arrangement of projections is quite specific: The orbital aspect is linked with the pars magnocellularis, the dorsolateral cortex with the pars parvocellularis. Other major subcortical connections are with the hippocampus by way of the cingulate and parahippocampal gyri, with the amygdala by way of the uncinate fasciculus, and with the hypothalamus, the septum, and the mesencephalon by direct pathways.

The prefrontal cortex thus receives input, by more than one channel, from the sensory association regions of the cortex; it is closely woven with the limbic system; and it can affect the motor system in multiple ways. The functionally central position of the frontal lobe can be made clearer by a brief review of its efferent and afferent connections in nonhuman primates.

The frontal lobe of the monkey is roughly comparable to that of the human in shape, limits, connections, and cytoarchitecture. Important differences, besides size, are apparent in the dorsolateral aspect where, instead of the three horizontally oriented gyri of the human frontal lobe, there are two fields placed in a dorsal and ventral position in relation to a single sulcus, the principalis (see Figure 14-2). One other major

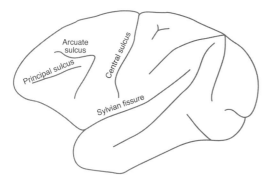

Figure 14–2. Lateral view of the brain of a rhesus monkey, with major frontal lobe sulci indicated.

sulcus, the arcuate, arch-shaped and roughly vertically oriented, marks the border between the monkey's prefrontal and premotor cortex. It is in this transition zone, particularly in the rostral bank of the sulcus, that Brodmann's field 8 is located. For a thorough comparison between the human frontal lobe and the frontal lobe of nonhuman primates, we recommend the pioneering investigation conducted by Semendeferi and H. Damasio using magnetic resonance imaging (MRI; Semendeferi, Lu, Schenker, & Damasio, 2002).

(Sources used in the following description of subcortical and cortical projections are Ward & McCulloch, 1947; Bailey & Von Bonin, 1951; Pribram & MacLean, 1953; Pribram et al., 1953; Whitlock & Nauta, 1956; Crosby et al., 1962; Nauta, 1962; Akert, 1964; De Vito & Smith, 1964; Nauta, 1964; Kuypers et al., 1965; Powell, et al., 1965; Valverde, 1965; Johnson et al., 1968; Nauta & Haymaker, 1969; Pandya et al., 1969; Pandya & Kuypers, 1969; Pandya & Vignolo, 1971; Pandya et al., 1971; Kievit & Kuypers, 1974; Chavis & Pandya, 1976; Rosene, et al., 1976; Goldman & Nauta, 1977; Yeterian & Van Hoesen, 1977; Goldman, 1978; Potter & Nauta, 1979; Damasio & Van Hoesen, 1980; Barbas & Mesulam, 1981; Porrino et al., 1981; Goldman-Rakic & Schwartz, 1982; Porrino & Goldman-Rakic, 1982; Petrides & Pandya, 1984, 1988; Barbas & Mesulam, 1985; Barbas & Pandya, 1987, 1989; Goldman-Rakic, 1987; Moran et al., 1987; Pandya & Barnes, 1987; Cavada & Goldman-Rakic, 1989; Seltzer & Pandya, 1989; Di Pellegrino & Wise, 1991; Goldman-Rakic & Friedman, 1991; Preuss & Goldman-Rakic,

1991; Morecraft & Van Hoesen, 1993; Barbas, 1995; Fuster, 1997; Price 1999a, 1999b; Öngur & Price, 2000).

SUBCORTICAL CONNECTIONS

Projections from the Hypothalamus

Direct projections from the hypothalamus have not been as easy to identify as those in the opposite direction, which may possibly reflect a different functional significance. At any rate, some evidence suggests that there are such projections to several regions above and below the arcuate sulcus and to the rostral part of the principal sulcus. These projections may be parallel to the monoaminergic projections arising in the mesencephalic tegmentum and may indeed be interwoven with them, since the latter are known to travel in the lateral hypothalamic region.

Projections from the Amygdala and the Hippocampus

There are strong projections from the amygdala and hippocampus to the orbital cortex, particularly in its most posterior and medial region, but the amygdala also projects to the mesial aspect of the frontal lobe, particularly into areas such as the gyrus rectus and the subcallosal portion of the cingulate gyrus and the anterior parts of the cingulate gyrus (Brodmann's areas 25 and 24, respectively). The amygdala, as does the hippocampus, projects to areas of the diencephalon and mesencephalon, to which the prefrontal lobe itself strongly projects.

Projections from the Thalamus

The afferent projections from the thalamus originate mostly in those regions where the efferent projections from the prefrontal cortex terminate, that is, in both the medial and lateral aspects of the dorsomedial nucleus. The medial thalamus thus appears as a transforming station for inputs from the prefrontal regions. Projections of the medial pulvinar to area 8 have also been described, and it is now known that other projections from the thalamic association nuclei, midline nuclei, and intralaminar nuclei exist. These link the prefrontal cortex to ascending reticular, visceral, and autonomic systems.

Projections to the Amygdala and Hippocampus

These arise mostly from the mesial and orbital aspects and partly from the inferior ventral dorsolateral aspect and travel in the cingulum and uncinate fasciculus. Many go directly to the amygdala, although others go to rostral temporal cortex, which in turn projects to the amygdala. Projection to the hippocampus is indirect via the limbic cortex of the cingulate and hippocampal gyri (retrosplenial and perirhinal cortices respectively).

Projections to the Hypothalamus

Direct connections to various hypothalamic nuclei have long been mentioned, but have been only recently described with certainty in monkeys. Almost in continuum with the latter, there are projections to the mesencephalic tegmentum, namely, to the anterior half of the periaqueductal gray matter. These are areas to which both the hippocampus and the amygdala send strong projections.

Projections to the Septum

In the monkey, these probably arise from the upper bank of the sulcus principalis. A reciprocal connection is probably involved. As with hypothalamic projections, further investigations of these potentially important prefrontal efferents are needed.

Projections to the Thalamus

Other than the well-known projections to the nucleus dorsalis medialis, fibers also terminate in the intralaminar thalamic complex and pulvinar.

Projections to the Striatum

Projections to the caudate and the putamen but not the pallidum have been identified. The projections from the cingulate gyrus and supplementary motor area are especially strong. It was once thought that the frontocaudate projection was limited to the head of the caudate, but it has recently been shown that the prefrontal cortex projects to the whole caudate. Of particular interest is the fact that regions of the cortex with which the frontal lobe is reciprocally innervated (e.g., the parietal lobe) seem to project to the caudate in approximately the same area. This integrates corticostriate neural systems with corticocortical neural systems.

Projections to the Claustrum, Subthalamic Regions, and Mesencephalon

Projections to the claustrum travel in the uncinate fasciculus and external capsule, and originate in the orbital and inferior dorsolateral aspects. Projections to the regions of the subthalamic nucleus and the red nucleus also seem to come primarily from the orbital aspects. Some projections to the central gray seem to come from the convexity, but a strong contingent arises from orbitofrontal and medial frontal cortices.

CORTICAL CONNECTIONS

Projections from Visual, Auditory, and Somatosensory Cortex

Practically all areas of the association cortex project to the frontal lobe. In the rhesus monkey, these projections have been studied in relation to two distinct regions: the periarcuate cortex, which surrounds the arcuate sulcus, and the prearcuate cortex, which includes all of the frontal pole lying anterior to the former region and which encompasses the region of the sulcus principalis.

Projections terminating in the periarcuate cortex arise from the caudal portion of the superior temporal gyrus, the lateral peristriate belt, the superior parietal lobule, and the anterior portion of the inferior parietal lobule. Projections terminating in the prearcuate cortex arise from the middle region of the superior temporal gyrus, the caudal and inferior temporal cortex, and the middle portion of the inferior bank of the intraparietal sulcus.

Direct projections to the orbital cortex come mainly from the anterior region of the superior temporal gyrus, but there are also indirect projections that reach this area by way of the mediodorsal thalamus: These originate in the middle and inferior temporal gyri and share the same route of projections from the olfactory cortex.

Considerable overlap takes place in relation to these connections, for instance, between the first-order visual and auditory projections in the periarcuate region and between second-order visual, auditory, and somatosensory projections in prearcuate cortex.

Projections from Olfactory Cortex and Olfactory Bulb

The piriform cortex projects to the frontal lobe indirectly by way of the mediodorsal nucleus of the thalamus. In this way, olfactory information joins that of the other senses to create a convergence absent in the posterior sensory cortex. There are direct connections from the olfactory bulb to the posterior orbitofrontal cortex.

Projections to Temporal Cortex

The temporal cortex receives projections from regions of the sulcus principalis in a well-organized fashion. The anterior third projects mainly to the anterior third of the superior temporal sulcus and the superior temporal gyrus. The middle third connects with both the anterior and the middle portions of the superior temporal sulcus. The posterior third projects mainly to the more caudal region of the superior temporal sulcus. The orbital aspect of the frontal lobe also projects to the rostral area of the temporal lobe and especially the temporal polar cortex.

Projections to Posterior Sensory Cortex

These projections are mainly directed to the inferior parietal lobule and originate in the posterior third of the sulcus principalis and in the arcuate sulcus.

Projections to Nonmotor Limbic Cortex

Both the anterior and middle thirds of the sulcus principalis project to the lower part of the cingulate gyrus, the latter in a more intense fashion, as do areas in the concavity of the arcuate sulcus. This is an interesting projection that courses all along the cingulate, distributing fibers to the overlying cortex but then continuing as a bundle to reach the parahippocampal gyrus.

PATHOPHYSIOLOGY

Traditionally, two main problems have complicated the evaluation of behavioral and cognitive manifestations of frontal lobe damage: the concept of a single "frontal lobe syndrome," and the failure to consider the multitude of pathophysiological, individual, and environmental variables that can influence the expression of frontal lobe dysfunction. The notion that there is a unitary frontal lobe syndrome is not supported by anatomical or neuropsychological evidence. The locus of a lesion within the frontal lobe is a crucial factor in the profile of frontal lobe signs. Side of lesion, for instance, is important, as there is evidence that some lesions of the left frontal lobe interfere with verbal behavior more so than do corresponding right-sided lesions (in persons with standard left language dominance), and certain emotional changes are also related to the left–right dichotomy. Gender may interact with side, as there is recent evidence that the functional asymmetry of the frontal lobes may be sex-related (e.g., Tranel, Damasio, Denburg, & Bechara, 2005). Bilateral lesions may produce yet a different clinical picture, both quantitatively and qualitatively. Regional effects within a lobe may determine distinctive clinical configurations and allow the prediction of whether the involvement is predominantly mesial, dorsolateral, or inferior orbital. Depth of lesion is also an important variable, probably as much so as surface extent of damage. Many signs of frontal lobe dysfunction result from severed subcortical connections, which a deep lesion has a better chance of producing.

Analysis of the behavioral effects of different loci of damage must also take account of the nature of the lesion. The clinical presentation of the various pathophysiological processes that can cause damage to the frontal lobes can be quite different from one another.

Vascular disorders, tumors, and traumatic injury are among the most common causes of structural damage in the frontal lobes.

The vascular syndromes are the most distinctive, particularly those related to the anterior cerebral artery. Bilateral as well as unilateral involvement is a common cause of mutism with or without akinesia. Personality changes are also frequently found, and a characteristic amnesic syndrome has been identified with lesions in this vascular distribution (Damasio et al., 1985). Damage is predominantly to the ventromedial and mesial aspects of the frontal lobe. The most common cause of those abnormalities is rupture of an aneurysm of the anterior communicating artery or of the anterior cerebral artery itself. In other cases, the frontal branches of the middle cerebral artery may be involved, the more frequent causes being embolism and thrombosis. Damage is almost always unilateral and predominantly affects the dorsolateral aspect of the lobe, giving rise to various speech and language impairments when the left hemisphere is involved and to affective and spatial alterations when the right hemisphere is injured.

The syndromes caused by tumors naturally vary with location and histological nature. Extrinsic tumors, such as meningiomas, are frequently located subfrontally or at the cerebral falx, where they involve the mesial aspect of the frontal lobes and often cause bilateral changes. They may also have a more lateral origin and compress the dorsolateral aspect of one frontal lobe only. Intrinsic tumors may show up unilaterally or bilaterally. The distinction often depends on time, as an originally unilateral glioma may invade the corpus callosum and cross to the opposite side.

Not uncommonly, patients with frontal lobe tumors present with major intellectual and affective impairment that justifies the use of the term "dementia," so pervasive is the disorganization of normal behavior (e.g., Strauss & Keschner, 1935). For this reason, the diagnosis of frontal lobe tumor should always be considered in the study of a dementia syndrome. Confusional states are also frequently associated with tumors of the frontal lobe, perhaps more so than with tumors anywhere else in the central nervous system (Hecaen, 1964). Disturbances of mood and character, although less frequent than confusion or dementia, were noted almost as frequently in Hecaen's study.

Wounds caused by head injury—whose clinical pictures were vividly described by Kleist (1936) and Goldstein (1948)—may have a preponderant frontal involvement and present with a combination of frontal lobe signs. The orbital surface of the frontal lobes and the frontal poles are particularly susceptible to damage from traumatic head injury, due to contact of these structures with the skull. Although the consequences of head injury typically reflect the combined effects of damage to multiple brain areas, many of the sequelae that prove to be most disruptive are similar to those seen following focal damage in frontal cortex, and are likely related to frontal damage per se.

The rate of development of a lesion and the time elapsed since peak development are additional factors that interact with lesion type to influence the clinical picture. Worsening, stabilization, or recovery depend on the nature of the underlying pathological process. Most patients with cerebrovascular lesions tend to stabilize and then improve gradually, whereas the course of patients with tumors is a function of the degree of cytological and mechanical malignancy of the tumor and of the nature of the surgical or medical management adopted. Patients with severe symptomatology from a vascular event or traumatic injury will often have a remarkable remission within a period of weeks. On the other hand, patients with slowly growing tumors that infiltrate neural tissue without grossly disrupting its function may fail to show measurable behavioral defects, in spite of the considerable size of their malignancies (Anderson et al., 1989).

Another important factor is the age at which the dysfunction begins. There is evidence that the effects of lesions starting in childhood or adolescence are different from those caused by lesions starting in adulthood (Grattan & Eslinger, 1991; Anderson et al., 1999). If these factors are not taken into account, it will not be possible to make an adequate clinical evaluation of patients, and clinical research may produce paradoxical results.

The results of prefrontal leucotomy and prefrontal lobotomy, which were a source of early information on frontal lobe physiology, have also been a source of controversy. Although Moniz (1936, 1949) was impressed by the lack of pronounced defects of motor, sensory, and language function in cases of frontal lobe lesion, he attributed several important functions to the frontal lobe. He reasoned that, in cases of schizophrenic thought disorder or of obsessive compulsive disease, the wrongly learned and abnormally repetitive thinking processes were dependent on frontal lobe (dys)function and based on reverberating circuitry connecting the frontal lobe to midline subcortical structures and to the posterior cortical areas. Such "repetitive linkages" called for surgical interruption. He also hypothesized a relation between the aberrant thought process and the accompanying emotional status of the patient, and he assumed that a lesion that altered one would also alter the other. He recalled the frequent observation of affective indifference in frontal lobe patients, as well as the remarkable affective changes shown in Jacobsen's chimpanzees (Fulton & Jacobsen, 1935) after frontal lobe surgery. It seems that Moniz conceived of the frontal lobes as important for higher cognition and for the regulation of emotion (Fulton, 1951). Far from designing an innocuous intervention, he intended to create particular defects that might benefit patients whose previous abnormality was thoroughly incapacitating.

Objective assessment of the results of prefrontal surgery is difficult to obtain. The original Moniz method, apparently one of the most effective and least damaging, was not used in the United States. Other surgical methods have been devised involving various amounts of damage to different structures. All cases suffered from preexisting psychiatric disease or intractable pain, generally of considerable severity and duration. Finally, the methods of behavioral assessment have been varied in scope and quality. It is evident, however, that bilateral, surgically controlled frontal lobe damage, particularly when it involves the mesial and inferior orbital cortices or their connections, causes modifications in the affective and emotional sphere. Leaving aside any discussion of the value of this approach in psychiatry, it is important for neuropsychologists to know that even minor psychosurgery may be a factor in

their patients' behavior. For an appraisal of the measurable neuropsychologic disturbances associated with leucotomy, the reader is referred to Stuss et al. (1981).

Frontal lobe damage also may play a prominent role in many progressive demential syndromes. For example, Van Hoesen et al. (2000) found extensive distribution of neurofibrillary tangles throughout the orbitofrontal cortex of patients with Alzheimer disease. It is likely that this damage contributes to some of the non–memory behavioral disorders that are common in Alzheimer disease. There is evidence, from functional neuroimaging cases, that patients with Alzheimer disease have diminished activation in the frontal cortices, especially in the medial sector. The reductions in activation can be identified early in the disease (Minoshima et al., 1997). In light of findings of orbitofrontal activation in normal adults during memory tasks (e.g., Frey & Petrides, 2000), it also is possible that neurofibrillary tangles in this region contribute to the memory defects in Alzheimer disease. In other demential syndromes, frontal lobe dysfunction is the most important feature. Progressive impairments of behavioral regulation, attention, and emotion, in the context of relatively preserved memory, characterize the frontal variant of frontotemporal dementia (e.g., Neary et al., 1988; Rahman et al., 1999; Perry & Hodges, 2000). The behavior of these patients gradually deteriorates to resemble that of persons with macroscopic lesions in the frontal lobes. The insidious onset of the behavioral abnormalities in the absence of an identifiable neurological event presents particular challenges for diagnosis and management.

NEUROLOGICAL FINDINGS

CHANGES IN AROUSAL AND ORIENTING RESPONSE

Patients who move little or not at all often pay limited attention to new stimuli. The possibility that akinesia associated with frontal lobe lesions goes pari passu with severe bilateral neglect is an interesting one. Thus, changes in motor and affective processing may be associated with changes in the mechanisms of arousal. The type of abnormality described by Fisher (1968) as "intermittent interruption of behavior" in cases of anterior cerebral artery infarction is another good example of the coexistence of such changes.

There is no doubt that orienting responses are impaired after dorsolateral and cingulate gyrus damage. The changes frequently appear in the setting of neglect to stimuli arriving in the space contralateral to the lesion, with associated hypomobility of the neglected side (Heilman & Valenstein, 1972; Damasio et al., 1980). Lesions in the arcuate region in primates cause unilateral neglect (Kennard & Ectors, 1938; Welch & Stuteville, 1958), not unlike that determined by lesions of multimodal parietal association areas (Heilman et al., 1971), and the same applies to the cingulate gyrus (Watson et al., 1973). Lesions in non–frontal lobe structures—including the thalamus, hypothalamus, and midbrain—can also cause neglect in both humans and animals (Segarra & Angelo, 1970; Marshall et al., 1971; Marshall & Teitelbaum, 1974; Watson et al., 1974). And, in human lesion studies, it has been shown that damage to the anterior cingulate region leads to marked impairments in psychophysiological orienting responses (Tranel & H. Damasio, 1994).

ABNORMAL REFLEXES

The more significant abnormal reflexes are the grasp reflex, the groping reflex, and the snout and sucking reflexes. Traditionally. these abnormal responses have been called *psychomotor signs*, calling attention to the fact that they almost invariably appear in the setting of an abnormal mental status.

The most useful of the group is the grasp reflex (the prehension reflex of Kleist, the forced grasping of Adie and Critchley), which may appear unilaterally or bilaterally, in the hands or in the feet. It consists of a more or less forceful prehension of an object that has come into contact with the palm or the sole. It can be elicited by touching or by stroking the skin, particularly in the region between the thumb and index finger. Most maneuvers used to elicit the plantar reflex may produce a grasp reaction of the foot and may even mask an abnormal

extensor response, which, in that case, may be obtained from stimulation of the lateral side of the foot. The degree of the grasp reflex varies from patient to patient and is generally more intense in cases with impaired mentation. In more alert states, it is characteristic that the patient cannot release the prehension even if told to do so and even if she or he wishes to do so. The reflex may extinguish after repeated stimulation and reappear after a period of rest. Classic descriptions used to refer to changes in lateralization induced by positioning of the head and body, but such changes are not reliable and should not be used for clinical localization.

The groping reflex is less frequent than the grasp reflex and generally appears in conjunction with the latter. The hand of the patient, as well as the eyes, tend to follow an object or the fingers of the examiner. For a brief period, the patient behaves as if stimulus-bound.

The sucking reflex is elicited by touching the lips of the patient with a cotton swab, and the snout reflex is obtained by tapping the skin of the upper perioral region with finger or hammer. These responses are often present in patients with disease confined to the frontal lobe, but, more so than the grasp reflex, they appear in a wide variety of dementia syndromes associated with more wide-ranging damage. Furthermore, the snout reflex, just like the palmomental reflex, may appear in patients with basal ganglia disorders and even in normal older individuals.

Traditionally, these signs have been interpreted as an indication of release of primitive forms of reflex response, kept in abeyance by normal inhibitory function of frontal lobe structures.

ABNORMAL TONE

Patients with lesions in the prefrontal areas often show changes in muscle tone. These may be more closely associated with lesions in the dorsolateral aspect of the frontal lobes, particularly near the premotor regions. The most characteristic sign is Kleist's *Gegenhalten*, also referred to as counterpull, paratonia, opposition, or the Mayer-Reisch phenomenon. This is another of the so-called psychomotor signs and may be wrongly interpreted as a deliberate negative attitude on the part of the patient. When the examiner tries to assess tone by passively moving the arm, he or she may find a sudden resistance to the extension maneuver and note that the counteracting flexion movement actually increases in intensity in an attempt to neutralize the action. The patient may or may not be aware of this development and, as with the grasp reflex, will be unable to suppress the reflex even if desiring to do so. Rigidity may also be present, but since it is not associated with tremor, it will not have "cogwheel" characteristics. The degree of rigidity may show little consistency and may vary between observations. It is best described as plastic. Periodic hypotonia resembling cataplexy is quite rare (Ethelberg, 1949).

ABNORMAL GAIT AND POSTURE

Patients with severe frontal lobe damage often show abnormalities of gait. A wide range of characteristic changes may be present, including walking with short steps but without festination, loss of balance with retropulsion, or inability to walk (as in cases of gait apraxia). The latter may be seen in a variety of conditions, most frequently in the syndrome of normal-pressure hydrocephalus, which is, in effect, a frontal lobe syndrome consequent to periodically raised intraventricular pressure. In diagnosing gait apraxia, an effort should be made to demonstrate that the patient can execute, in a recumbent position, the movements that he or she is unable to perform while standing.

The designation "frontal ataxia" probably does not cover a manifestation typical of frontal lobe lesions, as even Bruns admitted when he coined the term. A tendency to fall backward rather than to the side, and a predominance of deficits in the trunk rather than in the extremities are evident in some cases.

Abnormalities of posture are possible, although not pathognomic or frequent. In some cases, the examiner is able to place the arms of the patient in various bizarre positions and note the waxy flexibility with which the patient will remain in those unlikely positions. True catalepsy and sudden freezing of posture have also been described but seem rare.

CHANGES IN EYE MOVEMENT CONTROL

The control of eye and head movements is part of a highly developed system tuned to orient the organism toward possibly important stimuli and therefore aid perception of the environment. The frontal eye fields, located bilaterally in area 8 of Brodmann, are important in the control of these movements. The paucity of spontaneous head and eye movement toward new stimuli, which is commonly described in connection with the impairment of orienting responses of frontal lobe patients, is possibly related to eye field dysfunction. On the whole, however, the value of eye movement defects in the assessment of higher levels of behavior disturbance is limited.

Frontal seizures, originating in lesions in or near one eye field, may be characterized by a turning of the eye and head away from the side of the lesion. On the other hand, structural damage of one eye field, particularly if acute, produces a turning of eyes and head toward the side of the lesion.

Clear anomalies of conjugate gaze mechanism have their greatest value in the assessment of the comatose patient, where their relation to a concomitant paresis may decide whether the damage is in the frontal lobe or in the brainstem.

OLFACTORY DISTURBANCES

Anatomical and electrophysiological studies in the monkey have suggested that the prefrontal cortex may be involved in qualitative olfactory discrimination (Tanabe et al., 1975a, 1975b; Potter & Nauta, 1979). Potter and Butters (1980) have reported that damage to the orbital region of the frontal lobe can lead to impaired odor quality discrimination without a significant decrease in odor detection. Projections from the temporal lobe directly to orbitofrontal cortex, as well as by way of the thalamus, were hypothesized to carry olfactory information in a hierarchical system of "odor-quality analyzers." Damage to thalamic and prefrontal lobe structures has also been found to impair odor quality discrimination in nonprimates without influencing odor detection (Eichenbaum et al., 1980; Sapolsky & Eichenbaum, 1980). The findings suggest that selective frontal lobe damage can be associated with deficits in a cognitive task of odor quality discrimination without decreasing odor detection ability. Although olfactory identification impairments can arise from damage to right or left orbitofrontal cortex, lesions of the right orbitofrontal cortex may produce greater deficits in olfactory processing than comparable damage on the left (e.g., Zatorre & Jones-Gotman, 1991; Jones-Gotman & Zatorre, 1993). Recent functional imaging studies also have provided support for the notion that human frontal cortex, particularly pyriform and orbital regions, plays an integral role in olfaction (Kobal & Kettenmann, 2000; Zald & Pardo, 2000). The orbitofrontal cortex also may be important for taste, and representation of the reward value of taste and odors may be linked to more general representation of punishment and reward (Rolls, 2000).

CHANGES IN SPHINCTER CONTROL

It is often noted that patients with frontal lobe damage have disturbances of sphincter control. The patient shows little concern about urinating or even defecating in socially unacceptable situations. Bilateral involvement of the mesial aspect of the frontal lobe is the rule in these cases. Resection of an underlying tumor often improves sphincter disturbances, which tend to recover spontaneously in cases of stroke. Extensive lesions of the white matter may also produce incontinence, as the early techniques of frontal lobotomy demonstrated. This defect is probably the result of loss of the inhibitory action that the frontal lobe presumably exerts over the spinal detrusor reflex.

COGNITION AND BEHAVIOR

Although patients with frontal lobe damage may exhibit any of the neurologic signs noted above, it is not uncommon for the neurological examination to be entirely normal except for a history of behavioral disturbance. Evaluation of the consequences of frontal lobe damage is arguably the most challenging task faced by clinical neuropsychologists and behavioral neurologists, not only because the laboratory manifestations

of frontal lobe damage are often subtle, but because the nature of neuropsychological assessment—with its emphasis on highly structured tasks administered under carefully controlled laboratory conditions—tends to lack sensitivity to the most important defects associated with frontal lobe damage. Standard psychological or neuropsychological evaluations may reveal few unequivocal defects, even in patients who are no longer able to behave normally in real life. Nevertheless, comprehensive evaluations can disclose a variety of signs suggestive of dysfunction in frontal cortices, and neuropsychological assessment is an indispensable part of the evaluation of patients with frontal lobe damage.

INTELLIGENCE

When we consider the role of the frontal lobes in human intellect, it is necessary to distinguish between intelligence as a global capacity to engage in adaptive, goal-directed behavior, and intelligence as defined by performance on standard psychometric instruments. There is little controversy regarding the idea that the frontal cortices constitute a necessary anatomical substrate for human intelligence as a global adaptive capacity. By contrast, extensive frontal lobe damage may have little or no impact on the abilities measured by intelligence tests.

Although not originally designed as neuropsychological instruments, standardized intelligence tests, and the Wechsler Scales in particular, have evolved to become some of the most frequently administered measures of cognitive function (Benton, 1991b; Tranel, 2009). There is general agreement that summary IQ scores provide limited information for the purposes of most neuropsychological evaluations (Lezak, 1988), but the analysis of performances on selected subtests remains a cornerstone of clinical evaluation for neuropsychologists. Early indications that standardized intelligence tests do not address the type of cognitive ability lost by frontal lobe patients were provided by Hebb's patient, who obtained an IQ of 98, and by Brickner's patient A., who obtained an IQ of 80 on Terman's revision of the Binet-Simon 1 year after operation and an IQ of 99 when he was retested 12 months later. In all of

Table 14–1. Wechsler Adult Intelligence Scale (WAIS-III) data (means, standard deviations in parentheses) for participants in the Tranel et al. (2008) study

Group	N	Matrix Reasoning	Vocabulary	VIQ	PIQ	FSIQ
Prefrontal	80	10.5 (2.9)	10.5 (3.0)	100.1 (16.7)	98.7 (17.7)	99.5 (16.7)
DLPC	37	10.4 (2.9)	10.6 (3.4)	98.0 (17.9)	98.1 (16.0)	97.4 (16.3)
VMPC	25	10.7 (2.5)	11.1 (2.5)	105.7 (14.8)	102.6 (19.1)	105.7 (16.9)
DL+VM	18	10.6 (3.7)	9.6 (2.9)	96.6 (16.1)	94.8 (19.2)	95.6 (16.1)
BDC	80	10.4 (3.0)	10.2 (3.1)	101.8 (15.3)	100.1 (14.6)	101.2 (14.2)

Matrix Reasoning and Vocabulary are age-corrected scaled scores. VIQ, Verbal IQ; PIQ, Performance IQ; FSIQ, Full Scale IQ. DLPC, patients with lesions to dorsolateral prefrontal cortex; VMPC, patients with lesions to ventromedial prefrontal cortex; DL + VM, patients with lesions to dorsolateral and ventromedial prefrontal cortices; BDC, patients with damage outside the frontal lobes.

these cases, the IQ score fell in or near the average range, and was grossly out of line with the fact that these patients were egregiously *un*-intelligent in terms of their navigation in real-world settings.

The preservation of psychometric intelligence in patients with frontal lobe damage, in fact, is a common finding (albeit not true of every case). For example, Milner (1963) reported a mean loss of 7.2 IQ points following dorsolateral frontal lobectomies, with mean postoperative IQ scores remaining in the average range, and Black (1976) found a mean Wechsler Adult Intelligence Score (WAIS) Verbal IQ of 99.1 and a mean Performance IQ of 99.5 in a group of 44 Vietnam veterans who had sustained unilateral frontal lobe shrapnel injuries. Likewise, Janowski et al. (1989) described seven subjects with various focal frontal lobe lesions who obtained a mean WAIS-R Full Scale IQ of 101.

Standard tests of intelligence may be insensitive to deficits of frontal lobe function because they emphasize measures of "crystallized" (e.g., vocabulary, fund of information) more than "fluid" (e.g., novel problem solving) intelligence. We examined the possibility that the Matrix Reasoning subtest of the WAIS-III, as a measure of "fluid intelligence" (i.e., the ability to solve novel abstract problems), would provide a more sensitive index of frontal lobe dysfunction (Tranel, Manzel, & Anderson, 2008). Accordingly, we investigated Matrix Reasoning performances in 80 patients with damage to various sectors of the prefrontal cortex. The performances of the

prefrontal patients were contrasted with performances of 80 demographically matched patients with damage outside the frontal lobes. The results (see Table 14-1) failed to support the fluid intelligence hypothesis, as prefrontal damage did *not* disproportionately impair so-called "fluid" intelligence. We also divided the prefrontal patients into anatomic subgroups, and in every subgroup we studied (dorsolateral, ventromedial, dorsolateral + ventromedial), the Matrix Reasoning scores (as well as IQ scores more generally) were indistinguishable from those of the brain-damaged comparison group (Table 14-2). These findings do not support a connection between fluid intelligence and the frontal lobes. However, our study also leaves open the possibility that Matrix Reasoning is simply not measuring what it purports to measure; that is, it lacks construct validity as a measure of fluid intelligence.

It has long been taught that patients with damage to ventromedial frontal lobe (including orbitofrontal cortex) frequently lack impairments in psychometric—or what can be termed "cognitive"—intelligence (e.g., Bar-On, Tranel, Denburg, & Bechara, 2003). However, the failure of our study to find disproportionate defects in fluid intelligence associated with dorsolateral prefrontal cortex (DLPC) damage is more surprising. There is a fairly consistent literature, especially from studies using functional imaging, that has indicated a relationship between DLPC and "fluid" intelligence. For example, DLPC activation has been reported

Table 14–2. WAIS-III Subtest Performances of Patients with Frontal Lobe Damage

Subject	1	2	3	4	5	6	7
Age (years)	58	88	55	62	26	51	51
Education	16	16	8	12	16	14	16
Vocabulary	14	—	9	8	12	11	—
Similarities	12	—	8	9	9	11	—
Arithmetic	12	—	8	10	12	10	—
Digit Span	13	—	9	11	13	13	—
Information	16	—	7	10	15	10	—
Comprehension	12	—	8	8	12	14	—
Letter–Number	12	—	6	10	15	13	—
Picture Completion	6	9	12	11	11	9	11
Digit Symbol	5	7	8	5	7	14	6
Matrix Reasoning	13	11	8	10	11	10	15
Block Design	12	12	11	11	7	11	14
Picture Arranging	10	12	9	8	7	8	10
Symbol Search	6	—	10	8	15	14	9

Note: WAIS-III scores are age-corrected scaled scores. Subjects 2 and 7 were too aphasic to complete the verbal sub-tests.

in "high g" tasks that ostensibly require fluid intelligence, such as the Raven Progressive Matrices task and similar reasoning tasks (Prabhakaran, Smith, Desmond, Glover, & Gabrieli, 1997; Esposito, Kirkby, Van Horn, Ellmore, & Berman, 1999; Duncan, Seitz, Kolodny, Bar, et al., 2000; Gray, Chabris, & Braver, 2003; Njemanze, 2005). Waltz and colleagues (Waltz, Knowlton, Holyoak, Boone, et al., 1999) reported six patients with damage to prefrontal cortex caused by degenerative disease, who had severe damage in DLPC sectors and were selectively impaired on matrix-reasoning–like tasks. Also, there is evidence that performance on traditional "frontal" tasks (e.g., Wisconsin Card Sorting Test; Tower of London) is correlated with measures of fluid intelligence (Isingrini & Vazou, 1997; Parkin & Java, 1999).

We examined the neural underpinnings of "g," or what has traditionally been defined as "general intelligence" (Gläscher et al., 2010). This construct (g) captures the performance variance shared across cognitive tasks, and correlates reasonably highly with real-world success in all manner of endeavors. However, it remains unclear whether g reflects some kind of "global" brain function, or perhaps draws on more circumscribed neural regions. We investigated the neural substrates of g in 241 patients with focal brain damage using voxel–based lesion-symptom mapping. A robust measure of g was derived from a hierarchical factor analysis across multiple cognitive tasks. Statistically significant associations were found between g and damage to a distributed brain network that included frontal and parietal cortex, as well as white matter association tracts and the frontopolar cortex.

These findings can be taken to indicate that general intelligence draws on connections between regions that integrate verbal, visuospatial,

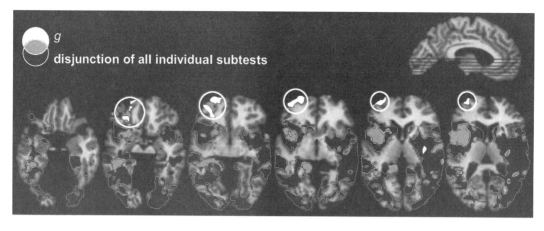

Figure 14–3. Overlap of g (*white*) and a disjunction (logical "OR") of nine Wechsler Adult Intelligence Scale (WAIS) subtests (*dark gray*) thresholded at 5% false discovery rate (FDR). A region in the left frontal pole (*white circles*) is unique to g and not captured by any other subtest. Immediately adjacent (left lateral OFC and underlying white matter) lies the significant lesion-deficit effect for Information, which partially overlaps with the unique frontal polar region for g (*two left-most circles*). From Gläscher, J., Rudrauf, D., Paul, L.K., Colom, R., Tranel, D., Damasio, H., & Adolphs, R. (2010). Lesion mapping of general intelligence.

working memory, and executive processes. Also, and of particular interest, the findings provide a hint that a sector of prefrontal cortex may play a unique role in g (Figure 14-3). This region (left lateral aspect of Brodmann's area 10) has been associated with increased brain oxygen level dependent (BOLD) activity during a variety of higher-order cognitive processes (Ramnani & Owen, 2004), including branching and subgoal processing (Koechlin, Basso, Pietrini, Panzer, & Grafman, 1999). Activation in this region has also been reported in connection with difficult problem-solving tasks that were derived from Raven's Advanced Progressive Matrices (e.g., Christoff et al., 2001), a test commonly used to measure general intelligence (Gray, Chabris, & Braver, 2003; Lee et al., 2006; Jung & Haier, 2007; Colom et al., 2009). In sum, the left anterior dorsolateral region may be a portion of a distributed network important for overall general intelligence, or g. In this context, it is interesting to recall a prediction from Kane and Engle (2002) who, after reviewing the relevant literature, concluded that further investigations would confirm a prominent role for the DLPC in novel reasoning and psychometric g.

Many of the real-life problems encountered by patients with frontal lobe lesions are in social situations, raising the possibility that frontal dysfunction may cause a selective defect in some aspect of "social intelligence." One possible mechanism for the impairment of social behavior is that frontal lobe damage alters the ability to generate an appropriate array of response options and an adequate representation of the future consequences. Another possible mechanism is that these patients are able to conjure up adequate response options and consequences, yet fail to select the most advantageous choice. Saver and Damasio (1991) administered to subject E.V.R. a series of standardized measures designed to examine the manipulation of response options and projected outcomes to social stimuli. E.V.R. demonstrated normal or superior performances on tasks that required the generation of response options to social situations, consideration of the future consequences of pursuing particular responses, and moral reasoning. These results were replicated in additional subjects with adult-onset damage to the frontal lobes (Anderson et al., 1999). These findings suggest that the defect in these patients does not result from deficient social knowledge or an inability to reason regarding social situations, although some patients with frontal lobe lesions have been found to be impaired in rating the effectiveness of solutions to social problems (Dimitrov et al., 1996).

The mismatch between intelligence measured in a laboratory and intelligence applied to real-life behaviors remains one of the most compelling challenges in frontal lobe research. It is evident that real-life intelligent behavior requires more than basic problem solving skills. In real-life problems, unlike most artificial problems posed by neuropsychological tasks, the relevant issues, rules of engagement, and endpoints are not always clearly identified. Real-life behaviors often introduce heavy time processing and working memory demands, and there is a requirement for the prioritization and weighing of multiple options and possible outcomes. Such factors seem to conspire against patients with frontal lobe damage, who, despite good IQ scores, cannot effectively deploy their intelligence in real-world, online situations.

ATTENTION AND MEMORY

Attention

Luria (e.g., 1966) emphasized the verbally mediated activating and regulatory role of the frontal lobes and their role in problem solving. He suggested that the orienting reaction, as measured by galvanic skin response or suppression of the α rhythm in the EEG, cannot be controlled in a "top-down" fashion in patients with frontal lobe lesions. In normal participants, the presentation of verbally meaningful instructions is expected to prevent habituation to stimuli and therefore prevent the orienting response from disappearing (Homskaya, 1966). In patients with frontal lobe lesions, however, the verbal signal does not prevent habituation. Luria argued that patients with damage to the frontal poles and to the mesial and basal aspects of the frontal lobes tend to be more affected than those with dorsolateral involvement. Additional evidence for altered orienting responses in frontal lobe patients comes from studies of visual potentials evoked by verbally tagged stimuli. Stimuli that would have increased the amplitude of visual evoked potentials in normal participants failed to do so in patients with frontal lobe damage (Simernitskaya & Homskaya, 1966; Simernitskaya, 1970). Animal studies have also supported the idea that frontal lobe damage produces changes in the processing of information by altering the orienting response (e.g., Grueninger et al., 1965, Kimble et al., 1965), but, as noted earlier, the impact of frontal lobe damage on attention is not limited to immediate orienting responses.

Patients with frontal lesions show heightened vulnerability to distracting stimuli in other modalities, as well as electrophysiological evidence of disinhibition in sensory regions. For example, Chao and Knight (1998) found that patients with frontal lesions generated enhanced event-related potentials in primary auditory cortex in response to distracting noises. It has been proposed that the dependency on immediately present environmental cues shown by some patients with frontal lobe damage may be due to release of parietal lobe activity resulting from loss of frontal lobe inhibition (Lhermitte et al., 1986). Dias et al. (1997) have provided evidence suggesting that dorsolateral prefrontal damage in primates may have a greater impact on inhibitory control of attention selection, whereas orbitofrontal damage may have a greater effect on affectively related inhibition. Impairment of inhibitory control following frontal lobe damage appears to be a common mechanism affecting not just allocation of attention, but several aspects of cognition and behavior.

Memory

Although frontal lobe damage usually does not cause amnesia in the conventional sense, it can disrupt mnemonic processes at several stages. Ever since Jacobsen's (1935) demonstration of impairments on a delayed response task by monkeys with frontal lobe ablations, investigators have been attempting to explicate the memory defects that follow damage to the frontal lobes. As reviewed earlier, the anatomical connections of the frontal lobes are certainly consistent with the notion that the frontal cortices are involved in memory. Bidirectional connections with sensory association cortices, thalamic nuclei, and the amygdalo-hippocampal region provide a neuroanatomical substrate by which the frontal cortices could play a role in the formation and activation of stored representations—i.e., memory.

Working Memory

Many of the reasoning abilities considered more or less uniquely characteristic of humans, such as long-term planning, hypothetical reasoning, and reorganization of complex concepts, require *working memory*, or the transient maintenance of representations in an activated or accessible state while the reasoning is taking place. Working memory is not a unitary process and likely is an essential function of many nonfrontal brain regions. Conceptually, working memory has at least some overlap with the construct of short-term (or immediate) memory, as both constructs emphasize limited storage capacity and a brief duration of processing. Based especially on work in nonhuman animals, the frontal cortex appears to be important for working memory tasks that involve bridging of temporally separate elements and the comparison or manipulation of several pieces of information (e.g., Goldman-Rakic, 1984; Petrides, 1995; Fuster, 1997; Kim & Shadlen, 1999).

Although the articulation of working memory as a psychological construct has been in place for some time (cf. Baddeley, 1986), most of the earlier work regarding the neural substrates of working memory was conducted in nonhuman animals, using the well-known delayed response paradigms (for review, see Goldman-Rakic, 1992, 1995). This work showed that dorsolateral prefrontal lesions impaired the ability of the animal to "hold" information for brief periods of time, for example, for the moment or two during which the animal had to remember which location or which object might be associated with a food reward. Curiously, lesion studies in humans have not made much of a contribution to this literature, and it is difficult to find compelling examples of human cases who developed profound working memory impairments in connection with dorsolateral prefrontal lesions. In sharp contrast, functional imaging studies have generated a rich and rapidly expanding body of evidence linking working memory to dorsolateral prefrontal structures. In one review, for example, Cabeza and Nyberg (2000) summarized more than 60 such studies. We summarize here some of the main findings from this literature (for other reviews, see Smith

& Jonides, 1998; Smith, Jonides, Marshuetz, & Koeppe, 1998; D'Esposito, 2000).

A typical paradigm for the investigation of working memory in functional imaging studies is the "N-back" task, in which subjects must indicate whether each item in a continuous stream of items matches an item that occurred one, two, or N items back in the series. For example, in one typical example (Smith et al., 1996), the investigators presented subjects a continuous stream of single letters that appeared at random locations around an imaginary circle centered on a fixation cross. Two conditions were utilized: In the verbal memory condition, subjects were asked to decide whether each letter matched the letter presented three stimuli previously—i.e., "three-back" (and regardless of location). In the spatial memory condition, subjects were asked to decide whether the position of each letter matched the position of the letter presented three stimuli previously, again, "three-back" (and regardless of letter identity). Examples of these tasks, taken from Smith et al. (1996), are shown in Figure 14-4.

Two main conclusions have emerged from studies of this type. First, performance of working memory tasks consistently activates structures in the DLPC, including Brodmann's areas 6, 44, 9, and 46. Second, a fairly consistent laterality effect exists: The left dorsolateral prefrontal sector is preferentially activated by verbal working memory tasks, whereas the right dorsolateral prefrontal sector is preferentially activated by spatial working memory tasks. In the task used by Smith et al. (1996), for example, the investigators found left-sided dorsolateral prefrontal activation in the verbal condition, and right-sided dorsolateral prefrontal activation in the spatial condition. The literature also contains some hints regarding other subdivisions within the dorsolateral sector: For example, activations in areas 9 and 46 seem to occur most consistently with tasks that require manipulation of the contents of working memory (such as the N-back task), whereas tasks requiring simple maintenance or "holding" of information over a short time interval may be more related to areas 6 and 44 (e.g., D'Esposito et al., 1998). Also, Smith and Jonides (1998; Smith et al., 1998) have

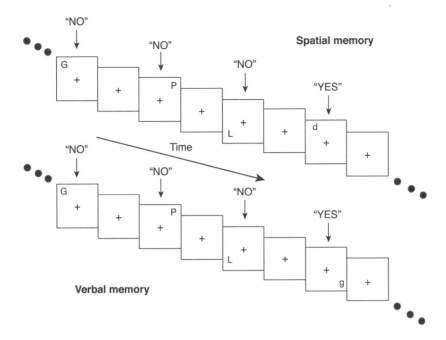

Figure 14–4. A typical working memory task paradigm requiring spatial (*top*) or verbal (*bottom*) processing. From Smith, E. E., Jonides, J., & Koeppe, J. R. A. (1996). Dissociating verbal and spatial working memory using PET. *Cerebral Cortex* 6:11–20, with permission of the authors and publisher.

addressed distinctions between, for example, storage and rehearsal processes, and executive functions that are believed to regulate the processing of working memory contents (see also Prabhakaran et al., 2000).

As noted, despite the abundant evidence of prefrontal involvement in working memory from functional imaging studies, patients with damage in this area generally do *not* have impairments on standard measures of working memory, such as verbal or spatial span, although delayed response performance can be impaired under certain conditions (e.g., Ghent et al., 1962; Chorover & Cole, 1966; D'Esposito & Postle, 1999). Milner et al. (1985) noted that the ability to solve such problems through verbal mediation so alters the task requirements that they may not be appropriate paradigms for human subjects. Also, there is growing reason to think that much of the contribution of the frontal lobes to working memory task performance may be in executive control over mnemonic processing, rather than working memory per se (Robbins, 1996; Postle et al., 1999). Consistent with this idea, activation of anterior dorsolateral frontal regions, on the left and

right, has been found in normal persons when the task requires both keeping in mind a main goal (working memory) and allocating attention during dual-task performance (Koechlin et al., 1999). Our work on the neural correlates of WAIS factors is also relevant here, inasmuch as we found that the Working Memory Index was associated with the left frontal and parietal cortex, but not the prefrontal cortices per se (Gläscher et al., 2009).

In one lesion study that is broadly consistent with the functional imaging literature, we examined performance on delayed response and delayed nonmatching to sample tasks in patients with lesions in ventromedial (VM) or dorsolateral/high mesial (DL/M) prefrontal areas (Bechara et al., 1998). Only patients with right DL/M or posterior VM lesions (with likely involvement of the basal forebrain) were impaired on these spatial working memory tasks. The posterior VM patients, but not the DL/M patients, were impaired on an experimental decision-making task, and patients with VM lesions were able to perform normally on the working memory tasks despite impairments of decision making. These findings suggest a dissociation of working memory and decision making in the human prefrontal cortex. Within the prefrontal region, damage to dorsolateral cortex appears to have the greatest impact on working memory, possibly through disrupted regulation of posterior regions more directly involved in memory encoding and storage. It also has been found that frontal lobe patients with impaired working memory may show impairments of procedural learning (Beldarrain et al., 1999).

Although aspects of working memory may be disturbed, anterograde memory tends to be less affected. When damage is limited to the frontal lobes, there typically appears to be little or no impairment on most standardized neuropsychological memory tests (e.g., Black, 1976; Janowsky et al., 1989; Stuss et al., 1982; Swick & Knight, 1996). However, in some instances, free recall of recently presented or remote information may be defective (e.g., Dimitrov et al., 1999). At least in part, this appears to be due to reduced executive control of active learning and recall strategies (Eslinger & Grattan, 1994; Gershberg & Shimamura, 1995; Mangels et al., 1996; Fletcher et al., 1998). Damage to the frontal lobes also has been linked to high rates of false recognition and confabulation (e.g., Stuss et al., 1978; Parkin et al., 1996; Schacter et al., 1996; Rapcsak et al., 1998), suggestive of a defect in monitoring or evaluating mnemonic operations. Positron emission tomography (PET) evidence from normal subjects has supported the notion that the posterior orbitomesial frontal region is involved in distinguishing between memories that are or are not relevant to ongoing reality (Schnider et al., 2000). Neural pathways exist that could provide a substrate for prefrontal influence on memory. Neurons in prefrontal cortex project to the hippocampal region via at least two distinct routes (Goldman-Rakic, 1984), and neurophysiological studies in monkeys have supported the concept of prefrontal top-down control of mesial temporal lobe memory functions (Tomita et al., 1999).

The relatives and caretakers of patients with frontal lobe damage often describe them as forgetful in the execution of daily activities, despite relatively normal scores on standard tests of anterograde memory. One factor contributing

to this discrepancy is impairment in various aspects of attention (e.g., Stuss et al., 1999; Metzler & Parkin, 2000). Norman and Shallice (1986) provided a detailed model of a supervisory attentional system based in the frontal lobes, which is involved primarily in allocating attention in nonroutine situations. As mentioned, there is evidence that frontal lobe damage results in diminished attention to novel events and increased susceptibility to distraction (Malmo, 1942; Milner, 1964; Stuss et al., 1982; Knight, 1984; Daffner et al., 2000). The acquisition of new, functionally relevant information requires the filtering or gating of irrelevant stimuli, and prefrontal cortex appears to contribute to this process by exerting inhibitory effects on posterior brain regions involved in perception. For example, Holmes (1938) argued that an important role of the frontal lobes was suppression of reflexive ocular behavior, and damage to inferior dorsolateral prefrontal cortex has been associated with impairments on the antisaccade paradigm, which requires inhibition of reflexive glances to peripheral stimuli (Guitton et al., 1985; Walker et al., 1998).

Defects in working memory, attention, or executive control may result in major dissociations between well-preserved memory capacity (as demonstrated by normal performances on standardized memory tests) and severely impaired utilization of those abilities in real-life situations. A telling example of this dissociation was provided by a patient studied in our laboratory following a large right dorsolateral frontal lobe lesion caused by stroke (subject #1331; see Figure 14-5). Six months after the event, this 56-year-old former industrial engineer obtained a Wechsler Memory Scale MQ of 132 and correctly identified 29 of 30 words (15 targets and 15 foils) on a 30-minute delayed recognition version of the Auditory-Verbal Learning Test. However, the patient's wife described him as extremely forgetful in his normal daily activities. In contrast to his formerly conscientious behavior, the patient would now repeatedly misplace his keys and other personal effects, and would regularly leave the television and lights on when he left a room. He was known to forget to turn off his car engine after parking and occasionally leave it running for hours. This "failure to remember" remained a constant

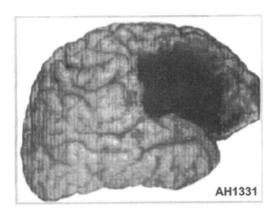

Figure 14–5. Three-dimensional reconstruction of the brain of subject #1331 obtained from thin-cut magnetic resonance imaging slices using Brainvox. From Frank, R. J., Damasio, H. & Grabowski, T.J. (1997). Brainvox: An interactive multimodal visualization and analysis system for neuroanatomical imaging. *Neuroimage* 5:13–30, with permission of the publisher.

feature of his behavior. The notion of "forgetting to remember," which seems to capture, at least intuitively, some of the fundamental "memory" problems exhibited by patients with frontal lobe damage, has been very difficult to operationalize (and measure) experimentally.

Temporal Aspects of Memory

The proximity of the basal forebrain region to the ventromedial frontal lobe makes it likely that both frontal and basal forebrain areas are damaged by the same lesion. The problem of distinguishing between the type of dysfunction caused by damage to these two areas is made more difficult by the fact that the basal forebrain region, due to its location and size, is often difficult to visualize on imaging studies. This region contains the largest concentration of cholinergic neurons (including those in the nucleus basalis of Meynert), along with major neurotransmitter projections en route from brainstem to cerebral cortex. Lesions of the basal forebrain result in an amnesic syndrome (Damasio et al., 1985) (see also Chapter 16). Such lesions are commonly caused by infarcts secondary to rupture of aneurysms of the anterior communicating or anterior cerebral arteries.

The frontal lobes may play a specific role in aspects of temporal contextual memory (see also Chapter 16). Studies of patients with frontal lobe damage have documented impairments in judgments of relative recency or frequency (e.g., Milner, 1971; Smith & Milner, 1988; Milner et al., 1991; Butters et al., 1994). For example, subjects with frontal cortical excisions for treatment of epilepsy were able to discriminate between novel and familiar items, but were impaired in the ability to judge the relative recency of two familiar items that had been previously presented sequentially (Corsi & Milner, reported in Milner, 1971; Milner et al., 1991). In contrast, subjects with unilateral temporal lobectomies show material-specific recognition problems, but normal recency judgements. The defect may primarily be due to defects in strategic, rather than automatic, processing of temporal information (Mangels, 1997). Impairment of the ability to judge the relative frequency of occurrence of nonverbal items has also been demonstrated in subjects with right frontal lobe damage (Smith & Milner, 1988). Impairments of memory for recency and frequency also can occur in the context of pathology outside of the frontal lobes (e.g., Parkin & Hunkin, 1993; Stanhope et al., 1998), although the defects do dissociate from standard anterograde memory impairments. For example, it has been shown that patient H.M., the patient who developed amnesia following bilateral mesial temporal lobe resection, has relatively preserved recency and frequency judgments despite severely impaired item recognition (Sagar et al., 1990).

SPEECH AND LANGUAGE

Aphasia

One of the most influential discoveries in the early history of brain–behavior relationships was Paul Broca's (1861) description of an infarction in left posterior inferior frontal cortex in a patient whose speech was limited to repetitive production of a single syllable. It is now known that various sectors of left inferior dorsolateral frontal lobe interface with posterior cortices and subcortical structures to provide the substrate for linguistic formulation and comprehension. The left posterior/inferior sector of the frontal lobe appears to play an important role in aspects of language processing that involve combinatorial assembly (e.g., the combination of phonemes into morphemes, and of morphemes into sentences) (Damasio, 1992). Other frontal regions, namely the cingulate gyrus and supplementary motor area, are involved in the affective and motor control of speech production. Although Broca's aphasia remains the best known language defect associated with frontal lobe damage, it is becoming increasingly evident that this clinical diagnostic category encompasses various interactions of several dissociable impairments, including defects of linguistic formulation, motor programming, and the initiation and maintenance of output (Alexander et al., 1989). Correspondingly, damage to posterior inferior frontal cortex alone does not produce the full syndrome, but rather Broca's aphasia is caused by extensive and varied damage to several neighboring brain areas (e.g., Mohr, 1976). Because discussion of Broca's aphasia, transcortical motor aphasia, and speech apraxia are provided elsewhere in this volume (see Chapters 2, 3, 4, and 10), we will not go into further detail here. There are, however, several other aspects of frontal lobe involvement in speech and language that warrant comment.

Mutism

Mutism, generally associated with some degree of both akinesia and bradykinesia, is a frequent sign of frontal lobe dysfunction. It denotes involvement of the mesial cortex of the frontal lobe or of its connections, unilaterally or bilaterally. Current evidence indicates that lesions in the cingulate gyrus or the supplementary motor area (often in both) are crucial for the appearance of mutism and akinesia. Bilateral damage tends to cause longer-lasting changes. Unilateral damage, in stroke or in surgical ablations, permits recovery in a matter of weeks. There is no evidence that side of lesion plays a major role here, and dominant as well as nondominant lesions cause much the same results. There is also evidence that these areas are related to affective and motor control but not to linguistic processing, and thus damage to these areas can interfere with speech (and all other movement, purposeful or automatic),

but not language. The most frequent cause for the lesions that cause mutism is impairment in the blood supply in the anterior cerebral artery territories. Rupture of aneurysms of the anterior communicating or anterior cerebral artery is the usual antecedent event. The patient is mostly silent and motionless or nearly so, but tracking movements of the eyes and blinking are almost always preserved. The ability to walk is maintained in patients who do not have concomitant paraparesis from involvement of the mesial aspect of the motor areas. Often patients make many purposeful movements, such as those needed to adjust clothes or eat. There is an absence of facial expression, and often the patient makes no effort to communicate verbally or by gesture. Rare isolated utterances may be produced, and repetition of single words and short sentences can occasionally be performed under coaxing. Whatever the amount of verbal output, patients do not produce paraphasias and have well-articulated, although often hypophonic speech (Damasio & Van Hoesen, 1980, 1983).

Patients with mutism are often diagnostically reminiscent of patients with psychiatric disease, and if it were not for a clarifying previous history, a primarily neurological disease could go unnoticed. Mutism must be distinguished from anarthria and aphemia, conditions in which the inability to speak (or to speak without phonetic errors) is accompanied by a frustrated intent to communicate verbally and in which attempts to communicate by gesture or facial expression are often successful. These features also help distinguish mutism from the transcortical motor aphasias, in which speech is sparse and nonfluent, and in which word and sentence repetition are preserved.

Verbal Fluency

Verbal fluency, as measured by verbal association tests, often is impaired by frontal lobe damage. This may be noted in the absence of any detectable change in speech output. A curious instance is Brickner's patient A. He spoke fluent and well-articulated speech, often at a high rate, manifesting a free flow of verbal association of almost manic nature. However, when given a certain word, his ability to produce morphologically similar words by changing a letter or letter positions was impaired.

Using Thurstone's Word Fluency Test, Milner (1964) showed that patients with left frontal lobectomies that spared Broca's area scored very poorly in this test, despite there being no evidence of aphasia. Controls with temporal lobectomies performed as well as patients with right frontal lobectomies. Patients with left frontal ablations performed a verbal memory test at the same level as did those with right frontal ablations, suggesting the relative independence of the mechanism underlying fluency and memory. Temporal lobe controls, however, did poorly on the verbal memory task.

Benton (1968) arrived at the same conclusions studying a group of patients with left, right, and bilateral frontal damage. The task used to test fluency was an oral version of the Thurstone test, in which the patient is requested to say as many words beginning with a given letter of the alphabet as come to mind. Not only did the left hemisphere patients do remarkably worse than the right hemisphere ones, but bilaterally damaged patients also performed more poorly than those with right hemisphere damage only. A number of subsequent studies have replicated this basic pattern, although fluency also may be affected by nonfrontal lesions in the left hemisphere or by diffuse damage. Baldo and Shimamura (1998) found that frontal lobe damage affected both letter and category fluency. Stuss et al. (1998) examined the effects on verbal fluency of damage to various subregions of the frontal lobes and found that left dorsolateral and superior mesial lesions on the left or right affected letter fluency. Category fluency was impaired by damage to these same regions, as well as by damage to right dorsolateral and inferior medial regions.

These findings generally support the classic views of Feuchtwanger (1923) and Kleist (1936), according to which "dominant" frontal lesions, but not "minor" (nondominant) frontal ones, interfere with verbal processes, particularly in respect to spontaneity and the ability to maintain a flow of verbal evocation without actually producing one of the typical aphasias. They are in opposition to the views of Jefferson (1937) and Rylander (1940), who denied any lateralization of defect after frontal lobectomies.

Several functional imaging studies have reported left inferior frontal gyrus activation when normal subjects are shown concrete nouns and required to generate semantically appropriate verbs (the so-called "verb generate" task), but the exact role of this brain region in the task has not been clear (e.g., Petersen et al., 1989; Raichle et al., 1994). Thompson-Schill et al. (1998) found that patients with lesions in the left inferior frontal gyrus were impaired on the verb generation task when there were high demands for selection among competing responses, but not when there were low selection demands (i.e., in response to nouns with only one commonly associated verb, such as "scissors"). This suggests that the role of the inferior frontal gyrus in verb generation tasks may not be in semantic retrieval per se, but rather in the process of selection among multiple competing sources of information, a function which may apply across a wider range of tasks.

Related to this are studies that have revealed an intriguing pattern of naming impairment associated with lesions in the premotor/prefrontal region, in and near the left frontal operculum. Patients with such lesions often demonstrate a disproportionate impairment in the ability to name actions (with verbs) and, by contrast, tend to have normal naming of concrete entities (with nouns) (Damasio & Tranel 1993; Tranel et al. 2001; Hillis et al. 2002; Hillis et al. 2003; Kemmerer & Tranel 2003). This has led to the notion that verb retrieval is associated with the left premotor/prefrontal region. The findings are consistent with other work that has shown a higher incidence of verb retrieval impairment in patients with agrammatic aphasia, who typically have lesions involving the left frontal operculum (e.g., Hillis & Caramazza 1995), and with studies using functional imaging with normal participants that have shown left prefrontal activation in connection with verb retrieval (e.g., Tranel et al. 2005). Moreover, the opposite pattern is associated with left temporal lobe lesions—such patients have defective retrieval of words for concrete entities (nouns) but normal retrieval of words for actions (verbs) (e.g., H. Damasio et al., 2004).

Together, such findings constitute a double dissociation with regard to both word type (nouns vs. verbs) and site of lesion (left temporal vs. left premotor/prefrontal).

Prosody

Lesions to the frontal operculum in the right hemisphere have been linked to defects in paralinguistic communication, whereas propositional speech and language are not affected (e.g., Ross 1981). For example, patients with right frontal opercular lesions may lose the ability to implement normal patterns of prosody and gesturing. Their communication is characterized by flat, monotone speech, loss of spontaneous gesturing, and impaired ability to repeat affective contours (e.g., to implement emotional tones in speech, such as happiness, sadness, etc.). The left frontal operculum also appears to play some role in the processing of emotional prosody, although not to the extent of right hemisphere structures (Adolphs et al. 2002). For a more detailed discussion of emotional communication, see Chapter 15.

Nonvocal Language

The role of the frontal lobes in language is not limited to the auditory–vocal channel. Impairments of visual–gestural language, reading comprehension, and writing have been documented in patients with focal damage in left premotor and prefrontal cortex. Damage to the left frontal lobe has been shown to result in breakdowns of signed language that have similarities to the patterns of aphasia in spoken language following damage to this area, with agrammatism and halting, effortful signing (Bellugi et al., 1989).

Damage to the left frontal lobe has long been associated with alexia in the setting of Broca's aphasia (Lichtheim, 1885; Dejerine & Mirallie, 1895; Nielsen, 1938, 1946). Benson (1977) reported that 51 of 61 patients (84%) with Broca's aphasia and no evidence of posterior lesions had at least mild alexia, and that these patients had particular difficulty in decoding words by grapheme-to-phoneme conversion. It has also been noted that oral reading and reading comprehension of Broca's aphasia may mirror the typical patterns of language breakdown in

these patients, in that concrete nouns may be more likely to be read correctly than function words such as conjunctions, prepositions, pronouns, and articles (Gardner & Zurif, 1975; Kaplan & Goodglass, 1981). For a further discussion of alexia, see Chapter 5.

Exner (1881) is usually credited with first describing agraphia following lesions in the superior aspect of the left premotor cortex ("Exner's area" in area 6, above areas 44 and 45). Other cases of agraphia associated with left dorsolateral frontal lesions have been described by Gordinier (1899), Penfield and Roberts (1959), and Rapscak et al. (1988). For additional discussion of agraphia, see Chapter 6.

We have studied a case with isolated alexia and agraphia associated with a circumscribed surgical lesion in Exner's area (Anderson et al., 1990). This patient was not aphasic or hemiparetic, but was virtually unable to write any words or letters, with her writing attempts showing severe spatial distortion. Reading of single letters, words, and sentences was also severely impaired, but she could occasionally recognize single words in a gestalt fashion. The impairments of reading and writing were limited to the domain of letters; she could read and write numbers and perform written calculations without difficulty.

Further evidence that Exner's area may be involved in reading is provided by a case of reading epilepsy associated with a focal lesion in this region (Rittacio et al., 1992). The patient was a 24-year-old college student who underwent removal of a left frontal arteriovenous malformation. He was left without neurologic or cognitive defects except for seizures that occurred only when reading. In a series of controlled laboratory experiments, silent reading while subvocalizing was the most reliable means of eliciting seizure activity. Electrophysiological studies suggested that the epileptogenic zone was just anterior to the postsurgical lesion in Exner's area.

MOTOR FUNCTION AND VISUAL PERCEPTION

Axons from neurons in primary motor cortex and premotor cortex run through the corticospinal tract, providing the major substrate for cortical control of movement. In addition to motor dysfunction due to primary motor cortex damage, lesion studies in humans and monkeys have documented a variety of motor impairments associated with frontal lobe damage, including motor neglect, hypokinesia, motor impersistence, and perseveration (for a review, see Heilman & Watson, 1991, as well as Chapter 12). There is evidence that the organization of posterior visual cortices into dorsal "where" pathways and ventral "what" pathways also extends into prefrontal organization (Nadeau & Heilman, 2007). For example, the planning of movement is dependent on connections from dorsal visual and somatosensory cortices to the dorsolateral frontal convexity, whereas response selection based on stimulus features, such as color or orthography, depend on projections from ventral aspects of the visual association cortices to ventral prefrontal cortex (Alexander et al., 2007). Lesions involving the dorsal premotor region can impair learning and performance of conditional sensorimotor tasks, where a cue prompts performance of a specific movement based on learned associations between sensory cues and motor responses (Petrides, 1987; Halsband & Freund, 1990).

Frontal lobe damage, especially involving the left hemisphere, has long been associated with ideomotor apraxia (Liepmann, 1908), although the deficits are generally of less severity and occur less frequently with frontal lobe damage than with parietal lobe damage (e.g., Kolb & Milner, 1981; De Renzi et al., 1983). Defects also can be found on other visuomotor tasks with significant demands for organization. For example, Benton (1968) demonstrated that patients with right frontal or bilateral frontal lobe lesions were inferior to patients with left frontal lobe lesions on tests of three-dimensional block construction and copying designs, and Jones-Gotman and Milner (1977) found that subjects with right frontal lobe damage were impaired relative to subjects with temporal lobe or left frontal lobe damage on a task requiring the rapid generation of original abstract drawings. Neuroimaging studies and electrophysiological studies in monkeys suggest that the anterior premotor regions may provide the critical substrate for planning and organizing complex motor behaviors (Abe & Hanakawa, 2009).

As discussed earlier, damage to DLPC can impair control of eye movements, including smooth pursuit of moving targets and control of saccades. Although higher-order visuoperceptual defects are more commonly associated with dysfunction in posterior cortical regions, it also is possible for various aspects of visuoperception to be affected by frontal lesions. Infarction of the middle cerebral artery often results in combined damage to the dorsolateral frontal lobe and the anterior parietal lobe, with a high probability of contralateral neglect if the damage is on the right. Damage limited to the frontal lobes has been shown to cause both contralateral and ipsilateral neglect (Heilman & Valenstein, 1972; Kwon & Heilman, 1991). In most cases of stroke or traumatic injury, these impairments resolve over a period of days or weeks.

Although focal frontal lobe damage usually results in little or no long-term impairment on most standardized clinical tests of visual perception, subtle deficits may be present. For example, circumscribed prefrontal lesions may impair control of perceptual processes, including the ability to intentionally switch between competing representations (Windmann et al., 2006), and the ability to integrate local elementary stimulus features into a holistic global percept (Ciaramelli et al., 2007). As discussed in the next section, damage to prefrontal cortex can have profound effects on emotion and social behavior. One aspect of this is impairment in the perception of relatively elementary social and emotional stimuli. For example, damage to ventromedial prefrontal regions can impair the recognition of facial emotional expressions (Heberlein et al., 2008), and damage to right prefrontal cortex, both ventromedial and dorsolateral regions, can lead to deficits in the recognition of negative social expressions, such as hostility or suspiciousness (Shaw et al., 2005).

EMOTION AND SOCIAL BEHAVIOR

Alterations of emotion and social behavior, including changes in characteristic emotional response patterns, mood, and interactions with others, are frequent consequences of frontal lobe damage and among the most difficult to evaluate. The assessment of changes at this level of behavior implies a notion of the limits or normal variations of several aspects of human personality. Naturally, only an approximation is possible, taking into account the patient's age, educational level, social and cultural group, and previous achievements. Alterations of emotion, social behavior, and personality following prefrontal damage are not independent of cognitive impairments. It is possible for elementary cognitive defects resulting from frontal lobe damage to impact on social interactions and other behaviors considered to be aspects of personality. For example, Deutsch et al. (1979) found that patients with frontal lobe damage who were rated as having a tendency toward social isolation showed defective orientation to other people who entered a room, and Daffner et al. (2000) found strong correlations between measures of visual attention to novel stimuli by a group of patients with frontal lobe damage and a rating of apathy in their daily activities. Also, disruption of emotion plays a key role in impairments of judgment, behavioral control, and decision making following prefrontal damage. We have found that ratings of emotional dysfunction, conducted by relatives of patients with ventromedial prefrontal damage, are highly predictive of these patients' real-world competencies in areas such social, financial, and occupational function (Anderson et al., 2006).

Affect

Butter et al. (1963, 1968) observed that monkeys with orbital ablations showed marked and long-lasting changes in emotional behavior that seemed to be related to an increase in aversive reactions and a concomitant decrease in aggressive reactions. They followed these observations with a careful study of aversive and aggressive behaviors in two groups of monkeys, one with orbital lesions, the other with temporal lesions (Butter et al., 1970). The orbital lesions produced a clear reduction in aggressive behaviors, a change that could still be seen after 10 months. This reduction seemed to be situational, as there were noticeable differences

in the way the animals reacted to different potentially threatening stimuli, and the animals could still demonstrate aggression when brought back to the colony in which they had been dominant figures. This suggests that a regulatory mechanism of aggression had been impaired and that the capacity to display aggression had not been eliminated. The authors point out that the dependence on environmental configuration and the variety of possible emotional responses are not consistent with a permanent state of "bluntness of affect" used to describe similar changes in animals or in patients, even if the animals do appear tame in many situations.

Anatomical study of the experimental lesions indicated that damage to the posterior and medial sector of the orbital frontal lobe was closely correlated with the reported changes. This area of the cortex is intimately connected to the amygdala, and along with the dorsomedial nucleus of the thalamus, the amygdala and posteromedial orbital cortex project to roughly the same regions of the hypothalamus. The combination of behavioral and anatomical data supports the conjecture that these structures are part of a system involved in certain types of emotional reaction.

The standard descriptions of affective and emotional changes in frontal lobe patients include *witzelsucht*, a term coined by Oppenheim (1889) to describe the facetiousness of these patients, and *moria*, a term coined by Jastrowitz (1888) to denote a sort of caustic euphoric state that is almost inseparable from *witzelsucht*. Phenomena resembling such descriptions are occasionally found, especially in the acute presentation of cases, but it should be understood that in no patient are such changes permanent. Patients who appear facetious and boastful will look apathetic and indifferent at some later time or else may show a sudden burst of short-lived anger. The instability of humor also applies to the traditional and somewhat misleading descriptions of "tameness" and "bluntness" of emotion, which may be quite changeable and actually give way to unbridled aggressive behavior against a background of flat affect. External circumstances, particularly if they are stressful, as during an examining session, may "set" the patient's emotional tone. Frequently, the reaction will be found inappropriate to the circumstances but not necessarily in a consistent or predictable manner.

When facetiousness is present, it may have a sexual content, but the inappropriate acts usually are verbal, and rarely does a patient attempt to behave according to the wishes or judgments expressed in his profane remarks. The lack of appreciation of social rules is usually evident, but even so there tends to be little or no intentional viciousness. Nor is there any indication that facetiousness produces pleasure: indeed, affect tends to be shallow. Limited ability to enjoy pleasurable stimulation, particularly if it involves social, intellectual, and aesthetic situations, is probably characteristic of such patients and accompanies a restricted response to punishment. Both of these underscore the elementary disorder of emotion.

The association of changes in affect and in emotional control with predominant involvement of a specific region of the frontal lobe is still unsettled. Nonetheless, there is little doubt that the ventral and medial aspects of the frontal lobe are especially involved in many patients presenting with emotional changes. Also, patients with mesial frontal lobe lesions often appear to have blunted emotional responses, as if their affect had been neutralized (Damasio & Van Hoesen, 1983). Damasio et al. (1990) found that subjects with bilateral ventromedial frontal lobe lesions had abnormal autonomic responses to socially meaningful stimuli, despite normal autonomic responses to elementary and unconditioned stimuli. These findings suggest that such stimuli failed to activate somatic states previously associated with specific social situations, and which marked the anticipated outcomes of response options as advantageous or not.

Although patients with ventral and medial frontal lobe damage rarely show the concern and preoccupation that depressed patients do, damage to the dorsolateral prefrontal region has been associated with depression (e.g., Koenigs et al., 2008). Blumer and Benson (1975) referred to a pseudodepressed syndrome with decreased self-initiation following dorsolateral frontal lobe damage, and Cummings (1985) described apathy, indifference, and psychomotor retardation as frequent

features. Depressive symptomatology and social unease were found to be common in patients 3 months after dorsolateral prefrontal damage from stroke or trauma (Paradiso et al., 1999). Patients with lesions on the left hemisphere appear to have the greatest chance to develop depression (Robinson et al., 1984, 1985). Damage to the left dorsolateral frontal region, for example, that resulting from stroke in the anterior distribution of the middle cerebral artery, often has devastating consequences (paresis of the dominant side, aphasia), and unlike comparable lesions on the right, generally does not impair awareness for the acquired impairments. However, during the acute phase following a stroke, depression cannot be fully explained by these factors, suggesting a neurophysiological basis for the relationship between left dorsolateral prefrontal damage and depression. Reaction to functional impairments is likely to play a more important role in depression that begins 6 months or more after a stroke (Robinson et al., 1987).

The emotional consequences of focal damage to the right dorsolateral frontal cortex have not been well characterized, but may include both restriction of affect and emotional dyscontrol. Damage to the right frontal lobe may also contribute to anosognosia for hemiparesis and unawareness of acquired cognitive impairments. Self-awareness has been described as the highest cognitive attribute of the frontal lobes (Stuss & Benson, 1987). A lack of awareness regarding alterations in behavior, emotions, and thought processes is a common consequence of frontal lobe dysfunction, and one that has major implications for assessment and rehabilitation. Interviews with patients may suggest that all is normal, in contrast to descriptions of marked behavioral dysfunction provided by relatives and caretakers. Impaired awareness or self-monitoring may contribute to a lack of appropriate emotional reactions to social transgressions (such as embarrassment), further worsening the social dysfunction due to failure to motivate socially reparative behavior (Beer et al., 2006). Frontal lobe damage may also impair other aspects of self-monitoring or insight on specific cognitive abilities. For example, Janowsky et al. (1989) found that subjects with frontal lobe lesions were impaired on a task in which they had to judge the probability that they would recognize the correct answer to a multiple choice question.

Patients with limited awareness of acquired impairments tend not to be motivated to improve their behavior in rehabilitation settings. A major component of interventions directed at impairments of social behavior, impulse control, and decision making involves training patients to become increasingly aware of their dysfunctional behaviors. These patients often have a more general problem with evaluating the consequences and implications of their own behavior. Patients with frontal lobe damage may fail to see the significance of their decisions for themselves and for those around them. Their behavior suggests difficulty assessing the value of each new action, or lack of action, in terms of goals that are not overtly specified in the immediate environment.

The perception or comprehension of emotional information also appears to be altered in some patients with frontal lobe damage (e.g., Grattan et al., 1994). As noted previously, recognition of emotional facial expressions may be impaired following prefrontal damage, although such impairments may also follow damage to right somatosensory cortex (Adolphs et al., 2000). Perception and interpretation of more complex social stimuli, such as judging the nature of relationships between people based on their interactions, also may become impaired following prefrontal damage (Mah et al., 2004). A loss of empathy is often reported by family members to be one of the most troubling consequences of prefrontal injury. It is possible that different parts of the prefrontal cortex may contribute to different aspects of empathic processing (Eslinger, 1998). Recent evidence has suggested that ventromedial frontal damage may impair a cognitive perspective-taking system, whereas damage to more lateral inferior frontal regions may impair an emotional contagion system (Shamay-Tsoory et al., 2009). In another example of disrupted processing of social-emotional information, damage to the right frontal lobe has been associated with impaired appreciation of humor, possibly through disruption of component processes such as emotional reactivity and abstract thought (Shammi & Stuss, 1999).

Hallmark Case Studies

A number of detailed case studies have helped to characterize the personality changes that can result from frontal lobe damage. The famous patient Gage, described by Harlow (1848, 1868), provides the first solid reference to specific injury of the frontal lobes and its relation to disturbances of complex behavior. The other important observations were added in this century. They include the case studies of Brickner (1934, 1936), Hebb (Hebb & Penfield, 1940), Benton (Ackerly & Benton, 1948), and Damasio (Eslinger & Damasio, 1985; Damasio et al., 1991; Saver & Damasio, 1991). For a review of the early history of clinical investigations into frontal lobe damage, see Benton (1991a).

Brickner's patient, known as A., was a 39-year-old New York stockbroker who, until 1 year before surgery, led a normal life. Slowly progressive headaches, which became more and more severe, and finally the sudden onset of mental obtundation brought him to medical attention. A diagnosis of frontal tumor was made, which, at surgery, proved to be a voluminous meningioma of the falx compressing both frontal lobes. The neurosurgeon Walter Dandy had to perform an extensive bilateral resection of frontal tissue in two stages. On the left side, all the frontal tissue rostral to Broca's area was removed. On the right, the excision was even larger and included all the brain anterior to the motor area. The patient's condition gradually stabilized, and no motor or sensory defect could be detected. For months, there were frequent periods of restlessness, but akinesia or changes in tone were never noted, nor were there any signs of motor perseveration. Orientation to person, place, and time seemed intact, as well as remote and recent memory. A. was able to understand the circumstances of his illness and the surgical intervention to which he had been subject, and he was aware of the efforts of his family and physician to have him recover as much as possible. The range of his intellectual ability could be inferred from his capacity to play checkers, sometimes at a quick and expert pace, to explain the meaning of proverbs, and, occasionally, to discuss with lucidity the meaning of his predicament for himself, his relatives, and his friends. On the negative side, his behavior had undergone a marked deterioration. He was unable to adjust his emotional reactions appropriately. Furthermore, his affect was shallow. He became boastful, constantly insisting on his professional, physical, and sexual prowess, and showed little restraint, not only in describing his mythical adventures but in verbalizing judgments about people and circumstances surrounding him. His train of thought was hypomanic, with facetious remarks to match, but he could suddenly become aggressive if frustrated. Frequently, he tried to be witty, generally at the expense of others. He was particularly nasty toward his wife. Prior to surgery, he had always been kind to her, although not unusually considerate. His sex life, which his wife described as normal before the operation, changed radically. He became impotent and after a few frustrated attempts at intercourse, never again sought her or indeed any other partner, although much of his conversation would revolve around his sexual exploits. Ability to plan daily activity meaningfully had been lost and so had his initiative and creativity. Although he constantly spoke of returning to work, he never made any effort to do so and continued living in close dependence on his relatives. Certain levels of learning ability, however, both verbal and nonverbal, seemed intact. For example, in the face of his constant distractibility and lack of interest, he was taught how to operate proficiently a complex printing machine, on which he produced visiting cards. When faced with strangers in a reasonably nondemanding situation, he would be charming, display impeccable manners, and be considerably restrained. Independent examiners, including neurologists, would then be unable to detect any abnormality even after fairly long conversations.

Brickner's painstaking description produced different impressions on the readers of the time. The overall view was that the intervention had a crippling effect on A.'s mental ability, but for Egas Moniz, the enterprising pioneer of frontal leucotomy (1936), A.'s case was remarkable in that it proved bilateral frontal damage to be compatible with maintenance of major operational abilities, and especially because it demonstrated a change in affect and emotional response with pronounced reduction of anxiety.

This view is likely to have played a role in the theorization behind the leucotomy project.

In view of the location and size of the tumor, damage to the septal and hypothalamic regions was a possibility, and although the autopsy report on this case (Brickner, 1952) mentioned no such evidence, there may have been microscopic basal forebrain changes. The report is clear in noting that the cortical territory of the anterior cerebral arteries was intact (which might have been predicted from the patient's lack of crural paresis). Nevertheless, the autopsy did becloud the issue by revealing several meningiomas, one of which was of significant size and located in the right occipital area. In retrospect, it seems clear that the latter tumor had not grown yet at the time of operation because the patient developed a new set of symptoms 6–7 years after surgery. Such findings should not be used to minimize the significance of this case, as it is unlikely that they played any role in the patient's behavior.

Hebb and Penfield (1940) described an example of relatively successful bilateral removal of frontal tissue with a more straightforward possibility of a clinical–anatomical correlation. This patient had been normal until age 16 and had then sustained a compounded frontal fracture that damaged both frontal lobes, produced the formation of scar tissue, and resulting in a severe convulsive disorder. At age 28, the patient was operated on and the frontal lobes were extensively resected bilaterally, exposing both orbital plates back to the lesser wing of the sphenoid and transecting the frontal horns of the lateral ventricles. The anterior cerebral arteries were spared. At least a third of the frontal lobes was removed. In terms of the anatomical result, the intervention was not very different from that of Brickner's patient, but, unlike A., this patient's brain had not been distorted and edematous prior to resection, and the ablation took place under optimal surgical circumstances. In the postoperative period, seizures practically stopped and the behavioral disturbances associated with interictal periods disappeared. The authors suggest that the patient's personality actually improved (from the time he had sustained the fracture) and that his intellectual ability was probably better than before the surgical intervention. We take this to mean that comparison with the period of convulsive disorder was favorable. Comparison with the period prior to the initial damage would certainly not be as favorable, as we believe this patient's intellectual and emotional maturation had been considerably affected by his frontal lobe lesion. Even if he is described as relatively independent, socially adequate, and intellectually intact, some observers have felt that his personality development seemed arrested at the age of the accident, and a certain resemblance with the patient of Ackerly and Benton has been indicated. In a later study, Hebb (1945) conceded that, in spite of the patient's apparently good adjustment, his long-term planning and initiative were impaired.

The patient of Ackerly and Benton (1948), on the other hand, sustained bilateral frontal lobe damage either at birth or during the perinatal period. A neurosurgical exploration was performed at age 20 and revealed cystic degeneration of the left frontal lobe and absence of the right one, probably as a result of atrophy. This patient's history was marked throughout childhood and adolescence by severe behavioral problems, in school and at home. He could not hold a job, generally because, after some days of being an obedient and even charming employee, he would suddenly show bursts of bad temper, lose interest in his activity, and often end up by stealing or being disorderly. He reacted badly to frustration, and departure from routine would easily frustrate him. Except for periods of frustration and catastrophic reaction, his docility, quietness, and polite manners were quite impressive. His general health seems to have been good. His sexual interests were dim, and he never had an emotional involvement with any partner although, for a time, he did have occasional sex with prostitutes. As a whole, his behavior was described as stereotyped, unimaginative, and lacking in initiative. He never developed any particular professional skill or hobby. He also failed to plan for the future, either immediate or long range, and reward and punishment did not seem to influence the course of his behavior. His memory was described as capricious, showing at times a remarkable capacity (such as his ability to remember the makes of automobiles) and

at other times an inaccurate representation of events. There was no evidence of the common varieties of neurotic disorder, of somatization or of deliberate antisocial behavior, or addictive behaviors. Apparently, he could not be described as being joyful or happy, and it looked like both pleasure and pain were short-lived and directly related to the presence or absence of frustration.

When he was reevaluated 15 years later, there had been no remarkable personality changes except for a higher frustration threshold. Intellectually, however, recent memory deficits were now noticeable and an inability to perform the Wisconsin Card Sorting Test was recorded. We have recently demonstrated that there is considerable consistency in the basic profile described by Ackerly and Benton following damage to prefrontal cortex in childhood (Anderson et al., 2009).

We have had the opportunity to study patient E.V.R. in detail for more than 20 years (Eslinger & Damasio, 1985). The patient grew up as the oldest of five children, an excellent student and a role model for many friends and siblings. After high school, he married and completed a business college degree in accounting. By age 30, he was the father of two children and a church elder, and had come through the ranks of his company to a supervisory post. In 1973, his family and employers began to notice a variety of personality changes. He became unreliable, could not seem to complete his usual work, and experienced marital difficulties. He was suspended from his job. In 1975, a large orbitofrontal meningioma compressing both frontal lobes was removed. After his postoperative recovery, E.V.R. returned to accounting with a small home construction business. He soon established a partnership with a man of questionable reputation and went into business, against sound advice. The venture proved catastrophic. E.V.R. had to declare bankruptcy, and he lost his entire personal investment. Next, he tried several different jobs (warehouse laborer, apartment complex manager, accountant) but was consistently fired from all of them when it became clear that he could not keep reliable standards. His wife left home with the children and filed for a divorce. When he was reevaluated 2 years later, a computed tomography (CT) scan excluded a recurrence of tumor, and the neurological examination was normal except for slight incoordination in the left upper extremity and bilateral anosmia. Psychometric evaluation at that time revealed a verbal IQ of 120 (91st percentile), a performance IQ of 108 (70th percentile), and a Wechsler memory quotient of 140. A Minnesota Multiphasic Personality Inventory was valid and entirely within the normal range.

E.V.R.'s problems persisted. He was fired from two additional jobs. The reasons given included tardiness and lack of productivity. He remarried within a month after his first divorce, against the advice of his relatives. The second marriage ended in divorce 2 years later. Further neurological and psychological evaluation of E.V.R. at a private psychiatric institution in September 1981 revealed "no evidence of organic brain syndrome or frontal dysfunction." Assessment with the WAIS disclosed a verbal IQ of 125 (95th percentile) and a performance IQ of 124 (94th percentile). His Wechsler memory quotient was 148, and the Halstead-Reitan battery revealed average to superior ability on every subtest. An Minnesota Multiphasic Personality Inventory (MMPI) was once again valid, with no evidence of psychopathology on the clinical scales. Psychiatric evaluation suggested only psychological adjustment problems that should be amenable to psychotherapy. To this day, E.V.R.'s basic neuropsychological test performances remain normal.

Neuroanatomical analysis of E.V.R.'s neuroimaging studies reveals the structural correlate of his behavioral defect. Computed tomography and MRI show clear evidence of bilateral damage to frontal cortices, especially marked in the ventromedial area, and more so on the right than on the left. The dorsolateral sectors, the cingulate gyri, and the motor and supplementary motor regions are intact.

Reflection on the shared behavioral characteristics of these patients provides an overview of the major real-world consequences of frontal lobe damage. The patients of Hebb and Benton shared a rigid, perseverative attitude in their approach to life, and both had the courteous manner described as "English valet politeness," although in the judgment of several examiners, Hebb's patient led a clearly more productive but not fully independent existence. The evolution of the personality in Hebb's patient seems to have been arrested at the time of his accident, when he was 16, whereas in Ackerly and Benton's patient, the defect came early in development. The patients of Brickner and of Damasio, on the other hand, had normal development and sustained frontal lobe damage in adult life. It is possible that differences in the age of onset may account for some differences of outcome. Nonetheless, the patients share a number of features: inability to organize future activity and hold gainful employment; tendency to present a favorable view of themselves; stereotyped but correct manners; diminished ability to respond to punishment and experience pleasure; diminished sexual and exploratory drives; lack of motor, sensory, or communication defects; and overall intelligence within expectations based on educational and occupational background. With the exception of Damasio's patient, all patients showed lack of originality and creativity, inability to focus attention, recent memory vulnerable to interference, and a tendency to display inappropriate emotional reactions. The cluster of these features constitutes one of the more typical frontal lobe syndromes, and perhaps the one that easily comes to mind when there is a reference to "frontal lobe syndrome." Let us point out again that many patients with frontal lobe damage have no such defects.

The generalizability of the conclusions regarding personality changes and frontal lobe damage drawn from the individual case studies and clinical lore is supported by findings from a recent group study. For a large sample of subjects with chronic, focal adult-onset lesions, Barrash et al. (2000) obtained standardized ratings of a wide range of personality characteristics from informants who knew the patients well both before and after lesion onset. It was found that bilateral lesions in the orbital and mesial frontal cortex were reliably associated with a number of specific, highly disruptive, and persistent emotional and personality alterations, including blunted emotional experience, low emotional expressivity, apathy, indecisiveness, poor judgment, lack of planning, lack of initiative, social inappropriateness, and lack of insight. (For a depiction of the typical lesion

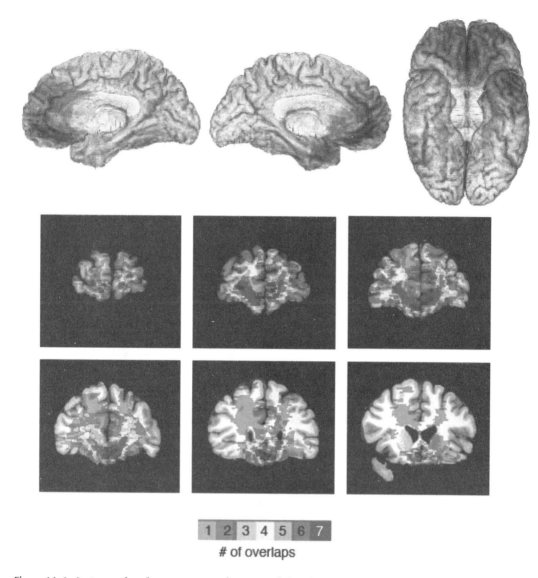

# of overlaps

Figure 14–6. Lesion overlap of seven patients with ventromedial prefrontal lesions The highest area of overlap (*see gray-scale bar*) is shown in dark gray. From Koenigs, M. & Tranel, D. (2007). Irrational economic decision-making after ventromedial prefrontal damage: Evidence from the Ultimatum Game. *The Journal of Neuroscience* 27:951–956, with permission of the publisher.

locations in ventromedial prefrontal patients, (see Figure 14-6.)

BEHAVIORAL GUIDANCE

As illustrated by the hallmark case studies, a major breakdown often occurs in the guidance of behavior following damage to prefrontal cortex. Although impairment of emotion is at the core of much of this difficulty, carrying particularly strong implications for social behavior, the impairments clearly extend to other aspects of behavioral guidance. Delineating the component cognitive deficits that contribute to impaired behavioral guidance, which often fall under the rubric of *executive dysfunction*, is one of the more challenging tasks facing clinical neuropsychology. Complicating this mission is the fact that these cognitive deficits are not independent of one another, but rather share core features and mechanisms, and interact with one another in their behavioral expression.

IMPULSE CONTROL AND DECISION MAKING

A key marker of frontal lobe dysfunction is difficulty in the willful direction and organization of thought processes, and of executing behaviors that are in the long-term best interests of the patient. Following frontal lobe injury, there is a tendency for behavior to be inordinately guided by immediate environmental circumstances or internal drive states. The terms *impulse control* or *response inhibition* refer to the suppression of prepotent actions that are inappropriate in a given context or that interfere with goal-directed behavior. Inhibitory processes, together with the initiation, amplification, or positive biasing of adaptive response options, are key aspects of the broader concept of cognitive control.

Several laboratory tasks have been employed to reveal impaired inhibition and its anatomical correlates. In go/no-go tasks, in which subjects are instructed to respond to one stimulus and not another, patients with frontal lobe lesions tend to show a high rate of false positive responses; that is, they fail to inhibit inappropriate or incorrect responses. Picton et al. (2007) found that damage to the left superior frontal cortex (area 6) was specifically related to deficits in withholding responses on this task. In stop-signal tasks, subjects are to respond rapidly with a button press to certain stimuli unless a stop signal occurs at the same time or immediately after these stimuli. Impairment on this task has been related to damage in the right ventrolateral and superior medial frontal regions (Aron et al., 2003; Floden & Stuss, 2006). Using a set of response selection tasks with varied levels of abstraction required for action decisions, Badre et al. (2009) found that patients with frontal lobe damage showed increasing impairment as the level of abstraction increased. It was found that the more rostral the damage within the prefrontal cortex, the greater the impairment on abstract tasks, whereas caudal damage affected more concrete decisions. These findings suggest that there may be a rostral–caudal axis of organization for cognitive control within the frontal lobes. One of the more frequently used clinical tests used to detect inhibitory deficits is the Stroop task. A recent study by Alexander et al. (2007) found the lesions of the left ventrolateral region resulted in a high number of incorrect responses to distractors.

In an interesting real-world example of failure to inhibit maladaptive responses following prefrontal damage, we found damage to mesial frontal regions, particularly on the right, to be associated with the development of pathological collecting behavior (Anderson, Damasio & Damasio, 2005). With no prior history of psychiatric disease or unusual collecting behavior, following prefrontal injury, these patients amassed large and disruptive accumulations of useless objects, seemingly unable to modulate the predisposition to acquire and collect.

Adaptive decision making depends on numerous cognitive processes in addition to inhibiting prepotent responses. For instance, to make a selection among multiple options with several possible outcomes, both immediate and future, it is necessary to operate on many premises, some just perceived, some recalled from previous experiences, and some recalled from imagined future scenarios. The process of analysis requires the relatively simultaneous holding of numerous sites of neural activity, in widespread regions of the cerebral cortex across long delays of many thousands of milliseconds (i.e., in working memory). However, significant decision making defects occur in patients with no apparent defect in other cognitive abilities, including working memory (e.g., Bechara et al., 1998).

In an effort to detect and measure this impairment, Bechara et al. (1994) developed a card task that mimics real-life decision making in the way it factors uncertainty, reward, and punishment. Subjects are given a loan of play money, shown four decks of cards (face down), and asked to draw cards in a manner to lose the least amount of money and win the most. Turning each card results in an immediate reward ($100 for decks A and B, and $50 for decks C and D). At unpredictable points, the turning of some cards results in a financial penalty (larger for decks A and B, and smaller in decks C and D). Playing mostly from the decks with the larger initial payoff (A and B) is disadvantageous over the long run because of the larger penalties. Playing mostly from decks C and D, with the smaller initial reward, turns out to be advantageous, because it leads to financial gain. There is no way for a subject to predict when a penalty will arise or to calculate with precision the net gain or loss from each deck. Normal subjects and subjects with damage to nonfrontal brain areas tend to initially sample from all decks, but choose significantly more from decks C and D while avoiding A and B over the course of 100 card selections. In contrast, subjects with frontal lobe damage select more from the disadvantageous decks (A and B) than from the advantageous decks (C and D). These findings suggest that performance on this task by patients with ventromedial frontal lobe damage is comparable to their real-life inability to guide behavior on the basis of previous mistakes, despite normal intelligence and memory. Functional imaging studies in persons without brain damage have supported the notion that this brain region is involved in decision making, particularly if uncertainty and reward are involved (Rogers et al., 1999; Elliot et al., 2000).

An important part of the mechanism underlying the impairment of decision making in patients with frontal lobe damage is tied to the disruption of emotion noted earlier. Damasio (1994; Damasio et al., 1991) has proposed that a major factor (albeit not the only one) in the appearance of the abnormal social conduct that repeatedly leads to punishing consequences is the defective activation of somatic states linked to punishment. The primary signal used to guide response selection is a somatic marker —a somatic state consisting of a combination of the state of viscera, internal milieu, and skeletal musculature—that is temporally correlated with a particular representation that is "marked" by it. Those states ought to have been reenacted in connection with the representation of negative future outcomes related to a given response option. The failure of their reactivation deprives patients of an alarm signal marking the representation of negative consequences for options that might, nonetheless, produce an immediate reward. (Note that positive somatic states may also mark future advantageous outcomes relative to responses that might bring immediate pain.) The activation of somatic markers works at both conscious and nonconscious levels. At the conscious level, it draws

attention to future negative consequences and promotes the deliberate suppression of options leading to a negative outcome. At nonconscious level, somatic markers or signals related to them, would trigger inhibition of response states. Subcortical neurotransmitter systems linked to appetitive or aversive behaviors would be involved in this covert level processing. The neural systems necessary for somatic state activation include the cortices in the ventromedial frontal region, whose damage is the main correlate of these behavioral changes.

In support of this model, it was found that patients with frontal lobe damage did not generate anticipatory skin conductance responses (SCRs) that normal subjects produced prior to making risky decisions in the Gambling Task (Bechara et al., 1997). When normal subjects performed the task, they developed anticipatory SCRs prior to choosing from the disadvantageous decks, even before they could explicitly identify these choices as risky. These covert biases appear to be important in avoiding disadvantageous behavior. Further evidence for the role of emotion regulation impairment in maladaptive decision making following frontal lobe damage comes from the performance of patients with ventromedial prefrontal lesions on the Ultimatum Game (Koenigs & Tranel, 2007). In this game, subjects respond to various offers, each from a different proposer, for splitting $10, ranging from fair (give $5, keep $5) to extremely unfair (give $1, keep $9). If the offer is accepted, both players get the money according to the offer. If the offer is rejected, neither player gets any money. A purely rational approach would be to accept all offers, but relatively low offers are often rejected by normal subjects, presumably due to an emotional reaction to unfair treatment. It was found that the rejection rate of patients with ventromedial prefrontal lesions was higher than that of normal subjects or brain-damaged comparison subjects for each of the most unfair offers, suggesting that emotional regulation subserved by this area is a key aspect of normal economic decision making.

There are many reasons, discussed elsewhere, why we place an emphasis on the role of emotion and somatic states in the guidance of behavior. Firstly, and most obvious, is that the human acquisition of appropriate behavioral guidance, especially in the social setting, occurs during the process of education and acculturation, under the control of punishment and reward. There are repeated interactions that occur during childhood and adolescence during which social events are paired with somatic states, at both the time of the event, and at the time at which future consequences take place. Second, it is apparent that event/somatic state conjunctions have been important for the behavior of nonhuman species, and that those species seem to have an automatic signaling system alerting individuals to immediate potential danger and immediate opportunities for food, sex, and shelter. Such a system has been especially important in those species in which representational capacity and intelligence are limited. We believe an equivalent automated device is present in humans, but that it is tuned to future outcomes. The human somatic markers would thus mark future outcome rather than immediate outcome. In subhuman species, the critical conjunction is between response option and immediate outcome, and the somatic marker thus tags immediate outcome. We also believe that in humans, such an automated decision making system is then overlaid by cognitive strategy systems that perform cost–benefit analyses but remain connected, neurophysiologically, to the primitive systems. In other words, the systems that humans use for deliberate decision making and planning of future are rooted in the primitive automated systems that other species have long used for their immediate decision making. The neural architecture of the former is connected to the neural architecture of the latter. When the primitive part of the system fails, superimposed levels cannot operate efficiently.

RESPONSE TO CHANGING CONTINGENCIES

Failure to adjust behavior adequately in response to environmental conditions may play an important role in the cognitive/behavioral defects seen after frontal lobe damage. Socially inappropriate behavior and nonadaptive decision making by patients with frontal lobe damage may reflect dysfunction of the neural system by which the consequences of past actions impact upon the online guidance of behavior. It has long been known that monkeys with frontal lobe ablations are unable to make normal adjustments of behavior in response to changing contingencies (Settlage et al., 1948). A large body of literature now demonstrates that impairment of reversal learning, or of adjusting behavior when stimulus-reinforcement associations change, is one of the key deficits resulting from frontal lobe damage (Rolls, 2004).

Testing for the ability to initiate, stop, and modify behavior in response to changing stimuli has traditionally been part of the evaluation for frontal lobe dysfunction. Depending on the circumstances, the evaluation may involve observation of performances on bedside go/no-go tasks or more sophisticated psychometric assessment. The Wisconsin Card Sorting Test (WCST) was developed by Berg (1948) and Grant and Berg (1948) to provide a measure of the ability to identify abstract categories and shift cognitive set, and it has been widely applied in the assessment of frontal lobe damage. The test requires patients to sort a deck of response cards according to various stimulus dimensions. The patient is not informed of the sorting principles, but rather must infer these from information given by the examiner after each response. Further complicating the patient's task is the fact that the sorting principles change throughout the test without any clue other than the changing pattern of feedback. Although there have been several variations on the original methodology, certain features have remained generally constant (see Heaton, 1981, for a complete description of the test). Each response card contains from one to four identical figures (stars, crosses, triangles, or circles), in one of four colors. These figures provide the basis for the three sorting principles: color, form, and number. At the beginning of the test, four stimulus cards are placed before the patient (one red triangle, two green stars, three yellow crosses, and four blue circles). The patient is instructed to place each consecutive response card in front of one of the stimulus cards, wherever it appears to match best. The patient is not informed of the correct sorting principle, but is told only if each response is right or wrong. After the patient has made ten consecutive correct sorts, the initial sorting principle (color) is changed (to form) without warning. Again, after ten correct sorts, the sorting principle is changed without warning from form to number. This procedure continues until either five shifts of sorting category have been completed, or the two decks of 64 cards have been sorted.

The requirements of the WCST for cognitive abstraction and flexibility in response to changing contingencies make it an attractive instrument for investigating the consequences of frontal lobe damage. In a pioneering study, Milner (1963) documented a consistent and severe impairment on the WCST in patients who had undergone prefrontal lobectomies for treatment of epilepsy. None of her subjects were able to complete more than two shifts of set (three categories). The findings were interpreted as suggesting that the ability to shift from one strategy to another in a sorting task is more compromised by frontal lobe damage than by rolandic or posterior sensory cortex damage. The manifest perseveration that made patients rigidly adhere to one criterion and ignore the examiner's guiding information was interpreted as an inability to overcome an established response set.

Although some subsequent studies also found that, as a group, frontal lobe–damaged subjects tended to perform worse than subjects with focal nonfrontal damage, these investigations showed substantial variability in WCST performance across subjects with frontal lobe damage (Heaton, 1981), and one study using a slightly modified procedure found that patients with posterior lesions performed worse than patients with anterior lesions (Teuber et al., 1951). We examined the WCST performances of 91 subjects with focal brain lesions caused by stroke or tumor resection, and found no differences between those subjects with frontal versus nonfrontal lesions (Anderson et al., 1991). Consistent with most prior studies, considerable variability existed in WCST performances across subjects with frontal damage. Some subjects with extensive frontal lobe damage performed the task with ease and made virtually no errors, whereas others with comparable lesions were severely defective. Likewise,

many subjects with nonfrontal lesions had defective performances. Within the frontal lobe group, performances on the WCST did not appear to be related to the specific area of damage (e.g., dorsolateral vs. ventromedial). Along similar lines, a large-scale study of Vietnam war veterans found no difference in WCST performances between subjects with frontal lobe damage versus posterior damage (Grafman et al., 1990). Regional cerebral blood flow studies have indicated that performance on the WCST is associated with relative increases in physiological activity in the prefrontal area, but that several other areas also show increased activity relative to a resting state (Weinberger et al., 1986). Clearly, scores on the WCST must be interpreted in a broad neuropsychological context. Performances are correlated with age, education, and IQ, and the combined findings of several studies suggest that time since onset is a critical factor, with considerable improvement occurring over time (see Stuss et al., 2000).

The number of perseverative errors committed has been the performance measure from the WCST that has proven most sensitive to prefrontal damage. Perseveration at multiple levels of behavioral organization may be observed in some patients with frontal lobe damage, but the localizing value of perseveration is limited (e.g., Goldberg, 1986). Decreased ability to inhibit repetition of ineffective responses appears to be one of the basic defects arising from frontal lobe damage, affecting performance on a variety of tasks. It is possible that variations in inhibitory control may underlie important cognitive differences between humans and other species, as well as differences that arise during the course of human development (Hauser, 1999).

Frontal lobe damage may cause impairments on conditional learning tasks other than the WCST. For example, patients with frontal lobe tumors were found to be impaired relative to those with posterior tumors on a task in which they were required to generate hypotheses regarding the relevance of certain stimulus dimensions, and then modify the hypotheses on the basis of repeated feedback (Cicerone et al., 1983). The subjects with frontal lobe tumors showed a tendency to repeat responses despite negative feedback. In a series of studies with nonhuman primates and human subjects with frontal lobe ablations, Petrides has investigated the ability to select, from a number of possible alternative responses, the correct response given the current stimulus. Each of the alternative responses is correct only in the presence of one particular stimulus, and the subject must discover on the basis of information given by the examiner after each response which is the appropriate response for each one of the set of stimuli. Petrides (1985) found that patients with unilateral frontal lobe excisions were impaired, relative to patients with temporal lobe excisions, on tasks that required the subject to point to different locations or display various hand shapes in response to specific stimuli. This basic finding was replicated with a task in which the subjects learned to associate various abstract designs with various colored lights (Petrides, 1990), suggesting that the defect in conditional learning following frontal damage is a general one not limited to situations requiring selection between distinct movements or spatial locations. The subjects involved in these studies had undergone extensive prefrontal lobectomies, with lesions generally involving dorsolateral as well as ventral or medial cortices. However, parallel research with nonhuman primates has suggested that the posterior dorsolateral frontal cortex may be the critical region for performance on the conditional association tasks (Petrides, 1987).

PLANNING AND SEQUENCING

The ability to plan short- and long-term future behaviors often seems to be devastated in patients with frontal lobe damage. In our experience, the modal response of these patients to questions regarding plans for the upcoming days or months is a recitation of the activities of the past several days. Consistent with this, their daily behavior often becomes a highly repetitious routine if left to their own devices. Other patients may describe, generally in vague terms, long-term goals that are typically fanciful, unrealistic, or illogical. These verbalizations provide scant evidence of planning, and seem to have little or no impact on the guidance of behavior.

The relationship of planning defects to frontal lobe damage is due in part to the major working memory and temporal sequencing demands of planning (Sirigu et al., 1995; Owen, 1997). Patients with frontal lobe damage have been shown to have impairments on a variety of sequencing tasks in which they are required to determine the most reasonable order of a series of actions or events, although they have no difficulty in recalling highly constrained sequences, such as the order of the months of the year (Zanini, 2008).

Neurophysiological evidence from monkeys also indicates that neurons in prefrontal cortex are involved in prospective coding of anticipated reward and expected objects (Rainer et al., 1999; Watanabe, 1996), and functional imaging in normal humans has suggested that anterior dorsolateral prefrontal cortex may play a unique role in maintaining goals in working memory while proceeding with subgoals (Koechlin et al., 1999).

Much of the evidence for an impairment of planning following prefrontal damage has been based on the Tower tasks (e.g., Tower of Hanoi, Tower of London), which require movement of a set of disks to a goal position, following certain rules that require planning of a series of steps (Shallice, 1982; Owen et al., 1990; Carlin et al., 2000). The linkage between performance on such tasks and frontal activity has been supported by functional imaging studies (e.g., Dagher et al., 1999). Goel and Grafman (1995) have pointed out that the Tower of Hanoi task may have different cognitive demands than the Tower of London, with the critical step in Tower of Hanoi being the ability to see and resolve a goal–subgoal conflict (i.e., to perform a counterintuitive backward move), rather than simple foresight or planning. Further evidence that the deficient planning abilities of patients with frontal lobe damage are due to impairment of ability to select responses most in keeping with a final goal, particularly when these are counterintuitive or less obvious responses, has come from the Water Jug task (Colvin et al., 2001). When the best response required looking beyond simply moving closer to the goal on the next step, patients with dorsolateral prefrontal damage showed the greatest impairment.

Although there appears to be an association between dorsolateral frontal damage and impairments on laboratory tests involving planning, Sarazin et al. (1998) have provided evidence that orbital prefrontal dysfunction is most highly correlated with planning defects in real-world activities. Planning clearly is not a single cognitive operation. Rather, planning involves conflation of multiple component processes and occurs over a broad range of circumstances involving widely divergent time frames, levels of complexity and intentionality, and methods of execution. It appears that broad sectors of the frontal lobes, including dorsolateral and orbital prefrontal regions, in addition to premotor cortex, are involved in aspects of planning. An important research challenge at this point is delineation of component cognitive processes and their linkage to specific regions of the prefrontal cortex (Goel et al., 1997).

Petrides and Milner (1982) contrasted the effect of lesions in the frontal lobe with the effect of lesions in the temporal lobe on four self-ordered tasks that required the organization of the sequence of pointing responses. In these sequential tasks, the subject is free to choose his or her own order of response but is prevented from giving the same response twice. Patients with frontal lobe excisions had significant impairments in all four tasks, whereas the patients with temporal excisions either had no impairment or, when their lesions encompassed the hippocampus, exhibited material-specific deficits. It is of interest that the patients with left frontal lobe excisions were impaired in both verbal and nonverbal tasks, whereas the patients with right frontal lobe excisions were impaired only in nonverbal ones. Petrides and Milner (1982) pointed out how this disparity is compatible with the notion of left hemisphere dominance for the programming of voluntary actions.

Learning to maneuver through a spatial maze requires that a sequence of behaviors be performed in a particular order, and subjects with frontal lobe lesions have been found to be defective in various maze learning tasks (e.g., Porteus et al., 1944; Milner, 1965; Canavan, 1983). Milner (1965) noted that the frontal lobe subjects repeatedly failed to return to the correct path despite feedback regarding their error. Consistent with this, Karnath et al. (1991) used a computerized maze task to demonstrate that, relative to normal control subjects, subjects with medial frontal lobe lesions showed greater rule breaking behavior on the second trial through the mazes. The finding that subjects with frontal lobe damage are slower to benefit from experience for the guidance of maze learning is reminiscent of Petrides' findings on learning conditional associations. Additional information regarding the effects of frontal lesions on maze learning comes from a recent study by Winocur and Moscovitch (1990). Rats with bilateral prefrontal lesions were impaired in learning the general skill of maze learning, despite good memory for information regarding the specific maze they had experience with. The opposite pattern was found in rats with bilateral hippocampal lesions.

STRATEGY APPLICATION

The complexity of real-world problem solving and decision making is not approximated by standard clinical or laboratory tasks, which typically are characterized by having a single explicit problem, brief trials, and clear cues for task initiation and completion. Problem solving and decision making in the real world involve integration of information from diverse sources over extended time frames, a seemingly unlimited choice of response options, and often an absence of specific criteria for adequate task performance. It appears likely that much of the dissociation between standardized test performance and real-world dysfunction may arise because prefrontal cortex damage leaves relatively preserved an ability to respond appropriately when sufficient constraints and structure are provided by immediately present environmental stimuli. Cummings (1995) has emphasized the role of increased environmental dependency as a key organizing theme for understanding frontal lobe dysfunction. In its most extreme form, environmental dependency can be expressed as a near compulsion to grasp and use immediately present items, the so-called "utilization behavior" (Lhermitte et al., 1986; Shallice et al., 1989; Brazzelli & Spinnier, 1998). In milder forms, environmental dependency may set the stage for deceptively good problem solving, provided the necessary components for the task are placed on the table in front of the patient. This factor introduces a fundamental conflict between the format of most standardized testing and the nature of the impairments that arise from prefrontal damage.

Goldberg and Podell (2000) have emphasized the additional distinction between veridical problem solving (tapped by most neuropsychological tests) and adaptive problem solving, which incorporates the organism's priorities and more closely resembles real-world activity. They have developed the Cognitive Bias Test, which requires response selection based on the subject's preferences rather than external criteria. Measures reflecting the extent to which responses in an ambiguous situation were guided by context appeared to be sensitive to hemispheric and gender differences.

Shallice and Burgess (1991) developed a quantifiable analog of the type of relatively unstructured, open-ended, multiple subgoal tasks that seem to cause so much difficulty in the daily life of patients with frontal lobe damage. Subjects were required to complete a set of everyday tasks (e.g., buy a certain item, meet someone at a given time, obtain basic meteorological and consumer information), which were designed to place limited demands on nonexecutive cognitive functions. They found that three patients with traumatic head injuries involving prefrontal damage approached the tasks inefficiently and tended to violate rules (task imposed and societal norms). These tasks and various modifications have subsequently been utilized by a number of researchers to investigate executive functioning in normal subjects and various patient populations (Burgess et al., 2006), and appear to provide a useful window into the real-world deficits associated with prefrontal dysfunction. To address the question of which prefrontal region is most specifically associated with impairment on these tasks, we replicated the initial Shallice and Burgess experiment in a group of 34 patients with focal brain lesions caused by stroke or surgery (nine ventromedial prefrontal, eight dorsolateral or orbitolateral, 17 nonfrontal) (Tranel et al., 2007). The tasks were performed in a complex real-world environment presenting myriad options (i.e., a shopping mall). We found that the behavior of patients with prefrontal lesions was marked by inefficiencies, failure to complete tasks, and rule infractions. The impairments tended to be most severe in patients with damage to ventromedial prefrontal regions, although dorsolateral lesions also resulted in impairments of lesser severity. These findings help substantiate the linkage between frontal lobe dysfunction and impairment meeting the exigencies of normal daily life, and highlight some of the behavioral and environmental factors that may contribute to the defect.

CONCLUSION

The manifestations of frontal lobe dysfunction are varied, ranging from akinesia and mutism to major changes in personality. Often, there are no apparent defects of movement, perception, or intelligence. Depending on the cause and location of the lesion, a variety of frontal lobe symptom clusters can thus appear. There is no single frontal lobe syndrome.

In general, the vast set of cerebral cortices collectively known as the frontal lobes appear to have evolved to guide response selection in order to offer the organism its best chance of long-term survival. It is probable that this overall goal was implemented first in simple social environments, dominated by the needs for food, sex, and the avoidance of predators. Other contingencies, in ever more complex environments, were later connected with those original contingencies, so that the basic neural mechanism for response selection was incorporated in the decision making mechanisms developed for newer and more challenging environments. Damage to this system disrupts many of the cognitive and behavioral abilities that have come to define humanity.

ACKNOWLEDGMENTS

Supported by NINDS Program Project Grant NS 19632 and NIDA DA022549. We thank Ashton McNutt for careful help with the reference list.

REFERENCES

Abe, M., & Hanakawa, T. (2009). Functional coupling underlying motor and cognitive functions of the dorsal premotor cortex. *Behavioural Brain Research*, 198, 13–23.

Ackerly, S. S., & Benton, A. L. (1948). Report of a case of bilateral frontal lobe defect. *Research Publication of the Association for Research in Nervous and Mental Disease*, 27, 479–504.

Adolphs, R., Damasio, H., & Tranel, D. (2002). Neural systems for recognition of emotional prosody: A 3-D lesion study. *Emotion*, 2, 23–51.

Adolphs, R., Damasio, H., Tranel, D., Cooper, G., & Damasio, A. R. (2000). A role for somatosensory cortices in the visual recognition of emotion as revealed by three-dimensional lesion mapping. *The Journal of Neuroscience*, 20, 2683–2690.

Akert, K. (1964). Comparative anatomy of frontal cortex and thalamofrontal connections. In J. M. Warren, & K. Akert (Eds.), *The frontal granular cortex and behavior*. New York: McGraw-Hill.

Alexander, M. P., Benson, D. F., & Stuss, D. T. (1989). Frontal lobes and language. *Brain and Language*, 37, 656–691.

Alexander, M. P., Stuss, D. T., Picton, T., Shallice, T., & Gillingham, S. (2007). Regional frontal injuries cause distinct impairments in cognitive control. *Neurology*, 68, 1515–1523.

Anderson, S. W., Barrash, J., Bechara, A., & Tranel, D. (2006). Impairments of emotion and real-world behavior following childhood- or adult-onset damage to ventromedial prefrontal cortex. *Journal of the International Neuropsychological Society*, 12, 224–235.

Anderson, S. W., Bechara, A., Damasio, H., Tranel, D., & Damasio, A. R. (1999). Impairment of social and moral behavior related to early damage in the human prefrontal cortex. *Nature Neuroscience*, 2, 1032–1037.

Anderson, S. W., Damasio, A. R., & Damasio, H. (1990). Troubled letters but not numbers: Domain specific cognitive impairments following focal damage in frontal cortex. *Brain*, 113, 749–766.

Anderson, S. W., Damasio, H., & Damasio, A. R. (2005). A neural basis for collecting behavior. *Brain*, 128, 201–212.

Anderson, S. W., Damasio, H., Jones, R. D., & Tranel, D. (1991). Wisconsin card sorting test performance as a measure of frontal lobe damage. *Journal of Clinical and Experimental Neuropsychology*, 13, 909–922.

Anderson, S. W., Damasio, H., & Tranel, D. (1989). Neuropsychological profiles associated with lesions caused by tumor or stroke. *Archives of Neurology*, 47, 397–405.

Anderson, S. W., Wisnowski, J. L., Barrash, J., Damasio, H., & Tranel, D. (2009). Consistency of neuropsychological outcome following damage to prefrontal cortex in the first years of life. *Journal of Clinical and Experimental Neuropsychology*, 31, 170–179.

Aron, A. R., Fletcher, P. C., Bullmore, T. T., Sahakian, B. J., & Robbins, T. W. (2003). Stop-signal inhibition disrupted by damage to the right inferior frontal gyrus in humans. *Nature Neuroscience*, 6, 115–116.

Baddeley, A. D. (1986). *Working memory*. New York: Oxford University Press.

Badre, D., Hoffman, J., Cooney, J. W., & D'Esposito, M. (2009). Hierarchical cognitive control deficits following damage to the human frontal lobe. *Nature Neuroscience*, 12, 515–522.

Bailey, P., & Von Bonin, G. (1951). *The isocortex of man*. Urbana, IL: University of Illinois Press.

Baldo, J. V., & Shimamura, A. P. (1998). Letter and category fluency in patients with frontal lobe lesions. *Neuropsychology*, 12, 259–267.

Barbas, H. (1995). Anatomic basis of cognitive-emotional interactions in the primate prefrontal cortex. *Neuroscience and Biobehavioral Reviews*, 19, 499–510.

Barbas, H., & Mesulam, M. M. (1981). Organization of afferent input of subdivisions of area 8 in the rhesus monkey. *Journal of Comparative Neurology*, 200, 407–431.

Barbas, H., & Mesulam, M. M. (1985). Cortical afferent input to the principalis region of the rhesus monkey. *Neuroscience*, 15, 619–637.

Barbas, H., & Pandya, D. N. (1987). Architecture and frontal cortical connections of the premotor cortex (area 6) in the rhesus monkey. *Journal of Comparative Neurology*, 256, 211–228.

Bar-On, R., Tranel, D., Denburg, N. L., & Bechara, A. (2003). Exploring the neurological substrate of emotional and social intelligence. *Brain*, 126, 1790–1800.

Barrash, J., Tranel, D., & Anderson, S. W. (2000). Acquired sociopathy: Characteristic personality changes following ventromedial frontal lobe damage. *Developmental Neuropsychology*, 18, 355–381.

Bechara, A., Damasio, A. R., Damasio, H., & Anderson, S. W. (1994). Insensitivity to future consequences following damage to prefrontal cortex. *Cognition*, 50, 7–15.

Bechara, A., Damasio, H., Tranel, D., & Anderson, S. W. (1998). Dissociation of working memory from decision-making within the human prefrontal cortex. *The Journal of Neuroscience*, *18*, 428–437.

Bechara, A., Damasio, H., Tranel, D., & Damasio, A. R. (1997). Deciding advantageously before knowing the advantageous strategy. *Science*, *275*, 1293–1295.

Beer, J. S., John, O. P., Scabini, D., & Knight, R. T. (2006). Orbitofrontal cortex and social behavior: Integrating self-monitoring and emotion-cognition interactions. *Journal of Cognitive Neuroscience*, *18*, 871–879.

Beldarrain, G., Grafman, J., Pascual-Leone, A., & Garcia-Monco, J. C. (1999). Procedural learning is impaired in patients with prefrontal lesions. *Neurology*, *52*, 1853–1860.

Bellugi, U., Poizner, H., & Klima, E. S. (1989). Language, modality and the brain. *Trends in Neurosciences*, *12*, 380–388.

Benton, A. L. (1968). Differential behavioral effects in frontal lobe disease. *Neuropsychologia*, *6*, 53–60.

Benton, A. L. (1991a). The prefrontal region: Its early history. In H. S. Levin, H. M Eisenberg, & A.L. Benton (Eds.), *Frontal lobe function and dysfunction*. New York: Oxford University Press.

Benton, A. L. (1991b). Basic approaches to neuropsychological assessment. In S.R. Steinhauer, J. J. Gruzelier, & J. Zubin (Eds.), *Handbook of schizophrenia* Vol. 5: *Neuropsychology, psychophysiology, and information processing*. Amsterdam: Elsevier.

Benson, D. F. (1977). The third alexia. *Archives of Neurology, Chicago*, *34*, 327–331.

Berg, E. A. (1948). A simple objective technique for measuring flexibility in thinking. *Journal of Genetic Psychology*, *39*, 15–22.

Black, F. W. (1976). Cognitive deficits in patients with unilateral war-related frontal lobe lesions. *Journal of Clinical Psychology*, *32*, 366–372.

Blumer, D., & Benson, D. F. (1975). Personality changes with frontal and temporal lobe lesions. In D. F. Benson, & D. Blumer (Eds.), *Psychiatric aspects of neurologic disease*. New York: Grune and Stratton.

Brazelli, M., & Spinnler, H. (1998). An example of lack of frontal inhibition: The "utilization behavior." *European Journal of Neurology*, *5*, 347–353.

Brickner, R. M. (1934). An interpretation of frontal lobe function based upon the study of a case of partial bilateral frontal lobectomy. *Research Publication of the Association for Research in Nervous and Mental Disease*, *13*, 259–351.

Brickner, R. M. (1936). *The intellectual functions of the frontal lobes: Study based upon observation of a man after partial bilateral frontal lobectomy*. New York: Macmillan.

Brickner, R. M. (1952). Brain of patient "A" after bilateral frontal lobectomy: Status of frontal lobe problem. *Archives of Neurology and Psychiatry*, *68*, 293–313.

Broca, P. (1861). Remarques sur le siege de la faculte du langage articule, suivies d'une observation d'aphemie (perte de la parole). *Bulletin de la Societe d'Anatomie (Paris)*, *36*, 330–357.

Burgess, P. W., Alderman, N., Forbes, C., Cosetllo, A., Coates, L. M., Dawson, D. R., et al. (2006). The case for the development and use of "ecologically valid" measures of executive function in experimental and clinical neuropsychology. *Journal of the International Neuropsychology Society*, *12*, 194–209.

Butter, C. M., Mishkin, M., & Mirsky, A. F. (1968). Emotional responses toward humans in monkeys with selective frontal lesions. *Physiology and Behavior*, *3*, 213–215.

Butter, C. M., Mishkin, M., & Rosvold, H. E. (1963). Conditioning and extinction of a food-rewarded response after selective ablations of frontal cortex in rhesus monkeys. *Experimental Neurology*, *7*, 65–75.

Butter, C. M., Snyder, D. R., & McDonald, J. A. (1970). Effects of orbital frontal lesions on aversive and aggressive behaviors in rhesus monkeys. *Journal of Comparative and Physiological Psychology*, *72*, 132–144.

Butters, M. A., Kaszniak, A. W., Glisky, E.L., Eslinger, P. J., & Schacter, D. L. (1994). Recency discrimination deficits in frontal lobe patients. *Neuropsychology*, *8*, 343–353.

Cabeza, R., & Nyberg, L. (2000). Imaging cognition II: An empirical review of 275 PET and fMRI studies. *Journal of Cognitive Neuroscience*, *12*, 1–47.

Canavan, A. G. M. (1983). Stylus-maze performance in patients with frontal-lobe lesions: Effects of signal valency and relationship to verbal and spatial abilities. *Neuropsychologia*, *21*, 375–382.

Carlin, D., Bonerba, J., Phipps, M., Alexander, G., Shapiro, M., & Grafman, J. (2000). Planning impairments in frontal lobe dementia and frontal lobe lesion patients. *Neuropsychologia*, *38*, 655–665.

Cavada, C., & Goldman-Rakic, P. S. (1989). Posterior parietal cortex in rhesus monkey: II. Evidence for segregated corticocortical networks linking sensory and limbic areas with the frontal lobe. *Journal of Comparative Neurology*, *287*, 422–445.

Chao, L. L., & Knight, R. T. (1998). Contribution of human prefrontal cortex to delay performance. *Journal of Cognitive Neuroscience*, *10*, 167–177.

Chavis, D. A., & Pandya, D. N. (1976). Further observations on corticofrontal connections in the rhesus monkey. *Brain Research, 117*, 369–386.

Chorover, S. L., & Cole, M. (1966). Delayed alternation performance in patients with cerebral lesions. *Neuropsychologia, 4*, 1–7.

Christoff, K., Prabhakaran, V., Dorfman, J., Zhao, Z., Kroger, J. K., Holyoak, K. J., et al. (2001). Rostrolateral prefrontal cortex involvement in relational integration during reasoning. *Neuroimage, 14*, 1136–1149.

Ciaramelli, E., Leo, F., Del Viva, M. M., Burr, D. C., & Ladavas, E. (2007). The contribution of prefrontal cortex to global perception. *Experimental Brain Research, 181*, 427–434.

Cicerone, K. D., Lazar, R. M., & Shapiro, W. R. (1983). Effects of frontal lobe lesions on hypothesis sampling during concept formation. *Neuropsychologia, 21*, 513–524.

Colom, R., Haier, R. J., Head, K., Alvarez-Linera, J., Angeles Quiroga, M., Chun Shih, P., & Jung, R. E. (2009). Gray matter correlates of fluid, crystallized, and spatial intelligence: Testing the P-FIT model. *Intelligence, 37*, 124–135.

Colvin, M. K., Dunbar, K., & Grafman, J. (2001). The effects of frontal lobe lesions on goal achievement in the Water Jug task. *Journal of Cognitive Neuroscience, 13*, 1129–1147.

Crosby, E. C., Humphrey, T., & Lauer, E. W. (1962). *Correlative anatomy of the nervous system.* New York: Macmillan.

Cummings, J. L. (1985). *Clinical neuropsychiatry.* New York: Grune & Stratton.

Cummings, J. L. (1995). Anatomic and behavioral aspects of frontal-subcortical circuits. In J. Grafman, K. J. Holyoak, & F. Boller (Eds.), *Structure and function of the human prefrontal cortex. Annals of the New York Academy of Sciences 769*:1–14.

Daffner, K. R., Mesulan, M. M., Scinto, L. F. M., Acar, D., Calvo, V., Faust, R., et al. (2000). The central role of the prefrontal cortex in directing attention to novel events. *Brain, 123*, 927–939.

Dagher, A., Owen, A. M., Boecker, H., & Brooks, D. J. (1999). Mapping the network for planning: A correlational PET activation study with the Tower of London task. *Brain, 122*, 1973–1987.

Damasio, A. R. (1992). Aphasia. *The New England Journal of Medicine, 326*, 531–539.

Damasio, A. R. (1994). *Descartes' error: Emotion, reason, and the human brain.* New York: Grosset/Putnam.

Damasio, A. R., Damasio, H., & Chui, H. C. (1980). Neglect following damage to frontal lobe or basal ganglia. *Neuropsychologia, 18*, 123–132.

Damasio, A. R., Eslinger, P., Damasio, H., Van Hoesen, G. W., & Cornell, S. (1985). Multimodal amnesic syndrome following bilateral temporal and basal forebrain damage. *Archives of Neurology, 42*, 252–259.

Damasio, A. R., & Tranel, D. (1993). Nouns and verbs are retrieved with differently distributed neural systems. *Proceedings of the National Academy of Sciences, 90*, 4957–60.

Damasio, A. R., Tranel, D., & Damasio, H. (1990). Individuals with sociopathic behavior caused by frontal damage fail to respond autonomically to social stimuli. *Behavioural Brain Research, 41*, 81–94.

Damasio, A. R., Tranel, D., & Damasio, H. (1991). Somatic markers and the guidance of behavior: Theory and preliminary testing. In H. S. Levin, H. M. Eisenberg, & A. L. Benton (Eds.), *Frontal lobe function and dysfunction.* New York: Oxford University Press.

Damasio, A. R., & Van Hoesen, G. W. (1980). Structure and function of the supplementary motor area. *Neurology, 30*, 359.

Damasio, A. R., & Van Hoesen, G. W. (1983). Emotional disturbances associated with focal lesions of the frontal lobe. In K. Heilman, & P. Satz (Eds.), *The neurophysiology of human emotion: Recent advances.* New York: Guilford Press.

Damasio, H., Tranel, D., Grabowski, T., Adolphs, R., & Damasio, A. (2004). Neural systems behind word and concept retrieval. *Cognition, 92*, 179–229.

Dejerine, J., & Mirallie, C. (1895). Sur les alterations de la lecture mentale chez les aphasiques moteurs corticaux. *Comptes Rendus des Seances et Memoires de la Societe de Biologie, Paris, 10th ser,* ii, 523–527.

DeRenzi, E. Faglioni, P., Lodesani, M., & Vecchi, A. (1983). Impairment of left brain-damaged patients on imitation of single movements and motor sequences: Frontal and parietal injured patients compared. *Cortex, 19*, 333–343.

D'Esposito, M. (2000). Functional neuroimaging of working memory. In R. Cabeza, & A. Kingstone (Eds.), *Handbook of functional neuroimaging of cognition* (pp. 293–327). Cambridge, MA: MIT Press.

D'Esposito, M., Aguirre, G. K., Zarahn, E., Ballard, D., Shin, R. K., & Lease, J. (1998). Functional MRI studies of spatial and nonspatial working memory. *Cognitive Brain Research, 7*, 1–13.

D'Esposito, M., & Postle, B. R. (1999). The dependence of span and delayed-response performance on prefrontal cortex. *Neuropsychologia, 37*, 1303–1315.

Deutsch, R. D., Kling, A., & Steklis, H. D. (1979). Influence of frontal lobe lesions on behavioral interactions in man. *Research Communications in Psychology, Psychiatry and Behavior, 4*, 415–431.

DeVito, J. L., & Smith, O. E. (1964). Subcortical projections of the prefrontal lobe of the monkey. *Journal of Comparative Neurology, 123*, 413.

Dias, R., Robbins, T. W., & Roberts, A. C. (1997). Dissociable forms of inhibitory control within prefrontal cortex with an analog of the Wisconsin card sort test: Restriction to novel situations and independence from "on-line" processing. *The Journal of Neuroscience, 17*, 9285–9297.

Dimitrov, M., Grafman, J., & Hollnagel, C. (1996). The effects of frontal lobe damage on everyday problem solving. *Cortex, 32*, 357–366.

Dimitrov, M., Granetz, J., Peterson, M., Hollnagel, C., Alexander, G., & Grafman, J. (1999). Associative learning impairments in patients with frontal lobe damage. *Brain and Cognition, 41*, 213–230.

Di Pellegrino, G., & Wise, S. P. (1991). A neurophysiological comparison of three distinct regions of the primate frontal lobe. *Brain, 114*, 951–978.

Duncan, J., Seitz, R. J., Kolodny, J., Bor, D., Herzog, H., Ahmed, A., et al. (2000). A neural basis for general intelligence. *Science, 289*, 457–460.

Eichenbaum, H., Shedlack, K. J., & Eckmann, K. W. (1980). Thalamocortical mechanisms in odor-guided behavior. I: Effects of lesions of the mediodorsal thalamic nucleus and frontal cortex on olfactory discrimination in the rat. *Brain Behavior and Evolution, 17*, 225–275.

Elliot, R., Dolan, R. J. & Frith, C. D. (2000). Dissociable functions in the medial and lateral orbitofrontal cortex: evidence from human neuroimaging studies. *Cerebral Cortex, 10*, 308–317.

Eslinger, P. J. (1998). Neurological and neuropsychological bases of empathy. *European Neurology, 39*, 193–199.

Eslinger, P. J., & Damasio, A. R. (1985). Severe disturbance of higher cognition after bilateral frontal lobe ablation: patient EVR. *Neurology, 35*, 1731–1741.

Eslinger, P. J., & Grattan, L. M. (1994). Altered serial position learning after frontal lobe lesion. *Neuropsychologia, 32*, 729–739.

Esposito, G., Kirkby, B. S., Van Horn, J. D., Ellmore, T. M., & Berman, K. F. (1999). Context-dependent, neural system-specific neurophysiological concomitants of ageing: Mapping PET correlates during cognitive activation. *Brain, 122*, 963–979.

Ethelberg, S. (1949). On "cataplexy" in a case of frontal lobe tumor. *Acta Psychiatrica et Neurologica Scandinavica, 24*, 421–427.

Exner, S. (1881). *Untersuchungen uber die localisation der functionen in der grosshirnrinde des menschen.* Wien: W. Braumuller.

Feuchtwanger, E. (1923). Die funktionen des stirnhirns. In O. Forster, & K. Willmanns (Eds.), *Monographien aus dem gesamtgebiete der neurologie und psychiatrie.* Berlin: Springer.

Fisher, C. M. (1968). Intermittent interruption of behavior. *Transactions of the American Neurological Association, 93*, 209–210.

Fletcher, P. C., Shallice, T., & Dolan, R. J. (1998). The functional roles of prefrontal cortex in episodic memory. *Brain, 121*, 1239–1248.

Floden, D., & Stuss, D. T. (2006). Inhibitory control is slowed in patients with right superior medial frontal damage. *Journal of Cognitive Neuroscience, 18*, 1843–1849.

Frank, R. J., Damasio, H., & Grabowski, T. J. (1997). Brainvox: An interactive multimodal visualization and analysis system for neuroanatomical imaging. *Neuroimage, 5*, 13–30.

Frey, S., & Petrides, M. (2000). Orbitofrontal cortex: A key prefrontal region for encoding information. *Proceedings of the National Academy of Sciences, 97*, 8723–8727.

Fulton, J. F. (1951). *Frontal lobotomy and affective behavior.* New York: Norton.

Fulton, J. F., & Jacobsen, C. F. (1935). The functions of the frontal lobes: A comparative study in monkeys, chimpanzees and man. *Advan. Mod. Biol. (Moscow), 4*, 113–123.

Fuster, J. M. (1997). *The prefrontal cortex: Anatomy, physiology, and neuropsychology of the frontal lobe.* New York: Lippincott-Raven.

Gardner, H., & Zurif, E. (1975). Bee but not be: Oral reading of single words in aphasia and alexia. *Neuropsychologia, 13*, 181–190.

Gershberg, F. B., & Shimamura, A. P. (1995). Impaired use of organizational strategies in free recall following frontal lobe damage. *Neuropsychologia, 13*, 1305–1333.

Ghent, L., Mishkin, M., & Teuber, H. L. (1962). Short-term memory after frontal-lobe injury in man. *Journal of Comparative and Physiological Psychology, 55*, 705–709.

Gläscher, J., Rudrauf, D., Paul, L. K., Colom, R., Tranel, D., Damasio, H., & Adolphs, R. (2010). Distributed neural system for general intelligence revealed by lesion mapping. *Proceedings of the National Academy of Sciences, USA, 107*, 4705–4709.

Gläscher, J., Tranel, D., Paul, L. K., Rudrauf, D., Rorden, C., Hornaday, A., et al. (2009). Lesion mapping of cognitive abilities linked to intelligence. *Neuron, 61*, 681–691.

Goel, V., & Grafman, J. (1995). Are the frontal lobes implicated in "planning" functions? Interpreting data from the Tower of Hanoi. *Neuropsychologia, 33,* 623–642.

Goel, V., Grafman, J., Tajik, J., Gana, S., & Danto, D. (1997). A study of the performance of patients with frontal lobe lesions in a financial planning task. *Brain, 120,* 1805–1822.

Goldberg, E. (1986). Varieties of perseveration: A comparison of two taxonomies. *Journal of Clinical and Experimental Neuropsychology, 8,* 710–726.

Goldberg, E., & Podell, K. (2000). Adaptive decision making, ecological validity, and the frontal lobes. *Journal of Clinical and Experimental Neuropsychology, 22,* 56–68.

Goldman, P. S. (1978). Neuronal plasticity in primate telencephalon: Anomalous projections induced by prenatal removal of frontal cortex. *Science, 202,* 768–770.

Goldman, P. S., & Nauta, W. J. H. (1977). An intricately patterned prefrontocaudate projection in the rhesus monkey. *Journal of Comparative Neurology, 171,* 369–386.

Goldman-Rakic, P. S. (1984). Modular organization of the prefrontal cortex. *Trends in Neuroscience, 7,* 419–424.

Goldman-Rakic, P. S. (1987). Circuitry of primate prefrontal cortex and regulation of behavior by representational memory. In F. Plum (Ed.), *Handbook of physiology: The nervous system* Vol. 5. Bethesda, MD: American Physiological Society.

Goldman-Rakic, P. S. (1992). Working memory and the mind. *Scientific American, 267,* 111–117.

Goldman-Rakic, P. S. (1995). Architecture of the prefrontal cortex and the central executive. In J. Grafman, K. Holyoak, & F. Boller (Eds.), *Structure and functions of the human prefrontal cortex* (pp. 71–83). New York: The New York Academy of Sciences.

Goldman-Rakic, P. S., & Friedman, H. R. (1991). The circuitry of working memory revealed by anatomy and metabolic imaging. In H. S. Levin, H. M. Eisenberg, & A. L. Benton (Eds.), *Frontal lobe function and dysfunction.* New York: Oxford University Press.

Goldman-Rakic, P. S., & Schwartz, M. L. (1982). Interdigitation of contralateral and ipsilateral columnar projections to frontal association cortex in primates. *Science, 216,* 755–757.

Goldstein, K. (1948). *Aftereffects of brain injuries in war.* New York: Grune & Stratton.

Gordinier, H. C. (1899). A case of brain tumor at the base of the second left frontal convolution. *American Journal of the Medical Sciences, 117,* 526–535.

Grafman, J., Jonas, B., & Salazar, A. (1990). Wisconsin card sorting test performance based on location and size of neuroanatomical lesion in Vietnam veterans with penetrating head injury. *Perceptual and Motor Skills, 71,* 1120–1122.

Grant, D. A., & Berg, E. A. (1948). A behavioral analysis of degree of reinforcement and ease of shifting to new responses in a Weigl-type card-sorting problem. *Journal of Experimental Psychology, 38,* 404–411.

Grattan, L. M., Bloomer, R. H. Archambault, F. X., & Eslinger, P. J. (1994). Cognitive flexibility and empathy after frontal lobe lesion. *Neuropsychiatry, Neuropsychology, and Behavioral Neurology, 7,* 251–259.

Grattan, L. M., & Eslinger, P. J. (1991). Frontal lobe damage in children and adults: A comparative review. *Developmental Neuropsychology, 7,* 283–326.

Gray, J. R., Chabris, C. F., & Braver, T. S. (2003). Neural mechanisms of general fluid intelligence. *Nature Neuroscience, 6,* 316–321.

Grueninger, W. E., Kimble, D. P., Grueninger, J., & Levine, S. E. (1965). GSR and corticosteroid response in monkeys with frontal ablations. *Neuropsychologia, 3,* 205–216.

Guitton, D., Buchtel, H. A., & Douglas, R. M. (1985). Frontal lobe lesions in man cause difficulties in suppressing reflexive glances and in generation of goal directed saccades. *Experimental Brain Research, 58,* 455–472.

Halsband, U., & Freund, H. J. (1990). Premotor cortex and conditional learning in man. *Brain, 113,* 207–222.

Harlow, J. M. (1848). Passage of an iron rod through the head. *Boston Medical and Surgical Journal, 39,* 389–393.

Harlow, J. M. (1868). Recovery from the passage of an iron bar through the head. *Publications of the Massachusetts Medical Society, 2,* 327–347.

Hauser, M. D. (1999). Perseveration, inhibition and the prefrontal cortex: A new look. *Current Opinion in Neurobiology, 9,* 214–222.

Heaton, R. K. (1981). *Wisconsin card sorting test manual.* Odessa, FL: Psychological Assessment Resources, Inc.

Hebb, D. O. (1945). Man's frontal lobes: A critical review. *Archives of Neurology and Psychiatry, 54,* 421–438.

Hebb, D. O., & Penfield, W. (1940). Human behavior after extensive bilateral removals from the frontal lobes. *Archives of Neurology and Psychiatry, 44,* 421–438.

Heberlein, A. S., Padon, A. A., Gillihan, S. J., Farah, M. J., & Fellows, L. K. (2008). Ventromedial frontal lobe plays a critical role in facial emotion recognition. *Journal of Cognitive Neuroscience*, *20*, 721–733.

Hecaen, H. (1964). Mental symptoms associated with tumors of the frontal lobe. In J. M. Warren, & K. Akert (Eds.), *The frontal granular cortex and behavior*. New York: McGraw-Hill.

Heilman, K. M., & Valenstein, E. (1972). Frontal lobe neglect in man. *Neurology*, *22*, 660–664.

Heilman, K. M., Pandya, D. N., Karol, E. A., & Geschwind, N. (1971). Auditory inattention. *Archives of Neurology*, *24*, 323–325.

Heilman, K. M., & Watson, R. T. (1991). Intentional motor disorders. In H. S. Levin, H. L. Eisenburg, & A. L. Benton (Eds.), *Frontal lobe function and dysfunction*. New York: Oxford University Press.

Hillis, A. E., & Caramazza, A. (1995). Representations of grammatical categories of words in the brain. *Journal of Cognitive Neuroscience*, *7*, 396–407.

Hillis, A. E., Tuffiash, E., Wityk, R. J., & Barker, P. B. (2002). Regions of neural dysfunction associated with impaired naming of actions and objects in acute stroke. *Cognitive Neuropsychology*, *19*, 523–534.

Hillis, A. E., Wityk, R. J., Barker, P. B., & Caramazza, A. (2003). Neural regions essential for writing verbs. *Nature Neuroscience*, *6*, 19–20.

Holmes, G. (1938). The cerebral integration of ocular movements. *British Medical Journal*, *2*, 107–112.

Homskaya, E. D. (1966). Vegetative components of the orienting reflex to indifferent and significant stimuli in patients with lesions of the frontal lobes. In A. R. Luria, & E. D. Homskaya (Eds.), *Frontal lobes and regulation of psychological processes*. Moscow: Moscow University Press.

Isingrini, M., & Vazou, F. (1997). Relation between fluid intelligence and frontal lobe in older adults. *International Journal of Aging and Human Development*, *45*, 99–109.

Jacobsen, C. F. (1935). Functions of the frontal association area in primates. *Archives of Neurology and Psychiatry*, *33*, 558–569.

Janowsky, J. S., Shimamura, A. P., Kritchevsky, M., & Squire, L. R. (1989). Cognitive impairments following frontal lobe damage and its relevance to human amnesia. *Behavioral Neuroscience*, *103*, 548–560.

Janowsky, J. S., Shimamura, A. P., & Squire, L. R. (1989). Memory and metamemory: Comparisons between patients with frontal lobe lesions and amnesic patients. *Psychobiology*, *17*, 3–11.

Jastrowitz, M. (1888). Beitrage zur localisation im grosshirn and uber deren praktische verwerthung. *Deutsch Medizinische Wochenschrift*, *14*, 81.

Jefferson, G. (1937). Removal of right or left frontal lobes in man. *British Medical Journal*, *2*, 199.

Johnson, T. N., Rosvold, H. E., & Mishkin, M. (1968). Projections from behaviorally defined sectors of the prefrontal cortex to the basal ganglia, septum, and diencephalon of the monkey. *Españolas Neurología*, *21*, 20.

Jones-Gotman, M., & Milner, B. (1977). Design fluency: The invention of nonsense drawings after focal cortical lesions. *Neuropsychologia*, *15*, 653–674.

Jones-Gotman, M., & Zatorre, R. J. (1993). Odor recognition memory in humans: Role of right temporal and orbitofrontal regions. *Brain and Cognition*, *22*, 182–198.

Jung, R. E., & Haier, R. J. (2007). The Parieto-Frontal Integration Theory (P-FIT) of intelligence: Converging neuroimaging evidence. *Behavioral and Brain Sciences*, *30*, 135–154.

Kane, M. J., & Engle, R. W. (2002). The role of prefrontal cortex in working-memory capacity, executive attention, and general fluid intelligence: An individual-differences perspective. *Psychonomic Bulletin Review*, *9*, 637–671.

Kaplan, E., & Goodglass, H. (1981). Aphasia related disorders. In M. T. Sarno (Ed.), *Acquired aphasia*. New York: Academic Press.

Karnath, H. O., Wallesch, C. W., & Zimmerman, P. (1991). Mental planning and anticipatory processes with acute and chronic frontal lobe lesions: A comparison of maze performance in routine and non-routine situations. *Neuropsychologia*, *29*, 271–290.

Kemmerer, D., & Tranel, D. (2003). A double dissociation between the meanings of action verbs and locative prepositions. *Neurocase*, *9*, 421–435.

Kennard, M. A., & Ectors, L. (1938). Forced circling movements in monkeys following lesions of the frontal lobes. *Journal of Neurophysiology*, *1*, 45–54.

Kievit, J., & Kuypers, H. G. J. M. (1974). Basal forebrain and hypothalamic connections to frontal and parietal cortex in the rhesus monkey. *Science*, *187*, 660–662.

Kim, J. -N., & Shadlen, M. N. (1999). Neural correlates of a decision in the dorsolateral prefrontal cortex of the macaque. *Nature Neuroscience*, *2*, 176–185.

Kimble, D. P., Bagshaw, M. H., & Pribram, K. H. (1965). The GSR of monkeys during orienting and habituation after selective partial ablations of the cingulate and frontal cortex. *Neuropsychologia*, *3*, 121–128.

Kleist, K. (1936). *Gehirnpatholgie*. Leipzig: Barth.

Knight, R. T. (1984). Decreased response to novel stimuli after prefrontal lesions in man. *Electroencephalography and Clinical Neurophysiology*, *59*, 9–20.

Kobal, G., & Kettenmann, B. (2000). Olfactory functional imaging and physiology. *International Journal of Psychophysiology, 36,* 157–163.

Koechlin, E., Basso, G., Peitrini, P., Panzer, S., & Grafman, J. (1999). The role of the anterior prefrontal cortex in human cognition. *Nature, 399,* 148–151.

Koenigs, M., Huey, E. D., Calamia, M., Raymont, V., Tranel, D., & Grafman, J. (2008). Distinct regions of prefrontal cortex mediate resistance and vulnerability to depression. *The Journal of Neuroscience, 28,* 12341–12348.

Koenigs, M., & Tranel, D. (2007). Irrational economic decision-making after ventromedial prefrontal damage: Evidence from the ultimatum game. *The Journal of Neuroscience, 27,* 951–956.

Kolb, B., & Milner, B. (1981). Performance of complex arm and facial movements after focal brain lesions. *Neuropsychologia, 19,* 491–503.

Kuypers, H. G. J. M., Szwarobart, M. K., & Mishkin, M. (1965). Occipitotemporal corticocortical connections in the rhesus monkey. *Experimental Neurology, 11,* 245.

Kwon, S. E., & Heilman, K. M. (1991). Ipsilateral neglect in a patient following a unilateral frontal lesion. *Neurology, 41,* 2001–2004.

Lee, K. H., Choi, Y. Y., Gray, J. R., Cho, S. H., Chae, J. H., Lee, S., & Kim, K. (2006). Neural correlates of superior intelligence: stronger recruitment of posterior parietal cortex. *Neuroimage, 29,* 578–586.

Lezak, M. D. (1988). IQ: RIP. *Journal of Clinical and Experimental Neuropsychology, 10,* 351–361.

Lhermitte, F., Pillon, B., & Serdaru, M. (1986). Human autonomy and the frontal lobes. Part 1: Imitation and utilization behavior. *Annals of Neurology, 19,* 326–334.

Lichtheim, L. (1885). On aphasia. *Brain, 7,* 433–484.

Liepmann, H. (1908). *Drei aufsatze aus dem apraxiegebiet.* Berlin: Karger.

Luria, A. R. (1966). *Human brain and psychological processes.* New York: Harper & Row.

Mah, L., Arnold, M. C., & Grafman, J. (2004). Impairment of social perception associated with lesions of the prefrontal cortex. *American Journal of Psychiatry, 161,* 1247–1255.

Malmo, R. B. (1942). Interference factors in delayed response in monkeys after removal of frontal lobes. *Journal of Neurophysiology, 5,* 295–308.

Mangels, J. A. (1997). Strategic processing and memory for temporal order in patients with frontal lobe lesions. *Neuropsychology, 11,* 207–221.

Mangels, J. A., Gershberg, F. B., Shimamura, A. P., & Knight, R. T. (1996). Impaired retrieval from remote memory in patients with frontal lobe damage. *Neuropsychology, 10,* 32–41.

Marshall, J. F., & Teitelbaum, P. (1974). Further analysis of sensory inattention allowing lateral hypothalamic damage in rats. *Journal of Comparative and Physiological Psychology, 86,* 375–395.

Marshall, J. F., Turner, B. H., & Teitelbaum, P. (1971). Sensory neglect produced by lateral hypothalamic damage. *Science, 174,* 523–525.

Metzler, C., & Parkin, A. J. (2000). Reversed negative priming following frontal lobe lesions. *Neuropsychologia, 38,* 363–379.

Milner, B. (1963). Effects of different brain lesions on card sorting. *Archives of Neurology, 9,* 90–100.

Milner, B. (1964). Some effects of frontal lobectomy in man. In J. M. Warren, & K. Akert (Eds.), *The frontal granular cortex and behavior.* New York: McGraw-Hill.

Milner, B. (1965). Visually-guided maze learning in man: Effects of bilateral hippocampal, bilateral frontal, and unilateral cerebral lesions. *Neuropsychologia, 3,* 317–338.

Milner, B. (1971). Interhemispheric differences in the localisation of psychological processes in man. *British Medical Bulletin, 27,* 272–277.

Milner, B., Corsi, P., & Leonard, G. (1991). Frontal-lobe contribution to recency judgements. *Neuropsychologia, 29,* 601–618.

Milner, B., Petrides, M., & Smith, M. L. (1985). Frontal lobes and the temporal organization of memory. *Human Neurobiology, 4,* 137–142.

Minoshima, S., Giordani, B., Berent, S., Frey, K. A., Foster, N. L., & Kuhl, D. E. (1997). Metabolic reduction in the posterior cingulate cortex in very early Alzheimer's disease. *Annals of Neurology, 42,* 85–94.

Mohr, J. P. (1976). Broca's area and Broca's aphasia. In H. Whitaker, & H. A. Whitaker (Eds.), *Studies in neurolinguistics* Vol. 1. New York: Academic Press.

Moniz, E. (1936). *Tentatives operatoires dans le traitement de certaines psychoses.* Paris: Masson et Cie.

Moniz, E. (1949). *Confidencias de um investigador cientifico.* Lisbon: Livraria Atica.

Moran, M. A., Mufson, E. J., & Mesulam, M. M. (1987). Neural inputs into the temporopolar cortex of the rhesus monkey. *Journal of Comparative Neurology, 256,* 88–103.

Morecraft, R. J., & Van Hoesen, G. W. (1993). Frontal granular cortex input to the cingulate (M3), supplementary (M2) and primary (M1) motor cortices in the rhesus monkey. *The Journal of Comparative Neurology, 337,* 669–689.

Nadeau, S. E., & Heilman, K. M. (2007). Frontal mysteries revealed. *Neurology*, 68, 1450–1453.

Nauta, W. J. H. (1962). Neural associations of the amygdaloid complex in the monkey. *Brain*, 85, 505–520.

Nauta, W. J. H. (1964). Some efferent connections of the prefrontal cortex in the monkey. In J. M. Warren, & K. Akert (Ed.), *The frontal granular cortex and behavior*. New York: McGraw-Hill.

Nauta, W. J. H., & Haymaker, W. (1969). *The hypothalamus*. Springfield, IL: Thomas.

Neary, D., Snowden, J. S., Northen, B., & Goulding, P. (1988). Dementia of frontal lobe type. *Journal of Neurology, Neurosurgery & Psychiatry*, 51, 353–361.

Nielsen, J. M. (1938). The unsolved problems in aphasia. I. Alexia in motor aphasia. *Bulletin of the Los Angeles Neurological Society*, 4, 114–122.

Nielsen, J. M. (1946). *Agnosia, apraxia, aphasia. Their value in cerebral localization*. New York: P. B. Hoeber.

Njemanze, P. C. (2005). Cerebral lateralization and general intelligence: Gender differences in a transcranial Doppler study. *Brain and Language*, 92, 234–239.

Norman, D. A., & Shallice, T. (1986). Attention to action: Willed and automatic control of behaviour. In R. J. Davidson, G. E. Schwartz, & D. Shapiro (Eds.), *Consciousness and self-regulation: Advances in research and theory* Vol. 4 (pp. 1–18). New York: Plenum.

Öngur, D., & Price, J. L. (2000). The organization of networks within the orbital and medial prefrontal cortex of rats, monkeys, and humans. *Cerebral Cortex*, 10, 206–219.

Oppenheim, H. (1889). Zur pathologie der grosshirngeschwulste. *Archives of Psychiatry*, 21, 560.

Owen, A. M. (1997). Cognitive planning in humans: Neuropsychological, neuroanatomical and neuropharmacological perspectives. *Progress in Neurobiology*, 53, 431–450.

Owen, A. M., Downes, J. D., Sahakian, B. J., Polkey, C. E., & Robbins, T. W. (1990). Planning and spatial working memory following frontal lobe lesions in man. *Neuropsychologia*, 28, 1021–1034.

Pandya, D. N., & Barnes, C. L. (1987). Architecture and connections of the frontal lobe. In E. Perecman (Ed.), *The frontal lobes revisited*. Hillsdale, N.J.: Lawrence Erlbaum Associates.

Pandya, D. N., Dye, P., & Butters, N. (1971). Efferent cortico-cortical projections of the prefrontal cortex in the rhesus monkey. *Brain Research*, 31, 35–46.

Pandya, D. N., Hallett, M., & Mukherjee, S. K. (1969). Intra- and interhemispheric connections of the neocortical auditory system in the rhesus monkey. *Brain Research*, 13, 49.

Pandya, D. N., & Kuypers, H. G. J. M. (1969). Cortico-cortical connections in the rhesus monkey. *Brain Research*, 13, 13.

Pandya, D. N., & Vignolo, L. A. (1971). Intra- and interhemispheric projections of the precentral, premotor and arcuate areas in the rhesus monkey. *Brain Research*, 26, 217–233.

Paradiso, S., Chemerinski, E., Yazici, K. M., Tartaro, A., & Robinson, R. G. (1999). Frontal lobe syndrome reassessed: comparison of patients with lateral or medial frontal brain damage. *Journal of Neurology, Neurosurgery, and Psychiatry*, 67, 664–667.

Parkin, A. J., Bindschaedler, C., Harsent, L., & Metzler, C. (1996). Pathological false alarm rates following damage to the left frontal cortex. *Brain and Cognition*, 32, 14–27.

Parkin, A. J., & Hunkin, N. M. (1993). Impaired temporal context memory on anterograde but not retrograde tests in the absence of frontal pathology. *Cortex*, 29, 267–280.

Parkin, A. J., & Java, R. I. (1999). Deterioration in frontal lobe function in normal aging: Influences of fluid intelligence versus perceptual speed. *Neuropsychology*, 13, 539–545.

Penfield, W., & Roberts, L. (1959). *Speech and brain mechanisms*. Princeton: Princeton University Press.

Perry, R. J., & Hodges, J. R. (2000). Differentiating frontal and temporal variant frontotemporal dementia from AD. *Neurology*, 54, 2277–2284.

Petersen, S. E., Fox, P. T., Posner, M. I., Mintun, M. A., & Raichle, M.A. (1989). Positron emission tomographic studies of the processing of single words. *Journal of Cognitive Neuroscience*, 1, 153–170.

Petrides, M. (1985). Deficits on conditional associative-learning tasks after frontal- and temporal-lobe lesions in man. *Neuropsychologia*, 23, 601–614.

Petrides, M. (1987). Conditional learning and the primate frontal cortex. In E. Perecman (Ed.), *The frontal lobes revisited*. Hillsdale, NJ: Lawrence Erlbaum Associates.

Petrides, M. (1990). Nonspatial conditional learning impaired in patients with unilateral frontal but not unilateral temporal lobe excisions. *Neuropsychologia*, 28, 137–149.

Petrides, M. (1995). Functional organization of the human frontal cortex for mnemonic processing. In J. Grafman, K. J. Holyoak, & F. Boller (Eds.), *Structure and functions of the human prefrontal* cortex. *Annals of the New York Academy of Science*, 769, 85–96.

Petrides, M., & Milner, B. (1982). Deficits on subject-ordered tasks after frontal- and temporal-lobe lesions in man. *Neuropsychologia*, 20, 259–262.

Petrides, M., & Pandya, D. N. (1984). Projections to the frontal cortex from the posterior parietal region in the rhesus monkey. *Journal of Comparative Neurology*, 228, 105–116.

Petrides, M., & Pandya, D. N. (1988). Association fiber pathways to the frontal cortex from the superior temporal region in the rhesus monkey. *Journal of Comparative Neurology*, 310, 507–549.

Picton, T. W., Stuss, D. T., Alexander, M. P., Shallice, T., Binns, M. A., & Gillingham, S. (2007). Effects of focal frontal lesions on response inhibition. *Cerebral Cortex*, 17, 826–838.

Porrino, J. J., & Goldman-Rakic, P. S. (1982). Brainstem innervation of prefrontal and anterior cingulate cortex in the rhesus monkey revealed by retrograde transport of HRP. *Journal of Comparative Neurology*, 205, 63–76.

Porrino, L. J., Craine, A. M., & Goldman-Rakic, P. S. (1981). Direct and indirect pathways from the amygdala to the frontal lobe in rhesus monkeys. *Journal of Comparative Neurology*, 198, 121–136.

Porteus, S. D., De Monbrun, R., & Kepner, M. D. (1944). Mental changes after bilateral prefrontal leucotomy. *Genetic Psychology Monographs*, 29, 3–115.

Postle, B.R., Berger, J. S., & D'Esposito, M. (1999). Functional neuroanatomical double dissociation of mnemonic and executive control processes contributing to working memory performance. *Proceedings of the National Academy of Science*, 96, 12959–12964.

Potter, H., & Butters, N. (1980). An assessment of olfactory deficits in patients with damage to prefrontal cortex. *Neuropsychologia*, 18, 621–628.

Potter, H., & Nauta, W. J. H. (1979). A note on the problem of olfactory associations of the orbitofrontal cortex in the monkey. *Neuroscience*, 4, 316–367.

Powell, T. P. S., Cowan, W. M., & Raisman, G. (1965). The central olfactory connexions. *Journal of Anatomy (London)*, 99, 791.

Prabhakaran, V., Narayanan, K., Zhao, Z., & Gabrieli, J. D. (2000). Integration of diverse information in working memory within the frontal lobe. *Nature Neuroscience*, 3, 85–90.

Prabhakaran, V., Smith, J. A. L., Desmond, J. E., Glover, G. H., & Gabrieli, J. D. E. (1997). Neural substrates of fluid reasoning: An fMRI study of neocortical activation during performance of the Raven's Progressive Matrices Test. *Journal of Cognitive Psychology*, 33, 43–63.

Preuss, T. M., & Goldman-Rakic, P. S. (1991). Ipsilateral cortical connections of the granular frontal cortex in the Strepsirhine primate Galago, with comparative comments on anthropoid primates. *Journal of Comparative Neurology*, 310, 507–549.

Pribram, K. H., & MacLean, P. D. (1953). Neuronographic analysis of medial and basal cerebral cortex. II: Monkey. *Journal of Neurophysiology*, 16, 324–340.

Pribram, K. H., Chow, K. L., & Semmes, J. (1953). Limit and organization of the cortical projection from the medial thalamic nucleus in monkey. *Journal of Comparative Neurology*, 98, 433–448.

Price, J. L. (1999a). Networks within the orbital and medial prefrontal cortex. *Neurocase*, 5, 231–241.

Price, J. L. (1999b). Prefrontal cortical networks related to visceral function and mood. *Annals of the New York Academy of Sciences*, 877, 383–396.

Rahman, S., Sahakian, B. J., Hodges, J. R., Rogers, R. D., & Robbins, T. W. (1999). Specific cognitive deficits in mild frontal variant frontotemporal dementia. *Brain*, 122, 1469–1493.

Raichle, M. E., Fiez, J. A., Videen, T. O., MacLeod, A. M., Pardo, J. V., Fox, P. T., & Petersen, S. E. (1994). Practice-related changes in human brain functional anatomy during nonmotor learning. *Cerebral Cortex*, 4, 8–26.

Rainer, G., Rao, S. C., & Miller, E. K. (1999). Prospective coding for object in primate prefrontal cortex. *The Journal of Neuroscience*, 19, 5493–5505.

Ramnani, N., & Owen, A. M. (2004). Anterior prefrontal cortex: Insights into function from anatomy and neuroimaging. *Nature Reviews Neuroscience*, 5, 184–194.

Rapcsak, S. Z., Arthur, S. A., & Rubens, A. B. (1988). Lexical agraphia from focal lesion of the left precentral gyrus. *Neurology*, 38, 1119–1123.

Rapcsak, S. Z., Kaszniak, A. W. Reminger, S. L., Glisky, M. L., Glisky, E. L. & Comer, J. F. (1998). Dissociation between verbal and autonomic measures of memory following frontal lobe damage. *Neurology*, 50, 1259–1265.

Ritacciao, A. L., Hickling, E. J., & Ramani, V. (1992). The role of dominant premotor cortex and grapheme to phoneme transformation in reading epilepsy. *Archives of Neurology*, 49, 933–939.

Robbins, T. W. (1996). Dissociating executive functions of the prefrontal cortex. *Philosophical*

Transactions of the Royal Society of London Biological Sciences, 351, 1463–1470.

Robinson, R. G., Kubos, K. L., Starr, L. B., Rao, K., & Price, T. R. (1984). Mood disorders in stroke patients. Importance of location of lesion. *Brain, 107,* 81–93.

Robinson, R. G., Starr, L. B., Lipsey, J. R., Rao, K., & Price, T. R. (1985). A 2-year longitudinal study of poststroke mood disorders: In-hospital prognostic factors associated with 6-month outcome. *Journal of Nervous and Mental Disease, 173,* 221–226.

Robinson, R. G., Bolduc, P. L., & Price, T. R. (1987). Two-year longitudinal study of poststroke mood disorders: Diagnosis and outcome at one and two years. *Stroke, 18,* 837–843.

Rogers, R. D., Owen, A. M., Middleton, H. C., Williams, E. J., Pickard, J. D., Sahakian, B. J. & Robbins, T. W. (1999). Choosing between small, likely rewards and large, unlikely rewards activates inferior and orbital prefrontal cortex. *The Journal of Neuroscience, 20,* 9029–9038.

Rolls, E. T. (2000). The orbitofrontal cortex and reward. *Cerebral Cortex, 10,* 284–294.

Rolls, E. T. (2004). The functions of the orbitofrontal cortex. *Brain and Cognition, 55,* 11–29.

Rosene, D. L., Mesulam, M. M., & Van Hoesen, G. W. (1976). Afferents to area FL of the medial frontal cortex from the amygdala and hippocampus of the rhesus monkey. In *neuroscience abstracts* Vol. 2, Part 1. Bethesda, MD: Society for Neuroscience.

Ross, E. D. (1981). The aprosodias: Functional-anatomic organization of the affective components of language in the right hemisphere. *Archives of Neurology, 38,* 561–569.

Rylander, G. (1940). *Personality changes after operations on the frontal lobes.* Copenhagen: Munksgaard.

Sagar, H. J., Gabrieli, J. D. E., Sullivan, E. V., & Corkin, S. (1990). Recency and frequency discrimination in the amnesic patient H.M. *Brain, 113,* 581–602.

Sapolsky, R. M., & Eichenbaum, H. (1980). Thalamocortical mechanisms in odor guided behavior. II: Effects of lesions of the mediodorsal thalamic nucleus and frontal cortex on odor preferences and sexual behavior in the hamster. *Brain, Behavior and Evolution, 17,* 276–290.

Sarazin, M., Pillon, B., Giannakopoulos, P., Rancurel, G., Samson, Y., & Dubois, B. (1998). Clinicometabolic dissociation of cognitive functions and social behavior in frontal lobe lesions. *Neurology, 51,* 142–148.

Saver, J. L., & Damasio, A. R. (1991). Preserved access and processing of social knowledge in a patient with acquired sociopathy due to ventromedial frontal damage. *Neuropsychologia, 29,* 1241–1249.

Schacter, D. L., Curran, T., Gallucio, L., Millberg, W. P., & Bates, J. F. (1996). False recognition and the right frontal lobe: A case study. *Neuropsychologia, 34,* 793–808.

Schnider, A., Treyer, V., & Buck, A. (2000). Selection of currently relevant memories by the human posterior medial orbitofrontal cortex. *The Journal of Neuroscience, 20,* 5880–5884.

Segarra, J., & Angelo, J. (1970). Anatomical determinants of behavioral change. In A. L. Benton (Ed.), *Behavioral change in cerebrovascular disease.* New York: Harper & Row.

Seltzer, B., & Pandya, D. N. (1989). Frontal lobe connections of the superior temporal sulcus in the rhesus monkey. *Journal of Comparative Neurology, 281,* 97–113.

Semendeferi, K., Lu, A., Schenker, N., & Damasio, H. (2002). Humans and great apes share a large frontal cortex. *Nature Neuroscience, 5,* 272–276.

Settlage, P., Zable, M., & Harlow, H. F. (1948). Problem solving by monkeys following bilateral removal of the prefrontal areas: VI. Performance on tests requiring contradictory reactions to similar and identical stimuli. *Journal of Experimental Psychology, 38,* 50–65.

Shallice, T. (1982). Specific impairments of planning. *Philosophical Transactions of the Royal Society of London, 298,* 199–209.

Shallice, T., & Burgess, W. P. (1991). Deficits in strategy application following frontal lobe damage in man. *Brain, 114,* 727–741.

Shallice, T., Burgess, W. P., Schon, F., & Baxter, M. D. (1989). The origin of utilization behaviour. *Brain, 112,* 1587–1598.

Shamay-Tsoory, S. G., Aharon-Peretz, J., & Perry, D. (2009). Two systems for empathy: A double dissociation between emotional and cognitive empathy in inferior frontal gyrus versus ventromedial prefrontal lesions. *Brain, 132,* 617–627.

Shammi, P., & Stuss, D. T. (1999). Humour appreciation: A role of the right frontal lobe. *Brain, 122,* 657–666.

Shaw, P., Bramham, J., Lawrence, E. G., Morris, R., Baron-Cohen, S., & David, A. S. (2005). The differential effects of lesions of the amygdala and prefrontal cortex on decoding facial expressions of complex emotions. *Journal of Cognitive Neuroscience, 17,* 1410–1419.

Simernitskaya, E. G. (1970). *Evoked potentials as an indicator of the active process.* Moscow: Moscow University Press.

Simernitskaya, E. G., & Homskaya, E. D. (1966). Changes in evoked potentials to significant stimuli in normal subjects and in lesions of the frontal lobes. In A. R. Luria, & E. D. Homskaya (Eds.), *Frontal lobes and regulation of psychological processes*. Moscow: Moscow University Press.

Sirigu, A., Zalla, T., Pillon, B., Grafman, J., Dubois, B., & Agid, Y. (1995). Planning and script analysis following prefrontal lobe lesions. In J. Grafman, K. Holyoak, & F. Boller (Eds.), *Structure and functions of the human prefrontal cortex. Annals of the New York Academy of Sciences, 769*, 277–288.

Smith, E. E., & Jonides, J. (1998). Neuroimaging analyses of human working memory. *Proceedings of the National Academy of Sciences USA, 95*, 12061–12068.

Smith, E. E., Jonides, J., Koeppe, J. R. A. (1996). Dissociating verbal and spatial working memory using PET. *Cerebral Cortex, 6*, 11–20.

Smith, E. E., Jonides, J., Marshuetz, C., & Koeppe, R. A. (1998). Components of verbal working memory: Evidence from neuroimaging. *Proceedings of the National Academy of Sciences USA, 95*, 876–882.

Smith, M. L., & Milner, B. (1988). Estimation of frequency of occurrence of abstract designs after frontal or temporal lobectomy. *Neuropsychologia, 26*, 297–306.

Stanhope, N., Guinan, E., & Kopelman, M. D. (1998). Frequency judgements of abstract designs by patients with diencephalic, temporal lobe or frontal lobe lesions. *Neuropsychologia, 26*, 1387–1396.

Strauss, I., & Keschner, M. (1935). Mental symptoms in cases of tumor of the frontal lobe. *Archives of Neurology and Psychiatry, 33*, 986–1007.

Stuss, D. T., Alexander, M. P., Hamer, L, Palumbo, C., Dempster, R., Binns, M., et al. (1998). The effects of focal anterior and posterior brain lesions on verbal fluency. *Journal of the International Neuropsychological Society, 4*, 265–278.

Stuss, D. T., Alexander, M. P., Lieberman, A., & Levine H. (1978). An extraordinary form of confabulation. *Neurology, 28*, 1166–1172.

Stuss, D. T., & Benson, D. F. (1987). The frontal lobes and control of cognition and memory. In E. Perecman (Ed.), *The frontal lobes revisited*. Hillsdale, NJ: Lawrence Erlbaum Associates.

Stuss, D. T., Kaplan, E. F., Benson, D. F., Weir, W. S., Chiulli, S., & Sarazin, F. F. (1982). Evidence for the involvement of orbitofrontal cortex in memory functions: An interference effect. *Journal of Comparative and Physiological Psychology, 96*, 913–925.

Stuss, D. T., Kaplan, E. F., Benson, D. F., Weir, W. S., Naeser, M. A., & Levine, H. L. (1981). Long-term effects of prefrontal leucotomy: An overview of neuropsychologic residuals. *Journal of Clinical Neuropsychology, 3*, 13–32.

Stuss, D. T., Levine, B., Alexander, M. P., Hong, J., Palumbo, C., Hamer, L., et al. (2000). Wisconsin card sorting test performance in patients with focal frontal and posterior brain damage: Effects of lesion location and test structure on separable cognitive process. *Neuropsychologia, 38*, 388–402.

Stuss, D. T., Toth, J. P., Franchi, D., Alexander, M. P., Tipper, S., & Craik, F. (1999). Dissociation of attentional processes in patients with focal frontal and posterior lesions. *Neuropsychologia, 37*, 1005–1027.

Swick, D., & Knight, R. T. (1996). Is prefrontal cortex involved in cued recall? A neuropsychological test of PET findings. *Neuropsychologia, 34*, 1019–1028.

Tanabe, T., Iino, M., & Takogi, S. F. (1975a). Discrimination of odors in olfactory bulb, pyriform-amygdaloid areas, and orbitofrontal cortex of the monkey. *Journal of Neurophysiology, 38*, 1284–1296.

Tanabe, T., Yarita, H., Iino, M., Ooshima, Y., & Takagi, S. F. (1975b). An olfactory projection area in orbitofrontal cortex of the monkey. *Journal of Neurophysiology, 38*, 1269–1283.

Teuber, H. L., Battersby, W. S., & Bender, M. B. (1951). Performance of complex visual tasks after cerebral lesions. *Journal of Nervous and Mental Disease, 114*, 413–429.

Thompson-Schill, S. L., Swick, D., Farah, M., D'Esposito, M., Kan, I. P., & Knight, R. T. (1998). Verb generation in patients with focal frontal lesions: a neuropsychological test of neuroimaging findings. *Proceedings of the National Academy of Science, 95*, 15855–15860.

Tomita, H., Ohbayashi, M., Nakahara, K., Hasegawa, I., & Miyashita, Y. (1999). Top-down signal from prefrontal cortex in executive control of memory retrieval. *Nature, 401*, 699–703.

Tranel, D. (2009). The Iowa-Benton school of neuropsychological assessment. In I. Grant, & K. M. Adams (Eds.), *Neuropsychological assessment of neuropsychiatric disorders* (3rd ed., pp. 66–83). New York: Oxford University Press.

Tranel, D., Adolphs, R., Damasio, H., & Damasio, A. R. (2001). A neural basis for the retrieval of words for actions. *Cognitive Neuropsychology, 18*, 655–670.

Tranel, D., Anderson, S. W., & Manzel, K. (2008). Is the prefrontal cortex important for "fluid" intelligence? A neuropsychological study using Matrix

Reasoning. *The Clinical Neuropsychologist, 22,* 242–261.

Tranel, D., & Damasio, H. (1994). Neuroanatomical correlates of electrodermal skin conductance responses. *Psychophysiology, 31,* 427–438.

Tranel, D., Hathaway-Nepple, J., & Anderson, S. W. (2007). Impaired behavior on real-world tasks following damage to the ventromedial prefrontal cortex. *Journal of Clinical and Experimental Neuropsychology, 29,* 319–332.

Tranel, D., Martin, C., Damasio, H., Grabowski, T., & Hichwa, R. (2005). Effects of noun-verb homonymy on the neural correlates of naming concrete entities and actions. *Brain and Language, 92,* 288–299.

Valverde, F. (1965). *Studies on the piriform lobe.* Cambridge, MA: Harvard University Press.

Van Hoesen, G. W., Parvizi, J., & Chu, C. -C. (2000). Orbitofrontal cortex pathology in Alzheimer's disease. *Cerebral Cortex, 10,* 243–251.

Walker, R., Husain, M., Hodgson, T. L., Harrison, J., & Kennard, C. (1998). Saccadic eye movement and working memory deficits following damage to human prefrontal cortex. *Neuropsychologia, 26,* 1141–1159.

Waltz, J. A., Knowlton, B. J., Holyoak, K. J., Boone, K. B., Mishkin, F. S., de Menezes Santos, M., et al. (1999). A system for relational reasoning in human prefrontal cortex. *Psychological Science, 10,* 119–125.

Ward, A. A., & McCulloch, W. S. (1947). The projection of the frontal lobe on the hypothalamus. *Journal of Neurophysiology, 10,* 309–314.

Watanabe, M. (1996). Reward expectancy in primate prefrontal neurons. *Nature, 382,* 629–632.

Watson, R. T., Heilman, K. M., Cauthen, J. C., & King, F. A. (1973). Neglect after cingulectomy. *Neurology, 23,* 1003–1007.

Watson, R. T., Heilman, K. M., Miller, B. D., & King, F. A. (1974). Neglect after mesencephalic reticular formation lesions. *Neurology, 24,* 294–298.

Weinberger, D. R., Berman, K. F., & Zec, R. F. (1986). Physiologic dysfunction of dorsolateral prefrontal cortex in schizophrenia. *Archives of General Psychiatry, 43,* 114–124.

Welch, K., & Stuteville, P. (1958). Experimental production of neglect in monkeys. *Brain, 81,* 341–347.

Whitlock, D. C., & Nauta, W. J. H. (1956). Subcortical projections from the temporal neocortex in Macaca mulatta. *Journal of Comparative Neurology, 106,* 183–212.

Windmann, S., Wehrmann, M., Calabrese, P., & Gunturkun, O. (2006). Role of the prefrontal cortex in attentional control over bistable vision. *Journal of Cognitive Neuroscience, 18,* 456–471.

Winocur, G., & Moscovitch, M. (1990). Hippocampal and prefrontal cortex contribution to learning and memory: Analysis of lesion and aging effects on maze learning in rats. *Behavioral Neuroscience, 104,* 544–551.

Yeterian, E. H., & Van Hoesen, G. W. (1977). Cortico-striate projections in the rhesus monkey. The organization of certain cortico-caudate connections. *Brain Research, 139,* 43–63.

Zald, D. H., & Pardo, J. V. (2000). Functional neuroimaging of the olfactory system in humans. *International Journal of Psychophysiology, 36,* 165–181.

Zanini, S. (2008). Generalized script sequencing deficits following frontal lobe lesions. *Cortex, 44,* 140–149.

Zatorre, R. J., & Jones-Gotman, M. (1991). Human olfactory discrimination after unilateral frontal or temporal lobectomy. *Brain, 114,* 71–84.

15

Emotional Disorders Associated with Neurological Diseases

KENNETH M. HEILMAN, LEE X. BLONDER, DAWN BOWERS, AND EDWARD VALENSTEIN

In this chapter, we discuss changes in emotional experience and behavior that are caused directly by diseases of the central nervous system (CNS). These disorders interfere with brain mechanisms that underlie emotion. There are other ways in which neurological disorders and emotions may interact: Patients with neurological diseases may have an emotional response to their illness (e.g., they may get depressed because they are disabled), emotional states may enhance neurological symptoms (e.g., anxiety may aggravate tremor), and emotional states may induce neurological symptoms (e.g., stress may cause headaches). Emotional response to disease, emotional enhancement of symptoms, and emotion-induced disorders are not unique to neurology, and are not discussed in this chapter. It has long been recognized that several disorders traditionally in the realm of psychiatry, such as schizophrenia, are probably caused by abnormalities in the brain. However, this chapter is limited to traditional neurological illnesses.

Our approach is primarily anatomic. We first consider emotional changes that result from lesions in the cerebral hemispheres. These may result from interference with specific neocortically mediated cognitive processes, such as stimulus appraisal, or from disruption of cortical modulation of limbic or other subcortical regions. The frontal lobes have particularly strong limbic connections, and frontal lobe lesions can cause prominent emotional changes. These are primarily treated in Chapter 14. After discussing emotional changes resulting from dysfunction of either cerebral hemisphere, we consider changes associated with limbic and basal ganglia disorders. Finally, we discuss the pseudobulbar state, in which inappropriate emotional expression occurs despite appropriate emotional experience.

Emotions can be divided into three major domains: emotional experiences, emotional memories, and emotional behaviors. Emotions may be transient or prolonged. Prolonged emotional experiences are called moods. Ross et al. (1994) also divides emotions into primary (e.g., happy, sad, angry, fearful) and social (e.g., embarrassed). Our discussion will mainly address the primary emotions. Throughout this chapter, we emphasize information gained from studies of humans with brain dysfunction because much of our knowledge comes from the investigation of pathological states in humans. We also consider animal studies when they pertain to observations on humans, but we do not attempt to summarize the extensive literature on animals.

HEMISPHERIC DYSFUNCTION

Hemispheric dysfunction may affect emotion in several ways. There may be behavioral changes including receptive and expressive communicative disorders, changes in the viscera, and autonomic nervous system alterations. Hemispheric dysfunction may cause changes in emotional experience and mood, as well as changes in emotional memory. Each of these will be discussed separately.

COMMUNICATIVE DEFECTS

Receptive

Visual Nonverbal Processes. The development of an appropriate emotional state may depend on perceiving and comprehending visual stimuli such as facial expressions, gestures, and scenes. DeKosky et al. (1980) gave facial affective recognition tasks to patients with left or right hemisphere lesions, as well as to control subjects without hemispheric disease. There were several subtests. Patients were asked to determine if a pair of neutral faces were of the same person or two different people, to name the emotion expressed by a face (happy, sad, angry, indifferent), to select from a multiple-choice array of faces a "target" emotion ("Point to the happy face"), and to determine whether two pictures of the same person's face expressed the same or a different emotion. When compared to control subjects, patients with right hemisphere disease were markedly impaired in their ability to discriminate between pairs of neutral faces, as previously reported by Benton and Van Allen (1968). Although both the right and left hemisphere–damaged patients had difficulty naming and selecting emotional faces, there was a trend for patients with right hemisphere disease to perform more poorly on these two tasks than patients with left hemisphere disease. In addition, patients with right hemisphere disease were more impaired in making same–different discriminations between emotional faces. When performance across these various emotional facial recognition tasks was covaried for neutral facial discrimination (a visuoperceptual nonemotional task), differences between the two groups disappeared.

This finding suggests that a visuoperceptual disturbance may underlie the poor performance of right hemisphere–damaged patients on facial affect tasks. However, the poor facial discrimination by the right hemisphere group did not entirely correlate with their ability to recognize and discriminate between emotional faces. Retrospective review of the individual cases revealed that about one-third of the patients with right hemisphere disease performed poorly on both the neutral facial task and the emotional faces tasks, whereas about one-third performed well on both. The remaining patients with right hemisphere disease, however, performed relatively well on neutral facial discrimination but poorly on the emotional faces tasks. This observation suggests that visuoperceptual deficits do not account for impaired affective processing in all right hemisphere–damaged patients and that some of these patients do have an impairment of processing emotional facial expressions.

Some of the facial emotion tasks used by the DeKosky group could be performed by using strategies that involved no knowledge of the emotion expressed on faces. One such task required subjects to judge whether two faces depicted the same or different emotions. Because the same actor was used for both pictures, subjects could have accurately made this determination merely by deciding whether the two faces had identical physiognomic/structural configurations, without any regard to emotionality on the face. This is what might be referred to as a "perceptual" rather than an "associative" emotion judgment. To circumvent the use of pure perceptual "template matching" in making judgments about the similarity of two facial expressions, two different actors are used, sometimes displaying the same emotion and sometimes displaying different emotions. The faces of two actors have inherently unique physiognomic properties (i.e., faceprints) and therefore must be matched by comparing the similarity of their emotional expressions.

Taking these considerations in mind, Bowers and coworkers (1985) assessed stroke patients with hemispheric lesions and control subjects across a series of seven perceptual and associative facial affect tasks. When the patient groups were statistically equated for visuoperceptual ability, the right hemisphere–damaged group was impaired on three of the facial affect tasks, including naming, selecting, and discriminating facial emotions across two different actors. The critical factor distinguishing these three tasks from those that did not give rise to hemispheric asymmetries was related to the underlying task demand of categorizing facial emotions. These findings suggest that the disorders of facial affect recognition among right hemisphere–damaged patients cannot be solely attributed to defects in visuoperceptual processing, and that a right hemisphere superiority for processing facial affect exists above and beyond its superiority for processing faces in general.

Investigators from other laboratories have also reported that right hemisphere–damaged stroke patients are more impaired than their left hemisphere counterparts in recognizing or categorizing facial emotions (Cicone et al., 1980; Etcoff, 1984; Borod et al., 1985, 1986, 2002; Blonder et al., 1991; Mandal et al., 1999; Adolphs et al., 1996, 2000; Charbonneau et al., 2003; Kucharska-Pietura et al., 2003, Harciarek et al., 2006; Harciarek & Heilman 2008). Borod et al. (2002) noted that 20 out of 23 published studies showed deficits in facial affect recognition associated with focal lesions in the right hemisphere. In general, these defects in identifying facial affect by right hemisphere–damaged patients are not valence dependent and extend to all categories of emotion (but see Mandel et al., 1991).

Hemispheric asymmetries in the evaluation of facial emotional expressions have also been described in split-brain patients and in individuals undergoing Wada testing. Benowitz and colleagues (1983) presented filmed facial expressions from the Profile of Nonverbal Sensitivity Test (PONS) to each hemisphere of a split-brain patient. This patient was fitted with special contact lens that restricted visual input to one hemisphere. The patient had no difficulty identifying facial expressions when they were directed to the isolated right hemisphere, but was impaired when the facial expressions were directed to the isolated left hemisphere. Comparable findings have also been reported in patients while undergoing intracarotid sodium amytal procedures (Ahern et al., 1991). Ahern and colleagues found that

affective faces were rated as less emotionally intense (as compared to baseline ratings) when they were shown to patients whose nondominant language hemisphere (usually right) was anesthetized. Such an effect was not observed with anesthetization of the language-dominant hemisphere. Studies of normal subjects have also implicated the right hemisphere in processing affective faces. Tachistoscopic studies have generally found that affective faces are responded to more accurately and/or more quickly when presented to the left visual field (right hemisphere) than to the right visual field (Suberi & McKeever, 1977; Ley & Bryden, 1979; Strauss & Moscovitch, 1981). Reuter-Lorenz and Davidson (1981) reported hemispheric-specific valence effects, in that happy faces were responded to more quickly in the right visual field and sad faces were responded to more quickly in the left visual field. Subsequent investigators have failed to replicate this finding (Duda & Brown, 1984; McLaren & Bryson, 1987; Bryson et al., 1991).

Other studies with normal subjects using chimeric and/or composite face stimuli have found that the side of the face on the viewer's left influences judgments of emotionality more than the side of the face on the viewer's right (Campbell, 1978; Heller & Levy, 1981). Based on these studies with both normal and neurologically impaired subjects, we believe that the right hemisphere is important for perceiving both faces and facial expressions. In particular, we have argued that the right hemisphere may contain a "store of facial emotion icons" or representations (Bowers & Heilman, 1984). Support for this representational hypothesis comes from the research of Blonder and colleagues (1991a) who found that right hemisphere–damaged patients were impaired relative to left hemisphere–damaged patients and normal controls in identifying the emotion associated with a verbal description of a nonverbal signal. The subjects were read brief sentences describing facial ("His face whitened"), vocal ("She raised her voice"), and gestural signals ("He shook his fist"). Because these signals were described verbally, the poor performance of the right hemisphere–damaged group could not be attributed to a perceptual disturbance. Further, their poor performance was not due to a general derangement in emotional knowledge in that these patients performed normally on another task in which they had to make inferences about emotions that are linked to various situational contexts (i.e., "The children track dirt over your white carpet"). Rather, the poor performance of the right hemisphere–damaged patients in assigning an emotion to a verbally described nonverbal signal is consistent with the view that the right hemisphere normally contains representations of species-typical facial expressions. Further evidence that the right hemisphere contains representations of species-typical facial expressions comes from a study in which right and left hemisphere–damaged patients were evaluated on two imagery tasks (Bowers et al., 1991). One involved imagery for facial emotional expressions and the other involved imagery for common objects. On both tasks, the subjects were asked to image a target (i.e., frowning face) and were then asked a series of yes–no questions regarding the structural characteristics of the face (i.e., "Are the outer lips pulled down?"). The right hemisphere–damaged group was more impaired on the facial emotion than on the object imagery task, whereas the left hemisphere group showed the opposite pattern. That some of these right hemisphere–damaged patients were also more impaired at recognizing visible facial emotions (i.e., a recognition task, rather than an imagery task) than were the left hemisphere–damaged group suggests that the right hemisphere contains a hypothetical "store of facial emotional representations" that had been destroyed in these individuals. Bowers et al. (1991) also described a patient with a ventral temporal-occipital lesion of the right hemisphere who could recognize emotional faces but could not image them. This case suggests that the mechanism underlying emotion imagery generation is at least in part mediated by the posterior ventral area, and that the facial emotional representations are anatomically distinct from the areas that either generate, display, or immediately inspect the image.

Some investigators have attempted to define more precisely the regions in the right hemisphere that are associated with facial affect processing deficits. Work from Roll's laboratory using single-cell recordings has identified visual neurons in the temporal cortex and amygdala of monkeys that respond selectively to faces and facial expressions (Baylis et al., 1985; Leonard et al., 1985). Similar findings have been reported during intraoperative recordings of awake humans while undergoing epilepsy surgery (Fried et al., 1982). Bowers and Heilman (1984) described a patient with a category-specific visual verbal discrimination deficit that was confined to facial emotion. The patient had a tumor in the region of the forceps major (the occipital white matter tract leading into the corpus callosum). This patient was unable both to name emotional facial displays and to point to the emotional faces named by the examiner. In contrast, the patient could determine if two faces displayed the same or different emotions, and performed normally across an array of other affect tasks including prosody, gesture, and narration. It was posited that the tumor induced a callosal disconnection such that the speech and language areas of the left hemisphere were unable to access the emotional facial icons (and vice versa), thus causing a verbal–emotional face disconnection. A similar case has been described by Rapcsak et al. (1989).

Rapcsak et al. (1993) reported two individuals who sustained selective impairments in naming facial emotion following lesions in the right middle temporal gyrus. Adolphs et al. (1996) performed lesion mapping in patients with focal brain damage and found a correlation between impaired facial affect recognition and damage in the right supramarginal gyrus and the right mesial anterior infracalcarine cortex. In a subsequent study, Adolphs et al. (2000) performed volumetric co-registration of lesions from 108 stable, neurologic patients in order to map the shared location associated with facial affect recognition disorders. They found that impaired recognition of emotional facial expressions was associated with damage to the right somatosensory cortices, the right anterior supramarginal gyrus, and the right insula. The investigators speculate that recognition of affective facial displays requires an individual to reactivate an internal somatic representation of the facial configuration associated with particular emotional expressions. More recently, Harciarek and Heilman (2008) compared facial affect recognition in anterior versus posterior right hemisphere–damaged stroke patients and found that, although both groups were impaired relative to normal controls, patients with anterior lesions performed significantly worse than those with posterior lesions, particularly when interpreting negative emotional expressions. The investigators conclude that activation of the somatosensory cortex is crucial for the recognition of facial affect, supporting the findings of Adolphs et al. (2000). These studies may help to explain the findings of Blonder et al. (1991) and Bowers et al. (1991) reported above. The failure of right hemisphere–damaged stroke patients to comprehend the emotional meaning of nonverbal descriptors, and imagine the facial configurations associated with emotional expressions, might stem in part from damage to circuits responsible for generating internal somatic representations of these displays.

Auditory Nonverbal Processes. "It was not what you said, but how you said it." Speech may simultaneously communicate propositional and emotional messages. The propositional message is conveyed by a complex code requiring semantic, lexical, syntactic, and phonemic decoding. Although prosody, which includes pitch, tempo, amplitude, and rhythm, may also convey linguistic content (e.g., declarative vs. interrogative sentences), prosody is more important in conveying emotional content (Paul, 1909; Monrad-Krohn, 1947). In more than 90% of people, the left hemisphere is superior to the right when decoding the propositional message. To learn if the right hemisphere was superior to the left in decoding the emotional prosody of speech, Heilman et al. (1975) and Tucker et al. (1977) presented sentences with propositionally neutral content using four different emotional prosodies (happy, sad, angry, and indifferent) to patients with right hemisphere infarctions and to aphasic patients with left hemisphere infarctions. The patients were asked to identify the emotional tone of the speaker based not on what was said, but rather how it was said. Patients with right hemisphere lesions performed worse on this task than those with left hemisphere lesions, suggesting that the right hemisphere is more involved in processing the

emotional intonations of speech than is the left hemisphere. Similar findings were reported by Ross (1981). Schlanger and colleagues (1976) failed to find any differences between right and left hemisphere–damaged patients in the comprehension of emotional prosody, but only three of the 20 right hemisphere patients in the Schlanger et al. study had lesions involving temporoparietal areas. Further evidence for the dominant role of the right hemisphere in comprehending affective intonation comes from studies that demonstrate preserved abilities in patients with left hemisphere lesions. We examined a patient with pure word deafness (normal speech output and reading but impaired speech comprehension) from a left hemisphere lesion. In patients with pure word deafness, the left auditory cortex is thought to be destroyed and the right auditory cortex is disconnected from Wernicke's area in the left hemisphere; however, the right auditory area and its connections to the right hemisphere are intact. Although this patient comprehended speech very poorly, he had no difficulty recognizing either environmental sounds or emotional intonations of speech.

Weintraub et al. (1981) reported that, relative to normal controls, right hemisphere–damaged patients had difficulty determining whether prosodically intoned sentences were statements, commands, or questions. Based on these findings, they suggested that a generalized prosodic disturbance might be associated with right hemisphere damage. However, a left hemisphere–damaged group was not tested in this study. Heilman and colleagues (1984) compared right and left hemisphere–damaged patients for comprehension of emotional (happy, sad, angry) or nonemotional prosody (questions, commands, statements). Compared to normal controls, both the right hemisphere–damaged and the left hemisphere–damaged groups were equally impaired on the nonemotional (syntactic-propositional) prosody task. However, on the emotional prosody task, the right hemisphere–damaged patients performed significantly worse than the left hemisphere–damaged patients. This finding suggests that, whereas both hemispheres may be important in comprehending syntactic-propositional prosody, the right hemisphere plays a dominant role in comprehending emotional prosody. Since these early studies, a large body of clinical research has shown impairments in emotional prosodic comprehension associated with damage to the right cerebral hemisphere (Charbonneau et al., 2003; Kucharska-Pietura et al., 2003; Harciarek et al., 2006; Pell, 2006). In a lesion-mapping study involving 60 patients, Adolphs et al. (2002) found that recognizing emotions from prosody involves the right frontoparietal operculum, the bilateral frontal pole, and the left frontal operculum.

The specific defect underlying the impaired ability of patients with right hemisphere disease to identify affective intonations in speech is not entirely clear. It may be related to a cognitive disability, whereby these patients fail to verbally denote or name prosodic stimuli. It could also be related to an inability to discriminate between different affective intonations in speech. Tucker et al. (1977) attempted to determine whether patients with right hemisphere disease could in fact discriminate between affective intonations of speech without having to verbally classify or denote these intonations. Patients were required to listen to identical pairs of sentences spoken with either the same or different emotional prosody. The patients did not have to verbally denote or name the emotional prosody, but had to indicate whether the prosody associated with the sentences sounded the same or different. Patients with right hemisphere disease performed more poorly on this task than did patients with left hemisphere disease. We suspect that the right hemisphere contains not only representations of species-typical facial expressions, but also contains representations of species-typical affective prosodic expressions. Destruction of these representations or an inability to access them could impair both comprehension and discrimination of emotional prosody.

In normal conversation and in experimental tasks, emotional prosody is often superimposed on propositional speech. Another possible explanation for the poor performance of right hemisphere–damaged patients on emotional prosody tasks is that these patients are "distracted" by the propositional semantic message of affectively intoned sentences. Findings from

studies of hemispheric asymmetries of attention in normal adults demonstrate that each hemisphere is more disrupted by stimuli it normally processes (Heilman et al., 1977), the left hemisphere being more disrupted by speech distractors (i.e., running conversation), and the right hemisphere being more disrupted by music distractors. After right hemisphere damage, perhaps the intact left hemisphere can comprehend emotional prosody, but in our tasks, it is distracted by the propositional semantic message. To test this hypothesis, we presented right and left hemisphere–damaged subjects an emotional prosody task that varied in the degree of conflict between the emotional message conveyed by the prosody and that conveyed by the propositional content (Bowers et al., 1987). If right hemisphere–damaged patients were distracted by the propositional content, then their comprehension of emotional prosody should be worse when the propositional content and prosody messages are strongly conflicting (i.e., "All the puppies are dead," said in a happy tone of voice). We found that the right hemisphere–damaged group was more disrupted when the propositional and prosodic emotional messages were highly conflicting than when they were less conflicting. The left hemisphere–damaged group was unaffected by increasing the discrepancy between the two messages. These results suggest that, at least in part, the defect in comprehending emotional prosody by right hemisphere–damaged patients is related to distraction, by which they are "pulled" to the propositional-semantic content of emotionally intoned sentences. However, this distraction defect cannot entirely account for their poor performance, in that right hemisphere–damaged patients remained impaired in identifying emotional prosody even when the semantic content was rendered completely unintelligible by speech filtering (Bowers et al., 1987).

In summary, these studies suggest that right hemisphere–damaged patients have both processing and distraction defects that contribute to their poor performance on emotional prosody comprehension tasks. The coexistence of these defects might emerge when a right hemisphere lesion induces defective processing/miscategorization of emotional prosody due to disruption of right hemisphere prosodic processors. Defective processing of emotional prosody may render the right hemisphere–damaged patients more susceptible to the distracting effects of propositional semantic stimuli. They may not hear "how it was said," but only "what was said."

Visual and Auditory Verbal Processes. Although the preceding sections dealt with the evaluation of nonverbal communicative signals of emotion, the focus here is on emotional meaning that is derived from verbal-propositional language. Emotional messages can be conveyed at the single-word level (i.e., fear, joy), by sentences, or by lengthier narratives that describe contextual situations that are associated with specific emotional states. One obvious question concerns whether the right hemisphere plays a critical role in deriving emotional meaning from propositional language, as it appears to do for nonverbal affective signals. Historically, this question has been addressed from several perspectives.

Reading and auditory comprehension by aphasic left hemisphere–damaged patients is improved when emotional words or phrases are used (Boller et al., 1979; Landis et al., 1982; Reuterskiold, 1991). Landis and colleagues (1982) reported that emotional words were read and written more accurately than nonemotional words by left hemisphere–damaged aphasic patients. Improvements in auditory comprehension have been reported for aphasic patients with severe comprehension defects when emotional versus nonemotional words (object names, actions) are presented (Reuterskiold, 1991). Such improvements may suggest that the right hemisphere has a lexical semantic system that can process emotional words.

Alternatively, the increased arousal that typically accompanies emotional stimuli may be the critical factor. Several studies have directly assessed the comprehension of emotional words, sentences, and narratives by patients with right hemisphere lesions. Borod and her coworkers (1992) tested right and left hemisphere–injured patients with emotional and nonemotional sentence and word discrimination tests. In the emotional condition, the right hemisphere–damaged subjects were more impaired than subjects with

left hemisphere damage. However, others could not find these asymmetries. For example, Morris and colleagues (1992) found no differences between right and left hemisphere–damaged patients in their ability to comprehend the denotative or connotative meaning of emotional versus nonemotional words. Etcoff (1984) presented pairs of emotional words to right and left hemisphere–damaged subjects who were required to judge the similarity of the emotional states conveyed by these words. Using multidimensional scaling techniques, she found that right hemisphere–damaged patients did not differ from controls in their scaling solutions for emotion words, nor in the strategies they described for judging the similarity of the emotions conveyed in words. Other studies have indicated that right hemisphere–damaged patients are not impaired in their understanding of the emotionality of short propositional sentences (Cicone et al., 1980; Heilman et al., 1984). This is true even when the sentences contain no specific emotion words and the emotional meaning must be derived from the situational context (e.g., "The children tracked over your white carpet") (Blonder et al., 1991a). A different pattern of findings emerges when right hemisphere–damaged patients are presented with lengthier and more complex narratives. Several investigators have found that these patients are impaired in understanding the affective-emotional content of stories and appreciating humor (Gardner et al.,1975; Brownell et al., 1983). Such problems, however, do not appear to be specific to "emotion" per se, but are related to more general difficulties that right hemisphere–damaged patients have in drawing inferences and logical reasoning (Brownell et al., 1986; McDonald & Wales, 1986; Blonder et al., 1991b; Cheang & Pell, 2006) and interpreting figures of speech (Winner & Gardner, 1977). Taken together, these studies suggest that lesions of the right hemisphere do not specifically disrupt lexical semantic knowledge about emotions or emotional situations, at least when conveyed by short verbal descriptions. Patients with right hemisphere lesions appear to have intact conceptual knowledge about emotions that are communicated verbally, as long as this communication does not involve verbal descriptions of nonverbal affect signals (Blonder et al., 1991a) or does not entail higher-level inferential processes (Brownell et al., 1986). Left hemisphere–damaged patients, especially those with word deafness or Wernicke's, global, transcortical sensory, or mixed transcortical aphasia, may have defects in comprehending propositional speech. If the development of an appropriate cognitive state were dependent on propositional language, patients with these aphasias might not be able to do so. Patients with Broca's and conduction aphasia may have difficulty comprehending emotional messages conveyed by propositional speech if these messages contain complex syntax or require a large memory store (see Chapter 2).

Although left hemisphere–damaged aphasic and word-deaf patients may have difficulty comprehending propositional speech, some of these patients can comprehend emotional intonations, and their comprehension of propositional speech may be aided by these intonations (Heilman et al., 1975; Coslett et al., 1984). Finally, some support for the role of the right hemisphere in comprehending emotional verbal language comes from studies of normal subjects. Graves et al., 1981 found a relative superiority in the left visual field for the recognition of emotional words over nonemotional words. However, Strauss (1983) was unable to replicate these findings. More recently, Landis (2006) reviewed visual half-field experiments conducted in normal subjects and suggested that the left visual cortex is less sensitive to emotional words than that of the right hemisphere.

EXPRESSIVE DEFECTS

Speech and Writing

We attempted to determine whether patients with right hemisphere disease could express emotionally intoned speech (Tucker et al., 1977). The patients were asked to say semantically neutral sentences (e.g., "The boy went to the store") using a happy, sad, angry, or indifferent prosody. These patients were severely impaired. Typically, they spoke the sentences in a flat monotone and often denoted the target affect (e.g., "The boy went to the store and he was sad"). Similar findings have been reported

by Borod et al. (1985). Ross and Mesulam (1979) described two patients who could not express affectively intoned speech but could comprehend affective speech. Ross (1981) also described patients who could not comprehend affective intonation but could repeat affectively intoned speech. He postulated that right hemisphere lesions might disrupt the comprehension, repetition, or production of affective speech in the same manner that left hemisphere lesions disrupt propositional speech. Since these early studies, a large body of clinical research has shown reductions in emotional prosodic expression associated with focal lesions in the right hemisphere (Ross, 1981, 1997; Weintraub et al., 1981; Hughes et al., 1983; Borod et al., 1985; Blonder et al., 1995; Charbonneau et al., 2003; Heilman et al., 2004). Acoustic analyses of right hemisphere–damaged patients' speech show abnormalities such as decreased variation in fundamental frequency (e.g., Kent & Rosenbek, 1982; Ross et al., 1988; Behrens, 1989; Blonder et al., 1995; Pell, 1999).

Some evidence suggests that patients with right hemisphere dysfunction are also impaired at expressing emotions using propositional speech. For example, Bloom et al. (1992) reported that right hemisphere–damaged patients used fewer words when denoting emotions in their spontaneous speech. Cimino et al. (1991) found that right hemisphere–damaged patients produced autobiographical memories that were judged as less emotional than those of normal volunteers, but left hemisphere–damaged patients were not assessed. Borod et al. (1996) had raters judge emotionality in monologues produced by right hemisphere–damaged, left hemisphere–damaged, and normal volunteers. Right hemisphere–damaged patients' monologues were rated as significantly less emotional than the monologues of normal controls. There was also a trend for right hemisphere–damaged patients' monologues to be rated as less emotional than left hemisphere–damaged patients. However, Blonder et al. (2005) found that aprosodic right hemisphere–damaged patients produced a greater percentage of emotion words relative to total words than did aphasic left hemisphere–damaged patients during interviews, suggesting that reduced emotional expressivity in right hemisphere–damaged patients is primarily limited to nonverbal channels.

Depending on the type of aphasia, patients with left hemisphere disease may have difficulty expressing emotions when these emotions are expressed as a spoken or written propositional message. Hughlings Jackson (1932), however, observed that even nonfluent aphasic patients could imbue their simple utterances with emotional content by using affective intonation. In addition, some nonfluent aphasics may be very fluent when using expletives. Jackson postulated that the right hemisphere might be mediating these activities. Roeltgen et al. (1983) demonstrated that aphasic patients with agraphia were able to write emotional words better than nonemotional words. Similar findings were reported by Landis et al. (1982). However, the role of the right hemisphere in these cases remains uncertain.

Normally, propositional speech is colored by affective intonation that is governed by mood. Whereas the left hemisphere is responsible for mediating the propositional aspect of speech, there is parallel processing in the right hemisphere that is responsible for the emotional prosodic element of speech. Speedie et al. (1984) provided evidence that this propositional and affective prosodic mixing occurs interhemispherically.

Expressive affective (emotional) aprosodia may respond to treatment. Rosenbek and co-investigators (2006) used an imitative treatment and a cognitive–linguistic treatment, and found that both treatments were effective.

FACIAL EXPRESSIONS

It is well established that lesions of the right hemisphere disrupt the perception and evaluation of nonverbal affective signals, and considerable evidence exists showing that the right hemisphere also plays a unique role in expressing facial emotions. Some investigators have found that right hemisphere–damaged patients are more impaired than left hemisphere–damaged patients in expressing facial emotions. In an initial study, Buck and Duffy (1980) reported that right hemisphere–damaged patients were less facially expressive than left

hemisphere–damaged patients when viewing slides of familiar people, unpleasant scenes, and unusual pictures. Subsequent research, much of it from Borod's laboratory, has replicated these right–left differences in facial expressiveness across a series of studies with focal lesion stroke patients involving both spontaneous and voluntarily expressed emotions (Borod et al., 1985, 1986, 1988; Kent et al., 1990; Richardson et al., 1992). Similar deficits have also been observed in more naturalistic settings outside the laboratory. Blonder and colleagues (Blonder et al., 1993) videotaped interviews with patients and their spouses in their homes and found that patients with right hemisphere damage were rated as less facially expressive than were left hemisphere–damaged patients and normal controls. They also smiled and laughed less. This work was replicated in a subsequent study comparing right hemisphere–damaged aprosodic patients with left hemisphere–damaged aphasic patients (Blonder et al., 2005). A study of deaf signers (Bellugi et al., 1988) found that right hemisphere lesions are associated with dramatic impairments in the spontaneous use of affective facial expressions in the context of preserved use of linguistic facial expressions. The opposite pattern is observed in deaf signers with left hemisphere lesions. In a review of the literature on emotional processing deficits in patients with unilateral brain damage, Borod et al. (2002) reported that nine of 13 studies of spontaneous facial expressivity found deficits associated with right hemisphere damage.

Some investigators have reported no differences in facial emotion expressiveness between right and left hemisphere–damaged patients using the Facial Action Scoring System (FACS; Mammucari et al., 1988; Caltagirone et al., 1989). Still others have found that lesions that extend into the frontal lobes, regardless of whether the right or left hemispheres are involved, are critical for a reduction of facial expression (Kolb & Milner, 1981; Weddell et al., 1990). The basis for these discrepant findings is unclear (see Buck, 1990). In part, they may relate to subject factors, intrahemispheric lesion location, as well as the different methods used across laboratories for quantifying facial expressions. Some systems involve scoring the movements of various muscle groups which appear pathognomic of certain emotional facial expressions (i.e., FACS, Ekman & Friesen, 1978), whereas others involve subjective judgments by raters about intended facial expressions, including their intensity and frequency. Another factor may relate to the manner by which facial expressions are elicited. Richardson and colleagues (1992) found that, although right hemisphere–damaged patients were overall less accurate than left hemisphere–damaged patients and normal control subjects in communicating target facial emotions, their expressive deficits were most salient in response to affective pictures, affective prosody, and other affective faces. There were no differences among the groups in producing facial expressions on verbal command or in response to the emotional meaning of sentences. These findings have direct implications for studies that use emotional scenes or films for eliciting spontaneous facial expressions, in that defects in fully evaluating the affective meaning of such stimuli could directly reduce one's responsivity to them. This observation, however, cannot readily account for the diminished facial expressiveness of right hemisphere–damaged patients in more naturalistic settings (Blonder et al., 1993, 2005) or the asymmetries seen in normal subjects. In general, normal subjects express emotions more intensely on the left side of the face (Sackheim et al., 1978; Campbell, 1978; Heller & Levy, 1981; Moreno et al., 1990).

Although there has been no research in the treatment of emotional facial expressive disorders, it might be worth treating patients with this disorder with both imitation and cognitive strategies, similar to those that were successful in treating disorders of prosody.

EMOTIONAL EXPERIENCES AND MOOD

Clinical Descriptions

Babinski (1914) noted that patients with right hemisphere disease often appeared indifferent or euphoric. Hecaen et al. (1951) and Denny-Brown et al. (1952) also noted that patients with right hemisphere lesions were often inappropriately indifferent. Gainotti's study (1972)

of 160 patients with lateralized brain damage supported these earlier clinical observations: Right hemisphere lesions were often associated with indifference. Terzian (1964) and Rossi and Rosadini (1967) studied the emotional reactions of patients recovering from barbiturate-induced hemispheric anesthesia produced by left or right carotid artery injections (the Wada test). They observed that right carotid injections were associated with a euphoric-manic response. Milner (1974), however, was unable to replicate these findings. In contrast to the flattened emotional response or inappropriate euphoric mood associated with right hemisphere damage, Goldstein (1948) noted that many patients with left hemisphere lesions and aphasia appeared anxious, agitated, and sad, which Goldstein called the "catastrophic reaction." Gainotti (1972) confirmed Goldstein's (1948) observations. Terzian (1964) and Rossi and Rosadini (1967) observed that barbiturate injections into the left carotid artery could induce a catastrophic reaction. Gainotti (1972) thought that the indifference reaction was an abnormal mood associated with denial of illness (anosognosia) but that the catastrophic reaction was a normal response to a serious physical or cognitive deficit. However, several studies and observations are incompatible with Gainotti's hypothesis. The Wada test causes only a transient aphasia with hemiparesis and would, therefore, be unlikely to cause a reactive depression in patients who are undergoing a diagnostic test. Anosognosia is the verbal explicit denial of a hemiplegia (see Chapter 9). We see right hemisphere–damaged patients in the clinic who also appear to be indifferent but do not demonstrate anosognosia. Critchley (1953) has termed this *anosodiaphoria*. It is not clear if these patients' propensity to be unconcerned about their own illness is related to a general emotional flattening, or if anosodiaphoria is a mild form of anosognosia and their indifference is related to defective evaluation of their own illness. The depressive reaction associated with left hemisphere disease is usually seen in nonfluent aphasic patients with anterior perisylvian lesions (Benson, 1979; Robinson & Sztela, 1981). As discussed, Hughlings Jackson (1932) noted that left hemisphere lesions induced deficits in propositional language, and the nonfluent aphasics who could not express themselves with propositional speech could express feelings by using expletives and by intoning simple verbal utterances. Hughlings Jackson postulated that the right hemisphere might be mediating this activity. His postulate was supported by the observations of Tucker et al. (1977) and Ross and Mesulam (1979). Because left hemisphere–damaged patients are unable to use propositional speech, they may rely more on right hemisphere nonpropositional affective systems by more heavily intoning their speech and by using more facial expression. As we discussed, patients with right hemisphere disease have more difficulty than do patients with left hemisphere disease in comprehending and expressing affectively intoned speech, as well as in comprehending and expressing emotional facial expressions. Patients with right hemisphere disease may also have more difficulty comprehending or remembering emotionally charged speech. These perceptual, cognitive, and expressive deficits might underlie and account for the flattened emotional reaction of patients with right hemisphere lesions (i.e., indifference reactions), as previously described by clinical investigators. Alternatively, these perceptual, cognitive, and expressive deficits may not reflect the patients' underlying mood.

Although defects of affective communication may account for some of the behavioral symptoms discussed by Goldstein (1948), Babinski (1914), and Gainotti (1972), they cannot explain the results of Gasparrini et al. (1978), who administered the Minnesota Multiphasic Inventory (MMPI) to patients with unilateral hemisphere lesions. The MMPI has been widely used as an index of underlying affective experience, and the completion of this inventory does not require the perception or expression of affectively intoned speech or the perception of facial expression. Patients with left hemisphere disease showed a marked elevation on the depression scale of this inventory, whereas patients with right hemisphere disease did not. This finding suggests that the differences in emotional reactions of patients with right versus left hemisphere disease cannot be attributed entirely to difficulties in perceiving or expressing affective stimuli.

Starkstein et al. (1987) have studied stroke and depression. They found that about one-third of stroke patients had a major depression and long-lasting depressions were associated with both cortical lesions and subcortical lesions. They also found that the left frontal and left caudate lesions were most frequently associated with severe depression: The closer to the frontal pole, the more severe the depression. Many of the patients with depression, and especially those with cortical lesions, were anxious. In contrast, in the acute poststroke period, right frontal lesions were associated with indifference and even euphoria. When patients with right hemisphere damage had depression, they were more likely to have parietal lesions.

Not all investigators agree that there are hemispheric asymmetries in depression. House et al. (1990) believe that depression associated with right hemisphere disease may be under-diagnosed because right hemisphere–damaged patients may have an emotional communicative disorder. Whyte and Mulsant (2002) reviewed the literature on post-stroke depression and reported that while left anterior lesions, left basal ganglia lesions, and lesions closer to the frontal pole have been associated with post-stroke depression, biopsychosocial factors combine to play a role in the development of this disorder.

POSSIBLE MECHANISMS OF THE CHANGES IN MOOD AND EMOTIONAL EXPERIENCE ASSOCIATED WITH HEMISPHERIC DYSFUNCTION

If the observation that left hemisphere–damaged patients are depressed (or anxious) and right hemisphere–damaged patients are indifferent (or euphoric) is correct, how can these asymmetries be explained? Unfortunately, the brain mechanisms underlying mood and memory have not been entirely elucidated. However, we will briefly review some of the major theories. We will also discuss their relative merits and how well they explain clinical observations. Theories of emotional experience can be divided into two major types: feedback theories and central theories. Because feedback and central theories both have explanatory value, we will discuss both.

Feedback Theories

Facial. Emotional experiences are also called emotional "feelings." In general, in order to feel something, one must have sensory or afferent input into the brain. Because emotional experience is associated with feelings, emotional experience may also require afferent input. However, emotional feelings are unlike traditional sensory experiences (e.g., visual, tactile, auditory) because they do not rely directly on the physical characteristics of the external stimulus. Rather, they may rely on the pattern of neural activity that the stimulus is eliciting. Emotional feelings may even occur in the absence of an external stimulus, suggesting that afferent activity must have been induced by efferent activity. This efferent activity may not only be important for emotional expression, but feedback of this expression to the brain may be responsible for emotional feelings.

There are two major feedback hypotheses: the facial theory of Charles Darwin and the visceral theory of William James. Darwin (1872) noted that the free expression by outward signs of an emotion intensifies it. On the other hand, the repression, as far as possible, of all outward signs softens our emotions: "He who gives violent gesture increases his rage." Darwin also thought that emotional expression is innate. Izard (1977) and Ekman (1969), using cross-cultural studies, provided support for Darwin's hypothesis that emotional expression is innate. Tomkins (1962, 1963) thought that sensory receptors in the face provide afferent activity to the brain and that it was self-perception of the facial expression that induced emotion. Laird (1974) experimentally manipulated facial expression, and these manipulations induced emotional experience. Studies by Adelmann and Zajonc (1989) and Levenson et al. (1990) have shown that producing an emotional facial expression through volitional contraction of facial muscles induces the emotional state normally associated with that expression. Because patients with right hemisphere lesions may be impaired in expressing emotions, including facial expression, they may have reduced facial feedback and therefore appear indifferent. However, the facial feedback theory cannot explain why patients with left hemisphere disease are anxious and depressed. There are many other unresolved problems with the facial feedback theory. When a person is feeling a strong emotion, such as sadness she cannot entirely change this emotion to happiness just by voluntarily smiling. Therefore, a person can express one emotion while feeling another. Patients with pseudobulbar affect (see the final section) may express strong facial emotions that they are not feeling. Although it is possible that feedback is interrupted in these patients, we reported a patient with no facial mobility from a polyneuritis (Guillain-Barré syndrome) who reported feeling emotions (Keillor et al., 2002). Therefore, while facial expressions may influence emotions as Darwin suggested, the facial feedback theory cannot alone account for emotional experience.

Visceral–Autonomic Feedback. William James (1890) proposed that emotion-provoking stimuli induced bodily changes and that the self-perception of these changes as they occur produced the emotional feeling or experience. James, however, noted that there were also "cerebral" forms of pleasure and displeasure that did not require bodily changes or perception of these changes. James's model was challenged by Cannon (1927), who argued that the separation of the viscera from the brain does not eliminate emotional feelings. This argument was supported by observations that patients with cervical spinal cord transections continued to experience emotions. However, Hohmann (1966) found that patients with either high or low spinal cord transections experienced emotions, but patients with lower lesions reported stronger emotions than those with high lesions. In addition, because the vagus nerve, which enters the brain in the medulla, bypassing the spinal cord, contains visceral afferents, cord transection at any level may not fully interfere with feedback. Cannon also noted that pharmacologically induced visceral activation does not produce emotion. Maranon (1924) injected epinephrine into subjects and then inquired whether or not these injections induced an emotion. He found that these injections produced only "as if" feelings. Schachter and Singer (1962) also found that pharmacologically induced visceral activation did not produce an emotion, unless this arousal was accompanied by a cognitive set. Based on his studies, Schachter modified William James's postulate and proposed the "cognitive-arousal" theory of emotions. According to this theory, the experience of emotion involves specific cognitive attributions superimposed on a state of diffuse physiologic arousal; that is, a primary determinant of felt emotion is the environmental context within which arousal occurs. Cannon thought that the visceral feedback theory could not account for a variety of emotions because the same visceral responses occur with different emotions. Although Schachter's modification of James's theory could also deal with this critique, Ax (1953) and Ekman et al. (1969) have demonstrated that different bodily reactions can be associated with different emotions. It has not been shown, however, that feedback of these different bodily reactions can induce different emotional experiences. Regarding Cannon's critique that the viscera have insufficient afferent input to the brain, contemporary research has examined the role of autonomic feedback in emotional experience using the heartbeat detection paradigm. Katkin et al. (1982) found that some normal subjects can accurately detect their heartbeats, and it was those individuals who had stronger emotional response to negative slides as determined by self-report (Hantas et al., 1982). Further support for the importance of autonomic feedback comes from other observations. Experiments in animals demonstrate that sympathectomy may retard aversive conditioning (DiGiusto & King, 1972), most likely because sympathectomy reduces fear. Taken together, not only do Cannon's critiques fail to refute the feedback theory, but there is also evidence that would support a role of visceral feedback in emotional experience.

For feedback to occur, there must be a means for the viscera and autonomic nervous system to become activated. We will use the term *feedforward* to refer to the brain's ability to activate the autonomic nervous system and viscera. In humans, the cortex plays a critical role in the analysis and interpretation of various stimuli, including those that induce emotional feeling and autonomic–visceral responses. Consequently, feedforward systems must exist

to enable the cortex to control the autonomic nervous system and the viscera such as the heart (visceral efferents). Similarly, if visceral activity can be detected by subjects, there must be neuronal pathways that support the feedback system and bring this information back to the brain (visceral afferents). As we briefly mentioned, the major nerve that carries visceral afferent information is the vagus. Vagus nerve afferents terminate in the medulla, primarily in the nucleus of the solitary tract. The nucleus of the solitary tract projects to the central nucleus of the amygdala (as well as to several hypothalamic nuclei), and the central nucleus of the amygdala in turn projects to other amygdala nuclei and to the insula. Electrical stimulation of the vagus nerve also produces excitation of the insula and amygdala. The amygdala and insula project to several cortical areas including temporal, parietal, and frontal regions. It is possible that the vagal-solitary tract nucleus-amygdala-insula-cortical pathway may be responsible for visceral feedback.

Emotions can be expressed by both the striated muscles and the autonomic nervous system–controlled viscera. We have already discussed the facial feedback theory. James did not believe that muscle and facial feedback were critical for emotional experience. Viscera, such as the heart, are controlled by the autonomic nervous system. The autonomic nervous system has two major components, the sympathetic and parasympathetic. The sympathetic nerves originate in the intermediolateral columns of the spinal cord. Most of the parasympathetic outflow to the viscera is through the vagus nerve that originates in the brainstem (dorsal motor nucleus). Sympathetic neurons in the spinal cord receive projections from the hypothalamus as well as from cells in the ventrolateral pons and medulla. However, the ventrolateral medulla also receives projections from the paraventricular and lateral nuclei of the hypothalamus. Whereas the hypothalamus receives projections from many "limbic" areas, the strongest projections come from the amygdala. The amygdala not only appears to influence the sympathetic nervous system via the hypothalamus, but also sends direct projections to the nucleus of the solitary tract and the dorsal motor nucleus of the vagus nerve, and may therefore also directly influence the parasympathetic system. Although there are more widespread projections from the amygdala to the cortex than vice versa, the amygdala does receive cortical input. The insula also receives projections from the neocortex, and stimulation of the insula induces autonomic and visceral changes. In humans, stimuli that induce emotional behavior must be analyzed and interpreted by the cortex, including such areas as the temporoparietal association cortex. Stimuli that induce emotion do cause changes in the autonomic nervous system and the viscera. Although it is not clear which limbic area or areas are critical for transcoding the knowledge gained from the emotional stimuli into changes of the autonomic nervous system and viscera, the amygdala and insula would appear to be ideal candidates. The visceral afferent and efferent pathways discussed above are bilateral; however, several studies suggest that asymmetries may exist both in the control of the autonomic nervous system and viscera as well as in the monitoring of the autonomic nervous system.

Regarding the efferent control of the autonomic nervous system (the feedforward system), Heilman et al. (1978) studied skin conductance responses (SCR) to mildly noxious stimuli in patients with right or left hemisphere lesions. The SCR, which results from phasic changes in eccrine sweat gland activity, is almost entirely mediated by the sympathetic branch of the autonomic nervous system. When compared to both normal controls and subjects with left hemisphere lesions, those with right hemisphere damage had decreased SCRs. In contrast, when compared to controls, the left hemisphere–damaged patients had increased responsivity. Although Morrow et al. (1981) also found decreased SCR to emotional stimuli in patients with right hemisphere damage they did not find an increased SCR in patients with left hemisphere damage. Yokoyama et al. (1987) measured heart rate changes in response to an attention-demanding task. These authors found that right hemisphere–damaged patients had reduced heart rate responses, whereas left hemisphere–damaged patients had increased responsivity. The exact parts of the brain that mediate these autonomic changes are not

known. Although Heilman et al. (1978) suspected that parietal and temporal cortex was involved, high-quality neuroimaging was not available when they did this study. In Yokoyama's study, the lesion loci were noted in the methods section, but no mention is made of the relationship between lesion locus and changes in heart rate. However, Schrandt et al. (1989) reported a study in which they measured SCR to emotional slides. Within the right hemisphere–damaged group, only those patients whose lesions involved the right parietal lobe showed reduced SCR.

Luria and Simernitskaya (1977) proposed that the right hemisphere might be more important than the left in perceiving visceral changes (i.e., feedback system), and several studies in normal subjects have suggested that the right hemisphere may play a special role in visceral perception. For example, Davidson and coworkers (1981) gave a variety of tapping tests to normal individuals in order to assess whether the left or right hand's tapping rate was more influenced by heartbeat. They found that the left hand was more influenced by heart rate than the right hand, suggesting that the right hemisphere might be superior at detecting heartbeat. Other investigators, however, could not replicate this left hand superiority in the detection of heartbeat. Hantas et al. (1984) used a signal detection technique to learn if normal subjects could detect their own heartbeat. They also assessed cerebral lateral preference by judging conjugate lateral eye movements and found that left movers (who were "right hemisphere preferent") were better at detecting their own heartbeat than were those who were right movers. If the right hemisphere plays a dominant role in visceral autonomic activation, and also has a dominant role in perceiving visceral changes, and if this feedback is critical to emotional experience, it would follow that right hemisphere lesions that damage critical cortical and limbic areas should be associated with reduced emotional feeling or indifference even in those patients who are aware of their deficits. Left hemisphere lesions may not only spare the right hemisphere feedforward and feedback systems, but the left hemisphere may help regulate or control the feedforward systems such that, with left hemisphere lesions, there is increased visceral–autonomic activation (Heilman et al., 1978; Yokoyama et al., 1987). Therefore, the heightened autonomic–visceral activity found in patients with left hemisphere injuries, together with their knowledge of their neurological deficits, may lead to the anxiety associated with left hemisphere lesions.

In a more recent study, Crucian et al. (2000) sought to examine the relationship between autonomic–visceral arousal and emotional experience. They exposed men, both neurologically intact and those with right and left hemisphere lesions, to emotionally provocative pictures that were paired with false cardiac feedback and examined the effects of this false feedback on their ratings of attractiveness of these pictures and their cardiac reactivity to this information. Subjects with left hemisphere damage, but not right hemisphere damage, showed significant changes in their emotional ratings to this false feedback. In contrast, control subjects showed marginal reactivity to false feedback in their emotional ratings. Subjects with left hemisphere damage also showed significant changes in their cardiac reactivity. This finding indicates that patients with left hemisphere lesions have an increased visceral–autonomic response to stimuli and is consistent with prior skin conductance studies (Heilman et al., 1978). These findings further provide support for the postulate that it is the cognitive interpretation of perceived physiological arousal, together with the cognitive interpretation of the stimulus, that is important in the development of emotional judgment and experience. These results do not support the approach-left hemisphere–avoidance-right hemisphere dichotomy of Davidson et al. (1979), but instead suggest that left hemisphere damage increases reactivity to false feedback, and that the intact right hemisphere integrates the cognitive interpretation of the emotional information and perceived arousal that lead to emotional judgments. That these subjects showed no consistent relationship between measures of cardiac reactivity and ratings of attractiveness does not support the James-Lange and attribution theories. These subjects also showed no consistent relationship between their knowledge of affective physiological reactivity and their ratings of attractiveness,

or between their knowledge of physiological reactivity and actual measures of cardiac reactivity, suggesting that other neuropsychological factors are involved in making an emotional judgment.

Central Theories

Diencephalic. One of the first central theories to explain emotional experience was that of Walter Cannon (1927), who proposed that stimuli that enter the brain by way of the thalamus activate the hypothalamus. The hypothalamus controls the endocrine systems and also controls the autonomic nervous system. The endocrine and autonomic nervous systems can induce physiological changes in almost all organ systems. Cannon posited that hypothalamic-induced changes in organ systems are adaptive in that they aid survival. Cannon also thought that the hypothalamus activated the cerebral cortex, and it was this cerebral activation that was responsible for the conscious experience of emotion. Although Cannon believed that the cortex normally inhibits the hypothalamus, and a loss of this inhibition was responsible for a loss of appropriate emotional control, such as seen in sham rage, he did not suggest a critical role for the cortex in the interpretation of stimuli.

Limbic System. In 1878, Broca designated a group of anatomically related structures on the medial wall of the cerebral hemisphere *le grand lobe limbique.* Because these structures are in proximity to structures of the olfactory system, it was at first assumed that they all had olfactory or related functions. But in 1901, Ramon y Cajal (1965) concluded on the basis of histological studies that portions of the limbic lobe (the hippocampal-fornix system) had no more than a neighborly relationship with the olfactory apparatus. After Bard (1934) demonstrated that the hypothalamus was important in mediating the rage response, Papez (1937) postulated that the hypothalamus was the effector of emotion. He proposed that a limbic lobe-hypothalamic circuit comprising the cingulate cortex, hippocampus, fornix, mammillary bodies, anterior thalamus, and back to the cingulate cortex, was an important component of the central mechanism subserving emotional feeling and expression. In 1948, Yakovlev added basolateral components (orbitofrontal, insular, and anterior temporal lobe cortex, the amygdala, and the dorsomedial nucleus of the thalamus) to Papez' medial system, and together these were designated as the limbic system (MacLean, 1952). Although the neocortex influences the hypothalamus, both inhibiting and activating it, the neocortex does not have strong, direct projections to the hypothalamus. Most neocortical projections that influence the hypothalamus are mediated by the limbic system. In addition, as we will discuss in a later section, patients who are stimulated in limbic areas or have seizures that emanate from limbic areas may experience an emotion. Monkeys with bilateral anterior temporal ablations including the amygdala have decreased emotions (Kluver & Bucy, 1937). LeDoux and coworkers (1990) studied fear in animals conditioned by associating a nociceptive stimulus with an auditory stimulus. Ablation of the auditory thalamus and amygdala interrupted the behavioral response to the conditioned stimulus. Ablation of the auditory cortex, however, did not disrupt this response, suggesting that nonlimbic cortex was not required for conditioned fear.

We agree with Cannon that emotions are adaptive, and many of the physiologic changes associated with adaptation are mediated by the hypothalamus. We also agree with LeDoux that conditioned fear may not require cortical mediation. However, as we pointed out earlier in this chapter, it is the cortex, rather than the thalamus or hypothalamus, that appears to be critical in the interpretation of the complex stimuli and it is complex stimuli that most commonly induce emotions in humans. The diencephalic theories of Cannon and the limbic-diencephalic theory of LeDoux also fail to explain how humans can experience a variety of emotions.

Modular Theory of Emotion. In 1903, Wundt proposed that emotional experiences vary in three dimensions: quality (good or bad), excitement (arousal), and activity. Osgood et al. (1957) had normal subjects verbally assess emotions and then performed a factor analysis on these judgments. These investigators found

three major factors that were similar to those of Wundt, but rather than activity, these investigators found that the third factor was control (in control/out of control). However Frijda (1987) who also explored the cognitive structure of emotion found, as Wundt posited, that action readiness, instead of control, was the third factor. This dimensional view of emotional experience was supported by psychophysiological studies (Greenwald et al., 1989). Based on this dimensional view of emotions, Heilman (1997) suggested that the conscious experience of emotion may be mediated by three anatomically distributed modular networks: one that determines quality or valence (positive or negative), a second that mediates arousal (high or low), and a third that mediates motor activation (approach or avoid).

VALENCE

In regard to valence or quality, we have previously discussed the observations that, after left hemisphere injury, patients appear to be more depressed than after right hemisphere injury. In addition to this clinical data, several functional imaging studies performed on patients with depression suggested the left hemisphere appeared hypoactive (Phelps et al., 1984; Bench et al., 1992). Using electrophysiological techniques, Davidson et al. (1979) and Tucker (1981) demonstrated in normal subjects that the left hemisphere mediates emotions with positive valence, whereas the right hemisphere mediates emotions with negative valence. The mechanism by which each hemisphere mediates valence is unknown. Since the time of Hippocrates, it has been postulated that body humors can influence mood. Tucker and Williamson (1984) suggested that hemispheric valence asymmetries might be related to asymmetrical control of neuropharmacologic systems. This hypothesis was supported by a study using positron emission tomography (PET) imaging. Robinson and Starkstein (1989) reported that, after left hemisphere stroke, there was reduced serotonergic receptor binding and that after right hemisphere stroke, there was increased serotonergic binding. They also found that the lower the serotonergic binding, the worse the depression. Although clinical psychiatry has provided strong evidence that depression is associated with a reduction of serotonin, it remains unclear how these neuropharmacological changes induce the emotional experiences associated with a depressed or happy mood.

AROUSAL

The term *arousal*, like the terms attention and emotion, is difficult to define. Behaviorally, an aroused organism is awake, alert, and prepared to process stimuli, whereas an unaroused organism is lethargic or comatose and not prepared to process stimuli. Physiologically arousal has several definitions. In the CNS, arousal usually refers to the excitatory state of neurons or the propensity of neurons to discharge when appropriately activated. In functional imaging, arousal is usually measured by increases of blood flow, and electrophysiologically it is measured by desynchronization of the electroencephalogram (EEG) or by the amplitude and latency of evoked potentials. Outside the CNS, arousal usually refers to activation of the sympathetic nervous system and to increased visceral activity such as heart rate.

The neural substrate of arousal and attention is discussed in detail in Chapter 12. Briefly, arousal and attention are intimately linked and appear to be mediated by a cortical limbic reticular modular network (Heilman, 1979; Watson, 1981; Mesulam, 1981). Sensory information relayed through the thalamus is processed in primary sensory cortices, and then in unimodal sensory association cortices, which in turn converge upon polymodal sensory cortex in frontal cortex and on both banks of the superior temporal sulcus (Pandya & Kuypers, 1969). Both of these sensory polymodal convergence areas project to the supramodal inferior parietal lobe (Mesulam et al., 1977). Whereas the determination of stimulus novelty may be mediated by modality-specific sensory association cortex, stimulus significance requires knowledge as to both the meaning of the stimulus and the motivational state of the organism. The motivational state is dependent on at least two factors: immediate biological needs and long-term goals. It has been demonstrated that portions of the limbic system together with the hypothalamus monitor the internal milieu and develop drive states. Therefore, limbic input into regions important in determining stimulus significance may provide information about immediate biological needs. Information about long-term goals that are not motivated by immediate biological needs is provided by the frontal lobes, which have been demonstrated to play a major role in goal-oriented behavior and set development (Stuss & Benson, 1986) (see Chapter 14). Studies of cortical connectivity in monkeys have demonstrated that the temporoparietal region has strong connections both with portions of the limbic system (cingulate gyrus) and with the frontal cortex.

Polymodal and supramodal cortex not only determine stimulus significance but also modulate arousal by influencing the mesencephalic reticular formation (MRF) (Segundo et al., 1955). Stimulation of the MRF in animals induces behavioral and physiological arousal (Moruzzi & Magoun, 1949). In contrast, bilateral lesions of the MRF induce coma, and unilateral lesions cause ipsilateral hemispheric hypoarousal (Watson et al., 1974). The exact means by which these cortical areas influence the MRF and the MRF influences the cortex remain unknown. There are at least three mechanisms by which the MRF may influence cortical processing. The first is by projections to the nucleus basalis of the basal forebrain, which has cholinergic projections to the entire cortex. These cholinergic projections appear to be important for increasing neuronal responsivity (Sato et al., 1987). Second, MRF stimulation activates specific thalamic nuclei such as centralis lateralis and paracentralis that project to widespread cortical regions (Steriade & Glenn, 1982). Third, gating of sensory input through thalamic relay nuclei is accomplished via the thalamic nucleus reticularis (NR). This thin nucleus envelops the thalamus and projects to all the sensory thalamic relay nuclei. Physiologically, NR inhibits the thalamic relay of sensory information (Scheibel & Scheibel, 1966). However, when cortical limbic networks determine that a stimulus is significant or novel, corticofugal projections may inhibit the inhibitory NR thereby allowing the thalamic sensory nuclei to relay sensory information to the cortex.

The level of arousal in the CNS is usually mirrored by activity of the peripheral autonomic nervous system. Hand sweating, as measured by the galvanic skin response (GSR), is one means of measuring peripheral autonomic arousal. Heilman et al. (1978) measured GSR in patients with right and left hemisphere damage, as well as in normal controls. Patients with right hemisphere lesions had a reduced GSR response to a nonpainful electric shock when compared to normal subjects and left hemisphere–damaged controls. Subsequently, other investigators reported similar findings (Morrow et al., 1981; Schrandt et al., 1989). However, Heilman and his coworkers reported another interesting finding. When compared to normal subjects, patients with left hemisphere lesions appear to have a greater autonomic response (Heilman et al., 1978). Using changes in heart rate as a peripheral measure of arousal, Yokoyama et al. (1987) obtained similar results. Using physiological imaging, Perani et al. (1993) found metabolic depression of the left hemisphere in cases of right hemisphere stroke. Unfortunately, left hemisphere–damaged control patients were not reported.

The mechanism underlying the asymmetrical hemispheric control of arousal remains unknown. Because lesions restricted to the right hemisphere could not directly interfere with the left hemisphere's corticofugal projections to the reticular systems or the reticular system's corticipetal influence of the left hemisphere, one would have to propose that the right hemisphere's control of arousal may be related to privileged communication that the right hemisphere has with the reticular activating system. Alternatively, portions of the right hemisphere may play a dominant role in computing stimulus significance. The increased arousal associated with left hemisphere lesions also remains unexplained. Perhaps the left hemisphere maintains inhibitory control over the right hemisphere or the reticular activating system.

MOTOR ACTIVATION

Some emotions do not call for action (e.g., sadness, satisfaction), but others do (e.g., anger, fear, joy, surprise). The stimulus that induces the emotion may be approached or avoided. In general, one would like to avoid situations that induce unpleasant emotions and approach situations that induce pleasant emotions. Thus, as a rule, we avoid stimuli that induce fear and approach stimuli that induce joy; however, sometimes we approach stimuli that induce negative emotions, as when we approach a stimulus that has made us angry. In the following discussion of approach and avoidance, we refer to the behavior associated with the emotion, rather than one's ideal plans for structuring behavior (which, for example, would be to avoid stimuli that induce anger).

We have posited that motor activation or intention is mediated by a modular network that includes portions of the cerebral cortex, basal ganglia, and limbic system (see Chapter 12 for a detailed review). The dorsolateral frontal lobe appears to be the fulcrum of this motor preparatory network (Watson et al., 1978, 1981). Physiological recording from cells in the dorsolateral frontal lobe reveal neurons that have enhanced activity when the animal is presented with a stimulus that is meaningful and predicts movement (Goldberg & Bushnell, 1981). The dorsolateral frontal lobes receive input from the cingulate gyrus and from unimodal, polymodal, and supramodal posterior cortical association areas. Input from these posterior neocortical areas may provide the frontal lobes information about the stimulus, including its meaning and spatial location. The cingulate gyrus, which is not only part of Papez' circuit but also receives input from Yakolov's basolateral circuit, may provide information as to the organism's motivational state. The dorsolateral frontal lobes participate in a cortical-basal ganglia-thalamo-cortical loop (dorsolateral frontal cortex → neostriatum (caudate and putamen) → globus pallidus → thalamus → frontal cortex) (Alexander, DeLong, & Strick, 1986), and also have extensive connections with the nonspecific intralaminar nuclei of the thalamus (centromedian and parafascicularis). The intralaminar nuclei may gait motor activation by their influence on the basal ganglia, especially the putamen, or by influencing the thalamic portion of motor circuits (ventralis lateralis pars oralis). Last, the dorsolateral frontal lobes have strong input into premotor areas. The observation that lesions of the dorsolateral frontal lobe, the cingulate gyrus, the basal ganglia, the intralaminar nuclei, and the ventrolateral thalamus may all cause akinesia support the postulate that this system mediates motor activation.

The right hemisphere appears to play a special role in motor activation or intention. Coslett and Heilman (1984) demonstrated that right hemisphere lesions are more likely to be associated with contralateral akinesia than are lesions of the left hemisphere. Howes and Boller (1975) measured reaction times (a measure of the time taken to initiate a response) of the hand ipsilateral to a hemispheric lesion and demonstrated that right hemisphere lesions were associated with slower reaction times than left hemisphere lesions. However, as previously discussed, this finding may be related to the important role of the right hemisphere in mediating attention–arousal. Heilman and Van Den Abell (1979) measured the reduction of reaction times of normal subjects who received warning stimuli directed to either their right or left hemisphere. They found that, independent of the hand used, warning stimuli delivered to the right hemisphere reduced reaction times to midline stimuli more than warning stimuli delivered to the left hemisphere.

Summary. In summary we propose, as did Wundt, that there are three major components of emotional experience: emotional cognition, arousal, and motor intention–activation. Emotional experience is a "top-down" process. Except in conditioned responses, in which direct thalamic–amygdala connections appear important (Iwata et al., 1986), cognitive interpretation of stimuli helps determine the type of emotion, including its valence (positive–negative). The valence decision is based on whether the stimulus is beneficial (positive) or detrimental (negative) to the well-being of the organism, its family, or species. Positive or negative emotions can be associated with high (joy, fear) or low (satisfaction, sadness) arousal. Certain negative emotions are associated with preparation for action (e.g., fear and anger), and others are associated with reduced intention–activation (e.g., sadness). Certain positive

emotions may also be associated with preparations for action (joy and surprise), and others may not (satisfaction). The negative emotions associated with high arousal are usually associated with action: Anger is associated with approach behaviors and fear with avoidance. As we have discussed, depending on the nature of the stimulus (e.g., verbal or nonverbal), the left or right hemisphere determines the type of emotion. The frontal lobes play a critical role in mediating valence, the left mediating positive valence, and the right negative. The right hemisphere and especially the parietal lobe appears to have a strong excitatory role in arousal, and the left hemisphere an inhibitory role. Arousal is mediated by the mesencephalic and diencephalic portions of the reticular activating system. However, the cortex, and especially the right inferior parietal cortex, appears to modulate these arousal systems. The dorsolateral and medial frontal lobes form a recurrent circuit with the basal ganglia and thalamus. This system appears to be important in motor activation, with the right frontal lobe playing a dominant role in motor activation.

The cortical areas we have mentioned are extensively interconnected. In addition, they are strongly connected with the limbic system (e.g., amygdala), basal ganglia, thalamus, and reticular system. Therefore, the anatomic modules that mediate valence, arousal, and activation systems are richly interconnected and form a modular network. Emotional experience depends upon the patterns of neural activation of this modular network.

EMOTIONAL MEMORY

Only a limited number of studies have examined the ability of right and left hemisphere–damaged patients to recall emotional memories. Wechsler (1973) studied right and left hemisphere–damaged patients' ability to recall neutral and emotionally charged stories. The left hemisphere–damaged patients recalled more portions of the emotional story than they did of the neutral story. The right hemisphere–damaged patients did not show this enhanced recall. Since the story was sad, this finding was compatible with both a valence–mood congruence and right hemisphere dominance hypotheses. Cimino and coworkers (1991) examined the ability of right hemisphere–damaged patients and normal controls to recall personal episodic memories. The autobiographical memories of the right hemisphere–damaged patients were less emotional and less detailed than those of the controls. There were no valence effects. Borod et al. (1996) also studied right and left hemisphere–damaged subject's recall of emotional experiences and found that the recall of right hemisphere–damaged patients was less intense than those with left hemisphere damage.

LIMBIC SYSTEM DYSFUNCTION

COMMUNICATIVE DEFICITS

It is unusual to observe communicative deficits in patients with limbic system dysfunction. However, bilateral injury to the amygdala is associated with impairment in processing emotional faces (Adolphs et al., 1994; Adolphs, 2008). Functional imaging studies also support a role of the amygdala in the processing of emotional faces (Breiter et al., 1996; Whalen et al., 1998).

EMOTIONAL EXPERIENCE

Animal Studies

One of the earliest and most important animal observations was that bilateral ablation of the anterior temporal lobe changes the aggressive rhesus monkey into a tame animal (Kluver & Bucy, 1937). Such animals also demonstrated hypersexuality and visual agnosia. Akert et al. (1961) demonstrated that the removal of the temporal lobe neocortex did not produce this tameness. Ursin (1960) stimulated the amygdaloid nucleus and produced a rage-like response and an increase in emotional behavior. Amygdala ablation (Woods, 1956) produced placid animals. Septal lesions in animals produce a rage-like state (Brady & Nauta, 1955), and septal stimulation produces what appears to be a pleasant state, in which animals stimulate themselves without additional reward

(Olds, 1958). Decortication in animals produces a state of pathological rage ("sham rage"). In a series of experiments, Bard (1934) demonstrated that the caudal hypothalamus was mediating this response. Both the amygdala (a component of the basolateral circuit) and the septal region (a portion of both limbic circuits) have strong input into the hypothalamus (Yakovlev, 1948). MacLean (1952) proposed that the septal pathway is important for species preservation (that is, social-sexual behavior), and the amygdala circuit is more important for self preservation (fight and flight).

Subsequent research has established the importance of limbic and related structures in the mediation of emotional behavior. The studies of LeDoux and colleagues demonstrating the critical role of the amygdala in mediating fear conditioning have been mentioned already (LeDoux et al., 1990; Wilensky et al., 2006). The amygdala may also be involved in the mediation of nonfear emotions, as shown by the responses of single neurons in the monkey amygdala during reinforcement learning using rewards and punishments (Paton et al., 2006). Functional imaging studies in humans have demonstrated emotion-related activity in the basolateral amygdala, anterior insula, caudal orbitomedial prefrontal cortex, and anterior cingulate gyrus, consistent with anatomical and behavioral studies in primates and other animals (see Heimer & Van Hoesen, 2006).

Human Studies

Lesions. Some of the findings in humans have been analogous to the results reported in animals. In humans, for example, tumors in the septal region have been reported to produce rage-like attacks and increased irritability (Zeman & King, 1958; Poeck & Pilleri, 1961). Bilateral temporal lobe lesions in humans entailing the destruction of the amygdala, uncus, and hippocampal gyrus have been reported to produce placidity (Poeck, 1969). In aggressive patients, stereotactic amygdaloidectomy has been reported to reduce rage (Mark et al., 1972). Anterior temporal lobectomy for seizure disorders has been reported to increase sexuality (Blumer & Walker, 1975). More discrete and selective amygdalar lesions have more subtle effects on the emotional modulation of behavior. For example, the patient described by Kennedy et al. (2009) with selective amygdalar degeneration from Urbach-Wiethe disease, showed reduced aversion to invasion of personal space, as well as reduced ability to understand emotion (especially fear) from faces.

Inflammation. Several inflammatory and viral diseases can affect the limbic system. Herpes simplex encephalitis has a predilection for the orbitofrontal and anterior temporal regions and thus selectively destroys much of the limbic system. Impulsivity, memory loss, and abnormalities of emotional behavior are frequently early manifestations of this infection. Limbic encephalitis may be a remote effect of cancer. In this condition, there is inflammation and injury to the amygdaloid nuclei, hippocampi, and cingulate gyri, as well as to other structures. Clinically, the picture is similar to that of herpes infection, with memory loss and abnormalities of emotional behavior, including depression, agitation, and anxiety (Corsellis et al., 1968). Rabies also has a predilection for limbic structures and may be associated with prominent emotional symptoms, including profound anxiety and agitation.

Seizures. Partial (focal) seizures with complex symptomatology (temporal lobe epilepsy, psychomotor epilepsy) are known to produce emotional symptoms. These symptoms may be seen with a seizure (ictal phenomena), immediately after a seizure (postictal phenomena), or between seizures (interictal behavior). We will discuss each of these separately.

Ictal phenomena. One of the strongest arguments supporting the notion that the limbic system is important in mediating emotional behavior is the observation that emotional change as a manifestation of a seizure discharge is highly correlated with foci in or near the limbic system, particularly with foci in the anteromedial temporal lobes.

Sexuality. Currier et al. (1971) described patients who had ictal behavior that resembled sexual intercourse. Undressing and exhibitionism have been described with temporal lobe seizures (Hooshmand & Brawley, 1969; Rodin, 1973). In general, however, ictal sexual behavior is not purposeful. Remillard et al. (1983) reported 12 women with temporal lobe epilepsy who had sexual arousal or orgasm as part of their seizures, and they reviewed 14 other cases. Most cases had right-sided foci, and most were women. Spencer et al. (1983) reported sexual automatisms in four patients with seizure foci in the orbitofrontal cortex. They proposed that sexual experiences were more likely to occur with temporal lobe foci, whereas sexual automatisms occurred with frontal foci.

Gelastic and Dacrystic Seizures. Gelastic epilepsy refers to seizures in which laughter is a prominent ictal event (Daly & Mulder, 1957). Sackeim et al. (1982) reviewed 91 reported cases of gelastic epilepsy and found that, of 59 cases with lateralized foci, 40 were left-sided. Gascon and Lombroso (1971) described ten patients with gelastic epilepsy; five had bilateral synchronous spike-and-wave abnormalities, and two of these had diencephalic pathology; the other five had right temporal lobe foci. Gascon and Lombroso thought they could differentiate two types of laughter. They thought that the diencephalic group appeared to have automatic laughter without affect and the temporal lobe group more affective components (including pleasurable auras). The diencephalic lesion most often associated with gelastic epilepsy is a hypothalamic hamartoma.

Crying as an ictal manifestation, termed *dacrystic epilepsy* (Offen et al., 1976), is much less common than laughing. Of the six cases reviewed by Offen et al., four probably had right-sided pathology, one had left-sided pathology, and in one the site of pathology was uncertain. Dacrystic epilepsy may also be associated with hypothalamic hamartomas (Kahane et al., 2003).

Aggression. Ictal aggression is rare. Ashford et al. (1980) documented nonpurposeful violent behavior as an ictal event. Although purposeful violence has been alleged to result from seizures themselves (Mark & Ervin, 1970; Pincus, 1980), careful analysis of larger groups of patients do not support this association

(Stevens & Hermann, 1981; Delgado-Escueta et al., 1981; Trieman & Delgado-Esqueta, 1983; Reuber & Mackay, 2008).

Fear and Anxiety. Fear is the affect most frequently associated with a temporal lobe seizure (Williams, 1956). Ictal fear may be found equally with right- and left-sided dysfunction (Williams, 1956; Strauss et al., 1982), although a preponderance of right-sided epileptic foci has also been reported (Guimond et al., 2008). A prolonged attack of fear has been associated with right-sided temporal lobe status (McLachlan & Blume, 1980). Although fear responses are usually associated with temporal lobe seizures, they may also be associated with seizures emanating from the cingulate gyrus (Daly, 1958). The amygdala appears to be the critical structure in the induction of the fear response (Gloor, 1972; Maletti et al., 2006), and volumetric MRI studies have associated ictal fear with amygdala atrophy (Cendes et al., 1994).

Depression and Euphoria. Williams (1956) describes patients who became very sad and others who had extreme feelings of well-being.

Postictal phenomena. Many patients are confused, restless, and combative after a seizure, especially after a temporal lobe seizure. Instances of aggression in this state are common but usually consist only of patients struggling with persons who are trying to restrain them. Depression may last for several days after a seizure.

Interictal phenomena. The postulate that seizures directly induce interictal behavioral changes has proved to be the most difficult of issues and has yet to be resolved.

Anxiety, Fear, and Depression. Currier et al. (1971) found that 44% of patients with temporal lobe epilepsy had psychiatric complications. The most common were anxiety and depression. Men with left-sided foci reported more fear than men with right-sided foci. Patients with left-sided foci reported more fear of social and sexual situations (Strauss et al., 1982). There is an increased risk of suicide in epileptics (Hawton et al., 1980). Flor-Henry (1969)

found a relationship between right temporal lobe seizure foci and affective disorders. McIntyre et al. (1976) and Bear and Fedio (1977) also showed that patients with right hemisphere foci are more likely to show emotional tendencies. However, according to some studies, patients with left-sided foci score higher on depression scales than do patients with right-sided foci (Robertson et al., 1987). Bear (1979) has suggested that a sensory–limbic hyperconnection may account for interictal behavioral aberrations. Hermann and Chhabria (1980) postulated that classical conditioning might mediate an overinvestment of affective significance. The unconditioned response is the emotion caused by the firing of a limbic focus. Environmental stimuli coincidentally paired with this firing result in the conditioned response of inappropriate emotional significance attributed to environmental stimuli. Recent studies have also shown a relationship of right temporal foci with depression; after seizure surgery, improvement in depression is correlated with seizure control (Witt, Hohlman, & Helmstaedter, 2008). Patients with temporal lobe epilepsy also have reduced ability to identify emotions in faces, particularly fear. This deficit is more pronounced in patients with bilateral and right temporal lobe foci than in patients with seizures emanating from the left temporal lobe (Miletti et al., 2009).

Sexuality. Hyposexuality has been associated with temporal lobe epilepsy (Gaustaut & Colomb, 1954). Taylor (1969) studied patients with temporal lobe seizures and found that 72% had a decreased sexual drive. Pritchard (1980) was able to confirm that reduced libido and impotence were associated with temporal lobe seizures. The side of the epileptic focus, drug therapy, and seizure control did not seem to be related to the hyposexuality. The location of the focus did, however, appear important. A seizure focus in the mesobasal area of the temporal lobe appears to be most often associated with decreased libido. However, increased libido has also been reported to be associated with seizures (Cogen et al., 1979).

The medial temporal lobe structures, including the amygdala, have a close anatomic and physiological relationship with the hypothalamus.

Pritchard (1980) found that endocrine changes could be demonstrated in patients with seizures, including eugonadotropic, hypogonadotropic, and hypergonadotropic hypogonadism. Herzog et al. (1982) also demonstrated endocrine changes and suggested that hypothalamic-pituitary control of gonadotropin secretion may be altered in patients with temporal lobe epilepsy. Further studies suggested a relationship between the laterality of discharge and the type of endocrine pathology (Herzog, 1993). Pritchard et al. (1981) found elevation of prolactin following complex partial seizures. Hyperprolactinemia may be associated with impotence in males. Taylor (1969) and Cogen et al. (1979) noted that temporal lobectomy may restore normal sexual function.

Aggressiveness. Interictal aggressiveness, like ictal aggressiveness, remains controversial and has many medicolegal implications. Taylor (1969) found that about one-third of patients with temporal lobe epilepsy were aggressive interictally. Williams (1969) reviewed the EEGs of aggressive criminals, many of whom had committed acts of violence. Abnormal EEGs were five times more common than in the general population. However, Stevens and Hermann (1981) note that this observation has not been validated by detailed controlled studies. Treiman (1991) notes that interictal violence tends to occur in young men of subnormal intelligence, with character disorders, a history of early and severe seizures, and associated neurological deficits. When patients with psychiatric disorders or subnormal intelligence are removed from a series, there is no evidence of increased violence.

Other Interictal Changes. Patients with temporal lobe epilepsy are said to have a dramatic, and possibly specific, disorder of personality (Blumer & Benson, 1975). Slater and Beard (1963) described "schizophreniform" psychosis in patients with temporal lobe epilepsy, but they described selected cases and could not comment on the incidence of this disorder in temporal lobe epileptics. Other studies (Currie et al., 1971) have failed to show a higher than expected incidence of psychosis in temporal lobe epileptics, but it can still be maintained

that less severe psychiatric abnormalities could have eluded these investigators. Studies that claim to show no difference in emotional makeup between temporal lobe and other epileptic patients (Guerrant et al., 1962; Stevens, 1966) have been reinterpreted (Blumer, 1975) to indicate that there is, in fact, a difference: those with temporal lobe epilepsy are more likely to have more serious forms of emotional disturbance. The "typical personality" of the temporal lobe epileptic patient has been described in roughly similar terms over many years (Blumer & Benson, 1975; Geschwind, 1975, 1977; Blumer, 1999; Devinsky & Schachter, 2009). These patients are said to have a deepening of emotions; they ascribe great significance to commonplace events. This can be manifested as a tendency to take a cosmic view; hyperreligiosity (or intensely professed atheism) is said to be common. Concern with minor details results in slowness of thought and circumstantiality, and can also be manifested by hypergraphia, a tendency of such patients to record in writing minute details of their lives (Waxman & Geschwind, 1974). In the extreme, psychosis, often with prominent paranoid qualities, can be seen (the schizophreniform psychosis noted above; but, unlike schizophrenics, these patients do not have a flat affect and tend to maintain interpersonal relationships. McIntyre et al. (1976) demonstrated that, whereas patients with left temporal lobe foci demonstrate a reflective conceptual approach, patients with right temporal lobe foci are more impulsive. Bear and Fedio (1977) designed a questionnaire specifically to detect personality features. They found that these personality changes are significantly more common among patients with temporal lobe epilepsy than among normal subjects. Patients with right hemisphere foci are more likely to show emotional tendencies and denial, and patients with left temporal lobe foci show ideational aberrations (paranoia, sense of personal destiny) and dyssocial behavior. Since a control population with seizure foci in other sites was not used, the specificity of these changes to limbic regions can still be questioned. Attempts to replicate Bear and Fedio's findings have failed to define a personality profile specific to temporal lobe epilepsy (Brandt et al., 1985;

Hermann & Riel, 1981; Mungas, 1982; Weiser, 1986). Several studies have suggested that patients with limbic temporal lobe foci are more likely to have abnormal personality traits than are patients with lateral temporal lobe foci (Nielsen & Kristensen, 1981; Hermann et al., 1982; Weiser, 1986). Much of this literature has been reviewed by Strauss (1989), Blumer (1999), and Devinsky and Najjar (1999).

BASAL GANGLIA DYSFUNCTION

Basal ganglia disorders are commonly thought to be primarily motor disorders; however, patients with basal ganglia disorders frequently have emotional, communicative and mood disorders.

PARKINSON DISEASE

Parkinson disease is a common neurodegenerative disorder involving loss of neurons in the substantia nigra pars compacta, dopamine depletion in the basal ganglia and the presence of Lewy bodies. Patients present with motor symptoms of tremor, akinesia, and rigidity. Although these motor symptoms are the hallmark features of the disease, cognitive and emotional changes are highly prevalent and can be some of the most disturbing, disabling, and complex aspects of Parkinson disease.

COMMUNICATIVE DEFECTS

Patients with Parkinson disease often demonstrate a paucity of spontaneous facial expressions, commonly known as the "masked face." Some, but not all neuropsychological studies have also reported that Parkinson disease patients have difficulties posing voluntary facial expressions as well (Borod, Welkowitz, Alpert, et al., 1990; Jacons, Shuren, Bowers, & Heilman, 1995; Smith et al., 1996). One real-world consequence of facial flattening relates to misinterpretation of how the Parkinson disease patient is actually feeling. This can range from misdiagnosis of depression to inaccurate impression formation by family members, spouses, and others. In fact, Pentland and colleagues (1987) found that health care providers

consistently rated Parkinson patients as more anxious, depressed, and suspicious than cardiac patients, even though the groups did not differ on objective indices of mood.

The mechanisms underlying the diminished expressivity in Parkinson patients are not clearly understood. Bowers and colleagues (2006) used computer digitizing methods and found that intentional facial expressions of Parkinson patients were slowed (bradykinetic) and involved less movement change (entropy) than healthy controls. These findings are consistent with the view that the basal ganglia play a role in modulating intentional facial movements. This may occur because of reduced efficiency and/or activation of face motor areas in the frontal cortical regions or because of movement based suppression secondary to dopaminergic reduction in frontostriatal pathways.

Some investigators have asked whether Parkinson patients are fully aware of the extent of their decreased ability to spontaneously portray emotional facial expressions. To address this question, Mikos et al. (2009) gave the Emotional Expressivity Questionnaire (EEQ) to 37 nondemented Parkinson disease patients and 21 healthy controls, along with their respective spouses The EEQ is a self-report measure of how demonstrative and expressive an individual is in overtly displaying and sharing emotions with others, including the use of facial expressions. Parkinson patients rated themselves as less facially expressive than did the control group and spousal ratings completely corresponded to those of the Parkinson patients. These findings suggest that nondemented PD patients demonstrate awareness of their deficits in emotional expressivity in line with that noted by family members. This observation adds to the growing literature that anosognosia is not a primary characteristic of nondemented patients with Parkinson disease.

In addition to masked faces, patients with Parkinson disease may have problems with discriminating emotional faces (Jacobs et al., 1995; Kan et al., 2002; Clark et al., 2008). However, Adolphs et al. (1998) and Pell and Leonard (2005) did not find that Parkinson patients had deficits in the ability to recognize facial expressions of emotion. Patients with Parkinson disease may also have impaired production and comprehension of emotional prosody (Blonder et al., 1989; Pell & Leonard, 2003).

EMOTIONAL EXPERIENCE

Parkinson (1938) noted that his patients were unhappy. Depression has subsequently been found to be a frequent part of the Parkinson disease complex and has been studied extensively over the years. Rates of depression in Parkinson disease vary and directly depend on whether strict clinical diagnostic criteria for depression are followed versus cut-scores on a depression scale are used (Slaughter, Slaughter, Nichols, Holmes, & Martens, 2001). A recent meta-analysis by Reijnders and colleagues (2009) reviewed 36 studies of depression in Parkinson disease and found the overall prevalence of major depressive disorder (MDD) to be 19% when strict diagnostic criteria from the *Diagnostic and Statistical Manual of Mental Disorders* (DSM-IV) were applied. This prevalence was much higher than the 2%–9% prevalence of MDD found in the general population. The prevalence of clinically significant depression in PD, whether or not there was a formal DSM diagnosis, was 35% (Reijnders et al., 2009). Depressive symptoms were a primary factor impacting quality of life (Phillips, 1999).

The basis for depression in Parkinson disease is unclear. The depression may be reactive or a part of the parkinsonian syndrome or both. Support for the hypothesis that it is not entirely reactive comes from the observation that the severity of motor impairment and depression symptoms correlate poorly. Patients who are more severely disabled are often less depressed (Robins, 1976), and in many patients, depression is noted prior to the onset of motor symptoms (Mindham, 1970; Mayeux et al., 1981). Patients with Parkinson disease may also have anxiety and panic associated with their depression. As might be expected from the poor correlation between depression and motor impairment, the depression in Parkinsonism responds poorly to the drugs that help the motor symptoms.

Many of the motor symptoms are primarily induced by deficits in the nigrostriatal dopaminergic system. Although L-dopa replacement therapy improves the motor symptoms, it may not reduce depression (Marsh & Markham, 1973; Mayeux et al., 1981). However, Maricle et al. (1995) reported patients who had elevation of mood with dopaminergic treatment. Another hypothesis is that depression in Parkinson disease is associated with defects in the serotonergic or noradrenergic systems secondary to cell loss in both the raphe nuclei and locus coeruleus. Currently, selective serotonin reuptake inhibitors (SSRIs) are the typical first-line choice for treatment of depression in Parkinson disease. A recent clinical trial of antidepressant treatment in 52 Parkinson disease patients reported that nortriptyline, a dual reuptake inhibitor of serotonin and norepinephrine, was more efficacious than either placebo or the SSRI paroxetine for remitting depressive symptoms (Menza et al., 2009).

Recently, attention has turned to the possibility that "apathy" may represent an integral aspect of Parkinson disease. As defined by Marin (1991), apathy refers to a primary lack of goal-directed behavior that can manifest in behavioral, cognitive, and affective domains. Although symptoms of apathy may overlap those of depression, apathy may also be its own syndrome and separable from depression (for review, see van Reekum et al., 2005). A key distinction between depression and apathy is that, with apathy, there is a lack of dysphoria that is symptomatic of depression. It has been argued that patients with pure apathy do not experience the sadness, helplessness, hopelessness, or suicidality that characterizes many patients with depression (Marin, 1991). Although apathy may accompany cognitive impairment and dementia in Parkinson disease, the lack of motivation in the apathy syndrome is viewed as primary and not explained by such impairments.

Emerging evidence indicates a high frequency of apathy in Parkinson disease, with estimates ranging from 38% to 51% across studies that have used validated apathy scales (Starkstein et al., 1992; Isella et al., 2002; Pluck & Brown, 2002; Kirsh-Darrow et al., 2006; Sockeel et al., 2006). A considerable portion of Parkinson disease patients also exhibit apathy in the absence of depression. In a series of 80 consecutive Parkinson disease patients, almost 30% were noted to have apathy alone, 4% had depression alone, and 22.5% exhibit both apathy and depression (Kirsch-Darrow et al, 2006). Thus, almost half the Parkinson disease patients in this study were identified as exhibiting apathy compared to 20% of patients in a control group of dystonia patients. Such findings raise questions as to whether apathy may be a core feature of Parkinson disease. Apathy appears to occur in all stages of the Parkinson disease, including in early drug-naive patients who have been recently diagnosed (Pedersen, Alves, et al., 2009). Zahodne et al. (2009) assessed 139 idiopathic Parkinson patients at two time points appropriately 24 months apart using standard apathy and depression scales. Apathy scores significantly worsened over time in these moderately affected patients, whereas depression scores remained stable. Other studies have focused on apathy following deep brain stimulation surgery for Parkinson disease (for review, see Kirsch-Darrow, Mikos, & Bowers, 2008). Other information about the longitudinal course of apathy is relatively unknown.

The pathophysiology of apathy is thought to involve a functional disturbance of the mesial frontal-anterior cingulate regions (Craig et al., 1996; Benoit et al., 2002; Sarazin et al., 2003; Lejeune, Drapier, Bourguignon, et al., 2009). This region has reciprocal connections with limbic, frontal cortices, and basal ganglia structures. Although dopaminergic reward systems have been implicated in the pathogenesis of apathy in PD, there is little evidence that apathy is actually improved by levodopa.

HUNTINGTON DISEASE

Communicative Deficits

Huntington disease, or Huntington's chorea, is characterized by involuntary movements and intellectual decline. Patients with Huntington disease may have impaired comprehension of emotional prosody (Speedie et al., 1990) and emotional faces (Jacobs et al., 1995; Sprengelmeyer et al., 1996). Several investigators have shown selective impairment in the recognition of disgust facial expressions among patients with Huntington disease (Sprengelmeyer et al., 1996;

Hennenlotter et al. 2004), but Johnson et al. (2007) found that recognition of all negative emotions declines early in the disease process. Evidence suggests that dysfunction in the insula and basal ganglia underlie these deficits.

EMOTIONAL EXPERIENCE

Huntington (1872) noted that many patients with this disease have severe emotional disorders and that there is a tendency toward suicide. Almost every patient who develops Huntington disease has emotional or psychiatric signs and symptoms (Mayeux, 1983). Although it is possible that some of the emotional signs and symptoms are a reaction to the disease, in many cases, they precede motor and cognitive dysfunction (Heathfield, 1967). The emotional changes are variable and include mania and depression (Folstein et al., 1979), apathy, aggressiveness, irritability, promiscuity, and irresponsibility. Different emotional symptoms may be manifested at different times during the course of the disease. In general, however, the apathy is usually seen later in the course, when there are signs of intellectual deterioration. The pathophysiology of the emotional disorders associated with Huntington disease is unclear. In general, patients have cell loss in the neostriatum and especially in the caudate. There is also cortical cell loss. However, other areas of the brain may also show degenerative changes. Many of the signs displayed by patients with Huntington disease are similar to those seen with frontal lobe dysfunction (e.g., apathy), and frontal lobe atrophy may be responsible for these signs (see Chapter 17). However, profound neurochemical changes are associated with Huntington disease. For example, γ-aminobutyric acid and acetylcholine levels are reduced in the basal ganglia. Mayberg et al. (1992) studied patients with Huntington disease using functional imaging. They found that patients with depression, when compared to patients who were not depressed, had reduced activation of the inferior and orbitofrontal portions of the frontal cortex. The frontal cortex modulates the activity of the locus ceruleus, the source of norepinephrine. Studies suggest that reduction of norepinephrine may be important in depression.

PSEUDOBULBAR PALSY

Wilson (1924) postulated a pontobulbar area responsible for emotional facial expression. Lesions that interrupt the corticobulbar motor pathways bilaterally release reflex mechanisms for facial expression from cortical control. This was called *pseudobulbar palsy*, to distinguish it from motor deficits (palsy) resulting from lower motor neuron (bulbar) dysfunction, a common occurrence when polio was prevalent. The syndrome consists of involuntary laughing or crying (or both). As with many forms of release phenomena, this excess of emotional expression is stereotypic, lacking variation in quality or modulation of intensity of expression. It can be triggered by a wide variety of stimuli but cannot be initiated or stopped voluntarily. Examination usually shows weakness of voluntary facial movements and increase in the facial and jaw stretch reflexes. The location of the centers for the control of facial expression is not known, and although Wilson postulated it to be in the lower brainstem, Poeck (1969) has postulated centers in the thalamus and hypothalamus. Although bilateral lesions are usually responsible, the syndrome has been described with unilateral lesions on either side (Bruyn & Gaithier, 1969).

Patients with pseudobulbar palsy usually consistently either laugh or cry (Schiffer & Pope, 2005). Sackeim et al. (1982) noted that, although most patients with pseudobulbar crying or laughing have bilateral lesions, the larger lesion is usually in the right hemisphere when there is laughter and in the left when there is crying. Patients with this syndrome report feeling normal emotions, despite the abnormality of expression. Commonly, their family and physicians speak of them as being emotionally labile, implying that they no longer have appropriate internal emotional feeling. It is important to make the distinction between true emotional lability (as may be seen with bilateral frontal lobe disturbance) and pseudobulbar lability of emotional expression (with normal inner emotions).

In regard to treatment of pseudobulbar palsy, prior studies have suggested that antidepressants, such as the tricyclic antidepressants as well as the serotonin uptake inhibitors, can reduce the production of pseudobulbar facial expressions. In addition, a combination of dextromethorphan and quinidine also appears to be effective (Brooks et al., 2004).

REFERENCES

Adolphs, R., Tranel, D., Damasio, H., & Damasio, A. (1994). Impaired recognition of emotion in facial expressions following bilateral damage to the human amygdala. *Nature*, 15, 669–672.

Adolphs, R., Damasio, H., & Tranel, D. (2002). Neural systems for recognition of emotional prosody: a 3-D lesion study. *Emotion*, 2, 23–51.

Adolphs, R. (2008). Fear, faces, and the human amygdala. *Current Opinion in Neurobiology*, 18, 166–172.

Adolphs, R., Damasio, H., Tranel, D., & Damasio, A. R. (1996). Cortical systems for the recognition of emotion in facial expressions. *Journal of Neuroscience*, 16, 7678–7687.

Adolphs, R., Schul, R., & Tranel, D. (1998). Intact recognition of facial emotion in Parkinson's disease. *Neuropsychology*, 12, 253–258.

Adolphs, R., Damasio, H., Tranel, D., Cooper, G., & Damasio, A. R. (2000). A role for somatosensory cortices in the visual recognition of emotion as revealed by three-dimensional lesion mapping. *Journal of Neuroscience*, 20, 2683–2690.

Adelmann, P. K., & Zajonc, R. B. (1989). Facial efference and the experience of emotion. *Annual Review of Psychology*, 40, 249–280.

Ahern, G., Schumer, D., Kleefield, J., Blume, H., Cosgrove, G., Weintraub, S., & Mesalum, M. (1991). Right hemisphere advantage in evaluating emotional facial expressions. *Cortex*, 27, 193–202.

Akert, K., Greusen, R. A., Woosley, C. N., & Meyer, D. R. (1961). Kluver-Bucy syndrome in monkeys with neocortical ablations of temporal lobe. *Brain*, 84, 480–498.

Alexander, G. E., DeLong, M. R., & Strick, P. L. (1986). Parallel organization of functionally segregated circuits linking basal ganglia and cortex. *Annual Review of Neuroscience*, 9, 357–381.

Ashford, J. W., Aabro, E., Gulmann, N., Hjelmsted, A., & Pedersen, H. E. (1980). Antidepressive treatment in Parkinson's disease. *Acta Neurologica Scandinavica*, 62, 210–219.

Ashford, J. W., Schulz, C., & Walsh, G. O. (1980). Violent automatism in a partial complex seizure. Report of a case. *Archives of Neurology*, 37, 120–122.

Ax, A. F. (1953). The physiological differentiation between fear and anger in humans. *Psychosomatic Medicine*, 15, 433–442.

Babinski, J. (1914). Contribution; aga l'etude des troubles mentaux dans l'hemisplegie organique cerebrale (anosognosie). *Revue Neurologique, 27,* 845–848.

Bard, P. (1934). Emotion. I: The neuro-humoral basis of emotional reactions. In C. Murchison (Ed.), *Handbook of general experimental psychology.* Worcester, MA: Clark University Press.

Baylis, G., Rolls, E., & Leonard, C. (1985). Selectivity between faces in the responses of a population of neurons in the superior temporal sulcus of the monkey. *Brain Research, 342,* 91–102.

Bear, D. M. (1979). Temporal lobe, epilepsy: a syndrome of sensory-limbic hyperconnection. *Cortex, 15,* 357–384.

Bear, D. M., & Fedio, P. (1977). Quantitative analysis of interictal behavior in temporal lobe epilepsy. *Archives of Neurology, 34,* 454–467.

Behrens, S. J. (1989). Characterizing sentence intonation in a right hemisphere-damaged population. *Brain and Language, 36*(2), 181–200.

Bellugi, U., Corina, D., Normal, F., Klima, E., & Reilly, J. (1988). *Differential specialization for linguistic facial expressions in left and right lesioned deaf singers.* Paper presented at the 27th annual meeting of the Academy of Aphasia, Santa Fe, NM.

Bench, C. J., Friston, K. J., Brown, R. G., Scott, L. C., Frackowiak, R. S., & Dolan, R. J. (1992). The anatomy of melancholia—focal abnormalities of cerebral blood flow in major depression. *Psychological Medicine, 22,* 607–615.

Benoit, M., Koulibaly, P. M., Darcout, J., Pringuey, D. J., & Robert, P. H. (2002). Brain perfusion in Alzheimer's disease with and without apathy: A SPECT study with statistical parametric mapping analysis. *Psychiatry Research, 114,* 103–111.

Benowitz, L., Bear, D., Mesulam, M., Rosenthal, R., Zaidel, E., & Sperry, W. (1983). Nonverbal sensitivity following lateralized cerebral injury. *Cortex, 19,* 5–12.

Benson, D. F. (1979). Psychiatric aspects of aphasia. In D. F. Benson (Ed.), *Aphasia, alexia, & agraphia.* New York: Churchill Livingstone.

Benton, A. L., & Van Allen, M. W. (1968). Impairment in facial recognition in patients with cerebral disease. *Cortex, 4,* 344–358.

Blonder, L. X., Bowers, D., & Heilman, K. M. (1991a). The role of the right hemisphere in emotional communication. *Brain, 114,* 1115–1127.

Blonder, L., Bowers, D., & Heilman, K. (1991b). Logical inferences following right hemisphere damage. [Abstract]. *Journal of Clinical and Experimental Neuropsychology, 13,* 39.

Blonder, L. X., Burns, A., Bowers, D., Moore, R. W., & Heilman, K. M. Right hemisphere facial expressivity during natural conversation. *Brain and Cognition, 21*(1), 44–56.

Blonder, L. X., Gur, R. E., & Gur, R. C. (1989). The effects of right and left hemiparkinsonism on prosody. *Brain and Language, 36,* 193–207.

Blonder, L. X., Pickering, J. E., Heath, R. L., Smith, C. D., & Butler, S. M. (1995). Prosodic characteristics of speech pre- and post-right hemisphere stroke. *Brain and Language, 51*(2), 318–335.

Blonder, L. X, Heilman, K. M., Ketterson, T., Rosenbek, J., Crosson, B., Raymer, S., et al. (2005). Affective facial and lexical expression in aprosodic versus aphasic stroke patients. *Journal of the International Neuropsychological Society, 11*(6), 677–685.

Bloom, R., Borod, J. C., Obler, L., & Gerstman, L. (1992). Impact of emotional content on discourse production in patients with unilateral brain damage. *Brain and Language, 42,* 153–164.

Blumer, D. (1975). Temporal lobe epilepsy and its psychiatric significance. In D. F. Benson, & D. Blumer (Eds.), *Psychiatric aspects of neurological disease.* New York: Grune and Stratton.

Blumer, D. (1999). Evidence supporting the temporal lobe epilepsy personality syndrome. *Neurology, 53*(Suppl 2), S9–S12.

Blumer, D., & Benson, D. F. (1975). Personality changes with frontal and temporal lobe lesions. In D. F. Benson, & D. Blumer (Eds.), *Psychiatric aspects of neurological disease.* New York: Grune & Stratton.

Blumer, D., & Walker, A. E. (1975). The neural basis of sexual behavior. In D. F. Benson, & D. Blumer (Eds.), *Psychiatric aspects of neurological disease.* New York: Grune and Stratton.

Boller, F., Cole, M., Vtunski, P., Patterson, M., & Kim, Y. (1979). Paralinguistic aspects of auditory comprehension in aphasia. *Brain and Language, 7,* 164–174.

Borod, J. C., Koff, E., Lorch, M. P., & Nicholas, M. (1985). Channels of emotional communication in patients with unilateral brain damage. *Archives of Neurology, 42,* 345–348.

Borod, J., & Koff, E. (1990). Lateralization for facial emotion behavior: a methodological perspective. *International Journal of Psychology, 25,* 157–177.

Borod, J. C., Bloom, R. L., Brickman, A. M., Nakhutina, L., & Curko, E. A. (2002). Emotional processing deficits in individuals with unilateral brain damage. *Applied Neuropsychology, 9,* 23–36.

Borod, J., Koff, E., Perlman-Lorch, J., & Nicholas, M. (1986). The expression and perception of facial emotions in brain damaged patients. *Neuropsychologia, 24,* 169–180.

Borod, J., Koff, E., Perlman-Lorch, M., Nicholas, M., & Welkowitz, J. (1988). Emotional and nonemotional facial behavior in patients with unilateral brain damage. *Journal of Neurology, Neurosurgery, and Psychiatry, 51,* 826–832.

Borod, J.C., Rorie, K. D., Haywood, C. S., Andelman, F., Obler, L. K., Welkowitz, J., Bloom, R. L., & Tweedy, J. R. (1996). Hemispheric specialization for discourse reports of emotional experiences: relationships to demographic, neurological, and perceptual variables. *Neuropsychologia. 34,* 351–359.

Borod, J., Welkowitz, J., Alpert, M., Brozgold, A., Martin, C., Peselow, E., & Diller, L. (1990). Parameters of emotional processing in neuropsychiatric disorders: Conceptual issues and a battery of tests. *Journal of Communicative Disorders, 23,* 247–271.

Bowers, D., & Heilman, K. M. (1984). Dissociation of affective and nonaffective faces: A case study. *Journal of Clinical Neuropsychology, 6,* 367–379.

Bowers, D., Bauer, R. M., Coslett, H. B., & Heilman, K. M. (1985). Processing of faces by patients with unilateral hemispheric lesions. I. Dissociation between judgments of facial affect and facial identity. *Brain and Cognition, 4,* 258–272.

Bowers, D., Blonder, L. X., Feinberg, T., & Heilman, K. M. (1991). Differential impact of right and left hemisphere lesions on facial emotion and object imagery. *Brain. 114,* 2593–2609.

Bowers, D., Coslett, H. B., Bauer, R. M., Speedie, L. J., & Heilman, K. M. (1987). Comprehension of emotional prosody following unilateral hemispheric lesions: processing defect vs. distraction defect. *Neuropsychologia, 25,* 317–328.

Bowers, D., Miller, K., Bosch, W., Gokcay, D., Springer, U., & Okun, M. S. (2006). Faces of emotion in Parkinson's disease: Digitizing the moving face during voluntary expressions. *Journal of International Neuropsychological Society, 12,* 1276–1273.

Brady, J. V., & Nauta, W. J. (1955). Subcortical mechanisms in control of behavior. *Journal of Comparative and Physiological Psychology, 48,* 412–420.

Brandt, J., Seidman, L. J., & Kohl, D. (1985). Personality characteristics of epileptic patients: a controlled study of generalized and temporal lobe cases. *Journal of Clinical and Experimental Neuropsychology, 7,* 25–38.

Breiter, H. C., Etcoff, N. L., Whalen, P. J., Kennedy, W. A., Rauch, S. L., Buckner, R. L., Strauss, M. M., Hyman, S. E., & Rosen, B. R. (1996). Response and habituation of the human amygdala during visual processing of facial expression. *Neuron 17,* 875–887.

Broca, P. (1878). Anatomie comparee des enconvolutions cerebrales: Le grand lobe limbique et al scissure limbique dans la seire des mammiferes. *Revue Anthropologique, 1,* 385–498.

Brooks, B. R., Thisted, R. A., Appel, S. H., Bradley, W. G., Olney, R. K., Berg, J. E., et al. (2004). Treatment of pseudobulbar affect in ALS with dextromethorphan/quinidine: A randomized trial. *Neurology, 63,* 1364–1370.

Brownell, H., Michel, D., Powelson, J., & Gardner, H. (1983). Surprise but not coherence: sensitivity to verbal humor in right hemisphere patients. *Brain and Language, 18,* 20–27.

Brownell, H., Potter, H., & Birhle, A. (1986). Inferences deficits in right brain damaged patients. *Brain and Language, 27,* 310–321.

Bruyn, G. W., & Gaither, J. C. (1969). The opercular syndrome. In P. J. Vincken, & G. W. Bruyn (Eds.), *Handbook of clinical neurology,* Vol. 1. Amsterdam: North-Holland.

Bryson, S., McLaren, J., Wadden, N., & Maclean, M. (1991). Differential asymmetries for positive and negative emotions: hemisphere or stimulus effects. *Cortex, 27,* 359–365.

Buck, R., & Duffy, R. J. (1980). Nonverbal communication of affect in brain damaged patients. *Cortex, 16,* 351–362.

Buck, R. (1990). Using FACS versus communication scores to measure spontaneous facial expression of emotion in brain damaged patients. *Cortex, 26,* 275–280.

Caltagirone, C., Ekman, P., Friesen, W., Gainotti, G., Mammucari, A., Pizzamiglio, L., & Zoccolatti, P. (1989). Posed emotional facial expressions in brain damaged patients. *Cortex, 25,* 653–663.

Campbell, R. (1978). Asymmetries in interpreting and expressing a posed facial expression. *Cortex, 14,* 327–342.

Cannon, W. B. (1927). The James-Lange theory of emotion: a critical examination and an alternative theory. *American Journal of Psychology, 39,* 106–124.

Celesia, G. G., & Wanamaker, W. M. (1972). Psychiatric disturbances in Parkinson's disease. *Diseases of the Nervous System, 33,* 577–583.

Cendes, F., Andermann, F., Gloor, P., Gambardella, A., Lopes-Cendes, I., Watson, C., et al. (1994). Relationship between atrophy of the amygdala and ictal fear in temporal lobe epilepsy. *Brain, 117,* 739–746.

Charbonneau, S., Scherzer, B. P., Aspirot, D., & Cohen, H. (2003). Perception and production of facial and prosodic emotions by chronic CVA patients. *Neuropsychologia, 41,* 605–613.

Cheang, H. S., & Pell, M. D. (2006). A study of humour and communicative intention following right hemisphere stroke. *Clinical Linguistics and Phonetics, 20*(6), 447–462.

Cicone, M., Waper, W., & Gardner, H. (1980). Sensitivity to emotional expressions and situations in organic patients. *Cortex, 16,* 145–158.

Cimino, C. R., Verfaellie, M., Bowers, D., & Heilman, K. M. (1991). Autobiographical memory with influence of right hemisphere damage on emotionality and specificity. *Brain and Cognition, 15,* 106–118.

Clark, U. S., Neargarder, S., Cronin-Golumb. A. (2008). Specific impairments in the recognition of emotional facial expressions in Parkinson's disease. *Neuropsychologia, 46* (9), 2300–2309.

Cogen, P. H., Antunes, J. L., & Correll, J. W. (1979). Reproductive function in temporal lobe epilepsy: the effect of temporal lobe lobectomy. *Surgical Neurology, 12,* 243–246.

Corsellis, J. A. N., Goldberg, G. J., & Norton, A. R. (1968). Limbic encephalitis and its association with carcinoma. *Brain, 91,* 481–496.

Coslett, H. B., Brasher, H. R., & Heilman, K. M. (1984). Pure word deafness after bilateral primary auditory cortex infarcts. *Neurology, 34,* 347–352.

Craig, A. H., Cummings, J. L., Fairbanks L., Itti, L., Miller, B. L., Li, J., & Mena, I. (1996). Cerebral blood flow correlates of apathy in Alzheimer's disease. *Archives of Neurology, 53,* 1116–1120.

Critchley, M. (1953). The parietal lobes. London: E. Arnold.

Crucian, G., Hughes, J., Barrett, A., Williamson, D., Bauer, R., Bowers, D., & Heilman, K. (2000). Emotional and physiological responses to false feedback. *Cortex, 36*(5), 623–647.

Currie, S., Heathfield, K. W. G., Henson, R. A., & Scott, D. F. (1971). Clinical course and prognosis of temporal lobe epilepsy: a survey of 666 patients. *Brain, 94,* 173–190.

Cummings, J. L. (1992). Depression and Parkinson's disease: A review. *American Journal of Psychiatry, 149,* 443–454.

Currier, R. D., Little, S. C., Suess, J. F., & Andy, O. J. (1971). Sexual seizures. *Archives of Neurology, 25,* 260–264.

Daly, D. (1958). Ictal affect. *American Journal of Psychiatry, 115,* 97–108.

Daly, D. D., & Mulder, D. W. (1957). Gelastic epilepsy. *Neurology, 7,* 189–192.

Davidson, R. J., Horowitz, M. E., Schwartz, G. E., & Goodman, D. M. (1981). Lateral differences in the latency between finger tapping and heart beat. *Psychophysiology, 18,* 36–41.

Davidson, R. J., Schwartz, G. E., Saron, C., Bennett, J., & Goldman, D. J. (1979). Frontal versus parietal EEG asymmetry during positive and negative affect. *Psychophysiology, 16,* 202–203.

DeKosky, S., Heilman, K. M., Bowers, D., & Valenstein, E. (1980). Recognition and discrimination of emotional faces and pictures. *Brain and Language, 9,* 206–214.

Delgade-Escueta, A. V., Mattson, R. H., King, L., Goldensohn, E. S., Spiegel, H., Madsen, J., et al. (1981). The nature of aggression during epileptic seizures. *New England Journal of Medicine, 305,* 711–716.

Denny-Brown, D., Meyer, J. S., & Horenstein, S. (1952). The significance of perceptual rivalry resulting from parietal lesions. *Brain, 75,* 434–471.

Darwin, C. (1872). *The expression of emotion in man and animals.* London: John Murray.

Devinsky, O., Najjar, S. (1999). Evidence against the existence of a temporal lobe epilepsy personality syndrome. *Neurology, 53*(Suppl 2), S13–S25.

Devinsky, J., & Schachter, S. (2009). Norman Geschwind's contribution to the understanding of behavioral changes in temporal lobe epilepsy: The February 1974 lecture. *Epilepsy & Behavior, 15,* 417–424.

DiGuisto, E. L., & King, M. G. (1972). Chemical sympathectomy and avoidance learning. *Journal of Comparative and Physiological Psychology, 81,* 491–500.

Duda, P., & Brown, J. (1984). Lateral asymmetry of positive and negative emotions. *Cortex, 20,* 253–261.

Ekman, P., Sorenson, E. R., & Friesen, W. V. (1969). Pancultural elements in facial displays of emotions. *Science, 164,* 86–88.

Ekman, P., & Friesen, W. V. (1978). Facial action coding system. Palo Alto, CA: Consulting Psychologists Press.

Etcoff, N. (1984). Perceptual and conceptual organization of facial emotions. *Brain Cognition, 3,* 385–412.

Flor-Henry, P. (1969). Psychosis and temporal lobe epilepsy: A controlled investigation. *Epilepsia, 10,* 363–395.

Folstein, S. E., Folstein, M. F., & McHugh, P. R. (1979). Psychiatric syndromes in Huntington's disease. *Advances in Neurology, 23,* 281–289.

Fox, N. A., & Davidson, R. J. (1984). Hemispheric substrates for affect: a developmental model. In N. A. Fox, & R. J. Davidson (Eds.), *The psychobiology of affective development*. Hillsdale, N.J. : Erlbaum.

Fried, I., Mateer, C., Ojemann, G., Wohns, R., & Fedio, P. (1982). Organization of visuospatial functions in human cortex. *Brain, 105*, 349–371.

Frijda, N. H. (1987). Emotion, cognitive structure and action tendency. *Cognition and Emotion 1*, 115–143.

Gainotti, G. (1972). Emotional behavior and hemispheric side of lesion. *Cortex, 8*, 41–55.

Gardner, H., Ling, P. K., Flam, I., & Silverman, J. (1975). Comprehension and appreciation of humorous material following brain damage. *Brain, 98*, 399–412.

Gascon, G. G., & Lombroso, C. T. (1971). Epileptic (gelastic) laughter. *Epilepsia, 12*, 63–76.

Gasparrini, W. G., Spatz, P., Heilman, K. M., & Coolidge, F. L. (1978). Hemispheric asymmetries of affective processing as determined by the Minnesota multiphasic personality inventory. *Journal of Neurology, Neurosurgery, and Psychiatry, 41*, 470–473.

Gaustaut, H., & Colomb, H. (1954). Etude du comportment sexuel chez les ipieptiques psychomoteurs. *Annales Médico-psychologiques (Paris), 112*, 659–696.

Geschwind, N. (1975). The clinical setting of aggression in temporal lobe epilepsy. In W. S. Fields, & W. H. Sweets (Eds.), *The neurobiology of violence*. St. Louis: Warren H. Green.

Geschwind, N. (1977). Behavioral changes in temporal lobe epilepsy. *Archives of Neurology, 34*, 453.

Gloor, P. (1972). Temporal lobe epilepsy. In B. Eleftheriou (Ed.), *Advances in behavioral biology*, Vol. 2. (pp. 423–427). New York: Plenum.

Goldberg, M. E., & Bushnell, B. C. (1981). Behavioral enhancement of visual responses in monkey cerebral cortex: II. Modulation in frontal eye fields specifically to related saccades. *Journal of Neurophysiology, 46*, 773–787.

Goldstein, K. (1948). Language and language disturbances. New York: Grune and Stratton.

Graves, R., Landis, T., & Goodglass, H. (1981). Laterality and sex differences for visual recognition of emotional and nonemotional words. *Neuropsychologia, 19*, 95–102.

Greenwald, M. K., Cook, E. W., & Lang, P. J. (1989). Affective judgement and psychophysiological response: Dimension co-variation in the evaluation of pictorial stimuli. *Journal of Psychophysiology, 3*, 51–64.

Guerrant, J., Anderson, W. W., Fischer, A., Weinstein, M. R., Janos, R. M., & Deskins, A.

(1962). *Personality in epilepsy*. Springfield, IL: Charles C. Thomas.

Guimond, A., Braun, C. M., Bélanger, E., & Rouleau, I. (2008). Ictal fear depends on the cerebral laterality of the epileptic activity. *Epileptic Disorders, 10*, 101–112.

Haggard, M. P., & Parkinson, A. M. (1971). Stimulus and task factors as determinants of ear advantages. *Quarterly Journal of Experimental Psychology, 23*, 168–177.

Hantas, M., Katkin, E. S., & Blasovich, J. (1982). Relationship between heartbeat discrimination and subjective experience of affective state. *Psychophysiology, 19*, 563.

Hantas, M., Katkin, E. S., & Reed, S. D. (1984). Heartbeat discrimination training and cerebral lateralization. *Psychophysiology, 21*, 274–278.

Harciarek, M., Heilman, K. M., & Jodzio, K. (2006). Defective comprehension of emotional faces and prosody as a result of right hemisphere stroke: Modality versus emotion-type specificity. *Journal of the International Neuropsychology Society, 12*(6), 774–781.

Harciarek, M., Heilman, K. M. (2008). The contribution of anterior and posterior regions of the right hemisphere to the recognition of emotional faces. *Journal of Clinical and Experimental Neuropsychology, 9*, 1–9.

Hawton, K., Fagg, J., & Marsack, P. (1980). Association between epilepsy and attempted suicide. *Journal of Neurology, Neurosurgery, and Psychiatry, 43*, 168–170.

Heathfield, K. W. G. (1967). Huntington's chorea. *Brain, 90*, 203–232.

Hecaen, H., Ajuriagurra, J., & de Massonet, J. (1951). Les troubles visuoconstuctifs par lesion parieto-occipitale droit. *Encephale, 40*, 122–179.

Heilman, K. M. (1997). The neurobiology of emotional experience. In S. Salloway, P. Malloy, & J.L. Cummings (Eds.), *The neuropsychiatry of limbic and subcortical disorders*. Washington: American Psychiatric Press, Inc.

Heilman, K. M. (1979). Neglect and related syndromes. In K. M. Heilman, & E. Valenstein (Eds.), Clinical neuropsychology. New York: Oxford University Press.

Heilman, K. M., Bowers, D., Rasbury, W., & Ray, R. (1977). Ear asymmetries on a selective attention task. *Brain and Language, 4*, 390–395.

Heilman, K.M., Leon, S.A., & Rosenbek, J.C. (2004). Affective aprosodia from a middle frontal stroke. Brain and Language, 89, 411–416.

Heilman, K. M., Schwartz, H., & Watson, R. T. (1978). Hypoarousal in patients with the neglect syndrome and emotional indifference. *Neurology*, 28, 229–232.

Heilman, K. M., Bowers, D., Speedie, L., & Coslett, B. (1984). Comprehension of affective and nonaffective speech. *Neurology*, 34, 917–921.

Heilman, K. M., Scholes, R., & Watson, R. T. (1975). Auditory affective agnosia: Disturbed comprehension of affective speech. *Journal of Neurology, Neurosurgery, and Psychiatry*, 38, 69–72.

Heimer, L., & Van Hoesen, G. W. (2006). The limbic lobe and its output channels: Implications for emotional functions and adaptive behavior. *Neuroscience and Biobehavioral Reviews*, 30, 126–147.

Heller, W. (1990). The neuropsychology of emotion: Developmental and complications for psychopathology. In N. L. Stein, B. Leventhal, & T. Trebasso (Eds.), Psychological and biological approaches to emotion. Hillsdale, NJ: Lawrence Erlbaum.

Heller, W., & Levy, J. (1981). Perception and expression of emotion in right handers and left handers. *Neuropsychologia*, 19, 263–272.

Hennenlotter, A., Schroeder, U., Erhard, P., Haslinger, B., Stahl, R., Weindl, A., et al. Neural correlates associated with impaired disgust processing in pre-symptomatic Huntington's disease. *Brain*, 127, 1446–1453.

Hermann, B. P., & Chhabria, S. (1980). Interictal psychopathology in patients with ictal fear: Examples of sensory-limbic hyperconnection? *Archives of Neurology*, 37, 667–668.

Hermann, B. P., Dikmen, S., & Wilensky, A. (1982). Increased psychopathology associated with multiple seizure types: Fact or artifact? *Epilepsia*, 23, 587–596.

Hermann, B. P., & Riel, P. (1981). Interictal personality and behavioral traits in temporal lobe and generalized epilepsy. *Cortex*, 17, 125–128.

Herzog, A. G. (1993). A relationship between particular reproductive endocrine disorders and the laterality of epileptiform discharges in women with epilepsy. *Neurology*, 43, 1907–1910.

Herzog, A. G., Russell, V., Vaitukatis, J. L., & Geschwind, N. (1982). Neuroendocrine dysfunction in temporal lobe epilepsy. *Archives of Neurology*, 39, 133–135.

Hohmann, G. (1966). Some effects of spinal cord lesions on experimental emotional feelings. *Psychophysiology*, 3, 143–156.

Hooshmand, H., & Brawley, B. W. (1969). Temporal lobe seizures and exhibitionism. *Neurology*, 19, 119–124.

House, A., Dennis, M., Warlow, C., Hawton, K., & Molyneux, A. (1990). Mood disorders after stroke and their relation to lesion location. *Brain*, 113, 1113–1129.

Howes, D., & Boller, F. (1975). Evidence for focal impairment from lesions of the right hemisphere. *Brain*, 98, 317–332.

Hughlings Jackson, J. (1932). *Selected writings of John Hughlings Jackson*. (J. Taylor, Ed.). London: Hodder and Stoughton.

Huntington, G. W. (1872). On chorea. *Medical Surgical Reports*, 26, 317–321.

Isella, V., Melzi, P., Grimaldi, M., et al. (2002). Clinical, neuropsychological, and morphometric correlates of apathy in Parkinson's disease. *Movement Disorders*, 17, 366–371.

Iwata, J., LeDoux, J. E., Meeley, M. P., Arneric, S., & Reis, D. J. (1986). Intrinsic neurons in the amygdaloid field projected to by the medial geniculate body mediate emotional responses conditioned to acoustic stimuli. *Brain Research*, 383, 195–214.

Izard, C. E. (1977). *Human emotions*. New York: Plenum Press.

James, W. (1950). *The principles of psychology*, Vol. 2. New York: Dover Publications. (Original work published 1890).

Jacobs, D., Shuren, J., Bowers, D., & Heilman, K. (1995). Emotional facial imagery, perception, and expression in Parkinson's disease. *Neurology*, 45, 1696–1702.

Johnson, S.A., Stout, J. C., Solomon, A. C., Langbehn, D. R., Aylward, E. H., Cruce, C. B., et al. (2007). Beyond disgust: Impaired recognition of negative emotions prior to diagnosis in Huntington's disease. *Brain*, 130(7), 1732–1744.

Kahane, P., Ryvlin, P., Hoffmann, D., Minotti, L., & Benabid, A.L. (2003). From hypothalamic hamartoma to cortex: What can be learnt from depth recordings and stimulation? *Epileptic Disorders*, 5, 205–217.

Kan, Y., Kawamura, M., Hasegawa, Y., Mochizuki, S., & Nakamura, K. (2002). Recognition of emotion from facial, prosodic and written verbal stimuli in Parkinson's disease. *Cortex*, 38, 623–630.

Katkin, E. S., Morrell, M. A., Goldband, S., Bernstein, G. L., & Wise, J. A. (1982). Individual differences in heartbeat discrimination. *Psychophysiology*, 19, 160–166.

Keillor, J. M., Barrett, A. M., Crucian, G. P., Kortenkamp, S., Heilman, K. M. (2002). Emotional experience and perception in the absence of facial feedback. *Journal of the International Neuropsychology Society*, 8(1), 130–135.

Kennedy, D. P., Glascher, J., Tyszka, J. M., Adolphs, R. (2009). Personal space regulation by the human amygdala. *Nature Neuroscience*, 12, 1226–1227.

Kent, J., Borod, J. C., Koff, E., Welkowitz, J., & Alpert, M. (1988). Posed facial emotional expression in brain-damaged patients. *International Journal of Neuroscience*, *43*, 81–87.

Kent, R. D., & Rosenbek, J. C. (1982). Prosodic disturbance and neurologic lesion. *Brain and Language*, *15*(2), 259–291.

Kimura, D. (1967). Functional asymmetry of the brain in dichotic listening. *Cortex*, *3*, 163–178.

Kirsch-Darrow, L., Fernandez, H. H., Marsiske, M., Okun, M. S., & Bowers, D. (2006). Dissociating apathy and depression in Parkinson disease. *Neurology*, *67*, 33–38.

Kirsch-Darrow, L., Mikos, A., & Bowers, D. (2008). Does deep brain stimulation induce apathy in Parkinson's disease? *Frontiers in Bioscience*, *13*, 5316–5322.

Klüver, H., & Bucy, P. C. (1937). "Psychic blindness" and other symptoms following bilateral temporal lobe lobectomy in rhesus monkeys. *American Journal of Physiology*, *119*, 352–353.

Kolb, B., & Milner, B. (1981). Observations on spontaneous facial expression after focal cerebral excisions and after intracarotid injection of sodium amytal. *Neuropsychologia*, *19*, 505–514.

Kucharska-Pietura, K., Phillips, M. L., Gernand, W., & David, A. S. (2003). Perception of emotions from faces and voices following unilateral brain damage. *Neuropsychologia*, *41*, 1082–1090.

Laird, J. D. (1974). Self-attribution of emotion: The effects of expressive behavior on the quality of emotional experience. *Journal of Personality and Social Psychology*, *29*, 475–486.

Landis, T., Graves, R., & Goodglass, H. (1982). Aphasic reading and writing: Possible evidence for right hemisphere participation. *Cortex*, *18*, 105–122.

Landis, T. (2006). Emotional words: What's so different from just words? *Cortex*, *42*, 823–830.

LeDoux, J. E., Cicchetti, P., Xagoraris, A., & Romanski, L. M. (1990). The lateral amygdaloid nucleus: Sensory interface of the amygdala in fear conditioning. *Journal of Neuroscience*, *10*, 1062–1069.

LeJeun, F., Drapier, D., Bourguignon, A., Peron, J., Nesbah, H., et al. (2009). Subthalamic stimulation in Parkinson's disease induces apathy: A PET study. *Neurology*, *73*, 1746–1751.

Leonard, C., Rolls, E., & Wilson, A. (1985). Neurons in the amygdala of the monkey with responses selective for faces. *Behavioral Brain Research*, *15*, 159–176.

Levenson, R. W., Ekman, P., & Friesen, W. V. (1990). Voluntary facial action generates emotion-specific autonomic nervous system activity. *Psychophysiology*, *27*, 363–384.

Ley, R., & Bryden, M. (1979). Hemispheric differences in recognizing faces and emotions. *Brain and Language*, *1*, 127–138.

Luria, A. R., & Simernitskaya, E. G. (1977). Inter-hemispheric relations and the functions of the minor hemisphere. *Neuropsychologia*, *15*, 175–178.

MacLean, P. D. (1952). Some psychiatric implications of physiological studies of the frontotemporal portion of the limbic system (visceral brain). *Electroencephalography and Clinical Neurophysiology*, *4*, 407–418.

Maletti, S., Tassi, L., Mai, R., Tassinari, C. A., & Russo, G. L. (2006). Emotions induced by intracerebral electrical stimulation of the temporal lobe. *Epilepsia*, *47*(Suppl. 5), 47–51.

Mammucari, A., Caltagirone, C., Ekman, P., Friesen, W., Gainotti, G., Pizzamiglio, L., & Zoccolatti, P. (1988). Spontaneous facial expression of emotions in brain damaged patients. *Cortex*, *24*, 521–533.

Mandel, M., Tandon, S., & Asthana, H. (1991). Right brain damage impairs recognition of negative emotions. *Cortex*, *27*, 247–253.

Maranon, G. (1924). Contribution a l'entude de l'action emotive de l'adrenaline. *Revue Française d'Endocrinologie*, *2*, 301–325.

Maricle, R. A., Nutt, J. G., Valentine, R. J., & Carter, J. H. (1995). Dose–response relationship of levodopa with mood and anxiety in fluctuating Parkinson's disease: a double-blind placebo-controlled study. *Neurology*, *45*, 1757–1760.

Marin, R. S. (1991). Apathy: A neuropsychiatric syndrome. *Journal of Neuropsychiatry and Clinical Neurosciences*, *3*(3), 243–254.

Marin, R. S., Biedrzycki, R. C., & Firinciogullari, S. (1991). Reliability and validity of the Apathy Evaluation Scale. *Psychiatry Research*, *38*(2), 143–162.

Mark, V. H., & Ervin, F. R. (1970). *Violence and the brain*. New York: Harper and Row.

Mark, V. H., Sween, W. H., & Ervin, F. R. (1972). The effect of amygdalectomy on violent behavior in patients with temporal lobe epilepsy. In E. Hitchcock, L. Laitinen, & K. Vernet (Eds.), *Psychosurgery*. Springfield, IL: Charles C. Thomas.

Marsh, G. G., & Markham, C. H. (1973). Does levodopa alter depression and psychopathology in parkinsonism patients? *Journal of Neurology, Neurosurgery, and Psychiatry*, *36*, 935.

Mayberg, H. S., Starkstein, S. E., Peyser, C. E., Brandt, J., Dannals, R. F., & Folstein, S. E. (1992). Paralimbic frontal lobe hypometabolism in depression associated with Huntington's disease. *Neurology*, *42*, 1791–1797.

Mayeux, R. (1983). Emotional changes associated with basal ganglia disorders. In K. M. Heilman, & P. Satz (Eds.), *Neuropsychology of human emotion*. New York: Guilford Press.

Mayeux, R., Stern, Y., Rosen, J., & Leventhal, J. (1981). Depression, intellectual impairment, and Parkinson disease. *Neurology, 31,* 645–650.

McDonald, S., & Wales, R. (1986). An investigation of the ability to process inferences in language following right hemisphere brain damage. *Brain and Language, 29,* 68.

McIntyre, M., Pritchard, P. B., & Lombroso, C. T. (1976). Left and right temporal lobe epileptics: A controlled investigation of some psychological differences. *Epilepsia, 17,* 377–386.

McLachlan, R. S., & Blume, W. T. (1980). Isolated fear in complex partial status epilepticus. *Annals of Neurology, 8,* 639–641.

McLaren, J., & Bryson, S. (1987). Hemispheric asymmetry in the perception of emotional and neutral faces. *Cortex, 23,* 645–654.

Menza, M., Dobkin, R. D., Marin, H., Mark, M. H., Gara, M., Buyske, S., et al. (2009). A controlled trial of antidepressants in patients with Parkinson's disease and depression. *Neurology, 72*(10), 886–892.

Mesulam, M. M. (1981). A cortical network for directed attention and unilateral neglect. *Annals of Neurology, 10,* 309–325.

Mesulam, M. M., Van Hesen, G. W., Pandya, D. N., et al. (1977). Limbic and sensory connections of the inferior parietal lobule (area PG) in the rhesus monkey: a study with a new method for horseradish peroxidase histochemistry. *Brain Research, 136,* 393–414.

Mikos, A., Springer, U. S., Nisenzon, A., Kellison, I., Fernandez, H. H., Okun, M. S., & Bowers, D. (2009). Awareness of expressivity deficits in non-demented Parkinson's disease: *The Clinical Neuropsychologist, 23*(5), 805–817.

Miletti, S., Benuzzi, F., Cantalupo, G., Rubboli, G., Tassinari, C.A., & Nichelli, P. (2009). Facial emotion recognition impairment in chronic temporal lobe epilepsy. *Epilepsia, 50,* 1547–1559.

Milner, B. (1974). Hemispheric specialization: Scope and limits. In F. O. Schmitt, & F. G. Worden (Eds.), *The neurosciences: Third study program.* Cambridge, MA: MIT Press.

Mindham, H. S. (1970). Psychiatric syndromes in Parkinsonism. *Journal of Neurology, Neurosurgery, and Psychiatry, 30,* 188–191.

Monrad-Krohn, G. (1947). The prosodic quality of speech and its disorders. *Acta Psychologica Scandinavica, 22,* 225–265.

Moreno, C. R., Borod, J., Welkowitz, J., & Alpert, M. (1990). Lateralization for the expression and perception of facial emotion as a function of age. *Neuropsychologia, 28,* 119–209.

Morris, M., Bowers, D., Verfaellie, M., Blonder, L., Cimino, C., Bauer, R., & Heilman, K. (1992).

Lexical denotation and connotation in right and left hemisphere damaged patients. [Abstract]. *Journal of Clinical and Experimental Neuropsychology, 14,* 105.

Morris, M. K., Bradley, M., Bowers, D., Lang, P. J., & Heilman, K. M. (1991). *Valence-specific hypoarousal following right temporal lobectomy.* Presented at the 19th annual meeting of the International Neuropsychology Society, San Antonio, TX.

Morrow, L., Vrtunski, P. B., Kim, Y., & Boller, F. (1981). Arousal responses to emotional stimuli and laterality of lesions. *Neuropsychologia, 19,* 65–71.

Moruzzi G., & Magoun, H. W. (1949). Brainstem reticular formation and activation of the EEG. *Electroencephalography and Clinical Neurophysiology,* 1:455–473.

Mungas, D. (1982). Interictal behavior abnormality in temporal lobe epilepsy: A specific syndrome or nonspecific psychopathology? *Archives of General Psychiatry, 39,* 108–111.

Murray, E. A. (2007). The amygdala, reward and emotion. *Trends in Cognitive Sciences, 11,* 489–497.

Nielsen, H., & Kristensen, O. (1981). Personality correlates of sphenoidal EEG foci in temporal lobe epilepsy. *Acta Neurologica Scandinavica, 64,* 289–300.

Offen, M. L., Davidoff, R. A., Troost, B. T., & Richey, E. T. (1976). Dacrystic epilepsy. *Journal of Neurology, Neurosurgery, and Psychiatry, 39,* 829–834.

Olds, J. (1958). Self-stimulation of the brain. *Science, 127,* 315–324.

Pandya, D. M., & Kuypers, H. G. (1969). Corticocortical connections in the rhesus monkey. *Brain Research, 13,*13–36.

Papez, J. W. (1937). A proposed mechanism of emotion. *Archives of Neurology and Psychiatry, 38,* 725–743.

Parkinson, J. (1938). An essay of the shaking palsy, 1817. *Medical Classics, 2,* 964–997.

Patton, J. J., Belova, M. A., Morrison, S. E., & Salzman, C. D. (2006). The primate amygdala represents the positive and negative value of visual stimuli during learning. *Nature, 439,* 865–870.

Paul, H. (1909). *Principien der sprachgeschichte,* 4th ed. Tübingen: Niemeyer.

Pell, M. D. (1999). Fundamental frequency encoding of linguistic and emotional prosody by right hemisphere-damaged speakers. *Brain and Language, 69*(2), 161–192.

Pell, M. D. (2006). Judging emotion and attitudes from prosody following brain damage. *Progress in Brain Research, 156,* 303 –317.

Pell, M. D., Leonard, C. L. (2003). Processing emotional tone from speech in Parkinson's disease: a role for the basal ganglia. *Cognitive, Affective, & Behavioral Neuroscience, 3*(4), 275–288.

Pell, M. D., & Leonard, C. L. (2005). Facial expression decoding in early Parkinson's disease. *Cognitive Brain Research, 23,* 327–340.

Pedersen, K. F., Alves, G., Bronnick, K., Aarsland, D., Tysnes, O. B., & Larsen, J. P. (2010). Apathy in drug-naive patients with incident Parkinson's disease: the Norwegian ParkWest study. *Journal of Neurology, 257*(2), 217–223.

Pedersen, K. F., Larsen, J. P., Alves, G., & Aarsland, D. (2009). Prevalence and clinical correlates of apathy in Parkinson's disease: A community-based study. *Parkinsonism & Related Disorders, 15*(4), 295–299.

Pentland, B, Pitcairn, T., Gray, J., et al. (1987). The effects of reduced expression in Parkinson's disease on concept formation by health professionals. *Clinical Rehabilitation, 1,* 307–131.

Perani, D., Vallar, G., Paulesu, E., et al. (1993). Left and right hemisphere contributions to recovery from neglect after right hemisphere damage. *Neuropsychologia, 31,* 115–125.

Phelps, M. E., Mazziotta, J. C., Baxter, L., & Gerner, R. (1984). Positron emission tomographic study of affective disorders: problems and strategies. *Annals of Neurology, 15*(Suppl), S149–S156.

Phillips, P. (1999). Keeping depression at bay helps patients with Parkinson's disease. *Journal of the American Medical Association, 282*(12), 1118–1119.

Pincus, J. H. (1980). Can violence be a manifestation of epilepsy? *Neurology, 30,* 304–307.

Pitcairn, T., Clemie, S., Gray, J., & Pentland, B. (1990). Non-verbal cues in the self presentation of parkinsonian people. *British Journal of Clinical Psychology, 29,* 177–184.

Pluck, G. C., & Brown, R. G. (2002). Apathy in Parkinson's disease. *Journal of Neurology, Neurosurgery, and Psychiatry, 73,* 636–642.

Poeck, K. (1969). Pathophysiology of emotional disorders associated with brain damage. In P. J. Vinken, & G. W. Bruyn (Eds.), *Handbook of neurology* Vol. 3. New York: Elsevier.

Poeck, K., & Pilleri, G. (1961). Wutverhalten and pathologischer schlaf bei tumor dervorderen mitellinie. *Archiv fur Psychiatrie und Nervenkrankheiten, 201,* 593–604.

Pontius, A. A., & Yudowitz, B. S. (1980). Frontal lobe system dysfunction in some criminal actions as shown in the narratives text. *Journal of Nervous and Mental Disease, 168,* 111–117.

Pritchard, P. B. (1980). Hyposexuality: A complication of complex partial epilepsy. *Transactions of the American Neurological Association, 105,* 193–195.

Pritchard, P. B., Wannamaker, B. B., Sagel, J., & deVillier, C. (1981). Post-ictal hyperprolactinemia in complex partial epilepsy. *Annals of Neurology, 10,* 81–82.

Ramon y Cajal, S. (1965). *Studies on the cerebral cortex (limbic structures).* (L. M. Kraft, Trans.). London: Lloyd-Luke.

Rapscak, S., Kasniak, A., & Rubins, A. (1989). Anomia for facial expressions: Evidence for a category specific visual verbal disconnection. *Neuropsychologia, 27,* 1031–1041.

Rapcsak, S. Z., Comer, J. F., & Rubens, A. B. (1993). Anomia for facial expressions. Neuropsychological mechanisms and anatomical correlates. *Brain and Language, 45,* 233–252.

Reijnders, J. S., Ehrt, U., Lousberg, R., Aarsland, D., & Leentjens, A. F. (2009). The association between motor subtypes and psychopathology in Parkinson's disease. *Parkinsonism & Related Disorders, 15*(5), 379–382.

Remillard, G. M., Andermann, F., Testa, G. F., Gloor, P., Aube, M., Martin, J. B., et al. (1983). Sexual manifestations predominate in a woman with temporal lobe epilepsy: A finding suggesting sexual dimorphism in the human brain. *Neurology, 33,* 3–30.

Reuber, M., & Mackay, R. D. (2008). Epileptic automatisms in the criminal courts: 13 cases tried in England and Wales between 1975 and 2001. *Epilepsia, 49,* 138–145.

Reuter-Lorenz, P., & Davidson, R. (1981). Differential contributions of the two cerebral hemispheres for perception of happy and sad faces. *Neuropsychologia, 19,* 609–614.

Reuterskiold, C. (1991). The effects of emotionality on auditory comprehension in aphasia. *Cortex, 27,* 595–604.

Richardson, C., Bowers, D., Eyeler, L., & Heilman, K. (1992). *Asymmetrical control of facial emotional expression depends on the means of elicitation.* Presented at the meeting of the International Neuropsychology Society, San Diego.

Robertson, M. M., Trimble, M. R., & Townsend, H. R. (1987). Phenomenology of depression in epilepsy. *Epilepsia, 28,* 364–372.

Robins, A. H. (1976). Depression in patients with Parkinsonism. *British Journal of Psychology, 128,* 141–145.

Robinson, R. G., & Sztela, B. (1981). Mood change following left hemisphere brain injury. *Annals of Neurology, 9,* 447–453.

Robinson, R. G., Starkstein, S. E. (1989). Mood disorders following stroke: new findings and future directions. *Journal of Geriatric Psychiatry, 22,* 1–15.

Rodin, E. A. (1973). Psychomotor epilepsy and aggressive behavior. *Archives of General Psychiatry, 28,* 210–213.

Roeltgen, D. P., Sevush, S., & Heilman, K. M. (1983). Phonological agraphia: Writing by the lexical semantic route. *Neurology, 33,* 755–765.

Rosenbek, J. C., Rodriguez, A. D., Hieber, B., Leon, S. A., Crucian, G. P., Ketterson, T. U., et al. (2006). Effects of two treatments for aprosodia secondary to acquired brain injury. *Journal of Rehabilitation Research and Development, 43*(3), 379–390.

Ross, E. D. (1981). The aprosodias: Functional-anatomic organization of the affective components of language in the right hemisphere. *Annals of Neurology, 38,* 561–589.

Ross, E. D., & Mesulam, M. M. (1979). Dominant language functions of the right hemisphere? Prosody and emotional gesturing. *Archives of Neurology, 36,*144–148.

Rossi, G. S., & Rodadini, G. (1967). Experimental analysis of cerebral dominance in man. In C. Millikan, & F. L. Darley (Eds.), *Brain mechanisms underlying speech and language.* New York: Grune & Stratton.

Ross, E. D., Homan, R. W., Buck, R. (1994). Differential hemispheric lateralization of primary and social emotions. *Neuropsychiatry Neuropsychology and Behavioral Neurology, 7,* 1–19.

Sackeim, H., Gur, R., & Saucy, M. (1978). Emotions are expressed more intensely on the left side of the face. *Science, 202,* 434–436.

Sackeim, H. A., Greenberg, M. S., Weiman, A. L., Gur, R. C., Hungerbuhler, J. P., & Geschwind, N. (1982). Hemispheric asymmetry in the expression of positive and negative emotion: Neurologic evidence. *Archives of Neurology, 39,* 210–218.

Sarazin, M., Michon, A., Pillon, B., Samson, Y., Canuto, A., Gold, G., Bouras, C., Dubois, B., & Giannakopoulos, P. (2003). Metabolic correlates of behavioral and affective disturbances in frontal lobe pathologies. *Journal of Neurology, 250,* 827–33.

Sato, H., Hata, Y., Hagihara, K., et al. (1987). Effects of cholinergic depletion on neuron activities in the cat visual cortex. *Journal of Neurophysiology, 58,* 781–794.

Schacter, S., & Singer, J. E. (1962). Cognitive, social, and physiological determinants of emotional state. *Psychological Review, 69,* 379–399.

Scheibel, M.E., & Scheibel, A. B. (1966). The organization of the nucleus reticularis thalami: a Golgi study. *Brain Research, 1,* 43–62.

Schiffer, R., & Pope, L. E. (2005). Review of pseudobulbar affect including a novel and poten-tial therapy. *Journal of Neuropsychiatry and Clinical Neurosciences, 17,* 447–454.

Schlanger, B. B., Schlanger, P., & Gerstmann, L. J. (1976). The perception of emotionally toned sentences by right-hemisphere damaged and aphasic subjects. *Brain and Language, 3,* 396–403.

Schrandt, N. J., Tranel, D., & Damasio, H. (1989). The effects of total cerebral lesions on skin conductance response to signal stimuli. *Neurology, 39*(Suppl. 1), 223.

Scott, S., Caird, B. I., & Williams, B. (1984). Evidence of apparent sensory speech disorder in Parkinson's disease. *Journal of Neurology, Neurosurgery, and Psychiatry, 47,* 840–843.

Slater, E., & Beard, A. W. (1963). The schizophrenia-like psychoses of epilepsy. *British Journal of Psychiatry, 109,* 95–150.

Slaughter, J. R., Slaughter, K. A., Nichols, D., Holmes, S. E., & Martens, M. P. (2001). Prevalence, clinical manifestations, etiology, and treatment of depression in Parkinson's disease. *Journal of Neuropsychiatry and Clinical Neuroscience, 13,* 187–196.

Sockeel, P., Dujardin, K., Devos, D., Denève, C., Destée, A., & Defebvre, L. (2006). The Lille Apathy Rating Scale (LARS), a new instrument for detecting and quantifying apathy: Validation in Parkinson's disease. *Journal of Neurology, Neurosurgery, & Psychiatry, 77,* 579–584.

Smith, M. C., Smith, M. K., & Ellgring, H. (1996). Spontaneous and posed facial expression in Parkinson's disease. *Journal of the International Neuropsychological Society, 2,* 383–391.

Speedie, L. J., Broke, N., Folstein, S. E., Bowers, D., & Heilman, K. M. (1990). Comprehension of prosody in Huntington's disease. *Journal of Neurology, Neurosurgery, and Psychiatry, 53,* 607–610.

Speedie, L. J., Coslett, H. B., & Heilman, K. M. (1984). Repetition of affective prosody in mixed transcortical aphasia. *Archives of Neurology, 41,* 268–270.

Spencer, S. S., Spencer, D. D., Williamson, P. D., & Mattson, R. H. (1983). Sexual automatisms in complex partial seizures. *Neurology, 33,* 527–533.

Sprengelmeyer, R., Young, A. W., Calder, A. J., Karnat, A., Lange, H., Homberg, V., Perrett, D. I., & Rowland, D. (1996). Loss of disgust. Perception of faces and emotions in Huntington's disease. *Brain, 118,* 1647–1665.

Starkstein, S. E., Mayberg, H. S., Preziosi, T. J., et al. (1992). Reliability, validity, and clinical correlates of apathy in Parkinson's disease.

Journal of Neuropsychiatry and Clinical Neuroscience, 4, 134–139.

Starkstein, S., & Robinson, R. (1990). Depression following cerebrovascular lesions. *Seminars in Neurology, 40*, 247.

Starkstein, S. E., Robinson, R. G., & Price, T. R. (1987). Comparison of cortical and subcortical lesions in the production of poststroke mood disorders. *Brain, 110*, 1045–1059.

Steriade, M., & Glenn, L. (1982). Neocortical and caudate projections of intralaminar thalamic neurons and their synaptic excitation from the midbrain reticular core. *Journal of Neurophysiology, 48*, 352–370.

Stevens, J. R. (1966). Psychiatric implications of psychomotor epilepsy. *Archives of General Psychiatry, 14*, 461–471.

Stevens, J. R., & Hermann, B. P. (1981). Temporal lobe epilepsy, psychopathology and violence: the state of evidence. *Neurology, 31*, 1127–1132.

Strauss, E. (1983). Perception of emotional words. *Neuropsychologia, 21*, 99–103.

Strauss, E. (1989). Ictal and interictal manifestations of emotions in epilepsy. In F. Boller, & J. Grafman (Eds.), *Handbook of neuropsychology* Vol. 3 (pp. 315–344). Amsterdam: Elsevier.

Strauss, E. & Moscovitch, M. (1981). Perception of facial expressions. *Brain Language, 13*, 308–332.

Strauss, E., Risser, A., & Jones, M. W. (1982). Fear responses in patients with epilepsy. *Neurology, 39*, 626–630.

Stuss, D. T., & Benson, D. F. (1986). *The Frontal Lobes*. New York: Raven Press.

Suberi, M., & McKeever, W. (1977). Differential right hemisphere memory storage of emotional and nonemotional faces. *Neuropsychologia, 15*, 757–768.

Taylor, D. C. (1969). Aggression and epilepsy. *Journal of Psychiatric Research, 13*, 229–236.

Tomkins, S. S. (1962). *Affect, imagery, consciousness* Vol. 1: *The positive affect*. New York: Springer.

Tomkins, S. S. (1963). *Affect, imagery, consciousness* Vol. 2: *The negative affects*. New York: Springer.

Terzian, H. (1964). Behavioral and EEG effects of intracarotid sodium amytal injections. *Acta Neurochirurgica (Vienna), 12*, 230–240.

Trieman, D. M. (1991). Psychobiology of ictal aggression. In D. Smith, D. Treiman, & M. Trimble (Eds.), *Advances in neurology* (p. 341). New York: Raven Press.

Trieman, D. M., & Delgado-Escueta, A. V. (1983). Violence and epilepsy: A critical review. In T. A. Pedley, & B. S. Meldrum (Eds.), *Recent advances in epilepsy*, Vol. 1 (pp. 179–209). London: Churchill Livingstone.

Tucker, D. M. (1981). Lateral brain function, emotion and conceptualization. *Psychological Bulletin, 89*, 19–46.

Tucker, D. M., Watson, R. T., & Heilman, K. M. (1977). Affective discrimination and evocation in patients with right parietal disease. *Neurology, 17*, 947–950.

Tucker, D. M., & Williamson, P. A. (1984). Asymmetric neural control in human self-regulation. *Psychological Review, 91*, 185–215.

Ursin, H. (1960). The temporal lobe substrate of fear and anger. *Acta Psychiatrica et Neurologica Scandinavica, 35*, 378–396.

van Reekum, R., Stuss, D. T., & Ostrander, L. (2005). Apathy: Why care? *Journal of Neuropsychiatry and Clinical Neurosciences, 17*(1), 7–19.

Veazey, C., Aki, S. O., Cook, K. F., Lai, E. C., & Kunik, M. E. (2005). Prevalence and treatment of depression in Parkinson's disease. *Journal of Neuropsychiatry and Clinical Neuroscience, 17*, 310–323.

Watson, R. T., Heilman, K. M., Miller, B. D., et al. (1974). Neglect after mesencephalic reticular formation lesions. *Neurology, 24*, 294–298.

Watson, R. T., Miller, B. D., & Heilman, K. M. (1978). Nonsensory neglect. *Annals of Neurology, 3*, 505–508.

Watson, R. T., Valenstein, E., & Heilman, K. M. (1981). Thalamic neglect: the possible role of the medial thalamus and nucleus reticularis thalami in behavior. *Arch. Neurol., 38*, 501–507.

Wapner, W., Harby, S., & Gardner, H. (1981). The role of the right hemisphere in the apprehension of complex linguistic stimuli. *Brain Cognition, 14*, 15–33.

Warburton, J. W. (1967). Depressive symptoms in Parkinson's patients referred for thalamotomy. *Journal of Neurology, Neurosurgery, and Psychiatry, 30*, 368–370.

Waxman, S. G., & Geschwind, N. (1974). Hypergraphia in temporal lobe epilepsy. *Neurology, 24*, 629–636.

Wechsler, A. F. (1973). The effect of organic brain disease on recall of emotionally charged versus neutral narrative texts. *Neurology, 23*, 130–135.

Weddell, R., Miller, R., & Trevarthen, C. (1990). Voluntary emotional facial expressions in patients with focal cerebral lesions. *Neuropsychologia, 28*, 49–60.

Weintraub, S., Mesulam, M. M., & Kramer, L. (1981). Disturbances in prosody. *Archives of Neurology, 38*, 742–744.

Wieser, H. G. (1986). Selective amygdalohippocampectomy: Indication, investigative technique and results. *Advances and Technical Standards in Neurosurgery, 13*, 39–133.

Wilensky, A. E., Schafe, G. E., Kristensen, M. P., & LeDoux, J. E. (2006). Rethinking the fear circuit: The central nucleus of the amygdala is required for the acquisition, consolidation, and expression of Pavlovian fear conditioning. *Journal of Neuroscience*, *26*, 12387–12396.

Williams, D. (1956). The structure of emotions reflected in epileptic experiences. *Brain*, *79*, 29–67.

Williams, D. (1969). Neural factors related to habitual aggression. *Brain*, *92*, 503–520.

Wilson, S.A.K. (1924).

Winner, E., & Gardner H. (1977). The comprehension of metaphor in brain-damaged patients. *Brain*, *100*, 717–29.

Witt, J.A., Hollmann, K., Helmstaedter, C. (2008). The impact of lesions and epilepsy on personality and mood in patients with symptomatic epilepsy: a pre- to postoperative follow-up study. *Epilepsy Research*, *82*, 139–46.

Whalen, P. J., Rauch, S. L., Etcoff, N. L., McInerney, S. C., Lee, M. B., & Jenike, M. A. (1998). Masked presentations of emotional facial expressions modulate amygdala activity without explicit knowledge. *Journal of Neuroscience*, *18*, 411–418.

Whyte, E. M., & Mulsant, B. H. (2002). Post-stroke depression: Epidemiology, pathophysiology, and biological treatment. *Biological Psychiatry*, *52*, 253–263.

Zahodne, L. B., Kirsch-Darrow, L., Fernandez, H. H., Okun, M. S., & Bowers, D. (2010). *Divergent trajectories of apathy and depression over two years in medically-managed, idiopathic Parkinson's disease*. Presented at the 62nd annual meeting of the American Academy of Neurology, Toronto, CAN. (*Neurology* 74, No. 9, Suppl. 2, A77).

Zahodne, L.B., Okun, M.S., Foote, K.D., Fernandez, H.H., Rodriguez, R.L., Wu, S.S., Kirsch-Darrow, L., Jacobson, C.E. 4th, Rosado, C., & Bowers, D. (2009). Greater improvement in quality of life following unilateral deep brain stimulation surgery in the globus pallidus as compared to the subthalamic nucleus. *Journal of Neurology*, *256*, 1321–1329.

Zeman, W., & King, F. A. (1958). Tumors of the septum pellucidum and adjacent structures with abnormal affective behavior: an anterior midline structure syndrome. *Journal of Nervous and Mental Disorders*, *127*, 490–502.

Zgaljardic, D. J., Borod, J. C., Foldi, N. S., Rocco, M., Mattis, P. J., Gordon, M. F., et al. (2007). Relationship between self-reported apathy and executive dysfunction in nondemented patients with Parkinson disease. *Cognitive and Behavioral Neurology*, *20*(3), 184–192.

16

Amnesic Disorders

RUSSELL M. BAUER, GILA Z. RECKESS, ABHAY KUMAR, AND EDWARD VALENSTEIN

In this chapter, the term *amnesic syndrome* refers to the behavioral characteristics of memory disorders that follow medial temporal lobe destruction, and to the substantially similar disorders associated with diencephalic and basal forebrain lesions. To facilitate discussion of clinical and research topics relevant to amnesia, we have divided this chapter into seven sections. The first section, Clinical Characteristics of the Amnesic Syndrome, provides an overview of the behavioral characteristics of amnesia. The second, Evaluating the Amnesic Patient, discusses the neuropsychological evaluation of memory. The third section, Anatomy, reviews the anatomic localization of lesions that cause amnesia. The fourth section, Theoretical Accounts of Amnesia, reviews theories of amnesia and their ability to account for the clinical and neuroanatomic findings reviewed in the previous sections. The fifth section, Functional Imaging Studies of Amnesia, discusses the role of functional neuroimaging in advancing our understanding of memory and amnesia. The sixth, Clinical Presentation of Disorders Associated with Amnesia, discusses neurological conditions that often present with impairment of memory, and the seventh, Rehabilitation of Memory Disorders, reviews the treatment and rehabilitation of patients with amnesia.

DEFINITIONS

Discussions of memory and amnesia are often complicated by the abundant, often overlapping, terms used to describe memory functions and processes. We will therefore begin by introducing the most important nomenclatures (see Roediger et al., 2008, for a more comprehensive overview).

First, memory processing has historically been divided into three distinct stages (cf. Klatzky, 1982): (a) *acquisition* or *encoding* of new information, (b) *maintenance and storage* during the retention interval, and (c) *retrieval* of information (Baddeley, 1982; Squire & Cohen, 1984; Cermak, 1997). These stages are hierarchical and broadly apply to all forms of memory.

Another distinction lies in the *type* of memory being processed. Cohen and Squire (1980) proposed the dichotomy between declarative memory (e.g., knowing *that* something was learned) and procedural learning (e.g., knowing *how* to perform a skill). More recently, the term *nondeclarative* has been used in place of procedural (cf. Squire, 1987) to encompass skills, priming, conditioning, and other phenomena, in agreement with the classification system proposed earlier by Cermak (Cermak,

Talbot, Chandler, & Wolbarst, 1985). Declarative memory operates on both episodic memory (memory for contextually specific events) and semantic memory (general world knowledge, linguistic skill, vocabulary) (Tulving, 1972, 1983). The term *episodic memory* is sometimes used interchangeably with other terms (e.g., autobiographical, source/contextual, recollective, or associative memory), each of which has a slightly different meaning.

Declarative and nondeclarative memory are often referred to as explicit and implicit memory, respectively. Explicit memory is tested directly by asking subjects questions that make specific reference to prior learning (e.g., "Was this word on the list you were shown?"). Implicit memory is measured using indirect or incidental tasks (Jacoby, 1984; Johnson & Hasher, 1987; Richardson-Klavehn & Bjork, 1988) that make no reference to prior learning episodes at the time of retrieval (e.g., skill learning, repetition priming, conditioning and discriminative physiological responses, and preference formation). There is no guarantee, however, that direct or indirect tests are process pure. For example, healthy adults may recall the learning episode and use conscious recall on indirect tests (Kelley & Jacoby, 2000) and may guess or otherwise use nonconscious recollection to succeed on direct tests (Cermak et al., 1997; Verfaellie & Cermak, 1999).

A final distinction relates to the *experience* of recalling a memory. One important distinction is that between recollection and familiarity. When a retrieval act is accompanied by an experience of direct, deliberate reference to a prior episode, it engenders a conscious "recollective" experience. In contrast, some successful acts of retrieval lack this experience and reflect nondeclarative aspects of learning. This experience is referred to as *familiarity* (Jacoby, 1991; Yonelinas, 2002). Methods to distinguish these two types of experiences, including the process dissociation procedure (Jacoby, 1991) and the remember-know-guess paradigm (Gardiner & Richardson-Klavehn, 2000) have been developed amidst debate regarding the degree to which recollection and familiarity reflect independent processes.

CLINICAL CHARACTERISTICS OF THE AMNESIC SYNDROME

Amnesias caused by various diseases or by lesions in different parts of the brain have common characteristics that comprise the "amnesic syndrome." In many cases, it is possible to provide relatively precise estimates of the date of onset of the illness based on patient history. Classic symptoms include (a) loss of memory for events occurring after illness onset, called *anterograde amnesia*; and (b) difficulty recalling some events that occurred prior to the onset of amnesia, called *retrograde amnesia* or *remote memory disturbance*. Many amnesic patients show preservation of certain cognitive abilities (e.g., attention span, measured IQ), and these preserved abilities also help to define the syndrome.

Anterograde Amnesia

The hallmark of the amnesic syndrome is a profound defect in new learning, called *anterograde amnesia*. In the literature, the deficit is variously described as involving recent or long-term memory; the essential problem is impaired conscious, deliberate recall of information initially learned after illness onset. The defect manifests in practically any situation in which the recall burden exceeds the immediate memory span, or in which a delay with distraction ensues between information exposure and the memory test. Anterograde memory loss prevents the patient from establishing new, permanent memories. Amnesic patients are severely impaired in everyday life, and their learning deficit is apparent on even casual observation. Patients may fail to learn the names of hospital staff and will fail to recognize newly encountered persons after brief delays. They may appear disoriented in place or time because they have failed to learn their location or have lost the ability to monitor and keep track of ongoing events. Amnesic patients are usually capable of maintaining adequate conversation, but their deficit may become obvious when they are asked to recall an event that occurred only hours or minutes before. Instructions to remember such events for later recall rarely result in measurable improvement. Although such deficits are apparent in the patient's everyday behavior, they may be more precisely documented by objective tests of delayed free recall, cued recall, and recognition.

Retrograde Amnesia and Remote Memory Disturbance

The amnesic patient usually also has difficulty recalling events that occurred prior to illness onset. This impairment is often worse for relatively recent events than for events that occurred in the very remote past. The deficit involves autobiographical information from the patient's personal past (e.g., the circumstances surrounding an important relative's death), as well as items from the generic knowledge base (e.g., what happened on September 11, 2001). It has been suggested (Kapur, 1999; Moscovitch, Rosenbaum, Gilboa, et al., 2005) that autobiographical memory for past personal events is distinct, both anatomically and functionally, from remote semantic knowledge and fact memory. Autobiographical defects are commonly seen after lesions to medial temporal and diencephalic structures, whereas defects in remote semantic memory suggest neocortical damage (Moscovitch et al., 2005).

Among subjects with amnesia, three patterns of remote memory impairment have been described. *Temporally limited impairments* primarily affect memories from the few years prior to the onset of amnesia and have been documented in the amnesic patient H.M. (Milner, Corkin, & Teuber, 1968; Marslen-Wilson & Teuber, 1974; Corkin, 1984), in patients having just completed electroconvulsive therapy (ECT) for depression (Squire et al., 1975; Squire & Fox, 1980), and in cases of remote memory impairment after language-dominant temporal lobectomy (Barr, Goldberg, Wasserstein, & Novelly, 1990). *Temporally graded impairments* affect all time periods but with greater impairment of memories derived from recent time periods. This pattern is typical of patients with alcoholic Korsakoff syndrome (Seltzer & Benson, 1974; Albert et al., 1979; Meudell et al., 1980; Squire & Cohen, 1984; Squire et al., 1989a) and has been reported in patients with basal forebrain damage (Gade & Mortensen, 1990).

Finally, *decade-nonspecific impairment* affects all time periods equally and has been described in patients surviving herpes simplex encephalitis (Cermak & O'Connor, 1983; Butters et al., 1984; Damasio et al., 1985; Kopelman, Stanhope, & Kingsley, 1999), patients with Huntington disease (Albert et al., 1981), and in certain other amnesic subjects (Sanders & Warrington, 1971).

Other Characteristic Deficits

Other cognitive deficits can be seen in some amnesic patients and may contribute to deficits in memory. A good example is that patients with alcoholic Korsakoff syndrome often have visuospatial and visuoperceptual deficits (Kapur & Butters, 1977) and impairment on tests of executive skill and strategy formation (Moscovitch, 1982; Squire, 1982b; Kopelman, 1995).

The anterograde and retrograde deficits that characterize the amnesic syndrome affect information from all sensory modalities. However, modality-specific impairments in new learning have been described in patients with circumscribed vascular lesions affecting corticocortical pathways linking sensory association cortices with the medial temporal memory system (Ross, 1980a,b). Also, patients with unilateral lesions may have a modality-independent amnesia that is nevertheless *material-specific*: Patients with language-dominant (usually left hemisphere) lesions usually have more difficulty with verbal than with nonverbal memory, whereas the reverse tends to be true (although less strongly) of patients with language-nondominant (usually right hemisphere) lesions (Barret al., 1997).

Spared Abilities

Even densely amnesic patients show certain spared memory capacities. A substantial literature has developed in the area of "memory dissociations": dissociations between classes of tasks amnesic patients can and cannot perform (cf. Squire, 1987; Schacter, Chiu, & Ochsner, 1993; Roediger, Guynn, & Jones, 1994; Gabrieli, 1998 for reviews). The following is an overview of key findings.

Preserved pre-illness memory. Although amnesic patients generally have some form of impairment in memory for events that occurred prior to the onset of amnesia, a substantial part of pre-illness memory is usually intact. In fact, most amnesic patients remember more from the time prior to illness onset than they forget. Preserved pre-illness memory can include knowledge structures, skills, and preferences.

Intact knowledge structures. The amnesic patient retains substantial intellectual, linguistic, and social skills. Performance on standardized intellectual tests is frequently normal or near normal. In the pure amnesic, social graces are almost always intact, and language is grossly normal. That is, amnesic patients can often use general knowledge despite significantly impaired memory and learning skills. Although amnesic patients perform poorly on conventional memory tests that require recollection of a specific episode or context, spared social and linguistic knowledge represents "context-free" retrieval without reference to the episode in which the information was originally learned.

Motor and cognitive skills. Amnesic patients show relatively good retention of previously acquired motor and cognitive skills, such as how to ride a bike, play the piano, or use appliances. Schacter (1983) provides a fascinating case study of an amnesic who retained his golf skills but who was unable to accurately remember his score or his preceding shots. Moments after teeing off, the patient would begin to tee another ball, forgetting that he had just taken a shot. As another example, Squire and colleagues (1984) taught a mirror-reading skill to depressed psychiatric inpatients prior to a scheduled course of ECT. After treatment was completed, the skill was retained despite marked retrograde amnesia for the training procedure itself.

Preferences. Although very little empirical data are available regarding the effects of amnesia on personality traits and emotional functioning, Johnson et al. (1985) suggest that feelings and personal preferences may be spared to the extent that they are based on memory for general sensory/perceptual features of stimuli as opposed to specific autobiographical memories.

Indeed, anecdotal information suggests that many amnesic patients continue to exhibit personal preferences for such things as color, clothes, food, and people, even though they may not remember the specific reasons for these feelings. They also retain *general* evaluative responses and emotional reactions. For example, they generally remember that fire is dangerous and respond physiologically to previously fearful stimuli, just as they appropriately express sadness and joy in response to stimuli.

Preserved new learning capacities. In general, amnesic patients can learn a wide range of new information even though they may have no conscious recollection for the experience upon which the learning is based. They demonstrate such knowledge as long as doing so does not require direct, conscious recollection. Such distinctions suggest that implicit memory is spared while explicit memory is not (Schacter, Chiu, & Ochsner, 1993; Toth, 2000).

Skill learning. Most amnesic patients can learn new perceptual, cognitive, and motor skills despite being unable to remember experiences that led to such learning (Schacter et al., 1993; Tranel, Damasio, Damasio, & Brandt, 1994; Rich, Bylsma, & Brandt, 1996; Gabrieli, 1998). For example, patient H.M. demonstrated consistent learning in rotary pursuit and bimanual tracking tasks (Corkin, 1968), a mirror-tracing task (Milner, 1962), and a short visual maze (Milner et al., 1968), although he could not remember having practiced these skills or having previously encountered the apparatus. Similar results have been documented with other amnesic patients (Eslinger & Damasio, 1986; Yamashita, 1993), including practice effects on jigsaw puzzles (Brooks & Baddeley, 1976), the Tower of Hanoi puzzle (Squire & Cohen, 1984), applying numerical rules (Wood, Ebert, & Kinsbourne, 1982), classifying novel patterns as instances of categories (Ashby, Alfonso Reese, Turken, & Waldron, 1998; Knowlton & Squire, 1993; Squire & Knowlton, 1995), learning stimulus presentation patterns (Nissen & Bullemer, 1987; Reber & Squire, 1998), and mirror-reading (Cohen & Squire, 1980; Schmidtke et al., 1996). Unlike normal subjects, amnesic patients do not show greater mirror-reading improvement with practiced items, presumably because normal subjects can also use explicit memory for these materials. Practice effects on skill learning tasks can endure for months (Cohen & Squire, 1980) or years (Cohen, 1984).

Repetition priming. Warrington and Weiskrantz (1970, 1974, 1978) demonstrated that amnesic patients who were severely impaired on tests of recall and recognition showed long-term learning and retention of new information when cued with partial information, such as stimulus fragments or word stems. Although these results were interpreted as support for a retrieval-deficit account of explicit memory impairment in amnesia, they can also be construed as the first experimental evidence of intact priming in amnesic patients.

Repetition priming is the facilitation in information processing that occurs following a prior exposure to the same or related stimulus. Performance facilitation in amnesic patients is revealed in decreased decision latency, increased identification accuracy, or increased likelihood of generating a previously exposed item to an ambiguous cue. This has been demonstrated on lexical decision tasks (Moscovitch, 1982; Duchek & Neeley, 1989; Smith & Oscar-Berman, 1990), object decision tasks (deciding whether previously shown and novel objects were geometrically possible; Schacter, et al., 1991), word (perceptual) identification (identifying previously presented words relative to new words; Cermak et al., 1988; Cermak, Hill, & Wong, 1998; Postle & Corkin, 1998), and word stem or fragment completion tasks (Diamond & Rozin, 1984; Shimamura & Squire, 1984; Graf & Schacter, 1985; Graf et al., 1985; Shimamura, 1986; Hamann & Squire, 1996; Cermak et al., 1997; Squire et al., 1985). These are indirect tests of memory because no direct reference to the study words is made. Warrington and Weiskrantz used a direct test in that they instructed their subjects to use the cues to recall previously studied items; however, their amnesic subjects probably used an implicit strategy by treating the memory test as a "guessing game." It has subsequently been demonstrated that amnesic patients perform normally only when indirect instructions are utilized (e.g., "Read this word," "Generate the first word that

comes to mind," etc.) with direct instructions (e.g., "Is this a word you studied?"). Performance by normal subjects is boosted by explicit recollection, whereas amnesic patients may be reluctant to guess (Squire et al., 1978; Graf, et al., 1984, 1985).

The examples described above reflect perceptual priming, in that processing of stimulus form leads to subsequent facilitation irrespective of stimulus meaning (Roediger & McDermott, 1993). In contrast, word meaning is important for conceptual priming (e.g., "What word goes with 'doctor'?" when "nurse" had been studied). Although some studies have failed to demonstrate conceptual priming in amnesia (Vaidya, Gabrieli, Demb, Keane, & Wetzel, 1996), many have shown normal conceptual priming (Shimamura & Squire, 1984; Graf, Shimamura, & Squire, 1985; Cermak & Wong, 1998), even in the context of impaired explicit memory for the priming cues (e.g., Gardner, Boller, Moreines, & Butters, 1973; Kihlstrom, 1980; Shimamura & Squire, 1984; Graf et al., 1985; Schacter, 1985). Thus, there is ample evidence that amnesic patients show conceptual priming, provided that the task allows for implicit retrieval.

Psychophysiological and electrophysiological correlates. In the 1980s, it was noted that patients with prosopagnosia showed a reliably stronger electrodermal response (EDR) to familiar faces than to unfamiliar faces in a multiple-choice paradigm, despite their inability to explicitly recognize the faces as familiar (Bauer, 1984; Tranel & Damasio, 1985; see Chapter 11). Schacter (1987, 1988) noted the conceptual similarities among spared implicit memory in amnesia and spared recognition in agnosia and hemianopia (blindsight). Bauer et al. (1992) hypothesized that EDR recognition may provide another index of this unconscious form of memory. In support of this hypothesis, Verfaellie, Bauer, and Bowers (1991) demonstrated that an amnesic patient with a left retrosplenial lesion showed normal EDR to targets despite greatly impaired overt recognition. Verbal recognition and EDR recognition were statistically independent. Similar effects have been demonstrated by Tranel and Damasio (1987) in a postencephalitic patient.

It remains unclear whether the psychological processes indexed by EDR are truly "unconscious" or whether they depend on variables that affect explicit memory. Bauer and Verfaellie (1992) showed that certain variables known to affect explicit memory do not affect EDR, including retention interval and levels of processing (Bauer et al., 1991). Although this supports the hypothesis that EDR recognition more closely resembles implicit phenomena, EDR has been linked to constructs such as orienting, significance detection, metamemory skills, and cognitive effort, which may correlate with aspects of explicit memory.

In addition to measures of autonomic activity such as EDR, electrophysiological investigations using event-related potentials (ERP) have shown that aspects of conscious and unconscious recollection can manifest in scalp-recorded electroencephalographs (EEG; Paller, Kutas, & Mayes, 1987; Rugg, Mark, & Walla, 1998; Curran, 1999). These studies have been of value in further elucidating cognitive components of recollective experience that might contribute to spared memory in amnesia (Paller, Kutas, & McIsaac, 1995; Allan, Wilding, & Rugg, 1998; Spencer, 2000; Stenberg, 2000).

Emotional and other evaluative responses. Anecdotal and formal experimental evidence indicates that new emotional responses can be preserved as implicit memories in the absence of conscious recollection of the experiences on which these reactions are based. Johnson, Kim, and Risse (1985) explored this idea formally with a study based on the "mere exposure" effect (Zajonc, 1968). Zajonc had shown that, in normal subjects, repeated exposure to an object tends to increase judgments of likability, even when exposures are subliminal (i.e., not consciously perceived; Kunst-Wilson & Zajonc, 1980; Zajonc, 1980). In the Johnson et al. study, patients with Korsakoff syndrome and controls preferred previously presented Korean melodies over new melodies; however, Korsakoff patients were significantly impaired for recognition of old melodies. In a second task, participants were shown pictures of two faces accompanied by fictional biographical information that depicted one face positively and the other negatively. Twenty days later, both groups showed strong

preference for the "good guy." Control subjects made this choice 100% of the time, and always based their judgment on explicit memory for the accompanying description. The amnesic subjects were unable to recall any of the biographical information, yet also showed a strong "good guy" preference (78%), and this preference was maintained at 1-year follow-up.

Damasio, Tranel, and Damasio (1989) performed a similar experiment with the postencephalitic patient Boswell. The experimenters set up a series of positive, negative, and neutral encounters with three confederates. When asked afterward to whom he would go for treats, Boswell strongly preferred the positive confederate over the negative one, with the neutral confederate falling in between. This occurred despite his inability to recall or demonstrate familiarity with the confederates. These preferences were maintained over a period of years.

These studies suggest that amnesic patients can learn new conceptual "emotional" associations that persist over long periods. They also suggest that emotional responses, as reflected by fairly complex behavioral interactions, can serve as another measure of spared memory function. Such research may provide insights on emotional functioning in memory-impaired individuals, about which little is currently known. It has been argued that emotional and amnestic function can be anatomically dissociated within the medial temporal lobe, with emotional functioning depending preferentially on the amygdala, and memory function depending more strongly on the hippocampal system (cf. Zola-Morgan, Squire, Alvarez Royo, & Clower, 1991).

Classical conditioning. It has long been known that amnesic patients may show intact classical conditioning of the eyeblink response when a conditioned stimulus (e.g., a tone or light) is paired with an unconditioned stimulus (airpuff applied to the open eye; Weiskrantz & Warrington, 1979). Amnesic patients with temporal lobe lesions (including patient H.M.) can readily show both delay- (Gabrieli et al., 1995) and trace-conditioning (Woodruff Pak, 1993), and can display the effects of conditioning over long periods (Schugens & Daum, 1999) even though they have no general recollection of the conditioned–unconditioned stimulus relationship or of the general experimental situation. However, one study (McGlinchey-Berroth, Carrillo, Gabrieli, Brawn, & Disterhoft, 1997) reported impaired eyeblink conditioning in patients with amnesia from bilateral medial temporal lobe damage, using the trace conditioning paradigm, whereas another (McGlinchey-Berroth, Brawn, & Disterhoft, 1999) showed that the timing of conditioned responses may be abnormal in these patients. Patients with diencephalic damage also appear to be impaired in classical eyeblink conditioning (McGlinchey et al., 1995) using the delay paradigm.

EVALUATING THE AMNESIC PATIENT

When evaluating the amnesic patient, the clinician should use a variety of memory measures with a range of difficulty and should incorporate both recall and recognition formats (Shimamura & Squire, 1986). Amnesic patients not only show substantial statistical discrepancies between general cognitive abilities and performance on memory measures, but also demonstrate functional impairment in everyday life. The two main assessment goals are (a) to establish the severity of the memory defect in the context of other cognitive complaints, and (b) to characterize the nature of the memory impairment and its basis in encoding, storage, and retrieval operations.

The first goal is best achieved by embedding memory testing in a comprehensive mental status or neuropsychological examination that includes assessment of general intellectual capacity, language functions, visuoperceptual/ visuospatial skill, frontal-executive skills, motor functions, psychopathology, and emotional dysfunction. Screening approaches typically are not sufficient. Historically, one approach has been the *global achievement model* (Delis, 1989), which is designed to quantify the severity of a memory deficit by representing memory performance as an overall score that can be compared to performance on intellectual or neuropsychological tests. For example, the original Wechsler Memory Scale (WMS; Wechsler, 1945) yielded an overall Memory Quotient (MQ) intended as an omnibus index of memory ability that could be compared with IQ.

Although this approach is sometimes useful for determining whether a memory disorder is present, detailed prescriptive and rehabilitative recommendations require the kind of data supplied only by comprehensive neuropsychological evaluation. For this reason, subsequent editions of the WMS have tended to de-emphasize the global achievement model because it fails to account for qualitative differences among patients who score at about the same level (Kaplan, 1983).

The second goal is achieved by performing in-depth evaluation of underlying memory functions relevant to the diagnostic or descriptive task faced by the clinician. The *cognitive science model* (Delis, 1989) incorporates concepts from cognitive psychology and psychometrics. It applies methods of memory assessment derived from the cognitive information-processing literature to the clinical evaluation of memory-disordered patients in an effort to better understand spared and impaired information processing capabilities. Such a battery should broadly evaluate immediate, recent, and remote memory (as defined below), incorporate different types of material (e.g., verbal and nonverbal) and testing formats (e.g., free recall, cued recall, recognition), and should evaluate the manner in which the patient learns complex material (e.g., short passages, word lists, complex nonverbal designs). A detailed description of available clinical memory tests is given in Lezak, Howieson, and Loring (2004); other reviews of memory assessment include Delis (1989) and O'Connor and Lafleche (2006).

IMMEDIATE MEMORY SPAN

The amnesic patient usually performs normally on tasks that require the repetition of information immediately after it is presented, in contrast to patients with impaired attention. Diseases that interfere with rehearsal, such as certain forms of aphasia, can also impair verbal immediate memory. The most widely used span tests are the Digit Span subtests of the Wechsler Intelligence Scales (WAIS) and the WMS. Although Digit Span Forward provides a relatively direct measure of immediate memory span, the backward trial adds a manipulation component that draws more heavily on working memory capacity. Other tests of working memory (Letter-Number Sequencing, Paced Auditory Serial Addition Test) are also available. Nonverbal pointing span can be evaluated with a modification of the Corsi Blocks (Kaplan, Delis, Fein, & Morris, 1991) that was first incorporated into the WMS-III (Wechsler, 1997). Tests evaluating memory for increasingly long sequences of words or sentences (e.g., Benton & Hamsher, 1976) are also available.

ANTEROGRADE LEARNING (RECENT MEMORY)

Memory for Word Lists and Stories

The most widely used clinical memory tests are those that require the patient to verbally recall or recognize information presented in list or story format. The most useful tests are those that include both immediate- and delayed-recall probes. Prominent examples of list-learning tasks include the Rey Auditory Verbal Learning Test (RAVLT; Rey, 1964), the California Verbal Learning Test-II (CVLT-II; Delis, Kaplan, Kramer, & Ober, 2000), the Selective Reminding Procedure (Bushke & Fuld, 1974), and the Hopkins Verbal Learning Test (Brandt, 1991). Each measure provides a number of performance indices that may help characterize the memory deficit. Examples of story recall tests include the WMS Logical memory subtest (Wechsler, 1945, and subsequent revisions), the Babcock-Levy Story (Babcock, 1930), and the Randt Memory Test (Randt & Brown, 1983). The Warrington Recognition Memory Test (RMT; Warrington, 1984) provides a relatively sensitive (but nonspecific) test of verbal (word) and nonverbal (face) recognition using a forced-choice format. This test shows some utility for documenting material-specificity (e.g., verbal vs. nonverbal memory deficits) in memory performance after unilateral brain lesions, and has been used in recent studies as one of an increasing number of tests sensitive to reduced effort by the examinee (Kim et al., 2009).

Nonverbal Memory Tests

A variety of tests using nonverbal stimuli are also available. These include drawing-from-memory tests such as Visual Reproduction subtests of the WMS (Wechsler, 1945, and subsequent revisions), Benton Visual Retention Test (VRT; Benton, 1974), and Rey Complex Figure (Myers REF) test. In addition to accuracy, the patient's drawing approach can also be evaluated for the degree of organization (Binder, 1982; Hamby, Wilkins, & Barry, 1993; Stern et al., 1994). A copy trial should be used to distinguish nonverbal memory deficits from constructional disability, visuoperceptual dysfunction, or planning difficulty. Unfortunately, it is difficult to assess nonverbal free recall without requiring construction in some form (e.g., drawing), and nonverbal memory is therefore often assessed with forced-choice recognition tests. Examples include multiple-choice alternatives for the Benton VRT (Benton, Hamsher, Varney, & Spreen, 1983) and WMS figures (Milberg, Hebben, & Kaplan, 1986), and yes–no recognition tests of faces (Warrington RMT and WMS tests) and designs (WMS VR, Brief Visual Memory Test). The Continuous Visual Memory Test (Trahan & Larrabee, 1986) provides a "recurring figures" type of recognition test with excellent normative data, a visuoperceptual check, and a method for calculating response bias in recognition performance.

RETROGRADE AND REMOTE MEMORY

The patient's ability to recall information acquired before the onset of amnesia can be assessed informally by planning an interview containing both autobiographical and general knowledge questions. Including the former type of material requires a knowledgeable informant and poses some difficulty regarding quantification of the severity and temporal parameters of any deficit that emerges. A number of more formal assessments of remote memory have been developed. The Boston Remote Memory Battery (Albert, Butters, & Levin, 1979) assesses memory for public events and famous faces, and it contains both easy and difficult questions about historical events from the 1930s to the 1990s. The test, and others like it, has been used extensively in clinical and experimental research documenting patterns of remote memory impairment in various clinical populations. Because this test assesses knowledge of well-known historical events, it is difficult to determine when knowledge about a specific public event or famous personality was actually acquired. This makes interpretation of temporal parameters of remote memory loss very difficult. In an attempt to deal with this problem, Squire and colleagues (Squire & Slater, 1975) developed the TV Test, which assesses memory for television shows that were broadcast for only one season. This test has been periodically updated and has been used widely in studies of amnesic patients. A similar test probing knowledge of transient news events is also available (O'Connor et al., 2000).

Tests of retrograde amnesia present substantial methodological and conceptual complexities (Sanders & Warrington, 1971; Squire, Haist, & Shimamura, 1989). Most of these tests make three important assumptions: (a) relevant information was learned at about the time it occurred (e.g., that the patient learned in late 1963 about the assassination of President Kennedy), (b) all items were learned with approximately equal strength, and (c) forgetting of specific details has proceeded at approximately the same rate since original learning. It is often difficult to determine when a patient learned about a specific event, and it is clear that the method by which the subject learned about the event (e.g., through high school history vs. personal experience) may affect the nature of the memory store. The field is still in need of further refinement of remote memory tests that address limitations of available instruments.

SPECIALIZED TESTS OF INFORMATION PROCESSING

Several experimental memory tests are available that are designed to evaluate specific aspects of memory-relevant information processing. Tests relevant to *encoding* ability include Wickens' release from proactive interference procedure (Wickens, 1970), comparison of recall and recognition performance on categorized versus uncategorized lists, and variations of the levels-of-processing approach (Craik & Lockhart, 1972), in which orienting questions at the point of learning directs processing to particular aspects of target stimuli. Encoding deficits are revealed by insensitivity to these manipulations and by impaired immediate memory performance.

Rate of forgetting from long-term memory may be evaluated with a variety of recognition paradigms based on the Huppert and Piercy (1979) procedure. The key feature of this approach is to equate initial learning with a control group in some meaningful way, and to then periodically probe recognition accuracy at specified delays after original learning. *Retrieval* processes can be evaluated by manipulating cues available during the memory test and making comparisons between free recall and recognition. Additionally, disproportionate improvement on recognition, when compared to free recall, is often taken as evidence of a retrieval deficit. However, this pattern may not be specific to retrieval impairment; it can also reflect weak memory due to poor initial encoding or a long study–test interval.

SPARED FUNCTIONS

The clinician should document domains of spared memory in amnesic patients. Semantic memory can be assessed with general information questions (e.g., Information subtest from the Wechsler Intelligence Scale family; e.g., Wechsler, 1981), vocabulary measures, and tests of controlled word association (Benton, Hamsher, Varney, & Spreen, 1983). Performance on indirect tests of memory can be assessed using variants of word-stem completion priming (Graf, Squire, & Mandler, 1984; Cermak, Mather, & Hill, 1997), perceptual identification (Jacoby & Dallas, 1981; Tulving & Schacter, 1990), motor skill learning (Milner, Corkin, & Teuber, 1968; Willingham, 1998), and other procedures relevant to the specific case.

ANATOMY: STRUCTURE, FUNCTION, AND CLINICAL CORRELATES

The amnesic syndrome in humans has classically been associated with damage to the hippocampus and adjacent medial temporal lobe structures (medial temporal amnesia), the hypothalamus and thalamus (diencephalic amnesia), and the basal forebrain (basal forebrain amnesia). These regions are extensively interconnected, and damage to connecting structures also can result in amnesia. Each of these three areas and their principal connections will be considered in turn. Other brain regions, such as the amygdala, the prefrontal cortex, parietal cortex, and basal ganglia, are also implicated in memory; however, selective lesions to these regions do not result in the complete amnesic syndrome. The amygdala will be briefly discussed; the other regions will not be considered here in any detail.

MEDIAL TEMPORAL LOBES: HIPPOCAMPUS, PARAHIPPOCAMPAL GYRUS, AND AMYGDALA

Anatomy of the Medial Temporal Lobes

Damage to the medial temporal lobes is a prominent cause of the amnesic syndrome. Structures involved include the parahippocampal gyrus, hippocampus, and amygdala (see Figure 16-1). Anteriorly, the parahippocampal gyrus consists of entorhinal and perirhinal cortex; posteriorly it comprises the parahippocampal cortex (see Table 16-1). As one pro-

Table 16–1. Anatomic Designations

Individual Designations	Collective Designations	
Ammon's horn (CA1-4) Dentate gyrus Subiculum		Hippocampus
Presubiculum Parasubiculum Entorhinal cortex Perirhinal cortex	Rhinal cortex	Parahippocampal gyrus
Parahippocampal cortex (areas TH, TF in macaque; post-rhinal cortex in rat).		

ceeds from temporal neocortex toward the more primitive three-layered hippocampal cortex, one encounters perirhinal and then entorhinal cortex, which is adjacent to para- and presubicular cortex, and then the subiculum of the hippocampus. The amygdala lies just anterior to the hippocampus. It is a largely subcortical structure, intimately related with the basal forebrain and often classified as one of the basal ganglia.

Hippocampal Anatomy and Connections.
Intrinsic connections: The trisynaptic circuit. Internal hippocampal connections were identified by Ramón y Cajal and his student Lorrente de Nó (cited by Van Hoesen, 1985), who first described the *trisynaptic circuit.* Neurons of the neighboring entorhinal cortex project via the *perforant pathway* (see Figure 16-2, pathway 1) to the dentate gyrus, which then projects to the CA3 region of Ammon's horn (*mossy fiber* projection, Figure 16-2, pathway 2). Axons in CA3 then bifurcate: One branch projects subcortically via the fimbria fornix; the second branch projects to CA1 (Shaffer collateral pathway, Figure 16-2, pathway 4), which not only projects to the fimbria but also to the subiculum. The subiculum is the major source of hippocampal efferents; it projects to cortical and subcortical structures, and projects back to the entorhinal cortex (Figure 16-2, pathway 6), thus completing the circuit (Rosene & Van Hoesen, 1977). Connections within the trisynaptic circuit

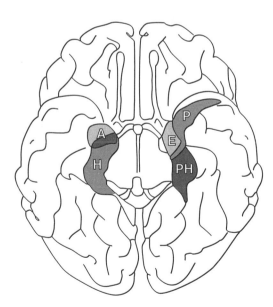

Figure 16–1. The amygdala, hippocampus, and parahippocampal cortex. The positions of the amygdala (A) and hippocampus (H) are indicated on the left. On the right, the overlying parahippocampal cortical structures are indicated; namely, the entorhinal cortex (E), perirhinal cortex (P), and parahippocampal cortex (PH).

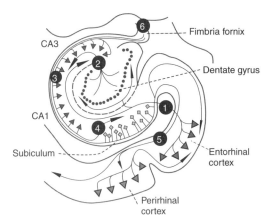

Figure 16–2. The internal structure of the hippocampus. The circled numbers indicate: (1) The perforant pathway; (2) projections from the dentate to CA3; (3) from CA3 to CA1; (4) from CA1 to the subiculum; (5) from the subiculum to the entorhinal and perirhinal cortices, and (6) the subcortical projections of CA3, CA1 and subiculum via the fimbria fornix.

are unidirectional, suggesting an orderly progression of information.

Cortical connections: The parahippocampal gyrus. Connections between the hippocampus and the parahippocampal gyrus are best characterized as a combination of hierarchical and parallel pathways (Figure 16-3). Hierarchically, afferents from sensory cortices project to the perirhinal and parahippocampal cortices, which project to the entorhinal cortex, which, in turn, projects to the hippocampus via the perforant path (Van Hoesen & Pandya, 1975). Thus, the entorhinal cortex receives indirect access to a variety of highly processed information (Van Hoesen, Pandya & Butters, 1972; Amaral, Insausti & Cowan, 1983; Van Hoesen, 1985; Insausti, Amaral & Cowan, 1987a). Unlike the intrinsic hippocampal connections, connections of the parahippocampal region are reciprocal (Rosene & Van Hoesen, 1977) and maintain the same hierarchical progression in reverse. That is, hippocampal output is relayed to the cortex via the entorhinal cortex, followed by the perirhinal and parahippocampal cortices (see Figure 16-3).

Within the context of this reciprocal hierarchy, there are two relatively distinct parallel circuits. The perirhinal cortex in primates receives input

predominately from the ventral visual stream and receives no auditory input; most polysensory information is relayed through the parahippocampal cortex, which is heavily innervated by afferents from the dorsal visual stream (Burwell, 2000; Bussey & Saksida, 2005). Reciprocal projections with the entorhinal cortex are also mostly segregated, with the perirhinal cortex almost exclusively projecting to the lateral entorhinal cortex and the parahippocampal cortex projecting to the medial entorhinal cortex (Burwell, 2000).

There are exceptions to the hierarchical and parallel circuitry. For example, reciprocal connections exist between the parahippocampal and perirhinal cortices, with those from the

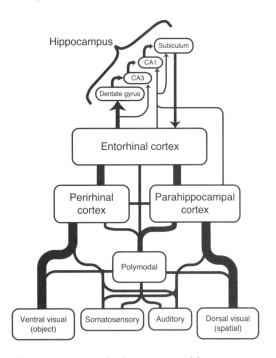

Figure 16–3. Hierarchical connectivity of the parahippocampal region. The entorhinal cortex is the principal gateway to the hippocampus. Much of the input to entorhinal cortex comes from perirhinal and entorhinal cortices. The visual object stream is preferentially directed to perirhinal cortex, whereas the visual spatial stream is directed to parahippocampal cortex. Lines without arrows indicate bidirectional connections. Adapted from Suzuki, W.I, & Eichenbaum, H. (2000). The neurophysiology of memory. In H. E. Scharfman, M. P. Witter, & R. Schwarcz (Eds.), *The parahippocampal region. Implications for neurological and psychiatric diseases. Annals of the New York Academy of Science*, 911, 175–191, with permission of the publisher.

former being more prominent (Burwell, 2000). Additionally, the hippocampus receives direct projections from the perirhinal and parahippocampal cortices (Witter et al., 2000).

Subcortical connections: Papez' circuit. Subcortical projections from the hippocampus form the first portion of a circuit described by Papez in 1937 to explain how emotional expression and feeling, mediated by the hypothalamus, could be coordinated with cognition, mediated by the cortex. The hippocampus projects via the post-commissural fornix to the mammillary bodies, which project via the mammillothalamic tract to the anterior nuclei of the thalamus. The circuit is completed by thalamic projections to the cingulate gyrus and cingulate projections, via the cingulate bundle or cingulum, to the hippocampus (Figure 16-4).

Subcortical hippocampal projections also exist outside of Papez' circuit. Fibers from CA1, CA3, and the subiculum project in the precommissural fornix to the lateral septal nucleus (Swanson & Cowan, 1979). The hippocampus also projects to the amygdala, nucleus accumbens, and other regions in the basal forebrain, and to the ventromedial hypothalamus (Swanson & Cowan, 1979; Amaral & Insausti, 1990).

The hippocampus also receives subcortical projections from midline, anterior, and laterodorsal thalamic nuclei, and from amygdala, hypothalamus, and central gray region of the midbrain. It receives cholinergic projections from the basal forebrain (medial septal nucleus and nucleus of the diagonal band of Broca), dopaminergic projections from the ventral tegmental area, serotonergic projections from the raphe nuclei, and noradrenergic projections from the locus coeruleus (Herkenham, 1978; Amaral & Cowan, 1980; Van Hoesen, 1985; Insuasti, Amaral, & Cowan, 1987b; Amaral & Insausti, 1990). The retrosplenial cortex also receives prominent projections from anterior thalamic nuclei, and has reciprocal connections with the hippocampus and entorhinal cortex (Morris, Petrides & Pandya, 1999).

Hippocampal Physiology. Physiological studies reveal cellular mechanisms that could subserve memory in the hippocampus. Although these mechanisms are not unique to the hippocampus, they may underlie the ability of the hippocampus to preserve the associations of disparate inputs. High-frequency stimulation of the perforant path enhances transmission at synapses in the

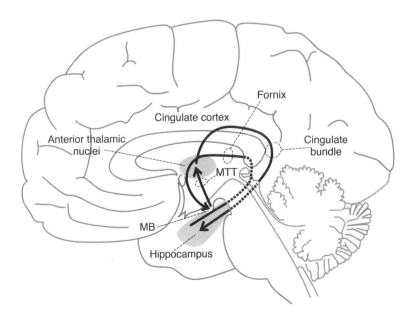

Figure 16–4. Papez' circuit. A schematic drawing of Papez' circuit, from the hippocampus via the fornix to the mammillary body (MB) of the hypothalamus, thence via the mamillothalamic tract (MMT) to the anterior thalamic nuclei, thence to the cingulate cortex and via the cingulate bundle to the hippocampus.

dentate gyrus. This enhancement, called *long-term potentiation* (LTP), can last weeks (Lomo, 1971; Bliss & Lomo 1973; Bliss & Gardner-Medwin, 1973). Long-term potentiation can be homosynaptic (caused by repetitive firing of one input), heterosynaptic (occurring when two particular inputs to a single neuron fire coincidently), or Hebbian (occurring when stimulation of a neuronal afferent occurs when a neuronal cell body is coincidentally depolarized; Bailey et al., 2000). The last two kinds of LTP could represent mechanisms by which two coincident stimuli are associated (see Kennedy, 1989). Further studies have identified cellular mechanisms underlying LTP (see Gustaffsson & Wigstrom, 1988; Kennedy, 1989; Matthies et al., 1990; Bailey et al., 2000). In the experimental setting, drugs that block specific kinds of glutamate receptors may interfere with both LTP and memory (see Izquierdo, 1991). Recently, it has been demonstrated that maintenance of LTP requires a protein kinase-C isoform, PKM-ζ (Hernandez et al., 2003). Injection a PKM-ζ-inhibitor into rat hippocampus abolishes spatial memories (Pastalkova et al., 2006).

Oscillatory EEG rhythms have been shown to correlate with memory encoding and recall. Oscillations in the θ (4–8 Hz) and fast γ (30–100 Hz) bands recorded from depth electrodes in humans with epilepsy predict memory formation (Sederberg et al., 2003, 2007). Synchronous firing of neurons may serve to bind disparate elements of a memory (Jensen, Kaiser, & Lachaux, 2007).

Additionally, multi-electrode recordings of hippocampal activity in rodents during inactivity and sleep reveal multiple rehearsals of brain activity that accompanied spatial exploration during the previous day (Wilson & McNaughton, 1994; O'Neill et al., 2006; O'Neill et al., 2010). Other studies provide evidence that sleep may have an important role in memory consolidation (reviewed in Diekelmann and Born, 2010).

Amygdala Anatomy and Connectivity. The amygdala is situated immediately anterior to the hippocampus, and deep to the periamygdaloid and perirhinal cortices. It can be broadly conceived as having two parts: a large basolateral group of nuclei, with extensive connections to limbic and association cortex and to dorsomedial thalamus, and a smaller corticomedial segment, which extends into the basal forebrain and has extensive connections with basal forebrain, hypothalamus, and brainstem (DeOlmos, 1990; Heimer & Alheid, 1991; Scott, DeKosky, & Scheff, 1991).

Both the amygdala and hippocampus are strongly interconnected with frontal and temporal limbic cortex, and thus have indirect access to polymodal and supramodal neocortical association areas (Herzog & Van Hoesen, 1976; Rosene & Van Hoesen, 1977). Both project to basal forebrain and hypothalamus. The amygdala and hippocampus also have direct interconnections (Insuausti, Amaral, & Cowen, 1987b; Saunders, Rosene, & Van Hoesen, 1988; Poletti, 1986).

However, there are also clear differences in connectivity. The amygdala is closely related to limbic and neocortical regions that are of pale-ocortical derivation, including the orbitofrontal and anterior temporal cortex (Porrino, Crane, & Goldman-Rakic, 1981), whereas the hippocampus is archicortical, and is more closely related to cortex of archicortical derivation such as the cingulate cortex (Pandya & Yeterian 1990). The amygdala projects to the dorsomedial nucleus of the thalamus (Nauta, 1961), whereas the hippocampus projects via the fornix and mamillary bodies to the anterior thalamic nuclei. Basal forebrain connections also differ: The hippocampus is related to more ventral portions of the septal nuclei, and the amygdala has more extensive connections with the bed nucleus of the stria terminalis. Cholinergic projections to the amygdala are from the nucleus basalis of Meynert, whereas the hippocampus receives input from the septal region and diagonal band of Broca (Mesulam et al., 1983). Finally, the amygdala has connections with brainstem autonomic centers (nucleus of the tractus solitarius), providing a direct pathway for limbic–autonomic interaction. A circuit from the anterior temporal lobe through amygdala to mediodorsal thalamus to orbitofrontal cortex and back to the anterior temporal cortex via the uncinate fasciculus is sometimes called the *lateral limbic circuit*, described by Yakovlev and Nauta (1962) and Livingston and Escobar (1971), and distinguished from Papez' medial limbic circuit.

Behavioral Studies of Medial Temporal Lobe Amnesia

Early Studies. Although there were previous reports of temporal lobe lesions in amnesic patients (von Bechterew, 1900; Grünthal 1947; Glees & Griffith, 1952), the importance of the temporal lobes in memory was established by reports of severe and permanent amnesia after bilateral resections of the medial aspects of the temporal lobes in humans (Scoville, 1954; Scoville & Milner, 1957). The aim of surgery was either to ameliorate psychotic behavior or to treat intractable focal epilepsy. H.M., who was treated for epilepsy, is the best-studied of such patients, having been the subject of numerous reports over nearly five decades. Early investigations of humans indicated that damage to the hippocampus was a prerequisite for medial temporal amnesia: Resections restricted to the uncus and amygdala did not result in amnesia (Scoville & Milner, 1957). The severity of the amnesia increased as the lesions extended posteriorly to involve the hippocampus (Scoville & Milner, 1957); this relationship also held for the selective verbal or nonverbal amnesias that followed, respectively, left or right temporal resections (Milner, 1972, 1974; Smith, 1989), although more recent work (Barr et al., 1997) has shown the relationship between language-nondominant resections and nonverbal memory impairment to be less robust. The importance of the hippocampus was also supported by Penfield and Milner (1958), who reported two patients with amnesia following unilateral temporal resections. They speculated that preexisting contralateral hippocampal damage explained the severe amnesia after unilateral resection. This was confirmed when one of the patients (P.B.) was found at autopsy to have hippocampal sclerosis in the unoperated temporal lobe, but no damage to other temporal cortical structures or to the amygdala (Penfield & Matheison, 1974).

The case for the importance of the hippocampus in memory was subsequently made even more convincingly by the study of patients who survived cardiopulmonary arrest with well-documented deficits in memory, and whose brains were carefully examined after they died from other causes (Cummings et al., 1984; Zola-Morgan, Squire, & Amaral, 1986; Victor & Agamanolis, 1990). In each case, damage was restricted almost entirely to the hippocampus, where the pyramidal neurons of CA1, exquisitely sensitive to hypoxia, were selectively destroyed.

Despite strong evidence implicating the hippocampus in human amnesia, it proved difficult to develop an animal model of human medial temporal amnesia. In the two decades that followed the documentation of medial temporal amnesia in humans with medial temporal resections, numerous studies showed that animals with medial temporal resections were not impaired on many learning tasks (see Zola-Morgan & Squire, 1983, 1984). In general, the tasks that animals performed well required the discrimination between two objects that were presented repeatedly over multiple trials. Both control and medial-temporal lobe lesioned animals easily learned to select the object that would be rewarded. Gaffan (1974) and Mishkin and Petri (1984) pointed out that these tasks allowed for the development of response habits, and therefore might be a form of procedural memory, which is spared in human medial temporal amnesia. They postulated such response habits could be avoided if a different set of objects was used in each trial. Gaffen (1974) described a delayed match to sample (DMS) task, and Mishkin and Petri (1984) a delayed non-match to sample (DNMS) task. In both tasks, the animal is presented with an object, and after a delay, is presented with the same object paired with a new object. On the DMS task, to receive a reward, the animal must chose which of two objects has been presented before, and on the DNMS task, the animal must select the novel stimulus. In both tasks, the lesioned animals were impaired. Human amnesic patients also have difficulty with DMS (Sidman, Stoddard, & Mohr, 1968) and DNMS tasks (Oscar-Berman & Bonner, 1985; Squire, Zola-Morgan, & Chen, 1988; Zola-Morgan & Squire, 1990a). Other tasks have also been developed that are sensitive to medial temporal lesions in monkeys, and that present difficulties for human amnesic patients (Squire, Zola-Morgan, & Chen, 1988; Zola-Morgan & Squire, 1990a).

Dual-system Theories of Amnesia. Armed with behavioral tasks that were thought to be relevant to human amnesia, investigators proceeded to investigate which regions within the medial temporal lobe were actually critical for memory. Mishkin (1978; 1982; Mishkin & Saunders, 1979; Mishkin et al., 1982) noted that lesions restricted to the hippocampus or its subcortical connections (Papez' circuit) appeared to produce a less severe memory deficit on DNMS tasks than did lesions that involved the hippocampus plus other mesial temporal structures. Mishkin first suggested that the amygdala might be the critical second component in the medial temporal lobe. The amygdala is a component of the lateral limbic circuit (Nauta, 1962). In primates, either temporal or subcortical lesions involving components of both the Papez' and the lateral limbic circuits produced more severe memory impairment than did damage restricted to either circuit alone (Aggleton & Mishkin, 1983; Bachevalier, Saunders, & Mishkin, 1985; Bachevalier, Parkinson, & Mishkin, 1985; Bachevalier & Mishkin, 1986). But Zola-Morgan, Squire, and Amaral (1989a) showed that stereotactic lesions of the amygdala sparing perirhinal cortex did not add to the memory deficit of animals with hippocampal and parahippocampal gyrus lesions. They suggested that memory deficits attributed to amygdalar lesions in fact resulted from collateral damage to the perirhinal cortex. Because both the amygdala and the perirhinal cortex project to dorsomedial thalamus, the dual-system theory could be easily modified by substituting perirhinal cortex for the amygdala. This theory has also been invoked to explain the pathogenesis of thalamic amnesia (see below).

Role of the Parahippocampal Gyrus. Zola-Morgan et al. (1989b) found that lesions involving both perirhinal and parahippocampal cortex, but not the hippocampus, cause severe memory impairment in the monkey. This is not explained entirely by interruption of cortical input to the hippocampus, because monkeys with this lesion had more severe memory deficits than did monkeys with lesions that only involved the hippocampus (Zola-Morgan & Squire, 1986; Squire & Zola-Morgan, 1991). Similar findings were reported by Meunier et al. (1993). This suggests that the perirhinal cortex not only conveys information to the hippocampus via entorhinal cortex, but that it contributes to memory in its own right.

Perirhinal cortical lesions affect performance on DNMS more than hippocampal lesions. In fact, isolated hippocampal lesions in monkeys produce little or no deficit in DNMS performance (Murray, Gaffen, & Mishkin, 1993; Murray & Mishkin, 1998; but see Alvarez, Zola-Morgan, & Squire, 1995), leading some to question whether there is a role for the hippocampus in memory (see, for example, Loring et al., 1991; Pigott & Milner, 1993). In animals, lesions of the hippocampus or fornix result in deficits in spatial memory tasks (Mahut & Moss, 1986; Parkinson Murray, & Mishkin, 1988; Angeli, Murray, & Mishkin, 1993; Malkova, Mishkin, & Bachevalier, 1995; Wan, Aggleton, & Brown, 1999), suggesting that perirhinal cortex and hippocampus may subserve different aspects of memory—the perirhinal cortex for memory of object identity, and the hippocampus for memory of spatial location. Hippocampal neurons in rodents respond to specific spatial location as an animal moves through an environment (O'Keefe & Dostrovsky, 1971). O'Keefe and Nadel (1978) proposed that episodic memory in humans may make use of brain mechanisms that originally evolved to map spatial relationships. Gaffen suggests that the relationship between the hippocampal spatial ability and episodic memory is in the ability to associate an object with a specific spatial background, defining an episodic event (Gaffen & Parker, 1996). Spatial information may reach the hippocampus by way of parietal projections to parahippocampal cortex (Suzuki & Amaral, 1994). The parahippocampal gyrus appears to be important for topographic orientation (see Chapter 7).

The perirhinal cortex, on the other hand, can be considered the last link in a chain of visual association cortices in the ventral visual stream critical for object identification. Murray and Bussey (1999) suggest that perirhinal cortex can encode objects in sufficient complexity as to allow recognition in the most varied circumstances. Monkeys with perirhinal cortical lesions lose the ability to make discriminations on DNMS tasks that they learned preoperatively, but they are nevertheless able to acquire similar discriminations postoperatively (Thorton, Rothblatt, & Murray, 1997). Murray and Bussey (1999) suggest that the preoperative discriminations were made on the basis of the most complex analysis of the properties of the object mediated by perirhinal cortex. Postoperatively, the animal can no longer make these kinds of discriminations, and fails the task; however, the animal can acquire new discriminations presumably based on less complex analysis mediated by remaining association cortex proximal to the perirhinal cortex. Murray and Bussey (1999) and others (Taylor, Moss, Stamatakis, & Tyler, 2006; Moses, Ryan, Bardouille, et al., 2009) have suggested that perirhinal cortex contributes to networks subserving semantic memory. If so, patients with lesions restricted to hippocampus might be able to acquire new semantic memories. The ability to acquire new knowledge is relatively preserved in patients with hypoxic damage to the hippocampus acquired in childhood, despite dramatic and long-lasting impairment of episodic memory (Vargha-Kardem et al., 1997). These children may continue to perform at grade level in school. Patients with hippocampal damage acquired in adult life have been shown to have familiarity with vocabulary that originated after the onset of amnesia (Verfaellie, Koseff, & Alexander, 2000), suggesting a retained ability to learn new material despite very poor episodic memory. It has also been proposed that patients with hippocampal damage may also have preservation of recognition memory based on familiarity (Aggleton et al., 2005). In this view, a complete recollection of an event, more than just familiarity, requires hippocampal processing.

Role of Temporal Neocortex. Some attention has been given to the role of anterior temporal neocortex, outside of parahippocampal cortex. Lesions of anterior temporal neocortex (temporal pole and portions of the inferotemporal cortex) in monkeys impair performance on DNMS (Spiegler & Mishkin, 1981) and DMS (Horel, Vyotko, & Salsbury, 1984; Cirillo, Horel, & George, 1989; George, Horel, & Cirillo, 1989). Horel and colleagues provide evidence that this cannot be accounted for by impairment in visual discrimination, and they argue that anterior and inferior temporal neocortex contribute to memory (George, Horel, & Cirillo, 1989; see also, Horel, 1978). Several lines of evidence suggest that temporal neocortex plays a role in semantic memory. The semantic dementias are associated with anterior temporal neocortical atrophy (see Chapter 17). Retrograde (remote) memories may be resistant to memory loss because they have become semantic (that is, part of knowledge structure divorced from experience of personal events). The extent of retrograde memory loss has been thought to correlate with anterior temporal neocortical damage. Damasio and colleagues (Damasio et al., 1985; Damasio et al., 1987; Damasio, Tranel, & Damasio, 1989) suggest that the temporally extensive retrograde amnesia of their postencephalitic patient, Boswell, might be attributed to anterior temporal neocortical destruction. Boswell's severe retrograde amnesia distinguished him from H.M., whose lesions spared most temporal neocortical areas. Kapur et al. (1992) described severe retrograde amnesia in a woman following closed head injury. Anterograde amnesia cleared nearly completely within 6 months of the injury, but the patient was left with severe retrograde amnesia. Magnetic resonance imaging (MRI) scans showed bilateral anterior temporal lesions sparing hippocampus. Head injury, however, typically causes more widespread damage, particularly to subcortical structures. Kapur et al.'s case did have acute frontal white matter changes on MRI. The documentation of severe retrograde amnesia with little or no persisting anterograde amnesia is significant; but localization to anterior temporal requires confirmation. Reed and Squire (1998) describe little or no retrograde general or autobiographical memory loss in two patients with moderately severe anterograde amnesia from presumed isolated hippocampal pathology, whereas two patients with postencephalitic amnesia, who had extensive temporal lobe damage not restricted to the hippocampus, had impairments of retrograde as well as anterograde memory.

The Amygdala. Amygdala lesions in primates do not impair performance on the DNMS task, and selective amygdala lesions in humans do not result in the full amnesic syndrome (Milner, 1960; Narabayashi et al., 1963; Lee et al., 1988). Many lines of evidence attest to the importance of the amygdala in emotional behavior.

Amygdala lesions in nonhuman primates have been associated with impairments in stimulus–reward association (Jones & Mishkin, 1972; Speigler & Mishkin, 1981), the association of affect with neutral stimuli (Iwata et al., 1986; LeDoux, 1987; Gaffan & Harrison, 1987; McGaugh et al., 1990), and with defects in social and emotional behavior (Kling & Stecklis, 1976; Zola-Morgan, Squire, & Amaral, 1989a). Stimulation of the amygdala in humans often elicits emotional experiences (Gloor, 1986; see also, Chapter 15).

Although early studies on the effects of selective amygdala lesions on memory in humans were negative or inconclusive (Narabayashi et al., 1963; Lee at al., 1988; Andersen, 1978), subsequent studies have shown an effect of amygdalar lesions on the normal enhancement of memory by emotion. Adolphs et al. (1997) studied two patients with bilateral amygdala calcifications secondary to lipoid proteinosis (Urbach-Wiethe disease). These patients failed to show enhanced memory for emotional stimuli that is seen in normal subjects and even in patients with pure hippocampal lesions (Hamann et al., 1997). Studies of patients with temporal lobe resections for epilepsy show less emotion-based memory enhancement for negatively charged memories in patients with right but not left temporal lobe resections relative to normal subjects. Functional MRI (fMRI) and positron emission tomography (PET) functional imaging studies have shown a correlation between amygdala activation during a learning task and recall of emotionally charged stimuli (Cahill et al., 1996; Hamann et al., 2002; Canli et al., 2000).

Papez' Circuit. The pathologic evidence of mammillary body damage in patients with Wernicke-Korsakoff disease combined with the evidence that medial temporal resections result in amnesia led to speculation that Papez' circuit (hippocampus → fornix → mammillary bodies → anterior thalamus → cingulate gyrus → hippocampus) forms the anatomic substrate of memory (Figure 16-4) (Delay & Brion, 1969). We have already discussed the role of the hippocampus. We will briefly consider the evidence that other components of Papez' circuit are important for memory.

Fornix. Although it was once widely held that fornix damage did not result in memory loss

(Dott, 1938; Cairns & Mosberg, 1951; Garcia Bengochea et al., 1954; Woolsey & Nelson, 1975), there is now ample evidence that fornix lesions in animals (Gaffan, 1974; Moss, Mahut, & Zola-Morgan, 1981; Owen & Butler, 1981; Carr, 1982; Bachevalier, Parkinson, & Mishkin, 1985; Bachevalier, Saunders, & Mishkin, 1985; Gaffen, 1993) and humans (Hassler & Riechert, 1957; Sweet, Talland, & Ervin, 1959; Heilman & Sypert, 1977; Aggleton et al., 2000; Calabrese et al., 1995; D'Esposito et al., 1995; Gaffan, Gaffan, & Hodges, 1991; Gaffan & Gaffan, 1991; Grafman et al., 1985; McMackin et al., 1995; Moudgil et al., 2000; Park et al., 2000) can result in memory impairment. Heilman and Sypert (1977) pointed out that lesions of the fornix posterior to the anterior commissure affect not only fibers destined for the mammillary bodies, but also disrupt connections between the hippocampus and the basal forebrain, and direct projections from the hippocampus to the anterior thalamic nuclei (Veazey, Amaral, & Cogan, 1982; Aggleton, Desimone, & Mishkin, 1986). They suggested that section of the columns of the fornix ventral to the anterior commissure may not cause amnesia, as it only affects projections to the mammillary bodies. The memory loss that sometimes follows section of the corpus callosum has been attributed to incidental damage to the fornix (Clark & Geffen, 1989). Tsvilis et al. (2008) have reported memory deficits in patients with fornix damage related to removal of colloid cysts of the third ventricle. Deficits in recall were correlated with the degree of damage to the fornix, and with subsequent mammillary body atrophy. Infarction of the fornix in humans is also reported to cause amnesia (Park, et al., 2000; Renou et al., 2008).

In primates, fornix damage, like hippocampal lesions, impairs spatial memory and memory for objects in a scene, a paradigm that Gaffan (Gaffan & Parker, 1996) suggests is related to episodic memory. In humans, fornix lesions have been found to affect recall more than recognition (familiarity) memory (Aggleton & Brown, 1999; Tsvilis et al., 2008), and to cause anterograde but not retrograde amnesia (but see Yasuno et al., 1999; Poreh et al., 2004).

Mammillary bodies. The mammillary bodies are visible as paired rounded protrusions on the inferior surface of the brain just rostral to the brainstem. Their anatomy and connections are summarized by Aggleton and Sahgal (1993) and Vann and Aggelton (2004). Both the medial and lateral mammillary nuclei receive input from the medial temporal lobe and project to the anterior thalamic nuclei; however, the connectivity differs. The medial nuclei receive projections from the subiculum and medial entorhinal cortex and project to the anteroventral and anteromedial thalamic nuclei, whereas the lateral mammillary nucleus receives input from presubicular, parasubicular, and postsubicular cortex, and projects to the anteroventral thalamic nucleus. The medial mammillary nuclei are more affected in Wernicke-Korsakoff disease.

The presence of prominent mammillary body damage in Wernicke-Korsakoff syndrome first suggested their importance in memory (Gamper, cited by Victor, Adams, & Collins, 1971). Victor, Adams, and Collins (1971) examined the mammillary bodies and the dorsomedial thalamic nucleus of 43 alcoholics. Five had had suffered Wernicke's encephalopathy but had recovered without evidence of memory loss; 38 had Wernicke-Korsakoff disease, with persistent amnesia. At autopsy, all had lesions of the mammillary bodies, but only the 38 patients with persistent memory loss had lesions involving the dorsomedial thalamic nucleus. The investigators concluded that memory loss could not be attributed solely to mammillary body damage, and was more likely to be associated with thalamic lesions. Mair, Warrington, and Weiskrantz (1979) and Mayes et al. (1988) each report two cases of Wernicke-Korsakoff syndrome with lesions in the thalamus restricted to a thin band of gliosis adjacent to the third ventricle, which affected the midline nuclei, but not the dorsomedial nucleus. Mair, Warrington, and Weiskrantz (1979) suggested that the mammillary body lesions (present in each of these patients) may account for the memory loss. Lesions restricted to the mammillary bodies have not been associated with deficits on DNMS tasks in monkeys (Aggleton & Mishkin, 1985); however, deficits have been found on spatial memory tasks in monkeys (Parker & Gaffan, 1997) and in rats (Sziklas & Petrides, 1998).

Human cases with selective mammillary body lesions are rare. Teuber, Milner, and Vaughan

(1967) report memory loss following a penetrating injury from a fencing foil; however, there was also thalamic damage. Dusoir et al. (1990) reported amnesia in a patient with MRI evidence of mammillary body lesions following a penetrating injury from a snooker cue (Dusoir et al., 1990). Loesch et al. (1995) report memory deficits in a patient with a cavernous malformation of the mammillary bodies, and Tanaka et al. (1997) report memory loss with mammillary body damage following removal of a cystic craniopharyngioma. It is difficult to exclude extramammillary lesions in these cases, especially to adjacent portions of the hypothalamus or to the basal forebrain. Kim et al. (2009) report that functional connectivity between the mammillary bodies and anterior thalamus measured in a resting state by fMRI correlates with memory loss in a small group of patients with Wernicke-Korsakoff disease. In a postmortem examination of patients with careful premortem clinical and psychological evaluation, Harding et al. (2000) compared subjects with Wernicke's encephalopathy with or without lasting amnesia (Korsakoff's psychosis), and found that whereas both amnesic and nonamnesic subjects had atrophy in mammillary bodies and mediodorsal thalamus, only amnesic subjects had significant atrophy in anterior thalamic nuclei.

Anterior thalamic nuclei. The anterior thalamic nuclei consist of anteromedial (am), anteroventral (av), anterodorsal (ad) and lateral dorsal (ld) nuclei. The medial mammillary nucleus projects ipsilaterally to am and av; whereas the lateral mammillary nucleus projects bilaterally to ad (see Aggleton & Sahgal, 1993). The anterior thalamic nuclei also receive a substantial direct projection from the hippocampus. Pre- and parasubiculum project to av, and subiculum to am, and the hippocampus also projects to ld. All of these hippocampal-thalamic projections are reciprocated.

The anterior thalamic nuclei project to the cingulate and retrosplenial cortices, among other locations. The lateral dorsal nucleus projects strongly to retrosplenial cortex, and shows specific degeneration in Alzheimer disease (Xuereb et al., 1991).

The contribution of the mammillothalamic tract and anterior thalamic nuclei to memory function is considered below, in the section on thalamic amnesia.

Cingulate and retrosplenial cortex. The major cortical connections of the anterior thalamic nuclei are with the cingulate gyrus. Bachevalier and Mishkin (1986) suggest that combined lesions of orbitofrontal and anterior cingulate cortex in monkeys damages both memory circuits, the orbitofrontal cortex being connected to the perirhinal-dorsomedial thalamic circuit, and the anterior cingulate to the hippocampal-anterior thalamic circuit. But extensive frontal lesions in man (Eslinger & Damasio, 1985) do not result in the classical amnesic syndrome. Meunier, Bachevalier, and Mishkin (1997) describe a spatial memory deficit in monkeys with anterior cingulate lesions; studies in rats (Aggleton et al., 1995) suggest that this may be due to damage to the underlying cingulate bundle. The anterior cingulate region appears to play a role in initiating movement, in motivation, and in goal-directed behaviors (Devinsky, Morrell, & Vogt (1995), but anterior cingulate gyrus lesions have not been associated with amnesia in humans.

The principal projections of the anterior thalamic nuclei, however, are to posterior cingulate cortex, and especially retrosplenial cortex. These cortical regions are also interconnected with the hippocampus (Morris, Petrides, & Pandya. 1999). Lesions in humans that involve retrosplenial cortex can result in a classical amnesic syndrome (Valenstein et al., 1987) but there remains some debate whether the cause of the amnesia is interruption of cingulate/hippocampal connections via the cingulate bundle, damage to the retrosplenial cortex itself, or damage to hippocampal-thalamic, hippocampal-basal forebrain (septal nuclei), or frontal lobe connections traveling in the fornix (Rudge & Warrington, 1991; von Cramon & Shuri, 1992). Additional cases of amnesia with retrosplenial lesions have been reported (Katai et al., 1992; Takayama et al., 1991; Iwasaki et al., 1993; Arita et al., 1995; Yasuda et al., 1997; Sato et al., 1998, MacDonald et al., 2001; Osawa, Maeshima, & Kunishio, 2008). Amnesia is usually associated with left retrosplenial lesions. Right retrosplenial lesions have been associated with topographic disorientation (Takahashi et al., 1999), a finding in keeping with

extensive connections of retrosplenial cortex with the parietal lobes (Kobayashi & Amara, 2007), and with clinical and functional imaging evidence that the retrosplenial cortex is involved in topographic navigation (Maguire, 2001; Wolbers & Büchel, 2005; Burgess, 2008) (see also Chapter 7).

THALAMIC AMNESIA

The relationship of anterior thalamic pathology to amnesia in Wernicke-Korsakoff amnesia has been mentioned above (Harding et al., 2000). Parker and Gaffen (1997) demonstrated deficits on a delayed matching to place task in monkeys with anterior thalamic lesions. Ghika-Schmid and Bogousslavsky (2000) report a series of 12 patients with anterior thalamic infarcts all of whom demonstrated anterograde amnesia (verbal with left and nonverbal with right hemisphere lesions) in combination with perseveration, transcortical motor aphasia, apathy, and executive dysfunction. They thought this combination of features was highly suggestive of this localization. The lesions involved the anterior thalamic nuclei and not the dorsomedial or ventrolateral nuclei. They also extended to involve the mamillothalamic tract and the internal medullary lamina. Cipolotti et al. (2008) report two cases with very small thalamic lesions involving the mediodorsal and anterior thalamic nuclei and mammillothalamic tract. More often, thalamic lesions in humans associated with severe amnesia spare the anterior thalamic nuclei.

Amnesia associated with tumors in the walls of the third ventricle (Foerster & Gagel, 1933; Grünthal, 1939; Lhermitte, Doussinet, & Ajuriaguerra, 1937; Sprofkin & Sciarra, 1952; Williams & Pennybacker, 1954) provided early evidence that medial thalamic structures may be important in memory. Early reports suggested that N.A., a patient who became amnesic after a fencing foil passed through his nose into the brain (Teuber, Milner, & Vaughan, 1968), had a relatively restricted lesion involving the left dorsomedial thalamic nucleus on CT scan (Squire & Moore, 1979), and that amnesic patients with thalamic strokes had CT evidence of dorsomedial lesions (Speedie & Heilman, 1982; Choi et al., 1983; Bogousslavsky,

Regli, & Assal, 1986). High-resolution imaging in N.A., however, revealed that his lesion affected only the ventral aspect of the dorsomedial nucleus, but severely damaged the intralaminar nuclei, mamillothalamic tract, and internal medullary lamina (Squire et al., 1989). N.A. also had lesions affecting the postcommissural fornix, mammillary bodies, and the right temporal tip. More restricted lesions in patients with thalamic infarctions suggest that thalamic amnesia best correlates with lesions affecting the internal medullary lamina and mamillothalamic tract (von Cramon, Hebel, & Schuri, 1985; Gentilini, DeRenzi, & Crisi, 1987; Graff-Radford et al., 1990; Malamut et al., 1992, Winocur et al., 1984). Lesions that involve portions of the dorsomedial nucleus but spare the internal medullary lamina and mamillothalamic tract are not associated with amnesia (von Cramon, Hebel, & Schuri, 1985; Kritchevsky, Graff-Radford, & Damasio, 1987; Graff-Radford et al., 1990). The modified dual pathway theory described above suggests that severe and lasting amnesia requires disruption of both Papez' circuit and the perirhinal/dorsomedial thalamic/frontal pathway. Graff-Radford et al. (1990) provided a clear anatomic demonstration in the monkey of the juxtaposition of the mamillothalamic tract and the ventral amygdalofugal pathway in the internal medullary lamina.

Alternative explanations of thalamic amnesia suggest a role for the midline thalamic nuclei, which include the parataenial, anterior paraventricular, centralis medialis, and reuniens nuclei. These nuclei have connections with the hippocampus (Herkenham, 1978; Amaral & Cowan, 1980; Van Hoesen, 1985; Insuasti, Amaral & Cowan, 1987b). They are quite consistently damaged in patients with Wernike-Korsakoff disease (Mair, Warrington, & Weiskrantz, 1979; Mayes et al. (1988). Another proposal is that thalamic lesions may disconnect thalamic connections with the frontal lobes. Warrington (Warrington & Weiskrantz, 1982; Warrington, 1985) proposed that restricted thalamic lesions found in their cases of Wernicke-Korsakoff disease (Mair, Warrington, & Weiskrantz, 1979) may disconnect mediodorsal-frontal connections important for coordinating posterior cortical regions subserving semantic memories with frontal structures that impose cognitive structure upon these memories. Kooistra and Heilman (1988) also suggested that thalamo-frontal disconnections might contribute to amnesia.

Aggleton and Brown (1999) proposed that the medial and lateral circuits subserve different aspects of memory. The medial circuit (hippocampus, fornix, mammillary bodies, anterior thalamic nuclei) subserves context-dependent recollection, whereas the lateral system (perirhinal cortex, internal medullary lamina, mediodorsal thalamic nuclei) supports context-independent familiarity judgments. Gold and Squire (2006) report postmortem examinations of three amnesic patients, two with diencephalic lesions. One had alcoholic Wernicke-Korsakoff disease with damage to the mammillary bodies, mediodorsal thalamic nuclei, and anterior thalamic nuclei, and one had bilateral strokes affecting the mediodorsal nucleus and internal medullary lamina but not the mammillothalamic tract. Contrary to the predictions of Aggleton and Brown's proposal, the three patients had qualitatively similar amnesia.

BASAL FOREBRAIN

The basal forebrain is at the junction of the diencephalon and the cerebral hemispheres, and has, at minimum, the following components: the septal area, diagonal band of Broca, nucleus accumbens septi, olfactory tubercle, substantia innominata (containing the nucleus basalis of Meynert), bed nucleus of the stria terminalis, and preoptic area (Figure 16-5). It is the third major region, after the temporal lobes and diencephalon, to be considered essential for normal memory function in man. It was known for many years that some patients developed memory loss after hemorrhage from aneurysms, particularly after rupture of anterior communicating artery aneurysms (Linqvist & Norlen, 1966; Talland, Sweet, & Ballantine, 1967); however, the pathogenesis of this amnesia was not understood. Several lines of evidence suggested that cholinergic neurons in the basal forebrain were involved in memory. Lewis and Shute (1967) documented a cholinergic projection from the medial septal region of the basal forebrain to the hippocampus. For many years, scopolamine, a centrally acting anticholinergic agent, had been used in obstetrics, in conjunction with analgesics, to induce a "twilight" state, after which women would have little recall of their deliveries.

Drachman and Leavitt (1974) demonstrated that normal subjects had difficulty with free recall of words when given scopolamine, and that this effect was reversed by physostigmine, a centrally acting anticholinesterase agent that prevents inactivation of acetylcholine. Mesulam and Van Hoesen (1976) documented a cholinergic projection from the basal nucleus of Meynert, and in subsequent studies Mesulam and his colleagues (Mesulam et al., 1983; Mesulam & Mufson, 1984) defined the connections of basal forebrain cholinergic neurons. Neurons in the medial septal nucleus and diagonal band of Broca project strongly to the hippocampus, as had been documented by Lewis and Shute (1967). Cholinergic neurons in the nucleus basalis of Meynert, however, project widely to limbic cortex and neocortex. In 1981, Whitehouse et al. documented selective loss of neurons in the nucleus basalis of Meynert in patients with Alzheimer's Disease. Cell loss in cholinergic neurons of the basal forebrain

(Arendt, Bigl, & Arendt, 1983) has also been found in Wernicke-Korsakoff syndrome (Butters, 1985; Butters & Stuss, 1989). All of these lines of evidence suggested a role for the basal forebrain in memory, and more specifically, suggested that the cholinergic projections of the basal forebrain may be of particular importance.

The complexity of basal forebrain anatomy makes it difficult to arrive at firm conclusions about the pathophysiology of amnesia associated with basal forebrain lesions (see Figure 16-5). In addition to structures containing cholinergic neurons (the substantia innominata, basal nucleus of Meynert, diagonal band of Broca, and septal nuclei), the basal forebrain encompasses pathways and systems that could conceivably participate in memory. The anterior commissure crosses the midline just posterior to the septal nuclei. The columns of the fornix descend through the basal forebrain on their way to the hypothalamus. The ventral amygdalofugal pathway both projects to the basal forebrain and traverses it on its way to the thalamus. Thus, basal forebrain lesions, if properly situated, may disrupt one or both of the pathways critical for

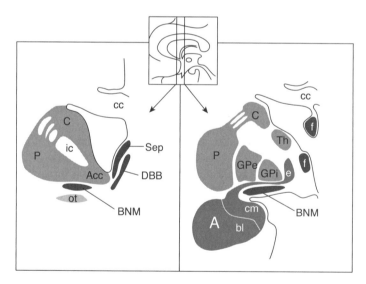

Figure 16–5. The basal forebrain. Two coronal sections through the basal forebrain are shown, as indicated in the midsagittal view in the box at the top of the Figure. BNM, basal nucleus of Meynert; DBB, diagonal band of Broca; Sep, septal nuclei. The amygdala (A) has basolateral (bl) and centromedial (cm) divisions, and it extends into the basal forebrain as the extended amygdala (e). Other structures indicated are the basal ganglia (putamen, P), caudate (C), nucleus accumbens (Acc), globus pallidus externa (GPe) and interna (GPi). Th, thalamus, and f, fornix, which is sectioned twice in the posterior (*right*) section, as it arcs anterior to and back into the section.

memory. The medial forebrain bundle, which interconnects brainstem, hypothalamic, and forebrain structures, travels through the lateral hypothalamus and the basal forebrain. Noradrenergic and dopaminergic pathways are represented in the median forebrain bundle. Dobkin and Hanlon (1993) report a patient with anterior basal forebrain and caudate nucleus injury whose amnesia improved with bromocriptine, a selective dopamine agonist. It is unknown whether other structures in the basal forebrain, including the extended amygdala (Heimer & Alheid, 1991), the ventral pallidum, and the preoptic area, play a role in memory.

Most basal forebrain lesions reported in human cases of amnesia have been large, and probably affect all or many of the above structures. Often, they also involve areas outside the basal forebrain, such as the orbitofrontal and medial frontal cortices, and the caudate nucleus. Irle et al. (1992) studied 30 patients with brain lesions associated with anterior cerebral artery aneurysm rupture. Severe memory loss was associated with combined lesions in the striatum (caudate) and basal forebrain, whereas lesions restricted to basal forebrain were not associated with memory disturbance. Morris et al. (1992), however, reported a patient with amnesia following removal of a very small glioma in the lamina terminalis, just posterior to the right gyrus rectus. Postoperative MRI scans demonstrated a lesion restricted to the diagonal band of Broca, anterior commissure, nucleus accumbens, and preoptic area. They postulated that destruction of the cholinergic projection to the hippocampus, most of which originates in the nucleus of the diagonal band of Broca, probably accounted for the amnesia, but they could not rule out contributions from other damaged areas. Hashimoto, Tanaka, and Nakano (2000) report an amnesic confabulatory syndrome from a small spontaneous right basal forebrain intracerebral hemorrhage. Benke et al. (2005) report improvement in performance on the California Verbal Learning Task after treatment with a centrally acting anticholinesterase medication (donepezil) in 11 patients with basal forebrain amnesia from aneurysm rupture, supporting a role for acetylcholine; however, a similar patient reported by Write, Boeve, and Malec (1999) failed to improve with donepezil.

LATERALITY OF LESIONS CAUSING AMNESIA IN HUMANS

Many of the best-studied patients with amnesia have bilateral lesions. When unilateral temporal lobectomy for epilepsy causes severe amnesia, it is usually assumed that there has been prior damage to the contralateral hippocampus. Otherwise, memory deficits are relatively mild and material-specific. More severe memory disturbances have been described, however, with unilateral lesions. Most often these are left sided, and cause more verbal than nonverbal memory disturbance. This has been reported for left posterior cerebral artery infarctions affecting the medial temporal region (Benson, Marsden, & Meadows, 1974; von Cramon, Hebel, & Schuri, 1988), for left retrosplenial lesions (Valenstein et al., 1987), and for left thalamic lesions (Speedie & Heilman, 1982; Goldenberg, Wimmer, & Maly, 1983; Graff-Radford et al., 1984; Mori, Yamadori, & Mitani, 1986). Less often, lesions causing relatively severe amnestic disturbances are right sided (Graff-Radford et al., 1984; Morris et al., 1992; Hashimotor, Tanaka, & Nakono, 2000).

SUMMARY OF THE ANATOMY OF MEMORY

Tulving (2002) suggests that episodic memory, which requires both self-awareness and a sense of time, is uniquely human. It may seem paradoxical that the amnesic syndrome, which predominately involves episodic memory, is caused by damage to the hippocampus, a phylogenetically ancient structure. But the anatomical connections of the hippocampus are ideal to gather information from multiple high-order sensory, polymodal, and supramodal cortices, and to selectively reactivate cortical regions that may store information relevant to specific memories. Whereas neocortical and paralimbic cortical regions may be able to mediate semantic memories and allow for recall based on familiarity, the hippocampus and/or its extensive subcortical network may be uniquely equipped to establish personal autobiographical memories. This ability may derive from several characteristics: its phylogenetic importance in mediating spatial orientation, its ability to encode temporal characteristics of memories; its access to both ventral pathways for object identification and dorsal pathways, via parahippocampal cortex, for spatial localization; and also to its unique wiring. The relative contributions of different temporal lobe structures to different types of memory remain to be worked out, but semantic memories, which may or may not depend on hippocampal mechanisms to be established, eventually are independent of hippocampal integrity. Although it cannot be doubted that the basal forebrain and subcortical components of Papez circuit, as well as the retrosplenial cortex, are also required for normal memory function, the nature of their contributions remains to be elucidated.

THEORETICAL ACCOUNTS OF AMNESIA

Theories of amnesia fall broadly into one of three categories: (a) information processing accounts, which propose that amnesia results from selective impairment in one stage of processing (i.e., encoding, storage, or retrieval); (b) multiple memory system accounts, which differentiate between types of memory disrupted in amnesia; and (c) anatomic accounts, which suggest that deficit patterns differ depending on whether the primary lesion is located in the medial temporal lobe, diencephalon, or basal forebrain.

INFORMATION PROCESSING ACCOUNTS OF AMNESIA

Each of the three stages of information processing (encoding, retention, and retrieval) has been theoretically implicated in the etiology of human amnesia. Validating these theories has proven to be a formidable task. As Squire and Cohen (1984) indicate, doing so requires demonstration that a selective processing defect is a cause, rather than a consequence, of amnesia (cf. Mayes, Meudell, & Som, 1981), and that amnesic patients are disproportionately affected by manipulations designed to affect the process in question (the "law of differential deficits"). Indeed, data exist in favor of defects within each of these stages, and it is increasingly clear that impairment of one (and only one) stage of

memory processing cannot explain the full range of deficits seen in amnesia. Instead, we prefer to view encoding, retention, and retrieval as dimensions (or sources of variance) that contribute to the strength and utility of a memory trace. Nonetheless, attempts to localize amnesic defects at specific cognitive loci have been valuable, not as ultimate explanations, but as *heuristics* in specifying the important dimensions on which amnesic syndromes may vary.

Amnesia As an Encoding Deficit

Evaluations of encoding deficits as a causative factor in amnesia were stimulated by the levels-of-processing approach to memory (Craik & Lockhart, 1972), which argued that memory is the natural result of cognitive operations applied to stimuli at the point of learning. Levels of processing theory predicts that "deeper," meaning-based, semantic analysis would lead to superior retention than would analysis of the "superficial" (orthographic or phonemic) characteristics of stimuli. Talland (1965) asserted that alcoholic Korsakoff patients engaged in a "premature closure of activation" that affected the dynamic processing required for full encoding of to-be-learned stimuli. Subsequent studies (Cermak & Butters, 1972; Cermak et al., 1973, 1974, 1976) showed that, when left to their own devices, amnesic Korsakoff patients spontaneously analyze only superficial features of verbal information, and strategies that promote deeper semantic analysis aided recall.

Support for the idea that superficial analysis leads to poor retrieval comes from results of a study (Cermak, et al., 1974) using Wickens' (1970) release from proactive interference (PI) technique. In this procedure, subjects are presented with a series of trials, each of which contains a different set of three words from the same semantic category. Word recall is tested after a delay. As trials proceed, practically all subjects recall fewer and fewer words. When, on a later trial, the category to which the words belong is changed, normal subjects typically improve their performance. Wickens attributed this to reduced PI and viewed it as confirmation that normal subjects were encoding information using a semantic strategy. In alcoholic Korsakoff patients, the amount of PI release varies with the nature of to-be-learned information. In the Cermak et al. study, normal release was seen when numbers were used as stimuli but not when words were used. They concluded that the patients' retrieval deficit was a result of an inability to spontaneously engage in semantic analysis.

Even when alcoholic Korsakoff patients are directed toward semantic analysis via appropriate orienting questions, their retention remains far below normal. This and similar findings (Thomson & Tulving, 1970) led to a modification of the original encoding deficits theory (Cermak, et al., 1980; cf. Verfaellie & Cermak, 1991), in which encoding is redefined as a product of analysis in which subjects cognitively manipulate features of information in order to permit differential storage. Thus, amnesic patients may be able to semantically analyze information, but they do not profit from such analysis because they fail to encode its products. Verfaellie and Cermak (1991) assert that this view bridges the gap between theories of amnesia that focus on encoding, consolidation, and retrieval deficits. Common to all these theories is the idea that amnesic patients cannot store new material because they cannot cognitively manipulate the features of the material to permit their assimilation into long-term memory.

Even as modified, encoding deficit theory is insufficient as an overall account of amnesia since the abnormal performances it seeks to explain are not found in all amnesic patients. For example, normal release from PI after a shift in semantic category has been found in patient N.A. (with diencephalic amnesia), patients undergoing bilateral ECT (Squire, 1982b), postencephalitic amnesic patients (Cermak, 1976), and a patient with amnesia secondary to a left retrosplenial lesion (Valenstein et al., 1986). Also, other studies have suggested that alcoholic Korsakoff patients may release from PI if they are provided with repeated exposure to the new category members (Kinsbourne & Wood, 1975) or if they are forewarned of the impending shift (Winocur et al., 1981).

Amnesia As a Retention Deficit

Retention/storage theories of amnesia propose a "postencoding" deficit in which memory representations are poorly maintained or poorly elaborated with the passage of time. Retention-deficit views are based on two main findings: (a) at least some forms of amnesia show an abnormally rapid rate of forgetting, and (b) the same patients tend to display a temporally limited retrograde defect, affecting only those time periods immediately preceding the onset of amnesia.

Retention theories have drawn support primarily from studies of patients with medial temporal lobe damage. Huppert and Piercy (1979) published an influential paper demonstrating abnormally rapid forgetting in the temporal lobe amnesic, H.M. Specifically, H.M.'s performance on a yes–no recognition task was similar to controls at a 10-minute delay but declined precipitously when tested 1 and 7 days later. H.M. also forgot more rapidly than did alcoholic Korsakoff patients.

Squire, Cohen, and Nadel (1984) suggested that temporally limited retrograde amnesia may result from a defect in consolidation of information. They proposed that consolidation is a gradual process, lasting for months or even years. When interrupted by brain impairment, premorbid memories still undergoing consolidation will be disrupted. Alvarez and Squire (1994) proposed a network model of consolidation in which the medial temporal system initially stores memory traces. The hippocampal system repeatedly reactivates representations in the neocortex, resulting in the binding between cortical regions and the creation of strong interconnections. Neocortical storage sites eventually become capable of being autonomously activated and able to retrieve memories independently of the hippocampal system. Squire and Alvarez (1995) suggest that the tendency for hippocampal synapses to change quickly permits this structure to store initial memory traces until the neocortical synapses have time to change and allow for the more permanent memory storage. If one supposes that this process takes place gradually (over a period of years), then retrieval of very remote memories is preserved in individuals with medial temporal amnesia because remote memories are fully consolidated and no longer depend upon the activity of the medial temporal system. This view predicts a strong relationship between temporally limited retrograde amnesia and anterograde amnesia since both result from the same process (Squire & Cohen, 1994).

However, consolidation theory has increasingly received criticism. For example, impaired consolidation cannot explain how retrograde amnesia recovers over time in some patients (Benson & Geschwind, 1967) and has difficulty explaining temporally graded and temporally limited remote memory disturbance. A contemporary alternative to consolidation theory is the *multiple trace theory* (MTT; Moscovitch, et al., 2005a, 2005b; 2006; Nadel & Moscovitch, 1997), which attempts to explain such findings in terms of impairment in a single underlying hippocampal/medial temporal lobe memory system (Moscovitch et al., 2005a, 2005b). The MTT posits that, as long as memories retain their episodic quality (e.g., vividness), they remain hippocampus-dependent. Each time an episodic memory is retrieved it is subsequently reencoded within the hippocampus and by dynamic activation of hippocampal and neocortical networks. This leads to formation of multiple traces in an increasingly distributed network. As a result, older episodic memories (i.e., those that have been retrieved numerous times) are distributed more widely within the medial temporal lobe than are more recent ones, and different structures/regions within the medial temporal lobe make their own contribution. As the distributed network strengthens via multiple episodes of encoding, it eventually can become independent of the hippocampus and supported solely by neocortex. These memories lose their context-dependency or autobiographic quality over time, to the extent to which they have been retrieved in multiple contexts. By this process, some episodic memories can gradually become semantic memories. Thus, semantic memory results at least in part from gradual transfer of memory from hippocampus-dependent networks to neocortical representations.

With respect to amnesia, MTT predicts that medial temporal lobe damage will result in both anterograde and retrograde impairment for episodic memories, with more extensive damage leading to more extensive impairment. Although early studies with amnesic patients such as H.M. found largely intact remote memory, more recent reevaluations support the existence of more extensive retrograde amnesia than previously thought (e.g., Steinvorth, Levine, & Corkin, 2005).

Amnesia As a Retrieval Deficit

Retrieval explanations of amnesia are based on two main findings: (a) retrieval cues or prompts can dramatically improve the memory performance of some amnesic patients, and (b) all amnesic patients exhibit some problem in the retrieval of remote memories. However, many studies comparing amnesic patients to normal subjects on cued recall (Mayes & Meudell, 1981; Wetzel & Squire, 1982) and recognition (Mayes, Meudell, & Neary, 1980) have shown that the pattern exhibited by amnesic patients was also shown by normal subjects during the course of natural forgetting. Such findings favor a "weak memory" interpretation of amnesia, rather than disproportionately impaired retrieval operations.

Retrieval Deficits in Anterograde Amnesia. Warrington and Weiskrantz (1970, 1973) proposed a retrieval deficit model of amnesia based on findings from studies using the *partial information technique*. In their experiments, amnesic participants were presented on each of five learning trials with a series of stimuli that were increasingly less fragmented until they could identify the stimulus. When the stimuli were re-presented after a 1-day delay, amnesic participants identified them sooner (when more fragmented) than on the initial presentation, implying that something was retained from initial stimulus exposure. Despite this facilitation, amnesic patients showed little evidence of retention on conventional tests of recall and recognition. Warrington and Weiskrantz concluded that retention by amnesic patients depended more on the method of retrieval than on the method of acquisition. They explained the amnesic deficit as resulting from abnormal susceptibility to interference from competing responses at the point of recall. Their model has therefore been referred to as the *retrieval-interference model of amnesia*.

To provide further support for the presumed effects of interference during retrieval, Warrington and Weiskrantz (1974, 1978) performed a series of experiments using a reversal-learning paradigm. In these experiments, subjects learned two different word lists constructed so that each word on List 1 began with the same three letters as a word on List 2. Participants studied List 1 once and made multiple attempts to learn List 2. After each trial, retention was assessed with a cued recall (stem completion) paradigm in which the first three letters of target words were provided. Both healthy controls and amnesic patients performed well on List 1 items, but had difficulty with List 2 due to interference from List 1. However, although control performance improved with repeated exposure to List 2, amnesic patients continued to exhibit a high incidence of intrusions from List 1. Warrington and Weiskrantz argued that storage of List 1 had occurred, and that it continued to interfere with retrieval of List 2 words through a process of response competition.

Subsequent research (Warrington & Weiskrantz, 1978) highlighted problems with a strict retrieval-interference interpretation of this data. They found that the amnesic patients did not show more susceptibility to interference on the initial List 2 trial, violating the principle of differential deficits. Second, amnesic participants did not demonstrate interference effects when response competition was reduced by creating word lists in which each pair of words (one from List 1 and one from List 2) were the only English words beginning with those initial letters. These results led Warrington and Weiskrantz to modify their view and to suggest that List 1 responses were so domineering as to actually impede the *learning* of List 2 words. This was an important statement, since it represents the first time that a retrieval-deficit theorist conceded the possibility of a deficit in acquisition. As a consequence, it was the beginning of an eventual merger between retrieval-deficit and encoding-deficit theories (Winocur, Kinsbourne, & Moscovitch, 1981; Cermak, 1982; Verfaellie & Cermak, 1991).

Retrieval Deficits in Retrograde Amnesia. Retrieval deficits are more securely invoked in explaining some forms of retrograde amnesia, including temporary retrograde impairments in transient global amnesia and after closed head injury. Recovery of retrograde memories (so-called "shrinking retrograde amnesia"; Benson

& Geschwind, 1967) must be attributed to a reversible retrieval deficit since memories of remote events must be intact during the amnesia if they are to be recalled afterward. Retrieval deficits are also consistent with decade-nonspecific remote memory impairment, since there would be no basis to suppose that a generalized retrieval deficit would favor certain time periods. Such an explanation has, in fact, been advanced to explain remote memory impairment in Huntington disease (Albert, Butters, & Brandt, 1981).

Some form of retrieval deficit may also help partially to explain the extensive, temporally graded retrograde amnesia seen in patients with alcoholic Korsakoff syndrome. It has been argued, however, that this retrograde amnesia may result from a progressively severe *acquisition* deficit (Albert, Butters, & Levin, 1980; Cohen & Squire, 1981). Detoxified non-Korsakoff alcoholics demonstrate anterograde learning defects, the severity of which correlates with duration of alcohol abuse (Ryan & Butters, 1980a, b). The temporal gradient in Korsakoff amnesia may thus reflect the fact that more recent information was never effectively learned. There is some evidence against this view, including the finding that Korsakoff patients, when compared to alcoholic controls, tend to be impaired at *all decades*—even those that predate the onset of abuse-related memory dysfunction (Albert et al., 1980; Cohen & Squire, 1981). However, there is also substantial support for the theory. For example, studies of amnesic patients with acute-onset diencephalic pathology (e.g., stroke, trauma) show comparatively mild retrograde amnesia (Cohen & Squire, 1981; Winocur, Oxbury, Roberts, Agnetti, & Davis, 1984). Additionally, Butters and Cermak (1986) reported the case of P.Z., an eminent scientist who had published an autobiography 3 years prior to the onset of Wernicke's encephalopathy in 1982. On Albert et al.'s remote memory test, P.Z., like other Korsakoff patients, had significant impairment across all time periods, with some relative sparing of the ability to recognize famous faces from the 1930s and 1940s. But on a remote memory test based on information derived from P.Z.'s autobiography, there was a striking temporal gradient in his memory, with dramatic and complete impairment of information from the 1960s and 1970s, and relative (although not complete) sparing of very remote memories. The fact that all questions were autobiographic eliminates the possibility that this information was never learned, although the possibility remains that it was somehow "less stable" and therefore more difficult to retrieve for more recent time periods.

These findings led Butters and Miliotis (1985) to propose that the temporally graded retrograde memory impairment in Korsakoff syndrome is the product of two separate factors: (a) an increasingly severe anterograde learning deficit that is gradually acquired through years of alcohol abuse, and (b) an impairment of memory retrieval that appears acutely with the Wernicke stage of the illness and affects all time periods equally. These two superimposed deficits result in the temporally graded retrograde amnesia affecting all time periods.

MULTIPLE MEMORY SYSTEMS ACCOUNTS

The existence of two (or more) memory "systems," each responsible for a different type of memory function and each operating according to different parameters (Sherry & Schacter, 1987; Schacter, Wagner, & Buckner, 2000), has by far been the most popular explanation for the pattern of impaired and spared memory in amnesia. The most prominent of these theories will be discussed below. It should be noted that each proposed dichotomy is not mutually exclusive.

Explicit Versus Implicit Memory

Sherry and Schacter (1987) suggested that separate explicit and implicit memory systems may have evolved in order to efficiently perform functionally incompatible memory processes. In more recent years, the distinction between explicit and implicit memory as reflecting different modes of retrieval has received increasing attention (Yonelinas, 2002; Wixted, 2007). Additionally, it has long been known that performance on various direct measures of explicit memory (free recall, cued recall, and recognition) are dissociable, and evidence now suggests that implicit memory may be similarly divisible into smaller "subsystems" (Heindel et al., 1989;

Witherspoon & Moscovitch, 1989; Vaidya et al., 1997).

Explicit and implicit memory may interact in traditional tasks of memory (cf. Jacoby & Dallas, 1981; Jacoby, Kelly, & Dywan, 1989). Jacoby and Dallas (1981) argued that performance on recognition tests can be based on two potentially independent processes known as *recollection* and *familiarity*. Thus, one may select an item on forced choice recognition because it is directly remembered or because it "just seems right" as a result of perceptual priming or apparent familiarity. Because both explicit and implicit memory operate in the same direction (i.e., both would increase the probability of selecting a target item), it has been difficult to specify the relative contribution each has to recognition memory in normal subjects and amnesic patients. Jacoby and colleagues have developed a "process-dissociation" method to measure the separate contributions of recollection and fluency/familiarity (Jacoby, 1991; Cermak, Verfaellie, Sweeney, & Jacoby, 1992; Kelley & Jacoby, 2000), although this has been criticized with respect to its assumption that recollection and familiarity are independent processes (Ratcliff, Van Zandt, & McKoon, 1995; Dodson & Johnson, 1996).

Declarative Versus Procedural (Nondeclarative) Memory

The declarative–nondeclarative distinction implies two separate memory systems that differ in their constituent contents and processes. For example, it has been argued that nondeclarative memory entails a knowledge base that cannot be inspected consciously and is not directly reflected in verbal report. In contrast, declarative memory entails explicit, verbal retrieval from a well-defined knowledge base: "it includes the facts, lists, and data of conventional memory experiments and everyday remembering" (Squire, 1987, p. 158).

Behavioral support for this distinction overlaps substantially with that invoked to validate/sustain the distinction between explicit and implicit memory and consists mainly of demonstrations that amnesic patients are capable of learning new perceptual and motor skills despite a nearly total lack of explicit recall of experiences that lead to such learning (Nissen & Bullemer, 1987; Squire & McKee, 1993; Knowlton, Squire, & Gluck, 1994; Hamann & Squire, 1995; Reber, Knowlton, & Squire, 1996; Cohen et al., 1997). Anatomic evidence comes from work by Zola-Morgan and Squire (1983, 1984) in the macaque, showing that medial temporal lesions impair declarative memory as assessed by delayed non-matching to sample, but in contrast, such monkeys do not show impaired motor skill learning and retain new motor skills over a 1-month interval. Human data also indicate that sensorimotor skill learning is intact in amnesic patients with basal forebrain lesions (Tranel et al., 1994), whereas patients with basal ganglia disease often show impaired skill learning in the absence of severe deficits in declarative memory (Heindel, Salmon, Shults, Walicke, & Butters, 1989; Knowlton, Mangels, & Squire, 1996; Poldrack et al., 1999; Price et al., 2009). These findings suggests that the memory system involved in declarative learning relies on anatomic structures different from those involved in learning "how" to perform certain tasks.

Episodic Versus Semantic Memory

Many authors have argued that selective impairment of episodic (vs. semantic) memory accounts for the finding that amnesic patients retain substantial intellectual, linguistic, and social skill despite profound impairments in the ability to recall specific information encountered in prior learning episodes (Kinsbourne & Wood, 1975; Weingartner, Grafman, Boutelle, Kaye, & Martin, 1983; Cermak, 1984; Tulving, 1998; Ferreira, et al., 2008). Kinsbourne and Wood (1975) were among the first to suggest this dissociation. Although influential, their report was based largely on clinical observation and a brief, uncontrolled experiment, in which they found that their amnesic patients could provide adequate definitions of common objects but could not recall specific autobiographical events related to those same objects (cf. Crovitz & Schiffman, 1974).

Cermak (1984) suggested that the episodic-semantic distinction could explain temporally graded retrograde amnesia. He suggested that, as biographical material ages, it becomes progressively more semantic. Through retelling, it becomes incorporated into personal history and becomes part of the personal or family "folklore." More recent memories are less likely to have been retold or elaborated, and thus may retain more of an episodic quality. If amnesia reflects a selective impairment in episodic memory, then memories from more remote time periods would be relatively spared as a result of this process.

If the episodic–semantic distinction reflects a general principle of brain organization, then these domains of memory should show double dissociation in cases of focal brain disease. Indeed, there have been several case reports demonstrating impaired semantic retrieval in the absence of a deficit in episodic/autobiographical retrieval (De Renzi, Liotti, & Nichelli, 1987; Grossi, Trojano, Grasso, & Orsini, 1988; Yasuda, Watanabe, & Ono, 1997); conversely, there is ample evidence that episodic memory can be impaired in the absence of a deficit in semantic memory, thus not precluding the acquisition of factual knowledge or language competence during development (Vargha-Khadem et al., 1997). However, many amnesic patients do suffer impairments of semantic as well as episodic memory (Cermak, Reale, & Baker, 1978; Cohen & Squire, 1981; Zola-Morgan, Cohen, & Squire, 1983; Butters, Granholm, Salmon, Grant, & Wolfe, 1987; Verfaellie & Cermak, 1994; Squire & Zola, 1998). For example, Cermak et al. (1978) found that Korsakoff patients had difficulty generating words from what Collins and Loftus (1975) called "conceptual" semantic memory ("Name a fruit that is red"). Butters and colleagues (1987) similarly found Korsakoff amnesic patients deficient on a verbal fluency task.

A fundamental problem is that episodic and semantic memories are not easily dissociable behaviorally (Squire & Zola, 1998) and seem to involve activation of the same or similar structures in functional imaging studies (Schacter et al., 2000). One confound is that they interact in complex ways (for example, episodic learning can have a stimulating effect on semantic search rate; Loftus & Cole, 1974).

Of relevance to the episodic–semantic distinction is the finding that amnesic patients can show repetition priming for novel information first encountered after illness onset.

Initial findings suggested that normal subjects did not show repetition priming for material like nonwords that had no preexisting semantic memory representation (Bentin & Moscovitch, 1988; Kersteen-Tucker, 1991), and early work suggested that this also held true for amnesic patients (Cermak, Talbot, Chandler, & Wolbarst, 1985). This led to the view that priming reflects activation or modification of semantic memory (Scarborough, Cortese, & Scarborough, 1977; Mandler, 1980; Diamond & Rozin, 1984). However, many studies have shown normal priming or learning of novel material (e.g., nonwords, novel line patterns and objects) in amnesic patients (Gabrieli, Milberg, Keane, & Corkin, 1990; Schacter, Cooper, Tharan, & Rubens, 1991; Gooding, van Eijk, Mayes, & Meudell, 1993; Keane, Gabrieli, Noland, & McNealy, 1995; Postle & Corkin, 1998), suggesting that patients are capable of acquisition of new experience-dependent (episodic) memories, not simply the activation of preexisting representations. As a result, it is now widely believed that some amnesic patients are capable of some forms of episodic learning but are generally unaware of the products of such learning. Amnesia severity may play a role in this effect.

Several well-described cases of focal retrograde amnesia (i.e., disproportionately impaired retrograde memory with relatively spared anterograde memory) have also contributed to our understanding of the relationship between episodic and semantic memory (Kapur, Young, Bateman, & Kennedy, 1989; Kapur, Ellison, Smith, McLellan, & Burrows, 1992; O'Connor, Butters, Miliotis, Eslinger, & Cermak, 1992; Hodges & McCarthy, 1995; Hunkin et al., 1995; Carlesimo, Sabbadini, Loasses, & Caltagirone, 1998; Markowitsch, Calabrese, Neufeld, Gehlen, & Durwen, 1999). In some cases (Markowitsch et al., 1999), a distinction within remote memory has been found in which the patient is impaired in retrieval of general knowledge but unimpaired in retrieval of remote autobiographical events. Damage to the anterior temporal cortex is involved in most cases of focal retrograde amnesia and damage to limbic-diencephalic structures contributes to impairment in remote autobiographical memory. However, not all cases of focal retrograde amnesia are clearly suggestive of an episodic–semantic distinction,

since careful analysis of the memory loss in some cases reveals equivalent impairments in remote autobiographical memory and factual knowledge (Kapur, 1999).

As indicated earlier, MTT provides a contemporary reformulation of the episodic–semantic memory distinction within a functional–anatomic account of the activity of the hippocampal system. From the perspective of multiple memory systems accounts of spared and impaired function, MTT offers a promising way to conceptualize episodic and semantic memory as points on a processing continuum. Of equal importance, it provides a neurobiologically realistic model of memory dissociations that accounts for a large amount of clinical and research data.

ACTIVATION ACCOUNTS

Activation accounts of the dissociation of memory disorders have suggested that normal performance on indirect memory tests such as word-stem completion result from temporary, automatic activation of preexisting memory representations, rather than new learning per se (Graf & Mandler, 1984). By this view, explicit memory requires additional (effortful, elaborative) processing that is selectively impaired in amnesia. The activation view is also relevant to the episodic–semantic memory distinction because priming was initially thought to involve activation of memory representations already resident in semantic memory. Activation views were originally advanced to account for the fact that repetition priming effects tend to dissipate rapidly (Graf, Squire, & Mandler, 1984; Cermak, Talbot, Chandler, & Wolbarst, 1985) and for early findings that, in normal subjects and amnesic patients, priming did not occur for stimuli which had no preexisting memory representations (Scarborough et al., 1977; Diamond & Rozin, 1984; Cermak et al., 1985; Bentin & Moscovitch, 1988; Kersteen-Tucker, 1991).

Two general findings have challenged the activation account. First, priming effects sometimes persist over several weeks or longer (Jacoby & Dallas, 1981; Schacter & Graf, 1986a), which pushes the concept of "activation" to unacceptable limits. Second, recent studies have shown normal priming of novel material (nonwords, novel line patterns, and new associations) in both normal subjects (Feustel et al., 1983; Jacoby, 1983a; Cermak et al., 1985, 1991; Musen & Triesman, 1990; Schacter et al., 1990; Rueckl, 1991; Goshen-Gottstein, Moskovitch, & Melo, 2000) and amnesic patients (Gabrieli et al., 1990; Haist et al., 1991; Musen & Squire, 1991; Schacter et al., 1991).

Further evidence that new learning may underlie at least some forms of priming is provided by experiments showing long-lasting priming of novel solutions to complex sentence puzzles (McAndrews, Glisky, & Schacter, 1987), new associations between words (Graf & Schacter, 1985; Schacter, 1985; Schacter & Graf, 1986; Goshen-Gottstein, Moscovitch, & Melo, 2000), new nonverbal patterns (Musen & Squire, 1992), and orthographically illegal nonwords that do not have preexisting orthographic representations (Keane et al., 1995). For example, McAndrews et al. showed a mixed group of amnesic patients a series of difficult-to-comprehend sentences like "The person was unhappy because the hole closed." Subjects were instructed that the sentence would become comprehensible if they could think of a specific key word or phrase (in this case, "pierced ears"). They had to come up with a solution within 1 minute and, if they did not, the experimenter presented the solution and asked the subject to explain it. Results revealed that amnesic patients were able to generate the key word/phrase needed to solve the sentence puzzles (for periods up to 1 week) after only one exposure to the problem. This convincingly demonstrates that amnesic patients can implicitly learn and remember, after even one trial, the meaning of novel sentences that require a new sentence–solution relationship to be formed (Bowers & Schacter, 1993).

In other studies (Graf & Schacter, 1985; Schacter & Graf, 1986), amnesic patients were exposed to unrelated word pairs (e.g., "window-reason"). In a subsequent test, subjects were presented with the stem of the second word preceded either by the word with which it was studied (e.g., window-rea___) or by a different word (e.g., officer-rea___). Subjects were asked to complete the stem with the first word that came to mind and were told that the preceding word might help them think of a completion. Amnesic patients with relatively mild memory problems demonstrated more priming when the stem was preceded by the word that originally accompanied it during the study phase than when it was preceded by a different word. Conscious, explicit memory could not account for the findings, since subjects were unable to use the cues to explicitly recall the target words. The fact that priming occurred only in mildly amnesic patients suggests that residual explicit memory may account for these effects (Bowers & Schacter, 1993; McKone & Slee, 1997).

TRANSFER-APPROPRIATE PROCESSING

An influential view of memory dissociations is that direct (e.g., free recall) and indirect (e.g., repetition priming) memory tasks differentially tap cognitive processes that tend to support explicit versus implicit memory, respectively. The *transfer-appropriate processing* (TAP) account of memory dissociations suggests that memory performance benefits to the extent that the cognitive operations needed to retrieve an item during the memory test overlap with the encoding operations performed during original learning (Blaxton, 1985; Roediger & Blaxton, 1987; Roediger, Weldon, & Challis, 1989; Blaxton, 1992, 1995; Roediger et al., 1994). The TAP approach thus emphasizes the concept of encoding specificity (Tulving & Pearlstone, 1966) and predicts better retrieval when encoding operations are recapitulated during the testing phase. Most tests of explicit recall rely on elaborative, semantic encoding, reflecting "conceptually driven" processing (Jacoby, 1983a, 1983b). In contrast, most tests of implicit memory depend upon the perceptual match between study and test, thus relying on what has been called "data-driven" processing. The resulting account of amnesia suggests that amnesic patients show normal data-driven processing, but are impaired in elaborative, conceptually driven processing.

Support for the TAP account comes from studies that show beneficial effects of study–test correspondence on memory performance (Blaxton, 1985; Roediger, 1990; Blaxton, 1992, 1995; Roediger et al., 1994). Blaxton (1985; Experiment 1) found that the relative strength of word-fragment completion and free recall depended upon the activities engaged in during the study phase. In this experiment, better word-fragment completion was seen when subjects simply read words (XXXX-COLD) than when they generated the words from associative cues (hot-????). In contrast, better free recall was seen in the generate condition. According to the TAP framework, word-fragment completion depends more strongly on visual processing (which was greater during simple reading than during generating), whereas free recall depends more strongly on conceptual processing (which was greater during generating than during reading).

The TAP approach has encouraged greater specificity regarding the information-processing demands imposed by specific tests of implicit and explicit memory. Although direct tests of memory typically utilize conceptual processes while indirect tests rely more heavily on data-driven processes, both are likely to have data-driven and conceptually driven components. For example, Blaxton (1985, Experiment 2) found that certain direct memory tests (e.g., graphemic cued recall, in which subjects are cued for a target word [SUNRISE] with a graphemically similar word [SURMISE]) are heavily data-driven, whereas certain indirect memory tests (e.g., where subjects study word pairs like "ESPIONAGE-treason," then answer questions like, "For what crime were the Rosenbergs executed"?) are conceptually driven. Thus, the important distinction is whether data- or conceptually driven processes are required, not whether the test nominally appears to tap explicit or implicit memory.

The assumption that impaired conceptual, but not perceptual, priming explains memory dissociations in amnesia, has been questioned. Some studies have shown amnesic patients to display impaired perceptual priming (Cermak, Verfaellie, & Letourneau, 1993; Gabrieli et al., 1994), and others have found sparing of conceptual priming (Keane, Gabrieli, Monti, Cantor, & Noland, 1993; Carlesimo, 1994; Cermak, Verfaellie, & Chase, 1995). However, there is evidence that the distinction between perceptual and conceptual processing has a basis in functional brain anatomy (Keane, Clarke, & Corkin, 1992; Gabrieli, Fleischman, Keane, Reminger, & Morrell, 1995). A combined view that incorporates both the implicit–explicit distinction and the perceptual–conceptual

distinction may be most fruitful (Schacter et al., 2000).

THE "THREE AMNESIAS"

Behavioral and neuropathologic heterogeneity in amnesic patients has fueled speculation that profound memory loss following temporal, diencephalic, and basal forebrain damage may represent different subtypes of amnesia (Lhermitte & Signoret, 1972; Huppert & Piercy, 1979; Squire, 1981; Parkin, 1984). One key question has been whether these subtypes can be distinguished on neuropsychological grounds. Data on this issue primarily come from comparisons between bitemporal and diencephalic (e.g., Korsakoff's) amnesia, and focuses on three main phenomena: rates of forgetting from long-term memory, patterns of retrograde amnesia, and deficits in spatiotemporal context.

Rate of Forgetting from Long-term Memory

Rate of forgetting has been commonly assessed in experimental studies of amnesic patients. Using retention intervals from 10 minutes to 7 days, several authors have argued that bitemporal amnesic patients (e.g., H.M., herpes encephalitic, bilateral ECT) show more rapid rate of forgetting than diencephalic amnesic patients or controls (Huppert & Piercy, 1979; Squire, 1981; Martone, Butters, & Trauner, 1986). However, diencephalic patients are typically given longer stimulus exposures in order to counteract an encoding deficit and achieve comparable recognition performance at the shortest delays (Mayes, Downes, Symons, & Shoqeirat, 1994). This, coupled with faster forgetting for bitemporals, initially led to the conclusion that bitemporal amnesia involves a defect in "consolidation," whereas diencephalic amnesia involves an earlier defect in stimulus "registration" or encoding (Huppert & Piercy, 1979; Squire, 1982a; Winocur, 1984).

However, this view has been questioned. Freed, Corkin, and Cohen (1987) retested H.M.'s recognition memory over intervals of 10 minutes, 24 hours, 72 hours, and 1 week with two recognition paradigms, taking pains to precisely equate his 10-minute recall with that of normal subjects. Using yes–no recognition probes,

H.M.'s performance was normal after 10 minutes but dropped significantly below controls after 24 hours and remained at that level at 1 week. Normal controls continued to forget over the entire week, such that their recognition performance declined to H.M.'s level after 72 hours. The authors suggested that this indicated a "normal rate of forgetting over a 1-week delay interval," although, as Crosson (1992) has indicated, an alternative explanation of these results is that H.M.'s lowest level of performance for the 1-week interval was raised above previous levels reported by Huppert and Piercy (1979) by virtue of additional stimulus exposure. That is, although Freed et al. focused on the equivalence between H.M. and normal subjects at the 72-hour and 1-week delays, the fact that H.M.'s performance leveled off more rapidly than did controls may, in fact, be taken to support, rather than refute, the notion that bitemporal amnesic patients forget at an abnormally rapid rate (Crosson, 1992).

In the second task reported by Freed et al. (1987), forgetting rates at the same four intervals were assessed via multiple-choice recognition rather than yes–no recognition. H.M.'s performance was not significantly different from controls at any interval, and in fact was slightly above that of the controls at 72 hours and 1 week. This is a more convincing demonstration that abnormally rapid forgetting does not necessarily characterize bitemporal amnesia. A similar conclusion was reached by McKee and Squire (1992), who directly compared rate-of-forgetting in bitemporal and diencephalic amnesic patients equated for amnesia severity. The authors found no group differences for any recognition test (e.g., delayed matching- and non-matching-to-sample) at any retention interval (10 minutes, 2 hours, and 30–32 hours).

Thus, although initial studies differentiated bitemporal and diencephalic amnesia on the basis of long-term forgetting rate, recent studies have tended to emphasize the similarities, rather than the differences, in rate of forgetting in these two groups. Recent evidence suggests that rapid forgetting exists in many amnesic patients and may vary with the extent to which the memory test taps intentional (recollection) versus automatic (familiarity) aspects of memory (Green & Kopelman, 2002). Some recent studies

suggest that there may be subtle differences in the shape of the forgetting curve when recognition probes are concentrated in the first 30 minutes, but there is little evidence of substantial differences thereafter (Mayes, Downes, Symons, & Shoqeirat, 1994; Downes, Holdstock, Symons, & Mayes, 1998). McKee and Squire (1992) suggest that, although it is reasonable to suppose that the medial temporal lobe and diencephalic systems should have different contributions to normal memory, "each region might also be an essential component of a larger functional system such that a similar amnesia might result from damage to any portion of that system." (p. 3771)

Patterns of Retrograde Amnesia

The three recognized patterns of retrograde amnesia (temporally limited, temporally graded, and decade-nonspecific) have been attributed at least in part to impairments in consolidation or retrieval that also produce anterograde learning deficits. Squire (1984) initially suggested that temporally limited retrograde amnesia was due to a defect in consolidation specifically related to dysfunction of the hippocampus (Zola-Morgan & Squire, 1990b), thus linking it specifically to bitemporal amnesia. However, Squire, Haist, and Shimamura (1989), using an updated version of Cohen and Squire's (1981) remote faces and events tests, found extensive, temporally limited retrograde amnesia in Korsakoff patients ($n = 7$) and in a group of patients with presumed medial temporal pathology secondary to anoxia or ischemia ($n = 3$). Although there were individual differences, their retrograde amnesias spanned about 15 years and were not detectable in more remote time periods. Gade and Mortensen (1990) found graded retrograde memory loss, supposedly typical of patients with bitemporal amnesia, in patients with basal forebrain and diencephalic amnesia. It is thus unlikely that differences in the degree or pattern of retrograde amnesia can reliably distinguish among anatomic amnesia subtypes, although there may still be reason to distinguish between temporally graded, temporally limited, and decade-nonspecific patterns in the individual case. Some clinical and experimental evidence suggests that the degree and pattern of retrograde deficit may depend on concomitant involvement of temporal (Reed & Squire, 1998; Kapur & Brooks, 1999) or frontal (Kopelman, 1991; Kopelman, Stanhope, & Kingsley, 1999; Winocur & Moscovitch, 1999) cortex that is adjacent to temporal or diencephalic damage. Kapur (1999) suggests that, although lesions of the hippocampus and diencephalon can produce limited retrograde amnesia, more extensive episodic or semantic retrograde amnesia generally requires neocortical damage. Kapur argues that cases with extensive retrograde amnesia from ostensibly localized damage must be interpreted in the context of more widespread metabolic effects on brain function.

Deficits in the Spatiotemporal Context of Memory

Several studies have suggested that certain cognitive abilities might be disproportionately impaired in diencephalic amnesia, particularly in patients with alcoholic Korsakoff syndrome. Early research on alcoholic Korsakoff syndrome revealed disproportionate impairments in the spatiotemporal aspects of memory. A critical issue is whether such impairments are an obligatory part of alcoholic Korsakoff syndrome amnesia, or whether they result from concomitant frontal involvement.

Memory for Temporal Order. The ability to discriminate when a target occurred in a study sequence is critical to maintain order in the flow of events (Huppert & Piercy, 1976; Hirst & Volpe, 1982; McAndrews & Milner, 1991). In a typical temporal order judgment paradigm, subjects are given a target list, followed after a brief delay by a second list. During later testing, subjects are asked whether they had seen each stimulus before (recognition judgment) and, if so, whether it belonged to the first or second list (temporal order judgment). Bitemporal and diencephalic amnesic patients both show defects in temporal order judgments, but it is unclear whether the underlying mechanisms are the same (Shimamura, Janowsky, & Squire, 1990; Downes, Mayes, MacDonald, & Hunkin, 2002). In an early study, Squire, Nadel, and Slater (1981) found that ECT (bitemporal) patients and N.A. (diencephalic) demonstrated

impairments in temporal order judgments, but their recognition judgments were also poor. When recognition performance was subsequently equated with normal subjects, no temporal ordering deficit remained. Thus, impaired temporal order judgments appeared to be similar across patient groups and were due to poor recognition memory.

In contrast, impaired temporal order judgment exhibited by alcoholic Korsakoff syndrome patients cannot, in most studies, be accounted for by poor recognition performance (Squire, 1982b; Bowers, Verfaellie, Valenstein, & Heilman, 1988; Shuren, Jacobs, & Heilman, 1997; but see Kopelman, 1997). Several authors have attributed temporal ordering impairment to concomitant frontal lobe pathology known to coexist with diencephalic damage (Moscovitch, 1982; Squire, 1982b; Schacter, 1987b; Shimamura, Janowsky, & Squire, 1990; Jernigan et al., 1991a,b). By this view, impairment in judging temporal order is a "neighborhood sign" rather than a core symptom of amnesia. Indeed, *nonamnesic* patients with frontal lesions and basal ganglia disease show impairment in temporal order judgments (Sagar, Sullivan, Gabrieli, Corkin, & Growdon, 1988; Shimamura et al., 1990; McAndrews & Milner, 1991).

Although the link to frontal lobe damage has been relatively consistent, there are reasons to keep the book open on this issue. First, results from a temporal ordering study with a retrosplenial amnesic suggest that a defect in temporal ordering can exist independently of both recognition ability and frontal lobe dysfunction (Bowers, Verfaellie, Valenstein, & Heilman, 1988; see also Parkin & Hunkin, 1993). Interestingly, this patient was dramatically impaired in temporal order judgments for newly acquired information but had no difficulty judging the temporal order of remote events. He performed normally on tests of frontal lobe function. These findings provide an initial clue that it may be important to distinguish between two kinds of temporal ordering deficits: (a) one that is part of a more general, frontally mediated strategic deficit (as in Korsakoff's syndrome; Squire, 1982b; Shimamura et al., 1990), and (b) one that reflects an anterograde impairment in "time tagging" new information, which is independent of frontal pathology (Bowers et al., 1988; Parkin & Hunkin, 1993; Yasuno et al., 1999).

Source Monitoring and Source Amnesia. The phenomenon of *source amnesia* illustrates that the content and source of recollected information are potentially dissociable (Shimamura & Squire, 1987). In source amnesia, recollection of the informational source of a memory item is lost despite intact item (content) memory. For example, patients might remember specific information about a book or movie but not remember where that information was learned.

Schacter, Harbluck, and McLachlan (1984) presented bogus facts (e.g., "Bob Hope's father was a fireman") to their amnesic patients and then gave a recall test. Many patients demonstrated recall of at least some of the facts, but frequently asserted that they had learned them from a source other than the experimental session. This finding could not be explained by poor memory, since normal subjects whose recall was lowered by a 1-week study–test interval did not commit source errors. In a similar study, Shimamura and Squire (1987) taught obscure (true) facts to a small group of Korsakoff patients and a smaller group of patients with amnesia secondary to anoxia. Severe source amnesia was observed in three of the six Korsakoff patients and in one of the three anoxic patients, and was not predicted by fact memory performance. In contrast, patients with bitemporal amnesia, including H.M., display severe defects in fact memory but often perform *better* at tests of recency and temporal order than do nonamnesic frontal patients (Sagar et al., 1990; Milner, Corsi & Leonard, 1991).

Some evidence suggests that the severity of source amnesia varies as a function of frontal lobe impairment (Schacter et al., 1984; Janowsky, Shimamura & Squire, 1989). Source monitoring tasks make variable demands on retrieval and cognitive estimation (Shallice & Evans, 1978), reality-monitoring (Johnson, 1991), attribution (Jacoby, Kelly, & Dywan, 1989), and temporal order memory (Hirst & Volpe, 1982; Olton, 1989). It is likely that reported source memory distinctions between bitemporal and diencephalic amnesic patients are due to the variable demands on these functions.

Deficits in Metamemory and "Feeling of Knowing". Another cognitive domain that some have thought to be differentially impaired in alcoholic Korsakoff syndrome has been referred to as *metamemory*. Metamemory involves knowledge about one's own memory capabilities, the memory demands of particular tasks or situations, and potentially useful strategies relevant to given tasks or situations (Flavell & Wellman, 1977; Gruneberg, 1983). It encompasses people's beliefs (e.g., "I will [or will not] be able to remember these words") as well as their knowledge about the memory system (e.g., rehearsal strategies that enhance recall). Hirst and colleagues (Hirst, 1982) were among the first to report differentially impaired metamemory in Korsakoff patients when compared to other etiologies of amnesia. Based on interviews, Korsakoff patients had less knowledge of mnemonic strategies than did patients with amnesia from other causes.

The most widely studied metamemorial capacity in amnesic patients is the feeling-of-knowing (FOK) phenomenon (cf. Hart, 1965; Gruneberg & Monks, 1974; Nelson, Leonesio, Shimamura, Landwehr, & Narens, 1982, Nelson, Gerler, & Narens, 1984). In a typical FOK experiment, subjects are asked to freely recall the answers to general information questions of varying difficulty (e.g., "What is the tallest mountain in South America?") until a certain number of failures occur. For unrecalled items, subjects are then asked to judge the likelihood that they would be able to recognize the correct answer if it was presented along with other likely but incorrect choices. The FOK predictions are then validated by a subsequent recognition test. In normal subjects, recognition performance is generally better for questions eliciting strong FOK than for questions eliciting weak or no FOK.

Shimamura and Squire (1986) evaluated the ability of FOK judgments to predict subsequent recognition performance in patients with Korsakoff syndrome, psychiatric patients undergoing bilateral ECT, a mixed group of amnesic patients that included N.A., and controls. Using general information questions (Study 1) and a sentence memory paradigm that assessed newly learned information (Study 2), they found that only the Korsakoff patients (and not the other diencephalic cases) displayed impaired FOK judgments. From these results, it appears that metamemory dysfunction is not an obligatory aspect of amnesia (or even diencephalic amnesia). The authors speculated that the disturbed FOK in Korsakoff patients might be a function of their frontal pathology, which would be expected to impair their ability on a variety of judgment and planning tasks.

Basal Forebrain Amnesia: Distinct from Bitemporal and Diencephalic Types?

Amnesia due to basal forebrain lesions most commonly results from a vascular lesion or aneurysm surgery in the region of the anterior communicating artery (Gade, 1982; Alexander & Freedman, 1983; Volpe & Hirst, 1983; Damasio, Graff-Radford, Eslinger, Damasio, & Kassell, 1985; Vilkki, 1985; Phillips, Sangalang, & Sterns, 1987; DeLuca & Cicerone, 1989; Okawa, Maeda, Nukui, & Kawafuchi, 1980). These patients exhibit extensive anterograde but variable retrograde amnesia. Temporal gradients similar to that seen in Korsakoff's syndrome have been described (Lindqvist & Norlen, 1966; Gade & Mortensen, 1990). Some authors have also described impairment in placing memories in proper chronological order (Lindqvist & Norlen, 1966; Talland, Sweet, & Ballantine, 1967; Damasio, Graff-Radford, Eslinger, Damasio & Kassell, 1985). Free, and sometimes wild, confabulation appears to be characteristic, particularly in the acute period (Lindqvist & Norlen, 1966; Talland, et al., 1967; Logue et al., 1968; Okawa et al., 1980; Alexander & Freedman, 1983; Damasio, et al., 1985) and probably relates to the extent of concomitant orbitofrontal involvement, particularly in those patients who show spontaneous or unprovoked confabulation (Damasio et al., 1985; Vilkki, 1985; Phillips, Sangalang, & Sterns, 1987; DeLuca & Cicerone, 1989; Fischer, Alexander, D'Esposito, & Otto, 1995). Some patients have difficulty distinguishing reality from dreaming. Although these behavioral abnormalities are distinctive, they may not be functionally related to the amnesia per se. Often, basal forebrain amnesia persists after dream–waking confusion and confabulation have subsided (Morris, Bowers, Chatterjee, & Heilman, 1992; Hashimoto, Tanaka, & Nakano, 2000).

Cueing seems to differentially improve memory performance in these patients, and anecdotal evidence suggests that many of these patients can recall specific information in one retrieval attempt, but not the next. These data have led to the general idea that these patients suffer from a problem in accessing information in long-term memory. However, further data are needed before accepting this proposition confidently. It has frequently been noted that these patients appear unaware (anosognosic) or unconcerned (anosodiaphoric) about their memory impairment (Talland et al., 1967; Alexander & Freedman, 1983; Phillips et al., 1987).

Are these patients distinct from amnesic patients with bitemporal or diencephalic damage? Interestingly, Talland regarded basal forebrain amnesic patients to show striking behavioral similarities to patients with Korsakoff syndrome, and Graff-Radford et al. (1990) saw similarities between these amnesic patients and patients with memory loss secondary to paramedian thalamic infarctions. Patients with basal forebrain amnesia often have damage to frontal lobes or to portions of the thalamus with frontal connections. Hence, these two forms of amnesia may share symptoms because they are both associated with frontal dysfunction. It may also be that such similarities arise because the large, vascular lesions that characterize these cases also involve structures or pathways destined for components of the medial temporal or diencephalic memory systems (Gade, 1982; Crosson, 1992). Currently, however, there is insufficient behavioral data on which to formally compare basal forebrain amnesic patients with amnesic patients of diencephalic or bitemporal origin.

FUNCTIONAL IMAGING STUDIES OF MEMORY

Functional neuroimaging has added significantly to the investigation of memory; however, a comprehensive review of this vast literature is beyond the scope of this chapter. Hence, this section highlights key findings in healthy adults that are most relevant to amnesia, with a focus on the medial temporal lobe. To date, functional neuroimaging studies of the memory contributions of the basal forebrain and thalamus are limited, and this area clearly warrants more attention. Our emphasis on the medial temporal lobe therefore is not intended to suggest that this is the only area important to memory, but rather is offered as a selective glimpse into the advances conferred by functional neuroimaging.

METHODOLOGICAL CONSIDERATIONS

Functional neuroimaging of the processes underlying memory presents significant methodological challenges. For example, the medial temporal lobe is particularly difficult to evaluate due to its location in the medial portion of the brain, the small size of each substructure, and the extensive, intricate nature of medial temporal lobe connectivity (Brewer & Moghekar, 2002; Ekstrom et al., 2009). In fact, many investigations continue to rely on crude distinctions between anterior (perirhinal/entorhinal cortices) and posterior (parahippocampal/entorhinal cortices) parahippocampal gyrus (Henson, 2005; Eichenbaum et al., 2007; Qin et al., 2009). Those that do try to differentiate between substructures must choose between several different techniques (Insausti et al., 1998; Kim et al., 2000; Ekstrom et al., 2009; Feczko, Augustinack, Fischl, & Dickerson, 2009; Pruessner et al., 2002), further confounding comparisons across studies. Nonetheless, there have been improvements thanks to some creative study designs, careful manipulation of imaging parameters, advanced methods of analysis, and focus on obtaining converging evidence across studies and research modalities (Brewer & Moghekar, 2002; Miller, 2008; Bandettini, 2009; Ekstrom et al., 2009).

EPISODIC MEMORY

Initial functional imaging studies of the medial temporal lobe memory system emphasized its role in episodic/declarative memory. More recently, studies have addressed more complex questions, including the nature and time course of episodic-semantic memory interactions. We will review three areas of active research on episodic memory: the timeframe of hippocampal involvement, functional differentiation between structures within the parahippocampal gyrus, and comparisons between encoding and retrieval.

Hippocampus

The hippocampus has a well-established role in associative and spatial learning and memory, the details of which are a continued focus of research (Sperling et al., 2003; Rosenbaum, Ziegler, Winocur, Grady, & Moscovitch, 2004; Meltzer & Constable, 2005; Doeller, King, & Burgess, 2008; Whitlock, Sutherland, Witter, Moser, & Moser, 2008; Ryan, Lin, Ketcham, & Nadel, 2009; Zalesak & Heckers, 2009). Learning associations between stimuli and/or the spatial context in which a stimulus was encountered contributes to formation and retrieval of episodic memories. A controversial topic is the timeframe of hippocampal involvement in this process. The two most prominent views are the traditional theory of system-level consolidation (Squire et al., 1994a) and the newer MTT (Nadel & Moscovitch, 1997; Moscovitch, et al., 2005; Moscovitch et al., 2006), which make different predictions about functional activation. The MTT predicts hippocampal activation with episodic (autobiographic) retrieval regardless of the age of the memory. In contrast, consolidation theory proposes a time-limited role, such that hippocampal activation will only be associated with recent but not remote episodic memory. Consolidation theory also predicts the opposite pattern of activation for neocortex, reflecting neocortical involvement in retrieval of remote memories that have already been consolidated.

Several recent neuroimaging studies present evidence for an overall decrease of hippocampal activity over time and a corresponding increase in neocortical activity (Takashima et al., 2006; Davis, Di Betta, Macdonald, & Gaskell, 2009; Takashima et al., 2009). However, remote intervals used in these studies are typically not more than 24 hours (Davis et al., 2009; Takashima et al., 2009) and 3 months (Takashima et al., 2006), which arguably falls within the realm of "recent" memory (Mayes & Roberts, 2001). Also, these studies assessed memory for material learned within the laboratory setting, which may not have the same salience or personal relevance as real-world memories. Decreased hippocampal activation therefore may have resulted from decreased vividness of the memory, rather than the length of delay. However, this explanation is challenged by the fact that decreased hippocampal activation often occurred in the context of stable performance accuracy.

Many studies comparing remote and recent memory use episodic autobiographic memory because of its inherent vividness and association with "mental time travel" and "re-experiencing" of the event, and because everyone has autobiographic memories ranging from very recent to very remote (Cabeza & St Jacques, 2007; Piolino, Desgranges, & Eustache, 2009). The majority of neuroimaging studies demonstrate hippocampal activation during autobiographic memory retrieval independent of remoteness (Maguire, Henson, Mummery, & Frith, 2001; Ryan et al., 2001; Addis, Moscovitch, Crawley, & McAndrews, 2004; Gilboa, 2004; P. Piolino et al., 2004; Steinvorth, Corkin, & Halgren, 2006; Viard et al., 2007; Svoboda & Levine, 2009) and support MTT's prediction that the extent of activation is most closely tied with the quality (e.g., vividness, richness) of a given recollective experience, independent of its age. This hippocampal activation effect held true even when there was no opportunity for reencoding remote memories during prescan interview (Ryan et al., 2001; Viard et al., 2007) and when the study design controlled for reencoding in the scanner (Gilboa, 2004). In fact, some studies have found *greater* hippocampal activation during retrieval of more remote autobiographical memories (Pascale Piolino et al., 2004; Rekkas & Constable, 2005). Still, it should be noted that others have failed to demonstrate time-independent hippocampal activation (Niki & Luo, 2002; Piefke, Weiss, Zilles, Markowitsch, & Fink, 2003). Since all studies of remote autobiographic memory seem to employ different methodologies, it is often difficult to determine necessary and sufficient conditions for hippocampal activation. For example, Niki and Lou (2002) specifically evaluated topographical autobiographic memories and Piefke et al. (2003) used memories with positive or negative valence, neither of which are typically the focus of autobiographic investigations. There also may be additional relevant factors not typically evaluated. For example, studies have noted differential activation in the right and left hippocampi, although the nature of these differences is not consistent across

studies and may vary depending on participant and/or memory age (Maguire & Frith, 2003a, 2003b; P. Piolino et al., 2004; Viard et al., 2007).

Functional Differentiation Within the Parahippocampal Gyrus

Animal literature suggests that functional specialization exists between, and possibly even within, substructures in the parahippocampal gyrus (i.e., perirhinal, entorhinal, and parahippocampal cortices), rather than a simple dissociation between the hippocampus and the parahippocampal gyrus (Aggleton & Brown, 2005; Brun et al., 2008; Hafting, Fyhn, Bonnevie, Moser, & Moser, 2008). Neuroimaging evidence now suggests there may be divisions of labor in the human parahippocampal gyrus as well.

Broadly, the hippocampus appears to serve a more general role in binding information to form a unitized episodic memory, whereas structures within the parahippocampal gyrus contribute in a more domain-specific manner (Davachi, 2006; Staresina & Davachi, 2006; Preston et al., 2009). The most compelling evidence for functional specificity comes from within-study contrasts. With respect to material type, several groups have found a double dissociation between preferential perirhinal activation during encoding of individual items, contrasted with activation in parahippocampal cortex during encoding of more complex stimulus information, such as source and context (Davachi, Mitchell, & Wagner, 2003; Tendolkar et al., 2008; Diana, Yonelinas, & Ranganath, 2009). More subtle dissociations have also been documented. For example, Aminoff and colleagues (2007) found overall increased activation in the parahippocampal cortex in response to stimulus arrays previously learned on the basis of context, regardless of whether that context was spatial in nature. However, they found a hierarchical pattern of activity such that the posterior portion of the parahippocampal cortex was preferentially active during spatial context conditions whereas the anterior portion (closer to the perirhinal cortex) was active during nonspatial context conditions. Although limitations in spatial resolution are clearly important to bear in mind when evaluating such small structural differentiations, Aminoff and colleagues provide at least preliminary evidence that, as in animals, the functional role of the parahippocampal gyrus may not be adequately captured by gross distinctions between its three main substructures.

Functional dissociations also have been demonstrated with respect to memory subprocesses. Based on a 6-point scale for confidence ratings (i.e., a participant's confidence that he or she had previously seen a test item), Daselaar and colleagues (2006) found that the anterior hippocampus and rhinal cortex were associated with novelty detection, measured as a linear decrease in activation as confidence ratings increased; conversely, the posterior parahippocampal gyrus (presumably corresponding to the parahippocampal cortex) was associated with familiarity, as demonstrated by a linear increase in activation as ratings increased. In contrast, the posterior hippocampus demonstrated a *nonlinear* pattern consistent with recollection, such that it was preferentially activated in association with the highest confidence rating.

Despite extensive evidence that functional dissociations do exist, the precise nature of these dissociations remains highly controversial and is an extremely active area of ongoing neuroimaging research. Several theories have been generated to try to account for findings to date. Eichenbaum, Yonelinas, and Ranganath (2007) recently proposed that the dual processes of recognition memory (recollection and familiarity) are subserved by different, yet interconnected, anatomic networks within the medial temporal lobe, and that the medial temporal lobe's role in recognition memory is best understood in the context of its combined hierarchical and parallel circuitry. Specifically, they proposed that the pathway through the parahippocampal cortex (dorsal ["where"] stream → parahippocampal cortex → medial entorhinal cortex) subserves memory for contextual information and therefore contributes to recollection; in contrast, the pathway through the perirhinal cortex (ventral ["what"] stream → perirhinal cortex → lateral entorhinal cortex) primarily subserves memory for individual items without contextual association, and therefore selectively contributes to familiarity judgment.

The hippocampus, which is at the apex of both pathways, associates item information from the perirhinal cortex with context information from the parahippocampal cortex. Diana, Yonelinas, and Ranganath (2007) refer to this as the *binding of item and context* (BIC) model and additionally suggest that contributions within the parahippocampal gyrus may vary depending on task demands.

There is compelling evidence in support of the BIC model (for reviews, see Diana et al., 2007; Eichenbaum et al., 2007). However, there is also counter-evidence, including studies that demonstrate functional activation in extrahippocampal medial temporal lobe structures during associative learning and memory (Law et al., 2005; Awipi & Davachi, 2008) or perirhinal activation during spatial memory formation (Bellgowan, Buffalo, Bodurka, & Martin, 2009). Discrepancies such as these have led to alternative theories. For example, Squire, Wixted, and Clark (2007) posit that the role of substructures within the medial temporal lobe is not defined by differences between recollection and familiarity but by the strength of the memory, which at times coincides with the recollection/familiarity distinction. In evaluating these competing theories and developing new models, it will be important to consider that a purely modular view of structure–function relationships may not adequately capture the complexities of recognition memory or the intricacies of medial temporal lobe connectivity.

Stages of Information Processing: Encoding and Retrieval

A distinct benefit of functional neuroimaging is that it permits evaluation of conditions that are difficult to dissociate behaviorally, although even neuroimaging contrasts are almost never process pure. The investigation of encoding and retrieval stages of episodic memory has particularly benefited from techniques such as PET and fMRI.

The prefrontal cortex plays an important role in episodic memory, including potentially unique contributions from three of its subdivisions (Cabeza & St Jacques, 2007). According to the hemispheric encoding–retrieval asymmetry (HERA) phenomenon, left-sided prefrontal cortex activation in healthy young adults is preferentially associated with encoding, whereas right-sided prefrontal cortex activation is associated with retrieval (Tulving, Kapur, Craik, Moscovitch, & Houle, 1994; Habib, Nyberg, & Tulving, 2003). Cabeza (2002) proposed that the HERA effect decreases with age—a model he termed *hemispheric asymmetry reduction in older adults* (HAROLD). There is also evidence of decreased functional asymmetry in clinical populations, suggesting that aging simply represents one condition in which neural reorganization and/or compensation results in contralateral activation, decreasing the strength of former asymmetries like HERA (Park & Reuter-Lorenz, 2009). Although less extensively studied, there is evidence for similar trends in the hippocampus: In young adults, Maguire and Frith (2003b) found that only left hippocampal activation was independent of remoteness of memory, whereas the right hippocampus demonstrated decreased activation with increasing remoteness; in contrast, older adults (2003a) demonstrated bilateral hippocampal activation regardless of memory age.

In contradiction to the generally accepted HERA model, a recent meta-analysis (Spaniol et al., 2009) discovered more evidence of left-lateralized prefrontal cortex activation for both encoding and retrieval. They found similar left-lateralization in the medial temporal lobe, with support for a shift from encoding to retrieval along an anterior–posterior gradient. In other words, the anterior hippocampus generally demonstrated preferential activation during successful encoding, whereas the posterior parahippocampal gyrus demonstrated more activation during successful retrieval. It should be noted, though, that activations during encoding and retrieval were not necessarily mutually exclusive and may vary by stimulus type. For example, Kennepohl et al. (2007) found right-lateralized activation changes in the posterior hippocampus during encoding of nonverbal but not verbal material, whereas the anterior hippocampus and entorhinal cortex demonstrated left-lateralized changes independent of material type. The shift from high to low material-specificity from posterior to anterior medial temporal lobe is consistent with Preston et al. (2009), who identified activation within the anterior medial

temporal lobe (specifically, the subiculum and perirhinal cortex) associated with successful encoding of both scenes and faces, whereas the parahippocampal cortex demonstrated preferential activation during encoding of scenes. These findings suggest a complex interplay between stage of processing, material type, age, and anatomy, the details of which warrant further inquiry.

IMPLICIT MEMORY

As imaging methods become increasingly refined, so too does our understanding of what now seems to be a complex relationship between explicit and implicit memory systems. Although early studies tended to separately investigate these processes or use different behavioral paradigms and imaging parameters to evaluate each (see Voss & Paller, 2008 for review), recent investigations facilitate more direct comparisons (e.g., Schott et al., 2006; Danckert et al., 2007; Zeithamova, Maddox, & Schnyer, 2008; Kim & Cabeza, 2009. For example, Schott and colleagues (2005, 2006) differentiated priming with and without conscious awareness. They asked participants to count the number of syllables in each word in a study list. Shortly thereafter, participants performed a word-stem completion task and, for each trial, indicated whether their response was a new or previously seen word. During encoding (Schott et al., 2006), bilateral medial temporal lobe activity increased for words that were subsequently remembered (i.e., correctly identified their response as a previously studied word) but not for words that demonstrated subsequent priming without conscious recollection (i.e., incorrect identification of their response as a new word). These findings are consistent with the traditional belief that the medial temporal lobe is selectively involved in explicit (autobiographical) memory. However, medial temporal lobe activation patterns during retrieval (Schott, et al., 2005) were less clearly dissociable: As expected, the hippocampus demonstrated increased activation during retrieval of consciously recollected items; however, hippocampal and perirhinal activation changes were also noted in association with priming-without-recognition. The authors interpret this finding as a reflection of the medial temporal lobe's role in novelty detection, which is supported by other neuroimaging evidence (Elliott & Dolan, 1998). However, even unconscious novelty detection challenges the strict interpretation that the medial temporal lobe is involved only in explicit retrieval.

Based in part on contemporary imaging data, several authors have recently questioned the traditional view of independent, clearly dissociable systems for implicit and explicit memory. For example, Bussey and Saksida (2007) propose that the hierarchical organization of cortical–medial temporal lobe connectivity corresponds to a hierarchical (vs. modular) organization of perceptual-mnemonic processes. Reder, Park, and Kieffaber (2009) also propose a departure from the pure dissociation; instead, they suggest the medial temporal lobe's role is best described in terms of formation of associations, independent of the extent of conscious awareness. Others argue that the neural systems subserving implicit and explicit memory are separate but not independent. Indeed, emerging evidence from functional neuroimaging in healthy adults (Albouy et al., 2008) and patient populations (Moody, Bookheimer, Vanek, & Knowlton, 2004) points to functional interactions between the medial temporal lobe memory system and the memory system implicated in implicit memory. The precise nature of these interactions is not yet clear, although it may be competitive in nature in at least some forms of implicit memory (Poldrack & Packard, 2003), or the degree of competition versus cooperation may shift across time (Albouy et al., 2008).

CONCLUSIONS

The preceding section is offered as a brief overview of current controversies in memory research to which functional neuroimaging has contributed. This nascent but rapidly growing field may seem to raise more questions than answers, but in so doing it has already constrained cognitive theories of amnesia and has helped guide interpretations of clinical findings. Our challenge in the decades ahead will be to capitalize on the unique perspective afforded by functional neuroimaging techniques while remaining cognizant of its methodological limitations and need for continued refinement.

CLINICAL PRESENTATION OF DISORDERS ASSOCIATED WITH AMNESIA

Memory loss is a common problem and has considerable localizing significance. It is also a helpful diagnostic finding since it is a distinguishing feature of several neurological disorders. The following is a brief review of some of the more important disorders.

MILD COGNITIVE IMPAIRMENT

Kral (1962) used the term *benign senescent forgetfulness* to describe adults whose memory was poorer than that of age-matched peers but who had no other evidence of progressive dementia. The term *age-associated memory impairment* (AAMI) was used to describe healthy persons over 50 who are not depressed or demented but who score at least 1 standard deviation below the mean for young adults on tests of memory (Crook et al., 1986, 1991). More recently, the concept of *mild cognitive impairment* (MCI) was introduced to describe older adults with a memory complaint and impairments on memory tests when compared with normal subjects, in the context of intact activities of daily living, generally intact cognitive function, and no dementia (Petersen, Stevens, Ganfuli, et al., 2001; Petersen, 2004). At least three subtypes of MCI are widely recognized, including amnestic, multidomain (encompassing more than one cognitive area), and single-domain nonamnestic forms (Petersen, 2004). The primary importance of the MCI concept concerns its role as a possible prodromic stage of dementia. Longitudinal studies indicate that approximately 10%–15% of patients with MCI convert to Alzheimer disease each year, compared to overall conversion rates of 1%–2% in normal elders (Petersen, 2000). Behavioral markers and concurrent presence of entorhinal and hippocampal atrophy appear to predict eventual conversion (Devanand et al., 2008). It is important to note that MCI encompasses both objective evidence and subjective report (often including an informant) of age-related decline. Many objectively normal adults may complain of memory loss, particularly if they are in intellectually demanding positions. The isolated presence of a memory complaint without objective evidence may indicate the presence of depression or adjustment difficulties worthy of independent clinical attention. By the same token, depression, anxiety, and other neuropsychiatric symptoms that may give rise to a subjective memory complaint are quite common in MCI (Monastero et al., 2009). MCI is discussed more fully in Chapter 17.

DEGENERATIVE DISORDERS

Many degenerative dementias such as Pick, Huntington, and Parkinson diseases eventually affect memory (see Chapter 17), but Alzheimer disease typically first manifests with memory impairment (Damasio, Tranel, & Damasio, 1989). As discussed above, nearly all of the neural systems thought to be important in memory are affected by Alzheimer disease, including the medial temporal lobe (Hyman et al., 1984, 1986; Scott, DeKosky & Scheff, 1991), basal forebrain (Whitehouse et al., 1981), thalamus (Xuereb et al., 1991), and neocortex. Unlike the pure amnestic syndrome, memory impairment in advancing Alzheimer disease affects not only new learning, but also results in the gradual loss of knowledge structures and semantic memory stores. Eventually, other cognitive domains become involved, including language, visuospatial/perceptual ability, personality, and affect. Alzheimer disease and other dementias are discussed more thoroughly in Chapter 17.

EFFECTS OF ANTICHOLINERGIC MEDICATION

Many commonly used medications have significant central anticholinergic actions, including antihistamines commonly used in nonprescription sleep and allergy medications, some antidepressants, and medications used to manage urinary incontinence and frequency. Anticholinergic drugs can impair memory (Drachman & Leavitt, 1974), and withdrawal of these medications in patients with memory deficits may result in dramatic improvement in memory (Womack & Heilman, 2003).

VASCULAR DISEASE

Stroke will manifest with amnesia when critical areas are infarcted. Strokes affecting the posterior cerebral artery territory (posterior medial temporal lobe and retrosplenial cortex; Benson, Marsden & Meadows, 1974) and the thalamic penetrating arteries (Graff-Radford, Tranel, Van Hoesen, & Brandt, 1990) have been implicated, as has basal forebrain amnesia from anterior communicating artery aneurysm hemorrhage or surgery (Volpe & Hirst, 1983). Infarction of the fornix with or without basal forebrain lesions can also present with isolated amnesia (Park et al., 2000; Renou et al., 2008). In vascular cases, the onset of amnesia is abrupt. Improvement is variable, and patients may be left with serious permanent deficits, even following small infarctions.

CEREBRAL ANOXIA

Depending upon the degree and duration of ischemia and/or hypoxia, neuronal loss may be widespread, or very focal. Amnesia has been reported following cardiac arrest in which the only pathological feature identified was loss of neurons in field CA1 of the hippocampus (Zola-Morgan, Squire & Amaral, 1986; Squire & Zola, 1996).

WERNICKE-KORSAKOFF SYNDROME

Alcoholic Korsakoff syndrome typically develops after years of alcohol abuse and nutritional deficiency (Butters & Cermak, 1980; Butters, 1984; Victor, Adams, & Collins, 1989). Patients first undergo an acute stage of the illness, Wernicke's encephalopathy, in which symptoms of confusion, disorientation, oculomotor dysfunction, and ataxia are present. After this resolves, amnesia can persist as a permanent symptom. Severe anterograde amnesia and an extensive, temporally graded retrograde amnesia are characteristic. Patients with this disorder often confabulate memories and are unaware of the memory loss (anosognosia for amnesia). Pathologically, there is damage to the mammillary bodies and medial nuclei of the thalamus, as discussed above. Although usually associated with chronic alcohol abuse, Korsakoff syndrome can rarely occur in nonalcoholic patients who suffer chronic avitaminosis secondary to malabsorption syndromes (Becker, Furman, Panisset, & Smith, 1990) or who refuse to eat in the context of a psychiatric disorder (Newman, Adityanjee, Sobolewski, & Jampala, 1998).

HERPES SIMPLEX AND HSV-6 ENCEPHALITIS

Herpes simplex causes inflammation and necrosis, particularly in the orbitofrontal and inferior temporal regions. It thus involves limbic structures, including the hippocampus, parahippocampal gyrus, amygdala and overlying cortex, the polar limbic cortex, cingulate gyrus, and the orbitofrontal cortex (Damasio, Tranel, & Damasio, 1989). Patients may present with personality change, confusion, headache, fever, and seizures, and they are often amnesic. Prompt treatment with antiviral agents can control the illness, and full recovery is possible. However, damage to the aforementioned structures often leaves the patient with severe anterograde and retrograde amnesia. The amnesic syndromes in patient D.R.B. (also known as Boswell; Damasio, Eslinger, Damasio, Van Hoesen, & Cornell, 1985) and patient S.S. (Cermak, 1976; Cermak & O'Connor, 1983) have been particularly well-characterized. Recent reports indicate that herpes simplex infection can occasionally lead to a syndrome of focal retrograde amnesia (Carlesimo et al., 1998; Fujii, Yamadori, Endo, Suzuki, & Fukatsu, 1999; Tanaka, Miyazawa, Hashimoto, Nakano, & Obayashi, 1999). Human herpes virus-6 (HHV-6) also can target the limbic system and present with amnesic syndromes, confusion, sleep disorders, and seizures (Wainwright et al., 2001). Hokkanen and Launes (2007) review other infectious agents that can leave residual neuropsychological sequelae, including memory loss.

AUTOIMMUNE LIMBIC ENCEPHALITIS

This condition usually presents with personality change, agitation, and amnestic dementia. It was first described as a paraneoplastic syndrome (Corsellis, Goldberg, & Norton, 1968; Khan & Wieser, 1994; Martin et al., 1996; Gultekin et al., 2000); however, it can also occur in patients without neoplasm (Bien et al., 2000).

Over the past decade, several autoantibodies have been associated with different forms of limbic encephalitis (see Dalmau & Bataller, 2006; Darnell & Posner, 2009). Neuronal antibodies (Hu, Ma2, CV2/CRMP5, amphiphysin, and atypical intracellular antibodies) in patients with various neoplasms (small-cell and non–small cell lung cancer, testicular tumors, thymomas and others) have been associated with an inflammatory disorder affecting neurons throughout the neuraxis, but often with particular intensity in limbic structures, including the hippocampus. Although the pathogenesis is autoimmune, response to immunotherapy is usually poor. But patients with Ma-2 antibodies in association with testicular cancers often improve after surgery. And patients with antibodies to voltage-gated potassium channels (VGKC), sometimes associated with thymoma or small-cell lung cancer but more often without known neoplasm, can have a more selective limbic encephalitis that often responds to immunotherapy with steroids, intravenous immunoglobulin (IVIG), or plasma exchange (Bien et al., 2000). A syndrome of amnesia, psychosis, seizures, central hypoventilation progressing to coma has been attributed to antibodies that react with N-methyl-D-aspartate (NMDA) receptors (Nokura et al., 1997), and this syndrome may respond dramatically to immunotherapy. Although first described in association with neoplasms, only 60% of a large series had cancer (Dalmau et al., 2008), and the same syndrome has now been reported in children, many without neoplasms (Florance et al., 2009). Similar autoantibodies have been identified in patients with epilepsy and systemic lupus (Levite & Ganor, 2008).

TRAUMA

Following closed head injury, patients may have an acute anterograde and retrograde amnesia, the duration of which correlates with the severity of the injury as measured by the Glasgow Coma Scale or the duration of unconsciousness (Levin, 1989). The retrograde amnesia typically improves along with improvement in anterograde amnesia, providing evidence that a retrieval deficit is responsible for the portion of the retrograde memory loss that recovers. Residual memory impairment is usually a feature of broader cognitive and attentional impairment, but it can be prominent with severe injuries (Russell & Nathan, 1946; Whitty & Zangwill, 1977). Pathological changes are variable and widespread. Memory dysfunction may be caused by anterior temporal lobe contusions, temporal lobe white matter necrosis, or diffuse axonal disruption (Levin, 1989). Cases of focal retrograde amnesia in the relative absence of a new learning defect have been reported after closed head trauma (Kapur et al., 1992; Hunkin et al., 1995).

TRANSIENT GLOBAL AMNESIA

Transient global amnesia (TGA) is a distinctive form of amnesia that begins suddenly and typically resolves within a day (Fisher & Adams, 1964; Caplan, 1985; Kritchevsky, 1987, 1989; Kritchevsky, Squire, & Zouzounis, 1988; Hodges & Warlow, 1990). A severe impairment in new learning and patchy loss of information learned prior to onset is seen. The patient often asks repetitive questions and may be aware of the memory deficit. After resolution, neuropsychological testing is normal except for amnesia for the episode (Kritchevsky, 1989). Etiologic roles have been proposed for epilepsy (Fisher & Adams, 1958; Fisher, 1982), emotional stress (Oleson & Jørgensen, 1986), occlusive cerebrovascular disease (Heathfield, Croft, & Swash, 1973; Shuping, Rollinson, & Toole, 1980), migrainous vasospasm (Caplan et al., 1981; Haas & Ross, 1986; Hodges & Warlow, 1990; Tosi & Righetti, 1997; Schmidtke & Ehmsen, 1998) vertebrobasilar dyscontrol (Caplan, 1985), and venous insufficiency (Lewis, 1998; Chung et al., 2006). There are now several reports of small diffusion-weighted imaging (DWI) abnormalities in CA1 of the hippocampus in patients with TGA within the first 48 hours (Woolfenden et al., 1997; Ay et al., 1998; see Sander & Sander, 2005); these lesions typically are transient (Sedlaczek et al., 2004; Toledo et al., 2008) and are more likely to be evident after 24–48 hours of symptom onset (and hence, after resolution of the amnesia in the majority of patients). The striking predilection of these punctate lesions for the lateral hippocampus leaves little doubt as to their relevance to the clinical findings; however, their pathogenesis remains enigmatic. Although the DWI characteristics are suggestive of ischemia, patients with TGA do not appear to be at greater risk for cerebrovascular disease than controls (Miller, Petersen, Metter, Millikan, & Yanagihara, 1987; Hodges & Warlow, 1990). Epileptic TGA (Kapur 1993; Butler, 2007) usually has a shorter duration, is more likely to recur, and may be associated with EEG abnormalities.

ELECTROCONVULSIVE THERAPY

Used for relief of depression, ECT can produce severe anterograde and temporally limited retrograde amnesia (cf. Squire, 1974; Miller & Marlin, 1979). More severe impairment is seen after bilateral versus unilateral application. The anterograde defect is related in severity to the number of treatments and is characterized by rapid forgetting and poor delayed recall (Squire, 1984). Substantial, often complete, recovery takes place in the few months after treatment ends (Squire & Chace, 1975; Squire & Slater, 1983). The retrograde amnesia appears to be temporally limited, involving only the few years prior to treatment onset. It, too, recovers almost completely in the months after treatment (Squire, Chace, & Slater, 1976; Squire, Slater, & Miller, 1981). The extent of memory loss appears unrelated to therapeutic efficacy (Small, Milstein, & Small, 1981; Welch, 1982), although it may be related to the extent of pretreatment cognitive impairment and posttreatment disorientation (Sobin et al., 1995). Although the data are by no means clear, some authors have suggested that ECT-induced memory loss models bilateral temporal lobe disease (Inglis, 1970; Squire, 1984), and several studies have used ECT patients as a surrogate for temporal lobe amnesic patients to compare with patient with diencephalic pathology.

PSYCHOGENIC AMNESIAS

Psychogenic amnesias are reviewed by Schacter and Kihlstrom (1989). Psychologically induced loss of memory may be normal, as in amnesia for events of childhood (Wetzler & Sweeney, 1986; Usher & Neisser, 1993; Eacott & Crawley, 1999) or for events during sleep (Roth, Roehrs, Zwyghuizen Doorenbos, Stepanski, & Wittig, 1988). Alternatively, they may be pathological, as in the amnesias associated with dissociative states, multiple personality, or with simulated amnesia (Kopelman, 1987; Kessler et al., 1997; Markowitsch, 1999). A striking loss of autobiographical memory is a hallmark of functional amnesia, and amnesia for one's own name (in the absence of aphasia or severe cognitive dysfunction in other spheres) is seen exclusively in this form of memory loss. Retrograde loss is often disproportionate to anterograde amnesia, and some patients will demonstrate loss of skills or other procedural memories typically retained by organic amnesic patients. Some studies have reported disproportionate loss of "personal" as opposed to "public" information in the retrograde compartment (Kapur, 1991).

REHABILITATION OF MEMORY DISORDERS

Historically, the field of memory rehabilitation has been guided by practical rather than theoretical concerns, although there are important attempts to formulate an underlying theoretical basis for therapeutic interventions (Baddeley, 1984; Wilson, 1987; Parente & DiCesare, 1991; Sohlberg & Mateer, 1991; Baddeley & Wilson, 1994). As Glisky and Schacter (1987) point out, most rehabilitative interventions have attempted to directly improve memory performance through repetitive practice or exercises (cf. Prigatano et al., 1984), or through teaching mnemonic strategies. They refer to this as the "restorative" approach since its goal is to restore a certain degree of memory skill in these patients. Depending on severity of the memory loss and the nature of material to be learned, some studies have found beneficial effects of rehearsal strategies (Schacter, Rich, & Stampp, 1985), organizational techniques (Gianutsos & Gianutsos, 1979), and imagery mnemonics (Patten, 1972; Crovitz, Harvey, & Horn, 1979). Although such techniques have proven useful in individual cases, empirical investigations have generally not supported their efficacy in producing long-term relief of memory impairment, particularly in patients with concomitant deficits in initiation or executive skills (Richardson, 1992; Tate, 1997). A variety of techniques have been used to

improve attention, including encoding (e.g., chunking, PQRST methods for reading and remembering text, imagery mnemonics; Butters et al., 1997) and retention/retrieval (e.g., spaced retrieval technique; Schacter, Rich, & Stampp, 1985). The field lacks well-controlled clinical trials of the efficacy of memory therapy, and this is a key need for future work (das Nair & Lincoln, 2009; Sherer, Roebuck-Spencer, & Davis, 2009).

In contrast to the restorative approach, the alternative "compensatory" approach seeks to teach the memory-impaired patient new techniques designed to close the gap between adaptive ability and life demands (Baeckman & Dixon, 1992; Wilson, 2000). This approach emphasizes the use of external memory aids and other assistive technology. Examples include the use of electronic timers or personal digital devices (Chute & Bliss, 1994; Kim, Burke, Dowds, & George, 1999; Kim, Burke, Dowds, Boone, & Park, 2000), paging systems that remind patients when to perform certain activities (Wilson, Evans, Emslie, & Malinek, 1997; Evans, Emslie, & Wilson, 1998), and memory notebooks that serve as tools for organizing information (Sohlberg & Mateer, 1989; Zencius, Wesolowski, Krankowski, & Burke, 1991; Burke, Danick, Bemis, & Durgin, 1994; Schmitter Edgecombe, Fahy, Whelan, & Long, 1995).

A third approach has been to utilize residual learning capacities (e.g., procedural or skill learning) in memory-disordered patients as a basis for teaching new facts or skills. For example, some amnesic patients can learn new computer skills (Glisky, Schacter, & Tulving, 1986a; Glisky & Schacter, 1988; Glisky, 1992) and computer-related vocabulary (Glisky, Schacter, & Tulving, 1986b) using the "method of vanishing cues," which capitalizes on intact priming capacity. With this method, the amnesic patient is given increasingly shorter versions of a rule such as "to save your file, press F10" or of a word such as "delete" (e.g., dele__) until they are able to perform the function or recall the word without the cue. Glisky and colleagues have shown that memory-disordered patients can be taught functional use of a microcomputer (Glisky, Schacter, & Tulving, 1986a) and that, when enhanced with extensive repetition and direct cueing, such learning could generalize to a real work environment (Glisky & Schacter, 1987). Although such procedures appear relatively labor intensive and may not lead to extensive explicit memory, they do demonstrate that it is possible to obtain generalization of a newly acquired skill to the natural environment. Butters, Glisky, and Schacter (1993) suggest that continued practice may enhance transfer to real-world situations by capitalizing on a semantic memory system that is capable of acquiring new information at a slower rate. It is important to recognize that the goal of this approach is not to restore or improve memory in any general sense; instead, it is designed to teach a specific skill in hopes of preparing the patient for gainful employment. Glisky and Schacter (1987; cf. also Schacter & Glisky, 1986) have called this the "domain-specific" approach to distinguish it from the larger body of restorative techniques.

A fourth rehabilitation technique is "errorless learning" (Baddeley & Wilson, 1994), which is based on the idea that learning from mistakes is largely a process of explicit memory, whereas response repetition is more aligned with implicit memory. Once an error is made, the incorrect response essentially has to be "unlearned" to prevent interference with correct responses. By this view, residual implicit memory capabilities in amnesia might better support the learning of new information if errors are eliminated such that every response is correct (Baddeley & Wilson, 1994). The technique of errorless learning has been used successfully to teach amnesic patients new lists of words (Hunkin, Squires, Parkin, & Tidy, 1998), a route through a complex maze (Evans et al., 2000), face–name associations (Komatsu, Mimura, Kato, Wakamatsu, & Kashima, 2000), and tasks of everyday memory functioning (Clare et al., 2000). There is some debate whether the benefits of errorless learning accrue from implicit memory (Baddeley & Wilson, 1994) or residual explicit memory (Hunkin et al., 1998), although data suggest that this technique is a promising area for future clinical and experimental investigation.

Pharmacologic agents have been demonstrated to affect memory. Cholinergic agents such as donepezil have been demonstrated to provide a modest improvement in memory for patients with Alzheimer disease (see Chapter 17). Although a benefit is also reported in nondemented patients with mild cognitive impairment (Birks & Flicker, 2006) and multiple sclerosis (Krupp et al., 2004), the benefit is slight, and side effects can be troublesome. There is no questions, however, that discontinuation of anticholinergic medication may significantly improve cognitive function (Womack & Heilman, 2003).

CONCLUSION

FUTURE DIRECTIONS

The interdisciplinary study of memory and amnesia represents one of the remarkable success stories of contemporary neuropsychology and cognitive neuroscience. Work continues from the clinic to the laboratory, from studies of higher cognitive function to membrane physiology, and from highly controlled experiments to analyses of everyday memory functioning. This remarkable diversity has led to rapid accumulation of important new data and new insights into the complex nature of memory. Five decades of research with amnesic subjects has led to an increased understanding of the role that specific brain regions and brain systems play in normal and disordered memory functions. The sparing of many memory functions in amnesia has led to structural ("systems") and functional ("process") distinctions among different types of memory that are only now receiving anatomic verification through behavioral and neuroimaging analysis.

Despite remarkable advances in our understanding of the neural basis of memory, some key questions remain unresolved:

• *Is there a "core amnesic syndrome"?* Although initial research tended to support the notion of "three amnesias" (bitemporal, diencephalic, and basal forebrain), more recent data have been less compelling and have tended to favor the notion that memory is supported by a distributed functional–anatomic system that subsumes these three functional systems. Many of the behavioral features that appear to discriminate these three amnesic subtypes can be attributable to "neighborhood" damage (e.g., frontal damage in basal forebrain amnesia) rather than intrinsic damage to the distributed memory system per se. Still, it is reasonable to expect that each component of the distributed system provides a unique contribution to memory function and that behavioral differences should exist accordingly. Still, the bulk of the evidence is consistent with the presence of a "core" syndrome of anterograde and retrograde amnesia.

- *What cognitive deficits are necessary and sufficient to produce amnesia?* Since amnesic disorders can result from diverse disease processes and may be seen in the context of a variety of cognitive deficits, it seems reasonable to attempt to distinguish between what is causative (central) and what is ancillary to the underlying memory disorder. A prominent example of how this issue complicates contemporary amnesia research is the controversy regarding the role of frontal lobe deficits in the memory impairment of diencephalic (and, perhaps, basal forebrain) amnesic patients. Traditionally, frontal contributions to memory have been considered to be relatively nonspecific, producing complex disturbances in attention and strategy formation that affect various domains of neuropsychological functioning in addition to memory. However, recent research has revealed that the frontal lobes play specific mnemonic roles and may mediate complex processes, such as working memory and memory for self-generated responses. Thus, frontal contributions to memory are receiving renewed attention, not as "nuisance variables," but as aspects of memory functioning worthy of assuming a central place in amnesia research.

- *How can we best understand distinctions between spared and impaired memory abilities in amnesia?* We have considered various ways of viewing these distinctions (e.g., multiple memory systems vs. transfer-appropriate processing), and have suggested that much of the data can be considered

as supportive of both approaches. That is, viewing memory dissociations as supportive of the idea of multiple memory systems as opposed to considering such dissociations as based on differences in cognitive processes applied at study and test are not necessarily mutually exclusive.

- *What is the relationship between implicit and explicit memory function?* It will be important to advance knowledge of how implicit phenomena (e.g., priming and perceptual fluency) contribute to performances on traditional (explicit) tests of recall and recognition. New strategies for empirically and statistically separating effects of direct recollection (e.g., recall) from the indirect effects of prior stimulus exposure (e.g., perceptual fluency and familiarity) hold significant promise in facilitating this understanding in normal subjects and amnesic patients.

- *How will experimental studies of amnesia continue to inform contemporary debates about memory function and dysfunction?* Current debates include the nature of traumatically induced memory failures (Loftus, 1993; Zola, 1998) and distortions of eyewitness recall in the courtroom (Loftus & Ketcham, 1991; Schacter, 1998). These important topics have already benefited from research on encoding–retrieval interactions, memory for emotional events, and the constructive nature of memory, and will continue to increase as knowledge of normal and abnormal memory phenomena accumulates (Roediger & McDermott, 2000).

- *What are effective approaches to the treatment of memory disorders?* Despite significant advances in research on cognitive and anatomic mechanisms of memory, it is still unclear how best to design and implement effective interventions and rehabilitative techniques. The field suffers from a lack of well-designed clinical trials; this will be a significant challenge for the future.

It could be said that we now have a good understanding of the components, or building blocks, upon which memory performance is based. The focus of the next decade will likely be on building and testing more comprehensive models of memory function at the network level, facilitated by continued interdisciplinary collaboration, the growing availability of sensitive and specific assessment tools, and the development of exciting new technologies. Historically, the interdisciplinary study of memory and memory dysfunction has been one of the great success stories in contemporary neural science, and the next decade offers great promise for continued advancement in our understanding of these fundamental abilities.

REFERENCES

Addis, D. R., Moscovitch, M., Crawley, A. P., & McAndrews, M. P. (2004). Recollective qualities modulate hippocampal activation during autobiographical memory retrieval. *Hippocampus, 14*, 752–762.

Adolphs, R., Cahill, L., Schul, R., & Babinsky, R. (1997). Impaired declarative memory for emotional material following bilateral amygdala damage in humans. *Learning and Memory, 4*, 51–54.

Aggleton, J. P., & Brown, M. W. (1999). Episodic memory, amnesia, and the hippocampal-anterior thalamic axis. *Behavioral and Brain Sciences, 22*, 425–444.

Aggleton, J. P., & Brown, M. W. (2005). Contrasting hippocampal and perirhinal cortex function using immediate early gene imaging. *Quarterly Journal of Experimental Psychology, 58*(3–4), 218–233.

Aggleton, J. P., & Brown, M. W. (2006). Interleaving brain systems for episodic and recognition memory. *Trends in Cognitive Sciences, 10*, 455–463.

Aggleton, J. P., Neave, N., Nagle, S., & Sahgal, A. (1995). A comparison of the effects of medial prefrontal, cingulate cortex, and cingulum bundle lesions on tests of spatial memory: Evidence of a double dissociation between frontal and cingulum bundle contributions. *Journal of Neuroscience, 15*, 7270–7281.

Aggleton, J. P., & Mishkin, M. (1983). Memory impairments following restricted medial thalamic lesions in monkeys. *Experimental Brain Research, 52*, 199–209.

Aggleton, J. P., & Mishkin, M. (1985). Mammillary-body lesions and visual recognition in monkeys. *Experimental Brain Research, 58*, 190–197.

Aggleton, J. P., & Sahgal, A. (1993), The contribution of the anterior thalamic nuclei to anterograde amnesia. *Neuropsychologia, 31*, 1001–1019.

Aggleton, J. P., Desimone, R., & Mishkin, M. (1986). The origin, course, and termination of the hippocampothalamic projections in the macaque. *Journal of Comparative Neurology, 243*, 409–421.

Aggleton, J. P., McMackin, D., Carpenter, K., Hornak, J., Kapur, N., Halpin, S., et al. (2000). Differential cognitive effects of colloid cysts in the third ventricle that spare or compromise the fornix. *Brain, 12*, 800–815.

Aggleton, J. P., Vann, S. D., Denby, C., Dix, S., Mayes, A. R., Roberts, N., & Yonelinas, A. P. (2005). Sparing of the familiarity component of recognition memory in a patient with hippocampal pathology. *Neuropsychologia, 43*, 1810–1823.

Albert, M. S., Butters, N., & Brandt, J. (1980). Memory for remote events in alcoholics. *Journal of Studies in Alcohol, 41*, 1071–1081.

Albert, M. S., Butters, N., & Brandt, J. (1981). Patterns of remote memory in amnesic and demented patients. *Archives of Neurology, 38*, 495–500.

Albert, M. S., Butters, N., & Levin, J. (1980). Memory for remote events in chronic alcoholics and alcoholic Korsakoff patients. *Advances in Experimental Medicine and Biology, 126*, 719–730.

Albert, M. S., Butters N., & Levin J. (1979). Temporal gradients in the retrograde amnesia of patients with alcoholic Korsakoff's disease. *Archives of Neurology, 36*, 211–216.

Albouy, G., Sterpenich, V., Balteau, E., Vandewalle, G., Desseilles, M., Dang-Vu, T., et al. (2008). Both the hippocampus and striatum are involved in consolidation of motor sequence memory. *Neuron, 58*(2), 261–272.

Alexander, M. P., & Freedman, M. (1983). Amnesia after anterior communicating artery rupture. *Neurology, 33*(Suppl. 2), 104.

Allan, K., Wilding, E. L., & Rugg, M. D. (1998). Electrophysiological evidence for dissociable processes contribution to recollection. *Acta Psychologica, 98*, 231–252.

Alvarez, P., & Squire, L. R. (1994). Memory consolidation and the medial temporal-lobe - A simple network model. *Proceedings of the National Academy of Sciences of the United States of America, 91*, 7041–7045.

Amaral, D. G., & Cowan, W. M. (1980). Subcortical afferents to the hippocampal formation in the monkey. *Journal of Comparative Neurology, 189*, 573–591.

Amaral, D. G., & Insausti, R. (1990). Hippocampal formation. In G. Paxinos (Ed.), *The human nervous system* (pp. 711–755). San Diego: Academic Press.

Amaral, D. G., Insausti, R., & Cowan, W. M. (1983). Evidence for a direct projection from the superior temporal gyrus to the entorhinal cortex in the monkey. *Brain Research, 275*, 263–277.

Aminoff, E., Gronau, N., & Bar, M. (2007). The parahippocampal cortex mediates spatial and nonspatial associations. *Cereb Cortex, 17*(7), 1493–1503.

Anderson, J. R. (1976). *Language, memory, and thought.* Hillsdale, NJ: Lawrence Erlbaum.

Andersen, R. (1978). Cognitive changes after amygdalotomy. *Neuropsychologia, 16*, 439–451.

Anderson, J. R., & Ross, B. H. (1980). Evidence against a semantic-episodic distinction. *Journal of Experimental Psychology: Human Learning and Memory, 6*, 441–465.

Anderson, S. W., Damasio, H., Jones, R. D., & Tranel, D. (1991). Wisconsin card sorting test performance as a measure of frontal lobe damage. *Journal of Clinical and Experimental Neuropsychology, 13*, 909–922.

Angeli, S. J., Murray, E. A., & Mishkin, M. (1993). Hippocampectomized monkeys can remember one place but not two. *Neuropsychologia, 31*, 1021–1030.

Arendt, T., Bigl., V., & Arendt, A. (1983). Loss of neurons in the nucleus basalis of Meynert in Alzheimer's disease, paralysis agitans and Korsakoff's disease. *Acta Neuropathologica, 61*, 101–108.

Arita, K., Uozumi, T., Ogasawara, H., Sugiyama, K., Ohba, S., Pant, B., et al. (1995). A case of pineal germinoma presenting with severe amnesia. *No Shinkei Geka, 23*, 271–275.

Ashby, F. G., Alfonso Reese, L. A., Turken, A. U., & Waldron, E. M. (1998). A neuropsychological theory of multiple systems in category learning. *Psychological Review, 105*(3), 442–481.

Ay, H., Furie, K. L., Yamada, K., & Koroshetz, W. J. (1998). Diffusion-weighted MRI characterizes the ischemic lesion in transient global amnesia. *Neurology, 51*, 901–903.

Bachevalier, J., & Mishkin, M. (1986). Visual recognition impairment follows ventromedial but not dorsolateral prefrontal lesions in monkeys. *Behavioral Brain Research, 20*, 249–261.

Bachevalier, J., Parkinson, J. K., & Mishkin, M. (1985). Visual recognition in monkeys: Effects of separate vs. combined transection of fornix and amygdalofugal pathways. *Experimental Brain Research, 57*, 554–561.

Bachevalier, J., Saunders, R. C., & Mishkin, M. (1985). Visual recognition in monkeys: Effects of

transection of the fornix. *Experimental Brain Research, 57*, 547–553.

Baddeley, A. (1998). Recent developments in working memory. *Current Opinion in Neurobiology, 8*(2), 234–238.

Baddeley, A. D. (1982). Implications of neuropsychological evidence for theories of normal memory. *Philosophical Transactions of the Royal Society of London B: Biological Sciences, 298*(1089), 59–72.

Baddeley, A., & Wilson, B. A. (1994). When implicit learning fails: Amnesia and the problem of error elimination. *Neuropsychologia, 32*(1), 53–68.

Baeckman, L., & Dixon, R. A. (1992). Psychological compensation: A theoretical framework. *Psychological Bulletin, 112*(2), 259–283.

Bailey, C. H., Giustetto, M., Huang, Y. -Y., Hawkins, R. D., & Kandel, E. R. (2000). Is heterosynaptic modulation essential for stabilizing Hebbian plasticity and memory? *Nature Reviews: Neuroscience, 1*, 11–20.

Bandettini, P. A. (2009). What's new in neuroimaging methods? *Annals of the New York Academy of Sciences, 1156*(1), 260–293.

Barr, W. B., Goldberg, E., Wasserstein, J., & Novelly, R. A. (1990). Retrograde amnesia following unilateral temporal lobectomy. *Neuropsychologia, 28*(3), 243–255.

Barr, W. B., Chelune, G. J., Hermann, B. P., et al. (1997). The use of figural reproduction tests as measures of nonverbal memory in epilepsy surgery candidates. *Journal of the International Neuropsychological Society, 3*, 435–443.

Bartus, R. T., Dean, R. L., Beer, B., Ponecorvo, M. J., & Flicker, C. (1985). The cholinergic hypothesis: An historical overview, current perspective, and future directions. *Annals of the New York Academy of Sciences, 444*, 332–358.

Beaunieux, H., Desgranges, B., Lalevee, C., de la Sayette, V., Lechevalier, B., & Eustache, F. (1998). Preservation of cognitive procedural memory in a case of Korsakoff's syndrome: Methodological and theoretical insights. *Perceptual and Motor Skills, 86*(3 Pt 2), 1267–1287.

Becker, J. T., Furman, J. M. R., Panisset, M., & Smith, C. (1990). Characteristics of the memory loss of a patient with Wernicke-Korsakoff's syndrome without alcoholism. *Neuropsychologia, 28*, 171–179.

Bellgowan, P. S. F., Buffalo, E. A., Bodurka, J., & Martin, A. (2009). Lateralized spatial and object memory encoding in entorhinal and perirhinal cortices. *Learning & Memory, 16*(7), 433–433.

Benke, T., Köylü, B., Delazer, M., Trinka, E., & Kemmler, G. (2005). Cholinergic treatment of amnesia following basal forebrain lesion due to aneurysm rupture–an open label pilot study. *European Journal of Neurology, 12,* 791–796.

Benson, D. F., & Geschwind, N. (1967). Shrinking retrograde amnesia. *Journal of Neurology, Neurosurgery, and Psychiatry, 30,* 539–544.

Benson, D. F., Marsden, C. D., & Meadows, J. C. (1974). The amnesic syndrome of posterior cerebral artery occlusion. *Acta Neurologica Scandinavica, 50,* 133–145.

Bentin, S., & Moscovitch, M. (1988). The time course of repetition effects for words and unfamiliar faces. *Journal of Experimental Psychology: General, 117,* 148–160.

Bien, C. G., Schulze-Bonhage, A., Deckert, M., Urbach, H., Helmstaedter, C., Grunwalt, T., et al. (2000). Limbic encephalitis not associated with neoplasm as a cause of temporal lobe epilepsy. *Neurology, 55,* 1823–1828.

Birks, J., Flicker, L. (2006). Donepezil for mild cognitive impairment. *Cochrane Database Systematic Reviews, 3,* CD006104.

Blaney, P. H. (1986). Affect and memory: A review. *Psychological Bulletin, 99,* 229–246.

Blaxton, T. A. (1985). Investigating dissociations among memory measures: Support for a transfer-appropriate processing framework. *Journal of Experimental Psychology: Learning, Memory, and Cognition, 15,* 657–668.

Blaxton, T. A. (1992). Dissociations among memory measures in memory-impaired subjects: Evidence for a processing account of memory. *Memory & Cognition, 20*(5), 549–562.

Blaxton, T. A. (1995). A process-based view of memory. *Journal of the International Neuropsychological Society, 1*(1), 112–114.

Blaxton, T. A., Bookheimer, S. Y., Zeffiro, T. A., Figlozzi, C. M., Gaillard, W. D., & Theodore, W. H. (1996). Functional mapping of human memory using PET: Comparisons of perceptual and conceptual tasks. *Canadian Journal of Experimental Psychology, 50,* 42–56.

Bliss, T. V. P., & Gardner-Medwin, A. R. (1973). Long-lasting potentiation of synaptic transmission in the dentate area of the unanesthetized rabbit following stimulation of the perforant path. *Journal of Physiology, 232,* 357–374.

Bliss, T. V. P., & Lomo, T. (1973). Long-lasting potentiation of synaptic transmission in the dentate area of the anesthetized rabbit following stimulation of the perforant path. *Journal of Physiology, 232,* 331–356.

Bogousslavsky, J., Regli, F., & Assal, G. (1986). The syndrome of tuberothalamic artery territory infarction. *Stroke, 17,* 434–441.

Bowers, D., Verfaellie, M., Valenstein, E., & Heilman, K. M. (1988). Impaired acquisition of temporal order information in amnesia. *Brain and Cognition, 8,* 47–66.

Bozeat, S., Lambon Ralph, M. A., Patterson, K., Garrard, P., & Hodges, J. R. (2000). Non-verbal semantic impairment in semantic dementia. *Neuropsychologia, 38,* 1207–1215.

Brandt, J. (1991). The Hopkins verbal learning test: Development of a new verbal memory test with six equivalent forms. *The Clinical Neuropsychologist, 5,* 125–142.

Braskie, M. N., Small, G. W., & Bookheimer, S. Y. (2009). Entorhinal cortex structure and functional MRI response during an associative verbal memory task. *Human Brain Mapping, 30,* 3981–3992.

Brewer, J. B., Zhao, Z., Desmond, J. E., Glover, G. H., & Gabrieli, J. D. (1998). Making memories: Brain activity that predicts how well visual experience will be remembered. *Science, 281*(5380), 1185–1187.

Brooks D. N., & Baddeley A. (1976). What can amnesics learn? *Neuropsychologia, 14,* 111–122.

Buckner, R. L. (1996). Beyond HERA: Contributions of specific prefrontal brain areas to long-term memory retrieval. *Psychonomic Bulletin & Review, 3*(2), 149–158.

Buckner, R. L., Goodman, J., Burock, M., Rott, M., Koustaal, W., Schacter, D., et al. (1998). Functional-anatomic correlates of object priming in humans revealed by rapid presentation event-related fMRI. *Neuron, 20,* 285–296.

Buckner, R. L., Kelley, W. M., & Petersen, S. E. (1999). Frontal cortex contributes to human memory formation. *Nature Neuroscience, 2*(4), 311–314.

Buckner, R. L., Koutstaal, W., Schacter, D. L., Dale, A. M., Rotte, M., & Rosen, B. R. (1998). Functional-anatomic study of episodic retrieval. II. Selective averaging of event-related fMRI trials to test the retrieval success hypothesis. *Neuroimage, 7*(3), 163–175.

Buckner, R. L., Koutstaal, W., Schacter, D. L., Wagner, A. D., & Rosen, B. R. (1998). Functional-anatomic study of episodic retrieval using fMRI. I. Retrieval effort versus retrieval success. *Neuroimage, 7*(3), 151–162.

Buckner, R. L., Petersen, S. E., Ojemann, G., Miezin, F. M., Squire, L. R., & Raichle, M. E. (1995). Functional anatomical studies of explicit and implicit memory retrieval tasks. *Journal of Neuroscience, 15,* 12–29.

Buckner, R. L., Raichle, M. E., Miezin, F. M., & Petersen, S. E. (1996). Functional anatomic studies of memory retrieval for auditory words and visual pictures. *Journal of Neuroscience,* *16*(19), 6219–6235.

Burgess, N. (2008). Spatial cognition and the brain. *Annals of the New York Academy of Sciences,* *1124,* 77–97.

Burke, J. M., Danick, J. A., Bemis, B., & Durgin, C. J. (1994). A process approach to memory book training for neurological patients. *Brain Injury,* *8*(1), 71–81.

Burwell, R. D. (2000). The parahippocampal region: Corticocortical connectivity. *Annals of the New York Academy of Sciences, 911,* 25–42.

Bussey, T. J., & Saksida, L. M. (2005). Object memory and perception in the medial temporal lobe: An alternative approach. *Current Opinion in Neurobiology, 15,* 730–737.

Bussey, T. J., & Saksida, L. M. (2007). Memory, perception, and the ventral visual-perirhinal-hippocampal stream: Thinking outside of the boxes. *Hippocampus, 17*(9), 898–898.

Butter, C. M., & Snyder, D. R. (1972). Alterations in aversive and aggressive behaviors following orbital frontal lesions in rhesus monkeys. *Acta Neurobiologiae Experimentalis, 32,* 525–565.

Butters, M. A., Soety, E., & Becker, J. T. (1997). Memory rehabilitation. In P. D. Nussbaum (Ed.), *Handbook of neuropsychology and aging* (pp. 515–527). New York: Plenum Press.

Butters, M. A., Glisky, E. L., & Schacter, D. L. (1993). Transfer of new learning in amnesic patients. *Journal of Clinical & Experimental Neuropsychology, 15,* 219–230.

Butters, N. (1985). Alcoholic Korsakoff syndrome: Some unresolved issues concerning etiology, neuropathology, and cognitive deficits. *Journal of Clinical and Experimental Neuropsychology,* *7,* 181–210.

Butters, N. (1984). Alcoholic Korsakoff's syndrome: An update. *Seminars in Neurology, 4,* 226–244.

Butters, N., & Cermak, L. S. (1986). A case study of the forgetting of autobiographical knowledge: Implications for the study of retrograde amnesia. In D. Rubin (Ed.), *Autobiographical memory* (pp. 253–272). New York: Cambridge University Press.

Butters N., Cermak, L.S. (1980). *Alcoholic Korsakoff's syndrome: An information processing approach to amnesia.* New York: Academic Press.

Butters, N., Granholm, E., Salmon, E., Grant, I., & Wolfe, J. (1987). Episodic and semantic memory: A comparison of amnesic and demented patients. *Journal of Experimental and Clinical Neuropsychology, 9,* 479–497.

Butters, N., & Miliotis, P. (1985). Amnesic disorders. In K. M. Heilman, & E. Valenstein (Eds.), *Clinical neuropsychology* (2nd ed., pp. 403–451). New York: Oxford University Press.

Butters, N., Miliotis, P., Albert, M. S., & Sax, D. S. (1984). Memory assessment: Evidence of the heterogeneity of amnesic symptoms. In G. Goldstein (Ed.), *Advances in clinical neuropsychology,* Vol. 1 (pp. 127–159). New York: Plenum Press.

Butters, N., & Stuss, D. T. (1989). Diencephalic amnesia. In F. Boller, & J. Grafman (Eds.), *Handbook of Neuropsychology* Vol. 3 (L. Squire, Section Ed.) (pp. 107–148). Amsterdam: Elsevier.

Cabeza, R. (2002). Hemispheric asymmetry reduction in older adults: The HAROLD model. *Psychology and Aging, 17*(1), 85–100.

Cabeza, R., & Nyberg, L. (2003). Special issue on functional neuroimaging of memory. *Neuropsychologia, 41*(3), 241–244.

Cabeza, R., Grady, C. L., Nyberg, L., McIntosh, A. R., Tulving, E., Kapur, S., et al. (1997). Age-related differences in neural activity during memory encoding and retrieval: A positron emission tomography study. *Journal of Neuroscience, 17*(1), 391–400.

Cabeza, R., & St. Jacques, P. (2007). Functional neuroimaging of autobiographical memory. *Trends in Cognitive Sciences, 11*(5), 219–227.

Cahill, L., Haier, R. J., Fallon, J., Alkire, M., Tang, C., et al. (1996). Amygdala activity at encoding correlated with long-term, free recall of emotional information. *Proceedings of the National Academy of Science USA, 93,* 8016–8021.

Cairns, H., & Mosberg, W. H. (1951). Colloid cyst of the third ventricle. *Surgery, Gynecology and Obstetrics, 92,* 545–570.

Calabrese, P., Markowitsch, H. J., Harders, A. G., Scholz, M., & Gehlen, W. (1995). Fornix damage and memory. A case report. *Cortex, 31,* 555–564.

Canli, T., Zhao, Z., Brewer, J., Gabrieli, J. D., & Cahill, L. (2000). Event-related activation in the human amygdala associates with later memory for individual emotional experience. *Journal of Neuroscience, 20,* RC99, 1–5.

Caplan, L. B. (1985). Transient global amnesia. In J. A. M. Frederiks (Ed.), *Handbook of clinical neurology* Vol. 1 (pp. 205–218). Amsterdam: Elsevier.

Caplan, L., Chedru, F., Lhermitte, F., & Mayman, C. (1981). Transient global amnesia and migraine. *Neurology, 31,* 1167–1170.

Carlesimo, G. A. (1994). Perceptual and conceptual priming in amnesic and alcoholic patients. *Neuropsychologia, 32,* 903–921.

Carlesimo, G. A., Sabbadini, M., Loasses, A., & Caltagirone, C. (1998). Analysis of the memory impairment in a post-encephalitic patient with focal retrograde amnesia. *Cortex, 34*(3), 449–460.

Carr, A. C. (1982). Memory deficit after fornix section. *Neuropsychologia, 20,* 95–98.

Cermak, L. S. (1997). A positive approach to viewing processing deficit theories of amnesia. *Memory, 5*(1–2), 89–98.

Cermak, L. S. (1984). The episodic-semantic distinction in amnesia. In L. Squire, & N. Butters (Eds.), *Neuropsychology of memory* (pp. 55–62). New York: Guilford Press.

Cermak, L. S. (1976). The encoding capacity of patients with amnesia due to encephalitis. *Neuropsychologia, 14,* 311–326.

Cermak, L. S., & Butters, N. (1972). The role of interference and encoding in the short-term memory deficits of Korsakoff patients. *Neuropsychologia, 10,* 89–96.

Cermak, L. S., Butters, N., & Gerrein, J. (1973). The extent of the verbal encoding ability of Korsakoff patients. *Neuropsychologia, 11,* 85–94.

Cermak, L. S., Butters, N., & Moreines, J. (1974). Some analyses of the verbal encoding deficit of alcoholic Korsakoff patients. *Brain and Language, 1,* 141–150.

Cermak, L. S., Hill, R., & Wong, B. (1998). Effects of spacing and repetition on amnesic patients' performance during perceptual identification, stem completion, and category exemplar production. *Neuropsychology, 12*(1), 65–77.

Cermak, L. S., Lewis, R., Butters, N., & Goodglass, H. (1973). Role of verbal mediation in performance of motor tasks by Korsakoff patients. *Perceptual and Motor Skills, 37,* 259–262.

Cermak, L. S., Naus. M., & Reale, L. (1976). Rehearsal and organizational strategies of alcoholic Korsakoff patients. *Brain and Language, 3,* 375–385.

Cermak, L. S., & O'Connor, M. (1983). The anterograde and retrograde retrieval ability of a patient with amnesia due to encephalitis. *Neuropsychologia, 21,* 213–234.

Cermak, L. S., Reale, L., & Baker, E. (1978). Alcoholic Korsakoff patients' retrieval from semantic memory. *Brain and Language, 5,* 215–226.

Cermak, L. S., Talbot, N., Chandler, K., & Wolbarst, L. R. (1985). The perceptual priming phenomenon in amnesia. *Neuropsychologia, 23,* 615–622.

Cermak, L. S., Uhly, B., & Reale, L. (1980). Encoding specificity in the alcoholic Korsakoff patient. *Brain and Language, 11,* 119–127.

Cermak, L., Verfaellie, M., & Chase, K. A. (1995). Implicit and explicit memory in amnesia: An analysis of data-driven and conceptually-driven processes. *Neuropsychology, 9,* 281–290.

Cermak, L., Verfaellie, M., & Letourneau, L. (1993). Episodic effects on picture identification for alcoholic Korsakoff patients. *Brain and Cognition, 22,* 85–97.

Cermak, L. S., Verfaellie, M., Milberg, W., Letourneau, L., & Blackford, S. (1991). A further analysis of perceptual identification priming in alcoholic Korsakoff patients. *Neuropsychologia, 29,* 725–736.

Cermak, L. S., Verfaellie, M., Sweeney, M., & Jacoby, L. L. (1992). Fluency versus conscious recollection in the word completion performance of amnesic patients. *Brain and Cognition, 20*(2), 367–377.

Cermak, L. S., & Wong, B. M. (1998). Amnesic patients' impaired category exemplar production priming. *Journal of the International Neuropsychological Society, 4*(6), 576–583.

Choi, D., Sudarsky, L., Schachter, S., Biber, M., & Burke, P. (1983). Medial thalamic hemorrhage with amnesia. *Archives of Neurology, 40,* 611–613.

Chung, C. -P., Hsu, H. -Y., Chao, A. -C., Chang, F. -C., Sheng, W. -Y, & Hu, H. -H. (2006). Detection of intracranial venous reflux in patients of transient global amnesia. *Neurology, 66,* 1873–1877.

Chute, D. L., & Bliss, M. E. (1994). ProsthesisWare: Concepts and caveats for microcomputer-based aids to everyday living. *Experimental Aging Research, 20*(3), 229–238.

Ciaramelli, E., Grady, C. L., & Moscovitch, M. (2008). Top-down and bottom-up attention to memory: A hypothesis (AtoM) on the role of the posterior parietal cortex in memory retrieval. *Neuropsychologia, 46*(7), 1828–1851.

Cipolotti, L., Husain, M., Crinion, J., Bird, C. M., Khan, S. S., Losseff, N., et al. (2008). The role of the thalamus in amnesia: A tractography, high-resolution MRI and neuropsychological study. *Neuropsychologia, 46,* 2745–2758.

Cirillo, R. A., Horel, J. A., & George, P. J. (1989). Lesions of the anterior temporal stem and the performance of delayed match-to-sample and visual discriminations in monkeys. *Behavioural Brain Research, 34,* 55–69.

Clare, L., Wilson, B. A., Carter, G., Breen, K., Gosses, A., & Hodges, J. R. (2000). Intervening with everyday memory problems in dementia of Alzheimer type: An errorless learning approach. *Journal of Clinical and Experimental Neuropsychology, 22*(1), 132–146.

Clark, C. R., & Geffen, G. M. (1989). Corpus callosum surgery and recent memory. A review. *Brain, 112,* 165–175.

Cohen, N. J., Poldrack, R. A., & Eichenbaum, H. (1997). Memory for items and memory for relations in the procedural/declarative memory framework. *Memory, 5*(1–2), 131–178.

Cohen, N. J., Poldrack, R. A., & Eichenbaum, H. (1997). Memory for items and memory for relations in the procedural/declarative memory framework. In A. R. Mayes, & J. J. Downes (Eds.), *Theories of organic amnesia* (pp. 131–178). Hove, UK: Psychology Press/Erlbaum (UK) Taylor & Francis.

Cohen, N. J., & Squire, L. R. (1980). Preserved learning and retention of pattern analyzing skill in amnesia: Dissociation of knowing how and knowing that. *Science, 210,* 207–209.

Cohen, N. J., & Squire, L. R. (1981). Retrograde amnesia and remote memory impairment. *Neuropsychologia, 19,* 337–356.

Collins, A. M., & Loftus, E. F. (1975). A spreading-activation theory of semantic processing. *Psychological Review, 82,* 407–428.

Corkin, S. (1968). Acquisition of motor skill after bilateral MTL excision. *Neuropsychologia, 6,* 225–265.

Corkin, S. (1984). Lasting consequences of bilateral medial temporal lobectomy: Clinical course and experimental findings in H.M. *Seminars in Neurology, 4,* 249–259.

Corkin, S., Cohen, N. J., & Sagar, H. J. (1983). Memory for remote personal and public events after bilateral MTLctomy. *Society for Neuroscience Abstracts, 9,* 28.

Corsellas, J. A., Goldberg, G. J., & Norton, A. R. (1968). "Limbic encephalitis" and its association with carcinoma. *Brain, 91,* 481–496.

Corsi, P. M. (1972). *Human memory and the medial temporal region of the brain.* Unpublished doctoral dissertation, McGill University, Montreal, CAN.

Cosentino, S. A., Jefferson, A. L., Carey, M., Price, C. C., Davis-Garrett, K., Swenson, R., & Libon, D. J (2004). The clinical diagnosis of vascular dementia: A comparison among four classification systems and a proposal for a new paradigm. *Clinical Neuropsychology, 18,* 6–21.

Courtney, S. M., Ungerleider, L. G., Keil, K., & Haxby, J. V. (1997). Transient and sustained activity in a distributed neural system for human working memory. *Nature, 386*(6625), 608–611.

Cowan, N. (1988). Evolving conceptions of memory storage, selective attention, and their mutual constraints within the human information-processing system. *Psychological Bulletin, 104,* 163–191.

Craik, F. I. M., & Lockhart, R. S. (1972). Levels of processing: A framework for memory research. *Journal of Verbal Learning and Verbal Behavior, 11,* 671–684.

Crook, T. H., & Larrabee, G. J. (1991). Diagnosis, assessment and treatment of age-associated memory impairment. *Journal of Neural Transmission. Supplementa, 33,* 1–6.

Crosson, B. (1992). *Subcortical functions in language and memory.* New York: Guilford Press.

Crovitz, H. F., & Schiffman, H. (1974). Frequency of episodic memories as a function of their age. *Bulletin of the Psychonomic Society, 4,* 517–518.

Cummings, J. L., Tomiyasu, U., Read, S., & Benson, D. F. (1984). Amnesia with hippocampal lesions after cardiopulmonary arrest. *Neurology, 42,* 263–271.

Curran, T. (1999). The electrophysiology of incidental and intentional retrieval: ERP old/new effects in lexical decision and recognition memory. *Neuropsychologia, 37,* 771–778.

Dalmau, J., & Bataller, L. (2006). Clinical and immunological diversity of limbic encephalitis: A model for paraneoplastic neurological disorders. *Hematology/Oncology Clinics of North America, 20,* 1319–1335.

Dalmau, J., Gleichman, A. J., Hughes, E. G., Rossi, J. E., Peng, X., Lai, M., et al. (2008). Anti-NMDA-receptor encephalitis: Case series and analysis of the effects of antibodies. *Lancet Neurology, 7,* 1091–1098.

Damasio, A. R. (1989). Time-locked multiregional retroactivation: A systems-level proposal for the neural substrates of recall and recognition. *Cognition, 33,* 25–62.

Damasio, A. R., Damasio, H., Tranel, D., Welsh, K., & Brandt, J. (1987). Additional neural and cognitive evidence in patient DRB. *Society for Neuroscience, 13,* 1452.

Damasio, A. R., Eslinger, P. J., Damasio, H., Van Hoesen, G. W., & Cornell, S. (1985). Multimodal amnesic syndrome following bilateral temporal and basal forebrain damage. *Archives of Neurology, 42,* 252–259.

Damasio, A. R., Graff-Radford, N. R., Eslinger, P. J., Damasio, H., & Kassell, N. (1985). Amnesia following basal forebrain lesions. *Archives of Neurology, 42,* 263–271.

Damasio, A. R., Tranel, D., & Damasio, H. (1989). Amnesia caused by herpes simplex encephalitis, infarctions in basal forebrain, Alzheimer's disease, and anoxia/ischemia. In F. Boller, & J. Grafman (Eds.), *Handbook of neuropsychology* (pp. 149–166). Amsterdam: Elsevier.

Danckert, S. L., Gati, J. S., Menon, R. S., & Kohler, S. (2007). Perirhinal and hippocampal contributions to visual recognition memory can be distinguished from those of occipito-temporal structures based on conscious awareness of prior occurrence. *Hippocampus*, *17*(11), 1081–1092.

Darnell, R. B., & Poser, J. B. (2009). Autoimmune encephalopathy (editorial). *Annals of Neurology*, *66*, 1–2.

das Nair, R., & Lincoln, N. (2007). Cognitive rehabilitation for memory deficits following stroke. *Cochrane Database of Systematic Reviews*, *3*, CD002293. DOI: 10.1002/14651858.CD002293.pub2.

Daselaar, S. M., Fleck, M. S., & Cabeza, R. (2006). Triple dissociation in the medial temporal lobes: Recollection, familiarity, and novelty. *Journal of Neurophysiology*, *96*(4), 1902–1911.

Davachi, L., Mitchell, J. P., & Wagner, A. D. (2003). Multiple routes to memory: Distinct medial temporal lobe processes build item and source memories. *Proceedings of the National Academy of Sciences USA*, *100*(4), 2157–2162.

Davies, R. R., Halliday, G. M., Xuereb, J. H., Kril, J. J., & Hodges, J. R. (2009). The neural basis of semantic memory: Evidence from semantic dementia. *Neurobiology of Aging*, *30*(12), 2043–2052.

Davis, M. H., Di Betta, A. M., Macdonald, M. J. E., & Gaskell, M. G. (2009). Learning and consolidation of novel spoken words. *Journal of Cognitive Neuroscience*, *21*(4), 803–820.

de Haan, M., Mishkin, M., Baldeweg, T., & Vargha-Khadem, F. (2006). Human memory development and its dysfunction after early hippocampal injury. *Trends in Neurosciences*, *29*(7), 374–381.

Delay, J., & Brion, S. (1969). *Le syndrome de Korsakoff*. Paris: Masson & Cie.

DeLuca, J., & Cicerone, K. (1989). Cognitive impairments following anterior communicating artery aneurysm. *Journal of Clinical and Experimental Neuropsychology*, *11*, 47.

DeOlmos, J. S. (1990). Amygdala. In G. Paxinos (Ed.), *The human nervous system* (pp. 583–710). San Diego: Academic Press.

De Renzi, E., Liotti, M., & Nichelli, P. (1987). Semantic amnesia with preservation of autobiographic memory. A case report. *Cortex*, *23*(4), 575–597.

Devinsky, O., Morrell, M. J., & Vogt, B. A. (1995). Contributions of anterior cingulate cortex to behaviour. *Brain*, *118*, 279–306.

Demb, J. B., Desmond, J. E., Wagner, A. D., Vaidya, C. J., Glover, G. H., & Gabrieli, J. D. (1995). Semantic encoding and retrieval in the left inferior prefrontal cortex: A functional MRI study of task difficulty and process specificity. *Journal of Neuroscience*, *15*(9), 5870–5878.

D'Esposito, M., Detre, J. A., Alsop, D. C., Shin, R. K., Atlas, S., & Grossman, M. (1995). The neural basis of the central executive system of working memory. *Nature*, *378*(6554), 279–281.

D'Esposito, M., Verfaellie, M., Alexander, M. P., & Katz, D. I. (1995). Amnesia following traumatic bilateral fornix transection. *Neurology*, *45*, 1546–1550.

Devanand, D. P., Liu, X., Tabert, M. H., Pradhaban, G., Cuasay, K., Bell, K., et al. (2008). Combining early markers strongly predicts conversion from mild cognitive impairment to Alzheimer's disease. *Biological Psychiatry*, *64*, 871–879.

Devlin, J. T., & Price, C. J. (2007). Perirhinal contributions to human visual perception. *Current Biology*, *17*(17), 1484–1488.

Diamond, R., & Rozin, P. (1984). Activation of existing memories in the amnesic syndrome. *Journal of Abnormal Psychology*, *93*, 98–105.

Diana, R. A., Yonelinas, A. P., & Ranganath, C. (2007). Imaging recollection and familiarity in the medial temporal lobe: A three-component model. *Trends in Cognitive Sciences*, *11*(9), 379–386.

Diekelmann, S. and Born, J. (2010). The memory function of sleep. Nature Reviews: Neuroscience, 11:114–126.

Dobkin, B. H., & Hanlon, R. (1993). Dopamine agonist treatment of antegrade amnesia from a mediobasal forebrain injury. *Annals of Neurology*, *33*, 313–316.

Dodson, C. S., & Johnson, M. K. (1996). Some problems with the process-dissociation approach to memory. *Journal of Experimental Psychology: General*, *125*(2), 181–194.

Doeller, C. F., King, J. A., & Burgess, N. (2008). Parallel striatal and hippocampal systems for landmarks and boundaries in spatial memory. *Proceedings of the National Academy of Sciences*, *105*(15), 5915–5920.

Dott, N. M. (1938). Surgical aspects of the hypothalamus. In W. E. le G. Clark, J. Beattie, G. Riddoch, & N. M. Dott (Eds.), *The hypothalamus: Morphological, functional, clinical and surgical aspects* (pp. 131–185). Edinburgh: Oliver and Boyd.

Downes, J. J., Holdstock, J. S., Symons, V., & Mayes, A. R. (1998). Do amnesics forget colours pathologically fast? *Cortex*, *34*(3), 337–355.

Doyon, J., Owen, A. M., Petrides, M., Sziklas, V., & Evans, A. C. (1996). Functional anatomy of visuomotor skill learning in human subjects examined with positron emission tomography. *European Journal of Neuroscience, 8*, 637–648.

Drachman, D. A., & Arbit, J. (1966). Memory and the hippocampal complex. *Archives of Neurology, 15*, 52–61.

Drachman, D. A., & Leavitt, J. (1974). Human memory and the cholinergic system. A relationship to aging? *Archives of Neurology, 30*, 113–121.

Duchek, J. M., & Neeley, J. H. (1989). A dissociative word-frequency x levels of processing interaction in episodic recognition and lexical decision tasks. *Memory and Cognition, 17*, 148–162.

Dusoir, H., Kapur, N., Byrnes, D. P., McKinstry, S., & Hoare, R. D. (1990). The role of diencephalic pathology in human memory disorder. Evidence from a penetrating paranasal brain injury. *Brain, 113*, 1695–1706.

Eacott, M. J., & Crawley, R. A. (1999). Childhood amnesia: On answering questions about very early life events. *Memory, 7*(3), 279–292.

Eich, E. (1989). Theoretical issues in state dependent memory. In H. L. Roediger, & F. I. M. Craik (Eds.), *Varieties of memory and consciousness: Essays in honour of Endel Tulving* (pp. 331–354). Hillsdale, NJ: Lawrence Erlbaum.

Eich, E., & Metcalfe, J. (1989). Mood dependent memory for internal versus external events. *Journal of Experimental Psychology: Learning, Memory, and Cognition, 15*, 443–455.

Eichenbaum, H., Yonelinas, A. P., & Ranganath, C. (2007). The medial temporal lobe and recognition memory. *Annual Review of Neuroscience, 30*, 123–152.

Elliott, R., & Dolan, R. J. (1998). Neural response during preference and memory judgments for subliminally presented stimuli: A functional neuroimaging study. *Journal of Neuroscience, 18*(12), 4697–4704.

Eslinger, P. J., & Damasio, A. R. (1985). Severe disturbance of higher cognition after bilateral frontal lobe ablation: Patient EVR. *Neurology, 35*, 1731–1741.

Eustache, F., Desgranges, B., & Messerli, P. (1996). [Edouard Claparede and human memory]. *Revue Neurologique (Paris), 152*(10), 602–610.

Evans, F. J., & Thorn, W. A. F. (1966). Two types of posthypnotic amnesia: Recall amnesia and source amnesia. *International Journal of Clinical and Experimental Hypnosis, 14*, 162–179.

Evans, J. J., Emslie, H., & Wilson, B. A. (1998). External cueing systems in the rehabilitation of executive impairments of action. *Journal of the International Neuropsychological Society, 4*(4), 399–408.

Evans, J. J., Winson, B. A., Schuri, U., Andrade, J., Baddeley, A., Bruna, O., et al. (2000). A comparison of "errorless" and "trial-and-error" learning methods for teaching individuals with acquired memory deficits. *Neuropsychological Rehabilitation, 10*(1), 67–101.

Feczko, E., Augustinack, J. C., Fischl, B., & Dickerson, B. C. (2009). An MRI-based method for measuring volume, thickness and surface area of entorhinal, perirhinal, and posterior parahippocampal cortex. *Neurobiology Aging, 30*(3), 420–431.

Fernandez, G., Weyerts, H., Schrader Bolsche, M., Tendolkar, I., Smid, H. G., Tempelmann, C., et al. (1998). Successful verbal encoding into episodic memory engages the posterior hippocampus: A parametrically analyzed functional magnetic resonance imaging study. *Journal of Neuroscience, 18*(5), 1841–1847.

Ferraro, I. R., Balota, D. A., & Connor, T. (1993). Implicit memory and the formation of new associations in nondemented Parkinson's disease individuals and individuals with senile dementia of the Alzheimer type: A serial reaction time (SRT) investigation. *Brain and Cognition, 21*, 163–180.

Ferreira, V. S., Bock, K., Wilson, M. P., & Cohen, N. J. (2008). Memory for syntax despite amnesia. *Psychological Science, 19*, 940–946.

Feustel, T. C., Shiffrin, R. M., & Salasoo, A. (1983). Episodic and lexical contributions to the repetition effect in word identification. *Journal of Experimental Psychology: General, 112*, 309–346.

Fibiger, H. C. (1991). Cholinergic mechanisms in learning, memory and dementia: A review of recent evidence. *Trends in Neurosciences, 14*, 220–223.

Fischer, R. S., Alexander, M. P., D'Esposito, M., & Otto, R. (1995). Neuropsychological and neuroanatomical correlates of confabulation. *Journal of Clinical and Experimental Neuropsychology, 17*(1), 20–28.

Fisher, C. M. (1982). Transient global amnesia: Precipitating activities and other observations. *Archives of Neurology, 39*, 605–608.

Fisher, C. M., & Adams, R. D. (1958). Transient global amnesia. *Transactions of the American Neurological Association, 83*, 143–145.

Flavell, J. H., & Wellman, H. M. (1977). Metamemory. In R. V. Kail, & J. W. Hagen (Eds.), *Perspectives on the development of memory and cognition* (pp. 3–33). Hillsdale, NJ: Lawrence Erlbaum.

Fleischman, D. A., Vaidya, C. J., Lange, K. L., & Gabrieli, J. D. (1997). A dissociation between perceptual explicit and implicit memory processes. *Brain Cognition, 35*(1), 42–57.

Fletcher, P. C., Frith, C. D., Grasby, P. M., Shallice, T., Frackowiak, R. S., & Dolan, R. J. (1995). Brain systems for encoding and retrieval of auditory-verbal memory. An in vivo study in humans. *Brain, 118*(Pt. 2), 401–416.

Florance, N. R., Davis, R. L., Lam, C., Szperka, C., Zhou, L., Ahmad, S., et al. (2009). Anti-N-methyl-D-aspartate receptor (NMDAR) encephalitis in children and adolescents. *Annals of Neurology, 66,* 11–18.

Foerster, O., & Gagel, O. (1933). Ein fall von ependymcyste des iii ventrikels. Ein beitrag zur frage der beziehungen psychischer störungen zum hirnstamm. *Zeitschrift fur der Gesamte Neurologie und Psychiatrie, 149,* 312–344.

Freed, D. M., Corkin, S., & Cohen, N. J. (1987). Forgetting in H. M.: A second look. *Neuropsychologia, 25,* 461–471.

Fujii, T., Yamadori, A., Endo, K., Suzuki, K., & Fukatsu, R. (1999). Disproportionate retrograde amnesia in a patient with herpes simplex encephalitis. *Cortex, 35*(5), 599–614.

Funahashi, S., Bruce, C. J., & Goldman-Rakic, P. S. (1989). Mnemonic coding of visual space in the monkey's dorsolateral prefrontal cortex. *Journal of Neurophysiology, 61,* 1–19.

Fuster, J. M. (1984). The cortical substrate of memory. In L.R. Squires, & N. Butters (Eds.), *Neuropsychology of memory* (pp. 279–286). New York: Guilford Press.

Fuster, J. M. (1997). Network memory. *Trends in Neurosciences, 20,* 451–459.

Fyhn, M., Hafting, T., Witter, M. P., Moser, E. I., & Moser, M. B. (2008). Grid cells in mice. *Hippocampus, 18*(12), 1230–1238.

Fyhn, M., Molden, S., Witter, M. P., Moser, E. I., & Moser, M. B. (2004). Spatial representation in the entorhinal cortex. *Science, 305*(5688), 1258–1264.

Gabrieli, J. D. (1998). Cognitive neuroscience of human memory. *Annual Review of Psychology, 49,* 87–115.

Gabrieli, J. D., Cohen, N. J., & Corkin, S. (1988). The impaired learning of semantic knowledge following bilateral medial temporal-lobe resection. *Brain Cognition, 7*(2), 157–177.

Gabrieli, J. D., Corkin, S., Mickel, S. F., & Growdon, J. H. (1993). Intact acquisition and long-term retention of mirror-tracing skill in Alzheimer's disease and in global amnesia. *Behavioral Neuroscience, 107*(6), 899–910.

Gabrieli, J. D., McGlinchey-Berroth, R., Carrillo, M. C., Gluck, M. A., Cermak, L. S., & Disterhoft, J. F. (1995). Intact delay-eyeblink classical conditioning in amnesia. *Behavioral Neuroscience, 109*(5), 819–827.

Gabrieli, J. D., Milberg, W., Keane, M. M., & Corkin, S. (1990). Intact priming of patterns despite impaired memory. *Neuropsychologia, 28*(5), 417–427.

Gabrieli, J. D., Poldrack, R. A., & Desmond, J. E. (1998). The role of left prefrontal cortex in language and memory. *Proceedings of the National Academy of Sciences USA, 95*(3), 906–913.

Gabrieli, J. D. E., Brewer, J. B., Desmond, J. E., & Glover, G. H. (1997). Separate neural bases of two fundamental memory processes in the human MTL. *Science, 276*(5310), 264–266.

Gabrieli, J. D. E., Fleischman, D. A., Keane, M. M., Reminger, S. L., & Morrell, F. (1995). Double dissociation between memory systems underlying explicit and implicit memory in the human brain. *Psychological Science, 6,* 76–82.

Gabrieli, J. D. E., Keane, M. M., Stanger, B. Z., Kjelgaard, M. M., Corkin, S., & Growdon, J. H. (1994). Dissociations among structural-perceptual, lexical-semantic, and event-fact memory systems in amnesic, Alzheimer's and normal subjects. *Cortex, 30,* 75–103.

Gabrieli, J. D. E., Stebbins, G. T., Singh, J., Willingham, D. B., & Goetz, C. G. (1997). Intact mirror tracing and impaired rotary-pursuit skill learning in patients with Huntington's disease: Evidence for dissociable memory systems in skill learning. *Neuropsychology, 11,* 272–281.

Gade, A. (1982). Amnesia after operations on aneurysms of the anterior communicating artery. *Surgical Neurology, 18,* 46–49.

Gade, A., & Mortensen, E. L. (1990). Temporal gradient in the remote memory impairment of amnesic patients with lesions in the basal forebrain. *Neuropsychologia, 28*(9), 985–1001.

Gaffan, D. (1974). Recognition impaired and association intact in the memory of monkeys after transection of the fornix. *Journal of Comparative and Physiological Psychology, 86,* 1100–1109.

Gaffan, D. (1993). Additive effects of forgetting and fornix transection in the temporal gradient of retrograde amnesia. *Neuropsychologia, 31,* 1055–1066.

Gaffan, D., & Gaffan, E. A. (1991). Amnesia in man following transection of the fornix: A review. *Brain, 114,* 2611–2618.

Gaffan, D., & Harrison, S. (1987). Amygdalectomy and disconnection in visual learning for auditory secondary reinforcement by monkeys. *Journal of Neuroscience, 7,* 2285–2292.

Gaffan, D., & Parker, A. (1996). Interaction of perirhinal cortex with the fornix-fimbria: Memory for objects and "object-in-place" memory. *Journal of Neuroscience, 16,* 5864–5869.

Gaffan, E. A., Gaffan, D., & Hodges, J. R. (1991). Amnesia following damage to the left fornix and to other sites: A comparative study. *Brain, 114,* 1297–1313.

Garcia Bencochea, F., De La Torre, O., Esquivel, O., Vieta, R., & Fernandec, C. (1954). The section of the fornix in the surgical treatment of certain epilepsies: A preliminary report. *Transactions of the American Neurological Association, 79,* 176–178.

Gardiner, J. M., & Richardson-Klavehn, A. (2000). Remembering and knowing. In E. Tulving, & F. I. M. Craik (Eds.), *The Oxford handbook of memory* (pp. 229–244). New York: Oxford University Press.

Gentilini, M., DeRenzi, E., & Crisi, G. (1987). Bilateral paramedian thalamic artery infarcts: Report of eight cases. *Journal of Neurology, Neurosurgery, and Psychiatry, 50,* 900–909.

George, P. J., Horel, J. A., & Cirillo, R. A. (1989). Reversible cold lesions of the parahippocampal gyrus in monkeys result in deficits on the delayed match-to-sample and other visual tasks. *Behavioural Brain Research, 34,*163–178.

Ghika-Schmid, F., & Bogousslavsky, J. (2000). The acute behavioral syndrome of anterior thalamic infarction: A prospective study of 12 cases. *Annals of Neurology, 48,* 220–227.

Gilboa, A. (2004). Autobiographical and episodic memory—one and the same? Evidence from prefrontal activation in neuroimaging studies. *Neuropsychologia, 42*(10), 1336–1349.

Glees, P., & Griffith, H. B. (1952). Bilateral destruction of the hippocampus (cornu ammonis) in a case of dementia. *Psychiatrie, Neurologie, und medizinische Psychologie, 123,* 193–204.

Glisky, E. L. (1992). Acquisition and transfer of declarative and procedural knowledge by memory-impaired patients: A computer data-entry task. *Neuropsychologia, 30*(10), 899–910.

Glisky, E. L., & Schacter, D. L. (1988). Long-term retention of computer learning by patients with memory disorders. *Neuropsychologia, 26*(1), 173–178.

Glisky, E. L., Schacter, D. L., & Tulving, E. (1986a). Computer learning by memory-impaired patients: Acquisition and retention of complex knowledge. *Neuropsychologia, 24*(3), 313–328.

Glisky, E. L., Schacter, D. L., & Tulving, E. (1986b). Learning and retention of computer-related vocabulary in memory-impaired patients: Method of vanishing cues. *Journal of Clinical and Experimental Neuropsychology,* 8(3), 292–312.

Gloor, P. (1986). Role of the human limbic system in perception, memory, and affect: Lessons from temporal lobe epilepsy. In B. K. Doane, & K. E. Livingston (Eds.), *The limbic system: Functional organization and clinical disorders* (pp. 159–169). New York: Raven Press.

Gold, J. J., & Squire, L. R. (2006). The anatomy of amnesia: Neurohistological analysis of three new cases. *Learning and Memory, 13,* 699–710.

Goldenberg, G., Wimmer, A., & Maly, J. (1983). Amnesic syndrome with a unilateral thalamic lesion: A case report. *Journal of Neurology, 229,* 79–86.

Goldman-Rakic, P. S. (1984). Modular organization of the prefrontal cortex. *Trends in Neuroscience, 7,* 419–424.

Goldman-Rakic, P. S. (1992). Prefrontal cortical dysfunction in schizophrenia: The relevance of working memory. In B. Carroll (Ed.), *Psychopathology and the brain.* New York: Raven Press.

Gooding, P. A., Mayes, A. R., & van Eijk, R. (2000). A meta-analysis of indirect memory tests for novel material in organic amnesics. *Neuropsychologia, 38*(5), 666–676.

Gooding, P. A., van Eijk, R., Mayes, A. R., & Meudell, P. (1993). Preserved pattern completion priming for novel, abstract geometric shapes in amnesics of several aetiologies. *Neuropsychologia, 31*(8), 789–810.

Goodwin, D. W., Powell, B., Bremer, D., Hoine, H., & Stern, J. (1969). Alcohol and recall: State dependent effects in man. *Science, 163,* 1358–1360.

Goshen-Gottstein, Y., Moscovitch, M., & Melo, B. (2000). Intact implicit memory for newly formed verbal associations in amnesic patients following single study trials. *Neuropsychology, 14*(4), 570–578.

Graf, P., Mandler, G., & Haden, P. E. (1982). Simulating amnesic symptoms in normal subjects. *Science, 218*(4578), 1243–1244.

Graf, P., & Schacter, D. L. (1985). Implicit and explicit memory for new associations in normal and amnesic subjects. *Journal of Experimental Psychology Learning Memory and Cognition, 11,* 501–518.

Graf, P., Shimamura, A. P., & Squire, L. R. (1985). Priming across modalities and priming across category levels: Extending the domain of preserved function in amnesia. *Journal of Experimental Psychology: Learning Memory and Cognition, 11*(2), 386–396.

Graff-Radford, N. R., Damasio, H., Yamada, T., Eslinger, P. J., & Damasio, A. R. (1985). Nonhaemmorhagic thalamic infarction: Clinical, neuropsychological, and electrophysiological findings in four anatomical groups defined by computerized tomography. *Brain, 108*, 458–516.

Graff-Radford, N. R., Eslinger, P. J., Damasio, A. R., & Yamada, T. (1984). Nonhemmorhagic infarction of the thalamus: Behavioral, anatomic, and physiological correlates. *Neurology, 34*, 14–23.

Graff-Radford, N. R., Tranel, D., Van Hoesen, G. W., & Brandt, J. P. (1990). Diencephalic amnesia. *Brain, 113*, 1–25.

Grafman, J., Salazar, A. M., Weingartner, J., Vance, S. C., & Ludlow, C. (1985). Isolated impairment of memory following a penetrating lesion of the fornix cerebri. *Archives of Neurology, 42*, 1162–1168.

Grafton, S. T., Mzaaiotta, J. C., Presty, S., Friston, K. J., Frackowiak, R. S. J., & Phelps, M. E. (1992). Functional anatomy of human procedural learning determined with regional cerebral blood flow and PET. *Journal of Neuroscience, 12*, 2242–2248.

Grossi, D., Trojano, L., Grasso, A., & Orsini, A. (1988). Selective "semantic amnesia" after closed-head injury. A case report. *Cortex, 24*(3), 457–464.

Gruneberg, M. M. (1983). Memory processes unique to humans. In A. Mayes (Ed.), *Memory in animals and man* (pp. 253–281). Cambridge, UK: Van Nostrand Reinhold.

Gruneberg, M. M., & Monks, J. (1974). Feeling of knowing and cued recall. *Acta Psychologica, 41*, 257–265.

Grünthal, E. (1939). Über das corpus mamillare und den Korsakowshcen symptomenkomplex. *Confinia Neurologica, 2*, 64–95.

Grünthal, E. (1947). Über das klinische bild nach umschriebenem beiderseitigem ausfall der ammonshornrinde. *Monatsschrift für Psychiatrie und Neurologie, 113*, 1–6.

Gultekin, S. H., Rosenfeld, M. R., Voltz, R., Eichen, J., Posner, J. B., & Dalmau, J. (2000). Paraneoplastic limbic encephalitis: Neurological symptoms, immunological findings and tumor association in 50 patients. *Brain, 123*, 1481–1494.

Gustafsson, B., & Wigstrom, H. (1988). Physiological mechanisms underlying long-term potentiation. *Trends in Neurosciences, 11*, 156–162.

Haas, D. C., & Ross, G. S. (1986). Transient global amnesia triggered by mild head trauma. *Brain, 109*, 251–257.

Habib, R., Nyberg, L., & Tulving, E. (2003). Hemispheric asymmetries of memory: The HERA model revisited. *Trends in Cognitive Sciences, 7*(6), 241–245.

Hafting, T., Fyhn, M., Bonnevie, T., Moser, M. B., & Moser, E. I. (2008). Hippocampus-independent phase precession in entorhinal grid cells. *Nature, 453*(7199), 1248–1252.

Hamann, S. B., Cahill, L., McGaugh, J. L., & Squire, L. (1997). Intact enhancement for declarative memory for emotional material in amnesia. *Learning and Memory, 4*, 301–309.

Hamann, S. B., Eli, T. D., Hoffman, J. M., & Kilts, C. D. (2002). Ecstasy and agony: Activation of the human amygdala in positive and negative emotions. *Psychological Science, 13*, 135–141.

Hamann, S. B., & Squire, L. R. (1996). Level-of-processing effects in word-completion priming: A neuropsychological study. *Journal of Experimental Psychology: Learning, Memory, and Cognition, 22*(4), 933–947.

Hamann, S. B., & Squire, L. R. (1995). On the acquisition of new declarative knowledge in amnesia. *Behavioral Neuroscience, 109*(6), 1027–1044.

Hamann, S. B., & Squire, L. R. (1997). Intact perceptual memory in the absence of conscious memory. *Behavioral Neuroscience, 111*, 850–854.

Hamby, S. L., Wilkins, J. W., & Barry, N. S. (1993). Organizational quality on the Rey-Osterrieth and Taylor complex figure tests: A new scoring system. *Psychological Assessment, 5*, 27–33.

Hampton, R. R. (2005). Monkey perirhinal cortex is critical for visual memory, but not for visual perception: Reexamination of the behavioural evidence from monkeys. *Quarterly Journal of Experimental Psychology, 58*(3–4), 283–299.

Harding, A., Halliday, G., Caine, D., & Kril, J. (2000). Degeneration of anterior thalamic nuclei differentiates alcoholics with amnesia. *Brain, 123*, 141–154.

Hart, J. T. (1965). Memory and the feeling-of-knowing experience. *Journal of Educational Psychology, 56*, 208–216.

Hashimoto, R., Tanaka, Y., & Nakano, I. (2000). Amnesic confabulatory syndrome after focal basal forebrain damage. *Neurology, 54*(4), 978–980.

Hassler, R., & Riechert, T. (1957). Über einen fall von doppelseitiger fornicotomie bei sogenannter temporaler epilepsie. *Acta Neurocuirurgica, 5*, 330–340.

Hazeltine, E., Grafton, S. T., & Ivry, R. (1997). Attention and stimulus characteristics determine the locus of motor-sequence encoding: A PET study. *Brain, 120,* 123–140.

Heathfield, K. W. G., Croft, P. B., & Swash, M. (1973). The syndrome of transient global amnesia. *Brain, 96,* 729–736.

Heilman, K. M., & Sypert, G. W. (1977). Korsakoff's syndrome resulting from bilateral fornix lesions. *Neurology, 27,* 490–493.

Heimer, L., & Alheid, G. F. (1991). Piecing together the puzzle of basal forebrain anatomy. In T. C. Napier, P. W. Kalivas, & I. Hanin (Eds.), *The basal forebrain,* New York: Plenum Press. [Referenced by Medline as: Advances in Experimental Medicine and Biology, 295, 1–42, 1991.]

Heindel, W. C., Salmon, D. P., Shults, C. W., Walicke, P. A., & Butters, N. (1989). Neuropsychological evidence for multiple implicit memory systems: A comparison of Alzheimer's, Huntington's, and Parkinson's disease patients. *Journal of Neuroscience, 9,* 582–587.

Henson, R. (2005). A mini-review of fMRI studies of human medial temporal lobe activity associated with recognition memory. *Quarterly Journal of Experimental Psychology, 58*(3), 340–360.

Herkenham, M. (1978). The connections of the nucleus reuniens thalami: Evidence for a direct thalmo-hippocampal pathway in the rat. *Journal of Comparative Neurology, 177,* 589–610.

Herzog, A. G., & Van Hoesen, G. W. (1976). Temporal neocortical afferent connections to the amygdala in the rhesus monkey. *Brain Research, 115,* 57–69.

Hirst, W. (1982). The amnesic syndrome: Descriptions of explanations. *Psychological Bulletin, 91,* 435–462.

Hirst, W., & Volpe, B. T. (1982). Temporal order judgements with amnesia. *Brain and Cognition, 1,* 294–306.

Hodges, J. R., Patterson, K., Oxbury, S., & Funnell, E. (1992). Semantic dementia: Progressive fluent aphasia with temporal lobe atrophy. *Brain, 115,* 1783–1806.

Hodges, J. R., & McCarthy, R. A. (1995). Loss of remote memory: A cognitive neuropsychological perspective. *Current Opinion in Neurobiology, 5*(2), 178–183.

Holtz, K. H. (1962). Über gehirn- und augenveränderunge bei hyalinosis cutis et mucosae (lipoid proteinose) mit autopsiebefund. *Archiv für Klinische und Experimentelle Dermatologie, 214,* 289–306.

Horel, J. A. (1978). The neuroanatomy of amnesia. A critique of the hippocampal memory hypothesis. *Brain, 101,* 403–445.

Horel, J. A., Voytko, M. L., & Salsbury, K. (1984). Visual learning suppressed by cooling of the temporal lobe. *Behavioral Neuroscience, 98,* 310–324.

Hunkin, N. M., & Parkin, A. J. (1995). The method of vanishing cues: An evaluation of its effectiveness in teaching memory-impaired individuals. *Neuropsychologia, 33*(10), 1255–1279.

Hunkin, N. M., Parkin, A. J., Bradley, V. A., Burrows, E. H., Aldrich, F. K., Jansari, A., & Burdon-Cooper, C. (1995). Focal retrograde amnesia following closed head injury: A case study and theoretical account. *Neuropsychologia, 33*(4), 509–523.

Hunkin, N. M., Squires, E. J., Parkin, A. J., & Tidy, J. A. (1998). Are the benefits of errorless learning dependent on implicit memory? *Neuropsychologia, 36*(1), 25–36.

Huppert, F. A., & Piercy, M. (1979). Normal and abnormal forgetting in organic amnesia: Effect of locus of lesion. *Cortex, 15,* 385–390.

Huppert, F. A., & Piercy, M. (1976). Recognition memory in amnesic patients: Effect of temporal context and familiarity of material. *Cortex, 12,* 3–20.

Hyman, B. T., Van Hoesen, G. W., Kromer, J. J., & Damasio, A. R. (1986). Perforant pathway changes and the memory impairment of Alzheimer's disease. *Annals of Neurology, 20,* 472–481.

Hyman, B. T., Van Hoesen, G. W., Damasio, A. R., & Barnes, C. L. (1984). Cell specific pathology isolates the hippocampal formation in Alzheimer's disease. *Science, 225,* 1168–1170.

Inglis, J. (1970). Shock, surgery, and cerebral asymmetry. *British Journal of Psychiatry, 117,* 143–148.

Insausti, R., Amaral, D. G., & Cowan, W. M. (1987a). The entorhinal cortex of the monkey: II. Cortical afferents. *Journal of Comparative Neurology, 264,* 356–395.

Insuasti, R., Amaral, D. G., & Cowan, W. M. (1987b). The entorhinal cortex of the monkey: III. Subcortical afferents. *Journal of Comparative Neurology, 264,* 396–408.

Insausti, R., Juottonen, K., Soininen, H., Insausti, A. M., Partanen, K., Vainio, P., et al. (1998). MR volumetric analysis of the human entorhinal, perirhinal, and temporopolar cortices. *American Journal of Neuroradiology, 19*(4), 659–671.

Irle, E., & Markowitsch, H. J. (1982). Widespread cortical projections of the hippocampal formation in the cat. *Neuroscience, 7,* 2637–2647.

Irle, E., Wowra, B., & Kunert, H. (1992). Memory disturbances following anterior communicating artery rupture. *Annals of Neurology, 31,* 473–480.

Iwasaki, S., Arihara, T., Torii, H., Hiraguti, M., Kitamoto, F., Nakagawa, A., & et al. (1993). A case of splenial astrocytoma with various neuropsychological symptoms. *No To Shinkei, 45,* 1067–1073.

Iwata, J., LeDoux, J. E., Meeley, M. P., Arneric, S., & Reis, D. J (1986). Intrinsic neurons in amygdaloid field projected to by the medial geniculate body mediate emotional responses conditioned to acoustic stimuli. *Brain Research, 383,* 195–214.

Izquierdo, I. (1991). Role of NMDA receptors in memory. *Trends in Pharmacological Sciences, 12,* 128–129.

Jacoby, L. L. (1991). A process dissociation framework: Separating automatic from intentional uses of memory. *Journal of Memory and Language, 30,* 513–541.

Jacoby, L. L. (1984). Incidental versus intentional retrieval: Remembering and awareness as separate issues. In L. R. Squire, & N. Butters (Eds.), *Neuropsychology of memory* (pp. 145–156). New York: Guilford.

Jacoby, L. L. (1983a). Analyzing interactive processes in reading. *Journal of Verbal Learning and Verbal Behavior, 22,* 485–508.

Jacoby, L. L. (1983b). Perceptual enhancement: Persistent effects of an experience. *Journal of Experimental Psychology: Learning Memory and Cognition, 9,* 21–38.

Jacoby, L. L., & Dallas, M. (1981). On the relationship between autobiographical memory and perceptual learning. *Journal of Experimental Psychology: General, 3,* 306–340.

Jacoby, L. L., Kelly, C. M., & Dywan, J. (1989). Memory attributions. In H. L. Roediger, & F. I. M. Craik (Eds.), *Varieties of memory and consciousness: Essays in honour of Endel Tulving* (pp. 391–422). Hillsdale, NJ: Erlbaum.

Jacoby, L. L., & Kelly, C. (1992). Unconscious influences of memory: Dissociations and automaticity. In A. D. Milner, & M. Rugg (Eds.), *Neuropsychology of consciousness* (pp. 201–233). New York: Academic Press.

Janowsky, J. S., Shimamura, A. P., & Squire, L. R. (1989). Memory and metamemory: Comparisons between patients with frontal lobe lesions and amnesic patients. *Psychobiology, 17,* 3–11.

Jenkins, I. H., Brooks, D. J., Nixon, P. D., Frackowiak, R. S. J., & Passingham, R. E. (1994). Motor sequence learning: A study with positron emission tomography. *Journal of Neuroscience, 18,* 5026–5034.

Jensen, O., Kaiser, J., & Lachaux, J. -P. (2007). Human gamma-frequency oscillations associated with attention and memory. *Trends in Neuroscience, 30,* 317–324.

Jernigan, T. L., Schafer, K., Butters, N., & Cermak, L. S. (1991a). Magnetic resonance imaging of alcoholic Korsakoff patients. *Neuropsychopharmacology, 4,* 175–186.

Jernigan, T. L., Butters, N., DiTraglia, G., Schafer, K., Smith, T., Irwin, M., et al. (1991b). Reduced cerebral grey matter observed in alcoholics using magnetic resonance imaging. *Alcoholism, Clinical and Experimental Research, 15*(3), 418–427.

Jerusalinsky, D., Kornisiuk, E., & Izquierdo, I. (1997). Cholinergic neurotransmission and synaptic plasticity concerning memory processing. *Neurochemical Research, 22,* 507–515.

Johns, C. A., Greenwald, B. S., Mohs, R. C., & Davis, K. L. (1983). The cholinergic treatment strategy in ageing and senile dementia. *Psychopharmacology Bulletin, 19,* 185–197.

Johnson, M. K. (1991). Reality monitoring: Evidence from confabulation in organic brain disease patients. In G. Prigatano, & D. L. Schacter (Eds.), *Awareness of deficit after brain injury* (pp.176–197). New York: Oxford University Press.

Johnson, M. K., Hashtroudi, S., & Lindsay, D. S. (1993). Source monitoring. *Psychological Bulletin, 114*(1), 3–28.

Johnson, M. K., O'Connor, M., & Cantor, J. (1997). Confabulation, memory deficits, and frontal dysfunction. *Brain Cognition, 34*(2), 189–206.

Jones, B., & Mishkin, M. (1972). Limbic lesions and the problem of stimulus-reinforcement associations. *Experimental Neurology, 36,* 362–377.

Jones-Gotman, M., & Milner, B. (1978). Right temporal-lobe contribution to image-mediated verbal learning. *Neuropsychologia, 16,* 61–71.

Kaplan, R. F., Meadows, M. E., Verfaellie, M., Kwan, E., Ehrenberg, B. L., Bromfield, E. B., & Cohen, R. A. (1994). Lateralization of memory for the visual attributes of objects: Evidence from the posterior cerebral artery amobarbital test. *Neurology, 44,* 1069–1073.

Kapur, N. (1991). Amnesia in relation to fugue states—Distinguishing a neurological from a psychogenic basis. *British Journal of Psychiatry, 159,* 872–877.

Kapur, N. (1999). Syndromes of retrograde amnesia: A conceptual and empirical synthesis. *Psychological Bulletin, 125*(6), 800–825.

Kapur, N., & Brooks, D. J. (1999). Temporally-specific retrograde amnesia in two cases of discrete bilateral hippocampal pathology. *Hippocampus*, 9(3), 247–254.

Kapur, N., & Butters, N. (1977). Visuoperceptive deficits in long-term alcoholics with Korsakoff's psychosis. *Journal of Studies in Alcohol, 38*, 2025–2035.

Kapur, S., Craik, F. I., Tulving, E., Wilson, A. A., Houle, S., & Brown, G. M. (1994). Neuro-anatomical correlates of encoding in episodic memory: Levels of processing effect. *Proceedings of the National Academy of Sciences USA, 91*(6), 2008–2011.

Kapur, N., Ellison, D., Smith, M. P., McLellan, D. L., & Burrows, E. H. (1992). Focal retrograde amnesia following bilateral temporal lobe pathology. A neuropsychological and magnetic resonance study. *Brain, 115*(Pt. 1), 73–85.

Kapur, N., Young, A., Bateman, D., & Kennedy, P. (1989). Focal retrograde amnesia: A long term clinical and neuropsychological follow-up. *Cortex, 25*(3), 387–402.

Karni, A., Meyer, G., Jezzard, P., Adams, M. M., Turner, R., & Ungerleider, L. G. (1995). Functional MRI evidence for adult motor cortex plasticity during motor skill learning. *Nature, 377*, 155–158.

Keane, M. M., Clarke, H., & Corkin, S. (1992). Impaired perceptual priming and intact concep-tual priming in a patient with bilateral posterior cerebral lesions. *Society for Neuroscience Abstracts, 18*, 386.

Keane, M. M., Gabrieli, J. D., Noland, J. S., & McNealy, S. I. (1995). Normal perceptual priming of orthographically illegal nonwords in amnesia. *Journal of the International Neuropsy-chological Society, 1*(5), 425–433.

Keane, M. M., Gabrieli, J. D. E., Monti, L. A., Cantor, J. M., & Noland, J. S. (1993). Amnesic patients show normal priming and a normal depth-of-processing effect in a conceptually driven implicit memory task. *Society for Neuro-science Abstracts, 19*, 1079.

Kelley, C. M., & Jacoby, L. L. (2000). Recollection and familiarity: Process-dissociation. In E. Tulving, & F. I. M. Craik (Eds.), *The Oxford handbook of memory* (pp. 215–228). New York: Oxford University Press.

Kennedy, M. B. (1989). Regulation of synaptic transmission in the central nervous system: Long-term potentiation. *Cell, 59*, 777–787.

Kennepohl, S., Sziklas, V., Garver, K. E., Wagner, D. D., & Jones-Gotman, M. (2007). Memory and the medial temporal lobe: Hemi-spheric specialization reconsidered. *Neuroimage, 36*(3), 969–978.

Kersteen-Tucker, Z. (1991). Long-term repetition priming with symmetrical polygons and words. *Memory and Cognition, 19*, 37–43.

Kessler, J., Markowitsch, H. J., Huber, M., Kalbe, E., Weber-Luxenburger, G., & Kock, P. (1997). Massive and persistent anterograde amnesia in the absence of detectable brain damage: Antero-grade psychogenic amnesia or gross reduction in sustained effort? *Journal of Clinical and Experimental Neuropsychology, 19*(4), 604–614.

Khan, N., & Wieser, H. G. (1994). Limbic encepha-litis: A case report. *Epilepsy Research, 17*(2), 175–181.

Kihlstrom, J. F. (1995). Memory and consciousness: An appreciation of Claparede and recognition et moiite. *Consciousness and Cognition, 4*(4), 379–386.

Kilgard, M. P., & Merzenich, M. M. (1998). Cortical map reorganization enabled by nucleus basalis activity. *Science, 279*, 1714–1718.

Kim, E., Ku, J., Namkoong, K., Lee, W., Lee, K. S., Park, J. -Y., et al. (2009). Mammillothalamic functional connectivity and memory function in Wernicke's encephalopathy. *Brain, 132*, 369–376.

Kim, H. J., Burke, D. T., Dowds, M. M., & George, J. (1999). Utility of a microcomputer as an external memory aid for a memory-impaired head injury patient during in-patient rehabilita-tion. *Brain Injury, 13*(2), 147–150.

Kim, H. J., Burke, D. T., Dowds, M. M., Jr., Boone, K. A., & Park, G. J. (2000). Electronic memory aids for outpatient brain injury: Follow-up findings. *Brain Injury, 14*(2), 187–196.

Kim, M. S., Boone, K. B., Victor, T., Marion, S. D., Armano, S., Cottingham, M. E., et al. (2009). The Warrington recognition memory test for words as a measure of response bias: Total score and response time cutoffs developed on "real world" credible and noncredible subjects. *Archives of Clinical Neuropsychology* [Epub ahead of print].

Kim, J. J., Crespo-Facorro, B., Andreasen, N. C., O'Leary, D. S., Zhang, B., Harris, G., et al. (2000). An MRI-based parcellation method for the temporal lobe. *Neuroimage, 11*(4), 271–288.

Kinsbourne, M., & Wood, F. (1975). Short-term memory processes and the amnesic syndrome. In D. Deutsch, & J. A. Deutsch (Eds.), *Short-term memory* (pp. 258–291). New York: Academic Press.

Klatzky, R. L. (1982). *Human memory* (2nd ed.). San Francisco: W. H. Freeman.

Kling, A., & Steklis, H. D. (1976). A neural substrate for affiliative behavior in non-human primates. *Brain, Behavior and Evolution, 13*, 216–238.

Knopman, D., & Nissen, M. J. (1991). Procedural learning is impaired in Huntington's disease: Evidence from the serial reaction time task. *Neuropsychologia, 29*(3), 245–254.

Knowlton, B. J., Mangels, J. A., & Squire, L. R. (1996). A neostriatal habit learning system in humans. *Science, 273*(5280), 1399–1402.

Knowlton, B. J., & Squire, L. R. (1993). The learning of categories: Parallel brain systems for item memory and category knowledge. *Science, 262*(5140), 1747–1749.

Knowlton, B. J., Squire, L. R., & Gluck, M. A. (1994). Probabilistic classification learning in amnesia. *Learning and Memory, 1*(2), 106–120.

Kobayashi, Y., & Amaral, D. G. (2007). Macaque monkey retrosplenial cortex: III. Cortical efferents. *Journal of Comparative Neurology, 502,* 810–833.

Komatsu, S., Mimura, M., Kato, M., Wakamatsu, N., & Kashima, H. (2000). Errorless and effortful processes involved in the learning of face-name associations by patients with alcoholic Korsakoff's syndrome. *Neuropsychological Rehabilitation, 10*(2), 113–132.

Kooistra, C. A., & Heilman, K. M. (1988). Memory loss from a subcortical white matter infarct. *Journal of Neurology, Neurosurgery and Psychiatry, 51,* 866–869.

Kopelman, M. D. (1995). The Korsakoff syndrome. *British Journal of Psychiatry, 166*(2), 154–173.

Kopelman, M. D. (1991). Frontal dysfunction and memory deficits in the alcoholic Korsakoff syndrome and Alzheimer-type dementia. *Brain, 114*(Pt. 1A), 117–137.

Kopelman, M. D. (1987). Amnesia: Organic and psychogenic. *British Journal of Psychiatry, 150,* 428–442.

Kopelman, M. D. (1986). The cholinergic neurotransmitter system in human memory and dementia: A review. *Quarterly Journal of Experimental Psychology, 38A,* 535–573.

Kopelman, M. D. (1985). Rates of forgetting in Alzheimer-type dementia and Korsakoff's syndrome. *Neuropsychologia, 23,* 623–638.

Kopelman, M. D., Bright, P., Fulker, H., Hinton, N., Morrison, A., & Verfaellie, M. (2009). Remote semantic memory in patients with Korsakoff's syndrome and herpes encephalitis. *Neuropsychology, 23,*144–157.

Kopelman, M. D., Stanhope, N., & Kingsley, D. (1999). Retrograde amnesia in patients with diencephalic, temporal lobe or frontal lesions. *Neuropsychologia, 37*(8), 939–958.

Krebs, H., Brasherskrug, T., Rauch, S., Savage, C., Hogan, N., Rubin, R., et al. (1998). Robot-aided functional imaging: Application to a motor learning study. *Human Brain Mapping, 6,* 59–72.

Kritchevsky, M. (1989). Transient global amnesia. In F. Boller, & J. Grafman (Eds.), *Handbook of neuropsychology,* Vol. 3 (pp. 167–182). Amsterdam: Elsevier.

Kritchevsky, M., Graff-Radford, N. R., & Damasio, A. R. (1987). Normal memory after damage to medial thalamus. *Archives of Neurology, 44,* 959–962.

Kritchevsky, M., Squire, L. R., & Zouzounis, J. A. (1988). Transient global amnesia: Characterization of anterograde and retrograde amnesia. *Neurology, 38,* 213–219.

Krupp, L. B., Christodoulou, C., Melville, P., Scherl, W. F., MacAlister, W. S., & Elkins, L. E. (2004). Donepezil improved memory in multiple sclerosis in a randomized clinical trial. *Neurology, 63,* 1579–1585.

Kunst-Wilson, W. R., & Zajonc, R. B. (1980). Affective discrimination of stimuli that cannot be recognized. *Science, 207,* 557–558.

Larrabee, G. J., & Crook, T. H., III. (1995). Assessment of learning and memory. In R. L. Mapou, & J. Spector (Eds.), *Clinical neuropsychological assessment: A cognitive approach* (pp. 185–213). New York: Plenum Press.

Law, J. R., Flanery, M. A., Wirth, S., Yanike, M., Smith, A. C., Frank, L. M., et al. (2005). Functional magnetic resonance imaging activity during the gradual acquisition and expression of paired-associate memory. *Journal of Neuroscience, 25*(24), 5720–5729.

LeDoux, J. E. (1987). Emotion. In V. B. Mountcastle, F. Plum, & S. R. Geiger (Eds.), *Handbook of physiology,* Vol. 5 (pp. 419–460). Bethesda, MD: American Physiological Society.

Lee, A. C., Barense, M. D., & Graham, K. S. (2005). The contribution of the human medial temporal lobe to perception: Bridging the gap between animal and human studies. *Quarterly Journal of Experimental Psychology, 58*(3–4), 300–325.

Lee, G. P., Meador, K. J., Smith, J. R., Loring, D. W., & Flanigin, H. F. (1988). Preserved crossmodal association following bilateral amygdalotomy in man. *International Journal of Neuroscience, 40,* 47–55.

Levin, H. S. (1989). Memory deficit after closed head injury. In F. Boller, & J. Grafman (Eds.), *Handbook of neuropsychology,* Vol. 3 (pp. 183–207). Amsterdam: Elsevier.

Levine, B., Turner, G. R., Tisserand, D., Hevenor, S. J., Graham, S. J., & McIntosh, A. R. (2004). The functional neuroanatomy of episodic and semantic autobiographical remembering: A prospective functional MRI study. *Journal of Cognitive Neuroscience, 16,* 1633–1646.

Levite, M., & Ganor, Y. (2008). Autoantibodies to glutamate receptors can damage the brain in epilepsy, systemic lupus erythematosus and encephalitis. *Expert Review of Neurotherapeutics, 8,* 1141–1160.

Lewis, P. R., & Shute, C. C. D. (1967). The cholinergic limbic system: Projections of the hippocampal formation, medial cortex, nuclei of the ascending cholinergic reticular system, and the subfornical organ and supra-optic crest. *Brain, 90,* 521–540.

Lezak, M. D. (1983). *Neuropsychological assessment* (2nd ed.). New York: Oxford University Press.

Lhermitte, J., Doussinet & Ajuriaguerra, J. (1937). Une observation de la forme Korsakowienne des tumeurs du 3 ᵉ ventricule. *Revue Neurologique, 68,* 709–711.

Lhermitte, F., & Signoret, J. -L. (1972). Analyse neuropsychologique et differenciation des syndromes amnesiques. *Revue Neurologique, 126,* 161–178.

Libon, D. J., Price, C. C., Giovanetti, T., Swenson, R., Bettcher, B. M., Heilman, K. M., & Pennisi, A. (2008). Linking MRI hyperintensities with patterns of neuropsychological impairment: Evidence for a threshold effect. *Stroke, 39,* 806–813.

Lindqvist, G., & Norlen, G. (1966). Korsakoff's syndrome after operation on ruptured aneurysm of the anterior communicating artery. *Acta Psychiatrica Scandanavica, 42,* 24–34.

Livingston, K. E., & Escobar, A. (1971). Anatomic bias of the limbic system concept: A proposed reorientation. *Archives of Neurology, 24,* 17–21.

Loesch, D. V., Gilman S., Del Dotto, J., & Rosenblum, M. L. (1995). Cavernous malformation of the mammillary bodies: Neuropsychological implications. Case report. *Journal of Neurosurgery, 83,* 354–358.

Loftus, E. F. (1993). The reality of repressed memories. *American Psychologist, 48,* 516–537.

Loftus, E. F., & Cole, W. (1974). Retrieving attribute and name information from semantic memory. *Journal of Experimental Psychology, 102,* 1116–1122.

Loftus, E. F., & Ketcham, K. (1991). *Witness for the defense: The accused, the eyewitness, and the expert who puts memory on trial.* New York: St. Martin's.

Logothetis, N. K., & Pfeuffer, J. (2004). On the nature of the BOLD fMRI contrast mechanism. *Magnetic Resonance Imaging, 22*(10), 1517–1531.

Logue, V., Durward, M., Pratt, R. T. C., Piercy, M., & Nixon, W. L. B. (1968). The quality of survival after rupture of an anterior cerebral aneurysm. *British Journal of Psychiatry, 114,* 137–160.

Lomo, T. (1971). Patterns of activation in a monosynaptic cortical pathway: The perforant path input to the dentate areas of the hippocampal formation. *Experimental Brain Research, 12,* 18–45.

Loring, D. W., Lee, G. P., Meador, K. J., et al. (1991). Hippocampal contribution to verbal memory following dominant-hemisphere temporal lobectomy. *Journal of Clinical and Experimental Neuropsychology, 13,* 575–586.

MacLean, H. J., & Douen, A. G. (2002). Severe amnesia associated with human herpesvirus 6 encephalitis after bone marrow transplantation. *Transplantation, 73,* 1086–1089.

Maguire, E. A., & Frith, C. D. (2003a). Aging affects the engagement of the hippocampus during autobiographical memory retrieval. *Brain, 126*(Pt. 7), 1511–1523.

Maguire, E. A., & Frith, C. D. (2003b). Lateral asymmetry in the hippocampal response to the remoteness of autobiographical memories. *Journal of Neuroscience, 23*(12), 5302–5307.

Maguire, E. A., Henson, R. N., Mummery, C. J., & Frith, C. D. (2001). Activity in prefrontal cortex, not hippocampus, varies parametrically with the increasing remoteness of memories. *Neuroreport, 12*(3), 441–444.

Mahut, H., & Moss, M. (1986). The monkey and the sea horse. In R. L. Isaacson, & K. H. Pripram (Eds.), *The hippocampus* (pp. 241–279). New York: Plenum.

Mair, W. G. P., Warrington, E. K., & Weiskrantz, L. (1979). Memory disorder in Korsakoff's psychosis: A neuropathological and neuropsychological investigation of two cases. *Brain, 102,* 749–783.

Malamut, B. L., Graff-Radford, N., Chawluk, J., Grossman, R. I., & Gur, R. C. (1992). Memory in a case of bilateral thalamic infarction. *Neurology, 42,* 163–169.

Malkova, L., Mishkin, M., & Bachevalier, J. (1995). Long-term effects of selective neonatal temporal lobe lesions on learning and memory in monkeys. *Behavioral Neuroscience, 109,* 212–226.

Mandler, G. (1980). Recognizing: The judgement of previous occurrence. *Psychological Review, 87,* 252–271.

Manns, J. R., Clark, R. E., & Squire, L. R. (2000). Awareness predicts the magnitude of single-cue trace eyeblink conditioning. *Hippocampus, 10*(2), 181–186.

Markowitsch, H. J. (1999). Functional neuroimaging correlates of functional amnesia. *Memory, 7*(5–6), 561–583.

Markowitsch, H. J., Calabrese, P., Neufeld, H., Gehlen, W., & Durwen, H. F. (1999). Retrograde amnesia for world knowledge and preserved memory for autobiographic events. A case report. *Cortex*, 35(2), 243–252.

Marslen-Wilson, W. D., & Teuber, H. -L. (1974). Memory for remote events in anterograde amnesia: Recognition of public figures from news photographs. *Neuropsychologia*, 13, 353–364.

Martin, A., & Fedio, P. (1983). Word production and comprehension in Alzheimer's disease: The breakdown of semantic knowledge. *Brain and Language*, 19, 124–141.

Martin, R. C., Haut, M. W., Goeta Kreisler, K., & Blumenthal, D. (1996). Neuropsychological functioning in a patient with paraneoplastic limbic encephalitis. *Journal of the International Neuropsychological Society*, 2(5), 460–466.

Martone, M., Butters, N., & Trauner, D. (1986). Some analyses of forgetting pictorial material in amnesic and demented patients. *Journal of Clinical and Experimental Neuropsychology*, 8, 161–178.

Matthies, H., Frey, U., Reymann, K., Krug, M., Jork, R., & Schroeder, H. (1990). Different mechanisms and multiple stages of LTP. In Y. Ben-Ari (Ed.), *Excitatory amino acids and neuronal plasticity* (pp. 359–368). New York: Plenum Press.

Mayes, A. R., Downes, J. J., McDonald, C., Poole, V., Rooke, S., Sagar, H. J., & Meudell, P. R. (1994). Two tests for assessing remote public knowledge: A tool for assessing retrograde amnesia. *Memory*, 2(2), 183–210.

Mayes, A. R., Downes, J. J., Symons, V., & Shoqeirat, M. (1994). Do amnesics forget faces pathologically fast? *Cortex*, 30(4), 543–563.

Mayes, A. R., & Meudell, P. (1981). How similar is immediate memory in amnesic patients to delayed memory in normal subjects? A replication, extension and reassessment of the amnesic cueing effect. *Neuropsychologia*, 18, 527–540.

Mayes, A. R., Meudell, P. R., Mann, D., & Pickering, A. (1988). Location of lesions in Korsakoff's syndrome: Neuropsychological and neuropathological data on two patients. *Cortex*, 24, 367–388.

Mayes, A. R., Meudell, P. R., & Neary, D. (1980). Do amnesics adopt inefficient encoding strategies with faces and random shapes? *Neuropsychologia*, 18, 527–540.

Mayes, A., Meudell, P., & Som, S. (1981). Further similarities between amnesia and normal attenuated memory: Effects of paired-associate learning and contextual shifts. *Neuropsychologia*, 18, 655–664.

Mayes, A. R., & Roberts, N. (2001). Theories of episodic memory. *Philosophical Transactions of the Royal Society of London. Series B, Biological Sciences*, 356(1413), 1395–1408.

McAndrews, M. P., Glisky, E. L., & Schacter, D. L. (1987). When priming persists: Long-lasting implicit memory for a single episode in amnesic patients. *Neuropsychologia*, 25, 497–506.

McDonald, C. R., Crosson, B., Valenstein, E., & Bowers, D. (2001). Verbal encoding deficits in a patient with a left retrosplenial lesion. *Neurocase*, 7, 407–417.

McGaugh, J. L. (2004). The amygdala modulates the consolidation of memories of emotionally arousing experiences. *Annual Review of Neuroscience*, 27, 1–28.

McGaugh, J. L., Introini-Collison, I. B., Nagahara, A. H., Cahill, L., Brioni, J. D., & Castellano, C. (1990). Involvement of the amygdaloid complex in neuromodulatory influences on memory storage. *Neuroscience and Biobehavioral Reviews*, 14, 425–431.

McGlinchey-Berroth, R., Brawn, C., & Disterhoft, J. F. (1999). Temporal discrimination learning in severe amnesic patients reveals an alteration in the timing of eyeblink conditioned responses. *Behavioral Neuroscience*, 113(1), 10–18.

McGlinchey-Berroth, R., Carrillo, M. C., Gabrieli, J. D., Brawn, C. M., & Disterhoft, J. F. (1997). Impaired trace eyeblink conditioning in bilateral, medial-temporal lobe amnesia. *Behavioral Neuroscience*, 111(5), 873–882.

McGlinchey-Berroth, R., Cermak, L. S., Carrillo, M. C., Armfield, S., Gabrieli, J. D., & Disterhoft, J. F. (1995). Impaired delay eyeblink conditioning in amnesic Korsakoff's patients and recovered alcoholics. *Alcoholism, Clinical and Experimental Research*, 19(5), 1127–1132.

McKee, R. D., & Squire, L. R. (1992). Both hippocampal and diencephalic amnesia result in normal forgetting for complex visual material. *Journal of Clinical and Experimental Neuropsychology*, 14, 103.

McKone, E., & Slee, J. A. (1997). Explicit contamination in "implicit" memory for new associations. *Memory & Cognition*, 25(3), 352–366.

McKoon, G., Ratcliff, R., & Dell, G. S. (1986). A critical evaluation of the semantic-episodic distinction. *Journal of Experimental Psychology: Learning Memory and Cognition*, 12, 295–306.

McMackin, D., Cockburn, J., Anslow, P., & Gaffan, D. (1995). Correlation of fornix damage with memory impairment in six cases of colloid cyst removal. *Acta Neurocuirurgica*, 135, 12–18.

Meltzer, J. A., & Constable, R. T. (2005). Activation of human hippocampal formation reflects success in both encoding and cued recall of paired associates. *Neuroimage, 24*(2), 384–397.

Mesulam, M. -M., & Mufson, E. J. (1984). Neural inputs into the nucleus basalis of the substantia innominata (Ch4) in the rhesus monkey. *Brain, 107*, 253–274.

Mesulam, M. -M., Mufson, E. J., Levey, E. J., & Wainer, B. H. (1983). Cholinergic innervation of cortex by the basal forebrain: Cytochemistry and cortical connections of the septal area, diagonal band nuclei, nucleus basalis (substantia innominata) and hypothalamus in the rhesus monkey. *Journal of Comparative Neurology, 214*, 170–197.

Mesulam, M. -M., & Van Hoesen, G. W. (1976). Acetylcholinesterase containing basal forebrain neurons in the rhesus monkey project to neocortex. *Brain Research, 109*, 152–157.

Meudell, P., & Mayes, A. (1981). The Claparede phenomenon: A further example in amnesics, a demonstration of a similar effect in normal people with attenuated memory, and a reinterpretation. *Current Psychological Research, 1*, 75–88.

Meudell, P. R., Northern, B., Snowden, J. S., & Neary, D. (1980). Long-term memory for famous voices in amnesic and normal subjects. *Neuropsychologia, 18*, 133–139.

Meunier, M., Bachevalier, J., Mishkin, M., & Murray, E. A. (1993). Effects on visual recognition of combined and separate ablations of the entorhinal and perirhinal cortex in rhesus monkeys. *Journal of Neuroscience, 13*, 5418–5432.

Meunier, M., Bachevalier, J., & Mishkin, M. (1997). Effects of orbitofrontal and anterior cingulate lesions on object and spatial memory in rhesus monkeys. *Neuropsychologia, 35*, 999–1016.

Miller, G. (2008). Neuroimaging: Growing Pains for fMRI. *Science, 320*(5882), 1412–1412.

Miller, J. W., Petersen, R. C., Metter, E. J., Millikan, C. H., & Yanagihara, T. (1987). Transient global amnesia: Clinical characteristics and prognosis. *Neurology, 37*, 733–737.

Milner, B. (1962). Les troubles de la memoire accompagnant des lesions hippocampiques bilaterales. In P. Passouant (Ed.), *Physiologie de l'hippocampe*. Paris: Centre National de la Recherche Scientifique.

Milner, B. (1966). Amnesia following operation on the temporal lobes. In C. W. M. Whitty, & O. L. Zangwill (Eds.), *Amnesia*. London: Butterworths.

Milner, B. (1972). Disorders of learning and memory after temporal lobe lesions in man. *Clinical Neurosurgery, 19*, 421–446.

Milner, B. (1974). Hemispheric specialization: Scope and limits. In F. O. Schmitt, & F. G. Worden (Eds.), *The neurosciences: Third study program* (pp. 75–89). Boston: MIT Press.

Milner, B., Corkin, S., & Teuber, H. -L. (1968). Further analysis of the hippocampal amnesic syndrome: 14-year follow-up study of H.M. *Neuropsychologia, 6*, 215–234.

Milner, B., & Petrides, M. (1984). Behavioural effects of frontal-lobe lesions in man. *Trends in Neuroscience, 7*, 403–407.

Mishkin, M. (1978). Memory in monkeys severely impaired by combined but not separate removal of the amygdala and hippocampus. *Nature, 273*, 297–298.

Mishkin, M. (1982). A memory system in the monkey. *Philosophical Transactions of the Royal Society of London, 298*, 85–95.

Mishkin, M., & Petri, H. L. (1984). Memories and habits: Some implications for the analysis of learning and retention. In L. R. Squire, & N. Butters (Eds.), *Neuropsychology of memory* (pp. 287–296). New York: Guilford Press.

Mishkin, M., & Saunders, R. C. (1979). Degree of memory impairment in monkeys related to amount of conjoint damage to amygdaloid and hippocampal systems. *Society of Neuroscience Abstracts, 5*, 320.

Mishkin, M., Spiegler, B. J., Saunders, R. C., & Malamut, B. L. (1982). An animal model of global amnesia. In S. Corkin, et al. (Eds.), *Alzheimer's disease: A report of progress* (pp. 235–247). New York: Raven Press.

Moccia, F., Aramini, A., Montobbio, P., Altomonte, F., & Greco, G. (1996). Transient global amnesia: Disease or syndrome? *Italian Journal of Neurological Sciences, 17*(3), 211–214.

Monastero, R., Mangialasche, F., Camarda, C., Ercolani, S., & Camarda, R. (2009). A systematic review of neuropsychiatric symptoms in mild cognitive impairment. *Journal of Alzheimer's Disease*, 2009 June 19 [Epub ahead of print].

Moody, T. D., Bookheimer, S. Y., Vanek, Z., & Knowlton, B. J. (2004). An implicit learning task activates medial temporal lobe in patients with Parkinson's disease. *Behavioral Neuroscience, 118*(2), 438–442.

Mori, E., Yamadori, A., & Mitani, Y. (1986). Left thalamic infarction and disturbance of verbal memory: A clinicoanatomical study with a new method of computed tomographic stereotaxic lesion localization. *Annals of Neurology, 20*, 671–676.

Morris, M. K., Bowers, D., Chatterjee, A., & Heilman, K. M. (1992). Amnesia following a discrete basal forebrain lesion. *Brain*, *115*, 1827–1847.

Morris, R., Petrides, M., & Pandya, D. N. (1999). Architecture and connections of retrosplenial area 30 in the rhesus monkey (Macaca mulatta). *European Journal of Neuroscience*, *11*(7), 2506–2518.

Moscovitch, M., Nadel, L., Winocur, G., Gilboa, A., & Rosenbaum, R. S. (2006). The cognitive neuroscience of remote episodic, semantic and spatial memory. *Current Opinion in Neurobiology*, *16*, 179–190.

Moscovitch, M., Rosenbaum, R. S., Gilboa, A., Addis, D. R., Westmacott, R., Grady, C. L., et al. (2005a). Functional neuroanatomy of remote episodic, semantic and spatial memory: A unified account based on multiple trace theory. *Journal of Anatomy*, *207*, 35–66.

Moscovitch, M., Westmacott, R., Gilboa, A., Addis, D. R., Rosenbaum, R. S., Viskontas, I., et al.(2005b). Hippocampal complex contribution to retention and retrieval of recent and remote episodic and semantic memories: Evidence from behavioural and neuroimaging studies of healthy and brain-damaged people. In N. Ohta, C. M. McClund, & B. Uttl (Eds.), *Dynamic cognitive processes* (pp. 333–380). New York: Springer-Verlag.

Moscovitch, M. (1982). Multiple dissociations of function in amnesia. In L. S. Cermak (Ed.), *Human memory and amnesia* (pp. 337–370). Hillsdale, NJ: Lawrence Erlbaum.

Moses, S. N., Ryan, J. D., Bardouille, T., Kovacevic, N., Hanlon, F. M., & McIntosh, A. R. (2009). Semantic information alters neural activation during transverse patterning performance. *NeuroImage*, *46*, 863–873.

Moss, M., Mahut, H., & Zola-Morgan, S. (1981). Concurrent discrimination learning of monkeys after hippocampal, entorhinal, or fornix lesions. *Journal of Neuroscience*, *1*, 227–240.

Moudgil, S. S., Azzouz, M., Al-Azzaz, A., Haut, M., & Guttmann, L. (2000). Amnesia due to fornix infarction. *Stroke*, *31*, 1418–1419.

Mufson, E. J., & Pandya, D. N. (1984). Some observations on the course and composition of the cingulum bundle in the rhesus monkey. *Journal of Comparative Neurology*, *225*, 31–43.

Murray, E. A., & Bussey, T. J. (1999). Perceptual-mnemonic functions of the perirhinal cortex. *Trends in Cognitive Sciences*, *3*, 142–151.

Murray, E. A., Gaffan, D., & Mishkin, M. (1993). Neural substrates of visual stimulus-stimulus association in rhesus monkeys. *Journal of Neuroscience*, *13*, 4549–4561.

Murray, E. A., & Mishkin, M. (1998). Object recognition and location memory in monkeys with excitotoxic lesions of the amygdala and hippocampus. *Journal of Neuroscience*, *18*, 6568–6582.

Murre, J. M. (1997). Implicit and explicit memory in amnesia: Some explanations and predictions by the TraceLink model. *Memory*, *5*(1–2), 213–232.

Murre, J. M. (1999). Interaction of cortex and hippocampus in a model of amnesia and semantic dementia. *Reviews in the Neurosciences*, *10*(3–4), 267–278.

Musen, G., & Triesman, A. (1990). Implicit and explicit memory for visual patterns. *Journal of Experimental Psychology: Learning Memory and Cognition*, *16*, 127–137.

Nadel, L., & Moskovitch, M. (1997). Memory consolidation, retrograde amnesia, and the hippocampal complex. *Current Opinion in Neurobiology*, *7*, 217–227.

Narabayashi, H., Nagao, T., Saito, Y., Yoshida, M., & Nagahata, M. (1963). Stereotaxic amygdalotomy for behavior disorders. *Archives of Neurology*, *9*, 1–16.

Nauta, W. J. H. (1961). Fibre degeneration following lesions of the amygdaloid complex in the monkey. *Journal of Anatomy*, *95*, 515–531.

Nauta, W. J. (1962). Neural associations of the amygdaloid complex in the monkey. *Brain*, *85*, 505–520.

Nelson, T. O., Gerler, D., & Narens, L. (1984). Accuracy of feeling-of-knowing judgements for predicting perceptual identification and relearning. *Journal of Experimental Psychology: General*, *113*, 282–300.

Nelson, T. O., Leonesio, R. J., Shimamura, A. P., Landwehr, R. F., & Narens, L. (1982). Overlearning and the feeling of knowing. *Journal of Experimental Psychology: Learning Memory and Cognition*, *8*, 279–288.

Newman, M. E., Adityanjee, Sobolewski, E., & Jampala, V. C. (1998). Wernicke-Korsakoff amnestic syndrome secondary to malnutrition in a patient with schizoaffective disorder. *Neuropsychiatry, Neuropsychology, and Behavioral Neurology*, *11*(4), 241–244.

Niki, K., & Luo, J. (2002). An fMRI study on the time-limited role of the medial temporal lobe in long-term topographical autobiographic memory. *Journal of Cognitive Neurosciences*, *14*(3), 500–507.

Nissen, M. J., & Bullemer, P. (1987). Attentional requirements of learning: Evidence from performance measures. *Cognitive Psychology*, *19*, 1–32.

Nokura, K., Yamamoto, H., Okawara, Y., Koga, H., Osawa, H., & Sakai, K. (1997). Reversible limbic encephalitis caused by ovarian teratoma. *Acta Neurologica Scandinavica*, 95, 367–373.

Nyberg, L., & Cabeza, R. (2000). Brain imaging of memory. In E. Tulving, & F. I. M. Craik (Eds.), *The Oxford handbook of memory* (pp. 501–519). New York: Oxford University Press.

Nyberg, L., McIntosh, A. R., Cabeza, R., Nilsson, L. G., Houle, S., Habib, R., & Tulving, E. (1996). Network analysis of positron emission tomography regional cerebral blood flow data: Ensemble inhibition during episodic memory retrieval. *Journal of Neuroscience*, 16(11), 3753–3759.

Nyberg, L., McIntosh, A. R., & Tulving, E. (1998). Functional brain imaging of episodic and semantic memory with positron emission tomography. *Journal of Molecular Medicine*, 76(1), 48–53.

O'Connor, M., Butters, N., Miliotis, P., Eslinger, P., & Cermak, L. S. (1992). The dissociation of anterograde and retrograde amnesia in a patient with herpes encephalitis. *Journal of Clinical and Experimental Neuropsychology*, 14(2), 159–178.

Ojemann, G. A., & Dodrill, C. B. (1985). Verbal memory deficits after left temporal lobectomy for epilepsy. *Journal of Neurosurgery*, 62, 101–107.

Okawa, M., Maeda, S., Nukui, H., & Kawafuchi, J. (1980). Psychiatric symptoms in ruptured anterior communicating aneurysms: Social prognosis. *Acta Psychiatrica Scandinavica*, 61, 306–312.

O'Keefe, J., & Dostrovsky, J. (1971). The hippocampus as a spatial map. Preliminary evidence from unit activity in the freely moving rat. *Brain Research*, 34, 171–175.

O'Keefe, J., & Nadel, L. (1978). *The hippocampus as a cognitive map*. London: Oxford University Press.

Olesen, J., & Jørgensen, M. B. (1986). Leao's spreading depression in the hippocampus explains transient global amnesia: A hypothesis. *Acta Neurologica Scandanavica*, 73, 219–220.

Olson, I. R., & Berryhill, M. (2009). Some surprising findings on the involvement of the parietal lobe in human memory. *Neurobiology of Learning and Memory*, 91(2), 155–165.

Olton, D. S. (1989). Inferring psychological dissociations from experimental dissociations: The temporal context of episodic memory. In H. L. Roediger, & F. I. M. Craik (Eds.), *Varieties of memory and consciousness: Essays in honour of Endel Tulving* (pp. 161–177). Hillsdale, NJ: Lawrence Erlbaum.

O'Neill, J. et al. (2006) Place-selective firing of CA1 pyramidal cells during sharp wave/ripple network patterns in exploratory behavior. Neuron. 49, 143–155.

O'Neil, E. B., Cate, A. D., & Kohler, S. (2009). Perirhinal cortex contributes to accuracy in recognition memory and perceptual discriminations. *Journal of Neuroscience*, 29(26), 8329–8334.

O'Neill, J., Pleydell-Bouverie, B, Dupret D, and Csicsvari J. (2010). Play it again: reactivation of waking experience and memory. Trends in Neuroscience, 33: 220–229.

Osawa, A., Maeshima, S., & Kunishio, K. (2008). Topographic disorientation and amnesia due to cerebral hemorrhage in the left retrosplenial region. *European Neurology*, 59, 79–82.

Oscar-Berman, M., & Bonner R. T. (1985). Matching- and delayed matching-to-sample performance as measures of visual processing, selective attention, and memory in aging and alcoholic individuals. *Neuropsychologia*, 23, 639–651.

Owen, M. J., & Butler, S. R. (1981). Amnesia after transection of the fornix in monkeys: Long-term memory impaired, short-term memory intact. *Behavioural Brain Research*, 3, 115–123.

Paller, K. A., Kutas, M., & Mayes, A. R. (1987). Neural correlates of encoding in an incidental learning paradigm. *Electroencephalography and Clinical Neurophysiology*, 67, 360–371.

Paller, K. A., Kutas, M., & McIsaac, H. K. (1995). Monitoring conscious recollection via the electrical activity of the brain. *Psychological Science*, 6, 107–111.

Pandya, D. N., & Yeterian, E. H. (1990). Architecture and connections of cerebral cortex: Implications for brain evolution and function. In A. B. Scheibel, & A. F. Wechsler (Eds.), *Neurobiology of higher cognitive function*. New York: The Guilford Press.

Papez, J. (1937). A proposed mechanism of emotion. *Archives of Neurological Psychiatry*, 39, 725–743.

Park, D. C., & Reuter-Lorenz, P. (2009). The adaptive brain: Aging and neurocognitive scaffolding. *Annual Review of Psychology*, 60, 173–196.

Park, S. A., Hahn, J. H., Kim, J. I., Na, D. L., & Huh, K. (2000). Memory deficits after bilateral anterior fornix infarction. *Neurology*, 54, 1379–1382.

Parker, A., & Gaffan, D. (1997). Mammillary body lesions in monkeys impair object-in-place memory: Functional unity of the fornix-mammillary system. *Journal of Cog Neurosciences*, 9, 512–521.

Parkin, A. J., & Hunkin, N. M. (1993). Impaired temporal context memory on anterograde but not retrograde tests in the absence of frontal pathology. *Cortex, 29*(2), 267–280.

Parkinson, J. K., Murray, E. A., Mishkin, M. (1988). A selective mnemonic role for the hippocampus in monkeys: Memory for the location of objects. *Journal of Neuroscience, 8*, 4159–4167.

Passingham, R. (1997). Functional organization of the motor system. In R. S. J. Frackowiak, K. J. Friston, C. D. Frith, R. J. Dolan, & J. C. Mazziota (Eds.), *Human brain function* (pp. 243–274). Toronto: Academic Press.

Penfield, W., & Mathieson, G. (1974). Memory. Autopsy findings and comments on the role of hippocampus in experiential recall. *Archives of Neurology, 31*, 145–154.

Penfield, W., & Milner, B. (1958). Memory deficit produced by bilateral lesions in the hippocampal zone. *Archives of Neurology and Psychiatry, 79*, 475–497.

Peters, B. H., & Levin, H. S. (1979). Effects of physostigmine and lecithin on memory in Alzheimer disease. *Annals of Neurology, 6*, 219–221.

Peters, B. H., & Levin, H. S. (1982). Chronic oral physostigmine and lecithin administration in memory disorders of aging. In S. Corkin, J. H. Davies, E. Growdon, & R. J. Writman (Eds.), *Alzheimer's disease: A report of progress in research* (pp. 421–426). New York: Raven Press.

Petersen, R. C.(2004). *Mild cognitive impairment: Aging to Alzheimer's disease*. New York: Oxford University Press.

Petersen, R. C. (2000). Mild cognitive impairment: Transition between aging and Alzheimer's disease. *Neurologia, 15*, 93–101.

Petersen, R. C., Stevens, J., Ganguli, M., Tangalos, E. G., Cummings, J. L., & DeKosky, S. T. (2001). Practice parameter: Early detection of dementia: Mild cognitive impairment (an evidence-based review): Report of the quality standards subcommittee of the American Academy of Neurology. *Neurology, 56*, 1133–1142.

Petrides, M., & Milner, B. (1982). Deficits on subject-ordered tasks after frontal- and temporal-lobe lesions in man. *Neuropsychologia, 20*, 249–262.

Phillips, S., Sangalang, V., & Sterns, G. (1987). Basal forebrain infarction: A clinicopathologic correlation. *Archives of Neurology, 44*, 1134–1138.

Piefke, M., Weiss, P. H., Zilles, K., Markowitsch, H. J., & Fink, G. R. (2003). Differential remoteness and emotional tone modulate the neural correlates of autobiographical memory. *Brain, 126*(Pt. 3), 650–668.

Pigott, S., & Milner, B. (1993). Memory for different aspects of complex visual scenes after unilateral temporal or frontal lobe resection. *Neuropsychologia, 31*, 1–15.

Piolino, P., Desgranges, B., & Eustache, F. (2009). Episodic autobiographical memories over the course of time: Cognitive, neuropsychological and neuroimaging findings. *Neuropsychologia, 47*(11), 2314–2329.

Piolino, P., Giffard-Quillon, G., Desgranges, B., Chételat, G., Baron, J. -C., & Eustache, F. (2004). Re-experiencing old memories via hippocampus: A PET study of autobiographical memory. *Neuroimage, 22*(3), 1371–1383.

Poldrack, R. A., & Foerde, K. (2008). Category learning and the memory systems debate. *Neuroscience and Biobehavioral Reviews, 37*, 197–205.

Poldrack, R., Desmond, J., Glover, G., & Gabrieli, J. (1998). The neural basis of visual skill learning: An fMRI study of mirror reading. *Cerebral Cortex, 8*, 1–10.

Poldrack, R. A., & Packard, M. G. (2003). Competition among multiple memory systems: Converging evidence from animal and human brain studies. *Neuropsychologia, 41*(3), 245–251.

Poldrack, R. A., Prabhakaran, V., Seger, C. A., & Gabrieli, J. D. (1999). Striatal activation during acquisition of a cognitive skill. *Neuropsychology, 13*, 564–574.

Poletti, C. E. (1986). Is the limbic system a limbic system? Studies of hippocampal efferents: Their functional and clinical implications. In B. K. Doane, & K. E. Livingston (Eds.), *The limbic system: Functional organization and clinical disorders* (pp. 79–94). New York: Raven Press.

Poreh, A., Winocur, G., Moscovitch, M., Backon, M., Goshen, E., Ram, Z., & Feldman, Z. (2006). Anterograde and retrograde amnesia in a person with bilateral fornix lesions following removal of a colloid cyst. *Neuropsychologia, 44*(12), 2241–2248.

Porrino, L. J., Crane, A. M., & Goldman-Rakic, P. S. (1981). Direct and indirect pathways from the amygdala to the frontal lobe in rhesus monkeys. *Journal of Comparative Neurology, 198*, 121–136.

Postle, B. R., & Corkin, S. (1998). Impaired word-stem completion priming but intact perceptual identification priming with novel words: Evidence from the amnesic patient H.M. *Neuropsychologia, 36*(5), 421–440.

Preston, A. R., Bornstein, A. M., Hutchinson, J. B., Gaare, M. E., Glover, G. H., & Wagner, A. D. (2009). High-resolution fMRI of content-sensitive subsequent memory responses in human medial temporal lobe. *Journal of Cognitive Neuroscience*, 2009 January 13 [Epub ahead of print].

Price, A., Filoteo, J. V., Maddox, W. T. (2009). Rule-based category learning in patients with Parkinson's disease. *Neuropsychologia*, *47*, 1213–1226.

Pruessner, J. C., Kohler, S., Crane, J., Pruessner, M., Lord, C., Byrne, A., et al. (2002). Volumetry of temporopolar, perirhinal, entorhinal and para-hippocampal cortex from high-resolution MR images: Considering the variability of the collateral sulcus. *Cerebral Cortex*, *12*(12), 1342–1353.

Ratcliff, R., Van Zandt, T., & McKoon, G. (1995). Process dissociation, single-process theories, and recognition memory. *Journal of Experimental Psychology: General*, *124*(4), 352–374.

Reber, P. J., Knowlton, B. J., & Squire, L. R. (1996). Dissociable properties of memory systems: Differences in the flexibility of declarative and nondeclarative knowledge. *Behavioral Neuroscience*, *110*(5), 861–871.

Reber, P. J., & Squire, L. R. (1998). Encapsulation of implicit and explicit memory in sequence learning. *Journal of Cognitive Neuroscience*, *10*(2), 248–263.

Reder, L. M., Park, H., & Kieffaber, P. D. (2009). Memory systems do not divide on consciousness: Reinterpreting memory in terms of activation and binding. *Psychological Bulletin*, *135*(1), 23–49.

Reed, J. M., & Squire, L. R. (1998). Retrograde amnesia for facts and events: Findings from four new cases. *Journal of Neuroscience*, *18*(10), 3943–3954.

Rekkas, P. V., & Constable, R. T. (2005). Evidence that autobiographic memory retrieval does not become independent of the hippocampus: An fMRI study contrasting very recent with remote events. *Journal of Cognitive Neuroscience*, *17*(12), 1950–1961.

Renou, P., Ducreux, D., Batouche, F., & Denier, C. (2008). Pure and acute Korsakoff syndrome due to a bilateral anterior fornix infarction: A diffusion tensor tractography study. *Archives of Neurology*, *65*, 1252–1253.

Rich, J. B., Bylsma, F. W., & Brandt, J. (1996). Item priming and skill learning in amnesia. *Journal of Clinical and Experimental Neuropsychology*, *18*(1), 148–158.

Richardson, J. T. (1992). Imagery mnemonics and memory remediation. *Neurology*, *42*, 283–286.

Richardson-Klavehn, A., & Bjork, R. A. (1988). Measures of memory. *Annual Review of Psychology*, *39*, 475–543.

Roediger, H. L. (2008). Relativity of remembering: Why the laws of memory vanished. *Annual Review of Psychology*, *59*, 225–254.

Roediger, H. L., III, Guynn, M. J., & Jones, T. C. (1994). Implicit memory: A tutorial review. In G. D'Ydewalle, & P. Eelen (Eds.), *Perspectives on psychological science* Vol. 2. *The state of the art* (pp. 67–94). Hove, UK: Lawrence Erlbaum.

Roediger, H. L. (1990). Implicit memory: Retention without remembering. *American Psychologist*, *45*, 1043–1056.

Roediger, H. L., & Blaxton, T. A. (1987). Effects of varying modality, surface features, and retention interval on priming in word fragment completion. *Memory and Cognition*, *15*, 379–388.

Roediger, H. L., & McDermott, K. B. (1993). Implicit memory in normal human subjects. In F. Boller, & J. Grafman (Eds.), *Handbook of neuropsychology* Vol. 8 (pp. 63–131). New York: Elsevier.

Roediger, H. L., & McDermott, K. B. (2000). Distortions of memory. In E. Tulving, & F. I. M. Craik (Eds.), *The Oxford handbook of memory* (pp. 149–162). New York: Oxford University Press.

Roediger, H. L., Weldon, M. S., & Challis, B. H. (1989). Explaining dissociations between implicit and explicit measures of retention: A processing account. In H. L. Roediger, & F. I. M. Craik (Eds.), *Varieties of memory: Essays in honour of Endel Tulving* (pp. 3–41). Hillsdale, NJ: Lawrence Erlbaum.

Rolls, E. T., Kesner, R. P. (2006). A computational theory of hippocampal function, and empirical tests of the theory. *Progress in Neurobiology*, *79*, 1–48.

Rosenbaum, R. S., Moscovitch, M., Foster, J. K., Schnyer, D. M., Gao, F., Kovacevic, N., et al. (2008). Patterns of autobiographical memory loss in medial-temporal lobe amnesic patients. *Journal of Cognitive Neurosciences*, *20*, 1490–1506.

Rosenbaum, R. S., Ziegler, M., Winocur, G., Grady, C. L., & Moscovitch, M. (2004). "I have often walked down this street before": fMRI studies on the hippocampus and other structures during mental navigation of an old environment. *Hippocampus*, *14*(7), 826–835.

Rosene, D. L., & Van Hoesen, G. W. (1977). Hippocampal efferents reach widespread areas of cerebral cortex and amygdala in the rhesus monkey. *Science*, *198*, 315–317.

Ross, E. D. (1980a). Sensory-specific and fractional disorders of recent memory in man. I: Isolated loss of visual recent memory. *Archives of Neurology*, *37*, 193–200.

Ross, E. D. (1982). Disorders of recent memory in humans. *Trends in Neuroscience*, *5*, 170–172.

Ross, E. D., & Stewart, R. M. (1981). Akinetic mutism from hypothalamic damage: Successful treatment with dopamine agonists. *Neurology*, *31*, 1435–1439.

Roth, T., Roehrs, T., Zwyghuizen Doorenbos, A., Stepanski, E., & Wittig, R. (1988). Sleep and memory. *Psychopharmacology Ser*, *6*, 140–145.

Rudge, P., & Warrington, E. K. (1991). Selective impairment of memory and visual perception in splenial tumours. *Brain*, *114*, 349–360.

Rueckl, J. G. (1991). Similarity effects in word and pseudoword repetition priming. *Journal of Experimental Psychology: Learning Memory and Cognition*, *16*, 374–391.

Rugg, M. D., Fletcher, P. C., Frith, C. D., Frackowiak, R. S., & Dolan, R. J. (1996). Differential activation of the prefrontal cortex in successful and unsuccessful memory retrieval. *Brain*, *119*, 2073–2083.

Rugg, M. D., Mark, R. E., Walla, P., Schloerscheidt, A. M., Burch, C. S., & Allan, K. (1998). Dissociation of the neural correlates of implicit and explicit memory. *Nature*, *392*, 595–598.

Russell, E. W. (1981). The pathology and clinical examination of memory. In S.B. Filskov, & T. J. Boll (Eds.), *Handbook of clinical neuropsychology* (pp. 287–319). New York: John Wiley & Sons.

Russell, W. R., & Nathan, P. W. (1946). Traumatic amnesia. *Brain*, *69*, 290–300.

Ryan, C., & Butters, N. (1980a). Further evidence for a continuum of impairment encompassing male alcoholic Korsakoff patients and chronic alcoholic men. *Alcoholism: Clinical and Experimental Research*, *4*, 190–197.

Ryan, C., & Butters, N. (1980b). Learning and memory impairments in young and old alcoholics: Evidence for the premature-aging hypothesis. *Alcoholism: Clinical and Experimental Research*, *4*, 288–293.

Ryan, L., Lin, C. Y., Ketcham, K., & Nadel, L. (2009). The role of medial temporal lobe in retrieving spatial and nonspatial relations from episodic and semantic memory. *Hippocampus*, *20*, 11–18.

Ryan, L., Nadel, L., Keil, K., Putnam, K., Schnyer, D., Trouard, T., & Moscovitch, M. (2001). Hippocampal complex and retrieval of recent and very remote autobiographical memories: Evidence from functional magnetic resonance imaging in neurologically intact people. *Hippocampus*, *11*, 707–714.

Sander, K., & Sander, D. (2005). New insights into transient global amnesia: Recent imaging and clinical findings. *Lancet Neurology*, *4*, 437–444.

Sanders, H. I., & Warrington, E. K. (1971). Memory for remote events in amnesic patients. *Brain*, *94*, 661–668.

Sanes, J. N., Dimitrov, B., & Hallett, M. (1990). Motor learning in patients with cerebellar dysfunction. *Brain*, *113*, 103–120.

Sato, K., Sakajiri, K., Komai, K., & Takamori, M. (1998). *No To Shinkei*, *50*, 69–73.

Saunders, R. C., Rosene, D. L., & Van Hoesen, G. W. (1988). Comparison of the efferents of the amygdala and the hippocampal formation in the Rhesus monkey: II. Reciprocal and non-reciprocal connections. *Journal of Comparative Neurology*, *271*, 185–207.

Scarborough, D. L., Cortese, C., & Scarborough, H. S. (1977). Frequency and repetition effects in lexical memory. *Journal of Experimental Psychology: Human Perception and Performance*, *3*, 1–17.

Schacter, D. L. (1998). Illusory memories: A cognitive neuroscience analysis. In G. Mazzoni, & T. O. Nelson (Eds.), *Metacognition and cognitive neuropsychology: Monitoring and control processes* (pp. 119–138). Mahwah, NJ: Lawrence Erlbaum.

Schacter, D. L. (1997). The cognitive neuroscience of memory: Perspectives from neuroimaging research. *Philosophical Transactions of the Royal Society of London B: Biological Sciences*, *352*(1362), 1689–1695.

Schacter, D. L. (1989a). Memory. In M. I. Posner (Ed.), *Foundations of cognitive science* (pp. 683–725). Cambridge, MA: MIT Press.

Schacter, D. L. (1989b). On the relation between memory and consciousness: Dissociable interactions and conscious experience. In H. L. Roediger, & F. I. M. Craik (Eds.), *Varieties of memory and consciousness: Essays in honour of Endel Tulving* (pp. 355–389). Hillsdale, NJ: Lawrence Erlbaum.

Schacter, D. L. (1987a). Implicit memory: History and current status. *Journal of Experimental Psychology: Learning Memory and Cognition*, *13*, 501–518.

Schacter, D. L. (1987b). Memory, amnesia, and frontal lobe dysfunction: A critique and interpretation. *Psychobiology*, *15*, 21–36.

Schacter, D. L. (1985). Priming of old and new knowledge in amnesic patients and normal subjects. *Annals of the New York Academy of Science*, *444*, 41–53.

Schacter, D. (1983). Amnesia observed: Remembering and forgetting in a natural environment. *Journal of Abnormal Psychology*, *92*, 236–242.

Schacter, D. L., & Buckner, R. L. (1998). On the relations among priming, conscious recollection, and intentional retrieval: Evidence from neuroimaging research. *Neurobiology Learning and Memory, 70*(1–2), 284–303.

Schacter, D. L., Chiu, C. Y. P., & Ochsner, K. N. (1993). Implicit memory: A selective review. *Annual Review of Neuroscience, 16*, 159–182.

Schacter, D. L., Cooper, L. A., & Delaney, S. M. (1990). Implicit memory for unfamiliar objects depends on access to structural descriptions. *Journal of Experimental Psychology: Generall, 119*, 5–24.

Schacter, D. L., Cooper, L. A., Tharan, M., & Rubens, A.B. (1991). Preserved priming of novel objects in patients with memory disorders. *J of Cog Neurosci, 3*, 118–131.

Schacter, D. L., & Graf, P. (1986). Preserved learning in amnesic patients: Perspectives from research on direct priming. *Journal of Clinical and Experimental Neuropsychology, 8*(6), 727–743.

Schacter, D.L., Harbluck, J., & McLachlan, D. (1984). Retrieval without recollection. An experimental analysis of source amnesia. *Journal of Verbal Learning and Verbal Behavior, 23*, 593–611.

Schacter, D. L., Koutstaal, W., & Norman, K. A. (1996). Can cognitive neuroscience illuminate the nature of traumatic childhood memories? *Current Opinion in Neurobiology, 6*(2), 207–214.

Schacter, D. L., Norman, K. A., & Koutstaal, W. (1998). The cognitive neuroscience of constructive memory. *Annual Review of Psychology, 49*, 289–318.

Schacter, D. L., Rich, S. A., & Stampp, M. S. (1985). Remediation of memory disorders: Experimental evaluation of the spaced-retrieval technique. *Journal of Clinical and Experimental Neuropsychology, 7*(1), 79–96.

Schacter, D. L., Wagner, A. D., & Buckner, R. L. (2000). Memory systems of 1999. In E. Tulving & F. I. M. Craik (Eds.), *The Oxford Handbook of Memory* (pp. 627–643). New York: Oxford University Press.

Scharfman, H.E., Witter, M. P., & Schwarcz, R. (2000). Preface to Scharfman, H.E., Witter, M. P., & Schwarcz, R. (Eds.). The parahippocampal region. implications for neurological and psychiatric diseases. *Annals of the New York Academy of Science, 911*, ix–xii.

Schmidtke, K., & Ehmsen, L. (1998). Transient global amnesia and migraine. A case control study. *European Neurology, 40*(1), 9–14.

Schmidtke, K., Handschu, R., & Vollmer, H. (1996). Cognitive procedural learning in amnesia. *Brain Cognition, 32*(3), 441–467.

Schmitter Edgecombe, M., Fahy, J. F., Whelan, J. P., & Long, C. J. (1995). Memory remediation after severe closed head injury: Notebook training versus supportive therapy. *Journal of Consulting Clinical Psychology, 63*(3), 484–489.

Schott, B. H., Henson, R. N., Richardson-Klavehn, A., Becker, C., Thoma, V., Heinze, H. J., et al. (2005). Redefining implicit and explicit memory: The functional neuroanatomy of priming, remembering, and control of retrieval. *Proceedings of the National Academy of Sciences, 102*(4), 1257–1262.

Schott, B. H., Richardson-Klavehn, A., Henson, R. N., Becker, C., Heinze, H. J., & Duzel, E. (2006). Neuroanatomical dissociation of encoding processes related to priming and explicit memory. *Journal of Neuroscience, 26*(3), 792–800.

Schramke, C. J., & Bauer, R. M. (1997). State-dependent learning in older and younger adults. *Psychology of Aging, 12*(2), 255–262.

Schugens, M. M., & Daum, I. (1999). Long-term retention of classical eyeblink conditioning in amnesia. *Neuroreport, 10*(1), 149–152.

Scott, S.A., DeKosky, S.T., & Scheff, S.W. (1991). Volumetric atrophy of the amygdala in Alzheimer's disease: Quantitative serial reconstruction. *Neurology, 41*, 351–356.

Scoville, W.B. (1954). The limbic lobe in man. *Journal of Neurosurgery, 11*, 64–66.

Scoville, W.B., & Milner, B. (1957). Loss of recent memory after bilateral hippocampal lesions. *J Neurology, Neurosurgery Psychiatry, 20*, 11–21.

Sederberg, P.B., Kahana, M.J., Howard, M.W., Donner, E.J., Madsen, J.R. (2003). Theta and gamma oscillations during encoding predict subsequent recall. *Journal of Neuroscience, 23*, 10809–10814.

Sederberg, P. B., Schulze-Bonhage, A., Madsen, J. R., Bromfield, E. B., McCarthy, D. C., Brandt, A., et al. (2007). Hippocampal and neocortical gamma oscillations predict memory formation in humans. *Cerebral Cortex, 17*, 1190–1196.

Sedlaczek, O., Hirsch, J. G., Grips, E., Peters, C. N., Gass, A. Wöhrle, J., & Hennerici, M. (2004). Detection of delayed focal MR changes in the lateral hippocampus in transient global amnesia. *Neurology, 62*, 2165–2170.

Seltzer, B., & Benson, D. F. (1974). The temporal pattern of retrograde amnesia in Korsakoff's disease. *Neurology, 24*, 527–530.

Shallice, T., & Evans, M. E. (1978). The involvement of the frontal lobes in cognitive estimation. *Cortex, 14*, 294–303.

Sherer, M., Roebuck-Spencer, T., & Davis, L. C. (2009). Outcome assessment in traumatic brain injury clinical trials and prognostic studies. *Journal of Head Trauma Rehabilitation*, 2009 December 29. [Epub ahead of print]

Sherry, D. F., & Schacter, D. L. (1987). The evolution of multiple memory systems. *Psychological Review*, 94, 439–454.

Sherwin, B. B. (2000). Mild cognitive impairment: Potential pharmacological treatment options. *Journal of the American Geriatric Society*, 48(4), 431–441.

Shiffrin, R. M., & Schnieder, W. (1977). Controlled and automatic human information processing II: Perceptual learning, automatic attending, and a general theory. *Psychological Review*, 84, 127–190.

Shimamura, A. P. (1986). Priming effects in amnesia: Evidence for a dissociable memory function. *Quarterly Journal of Experimental Psychology*, 38A, 619–644.

Shimamura, A. P. Disorders of memory: The cognitive science perspective. In F. Boller, & J. Grafman (Eds.), *Handbook of neuropsychology*, Vol. 3 (pp. 35–73). Amsterdam: Elsevier.

Shimamura, A. P., Janowsky, J. S., & Squire, L. R. (1990). Memory for the temporal order of events in patients with frontal lobe lesions and amnesic patients. *Neuropsychologia*, 28(8), 803–813.

Shimamura, A. P., Jernigan, T. L., & Squire, L. R. (1988). Korsakoff's syndrome: Radiologic (CT) findings and neuropsychological correlates. *Journal of Neuroscience*, 8, 4400–4410.

Shimamura, A. P., & Squire, L. R. (1987). A neuropsychological study of fact memory and source amnesia. *Journal of Experimental Psychology Learning Memory and Cognition*, 13, 464–473.

Shimamura, A. P., & Squire, L. R. (1986). Memory and metamemory: A study of the feeling-of-knowing phenomenon in amnesic patients. *Journal of Experimental Psychology, Learning, Memory, and Cognition*, 12, 452–460.

Shimamura, A. P., & Squire, L. R. (1984). Paired-associate learning and priming effects in amnesia: A neuropsychological study. *Journal of Experimental Psychology: General*, 113, 556–570.

Shuping, J. R., Rollinson, R. D., & Toole, J. F. (1980). Transient global amnesia. *Annals of Neurology*, 7, 281–285.

Shuren, J. E., Jacobs, D. H., & Heilman, K. M. (1997). Diencephalic temporal order amnesia. *Journal of Neurology, Neurosurgery, and Psychiatry*, 62(2), 163–168.

Sidman, M., Stoddard, L. T., & Mohr, J. P. (1968). Some additional observations of immediate memory in a patient with bilateral hippocampal lesions. *Neuropsychologia*, 6, 245–254.

Small, I. F., Milstein, V., & Small, J. G. (1981). Relationship between clinical and cognitive change with bilateral and unilateral ECT. *Biological Psychiatry*, 16, 793–794.

Smith, M. L. (1989). Memory disorders associated with temporal-lobe lesions. In F. Boller., & J. Grafman J. (Eds.), *Handbook of neuropsychology* Vol. 3 (pp. 91–106). Amsterdam: Elsevier.

Smith, E. E., & Jonides, J. (1998). Neuroimaging analyses of human working memory. *Proceedings of the National Academy of Sciences USA*, 95(20), 12061–12068.

Sobin, C., Sackeim, H. A., Prudic, J., Devanand, D. P., Moody, B. J., & McElhiney, M. C. (1995). Predictors of retrograde amnesia following ECT. *American Journal of Psychiatry*, 152(7), 995–1001.

Sohlberg, M. M., & Mateer, C. A. (1989). Training use of compensatory memory books: A three stage behavioral approach. *Journal of Clinical and Experimental Neuropsychology*, 11(6), 871–891.

Spaniol, J., Davidson, P. S. R., Kim, A. S. N., Han, H., Moscovitch, M., & Grady, C. L. (2009). Event-related fMRI studies of episodic encoding and retrieval: Meta-analyses using activation likelihood estimation. *Neuropsychologia*, 47(8–9), 1765–1779.

Speedie, L., & Heilman, K. M. (1982). Amnesic disturbance following infarction of the left dorsomedial nucleus of the thalamus. *Neuropsychologia*, 20, 597–604.

Speedie, L., & Heilman, K. M. (1983). Anterograde memory deficits for visuospatial material after infarction of the right thalamus. *Archives of Neurology*, 40, 183–186.

Spiegler, B. J., & Mishkin, M. (1981). Evidence for the sequential participation of inferior temporal cortex and amygdala in the acquisition of stimulus-reward associations. *Behavioral Brain Research*, 3, 303–317.

Spencer, K. M. (2000). On the search for the neurophysiological manifestation of recollective experience. *Psychophysiology*, 37, 494–506.

Sperling, R., Chua, E., Cocchiarella, A., Rand-Giovannetti, E., Poldrack, R., Schacter, D. L., et al. (2003). Putting names to faces: Successful encoding of associative memories activates the anterior hippocampal formation. *Neuroimage*, 20(2), 1400–1410.

Sprofkin, B. E., & Sciarra, D. (1952). Korsakoff's psychosis associated with cerebral tumors. *Neurology*, 2, 427–434.

Squire, L. R. (1987). *Memory and brain*. New York: Oxford University Press.

Squire, L. R. (1984). ECT and memory dysfunction. In B. Lerer, R. D. Weiner, & R. H. Belmaker

(Eds.), *ECT: Basic mechanisms* (pp. 156–163). Washington, DC: American Psychiatric Press.

Squire, L. R. (1982a). The neuropsychology of human memory. *Annual Review of Neuroscience*, 5, 241–273.

Squire, L. R. (1982b). Comparison between forms of amnesia: Some deficits are unique to Korsakoff syndrome. *Journal of Experimental Psychology: Learning, Memory, and Cognition*, 8, 560–571.

Squire, L. R. (1981). Two forms of human amnesia: An analysis of forgetting. *Journal of Neuroscience*, 1, 635–640.

Squire, L. R., & Alvarez, P. (1995). Retrograde amnesia and memory consolidation: A neurobiological perspective. *Current Opinion in Neurobiology*, 5, 169–177.

Squire, L. R., Amaral, D. G., Zola-Morgan, S., Kritchevsky, M., & Press, G. (1989). Description of brain injury in the amnesic patient N.A. based on magnetic resonance imaging. *Experimental Neurology*, 105, 23–35.

Squire, L. R., & Chace, P. M. (1975). Memory functions six to nine months after electroconvulsive therapy. *Archives of General Psychiatry*, 32, 1157–1164.

Squire, L. R., Chace, P. M., & Slater, P. C. (1976). Retrograde amnesia following electroconvulsive therapy. *Nature*, 260, 775–777.

Squire, L. R., & Cohen, N. J. (1984). Human memory and amnesia. In G. Lynch, J. L. McGaugh, & N. M. Weinberger (Eds.), *Neurobiology of learning and memory* (pp. 3–64). New York: Guilford Press.

Squire, L. R., Cohen, N. J., & Nadel, L. (1984a). The medial temporal region and memory consolidation: A new hypothesis. In H. Weingartner, & E. Parker (Eds.), *Memory consolidation*. Hillsdale, NJ: Lawrence Erlbaum.

Squire, L. R., Cohen, N. J., & Zouzounis, J. A. (1984b). Preserved memory in retrograde amnesia: Sparing of a recently acquired skill. *Neuropsychologia*, 22(2), 145–152.

Squire, L. R., & Fox, M. M. (1980). Assessment of remote memory: Validation of the television test by repeated testing during a seven-day period. *Behavior Research Methods and Instrumentation*, 12, 583–586.

Squire, L. R., Haist, F., & Shimamura, A. P. (1989). The neurology of memory: Quantitative assessment of retrograde amnesia in two groups of amnesic patients. *Journal of Neuroscience*, 9, 828–839.

Squire, L. R., & Knowlton, B. J. (1995). Learning about categories in the absence of memory. *Proceedings of the National Academy of Sciences USA*, 92(26), 12470–12474.

Squire, L. R., & McKee, R. D. (1993). Declarative and nondeclarative memory in opposition: When prior events influence amnesic patients more than normal subjects. *Memory & Cognition*, 21(4), 424–430.

Squire, L. R., & Moore, R. Y. (1979). Dorsal thalamic lesion in a noted case of chronic memory dysfunction. *Annals of Neurology*, 6, 503–506.

Squire, L. R., Nadel, L., & Slater, P. C. (1981). Anterograde amnesia and memory for temporal order. *Neuropsychologia*, 19, 141–145.

Squire, L. R., & Shimamura, A. P. (1986). Characterizing amnesic patients for neurobehavioral study. *Behavioral Neuroscience*, 100, 866–877.

Squire, L. R., & Slater, P. C. (1983). Electroconvulsive therapy and complaints of memory dysfunction: A prospective three-year follow-up study. *British Journal of Psychiatry*, 142, 1–8.

Squire, L. R., Slater, P., & Chace, P. M. (1975). Retrograde amnesia: Temporal gradient in very long-term memory following electroconvulsive therapy. *Science*, 187, 77–79.

Squire, L. R., Slater, P. C., & Miller, P. (1981). Retrograde amnesia following ECT: Long-term follow-up studies. *Archives of General Psychiatry*, 38, 89–95.

Squire, L. R., Stark, C. E., & Clark, R. E. (2004). The medial temporal lobe. *Annual Review of Neuroscience*, 27, 279–306.

Squire, L. R., Wetzel, C. D., & Slater, P. C. (1978). Anterograde amnesia following ECT: An analysis of the beneficial effect of partial information. *Neuropsychologia*, 16, 339–347.

Squire, L. R., Wixted, J. T., & Clark, R. E. (2007). Recognition memory and the medial temporal lobe: A new perspective. *Nature Reviews Neuroscience*, 8(11), 872–883.

Squire, L. R., & Zola, S. M. (1996). Ischemic brain damage and memory impairment: A commentary. *Hippocampus*, 6(5), 546–552.

Squire, L. R., & Zola, S. M. (1998). Episodic memory, semantic memory, and amnesia. *Hippocampus*, 8(3), 205–211.

Squire, L. R., & Zola-Morgan, S. (1991). The MTL memory system. *Science*, 253, 1380–1386.

Squire, L. R., Zola-Morgan, S., & Chen, K. (1988). Human amnesia and animal models of amnesia: Performance of amnesic patients on tests designed for the monkey. *Behavioral Neuroscience*, 102, 210–211.

Stark, C. E. L., Squire, L. R. (2000). fMRI activity in the MTL during recognition memory as a function of study-test interval. *Hippocampus*, *10*, 329–337.

Steinvorth, S., Corkin, S., & Halgren, E. (2006). Ecphory of autobiographical memories: An fMRI study of recent and remote memory retrieval. *Neuroimage, 30*(1), 285–298.

Steinvorth, S., Levine, B., & Corkin, S. (2005). Medial temporal lobe structures are needed to re-experience remote autobiographical memories: Evidence from H.M., & W.R. *Neuropsychologia, 43*, 479–496.

Stenberg, G. (2000). Semantic processing without conscious identification: Evidence from event-related potentials. *Journal of Experimental Psychology: Learning, Memory, and Cognition, 26*, 973–1004.

Stern, C. E., Corkin, S., Gonzalez, R. G., Guimaraes, A. R., Baker, J. R., Jennings, P. J., et al. (1996). The hippocampal formation participates in novel picture encoding: Evidence from functional magnetic resonance imaging. *Proceedings of the National Academy of Sciences USA, 93*, 8660–8665.

Stern, R. A., Singer, E. A., Duke, L. M., & Singer, N. G. (1994). The Boston qualitative scoring system for the Rey-Osterrieth complex figure: Description and interrater reliability. *Clinical Neuropsychology, 8*, 309–322.

Stuss, D. T, Kaplan, E. F., Benson, D. F., Weir, W. S., Chiulli, S., & Sarazin, F. F. (1982). Evidence for the involvement of orbitofrontal cortex in memory functions: An interference effect. *Journal of Comparative & Physiological Psychology, 96*, 913–925.

Sullivan, E., Sagar, H., Gabrieli, J., Corkin, S., & Growdon, H. (1985). Sequencing deficits in Parkinson's disease. *Journal of Clinical and Experimental Neuropsychology, 2*, 160.

Suzuki, W. A. (2009). Perception and the medial temporal lobe: Evaluating the current evidence. *Neuron, 61*(5), 657–666.

Suzuki, W. A., & Amaral, D. G. (1994). Perirhinal and parahippocampal cortices of the macaque monkey: Cortical afferents. *Journal of Comparative Neurology, 350*, 497–533.

Suzuki, W. I., & Eichenbaum, H. (2000). The neurophysiology of memory. In H. E. Scharfman, M. P. Witter, & R. Schwarcz (Eds.), *The Annals of the New York Academy of Sciences* Vol. 911: *The parahippocampal region. Implications for neurological and psychiatric diseases* (pp. 175–191). New York: New York Academy of Sciences.

Svoboda, E., & Levine, B. (2009). The effects of rehearsal on the functional neuroanatomy of episodic autobiographical and semantic remembering: A functional magnetic resonance imaging study. *Journal of Neuroscience, 29*(10), 3073–3082.

Swanson, L. (1987). The hypothalamus. In A. Bjorklund, T. Holfelt, & L. Swanson (Eds.), *Handbook of chemical neuroanatomy: Integrate systems of the CNS. Part I - Hypothalamus, hippocampus, amygdala, retina* Vol. 5 (pp. 1–124). Amsterdam: Elsevier.

Swanson, L. W., & Cowan, W. M. (1979). An autoradiographic study of the organization of the efferent connections of the hippocampal formation in the rat. *Journal of Comparative Neurology, 172*, 49–84.

Sweet, W. H., Talland, G. A., & Ervin, F. R. (1959). Loss of recent memory following section of fornix. *Transactions of the American Neurological Association, 84*, 76–82.

Sziklas, V., & Petrides, M. (1998). Memory and the region of the mammillary bodies. *Progress in Neurobiology, 54*, 55–70.

Takahashi, N., Kawamura, M., Shiota, J., Kasahata, N., & Hirayama, K. (1997). Pure topographic disorientation due to right retrosplenial lesion. *Neurology, 49*, 464–469.

Takashima, A., Nieuwenhuis, I. L. C., Jensen, O., Talamini, L. M., Rijpkema, M., & Fernandez, G. (2009). Shift from hippocampal to neocortical centered retrieval network with consolidation. *Journal of Neuroscience, 29*(32), 10087–10093.

Takashima, A., Petersson, K. M., Rutters, F., Tendolkar, I., Jensen, O., Zwarts, M. J., et al. (2006). Declarative memory consolidation in humans: A prospective functional magnetic resonance imaging study. *Proceedings of the National Academy of Sciences USA,103*(3), 756–761.

Takayama, Y., Kamo, H., Ohkawa, Y., Akiguchi, I., & Kimura, J. (1991). A case of retrosplenial amnesia. *Rinsho Shinkeigaku, 31*, 331–333.

Talland, G. (1965). *Deranged memory*. New York: Academic Press.

Talland, G., Sweet, W. H., & Ballantine, H. T. (1967). Amnesic syndrome with anterior communicating artery aneurysm. *Journal of Nervous and Mental Disease, 145*, 179–192.

Tanaka, Y., Miyazawa, Y., Akaoka, F., & Yamada, T. (1997). Amnesia following damage to the mammillary bodies. *Neurology, 48*, 160–165.

Tanaka, Y., Miyazawa, Y., Hashimoto, R., Nakano, I., & Obayashi, T. (1999). Postencephalitic focal retrograde amnesia after bilateral anterior temporal lobe damage. *Neurology, 53*(2), 344–350.

Tate, R. L. (1997). Beyond one-bun, two-shoe: Recent advances in the psychological rehabilitation of memory disorders after acquired brain injury. *Brain Injury, 11*(12), 907–918.

Taylor, K. I., Moss, H. E., Stamatakis, E. A., & Tyler, L. K., 2006. Binding crossmodal object features in perirhinal cortex. *Proceedings of the National Academy of Sciences USA, 21,* 8239–8244.

Teuber, H. -L., Milner, B., & Vaughan, H. G. (1968). Persistent anterograde amnesia after stab wound to the basal brain. *Neuropsychologia, 6,* 267–282.

Thal, L. J., Fuld, P. A., Masure, D. M., & Sharpless, N. S. (1983). Oral physostigmine and lecithin improves memory in Alzheimer's disease. *Annals of Neurology, 113,* 491–496.

Thoene, A. I., & Glisky, E. L. (1995). Learning of name-face associations in memory impaired patients: A comparison of different training procedures. *Journal of the International Neuropsychological Society, 1*(1), 29–38.

Thomson, D. M., & Tulving, E. (1970). Associative encoding and retrieval: Weak and strong cues. *Journal of Experimental Psychology, 86,* 255–262.

Thornton, J. A., Rothblat, L. A., & Murray, E. A. (1997). Rhinal cortex removal produces amnesia for preoperatively learned discrimination problems but fails to disrupt postoperative acquisition and retention in rhesus monkeys. *Journal of Neuroscience, 17,* 8536–8549.

Toledo, M., Pujadas, R., Grivé, E., Álvarez-Sabin, J., Quintana, M., & Rovira A. (2008). Lack of evidence for arterial ischemia in transient global amnesia. *Stroke, 39,* 476–479.

Tosi, L., & Righetti, C. A. (1997). Transient global amnesia and migraine in young people. *Clinical Neurology and Neurosurgery, 99*(1), 63–65.

Tranel, D., & Hyman, B. T. (1990). Neuropsychological correlates of bilateral amygdala damage. *Archives of Neurology, 47,* 349–355.

Tranel, D., Damasio, A. R., Damasio, H., & Brandt, J. P. (1994). Sensorimotor skill learning in amnesia: Additional evidence for the neural basis of nondeclarative memory. *Learning & Memory, 1*(3), 165–179.

Tulving, E. (1998). Neurocognitive processes of human memory. In C. von Euler, I. Lundberg, & R. Llinas (Eds.), *Basic mechanisms in cognition and language* (pp. 261–281). Amsterdam: Elsevier.

Tulving, E. (1983). *Elements of episodic memory.* New York: Oxford University Press.

Tulving, E. (1972). Episodic and semantic memory. In E. Tulving, & W. Donaldson (Eds.), *Organization of memory* (pp. 381–403). New York: Academic Press.

Tulving, E. (2002). Episodic memory: From mind to brain. *Annual Review of Psychology, 53,* 1–25.

Tulving, E., Kapur, S., Craik, F. I., Moscovitch, M., & Houle, S. (1994). Hemispheric encoding/retrieval asymmetry in episodic memory: Positron emission tomography findings. *Proceedings of the National Academy of Sciences USA, 91*(6), 2016–2020.

Tulving, E., & Markowitsch, H. J. (1997). Memory beyond the hippocampus. *Current Opinion in Neurobiology, 7*(2), 209–216.

Tulving, E., Markowitsch, H. J., Kapur, S., Habib, R., & Houle, S. (1994). Novelty encoding networks in the human brain: Positron emission tomography data. *Neuroreport, 5*(18), 2525–2528.

Tulving, E., & Pearlstone, Z. (1966). Availability versus accessibility of information in memory for words. *Journal of Verbal Learning and Verbal Behavior, 5,* 381–391.

Tulving, E., & Schacter, D. L. (1990). Priming and human memory systems. *Science, 247*(4940), 301–306.

Tulving, E., Schacter, D., & Stark, H. A. (1982). Priming effects in word-fragment completion are independent of recognition memory. *Journal of Experimental Psychology, Learning, Memory, and Cognition, 8,* 336–342.

Turk-Browne, N. B., Yi, D. J., & Chun, M. M. (2006). Linking implicit and explicit memory: Common encoding factors and shared representations. *Neuron, 49*(6), 917–927.

Uncapher, M. R., & Wagner, A. D. (2009). Posterior parietal cortex and episodic encoding: Insights from fMRI subsequent memory effects and dual-attention theory. *Neurobiology of Learning and Memory, 91*(2), 139–154.

Ungerleider, L. G. (1995). Functional brain imaging studies of cortical mechanisms for memory. *Science, 270*(5237), 769–775.

Ungerleider, L. G., Courtney, S. M., & Haxby, J. V. (1998). A neural system for human visual working memory. *Proceedings of the National Academy of Sciences USA, 95*(3), 883–890.

Usher, J. A., & Neisser, U. (1993). Childhood amnesia and the beginnings of memory for four early life events. *Journal of Experimental Psychology: General, 122*(2), 155–165.

Vaidya, C. J., Gabrieli, J. D., Verfaellie, M., Fleischman, D., & Askari, N. (1998). Font-specific priming following global amnesia and occipital lobe damage. *Neuropsychology, 12*(2), 183–192.

Vaidya, C. J., Gabrieli, J. D. E., Demb, J. B., Keane, M. M., & Wetzel, L. C. (1996). Impaired priming on the general knowledge task in amnesia. *Neuropsychology, 10,* 529–537.

Vaidya, C. J., Gabrieli, J. D. E., Keane, M. M., Monti, L. A., Gutierrez-Rivas, H., & Zarella, M. M. (1997). Evidence for multiple mechanisms of conceptual priming on implicit memory tests. *Journal of Experimental Psychology, Learning, Memory, and Cognition, 23*(6), 1324–1343.

Valenstein, E., Bowers, D., Verfaellie, M., Heilman, K. M., Day, A., & Watson, R. T. (1986). Retrosplenial amnesia. *Brain, 110,* 1631–1646.

Valenstein, E., Bowers, D., Verfaellie, M., Heilman, K. M., Day, A., & Watson, R. T. (1987). Retrosplenial amnesia. *Brain, 110,*1631–1646.

Van Hoesen, G. W. (1985). Neural systems of the non-human primate forebrain implicated in memory. *Annals of the New York Academy of Sciences, 444,* 97–112.

Van Hoesen, G. W., & Pandya, D. N. (1975). Some connections of the entorhinal (area 28) and perirhinal (area 35) cortices of the rhesus monkey. I. Temporal lobe afferents. *Brain Research, 95,* 25–38.

Van Hoesen, G. W., Pandya, D. N., & Butters, N. (1972). Cortical afferents to the entorhinal cortex of the rhesus monkey. *Science, 175,* 1471–1473.

Van Hoesen, G. W., Rosene, D. L., & Mesulam, M. -M. (1979). Subicular input from temporal cortex in the rhesus monkey. *Science, 205,* 608–610.

Vann, S. D., & Aggleton, J. P. (2004). The mammillary bodies: Two memory systems in one? *Nature Reviews Neuroscience, 5,* 35–44.

Veazey, R. B., Amaral, D. G., & Cowan, W. M. (1982). The morphology and connections of the posterior hypothalamus in the cynomolgus monkey (*Maccaca fascicularis*). II. Efferent connections. *Journal of Comparative Neurology, 207,* 135–156.

Verfaellie, M., Bauer, R. M., & Bowers, D. (1991). Autonomic and behavioral evidence of "implicit" memory in amnesia. *Brain and Cognition, 15,* 10–25.

Verfaellie, M., Koseff, P., & Alexander, M. P. (2000). Acquisition of novel semantic information in amnesia: Effects of lesion location. *Neuropsychologia, 38,* 484–492.

Vargha-Khadem, F., Gadian, D. G., Watkins, K. E., Connelly, A., Van Paesschen, W., & Mishkin, M. (1997). Differential effects of early hippocampal pathology on episodic and semantic memory. *Science, 277*(5324), 376–380.

Verfaellie, M., & Cermak, L. S. (1999). Perceptual fluency as a cue for recognition judgments in amnesia. *Neuropsychology, 13*(2), 198–205.

Verfaellie, M., & Cermak, L. S. (1994). Acquisition of generic memory in amnesia. *Cortex, 30*(2), 293–303.

Verfaellie, M., & Cermak, L. S. (1991). Neuropsychological issues in amnesia. In J. L. Martinez, & R. P. Kesner (Eds.), *Learning and memory: A biological view* (pp. 467–497). New York: Elsevier.

Verfaellie, M., Koseff, P., & Alexander, M. P. (2000). Acquisition of novel semantic information in amnesia: Effects of lesion location. *Neuropsychologia, 38*(4), 484–492.

Viard, A., Piolino, P., Desgranges, B., Chetelat, G., Lebreton, K., Landeau, B., et al. (2007). Hippocampal activation for autobiographical memories over the entire lifetime in healthy aged subjects: An fMRI study. *Cerebral Cortex, 17*(10), 2453–2467.

Victor, M., Adams, R. D., & Collins, G. H. (1971). *The Wernicke-Korsakoff syndrome.* Philadelphia, PA: F. A. Davis Co.

Victor, M., Adams, R. D., & Collins, G. H. (1989). *The Wernicke-Korsakoff syndrome and related neurologic disorders due to alcoholism and malnutrition* (2nd ed.). Philadelphia, PA: Davis.

Victor, M., & Agamanolis, D. (1990). Amnesia due to lesions confined to the hippocampus: A clinical-pathologic study. *Journal of Cognitive Neuroscience, 2,* 246–257.

Vilkki, J. (1985). Amnesic syndromes after surgery of anterior communicating artery aneurysms. *Cortex, 21,* 431–444.

Viskontas, I. V., McAndrews, M. P., & Moscovtich, M. (2000). Remote episodic memory deficits in patients with unilateral temporal lobe epilepsy and excisions. *Journal of Neuroscience, 20,* 5853–5857.

Visser, A. M., van Doornum, G. J., Cornelissen, J. J., & van den Bent, M. J. (2005). Severe amnesia due to HHV-6 encephalitis after allogenic stem cell transplantation. *European Neurology, 54,* 233–234.

Vitay, J., & Hamker, F. H. (2008). Sustained activities and retrieval in a computational model of the perirhinal cortex. *Journal of Cognitive Neuroscience, 20,* 1993–2005.

Volpe, B. T., & Hirst, W. (1983). Amnesia following the rupture and repair of an anterior communicating artery aneurysm. *Journal of Neurology, Neurosurgery, and Psychiatry, 46,* 704–709.

von Bechterew, W. (1900). Demonstration eines gehirns mit zerstörung der vorderen und inneren theile der hirnrinde beider schläfenlappen. *Neurologish Zentralblatt, 19,* 990–991.

von Cramon, D. Y., Hebel, N., & Schuri, U. (1985). A contribution to the anatomical basis of thalamic amnesia. *Brain, 108,* 993–1008.

von Cramon, D. Y., Hebel, N., & Schuri, U. (1988). Verbal memory and learning in unilateral posterior cerebral infarction. A report on 30 cases. *Brain, 111*, 1061–1077.

von Cramon, D. Y., & Schuri, U. (1992). The septo-hippocampal pathways and their relevance to human memory: A case report. *Cortex, 28*,411–422.

Voss, J. L., & Paller, K. A. (2008). Brain substrates of implicit and explicit memory: The importance of concurrently acquired neural signals of both memory types. *Neuropsychologia, 46*(13), 3021–3029.

Wagner, A. D., Desmond, J. E., Glover, G. H., & Gabrieli, J. D. (1998). Prefrontal cortex and recognition memory. Functional-MRI evidence for context-dependent retrieval processes. *Brain, 121*(Pt. 10), 1985–2002.

Wagner, A. D., Poldrack, R. A., Eldridge, L. L., Desmond, J. E., Glover, G. H., & Gabrieli, J. D. (1998). Material-specific lateralization of prefrontal activation during episodic encoding and retrieval. *Neuroreport, 9*(16), 3711–3717.

Wagner, A. D., Schacter, D. L., Rotte, M., Koutstaal, W., Maril, A., Dale, A. M., et al. (1998). Verbal memory encoding: Brain activity predicts subsequent remembering and forgetting. *Science, 281*, 1188–1191.

Wainwright, M. S., Martin, P. L., Morse, R. P., Lacaze, M., Provenzale, J. M., Coleman, R. E., et al. (2001). Human herpesvirus 6 limbic encephalitis after stem cell transplantation. *Annals of Neurology, 50*, 612–619.

Wan, H., Aggleton, J. P., & Brown, M. W. (1999). Different contributions of the hippocampus and perirhinal cortex to recognition memory. *Journal of Neuroscience, 19*, 1142–1148.

Warrington, E. K. (1985). A disconnection analysis of amnesia. *Annals of the New York Academy of Sciences, 444*, 72–77.

Warrington, E. K., & Weiskrantz, L. (1978). Further analysis of the prior learning effect in amnesic patients. *Neuropsychologia, 16*, 169–177.

Warrington, E. K., & Weiskrantz, L. (1974). The effect of prior learning on subsequent retention in amnesic patients. *Neuropsychologia, 12*, 419–428.

Warrington, E. K., & Weiskrantz, L. (1973). An analysis of short-term and long-term memory defects in man. In J. A. Deutsch (Ed.), *The physiological basis of memory*. New York: Academic Press.

Warrington, E. K., & Weiskrantz, L. (1970). The amnesic syndrome: Consolidation or retrieval? *Nature, 228*, 628–630.

Warrington, E. K., & Weiskrantz, L. (1982). Amnesia: A disconnection syndrome? *Neuropsychologia, 20*, 233–248.

Weingartner, H., Grafman, J., Boutelle, W., Kaye, W., & Martin, P. (1983). Forms of cognitive failure. *Science, 221*, 380–382.

Weiskrantz, L., & Warrington, E. K. (1979). Conditioning in amnesic patients. *Neuropsychologia, 17*(2), 187–194.

Welch, C. A. (1982). The relative efficacy of unilateral nondominant and bilateral stimulation. *Psychopharmotherapy Bulletin, 18*, 68–70.

Westwater, H., McDowall, J., Siegert, R., Mossman, S., & Abernethy, D. (1998). Implicit learning in Parkinson's disease: Evidence from a verbal version of the serial reaction time task. *Journal of Clinical and Experimental Neuropsychology, 20*(3), 413–418.

Wetzel, C. D., & Squire, L. R. (1982). Cued recall in anterograde amnesia. *Brain and Language, 15*, 70–81.

Wetzler, S. E., & Sweeney, J. A. (1986). Childhood amnesia: A conceptualization in cognitive-psychological terms. *Journal of the American Psychoanalytical Association, 34*(3), 663–685.

Whitehouse, P. J., Price, D. L., Clark, A. W., Coyle, J. T., & DeLong, M. R. (1981). Alzheimer disease: Evidence for selective loss of cholinergic neurons in the nucleus basilis. *Annals of Neurology, 10*, 122–126.

Whitlock, J. R., Sutherland, R. J., Witter, M. P., Moser, M. B., & Moser, E. I. (2008). Navigating from hippocampus to parietal cortex. *Proceedings of the National Academy of Sciences USA, 105*(39), 14755–14762.

Whitty, C. D., & Zangwill, O. L. (Eds.) (1977). *Amnesia*. London: Butterworths.

Wickelgren, W. A. (1979). Chunking and consolidation: A theoretical synthesis of semantic networks, configuring in condition, S-R versus cognitive learning, normal forgetting, the amnesic syndrome, and the hippocampal arousal system. *Psychological Review, 86*, 44–60.

Wickens, D. D. (1970). Encoding strategies of words: An empirical approach to meaning. *Psychological Review, 22*, 1–15.

Williams, M., & Pennybacker, J. (1954). Memory disturbances in third ventricle tumours. *Journal of Neurology, Neurosurgery, and Psychiatry, 17*, 115–123.

Willingham, D. B. (1998). A neuropsychological theory of motor skill learning. *Psychological Review, 105*(3), 558–584.

Wilson, B. A. (1999). Memory rehabilitation in brain-injured people. In D. T. Stuss, &

G. Winocur (Eds.), *Cognitive neurorehabilitation* (pp. 333–346). New York: Cambridge University Press.

Wilson, B. A. (2000). Compensating for cognitive deficits following brain injury. *Neuropsychology Review, 10*(4), 233–243.

Wilson, B. A., Evans, J. J., Emslie, H., & Malinek, V. (1997). Evaluation of NeuroPage: A new memory aid. *Journal of Neurology, Neurosurgery, and Psychiatry, 63*(1), 113–115.

Wilson, M.A. and McNaughton, B.L. (1994) Reactivation of hippocampal ensemble memories during sleep. Science 265, 676–679.

Winocur, G. (1990). Anterograde and retrograde amnesia in rats with dorsal hippocampal or dorsomedial thalamic lesions. *Behavioral Brain Research, 38*(2), 145–154.

Winocur, G. (1984). Memory localization in the brain. In L. R. Squire, & N. Butters (Eds.), *Neuropsychology of memory* (pp. 122–133). New York: Guilford Press.

Winocur, G., Kinsbourne, M., & Moscovitch, M. (1981). The effect of cueing on release from proactive interference in Korsakoff amnesic patients. *Journal Experimental Psychology: Human Learning and Memory, 7*, 56–65.

Winocur, G., & Moscovitch, M. (1999). Anterograde and retrograde amnesia after lesions to frontal cortex in rats. *Journal of Neuroscience, 19*(21), 9611–9617.

Winocur, G., Oxbury, S., Roberts, R., Agnetti, V., & Davis, C. (1984). Amnesia in a patient with bilateral lesions to the thalamus. *Neuropsychologia, 22*, 123–143.

Winograd, T. (1975). Understanding natural language. In D. Bobrow, & A. Collins (Eds.), *Representation and understanding*. New York: Academic Press.

Witherspoon, D., & Moscovitch, M. (1989). Stochastic independence between two implicit memory tests. *Journal of Experimental Psychology: Learning, Memory, and Cognition, 15*, 22–30.

Witter, M. P., & Moser, E. I. (2006). Spatial representation and the architecture of the entorhinal cortex. *Trends in Neuroscience, 29*(12), 671–678.

Witter, M. P., Naber, P.A., van Haeften, T., Machielsen, W. C., Rombouts, S. A., Barkhof, F., et al. (2000). Cortico-hippocampal communication by way of parallel parahippocampal-subicular pathways. *Hippocampus, 10*, 398–410.

Wixted, J. T. (2007). Dual-process theory and signal-detection theory of recognition memory. *Psychological Review, 114*, 152–176.

Wolbers, T., & Büchel, C. (2005). Dissociable retrosplenial and hippocampal contributions to successful formation of survey representations. *Journal of Neuroscience, 25*, 3333–3340.

Womack, K. B., Heilman, K. M. (2003). Tolterodine and memory: Dry but forgetful. *Archives of Neurology, 60*, 771–773.

Wood, F., Ebert, V., & Kinsbourne, M. (1982). The episodic-semantic memory distinction in memory and amnesia: Clinical and experimental observations. In L. S. Cermak (Ed.), *Human memory and amnesia* (pp. 167–194). Hillsdale, NJ: Lawrence Erlbaum.

Woodruff Pak, D. S. (1993). Eyeblink classical conditioning in H.M.: Delay and trace paradigms. *Behavioral Neuroscience, 107*(6), 911–925.

Woolfenden, A. R., O'Brien, M. W., Schwartzberg, R. E., Norbash, A. M., & Tong, D. C. (1997). Diffusion-weighted MRI in transient global amnesia precipitated by cerebral angiography. *Stroke, 28*, 2311–2314.

Woolsey, R. M., & Nelson, J. S. (1975). Asymptomatic destruction of the fornix in man. *Archives of Neurology, 32*, 566–568.

Wright, R. A., Boeve, B. F., & Malec, J. F. (1999). Amnesia after basal forebrain damage due to anterior communicating artery rupture. *Journal of Clinical Neuroscience, 6*, 511–515.

Xuereb, J. H., Perry, R. H., Candy, J. M., Perry, E. K., Marshall, E., & Bonham, J. R. (1991). Nerve cell loss in the thalamus in Alzheimer's disease and Parkinson's disease. *Brain, 114*, 1363–1379.

Yamashita, H. (1993). Perceptual-motor learning in amnesic patients with MTL lesions. *Perceptual and Motor Skills, 77*(3 Pt. 2), 1311–1314.

Yasuda, K., Watanabe, O., & Ono, Y. (1997). Dissociation between semantic and autobiographic memory: A case report. *Cortex, 33*(4), 623–638.

Yasuno, F., Hirata, M., Takimoto, H., Taniguchi, M., Nakagawa, Y., Ikejiri, Y., et al. (1999). Retrograde temporal order amnesia resulting from damage to the fornix. *Journal of Neurology, Neurosurgery, and Psychiatry, 67*(1), 102–105.

Yonelinas, A. P. (2002). The nature of recollection and familiarity: A review of 30 years of research. *Journal of Memory and Language, 46*, 441–517.

Zalesak, M., & Heckers, S. (2009). The role of the hippocampus in transitive inference. *Psychiatry Research: Neuroimaging, 172*(1), 24–30.

Zencius, A., Wesolowski, M. D., Krankowski, T., & Burke, W. H. (1991). Memory notebook training with traumatically brain-injured clients. *Brain Injury, 5*(3), 321–325.

Zola-Morgan, S., Cohen, N. J., & Squire, L. R. (1983). Recall of remote episodic memory in amnesia. *Neuropsychologia, 21*, 487–500.

Zola-Morgan, S., Squire, L. R., Alvarez Royo, P., & Clower, R. P. (1991). Independence of memory functions and emotional behavior: Separate contributions of the hippocampal formation and the amygdala. *Hippocampus*, *1*(2), 207–220.

Zola, S. M. (1998). Memory, amnesia, and the issue of recovered memory: Neurobiological aspects. *Clinical Psychology Review*, *18*(8), 915–932.

Zola-Morgan, S., Squire, L. R., & Amaral, D. G. (1986). Human amnesia and the medial temporal region: Enduring memory impairment following a bilateral lesion limited to field CA1 of the hippocampus. *Journal of Neuroscience*, *6*, 2950–2967.

Zola-Morgan, S., Squire, L. R., & Amaral, D. G. (1989a). Lesions of the amygdala that spare adjacent cortical regions do not impair memory or exacerbate the impairment following lesions of the hippocampal formation. *Journal of Neuroscience*, *9*, 1922–1936.

Zola-Morgan, S., Squire, L. R., Amaral, D. G., & Suzuki, W. A. (1989b). Lesions of perirhinal and parahippocampal cortex that spare the amygdala and hippocampal formation produce severe memory impairment. *Journal of Neuroscience*, *9*, 4355–4370.

Zola-Morgan, S., & Squire, L. R. (1990a). The neuropsychology of memory: Parallel findings in human and nonhuman primates. *Annals of the New York Academy of Sciences*, *608*, 434–450.

Zola-Morgan, S., & Squire, L. R. (1990b). The primate hippocampal formation: Evidence for a time-limited role in memory storage. *Science*, *250*, 288–290.

Zola-Morgan, S., & Squire, L. R. (1986). Memory impairment in monkeys following lesions restricted to the hippocampus. *Behavioral Neuroscience*, *100*, 155–160.

Zola-Morgan S., & Squire, L. R. (1984). Preserved learning in monkeys with medial temporal lesions: Sparing of motor and cognitive skills. *Journal of Neuroscience*, *4*, 1072–1085.

Zola-Morgan, S., & Squire, L. R. (1983). Intact perceptuo-motor skill learning in monkeys with MTL lesions. *Society for Neuroscience Abstracts*, *9*, 27.

17

Neuropsychology of Dementia

DAVID KNOPMAN AND OLA SELNES

Dementia is a syndrome defined by a nonacute decline in cognition that interferes with functioning in everyday living (American Psychiatric Association, 1994). Dementia, in contrast to disorders defined by deficits in only one cognitive or behavioral domain, is diagnosed when there are deficits in multiple domains. Memory dysfunction, abnormalities in speech/language, abnormalities in visuospatial function, deficits in abstract reasoning/executive function, and mood/personality changes are the principal manifestations of the dementia syndrome. The most common dementia, Alzheimer disease (AD), almost invariably includes striking early deficits in new learning and recent memory. Alzheimer disease has an insidious onset and virtually always exhibits a declining course. Other common dementing disorders may have prominent dysfunction in other cognitive domains, but typically also lead to functional deterioration. In common usage, the term "dementia" is often used for nonprogressive conditions, but most dementing illnesses in the elderly are of neurodegenerative or cerebrovascular types, and, in fact, worsen over time.

HISTORICAL CONTEXT

Decline in intellectual function as a disorder of the elderly was recognized in antiquity.

Throughout most of history, the disorder that we now think of as dementia was viewed as an inevitable consequence of aging (Berchtold & Cotman, 1998). The distinction between the aging process and dementia is a recent conceptual development. The term "dementia" was first used in a clinical context similar to its current form in the 18th century by Pinel and Esquirol (Berchtold & Cotman, 1998). The linkage of a neuropathological state and a clinical dementia was first made by Alois Alzheimer in 1907. However, Blessed, Tomlinson, and Roth (Blessed et al., 1968), in their landmark article on the quantitative relationships between the histopathological findings and cognition in AD, also deserve credit for opening the modern study of dementia. Since their 1968 report, the field of dementia evolved from a backwater to one of the premier areas of neuroscientific investigation. The methodology that Blessed, Tomlinson, and Roth used to make their seminal observations represents the foundation of a rich collaboration between cognitive neuroscientists and clinicians. The fundamental principles established by these pioneers—that components of cognitive function important to dementia can be identified and that these components can be quantitated—are the basis of this chapter.

THE DIAGNOSIS OF DEMENTIA

The diagnosis of dementia has traditionally included requirements for both cognitive impairment and substantial impairment in daily functioning (National Institute of Neurological and Communicative Disorders and Stroke/Alzheimer's Disease and Related Disorders Association (NINCDS-ADRDA) criteria (McKhann et al., 1984) and *Diagnostic and Statistical Manual of Mental Disorders* (DSM-IV; American Psychiatric Association, 1994). The International Classification of Diseases 10th revision (ICD-10) (World Health Organization, 1992) offers a slightly different formulation that is not used widely in clinical practice or research in North America. The definition of all-cause dementia has been updated in the National Institute on Aging and Alzheimer's Association (NIA-AA) criteria (McKhann et al., 2011). That definition of dementia from the NIA-AA criteria are given in Table 17-1.

The NIA-AA definition of dementia requires that the deficits "interfere with the ability to function at work or at usual activities," and "represent a decline from previous levels of functioning and performing."

The second core aspect of the diagnosis of dementia is the pattern of cognitive impairment.

Dementia involves dysfunction in multiple cognitive domains, but often one domain exhibits the initial manifestations. The cognitive and behavioral domain affected by dementia include (1) Memory domain; (2) Executive domain; (3) Visuospatial domain: (4) Language domain, and (5) Personal behavior domain. The NIA-AA criteria require that at least two domains be affected to support a diagnosis of dementia. When only one domain is affected, a diagnosis of mild cognitive impairment may be the more appropriate syndromic label.

The new NIA-AA definition of dementia has greater generality than the older DSM-IV and NINCDS-ADRDA definitions because the older criteria required memory impairment as one of the involved domains. Such a definition did not accommodate many non-Alzheimer dementias.

The third core component of the diagnosis of dementia is the exclusions, in particular, of delirium. The temporal profile of the vast majority of dementia is that of a gradually appearing condition, and one in which symptoms steadily worsen. The prototypical exception would be a patient who experiences a episode of anoxic encephalopathy or traumatic brain injury—brain lesions of acute onset—who never regains his premorbid cognitive integrity.

Table 17–1. Definition of Dementia (NIA-AA Workgroup, McKhann et al., 2011)

Dementia is diagnosed when there are cognitive or behavioral symptoms that:

1. Interfere with the ability to function at work or at usual activities; and

2. Represent a decline from prior levels of functioning and performing; and

3. Are not explained by delirium or major psychiatric disorder;

4. Cognitive impairment is detected and diagnosed through a combination of (a) History-taking from the patient and a knowledgeable informant, and (b) Objective cognitive assessment, either a "bedside" mental status examination or neuropsychological testing.

5. The cognitive or behavioral impairment involves at least two of the following domains:

    a. Impaired ability to acquire and remember new information

    b. Impaired reasoning and handling of complex tasks, poor judgment

    c. Impaired visuospatial abilities

    d. Impaired language functions (speaking, reading, writing)

    e. Changes in personality, behavior or comportment

Table copyright Alzheimer's Association, 2011

In community-based ambulatory settings, the diagnosis of dementia is moderately reliable (Fratiglioni et al., 1992; Graham et al., 1996; Larson et al., 1998). The diagnostic problems with the definition of dementia mainly arise with cases that are neither clearly normal nor clearly demented (Fratiglioni et al., 1992; Graham et al., 1996). These latter individuals typically exhibit a discordance between cognitive–neuropsychologically derived evidence regarding their cognitive status and informant-based assessments of their daily functioning (Pittman et al., 1992; Herlitz et al., 1997). The recognition of such individuals with cognitive impairment without apparent functional impairment was one of the motivations for the development of the concept of mild cognitive impairment.

MILD COGNITIVE IMPAIRMENT

The term *mild cognitive impairment* (MCI) is the one most widely used to describe individuals who are neither cognitively normal nor demented (Petersen et al., 2001). Mild cognitive impairment is similar but not identical to the terms "cognitively impaired, not demented" and "dementia prodrome." MCI has gained traction as a diagnosis because it serves a useful purpose to clinicians who care for patients with a spectrum of cognitive impairment, and because researchers need a designation for those individuals often encountered in epidemiological investigations of the elderly who were neither normal nor demented. The importance of adding the concept of MCI to that of dementia comes because of the clear need to expand our appreciation of the earliest manifestations of cognitive impairment in chronic neurodegenerative and cerebrovascular diseases.

Cognitive impairment is the core deficit in dementia and its prodromal state, MCI. Whereas persons with dementia are impaired in daily functioning and eventually, become dependent on others because of cognitive impairment, persons who meet criteria for MCI are not substantially or significantly impaired in daily functioning. Like the diagnosis of dementia, MCI is a clinical diagnosis that can be established only through history and examination.

Mild cognitive impairment has been defined by the NIA-AA workgroup (Albert et al., 2011) to include the four core features: (1) There is a concern regarding change in cognition by the patient, someone who knows the patient well, or a skilled clinician; (2) Impairment in one or more cognitive domains, that were described above in the section on the diagnosis of dementia; (3) Preservation of independence in daily functioning; and (4) Does not meet criteria for dementia.

A key underlying motivation for diagnosing MCI is that it is a risk state for progression to dementia. There is no question that persons diagnosed with MCI are at a substantially greater risk to develop dementia in the following several years (Boyle et al., 2006; Manly et al., 2008). Using standard criteria, one multicenter clinical trial observed a roughly 15% rate of the development of dementia (Petersen et al., 2005), whereas other multicenter trials that claimed to use the same criteria but in fact allowed somewhat more mildly affected persons to participate observed lower rates of conversion to dementia (Thal et al., 2005; Feldman et al., 2007; Winblad et al., 2008).

There has been considerable controversy about how to define "evidence of cognitive deterioration" in MCI (Petersen & Knopman, 2006; Visser & Brodaty, 2006). Ideally, prior cognitive and neuropsychological testing would be available, and demonstrable declines would therefore serve as the objective basis for the determination of deterioration of cognitive functioning. Even in this ideal situation, how much decline would be sufficient is difficult to specify a priori. In practice, the vast majority of persons encountered either in clinical practice or in research contexts have no prior documented cognitive testing. Impaired performance relative to expectations based on age and education is the actual basis for a determination of cognitive impairment. Use of a standard for the diagnosis of MCI that depends on the inference that decline has occurred results in more diagnostic variability than a definition based on more objective data. Although there are age- and education-based norms for mental status examinations and many cognitive tests, those norms are of limited use in regions that are ethnically and culturally different from the localities where the normative data were generated.

There is also controversy as to whether age-corrected norms are appropriate for use in the diagnosis of MCI. If used, age-corrected norms make the diagnosis of cognitive impairment heavily dependent upon chronological age, and ignore many other aspects of health and behavior that are important. There is an empiric basis for choosing to define abnormal cognition as 1 or 1.5 standard deviations below age and education-normed test scores, but the predictive accuracy for future cognitive impairment of low neuropsychological test scores is quite limited. At this time, it is not possible to define absolute levels of impaired performance that are either age-dependent or age-independent. These challenges in definitions are not so much intrinsic to the particular formulation of MCI, but rather reflect the broader problem of defining a very complex activity.

The nature of the cognitive impairment in MCI may involve only amnestic difficulties or instead may include executive, attentional, visuospatial, or language deficits. Amnestic MCI is the most common MCI subtype with or without other nonamnestic deficits (Manly et al., 2005). The amnestic deficit in MCI closely resembles that of AD, albeit in slightly milder forms (Greenaway et al., 2006). In MCI patients recruited for clinical trials, their performance on tests of learning and recall is worse than those of normal subjects but not quite as impaired as patients diagnosed with very mild or mild AD (Grundman et al., 2004). Mild cognitive impairment involving a single nonmemory domain such as executive dysfunction, visuospatial dysfunction, or language dysfunction can also occur but is rare. Amnestic MCI is the most likely precursor of AD (DeCarli et al., 2004), whereas the nonamnestic MCI subtypes with executive or language dysfunction are more likely to represent the prodromes of other dementias, such as vascular dementia (Zanetti et al., 2006), dementia with Lewy Bodies, behavioral variant frontotemporal dementia (FTD), and the primary progressive aphasias. Mild cognitive impairment with prominent visuospatial impairment also might be associated with AD (Mapstone et al., 2003). Patients with MCI may also experience a variety of neuropsychiatric symptoms, especially apathy, anxiety, and depression (Lyketsos et al.,

2002; Geda et al., 2004). The presence of depression in MCI patients increases the risk of subsequent AD (Modrego & Ferrandez, 2004).

A core element of the diagnosis of MCI is that persons with the diagnosis should be "intact or minimally impaired" in their daily activities. Although such a definition may seem easily applicable in a routine clinical setting, closer and quantitative scrutiny often has shown that persons with MCI are clearly inferior to persons diagnosed as normal on tasks involving financial judgment (Griffith et al., 2003; Okonkwo et al., 2006); understanding complicated situations, such as possible participation in clinical trials; and in other higher-level tasks (Royall et al., 2004). Nonetheless, for the majority of patients, a commonsense approach to the determination of "intact or nearly intact" daily living independence allows a clinician to make the diagnosis of MCI.

Mild cognitive impairment represents a spectrum of persons who have variable probabilities of progressing to dementia over the ensuing several years (Petersen et al., 1999). From a clinical and neurocognitive perspective, it should not be surprising that the more impaired an MCI patient is, the greater his likelihood of progressing to dementia in a shorter period of time (Petersen et al., 1999; Tabert et al., 2006; Dickerson et al., 2007).

DISTINGUISHING MILD COGNITIVE IMPAIRMENT AND DEMENTIA FROM OTHER SYNDROMES

Genuine cognitive impairment must be distinguished from other states. Traditionally, delirium, aphasia, auditory or visual deficits, depression, and psychosis dominated this list. We add aging and low educational attainment to this list because, in practice, clinicians and laypeople have a great deal of difficulty in distinguishing genuine cognitive impairment from "normal" aging.

Dementia is underdiagnosed in clinical practice (Callahan et al., 1995; Eefsting et al., 1996; Ross et al., 1997; Sternberg et al., 2000; Valcour et al., 2000). "Normal" aging, rather than other neurological or psychiatric condition, is the diagnosis most often given if any alternative is offered at all (Knopman et al., 2000). Given the pervasive nature of cognitive complaints in the elderly, even the most diligent clinician, well aware of the predictors of incident dementia, will not be able to predict which elderly individual with subjective cognitive complaints, but without objective evidence of cognitive decline, will go on to develop dementia. As the concept of MCI is relatively new, there are no data on how the diagnosis is used in clinical practice.

AGING

Beliefs about the cognitive changes that occur with aging make early diagnosis of dementia difficult. Recognizing that a patient is experiencing lapses in memory, visuospatial function, judgment, or language that are outside the normal variability of everyday life is a challenge for both laypeople and health care professionals.

Genuine declines in mental speed occur even in optimally healthy elderly. In cross-sectional studies, a small number of individuals with undiagnosed incipient dementia will be present (Sliwinski et al., 1996; Wilson et al., 1999). Thus, unselected samples of elders perform less well than comparison groups who are in their 20s. In longitudinal studies and in studies in which only the healthiest of elderly were studied, the only consistent finding across the age spectrum (at least up to about age 75) is slowing of performance (Schaie, 1989). Several longitudinal studies of individuals over age 65 have demonstrated only slight declines of cognitive performance in large population samples of nondemented elderly (Colsher & Wallace, 1991; Ganguli et al., 1996; Haan et al., 1999; Wilson et al., 1999; Lamar et al., 2003). In one of the few studies that longitudinally examined nondemented individuals over age 75, persons who were over 75 declined more on cognitive testing than did 65- to 75-year-olds (Brayne et al., 1999). Nondemented elders decline on examinations such as the Mini-Mental State Exam (Chatfield et al., 2007); those scoring lower at baseline decline more than do those scoring at the highest levels.

The domains of learning and memory are usually considered to show the greatest changes with typical aging (Salthouse, 2003). Decline in learning with aging might be mediated by slowing of cognitive processing, but the end result is impaired new learning. Several types of learning

and memory come into play in day-to-day affairs, but rote retention of something like a phone number for less than a minute or longer-term retention of a several sentence message are two prototypical memory tasks. On tasks that involve immediate recall of a large number of items (e.g., seven or more words or digits), older adults have a lower learning rate (Drachman & Leavitt, 1972). Performance by older adults on verbal learning tasks from the neuropsychology laboratory offer insights into those functions (Geffen et al., 1990; Mitrushina et al., 1991; Petersen et al., 1992). In a test such as the auditory verbal learning task, the subject is asked to learn a list of 15 words over five trials and then recall them 30 minutes later. In the learning phase, older adults are clearly less successful as the length of the list of items to be remembered increases (Geffen et al., 1990). On delayed recall, however, older individuals are nearly as effective as younger individuals in recalling words after a delay, as a percentage of words successfully learned initially. Delayed recall performance in healthy elders is preserved into the tenth decade (Petersen et al., 1992). In contrast, delayed recall performance is severely impaired in AD patients.

Language functions decline very little with normal aging (Schaie, 1989; Howieson et al., 1993). Once people reach middle age, vocabulary levels remain stable thereafter. Naming and comprehension abilities also change very little over the lifespan, well into the eighth or ninth decades of life. Even verbal fluency declines only slightly with age when speed of processing is taken into account (Schaie, 1989).

In contrast, abstract reasoning declines with normal aging (Schaie, 1989; Schaie, 1989; Albert et al., 1990; Howieson et al., 1993). As mental speed drops, healthy elders may be less adept at performing concentration-demanding tasks without the benefit of paper and pencil. Consequently, typical elders do worse on tests of abstract reasoning than do younger individuals. However, the declines evident in the laboratory setting may not be obvious in daily affairs because individuals are able to compensate for reduced mental speed by experience and acumen acquired over a lifetime. Just as in memory disorder, when deficits in abstract reasoning appear, brain disease rather than normal aging is, by far, the likely etiology.

An axiom of assessment of mental function in the elderly is that clinically significant cognitive decline from a previously higher level is simply not compatible with a diagnosis of "normal aging." In general, low cognitive performance (without respect to whether decline has been documented) is also suggestive of dementia rather than typical aging. However, the possibility that life-long intellectual disability is the cause of poor memory and abstract reasoning abilities must be first ruled out.

Both neuropathological and imaging investigations have added complexity to the issue of what constitutes normal aging. Both show that a sizable minority of elderly persons have the pathology (Schmitt et al., 2000; Knopman et al., 2003) or molecular imaging features of AD (Pike et al., 2007; Rowe et al., 2007), even though cognitive testing and clinical impressions clearly show them to be normal. What to call persons with evidence of AD pathology but without clinical cognitive impairment is unresolved at this time.

LOW EDUCATION

Low educational achievement confounds cognitive assessment and makes a diagnosis of cognitive impairment more difficult. Low educational achievement usually implies that a subject was never exposed to the kinds of cognitive assessment experiences that become increasingly rigorous from elementary education to secondary education to postsecondary education. Many procedures used in both bedside and laboratory assessment of cognition utilize procedures and materials that are very similar to those used in aptitude testing for postsecondary education. As a consequence, individuals with less than a ninth-grade education may simply not have experience with some test procedures that are commonplace for college-educated individuals. In addition, educational achievement is a proxy for innate intelligence. Although the correlation is grossly imperfect, a relationship does exist between educational achievement, the educational achievement of one's parents, the occupation of one's parents, the socioeconomic circumstances of one's childhood and adulthood, and other factors that affect health status in general and cognition in particular. Education may be a useful proxy for academic achievement within

relatively homogeneous populations, but fails when comparing African Americans and whites because of the marked differences in educational quality in years past (Shadlen et al., 2006). Although more extensive discussion of the impact of education on cognition is beyond the scope of this chapter, the importance of education as a risk factor and as a confound in diagnosis should always be respected.

In normal individuals, prior educational achievement has a powerful effect on cognitive performance (Ganguli et al., 1991; Stern et al., 1992; Welsh et al., 1994; Cerhan et al., 1998). For example, in a very large population based sample from the Atherosclerosis Risk in Communities study (Cerhan et al., 1998), there was almost a twofold difference in the number of symbols completed on the Digit Symbol Substitution Subtest of the Wechsler Adult Intelligence Scale-Revised (WAIS-R) between individuals with less than a ninth-grade education and those with at least some college education. The difference was observed in both men and women, and in individuals between the ages of 45 and 59 as well as 60 and 69. A similar phenomenon was observed on the word fluency test. Educational achievement also had an impact on word recall in the ten-word Delayed Word Recall task, but the difference between those with a less than ninth-grade education and at least some college education was smaller, with the better educated individuals performing at most only 25% better than the lower educated subgroup.

In attempting to create criterion-based diagnoses of dementia based on neuropsychological (Stern et al., 1992; Welsh et al., 1994) or bedside mental status assessments (Crum et al., 1993), the education effect on test scores creates considerable difficulty. Dividing subjects into low, middle, and high education strata allows the test criteria to be applied in a strata-specific manner. Unfortunately, any form of education-based correction of raw test scores may worsen diagnostic accuracy rather than improve it.

VISUAL AND AUDITORY DEFICITS

Visual loss and impaired hearing adversely affect function especially in the elderly (Keller et al., 1999). Sensory deficits may not affect cognition, per se, but they can lead to decline in independence in daily living abilities in a way that may mimic dementia.

Visual changes in the elderly are very common (Rahmani et al., 1996). Glaucoma, cataracts, and macular degeneration affect a large proportion of elderly individuals. The consequences of visual loss include social isolation, visual misperceptions, and dependence on others that can mimic some of the manifestations of dementia. When assessing a patient with apparent functional impairment, it is essential to ask whether degraded vision could account for some or all of the deficits.

Similarly, hearing loss (Ives et al., 1995; Jerger et al., 1995) is common in the elderly and may also lead to social isolation. In addition, hearing loss can mimic memory loss by giving the appearance of inattentiveness or failure to recall conversations. As with visual loss, loss of auditory acuity at levels that interfere with processing ordinary conversations should be considered as part of the evaluation of a patient with memory loss. Unlike cognitively normal elders who typically have peripheral hearing loss with good compensatory abilities, patients with mild dementia also have evidence of central auditory dysfunction, in which their functional hearing is worse than expected based on pure tone hearing loss (Gates et al., 1995).

APHASIA

Patients with severe expressive or receptive aphasia can be very difficult to evaluate cognitively, and it is often not clear whether they are impaired in cognitive domains outside of language. Thus, persons who develop chronic aphasia following a cerebral infarction, hemorrhage, or brain trauma, cognitive assessment may be compromised. If writing is as impaired as speaking in an aphasic patient, there may be no way to test memory or reasoning abilities. Similarly, if auditory comprehension is severely impaired, such that only one-step commands can be executed, and reading comprehension is not substantially better, further cognitive testing may be fruitless. Functional ability may be the only yardstick for understanding an aphasic patient's cognitive capabilities.

DELIRIUM

Delirium by definition is acute or subacute in onset, occurring over hours to days. Delirium is a common disorder in hospitalized elderly (Francis et al., 1990; Inouye & Charpentier, 1996; Inouye, 2006). Although dementia may not be commonly mistaken for delirium, delirium (also referred to as *acute confusional state*) may be misdiagnosed as dementia if the clinician fails to appreciate the onset and progression of the cognitive disorder. Delirium and dementia are also distinguished by the impairment of level of arousal and attention in delirium, and its relative preservation in dementia. Patients with delirium experience fluctuations in their levels of consciousness and also have impaired attention and concentration. Most patients with dementia, in contrast, do not have fluctuations in their level of consciousness and often have virtually normal attention and concentration in the mild stages of the illness. The most common risk factors for delirium include advanced age, preexisting cognitive impairment, and polypharmacy.

The diagnosis of delirium is a clinical one. The confusion assessment method (CAM) is one of the most common screening tests in use for detection and diagnosis of delirium in both clinical and research settings (Wei et al., 2008). A simple but underutilized bedside tool for detecting delirium is narrative writing. Perhaps because writing involves multiple functions—language, visuo-constructional ability and the ability to plan and initiate action—it is particularly sensitive to global cognitive impairment (Chedru & Geschwind, 1972). A patient who is mildly to moderately demented but not delirious may still be able to compose and write a sentence on command.

When the two disorders overlap, diagnosis may be more difficult. Dementia patients are at greater risk for delirium in the setting of acute medical illnesses (Francis et al., 1990; Lerner et al., 1997). Longitudinal follow-up studies of patients who experience delirium have shown that they do not always have a complete cognitive recovery (Murray et al., 1993), perhaps because the episode of delirium unmasked incipient or unrecognized dementia. Thus, dementia should be a consideration to be addressed during post-hospitalization follow-up in an elderly patient who experiences delirium. Delaying assessment until several weeks after resolution of the acute illness is advisable, so that the patient's performance is not adversely affected by a resolving delirium.

DEPRESSION

The symptomatology of dementia and depression often overlap. Low mood, apathy, and loss of initiative may be presenting symptoms of dementia (Kramer & Reifler, 1992; Oppenheim, 1994). Patients with depression without dementia may have complaints of impaired memory and concentration, but they typically perform better than expected on mental status testing. Patients with pure depression are more likely than dementia patients to complain spontaneously of memory problems, but that difference is not always a reliable discriminator. Depressed patients will volunteer that they are sad or despondent, but spontaneous or elicited complaints of being sad do not rule out dementia either. Objective cognitive impairment, usually but not always, differentiates dementia from depression (La Rue, 1989; Bieliauskas, 1993), although patients with depression perform more poorly than do normal persons, particularly on tests that place demands on mental speed (Butters et al., 2004). Executive dysfunction and slowed mental processing are the hallmarks of cognitive dysfunction in late-life depression (Herrmann et al., 2007). The executive dysfunction may account for the apparent deficits in learning and recall (Elderkin-Thompson et al., 2007). Competent bedside mental status or neuropsychological assessments are necessary to characterize cognitive function adequately in order to make a diagnosis in a patient with depression and cognitive complaints.

Even when patients are thought to have depression as their primary diagnosis, the new onset of depression in late life carries an increased risk for subsequently developing dementia (Geerlings et al., 2000; Green et al., 2003). Depression is also a risk factor for MCI (Geda et al., 2006) and AD (Geerlings et al., 2000; Modrego & Ferrandez, 2004).

PSYCHOSIS

When "psychotic" symptoms such as hallucinations, delusions, paranoia, or bizarre behaviors occur in late middle-aged or elderly individuals who have no prior history of psychiatric disease, it is highly likely that these behaviors are manifestations of an underlying dementing disorder. Thus, schizophrenia should not be a serious diagnostic consideration in older patients with new-onset psychotic symptoms. On the other hand, persons with life-long histories of schizophrenia, who then appear to decompensate in later life, can be a challenge in diagnosis.

EPIDEMIOLOGY OF MILD COGNITIVE IMPAIRMENT AND DEMENTIA

DIAGNOSIS OF DEMENTIA IN POPULATION SAMPLES

Alzheimer disease, cerebrovascular disease, Lewy body disease, and their combinations account for the vast majority of dementia in the elderly. Other conditions are numerically less common, but still occur often in clinical practice. By autopsy studies (Wade et al., 1987; Joachim et al., 1988; Boller et al., 1989; Jellinger et al., 1990; Risse et al., 1990; Galasko et al., 1994; Holmes et al., 1999; Lim et al., 1999), clinical series (Larson et al., 1985; Thal et al., 1988), and population-based surveys (Pfeffer et al., 1987; Evans et al., 1989; Kokmen et al., 1989; Bachman et al., 1992; Canadian Study of Health and Aging Working Group, 1994; Hendrie et al., 1995; Ott et al., 1995; Graves et al., 1996; White et al., 1996; Hofman et al., 1997; Fillenbaum et al., 1998; Lobo et al., 2000), AD is the most common dementia in North America and Europe. At least 60% to as many as 80% of dementia patients have AD pathology. Dementia due to cerebrovascular disease is the second most common etiology, whereas dementia with Lewy bodies is the next most common dementia. Considerable pathological overlap exists between these three disorders (Barker et al., 2002), which may be very difficult to differentiate clinically.

PREVALENCE

Dementia is largely but not exclusively a diagnosis of the elderly. The prevalence of dementia and AD increases with advancing age (Pfeffer et al., 1987; Evans et al., 1989; Kokmen et al., 1989; Bachman et al., 1992; Canadian Study of Health and Aging Working Group, 1994; Hendrie et al., 1995; Ott et al., 1995; Graves et al., 1996; White et al., 1996; Hofman et al., 1997; Fillenbaum et al., 1998; Lobo et al., 2000). There is considerable consistency across prevalence surveys in North America and Europe, especially when case-finding methods for mild dementia are similar. In 65- to 70-year-olds, the prevalence of dementia is approximately 1 per 100 individuals. With each subsequent 5-year increment, the prevalence of dementia and AD doubles. Over age 85 years, estimates of the prevalence of dementia vary between 20% to nearly 50%. Beyond age 85, it appears that dementia prevalence continues to rise. Some earlier studies found a decrease above this age, but most studies have confirmed that the proportion of individuals with dementia continues to rise over this age. At the younger end of the age spectrum, dementia is quite rare in terms of numbers of cases in the population, but nonetheless dementia in young and middle-aged adults represents an important group of diseases for neuropsychologists, neurologists, and psychiatrists.

The prevalence of MCI has been more variable, perhaps not surprising because of the controversies over diagnostic criteria. Estimates of amnestic MCI in community-based studies using conservative criteria have ranged from 3% to 9% (Kivipelto et al., 2001; Ritchie et al., 2001; Lopez et al., 2003; Ganguli et al., 2004).

INCIDENCE

The number of newly diagnosed cases of dementia also rises dramatically with advancing age (Bachman et al., 1993; Stern et al., 1994; Hebert et al., 1995; Fillenbaum et al., 1998; Gao et al., 1998; Jorm & Jolley, 1998; Ott et al., 1998; Rocca et al., 1998). Incident dementia is very rare under age 65: rates of less than 0.1 and 0.5 per 1,000 cases per year in the 40–49 and 50–64 age ranges have been reported (Knopman et al., 2006). The number of new cases of dementia, mainly AD, begins to exceed 1 per 100 individuals per year as early as the early 70s to the early 80s. It is not until the late 70s or mid 80s that the rate of new cases reaches 2 per 100 individuals per year. The differences in definitions of dementia account for the variability in estimates of incidence rates between studies, with those studies using definitions that admit milder cases showing the higher incidence rates. Because patients diagnosed with dementia tend to live for several years to as long as a decade or more, incidence rates are considerably lower than prevalence rates.

There are very little data at present on the incidence of MCI. A study from North Manhattan of persons aged 65 years and older yielded an incidence rate of 5% (Manly et al., 2008).

RISK FACTORS FOR COGNITIVE IMPAIRMENT AND DEMENTIA

CONDITIONS THAT ARE ASSOCIATED WITH INCREASE RISK

The two most prominent risk factors for dementia are advancing age and a family history of dementia. In this chapter, we will focus on those risk factors and risk states that are of neuropsychological interest.

Family history is an important risk factor for early-onset AD (Lautenschlager et al., 1996) and frontotemporal lobar degenerations (FTLDs). Three genes are associated with early-onset AD, the Alzheimer precursor protein gene on chromosome 21, the presenilin 1 gene on chromosome 14, and the presenilin 2 gene on chromosome 1. The majority of early-onset cases (30%–70%) have been found to have mutations in the presenilin 1 gene. Interestingly, other than age of onset, there are no consistent clinical differences between familial and non-familial AD (Swearer et al., 1992; Farlow et al., 1994; Campion et al., 1995; Lopera et al., 1997). Two genes have been shown to produce one of the FTLDs, both on chromosome 17, one that codes for the tau protein (Hutton et al., 1998) and the other for progranulin (Baker et al., 2006). In AD, the apolipoprotein E (APOE) genotype is a major element of genetic risk for AD with onset between roughly age 50 and age 75 (Farrer et al., 1997; Green et al., 2002). The association of the APOEε4 allele with AD appears to be stronger among women than among men.

In addition to acting as a confound in diagnosis, very low educational achievement (less than eighth-grade education) has also been a consistently observed risk factor that increases a person's odds of developing AD by two- to threefold (Zhang et al., 1990; Friedland, 1993; Katzman, 1993; Stern et al., 1994; Cobb et al., 1995; Ott et al., 1995; Stern et al., 1995; Callahan et al., 1996; Kukull et al., 2002; Caamano-Isorna et al., 2006). The basis for its impact on risk for dementia could relate to education's proxy role for early childhood environment and brain reserve (Roe et al., 2007).

In a group of Catholic nuns, cognitive performance at age 20 years was predictive of the subsequent development of dementia roughly 50 years later (Snowdon et al., 1996). As the women were entering the Order, they completed essays. The cognitive complexity of the essays had a strong inverse association with the subsequent development of dementia. Several hypotheses related to early childhood experiences have been proposed to account for the findings. Better childhood brain "nurturing" presumably leads to better brain function, which in turn acts as a buffer in ameliorating the deleterious effects of AD pathology later in life. In general, enriched childhood environments will be associated with higher educational attainment, but it may be the sum of all enriching experiences, not the least of which is good childhood nutrition, that protects from the subsequent development of dementia (Snowdon et al., 1996). Another example of the relationship between early-life cognitive performance and later-life dementia comes from Scotland. Low scores on intelligence testing in grade school (at age 11) were associated with dementia in later life (Whalley et al., 2000). These findings have been extended to dementia subtypes and appear to be more specific for a dementia with cerebrovascular disease (McGurn et al., 2008).

Participation in cognitively stimulating activities in midlife has been suggested as being protective against later-life dementia (Verghese et al., 2003; Wilson et al., 2003; Wilson et al., 2007; Carlson et al., 2008) and MCI (Verghese et al., 2006). A study in monozygotic twins discordant for dementia onset is a particularly convincing demonstration that genetics and early life experience cannot explain the risk reduction (Carlson et al., 2008).

Cognitive complaints among normal elderly predict subsequent dementia (Jorm et al., 2004), although the specificity of such observations is low. In many studies, the most consistent predictor of subjective memory complaints has been depression. Subjective cognitive complaints do not constitute a risk factor for dementia, but rather may be an early manifestation of cognitive impairment.

NEUROPSYCHOLOGICAL AND CLINICAL ASSESSMENT IN COGNITIVE IMPAIRMENT AND DEMENTIA IN THE ELDERLY

INFORMATION FROM THE INFORMANT

The historical and functional information needed to diagnose dementia is gained by querying a knowledgeable informant and performing a cognitive assessment of the patient. Instruments that have been validated for informant interviews for diagnosing dementia include the Dementia Questionnaire (DQ) (Kawas et al., 1994; Ellis et al., 1998), the Informant Questionnaire on Cognitive Decline in the Elderly (IQCODE) (Jorm, 1994), or the Functional Activities Questionnaire (FAQ) (Pfeffer et al., 1982). The Clinical Dementia Rating Scale (Morris, 1993) also includes a semistructured interview that covers most of the major domains that are queried with informants.

Informant input for determining impairment in social function will increase specificity of the diagnosis of dementia compared to a diagnosis based solely on neuropsychological criteria (Pittman et al., 1992; Callahan et al., 1996). Particularly for individuals with low educational achievement, informant histories provide an external validation of the cognitive assessments. The trade-off is that informants may overlook substantial impairment in social and occupational functioning on the part of the patient, which will result in loss of sensitivity, particularly for mild dementia. For the practicing clinician, the interpretation of the history as reported by informants must be subjected to the same critical scrutiny as the cognitive testing data. For example, cognitive test norms might not be valid when culturally and educationally diverse populations are being evaluated. Clinicians must weigh all sources of data in drawing diagnostic conclusions.

BEDSIDE COGNITIVE ASSESSMENT TOOLS

Cognitive assessments that have been validated for bedside use include the Mini-Mental State examination (MMSE) (Folstein et al., 1975), the modified Mini-Mental State (3MS; Teng & Chui, 1987), the Orientation-Memory-Concentration test (Katzman et al., 1983), the Short Test of Mental Status (Kokmen et al., 1991; Tang-Wai et al., 2003), the Montreal Cognitive Assessment (Nasreddine et al., 2005), Addenbrook Cognitive Assessment (Mathuranath et al., 2000), and the Mini-Cog (Borson et al., 2003; Borson et al., 2005).

It is beyond the scope of this chapter to consider the composition of mental status examinations in detail. They all contain questions about orientation, but beyond that common feature, there is quite a range of coverage of different cognitive domains. Bedside cognitive assessments, such as the MMSE, have imperfect sensitivity as stand-alone instruments (Anthony et al., 1982; O'Connor et al., 1989; Kukull et al., 1994). For the diagnosis of dementia, a test like the MMSE is overweighted for language testing and underweighted for recent memory and executive function assessments. The three-word recall task in the MMSE may be useful for screening, but it is imperfectly correlated with neuropsychologically validated tests of recent memory (Cullum et al., 1993). There is no one "cut-score" on the MMSE that can be used to diagnose dementia. Because the MMSE is so highly dependent on educational level, a score of 27 (out of 30 correct) on the MMSE could indicate dementia in a highly educated person (O'Bryant et al., 2008), whereas scores under 24 correct could be found in cognitively normal persons with very low education (Crum et al., 1993; Tangalos et al., 1996). The Orientation-Memory-Concentration test (Katzman et al., 1983) provides somewhat greater weight for memory dysfunction and executive dysfunction. The "months backwards" item of this instrument may provide a sensitive measure of the constructs of mental agility and

working memory that we have included under the category of executive function (Ball et al., 1999).

A stand-alone battery of items sensitive to executive function has also been developed (Royall et al., 1992), one that its developers intended to be used in conjunction with a standard mental status instrument. The bedside battery of executive function includes such tasks as imitating sequences of hand movements ("fist-edge-palm"), echopraxia avoidance (inhibiting certain behaviors despite implicit prompts to do so), and other activities requiring sustained attention, such as reciting the months backwards or generating a list of words of a particular semantic category or first letter (word fluency). The Frontal Assessment Battery is another bedside instrument meant to measure mental flexibility and freedom from distraction (Dubois et al., 2000).

For patients who are not native English speakers, analysis of performance on these tests administered through an interpreter must be interpreted with considerable caution. In addition, educational and occupational background affects performance on these tests and diagnosis (Pittman et al., 1992; Stern et al., 1994; Herlitz et al., 1997; MacKnight et al., 1999). Both low socioeconomic status (Pittman et al., 1992) and very high prior intellectual achievement (Inouye et al., 1993; Rentz et al., 2004) present challenges to diagnosis. Persons of superior premorbid intellect can score in the "normal" range, yet such scores could represent important clinical decline for them.

Mental status examinations are also moderately correlated with assessments of daily functioning in dementia (Galasko et al., 1997; Gelinas et al., 1999). The remarkable degree of relationship between synaptic density in AD (DeKosky & Scheff, 1990; Terry et al., 1991) and mental status previously mentioned, and functional measures and mental status, are powerful validators of bedside cognitive assessment.

LABORATORY COGNITIVE NEUROPSYCHOLOGICAL ASSESSMENT

In patients with mild symptoms, in patients with possible dysexecutive syndrome, and in those in whom depression might be playing a role, neuropsychological testing is a necessary part of the evaluation for suspected dementia. Bedside testing of executive functions, memory function, or visuospatial function is usually not as informative, discriminating, or reliable as laboratory-based tests. Neuropsychological testing can evaluate the severity of impairment in different cognitive domains with greater precision than can bedside tests, and thus establish specific patterns or profiles of cognitive impairment (Pasquier, 1999). Even though no cognitive profiles are perfectly specific or sensitive to a given dementia diagnosis, establishing a profile that is *consistent* with a given dementia subtype is quite helpful. For example, in a patient with prominent behavioral disturbances, such as agitation and disinhibition, that might point to behavioral variant FTD, a neuropsychological test profile that documents severe recent memory and visuospatial disturbances would keep AD in the differential diagnosis.

In patients with severe dementia, neuropsychological testing may offer very little beyond a competent mental status examination and history. Once a person scores below roughly 15–20 on the MMSE or like examination, scores on neuropsychological measures tend to be very close to floor levels.

A number of studies have examined the role of neuropsychological assessment in the diagnosis of dementia compared to clinical diagnoses (Pittman et al., 1992; Monsch et al., 1995; Stuss et al., 1996; Tierney et al., 1996; Herlitz et al., 1997). These studies used expert clinicians to generate the clinical diagnoses. Consequently, the fact that neuropsychological assessment had relatively modest additional value above and beyond a skilled clinician's assessment in these studies does not generalize to routine practice. With increasing emphasis on early detection of cognitive impairment and dementia, the value of neuropsychological testing in routine clinical practice may be quite high for physicians who have little training in cognitive assessment beyond screening examinations. Neurologists and other physicians with less experience and expertise in bedside cognitive assessment skills should also make broader use of neuropsychological consultations. Those physicians who are comfortable with and skilled in bedside cognitive assessment may have more selective uses for neuropsychological assessments.

MEMORY

The neuropsychological assessment of recent verbal memory has definite advantages over bedside testing. The key features of neuropsychological assessment of memory in dementia evaluations include the use of supraspan length material, appropriate learning format (either multiple learning trials or elaborative encoding), delayed free recall, and delayed recognition. The widely used laboratory tests—such as the Auditory Verbal Learning Test (Ivnik et al., 1992; Crossen & Wiens, 1994; Lezak, 1995), Hopkins Verbal Learning Test (Brandt et al., 1992; Shapiro et al., 1999), the California Verbal Learning Test (Delis et al., 1988; Crossen & Wiens, 1994; Elwood, 1995; Lezak, 1995), the Wechsler Memory Scale, Revised or 3rd Edition Logical Memory subtest (Wechsler, 1987), the CERAD word recall test (Welsh et al., 1994), or the Free and Cued Recall (Grober et al., 1988)—allow for much better separation of normal and abnormal performance. Confounding effects of immediate recall are also minimized with longer delay intervals and longer lists. In patients in whom bedside assessment of recent memory function yields conflicting or inconclusive data, neuropsychological assessment of recent memory is very useful. The usefulness of visual memory testing is uncertain. Visual memory tests do not appear to have the same diagnostic accuracy; visual memory deficits (at least those measured by the Wechsler Memory Scale-Revised visual memory subtests) may be confounded by visuo-constructional deficits (Leonberger et al., 1991).

LANGUAGE FUNCTIONS

Quantitation of performance on naming to confrontation and comprehension of spoken language are important reasons for neuropsychological consultation in dementia patients. The Boston Naming test is widely used in North America for assessing confrontation naming. The Token Test is widely used for formal assessment of auditory comprehension (DeRenzi & Vignolo, 1982).

Verbal fluency is a frequently used task that assesses both verbal expressive abilities and executive functions. Several studies have shown that category or letter fluency tests are useful in early detection of dementia due to AD (Monsch et al., 1992; Welsh et al., 1994). Moreover, verbal fluency tests are useful for identifying patients with behavioral FTD and progressive aphasic disorders (Kramer et al., 2003; Libon et al., 2007). Assessment of vocabulary level and other measures of verbal ability can be particularly useful in estimating a patient's premorbid level of cognitive function. The Vocabulary subtests of the WAIS-R or WAIS-III are useful for evaluating premorbid verbal abilities. The National Adult Reading Test-Revised (NART-R) has also been used for the purpose of estimating premorbid verbal intelligence. Its advantage over the WAIS-vocabulary test in this context is that the NART simply requires correct pronunciation of the test words. It may be superior to educational level for quantitating premorbid intellectual level (Pavlik et al., 2006). In contrast, the vocabulary test requires not only recognizing the test word but also explaining its meaning, a function that may be impaired even in early dementia (Maddrey et al., 1996).

VISUOSPATIAL FUNCTION

Testing of visuospatial function with tests such as the Block Design subtest of the WAIS-R (Wechsler, 1981; Lezak, 1995) in the neuropsychological laboratory is considerably more detailed than is feasible with bedside testing. Other tests used include copying and then later drawing from memory the Rey-Osterreith figure.

Because visuospatial function draws on limb motor performance, the ability to sustain attention, and executive function, it is abnormal in many forms of dementia, even when patients are able to copy intersecting pentagons or draw a clock. Furthermore, bedside testing of visuospatial function usually requires intact dominant limb function. In patients with hemiparesis or other causes of dysfunction of the dominant hand or arm, neuropsychological tests such as Benton Judgment of Line Orientation (Lezak, 1995) may be used to evaluate visuospatial reasoning with

minimal need for limb motor function. A quick screening test of visuospatial abilities that requires little motor input is the Clock Reading test (Schmidtke & Olbrich, 2007).

EXECUTIVE FUNCTION AND ABSTRACT REASONING

Lateral and medial frontal brain regions are involved with attention, working memory, and the categorization of contingent relationships. In non–brain-damaged individuals, the separate frontal regions are interconnected and act cooperatively to support reasoning and decision making. We use the term *executive function* to encompass broadly the functions that are supported by the frontal lobes. The neuropsychology laboratory assessment of executive function—mental agility, foresight, planning, freedom from distraction, ability to shift mental set—has several advantages over the kinds of executive tasks that can be assessed with bedside techniques. The laboratory tests utilize specialized test materials. The instruments used to assess executive function take considerable time to administer. Because they are intensely demanding of concentration, testing situations that are optimally quiet and free from distractions are necessary.

Widely used tests such as the Wisconsin Card Sorting Test (Anderson et al., 1991), part B of the Trailmaking test, and the Porteus Mazes (Lezak, 1995) assess ability to shift set, recognize patterns, and alter behavior. The Tower Test measures the ability to problem solve and follow rules (Carey et al., 2008). Patients with frontal lesions commit excessive rule violations. Impaired performance on tests of executive function does not always signify a frontal lobe lesion. Patients with low educational achievement typically score worse on tests of executive function (Ganguli et al., 1991; Welsh et al., 1994; Cerhan et al., 1998), as do patients with depression (Beats et al., 1996). Patients with prominent visuospatial deficits will do poorly on the Wisconsin Card Sorting Test, Porteus Mazes, and Trailmaking because those tasks are visually based.

Some aspects of executive function are not captured by currently available instruments. Although the work is still experimental and not yet suitable for clinical use, newer tests of executive functioning are being developed. For example, the Iowa Gambling Test (Bechara et al., 1998; Torralva et al., 2007) measures decision making in the context of balancing risks and rewards. The multiple errands test (Alderman et al., 2003) involves a series of activities that gauge the patient's ability to stay on task, follow rules, and work efficiently. The Hotel task (Manly et al., 2002) is similarly geared towards measuring a patient's ability to develop a strategy to complete a number of tasks in as efficient a manner as possible.

OTHER DEMENTIA ASSESSMENT TOOLS

Increasingly, clinicians have come to rely on standardized assessment instruments for diagnosis and management of dementia patients. The MMSE and other standardized mental status exams have already been discussed. Other aspects of dementia are equally important to capture quantitatively, such as behavior, function, and also staging of the disease.

BEHAVIOR

A wide variety of neuropsychiatric symptoms occur in AD and other dementias. These behaviors may be challenging to quantitate because the symptoms may vary in frequency and severity. Rare behaviors may be catastrophically severe, whereas frequent behaviors may be minor nuisances. The Neuropsychiatric Inventory (Cummings et al., 1994) rates 12 behaviors that are common in AD and other dementias. Other tests used for assessment of behavior in dementia include the Behavioral Pathology in Alzheimer's Disease Rating Scale (Reisberg et al., 1987), the Frontal Systems Behavior Scale (Malloy & Grace, 2005), and the Frontal Behavioral Inventory (Kertesz et al., 1997).

FUNCTION

Activities of daily living (ADL) as they relate to dementia can be conveniently divided into two categories, basic and instrumental. Basic activities of daily living (Lawton & Brody, 1969) are included as queries. Basic ADLs are typically impaired in more severely demented patients. Pfeffer et al. (1982) developed a functional activities

questionnaire (FAQ) for instrumental daily living activities that is particularly useful for the assessment of patients with mild dementia. The FAQ is not useful for moderately demented individuals. Galasko et al. (1997) have developed a scale for use in clinical trials that has a broad range of performance. Other scales that have been used in AD clinical trials include the Interview for Deterioration in Daily functioning activities in dementia (IDDD) (Teunisse et al., 1991), which contains 33 items, of which 17 involve complex or instrumental activities, and the Disability Assessment in Dementia (DAD) (Gelinas et al., 1999).

GLOBAL DISEASE SEVERITY SCALES

Clinicians often find it helpful to rate patients for overall severity with an instrument that includes information from both caregiver impressions and direct mental status assessments of patients. Several global scales have been developed for that purpose. The Clinical Dementia Rating (CDR) Scale (Hughes et al., 1982; Morris, 1993) is one that includes most aspects of dementia and also provides explicit descriptions of each stage. Six different domains are rated separately: orientation, memory, judgment/problem-solving, function in home/hobbies, function in community affairs, and basic ADLs. Each domain is rated on a 5-point scale. A scoring algorithm (Morris, 1993) allows derivation of an overall rating. Two additional domains, one for language and another for behavior, comportment, and personality have been developed to supplement the standard six-domain CDR for use in patients with prominent behavioral or language difficulties (Knopman et al., 2008). Another scale that is also widely used is the Global Deterioration Scale (Reisberg et al., 1982). It uses eight rating points, ranging from normal through the various stages of severity.

LABORATORY ASSESSMENT IN MILD COGNITIVE IMPAIRMENT AND DEMENTIA

Laboratory assessments play a role in the evaluation of MCI and dementia. The American Academy of Neurology's Practice Parameter on dementia (Knopman et al., 2001) recommended measurement of B_{12} and thyrotropin levels, as well as electrolytes, complete blood count, and renal and hepatic function tests in typical elderly dementia patients. Other than delirium, the nature of the cognitive impairment in B_{12} deficiency and hypothyroidism is poorly understood because cases of deficiencies of either in association with cognitive impairment are very rare in the modern era.

Other laboratory tests should be reserved for patients with specific triggers. Patients with cognitive impairment and systemic symptoms or signs such as anemia, weight loss, or organ dysfunction should also be screened for systemic diseases such as human immunodeficiency virus (HIV) disease (see below); autoimmune diseases, such as potassium channel antibody disease (Thieben et al., 2004); systemic lupus erythematosus (Carlomagno et al., 2000; Loukkola et al., 2003; McLaurin et al., 2005; Kozora et al., 2008); Sjögren syndrome (Caselli et al., 1991); or occult cancer (Gultekin et al., 2000).

In patients with rapidly progressive dementia, a cerebrospinal fluid (CSF) examination should be performed to screen for central nervous system infections, cancer, and Creutzfeldt-Jakob disease (CJD).

Finally, in patients with cognitive impairment who are under age 60 years, additional studies looking for inherited metabolic disorders such as Wilson disease (Akil & Brewer, 1995), metachromatic leukodystrophy (Shapiro et al., 1994), adrenoleukodystrophy (Moser, 1997), and other very rare diseases such as Niemann-Pick type C (Coker, 1991) should be undertaken.

NEUROPSYCHOLOGICAL SYNDROMIC SUBTYPES OF MILD COGNITIVE IMPAIRMENT AND DEMENTIA

A few major clinical-neuropsychological patterns in the dementias correspond to the principal domains of dysfunction. The predominance of one particular domain of impairment may be of use diagnostically.

The *anterograde amnesic syndrome* is the most common, and AD dementia is its prototypical example. Alzheimer disease dementia patients almost always have other cognitive deficits, but typically, the symptoms of memory loss

and forgetfulness stand out. Hippocampal sclerosis is a pathologically defined entity that resembles AD in its profound anterograde amnesic presentation (Ala et al., 2000; Leverenz et al., 2002). Many of the non-AD dementias, such as vascular dementia (Reed et al., 2007), may, on occasion, feature anterograde amnesia as the dominant symptom, so that this syndrome is not specific for AD. The hippocampal system is the anatomic region implicated by anterograde amnesia in dementia, but the fact that the pathology of AD includes both hippocampal as well as neocortical regions makes the link with AD and anterograde amnesia more of a clinical-diagnostic link rather than a clinical association with a discrete anatomic region.

The syndrome of disproportionate abnormalities in executive cognitive dysfunction and behavioral dysregulation is termed *behavioral variant FTD* (Neary et al., 1998). Milder variants with associated executive-type cognitive deficits could be referred to as executive- type MCI. This syndrome is usually not due to AD. However, AD patients have prominent executive deficits along with equally intense anterograde amnesia. The neuropsychological syndrome of behavioral variant FTD is usually associated with pathology in prefrontal, medial frontal, and anterior temporal neocortical regions. Tauopathic and non-tauopathic FTLDs both cause this syndrome. However, lesions in subcortical regions such as the thalamus, the neostriatum, or the white matter pathways linking them to the prefrontal and anterior temporal regions may also produce a similar pattern of cognitive and behavioral deficits.

Disturbances of language function may also occur out of proportion to other cognitive deficits. They may be one of three prominent subtypes of primary progressive aphasia (Neary et al., 1998; Mesulam, 2001). When prominent anomia and loss of word meaning are the core deficits, the syndrome is referred to as *primary progressive aphasia, semantic type (previously known as semantic dementia)*. Primary progressive aphasia, semantic type usually, although not always, is due to the non-tauopathic form of FTLD. The disorder with prominent speech apraxia, agrammatism, labored speech, and reduced number of words per utterance is another distinct syndrome and is referred to as *primary progressive aphasia, nonfluent/agram-matic type (previously known as progressive nonfluent aphasia)*. This variant of primary progressive aphasia is often due to a tauopathic form of FLTD. There is also a disorder of expressive language in which anomia is the dominant symptom, without the difficulties with labored articulation. This latter disorder is referred to as *primary progressive aphasia, logopenic type* (Gorno-Tempini et al., 2004). Primary progressive aphasia, logopenic type may be due to either AD or FLTD.

When visuospatial impairment is the principal or presenting symptomatology, the brunt of the pathology, usually of the Alzheimer type, is seen in the parietal and occipital lobes. Clinically, the syndrome is sometimes referred to *as posterior cortical atrophy* (Mendez et al., 2002; Renner et al., 2004; Tang-Wai et al., 2004) or the *visual variant of AD* (Levine et al., 1993) the former being preferred because non-AD dementias are also occasionally seen in patients with prominent visuospatial impairment.

Finally, there are several dementias in whicht prominent motor and psychomotor slowing occurs in the setting of relative preservation of cortical functions such as language, calculations, and praxis. This pattern of *dementia with psychomotor slowing* occurs in patients with normal-pressure hydrocephalus, in a subset of patients with HIV infection (Navia et al., 1986), and in degenerative disorders such as progressive supranuclear palsy (PSP) or Huntington disease (HD). The pattern of cognitive dysfunction in such a condition as HIV dementia, is distinguished from FTD based on the prominence of cognitive slowing compared to impaired judgment. HIV dementia occurs only during the late stages of acquired immune deficiency syndrome (AIDS), and modern antiretroviral therapies have resulted in a reduced incidence of this dementia.

NEUROPSYCHOLOGICAL ASPECTS OF ALZHEIMER DISEASE

The diagnosis of dementia due to AD is based on the NINCDS-ADRDA criteria (McKhann et al., 1984) that were revised in 2011 (McKhann et al., 2011) (Table 17-2). The revised criteria have taken advantage of the progress made since

---

Table 17–2. Definition of Alzheimer's Disease Dementia (NIA-AA Workgroup, McKhann et al., 2011)

A. Probable AD Dementia is diagnosed when the patient:

1. Meets criteria for dementia (see Table 17-2), and has the following characteristics:

2. Insidious onset. Symptoms have a gradual onset over months to years; and

3. Clear-cut history of worsening of cognition by report or observation; and

4. The initial and most prominent cognitive deficits are evident on history and examination in one of the following categories.

   (1) *Amnestic disorder*: The most common syndromic presentation of AD dementia.

   (2) *Non-amnestic disorders*:

     • Language disorder

     • Visuospatial disorder

     • Executive and behavioral disorder

5. Exclusions: The diagnosis of Probable AD Dementia *should not* be applied when there is evidence of:

   (a) substantial concomitant cerebrovascular disease or

   (b) core features of Dementia with Lewy Bodies other than dementia itself; or

   (c) prominent features of behavioral variant frontotemporal dementia; or

   (d) prominent features of semantic variant primary progressive aphasia or non-fluent/agrammatic variant primary progressive aphasia; or

   (e) evidence for another concurrent, active neurological disease, or a non-neurological medical co-morbidity or medication use that could have a substantial impact on cognition.

(Continued)

Table 17–2. *(Cont'd)* Definition of Alzheimer's Disease Dementia (NIA-AA Workgroup, McKhann et al., 2011)

B. Possible AD dementia is diagnosed when the patient meets one of the two following criteria:

1. *Atypical Course*: Meets the Core Clinical Criteria (1) and (4) (above) for probable AD Dementia, but either had a sudden onset of cognitive impairment or demonstrates insufficient historical detail or objective cognitive documentation of progressive decline, or

2. *Etiologically Mixed Presentation*: Meets all Core Clinical Criteria (1) through (4) (above) for probable AD Dementia but has evidence of:

    (a) concomitant cerebrovascular disease or

    (b) features of Dementia with Lewy Bodies other than the dementia itself; or

    (c) evidence for another neurological disease or a non-neurological medical co-morbidity or medication use that could have a substantial impact on cognition

C. Research Definition of Probable AD dementia with biomarkers*

1. Meets clinical criteria (1) through (5) for Probable AD dementia and has the following levels of probability of AD pathophysiology based on the profile of neuroimaging and cerebrospinal fluid (CSF) biomarkers:

    a. Highest probability: β-amyloid marker (CSF or imaging) "positive" *and* neuronal injury marker (CSF tau, FDG-PET or structural MR) "positive"

    b. Intermediate probability: β-amyloid marker "positive" *or* neuronal injury marker "positive"

    c. Uninformative: Biomarkers unavailable, conflicting or indeterminate

D. Research Definition of Possible AD dementia with biomarkers

1. Meets clinical criteria for Possible AD dementia (above) dementia and has the following levels of probability of AD pathophysiology based on the profile of neuroimaging and CSF biomarkers:

    a. High, but does not rule out second etiology: β-amyloid marker "positive" and neuronal injury marker "positive"

    b. Uninformative: Any other configuration of biomarkers

---

*A biomarker is considered "positive" if it has a value that is regarded as diagnostic AD pathophysiology. As of 2011, there are no universally accepted standards for what is considered diagnostic of AD pathophysiology for any of the biomarkers listed in this Table. Therefore, standards based on local experience would be used.

Table copyright Alzheimer's Association, 2011

1984 in dementia research. The distinguishing features of the clinical diagnosis of AD dementia are a typical temporal profile, a typical spectrum of cognitive deficits, and the absence of features known to be linked to other dementing illnesses. The revised category of "probable AD dementia" is identical to the original formulation in specifying the appropriate temporal profile. The new criteria expand the definition of appropriate cognitive presentations of AD pathology. While the amnestic presentation is still, by far, the most common presentation for AD dementia, non-amnestic presentations such as logopenic primary progressive aphasia and posterior cortical atrophy, discussed later in this chapter, are also recognized. The revised criteria are also more explicit about the distinctions and overlap of AD dementia with other dementias,

especially those due to cerebrovascular disease and Lewy Body disease.

In the revised criteria, AD dementia remains a clinical diagnosis based on the combination of historical information plus objective evidence of cognitive impairment from brief examinations used at the bedside or neuropsychological testing.

In the new criteria, the category of "possible AD dementia" has been refined and focussed on patients who meet some criteria for probable AD dementia but who have atypical temporal profiles (abrupt onset or long plateaus) or evidence for a second etiology for the cognitive disorder.

In the older criteria, persons with MCI were sometimes classified as possible AD, but that inconsistency has been corrected in the revised

NIA-AA criteria. The NIA-AA criteria distinguish between the syndromes of MCI (Albert et al., 2011)and dementia based on differences in severity and extent of cognitive and functional deficits.

The revised AD dementia (McKhann et al., 2011) and AD due to MCI (Albert et al., 2011) criteria also introduce the use of biomarkers in research settings to increase certainty about the presence of underlying AD pathophysiology. The principal biomarkers include those from imaging and cerebrospinal fluid (CSF) (Table 17-2). Different levels of certainty are associated with the pattern of biomarker abnormalities. The highest level of certainty occurs when there is evidence both of β-amyloid marker abnormalities (CSF or positron emission tomography (PET) amyloid imaging) and neuronal injury marker abnormalities (CSF tau, [18]fluorodeoxyglucose-PET or structural MR). The diagnosis of AD dementia with biomarker support is intended to be limited to research settings until the AD biomarkers can be both validated and shown to add value for patients.

A variation on this approach was previously suggested as a way of logically ascribing an etiological basis to MCI (Dubois et al., 2007). The NIA-AA criteria for MCI due to AD differ from prior approaches by defining a hierarchy of biomarkers of the AD pathophysiological basis for MCI due to AD that distinguishes between amyloidogenic and neuronal degeneration processes. See Table 17-2.

Overall dementia severity in AD dementia is well correlated with the burden of neuritic plaques and neurofibrillary tangle pathology (Tiraboschi et al., 2004; Nelson et al., 2007; Haroutunian et al., 2008). Cognitive function in AD dementia, as measured by a test such as the MMSE, is remarkably well correlated with pathological markers of the disease. In a study that involved a brain biopsy 1 day after the MMSE had been administered, the number of synapses as counted in electron microscopic sections had a correlation coefficient of 0.77 with the MMSE (DeKosky & Scheff, 1990). An autopsy-based study that used mental status examinations performed 2 weeks to 3 years prior to death showed a similarly very high correlation between synaptic density and mental status examinations (Terry et al., 1991). From diagnostic and management

perspectives, evaluation of specific cognitive domains adds considerable information beyond what can be obtained from a global assessment.

The neuroimaging correlates of AD include atrophy of the medial temporal lobe, and the hippocampus in particular (Jack et al., 1992; Killiany et al., 1993; de Leon et al., 1997; Xu et al., 2000). The hippocampal changes can be appreciated qualitatively (DeCarli et al., 2007). As the pathological process of AD evolves, quantitative volumetric analyses show that the heteromodal association areas in the frontal, parietal, and temporal lobes undergo atrophy (Du et al., 2007; Dickerson et al., 2008; Whitwell et al., 2008). In contrast, primary visual, auditory, and somatosensory cortices and primary motor cortex are spared. The process may be asymmetric, leading to variations in the magnitude of behavioral, executive, linguistic, and visuospatial deficits in AD.

DECLARATIVE MEMORY AND EXPLICIT LEARNING

Both the NINCDS-ADRDA and DSM-IV definitions require memory impairment for a diagnosis of AD dementia. The amnestic form of MCI is also characterized by deficits in learning and recall. The deficit in "memory" in amnestic MCI and AD dementia is best characterized as a deficit in new learning and encoding of information when there is the intention to learn (Storandt et al., 1984; Knopman & Ryberg, 1989; Welsh et al., 1991; Petersen et al., 1994; Tierney et al., 1996; Grober & Kawas, 1997). Deficits in new learning and delayed recall of newly learned material in otherwise mildly affected persons are highly predictive of the pathological diagnosis of AD (Salmon et al., 2002).

The DSM-IV criteria for AD dementia include both new learning and remote memory under the heading of memory, which is conceptually incorrect, unfortunately. The anatomic and cognitive basis of remote memory is distinct from that of recent memory function. Remote autobiographical and worldly memories are part of semantic memory, which, although impaired in AD dementia patients, is not as profoundly impaired as new learning (Kopelman et al., 1989; Greene et al., 1995). In many mildly demented AD patients, retrieval of information from the remote past is minimally impaired (Storandt et al., 1998). In the

Canadian Study of Health and Aging, the deletion of the requirement for deficits in "remote" memory nearly doubled the number of subjects considered to have a memory problem (Erkinjuntti et al., 1997). Moreover, quantitative evaluation of "previously learned material" (remote memory, or information acquired years before) is difficult in many mildly or even moderately demented individuals.

The memory disorder in AD dementia is best demonstrated on list-learning tasks such as the Auditory Verbal Learning Task, the California Verbal Learning Test, or the Consortium to Establish a Registry for Alzheimer's Disease ten-word list, all of which involve learning new material and testing by free recall after a delay of 20–60 minutes. In MCI and during the earliest stages of AD dementia (which may be one and the same), acquisition of new information may be relatively normal, but delayed recall will nonetheless be impaired (Fox et al., 1998; Petersen et al., 1999). In slightly more impaired but still mild AD dementia patients, there is impaired initial learning of supraspan length material, impairment in free recall after a delay of 30 minutes, impairment in cued recall, and to a lesser extent, impairment in recognition memory. Alzheimer disease patients exhibit much more impairment for items at the beginning of the list (reduced primacy effect) than at the end of the list (less impairment of "recency" effect) (Martin et al., 1985). On subsequent trials, they show a flatter learning curve than do normal subjects in that they learn fewer additional words.

Another paradigm that captures other aspects of the memory impairment in AD dementia (Kopelman, 1985) involves the presentation of three numbers or words followed by free recall after delays of 0, 2, 5, 10, and 15 seconds (a variant of the Brown Peterson paradigm). The delay interval is filled with a distractor task, usually counting backwards by 2's or 3's. Compared to normal subjects, who ordinarily exhibit a 50% decay in recall after 15 seconds, AD dementia patients are at that level within 5 seconds and have virtually no recall at 15 seconds. Even though the amount of material is subspan in quantity (i.e., three items), the imposition of a distractor task substantially interferes with recall in AD dementia patients.

Learning and free recall are most useful for diagnosis of mild AD dementia, but are less useful for defining the different stages of AD dementia. Learning and recall performance are already quite poor in mild AD dementia, and it is difficult to demonstrate further decline as patients move into the moderate stages of the disease. On the other hand, recognition memory, which is often nearly intact in mild AD dementia patients, declines more slowly over the course of the disease (Welsh et al., 1992).

It is widely accepted that the memory deficit in AD dementia patients can be accounted for by the neuropathological changes involving of the hippocampus, subiculum, and entorhinal cortex (Hyman et al., 1984; Braak & Braak, 1991; Gosche et al., 2002). All three regions are heavily involved early in the disease. Magnetic resonance imaging (MRI) scanning studies confirm that brain atrophy in the hippocampal regions is often observable at the time of diagnosis (de Leon et al., 1997; Jack et al., 1997) and is correlated with the degree of memory impairment (Petersen et al., 2000). Neuroimaging shows that the anatomic basis of impaired learning and free recall in AD dementia includes the medial temporal lobe but other structures as well, such as the medial thalamus and posterior cingulate (Nestor et al., 2006). The relationship between the learning deficits (impaired primacy effect, flat learning curve, impaired delayed recall) and the pathology in the hippocampal system in AD dementia is entirely consistent with our understanding, from other disease states, of the anatomic basis of learning.

Further evidence for the central relationship between hippocampal integrity and AD dementia comes from studies of the natural history of MCI. The degree of hippocampal atrophy in MCI patients predicts the likelihood of conversion from MCI to dementia (Jack et al., 1999; Killiany et al., 2002; DeCarli et al., 2007; Devanand et al., 2007; Smith et al., 2007). Atrophy of entorhinal cortex and posterior cingulate cortex might also predict conversion from MCI to dementia (Barnes et al., 2007). Although hippocampal volume loss cannot be used for accurate clinical prediction of subsequent course, elderly persons with hippocampal atrophy diagnosed as normal are also at increased risk for subsequently developing AD dementia (Jack et al., 2005; Jagust et al., 2006).

The cholinergic projection neurons in the nucleus basalis, diagonal band, and septum are almost always subjected to neurofibrillary tangle formation (Saper et al., 1985). Dysfunction in cholinergic input to the hippocampus probably also plays a role in the memory disorder of AD (Hyman et al., 1987). A moderately strong correlation exists between performance on mental status examinations and the degree of cholinergic dysfunction (Francis et al., 1985; DeKosky et al., 1992).

IMPLICIT LEARNING

"Unaware" learning of certain tasks in the presence of dense anterograde amnesia occurs in AD. Several paradigms have been devised to tap into this function, such as various types of semantic priming tasks (Grafman et al., 1990; Heindel et al., 1997; Grossman et al., 2007) and several motor learning tasks (Grafman et al., 1990; Knopman, 1991; Willingham et al., 1997; van Halteren-van Tilborg et al., 2007). In one study that examined the neuropathological basis of implicit learning, the burden of AD pathology was linked to semantic but not perceptual priming (Fleischman et al., 2005).

ORIENTATION

Orientation is impaired in patients with AD dementia, although not invariably in mild patients. Orientation for time and place are mediated by memory, attention, language, visual function, and even executive functions; its impairment is a proxy for dysfunction in one or more of those domains. Orientation is virtually always impaired in dementia patients eventually.

LANGUAGE

Disturbances of language function are common in AD dementia. Although empiric studies confirm subtle language impairment even in the mild stages of AD dementia, frank aphasia is uncommon as a presenting syndrome of AD dementia, although it definitely occurs (Galton et al., 2000; Alladi et al., 2007; Mendez et al., 2007). In typical AD dementia, anomia and other aphasic disturbances occur only during the later stages of the illness. On rare occasions, patients who eventually prove to have AD pathologically may present initially with word-finding

problems that are out of proportion to other cognitive symptoms. This syndrome, *logopenic progressive aphasia* (Gorno-Tempini et al., 2004) can also occur with the FTLD, however.

By far, the most common language abnormality during early stages of dementia is word-finding difficulty or dysnomia. The dysnomia is sensitive to word frequency (Shuttleworth & Huber, 1988). A deficit in semantic processing is thought to be in part responsible for naming deficit in AD dementia (Grossman et al., 1998; Salmon et al., 1999), but studies examining naming errors in AD dementia suggest that lexical access problems and impaired activation of output phonology may be contributory (Nicholas et al., 1996). Category-specific naming deficits are not typically seen with AD dementia. Comprehension of conversational speech is thought to be relatively preserved during early stages of the disease, although formal testing may reveal some deficits even in milder patients (Grossman et al., 1996; Grossman & White-Devine, 1998; Croot et al., 1999).

Disorders of writing tend to occur relatively early in patients with AD dementia, consistent with relatively early involvement of the parietal lobes (Croisile, 1999). Poor performance of writing by AD dementia patients probably arises from multiple sources, including impairment in lexicosemantic systems (Lambert et al., 1996) as well as perseveration, executive dysfunction, and apraxia (Glosser et al., 1999).

Reduction in the number of words produced in tasks of verbal fluency is highly discriminating for mild AD dementia (Monsch et al., 1992; Welsh et al., 1992). Verbal fluency continues to deteriorate with increasing severity of AD dementia. This verbal task is typically thought of as a measure of executive function. Repetition deficits rarely occur in mild AD dementia with typical anterograde amnesic deficits. However, in the rare AD dementia patients who present with logopenic aphasia, repetition may be prominently impaired.

In contrast, some language tasks are relatively resistant to dysfunction in mild or even moderate AD dementia. Longitudinal studies suggest that language functions, such as reading, are relatively preserved (Paque & Warrington, 1995). Tests of reading of uncommon, irregularly spelled words, such as the New Adult Reading Test, can be used to determine premorbid intellectual levels in AD dementia (Willshire et al., 1991; Maddrey et al., 1996).

VISUOSPATIAL FUNCTION

Disturbances of visuospatial function commonly occur in AD dementia. In rare cases, the dominant presentation of the dementia is a gradually developing simultanagnosia (Balint syndrome), now usually referred to as *posterior cortical atrophy* (Mendez et al., 2002; Renner et al., 2004; Tang-Wai et al., 2004) (see below).

Unfortunately, visual-spatial function is one area in which the standard definitions of AD dementia lack clarity. The DSM-IV criteria include "agnosia," which is a severe disturbance of visual recognition rarely present in early stages of AD or other types of dementia. There is no specific reference to milder dysfunction of higher visual and spatial functions. The NINCDS-ADRDA criteria (McKhann et al., 1984) refers to visual perception and to "praxis" but describes the latter as visual constructional ability.

There is little evidence of impairment at the level of elemental visual perception during the early stages. Patients with early AD dementia tend not to have difficulties with identifying the common objects in line drawings such as on the Boston Naming Test. However, the perception of spatial relationships on a measure such as the Judgment of Line Orientation can be impaired relatively early (Finton et al., 1998).

In mild AD dementia, tests of visual constructions that involve copying of simple figures may not be substantially impaired (Welsh et al., 1992). Patients with AD dementia, as well as patients with vascular dementia or dementia with Lewy bodies of mild severity or greater, tend to be impaired on more complex tests of visuo-construction, such as clock drawing (Esteban-Santillan et al., 1998; Cahn-Weiner et al., 1999), the Rey Complex Figure, or Block Design from the WAIS-III. With progression of the disease, more severe forms of visuospatial synthesis, such as difficulties recognizing familiar faces or familiar environments, begin to emerge. It is therefore not surprising that patients with AD dementia have difficulty with tasks that combine perception of spatial relationships with numbers, such as clock drawing and perception of time from analog

clocks. Alzheimer disease patients are impaired on tasks that involve figure–ground discriminations or discrimination of complex visual scenes (Mendez et al., 1990). Patients with AD dementia have difficulty in geographic orientation (Monacelli et al., 2003). With advances in technology, testing of spatial and geographic cognition in virtual reality environments is feasible and can be shown to detect deficits in AD dementia patients (Cushman et al., 2008).

EXECUTIVE FUNCTIONS

Early in the dementia of AD, executive deficits are readily apparent, and distinguish mild patients from normal subjects (Kopelman, 1991; Lafleche & Albert, 1995; Mohs et al., 1997; Kanne et al., 1998; Collette et al., 1999; Albert et al., 2001), and the consequences of deficits in problem-solving, judgment, foresight and mental agility lead to loss of competence in daily living (Marson et al., 1995). Judgment and abstract reasoning are invariably affected even in mildly demented patients, and by the moderate stages of AD dementia, may be untestable. Verbal fluency, trailmaking, maze solving, or card sorting tasks all demonstrate these findings. In a subset of AD dementia patients, executive deficits are very prominent (Johnson et al., 1999). Alzheimer disease patients are generally impaired on measures of competency. Their ability to understand the consequences of medical decisions tends to correlate with several cognitive measures, including executive function tasks (Marson et al., 1996; Marson et al., 1999). The NINCDS-ADRDA definition of AD dementia refers to "problem-solving" in citing executive function.

More specifically, working memory, mental agility, and set shifting are prominently impaired (Perry & Hodges, 1999). On tests measuring sustained or divided attention (Greene et al., 1995; Johannsen et al., 1999; Perry & Hodges, 1999) or habituation and inhibition (Langley et al., 1998), AD dementia patients show substantial impairment. For example, experiments that require patients to divide attention between two tasks show that this manipulation results in more dysfunction for AD dementia patients than does sustaining attention on one task (Johannsen et al., 1999). Because attention is an important component of the performance of many neuropsychological tests, impaired attention may result in poor results in other cognitive domains. Disproportionately poor performance on simple tests of attention, such as digit span, may indicate that the patient is suffering from delirium rather than dementia.

Simpler tasks that can be used at the bedside, such as reciting the months of the year backward, solving arithmetic problems (in someone with known prior basic arithmetic skills), clock drawing, or verbal similarities and differences also bring out executive deficits in AD dementia patients. Ability to inhibit inappropriate actions and to carry out two cognitive tasks simultaneously (holding the result of one calculation in one's mind while carrying out a second calculation, and then adding the result together) may be two of the most important underlying executive functions to be impaired in AD dementia (Collette et al., 1999).

Deficits in executive function can influence performance in multiple cognitive domains. For example, poor organizational strategies on tests of verbal learning and lack of a consistent strategy on tests of visuo-constructional abilities have been reported with frontal lobe dysfunction.

In contrast to AD dementia, behavioral variant FTDs have executive dysfunction as their principal deficits (see below). In addition, dementias without hippocampal involvement but with predominant striatal, thalamic, or white matter (subcortical) involvement, such as PSP, HIV dementia, and vascular dementia, tend to be characterized by disproportionate psychomotor slowing and executive dysfunction (see below).

APRAXIA

Clinically significant ideomotor apraxia is often inapparent or modest in mild AD dementia (Rapcsak et al., 1989; Travniczek-Marterer et al., 1993; Mohs et al., 1997). Limb-transitive actions (e.g., "Show me how you would use a comb") elicit the greatest impairment in AD dementia patients (Rapcsak et al., 1989). Extremely rarely, AD may present with symptoms of apraxia as the earliest symptoms (Green et al., 1995). The role of apraxia as a symptom of dementia has been confounded by imprecision

in the use of the term. In the DSM-IV definition of dementia, ideomotor apraxia is specified. The NINCDS-ADRDA criteria broadened the intent of the word "apraxia" to include visuo-constructional deficits, but we would prefer to maintain the traditional use of the word "apraxia." There is some evidence that measuring response latency for executing gestures may provide a more sensitive measure of early (subclinical) apraxia in AD (Willis et al., 1998). It has also been suggested that imitation of meaningless gestures may be a more sensitive measure of early apraxia in AD than the traditional approach using purposeful actions (Dobigny-Roman et al., 1998). Ideomotor apraxia observed in some patients with AD is unrelated to impaired motor learning skills on tasks such as the rotor pursuit task (Jacobs et al., 1999).

Even though ideational apraxia was first described in patients with dementia and confusional states, only a few contemporary studies have compared ideational and ideomotor praxis. Ideational praxis, as defined by tool–action relationships and tool–object associations, could be disturbed in some AD dementia patients who had relatively preserved ideomotor praxis and relatively preserved language function (Ochipa et al., 1992). Scores for performance on ideomotor and ideational praxis tasks were highly correlated in AD dementia (Rapcsak et al., 1989).

Apraxia is not a more prominent symptom in patients with early-onset familial AD compared to late-onset sporadic AD (Swearer et al., 1992).

MOTOR AND PSYCHOMOTOR

Although performance on tests of simple motor function, such as finger tapping, pegboard, or reaction time, may be mildly slowed in patients with AD dementia when compared with neurologically intact individuals (Goldman et al., 1999), these deficits are nonetheless very mild when compared with the changes in memory and other cognitive functions. By contrast, patients with dementias of predominantly subcortical involvement, such as Parkinson disease, HIV dementia, and cerebrovascular dementia, tend to have early and more prominent impairment in areas of motor and psychomotor speed. Therefore, tests of motor speed are very important for distinguishing cortical dementias from subcortical dementias.

ANOSOGNOSIA

Anosognosia, unawareness of disability, is nearly universal among individuals with AD dementia (Grut et al., 1993; Lopez et al., 1994; Starkstein et al., 1996; Seltzer et al., 1997). The anosognosia for the memory problems and other disabilities is not complete, in that occasional patients will readily admit to their problems (Grut et al., 1993), although these individuals almost never are able to act on their concerns. The majority of patients tend to dismiss or minimize the memory failures, errors in judgment, or other lapses when queried about them by family or physicians. The lack of motivation on the part of the patient to seek medical attention is one of the major impediments to the diagnosis since the burden falls on others to recognize the problem, seek to act on the problem, and then convince the patient to accede.

BEHAVIORAL AND AFFECTIVE CHANGES

Disturbances of behavior or changes in comportment are among the core symptoms of AD dementia (Oppenheim, 1994), but also occur in most of the other degenerative and vascular dementias. The spectrum of changes is protean in AD dementia, ranging from increased apathy and social withdrawal to disinhibition or irritability (Reisberg et al., 1987; Teri et al., 1988; Mega et al., 1996; Reichman et al., 1996; Devanand et al., 1997; Gilley et al., 1997; Patterson et al., 1997; Lyketsos et al., 2002). Apathy is the most common neuropsychiatric symptom of AD dementia patients, followed by agitation, anxiety, irritability, and depression (Mega et al., 1996). None of these is specific for AD dementia, and may also occur in patients with subcortical disease. On the other hand, flamboyant, disinhibited, socially inappropriate behavior that typifies behavioral variant FTD rarely occurs in AD dementia.

LONGITUDINAL EVOLUTION OF COGNITIVE DECLINE IN ALZHEIMER DISEASE AND AMNESTIC MILD COGNITIVE IMPAIRMENT

Many patients with MCI decline and eventually receive a diagnosis of dementia, but the rate of global decline while still in MCI is slow, much slower than is seen once patients develop AD dementia (Smith et al., 2007). The stage of MCI may, in fact, be prolonged by compensatory processes that mitigate the neuropathological changes of incipient dementia. The small magnitude of change in patients with MCI has made trials in MCI quite challenging as large numbers of subjects are needed to detect it (Petersen et al., 2005; Feldman et al., 2007; Winblad et al., 2008).

In typical practice situations, clinicians rely on bedside mental status examinations and serial discussions with caregivers to determine rate of progression of dementia and to make predictions about future problems. In AD dementia patients, the rate of change on the MMSE is about 3 + 4 points per year (Salmon et al., 1990; Galasko et al., 1991; Schneider, 1992; Kraemer et al., 1994). Although that small amount of change may strike some clinicians as insensitive, the rate of change on the MMSE is probably a reasonable reflection of the global decline of an AD dementia patient. At some times, the MMSE seems even too sensitive. On an individual level, the rate of decline over one 6-month or 1-year period does not predict the rate over the next interval (Salmon et al., 1990).

The rate of decline in patients with typical AD dementia depends upon where the patient performs on initial assessment. Although substantial interindividual variability exists, cognitive decline on a test like the MMSE or an expanded instrument like the Alzheimer's Disease Assessment Scale - cognitive portion (ADAS-cog) (Rosen et al., 1984; Mohs & Cohen, 1988) exhibits a curvilinear relationship between baseline cognitive status and rate of decline over 6 months to 1 year (Morris et al., 1993; Stern et al., 1994). The smallest changes occur at the mildest and more severe ends of the spectrum. The reasons for this pattern could relate to the properties of the tests, or could relate to the disease progression itself. It is nearly impossible to distinguish which explanation is correct. The point may be an academic one, because from a clinical perspective, the observation of less decline in milder or more severe patients has been repeatedly observed. Experience with clinical trials of patients with mild to moderate AD dementia (MMSE scores between roughly 12 and 26) has shown that placebo-treated patients with AD dementia lose about 5–6 points per year on the ADAS-cog (Aisen et al., 2003; Reines et al., 2004).

Bedside mental status examinations are usually well suited for longitudinal follow-up, with some exceptions. For patients who are not very mild, the MMSE functions quite well for detecting change over the course of the disease. In some circumstances, a test like the MMSE may be inadequate for longitudinal follow-up. Patients with mild FTD, for example, may score near perfect on the MMSE, and may fail to show decline on the MMSE in the early stages of the disease. Patients with progressive aphasia may also not be the best candidates for the use of a test like the MMSE. In these instances, individual selection of cognitive measures, such as tests of verbal fluency or tests of reasoning and mental agility, may be more valuable. Similarly, in patients with the visual variant of AD, additional drawing and construction tasks should be used.

Factors that influence rate of cognitive decline in AD dementia may include education (Scarmeas et al., 2006) and prior participation in cognitive-stimulating leisure activities (Helzner et al., 2007). The observation of the association of higher educational attainment with more rapid cognitive decline in established AD dementia has suggested that more highly educated individuals may be exhausting their cognitive reserve once dementia appears. The APOE genotype appears to play a relatively small role in rate of decline in AD dementia (Dal Forno et al., 1996; Cosentino et al., 2008).

NEUROPSYCHOLOGICAL ASPECTS OF OTHER DEMENTIAS

POSTERIOR CORTICAL ATROPHY

Posterior cortical atrophy (PCA) may be a variant of AD pathology. It is characterized by disproportionate impairment in visuospatial function, relatively preserved memory, and relatively preserved insight. Visual impairment may occur in the context of reading (alexia), object recognition (associative visual agnosia), or face recognition (prosopagnosia), but it almost always causes simultanagnosia (Balint syndrome) (Graff-Radford et al., 1993; Mendez et al., 2002;

Tang-Wai et al., 2004; McMonagle et al., 2006). The syndrome of PCA probably overlaps with AD dementia when it is associated with some visuospatial impairment. The syndromic differences are in the degree of preservation of memory and insight in PCA compared to AD dementia. Rarely, PCA may be due to corticobasal degeneration, but the dominant pathology is AD (Renner et al., 2004; Tang-Wai et al., 2004). Patients with PCA typically show disproportionate atrophy of the occipital lobes and visual association cortices with obvious concomitant enlargement of the occipital horn of the lateral ventricles (Mendez et al., 2002; Tang-Wai et al., 2004). The hippocampal formations may be spared in PCA.

VASCULAR COGNITIVE IMPAIRMENT AND VASCULAR DEMENTIA

The term *vascular cognitive impairment* is used here to encompass the cognitive deficits attributable to cerebrovascular disease that span the range of MCI to frank dementia. In population-based studies, vascular dementia is about one-fifth as common as AD dementia (Fratiglioni et al., 2000). In a series of European studies, the pooled prevalence of vascular dementia defined by various criteria was 1.6% in the over-65 population (compared to AD dementia prevalence of 4.4% in the same studies) (Lobo et al., 2000). The additional burden of vascular cognitive impairment short of dementia is unknown.

Diagnostic criteria for vascular dementia are widely regarded as flawed. Current clinical diagnostic criteria for vascular dementia (Roman et al., 1993; American Psychiatric Association, 1994; Chui et al., 2000) cannot distinguish between "pure" vascular dementia and the combination of cerebrovascular and neurodegenerative etiologies. The best that the published criteria can do are to present reasonable specificity for dementing illness with a strong cerebrovascular component, while having a very poor sensitivity (Holmes et al., 1999; Gold et al., 2002; Knopman et al., 2003).

The clinical circumstances that can lead to cognitive impairment of cerebrovascular etiology are varied, reflecting the diversity of pathology that occurs in atherosclerosis and arteriolosclerotic brain injury. Usually, but not always, patients with vascular cognitive impairment have other typical symptoms and signs of cerebrovascular disease, such as gait disturbances, hemiparesis, or hemianopia. Patients with cerebrovascular disease may develop the syndromes of MCI or dementia in the presence of cerebral infarctions with single strategically placed lesions in such regions as the hippocampus, thalamus, or parietal lobes. Vascular dementia can also be seen in patients with multiple large-vessel cortical infarctions or smaller-vessel, deep, lacunar-type infarctions. There almost certainly is a dementia of cerebrovascular origin in which there is no history of stroke and no one obvious infarction on imaging (White et al., 2002; Schneider et al., 2004); this latter condition is a microvascular disorder.

Patients with focal right hemisphere lesions such as infarctions (Mesulam et al., 1976) may develop delirium acutely that can sometimes evolve into a clinical state that mimics dementia. Similarly, patients who sustain lesions in other cognitively eloquent locations in the brain, such as the left parietal lobe (Devinsky et al., 1988), thalamus (Graff-Radford et al., 1990), caudate nuclei (Mendez et al., 1989; Caplan et al., 1990), or hippocampus (Zola-Morgan et al., 1986; Ott & Saver, 1993), may have cognitive impairment in more than one domain in a pattern that overlaps with a dementia syndrome. Even small subcortical infarcts in "strategic" subcortical locations can sometimes produce surprisingly widespread cognitive and personality changes that can mimic the cognitive profile of a dementia syndrome (Tatemichi et al., 1992). Small, strategic lesions such as these constitute a small minority of the total number of patients with cerebrovascular disease that relates to their dementia.

White matter hyperintensities (WMH) or leukoaraiosis can be associated with cognitive impairment (de Groot et al., 2000) and increased risk for cognitive decline (De Groot et al., 2002). White matter hyperintensity is a predictor of cognitive decline (Mungas et al., 2001). Severe WMH in nondemented individuals is also a risk factor for dementia (Prins et al., 2004). Patients who have no prior history of stroke but who have infarcts on imaging had greater cognitive decline compared to those with no silent infarcts (Longstreth et al., 2002). Silent infarcts are associated with a greater than twofold risk for subsequent dementia (Vermeer et al., 2003).

Longitudinal studies have shown that stroke is a strong risk factor for cognitive decline and dementia within 1 year of the stroke (Tatemichi et al., 1994; Kokmen et al., 1996; Pohjasvaara et al., 2000; Henon et al., 2001; Gamaldo et al., 2006). Even a remote history of stroke increases the risk for MCI and dementia (Kalmijn et al., 1996; Petrovitch et al., 1998; Dik et al., 2000; Qiu et al., 2006; Reitz et al., 2006; Mariani et al., 2007). Neuropathologically, cerebrovascular pathology in a patient with slowly evolving dementia plays an important supporting role behind AD pathology (Snowdon et al., 1997; Heyman et al., 1998; Schneider et al., 2004; Troncoso et al., 2008).

Most commonly, however, dementia in the setting of vascular disease is associated with a mixture of AD neuropathological changes and infarctions (Galasko et al., 1994; Hulette et al., 1997; Holmes et al., 1999; Lim et al., 1999; Knopman et al., 2003). Pure vascular pathology sufficient to account for dementia is only approximately one-fourth as common as vascular pathology mixed with AD (Holmes et al., 1999; Lim et al., 1999; Knopman et al., 2003).

Given the variability inherent in the diagnostic criteria for vascular dementia, it is not surprising that a diagnostic neuropsychological pattern for vascular dementia has yet to be identified (Looi & Sachdev, 1999; Reed et al., 2007), and probably does not exist. However, the most common observation is that cerebrovascular disease is associated with impairment in nonmemory cognitive domains (Bowler, 2002), especially alterations in motor speed, attention, and executive dysfunction (Looi & Sachdev, 1999). Consistent with these observations are imaging studies of persons with WMH on MRI that have found that nonmemory cognitive dysfunction was more prominent than anterograde amnesia (de Groot et al., 2000; Tullberg et al., 2004; Prins et al., 2005). Analyses of patients with small-vessel disease also have found more prominent associations between evidence of infarction and nonamnesic cognitive functions than with memory impairment (Mungas et al., 2005). Disruption of subcortical white matter pathways linking frontal cortex to other regions by ischemic mechanisms is an attractive explanation as it accounts for both the clinical observations, as well as the evidence from imaging linking WMH and lacunar infarcts to executive deficits (Reed et al., 2004; Tullberg et al., 2004). Unfortunately, many neuropsychological studies of patients with cerebrovascular disease fail to include measures of motor speed, so that the relationship of that domain to the other measured ones is not fully understood.

The cognitive impairment that occurs with cerebrovascular disease poses a challenge for diagnosis and treatment because cerebrovascular disease is rarely the sole cause. It usually plays a supporting, albeit nontrivial role to AD. Less commonly, it is the principal pathological process in a cognitive disorder.

LEWY BODY DEMENTIA

Lewy body dementia comprises two clinical entities, *dementia with Lewy bodies* (DLB) and *Parkinson disease dementia*. These two conditions differ in the temporal profiles of dementia and parkinsonism. In the former, the dementia either precedes or occurs within 1 year of the onset of parkinsonism. Parkinson disease dementia, on the other hand, is the label given to the syndrome in which parkinsonism precedes the dementia by more than 1 year (McKeith et al., 2005). The probability of developing dementia among Parkinson disease patients with long-term survival appears to be quite high (Hely et al., 2008).

Prevalence studies suggest that Lewy body disease is the second or third most common etiology of dementing illness. It might comprise up to 20% of cases (Aarsland et al., 2005).

Criteria for DLB were published in 2005 (McKeith et al., 2005). These criteria include gait and balance disturbances, dementia, prominent visual hallucinations and delusions, fluctuations in cognitive status or arousal, sensitivity to dopaminergic blocking drugs (such as first-generation antipsychotics), and other less consistently seen symptoms and signs.

The cognitive disorder of DLB can be distinct from AD dementia (Salmon et al., 1996; Kraybill et al., 2005; Ferman et al., 2006; Galvin et al., 2006). The differences may be subtle, however. It is difficult to distinguish DLB and AD dementia with certainty on neurocognitive grounds, particularly in more severely demented patients. Patients with DLB have slightly better memory performance (Kraybill et al., 2005) but worse executive functions than do AD dementia patients. Patients with DLB exhibit prominent cognitive slowing (Ballard et al., 2001) that is either the basis for, or interacts with, the attentional and executive deficits in the disorder. For example, DLB patients are likely to do worse on word fluency tasks than are AD dementia patients at the same global severity level. Patients with DLB have some of the cognitive deficits seen in behavioral variant FTD, including lack of initiative and apathy. Both AD dementia and DLB have impairment of visuospatial processing and constructions, but these symptoms may appear earlier in DLB patients and may be somewhat worse. The visual hallucinations in DLB patients are dramatic, elaborate, and often quite outrageous. Delusional thinking often occurs. Psychomotor and motor slowing tends to be more prominent in DLB than in AD dementia (Salmon et al., 1996).

Dementia with Lewy bodies has some other unique manifestations as well. From day to day, many DLB patients experience marked fluctuations in how alert they are. A DLB patient may seem very confused one day and very sharp the next (Ferman et al., 2004). Many patients with DLB experience dramatic, detailed visual hallucinations. They resemble dreams in their vividness and their detachment from reality. Patients with DLB also experience a peculiar sleep disorder called *rapid eye movement sleep behavior disorder*. This particular sleep disorder can precede the diagnosis of DLB by years (Boeve et al., 2003).

The combination of parkinsonism and dementia confers a worse prognosis than that associated with typical AD dementia. Several studies, using different methods of case identification, have shown that patients with extrapyramidal features and dementia progress more rapidly than do patients with dementia due to AD alone (Olichney et al., 1998).

Dementia with Lewy bodies usually represents a mixture of AD and Lewy body pathology at autopsy (Hulette et al., 1995; Hansen & Samuel, 1997). In general, patients with Lewy body pathology have less intense neurofibrillary tangle pathology than do patients with pure AD. Patients with Parkinson disease with dementia have the least AD pathology and those with DLB more. In DLB, the links between neurochemical (Sabbagh et al., 1999) and neuropathological markers (Samuel et al., 1996) on the one hand, and cognition, on the other, are weak.

The 2005 Consortium criteria (McKeith et al., 2005) have excellent positive predictive value and probable specificity for Lewy body pathology (Fujishiro et al., 2008). Sensitivity for DLB (87%) was also higher using the revised criteria. Because Lewy body pathology is common in people with concomitant AD, there may be no simple answer to the sensitivity of clinical criteria for Lewy body disease.

CLINICAL SYNDROME OF BEHAVIORAL VARIANT FRONTOTEMPORAL DEMENTIA

Behavioral variant FTD (bvFTD) as a syndrome differs from the syndrome of anterograde amnesia (i.e., the clinical diagnosis of AD) in the disproportionate impairment of judgment and reasoning compared to recent memory. As the name implies, bvFTD usually presents as a change in personality and an alteration in behavior. Cognitive changes are usually but not always detectable in the earliest stages of bvFTD. The term *dysexecutive syndrome* has been applied to the cognitive syndrome of patients with bvFTD who have grossly disturbed abstract reasoning, poor judgment, and reduced mental flexibility (Neary et al., 1998). In many instances, bvFTD patients can recall minute details of recent events and conversations, even though they cannot use the memories in socially appropriate or functionally productive ways. Yet, caregivers complain that the patients' day-to-day memory functioning is impaired. Inattention, inability to focus on one task, and easy distractibility may account for the impairment of memory in daily activities ("strategic failure" rather than "amnesic failure" in Neary and Snowden's terms) (Neary & Snowden, 1991).

bvFTD constitutes about half of the FTLD in a clinic sample (Johnson et al., 2005; Knopman et al., 2008). A study in Cambridgeshire, U.K.,

found a prevalence of FTLD of 15 per 100,000 in the 45- to 64-year-old age range, whereas a survey in the Netherlands found a lower rate (Ratnavalli et al., 2002; Rosso et al., 2003). An incidence study of all FTLD from Rochester, Minnesota, found a rate of 4.1 per 100,000 population in the 40- to 69-year-old age range (Knopman et al., 2004), a rate that is only slightly less than AD in that age range.

bvFTD patients have a disturbance of personality, behavioral control, comportment, and social awareness that is as intense or exceeds the magnitude of the cognitive deficits. Patients may become socially inappropriate, excessively ebullient, inappropriately aggressive, or may get themselves into trouble because of grossly impaired judgment. Loss of insight and disinhibition contribute to the burden that these patients pose to caregivers. These deficits also highlight the functions of the prefrontal and anterior temporal lobes by showing the consequences of pathology in these regions. The behavioral disturbances are often initially attributed to primary psychiatric diseases, such as mania or psychosis. Alternatively, in patients who primarily demonstrate apathy and inertia, their social withdrawal may lead to a diagnosis of depression, but shows no improvement on antidepressants.

Motor deficits in patients with the syndrome of bvFTD are variable. In some patients, FTD is associated with corticobasal degeneration, and unilateral limb apraxia may result. In other patients who may later prove to have PSP pathologically, rigidity and bradykinesia may be prominent. Some patients with bvFTD will go on to develop motor neuron disease.

The syndrome of bvFTD is almost invariably due to one of the FTLDs. Either the tauopathic or non-tauopathic forms are possible. The tauopathic form is roughly synonymous with the pathological condition of Pick disease, in which there are argyrophilic intracellular inclusions. The non-tauopathic forms of bvFTD include a disease associated with mutations in the gene for progranulin, a sporadic disease with accumulation of the protein TDP-43, a disease associated with motor neuron disease, and some very rare degenerative conditions (Bigio, 2008). Alzheimer disease is an extremely rare cause of bvFTD.

Criteria for bvFTD from a consensus conference (Neary et al., 1998) are currently the standard for diagnosis. The diagnostic criteria reflect the cognitive and behavioral characteristics of FTD observed in pathologically verified cases. The clinical syndrome of bvFTD can be diagnosed with reasonable certainty based on a combination of clinical, neuropsychological, and imaging features (Knopman et al., 2005).

Psychometric testing plays an essential role in the diagnosis of bvFTD because the bedside mental status examination lacks sensitivity for early signs of executive dysfunction (Rascovsky et al., 2002; Kramer et al., 2003; Libon et al., 2007). Patients with bvFTD may be fully oriented and score in the nominally normal range on a test such as the MMSE. At the time of presentation, the typical patient with bvFTD will show either no impairment or mild impairment on tests of recent memory. For example, a bvFTD patient may recall between six and nine words on a 15-word list learning task after a 30-minute delay. The patient may similarly perform at or just below the normal range on tests such as the Block design subtest of the WAIS-R, and may have no difficulty with copying figures, such as the intersecting pentagons of the MMSE. In contrast, the same patient may be able to produce fewer than five words per letter in a letter fluency task over 60 seconds. The bvFTD patient may score poorly on the digit symbol substitution task, be unable to perform Part B of the Trailmaking task, be able to solve only the simplest of mazes, and be unable to complete even one category on the Wisconsin card sorting task. Patients with bvFTD exhibit a remarkable tendency in decision-making tasks to take higher risks than control subjects, seemingly separate from simple impulsiveness (Rahman et al., 1999; Torralva et al., 2007).

Patients with bvFTD have a pervasive impairment in personality and in comportment. The latter includes such behaviors as loss of modesty, inappropriate touching of other people, making off-color or caustic comments about other people, and lacking empathy for the feelings or needs of others. The Frontal-Behavioral Inventory (Kertesz et al., 1997; Kertesz et al., 2000) is a 24-item questionnaire that can be helpful in an inventory of the array of behavioral changes that occur in bvFTD. The ability to understand how other people feel, called *theory of mind*, is a fundamental deficit in patients with bvFTD (Gregory et al., 2002; Lough et al., 2006). Impairment in social cognition seems to be most strongly associated with pathology in the orbital frontal regions. In some bvFTD patients, neuropsychological testing abnormalities may lag behind prominent behavioral changes (Gregory et al., 1999). Thus, the clinical diagnosis of bvFTD does not require abnormal neuropsychological testing.

Magnetic resonance imaging in bvFTD usually shows prominent atrophy of the anterior temporal lobes or the frontal lobes. The frontal atrophy may involve the posterior orbital regions, anterior cingulate cortex, ventromedial regions, insulae, and lateral convexity (dorsolateral and premotor) regions (Rosen et al., 2002; Du et al., 2007; Whitwell et al., 2007). Functional imaging with single-proton emission computed tomography (SPECT) or PET may be more sensitive for the early diagnosis of FTD (Read et al., 1995; Talbot et al., 1998; Foster et al., 2007), but imaging should be best thought of as useful in cases with ambiguous clinical or neuropsychological evidence for or against bvFTD versus AD, rather than as a necessary part of the routine diagnostic process.

DEMENTIAS WITH PROMINENT LANGUAGE DISTURBANCES

The nosology of the neurodegenerative aphasias is in flux at the present time. It has been recognized that the entity of primary progressive aphasia (Mesulam, 1982) includes a number of distinct clinical syndromes that are each associated with differing neuropathological bases.

PRIMARY PROGRESSIVE APHASIA, NONFLUENT/AGRAMMATIC TYPE

Patients with primary progressive aphasia, nonfluent/agrammatic type (PPA-NF/G) are characterized by labored speech that is hesitant, telegraphic, often agrammatic, and anomic. The number of words per utterance in PPA-NF/G patients is markedly reduced, and hence the designation of their speech as nonfluent. Progressive nonfluent aphasia may represent a spectrum of a primary motor speech disturbance plus an aphasic disturbance. The majority of PPA-NF/G patients have a FTLD, and the majority of those have a tauopathic disorder (Hodges et al., 2004; Forman et al., 2006; Josephs et al., 2006). The pathology of patients dying with PPA-NF/G often includes elements that are part of the pathological spectrum of corticobasal degeneration or PSP. This disorder was previously referred to as progressive nonfluent aphasia (Neary et al., 1998), but the term PPA-NF/G is now preferred.

Compared to bvFTD, PNFA is about half as common (Johnson et al., 2005). Patients with PPA-NF/G are typically in their 60s or less commonly in their early 70s. The disorder is quite rare by the ninth decade of life.

The cognitive profile of PPA-NF/G may include other cognitive deficits beyond those directly associated with the speech disorder (Josephs et al., 2006; Knopman et al., 2008). Patients with PPA-NF/G have particular difficulty in tasks that involve processing of phonetic information (Graham et al., 2003; Mendez et al., 2003; Libon et al., 2007). Executive dysfunction is present, although not of the same magnitude as in bvFTD. They may have relatively preserved verbal memory, visuospatial abilities.

The neuroimaging profile of PPA-NF/G usually includes loss of brain volume in the left frontal lobe, centered either on the inferior frontal gyrus or the anterior insula (Nestor et al., 2003; Gorno-Tempini et al., 2004).

Patients with PPA-NF/G typically show progressive reduction in speech output, even though they may remain apparently nondemented. Eventually, cognitive and functional impairment appears.

PRIMARY PROGRESSIVE APHASIA, SEMANTIC TYPE

Patients with primary progressive aphasia, semantic type (PPA-S) are characterized by a distinctive loss of semantic knowledge, even though their speech retains its normal melody and prosody. Anomia is also an integral part of PPA-S, but the core loss of knowledge of the meaning of words and objects distinguishes PPA-S from primary progressive aphasia, logopenic type (Hodges et al., 1992, 1999). The prototypical observation by the patient in the course of a clinical interview is to express an unawareness of the meaning of a common noun when queried. This disorder was previously known as semantic dementia, but the term PPA-S is now preferred, in order to reflect its commonality with other PPA syndromes and the fact that not all PPA-S patients meet criteria for dementia.

PPA-S is also about half as common as bvFTD (Johnson et al., 2005). Patients with PPA-S are typically in their 50s and 60s. It is distinctly uncommon to encounter PPA-S patients who are over age 70 at onset of their illness.

The neuropathology of PPA-S is almost always that of a FTLD, but in contrast to PPA-NF/G is usually of the non-tauopathic type, now called TDP-43 proteinopathy (Knibb et al., 2006). The anatomic basis for PPA-S is the left anterior temporal lobe (Nestor et al., 2006).

Patients with PPA-S often exhibit some of the behavioral abnormalities described under bvFTD. They may not exhibit the executive deficits seen in bvFTD, however (Kramer et al., 2003; Rogers et al., 2006; Knopman et al., 2008). Visuospatial functions are often preserved. Language testing is distinct. They may be profoundly anomic on confrontation naming, and errors are often concrete descriptions of the object rather than the name, such as referring to a kitchen counter as a "platform." Their category fluency performance is typically quite poor even while letter fluency performance is only modestly impaired. Patients with PPA-S typically exhibit surface dyslexia, which is illustrated by their inability to pronounce or recognize orthographically irregular words.

The MRI profile of PPA-S is distinctive. There is a profound loss of brain volume in the anterior portions, both laterally and medially, of the left temporal lobe (Gorno-Tempini et al., 2004; Davies et al., 2008). There is usually involvement of the right anterior temporal lobe as well.

PRIMARY PROGRESSIVE APHASIA, LOGOPENIC TYPE

The clinical entity of primary progressive aphasia, logopenic type (PPA-L) is the most recent to be distinguished from among other degenerative aphasic syndromes. It was recognized both through comparative neuroimaging studies (Gorno-Tempini et al., 2004) and clinical pathological studies (Hodges et al., 2004; Forman et al., 2006; Josephs et al., 2006) that patients with prominent anomic speech patterns—that lacked the agrammatic, labored, dysarthric type described for PPA-NF/G—characterized mainly by word finding pauses in otherwise melodic and euprosodic speech, were different from both PPA-NF/G and PPA-S. A distinctive abnormality in PPA-L patients is a severe difficulty with word and sentence repetition. The likely reason for the difficulties with sentence repetition in PPA-L patients is impaired auditory–verbal short-term memory ("impaired phonological loop function") (Gorno-Tempini et al., 2008). Patients with PPA-L showed brain volume loss in the inferior parietal lobes. Autopsy studies have shown that AD is the more common pathological cause of the syndrome of PPA-L (Alladi et al., 2007; Mesulam et al., 2008).

PROGRESSIVE SUPRANUCLEAR PALSY AND CORTICOBASAL DEGENERATION

The syndrome of PSP was first labeled as a subcortical dementia (Albert et al., 1974) because PSP patients had somewhat better recognition and recent memory than AD patients, but very poor executive function, apathy, and loss of initiative (Albert et al., 1974; Gearing et al., 1994; Grafman et al., 1995; Litvan et al., 1996). Patients with PSP also have substantial motoric deficits, including the diagnostic vertical eye movement disorder, extrapyramidal signs, and brainstem nuclear motor dysfunction. Although they often show profound deficits on such tasks as verbal fluency, trailmaking, or digit symbol substitution, PSP patients perform in only a mildly impaired range on tests of recall and language (Milberg & Albert, 1989; Grafman et al., 1995; Pillon et al., 1995). Most but not all patients with the syndrome of PSP have a tauopathy, which is now recognized as part of the family of the FTLDs (Boeve et al., 2003).

The corticobasal syndrome (CBS) often exhibits a pattern of prominent executive deficits (Pillon et al., 1995; Bergeron et al., 1998) similar to that of the syndrome of PSP. About half of patients with CBS will have corticobasal degeneration pathologically, hence the importance of the distinction between the "syndrome" and the actual neuropathological diagnosis. Corticobasal degeneration is also a tauopathy, and like PSP is regarded as a member of the FTLDs (Kertesz et al., 2000; Boeve et al., 2003). The clinical syndrome of CBS is characterized by unilateral ideomotor apraxia, limb dystonia, myoclonus, and cortical sensory deficits (Gibb et al., 1989; Rinne et al., 1994; Pillon et al., 1995; Litvan et al., 1997). The cognitive profile of CBS includes prominent executive/attentional deficits as well as impairment in visuospatial function (Murray et al., 2007). Many patients with corticobasal degeneration on neuropathological examination have language difficulty that is similar to PNFA, although often milder (Graham et al., 2003). One comparative study noted that CBS patients are more likely than PSP patients to experience depression than apathy (Litvan et al., 1998).

HUNTINGTON DISEASE

Huntington disease is the most common autosomal dominant neurological disease of adults. It is a disorder whose gene mutation involves an excessive number of trinucleotide repeats. The gene for HD, *IT15*, is located on chromosome 4 and codes for a protein known at huntingtin (Reddy et al., 1999).

The disorder may occur prior to age 20, but most cases occur between the ages of 20 and 40 years. The movement disorder and the cognitive disorder usually have onset more or less simultaneously, but they may be dissociated. Huntington disease is also complicated by multiple psychiatric symptoms, including mood disorders, psychotic behavior, anxiety, irritability, and aggression. Some observers have commented upon the association between affective disturbances in HD patients and the disordered family environments that so often occur in the disease (Mindham et al., 1985; Folstein, 1991). The neuropathology of HD appears to be limited to the caudate and putamen, with the cerebral cortex only mildly affected (Vonsattel & DiFiglia, 1998). The prominent motor symptoms are chorea, athetosis, ataxia, rigidity, and dysarthria, which may eventually have a substantial impact on upper limb function as well as gait.

The cognitive disorder of HD is another of the disorders to which the term "subcortical dementia" was applied to draw attention to the cognitive and behavioral distinctions between HD and AD (Paulsen & Conybeare, 2005). Indeed, HD patients have predominantly sub-cortical pathology (Vonsattel & DiFiglia, 1998), but growing understanding of the relationship between the caudate nucleus and the frontal lobes (Cummings, 1993) provides an alternative and unifying account of the dysexecutive deficits in HD. Huntington disease patients exhibit prominent cognitive slowing (Brandt et al., 1988; Bamford et al., 1989; Bamford et al., 1995; Jason et al., 1997). They also show substantial dysexecutive deficits (Lange et al., 1995; Paulsen & Conybeare, 2005). Such defi-cits may also be seen in asymptomatic individu-als who are carriers of the abnormal HD gene (Lawrence et al., 1998). Patients with HD often do reasonably well on delayed recall (Paulsen & Conybeare, 2005). Over time, patients with HD decline in all cognitive domains, but especially on tests of attention and executive function (Lemiere et al., 2004). The behavioral correlates of the dysexecutive syndrome in HD are well known; some HD patients exhibit poor judgment, socially inappropriate behavior, and impulsive-ness, while other are apathetic and abulic (Caine et al., 1978). On the other hand, language func-tions deteriorate only very late in the course of HD, and may be unaffected in early HD.

Neuroimaging has confirmed the impor-tance of striatal atrophy in the motor and cog-nitive deficits that occur in HD, but has also demonstrated cortical thinning in multiple regions, including the motor and premotor cor-tices, medial frontal cortex, and the occipital poles (Kassubek et al., 2004; Peinemann et al., 2005; Rosas et al., 2008).

HIV-RELATED DEMENTIA

HIV-related dementia, also known as AIDS dementia complex, is a complication of HIV infection that occurs in the setting of severe immunosuppression during advanced HIV dis-ease. Before the availability of highly active anti-retroviral medications (HAART), the incidence

of HIV-related dementia was estimated at approximately 7% per year after the first AIDS-defining illness (McArthur et al., 1993). In the post-HAART era, the incidence of dementia related to HIV has seen a dramatic reduction.

The prevalence of a milder form of HIV-related cognitive disorder, designated as HIV-1 associated minor cognitive/motor deficit, may be increasing among patients with AIDS, how-ever. Definitional criteria for both of these con-ditions have been provided by the American Academy of Neurology AIDS Task Force (1991). The nosology of HIV-associated cognitive disor-ders now includes the category of asymptomatic neurocognitive impairment (ANI). Similar to the MCI diagnosis, this refers to patients with an acquired impairment of cognition that is not severe enough to interfere with everyday func-tioning (Antinori et al., 2007). The exact preva-lence and clinical significance of the milder forms of HIV-related cognitive impairment have been controversial. Early studies with small sample sizes found evidence of a high frequency of cognitive impairment during the early, asymp-tomatic stages of HIV infection. However, larger cohort studies did not report significant differ-ences in neuropsychological test performance between asymptomatic HIV-infected patients and seronegative controls (Selnes et al., 1990).

Although there is some variability in the neu-ropsychological test profile associated with early HIV-related dementia, certain key neuropsycho-logical features can help determine whether the cognitive changes are likely to be HIV-related or not. The principal feature is psychomotor and motor slowing. On measures such as the Grooved Pegboard, the slowing is typically most pro-nounced in the nondominant hand. The second feature is a mild-moderate memory disturbance. Although free recall may be moderately impaired, recognition memory tends to be relatively pre-served during the early stages. Mild to moderate constructional impairment on tasks such as copy-ing a three-dimensional cube, a clock, or the Rey Complex Figure, is a third feature. A relative absence of significant dysnomia, dyscalculia, or other parietal lobe findings is also characteristic of the subcortical dementia of HIV. The HIV Dementia Scale is a screening test designed to be particularly sensitive to this subcortical profile (Power et al., 1995; Berghuis et al., 1999).

Several authors have noted that the profile of cognitive test abnormalities in HIV-positive persons may be changing in the post-HAART era. Rather than a predominantly subcortical profile, there is now evidence of additional cortical features (Cysique et al., 2006). Whether this is due to specific effects of HAART or the increasing frequency of active coinfections, such as hepatitis B or C, is not known. The epidemiology of HIV infection has also changed dramatically over recent years, with a significant increase in new infections in persons over the age of 50 years. There is thus a higher frequency of comorbid conditions (e.g., cerebrovascular disease) that can potentially affect the profile of cognitive manifestations. Most of the information about the pattern of neuropsychological abnormalities associated with symptomatic HIV infection was obtained from studies of relatively young individuals. When evaluating older HIV-infected patients, it is important to consider other causes of a predominantly dysexecutive or subcortical pattern of cognitive impairment, such as vascular dementia or FTLDs.

Cognitive dysfunction and brain atrophy, particularly of the caudate nucleus, are related (Hall et al., 1996; Kieburtz et al., 1996; Stout et al., 1998). Neuropathologically, findings are somewhat bland, given the severity of the clinical deficits. Multinucleated giant cells are seen in multiple brain regions, as are microglial nodules containing macrophages, lymphocytes, and microglia. Perivascular inflammation, cortical spongiform changes, and synaptic loss occur (Price et al., 1988). The details of the pathophysiology of HIV dementia are still being worked out. The virus gains entry to the central nervous system soon after infection, but the dementia develops only after years of progressive immunosuppression. There is increasing evidence that the brain injury is due to the indirect effects of immune activation rather than to primary infection of neurons by the HIV virus (Zink et al., 1999).

Because of the success of HAART in reducing the incidence of HIV-related dementia, therapy recommendations for HIV-associated cognitive disorders are closely linked with more general recommendations for treating the underlying infection. Newer recommendations for when to initiate therapy and how to handle treatment failures emphasize the importance of individualized regimens, particularly in patients with active coinfections and those with risk factors for cardiovascular and renal disease (Hammer et al., 2006).

CREUTZFELDT-JAKOB DISEASE

Creutzfeldt-Jakob disease is the prototypical neurological disease that produces a rapidly progressive dementia. The vast majority of CJD patients are deceased in less than 1 year. The diagnosis of CJD is established based on the rapid onset of cognitive impairment (World Health Organization, 1998). The dementia of CJD is pleomorphic. Anterograde amnesia, major affective disturbances, major behavioral disturbances, or progressive visual agnosia are common syndromes that may herald the onset of CJD. Global cognitive impairment rapidly ensues within months of onset. Creutzfeldt-Jakob disease is usually accompanied by motor deficits (cerebellar, pyramidal, or extrapyramidal) and eventually by seizures and EEG abnormalities (Brown, 1994). The diagnosis can be established with moderately high confidence on clinical grounds, but EEG (Steinhoff et al., 1996), MRI (Schroter et al., 2000; Meissner et al., 2004), and CSF assessments (Aksamit et al., 2001) are very helpful in confirming the diagnosis.

NORMAL PRESSURE HYDROCEPHALUS

Normal pressure hydrocephalus (NPH) is a potentially reversible syndrome characterized by the triad of symptoms of gait instability, urinary incontinence, and cognitive decline occurring in the context of radiologically defined ventricular enlargement (Relkin et al., 2005). The cognitive profile of patients with NPH is nonspecific and is similar to that of patients with other forms of dementia. It includes prominent motor slowing, memory retrieval deficits, and some executive deficits (Hellstrom et al., 2007). It can often be a diagnostic challenge to differentiate patients with vascular cognitive impairment from those with NPH. Treatment of patients with NPH involves some form of CSF-shunting, and may improve gait stability and urinary symptoms, whereas cognitive symptoms do not always improve.

TREATMENT OF DEMENTIA

Progress in developing treatments for the neurodegenerative and vascular dementias has been frustrating. Treatment of HIV-related dementia, and most importantly prevention of HIV-related dementia, has been much more effective, particularly in the era of the HAART medications.

The only treatments for AD dementia that have been shown to be effective in well-designed clinical trials are those based on neurotransmitter-based approaches. Three cholinesterase inhibitors have been approved for the treatment of mild to moderate AD dementia: donepezil (Rogers et al., 1998; Burns et al., 1999; Seltzer et al., 2004), galantamine (Raskind et al., 2000; Tariot et al., 2000; Wilcock et al., 2000), and rivastigmine (Corey-Bloom et al., 1998; Rosler et al., 1999). A fourth (tacrine) is no longer marketed. A glutamate modulator (memantine) (Reisberg et al., 2003; Tariot et al., 2004) has also been approved for the treatment of moderate to severe AD dementia. Regulatory approval of anti-AD drugs in the United States is based on the demonstration of benefits on cognitive assessments and clinician's global impressions. For the cholinesterase inhibitors, the cognitive assessment that served as the primary outcome measure was the ADAScog (Rosen et al., 1984). Memantine, on the other hand, utilized the Severe Impairment Battery (Schmitt et al., 1997), a cognitive assessment tool specifically developed for patients who were in the moderate to severe stages of AD.

There have been several trials of cholinesterase inhibitors in MCI patients (Salloway et al., 2004; Petersen et al., 2005; Feldman et al., 2007; Winblad et al., 2008), but none has been positive as of early 2009. None of these four drugs has received regulatory approval for the treatment of MCI.

Although there has been considerable progress in understanding the neurobiology of AD, the advances in our understanding of the molecular biology of β-amyloid and tau protein pathways has not, as of 2010, led to effective therapies. Hopefully, this will change in the next few years.

Treatment of Lewy body dementia has also made only modest progress. Although there is some evidence that cholinesterase inhibitors might have efficacy in treating the cognitive disorder in this condition, no agent has regulatory approval for this indication. The treatment of Lewy body dementia often goes well beyond managing the cognitive dysfunction, however. Treatment of the movement disorder, the often-present depression, the often-present psychosis, and the associated disorders of sleep and wakefulness often are more pressing concerns to the patient, family, and physician.

REFERENCES

Anonymous. (1991). Nomenclature and research case definitions for neurologic manifestations of human immunodeficiency virus-type 1 (HIV-1) infection. Report of a working group of the American Academy of Neurology AIDS task force. *Neurology, 41*, 778–785.

Aarsland, D., Zaccai, J., & Brayne, C. (2005). A systematic review of prevalence studies of dementia in Parkinson's disease. *Movement Disorders, 20*, 1255–1263.

Aisen, P. S., Schafer, K. A., Grundman, M., Pfeiffer, E., Sano, M., Davis, K. L., et al. (2003). Effects of rofecoxib or naproxen vs placebo on Alzheimer disease progression: A randomized controlled trial. *Journal of the American Medical Association, 289*, 2819–2826.

Akil, M., & Brewer, G. J. (1995). Psychiatric and behavioral abnormalities in Wilson's disease. *Advances in Neurology, 65*, 171–178.

Aksamit, A. J., Jr., Preissner, C. M., & Homburger, H. A. (2001). Quantitation of 14-3-3 and neuron-specific enolase proteins in CSF in Creutzfeldt-Jakob disease. *Neurology, 57*, 728–30.

Ala, T. A., Beh, G. O., & Frey, W. H., 2nd. (2000). Pure hippocampal sclerosis: A rare cause of dementia mimicking Alzheimer's disease. *Neurology, 54*, 843–848.

Albert, M. L., Feldman, R. G., & Willis, A. L. (1974). The "subcortical dementia" of progressive supranuclear palsy. *Journal of Neurology, Neurosurgery, and Psychiatry, 37*, 121–130.

Albert, M. S., Moss, M. B., Tanzi, R., & Jones, K. (2001). Preclinical prediction of AD using neuropsychological tests. *Journal of the International Neuropsychological Society, 7,* 631–639.

Albert, M. S., Wolfe, J., & Lafleche, G. (1990). Differences in abstraction ability with age. *Psychology and Aging, 5,* 94–100.

Albert, M., DeKosky, S. T., Dickson, D., Dubois, B., Feldman, H., Fox, N. C., et al. (2011). The diagnosis of mild cognitive impairment due to Alzheimer's disease: Report of the National Institute on Aging and the Alzheimer's Association Workgroup. Alzheimer's & Dementia. *Journal of the Alzheimer's Association, 7,* epub April 19.

Alderman, N., Burgess, P. W., Knight, C., & Henman, C. (2003). Ecological validity of a simplified version of the multiple errands shopping test. *Journal of the International Neuropsychological Society, 9,* 31–44.

Alladi, S., Xuereb, J., Bak, T., Nestor, P., Knibb, J., Patterson, K., et al. (2007). Focal cortical presentations of Alzheimer's disease. *Brain, 130,* 2636–2645.

American Psychiatric Association. (1994). *Diagnostic and Statistical Manual of Mental Disorders.* Washington, DC: American Psychiatric Association.

Anderson, S. W., Damasio, H., Jones, R. D., & Tranel, D. (1991). Wisconsin card sorting test performance as a measure of frontal lobe damage. *Journal of Clinical and Experimental Neuropsychology, 13,* 909–922.

Anthony, J. C., LeResche, L., Niaz, U., von Korff, M. R., & Folstein, M. F. (1982). Limits of the "mini-mental state" as a screening test for dementia and delirium among hospital patients. *Psychological Medicine, 12,* 397–408.

Antinori, A., Arendt, G., Becker, J. T., Brew, B. J., Byrd, D. A., Cherner, M., et al. (2007). Updated research nosology for HIV-associated neurocognitive disorders. *Neurology, 69,* 1789–1799.

Bachman, D. L., Wolf, P. A., Linn, R., Knoefel, J. E., Cobb, J., Belanger, A., et al. (1992). Prevalence of dementia and probable senile dementia of the Alzheimer type in the Framingham study. *Neurology, 42,* 115–119.

Bachman, D. L., Wolf, P. A., Linn, R. T., Knoefel, J. E., Cobb, J. L., Belanger, A. J., et al. (1993). Incidence of dementia and probable Alzheimer's disease in a general population: The Framingham study. *Neurology, 43,* 515–519.

Baker, M., Mackenzie, I. R., Pickering-Brown, S. M., Gass, J., Rademakers, R., Lindholm, C., et al. (2006). Mutations in progranulin cause tau-negative frontotemporal dementia linked to chromosome 17. *Nature, 442,* 916–919.

Ball, L. J., Bisher, G. B., & Birge, S. J. (1999). A simple test of central processing speed: An extension of the Short Blessed test. *Journal of the American Geriatric Society, 47,* 1359–1363.

Ballard, C., O'Brien, J., Gray, A., Cormack, F., Ayre, G., Rowan, E., et al. (2001). Attention and fluctuating attention in patients with dementia with Lewy bodies and Alzheimer disease. *Archives of Neurology, 58,* 977–982.

Bamford, K. A., Caine, E. D., Kido, D. K., Cox, C., & Shoulson, I. (1995). A prospective evaluation of cognitive decline in early Huntington's disease: Functional and radiographic correlates. *Neurology, 45,* 1867–1873.

Bamford, K. A., Caine, E. D., Kido, D. K., Plassche, W. M., & Shoulson, I. (1989). Clinical-pathologic correlation in Huntington's disease: A neuropsychological and computed tomography study. *Neurology, 39,* 796–801.

Barker, W. W., Luis, C. A., Kashuba, A., Luis, M., Harwood, D. G., Loewenstein, D., et al. (2002). Relative frequencies of Alzheimer disease, Lewy body, vascular and frontotemporal dementia, and hippocampal sclerosis in the state of Florida brain bank. *Alzheimer Disease and Associated Disorders, 16,* 203–212.

Barnes, J., Godbolt, A. K., Frost, C., Boyes, R. G., Jones, B. F., Scahill, R. I., et al. (2007). Atrophy rates of the cingulate gyrus and hippocampus in AD and FTLD. *Neurobiology of Aging, 28,* 20–28.

Beats, B. C., Sahakian, B. J., & Levy, R. (1996). Cognitive performance in tests sensitive to frontal lobe dysfunction in the elderly depressed. *Psychological Medicine, 26,* 591–603.

Bechara, A., Damasio, H., Tranel, D., & Anderson, S. W. (1998). Dissociation of working memory from decision making within the human prefrontal cortex. *Journal of Neuroscience, 18,* 428–437.

Berchtold, N. C., & Cotman, C. W. (1998). Evolution in the conceptualization of dementia and Alzheimer's disease: Greco-Roman period to the 1960s. *Neurobiology of Aging, 19,* 173–189.

Bergeron, C., Davis, A., & Lang, A. E. (1998). Corticobasal ganglionic degeneration and progressive supranuclear palsy presenting with cognitive decline. *Brain Pathology, 8,* 355–365.

Berghuis, J. P., Uldall, K. K., & Lalonde, B. (1999). Validity of two scales in identifying HIV-associated dementia. *Journal of Acquired Immune Deficiency Syndrome, 21,* 134–140.

Bieliauskas, L. A. (1993). Depressed or not depressed? That is the question. *Journal of Clinical and Experimental Neuropsychology, 15,* 119–134.

Bigio, E. H. (2008). Update on recent molecular and genetic advances in frontotemporal lobar degeneration. *Journal of Neuropathology and Experimental Neurology, 67,* 635–648.

Blessed, G., Tomlinson, B. E., & Roth, M. (1968). The association between quantitative measures of dementia and of senile change in the cerebral grey matter of elderly subjects. *British Journal of Psychiatry, 114,* 797–811.

Boeve, B. F., Lang, A. E., & Litvan, I. (2003). Corticobasal degeneration and its relationship to progressive supranuclear palsy and frontotemporal dementia. *Annals of Neurology, 54,* S15–19.

Boeve, B. F., Silber, M. H., Parisi, J. E., Dickson, D. W., Ferman, T. J., Benarroch, E. E., et al. (2003). Synucleinopathy pathology and REM sleep behavior disorder plus dementia or parkinsonism. *Neurology, 61,* 40–45.

Boller, F., Lopez, O. L., & Moossy, J. (1989). Diagnosis of dementia: Clinicopathologic correlations. *Neurology, 39,* 76–79.

Borson, S., Scanlan, J. M., Chen, P., & Ganguli, M. (2003). The mini-cog as a screen for dementia: Validation in a population-based sample. *Journal of the American Geriatric Society, 51,* 1451–1454.

Borson, S., Scanlan, J. M., Watanabe, J., Tu, S. P., & Lessig, M. (2005). Simplifying detection of cognitive impairment: Comparison of the mini-cog and mini-mental state Examination in a multiethnic sample. *Journal of the American Geriatric Society, 53,* 871–874.

Bowler, J. V. (2002). The concept of vascular cognitive impairment. *Journal of the Neurological Sciences, 203–204,* 11–15.

Boyle, P. A., Wilson, R. S., Aggarwal, N. T., Tang, Y., & Bennett, D. A. (2006). Mild cognitive impairment: Risk of Alzheimer disease and rate of cognitive decline. *Neurology, 67,* 441–445.

Braak, H., & Braak, E. (1991). Neuropathological staging of Alzheimer-related changes. *Acta Neuropathologica, 82,* 239–259.

Brandt, J., Corwin, J., & Krafft, L. (1992). Is verbal recognition memory really different in Huntington's and Alzheimer's disease. *Journal of Clinical and Experimental Neuropsychology, 14,* 773–784.

Brandt, J., Folstein, S. E., & Folstein, M. F. (1988). Differential cognitive impairment in Alzheimer's disease and Huntington's disease. *Annals of Neurology, 23,* 555–561.

Brayne, C., Spiegelhalter, D. J., Dufouil, C., Chi, L. Y., Dening, T. R., Paykel, E. S., et al. (1999). Estimating the true extent of cognitive decline in the old old. *Journal of the American Geriatric Society, 47,* 1283–1288.

Brown, P. (1994). Infectious cerebral amyloidoses: Creutzfeldt-Jakob disease and the Gerstmann-Straussler-Scheinker syndrome. In J. C. Morris (Ed.), *Handbook of dementing illnesses* (pp. 353–376). New York: Marcel Dekker Inc.

Burns, A., Rossor, M., Hecker, J., Gauthier, S., Petit, H., H., M., et al. (1999). The effects of donepezil in Alzheimer's Disease - Results from a multinational trial. *Dementia and Geriatric Cognitive Disorders, 10,* 237–244.

Butters, M. A., Whyte, E. M., Nebes, R. D., Begley, A. E., Dew, M. A., Mulsant, B. H., et al. (2004). The nature and determinants of neuropsychological functioning in late-life depression. *Archives of General Psychiatry, 61,* 587–595.

Caamano-Isorna, F., Corral, M., Montes-Martinez, A., & Takkouche, B. (2006). Education and dementia: A meta-analytic study. *Neuroepidemiology, 26,* 226–232.

Cahn-Weiner, D. A., Sullivan, E. V., Shear, P. K., Fama, R., Lim, K. O., Yesavage, J. A., et al. (1999). Brain structural and cognitive correlates of clock drawing performance in Alzheimer's disease. *Journal of the International Neuropsychological Society, 5,* 502–509.

Caine, E. D., Hunt, R. D., Weingartner, H., & Ebert, M. H. (1978). Huntington's dementia. Clinical and neuropsychological features. *Archives of General Psychiatry, 35,* 377–384.

Callahan, C. M., Hall, K. S., Hui, S. L., Musick, B. S., Unverzagt, F. W., & Hendrie, H. C. (1996). Relationship of age, education, and occupation with dementia among a community-based sample of African Americans. *Archives of Neurology, 53,* 134–140.

Callahan, C. M., Hendrie, H. C., & Tierney, W. M. (1995). Documentation and evaluation of cognitive impairment in elderly primary care patients. *Annals of Internal Medicine, 122,* 422–429.

Campion, D., Brice, A., Hannequin, D., Tardieu, S., Dubois, B., Calenda, A., et al. (1995). A large pedigree with early-onset Alzheimer's disease: Clinical, neuropathologic, and genetic characterization. *Neurology, 45,* 80–85.

Canadian Study of Health and Aging Working Group. (1994). Canadian study of health and aging: Study methods and prevalence of dementia. *Canadian Medical Association Journal, 150,* 899–913.

Caplan, L. R., Schmahmann, J. D., Kase, C. S., Feldmann, E., Baquis, G., Greenberg, J. P., et al. (1990). Caudate infarcts. *Archives of Neurology, 47,* 133–143.

Carey, C. L., Woods, S. P., Damon, J., Halabi, C., Dean, D., Delis, D. C., et al. (2008). Discriminant validity and neuroanatomical correlates of rule monitoring in frontotemporal dementia and Alzheimer's disease. *Neuropsychologia, 46,* 1081–1087.

Carlomagno, S., Migliaresi, S., Ambrosone, L., Sannino, M., Sanges, G., & Di Iorio, G. (2000). Cognitive impairment in systemic lupus erythematosus: A follow-up study. *Journal of Neurology, 247*, 273–279.

Carlson, M. C., Helms, M. J., Steffens, D. C., Burke, J. R., Potter, G. G., & Plassman, B. L. (2008). Midlife activity predicts risk of dementia in older male twin pairs. *Alzheimer's and Dementia, 4*, 324–331.

Caselli, R. J., Scheithauer, B. W., Bowles, C. A., Trenerry, M. R., Meyer, F. B., Smigielski, J. S., et al. (1991). The treatable dementia of Sjögren's syndrome. *Annals of Neurology, 30*, 98–101.

Cerhan, J. R., Folsom, A. R., Mortimer, J. A., Shahar, E., Knopman, D. S., McGovern, P. G., et al. (1998). Correlates of cognitive function in middle-aged adults. Atherosclerosis risk in communities (ARIC) study investigators. *Gerontology, 44*, 95–105.

Chatfield, M., Matthews, F. E., & Brayne, C. (2007). Using the mini-mental state examination for tracking cognition in the older population based on longitudinal data. *Journal of the American Geriatric Society, 55*, 1066–1071.

Chedru, F., & Geschwind, N. (1972). Writing disturbances in acute confusional states. *Neuropsychologia, 10*, 343–353.

Chui, H. C., Mack, W., Jackson, J. E., Mungas, D., Reed, B. R., Tinklenberg, J., et al. (2000). Clinical criteria for the diagnosis of vascular dementia: A multicenter study of comparability and interrater reliability. *Archives of Neurology, 57*, 191–196.

Cobb, J. L., Wolf, P. A., Au, R., White, R., & D'Agostino, R. B. (1995). The effect of education on the incidence of dementia and Alzheimer's disease in the Framingham study. *Neurology, 45*, 1707–1712.

Coker, S. B. (1991). The diagnosis of childhood neurodegenerative disorders presenting as dementia in adults. *Neurology, 41*, 794–798.

Collette, F., Van der Linden, M., & Salmon, E. (1999). Executive dysfunction in Alzheimer's disease. *Cortex, 35*, 57–72.

Colsher, P. L., & Wallace, R. B. (1991). Longitudinal application of cognitive function measures in a defined population of community-dwelling elders. *Annals of Epidemiology, 1*, 215–230.

Corey-Bloom, J., Anand, R., & Veach, J., for the ENA 713 B352 Study Group. (1998). A randomized trial evaluating the efficacy and safety of ENA 713 (rivastigmine tartrate), a new acetylcholinesterase inhibitor, in patients with mild to moderately severe Alzheimer's disease. *International Journal of Geriatric Psychopharmacology, 1*, 55–65.

Cosentino, S., Scarmeas, N., Helzner, E., Glymour, M. M., Brandt, J., Albert, M., et al. (2008). APOE epsilon 4 allele predicts faster cognitive decline in mild Alzheimer disease. *Neurology, 70*, 1842–1849.

Croisile, B. (1999). Agraphia in Alzheimer's disease. *Dementia and Geriatric Cognitive Disorders, 10*, 226–230.

Croot, K., Hodges, J. R., & Patterson, K. (1999). Evidence for impaired sentence comprehension in early Alzheimer's disease. *Journal of the International Neuropsychological Society, 5*, 393–404.

Crossen, J. R., & Wiens, A. N. (1994). Comparison of the auditory-verbal learning test (AVLT) and California verbal learning test (CVLT) in a sample of normal subjects. *Journal of Clinical and Experimental Neuropsychology, 16*, 190–194.

Crum, R. M., Anthony, J. C., Bassett, S. S., & Folstein, M. F. (1993). Population-based norms for the mini-mental state examination by age and educational level. *Journal of the American Medical Association, 269*, 2386–2391.

Cullum, C. M., Thompson, L. L., & Smernoff, E. N. (1993). Three word recall as a measure of memory. *Journal of Clinical and Experimental Neuropsychology, 15*, 321–329.

Cummings, J. L. (1993). Frontal-subcortical circuits and human behavior. *Archives of Neurology, 50*, 873–880.

Cummings, J. L., Mega, M., Gray, K., Rosenberg-Thompson, S., Carusi, D. A., & Gornbein, J. (1994). The Neuropsychiatric Inventory: Comprehensive assessment of psychopathology in dementia. *Neurology, 44*, 2308–2314.

Cushman, L. A., Stein, K., & Duffy, C. J. (2008). Detecting navigational deficits in cognitive aging and Alzheimer disease using virtual reality. *Neurology, 71*, 888–895.

Cysique, L. A., Maruff, P., & Brew, B. J. (2006). The neuropsychological profile of symptomatic AIDS and ADC patients in the pre-HAART era: A meta-analysis. *Journal of the International Neuropsychological Society, 12*, 368–382.

Dal Forno, G., Rasmusson, D. X., Brandt, J., Carson, K. A., Brookmeyer, R., Troncoso, J., et al. (1996). Apolipoprotein E genotype and rate of decline in probable Alzheimer's disease. *Archives of Neurology, 53*, 345–350.

Davies, R. R., Halliday, G. M., Xuereb, J. H., Kril, J. J., & Hodges, J. R. (2008). The neural basis of semantic memory: Evidence from semantic dementia. *Neurobiology of Aging* (epub 2008, March 24).

de Groot, J. C., de Leeuw, F. E., Oudkerk, M., van Gijn, J., Hofman, A., Jolles, J., et al. (2000). Cerebral white matter lesions and cognitive function: The Rotterdam scan study. *Annals of Neurology, 47,* 145–151.

De Groot, J. C., De Leeuw, F. E., Oudkerk, M., Van Gijn, J., Hofman, A., Jolles, J., et al. (2002). Periventricular cerebral white matter lesions predict rate of cognitive decline. *Annals of Neurology, 52,* 335–341.

de Leon, M. J., George, A. E., Golomb, J., Tarshish, C., Convit, A., Kluger, A., et al. (1997). Frequency of hippocampal formation atrophy in normal aging and Alzheimer's disease. *Neurobiology of Aging, 18,* 1–11.

DeCarli, C., Frisoni, G. B., Clark, C. M., Harvey, D., Grundman, M., Petersen, R. C., et al. (2007). Qualitative estimates of medial temporal atrophy as a predictor of progression from mild cognitive impairment to dementia. *Archives of Neurology, 64,* 108–15.

DeCarli, C., Mungas, D., Harvey, D., Reed, B., Weiner, M., Chui, H., et al. (2004). Memory impairment, but not cerebrovascular disease, predicts progression of MCI to dementia. *Neurology, 63,* 220–227.

DeKosky, S. T., Harbaugh, R. E., Schmitt, F. A., Bakay, R. A., Chui, H. C., Knopman, D. S., et al. (1992). Cortical biopsy in Alzheimer's disease: Diagnostic accuracy and neurochemical, neuropathological, and cognitive correlations. Intraventricular bethanechol study group. *Annals of Neurology, 32,* 625–632.

DeKosky, S. T., & Scheff, S. W. (1990). Synapse loss in frontal cortex biopsies in Alzheimer's disease: Correlation with cognitive severity. *Annals of Neurology, 27,* 457–464.

Delis, D. C., Freeland, J., Kramer, J. H., & Kaplan, E. (1988). Integrating clinical assessment with cognitive neuroscience: Construct validation of the California verbal learning test. *Journal of Consulting and Clinical Psychology, 56,* 123–130.

DeRenzi, E., & Vignolo, L. A. (1982). The token test: A sensitive test to detect receptive disturbances in aphasics. *Brain, 103,* 337–350.

Devanand, D. P., Jacobs, D. M., Tang, M. X., Del Castillo-Castaneda, C., Sano, M., Marder, K., et al. (1997). The course of psychopathologic features in mild to moderate Alzheimer disease. *Archives of General Psychiatry, 54,* 257–263.

Devanand, D. P., Pradhaban, G., Liu, X., Khandji, A., De Santi, S., Segal, S., et al. (2007). Hippocampal and entorhinal atrophy in mild cognitive impairment: Prediction of Alzheimer disease. *Neurology, 68,* 828–836.

Devinsky, O., Bear, D., & Volpe, B. T. (1988). Confusional states following posterior cerebral artery infarction. *Archives of Neurology, 45,* 160–163.

Dickerson, B. C., Bakkour, A., Salat, D. H., Feczko, E., Pacheco, J., Greve, D. N., et al. (2008). The cortical signature of Alzheimer's disease: Regionally specific cortical thinning relates to symptom severity in very mild to mild AD dementia and is detectable in asymptomatic amyloid-positive individuals. *Cerebral Cortex, 19,* 497–510.

Dickerson, B. C., Sperling, R. A., Hyman, B. T., Albert, M. S., & Blacker, D. (2007). Clinical prediction of Alzheimer disease dementia across the spectrum of mild cognitive impairment. *Archives of General Psychiatry, 64,* 1443–1450.

Dik, M. G., Deeg, D. J., Bouter, L. M., Corder, E. H., Kok, A., & Jonker, C. (2000). Stroke and apolipoprotein E epsilon4 are independent risk factors for cognitive decline: A population-based study. *Stroke, 31,* 2431–2436.

Dobigny-Roman, N., Dieudonne-Moinet, B., Tortrat, D., Verny, M., & Forette, B. (1998). Ideomotor apraxia test: A new test of imitation of gestures for elderly people. *European Journal of Neurology, 5,* 571–578.

Drachman, D. A., Leavitt, J. (1972). Memory impairment in the aged: Storage versus retrieval deficit. *Journal of Experimental Psychology, 93,* 302–308.

Du, A. T., Schuff, N., Kramer, J. H., Rosen, H. J., Gorno-Tempini, M. L., Rankin, K., et al. (2007). Different regional patterns of cortical thinning in Alzheimer's disease and frontotemporal dementia. *Brain, 130,* 1159–1166.

Dubois, B., Feldman, H. H., Jacova, C., Dekosky, S. T., Barberger-Gateau, P., Cummings, J., et al. (2007). Research criteria for the diagnosis of Alzheimer's disease: Revising the NINCDS-ADRDA criteria. *Lancet Neurology, 6,* 734–746.

Dubois, B., Slachevsky, A., Litvan, I., & Pillon, B. (2000). The FAB: A frontal assessment battery at bedside. *Neurology, 55,* 1621–6.

Eefsting, J. A., Boersma, F., Van den Brink, W., & Van Tilburg, W. (1996). Differences in prevalence of dementia based on community survey and general practitioner recognition. *Psychological Medicine, 26,* 1223–1230.

Elderkin-Thompson, V., Mintz, J., Haroon, E., Lavretsky, H., & Kumar, A. (2007). Executive dysfunction and memory in older patients with major and minor depression. *Archives of Clinical Neuropsychology, 22,* 261–270.

Ellis, R. J., Jan, K., Kawas, C., Koller, W. C., Lyons, K. E., Jeste, D. V., et al. (1998). Diagnostic validity of the dementia questionnaire for Alzheimer disease. *Archives of Neurology, 55,* 360–365.

Elwood, R. W. (1995). The California Verbal Learning Test: Psychometric characteristics and clinical application. *Neuropsychology Review, 5,* 173–201.

Erkinjuntti, T., Ostbye, T., Steenhuis, R., & Hachinski, V. (1997). The effect of different diagnostic criteria on the prevalence of dementia. *New England Journal of Medicine, 337,* 1667–1674.

Esteban-Santillan, C., Praditsuwan, R., Ueda, H., & Geldmacher, D. S. (1998). Clock drawing test in very mild Alzheimer's disease. *Journal of the American Geriatric Society, 46,* 1266–1269.

Evans, D. A., Funkenstein, H. H., Albert, M. S., Scherr, P. A., Cook, N. R., Chown, M. J., et al. (1989). Prevalence of Alzheimer's disease in a community population of older persons. Higher than previously reported. *Journal of the American Medical Association, 262,* 2551–2516.

Farlow, M., Murrell, J., Ghetti, B., Unverzagt, F., Zeldenrust, S., & Benson, M. (1994). Clinical characteristics in a kindred with early-onset Alzheimer's disease and their linkage to a G—>T change at position 2149 of the amyloid precursor protein gene. *Neurology, 44,* 105–111.

Farrer, L. A., Cupples, L. A., Haines, J. L., Hyman, B., Kukull, W. A., Mayeux, R., et al. (1997). Effects of age, sex, and ethnicity on the association between apolipoprotein E genotype and Alzheimer disease. A meta-analysis. APOE and Alzheimer Disease Meta Analysis Consortium. *Journal of the American Medical Association, 278,* 1349–1356.

Feldman, H. H., Ferris, S., Winblad, B., Sfikas, N., Mancione, L., He, Y., et al. (2007). Effect of rivastigmine on delay to diagnosis of Alzheimer's disease from mild cognitive impairment: The InDDEx study. *Lancet Neurology, 6,* 501–12.

Ferman, T. J., Smith, G. E., Boeve, B. F., Graff-Radford, N. R., Lucas, J. A., Knopman, D. S., et al. (2006). Neuropsychological differentiation of dementia with Lewy bodies from normal aging and Alzheimer's disease. *Clinical Neuropsychology, 20,* 623–636.

Ferman, T. J., Smith, G. E., Boeve, B. F., Ivnik, R. J., Petersen, R. C., Knopman, D., et al. (2004). DLB fluctuations: Specific features that reliably differentiate DLB from AD and normal aging. *Neurology, 62,* 181–187.

Fillenbaum, G. G., Heyman, A., Huber, M. S., Woodbury, M. A., Leiss, J., Schmader, K. E., et al. (1998). The prevalence and 3-year incidence of dementia in older Black and White community residents. *Journal of Clinical Epidemiology, 51,* 587–595.

Finton, M. J., Lucas, J. A., Graff-Radford, N. R., & Uitti, R. J. (1998). Analysis of visuospatial errors in patients with Alzheimer's disease or Parkinson's disease. *Journal of Clinical and Experimental Neuropsychology, 20,* 186–193.

Fleischman, D. A., Wilson, R. S., Gabrieli, J. D., Schneider, J. A., Bienias, J. L., & Bennett, D. A. (2005). Implicit memory and Alzheimer's disease neuropathology. *Brain, 128,* 2006–2015.

Folstein, M. F., Folstein, S. E., & McHugh, P. R. (1975). "Mini-mental state." A practical method for grading the cognitive state of patients for the clinician. *Journal of Psychiatric Research, 12,* 189–198.

Folstein, S. E. (1991). The psychopathology of Huntington's disease. *Research Publications, Association for Research in Nervous and Mental Disorders, 69,* 181–191.

Forman, M. S., Farmer, J., Johnson, J. K., Clark, C. M., Arnold, S. E., Coslett, H. B., et al. (2006). Frontotemporal dementia: Clinicopathological correlations. *Annals of Neurology, 59,* 952–962.

Foster, N. L., Heidebrink, J. L., Clark, C. M., Jagust, W. J., Arnold, S. E., Barbas, N. R., et al. (2007). FDG-PET improves accuracy in distinguishing frontotemporal dementia and Alzheimer's disease. *Brain, 130,* 2616–2635.

Fox, N. C., Warrington, E. K., Seiffer, A. L., Agnew, S. K., Rossor, M. N. (1998). Presymptomatic cognitive deficits in individuals at risk of familial Alzheimer's disease. A longitudinal prospective study. *Brain, 121,* 1631–1639.

Francis, J., Martin, D., Kapoor, W. N. (1990). A prospective study of delirium in hospitalized elderly. *Journal of the American Medical Association, 263,* 1097–1101.

Francis, P. T., Palmer, A. M., Sims, N. R., Bowen, D. M., Davison, A. N., Esiri, M. M., et al. (1985). Neurochemical studies of early-onset Alzheimer's disease. Possible influence on treatment. *New England Journal of Medicine, 313,* 7–11.

Fratiglioni, L., Grut, M., Forsell, Y., Viitanen, M., & Winblad, B. (1992). Clinical diagnosis of Alzheimer's disease and other dementias in a population survey. Agreement and causes of disagreement in applying Diagnostic and Statistical Manual of Mental Disorders, Revised Third Edition, Criteria. *Archives of Neurology, 49,* 927–932.

Fratiglioni, L., Launer, L. J., Andersen, K., Breteler, M. M., Copeland, J. R., Dartigues, J. F., et al. (2000). Incidence of dementia and major subtypes in Europe: A collaborative study of population-based cohorts. Neurologic Diseases in the Elderly Research Group. *Neurology, 54,* S10–15.

Friedland, R. P. (1993). Epidemiology, education, and the ecology of Alzheimer's disease. *Neurology, 43,* 246–249.

Fujishiro, H., Ferman, T. J., Boeve, B. F., Smith, G. E., Graff-Radford, N. R., Uitti, R. J., et al. (2008). Validation of the neuropathologic criteria of the third consortium for dementia with Lewy bodies for prospectively diagnosed cases. *Journal of Neuropathology and Experimental Neurology*, *67*, 649–656.

Galasko, D., Bennett, D., Sano, M., Ernesto, C., Thomas, R., Grundman, M., et al. (1997). An inventory to assess activities of daily living for clinical trials in Alzheimer's disease. The Alzheimer's Disease Cooperative Study. *Alzheimer Disease and Associated Disorders*, *11* Suppl 2, S33–39.

Galasko, D., Corey-Bloom, J., & Thal, L. J. (1991). Monitoring progression in Alzheimer's disease. *Journal of the American Geriatric Society*, *39*, 932–941.

Galasko, D., Hansen, L. A., Katzman, R., Wiederholt, W., Masliah, E., Terry, R., et al. (1994). Clinical-neuropathological correlations in Alzheimer's disease and related dementias. *Archives of Neurology*, *51*, 888–895.

Galton, C. J., Patterson, K., Xuereb, J. H., & Hodges, J. R. (2000). Atypical and typical presentations of Alzheimer's disease: A clinical, neuropsychological, neuroimaging and pathological study of 13 cases. *Brain*, *123*, 484–498.

Galvin, J. E., Pollack, J., & Morris, J. C. (2006). Clinical phenotype of Parkinson disease dementia. *Neurology*, *67*, 1605–1611.

Gamaldo, A., Moghekar, A., Kilada, S., Resnick, S. M., Zonderman, A. B., & O'Brien, R. (2006). Effect of a clinical stroke on the risk of dementia in a prospective cohort. *Neurology*, *67*, 1363–9.

Ganguli, M., Dodge, H. H., Shen, C., & DeKosky, S. T. (2004). Mild cognitive impairment, amnestic type: An epidemiologic study. *Neurology*, *63*, 115–121.

Ganguli, M., Ratcliff, G., Huff, F. J., Belle, S., Kancel, M. J., Fischer, L., et al. (1991). Effects of age, gender, and education on cognitive tests in a rural elderly community sample: Norms from the Monongahela Valley Independent Elders Survey. *Neuroepidemiology*, *10*, 42–52.

Ganguli, M., Seaberg, E. C., Ratcliff, G. G., Belle, S. H., & DeKosky, S. T. (1996). Cognitive stability over 2 years in a rural elderly population: The MoVIES project. *Neuroepidemiology*, *15*, 42–50.

Gao, S., Hendrie, H. C., Hall, K. S., & Hui, S. (1998). The relationships between age, sex, and the incidence of dementia and Alzheimer disease: A meta-analysis. *Archives of General Psychiatry*, *55*, 809–815.

Gates, G. A., Karzon, R. K., Garcia, P., Peterein, J., Storandt, M., Morris, J. C., et al. (1995). Auditory dysfunction in aging and senile dementia of the Alzheimer's type. *Archives of Neurology*, *52*, 626–634.

Gearing, M., Olson, D. A., Watts, R. L., & Mirra, S. S. (1994). Progressive supranuclear palsy: Neuropathologic and clinical heterogeneity. *Neurology*, *44*, 1015–1024.

Geda, Y. E., Knopman, D. S., Mrazek, D. A., Jicha, G. A., Smith, G. E., Negash, S., et al. (2006). Depression, apolipoprotein E genotype, and the incidence of mild cognitive impairment: A prospective cohort study. *Archives of Neurology*, *63*, 435–440.

Geda, Y. E., Smith, G. E., Knopman, D. S., Boeve, B. F., Tangalos, E. G., Ivnik, R. J., et al. (2004). De novo genesis of neuropsychiatric symptoms in mild cognitive impairment (MCI). *International Psychogeriatrics*, *16*, 51–60.

Geerlings, M. I., Schmand, B., Braam, A. W., Jonker, C., Bouter, L. M., & van Tilburg, W. (2000). Depressive symptoms and risk of Alzheimer's disease in more highly educated older people. *Journal of the American Geriatric Society*, *48*, 1092–1097.

Geffen, G., Moar, K. J., O'Hanlon, A. P., Clark, C. R., & Geffen, L. B. (1990). Performance measures of 16- to 86-year-old males and females on the auditory verbal learning test. *Clinical Neuropsychologist*, *4*, 45–63.

Gelinas, I., Gauthier, L., McIntyre, M., & Gauthier, S. (1999). Development of a functional measure for persons with Alzheimer's disease: The disability assessment for dementia. *American Journal of Occupational Therapy*, *53*, 471–481.

Gibb, W. R., Luthert, P. J., & Marsden, C. D. (1989). Corticobasal degeneration. *Brain*, *112*, 1171–1192.

Gilley, D. W., Wilson, R. S., Beckett, L. A., & Evans, D. A. (1997). Psychotic symptoms and physically aggressive behavior in Alzheimer's disease. *Journal of the American Geriatric Society*, *45*, 1074–1079.

Glosser, G., Kohn, S. E., Sands, L., Grugan, P. K., & Friedman, R. B. (1999). Impaired spelling in Alzheimer's disease: A linguistic deficit? *Neuropsychologia*, *37*, 807–815.

Gold, G., Bouras, C., Canuto, A., Bergallo, M. F., Herrmann, F. R., Hof, P. R., et al. (2002). Clinicopathological validation study of four sets of clinical criteria for vascular dementia. *American Journal of Psychiatry*, *159*, 82–87.

Goldman, W. P., Baty, J. D., Buckles, V. D., Sahrmann, S., & Morris, J. C. (1999). Motor dysfunction in mildly demented AD individuals without extrapyramidal signs. *Neurology*, *53*, 956–962.

Gorno-Tempini, M. L., Brambati, S. M., Ginex, V., Ogar, J., Dronkers, N. F., Marcone, A., et al. (2008). The logopenic/phonological variant of primary progressive aphasia. *Neurology, 71,* 1227–1234.

Gorno-Tempini, M. L., Dronkers, N. F., Rankin, K. P., Ogar, J. M., Phengrasamy, L., Rosen, H. J., et al. (2004). Cognition and anatomy in three variants of primary progressive aphasia. *Annals of Neurology, 55,* 335–346.

Gosche, K. M., Mortimer, J. A., Smith, C. D., Markesbery, W. R., & Snowdon, D. A. (2002). Hippocampal volume as an index of Alzheimer neuropathology: Findings from the Nun Study. *Neurology, 58,* 1476–1482.

Graff-Radford, N. R., Bolling, J. P., Earnest, F. t., Shuster, E. A., Caselli, R. J., & Brazis, P. W. (1993). Simultanagnosia as the initial sign of degenerative dementia. *Mayo Clinic Proceedings, 68,* 955–964.

Graff-Radford, N. R., Tranel, D., Van Hoesen, G. W., & Brandt, J. P. (1990). Diencephalic amnesia. *Brain, 113,* 1–25.

Grafman, J., Litvan, I., & Stark, M. (1995). Neuropsychological features of progressive supranuclear palsy. *Brain and Cognition, 28,* 311–20.

Grafman, J., Weingartner, H., Newhouse, P. A., Thompson, K., Lalonde, F., Litvan, I., et al. (1990). Implicit learning in patients with Alzheimer's disease. *Pharmacopsychiatry, 23,* 94–101.

Graham, J. E., Rockwood, K., Beattie, B. L., McDowell, I., Eastwood, R., & Gauthier, S. (1996). Standardization of the diagnosis of dementia in the Canadian Study of Health and Aging. *Neuroepidemiology, 15,* 246–256.

Graham, N. L., Bak, T., Patterson, K., & Hodges, J. R. (2003). Language function and dysfunction in corticobasal degeneration. *Neurology, 61,* 493–499.

Graves, A. B., Larson, E. B., Edland, S. D., Bowen, J. D., McCormick, W. C., McCurry, S. M., et al. (1996). Prevalence of dementia and its subtypes in the Japanese American population of King County, Washington state. The Kame Project. *American Journal of Epidemiology, 144,* 760–771.

Green, R. C., Cupples, L. A., Go, R., Benke, K. S., Edeki, T., Griffith, P. A., et al. (2002). Risk of dementia among white and African American relatives of patients with Alzheimer disease. *Journal of the American Medical Association, 287,* 329–336.

Green, R. C., Cupples, L. A., Kurz, A., Auerbach, S., Go, R., Sadovnick, D., et al. (2003). Depression as a Risk Factor for Alzheimer Disease: The MIRAGE Study. *Archives of Neurology, 60,* 753–759.

Green, R. C., Goldstein, F. C., Mirra, S. S., Alazraki, N. P., Baxt, J. L., & Bakay, R. A. (1995). Slowly progressive apraxia in Alzheimer's disease. *Journal of Neurology, Neurosurgery, and Psychiatry, 59,* 312–315.

Greenaway, M. C., Lacritz, L. H., Binegar, D., Weiner, M. F., Lipton, A., & Munro Cullum, C. (2006). Patterns of verbal memory performance in mild cognitive impairment, Alzheimer disease, and normal aging. *Cognitive Behavioral Neurology, 19,* 79–84.

Greene, J. D., Hodges, J. R., & Baddeley, A. D. (1995). Autobiographical memory and executive function in early dementia of Alzheimer type. *Neuropsychologia, 33,* 1647–1670.

Gregory, C., Lough, S., Stone, V., Erzinclioglu, S., Martin, L., Baron-Cohen, S., et al. (2002). Theory of mind in patients with frontal variant frontotemporal dementia and Alzheimer's disease: Theoretical and practical implications. *Brain, 125,* 752–764.

Gregory, C. A., Serra-Mestres, J., & Hodges, J. R. (1999). Early diagnosis of the frontal variant of frontotemporal dementia: How sensitive are standard neuroimaging and neuropsychologic tests? *Neuropsychiatry Neuropsychology and Behavioral Neurology, 12,* 128–35.

Griffith, H. R., Belue, K., Sicola, A., Krzywanski, S., Zamrini, E., Harrell, L., et al. (2003). Impaired financial abilities in mild cognitive impairment: A direct assessment approach. *Neurology, 60,* 449–457.

Grober, E., Buschke, H., Crystal, H., Bang, S., & Dresner, R. (1988). Screening for dementia by memory testing. *Neurology, 38,* 900–903.

Grober, E., & Kawas, C. (1997). Learning and retention in preclinical and early Alzheimer's disease. *Psychology and Aging, 12,* 183–188.

Grossman, M., D'Esposito, M., Hughes, E., Onishi, K., Biassou, N., White-Devine, T., et al. (1996). Language comprehension profiles in Alzheimer's disease, multi-infarct dementia, and frontotemporal degeneration. *Neurology, 47,* 183–189.

Grossman, M., Murray, R., Koenig, P., Ash, S., Cross, K., Moore, P., et al. (2007). Verb acquisition and representation in Alzheimer's disease. *Neuropsychologia, 45,* 2508–2518.

Grossman, M., Robinson, K., Biassou, N., White-Devine, T., & D'Esposito, M. (1998). Semantic memory in Alzheimer's disease: Representativeness, ontologic category, and material. *Neuropsychology, 12,* 34–42.

Grossman, M., & White-Devine, T. (1998). Sentence comprehension in Alzheimer's disease. *Brain and Language*, *62*, 186–201.

Grundman, M., Petersen, R. C., Ferris, S. H., Thomas, R. G., Aisen, P. S., Bennett, D. A., et al. (2004). Mild cognitive impairment can be distinguished from Alzheimer disease and normal aging for clinical trials. *Archives of Neurology*, *61*, 59–66.

Grut, M., Jorm, A. F., Fratiglioni, L., Forsell, Y., Viitanen, M., & Winblad, B. (1993). Memory complaints of elderly people in a population survey: Variation according to dementia stage and depression. *Journal of the American Geriatric Society*, *41*, 1295–1300.

Gultekin, S. H., Rosenfeld, M. R., Voltz, R., Eichen, J., Posner, J. B., & Dalmau, J. (2000). Paraneoplastic limbic encephalitis: Neurological symptoms, immunological findings and tumour association in 50 patients. *Brain*, *123* Pt 7, 1481–1494.

Haan, M. N., Shemanski, L., Jagust, W. J., Manolio, T. A., & Kuller, L. (1999). The role of APOE epsilon4 in modulating effects of other risk factors for cognitive decline in elderly persons. *Journal of the American Medical Association*, *282*, 40–46.

Hall, M., Whaley, R., Robertson, K., Hamby, S., Wilkins, J., & Hall, C. (1996). The correlation between neuropsychological and neuroanatomic changes over time in asymptomatic and symptomatic HIV-1-infected individuals. *Neurology*, *46*, 1697–1702.

Hammer, S. M., Saag, M. S., Schechter, M., Montaner, J. S., Schooley, R. T., Jacobsen, D. M., et al. (2006). Treatment for adult HIV infection: 2006 recommendations of the International AIDS Society-USA panel. *Journal of the American Medical Association*, *296*, 827–843.

Hansen, L. A., & Samuel, W. (1997). Criteria for Alzheimer's disease and the nosology of dementia with Lewy bodies. *Neurology*, *48*, 126–132.

Haroutunian, V., Schnaider-Beeri, M., Schmeidler, J., Wysocki, M., Purohit, D. P., Perl, D. P., et al. (2008). Role of the neuropathology of Alzheimer disease in dementia in the oldest-old. *Archives of Neurology*, *65*, 1211–1217.

Hebert, L. E., Scherr, P. A., Beckett, L. A., Albert, M. S., Pilgrim, D. M., Chown, M. J., et al. (1995). Age-specific incidence of Alzheimer's disease in a community population. *Journal of the American Medical Association*, *273*, 1354–1359.

Heindel, W. C., Cahn, D. A., & Salmon, D. P. (1997). Non-associative lexical priming is impaired in Alzheimer's disease. *Neuropsychologia*, *35*, 1365–1372.

Hellstrom, P., Edsbagge, M., Archer, T., Tisell, M., Tullberg, M., & Wikkelso, C. (2007). The neuropsychology of patients with clinically diagnosed idiopathic normal pressure hydrocephalus. *Neurosurgery*, *61*, 1219–26; discussion 1227–1228.

Hely, M. A., Reid, W. G., Adena, M. A., Halliday, G. M., & Morris, J. G. (2008). The Sydney multicenter study of Parkinson's disease: The inevitability of dementia at 20 years. *Movement Disorders*, *23*, 837–844.

Helzner, E. P., Scarmeas, N., Cosentino, S., Portet, F., & Stern, Y. (2007). Leisure activity and cognitive decline in incident Alzheimer disease. *Archives of Neurology*, *64*, 1749–1754.

Hendrie, H. C., Osuntokun, B. O., Hall, K. S., Ogunniyi, A. O., Hui, S. L., Unverzagt, F. W., et al. (1995). Prevalence of Alzheimer's disease and dementia in two communities: Nigerian Africans and African Americans. *American Journal of Psychiatry*, *152*, 1485–1492.

Henon, H., Durieu, I., Guerouaou, D., Lebert, F., Pasquier, F., & Leys, D. (2001). Poststroke dementia: Incidence and relationship to prestroke cognitive decline. *Neurology*, *57*, 1216–1222.

Herlitz, A., Small, B. J., Fratiglioni, L., Almkvist, O., Viitanen, M., & Backman, L. (1997). Detection of mild dementia in community surveys. Is it possible to increase the accuracy of our diagnostic instruments? *Archives of Neurology*, *54*, 319–324.

Herrmann, L. L., Goodwin, G. M., & Ebmeier, K. P. (2007). The cognitive neuropsychology of depression in the elderly. *Psychological Medicine*, *37*, 1693–1702.

Heyman, A., Fillenbaum, G. G., Welsh-Bohmer, K. A., Gearing, M., Mirra, S. S., Mohs, R. C., et al. (1998). Cerebral infarcts in patients with autopsy-proven Alzheimer's disease: CERAD, part XVIII. Consortium to Establish a Registry for Alzheimer's Disease. *Neurology*, *51*, 159–162.

Hodges, J. R., Davies, R. R., Xuereb, J. H., Casey, B., Broe, M., Bak, T. H., et al. (2004). Clinicopathological correlates in frontotemporal dementia. *Annals of Neurology*, *56*, 399–406.

Hodges, J. R., Patterson, K., Oxbury, S., & Funnell, E. (1992). Semantic dementia. Progressive fluent aphasia with temporal lobe atrophy. *Brain*, *115*, 1783–1806.

Hodges, J. R., Patterson, K., Ward, R., Garrard, P., Bak, T., Perry, R., et al. (1999). The differentiation of semantic dementia and frontal lobe dementia (temporal and frontal variants of fron-totemporal dementia) from early Alzheimer's disease: A comparative neuropsychological study. *Neuropsychology, 13,* 31–40.

Hofman, A., Ott, A., Breteler, M. M., Bots, M. L., Slooter, A. J., van Harskamp, F., et al. (1997). Atherosclerosis, apolipoprotein E, and prevalence of dementia and Alzheimer's disease in the Rotterdam Study. *Lancet, 349,* 151–154.

Holmes, C., Cairns, N., Lantos, P., & Mann, A. (1999). Validity of current clinical criteria for Alzheimer's disease, vascular dementia and dementia with Lewy bodies. *British Journal of Psychiatry, 174,* 45–50.

Howieson, D. B., Holm, L. A., Kaye, J. A., Oken, B. S., & Howieson, J. (1993). Neurologic function in the optimally healthy oldest old. Neuropsychological evaluation. *Neurology, 43,* 1882–1886.

Hughes, C. P., Berg, L., Danziger, W. L., Coben, L. A., & Martin, R. L. (1982). A new clinical scale for the staging of dementia. *British Journal of Psychiatry, 140,* 566–572.

Hulette, C., Mirra, S., Wilkinson, W., Heyman, A., Fillenbaum, G., & Clark, C. (1995). The Consortium to Establish a Registry for Alzheimer's Disease (CERAD). Part IX. A prospective clini-coneuropathologic study of Parkinson's features in Alzheimer's disease. *Neurology, 45,* 1991–1995.

Hulette, C., Nochlin, D., McKeel, D., Morris, J. C., Mirra, S. S., Sumi, S. M., et al. (1997). Clinical-neuropathologic findings in multi-infarct dementia: A report of six autopsied cases. *Neurology, 48,* 668–672.

Hutton, M., Lendon, C. L., Rizzu, P., Baker, M., Froelich, S., Houlden, H., et al. (1998). Association of missense and 5'-splice-site mutations in tau with the inherited dementia FTDP-17. *Nature, 393,* 702–705.

Hyman, B. T., Kromer, L. J., & Van Hoesen, G. W. (1987). Reinnervation of the hippocampal perforant pathway zone in Alzheimer's disease. *Annals of Neurology, 21,* 259–267.

Hyman, B. T., Van Horsen, G. W., Damasio, A. R., & Barnes, C. L. (1984). Alzheimer's disease: Cell-specific pathology isolates the hippocampal formation. *Science, 225,* 1168–1170.

Inouye, S. K. (2006). Delirium in older persons. *New England Journal of Medicine, 354,* 1157–1165.

Inouye, S. K., Albert, M. S., Mohs, R., Sun, K., & Berkman, L. F. (1993). Cognitive performance in a high-functioning community-dwelling elderly population. *Journal of Gerontology, 48,* M146–151.

Inouye, S. K., & Charpentier, P. A. (1996). Precipitating factors for delirium in hospitalized elderly persons. Predictive model and interrelationship with baseline vulnerability. *Journal of the American Medical Association, 275,* 852–857.

Ives, D. G., Bonino, P., Traven, N. D., & Kuller, L. H. (1995). Characteristics and comorbidities of rural older adults with hearing impairment. *Journal of the American Geriatric Society, 43,* 803–806.

Ivnik, R. J., Malec, J. F., & Smith, G. E. (1992). WAIS-R, WMS-R and AVLT norms for ages 56 through 97. *Clinical Neuropsychology, 6 (suppl),* 1–104.

Jack, C. R., Jr., Petersen, R. C., O'Brien, P. C., & Tangalos, E. G. (1992). MR-based hippocampal volumetry in the diagnosis of Alzheimer's disease. *Neurology, 42,* 183–188.

Jack, C. R., Jr., Petersen, R. C., Xu, Y. C., Waring, S. C., O'Brien, P. C., Tangalos, E. G., et al. (1997). Medial temporal atrophy on MRI in normal aging and very mild Alzheimer's disease. *Neurology, 49,* 786–794.

Jack, C. R., Jr., Shiung, M. M., Weigand, S. D., O'Brien, P. C., Gunter, J. L., Boeve, B. F., et al. (2005). Brain atrophy rates predict subsequent clinical conversion in normal elderly and amnestic MCI. *Neurology, 65,* 1227–1231.

Jack, C. R., Petersen, R. C., Xu, Y. C., O'Brien, P. C., Smith, G. E., Ivnik, R. J., et al. (1999). Prediction of AD with MRI-based hippocampal volume in mild cognitive impairment. *Neurology, 52,* 1397–1403.

Jacobs, D. H., Adair, J. C., Williamson, D. J., Na, D. L., Gold, M., Foundas, A. L., et al. (1999). Apraxia and motor-skill acquisition in Alzheimer's disease are dissociable. *Neuropsychologia, 37,* 875–880.

Jagust, W., Gitcho, A., Sun, F., Kuczynski, B., Mungas, D., & Haan, M. (2006). Brain imaging evidence of preclinical Alzheimer's disease in normal aging. *Annals of Neurology, 59,* 673–681.

Jason, G. W., Suchowersky, O., Pajurkova, E. M., Graham, L., Klimek, M. L., Garber, A. T., et al. (1997). Cognitive manifestations of Huntington disease in relation to genetic structure and clinical onset. *Archives of Neurology, 54,* 1081–1088.

Jellinger, K., Danielczyk, W., Fischer, P., & Gabriel, E. (1990). Clinicopathological analysis of dementia disorders in the elderly. *Journal of the Neurological Sciences, 95,* 239–258.

Jerger, J., Chmiel, R., Wilson, N., & Luchi, R. (1995). Hearing impairment in older adults: New concepts. *Journal of the American Geriatric Society, 43,* 928–35.

Joachim, C. L., Morris, J. H., &Selkoe, D. J. (1988). Clinically diagnosed Alzheimer's disease: Autopsy results in 150 cases. *Annals of Neurology*, *24*, 50–56.

Johannsen, P., Jakobsen, J., Bruhn, P., & Gjedde, A. (1999). Cortical responses to sustained and divided attention in Alzheimer's disease. *Neuroimage*, *10*, 269–281.

Johnson, J. K., Diehl, J., Mendez, M. F., Neuhaus, J., Shapira, J. S., Forman, M., et al. (2005). Frontotemporal lobar degeneration: Demographic characteristics of 353 patients. *Archives of Neurology*, *62*, 925–930.

Johnson, J. K., Head, E., Kim, R., Starr, A., & Cotman, C. W. (1999). Clinical and pathological evidence for a frontal variant of Alzheimer disease. *Archives of Neurology*, *56*, 1233–1239.

Jorm, A. F. (1994). A short form of the Informant Questionnaire on Cognitive Decline in the Elderly (IQCODE): Development and cross-validation. *Psychological Medicine*, *24*, 145–153.

Jorm, A. F., & Jolley, D. (1998). The incidence of dementia: A meta-analysis. *Neurology*, *51*, 728–733.

Jorm, A. F., Masaki, K. H., Davis, D. G., Hardman, J., Nelson, J., Markesbery, W. R., et al. (2004). Memory complaints in nondemented men predict future pathologic diagnosis of Alzheimer disease. *Neurology*, *63*, 1960–1961.

Josephs, K. A., Duffy, J. R., Strand, E. A., Whitwell, J. L., Layton, K. F., Parisi, J. E., et al. (2006). Clinicopathological and imaging correlates of progressive aphasia and apraxia of speech. *Brain*, *129*, 1385–1398.

Josephs, K. A., Petersen, R. C., Knopman, D. S., Boeve, B. F., Whitwell, J. L., Duffy, J. R., et al. (2006). Clinicopathologic analysis of frontotemporal and corticobasal degenerations and PSP. *Neurology*, *66*, 41–48.

Kalmijn, S., Feskens, E. J., Launer, L. J., & Kromhout, D. (1996). Cerebrovascular disease, the apolipoprotein e4 allele, and cognitive decline in a community-based study of elderly men. *Stroke*, *27*, 2230–2235.

Kanne, S. M., Balota, D. A., Storandt, M., McKeel, D. W., Jr., & Morris, J. C. (1998). Relating anatomy to function in Alzheimer's disease: Neuropsychological profiles predict regional neuropathology 5 years later. *Neurology*, *50*, 979–985.

Kassubek, J., Juengling, F. D., Kioschies, T., Henkel, K., Karitzky, J., Kramer, B., et al. (2004). Topography of cerebral atrophy in early Huntington's disease: A voxel based morphometric MRI study. *Journal of Neurology, Neurosurgery, and Psychiatry*, *75*, 213–220.

Katzman, R. (1993). Education and the prevalence of dementia and Alzheimer's disease. *Neurology*, *43*, 13–20.

Katzman, R., Brown, T., Fuld, P., Peck, A., Schechter, R., & Schimmel, H. (1983). Validation of a short Orientation-Memory-Concentration Test of cognitive impairment. *American Journal of Psychiatry*, *140*, 734–9.

Kawas, C., Segal, J., Stewart, W. F., Corrada, M., & Thal, L. J. (1994). A validation study of the Dementia Questionnaire. *Archives of Neurology*, *51*, 901–906.

Keller, B. K., Morton, J. L., Thomas, V. S., & Potter, J. F. (1999). The effect of visual and hearing impairments on functional status. *Journal of the American Geriatric Society*, *47*, 1319–1325.

Kertesz, A., Davidson, W., & Fox, H. (1997). Frontal behavioral inventory: Diagnostic criteria for frontal lobe dementia. *Canadian Journal of the Neurological Sciences*, *24*, 29–36.

Kertesz, A., Martinez-Lage, P., Davidson, W., & Munoz, D. G. (2000). The corticobasal degeneration syndrome overlaps progressive aphasia and frontotemporal dementia. *Neurology*, *55*, 1368–1375.

Kertesz, A., Nadkarni, N., Davidson, W., & Thomas, A. W. (2000). The Frontal Behavioral Inventory in the differential diagnosis of frontotemporal dementia. *Journal of the International Neuropsychological Society*, *6*, 460–468.

Kieburtz, K., Ketonen, L., Cox, C., Grossman, H., Holloway, R., Booth, H., et al. (1996). Cognitive performance and regional brain volume in human immunodeficiency virus type 1 infection. *Archives of Neurology*, *53*, 155–158.

Killiany, R. J., Hyman, B. T., Gomez-Isla, T., Moss, M. B., Kikinis, R., Jolesz, F., et al. (2002). MRI measures of entorhinal cortex vs hippocampus in preclinical AD. *Neurology*, *58*, 1188–1196.

Killiany, R. J., Moss, M. B., Albert, M. S., Sandor, T., Tieman, J., & Jolesz, F. (1993). Temporal lobe regions on magnetic resonance imaging identify patients with early Alzheimer's disease. *Archives of Neurology*, *50*, 949–954.

Kivipelto, M., Helkala, E. L., Hanninen, T., Laakso, M. P., Hallikainen, M., Alhainen, K., et al. (2001). Midlife vascular risk factors and late-life mild cognitive impairment: A population-based study. *Neurology*, *56*, 1683–1689.

Knibb, J. A., Xuereb, J. H., Patterson, K., & Hodges, J. R. (2006). Clinical and pathological characterization of progressive aphasia. *Annals of Neurology*, *59*, 156–165.

Knopman, D. (1991). Long-term retention of implicitly acquired learning in patients with Alzheimer's disease. *Journal of Clinical and Experimental Neuropsychology*, *13*, 880–894.

Knopman, D., Donohue, J. A., & Gutterman, E. M. (2000). Patterns of care in the early stages of

Alzheimer's disease: Impediments to timely diagnosis. *Journal of the American Geriatric Society, 48,* 300–304.

Knopman, D., Parisi, J. E., Boeve, B. F., Rocca, W. A., Cha, R. H., Apaydin, H., et al. (2003). Vascular Dementia in a Population-based autopsy study. *Archives of Neurology, 60,* 569–576.

Knopman, D., Petersen, R., Edland, S., Cha, R., & Rocca, W. A. (2004). The incidence of frontotemporal lobar degeneration in Rochester, Minnesota, 1990–1994. *Neurology, 62,* 506–508.

Knopman, D. S., Boeve, B. F., Parisi, J. E., Dickson, D. W., Smith, G. E., Ivnik, R. J., et al. (2005). Antemortem diagnosis of frontotemporal lobar degeneration. *Annals of Neurology, 57,* 480–488.

Knopman, D. S., DeKosky, S. T., Cummings, J. L., Chuit, H., Corey-Bloom, J., Relkin, N., et al. (2001). Practice parameter: Diagnosis of dementia (an evidence-based review). *Neurology, 56,* 1143–1153.

Knopman, D. S., Kramer, J. H., Boeve, B. F., Graff-Radford, N. R., Mendez, M. F., Miller, B. L., et al. (2008). Development of methodology for conducting clinical trials in frontotemporal lobar degeneration. *Brain, 131,* 2957–2968.

Knopman, D. S., Parisi, J. E., Salviati, A., Floriach-Robert, M., Boeve, B. F., Ivnik, R. J., et al. (2003). Neuropathology of cognitively normal elderly. *Journal of Neuropathology and Experimental Neurology, 62,* 1087–1095.

Knopman, D. S., Petersen, R. C., Cha, R. H., Edland, S. D., & Rocca, W. A. (2006). Incidence and causes of nondegenerative nonvascular dementia: A population-based study. *Archives of Neurology, 63,* 218–221.

Knopman, D. S., & Ryberg, S. (1989). A verbal memory test with high predictive accuracy for dementia of the Alzheimer type. *Archives of Neurology, 46,* 141–145.

Kokmen, E., Beard, C. M., Offord, K. P., & Kurland, L. T. (1989). Prevalence of medically diagnosed dementia in a defined United States population: Rochester, Minnesota, January 1, 1975. *Neurology, 39,* 773–776.

Kokmen, E., Smith, G. E., Petersen, R. C., Tangalos, E., & Ivnik, R. C. (1991). The short test of mental status. Correlations with standardized psychometric testing. *Archives of Neurology, 48,* 725–728.

Kokmen, E., Whisnant, J. P., O'Fallon, W. M., Chu, C. P., & Beard, C. M. (1996). Dementia after ischemic stroke: A population-based study in Rochester, Minnesota (1960–1984). *Neurology, 46,* 154–159.

Kopelman, M. D. (1985). Rates of forgetting in Alzheimer-type dementia and Korsakoff's syndrome. *Neuropsychologia, 23,* 623–638.

Kopelman, M. D. (1991). Frontal dysfunction and memory deficits in the alcoholic Korsakoff syndrome and Alzheimer-type dementia. *Brain, 114,* 117–137.

Kopelman, M. D., Wilson, B. A., & Baddeley, A. D. (1989). The autobiographical memory interview: A new assessment of autobiographical and personal semantic memory in amnesic patients. *Journal of Clinical and Experimental Neuropsychology, 11,* 724–744.

Kozora, E., Arciniegas, D. B., Filley, C. M., West, S. G., Brown, M., Miller, D., et al. (2008). Cognitive and neurologic status in patients with systemic lupus erythematosus without major neuropsychiatric syndromes. *Arthritis Rheumatism, 59,* 1639–1646.

Kraemer, H. C., Tinklenberg, J., & Yesavage, J. A. (1994). "How far" vs "how fast" in Alzheimer's disease. The question revisited. *Archives of Neurology, 51,* 275–279.

Kramer, J. H., Jurik, J., Sha, S. J., Rankin, K. P., Rosen, H. J., Johnson, J. K., et al. (2003). Distinctive neuropsychological patterns in frontotemporal dementia, semantic dementia, and Alzheimer disease. *Cognitive Behavioral Neurology, 16,* 211–218.

Kramer, S. I., & Reifler, B. V. (1992). Depression, dementia, and reversible dementia. *Clinical Geriatric Medicine, 8,* 289–297.

Kraybill, M. L., Larson, E. B., Tsuang, D. W., Teri, L., McCormick, W. C., Bowen, J. D., et al. (2005). Cognitive differences in dementia patients with autopsy-verified AD, Lewy body pathology, or both. *Neurology, 64,* 2069–2073.

Kukull, W. A., Higdon, R., Bowen, J. D., McCormick, W. C., Teri, L., Schellenberg, G. D., et al. (2002). Dementia and Alzheimer disease incidence: A prospective cohort study. *Archives of Neurology, 59,* 1737–1746.

Kukull, W. A., Larson, E. B., Teri, L., Bowen, J., McCormick, W., & Pfanschmidt, M. L. (1994). The Mini-Mental State Examination score and the clinical diagnosis of dementia. *Journal of Clinical Epidemiology, 47,* 1061–1067.

La Rue, A. (1989). Patterns of performance on the Fuld Object Memory Evaluation in elderly inpatients with depression or dementia. *Journal of Clinical and Experimental Neuropsychology, 11,* 409–422.

Lafleche, G., & Albert, M. S. (1995). Executive function deficits in mild Alzheimer's disease. *Neuropsychology, 9,* 313–320.

Lamar, M., Resnick, S. M., & Zonderman, A. B. (2003). Longitudinal changes in verbal memory in older adults: Distinguishing the effects of age from repeat testing. *Neurology, 60,* 82–86.

Lambert, J., Eustache, F., Viader, F., Dary, M., Rioux, P., Lechevalier, B., et al. (1996). Agraphia in Alzheimer's disease: An independent lexical impairment. *Brain and Language*, 53, 222–233.

Lange, K. W., Sahakian, B. J., Quinn, N. P., Marsden, C. D., & Robbins, T. W. (1995). Comparison of executive and visuospatial memory function in Huntington's disease and dementia of Alzheimer type matched for degree of dementia. *Journal of Neurology, Neurosurgery, and Psychiatry*, 58, 598–606.

Langley, L. K., Overmier, J. B., Knopman, D. S., & Prod'Homme, M. M. (1998). Inhibition and habituation: Preserved mechanisms of attentional selection in aging and Alzheimer's disease. *Neuropsychology* 12, 353–366.

Larson, E. B., McCurry, S. M., Graves, A. B., Bowen, J. D., Rice, M. M., & McCormick, W. C. (1998). Standardization of the clinical diagnosis of the dementia syndrome and its subtypes in a cross-sectional study: The Ni-Hon-Sea experience. *Journal of Gerontology A Biological Sciences, Medical Sciences*, 53A, M313–M319.

Larson, E. B., Reifler, B. V., Sumi, S. M., Canfield, C. G., & Chinn, N. M. (1985). Diagnostic evaluation of 200 elderly outpatients with suspected dementia. *Journal of Gerontology*, 40, 536–543.

Lautenschlager, N. T., Cupples, L. A., Rao, V. S., Auerbach, S. A., Becker, R., Burke, J., et al. (1996). Risk of dementia among relatives of Alzheimer's disease patients in the MIRAGE study: What is in store for the oldest old? *Neurology*, 46, 641–650.

Lawrence, A. D., Hodges, J. R., Rosser, A. E., Kershaw, A., Ffrench-Constant, C., Rubinsztein, D. C., et al. (1998). Evidence for specific cognitive deficits in preclinical Huntington's disease. *Brain*, 121, 1329–1341.

Lawton, M. P., & Brody, E. M. (1969). Assessment of older people: Self-maintaining and instrumental activities of daily living. *Gerontologist*, 9, 179–86.

Lemiere, J., Decruyenaere, M., Evers-Kiebooms, G., Vandenbussche, E., & Dom, R. (2004). Cognitive changes in patients with Huntington's disease (HD) and asymptomatic carriers of the HD mutation—a longitudinal follow-up study. *Journal of Neurology*, 251, 935–942.

Leonberger, T. F., Nicks, S. D., Goldfader, P. R., & Munz, D. C. (1991). Factor analysis of the Wechsler Memory Scale-Revised and the Halstead-Reitan Neuropsychological battery. *Clinical Neuropsychologist*, 5, 83–88.

Lerner, A. J., Hedera, P., Koss, E., Stuckey, J., & Friedland, R. P. (1997). Delirium in Alzheimer disease. *Alzheimer Disease and Associated Disorders*, 11, 16–20.

Leverenz, J. B., Agustin, C. M., Tsuang, D., Peskind, E. R., Edland, S. D., Nochlin, D., et al. (2002). Clinical and neuropathological characteristics of hippocampal sclerosis: A community-based study. *Archives of Neurology*, 59, 1099–1106.

Levine, D. N., Lee, J. M., & Fisher, C. M. (1993). The visual variant of Alzheimer's disease: A clinico-pathologic case study. *Neurology*, 43, 305–313.

Lezak, M. D. (1995). *Neuropsychological Assessment*. New York: Oxford University Press.

Libon, D. J., Xie, S. X., Moore, P., Farmer, J., Antani, S., McCawley, G., et al. (2007). Patterns of neuropsychological impairment in frontotemporal dementia. *Neurology*, 68, 369–375.

Lim, A., Tsuang, D., Kukull, W., Nochlin, D., Leverenz, J., McCormick, W., et al. (1999). Clinico-neuropathological correlation of Alzheimer's disease in a community-based case series. *Journal of the American Geriatric Society*, 47, 564–569.

Litvan, I., Agid, Y., Goetz, C., Jankovic, J., Wenning, G. K., Brandel, J. P., et al. (1997). Accuracy of the clinical diagnosis of corticobasal degeneration: A clinicopathologic study. *Neurology*, 48, 119–125.

Litvan, I., Cummings, J. L., & Mega, M. (1998). Neuropsychiatric features of corticobasal degeneration. *Journal of Neurology, Neurosurgery, and Psychiatry*, 65, 717–721.

Litvan, I., Mega, M. S., Cummings, J. L., & Fairbanks, L. (1996). Neuropsychiatric aspects of progressive supranuclear palsy. *Neurology*, 47, 1184–1189.

Lobo, A., Launer, L. J., Fratiglioni, L., Andersen, K., Di Carlo, A., Breteler, M. M., et al. (2000). Prevalence of dementia and major subtypes in Europe: A collaborative study of population-based cohorts. Neurologic Diseases in the Elderly Research Group. *Neurology*, 54, S4–9.

Longstreth, W. T., Jr., Dulberg, C., Manolio, T. A., Lewis, M. R., Beauchamp, N. J., Jr., O'Leary, D., et al. (2002). Incidence, manifestations, and predictors of brain infarcts defined by serial cranial magnetic resonance imaging in the elderly: The Cardiovascular Health Study. *Stroke*, 33, 2376–2382.

Looi, J. C., & Sachdev, P. S. (1999). Differentiation of vascular dementia from AD on neuropsychological tests. *Neurology*, 53, 670–678.

Lopera, F., Ardilla, A., Martinez, A., Madrigal, L., Arango-Viana, J. C., Lemere, C. A., et al. (1997). Clinical features of early-onset Alzheimer disease in a large kindred with an E280A presenilin-1 mutation. *Journal of the American Medical Association, 277*, 793–799.

Lopez, O. L., Becker, J. T., Somsak, D., Dew, M. A., & DeKosky, S. T. (1994). Awareness of cognitive deficits and anosognosia in probable Alzheimer's disease. *European Neurology, 34*, 277–282.

Lopez, O. L., Jagust, W. J., DeKosky, S. T., Becker, J. T., Fitzpatrick, A., Dulberg, C., et al. (2003). Prevalence and classification of mild cognitive impairment in the cardiovascular health study cognition study: Part 1. *Archives of Neurology, 60*, 1385–1389.

Lough, S., Kipps, C. M., Treise, C., Watson, P., Blair, J. R., & Hodges, J. R. (2006). Social reasoning, emotion and empathy in frontotemporal dementia. *Neuropsychologia, 44*, 950–958.

Loukkola, J., Laine, M., Ainiala, H., Peltola, J., Metsanoja, R., Auvinen, A., et al. (2003). Cognitive impairment in systemic lupus erythematosus and neuropsychiatric systemic lupus erythematosus: A population-based neuropsychological study. *Journal of Clinical and Experimental Neuropsychology, 25*, 145–151.

Lyketsos, C. G., Lopez, O., Jones, B., Fitzpatrick, A. L., Breitner, J., & DeKosky, S. (2002). Prevalence of neuropsychiatric symptoms in dementia and mild cognitive impairment: Results from the cardiovascular health study. *Journal of the American Medical Association, 288*, 1475–1483.

MacKnight, C., Graham, J., & Rockwood, K. (1999). Factors associated with inconsistent diagnosis of dementia between physicians and neuropsychologists. *Journal of the American Geriatric Society, 47*, 1294–1299.

Maddrey, A. M., Cullum, C. M., Weiner, M. F., & Filley, C. M. (1996). Premorbid intelligence estimation and level of dementia in Alzheimer's disease. *Journal of the International Neuropsychological Society, 2*, 551–555.

Malloy, P., & Grace, J. (2005). A review of rating scales for measuring behavior change due to frontal systems damage. *Cognitive Behavioral Neurology, 18*, 18–27.

Manly, J. J., Bell-McGinty, S., Tang, M. X., Schupf, N., Stern, Y., & Mayeux, R. (2005). Implementing diagnostic criteria and estimating frequency of mild cognitive impairment in an urban community. *Archives of Neurology, 62*, 1739–1746.

Manly, J. J., Tang, M. X., Schupf, N., Stern, Y., Vonsattel, J. P., & Mayeux, R. (2008). Frequency and course of mild cognitive impairment in a multiethnic community. *Annals of Neurology, 63*, 494–506.

Manly, T., Hawkins, K., Evans, J., Woldt, K., & Robertson, I. H. (2002). Rehabilitation of executive function: Facilitation of effective goal management on complex tasks using periodic auditory alerts. *Neuropsychologia, 40*, 271–281.

Mapstone, M., Steffenella, T. M., & Duffy, C. J. (2003). A visuospatial variant of mild cognitive impairment: Getting lost between aging and AD. *Neurology, 60*, 802–808.

Mariani, E., Monastero, R., Ercolani, S., Mangialasche, F., Caputo, M., Feliziani, F. T., et al. (2007). Vascular risk factors in mild cognitive impairment subtypes. Findings from the ReGAl project. *Dementia and Geriatric Cognitive Disorders, 24*, 448–456.

Marson, D. C., Annis, S. M., McInturff, B., Bartolucci, A., & Harrell, L. E. (1999). Error behaviors associated with loss of competency in Alzheimer's disease. *Neurology, 53*, 1983–1992.

Marson, D. C., Chatterjee, A., Ingram, K. K., & Harrell, L. E. (1996). Toward a neurologic model of competency: Cognitive predictors of capacity to consent in Alzheimer's disease using three different legal standards. *Neurology, 46*, 666–672.

Marson, D. C., Cody, H. A., Ingram, K. K., & Harrell, L. E. (1995). Neuropsychologic predictors of competency in Alzheimer's disease using a rational reasons legal standard. *Archives of Neurology, 52*, 955–959.

Martin, A., Brouwers, P., Cox, C., & Fedio, P. (1985). On the nature of the verbal memory deficit in Alzheimer's disease. *Brain and Language, 25*, 323–241.

Mathuranath, P. S., Nestor, P. J., Berrios, G. E., Rakowicz, W., & Hodges, J. R. (2000). A brief cognitive test battery to differentiate Alzheimer's disease and frontotemporal dementia. *Neurology, 55*, 1613–1620.

McArthur, J. C., Hoover, D. R., Bacellar, H., Miller, E. N., Cohen, B. A., Becker, J. T., et al. (1993). Dementia in AIDS patients: Incidence and risk factors. Multicenter AIDS cohort study. *Neurology, 43*, 2245–2252.

McGurn, B., Deary, I. J., & Starr, J. M. (2008). Childhood cognitive ability and risk of late-onset Alzheimer and vascular dementia. *Neurology, 71*, 1051–6.

McKeith, I. G., Dickson, D. W., Lowe, J., Emre, M., O'Brien, J. T., Feldman, H., et al. (2005). Diagnosis and management of dementia with Lewy bodies: Third report of the DLB consortium. *Neurology, 65*, 1863–1872.

McKhann, G., Drachman, D., Folstein, M., Katzman, R., Price, D., & Stadlan, E. M. (1984). Clinical diagnosis of Alzheimer's disease: Report of the NINCDS-ADRDA work group under the auspices of Department of Health and Human

Services task force on Alzheimer's disease. *Neurology*, *34*, 939–944.

McKhann, G. M., Knopman, D. S., Chertkow, H., Hyman, B. T., Jack, C. R. J, Kawas, C. H., et al. (2011). The diagnosis of dementia due to Alzheimer's disease: Recommendations from the National Institute on Aging and the Alzheimer's Association workgroup. Alzheimer's & Dementia:. *Journal of the Alzheimer's Association*, *7*, epub April 19.

McLaurin, E. Y., Holliday, S. L., Williams, P., & Brey, R. L. (2005). Predictors of cognitive dysfunction in patients with systemic lupus erythematosus. *Neurology*, *64*, 297–303.

McMonagle, P., Deering, F., Berliner, Y., & Kertesz, A. (2006). The cognitive profile of posterior cortical atrophy. *Neurology*, *66*, 331–338.

Mega, M. S., Cummings, J. L., Fiorello, T., & Gornbein, J. (1996). The spectrum of behavioral changes in Alzheimer's disease. *Neurology*, *46*, 130–135.

Meissner, B., Kortner, K., Bartl, M., Jastrow, U., Mollenhauer, B., Schroter, A., et al. (2004). Sporadic Creutzfeldt-Jakob disease: Magnetic resonance imaging and clinical findings. *Neurology*, *63*, 450–456.

Mendez, M. F., Adams, N. L., & Lewandowski, K. S. (1989). Neurobehavioral changes associated with caudate lesions. *Neurology*, *39*, 349–354.

Mendez, M. F., Clark, D. G., Shapira, J. S., & Cummings, J. L. (2003). Speech and language in progressive nonfluent aphasia compared with early Alzheimer's disease. *Neurology*, *61*, 1108–1113.

Mendez, M. F., Ghajarania, M., & Perryman, K. M. (2002). Posterior cortical atrophy: Clinical characteristics and differences compared to Alzheimer's disease. *Dementia and Geriatric Cognitive Disorders*, *14*, 33–40.

Mendez, M. F., Mendez, M. A., Martin, R., Smyth, K. A., & Whitehouse, P. J. (1990). Complex visual disturbances in Alzheimer's disease. *Neurology*, *40*, 439–443.

Mendez, M. F., Shapira, J. S., McMurtray, A., Licht, E., & Miller, B. L. (2007). Accuracy of the clinical evaluation for frontotemporal dementia. *Archives of Neurology*, *64*, 830–835.

Mesulam, M., Wicklund, A., Johnson, N., Rogalski, E., Leger, G. C., Rademaker, A., et al. (2008). Alzheimer and frontotemporal pathology in subsets of primary progressive aphasia. *Annals of Neurology*, *63*, 709–719.

Mesulam, M. M. (1982). Slowly progressive aphasia without generalized dementia. *Annals of Neurology*, *11*, 592–598.

Mesulam, M. M. (2001). Primary progressive aphasia. *Annals of Neurology*, *49*, 425–432.

Mesulam, M. M., Waxman, S. G., Geschwind, N., & Sabin, T. D. (1976). Acute confusional states with right middle cerebral artery infarctions. *Journal of Neurology, Neurosurgery, and Psychiatry*, *39*, 84–89.

Milberg, W., & Albert, M. (1989). Cognitive differences between patients with progressive supranuclear palsy and Alzheimer's disease. *Journal of Clinical and Experimental Neuropsychology*, *11*, 605–614.

Mindham, R. H., Steele, C., Folstein, M. F., & Lucas, J. (1985). A comparison of the frequency of major affective disorder in Huntington's disease and Alzheimer's disease. *Journal of Neurology, Neurosurgery, and Psychiatry*, *48*, 1172–1174.

Mitrushina, M., Satz, P., Chervinsky, A., & D'Elia, L. (1991). Performance of four age groups of normal elderly on the Rey auditory- verbal learning test. *Journal Clinical Psychology*, *47*, 351–357.

Modrego, P. J., & Ferrandez, J. (2004). Depression in patients with mild cognitive impairment increases the risk of developing dementia of Alzheimer type: A prospective cohort study. *Archives of Neurology*, *61*, 1290–1293.

Mohs, R. C., & Cohen, L. (1988). Alzheimer's disease assessment scale (ADAS). *Psychopharmacology Bulletin*, *24*, 627–628.

Mohs, R. C., Knopman, D., Petersen, R. C., Ferris, S. H., Ernesto, C., Grundman, M., et al. (1997). Development of cognitive instruments for use in clinical trials of antidementia drugs: Additions to the Alzheimer's disease assessment scale that broaden its scope. The Alzheimer's disease cooperative study. *Alzheimer Disease and Associated Disorders*, *11* (Suppl. 2), S13–S21.

Monacelli, A. M., Cushman, L. A., Kavcic, V., & Duffy, C. J. (2003). Spatial disorientation in Alzheimer's disease: The remembrance of things passed. *Neurology*, *61*, 1491–1497.

Monsch, A. U., Bondi, M. W., Butters, N., Salmon, D. P., Katzman, R., & Thal, L. J. (1992). Comparisons of verbal fluency tasks in the detection of dementia of the Alzheimer type. *Archives of Neurology*, *49*, 1253–1258.

Monsch, A. U., Bondi, M. W., Salmon, D. P., Butters, N., Thal, L. J., Hansen, L. A., et al. (1995). Clinical validity of the Mattis dementia rating scale in detecting dementia of the Alzheimer type. A double cross-validation and application to a community-dwelling sample. *Archives of Neurology*, *52*, 899–904.

Morris, J. C. (1993). The clinical dementia rating (CDR): Current version and scoring rules. *Neurology*, *43*, 2412–2414.

Morris, J. C., Edland, S., Clark, C., Galasko, D., Koss, E., Mohs, R., et al. (1993). The consortium to establish a registry for Alzheimer's disease (CERAD). Part IV. Rates of cognitive change in the longitudinal assessment of probable Alzheimer's disease. *Neurology, 43*, 2457–2465.

Moser, H. W. (1997). Adrenoleukodystrophy: Phenotype, genetics, pathogenesis and therapy. *Brain, 120*, 1485–1508.

Mungas, D., Harvey, D., Reed, B. R., Jagust, W. J., DeCarli, C., Beckett, L., et al. (2005). Longitudinal volumetric MRI change and rate of cognitive decline. *Neurology, 65*, 565–571.

Mungas, D., Jagust, W. J., Reed, B. R., Kramer, J. H., Weiner, M. W., Schuff, N., et al. (2001). MRI predictors of cognition in subcortical ischemic vascular disease and Alzheimer's disease. *Neurology, 57*, 2229–2235.

Murray, A. M., Levkoff, S. E., Wetle, T. T., Beckett, L., Cleary, P. D., Schor, J. D., et al. (1993). Acute delirium and functional decline in the hospitalized elderly patient. *Journal of Gerontology, 48*, M181–M186.

Murray, R., Neumann, M., Forman, M. S., Farmer, J., Massimo, L., Rice, A., et al. (2007). Cognitive and motor assessment in autopsy-proven corticobasal degeneration. *Neurology, 68*, 1274–1283.

Nasreddine, Z. S., Phillips, N. A., Bedirian, V., Charbonneau, S., Whitehead, V., Collin, I., et al. (2005). The Montreal cognitive assessment, MoCA: A brief screening tool for mild cognitive impairment. *Journal of the American Geriatric Society, 53*, 695–699.

Navia, B. A., Jordan, B. D., & Price, R. W. (1986). The AIDS dementia complex: I. Clinical features. *Annals of Neurology, 19*, 517–524.

Neary, D., & Snowden, J. S. (1991). Dementia of the frontal lobe type. In H. S. Levin, H. Eisenberg, & A. L. Benton (Eds.), *Frontal lobe function and dysfunction* (pp. 304–317). New York: Oxford University Press.

Neary, D., Snowden, J. S., Gustafson, L., Passant, U., Stuss, D., Black, S., et al. (1998). Frontotemporal lobar degeneration: A consensus on clinical diagnostic criteria. *Neurology, 51*, 1546–1554.

Nelson, P. T., Jicha, G. A., Schmitt, F. A., Liu, H., Davis, D. G., Mendiondo, M. S., et al. (2007). Clinicopathologic correlations in a large Alzheimer disease center autopsy cohort: Neuritic plaques and neurofibrillary tangles "do count" when staging disease severity. *Journal of Neuropathology and Experimental Neurology, 66*, 1136–1146.

Nestor, P. J., Fryer, T. D., & Hodges, J. R. (2006). Declarative memory impairments in Alzheimer's disease and semantic dementia. *Neuroimage, 30*, 1010–1020.

Nestor, P. J., Graham, N. L., Fryer, T. D., Williams, G. B., Patterson, K., & Hodges, J. R. (2003). Progressive non-fluent aphasia is associated with hypometabolism centred on the left anterior insula. *Brain, 126*, 2406–2418.

Nicholas, M., Obler, L. K., Au, R., & Albert, M. L. (1996). On the nature of naming errors in aging and dementia: A study of semantic relatedness. *Brain and Language, 54*, 184–195.

O'Bryant, S. E., Humphreys, J. D., Smith, G. E., Ivnik, R. J., Graff-Radford, N. R., Petersen, R. C., et al. (2008). Detecting dementia with the mini-mental state examination in highly educated individuals. *Archives of Neurology, 65*, 963–967.

O'Connor, D. W., Pollitt, P. A., Hyde, J. B., Fellows, J. L., Miller, N. D., Brook, C. P., et al. (1989). The reliability and validity of the mini-mental state in a British community survey. *Journal of Psychiatric Research, 23*, 87–96.

Ochipa, C., Rothi, L. J., & Heilman, K. M. (1992). Conceptual apraxia in Alzheimer's disease. *Brain, 115*, 1061–1071.

Okonkwo, O. C., Wadley, V. G., Griffith, H. R., Ball, K., & Marson, D. C. (2006). Cognitive correlates of financial abilities in mild cognitive impairment. *Journal of the American Geriatric Society, 54*, 1745–1750.

Olichney, J. M., Galasko, D., Salmon, D. P., Hofstetter, C. R., Hansen, L. A., Katzman, R., et al. (1998). Cognitive decline is faster in Lewy body variant than in Alzheimer's disease. *Neurology, 51*, 351–357.

Oppenheim, G. (1994). The earliest signs of Alzheimer's disease. *Journal of Geriatric Psychiatry and Neurology, 7*, 116–120.

Ott, A., Breteler, M. M., van Harskamp, F., Claus, J. J., van der Cammen, T. J., Grobbee, D. E., et al. (1995). Prevalence of Alzheimer's disease and vascular dementia: Association with education. The Rotterdam study. *British Medical Journal, 310*, 970–973.

Ott, A., Breteler, M. M., van Harskamp, F., Stijnen, T., & Hofman, A. (1998). Incidence and risk of dementia. The Rotterdam study. *American Journal of Epidemiology, 147*, 574–580.

Ott, B. R., & Saver, J. L. (1993). Unilateral amnesic stroke. Six new cases and a review of the literature. *Stroke, 24*, 1033–1042.

Paque, L., & Warrington, E. K. (1995). A longitudinal study of reading ability in patients suffering from dementia. *Journal of the International Neuropsychological Society, 1*, 517–524.

Pasquier, F. (1999). Early diagnosis of dementia: Neuropsychology. *Journal of Neurology, 246,* 6–15.

Patterson, M. B., Mack, J. L., Mackell, J. A., Thomas, R., Tariot, P., Weiner, M., et al. (1997). A longitudinal study of behavioral pathology across five levels of dementia severity in Alzheimer's disease: The CERAD behavior rating scale for dementia. The Alzheimer's disease cooperative study. *Alzheimer Disease and Associated Disorders, 11* (Suppl. 2), S40–S44.

Paulsen, J. S., & Conybeare, R. A. (2005). Cognitive changes in Huntington's disease. *Advances in Neurology, 96,* 209–225.

Pavlik, V. N., Doody, R. S., Massman, P. J., & Chan, W. (2006). Influence of premorbid IQ and education on progression of Alzheimer's disease. *Dementia and Geriatric Cognitive Disorders, 22,* 367–377.

Peinemann, A., Schuller, S., Pohl, C., Jahn, T., Weindl, A., & Kassubek, J. (2005). Executive dysfunction in early stages of Huntington's disease is associated with striatal and insular atrophy: A neuropsychological and voxel-based morphometric study. *Journal of the Neurological Sciences, 239,* 11–19.

Perry, R. J., & Hodges, J. R. (1999). Attention and executive deficits in Alzheimer's disease. A critical review. *Brain, 122,* 383–404.

Petersen, R. C. (2004). Mild cognitive impairment as a diagnostic entity. *Journal of Internal Medicine, 256,* 183–194.

Petersen, R. C., Doody, R., Kurz, A., Mohs, R. C., Morris, J. C., Rabins, P. V., et al. (2001). Current concepts in mild cognitive impairment. *Archives of Neurology, 58,* 1985–1992.

Petersen, R. C., Jack, C. R., Jr., Xu, Y. C., Waring, S. C., O'Brien, P. C., Smith, G. E., et al. (2000). Memory and MRI-based hippocampal volumes in aging and AD. *Neurology, 54,* 581–587.

Petersen, R. C., & Knopman, D. S. (2006). MCI is a clinically useful concept. *International Psychogeriatrics, 18,* 394–402; discussion 409–414.

Petersen, R. C., Smith, G., Kokmen, E., Ivnik, R. J., & Tangalos, E. G. (1992). Memory function in normal aging. *Neurology, 42,* 396–401.

Petersen, R. C., Smith, G. E., Ivnik, R. J., Kokmen, E., & Tangalos, E. G. (1994). Memory function in very early Alzheimer's disease. *Neurology, 44,* 867–872.

Petersen, R. C., Smith, G. E., Waring, S. C., Ivnik, R. J., Tangalos, E. G., & Kokmen, E. (1999). Mild cognitive impairment: Clinical characterization and outcome. *Archives of Neurology, 56,* 303–308.

Petersen, R. C., Thomas, R. G., Grundman, M., Bennett, D., Doody, R., Ferris, S., et al. (2005). Vitamin E and donepezil for the treatment of mild cognitive impairment. *New England Journal of Medicine, 352,* 2379–2388.

Petrovitch, H., White, L., Masaki, K. H., Ross, G. W., Abbott, R. D., Rodriguez, B. L., et al. (1998). Influence of myocardial infarction, coronary artery bypass surgery, and stroke on cognitive impairment in late life. *American Journal of Cardiology, 81,* 1017–1021.

Pfeffer, R. I., Afifi, A. A., & Chance, J. M. (1987). Prevalence of Alzheimer's disease in a retirement community. *American Journal of Epidemiology, 125,* 420–436.

Pfeffer, R. I., Kurosaki, T. T., Harrah, C. H., Jr., Chance, J. M., & Filos, S. (1982). Measurement of functional activities in older adults in the community. *Journal of Gerontology, 37,* 323–329.

Pike, K. E., Savage, G., Villemagne, V. L., Ng, S., Moss, S. A., Maruff, P., et al. (2007). Beta-amyloid imaging and memory in non-demented individuals: Evidence for preclinical Alzheimer's disease. *Brain, 130,* 2837–2844.

Pillon, B., Blin, J., Vidailhet, M., Deweer, B., Sirigu, A., Dubois, B., et al. (1995). The neuropsychological pattern of corticobasal degeneration: Comparison with progressive supranuclear palsy and Alzheimer's disease. *Neurology, 45,* 1477–1483.

Pittman, J., Andrews, H., Tatemichi, T., Link, B., Struening, E., Stern, Y., et al. (1992). Diagnosis of dementia in a heterogeneous population. A comparison of paradigm-based diagnosis and physician's diagnosis. *Archives of Neurology, 49,* 461–467.

Pohjasvaara, T., Mantyla, R., Salonen, O., Aronen, H. J., Ylikoski, R., Hietanen, M., et al. (2000). MRI correlates of dementia after first clinical ischemic stroke. *Journal of the Neurological Sciences, 181,* 111–117.

Power, C., Selnes, O. A., Grim, J. A., & McArthur, J. C. (1995). HIV dementia scale: A rapid screening test. *Journal of Acquired Immune Deficiency Syndrome, Human Retrovirology, 8,* 273–278.

Price, R. W., Brew, B., Sidtis, J., Rosenblum, M., Scheck, A. C., & Cleary, P. (1988). The brain in AIDS: Central nervous system HIV-1 infection and AIDS dementia complex. *Science, 239,* 586–592.

Prins, N. D., van Dijk, E. J., den Heijer, T., Vermeer, S. E., Jolles, J., Koudstaal, P. J., et al. (2005). Cerebral small-vessel disease and decline in information processing speed, executive function and memory. *Brain, 128,* 2034–2041.

Prins, N. D., van Dijk, E. J., den Heijer, T., Vermeer, S. E., Koudstaal, P. J., Oudkerk, M., et al. (2004). Cerebral white matter lesions and the risk of dementia. *Archives of Neurology, 61,* 1531–1534.

Qiu, C., Winblad, B., & Fratiglioni, L. (2006). Cerebrovascular disease, APOE epsilon4 allele and cognitive decline in a cognitively normal population. *Neurology Research, 28,* 650–656.

Rahman, S., Sahakian, B. J., Hodges, J. R., Rogers, R. D., & Robbins, T. W. (1999). Specific cognitive deficits in mild frontal variant frontotemporal dementia. *Brain, 122,* 1469–1493.

Rahmani, B., Tielsch, J. M., Katz, J., Gottsch, J., Quigley, H., Javitt, J., et al. (1996). The cause-specific prevalence of visual impairment in an urban population. The Baltimore eye survey. *Ophthalmology, 103,* 1721–1726.

Rapcsak, S. Z., Croswell, S. C., & Rubens, A. B. (1989). Apraxia in Alzheimer's disease. *Neurology, 39,* 664–668.

Rascovsky, K., Salmon, D. P., Ho, G. J., Galasko, D., Peavy, G. M., Hansen, L. A., et al. (2002). Cognitive profiles differ in autopsy-confirmed frontotemporal dementia and AD. *Neurology, 58,* 1801–1808.

Raskind, M. A., Peskind, E. R., Wessel, T., & Yuan, W. (2000). Galantamine in AD: A 6-month randomized, placebo-controlled trial with a 6-month extension. *Neurology, 54,* 2261–2268.

Ratnavalli, E., Brayne, C., Dawson, K., & Hodges, J. R. (2002). The prevalence of frontotemporal dementia. *Neurology, 58,* 1615–1621.

Read, S. L., Miller, B. L., Mena, I., Kim, R., Itabashi, H., & Darby, A. (1995). SPECT in dementia: Clinical and pathological correlation. *Journal of the American Geriatric Society, 43,* 1243–1247.

Reddy, P. H., Williams, M., & Tagle, D. A. (1999). Recent advances in understanding the pathogenesis of Huntington's disease. *Trends in Neuroscience, 22,* 248–255.

Reed, B. R., Eberling, J. L., Mungas, D., Weiner, M., Kramer, J. H., & Jagust, W. J. (2004). Effects of white matter lesions and lacunes on cortical function. *Archives of Neurology, 61,* 1545–1550.

Reed, B. R., Mungas, D. M., Kramer, J. H., Ellis, W., Vinters, H. V., Zarow, C., et al. (2007). Profiles of neuropsychological impairment in autopsy-defined Alzheimer's disease and cerebrovascular disease. *Brain, 130,* 731–739.

Reichman, W. E., Coyne, A. C., Amirneni, S., Molino, B., Jr., & Egan, S. (1996). Negative symptoms in Alzheimer's disease. *American Journal of Psychiatry, 153,* 424–426.

Reines, S. A., Block, G. A., Morris, J. C., Liu, G., Nessly, M. L., Lines, C. R., et al. (2004). Rofecoxib: No effect on Alzheimer's disease in a 1-year, randomized, blinded, controlled study. *Neurology, 62,* 66–71.

Reisberg, B., Borenstein, J., Salob, S. P., Ferris, S. H., Franssen, E., & Georgotas, A. (1987). Behavioral symptoms in Alzheimer's disease: Phenomenology and treatment. *Journal of Clinical Psychiatry, 48*(Suppl.), 9–15.

Reisberg, B., Doody, R., Stoffler, A., Schmitt, F., Ferris, S., & Mobius, H. J. (2003). Memantine in moderate-to-severe Alzheimer's disease. *New England Journal of Medicine, 348,* 1333–1341.

Reisberg, B., Ferris, S. H., de Leon, M. J., & Crook, T. (1982). The global deterioration scale for assessment of primary degenerative dementia. *American Journal of Psychiatry, 139,* 1136–1139.

Reitz, C., Luchsinger, J. A., Tang, M. X., Manly, J., & Mayeux, R. (2006). Stroke and memory performance in elderly persons without dementia. *Archives of Neurology, 63,* 571–576.

Relkin, N., Marmarou, A., Klinge, P., Bergsneider, M., & Black, P. M. (2005). Diagnosing idiopathic normal-pressure hydrocephalus. *Neurosurgery, 57,* S4–S16; discussion ii-v.

Renner, J. A., Burns, J. M., Hou, C. E., McKeel, D. W., Jr., Storandt, M., & Morris, J. C. (2004). Progressive posterior cortical dysfunction: A clinicopathologic series. *Neurology, 63,* 1175–1180.

Rentz, D. M., Huh, T. J., Faust, R. R., Budson, A. E., Scinto, L. F., Sperling, R. A., et al. (2004). Use of IQ-adjusted norms to predict progressive cognitive decline in highly intelligent older individuals. *Neuropsychology, 18,* 38–49.

Rinne, J. O., Lee, M. S., Thompson, P. D., & Marsden, C. D. (1994). Corticobasal degeneration. A clinical study of 36 cases. *Brain, 117,* 1183–1196.

Risse, S. C., Raskind, M. A., Nochlin, D., Sumi, S. M., Lampe, T. H., Bird, T. D., et al. (1990). Neuropathological findings in patients with clinical diagnoses of probable Alzheimer's disease. *American Journal of Psychiatry, 147,* 168–172.

Ritchie, K., Artero, S., & Touchon, J. (2001). Classification criteria for mild cognitive impairment: A population-based validation study. *Neurology, 56,* 37–42.

Rocca, W. A., Cha, R. H., Waring, S. C., & Kokmen, E. (1998). Incidence of dementia and Alzheimer's disease: A reanalysis of data from Rochester, Minnesota, 1975–1984. *American Journal of Epidemiology, 148,* 51–62.

Roe, C. M., Xiong, C., Miller, J. P., & Morris, J. C. (2007). Education and Alzheimer disease without dementia: Support for the cognitive reserve hypothesis. *Neurology, 68,* 223–228.

Rogers, S. L., Farlow, M. R., Doody, R. S., Mohs, R., & Friedhoff, L. T. (1998). A 24-week, double-blind, placebo-controlled trial of donepezil in patients with Alzheimer's disease. *Neurology, 50,* 136–145.

Rogers, T. T., Ivanoiu, A., Patterson, K., & Hodges, J. R. (2006). Semantic memory in Alzheimer's disease and the frontotemporal dementias: A longitudinal study of 236 patients. *Neuropsychology, 20,* 319–335.

Roman, G. C., Tatemichi, T. K., Erkinjuntti, T., Cummings, J. L., Masdeu, J. C., Garcia, J. H., et al. (1993). Vascular dementia: Diagnostic criteria for research studies. Report of the NINDS-AIREN international workshop. *Neurology, 43,* 250–260.

Rosas, H. D., Salat, D. H., Lee, S. Y., Zaleta, A. K., Pappu, V., Fischl, B., et al. (2008). Cerebral cortex and the clinical expression of Huntington's disease: Complexity and heterogeneity. *Brain, 131,* 1057–1068.

Rosen, H. J., Gorno-Tempini, M. L., Goldman, W. P., Perry, R. J., Schuff, N., Weiner, M., et al. (2002). Patterns of brain atrophy in frontotemporal dementia and semantic dementia. *Neurology, 58,* 198–208.

Rosen, W. G., Mohs, R. C., & Davis, K. L. (1984). A new rating scale for Alzheimer's disease. *American Journal of Psychiatry, 141,* 1356–1364.

Rosler, M., Anand, R., Cicin-Sain, A., Gauthier, S., Agid, Y., Dal-Bianco, P., et al. (1999). Efficacy and safety of rivastigmine in patients with Alzheimer's disease: International randomised controlled trial. *British Medical Journal, 318,* 633–640.

Ross, G. W., Abbott, R. D., Petrovitch, H., Masaki, K. H., Murdaugh, C., Trockman, C., et al. (1997). Frequency and characteristics of silent dementia among elderly Japanese-American men. The Honolulu-Asia aging study. *Journal of the American Medical Association, 277,* 800–805.

Rosso, S. M., Donker Kaat, L., Baks, T., Joosse, M., de Koning, I., Pijnenburg, Y., et al. (2003). Frontotemporal dementia in The Netherlands: Patient characteristics and prevalence estimates from a population-based study. *Brain, 126,* 2016–2022.

Rowe, C. C., Ng, S., Ackermann, U., Gong, S. J., Pike, K., Savage, G., et al. (2007). Imaging beta-amyloid burden in aging and dementia. *Neurology, 68,* 1718–1725.

Royall, D. R., Chiodo, L. K., & Polk, M. J. (2004). Misclassification is likely in the assessment of mild cognitive impairment. *Neuroepidemiology, 23,* 185–191.

Royall, D. R., Mahurin, R. K., & Gray, K. F. (1992). Bedside assessment of executive cognitive impairment: The executive interview. *Journal of the American Geriatric Society, 40,* 1221–1226.

Sabbagh, M. N., Corey-Bloom, J., Tiraboschi, P., Thomas, R., Masliah, E., & Thal, L. J. (1999). Neurochemical markers do not correlate with cognitive decline in the Lewy body variant of Alzheimer disease. *Archives of Neurology, 56,* 1458–1461.

Salloway, S., Ferris, S., Kluger, A., Goldman, R., Griesing, T., Kumar, D., et al. (2004). Efficacy of donepezil in mild cognitive impairment: A randomized placebo-controlled trial. *Neurology, 63,* 651–657.

Salmon, D. P., Butters, N., & Chan, A. S. (1999). The deterioration of semantic memory in Alzheimer's disease. *Canadian Journal of Experimental Psychology, 53,* 108–117.

Salmon, D. P., Galasko, D., Hansen, L. A., Masliah, E., Butters, N., Thal, L. J., et al. (1996). Neuropsychological deficits associated with diffuse Lewy body disease. *Brain and Cognition, 31,* 148–165.

Salmon, D. P., Thal, L. J., Butters, N., & Heindel, W. C. (1990). Longitudinal evaluation of dementia of the Alzheimer type: A comparison of 3 standardized mental status examinations. *Neurology, 40,* 1225–1230.

Salmon, D. P., Thomas, R. G., Pay, M. M., Booth, A., Hofstetter, C. R., Thal, L. J., et al. (2002). Alzheimer's disease can be accurately diagnosed in very mildly impaired individuals. *Neurology, 59,* 1022–1028.

Salthouse, T. A. (2003). Memory aging from 18 to 80. *Alzheimer Disease and Associated Disorders, 17,* 162–167.

Samuel, W., Galasko, D., Masliah, E., & Hansen, L. A. (1996). Neocortical Lewy body counts correlate with dementia in the Lewy body variant of Alzheimer's disease. *Journal of Neuropathology and Experimental Neurology, 55,* 44–52.

Saper, C. B., German, D. C., & White, C. L. (1985). Neuronal pathology in the nucleus basalis and associated cell groups in senile dementia of the Alzheimer's type: Possible role in cell loss. *Neurology, 35,* 1089–1095.

Scarmeas, N., Albert, S. M., Manly, J. J., & Stern, Y. (2006). Education and rates of cognitive decline in incident Alzheimer's disease. *Journal of Neurology, Neurosurgery, and Psychiatry, 77,* 308–316.

Schaie, K. W. (1989). The hazards of cognitive aging. *Gerontologist, 29,* 484–493.

Schaie, K. W. (1989). Perceptual speed in adulthood: Cross-sectional and longitudinal studies. *Psychology and Aging, 4,* 443–453.

Schmidtke, K., & Olbrich, S. (2007). The clock reading test: Validation of an instrument for the diagnosis of dementia and disorders of visuo-spatial cognition. *International Psychogeriatrics, 19,* 307–321.

Schmitt, F. A., Ashford, W., Ernesto, C., Saxton, J., Schneider, L. S., Clark, C. M., et al. (1997). The severe impairment battery: Concurrent validity and the assessment of longitudinal change in Alzheimer's disease. The Alzheimer's disease cooperative study. *Alzheimer Disease and Associated Disorders, 11*(Suppl. 2), S51–S56.

Schmitt, F. A., Davis, D. G., Wekstein, D. R., Smith, C. D., Ashford, J. W., & Markesbery, W. R. (2000). "Preclinical" AD revisited: Neuropathology of cognitively normal older adults. *Neurology, 55,* 370–376.

Schneider, J. A., Wilson, R. S., Bienias, J. L., Evans, D. A., & Bennett, D. A. (2004). Cerebral infarctions and the likelihood of dementia from Alzheimer disease pathology. *Neurology, 62,* 1148–1155.

Schneider, L. S. (1992). Tracking dementia by the IMC and the MMSE. *Journal of the American Geriatric Society, 40,* 537–538.

Schroter, A., Zerr, I., Henkel, K., Tschampa, H. J., Finkenstaedt, M., & Poser, S. (2000). Magnetic resonance imaging in the clinical diagnosis of Creutzfeldt-Jakob disease. *Archives of Neurology, 57,* 1751–1757.

Selnes, O. A., Miller, E., McArthur, J., Gordon, B., Munoz, A., Sheridan, K., et al. (1990). HIV-1 infection: No evidence of cognitive decline during the asymptomatic stages. The multicenter AIDS cohort study. *Neurology, 40,* 204–208.

Seltzer, B., Vasterling, J. J., Yoder, J. A., & Thompson, K. A. (1997). Awareness of deficit in Alzheimer's disease: Relation to caregiver burden. *Gerontologist, 37,* 20–24.

Seltzer, B., Zolnouni, P., Nunez, M., Goldman, R., Kumar, D., Ieni, J., et al. (2004). Efficacy of donepezil in early-stage Alzheimer disease: A randomized placebo-controlled trial. *Archives of Neurology, 61,* 1852–1856.

Shadlen, M. F., Siscovick, D., Fitzpatrick, A. L., Dulberg, C., Kuller, L. H., & Jackson, S. (2006). Education, cognitive test scores, and black-white differences in dementia risk. *Journal of the American Geriatric Society, 54,* 898–905.

Shapiro, A. M., Benedict, R. H., Schretlen, D., & Brandt, J. (1999). Construct and concurrent validity of the Hopkins verbal learning test-revised. *Clinical Neuropsychology, 13,* 348–358.

Shapiro, E. G., Lockman, L. A., Knopman, D., & Krivit, W. (1994). Characteristics of the dementia in late-onset metachromatic leukodystrophy. *Neurology, 44,* 662–665.

Shuttleworth, E. C., & Huber, S. J. (1988). The naming disorder of dementia of Alzheimer type. *Brain and Language, 34,* 222–234.

Sliwinski, M., Lipton, R. B., Buschke, H., & Stewart, W. (1996). The effects of preclinical dementia on estimates of normal cognitive functioning in aging. *Journal of Gerontology, B Psychological Sciences and Social Sciences, 51,* 217–225.

Smith, C. D., Chebrolu, H., Wekstein, D. R., Schmitt, F. A., Jicha, G. A., Cooper, G., et al. (2007). Brain structural alterations before mild cognitive impairment. *Neurology, 68,* 1268–1273.

Smith, G. E., Pankratz, V. S., Negash, S., Machulda, M. M., Petersen, R. C., Boeve, B. F., et al. (2007). A plateau in pre-Alzheimer memory decline: Evidence for compensatory mechanisms? *Neurology, 69,* 133–139.

Snowdon, D. A., Greiner, L. H., Mortimer, J. A., Riley, K. P., Greiner, P. A., & Markesbery, W. R. (1997). Brain infarction and the clinical expression of Alzheimer disease. The nun study. *Journal of the American Medical Association, 277,* 813–817.

Snowdon, D. A., Kemper, S. J., Mortimer, J. A., Greiner, L. H., Wekstein, D. R., & Markesbery, W. R. (1996). Linguistic ability in early life and cognitive function and Alzheimer's disease in late life. Findings from the nun study. *Journal of the American Medical Association, 275,* 528–532.

Starkstein, S. E., Sabe, L., Chemerinski, E., Jason, L., & Leiguarda, R. (1996). Two domains of anosognosia in Alzheimer's disease. *Journal of Neurology, Neurosurgery, and Psychiatry, 61,* 485–490.

Steinhoff, B. J., Racker, S., Herrendorf, G., Poser, S., Grosche, S., Zerr, I., et al. (1996). Accuracy and reliability of periodic sharp wave complexes in Creutzfeldt-Jakob disease. *Archives of Neurology, 53,* 162–166.

Stern, R. G., Mohs, R. C., Davidson, M., Schmeidler, J., Silverman, J., Kramer-Ginsberg, E., et al. (1994). A longitudinal study of Alzheimer's disease: Measurement, rate, and predictors of cognitive deterioration. *American Journal of Psychiatry, 151,* 390–396.

Stern, Y., Andrews, H., Pittman, J., Sano, M., Tatemichi, T., Lantigua, R., et al. (1992).

Diagnosis of dementia in a heterogeneous population. Development of a neuropsychological paradigm-based diagnosis of dementia and quantified correction for the effects of education. *Archives of Neurology, 49*, 453–460.

Stern, Y., Gurland, B., Tatemichi, T. K., Tang, M. X., Wilder, D., & Mayeux, R. (1994). Influence of education and occupation on the incidence of Alzheimer's disease. *Journal of the American Medical Association, 271*, 1004–1010.

Stern, Y., Tang, M. X., Denaro, J., & Mayeux, R. (1995). Increased risk of mortality in Alzheimer's disease patients with more advanced educational and occupational attainment. *Annals of Neurology, 37*, 590–595.

Sternberg, S. A., Wolfson, C., & Baumgarten, M. (2000). Undetected dementia in community-dwelling older people: The Canadian study of health and aging. *Journal of the American Geriatric Society, 48*, 1430–1434.

Storandt, M., Botwinick, J., Danziger, W. L., Berg, L., & Hughes, C. P. (1984). Psychometric differentiation of mild senile dementia of the Alzheimer type. *Archives of Neurology, 41*, 497–499.

Storandt, M., Kaskie, B., & Von Dras, D. D. (1998). Temporal memory for remote events in healthy aging and dementia. *Psychology and Aging, 13*, 4–7.

Stout, J. C., Ellis, R. J., Jernigan, T. L., Archibald, S. L., Abramson, I., Wolfson, T., et al. (1998). Progressive cerebral volume loss in human immunodeficiency virus infection: A longitudinal volumetric magnetic resonance imaging study. HIV neurobehavioral research center group. *Archives of Neurology, 55*, 161–168.

Stuss, D. T., Meiran, N., Guzman, D. A., Lafleche, G., & Willmer, J. (1996). Do long tests yield a more accurate diagnosis of dementia than short tests? A comparison of 5 neuropsychological tests. *Archives of Neurology, 53*, 1033–1039.

Swearer, J. M., O'Donnell, B. F., Drachman, D. A., & Woodward, B. M. (1992). Neuropsychological features of familial Alzheimer's disease. *Annals of Neurology, 32*, 687–694.

Tabert, M. H., Manly, J. J., Liu, X., Pelton, G. H., Rosenblum, S., Jacobs, M., et al. (2006). Neuropsychological prediction of conversion to Alzheimer disease in patients with mild cognitive impairment. *Archives of General Psychiatry, 63*, 916–924.

Talbot, P. R., Lloyd, J. J., Snowden, J. S., Neary, D., & Testa, H. J. (1998). A clinical role for 99mTc-HMPAO SPECT in the investigation of dementia? *Journal of Neurology, Neurosurgery, and Psychiatry, 64*, 306–313.

Tang-Wai, D. F., Graff-Radford, N. R., Boeve, B. F., Dickson, D. W., Parisi, J. E., Crook, R., et al. (2004). Clinical, genetic, and neuropathologic characteristics of posterior cortical atrophy. *Neurology, 63*, 1168–1174.

Tang-Wai, D. F., Knopman, D. S., Geda, Y. E., Edland, S. D., Smith, G. E., Ivnik, R. J., et al. (2003). Comparison of the short test of mental status and the mini-mental state examination in mild cognitive impairment. *Archives of Neurology, 60*, 1777–1781.

Tangalos, E. G., Smith, G. E., Ivnik, R. J., Petersen, R. C., Kokmen, E., Kurland, L. T., et al. (1996). The mini-mental state examination in general medical practice: Clinical utility and acceptance. *Mayo Clinical Proceedings, 71*, 829–837.

Tariot, P. N., Farlow, M. R., Grossberg, G. T., Graham, S. M., McDonald, S., & Gergel, I. (2004). Memantine treatment in patients with moderate to severe Alzheimer disease already receiving donepezil: A randomized controlled trial. *Journal of the American Medical Association, 291*, 317–324.

Tariot, P. N., Solomon, P. R., Morris, J. C., Kershaw, P., Lilienfeld, S., & Ding, C. (2000). A 5-month, randomized, placebo-controlled trial of galantamine in AD. *Neurology, 54*, 2269–2276.

Tatemichi, T. K., Desmond, D. W., Prohovnik, I., Cross, D. T., Gropen, T. I., Mohr, J. P., et al. (1992). Confusion and memory loss from capsular genu infarction: A thalamocortical disconnection syndrome? *Neurology, 42*, 1966–1979.

Tatemichi, T. K., Desmond, D. W., Stern, Y., Paik, M., Sano, M., & Bagiella, E. (1994). Cognitive impairment after stroke: Frequency, patterns, and relationship to functional abilities. *Journal of Neurology, Neurosurgery, and Psychiatry, 57*, 202–207.

Teng, E. L., & Chui, H. C. (1987). The modified mini-mental state (3MS) examination. *Journal of Clinical Psychiatry, 48*, 314–318.

Teri, L., Larson, E. B., & Reifler, B. V. (1988). Behavioral disturbance in dementia of the Alzheimer's type. *Journal of the American Geriatric Society, 36*, 1–6.

Terry, R. D., Masliah, E., Salmon, D. P., Butters, N., DeTeresa, R., Hill, R., et al. (1991). Physical basis of cognitive alterations in Alzheimer's disease: Synapse loss is the major correlate of cognitive impairment. *Annals of Neurology, 30*, 572–580.

Teunisse, S., Derix, M. M., & van Crevel, H. (1991). Assessing the severity of dementia. Patient and caregiver. *Archives of Neurology, 48*, 274–277.

Thal, L. J., Ferris, S. H., Kirby, L., Block, G. A., Lines, C. R., Yuen, E., et al. (2005). A randomized, double-blind, study of Rofecoxib in patients with mild cognitive impairment. *Neuropsychopharmacology, 30,* 1204–1215.

Thal, L. J., Grundman, M., & Klauber, M. R. (1988). Dementia: Characteristics of a referral population and factors associated with progression. *Neurology, 38,* 1083–1090.

Thieben, M. J., Lennon, V. A., Boeve, B. F., Aksamit, A. J., Keegan, M., & Vernino, S. (2004). Potentially reversible autoimmune limbic encephalitis with neuronal potassium channel antibody. *Neurology, 62,* 1177–1182.

Tierney, M. C., Szalai, J. P., Snow, W. G., Fisher, R. H., Nores, A., Nadon, G., et al. (1996). Prediction of probable Alzheimer's disease in memory-impaired patients: A prospective longitudinal study. *Neurology, 46,* 661–665.

Tiraboschi, P., Hansen, L. A., Thal, L. J., & Corey-Bloom, J. (2004). The importance of neuritic plaques and tangles to the development and evolution of AD. *Neurology, 62,* 1984–1989.

Torralva, T., Kipps, C. M., Hodges, J. R., Clark, L., Bekinschtein, T., Roca, M., et al. (2007). The relationship between affective decision-making and theory of mind in the frontal variant of fronto-temporal dementia. *Neuropsychologia, 45,* 342–349.

Travniczek-Marterer, A., Danielczyk, W., Simanyi, M., & Fischer, P. (1993). Ideomotor apraxia in Alzheimer's disease. *Acta Neurologica Scandinavica, 88,* 1–4.

Troncoso, J. C., Zonderman, A. B., Resnick, S. M., Crain, B., Pletnikova, O., & O'Brien, R. J. (2008). Effect of infarcts on dementia in the Baltimore longitudinal study of aging. *Annals of Neurology, 64,* 168–176.

Tullberg, M., Fletcher, E., DeCarli, C., Mungas, D., Reed, B. R., Harvey, D. J., et al. (2004). White matter lesions impair frontal lobe function regardless of their location. *Neurology, 63,* 246–253.

Valcour, V. G., Masaki, K. H., Curb, J. D., & Blanchette, P. L. (2000). The detection of dementia in the primary care setting. *Archives of Internal Medicine, 160,* 2964–2968.

van Halteren-van Tilborg, I. A., Scherder, E. J., & Hulstijn, W. (2007). Motor-skill learning in Alzheimer's disease: A review with an eye to the clinical practice. *Neuropsychological Review, 17,* 203–212.

Verghese, J., LeValley, A., Derby, C., Kuslansky, G., Katz, M., Hall, C., et al. (2006). Leisure activities and the risk of amnestic mild cognitive impairment in the elderly. *Neurology, 66,* 821–827.

Verghese, J., Lipton, R. B., Katz, M. J., Hall, C. B., Derby, C. A., Kuslansky, G., et al. (2003). Leisure activities and the risk of dementia in the elderly. *New England Journal of Medicine, 348,* 2508–2516.

Vermeer, S. E., Prins, N. D., den Heijer, T., Hofman, A., Koudstaal, P. J., & Breteler, M. M. (2003). Silent brain infarcts and the risk of dementia and cognitive decline. *New England Journal of Medicine, 348,* 1215–1222.

Visser, P. J., Brodaty, H. (2006). MCI is not a clinically useful concept. *International Psychogeriatrics, 18,* 402–409; discussion 409–14.

Vonsattel, J. P., & DiFiglia, M. (1998). Huntington disease. *Journal of Neuropathology and Experimental Neurology, 57,* 369–384.

Wade, J. P., Mirsen, T. R., Hachinski, V. C., Fisman, M., Lau, C., & Merskey, H. (1987). The clinical diagnosis of Alzheimer's disease. *Archives of Neurology, 44,* 24–29.

Wechsler, D. (1981). *Wechsler adult intelligence scale-Revised.* New York: The Psychological Corporation.

Wechsler, D. A. (1987). *Wechsler memory scale-Revised.* New York: Psychological Corporation.

Wei, L. A., Fearing, M. A., Sternberg, E. J., & Inouye, S. K. (2008). The confusion assessment method: A systematic review of current usage. *Journal of the American Geriatric Society, 56,* 823–830.

Welsh, K., Butters, N., Hughes, J., Mohs, R., & Heyman, A. (1991). Detection of abnormal memory decline in mild cases of Alzheimer's disease using CERAD neuropsychological measures. *Archives of Neurology, 48,* 278–281.

Welsh, K. A., Butters, N., Hughes, J. P., Mohs, R. C., & Heyman, A. (1992). Detection and staging of dementia in Alzheimer's disease. Use of the neuropsychological measures developed for the consortium to establish a registry for Alzheimer's disease. *Archives of Neurology, 49,* 448–452.

Welsh, K. A., Butters, N., Mohs, R. C., Beekly, D., Edland, S., Fillenbaum, G., et al. (1994). The consortium to establish a registry for Alzheimer's disease (CERAD). Part V. A normative study of the neuropsychological battery. *Neurology, 44,* 609–614.

Whalley, L. J., Starr, J. M., Athawes, R., Hunter, D., Pattie, A., & Deary, I. J. (2000). Childhood mental ability and dementia. *Neurology, 55,* 1455–1459.

White, L., Petrovitch, H., Hardman, J., Nelson, J., Davis, D. G., Ross, G. W., et al. (2002). Cerebrovascular pathology and dementia in autopsied Honolulu-Asia aging study participants.

Annals of the New York Academy of Sciences,
977, 9–23.

White, L., Petrovitch, H., Ross, G. W., Masaki, K. H., Abbott, R. D., Teng, E. L., et al. (1996). Prevalence of dementia in older Japanese-American men in Hawaii: The Honolulu-Asia aging study. *Journal of the American Medical Association,* *276,* 955–960.

Whitwell, J. L., Jack, C. R., Jr., Baker, M., Rademakers, R., Adamson, J., Boeve, B. F., et al. (2007). Voxel-based morphometry in frontotemporal lobar degeneration with ubiquitin-positive inclusions with and without progranulin mutations. *Archives of Neurology, 64,* 371–376.

Whitwell, J. L., Josephs, K. A., Murray, M. E., Kantarci, K., Przybelski, S. A., Weigand, S. D., et al. (2008). MRI correlates of neurofibrillary tangle pathology at autopsy: A voxel-based morphometry study. *Neurology, 71,* 743–749.

Wilcock, G. K., Lilienfeld, S., & Gaens, E. (2000). Efficacy and safety of galantamine in patients with mild to moderate Alzheimer's disease: Multicentre randomised controlled trial. *British Medical Journal, 321,* 1445–1449.

Willingham, D. B., Peterson, E. W., Manning, C., & Brashear, H. R. (1997). Patients with Alzheimer's disease who cannot perform some motor skills show normal learning of other motor skills. *Neuropsychology, 11,* 261–271.

Willis, L., Behrens, M., Mack, W., & Chui, H. (1998). Ideomotor apraxia in early Alzheimer's disease: Time and accuracy measures. *Brain and Cognition, 38,* 220–233.

Willshire, D., Kinsella, G., & Prior, M. (1991). Estimating WAIS-R IQ from the national adult reading test: A cross- validation. *Journal of Clinical and Experimental Neuropsychology, 13,* 204–216.

Wilson, R. S., Beckett, L. A., Bennett, D. A., Albert, M. S., & Evans, D. A. (1999). Change in cognitive function in older persons from a community population: Relation to age and Alzheimer disease. *Archives of Neurology, 56,* 1274–1279.

Wilson, R. S., Bennett, D. A., Bienias, J. L., Mendes De Leon, C. F., Morris, M. C., & Evans, D. A. (2003). Cognitive activity and cognitive decline in a biracial community population. *Neurology, 61,* 812–816.

Wilson, R. S., Scherr, P. A., Schneider, J. A., Tang, Y., & Bennett, D. A. (2007). The relation of cognitive activity to risk of developing Alzheimer's disease. *Neurology, 69*(20), 1911–1920.

Winblad, B., Gauthier, S., Scinto, L., Feldman, H., Wilcock, G. K., Truyen, L., et al. (2008). Safety and efficacy of galantamine in subjects with mild cognitive impairment. *Neurology, 70,* 2024–2035.

World Health Organization. (1992). Mental and behavioral disorders (F00-F99). In *The international classification of diseases* 10th rev.: ICD-10 (pp. 311–388). Geneva: World Health Organization.

World Health Organization. (1998). Human transmissible spongiform encephalopathies. *Weekly Epidemiological Review, 73,* 361–365.

Xu, Y., Jack, C. R., Jr., O'Brien, P. C., Kokmen, E., Smith, G. E., Ivnik, R. J., et al. (2000). Usefulness of MRI measures of entorhinal cortex versus hippocampus in AD. *Neurology, 54,* 1760–1767.

Zanetti, M., Ballabio, C., Abbate, C., Cutaia, C., Vergani, C., & Bergamaschini, L. (2006). Mild cognitive impairment subtypes and vascular dementia in community-dwelling elderly people: A 3-year follow-up study. *Journal of the American Geriatric Society, 54,* 580–586.

Zhang, M. Y., Katzman, R., Salmon, D., Jin, H., Cai, G. J., Wang, Z. Y., et al. (1990). The prevalence of dementia and Alzheimer's disease in Shanghai, China: Impact of age, gender, and education. *Annals of Neurology, 27,* 428–437.

Zink, W. E., Zheng, J., Persidsky, Y., Poluektova, L., & Gendelman, H. E. (1999). The neuropathogenesis of HIV-1 infection. *FEMS Immunology and Medical Microbiology, 26,* 233–241.

Zola-Morgan, S., Squire, L. R., & Amaral, D. G. (1986). Human amnesia and the medial temporal region: Enduring memory impairment following a bilateral lesion limited to field CA1 of the hippocampus. *Journal of Neuroscience, 6,* 2950–2967.

18

Creativity

VALERIA DRAGO, BRUCE MILLER, AND
KENNETH M. HEILMAN

In this chapter, we will review the concept of creativity, how the brain might mediate creativity, and how neurological diseases can affect creativity. Creativity is a very important human attribute, and the construct of creativity has interested people in a variety of disciplines, including educators, psychologists, and neuroscientists. However, creativity is difficult to study—there is little agreement even about its definition—and it therefore remains poorly understood.

How do we define creativity? What do we mean when we say that something is a creative product or someone is a creative person? Webster's II University Dictionary (1988) gives several definitions of creativity: "having the power or ability to create," "productive," "marked by originality," "new." These definitions are incomplete. There are many examples of individuals who are extremely productive, but their products are not creative. As for originality or novelty, if a person typed a list of nonwords or randomly applied different color paints to a canvas, the products might be very novel, but many would not consider these productions to be creative.

Another definition of creativity is that of Bronowski (1972) who stated, "Creativity is finding unity in what appears to be diversity."

Great paintings have a myriad of colors and forms, and great musical works have a variety of melodies and rhythms, but in both paintings and symphonies the artist is able to develop a thread that unites diverse elements and displays order. Copernicus was able to see order in what appeared to be disorderly planetary motions, and he developed a construct of the solar system that subsequently was confirmed by Galileo. More recently, Einstein was able to see the thread that united matter and energy. Although Bronowski's definition of creativity focuses on the crucial importance of a "global approach," it is incomplete, lacking the critical aspects of originality (novelty) and productivity.

Within the concept of novelty two aspects need to be distinguished, novelty for a person versus novelty for the world. Many times researchers develop new ideas for future studies, only to learn that a study testing this idea has already been conducted. Were they creative? From the personal perspective, yes, their idea was creative; but from the world's perspective, no, since someone else already developed the same idea, tested it, and produced results.

Many investigators believe that a creative product, in addition to being novel, also has to be of value (Sternberg, 1999a). Thus, an invention must carry out the task for which it was designed, a scientific theory must help us understand the domain in question, and a creative work of art, music, or literature must be appreciated by some audience beyond the artist. Csikszentmihalyi (1988, 1996, 1999) has presented a detailed analysis of how novelty and value are both relevant to creativity. According to Csikszentmihalyi, a novel product becomes creative only after it has been positively valued by knowledgeable judges. If a product is rejected by the experts in that field, that product is not creative, whether or not it is novel.

Other researchers, however, like Heilman (2004), disagree with this "value" concept of creativity. Sometimes a product is not valued when it is first produced but becomes valued by later generations, or vice versa. For example, many of the Impressionists' paintings were not valued for years. If all Van Gogh's paintings were stored in a warehouse and this warehouse burned down, would Van Gogh no longer be an artistic creative genius? In 1633, when Galileo Galilee first provided support for the heliocentric theory of Copernicus, he was accused of being a heretic and confined in jail. It was only 180 years later that the Catholic Church recognized the Copernican theory as compatible with the Christian faith, and it was only in 1992 that Cardinal Poupard wrote that the persecution of Galileo Galilei was a mistake. It might therefore also be a mistake to judge creativity based on value.

Productivity is another important aspect of creativity. To conclude that a work is creative, it needs to be available. For this reason, great ideas are not creative if they are not followed by objective verification of the idea, independently of the value of the idea itself. If an idea remains solely in the mind of the researcher or the artist and never becomes a research study or a painting, we will never know if that idea was indeed creative. Having creative ideas without developing a product, such as scientific papers and works of art, is like leaving a treasure under the sea. Thus, in this chapter, we will define creativity as the ability to understand, develop, and express in a systematic fashion, novel orderly relationships (Heilman, 2004).

STAGES OF CREATIVITY

In ancient times, many people believed in "inspired thinking," which is a gift from the divinities. For example, Socrates thought that inspired thinking came from the muses, the nine daughters of Zeus, each of whom was in charge of a separate domain. The inspired savant is the instrument through which nature reveals its secrets to humanity. Nowadays, creative ideas are thought to come from within rather than from outside, and cognitive neuroscience studies focus on the processes within the brain that might help explain creativity (Heilman, 2004; Weisberg, 2006).

Helmholtz (1826) and Wallas (1926) have suggested that the creative process has four main stages: preparation, incubation, illumination, and verification. To be creative, an individual needs to be prepared, and thus the first step of the creative process is learning the background knowledge and skills that allow or enable a person to develop creative ideas and produce a creative product. Kuhn (1996) noted that many important discoveries are initiated by the observation of an anomaly (e.g., when a scientist perceives significance in an accidental occurrence, such as Alexander Fleming's discovery of penicillin). Although these discoveries are based on an anomaly, it is the "prepared mind" that enables these scientists to recognize the importance of the phenomenon they have observed. Geniuses such as Einstein have stated that imagination was a very important aspect of the creative thought process. Imagination allows our brain to alter life events and knowledge into new and original forms. The more rich and varied the experiences of a person are, the more his or her imagination will have the working material for creative productivity.

According to Hemholtz (1826) and Wallas (1926), the next step in the creative process is incubation. During this process, people are unconsciously thinking about the means by which they can develop a creative solution to a problem. When they suddenly become aware of this solution, they have what has been termed an "Aha!" experience. It is this "Aha" experience or epiphany that Hemholtz (1826) and Wallas (1926) termed *illumination*. One of the best known stories about the "Aha" experience was Archimedes discovery of the law of buoyancy when he exclaimed, "Eureka!" Henri Pioncaré (1854–1912), a world renowned mathematician reported several illuminations when describing his creative achievements. Wallas (1926) elaborated on Poincaré's self-observations and took the occurrence of illuminations as evidence for unconscious processing. If "Aha!" experiences do not come from conscious thinking and reasoning, then there has to be an unconscious incubation as an explanation for this sudden illumination.

The constructs of incubation and illumination have, however, received much criticism. For example, Metcalfe and Wiebe (1987) demonstrated that the subjective feeling of knowing (illumination) did not predict performance on insight problems. Weisberg (1986) suggested that creativity does not require great leaps (e.g., illumination), and instead, the processes that lead to many great discoveries might not be subconscious incubation, but rather a series of conscious steps. Even according to Helmholtz and Wallas, illumination, rather than being an independent factor, appears to be the culmination of the incubation process. Since consensus does not exist on these stages of creativity, instead of discussing incubation and illumination as independent stages, the term *creative innovation* will be used to include both of these theoretical processes.

After innovation, creative scientists perform experiments that attempt to test (refute) their hypothesis, and based on these experiments, present papers and write journal articles about their findings. Authors write books, poems, and plays; artists paint, draw, or sculpt; and composers write or play their music. This final stage of creativity is the process of scientific verification or artistic production.

INTELLIGENCE AND CREATIVITY

Many of the psychologists who, in the late 19th and early 20th centuries, helped to develop tests of intelligence thought that these tests were measures of creativity. For example, Alfred Binet, one of the founders of intelligence tests,

initially thought that creativity and intelligence were the same or closely related or overlapping constructs, because in the first intelligence test he devised in 1896, he used inkblots to explore the imagination of children. There was, however, a significant change in the direction of research on creativity around 1950, when Guilford, an expert on intelligence testing, surprised many people by proposing that psychology had not spent enough time examining a form of thinking or reasoning that went beyond the kind of thinking measured by IQ tests, that is, creative thinking.

There are many definitions of intelligence, but to most psychologists, intelligence is the measure of a person's ability to acquire and apply knowledge. Although the purpose of this chapter is not to discuss and analyze the construct of intelligence, many people continue to believe that intelligence is a measure of creative ability. A person with a high intelligence quotient is often called a "genius." However, the term genius is often used to describe people who were so creative that they produced a great advancement or what Kuhn (1996) termed a "paradigmatic shift." Thus, in this section, we briefly discuss the relationship between the constructs of intelligence and creativity.

Sternberg and O'Hara (1999) suggest several possible relationships between intelligence and creativity, including that they are the same, or that creativity is a subset of intelligence, or creativity and intelligence are overlapping but independent constructs. We have discussed the definition of creativity above. The possible relationship of intelligence and creativity also depends on the definition of intelligence. If intelligence is the measure of a person's cognitive ability to adapt, creativity is a gift that might allow one to better adapt; however this would only be true of certain forms of creativity (e.g., medical science) but not of other forms (e.g., painting).

Guilford and Christensen (1973) thought that creativity was a subset of intelligence, and since there were psychometric tests to measure intelligence, they attempted to develop psychometric tests that could measure creativity. These tests primarily assess subjects' ability to develop novel uses of common objects.

For example, subjects would be asked to name in a fixed time interval the different ways in which they might be able to use a brick. Guilford found that students with low IQ consistently performed poorly on these tests, but the performance on this divergent thinking test by those students with high IQs did not strongly correlate with their scores on IQ tests.

Another means of studying the relationship between creativity and intelligence is to study the intelligence of creative people. Barron and Harrington (1981) studied architects and found a weak relationship between their creativity and their IQ. They found that IQs above 120 did not predict creativity as much IQs below 120. Combined with Guilford's results (mentioned above), this suggests that there may be an IQ threshold that must be exceeded to have sufficient intelligence to acquire the knowledge and skills required for creativity. Thus, intelligence is a necessary but not sufficient component of creativity. Although they are unlikely to produce a paradigmatic shift, even people with average intelligence can be creative, and many people with learning disabilities have made paradigmatic shifts. Einstein might be one of the best examples. He did not speak until the age of 3, and he remained dyslexic throughout his life.

Whereas Simonton (1994) and other investigators (e.g., Herr et al., 1965) also found that the correlation between intelligence and creativity is weak, this weak correlation might be related to the types of tests that were used to measure intelligence.

Cattell (1963) posited that there are two types of intelligence, one he termed, "crystallized" and the other "fluid." Crystallized intelligence is basically declarative memories, such as knowing that Rome is the capital of Italy, or lexical-semantic knowledge, such as knowing the meaning of "impale." Fluid intelligence, in contrast, is the ability to solve problems. Most intelligence tests, such as the Wechsler Adult Intelligence Scale (WAIS), assess both crystallized (e.g., vocabulary definitions) and fluid intelligence (e.g., "How are a fly and tree similar?"). Cattell thought that, although crystallized knowledge can be an important factor in creativity, it is fluid intelligence that determines creativity. Although fluid intelligence may be

the best predictor of creativity, we know of no formal studies that have studied this relationship. In addition, on most IQ tests, the subtests that measure fluid intelligence assess convergent reasoning. Although convergent reasoning may be an important component of many creative activities, divergent reasoning is also an important component of creativity, and divergent reasoning is not assessed on most IQ tests. It is tested in the alternative-uses task mentioned above. In the next section, we will discuss these two different forms of reasoning.

DIVERGENT AND CONVERGENT THINKING IN THE ASSESSMENT OF CREATIVITY

Guilford posited that divergent thinking is an important step in the creative process. Guilford's (1950) work stimulated psychometric creativity research, which focused on measuring the psychological characteristics of creative people (Plucker & Renzulli, 1999). Guilford and others used his test in attempts to measure the thought processes underlying creative thinking, and other investigators (e.g., Torrance, 1974) developed additional tests that assessed both verbal and visuospatial divergent and convergent thinking. As mentioned above, creative endeavors require preparation, innovation, and production. Innovation has three major subcomponents. The first step is usually disengagement, when the creative person breaks away from prior theories, methods, beliefs, and styles. The second step is often divergent thinking, when the scientist or artist considers alternative solutions, theories, and styles. The last stage in the innovative process is convergent thinking, when the creative person attempts to find or develop unity in what appears to be diversity.

In this section, we briefly describe some of the tests that have been used and are currently used to study creative thinking, with the understanding that different tests explore different components of the creative process. The tests mentioned here are not an exhaustive list, and other tests have been used (see Guilford, 1967; Abraham, 2007).

TESTS ASSESSING DISENGAGEMENT AND DIVERGENT THINKING

The Constraining Examples Test (Smith et al., 1993) is one test of disengagement. Subjects are asked to create new ideas for toys. They are then given 5 minutes to draw a new toy. Prior to drawing the toy, the subjects are presented with examples of three toys, one with a ball, one with electronics, and the third demonstrating some physical activity. If the subjects' drawings contain any of the three examples, it suggests a failure of disengagement.

The Wisconsin Cart Sorting Test is one of the most frequently used neuropsychological tests (Berg 1948). This test can assess two elements of innovative thinking: disengagement and divergent thinking. In this test, subjects are presented with a series of cards, and each card has a figure or figures with the attributes of shape, quantity, and color. The subjects are asked to sort the cards such that cards with a similar characteristic are sorted together, but they are not told which characteristic they are to use. The subjects are, however, told that the examiner will indicate to them whether the sorting principle is correct or incorrect. When the participant makes the correct choice, they are told the sorting principle is correct; but, after the subject achieves ten consecutive correct responses, the rules are changed, and the examiner indicates that the sorting principle is now incorrect. The subject will then have to disengage from this strategy and use divergent thinking to find an alternative sorting strategy until the examiner again indicates that this new strategy (e.g., color) is correct. This process is repeated until all the cards are sorted. The time taken for the participant to learn the new rules, and the mistakes made during this task, are used to score performance. The score represents the ability of the subject to successfully disengage and use divergent thinking. Patients with frontal lobe damage are often impaired at this test (Zangwell 1966; Milner 1984) in that, once they find a successful strategy, they have difficulty disengaging from this strategy. This is called *perseveration* or "stuck in set" or a "conceptual grasp reflex."

The Alternative Use of Objects Test (Guilford, 1978) is also a test for disengagement and divergent thinking. The subjects are presented with three different objects, one at a time, and after each presentation, they are asked to name as many things as they possibly can do with that object in 2 minutes. Before starting the test, the subjects are told that they will be scored based on the number of solutions produced, as well as the degree of novelty or innovation of these solutions. Each of the subject's productions is scored 1 for common use (e.g., if the object is a brick, to build), 2 for minimally innovative (e.g., use it as a door stop or book end), 3 for moderately to greatly innovative (e.g., grind it up and use it as a cleaning abrasive or as a rouge like make-up). The total score is the sum of these item scores.

Using functional imaging, Carlsson (2000) examined the cerebral perfusion in low versus high creative individuals during the Alternate Use of Object Test. The results of this study indicated that the highly creative subjects had bilateral frontal activation, and those with low creativity had an activation response that was limited to the left hemisphere.

Another test used to assess for disengagement is the Alternative Meanings Test (Gorfein et al., 2000). Many words in English have multiple meanings. For example, the word "pen" can mean a writing instrument or a place where animals (e.g., pigs) are kept. When performing this test, subjects are given a series of five words. Before each word is given, the subject is asked to provide two sentences using this word, stipulating that in each sentence the word should have a different meaning. After the subject produces two sentences, a new word is given by the examiner. If two sentences are not given in 60 seconds, the examiner will provide the next word. The score is the time taken to complete the test, and the more adept a person is at disengaging from one meaning and finding the alternative meaning the better that person will do on this test.

TESTS ASSESSING CONVERGENT THINKING

The Verbal-Word Anagram Task provides subjects with a series of words in which the letters are out of order, and their task is to recognize the word that all these letters could spell if their order is rearranged. This task has been used in several studies in our laboratories, in which we looked at the effects of central norepinephrine blockade on creativity (Beversdorf et al., 1999). This anagram test is composed of ten words and contains five five-letter words, three six-letter words, and two seven-letter words. Subjects are shown the scrambled letters of a word printed on a sheet of paper and asked to write down on an answer sheet the word that these letters spell when rearranged. The score for each word was the number of seconds it took the subject to come up with a correct word. If the subject makes an error or does not write the correct word in 100 seconds, a maximum score of 100 is given.

The Verbal-Remote Associates Test requires respondents to access the semantic representations for three words and find the one correct fourth word that is linked with all three. The words may be related to the solution words in a number of ways: They can be semantically or associatively related; they may be two parts of a compound word; or they may be words used as synonyms. For example, the three words, falling, actor, and dust have as its solution the word "star." "Falling" and "star" are associatively linked, "actor" and "star" are synonyms, and "stardust" is a compound word. There are usually 20 items in this task; response to each item is scored for accuracy and time to respond.

Insight Problems

Insight problems are problems that are simple to state but relatively difficult to solve, and the solution to these problems require some sort of "insight" (unconscious creative thinking) (Dow & Mayer, 2004). Such problems initially seem overwhelming and without solution; however, unconscious processing may take place and insight may suddenly occur—the "Aha" experience. There are different kinds of insight problems: some are verbal problems, some are based on mathematical or spatial tasks.

The concept of insight began with the development of Gestalt psychology. Often, convergent thinking takes place at a conscious level when the person attempting to find a solution deliberates and focuses attention on the problem. However, a person can also solve problems when he "takes his mind off the problem." Dijsterhuis and coworkers (2006a, 2006b) call this the "deliberation-without attention effect." When a person focuses his attention, he limits the amount of data that he can process. These investigators have noted that conscious attention does not allow a person to fully assess the importance of all of the attributes of the stimuli when "making the right choice."

To test this hypothesis, Dijsterhuis et al. (2006a,b) had normal subjects make choices about small sets of data (selecting a towel to buy) versus choices that were complex, with much data (selecting which house to buy). They found that consumers made simple choices well with conscious attention, but with complex data, their subjects made better choices after they were distracted.

A TEST ASSESSING BOTH DIVERGENT AND CONVERGENT THINKING

The Revised Abbreviated Torrance Test of Creativity for Adults (ATTA) (Goff, 2002) consists of three activities: one verbal and two visual. During the verbal activity, the subject is asked the following question. "Just suppose you could walk on air or fly without being in an airplane or similar vehicle. What problems might this create? List as many as you can." The subjects are then given 3 minutes to write down all the ideas they could create.

The second activity consists of giving the subject a paper on which there are two incomplete drawings. The subjects are then asked to create meaningful drawings that incorporate these incomplete figures, and to title their drawings. The subjects are given 3 minutes to complete this task. The third activity consists of giving the subjects a sheet of paper that contains nine isosceles triangles. The subjects are asked to make as many pictures as possible using these triangles or lines. The subjects are told that every picture should have a meaning and a title. Again, the subjects are given 3 minutes to complete this activity. The divergent part of this test is thinking of the problems that flying would create, or changing triangles into new pictures. The convergent part is finding the best title.

CREATIVITY AND
NEUROLOGICAL DISEASES

The study of patients with brain lesions has been crucial to neurologists, neuropsychologists, and cognitive neuroscientists in their attempt to understand the modular organization of the brain. From the time of Paul Broca's and Karl Wernicke's papers, published in the 19th century, it has been known that specific areas of the brain store different forms of information and mediate specific functions and skills. In the past 20 years, functional imaging has brought converging evidence for the concept of modularity or localization of function. Additionally, studies of the behavioral changes associated with lesions of the brain have allowed scientists to fractionate many of these complex functions into their component parts. Focal lesions, as well as degenerative diseases, often cause the loss of specific forms of knowledge and skill. If this knowledge or skill was important for a certain aspect of a person's creative endeavors, this brain damage might reduce or even end productivity in that domain. For example, if a creative writer of fiction becomes globally aphasic from a left perisylvian cerebral infarction, it would doubtful that he or she could continue to be a creative author. In contrast, specific portions of the brain not only store certain forms of knowledge and mediate the performance of certain activities, but they may also inhibit other areas that store different forms of knowledge and perform different activities. Thus, brain damage to a focal area may disinhibit or release other forms of knowledge or functions. The types of knowledge stored and the skills mediated by different portions of the brain are discussed in other chapters, and will not be reviewed here. In the sections below, we discuss how diseases of the brain influence creative processes that are not specific to domains discussed in other chapters.

RIGHT HEMISPHERE

One of the neuroscientific theories of creativity is the hemispheric lateralization model that was developed about four decades ago. Investigators postulated that the nondominant right hemisphere was specialized for creative activity, such as holistic pattern recognition, art, and music.

At the beginning of the chapter, when we defined creativity, we raised the concept of "finding the thread that unites," or "finding unity in what appears to be diversity" (Bronowski, 1972). The right hemisphere appears to be more important in global than local processing (Robertson et al., 1988), and a global approach is often important in finding the thread that unites. The right hemisphere is also important in mediating visual-spatial functions (Benton & Tranel, 1993), and many extremely creative people claim to have used visual-spatial strategies to help find creative solutions. Thus, the hemispheric lateralization model suggests that right hemisphere–mediated functions are crucial for creative processing.

An electroencephalographic (EEG) study conducted by Jausovec (2000) found that when 115 normal individual were stratified across measures of creativity and intelligence, EEG coherence (during "rest" with eye open) was significantly related to creativity scores, particularly across the right hemisphere.

Miller and his coworkers (Miller et al., 1998; Miller, Boone, Cummings, Read, & Mishkin, 2000) wrote a series of reports on the emergence of artistic talents in patients affected by frontotemporal lobar degeneration (FTLD). The two most common forms of degenerative dementia seen in our clinics are Alzheimer disease (AD) and frontotemporal lobar degeneration FTLD. As discussed in Chapter 17, most patients with AD start off with memory loss and then develop other cognitive deficits, such as problems with naming, route finding, drawing, copying, and even performing learned skilled movements (ideomotor apraxia). In contrast, patients with FTLD usually present in one of three ways, with either behavioral-executive deficits (frontotemporal dementia), a progressive nonfluent aphasia, or semantic dementia with impaired comprehension and naming.

It is often difficult to know when a dementing disease has started. Several of the artists described by Miller and his coworkers (1998–2000), however, appeared to have started drawing or painting just prior to the time they had the symptoms and signs FTLD, or just as the disease was beginning. What was remarkable was that these patients continued to draw and paint in spite of their dementia, and their artistic skills even improved as the dementia advanced.

Whereas the left hemisphere primarily mediates verbal activities, the right hemisphere mediates the type of visual-spatial skills important in artistic productions such as drawing and painting. Miller and his coworkers (1998) noted that the brain atrophy in these people who developed artistic skills was primarily limited to the left frontal and anterior temporal regions, relatively sparing the right hemisphere. Because the patients described by Miller et al. started their painting shortly before or at the onset of their dementia, we do not know if they had talent before the onset of the dementia, or how the dementia might have influenced their art. In contrast, Finney and Heilman (2007) described a patient who was an artist before the onset of progressive nonfluent aphasia, which is a form of FTLD that causes degeneration of the left frontal lobe. To learn how this patient's disease influenced his artistic production, they had independent judges score the different qualities of his painting including novelty, "How original is this painting?"; aesthetic value, "How beautiful or attractive is this painting?"; representation: "How well is the subject of this painting rendered?"; and closure: "How complete the does this painting appear?" Seven paintings done before and seven painting done after disease onset were evaluated. The results of this study indicated that the patient's artistic ability neither diminished nor improved with the onset of his disease.

A recent functional magnetic resonance imaging study (fMRI) performed by Asari et al. (2008) supported this right hemisphere hypothesis of artistic creativity. During the study, 68 normal subjects were asked to look at ten ambiguous figures (Rorschach, 1921) and say what each of these figures looked like. The responses were then classified by judges into frequent, infrequent, and unique. During the times when the subjects gave unique responses, there was greater activity in the right temporopolar region than when they produced more common responses. These results support the postulate that the right hemisphere has a critical role in the novelty aspect of the creative process.

Drago et al. (2008) studied an artist affected by Parkinson disease (PD) who had a deep brain stimulator (DBS) placed in the left ventral subthalamic/substantia nigra pars reticularis (STN/SNr). Unilateral DBS in this region can induce ipsilateral hemispheric activation. Thus, the purpose of the study was to learn if DBS of the left hemisphere, potentially inducing left hemisphere activation and perhaps also inhibition of the right hemisphere, would alter the creativity of a professional artist, as well as her ability to judge somebody else's art. This patient performed a creativity test with the stimulator being either on or off. In addition, this patient was asked to judge the paintings of another artist when the stimulator was on or off. The results suggest that DBS of the left ventral STN/SNr reduced this patient's creativity, as well as her appreciation of art. The reason for these alterations is not known, but might be related to enhanced activation of the left hemisphere and reciprocal deactivation of the right hemisphere, which mediates both visuospatial skills and global attention, both of which might be important in artistic creativity and appreciation.

THE FRONTAL LOBES

To be successful in developing the skills and knowledge that are need to be creative, as well as to produce creative works, creative people need to have perseverance. According to Beals (1996), Thomas Edison said that being a creative genius required "ninety nine percent perspiration and one percent inspiration." Many of the most creative works in science and in the arts were frequently not appreciated at the time they were produced. Several creative geniuses died without ever knowing that their creations were appreciated. However, many of the most creative people continue to produce, even in the absence of rewards. Thus, creative people, independent of the domain in which they create, must persevere and persist if they are ever to achieve acceptance and be appreciated.

The major organ of volition appears to be the frontal lobes (see Chapter 14). In the clinic, we see people who have injury, disease, and degeneration of their frontal lobes. Often, these patients have lost their initiative and drive, and this loss is called *abulia*. They often show signs of impersistence, quitting prematurely, giving up "without a fight."

The ability to have long-term goals and to suppress biological drives when they interfere with long-term goals, as well as the ability to persist and not be distracted, is what Heilman calls "frontal intelligence" (Heilman, 2005). Frontal intelligence is one of the major factors underlying success in any profession, including those that require creativity. For example, patients who have orbitofrontal damage will give up larger "delay" rewards for lesser immediate rewards (Mobini et al., 2002), and thus orbitofrontal damage might interfere with some forms of creativity.

The frontal lobe networks, however, have two other functions that appear to be important for creativity: the ability to disengage and to perform divergent thinking. Disengagement can be physical and mental. Physically, infants and patients with damage to the frontal lobes have a release of ontologically primitive adherent behaviors and will grasp an item that touches their hand, or even items that they see (magnetic apraxia). When something comes near their face, they will root, and when something touches their lips they will suck. Frontal lobe function enables disengagement from the tendency to grasp and suck. Even in the absence of primitive reflexes, such as the suck and grasp, patients with frontal dysfunction may have deficits of sensorimotor disengagement. Bedside tests for sensorimotor disengagement include the crossed-response tasks. In the manual task, the subject is asked to close his eyes and to elevate the hand opposite to that which the examiner touched (Crucian et al., 2007). In the visual task (inhibition of the fixation reflex), the examiner places one of his or her hands in each visual field and tells the patient that when he sees the right hand wiggle, he is to look at the left hand and vice versa (Butter et al., 1988). In a test for echopraxia, such as Luria 2-1 task, the examiner instructs the subject that when the examiner puts up two fingers, the subject puts up one and vice versa. People who cannot disengage will raise the hand that was touched, look at the hand that has moved, and put up the same number of fingers as the examiner. After they make this initial error, patients will often correct their error.

Mental disengagement is the ability to question and reject currently accepted thoughts, concepts, and practices, and is a prerequisite for creativity. There are several tests for mental disengagement. One of the best is the Stroop test (Stroop, 1935). In this test, subjects are presented with printed words that denote colors, but the words are typed in a print color that does not match the word (e.g., the word "blue" printed in red ink). The subjects are asked to name as rapidly and accurately as possible the color of the print. Patients with frontal injury often have trouble disengaging, and read the word rather than naming the color of the print. They also often take longer to complete the test.

According to William James (1890), divergent thinking is the ability to take a different direction from current and past modes of thought or expression. Zangwell (1966) and Miller (1984) suggested that frontal lobe damage or dysfunction would disrupt divergent thinking. The Wisconsin Card Sorting Task, discussed earlier, is a test of disengagement and divergent thinking. Milner (1984) demonstrated that patients who have had portions of their frontal lobes removed do poorly on this test because they cannot disengage and use divergent thinking. Thus, these patients "get stuck in set." Comparing subjects with high and low creativity has revealed that highly creative subjects have a higher baseline frontal lobe regional cerebral blood flow and greater frontal increase in blood flow while performing creative tasks (Carlsson, 2000). In addition, there is preliminary evidence that rapid transcranial magnetic stimulation over the frontal lobes can increase creativity in normal subjects during both drawing and writing tasks (Snyder, 2004).

AMYGDALA, BASAL GANGLIA, AND DOPAMINE

The ventral medial frontal lobes have strong connections with the ventral striatum, a portion of the basal ganglia that contains the nucleus accumbens. The nucleus accumbens also receives input from orbitofrontal cortex, as well as from the basolateral nucleus of the amygdala, a portion of the limbic system that also projects to the frontal lobes. Input from the frontal neocortex, and olfactory as well as portions of the limbic system makes the nucleus accumbens very important in reward-based decisions.

In regard to the limbic system's influence on creativity, Bechara et al. (1999) and Brand et al. (2007) have demonstrated that patients with injury to the amygdala are more likely to have a propensity to select activities that might have larger awards but also involve more risk. Thus, amygdala damage might enhance creativity, but creativity in people with amygdala damage has not been studied.

The ventral striatum, including the nucleus accumbens, receives dopaminergic input primarily from the ventral tegmental area of the mesencephalon. Alterations of dopaminergic input can influence decision making. Dopamine mediates reward-seeking activity ranging from gambling and cocaine addiction to the appreciation of physical beauty and music (Aharon et al. 2001; Breiter et al., 2001). On the other hand, too much dopamine may cause excessively focused, highly complex motor stereotypes, such as repeatedly disassembling and reassembling flashlights (Fernandez & Friedman, 1999). Dopamine may also play a role in creative discovery through its effect on novelty seeking. An allele of the D_4 receptor has been postulated, somewhat controversially, to be a novelty-seeking gene (Keltikangas-Jarvinen et al. 2003; Savitz & Ramesar, 2004).

There are multiple reports of patients with PD who have demonstrated an increase in risk-taking behaviors after taking dopamine agonists (Voon et al., 2006). Kulisevsky et al. (2009) reported a patient with PD in whom dopamine agonists awakened a hidden creativity that led to a gradual increase in painting productivity. These behavioral changes might be related to alterations in dopaminergic uptake in the nucleus accumbens.

Many drugs abused by highly creative people, such as amphetamines, appear to excite the nucleus accumbens and ventral striatum (Floresco et al., 2008) and enhance the type of risk-taking behavior that might be important in creativity. Consistent with this hypothesis are case reports of patients whose creativity increased after receiving subcortical deep brain stimulation with electrodes near the nucleus accumbens (Gabriels, 2003; Flaherty et al., 2005). Creative subjects have higher baseline arousal and greater response to sensory stimulation (Martindale, 1999). Dopamine decreases latent inhibition, a behavioral index of the ability to habituate to sensation (Ellenbroek et al., 1996; Swerdlow et al., 2003), and raises baseline arousal. Thus, the focused aspect of creative drive may be driven by mesolimbic dopaminergic activity.

Patients with PD have reduced activity in the ventral tegmental, mesocortical, and mesolimbic dopaminergic systems. Drago et al. (2009) studied the performance of patients with PD on tests of creativity. These patients were divided into right- and left-onset groups. Since the left hemisphere mediates language, including speech, reading, and writing, and the right mediates visuospatial skills, these investigators posited that when compared to healthy control participants, patients with a right hemibody onset of PD would be more impaired in verbal creativity, and patients with left hemibody onset would have more problem with tests of visuospatial creativity. The results of this study indicated that patients affected by PD disease with a right hemibody onset had a reduction of verbal creativity. Many forms of creativity require persistence, and patients with PD disease are often abulic. Abulia would reduce creative productivity. Patients with PD can also have frontal executive deficits and, as mentioned previously, frontal dysfunction can decrease divergent thinking.

WHITE MATTER CONNECTIVITY

Creativity was defined in the beginning of this chapter as the ability to understand, develop, and express in a systematic fashion novel orderly relationships. The understanding, development, and expression of orderly relationships require communication between several cortical and subcortical modules that store different types of information. Works of scientific or artistic creativity often require the skills and knowledge mediated by both the right and left cerebral hemispheres. For example, the novelist who is writing about an emotional response of a character may use the knowledge of facial emotional expressions stored in the right hemisphere, together with the verbal lexicon stored in the left hemisphere. Like William James (1890), who suggested that creativity requires an "unheard of combination of elements and the subtlest associations . . .," Spearman (1931) suggested that creative ideas result from the combination of two or more ideas that have been previously isolated. Because the right and left hemispheres store different forms of knowledge and mediate different forms of cognitive activity, homologous association cortices may have different neuronal architectures. Resolving a previously unsolved problem may require seeing it "in a new light." One way of seeing a problem in a new light would be to use the different forms of knowledge and cognitive strategies mediated by the opposite hemisphere.

The largest structure connecting independent hemispheric modular systems is the corpus callosum. Lewis (1979) administered the Rorschach test to eight patients before and after they had cerebral commissurotomy for treatment of intractable epilepsy. They noted that disconnection of the two cerebral hemispheres reduced the patients' creativity, as measured by their interpretation of Rorschach patterns.

Intrahemispheric communication might also be important for creative innovation. Intrahemispheric white matter connections, which include connections between the frontal lobes and the posterior association areas in the temporal and parietal lobes, might allow the selective activation or inhibition of cognitive modules.

White matter connections enable distributed regions of the brain to function as neural networks. According to neural network theory, information in parallel distributed (PDP) networks is stored by the strengths of connections between units, and concepts are represented as patterns of activity involving many units (i.e., as distributed representations) (Rumelhart et al., 1986). A large number of units linked by a set of connections define a domain of knowledge from which any one of a large number of

concepts can be generated. It is thought that PDP systems emulate the fundamental properties of neural networks in the brain.

Mednick (1962) suggested that highly creative individuals have the ability to activate more highly distributed networks and thus are characterized by a flatter associative hierarchy than are less creative individuals. This ability to activate highly distributed networks permits creative people to perform discretionary-intentional activation of remote networks, thereby producing novel patterns of activation corresponding to novel concepts. Subjectively, solving a problem using a distant network is like using a metaphor. Here, one uses networks representing knowledge in one domain to help organize a different domain. Creativity by metaphor might involve the recruitment of networks of substantially different architecture in order to escape the constraints of existing (learned) internal models represented in the networks usually used for thinking in a particular domain. The manipulation of concepts in a network of a completely different architecture might allow a creative person to see a problem "in a new light." For example, both Albert Einstein and Richard Feynman, Nobel Prize–winning physicists, used abstract visual representations and imagery that they subsequently translated into mathematical terms. Apparently, the architecture of the networks supporting their visual representations permitted them the manipulative freedom to escape conventional language and mathematical formulations, thereby enhancing creative innovation.

Mednick's (1962) theory that creative innovation is related to the recruitment of highly distributed networks is supported by EEG studies of normal subjects who, during creative thought, demonstrated an increase of anatomically distributed coherence of EEG oscillations (Petsche, 1996; Jausovec & Jausovec, 2000).

Many diseases degrade white matter connectivity, including vascular dementia, multiple sclerosis, and the leukodystrophies. Although there have not been extensive studies of creativity in patients with these disorders, we suspect that many patients with these and similar disorders may have a loss of creativity. Future studies, however, will have to test this postulate.

EPILEPSY

The relationship between epilepsy and creativity is unclear. Some authors believe that epilepsy interferes with creativity. For example, Trimble (2000) writes about the life of Charles Lloyd, a poet who developed an epilepsy-related psychosis that destroyed his career. One of America's greatest authors, Edgar Allen Poe, had episodes of confusion and unconsciousness. He was expelled from the University of Virginia (UVa) because it was thought that these periods of confusion were induced by using drugs, such as opiates and alcohol. However, at the time Poe was a student at UVa, little was known about partial seizures and some now believe that Poe actually suffered with partial complex seizures (Bazil, 1999). Many other great authors have also been thought to have epilepsy, such as Machado de Assis (1839–1908), considered one of the most important Brazilian writers, and two of Europe's greatest writers, Gustave Flaubert and Fyodor Dostoevsky. In addition to writers, many people who have been creative in other domains have also had epilepsy. Chatterjee (2004) and Schachter (2006) write about visual artists who had epilepsy.

We know of no systematic studies that investigate whether epilepsy enhances or disturbs creativity. As mentioned above, however, during creative innovation, enhanced communication may occur between modular networks and this enhanced communication allows creative people to combine representations of ideas that have been previously isolated. Electroencephalographic studies of normal subjects have demonstrated an increase of anatomically distributed coherence of EEG oscillations during creative thinking (Petsche, 1996; Jausovec & Jausovec, 2000). Physiological connectivity is associated with enhanced concordance, and people with epilepsy have EEG evidence for increased concordance (functional coupling among cortical areas that is achieved by the synchronization of oscillatory activity).

As will be discussed below, emotional disorders such as depression may be associated with creativity, and there is a high incidence of mood disorders associated with epilepsy, particularly in patients with epileptic foci in the temporal or frontal lobes. The treatment of epilepsy with vagus nerve stimulation reduces creativity (Ghacibeh et al., 2006), but it also reduces depression, probably because it increases the release of norepinephrine.

RELAXATION, ANXIETY, AND DEPRESSION

Several scientists have reported that they were able to solve a difficult scientific problem either during sleep, when they were falling asleep, or when awakening from sleep. August Kekulè, in 1865, while attempting to learn the structure of benzene, described that he was in a dreamy state when had a vision of a snake chasing its own tail. This vision gave Kekulè the idea that benzene had a ring-like structure.

Before and after sleep, people who are actively working on a problem describe moments of insight when they were able to solve previously insoluble problems. Often, these moments of insight come at time when the person is relaxed and at rest.

Eysenck (1995) suggested that, during conscious problem solving, cortical arousal is high. A high level of cortical arousal narrows the associative field and suppresses the ability to make remote associations. Lowered arousal might allow these remote associations to emerge. During states of anxiety, there are high levels of cortical arousal. Studies have revealed that when people are anxious, they have a reduction of creativity (Baas, De Dreu, & Nijstad, 2008). In addition, patients with a generalized anxiety disorder also have reduced creativity (Henning et al., 2007).

Support for the postulate that the level of arousal might determine the size of neural networks comes from recent research by Contreras and Llinas (2001). Using high-speed optical imaging, they electrically stimulated subcortical white matter in slices of guinea pig brain and recorded the area of activated neocortex. They found that, with low-frequency stimulation, cortical activation is at first somewhat limited, but after few milliseconds this activation spreads to nearby areas. After high-frequency stimulation, however, the cortical excitation remained fixed to a small column of neurons that were directly above the stimulating electrode. Intracellular recording from the neurons around this excited column during the rapid stimulation revealed increased inhibitory synaptic activity that probably inhibited the spread of activation to other areas.

Several researchers have investigated the relationship of depression or depressive psychosis to creativity (Kraepelin, 1921; Post, 1996). These investigators found that many of the most creative composers, scientists, artists, and writers had depressive or bipolar disorders, and that there is a high incidence of affective disorders in this population.

It has been hypothesized that alteration of the brain's neurotransmitter systems, primarily a reduction of catecholamines including norepinephrine, might increase creative thinking (McCarley, 1982).

Behavioral support for the postulate that catecholamine modulates the size of neuronal networks comes from the priming study of Kischka and coworkers (1996). These investigators used a lexical priming task in which either real words or pseudowords were flashed on a screen, and the participants were asked to press a computer key as rapidly as possible when they determined that the word on the screen was a real word, but they were asked not to press the key if a pseudoword was seen. Sometimes the real and pseudowords were preceded by another word, called "a prime." When the preceding word was related to the real target word, the response time to the target word was reduced and the greater the association between the prime and the target words (direct priming), the more rapid the recognition of the real target word. In contrast, the less strongly the two real words are related (indirect priming), the less the influence of the prime on word recognition and response time. When Kischa et al. (1996) administered levodopa to normal participants, the indirect priming effect decreased, suggesting that dopamine reduces the spread of semantic activation. Although Kischka et al. attributed this effect to the dopaminergic system, levodopa is a precursor of both dopamine and norepinephrine, and the administration of L-dopa to these individuals may have also increased the level of norepinephrine.

To test the influence of norepinephrine on cognitive flexibility Beversdorf et al. (1999) tested normal participants' ability to solve anagrams when treated with placebo, ephedrine, and propanolol. Ephedrine increases the level of norepinephrine, whereas propanolol (a β-noradrenergic blocker) interferes with norepinephrine's influence on the brain. Beversdorf et al. found that the anagrams task was performed better after participants took propanolol then after they took ephedrine.

Further support for the postulate that high levels of catecholamine might reduce cognitive performances comes from a study of students with test anxiety, whose scores on the Scholastic Aptitude Test (SAT) improved when they took the β-adrenergic blocker propanolol (Faigel, 1991). In addition, during stressful conditions performance on the Remote Association Test also declines (Martindale, 1973).

Ghacibeh et al. (2006) studied the creativity of patients who had vagus nerve stimulation for medically intractable partial epilepsy. They hypothesized that since vagus nerve stimulation may activate the neurons in the locus coeruleus (LC), and this may result in increase release of brain norepinephrine, vagus nerve stimulation should reduce creativity and cognitive flexibility. Their findings were consistent with their hypothesis.

In depression, lower brain levels of norepinephrine are also present, and many drugs used to treat depression elevate the brain's levels of norepinephrine. Vagus nerve stimulation also alleviates depression (Milby, 2008) and, based on this literature, it would be reasonable to assume that depression might facilitate creative innovation because it is associated with reduced levels of norepinephrine. In contrast, anxiety might diminish innovation because it is associated with increased brain levels of norepinephrine. Brain norepinephrine changes the signal-to-noise-ratio. It suppresses intrinsic excitatory synaptic potentials and enhances potentials elicited by afferent input (Hasselmo et al., 1997). This bias for external input with high norepinephrine states might be important for "flight-or-fight" activities. Suppressing intrinsic excitatory potentials may prevent many association neurons that do not receive direct afferent input from achieving firing threshold, therefore increased norepinephrine activity may lead to the constriction of activated associative networks. Creativity, as mentioned, depends on the activation of highly distributed representations. Thus, high levels of norepinephrine in the cortex favors "bottom-up" processing, important when attending to external stimuli and increasing behavioral responsiveness to unexpected or novel stimuli (Aston-Jones et al., 1991). In contrast, low levels of locus coeruleus activity and norepinephrine might be important in "top-down" processing, critical for the creative innovation.

Many highly creative people have noted that moments of insight come at times when they are relaxed. In 1897, Ramon Cajal (1999) in his book *Advice for a Young Investigator*, wrote, "If a solution fails to appear after all of this, and yet we feel success is just around the corner, try resting for a while." Easterbrook (1959) and Eysenck (1995) each suggested that stress causes high cortical arousal and this high arousal might suppress the emergence of remote associations. As mentioned above, this stress induced suppression may be related to high level of norepinephrine. With reduced degrees of stress and cortical arousal, unusual associations are more like to become manifest.

Although depression, relaxation, and rest might all enhance innovation, the verification and productivity portions of the creative process do need high levels of arousal. Thus, it might be that depressed individuals have very creative ideas during their depression, but have difficulty producing creative products until their depression has abated.

CONCLUSION

In this chapter, we have defined creativity as the ability to understand, develop, and express, in a systematic fashion, novel orderly relationships. Helmholtz (1826) suggested that the creative process has four main stages: preparation, incubation, illumination, and verification (production). In the preparation stage, people develop the knowledge and skills need to be creative. The specific skills required are heavily dependent on the type or form of creative activity (e.g., writing fiction vs. composing music). Many psychologists have proposed a relationship between intelligence (the measure of a person's ability to acquire and apply knowledge)

and creativity. Several studies, however, suggest that intelligence is a necessary but not sufficient component of creativity. Independent of domain, developing creative ideas (innovation) requires disengagement and divergent reasoning, as well as insight and convergent thinking. Clinical, as well as functional imaging studies, suggest that the frontal lobes are important for disengagement. In addition, the frontal lobes have strong connections with the polymodal and supramodal regions of the temporal and parietal lobes where concepts and knowledge are stored. Frontal connections with these areas may selectively inhibit and activate portions of posterior neocortex and thus be important for developing alternative solutions. Convergent thinking or finding "the thread that unites" requires the binding of different forms of knowledge, stored in separate cortical modules that have not been previously associated. Thus, creativity requires the coactivation of and communication between regions of the brain that ordinarily are not strongly connected.

Neurological diseases can strongly influence creativity. Other chapters in this book discuss the different forms of knowledge and, depending on the domain of creativity, diseases that reduce a person's ability to use this knowledge and skill can reduce a person's creativity. Injury to the frontal lobes can interfere with disengagement and divergent thinking. Convergent reasoning requires communication among cortical modules and diseases that cause disconnection, such as diseases of the white matter, can also impair creativity. Although with degenerative diseases there may be a loss of some skills, others may be released. For example, in primary progressive aphasia, degradation of the left hemisphere language networks may release visuospatial skills mediated by the right hemisphere and enhance artistic creativity.

Creative innovation often occurs during levels of low arousal, when people are relaxed. In addition, many people with depression and bipolar disorders are highly creative. These observations suggest that alterations of neurotransmitters such as norepinephrine might be important in creative innovation. High levels of norepinephrine restrict the breadth of conceptual representations, whereas low levels of norepinephrine shift the brain toward intrinsic neuronal activation and increase in the size of distributed concept representations with coactivation across modular networks.

Although much has been learned about the brain mechanisms that may account for creativity and how neurological diseases might influence creativity, the neuropsychology of creativity is still in the early stages of development and much more has to be learned.

REFERENCES

Abraham, A., & Windmann, S. (2007). Creative cognition: The diverse operations and the prospect of applying a cognitive neuroscience perspective. *Methods, 42,* 38–48.

Aharon, I., Etcoff, N., Ariely, D., Chabris, C. F., O'Connor, E., & Breiter, H. C. (2001). Beautiful faces have variable reward value: fMRI and behavioral evidence. *Neuron, 32*(3), 537–551.

Asari, T., Konishi, S., Jimura, K., Chikazoe, J., Nakamura, N., & Miyashita, Y. (2008). Right temporal activation associated with unique perception. *Neuroimage, 41,* 142–152.

Aston-Jones, G., Chiang, C., & Alexinsky, T. (1991). Discharge of noradrenergic locus coeruleus neurons in behaving rats and monkeys suggests a role in vigilance. *Progress in Brain Research, 88,* 501–520.

Baas, M., De Dreu, C. K., & Nijstad, B. A. (2008). A meta-analysis of 25 years of mood-creativity research: Hedonic tone, activation, or regulatory focus? *Psychology Bulletin, 134*(6), 779–806.

Barron, F., & Harrington, D. M. (1981). Creativity, intelligence and personality. *Annual Review of Psychology, 32,* 439–476.

Bazil, C. W. (1999). Seizures in the life and work of Edgar Allan Poe. *Archives of Neurology, 56,* 740–743.

Beals, G. (1996). *Thomas Edison's home page.* Retrieved from www.thomasedison.com.

Bechara, A., Damasio, H., Damasio, A. R., & Lee, G. P. (1999). Different contributions of the human amygdala and ventromedial prefrontal cortex to decision-making. *Journal of Neuroscience, 19,* 5473–5481.

Berg, E. A. (1948). A simple objective test for measuring flexibility in thinking. *Journal of General Psychology, 39,* 15–22.

Benton, A., & Tranel, D. (1993). Visuoperceptual, visuospatial, and visuoconstructive disorders. In K. M. Heilman, & E. Valenstein (Eds.), *Clinical neuropsychology:* New York: Oxford University Press.

Beversdorf, D. Q., Hughes, J. D., Steinberg, B. A., Lewis, L. D., & Heilman, K. M. (1999). Noradrenergic modulation of cognitive flexibility in problem solving. *Neuroreport, 10,* 2763–2767.

Binet, A. (1886). *La psychologie du raisonnement.* Paris, Alcan. (Published in English as *The psychology of reasoning.* Chicago, IL: Open Court, 1896).

Brand, M., Grabenhorst, F., Starcke, K., Vandekerckhove, M. M., & Markowitsch, H. J. (2007). Role of the amygdala in decision under ambiguity and decisions under risk: Evidence from patients with Urbach-Wiethe disease. *Neuropsychologia, 45,* 1305–1317.

Breiter, H. C., Aharon, I., Kahneman, D., Dale, A., & Shizgal, P. (2001). Functional imaging of neural responses to expectancy and experience of monetary gains and losses. *Neuron, 30*(2), 619–639.

Bronowski, J. (1972). *Science and human values.* New York: Harper & Row.

Butter, C. M., Rapcsak, S., Watson, R. T., & Heilman, K. M. (1988). Changes in sensory inattention, directional motor neglect and "release" of the fixation reflex following a unilateral frontal lesion: A case report. *Neuropsychologia, 26*(4), 533–545.

Carlsson, I., Wendt, P.E., & Risberg, J. (2000). On the neurobiology of creativity. Differences in frontal activity between high and low creative subjects. *Neuropsychologia, 38,* 873–885.

Cattel, R. B. (1963). The theory of fluid and crystallized intelligence: A critical experiment. *Journal of Educational Psychology, 54,* 1–22.

Chatterjee, A. (2004). The neuropsychology of visual artistic production. *Neuropsychologia, 42,* 1568–1583.

Contreras, D., & Llinas, R. (2001). Voltage-sensitive dye imaging of neocortical spatiotemporal dynamics to afferent activation frequency. *Journal of Neuroscience, 21*(23), 9403–9413.

Crucian, G. P., Heilman, K., Junco, E., Maraist, M., Owens, W. E., Foote, K. D., & Okun, M. S. (2007). The crossed response inhibition task in Parkinson's disease: Disinhibition hyperkinesia. *Neurocase, 13,* 158–164.

Csikszentmihalyi, M. (1996). *Creativity: Flow and the psychology of discovery and invention.* New York: Harper Collins.

Dijksterhuis, A., Bos, M. W., Nordgren, L. F., & Van Baaren, R. B. (2006). On making the right choice: The deliberation-without attention effect. *Science, 311,* 1005–1007.

Dijksterhuis, A., & Meurs, T. (2006b). Where creativity resides: The generative power of unconscious thought. *Consciousness and Cognition, 15,* 135–146.

Dow, G. T., & Mayer, R. E. (2004). Teaching students to solve insight problems. Evidence for domain specificity in training. *Creativity Research Journal, 16*(4), 389–402.

Drago, V., Foster, P. S., Okun, M. S., Haq, I., Sudhyadhom, A., Skidmore, F. M., & Heilman, K. M. (2009). Artistic creativity and DBS: A case report. *Journal of the Neurological Sciences, 276,* 138–142.

Drago, V., Foster, P. S., Skidmore, F. M., & Heilman, K. M. (2009). Creativity in Parkinson's disease as a function of right versus left hemibody onset. *Journal of the Neurological Sciences, 276*(1–2), 179–183.

Easterbrook, J. A. (1959). The effect of emotion on cue utilization and the organization of behavior. *Psychological Review, 66,* 183–201.

Ellenbroek, B. A., Budde, S., & Cools, A. R. (1996). Prepulse inhibition and latent inhibition: The role of dopamine in the medial prefrontal cortex. *Neuroscience, 75*(2), 535–542.

Eysenck, H. L. (1995). *Genius.* New York and Cambridge: Cambridge University Press.

Faigel, H. C. (1991). The effect of beta blockade on stress-induced cognitive dysfunction in adolescents. *Clinical Pediatrics, 30,* 441–445.

Flaherty, A. W. (2005). Frontotemporal and dopaminergic control of idea generation and creative drive. *Journal of Comparative Neurology, 493,* 147–153.

Fernandez, H. H., & Friedman, J. H. (1999). Punding on L-dopa. *Movement Disorders, 14,* 836–838.

Finney, G. R., & Heilman, K. M. (2007). Artwork before and after onset of progressive nonfluent aphasia. *Cognitive and Behavioral Neurology, 20,* 7–10.

Floresco, S. B., McLaughlin, R. J., & Haluk, D. M. (2008). Opposing roles for the nucleus accumbens core and shell in cue-induced reinstatement of food-seeking behavior. *Neuroscience, 154,* 877–884.

Gabriëls, L., Cosyns, P., Nuttin, B., Demeulemeester, H., & Gybels, J. (2003). Deep brain stimulation for treatment-refractory obsessive-compulsive disorder: Psychopathological and neuropsychological outcome in three cases. *Preview. Acta Psychiatrica Scandinavica, 107*(4), 275–282.

Ghacibeh, G. A., Shenker, J. I., Shenal, B., Uthman, B. M., & Heilman, K. M. (2006). Effect of vagus nerve stimulation on creativity and cognitive flexibility. *Epilepsy and Behavior, 8*(4), 720–725.

Goff, K., & Torrance, E. P. (2002). *Abbreviated Torrance test for adults manual.* Bensenville, IL: Scholastic Testing Service.

Gorfein, D. S., Berger, S., & Bubka, A. (2000). The selection of homograph meanings: Word associations when context changes. *Memory and Cognition, 28,* 766–773.

Guilford, J. P. (1950). Creativity research: Past, present, and future. *American Psychologist, 5,* 444–454.

Guilford, J. P., & Christensen, P. W. (1973). The one way relationship between creative potential and IQ. *Journal of Creative Behavior, 7,* 247–252.

Hasselmo, M. E., Linster, C., Patil, M., Ma, D., & Cekic, M. (1997). Noradrenergic suppression of synaptic transmission may influence cortical signal-to-noise ratio. *Journal of Neurophysiology, 77,* 3326–3339.

Heilman, K. M. (2004). *Creativity and the brain.* New York: Oxford.

Helmholtz, H. (1826/1995). Vortrage und reden. In H. Eysenck (Ed.), *Genius. The natural history of creativity.* Cambridge, UK: Cambridge University Press.

Henning, E. R., Turk, C. L., Mennin, D. S., Fresco, D. M., & Heimberg, R. G. (2007). Impairment and quality of life in individuals with generalized anxiety disorder. *Depression and Anxiety, 24,* 342–349.

James, W. (1890). *The principles of psychology.* New York: Dover.

Jausovec, N., & Jausovec, K. (2000). Differences in resting EEG related to ability. *Brain Topography, 12,* 229–240.

Keltikangas-Järvinen, L., Elovainio, M., Kivimäki, M., Lichtermann, D., Ekelund, J., & Peltonen, L. (2003). Association between the type 4 dopamine receptor gene polymorphism and novelty seeking. *Psychosomatic Medicine, 65,* 471–476.

Kischka, U., Kammer, T., Maier, S., Weisbrod, M., Thimm, M., & Spitzer, M. (1996). Dopaminergic modulation of semantic network activation. *Neuropsychologia, 34,* 1107–1113.

Kraepelin, E. (1921). *Maniac-depressive insanity* (R. M. Barclay, Trans.). Edinburgh: E. & S. Livingstone.

Kuhn, T. S. (1996). *The structure of scientific revolutions* (3rd ed.). Chicago: University of Chicago Press.

Lewis, R. T. (1979). Organic sign, creativity, and personality characteristic of patients following cerebral commissurotomy. *Clinical Neuropsychologist, 1,* 29–33.

Martindale, C. (1999). Biological bases of creativity. In R. J. Sternberg (Ed.), *Handbook of creativity* (pp. 137–152). New York, NY: Cambridge University Press.

Martindale C., & Greenough, J. (1973). The differential effect of increased arousal on creative and intellectual performance. *Journal of Genetic Psychology, 123*, 392–335.

McCarley, R. W. (1982). REM sleep and depression: Common neurobiological control mechanisms. *American Journal of Psychiatry, 139*, 565–570.

Mednick, S. A. (1962). The associative basis of the creative process. *Psychological Review, 9*, 220–232.

Metcalfe, J., & Wiebe, D. (1987). Intuition in insight and noninsight problem solving, *Memory & Cognition, 15*, 238–246.

Milby, A. H., Halpern, C. H., & Baltuch, G. H. (2008). Vagus nerve stimulation for epilepsy and depression. *Neurotherapeutics, 5*, 75–85.

Miller, B. L., Boone, K., Cummings, J. L., Read, S. L., & Mishkin, F. (2000). Functional correlates of musical and visual ability in frontotemporal dementia. *British Journal of Psychiatry, 176*, 458–463.

Miller B. L., Cummings J., Mishkin, F., Boone K., Prince F., Poton, M., & Cotman, C. (1998). Emergence of artistic talent in frontotemporal dementia. *Neurology, 51*, 978–982.

Milner, B. (1984). Behavioural effects of frontal-lobe lesions in man. *Trends in Neurosciences, 7*, 403–407.

Mobini, S., Body, S., Ho, M. Y., Bradshaw, C. M., Szabadi, E., Deakin, J. F., & Anderson, I. M. (2002). Effects of lesions of the orbitofrontal cortex on sensitivity to delayed and probabilistic reinforcement. *Psychopharmacology, 160*, 290–298.

Petsche, H. (1996). Approaches to verbal, visual and musical creativity by EEG coherence analysis. *International Journal of Psychophysiology, 24*(1–2), 145–159.

Plucker, J. A., & Renzulli, J. S. (1999). Experimental studies of creativity. In R. J. Stenberg (Ed.), *Handbook of creativity*. Cambridge, UK: Cambridge University Press.

Post, F. (1996). Verbal creativity, depression and alcoholism. An investigation of one hundred American and British writers. *British Journal of Psychiatry, 168*, 545–555.

Ramon y Cajal, S. (1999). *Advice for a young investigator* (N. Swanson, & L. W. Swanson, Trans.). Cambridge, MA: MIT Press.

Robertson, L. C., Lamb, M. R., & Knight, R. T. (1988). Effects of lesions of temporal parietal junction on perceptual and attentional processing in humans. *Journal of Neurosciences, 8*, 3757–3769.

Rorschach, H. (1921). *Psychodiagnostik: Methodik und ergebnisse eines wahrnehmungsdiagnostischen experiments*. Bern: Ernst Bircher.

Rumelhart, D. E., & McClelland, J. L. (1986). *Parallel distributed processing: Explorations in the microstructure of cognition*, Vols. 1 and 2. Cambridge, MA: MIT Press.

Savitz, J. B., & Ramesar, R. S. (2004). Genetic variants implicated in personality: A review of the more promising candidates. *American Journal of Medical Genetics B Neuropsychiatric Genetics, 131B*(1), 20–32.

Schachter, S. C. (2006). The visual art of contemporary artists with epilepsy. *International Review of Neurobiology, 74*, 119–131.

Simonton, D. K. (1994). *Greatness: Who makes history and why?* New York: Guilford Press.

Smith, S. M., Ward, T. B., & Schumacher, J. S. (1993). Constraining effects of examples in a creative generation task. *Memory & Cognition, 21*, 837–845.

Snyder, A., Bossomaier, T., & Mitchell, D. J. (2004). Concept formation: "Object" attributes dynamically inhibited from conscious awareness. *Journal of Integrated Neurosciences, 3*, 31–46.

Soukhanov, A. H. (1988). *Webster's II, new Riverside University dictionary*. Boston, Mass. The Riverside Publishing Company.

Spearman, C. (1931). Our need of some science in place of the word "intelligence." *Journal of Educational Psychology, 22*, 401–411.

Sternberg, R. J., & O'Hara, L. A. (1999). Creativity and intelligence. In R. J. Sternberg (Ed.), *Handbook of creativity* (pp. 251–272). New York: Cambridge University Press.

Sternberg, R. J. (Ed.). (1999a). *Handbook of creativity*. New York: Cambridge University Press.

Stroop, J. R. (1935). Studies of interference in serial verbal reactions. *Journal of Experimental Psychology, 18*, 643–662.

Swerdlow, N. R., Stephany, N., Wasserman, L. C., Talledo, J., Sharp, R., & Auerbach, P. P. (2003). Dopamine agonists disrupt visual latent inhibition in normal males using a within-subject paradigm. *Psychopharmacology* (Berl), *169*, 314–320.

Torrance, E.P. (1974). *The Torrance test of creative thinking*. Bensenville: Scholastic Testing Service.

Trimble, M. R. (2000). Charles Lloyd: Epilepsy and poetry. *History of Psychiatry, 11*(43, Pt. 3), 273–289.

Wallas, G. (1926). *The art of thought*. New York: Harcourt Brace.

Weisberg, R. W. (1986). *Creativity: Genius and other myths*. New York: W. H. Freeman.

Weisberg, R. W. (2006). *Creativity: Understanding innovation in problem solving, science, invention, and the arts*. Hoboken, NJ: John Wiley.

Voon, V., Hassan, K., Zurowski, M., de Souza, M., Thomsen, T., Fox, S., et al. (2006). Prevalence of repetitive and reward-seeking behaviors in Parkinson disease. *Neurology*, 67, 1254–1257.

Zangwell, O. L. (1966). Psychological deficits associated with frontal lobe lesions. *International Journal of Neurology*, 5, 395–402.

Subject Index

Note: Page numbers followed by *f* or *t* indicate figures and tables

Author Index

Antinori, A., 612
Anton, G., 243, 298
Antoun, N., 257
Anzola, G. P., 322
Apostolos, G. T., 217
Appelros, P., 204
Arai, T., 334
Arbib, M. A., 33
Arbuthnott, G. W., 320
Archer, C. R., 243
Archibald, Y., 222
Ardila, A., 141, 171, 174, 245
Arduino, L. S., 119
Arendt, A., 524
Arendt, T., 524
Arguin, M., 117, 376, 395
Arita, K., 522
Arnault, P., 311
Aron, A. R., 447
Artner, C., 165, 166
Arzy, S., 169, 181
Asari, T., 644
Ash, S., 63
Ashby, F. G., 507
Ashcraft, M. H., 180
Ashford, J. W., 486
Ashkenazi, S., 172
Assal, G., 133, 263, 373, 523
Astafiev, S. V., 181
Aston-Jones, G., 310, 650
Audet, T., 171
Auer, T., 190
Auerbach, S. A., 29, 264, 265, 266
Augustinack, J. C., 539
Avanzi, S., 184
Ax, A. F., 478

Baars, B. J., 43, 45
Baas, M., 648
Babinski, J., 198, 354, 475, 476
Bachevalier, J., 518, 520, 522
Bachman, D. L., 589, 590
Bachoud Levi, A. C., 142, 261
Baddeley, A. D., 49, 94, 432, 504, 507, 547–548
Badre, D., 447
Baeckman, L., 547
Baier, B., 199, 200, 204
Bailey, C. H., 516
Bailey, P. L., 266, 420
Bak, T. H., 143
Bakchine, S., 201
Baker, C., 201
Baker, E., 48, 531
Baker, M., 590
Balasubramanian, V., 133
Baldo, J. V., 437
Baleydier, C., 313, 318
Balint, R., 70, 245, 331
Ball, L. J., 592
Ballantine, H. T., 523, 538
Ballard, C., 607

Balsamo, M., 188
Bamford, K. A., 612
Banich, M. T., 392
Banker, B. Q., 303, 306, 307
Banks, G., 355
Bar, M., 429
Barbas, H., 420
Barbizet, J., 355
Bard, P., 480, 485
Bardouille, T., 519
Barker, A. T., 10
Barker, W. W., 589
Barnes, C. L., 420
Barnes, J., 600
Baron, J. C., 124
Bar-On, R., 428
Barr, W. B., 506, 517
Barrash, J., 445
Barrett, A. M., 169, 198, 225, 335, 336
Barrett, J., 165
Barron, F., 640
Barry, C., 141
Barry, N. S., 511
Bartels, A., 181
Bartha, L., 48, 49, 61
Bartolomeo, P., 163, 166, 331
Barton, J. J., 47, 242
Barton, M. I., 256
Basaglia, N., 275
Basili, A. G., 171, 180
Bassett, S. S., 33
Basso, A., 29, 174, 180, 226, 232, 233, 430
Bastiaanse, R., 102
Bastian, H. C., 4, 5
Bataller, L., 545
Bateman, D., 532
Bates, E.B., 90, 101
Battersby, W. S., 302, 307, 328
Bauer, R. M., 238, 239, 256, 257, 277, 504, 508, 509
Bavelier, D., 104
Baxter, D. M., 132, 141
Baylis, G. C., 259, 469
Baynes, K., 355, 357, 368, 381
Bazil, C. W., 648
Beals, G., 644
Beard, A. W., 488
Beardsworth, E., 382
Beats, B. C., 594
Beauvois, M. F., 120, 133, 161, 251, 252, 253, 275
Bechara, A., 422, 428, 433, 447, 448, 595, 646
Becker, E., 328
Becker, J. T., 545
Beer, J. S., 441
Beeson, P. M., 132, 133, 144
Behrens, S. J., 473
Behrmann, M., 125, 133, 144, 163, 164, 256
Behrmann, N., 118
Beldarrain, G., 434
Belger, A., 392
Bellgowan, P. S. F., 541
Bellugi, U., 438, 474